D0242161

# Greens Sheriff Court and Sheriff Appeal Court Rules 2016/2017

# Greens Sheriff Court and Sheriff Appeal Court Rules 2016/2017

## REPRINTED FROM DIVISION D (COURTS, LOWER), DIVISION K (FAMILY LAW) AND DIVISION S (SHERIFF APPEAL COURT PRACTICE) OF THE PARLIAMENT HOUSE BOOK

**W. GREEN**

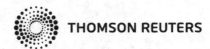

THOMSON REUTERS

Published in 2016 by
W. Green, 21 Alva Street, Edinburgh EH2 4PS
Part of Thomson Reuters (Professional) UK Limited
(Registered in England & Wales, Company No 1679046.
Registered Office and address for service:
2nd Floor, 1 Mark Square, Leonard Street, London EC2A 4EG)
*Printed and bound by CPI Group (UK) Ltd, Croydon, CR0 4YY*
No natural forests were destroyed to make this product;
only farmed timber was used and replanted
A CIP catalogue record for this book is available from the British Library

ISBN 9780414055926

Thomson Reuters and the Thomson Reuters Logo are trademarks of Thomson
Reuters.
All rights reserved. UK statutory material in this publication is acknowledged as
Crown copyright. No part of this publication may be reproduced or transmitted in
any form or by any means, or stored in any retrieval system of any nature, without
prior written permission of the copyright holder and publisher, except for permitted
fair dealing under the Copyright, Designs and Patents Act 1988, or in accordance
with the terms of a licence issued by the Copyright Licensing Agency in respect of
photocopying and/or reprographic reproduction. Full acknowledgment of publisher
and source must be given. Material is contained in this publication for which
publishing permission has been sought, and for which copyright is acknowledged.
Permission to reproduce such material cannot be granted by the publishers and application must be made to the copyright holders.

© 2016 Thomson Reuters (Professional) UK Limited

Reprinted from the *Parliament House Book*, published in looseleaf form and updated five times a year by W. Green, the Scottish Law Publisher

*The following paperback titles are also available in the series:*

Annotated Rules of the Court of Session 2016/2017

Solicitors Professional Handbook 2016/2017

*Parliament House Book consists of the following Divisions:*

A Fees and Stamps

B Courts, Upper

C Court of Session Practice

D Courts, Lower

E Licensing

F Solicitors

G Legal Aid

H Bankruptcy and other Mercantile Statutes

I Companies

J Conveyancing, Land Tenure and Registration

K Family Law

L Landlord and Tenant

M Succession, Trusts, Liferents and Judicial Factors

S Sheriff Appeal Court Practice

# MAIN TABLE OF CONTENTS

## COURTS, LOWER

### COURTS, LOWER: STATUTES

| | |
|---|---|
| Sheriff Courts (Scotland) Act 1907 | 3 |
| Sheriff Courts (Civil Jurisdiction and Procedure) (Scotland) Act 1963 | 431 |
| Sheriff Courts (Scotland) Act 1971 | 433 |
| District Courts (Scotland) Act 1975 | 439 |
| Fatal Accidents and Sudden Deaths Inquiry (Scotland) Act 1976 | 441 |
| Vulnerable Witnesses (Scotland) Act 2004 | 449 |
| Courts Reform (Scotland) Act 2014 | 459 |

### COURTS, LOWER: ACTS OF SEDERUNT, ETC

| | |
|---|---|
| Summary Suspension 1993 | 537 |
| Act of Sederunt (Child Care and Maintenance Rules) 1997 | 539 |
| Act of Sederunt (Summary Applications, Statutory Applications and Appeals etc. Rules) 1999 | 689 |
| Act of Sederunt (Proceedings for Determination of Devolution Issues Rules) 1999 | 871 |
| Act of Sederunt (Summary Cause Rules) 2002 | 879 |
| Act of Sederunt (Small Claim Rules) 2002 | 1041 |
| Act of Sederunt (Sheriff Court Caveat Rules) 2006 | 1127 |
| Act of Sederunt (Simple Procedure) 2016 | 1131 |

# SHERIFF APPEAL COURT PRACTICE

| | |
|---|---|
| Act of Sederunt (Sheriff Appeal Court Rules) 2015 | 1381 |
| Practice Note No.1 of 2016 | 1485 |

# SHERIFF COURTS (SCOTLAND) ACT 1907

(7 EDW. 7 C. 51)

An Act to regulate and amend the laws and practice relating to the civil procedure in sheriff courts in Scotland, and for other purposes.[1,2]

[28th August 1907]

*Preliminary*

**Short title**

**1.** This Act may be cited for all purposes as the Sheriff Courts (Scotland) Act 1907.

**2.** *[Repealed by the Statute Law Revision Act 1927, (c.42).]*

**Interpretation**

**3.** In construing this Act (unless where the context is repugnant to such construction)—

(a)[3] "Sheriff principal" includes sheriff;

(b) "Tenant" includes sub-tenant;

(c) "Lease" includes sub-lease;

(d)[4] "Action" or "cause" includes every civil proceeding competent in the ordinary sheriff court;

(e) "Person" includes company, corporation, or association and firm of any description nominate or descriptive, or any Board corporate or unincorporate;

(f) "Sheriff-clerk" includes sheriff-clerk depute;

(g) "Agent" means a law-agent enrolled in terms of the Law Agents (Scotland) Act 1873;

(h) "Final judgment" means an interlocutor which, by itself, or taken along with previous interlocutors, disposes of the subject-matter of the cause, notwithstanding that judgment may not have been pronounced on every question raised, and that the expenses found due may not have been modified, taxed or decerned for;

(i) *[Repealed by the Sheriff Courts (Scotland) Act 1971 (c.58), Sch.2.]*

(j) "Small Debt Acts" means and includes the Small Debt (Scotland) Acts 1887 to 1889, and Acts explaining or amending the same;

(k) "Initial writ" means the statement of claim, petition, note of appeal, or other document by which the action is initiated;

(l) "Procurator-Fiscal" means procurator-fiscal in the sheriff court;

(m) *[Repealed by the Statute Law (Repeals) Act 1989 (c.43), Sch.1, Pt I.]*

(n) "Pursuer" means and includes any person making a claim or demand, or seeking any warrant or order competent in the sheriff court;

---

[1] As amended by the Sheriff Courts (Scotland) Act 1913 (2 & 3 Geo. V, c. 28). Applied by the Agricultural Holdings (Scotland) Act 1991 (c.55), s.21(4), (5).

[2] For the interpretation of the terms "sheriff" and "sheriff-substitute" throughout this Act, see now the Sheriff Courts (Scotland) Act 1971 (c.58), s.4, and the Interpretation Act 1978 (c.30), Sched. 1.

[3] As substituted by the Sheriff Courts (Scotland) Act 1971 (c.58), s.4.

[4] As amended by the Sheriff Courts (Scotland) Act 1913 (c.28), Sch.1.

(o) "Defender" means and includes any person who is required to be called in any action;

(p)[1] "Summary application" means and includes all applications of a summary nature brought under the common law jurisdiction of the sheriff principal, and all applications, whether by appeal or otherwise, brought under any Act of Parliament which provides, or, according to any practice in the sheriff court, which allows that the same shall be disposed of in a summary manner, but which does not more particularly define in what form the same shall be heard, tried, and determined;

(q) *[Repealed by the Law Reform (Miscellaneous Provisions) (Scotland) Act 1980 (c.55), Sch.3.]*

*Jurisdiction*

## Jurisdiction

**4.** *[Repealed by the Courts Reform (Scotland) Act 2014 (asp 18) Sch.5 para.4 (effective April 1, 2015).]*

## Extension of jurisdiction

**5.** *[Repealed by the Courts Reform (Scotland) Act 2014 (asp 18) Sch.5 para.4 (effective April 1, 2015).]*

## Power of sheriff to order sheriff clerk to execute deeds relating to heritage

**5A.** *[Repealed by the Courts Reform (Scotland) Act 2014 (asp 18) Sch.5 para.4 (effective April 1, 2015).]*

## Action competent in sheriff court

**6.** *[Repealed by the Courts Reform (Scotland) Act 2014 (asp 18) Sch.5 para.4 (effective April 1, 2015).]*

(a)

## Privative jurisdiction in causes under one thousand five hundred pounds value

**7.** *[Repealed by the Courts Reform (Scotland) Act 2014 (asp 18) Sch.5 para.4 (effective April 1, 2015).]*

**8.** *[Repealed by the Sheriff Courts (Scotland) Act 1971 (c.58) Sch.2.]*

**9.** *[Repealed by the Sheriff Courts (Scotland) Act 1971 (c.58) Sch.2.]*

## Privilege not to exempt from jurisdiction

**10.** *[Repealed by the Courts Reform (Scotland) Act 2014 (asp 18) Sch.5 para.4 (effective April 1, 2015).]*

*Sheriffs*

## Appointment of sheriffs and salaried sheriffs-substitute

**11.** *[Repealed by the Courts Reform (Scotland) Act 2014 (asp 18) Sch.5 para.4 (effective April 1, 2015).]*

---

[1] As substituted by the Sheriff Courts (Scotland) Act 1971 (c.58), s.4.

**12, 13.** *[Repealed by the Sheriff Courts (Scotland) Act 1971 (c.58), Sch.2.]*

### Salaries of sheriffs and sheriffs-substitute

**14.** *[Repealed by the Courts Reform (Scotland) Act 2014 (asp 18) Sch.5 para.4 (effective April 1, 2015).]*

**15, 16.** *[Repealed by the Sheriff Courts (Scotland) Act 1971 (c.58), Sch.2.]*

### Honorary sheriff-substitute

**17.**[1]  The sheriff principal may by writing under his hand appoint such persons as he thinks proper to hold the office of honorary sheriff within his sheriffdom during his pleasure, and for whom he shall be answerable. An honorary sheriff, during the subsistence of his commission, shall be entitled to exercise the powers and duties appertaining to the office of sheriff. An honorary sheriff shall hold office, notwithstanding the death, resignation, or removal of the sheriff principal, until his commission shall be recalled by a succeeding sheriff principal. In this section "sheriff principal" does not include sheriff.

**18, 19.** *[Repealed by the Sheriff Courts (Scotland) Act 1971 (c.58), Sch.2.]*

**20.** *[Repealed by the Sheriffs' Pensions (Scotland) Act 1961 (c.42), Sch.2.]*

**21.** *[Repealed by the Sheriff Courts (Scotland) Act 1971 (c.58), Sch.2.]*

**22–24.** *[Repealed by the Sheriff Courts and Legal Officers (Scotland) Act 1927 (c.35), Sch.]*

**25, 26.** *[Repealed by the Sheriff Courts (Scotland) Act 1971 (c.58), Sch.2.]*

*Appeals*

### Appeal to sheriff

**27.** *[Repealed by the Courts Reform (Scotland) Act 2014 (asp 18) Sch.5 para.4 1 January 2016; as to savings see SSI 2015/378 art.3).]*

### Appeal to the Court of Session

**28.** *[Repealed by the Courts Reform (Scotland) Act 2014 (asp 18) Sch.5 para.4 1 January 2016; as to savings see SSI 2015/378 art.3).]*

### Effect of appeal

**29.** *[Repealed by the Courts Reform (Scotland) Act 2014 (asp 18) Sch.5 para.4 1 January 2016; as to savings see SSI 2015/378 art.3).]*

**30.** *[Repealed by the Law Reform (Miscellaneous Provisions) (Scotland) Act 1980 (c.55), Sch.3.]*

**31.** *[Repealed by the Law Reform (Miscellaneous Provisions) (Scotland) Act 1980 (c.55), s.11 and Sch.3.]*

---

[1] As substituted by the Sheriff Courts (Scotland) Act 1971 (c.58), s.4.

**32.** *[Repealed by the Sheriff Courts (Scotland) Act 1913 (2 & 3 Geo. V, c.28),s.1.]*

**33.** *[Repealed by the Juries Act 1949 (c.27), Sch.3.]*

*Removings[1]*

**Removings**

**34.**[2] Where lands exceeding two acres in extent are held under a probative lease specifying a term of endurance, and whether such lease contains an obligation upon the tenant to remove without warning or not, such lease, or an extract thereof from the books of any court of record shall have the same force and effect as an extract decree of removing obtained in an ordinary action at the instance of the lessor, or any one in his right, against the lessee or any party in possession, and such lease or extract shall along with authority in writing signed by the lessor or any one in his right or by his factor or law agent be sufficient warrant to any sheriff-officer or messenger-at-arms of the sheriffdom within which such lands or heritages are situated to eject such party in possession, his family, sub-tenants, cottars, and dependants, with their goods, gear, and effects, at the expiry of the term or terms of endurance of the lease: Provided that previous notice in writing to remove shall have been given—

    (a)  When the lease is for three years and upwards not less than one year and not more than two years before the termination of the lease; and

    (b)  In the case of leases from year to year (including lands occupied by tacit relocation) or for any other period less than three years, not less than six months before the termination of the lease (or where there is a separate ish as regards land and houses or otherwise before that ish which is first in date):

Provided that if such written notice as aforesaid shall not be given the lease shall be held to be renewed by tacit relocation for another year, and thereafter from year to year: Provided further that nothing contained in this section shall affect the right of the landlord to remove a tenant who has been sequestrated under the Bankruptcy (Scotland) Act 1913, or against whom a decree of cessio has been pronounced under the Debtors (Scotland) Act 1880, or who by failure to pay rent has incurred any irritancy of his lease or other liability to removal: Provided further that removal or ejectment in virtue of this section shall not be competent after six weeks from the date of the ish last in date: Provided further that nothing herein contained shall be construed to prevent proceedings under any lease in common form; and that the foregoing provisions as to notice shall not apply to any stipulations in a lease entitling the landlord to resume land for building, planting, feuing, or other purposes or to subjects let for any period less than a year.

---

[1] The provisions of this Act relating to removings are, in the case of an agricultural holding, subject to the Agricultural Holdings (Scotland) Act 1991 (c.55), s.21: see subs. (4).

[2] Reference to the Bankruptcy (Scotland) Act 1913 inserted by virtue of the Interpretation Act 1889 (c.63), s.38 (1). The 1913 Act was repealed by the Bankruptcy (Scotland) Act 1985 (c.66): see s.5(1) and Sch.8.

## Letter of removal

**35.**[1] Where any tenant in possession of any lands exceeding two acres in extent (whether with or without a written lease) shall, either at the date of entering upon the lease or at any other time, have granted a letter of removal, such letter of removal shall have the same force and effect as an extract decree of removing, and shall be a sufficient warrant for ejection to the like effect as is provided in regard to a lease or extract thereof, and shall be operative against the granter of such letter of removal or any party in his right within the same time and in the same manner after the like previous notice to remove: Provided always that where such letter is dated and signed within twelve months before the date of removal or before the first ish, if there be more than one ish, it shall not be necessary that any notice of any kind shall be given by either party to the other.

## Notice to remove

**36.** Where lands exceeding two acres in extent are occupied by a tenant without any written lease, and the tenant has given to the proprietor or his agent no letter of removal, the lease shall terminate on written notice being given to the tenant by or on behalf of the proprietor, or to the proprietor by or on behalf of the tenant not less than six months before the determination of the tenancy, and such notice shall entitle the proprietor, in the event of the tenant failing to remove, to apply for and obtain a summary warrant of ejection against the tenant and every one deriving right from him.

## Notice of termination of tenancy

**37.**[2] In all cases where houses, with or without land attached, not exceeding two acres in extent, lands not exceeding two acres in extent let without houses, mills, fishings, shootings, and all other heritable subjects (excepting land exceeding two acres in extent) are let for a year or more, notice of termination of tenancy shall be given in writing to the tenant by or on behalf of the proprietor or to the proprietor by or on behalf of the tenant: Provided always that notice under this section shall not warrant summary ejection from the subjects let to a tenant, but such notice, whether given to or by or on behalf of the tenant, shall entitle the proprietor to apply to the sheriff principal for a warrant for summary ejection in common form against the tenant and every one deriving right from him: Provided further that the notice provided for by this section shall be given at least forty days before the fifteenth day of May when the termination of the tenancy is the term of Whit-sunday, and at least forty days before the eleventh day of November when the termination of the tenancy is the term of Martinmas.

## Exception for certain tenancies

**37A.**[3] The provisions of this Act relating to removings (including summary removings) shall not apply to or in relation to short limited duration tenancies or limited duration tenancies within the meaning of the Agricultural Holdings (Scotland) Act 2003 (asp 11).

---

[1] As amended by the Requirements of Writing (Scotland) Act 1995 (c.7) Sch.5 (effective August 1, 1995: s.15(2)).

[2] As substituted by the Sheriff Courts (Scotland) Act 1971 (c.58), s.4.

[3] As inserted by the Agricultural Holdings (Scotland) Act 2003 (asp 11), Sch., para.1 and brought into force by the Agricultural Holdings (Scotland) Act 2003 (Commencement No.3, Transitional and Savings Provisions) Order 2003 (SSI 2003/548), reg.2(i) (effective November 23, 2003).

*Summary Removings*

## Summary removing

**38.**[1,2]    Where houses or other heritable subjects are let for a shorter period than a year, any person by law authorised may present to the sheriff principal a summary application for removing, and a decree pronounced in such summary cause shall have the full force and effect of a decree of removing and warrant of ejection. Where such a let is for a period not exceeding four months, notice of removal therefrom shall, in the absence of express stipulation, be given as many days before the ish as shall be equivalent to at least one-third of the full period of the duration of the let; and where the let exceeds four months, notice of removal shall, in the absence of express stipulation, be given at least forty days before the expiry of the said period. Provided that in no case shall notice of removal be given less than twenty-eight days before the date on which it is to take effect.

## Notice of termination in respect of dwelling-houses

**38A.**[3]    Any notice of termination of tenancy or notice of removal given under sections 37 and 38 above in respect of a dwelling-house, on or after the date of the coming into operation of section 123 of the Housing Act 1974, shall be in writing and shall contain such information as may be prescribed by virtue of section 131 of the Rent (Scotland) Act 1971, and Rule 112 of Schedule 1 to this Act shall no longer apply to any such notice under section 37 above.

## Lord Advocate as party to action for divorce

**38B.**    *[Repealed by the Family Law (Scotland) Act 2006 (asp.2), Sch.3 (effective May 4, 2006).]*

**38C.**    *[Repealed by the Children (Scotland) Act 1995 (c.36), Sch.5 (effective November 1, 1996).]*

*Procedure Rules*

## Procedure rules

**39.**    *[Repealed by the Courts Reform (Scotland) Act 2014 (asp 18) Sch.5 para.4 (effective April 1, 2015).]*

## Court of Session to regulate fees, etc.

**40.**    *[Repealed by the Courts Reform (Scotland) Act 2014 (asp 18) Sch.5 para.4 (effective April 1, 2015).]*

*Postal Charge*

**41.**    *[Repealed by the Administration of Justice (Scotland) Act 1933 (c.41), Sch.]*

---

[1] Proviso added by the Rent (Scotland) Act 1971 (c.28), Sch.18.

[2] As substituted by the Sheriff Courts (Scotland) Act 1971 (c.58) s.4. In terms of s.3(a) of the 1907 Act, the meaning of the term "sheriff principal" includes "sheriff".

[3] As inserted by the Housing Act 1974 (c.44), Sch.13, para.1. For rule 112 read rule 105 of the rules substituted by SI 1983/747, and rule 34.7 of the rules substituted by SI 1993/1956.

*Small Debts Acts*

**42–48.** *[Repealed by the Sheriff Courts (Scotland) Act 1971 (c.58), Sch.2]*

**49.** *[Repealed by the Execution of Diligence (Scotland) Act 1926 (c.16), s.7.]*

*Summary Applications*

## Summary applications

**50.**[1] In summary applications (where a hearing is necessary) the sheriff principal shall appoint the application to be heard at a diet to be fixed by him, and at that or any subsequent diet (without record of evidence unless the sheriff principal shall order a record) shall summarily dispose of the matter and give his judgment in writing: Provided that wherever in any Act of Parliament an application is directed to be heard, tried, and determined summarily or in the manner provided by section 52 of the Sheriff Courts (Scotland) Act 1876, such direction shall be read and construed as if it referred to this section of this Act: Provided also that nothing contained in this Act shall affect any right of appeal provided by any Act of Parliament under which a summary application is brought.

*The Poor's Roll*

**51.** *[Repealed by the Statute Law (Repeals) Act 1973 (c.39).]*

*Repeal*

**52.** *[Repealed by the Statute Law Revision Act 1927 (c.42).]*

SCHEDULES

FIRST SCHEDULE[2]

ORDINARY CAUSE RULES 1993[3]

Ordinary Cause Rules 1993

Arrangement of Ordinary Cause Rules
Initiation and Progress of Causes
*Chapter 1*
*Citation, Interpretation, Representation and Forms*

Rule
1.1       Citation.
1.2       Interpretation.
1.3       Representation.
1.3A      Lay support.

---

[1] As substituted by the Sheriff Courts (Scotland) Act 1971 (c.58) s.4. In terms of s.3(a) of the 1907 Act, the meaning of the term "sheriff principal" includes "sheriff".

[2] As substituted by SI 1983/747, affecting any action or proceedings commenced on or after September 1, 1983. New First Schedule substituted in respect of causes commenced on or after January 1, 1994 by SI 1993/1956: see pp.D 44/29 et seq. Please note that we have now removed the pre-1993 Ordinary Cause Rules from this volume.

[3] The Ordinary Cause Rules were amended inter alia by SI 1996/2445, effective November 1, 1996. The amendments made thereby apply equally to causes commenced before that date: see SI 1996/2586

1.4        Forms.

*Chapter 1A*

*Lay Representation*

1A.1      Application and interpretation

1A.2      Lay representation for party litigants

*Chapter 2*

*Relief from Compliance with Rules*

2.1        Relief from failure to comply with rules.

*Chapter 3*

*Commencement of Causes*

3.1        Form of initial writ.

3.2        Actions relating to heritable property.

3.2A      Actions relating to regulated agreements.

3.3        Warrants of citation.

3.4        Warrants for arrestment to found jurisdiction.

3.5        Warrants and precepts for arrestment on dependence.

3.6        Period of notice after citation.

*Chapter 4*

*Caveats*

[omitted by SSI 2006/198]

*Chapter 5*

*Citation, Service and Intimation*

5.1        Signature of warrants.

5.2        Form of citation and certificate.

5.3        Postal service or intimation.

5.4        Service within Scotland by sheriff officer.

5.5        Service on persons furth of Scotland.

5.6        Service where address of person is not known.

5.7        Persons carrying on business under trading or descriptive name.

5.8        Endorsation unnecessary.

5.9        Re-service.

5.10      No objection to regularity of citation, service or intimation.

*Chapter 6*

*Arrestment*

6.A1      Interpretation.

6.A2      Application for interim diligence.

6.A4      Recall etc. of arrestment or inhibition.

6.A5      Incidental applications in relation to interim diligence, etc.

6.A6      Form of schedule of inhibition on the dependence.

6.A7      Service of inhibition on the dependence where address of defender not known.

6.1        Service of schedule of arrestment.

6.2        Arrestment on dependence before service.

6.3        Movement of arrested property.

*Chapter 7*

*Undefended Causes*

| | |
|---|---|
| 7.1 | Application of this Chapter. |
| 7.2 | Minute for granting of decree without attendance. |
| 7.3 | Applications for time to pay directions in undefended causes. |
| 7.4 | Decree for expenses. |
| 7.5 | Finality of decree in absence. |
| 7.6 | Amendment of initial writ. |
| 7.7 | Disapplication of certain rules. |

*Chapter 8*

*Reponing*

| | |
|---|---|
| 8.1 | Reponing. |

*Chapter 9*

*Standard Procedure in Defended Causes*

| | |
|---|---|
| 9.1 | Notice of intention to defend. |
| 9.2 | Fixing date for Options Hearing. |
| 9.2A | Second or subsequent Options Hearing. |
| 9.3 | Return of initial writ. |
| 9.4 | Lodging of pleadings before Options Hearing. |
| 9.5 | Process folder. |
| 9.6 | Defences. |
| 9.7 | Implied admissions. |
| 9.8 | Adjustment of pleadings. |
| 9.9 | Effect of sist on adjustment. |
| 9.10 | Open record. |
| 9.11 | Record for Options Hearing. |
| 9.12 | Options Hearing. |
| 9.13–9.15 | [Omitted by SSI 2004/197.] |

*Chapter 9A*

*Documents and Witnesses*

| | |
|---|---|
| 9A.1 | Application of this chapter |
| 9A.2 | Inspection and recovery of documents |
| 9A.3 | Exchange of lists and witnesses |
| 9A.4 | Applications in respect of time to pay directions and arrestments |

*Chapter 10*

*Additional Procedure*

| | |
|---|---|
| 10.1 | Additional period for adjustment. |
| 10.2 | Effect of sist on adjustment period. |
| 10.3 | Variation of adjustment period. |
| 10.4 | Order for open record. |
| 10.5 | Closing record. |
| 10.6 | Procedural Hearing. |

*Chapter 11*

*The Process*

| | |
|---|---|
| 11.1 | Form and lodging of parts of process. |
| 11.2 | Custody of process. |

11.3    Borrowing and returning of process.

11.4    Failure to return parts of process.

11.5    Replacement of lost documents.

11.6    Intimation of parts of process and adjustments.

11.7    Retention and disposal of parts of process by sheriff clerk.

11.8    Uplifting of productions from process.

*Chapter 12*

*Interlocutors*

12.1    Signature of interlocutors by sheriff clerk.

12.2    Further provisions in relation to interlocutors.

*Chapter 13*

*Party Minuter Procedure*

13.1    Person claiming title and interest to enter process as defender.

13.2    Procedure following leave to enter process.

*Chapter 13A*

*Interventions by the Commission for Equality and Human Rights*

13A.1    Interpretation

13A.2    Interventions by the CEHR

13A.3    Applications to intervene

13A.4    Form of intervention

*Chapter 13B*

*Interventions by the Scottish Commission for Human Rights*

13B.1    Interpretation

13B.2    Application to intervene

13B.3    Invitation to intervene

13B.4    Form of intervention

*Chapter 14*

*Applications by Minute*

14.1    Application of this Chapter.

14.2    Form of minute.

14.3    Lodging of minutes.

14.4    Intimation of minutes.

14.5    Methods of intimation.

14.6    Return of minute with evidence of intimation.

14.7    Opposition where no order for answers made.

14.8    Hearing of minutes where no opposition or no answers lodged.

14.9    Intimation of interlocutor.

14.10    Notice of opposition or answers lodged.

14.11    Procedure for hearing.

14.12    Consent to minute.

14.13    Procedure following grant of minute.

*Chapter 15*

*Motions*

15.A1    Application of this Chapter.

15.1    Lodging of motions.

| | |
|---|---|
| 15.2 | Intimation of motions. |
| 15.3 | Opposition to motions. |
| 15.4 | Consent to motions. |
| 15.5 | Hearing of motions. |
| 15.6 | Motions to sist. |

### Chapter 15A
### *Motions Intimated and Lodged by Email*

| | |
|---|---|
| 15A.1 | Application of this Chapter. |
| 15A.2 | Interpretation of this Chapter. |
| 15A.2 | Provision of email addresses to sheriff clerk. |
| 15A.3 | Making of motions. |
| 15A.4 | Intimation of motions by email. |
| 15A.5 | Opposition to motions by email. |
| 15A.6 | Consent to motions by email. |
| 15A.7 | Lodging unopposed motions by email. |
| 15A.8 | Lodging opposed motions by email. |
| 15A.9 | Issuing of interlocutor by email. |
| 15A.10 | Other periods of intimation etc. under these Rules. |
| 15A.11 | Motions to sist. |
| 15A.12 | Dismissal of action due to delay. |

### Chapter 16
### *Decrees by Default*

| | |
|---|---|
| 16.1 | Application of this Chapter. |
| 16.2 | Decrees where party in default. |
| 16.3 | Prorogation of time where party in default. |

### Chapter 17
### *Summary Decrees*

| | |
|---|---|
| 17.1 | Application of this Chapter. |
| 17.2 | Applications for summary decree. |
| 17.3 | Application of summary decree to counterclaims etc. |

### Chapter 18
### *Amendment of Pleadings*

| | |
|---|---|
| 18.1 | Alteration of sum sued for. |
| 18.2 | Powers of sheriff to allow amendment. |
| 18.3 | Applications to amend. |
| 18.4 | Applications for diligence on amendment. |
| 18.5 | Service of amended pleadings. |
| 18.6 | Expenses and conditions of amendment. |
| 18.7 | Effect of amendment on diligence. |
| 18.8 | Preliminary pleas inserted on amendment. |

### Chapter 19
### *Counterclaims*

| | |
|---|---|
| 19.1 | Counterclaims. |
| 19.2 | Warrants for diligence on counterclaims. |
| 19.2A | Form of record where counterclaim lodged. |

19.3      Effect of abandonment of cause.
19.4      Disposal of counterclaims.

### Chapter 20
#### Third Party Procedure

20.1      Applications for third party notice.
20.2      Averments where order for service of third party notice sought.
20.3      Warrants for diligence on third party notice.
20.4      Service on third party.
20.5      Answers to third party notice.
20.5A      Consequences of failure to amend pleadings.
20.6      Procedure following answers.

### Chapter 21
#### Documents Founded on or Adopted in Pleadings

21.1      Lodging documents founded on or adopted.
21.2      Consequences of failure to lodge documents founded on or adopted.
21.3      Objection to documents founded on.

### Chapter 22
#### Preliminary Pleas

22.1      Note of basis of preliminary plea.

### Chapter 23
#### Abandonment

23.1      Abandonment of causes.
23.2      Application of abandonment to counterclaims.

### Chapter 24
#### Withdrawal of Solicitors

24.1      Intimation of withdrawal to court.
24.2      Intimation to party whose solicitor has withdrawn.
24.3      Consequences of failure to intimate intention to proceed.

### Chapter 25
#### Minutes of Sist and Transference

25.1      Minutes of sist.
25.2      Minutes of transference.

### Chapter 26
#### Transfer and Remit of Causes

26.1      Transfer to another sheriff court.
26.2      Remit to Court of Session.
26.3      Remit from Court of Session.

### Chapter 27
#### Caution and Security

27.1      Application of this Chapter.
27.2      Form of applications.
27.3      Orders.
27.4      Methods of finding caution or giving security.
27.5      Cautioners and guarantors.
27.6      Forms of bonds of caution and other securities.

27.7      Sufficiency of caution or security and objections.

27.8      Insolvency or death of cautioner or guarantor.

27.9      Failure to find caution or give security.

*Chapter 28*

*Recovery of Evidence*

28.1      Application and interpretation of this Chapter.

28.2      Applications for commission and diligence for recovery of documents or for orders under section 1 of the Act of 1972.

28.3      Optional procedure before executing commission and diligence.

28.4      Execution of commission and diligence for recovery of documents.

28.5      Execution of orders for production or recovery of documents or other property under section 1(1) of the Act of 1972.

28.6      Execution of orders for inspection etc. of documents or other property under section 1(1) of the Act of 1972.

28.7      Execution of orders for preservation etc. of documents or other property under section 1(1) of the Act of 1972.

28.8      Confidentiality.

28.9      Warrants for production of original documents from public records.

28.10     Commissions for examination of witnesses.

28.11     Commissions on interrogatories.

28.12     Commissions without interrogatories.

28.13     Evidence taken on commission.

28.14     Letters of request.

28.14A    Taking of evidence in the European Community.

28.15     Citation of witnesses and havers.

*Chapter 28A*

*Pre-Proof Hearing*

28.A.1    Pre-proof hearing

*Chapter 29*

*Proof*

29.1      Reference to oath.

29.2      Remit to person of skill.

29.3      Evidence generally.

29.4      Renouncing probation.

29.5      Orders for proof.

29.6      Hearing parts of proof separately.

29.7      Citation of witnesses.

29.8      Citation of witnesses by party litigants.

29.9      Second diligence against a witness.

29.10     Failure of witness to attend.

29.11     Lodging productions.

29.12     Copy productions.

29.13     Returning borrowed parts of process and productions before proof.

29.14     Notices to admit and notices of non-admission.

29.15     Instruction of shorthand writer.

29.16    Administration of oath or affirmation to witnesses.

29.17    Proof to be taken continuously.

29.18    Recording of evidence.

29.19    Incidental appeal against rulings on confidentiality of evidence and production of documents.

29.20    Parties to be heard at close of proof.

*Decrees, Extracts and Execution*

30.1    Interpretation of this Chapter.

30.2    Taxes on money under control of the court.

30.3    Decrees for payment in foreign currency.

30.4    When decrees extractable.

30.5    Extract of certain awards notwithstanding appeal.

30.6    Form of extract decree.

30.7    Form of warrant for execution.

30.8    Date of decree in extract.

30.9    Service of charge where address of defender not known.

*Chapter 31*

*Appeals*

31.1    Time limit for appeal.

31.2    Applications for leave to appeal.

31.3    Form of appeal to Court of Session.

31.4    Form of appeal to the sheriff principal.

31.5    Transmission of process and notice to parties.

31.6    Record of pleadings etc.

31.7    Determination of appeal.

31.8    Fixing of Options Hearing or making other order following appeal.

31.9    Appeals in connection with orders under section 11 of the Children (Scotland) Act 1995 or aliment.

31.10   Interim possession etc. pending appeal.

31.11   Abandonment of appeal.

*Chapter 32*

*Taxation of Expenses*

32.1    Taxation before decree for expenses.

32.1A   Order to lodge account of exenses

32.2    Decree for expenses in name of solicitor.

32.3    Procedure for taxation.

32.4    Objections to auditor's report.

*Chapter 32A*

*Live Links*

32.A.1   Live links

Special Provisions in Relation to Particular Causes

*Chapter 33*

*Family Actions*

*Part I*

*General Provisions*

| | |
|---|---|
| 33.1 | Interpretation of this Chapter. |
| 33.2 | Averments in actions of divorce or separation about other proceedings. |
| 33.3 | Averments where section 11 order sought. |
| 33.4 | Averments where identity or address of person not known. |
| 33.5 | Averments about maintenance orders. |
| 33.6 | Averments where aliment or financial provision sought. |
| 33.7 | Warrants and forms for intimation. |
| 33.8 | Intimation where improper association. |
| 33.9 | Productions in action of divorce or where section 11 order may be made. |
| 33.9A | Productions in action of divorce on ground of issue of interim gender recognition certificate |
| 33.9B | Application for corrected gender recognition certificate |
| 33.10 | Warrant of citation. |
| 33.11 | Form of citation and certificate. |
| 33.12 | Intimation to local authority. |
| 33.13 | Service in cases of mental disorder of defender. |
| 33.14 | Notices in certain actions of divorce or separation. |
| 33.15 | Orders for intimation. |
| 33.16 | Appointment of curators ad litem to defenders. |
| 33.17 | Applications for sist. |
| 33.18 | Notices of consent to divorce or separation. |
| 33.19 | Procedure in respect of children. |
| 33.20 | Recording of views of the child. |
| 33.21 | Appointment of local authority or reporter to report on a child. |
| 33.22 | Referral to family mediation. |
| 33.22A | Child Welfare Hearing. |
| 33.23 | Applications for orders to disclose whereabouts of children. |
| 33.24 | Applications in relation to removal of children. |
| 33.25 | Intimation to local authority before supervised contact order. |
| 33.26 | Joint minutes. |
| 33.27 | Affidavits. |
| 33.27A | Applications for postponement of decree under section 3A of the Act of 1976 |

## Part II
### Undefended Family Actions

| | |
|---|---|
| 33.28 | Evidence in certain undefended family actions. |
| 33.29 | Procedure for decree in actions under rule 33.28. |
| 33.30 | Extracts of undefended decree. |
| 33.31 | Procedure in undefended family action for section 11 order. |
| 33.32 | No recording of evidence. |
| 33.33 | Disapplication of Chapter 15. |
| 33.33A | Late appearance and application for recall by defenders |

## Part III

*Defended Family Actions*

33.34     Notice of intention to defend and defences.

33.35     Abandonment by pursuer.

33.36     Attendance of parties at Options Hearing.

33.37     Decree by default.

*Part IV*

*Applications and Orders Relating to Children in Certain Actions*

33.38     Application and interpretation of this Part.

33.39     Applications in actions to which this Part applies.

33.40     [Repealed.]

33.41     [Repealed.]

33.42     [Repealed.]

33.43     Applications in depending actions by motion.

33.44     Applications after decree relating to a section 11 order.

33.45     Applications after decree relating to aliment.

33.46     Applications after decree by persons over 18 years for aliment.

*Part V*

*Orders Relating to Financial Provision*

33.47     Application and interpretation of this Part.

33.48     Applications in actions to which this Part applies.

33.49     Applications in depending actions relating to incidental orders.

33.50     Applications relating to interim aliment.

33.51     Applications relating to orders for financial provision.

33.51A    Pension Protection Fund notification

33.52     Applications after decree relating to agreements and avoidance transactions.

*Part VI*

*Applications Relating to Avoidance Transactions*

33.53     Form of applications.

*Part VII*

*Financial Provision After Overseas Divorce or Annulment*

33.54     Interpretation of this Part.

33.55     Applications for financial provision after overseas divorce or annulment.

*Part VIII*

*Actions of Aliment*

33.56     Interpretation of this Part.

33.57     Undefended actions of aliment.

33.58     Applications relating to aliment.

33.59     Applications relating to agreements on aliment.

*Part IX*

*Applications for Orders under Section 11 of the Children (Scotland) Act 1995*

33.60     Application of this Part.

33.61     Form of applications.

33.62     Defenders in action for section 11 order.

33.63    Applications relating to interim orders in depending actions.
33.64    [Repealed.]
33.65    Applications after decree.

### Part X

*Actions under the Matrimonial Homes (Family Protection) (Scotland) Act 1981*

33.66    Interpretation of this Part.
33.67    Form of applications.
33.68    Defenders.
33.69    Applications by motion.
33.70    Applications by minute.
33.71    Sist of actions to enforce occupancy rights.
33.72    [Repealed.]

### Part XI
#### Simplified Divorce Applications

33.73    Application and interpretation of this Part.
33.74    Form of applications.
33.75    Lodging of applications.
33.76    Citation and intimation.
33.77    Citation where address not known.
33.78    Opposition to applications.
33.79    Evidence.
33.80    Decree.
33.81    Appeals.
33.82    Applications after decree.

### Part XII
#### Variation of Court of Session Decrees

33.83    Application and interpretation of this Part.
33.84    Form of application and intimation to Court of Session.
33.85    Defended actions.
33.86    Transmission of process to Court of Session.
33.87    Remit of applications to Court of Session.

### Part XIII
#### Child Support Act 1991

33.88    Interpretation of this Part.
33.89    Restriction of expenses.
33.90    Effect of maintenance assessments.
33.91    Effect of maintenance assessments on extracts relating to aliment.

### Part XIV
#### Referrals to Principal Reporter

33.92    Application and interpretation of this Part.
33.93    Intimation to Principal Reporter.
33.94    Intimation of decision by Principal Reporter.

### Part XV
#### Management of Money Payable to Children

33.95    Management of money payable to children.

*Part XVI*

*Action of Declarator of Recognition or Non-recognition of a Foreign Decree*

33.96 Action of declarator in relation to certain foreign decrees

*Chapter 33A*

*Civil Partnership Actions*

*Part I*

*General Provisions*

33A.1 Interpretation of this Chapter

33A.2 Averments in certain civil partnership actions about other proceedings

33A.3 Averments where section 11 order sought

33A.4 Averments where identity or address of person not known

33A.6 Averments where aliment or financial provision sought

33A.7 Warrants and forms for intimation

33A.8 Intimation where alleged association

33A.9 Productions in action of dissolution of civil partnership or where section 11 order may be made

33A.10 Warrant of citation

33A.11 Form of citation and certificate

33A.12 Intimation to local authority

33A.13 Service in cases of mental disorder of defender

33A.14 Notices in certain actions of dissolution of civil partnership or separation of civil partners

33A.15 Orders for intimation

33A.16 Appointment of curators ad litem to defenders

33A.17 Applications for sist

33A.18 Notices of consent to dissolution of civil partnership or separation of civil partners

33A.19 Procedure in respect of children

33A.20 Recording of views of the child

33A.21 Appointment of local authority or reporter to report on a child

33A.22 Referral to family mediation

33A.23 Child Welfare Hearing

33A.24 Applications for orders to disclose whereabouts of children

33A.25 Applications in relation to removal of children

33A.26 Intimation to local authority before supervised contact order

33A.27 Joint minutes

33A.28 Affidavits

*Part II*

*Undefended Civil Partnership Actions*

33A.29 Evidence in certain undefended civil partnership actions

33A.30 Procedure for decree in actions under rule 33A.29

33A.31 Extracts of undefended decree

33A.32 No recording of evidence

33A.33 Disapplication of Chapter 15

33A.33A    Late appearance and application for recall by defenders

*Part III*

*Defended Civil Partnership Actions*

33A.34    Notice of intention to defend and defences

33A.35    Abandonment by pursuer

33A.36    Attendance of parties at Options Hearing

33A.37    Decree by default

*Part IV*

*Applications And Orders Relating To Children In Certain Actions*

33A.38    Application and interpretation of this Part

33A.39    Applications in actions to which this Part applies

33A.40    Applications in depending actions by motion

33A.41    Applications after decree relating to a section 11 order

33A.42    Applications after decree relating to aliment

33A.43    Applications after decree by persons over 18 years for aliment

*Part V*

*Orders Relating To Financial Provisions*

33A.44    Application and interpretation of this Part

33A.45    Applications in actions to which this Part applies

33A.46    Applications in depending actions relating to incidental orders

33A.47    Applications relating to interim aliment

33A.48    Applications relating to orders for financial provision

33A.49    Applications after decree relating to agreements and avoidance transactions

*Part VI*

*Applications Relating To Avoidance Transactions*

33A.50    Form of applications

*Part VII*

*Financial Provision After Overseas Proceedings*

33A.51    Interpretation of this Part

33A.52    Applications for financial provision after overseas proceedings

*Part VIII*

*Actions In Respect Of Aliment*

33A.53    Applications relating to agreements on aliment

*Part IX*

*Applications For Orders Under* Section 11 Of The Children (Scotland) Act 1995

33A.54    Application of this Part

33A.55    Form of applications

33A.56    Applications relating to interim orders in depending actions

33A.57    Applications after decree

*Part X*

*Actions Relating To Occupancy Rights And Tenancies*

33A.58    Application of this Part

33A.59    Interpretation of this Part

33A.60    Form of application

| | |
|---|---|
| 33A.61 | Defenders |
| 33A.62 | Applications by motion |
| 33A.63 | Applications by minute |
| 33A.64 | Sist of actions to enforce occupancy rights |
| 33A.65 | [Repealed] |

*Part XI*

*Simplified Dissolution Of Civil Partnership Applications*

| | |
|---|---|
| 33A.66 | Application and interpretation of this Part |
| 33A.67 | Form of applications |
| 33A.68 | Lodging of applications |
| 33A.69 | Citation and intimation |
| 33A.70 | Citation where address not known |
| 33A.71 | Opposition to applications |
| 33A.72 | Evidence |
| 33A.73 | Decree |
| 33A.74 | Appeals |
| 33A.75 | Applications after decree |

*Part XII*

*Referrals To Principal Reporter*

| | |
|---|---|
| 33A.76 | Application and interpretation of this Part |
| 33A.77 | Intimation to Principal Reporter |
| 33A.78 | Intimation of decision by Principal Reporter |

*Part XIII*

*Sisting Of Civil Partnership Actions*

| | |
|---|---|
| 33A.79 | Application and interpretation of this Part |
| 33A.80 | Duty to furnish particulars of concurrent proceedings |
| 33A.81 | Mandatory sists |
| 33A.82 | Discretionary sists |
| 33A.83 | Recall of sists |
| 33A.84 | Orders in sisted actions |

*Chapter 33AA*

*Expeditious Resolution of Certain Causes*

| | |
|---|---|
| 33AA.1 | Application of Chapter |
| 33AA.2 | Fixing Date for Case Management Hearing |
| 33AA.3 | Pre-hearing conference |
| 33AA.4 | Case Management Hearing |

*Chapter 33B*

*Financial Provision for Former Cohabitants*

| | |
|---|---|
| 33B. | Interpretation of this Chapter |

*Chapter 34*

*Actions Relating to Heritable Property*

*Part I*

*Sequestration for Rent*

| | |
|---|---|
| 34.1 | Actions craving payment of rent. |
| 34.2 | Warrant to inventory and secure. |

| | |
|---|---|
| 34.3 | Sale of effects. |
| 34.4 | Care of effects. |

*Part II*
*Removing*

| | |
|---|---|
| 34.5 | Action of removing where fixed term of removal. |
| 34.6 | Form of notice of removal. |
| 34.7 | Form of notice under section 37 of the Act of 1907. |
| 34.8 | Giving notice of removal. |
| 34.9 | Evidence of notice to remove. |
| 34.10 | Disposal of applications under Part II of the Conveyancing and Feudal Reform (Scotland) Act 1970 for non-residential purposes. |
| 34.11 | Service on unnamed occupiers |
| 34.12 | Applications under the Mortgage Rights (Scotland) Act 2001 |

*Chapter 35*
*Actions of Multiplepoinding*

| | |
|---|---|
| 35.1 | Application of this Chapter. |
| 35.2 | Application of Chapters 9 and 10. |
| 35.3 | Parties. |
| 35.4 | Condescendence of fund *in medio*. |
| 35.5 | Warrant of citation in multiplepoindings. |
| 35.6 | Citation. |
| 35.7 | Advertisement. |
| 35.8 | Lodging of notice of appearance. |
| 35.9 | Fixing date for first hearing. |
| 35.10 | Hearings. |
| 35.11 | Lodging defences, objections and claims. |
| 35.12 | Disposal of defences. |
| 35.13 | Objections to fund *in medio*. |
| 35.14 | Preliminary pleas in multiplepoindings. |
| 35.15 | Consignation of the fund and discharge of holder. |
| 35.16 | Further service or advertisement. |
| 35.17 | Ranking of claims. |
| 35.18 | Remit to reporter. |

*Chapter 36*
*Actions of Damages*
*Part I*
*Intimation to Connected Persons in Certain Actions of Damages*

| | |
|---|---|
| 36.1 | Application and interpretation of this Part. |
| 36.2 | Averments. |
| 36.3 | Warrants for intimation. |
| 36.4 | Applications to dispense with intimation. |
| 36.5 | Subsequent disclosure of connected persons. |
| 36.6 | Connected persons entering process. |
| 36.7 | Failure to enter process. |

*Chapter 36A*

*Case Management of Certain Personal Injuries Actions*

36A.1    Application and interpretation of this Chapter.
36A.2    Form of initial writ.
36A.3    Averments of medical treatment.
36A.4    Making up open record.
36A.5    Period for adjustment.
36A.6    Variation of adjustment period.
36A.7    Closing record.
36A.8    Lodging of written statements.
36A.9    Procedural Hearing.
36A.10   Pre-proof timetable.
36A.11   Power of sheriff to make orders.

*Chapter 36B*
*Jury Trials*

36B.1    Application and interpretation of this Chapter.
36B.2    Applications for jury trial.
36B.3    Citation of jurors.
36B.4    Ineligibility for, and excusal from, jury service.
36B.5    Application of certain rules relating to proofs.
36B.6    Failure of party to appear at jury trial.
36B.7    Administration of oath or affirmation to jurors.
36B.8    Exceptions to sheriff's charge.
36B.9    Further questions for jury.
36B.10   Application of verdicts.
36A.11

*Part II*
*Interim Payments of Damages*

36.8     Application and interpretation of this Part.
36.9     Applications for interim payment of damages.
36.10    Adjustment on final decree.

*Part III*
*Provisional Damages for Personal Injuries*

36.11    Application and interpretation of this Part.
36.12    Applications for provisional damages.
36.13    Applications for further damages.

*Part IV*
*Management of Damages Payable to Persons under Legal Disability*

36.14    Orders for payment and management of money.
36.15    Methods of management.
36.16    Subsequent orders.
36.17    Management of money paid to sheriff clerk.

*Part IV A*
*Productions in Certain Actions of Damages*

36.17A   Application of this Part
36.17B   Averments of medical treatment

36.17C      Lodging of medical reports
*Part V*
Sex Discrimination Act 1975
36.18      *[Omitted by SSI 2006/509.]*
*Chapter 37*
Causes under the Presumption of Death (Scotland) Act 1977
37.1      Interpretation of this Chapter.
37.2      Parties to, and service and intimation of, actions of declarator.
37.3      Further advertisement.
37.4      Applications for proof.
37.5      Applications for variation or recall of decree.
37.6      Appointment of judicial factors.
*Chapter 38*
*European Court*
38.1      Interpretation of this Chapter.
38.2      Applications for reference.
38.3      Preparation of case for reference.
38.4      Sist of cause.
38.5      Transmission of reference.
*Chapter 39*
*Provisions in Relation to Curators Ad Litem*
39.1      Fees and outlays of curators *ad litem* in respect of children.
*Chapter 40*
*Commercial Actions*
40.1      Application and interpretation of the Chapter.
40.2      Proceedings before a nominated sheriff.
40.3      Procedure in commercial actions.
40.4      Election of procedure for commercial actions.
40.5      Transfer of action to be a commercial action.
40.6      Appointment of a commercial action as an ordinary cause.
40.7      Special requirements for initial writ in a commercial action.
40.8      Notice of Intention to Defend.
40.9      Defences.
40.10      Fixing date for Case Management Conference.
40.11      Applications for summary decree in a commercial action.
40.12      Case Management Conference.
40.13      Lodging of productions.
40.14      Hearing for further procedure.
40.15      Failure to comply with rule or order of sheriff.
40.16      Determination of action.
40.17      Parts of Process.
*Chapter 41*
*Protection from Abuse (Scotland) Act 2001*
41.1      Interpretation
41.2      Attachment of power to arrest to interdict

| | |
|---|---|
| 41.3 | Extension or recall of power to arrest |
| 41.4 | Documents to be delivered to chief constable in relation to recall or variation of interdict |
| 41.5 | Certificate of delivery of documents to chief constable |

*Chapter 42*

*Competition Appeal Tribunal*

| | |
|---|---|
| 42.1 | Interpretation |
| 42.1 | Transfer of proceedings to the tribunal |

*Chapter 43*

*Causes Relating to Articles 81 and 82 of the Treaty Establishing the European Community*

| | |
|---|---|
| 43.1 | Intimation of actions to the Office of Fair Trading |

*Chapter 44*

*The Equality Act 2010*

| | |
|---|---|
| 44.1 | Interpretation and application |
| 44.2 | Intimation to Commission |
| 44.3 | Assessor |
| 44.4 | Taxation of Commission expenses |
| 44.5 | National security |
| 44.6 | Transfer to Employment Tribunal |
| 44.7 | Transfer from Employment Tribunal |

*Chapter 45*

*Vulnerable Witnesses (Scotland) Act 2004*

| | |
|---|---|
| 45.1 | Interpretation |
| 45.2 | Child witness notice |
| 45.3 | Vulnerable witness application |
| 45.4 | Intimation |
| 45.5 | Procedure on lodging child witness notice or vulnerable witness application |
| 45.6 | Review of arrangements for vulnerable witnesses |
| 45.7 | Intimation of review application |
| 45.8 | Procedure on lodging a review application |
| 45.9 | Determination of special measures |
| 45.10 | Intimation of an order under section 12(1) or (6) or 13(2) |
| 45.11 | Taking of evidence by commissioner |
| 45.12 | Commission on interrogatories |
| 45.13 | Commission without interrogatories |
| 45.14 | Lodging of video record and documents |
| 45.15 | Custody of video record and documents |
| 45.16 | Application for leave for party to be present at the commission |

*Chapter 46*

*Companies Act 2006*

| | |
|---|---|
| 46.1 | Leave to raise derivative proceedings |
| 46.2 | Application to continue proceedings as derivative proceedings |

*Chapter 47*

*Actions of Division and Sale and Orders for Division and/or Sale of Property*
47.1        Remit to reporter to examine heritable property
47.2        Division and/or sale of property
*Chapter 48*
*Reporting Restrictions under the Contempt of Court Act 1981*
48.1        Interpretation and application of this Chapter
48.2        Interim orders: notification to interested persons
48.3        Interim orders: representations
48.4        Notification of reporting restrictions
48.5        Applications for variation or revocation
*Chapter 49*
*Admiralty Actions*
49.1        Interpretation of this Chapter
49.2        Forms of action
49.3        Actions in rem
49.4        Actions in personam
49.5        Sale of ship or cargo
49.6        Ship collisions and preliminary acts
49.7        Applications to dispense with preliminary acts
49.8        Ship collision and salvage actions
49.9        Arrestment of ships and arrestment in rem of cargo on board ship
49.10       Arrestment of cargo
49.11       Forms for diligence in admiralty actions
49.12       Movement of arrested property
49.13       Arrestment before service
*Chapter 50*
*Lodging Audio or Audio-visual Recordings of Children*
50.1        Interpretation
50.2        Lodging an audio or audio-visual recording of a child
50.3        Separate inventory of productions
50.4        Custody of a recording of a child
50.5        Access to a recording of a child
50.6        Incidental appeal against rulings on access to a recording of a child
50.7        Exceptions
50.8        Application of other rules
*Chapter 51*
*Land Registration etc.*
51.1        Interpretation of this Chapter
51.2        Applications under Part 6 of the 2012 Act
51.3        Form of orders under Part 6 of the 2012 Act
51.4        Effect of warrant to place or renew caveat
51.5        Form of order for rectification of a document
*Chapter 52*
*Mutual Recognition of Protection Measures in Civil Matters*
52.1        Interpretation

| | |
|---|---|
| 52.2 | Form of application for Article 5 certificate |
| 52.3 | Issue of Article 5 certificate |
| 52.4 | Conditions for issue of Article 5 certificate |
| 52.5 | Notice of issue of Article 5 certificate |
| 52.6 | Effect of variation of order |
| 52.7 | Application for rectification or withdrawal of Article 5 certificate |
| 52.8 | Issue of Article 14 certificate |

*Chapter 53*

*Proving the Tenor*

| | |
|---|---|
| 53.1 | Application of this Chapter |
| 53.2 | Parties |
| 53.3 | Supporting evidence |
| 53.4 | Undefended actions |

*Chapter 54*

*Reduction*

| | |
|---|---|
| 54.1 | Application of this Chapter |
| 54.2 | Craves for suspension and interdict |
| 54.3 | Production: objection by defender |
| 54.4 | Production: no objection by defender |
| 54.5 | Production: pursuer to satisfy |
| 54.6 | Production: joint minute for reduction |
| 54.7 | Production: satisfaction by a copy |

## INITIATION AND PROGRESS OF CAUSES

### Chapter 1

### Citation, Interpretation, Representation and Forms

**Citation**

These Rules may be cited as the Ordinary Cause Rules 1993.

**Interpretation**

**1.2.**[1](1)   In these Rules, unless the context otherwise requires—

"document" has the meaning assigned to it in section 9 of the Civil Evidence (Scotland) Act 1988;

"enactment" includes an enactment comprised in, or in an instrument made under, an Act of the Scottish Parliament;[2]

"period of notice" means the period determined under rule 3.6 (period of notice after citation).

"the Act of 2004" means the Vulnerable Witnesses (Scotland) Act 2004.[3]

"the 2014 Act" means the Courts Reform (Scotland) Act 2014;

---

[1] As amended by the Act of Sederunt (Rules of the Court of Session 1994 and Sheriff Court Rules Amendment) (No. 2) (Personal Injury and Remits) 2015 r.8 (effective September 22, 2015).

[2] As inserted by the Act of Sederunt (Ordinary Cause, Summary Application, Summary Cause and Small Claim Rules) Amendment (Miscellaneous) 2007 (SSI 2007/6), para.2(2) (effective January 29, 2007).

[3] As inserted by the Act of Sederunt (Ordinary Cause, Summary Application, Summary Cause and Small Claim Rules) Amendment (Vulnerable Witnesses (Scotland) Act 2004) 2007 (SSI 2007/463), r.2(2) (effective November 1, 2007).

"the all-Scotland sheriff court" means the sheriff court specified in the All-Scotland Sheriff Court (Sheriff Personal Injury Court) Order 2015(c) so far as the court is constituted by a sheriff sitting in the exercise of the sheriff's all-Scotland jurisdiction for the purpose of dealing with civil proceedings of a type specified in that Order.

(2)  For the purposes of these Rules—

(a)  "affidavit" includes an affirmation and a statutory or other declaration; and

(b)  an affidavit shall be sworn or affirmed before a notary public or any other competent authority.

(3)  Where a provision in these Rules requires a party to intimate or send a document to another party, it shall be sufficient compliance with that provision if the document is intimated or sent to the solicitor acting in the cause for that party.

(4)  Unless the context otherwise requires, anything done or required to be done under a provision in these Rules by a party may be done by the agent for that party acting on his behalf.

(5)  Unless the context otherwise requires, a reference to a specified Chapter, Part, rule or form, is a reference to the Chapter, Part, rule, or form in Appendix 1, so specified in these Rules; and a reference to a specified paragraph, sub-paragraph or head is a reference to that paragraph of the rule or form, that sub-paragraph of the paragraph or that head of the sub-paragraph, in which the reference occurs.

(6)[1]  In these Rules, references to a solicitor include a reference to a member of a body which has made a successful application under section 25 of the Law Reform (Miscellaneous Provisions) (Scotland) Act 1990 but only to the extent that the member is exercising rights acquired by virtue of section 27 of that Act.

(7)  In these Rules—

(a)  references to a sheriff's all-Scotland jurisdiction are to be construed in accordance with section 42(3) of the 2014 Act;

(b)  references to a sheriff's local jurisdiction are to be construed in accordance with section 42(4) of the 2014 Act.

## Representation

**1.3.**—(1)  Subject to paragraph (2), a party to any proceedings arising solely under the provisions of the Debtors (Scotland) Act 1987 shall be entitled to be represented by a person other than a solicitor or an advocate provided that the sheriff is satisfied that such person is a suitable representative and is duly authorised to represent that party.

(2)  *[Repealed by the Act of Sederunt (Rules of the Court of Session, Sheriff Appeal Court Rules and Sheriff Court Rules Amendment) (Sheriff Appeal Court) 2015 (SSI 2015/419) r.5 (effective 1 January 2016).]*

(3)[2]  A party may be represented by any person authorised under any enactment to conduct proceedings in the sheriff court in accordance with the terms of that enactment.

---

[1] As inserted by the Act of Sederunt (Sheriff Court Rules Amendment) (Sections 25 to 29 of the Law Reform (Miscellaneous Provisions) (Scotland) Act 1990) 2009 (SSI 2009/164) r.2 (effective May 20, 2009).

[2] As inserted by the Act of Sederunt (Ordinary Cause, Summary Application, Summary Cause and Small Claim Rules) Amendment (Miscellaneous) 2007 (SSI 2007/6), para.2(3) (effective January 29, 2007).

(4)[1]  The person referred to in paragraph (3) may do everything for the preparation and conduct of an action as may have been done by an individual conducting his own action.

## Lay support

**1.3A.**—[2](1)  At any time during proceedings the sheriff may, on the request of a party litigant, permit a named individual to assist the litigant in the conduct of the proceedings by sitting beside or behind (as the litigant chooses) the litigant at hearings in court or in chambers and doing such of the following for the litigant as he or she requires—

    (a)  providing moral support;

    (b)  helping to manage the court documents and other papers;

    (c)  taking notes of the proceedings;

    (d)  quietly advising on—

        (i)  points of law and procedure;

        (ii)  issues which the litigant might wish to raise with the sheriff;

        (iii)  questions which the litigant might wish to ask witnesses.

(2)  It is a condition of such permission that the named individual does not receive from the litigant, whether directly or indirectly, any remuneration for his or her assistance.

(3)  The sheriff may refuse a request under paragraph (1) only if—

    (a)  the sheriff is of the opinion that the named individual is an unsuitable person to act in that capacity (whether generally or in the proceeding concerned); or

    (b)  the sheriff is of the opinion that it would be contrary to the efficient administration of justice to grant it.

(4)  Permission granted under paragraph (1) endures until the proceedings finish or it is withdrawn under paragraph (5); but it is not effective during any period when the litigant is represented.

(5)  The sheriff may, of his or her own accord or on the motion of a party to the proceedings, withdraw permission granted under paragraph (1); but the sheriff must first be of the opinion that it would be contrary to the efficient administration of justice for the permission to continue.

(6)  Where permission has been granted under paragraph (1), the litigant may—

    (a)  show the named individual any document (including a court document) or

    (b)  impart to the named individual any information,

which is in his or her possession in connection with the proceedings without being taken to contravene any prohibition or restriction on the disclosure of the document or the information; but the named individual is then to be taken to be subject to any such prohibition or restriction as if he or she were the litigant.

(7)  Any expenses incurred by the litigant as a result of the support of an individual under paragraph (1) are not recoverable expenses in the proceedings.

---

[1] As inserted by the Act of Sederunt (Ordinary Cause, Summary Application, Summary Cause and Small Claim Rules) Amendment (Miscellaneous) 2007 (SSI 2007/6), para.2(3) (effective January 29 2007).

[2] As inserted by the Act of Sederunt (Sheriff Court Rules) (Miscellaneous Amendments) (No.2) 2010 (SSI 2010/416) r.2 (effective January 1, 2011).

**Forms**

**1.4.** Where there is a reference to the use of a form in these Rules, that form in Appendix 1 or Appendix 2, as the case may be, to these Rules, or a form substantially to the same effect, shall be used with such variation as circumstances may require.

Chapter 1A[1]

Lay Representation

**Application and interpretation**

**1A.1.**—(1) This Chapter is without prejudice to any enactment (including any other provision in these Rules) under which provision is, or may be, made for a party to a particular type of case before the sheriff to be represented by a lay representative.

(2) In this Chapter, a "lay representative" means a person who is not—

(a) a solicitor;

(b) an advocate, or

(c) someone having a right to conduct litigation, or a right of audience, by virtue of section 27 of the Law Reform (Miscellaneous Provisions) (Scotland) Act 1990.

**Lay representation for party litigants**

**1A.2.**—(1) In any proceedings in respect of which no provision as mentioned in rule 1A.1(1) is in force, the sheriff may, on the request of a party litigant, permit a named individual (a "lay representative") to appear, along with the litigant, at a specified hearing for the purpose of making oral submissions on behalf of the litigant at that hearing.

(2) An application under paragraph (1)—

(a) is to be made orally on the date of the first hearing at which the litigant wishes a named individual to make oral submissions; and

(b) is to be accompanied by a document, signed by the named individual, in Form 1A.2.

(3) The sheriff may grant an application under paragraph (1) only if the sheriff is of the opinion that it would assist his or her consideration of the case to grant it.

(4) It is a condition of permission granted by the sheriff that the lay representative does not receive directly or indirectly from the litigant any remuneration or other reward for his or her assistance.

(5) The sheriff may grant permission under paragraph (1) in respect of one or more specified hearings in the case; but such permission is not effective during any period when the litigant is legally represented.

(6) The sheriff may, of his or her own accord or on the motion of a party to the proceedings, withdraw permission granted under paragraph (1).

(7) Where permission has been granted under paragraph (1), the litigant may—

(a) show the lay representative any document (including a court document); or

(b) impart to the lay representative any information,

which is in his or her possession in connection with the proceedings without being taken to contravene any prohibition or restriction on the disclosure of the document or the information; but the lay representative is then to be taken to be subject to any

---

[1] As inserted by the Act of Sederunt (Sheriff Court Rules) (Lay Representation) 2013 (SSI 2013/91) r.2 (effective April 4, 2013).

such prohibition or restriction as if he or she were the litigant.

(8)  Any expenses incurred by the litigant in connection with lay representation under this rule are not recoverable expenses in the proceedings.

## Chapter 2

## Relief from Compliance with Rules

**Relief from failure to comply with rules**

**2.1.**—(1)  The sheriff may relieve a party from the consequences of failure to comply with a provision in these Rules which is shown to be due to mistake, oversight or other excusable cause, on such conditions as he thinks fit.

(2)  Where the sheriff relieves a party from the consequences of a failure to comply with a provision in these Rules under paragraph (1), he may make such order as he thinks fit to enable the cause to proceed as if the failure to comply with the provision had not occurred.

## Chapter 3

## Commencement of Causes

**Form of initial writ**

**3.1.**[1](1)[2]  A cause shall be commenced—
- (a)  in the case of an ordinary cause, by initial writ in Form G1; or
- (b)  in the case of a commercial action within the meaning of Chapter 40, by initial writ in Form G1A.

or
- (c)[3]  in the case of a personal injuries action within the meaning of Part AI of Chapter 36, by initial writ in Form PI1.
- (d)  in the case of a personal injuries action appointed to proceed in accordance with Chapter 36A under rule 36.C1, by initial writ in Form G1 which includes an interlocutor in Form PI4.

(2)  The initial writ shall be written, typed or printed on A4 size paper of durable quality and shall not be backed.

(3)  Where the pursuer has reason to believe that an agreement exists prorogating jurisdiction over the subject matter of the cause to another court, the initial writ shall contain details of that agreement.

(4)  Where the pursuer has reason to believe that proceedings are pending before another court involving the same cause of action and between the same parties as those named in the instance of the initial writ, the initial writ shall contain details of those proceedings.

(5)  An article of condescendence shall be included in the initial writ averring—
- (a)  the ground of jurisdiction; and
- (b)  the facts upon which the ground of jurisdiction is based.

(5A)  Where a personal injuries action within the meaning of Part A1 of Chapter 36 is raised in Edinburgh Sheriff Court the initial writ must include an averment

---

[1] As amended by the Act of Sederunt (Rules of the Court of Session 1994 and Sheriff Court Rules Amendment) (No. 2) (Personal Injury and Remits) 2015 r.8 (effective September 22, 2015).

[2] As inserted by the Act of Sederunt (Ordinary Cause Rules) Amendment (Commercial Actions) 2001 (SSI 2001/8) (effective March 1, 2001).

[3] As inserted by the Act of Sederunt (Ordinary Cause Rules Amendment) (Personal Injuries Actions) 2009 (SSI 2009/285) r.2 (effective November 2, 2009).

indicating whether the proceedings are for determination in the exercise of the sheriff's all-Scotland jurisdiction or the sheriff's local jurisdiction.

(5B) Where an averment is included indicating that the proceedings are for determination in the exercise of the sheriff's all-Scotland jurisdiction, the heading of the initial writ must state that the action is being raised in the all-Scotland sheriff court.

(6) Where the residence, registered office or place of business, as the case may be, of the defender is not known and cannot reasonably be ascertained, the pursuer shall set out in the instance that the whereabouts of the defender are not known and aver in the condescendence what steps have been taken to ascertain his present whereabouts.

(7) The initial writ shall be signed by the pursuer or his solicitor (if any) and the name and address of that solicitor shall be stated on the back of every service copy of that writ.

### Actions relating to heritable property

**3.2.**—(1) In an action relating to heritable property, it shall not be necessary to call as a defender any person by reason only of any interest he may have as the holder of a heritable security over the heritable property.

(2) Intimation of such an action shall be made to the holder of the heritable security referred to in paragraph (1)—

    (a)   where the action relates to any heritable right or title; and

    (b)   in any other case, where the sheriff so orders.

(3) *[Repealed by the Act of Sederunt (Sheriff Court Rules) (Enforcement of Securities over Heritable Property) 2010 (SSI 2010/324) para.2 (effective September 30, 2010).]*

### Actions relating to regulated agreements

**3.2A.**[1] In an action which relates to a regulated agreement within the meaning given by section 189(1) of the Consumer Credit Act 1974 the initial writ shall include an averment that such an agreement exists and details of that agreement.

### Warrants of citation

**3.3.**—[2,3](1) The warrant of citation in any cause other than—

    (a)   a family action within the meaning of rule 33.1(1),

    (b)   an action of multiplepoinding,

    (c)   an action in which a time to pay direction under the Debtors (Scotland) Act 1987 or a time order under the Consumer Credit Act 1974 may be applied for by the defender,

    (d)   *[Repealed by the Act of Sederunt (Sheriff Court Rules) (Enforcement of Securities over Heritable Property) 2010 (SSI 2010/324) para.2 (effective September 30, 2010).]*

---

[1] As inserted by the Act of Sederunt (Sheriff Court Rules) (Miscellaneous Amendments) 2009 (SSI 2009/294) r.2 (effective December 1, 2009) as substituted by the Act of Sederunt (Amendment of the Act of Sederunt (Sheriff Court Rules) (Miscellaneous Amendments) 2009) 2009 (SSI 2009/402) (effective November 30, 2009).

[2] Inserted by the Act of Sederunt (Amendment of Ordinary Cause Rules and Summary Applications, Statutory Applications and Appeals etc. Rules) (Applications under the Mortgage Rights (Scotland) Act 2001) 2002 (SSI 2002/7), para.2(3).

[3] As amended by the Act of Sederunt (Ordinary Cause, Summary Application, Summary Cause and Small Claim Rules) Amendment (Miscellaneous) 2007 (SSI 2007/6), para.2(4) (effective January 29, 2007).

(e)[1]   a civil partnership action within the meaning of rule 33A.1(1) shall be in Form O1.

(2)   In a cause in which a time to pay direction under the Debtors (Scotland) Act 1987 or a time order under the Consumer Credit Act 1974 may be applied for by the defender, the warrant of citation shall be in Form O2.

(3)   In a cause in which a warrant for citation in accordance with Form O2 is appropriate, there shall be served on the defender (with the initial writ and warrant) a notice in Form O3.

(4)   *[Repealed by the Act of Sederunt (Sheriff Court Rules) (Enforcement of Securities over Heritable Property) 2010 (SSI 2010/324) para.2 (effective September 30, 2010).]*

**Warrants for arrestment to found jurisdiction**

**3.4.**—(1)   Where an application for a warrant for arrestment to found jurisdiction may be made, it shall be made in the crave of the initial writ.

(2)   Averments to justify the granting of such a warrant shall be included in the condescendence.

**Warrants and precepts for arrestment on dependence**

**3.5.**   *[Repealed by the Act of Sederunt (Sheriff Court Rules Amendment) (Diligence) 2008 (SSI 2008/121) r.5(2) (effective April 1, 2008).]*

**Period of notice after citation**

**3.6.**—(1)   Subject to rule 5.6(1) (service where address of person is not known) and to paragraph (2) of this rule, a cause shall proceed after one of the following periods of notice has been given to the defender:—

(a)   where the defender is resident or has a place of business within Europe, 21 days after the date of execution of service; or

(b)   where the defender is resident or has a place of business outside Europe, 42 days after the date of execution of service.

(2)   Subject to paragraph (3), the sheriff may, on cause shown, shorten or extend the period of notice on such conditions as to the method or manner of service as he thinks fit.

(3)   A period of notice may not be reduced to a period of less than 2 days.

---

[1] As amended by Act of Sederunt (Ordinary Cause Rules) Amendment (Family Law (Scotland) Act 2006 etc.) 2006 (SSI 2006/207), para.2 (effective May 4, 2006).

(4)   Where a period of notice expires on a Saturday, Sunday, or public or court holiday, the period of notice shall be deemed to expire on the next day on which the sheriff clerk's office is open for civil court business.

## Chapter 4

### Caveats

*[Omitted by Act of Sederunt (Sheriff Court Caveat Rules) 2006 (SI 2006/198), effective April 28, 2006]*

## Chapter 5

### Citation, Service and Intimation

**Signature of warrants**

**5.1.**—(1)[1]   Subject to paragraph (2), a warrant for citation or intimation may be signed by the sheriff or sheriff clerk.

(2)   The following warrants shall be signed by the sheriff:—

(a)   a warrant containing an order shortening or extending the period of notice or any other order other than a warrant which the sheriff clerk may sign;

(b)[2, 3]   a warrant for arrestment to found jurisdiction (including the arrestment of a ship);

(ba)[4, 5]   a warrant for arrestment on the dependence;

(c)   a warrant for intimation ordered under rule 33.8 (intimation where alleged association).

(d)[6]   a warrant for intimation ordered under rule 33A.8 (intimation where alleged association).

(e)[7]   a warrant for arrestment of a ship to found jurisdiction;

(f)[8]   a warrant for arrestment of a ship or cargo in rem;

(g)[9]   a warrant for arrestment of cargo.

(3)   Where the sheriff clerk refuses to sign a warrant which he may sign, the party presenting the initial writ may apply to the sheriff for the warrant.

---

[1] As inserted by the Act of Sederunt (Ordinary Cause, Summary Application and Small Claim Rules) Amendment (Miscellaneous) 2004 (SSI 2004/197) para.2(3) (effective May 21, 2004).

[2] As inserted by the Act of Sederunt (Ordinary Cause, Summary Application and Small Claim Rules) Amendment (Miscellaneous) 2004 (SSI 2004/197) para.2(3) (effective May 21, 2004).

[3] As amended by the Act of Sederunt (Sheriff Court Rules) (Miscellaneous Amendments) 2012 (SSI 2012/188) para.10 (effective August 1, 2012).

[4] As inserted by the Act of Sederunt (Ordinary Cause, Summary Application and Small Claim Rules) Amendment (Miscellaneous) 2004 (SSI 2004/197) para.2(3) (effective May 21, 2004).

[5] As amended by Act of Sederunt (Ordinary Cause Rules) Amendment (Family Law (Scotland) Act 2006 etc.) 2006 (SSI 2006/207) para.2 (effective May 4, 2006).

[6] As inserted by Act of Sederunt (Ordinary Cause Rules) Amendment (Family Law (Scotland) Act 2006 etc.) 2006 (SSI 2006/207) para.2 (effective May 4, 2006).

[7] As inserted by the Act of Sederunt (Sheriff Court Rules) (Miscellaneous Amendments) 2012 (SSI 2012/188) para.10 (effective August 1, 2012).

[8] As inserted by the Act of Sederunt (Sheriff Court Rules) (Miscellaneous Amendments) 2012 (SSI 2012/188) para.10 (effective August 1, 2012).

[9] As inserted by the Act of Sederunt (Sheriff Court Rules) (Miscellaneous Amendments) 2012 (SSI 2012/188) para.10 (effective August 1, 2012).

## Form of citation and certificate

**5.2.**—[1,2](1)  Subject to rule 5.6 (service where address of person is not known), in any cause other than—

   (a)   a family action within the meaning of rule 33.1(1),

   (aa)[3]   a civil partnership action within the meaning of rule 33A.1(1);

   (b)   an action of multiplepoinding,

   (c)   an action in which a time to pay direction under the Debtors (Scotland) Act 1987 or a time order under the Consumer Credit Act 1974 may be applied for by the defender, or

   (d)   *[Repealed by the Act of Sederunt (Sheriff Court Rules) (Enforcement of Securities over Heritable Property) 2010 (SSI 2010/324) para.2 (effective September 30, 2010).]*

citation by any person shall be in Form O4 which shall be attached to a copy of the initial writ and warrant of citation and shall have appended to it a notice of intention to defend in Form O7.

   (2)  In a cause in which a time to pay direction under the Debtors (Scotland) Act 1987 or a time order under the Consumer Credit Act 1974 may be applied for by the defender, citation shall be in Form O5 which shall be attached to a copy of the initial writ and warrant of citation and shall have appended to it a notice of intention to defend in Form O7.

   (2A)  *[Repealed by the Act of Sederunt (Sheriff Court Rules) (Enforcement of Securities over Heritable Property) 2010 (SSI 2010/324) para.2 (effective September 30, 2010).]*

   (3)  The certificate of citation in any cause other than a family action within the meaning of rule 33.1(1) or an action of multiplepoinding shall be in Form O6 which shall be attached to the initial writ.

   (4)  Where citation is by a sheriff officer, one witness shall be sufficient for the execution of citation.

   (5)  Where citation is by a sheriff officer, the certificate of citation shall be signed by the sheriff officer and the witness and shall state—

   (a)   the method of citation; and

   (b)   where the method of citation was other than personal or postal citation, the full name and designation of any person to whom the citation was delivered.

   (6)  Where citation is executed under paragraph (3) of rule 5.4 (depositing or affixing by sheriff officer), the certificate shall include a statement—

   (a)   of the method of service previously attempted;

   (b)   of the circumstances which prevented such service being executed; and

   (c)   that a copy was sent in accordance with the provisions of paragraph (4) of that rule.

---

[1] As amended by SI 1996/2445 (effective November 1, 1996) (clerical error) and further amended by the Act of Sederunt (Amendment of Ordinary Cause Rules and Summary Applications, Statutory Applications and Appeals etc. Rules) (Applications under the Mortgage Rights (Scotland) Act 2001) 2002 (SSI 2002/7), para.2(4).

[2] As amended by the Act of Sederunt (Ordinary Cause, Summary Application, Summary Cause and Small Claim Rules) Amendment (Miscellaneous) 2007 (SSI 2007/6), para.2(5) (effective January 29, 2007).

[3] As inserted by Act of Sederunt (Ordinary Cause Rules) Amendment (Family Law (Scotland) Act 2006 etc.) 2006, para.2 (SSI 2006/207) (effective May 4, 2006).

**Postal service or intimation**

**5.3.**—(1)  In any cause in which service or intimation of any document or citation of any person may be by recorded delivery, such service, intimation or citation shall be by the first class recorded delivery service.

(2)  Notwithstanding the terms of section 4(2) of the Citation Amendment (Scotland) Act 1882 (time from which period of notice reckoned), where service or intimation is by post, the period of notice shall run from the beginning of the day after the date of posting.

(3)  On the face of the envelope used for postal service or intimation under this rule there shall be written or printed the following notice:—

> "This envelope contains a citation to or intimation from (*specify the court*). If delivery cannot be made at the address shown it is to be returned immediately to:— The Sheriff Clerk (*insert address of sheriff clerk's office*)".

(4)  The certificate of citation or intimation in the case of postal service shall have attached to it any relevant postal receipts.

**Service within Scotland by sheriff officer**

**5.4.**—(1)  An initial writ, decree, charge, warrant or any other order or writ following upon such initial writ or decree served by a sheriff officer on any person shall be served—

    (a)  personally; or

    (b)  by being left in the hands of a resident at the person's dwelling place or an employee at his place of business.

(2)  Where service is executed under paragraph (1)(b), the certificate of citation or service shall contain the full name and designation of any person in whose hands the initial writ, decree, charge, warrant or other order or writ, as the case may be, was left.

(3)  Where a sheriff officer has been unsuccessful in executing service in accordance with paragraph (1), he may, after making diligent enquiries, serve the document in question—

    (a)  by depositing it in that person's dwelling place or place of business; or

    (b)[1]  by leaving it at that person's dwelling place or place of business in such a way that it is likely to come to the attention of that person.

(4)  Subject to rule 6.1 (service of schedule of arrestment), where service is executed under paragraph (3), the sheriff officer shall, as soon as possible after such service, send a letter containing a copy of the document by ordinary first class post to the address at which he thinks it most likely that the person on whom service has been executed may be found.

(5)[2]  Where the firm which employs the sheriff officer has in its possession—

    (a)  the document or a copy of it certified as correct by the pursuer's solicitor, the sheriff officer may serve the document upon the defender without having the document or certified copy in his possession, in which case he shall if required to do so by the person on whom service is executed and within a reasonable time of being so required, show the document or certified copy to the person; or

---

[1]  As substituted by the Act of Sederunt (Sheriff Court Rules) (Miscellaneous Amendments) 2011 (SSI 2011/193) r.2 (effective April 4, 2011).

[2]  As inserted by the Act of Sederunt (Ordinary Cause, Summary Application, Summary Cause and Small Claim Rules) Amendment (Miscellaneous) 2003 (SSI 2003/26), para.2(3) (effective January 24, 2003).

    (b)   a certified copy of the interlocutor pronounced allowing service of the document, the sheriff officer may serve the document without having in his possession the certified copy interlocutor if he has in his possession a facsimile copy of the certified copy interlocutor (which he shall show, if required, to the person on whom service is executed).

(6)[1]  Where service is executed under paragraphs (1)(b) or (3), the document and the citation or notice of intimation, as the case may be, must be placed in an envelope bearing the notice "This envelope contains a citation to or intimation from (*insert name of sheriff court*)"and sealed by the sheriff officer.

### Service on persons furth of Scotland

**5.5.**—[2](1)  Subject to the following provisions of this rule, an initial writ, decree, charge, warrant or any other order or writ following upon such initial writ or decree on a person furth of Scotland shall be served—

    (a)   at a known residence or place of business in England, Wales, Northern Ireland, the Isle of Man, the Channel Islands or any country with which the United Kingdom does not have a convention providing for service of writs in that country—

        (i)   in accordance with the rules for personal service under the domestic law of the place in which service is to be executed; or

        (ii)  by posting in Scotland a copy of the document in question in a registered letter addressed to the person at his residence or place of business;

    (b)[3]  in a country which is a party to the Hague Convention on the Service Abroad of Judicial and Extra-Judicial Documents in Civil and Commercial Matters dated 15th November 1965 or the Convention in Schedule 1 or 3C to the Civil Jurisdiction and Judgments Act 1982—

        (i)   by a method prescribed by the internal law of the country where service is to be executed for the service of documents in domestic actions upon persons who are within its territory;

        (ii)[4]  by or through the central, or other appropriate, authority in the country where service is to be executed at the request of the Scottish Ministers;

        (iii)  by or through a British Consular Office in the country where service is to be executed at the request of the Secretary of State for Foreign and Commonwealth Affairs;

        (iv)  where the law of the country in which the person resides permits, by posting in Scotland a copy of the document in a registered letter addressed to the person at his residence; or

        (v)  where the law of the country in which service is to be executed permits, service by an huissier, other judicial officer or competent official of the country where service is to be executed; or

---

[1] As inserted by the Act of Sederunt (Sheriff Court Rules) (Miscellaneous Amendments) 2011 (SSI 2011/193) r.2 (effective April 4, 2011).

[2] As amended by SI 1996/2445 (effective November 1, 1996) and the Act of Sederunt (Ordinary Cause, Summary Application, Summary Cause and Small Claim Rules) Amendment (Miscellaneous) 2003 (SSI 2003/26), para.2(4) (effective January 24, 2003).

[3] As amended by the Act of Sederunt (Ordinary Cause, Summary Application and Small Claim Rules) Amendment (Miscellaneous) 2004 (SSI 2004/197) (effective May 21, 2004), para.2(4).

[4] As substituted by the Act of Sederunt (Sheriff Court Rules) (Miscellaneous Amendments) 2011 (SSI 2011/193) r.6 (effective April 4, 2011).

   (c)   in a country with which the United Kingdom has a convention on the service of writs in that country other than the conventions mentioned in sub-paragraph (b), by one of the methods approved in the relevant convention.

   (d)   *[Repealed by the Act of Sederunt (Ordinary Cause, Summary Application, Summary Cause and Small Claim Rules) Amendment (Miscellaneous) 2004 (SSI 2004/197) r.24(a) (effective May 21, 2004).]*

(1A)[1, 2]   In a country to which the EC Service Regulation applies, service—

   (a)   may be effected by the methods prescribed in paragraph (1)(b)(ii) and (iii) only in exceptional circumstances; and

   (b)   is effected only if the receiving agency has informed the person that acceptance of service may be refused on the ground that the document has not been translated in accordance with paragraph (6).

(2)   Any document which requires to be posted in Scotland for the purposes of this rule shall be posted by a solicitor or a sheriff officer; and on the face of the envelope there shall be written or printed the notice set out in rule 5.3(3).

(3)   In the case of service by a method referred to in paragraph (1)(b)(ii) and (iii), the pursuer shall—

   (a)[3]   send a copy of the writ and warrant for service with citation attached, or other document, as the case may be, with a request for service by the method indicated in the request to the Scottish Ministers or, as the case may be, the Secretary of State for Foreign and Commonwealth Affairs; and

   (b)   lodge in process a certificate signed by the authority which executed service stating that it has been, and the manner in which it was, served.

(4)   In the case of service by a method referred to in paragraph (1)(b)(v), the pursuer or the sheriff officer, shall—

   (a)   send a copy of the writ and warrant for service with citation attached, or other document, as the case may be, with a request for service by the method indicated in the request to the official in the country in which service is to be executed; and

   (b)   lodge in process a certificate of the official who executed service stating that it has been, and the method in which it was, served.

(5)   Where service is executed in accordance with paragraph (1)(a)(i) or (1)(b)(i) other than on another party in the United Kingdom, the Isle of Man or the Channel Islands, the party executing service shall lodge a certificate by a person who is conversant with the law of the country concerned and who practises or has practised law in that country or is a duly accredited representative of the Government of that country, stating that the method of service employed is in accordance with the law of the place where service was executed.

(6)   Every writ, document, citation or notice on the face of the envelope mentioned in rule 5.3(3) shall be accompanied by a translation in—

---

[1] As inserted by the Act of Sederunt (Ordinary Cause, Summary Application and Small Claim Rules) Amendment (Miscellaneous) 2004 (SSI 2004/197) (effective May 21, 2004), para.2(4) and substituted by the Act of Sederunt (Sheriff Court Ordinary Cause, Summary Application, Summary Cause and Small Claims Rules) Amendment (Council Regulation (EC) No. 1348 of 2000 Extension to Denmark) 2007 (SSI 2007/440) r.2(2) (effective October 9, 2007).

[2] As substituted by the Act of Sederunt (Sheriff Court Rules) (Miscellaneous Amendments) (No.2) 2008 (SSI 2008/365) r.7 (effective November 13, 2008).

[3] As amended by the Act of Sederunt (Sheriff Court Rules) (Miscellaneous Amendments) 2011 (SSI 2011/193) r.7 (effective April 4, 2011).

(a)[1]   an official language of the country in which service is to be executed; or

(b)[2]   in a country to which the EC Service Regulation applies, a language of the member state of transmission that is understood by the person on whom service is being executed.

(7)   A translation referred to in paragraph (6) shall be certified as correct by the person making it; and the certificate shall—

(a)   include his full name, address and qualifications; and

(b)   be lodged with the execution of citation or service.

(8)[3]   In this rule "the EC Service Regulation" means Regulation (EC) No. 1393/2007 of the European Parliament and of the Council of 13th November 2007 on the service in the Member States of judicial and extrajudicial documents in civil or commercial matters (service of documents), and repealing Council Regulation (EC) No. 1348/2000, as amended from time to time.

## Service where address of person is not known

**5.6.**—(A1)[4]   Subject to rule 6.A7 this rule applies to service where the address of a person is not known.

(1)   Where the address of a person to be cited or served with a document is not known and cannot reasonably be ascertained, the sheriff shall grant warrant for citation or service upon that person—

(a)   by the publication of an advertisement in Form G3 in a specified newspaper circulating in the area of the last known address of that person, or

(b)   by displaying on the walls of court a copy of the instance and crave of the initial writ, warrant of citation and a notice in Form G4;

and the period of notice fixed by the sheriff shall run from the date of publication of the advertisement or display on the walls of court, as the case may be.

(2)   Where service requires to be executed under paragraph (1), the pursuer shall lodge a service copy of the initial writ and a copy of any warrant of citation with the sheriff clerk from whom they may be uplifted by the person for whom they are intended.

(3)   Where a person has been cited or served in accordance with paragraph (1) and, after the cause has commenced, his address becomes known, the sheriff may allow the initial writ to be amended subject to such conditions as to re-service, intimation, expenses, or transfer of the cause as he thinks fit.

(4)   Where advertisement in a newspaper is required for the purpose of citation or service under this rule, a copy of the newspaper containing the advertisement shall be lodged with the sheriff clerk by the pursuer.

(5)   Where display on the walls of court is required under paragraph (1)(b), the pursuer shall supply to the sheriff clerk for that purpose a certified copy of the instance and crave of the initial writ and any warrant of citation.

---

[1] As inserted by the Act of Sederunt (Ordinary Cause, Summary Application and Small Claim Rules) Amendment (Miscellaneous) 2004 (SSI 2004/197) (effective May 21, 2004), para.2(4) and substituted by the Act of Sederunt (Sheriff Court Ordinary Cause, Summary Application, Summary Cause and Small Claims Rules) Amendment (Council Regulation (EC) No. 1348 of 2000 Extension to Denmark) 2007 (SSI 2007/440) r.2(2) (effective October 9, 2007).

[2] As substituted by the Act of Sederunt (Sheriff Court Rules) (Miscellaneous Amendments) (No.2) 2008 (SSI 2008/365) r.7 (effective November 13, 2008).

[3] As substituted by the Act of Sederunt (Sheriff Court Rules) (Miscellaneous Amendments) (No.2) 2008 (SSI 2008/365) r.7 (effective November 13, 2008).

[4] As inserted by the Act of Sederunt (Sheriff Court Rules Amendment) (Diligence) 2008 (SSI 2008/121) r.5(3) (effective April 1, 2008).

*(unincorporated associations)*

## Persons carrying on business under trading or descriptive name

**5.7.**—[1](1)  A person carrying on a business under a trading or descriptive name may sue or be sued in such trading or descriptive name alone; and an extract—

(a)  of a decree pronounced in the sheriff court, or

(b)  of a decree proceeding upon any deed, decree arbitral, bond, protest of a bill, promissory note or banker's note or upon any other obligation or document on which execution may proceed, recorded in the sheriff court books,

against such person under such trading or descriptive name shall be a valid warrant for diligence against such person.

(2)  An initial writ, decree, charge, warrant or any other order or writ following upon such initial writ or decree in a cause in which a person carrying on business under a trading or descriptive name sues or is sued in that name may be served—

(a)  at any place of business or office at which such business is carried on within the sheriffdom of the sheriff court in which the cause is brought; or

(b)  where there is no place of business within that sheriffdom, at any place where such business is carried on (including the place of business or office of the clerk or secretary of any company, corporation or association or firm).

## Endorsation unnecessary

**5.8.**  An initial writ, decree, charge, warrant or any other order or writ following upon such initial writ or decree may be served, enforced or otherwise lawfully executed anywhere in Scotland without endorsation by a sheriff clerk; and, if executed by a sheriff officer, may be so executed by a sheriff officer of the court which granted it or by a sheriff officer of the sheriff court district in which it is to be executed.

## Re-service

**5.9.**  Where it appears to the sheriff that there has been any failure or irregularity in citation or service on a person, he may order the pursuer to re-serve the initial writ on such conditions as he thinks fit.

## No objection to regularity of citation, service or intimation

**5.10.**—(1)  A person who appears in a cause shall not be entitled to state any objection to the regularity of the execution of citation, service or intimation on him; and his appearance shall remedy any defect in such citation, service or intimation.

(2)  Nothing in paragraph (1) shall preclude a party from pleading that the court has no jurisdiction.

Chapter 6

Interim Diligence[2]

*Annotations to Chapter 6 are by Tim Edward.*

GENERAL NOTE

The procedure for obtaining warrant to arrest to found jurisdiction is dealt with at rule 3.4.

---

[1] As amended by SI 1996/2445 (effective November 1, 1996).

[2] Chapter renamed by the Act of Sederunt (Sheriff Court Rules Amendment) (Diligence) 2008 (SSI 2008/121) r.5(4) (effective April 1, 2008).

The procedure for obtaining warrant for diligence on the dependence of an action is dealt with by Rule 6.A2, and by Part 1A of the Debtors (Scotland) Act 1987 (as inserted by the Bankruptcy and Diligence etc. (Scotland) Act 2007).

The 1987 Act, as amended, provides that the court may make an order granting warrant for diligence on the dependence of an action if it is satisfied, having had a hearing on the matter, that: the creditor has a prima facie case on the merits of the action; there is a real and substantial risk that enforcement by the creditor of any decree in the action would be defeated or prejudiced by reason of the debtor being insolvent or verging on insolvency or the likelihood of the debtor removing, disposing of, burdening, concealing or otherwise dealing with all or some of his assets; and that it is reasonable in all the circumstances to do so. An application for an order granting warrant for diligence must be intimated to the debtor and any other person having an interest (unless the application is for warrant to be granted before a hearing, as described below). Before making such an order, the court must give an opportunity to be heard to (a) any person to whom intimation of the date of the hearing was made; and (b) any other person the court is satisfied has an interest.

The court may make an order granting warrant for diligence without a hearing if it is satisfied that the creditor has a prima facie case, that it is reasonable to grant such an order, and that that there is a real and substantial risk that enforcement of any decree in the action in favour of the creditor would be defeated or prejudiced (again, due to insolvency or the risk of the debtor removing or otherwise dealing with his assets) if warrant were not granted in advance of a hearing.

In both cases, the onus is on the creditor to satisfy the court that the order should be made.

The 1987 Act now specifically provides that it is competent for the court to grant warrant for arrestment or inhibition on the dependence where the sum concluded for is a future or contingent debt. At common law, there had to be special circumstances justifying diligence in respect of a future or contingent debt, such as that the debtor was at significant risk of insolvency or was contemplating flight from the jurisdiction. However such special circumstances, as set out above, now have to be demonstrated in respect of all debts. Common law cases on future and contingent debts may now be of assistance in interpreting the rules applying to all cases under the new provisions.

Rule 6 sets out the procedure for execution of such arrestments and Rule 6.A4 deals with the recall of an arrestment.

## Interpretation

**6.A1.**[1]  In this Chapter—

"the 1987 Act" means the Debtors (Scotland) Act 1987; and

"the 2002 Act" means the Debt Arrangement and Attachment (Scotland) Act 2002.

## Application for interim diligence

**6.A2.**—[2](1)  The following shall be made by motion—

(a)  an application under section 15D(1) of the 1987 Act for warrant for diligence by arrestment or inhibition on the dependence of an action or warrant for arrestment on the dependence of an admiralty action;

(b)  an application under section 9C of the 2002 Act for warrant for interim attachment.

(2)  Such an application must be accompanied by a statement in Form G4A.

(3)  A certified copy of an interlocutor granting a motion under paragraph (1) shall be sufficient authority for the execution of the diligence concerned.

## Effect of authority for inhibition on the dependence

**6.A3.**—[3](1)  Where a person has been granted authority for inhibition on the dependence of an action, a certified copy of the interlocutor granting the motion may be registered with a certificate of execution in the Register of Inhibitions and Adjudications.

---

[1]  As inserted by the Act of Sederunt (Sheriff Court Rules Amendment) (Diligence) 2008 (SSI 2008/121) r.5(5) (effective April 1, 2008).

[2]  As inserted by the Act of Sederunt (Sheriff Court Rules Amendment) (Diligence) 2008 (SSI 2008/121) r.5(5) (effective April 1, 2008).

[3]  As inserted by the Act of Sederunt (Sheriff Court Rules Amendment) (Diligence) 2008 (SSI 2008/121) r.5(5) (effective April 1, 2008).

(2)[1]  A notice of a certified copy of an interlocutor granting authority for inhibition under rule 6.A2 may be registered in the Register of Inhibitions and Adjudications; and such registration is to have the same effect as registration of a notice of inhibition under section 155(2) of the Titles to Land Consolidation (Scotland) Act 1868.

### Recall etc. of arrestment or inhibition

**6.A4.**[2](1)  An application by any person having an interest—
    (a)   to loose, restrict, vary or recall an arrestment or an interim attachment; or
    (b)   to recall, in whole or in part, or vary, an inhibition,
shall be made by motion.
    (2)   A motion under paragraph (1) shall—
    (a)   specify the name and address of each of the parties;
    (b)   where it relates to an inhibition, contain a description of the inhibition including the date of registration in the Register of Inhibitions and Adjudications.

### Incidental applications in relation to interim diligence, etc

**6.A5.**[3]  An application under Part 1A of the 1987 Act or Part 1A of the 2002 Act other than mentioned above shall be made by motion.

### Form of schedule of inhibition on the dependence

**6.A6.**  *[Revoked by the Act of Sederunt (Sheriff Court Rules Amendment) (Diligence) 2009 (SSI 2009/107) r.3 (effective April 22, 2009).]*

### Service of inhibition on the dependence where address of defender not known

**6.A7.**—[4](1)  Where the address of a defender is not known to the pursuer, an inhibition on the dependence shall be deemed to have been served on the defender if the schedule of inhibition is left with or deposited at the office of the sheriff clerk of the sheriff court district where the defender's last known address is located.

    (2)   Where service of an inhibition on the dependence is executed under paragraph (1), a copy of the schedule of inhibition shall be sent by the sheriff officer by first class post to the defender's last known address.

### Form of schedule of arrestment on the dependence[5]

**6.A8.**—(1)  An arrestment on the dependence shall be served by serving the schedule of arrestment on the arrestee in Form G4B.

    (2)   A certificate of execution shall be lodged with the sheriff clerk in Form G4C.

---

[1] As substituted by the Act of Sederunt (Sheriff Court Rules Amendment) (Diligence) 2009 (SSI 2009/107) r.3 (effective April 22, 2009).

[2] As inserted by the Act of Sederunt (Sheriff Court Rules Amendment) (Diligence) 2008 (SSI 2008/121) r.5(5) (effective April 1, 2008).

[3] As inserted by the Act of Sederunt (Sheriff Court Rules Amendment) (Diligence) 2008 (SSI 2008/121) r.5(5) (effective April 1, 2008).

[4] As inserted by the Act of Sederunt (Sheriff Court Rules Amendment) (Diligence) 2008 (SSI 2008/121) r.5(5) (effective April 1, 2008).

[5] As inserted by the Act of Sederunt (Sheriff Court Rules Amendment) (Diligence) 2009 (SSI 2009/107) r.3 (effective April 22, 2009).

## Service of schedule of arrestment

**6.1**  If a schedule of arrestment has not been personally served on an arrestee, the arrestment shall have effect only if a copy of the schedule is also sent by registered post or the first class recorded delivery service to—

(a)  the last known place of residence of the arrestee, or

(b)  if such place of residence is not known, or if the arrestee is a firm or corporation, to the arrestee's principal place of business if known, or, if not known, to any known place of business of the arrestee;

and the sheriff officer shall, on the certificate of execution, certify that this has been done and specify the address to which the copy of the schedule was sent.

"SCHEDULE OF ARRESTMENT"

What is delivered to the arrestee is the "schedule" of arrestment. This is a short copy of the warrant. The sheriff officer will then return an "execution" or report of arrestment which states that the arrestment was duly executed.

Both the schedule and the execution narrate the warrant for the arrestment, (giving its date and the designation of the parties), the arrestee, the sum or subjects arrested and the date of execution. These must conform to the warrant and craves of the initial writ (*Mactaggart v MacKillop* , 1938 S.L.T. 100).

A high degree of precision is required in the schedule. By statute, the schedule must be signed by the officer, and must contain such information as the date and time of the execution and the name, occupation and address of the witness: Citation Acts 1592 and 1693.

Erroneous or defective execution, if in the essentials, can be fatal. Misnaming the pursuer, for example, may be fatal: *Richards & Wallington (Earthmoving) Limited v Whatlings Limited* , 1982 S.L.T. 66. Here the Lord Ordinary (Maxwell) held that "(a) trivial spelling mistake, for example, might not invalidate, but … I think that a high degree of accuracy in this field is required."

The same rule applies to naming the arrestee (*Henderson's Trs* (1831) 9 S. 618) and to the description of the capacity in which the funds or subjects are due to the common debtor: *Wilson v Mackie* (1875) 3 R. 18. So too does it apply to ambiguity in the description of the funds intended to be attached: *Lattimore v Singleton, Dunn & Co.* , 1911 2 S.L.T. 360.

It has been held that misnomer of the common debtor is not fatal if there is no risk of misunderstanding: *Pollock, Whyte & Waddell v Old Park Forge Limited* (1907) 15 S.L.T. 3. Similarly, misdescription of the capacity in which the arrestee holds any sum arrested need not be fatal if there is no difficulty in identifying the sums in the hands of the arrestee: *Huber v Banks* , 1986 S.L.T. 58.

Furthermore, a defective execution to a summons can be replaced by a correct one before being produced in judgement: *Henderson v Richardson* (1848) 10 D. 1035; *Hamilton v Monkland Iron & Steel Co.* (1863) 1 M. 672.

Where an arrestment has been made on the dependence of an action and subsequently decree is granted in favour of the arresting creditor, the arrestment is automatically transformed into an arrestment in execution and no further service of a schedule of arrestment is required: *Abercrombie v Edgar and Crerar Ltd.* , 1923 S.L.T. 271. In contrast to the diligence of poinding and sale, and arrestment against earnings, an arrestment on the dependence of an action or in execution proceeds without a charge having been served on the debtor.

"…PERSONALLY SERVED…"

(i)      Where the arrestee is an individual, the schedule of arrestment need not be served personally; it may also be served at his dwelling-place: *Campbell v Watson Trustees* (1898) 25 R. 690. Rule 6.1 provides that if the latter course is taken then the arrestment shall have effect only if a copy of the schedule of arrestment is also sent by registered post or the first class recorded delivery service to the last known place of residence of the arrestee, or, if such place of residence is not known, or if the arrestee is a firm or corporation, to the arrestee's principal place of business if known, or, if not known, to any known place of business of the arrestee. Postal service alone is incompetent, except in summary cause actions: Execution of Diligence (S) Act 1926, s.2 and *Dick Bros v Thomas C Gray Ltd* , 1958 S.L.T. (Sh. Ct.) 66.

(ii)     If the arrestee is a bank, the service of the arrestment should be made at its registered office, or the schedule should be delivered to an official at head office (see Macphail, *Sheriff Court Practice*, at 11.21. He also states that in all cases, notice by way of another schedule should be served at the branch where the account of the common debtor is kept).

(iii)    Where the arrestee is a corporation, the arrestment should name the corporation, and can be delivered to the hands of an employee: *Campbell v Watson's Trustee* (1898) 25 R. 690; *Gall v Stirling Water Commissioners* (1901) 9 S.L.T. (Sh. Ct.) 13. Service on a superior officer of a company does not appear to be essential, although it is a proper precaution according to Lord Young in *Campbell v Watson's Trustees* (1898) 25 R. 690. Delivery to the registered office is certainly competent, by virtue of the Companies Act 2006 s.1139(1).

In *McIntyre v Caledonian Railway Co.* (1909), 25 Sh. Ct Rep. 529, it was held that an arrestment by handing a schedule to a servant of a corporation within one of its branch offices was effectual, and rendered unnecessary the posting of a schedule to the corporation. However, this is authority only for the proposition that service at a branch office is only good in respect of subjects held at that branch.

It should be noted that in *Corson v Macmillan* , 1927 S.L.T. (Sh. Ct.) 13 it was found that service on a director at a place that was not a place of business was bad. This tends to suggest service at the registered office is the safest option. This should also attach subjects at branch offices.

(iv)    For a firm with a social name the arrestment should name the firm and be served at the place of business in the hands of an employee. Should the firm have a descriptive name then the arrestment should be served at its place of business and personally on or at the dwelling- places of three partners, should there be as many.

(v)    Where the arrestees are trustees, the schedule should be served on such trustees as are entitled to act (*Gracie v Gracie* , 1910 S.C. 899). The schedule should also state that the arrestment is served on each as a trustee and not as an individual: *Burns v Gillies* (1906) 8 F. 460.

Where the arrestment is not executed personally, and the arrestee in justifiable ignorance of it has paid away the arrested fund, he cannot be called upon to refund the money (*Laidlaw v Smith* 1838, 16 S. 367, aff'g. 2 Rob. App. 490; *Leslie v Lady Ashburton* , 1827, 6 S. 165)

## Arrestment on dependence before service

**6.2.** *[Repealed by the Act of Sederunt (Sheriff Court Rules Amendment) (Diligence) 2008 (SSI 2008/121) r.5(6) (effective April 1, 2008).]*

RULE 6.2

Rule 6.2 dealt with arrestment on the dependence of an action before service of the initial writ. This was repealed by the Act of Sederunt (Sheriff Court Rules Amendment) (Diligence) 2008 (SSI 2008/121) r.5(6) (effective 1 April 2008) and this area is now dealt with by Section 15G of the Debtors (Scotland) Act 1987.

## Movement of arrested property

**6.3.** [Omitted by the Act of Sederunt (Sheriff Court Rules) (Miscellaneous Amendments) 2012 (SSI 2012/188) para.10 (effective August 1, 2012).]

RULE 6.3

Rule 6.3, which allowed for an application to be made for a warrant authorising the movement of a vessel or cargo which is the subject of an arrestment, was omitted by the Act of Sederunt (Sheriff Court Rules) (Miscellaneous Amendments) 2012 (SSI 2012/188) para.10 (effective 1 August 2012). Admiralty Actions are now dealt with by Rule 49 and section 47 of the Administration of Justice Act 1956.

Chapter 7

Undefended Causes

## Application of this Chapter

**7.1.** This Chapter applies to any cause other than an action in which the sheriff may not grant decree without evidence.

## • Minute for granting of decree without attendance

**7.2.**—(1)[1]  Subject to the following paragraphs, where the defender—

(a)    does not lodge a notice of intention to defend,

(b)    does not lodge an application for a time to pay direction under the Debtors (Scotland) Act 1987 or a time order under the Consumer Credit Act 1974,

(c)    has lodged such an application for a time to pay direction or time order and the pursuer does not object to the application or to any recall or restriction of an arrestment sought in the application,

---

[1] As amended by the Act of Sederunt (Ordinary Cause, Summary Application, Summary Cause and Small Claim Rules) Amendment (Miscellaneous) 2007 (SSI 2007/6) r.2(6) (effective January 29, 2007).

the sheriff may, on the pursuer endorsing a minute for decree on the initial writ, at any time after the expiry of the period for lodging that notice or application, grant decree in absence or other order in terms of the minute so endorsed without requiring the attendance of the pursuer in court.

(2) The sheriff shall not grant decree under paragraph (1)—

    (a) unless it appears ex facie of the initial writ that a ground of jurisdiction exists under the Civil Jurisdiction and Judgments Act 1982; and

    (b) the cause is not a cause—

        (i) in which decree may not be granted without evidence;

        (ii) to which paragraph (4) applies; or

        (iii)[1] to which rule 33.31 (procedure in undefended family action for a section 11 order) applies.

(3) Where a defender is domiciled in another part of the United Kingdom or in another Contracting State, the sheriff shall not grant decree in absence until it has been shown that the defender has been able to receive the initial writ in sufficient time to arrange for his defence or that all necessary steps have been taken to that end; and for the purposes of this paragraph—

    (a) the question whether a person is domiciled in another part of the United Kingdom shall be determined in accordance with sections 41 and 42 of the Civil Jurisdiction and Judgments Act 1982;

    (b) the question whether a person is domiciled in another Contracting State shall be determined in accordance with Article 52 of the Convention in Schedule 1 or 3C to that Act; and

    (c) the term "Contracting State" has the meaning assigned in section 1 of that Act.

(4) Where an initial writ has been served in a country to which the Hague Convention on the Service Abroad of Judicial and Extra-Judicial Documents in Civil or Commercial Matters dated 15th November 1965 applies, decree shall not be granted until it is established to the satisfaction of the sheriff that the requirements of Article 15 of that Convention have been complied with.

### Applications for time to pay directions or time orders in undefended causes

7.3.—(1) This rule applies to a cause in which—

    (a)[2] a time to pay direction may be applied for under the Debtors (Scotland) Act 1987; or

    (b) a time order may be applied for under the Consumer Credit Act 1974.

(2) A defender in a cause which is otherwise undefended, who wishes to apply for a time to pay direction or time order, and where appropriate, to have an arrestment recalled or restricted, shall complete and lodge with the sheriff clerk the appropriate part of Form O3 before the expiry of the period of notice.

(2A)[3] As soon as possible after the application of the defender is lodged, the sheriff clerk shall send a copy of it to the pursuer by first class ordinary post.

(3) Where the pursuer does not object to the application of the defender made in accordance with paragraph (2), he shall minute for decree in accordance with rule

---

[1] As amended by SI 1996/2167 (effective November 1, 1996) and SI 1996/2445 (effective November 1, 1996).

[2] As amended by the Act of Sederunt (Ordinary Cause, Summary Application, Summary Cause and Small Claim Rules) Amendment (Miscellaneous) 2007 (SSI 2007/6) r.2(7) (effective January 29, 2007).

[3] As inserted by the Act of Sederunt (Sheriff Court Rules) (Miscellaneous Amendments) 2009 (SSI 2009/294) r.2 (effective December 1, 2009).

7.2; and the sheriff may grant decree or other order in terms of the application and minute.

(4)[1]  Where the pursuer objects to the application of the defender made in accordance with paragraph (2) he shall on the same date—

(a)   complete and lodge with the sheriff clerk Form O3A;

(b)   minute for decree in accordance with rule 7.2; and

(c)   send a copy of Form O3A to the defender.

(4A)[2]  The sheriff clerk shall then fix a hearing on the application of the defender and intimate the hearing to the pursuer and the defender.

(4B)[3]  The hearing must be fixed for a date within 28 days of the date on which the Form O3A and the minute for decree are lodged.

(5)   The sheriff may determine an application in which a hearing has been fixed under paragraph (4) whether or not any of the parties appear.

## Decree for expenses

**7.4.**   On granting decree in absence or thereafter, the sheriff may grant decree for expenses.

## Finality of decree in absence

**7.5.**[4]  Subject to section 9(7) of the Land Tenure Reform (Scotland) Act 1974 (decree in action of removing for breach of condition of long lease to be final when extract recorded in Register of Sasines), a decree in absence which has not been recalled or brought under review by suspension or by reduction shall become final and shall have effect as a decree *in foro contentioso*—

(a)   on the expiry of six months from the date of the decree or from the date of a charge made under it, as the case may be, where the service of the initial writ or of the charge has been personal; and

(b)   in any event, on the expiry of 20 years from the date of the decree.

## Amendment of initial writ

**7.6.**—(1)   In an undefended cause, the sheriff may—

(a)   allow the pursuer to amend the initial writ in any way permitted by rule 18.2 (powers of sheriff to allow amendment); and

(b)   order the amended initial writ to be re-served on the defender on such period of notice as he thinks fit.

(2)   The defender shall not be liable for the expense occasioned by any such amendment unless the sheriff so orders.

(3)   Where an amendment has been allowed under paragraph (1), the amendment—

(a)   shall not validate diligence used on the dependence of a cause so as to prejudice the rights of creditors of the party against whom the diligence has been executed who are interested in defeating such diligence; and

(b)   shall preclude any objection to such diligence stated by a party or any

---

[1] Para.(4) substituted for paras (4)–(4B) by the Act of Sederunt (Sheriff Court Rules) (Miscellaneous Amendments) 2009 (SSI 2009/294) r.2 (effective December 1, 2009).

[2] Para.(4) substituted for paras (4)–(4B) by the Act of Sederunt (Sheriff Court Rules) (Miscellaneous Amendments) 2009 (SSI 2009/294) r.2 (effective December 1, 2009).

[3] Para.(4) substituted for paras (4)–(4B) by the Act of Sederunt (Sheriff Court Rules) (Miscellaneous Amendments) 2009 (SSI 2009/294) r.2 (effective December 1, 2009).

[4] As amended by SI 1996/2445 (effective November 1, 1996).

person by virtue of a title acquired or in right of a debt contracted by him subsequent to the execution of such diligence.

## Disapplication of certain rules

**7.7**[1]  The following rules in Chapter 15 (motions) shall not apply to an action in which no notice of intention to defend has been lodged or to any action in so far as it proceeds as undefended—

rule 15.2 (intimation of motions),

rule 15.3 (opposition to motions),

rule 15.5 (hearing of motions).

Chapter 8

Reponing

## Reponing

**8.1.**—(1)  In any cause other than—

   (a)[2]  a cause mentioned in rule 33.1(a) to (h) or (n) to (p), (certain family actions), or

  (aa)[3]  a cause mentioned in rule 33A.1(a), (b) or (f) (certain civil partnership actions);

   (b)  a cause to which Chapter 37 (causes under the Presumption of Death (Scotland) Act 1977) applies,

the defender or any party with a statutory title or interest may apply to be reponed by lodging with the sheriff clerk, before implement in full of a decree in absence, a reponing note setting out his proposed defence or the proposed order or direction and explaining his failure to appear.

(2)  A copy of the note lodged under paragraph (1) shall be served on the pursuer and any other party—

(3)  The sheriff may, on considering the reponing note, recall the decree so far as not implemented subject to such order as to expenses as he thinks fit; and the cause shall thereafter proceed as if—

   (a)  the defender had lodged a notice of intention to defend and the period of notice had expired on the date on which the decree in absence was recalled; or

  (b)[4]  the party seeking the order or direction had lodged the appropriate application on the date when the decree was recalled.

(4)  A reponing note, when duly lodged with the sheriff clerk and served upon the pursuer, shall have effect to sist diligence.

(4A)[5]  Where an initial writ has been served on a defender furth of the United Kingdom under rule 5.5(1)(b) (service on persons furth of Scotland) and decree in absence has been pronounced against him as a result of his failure to enter appearance, the court may, on the defender applying to be reponed in accordance with paragraph (1) above, recall the decree and allow defences to be received if—

---

[1] Inserted by SI 1996/2445 (effective November 1, 1996).

[2] As amended by Act of Sederunt (Ordinary Cause Rules) Amendment (Family Law (Scotland) Act 2006 etc.) 2006 (SSI 2006/207) r.2 (effective May 4, 2006) and by the Act of Sederunt (Sheriff Court Rules) (Miscellaneous Amendments) (No.2) 2010 (SSI 2010/416) r.8 (effective January 1, 2011).

[3] Inserted by Act of Sederunt (Ordinary Cause Rules) Amendment (Family Law (Scotland) Act 2006 etc.) 2006 (SSI 2006/207) r.2 (effective May 4, 2006).

[4] Inserted by the Act of Sederunt (Ordinary Cause, Summary Application and Small Claim Rules) Amendment (Miscellaneous) 2004 (SSI 2004/197) r.2(5) (effective May 21, 2004).

[5] Inserted by SSI 2000/239 (effective October 2, 2000).

(a) without fault on his part, he did not have knowledge of the initial writ in sufficient time to defend;

(b) he has disclosed a prima facie defence to the action on the merits; and

(c) the reponing note is lodged within a reasonable time after he had knowledge of the decree or in any event before the expiry of one year from the date of decree.

(5) Any interlocutor or order recalling, or incidental to the recall of, a decree in absence shall be final and not subject to appeal.

## Chapter 9

| Standard Procedure in Defended Causes |

### Notice of intention to defend

**9.1.**—(1)[1,2] Subject to rules 33.34 (notice of intention to defend and defences in family action)33A.34 (notice of intention to defend and defences in civil partnership action) and 35.8 (lodging of notice of appearance in action of multiplepoinding), where the defender intends to—

(a) challenge the jurisdiction of the court,

(b) state a defence, or

(c) make a counterclaim,

he shall, before the expiry of the period of notice, lodge with the sheriff clerk a notice of intention to defend in Form O7 and, at the same time, send a copy to the pursuer.

(2) The lodging of a notice of intention to defend shall not imply acceptance of the jurisdiction of the court.

(3)[3] This Chapter shall not apply to a commercial action within the meaning of Chapter 40.

### Fixing date for Options Hearing

**9.2.**—(1)[4] Subject to paragraph (1A), on the lodging of a notice of intention to defend, the sheriff clerk shall fix a date and time for an Options Hearing which date shall be on the first suitable court day occurring not sooner than 10 weeks after the expiry of the period of notice.

(1A)[5,6] Where in a family action or a civil partnership action—

(i) the only matters in dispute are an order in terms of section 11 of the Children (Scotland) Act 1995 (court orders relating to parental responsibilities etc.); or

(ii) the matters in dispute include an order in terms of section 11 of that Act,

---

[1] As amended by the Act of Sederunt (Family Proceedings in the Sheriff Court) 1996 (SI 1996/2167) (effective November 1, 2000).

[2] As amended by Act of Sederunt (Ordinary Cause Rules) Amendment (Family Law (Scotland) Act 2006 etc.) 2006 (SSI 2006/207) r.2 (effective May 4, 2006).

[3] Inserted by the Act of Sederunt (Ordinary Cause Rules) Amendment (Commercial Actions) 2001 (SSI 2001/8) (effective March 1, 2001).

[4] As amended by the Act of Sederunt (Sheriff Court Ordinary Cause Rules Amendment) (Miscellaneous) 2000 (SSI 2000/239) (effective October 2, 2000).

[5] Added by the Act of Sederunt (Sheriff Court Ordinary Cause Rules Amendment) (Miscellaneous) 2000 (SSI 2000/239) (effective October 2, 2000).

[6] As amended by Act of Sederunt (Ordinary Cause Rules) Amendment (Family Law (Scotland) Act 2006 etc.) 2006 (SSI 2006/207) (effective May 4, 2006).

there shall be no requirement to fix an Options Hearing in terms of paragraph (1) above insofar as the matters in dispute relate to an order in terms of section 11(2) of the Children (Scotland) Act 1995.

(1B)[1]  In paragraph (1A) above—

    (a)  "family action" has the meaning given in rule 33.1(1); and

    (b)  "civil partnership action" has the meaning given in rule 33A.1(1).

(2)  On fixing the date for the Options Hearing, the sheriff clerk shall—

    (a)  forthwith intimate to the parties in Form G5—

        (i)  the last date for lodging defences;

        (ii)  the last date for adjustment; and

        (iii)  the date of the Options hearing; and

    (b)  prepare and sign an interlocutor recording those dates.

(3)[2]  The fixing of the date for the Options Hearing shall not affect the right of a party to make any incidental application to the court.

## Alteration of date for Options Hearing

**9.2A.**—[3](1)  Subject to paragraph (2), at any time before the date and time fixed under rule 9.2 (fixing date for Options Hearing) or under this rule, the sheriff—

    (a)  may, of his own motion or on the motion of any party—

        (i)  discharge the Options Hearing; and

        (ii)  fix a new date and time for the Options Hearing; or

    (b)  shall, on the joint motion of the parties—

        (i)  discharge the Options Hearing; and

        (ii)  fix a new date and time for the Options Hearing.

(2)  The date and time to be fixed—

    (a)  under paragraph (1)(a)(ii) may be earlier or later than the date and time fixed for the discharged Options Hearing;

    (b)  under paragraph (1)(b)(ii) shall be earlier than the date and time fixed for the discharged Options Hearing.

(3)  Where the sheriff is considering making an order under paragraph (1)(a) of his own motion and in the absence of the parties, the sheriff clerk shall—

    (a)  fix a date, time and place for the parties to be heard; and

    (b)  inform the parties of that date, time and place.

(4)  The sheriff may discharge a hearing fixed under paragraph (3) on the joint motion of the parties.

(5)  On the discharge of the Options Hearing under paragraph (1), the sheriff clerk shall forthwith intimate to all parties—

    (a)  that the Options Hearing has been discharged under paragraph (1)(a) or (b), as the case may be;

    (b)  the last date for lodging defences, if appropriate;

    (c)  the last date for adjustment, if appropriate; and

---

[1] Inserted by Act of Sederunt (Ordinary Cause Rules) Amendment (Family Law (Scotland) Act 2006 etc.) 2006 (SSI 2006/207) (effective May 4, 2006).

[2] As amended by the Act of Sederunt (Sheriff Court Ordinary Cause Rules Amendment) (Miscellaneous) 1996 (SI 1996/2445) (effective November 1, 1996).

[3] Inserted by the Act of Sederunt (Sheriff Court Ordinary Cause Rules Amendment) (Miscellaneous) 1996 (SI 1996/2445) (effective November 1, 1996) and substituted by the Act of Sederunt (Ordinary Cause and Summary Application Rules) Amendment (Miscellaneous) 2006 (SI 2006/410) (effective August 18, 2006).

(d)   the new date and time fixed for the Options Hearing under paragraph (1)(a) or (b), as the case may be.

(6)   Any reference in these Rules to the Options Hearing or a continuation of it shall include a reference to an Options Hearing for which a date and time has been fixed under this rule.

### Return of initial writ

**9.3.**   Subject to rule 9.4 (lodging of pleadings before Options Hearing), the pursuer shall return the initial writ, unbacked and unfolded, to the sheriff clerk within 7 days after the expiry of the period of notice.

### Lodging of pleadings before Options Hearing

**9.4.**   Where any hearing, whether by motion or otherwise, is fixed before the Options Hearing, each party shall lodge in process a copy of his pleadings, or, where the pleadings have been adjusted, the pleadings as adjusted, not later than 2 days before the hearing.

### Process folder

**9.5.**—(1)   On receipt of the notice of intention to defend, the sheriff clerk shall prepare a process folder which shall include—

(a)   interlocutor sheets;
(b)   duplicate interlocutor sheets;
(c)   a production file;
(d)   a motion file; and
(e)   an inventory of process.

(2)   Any production or part of process lodged in a cause shall be placed in the process folder.

### Defences

**9.6.**—(1)   Where a notice of intention to defend has been lodged, the defender shall (subject to paragraph (3)) lodge defences within 14 days after the expiry of the period of notice.

(2)   Subject to rule 19.1(3) (form of defences where counterclaim included), defences shall be in the form of answers in numbered paragraphs corresponding to the articles of the condescendence, and shall have appended a note of the pleas-in-law of the defender.

(3)[2]   In a family action (within the meaning of rule 33.1(1)) or a civil partnership action (within the meaning of rule 33A.1(1)), neither a crave nor averments need be made in the defences which relate to any order under section 11 of the Children (Scotland) Act 1995.

### Implied admissions

**9.7.**   Every statement of fact made by a party shall be answered by every other party, and if such a statement by one party within the knowledge of another party is not denied by that other party, that other party shall be deemed to have admitted that statement of fact.

---

[1]   Inserted by the Act of Sederunt (Family Proceedings in the Sheriff Court) 1996 (SI 1996/ 2167) (effective November 1, 2000).

[2]   As amended by Act of Sederunt (Ordinary Cause Rules) Amendment (Family Law (Scotland) Act 2006 etc.) 2006 (SSI 2006/207) (effective May 4, 2006).

**Adjustment of pleadings**

9.8.—(1)  Parties may adjust their pleadings until 14 days before the date of the Options Hearing or any continuation of it.

(2)  Any adjustments shall be exchanged between parties and not lodged in process.

(3)  Parties shall be responsible for maintaining a record of adjustments made during the period for adjustment.

(4)  No adjustments shall be permitted after the period mentioned in paragraph (1) except with leave of the sheriff.

**Effect of sist on adjustment**

9.9.—(1)  Where a cause has been sisted, any period for adjustment before the sist shall be reckoned as a part of the period for adjustment.

(2)  On recall of the sist of a cause, the sheriff clerk shall—

    (a)  fix a new date for the Options Hearing;

    (b)  prepare and sign an interlocutor recording that date; and

    (c)  intimate that date to each party.

**Open record**

9.10.  The sheriff may, at any time before the closing of the record in a cause to which this Chapter applies, of his own motion or on the motion of a party, order any party to lodge a copy of the pleadings in the form of an open record containing any adjustments and amendments made as at the date of the order.

**Record for Options Hearing**

9.11.—(1)  The pursuer shall, at the end of the period for adjustment referred to in rule 9.8(1), and before the Options Hearing, make a copy of the pleadings and any adjustments and amendments in the form of a record.

(2)  Not later than 2 days before the Options Hearing, the pursuer shall lodge a certified copy of the record in process.

(3)[1]  Where the Options Hearing is continued under rule 9.12(5), and further adjustment or amendment is made to the pleadings, a copy of the pleadings as adjusted or amended, certified by the pursuer, shall be lodged in process not later than 2 days before the Options Hearing so continued.

**Options Hearing**

9.12.—(1)  At the Options Hearing the sheriff shall seek to secure the expeditious progress of the cause by ascertaining from parties the matters in dispute and information about any other matter referred to in paragraph (3).

(2)  It shall be the duty of parties to provide the sheriff with sufficient information to enable him to conduct the hearing as provided for in this rule.

(3)  At the Options Hearing the sheriff shall, except where the cause is ordered to proceed under the procedure in Chapter 10 (additional procedure), close the record and—

    (a)  appoint the cause to a proof and make such orders as to the extent of proof, the lodging of a joint minute of admissions or agreement, or such other matter as he thinks fit;

    (b)  after having heard parties and considered any note lodged under rule 22.1

---

[1] Inserted by SI 1996/2445 (effective November 1, 1996).

(note of basis of preliminary plea), appoint the cause to a proof before answer and make such orders as to the extent of proof, the lodging of a joint minute of admissions or agreement, or such other matter as he thinks fit; or

(c)[1] after having heard parties and considered any note lodged under rule 22.1, appoint the cause to debate if satisfied that there is a preliminary matter of law which if established following debate would lead to decree in favour of any party, or to limitation of proof to any substantial degree.

(d)[2] consider any child witness notice or vulnerable witness application that has been lodged where no order has been made, or

(e)[3] ascertain whether there is or is likely to be a vulnerable witness within the meaning of section 11(1) of the Act of 2004 who is to give evidence at any proof or hearing and whether any order under section 12(1) of the Act of 2004 requires to be made.

(f)[4] where the cause has been appointed to proof or proof before answer and Chapter 33AA applies, assign a case management hearing.

(4) At the Options Hearing the sheriff may, having heard parties—

(a) of his own motion or on the motion of any party, and

(b) on being satisfied that the difficulty or complexity of the cause makes it unsuitable for the procedure under this Chapter,

order that the cause proceed under the procedure in Chapter 10 (additional procedure).

(5) The sheriff may, on cause shown, of his own motion or on the motion of any party, allow a continuation of the Options Hearing on one occasion only for a period not exceeding 28 days or to the first suitable court day thereafter.

(6) On closing the record—

(a) where there are no adjustments made since the lodging of the record under rule 9.11(2), that record shall become the closed record; and

(b) where there are such adjustments, the sheriff may order that a closed record including such adjustments be lodged within 7 days after the date of the interlocutor closing the record.

(7)[5] For the purposes of rules 16.2 (decrees where party in default), 33.37 (decree by default in family action) and 33A.37 (decree by default in civil partnership action), an Options Hearing shall be a diet in accordance with those rules.

(8)[6] Where the cause is appointed, under paragraph (3), to a proof or proof before answer, the sheriff shall consider whether a pre-proof hearing should be fixed under rule 28A.1.

---

[1] As amended by the Act of Sederunt (Ordinary Cause, Summary Application and Small Claim Rules) Amendment (Miscellaneous) 2004 (SSI 2004/197) (effective May 21, 2004).

[2] As inserted by the Act of Sederunt (Ordinary Cause, Summary Application, Summary Cause and Small Claim Rules) Amendment (Vulnerable Witnesses (Scotland) Act 2004) 2007 (SSI 2007/463) r.2(3) (effective November 1, 2007).

[3] As inserted by the Act of Sederunt (Ordinary Cause, Summary Application, Summary Cause and Small Claim Rules) Amendment (Vulnerable Witnesses (Scotland) Act 2004) 2007 (SSI 2007/463) r.2(3) (effective November 1, 2007).

[4] As inserted by the Act of Sederunt (Sheriff Court Rules)(Miscellaneous Amendments) (No.2) 2013 (SI 2013/139) para.2 (effective June 3, 2013).

[5] As amended by Act of Sederunt (Ordinary Cause Rules) Amendment (Family Law (Scotland) Act 2006 etc.) 2006 (SSI 2006/207) (effective May 4, 2006).

[6] Inserted by the Act of Sederunt (Ordinary Cause and Summary Application Rules) Amendment (Miscellaneous) 2006 (SSI 2006/410) (effective August 18, 2006).

(9)[1]  Paragraph (8) does not apply where Chapter 33AA applies.

**9.13.–9.15.**  *[Omitted by the Act of Sederunt (Ordinary Cause, Summary Application and Small Claim Rules) Amendment (Miscellaneous) 2004 (SSI 2004/197) (effective May 21, 2004), r.2(7).]*

Chapter 9A[2]

Documents and Witnesses

**Application of this Chapter**

**9A.1.**  This Chapter applies to any cause proceeding under Chapters 9 and 10.

**Inspection and recovery of documents**

**9A.2.**—(1)  Each party shall, within 14 days after the date of the interlocutor allowing proof or proof before answer, intimate to every other party a list of the documents, which are or have been in his possession or control and which he intends to use or put in evidence at the proof, including the whereabouts of those documents.

(2)  A party who has received a list of documents from another party under paragraph (1) may inspect those documents which are in the possession or control of the party intimating the list at a time and place fixed by that party which is reasonable to both parties.

(3)  A party who seeks to use or put in evidence at a proof a document not on his list intimated under paragraph (1) shall, if any other party objects to such document being used or put in evidence, seek leave of the sheriff to do so; and such leave may be granted on such conditions, if any, as the sheriff thinks fit.

(4)  Nothing in this rule shall affect—

   (a)  the law relating, or the right of a party to object, to the inspection of a document on the ground of privilege or confidentiality; or

   (b)  the right of a party to apply under rule 28.2 for a commission and diligence for recovery of documents or an order under section 1 of the Administration of Justice (Scotland) Act 1972.

**Exchange of lists of witnesses**

**9A.3.**—(1)  Within 28 days after the date of the interlocutor allowing a proof or proof before answer, each party shall—

   (a)  intimate to every other party a list of witnesses, including any skilled witnesses, on whose evidence he intends to rely at proof; and

   (b)  lodge a copy of that list in process.

(2)  A party who seeks to rely on the evidence of a person not on his list intimated under paragraph (1) shall, if any other party objects to such evidence being admitted, seek leave of the sheriff to admit that evidence whether it is to be given orally or not; and such leave may be granted on such conditions, if any, as the sheriff thinks fit.

---

[1] As inserted by the Act of Sederunt (Sheriff Court Rules)(Miscellaneous Amendments) (No.2) 2013 (SI 2013/139) para.2 (effective June 3, 2013).

[2] Inserted by the Act of Sederunt (Ordinary Cause, Summary Application and Small Claim Rules) Amendment (Miscellaneous) 2004 (SSI 2004/197) (effective May 21, 2004) and substituted by the Act of Sederunt (Ordinary Cause, Summary Application, Summary Cause and Small Claim Rules) Amendment (Miscellaneous) 2007 (SSI 2007/6) (effective January 29, 2007).

(3)[1]   The list of witnesses intimated under paragraph (1) shall include the name, occupation (where known) and address of each intended witness and indicate whether the witness is considered to be a vulnerable witness within the meaning of section 11(1) of the Act of 2004 and whether any child witness notice or vulnerable witness application has been lodged in respect of that witness.

### Applications in respect of time to pay directions, arrestments and time orders

**9A.4.**   An application for—

(a)   a time to pay direction under section 1(1) of the Debtors (Scotland) Act 1987;

(b)   the recall or restriction of an arrestment under section 2(3) or 3(1) of that Act; or

(c)   a time order under section 129 of the Consumer Credit Act 1974,

in a cause which is defended, shall be made by motion lodged before the sheriff grants decree.

### Chapter 10

### Additional Procedure

### Additional period for adjustment

**10.1.**—(1)   Where, under rule 9.12(4) (order at Options Hearing to proceed under Chapter 10), the sheriff orders that a cause shall proceed in accordance with the procedure in this Chapter, he shall continue the cause for adjustment for a period of 8 weeks.

(2)   Paragraphs (2) and (3) of rule 9.8 (exchange and record of adjustments) shall apply to a cause in which a period for adjustment under paragraph (1) of this rule has been allowed as they apply to the period for adjustment under that rule.

### Effect of sist on adjustment period

**10.2.**   Where a cause has been sisted, any period for adjustment before the sist shall be reckoned as part of the period for adjustment.

### Variation of adjustment period

**10.3.**—(1)   At any time before the expiry of the period for adjustment the sheriff may close the record if parties, of consent or jointly, lodge a motion seeking such an order.

(2)   The sheriff may, if satisfied that there is sufficient reason for doing so, extend the period for adjustment for such period as he thinks fit, if any party—

(a)   lodges a motion seeking such an order; and

(b)   lodges a copy of the record adjusted to the date of lodging of the motion.

(3)   A motion lodged under paragraph (2) shall set out—

(a)   the reasons for seeking an extension of the period for adjustment; and

(b)   the period for adjustment sought.

### Order for open record

**10.4.**   The sheriff may, at any time before the closing of the record in a cause to which this of his own motion or on the motion of a party, order any party to lodge a

---

[1] As amended by the Act of Sederunt (Ordinary Cause, Summary Application, Summary Cause and Small Claim Rules) Amendment (Vulnerable Witnesses (Scotland) Act 2004) 2007 (SSI 2007/463) r.2(4) (effective November 1, 2007).

copy of the pleadings in the form of an open record containing any adjustments and amendments made as at the date of the order.

## Closing record

**10.5.**—(1)  On the expiry of the period for adjustment, the record shall be closed and, without the attendance of parties, the sheriff clerk shall forthwith—

    (a)  prepare and sign an interlocutor recording the closing of the record and fixing the date of the Procedural Hearing under rule 10.6, which date shall be on the first suitable court day occurring not sooner than 21 days after the closing of the record; and

    (b)  intimate the date of the hearing to each party.

(2)  The pursuer shall, within 14 days after the date of the interlocutor closing the record, lodge a certified copy of the closed record in process.

(3)  The closed record shall contain only the pleadings of the parties.

## Procedural Hearing

**10.6.**—(1)  At the Procedural Hearing, the sheriff shall seek to secure the expeditious progress of the cause by ascertaining from parties the matters in dispute and information about any other matter referred to in paragraph (3).

(2)  It shall be the duty of parties to provide the sheriff with sufficient information to enable him to conduct the hearing as provided for in this rule.

(3)  At the Procedural Hearing the sheriff shall—

    (a)  appoint the cause to a proof and make such orders as to the extent of proof, the lodging of a joint minute of admissions or agreement, or such other matter as he thinks fit;

    (b)  after having heard the parties and considered any note lodged under rule 22.1 (note of basis of preliminary plea), appoint the cause to a proof before answer and make such orders as to the extent of proof, the lodging of a joint minute of admissions or agreement, or such other matter as he thinks fit; or

    (c)[1]  after having heard parties and considered any note lodged under rule 22.1, appoint the cause to a debate if satisfied that there is a preliminary matter of law which if established following debate would lead to decree in favour of any party, or to limitation of proof to any substantial degree.

    (d)[2]  consider any child witness notice or vulnerable witness application that has been lodged where no order has been made, or

    (e)[3]  ascertain whether there is or is likely to be a vulnerable witness within the meaning of section 11(1) of the Act of 2004 who is to give evidence at any proof or hearing and whether any order under section 12(1) of the Act of 2004 requires to be made.

    (f)[4]  where the cause has been appointed to proof or proof before answer and Chapter 33AAapplies, assign a case management hearing.

---

[1]  As amended by the Act of Sederunt (Ordinary Cause, Summary Application and Small Claim Rules) Amendment (Miscellaneous) 2004 (SSI 2004/197) r.2(9) (effective May 21, 2004).

[2]  As inserted by the Act of Sederunt (Ordinary Cause, Summary Application, Summary Cause and Small Claim Rules) Amendment (Vulnerable Witnesses (Scotland) Act 2004) 2007 (SSI 2007/463) r.2(5) (effective November 1, 2007).

[3]  As inserted by the Act of Sederunt (Ordinary Cause, Summary Application, Summary Cause and Small Claim Rules) Amendment (Vulnerable Witnesses (Scotland) Act 2004) 2007 (SSI 2007/463) r.2(5) (effective November 1, 2007).

[4]  As inserted by the Act of Sederunt (Sheriff Court Rules) (Miscellaneous Amendments) (No.2) 2013 (SSI 2013/139) para.2 (effective June 3, 2013).

(4)[1]   For the purposes of rules 16.2 (decrees where party in default), 33.37 (decree by default in family action) and 33A.37 (decree by default in civil partnership action), a Procedural Hearing shall be a diet in accordance with those rules.

(5)[2]   Where the cause is appointed, under paragraph (3), to a proof or proof before answer, the sheriff shall consider whether a pre-proof hearing should be fixed under rule 28A.1.

(6)[3]   Paragraph (5) does not apply where Chapter 33AA applies.

Chapter 11

The Process

## Form and lodging of parts of process

**11.1.**   All parts of process shall be written, typed or printed on A4 size paper of durable quality and shall be lodged, unbacked and unfolded, with the sheriff clerk.

## Custody of process

**11.2.**—(1)   The initial writ, and all other parts of process lodged in a cause, shall be placed by the sheriff clerk in the process folder.

(2)   The initial writ, interlocutor sheets, borrowing receipts and the process folder shall remain in the custody of the sheriff clerk.

(3)   The sheriff clerk may, on cause shown, authorise the initial writ to be borrowed by the pursuer, his solicitor or the solicitor's authorised clerk.

## Borrowing and returning of process

**11.3.**—(1)   Subject to paragraph (3), a process, or any part of a process which may be borrowed, may be borrowed only by a solicitor or by his authorised clerk.

(2)   All remedies competent to enforce the return of a borrowed process may proceed on the warrant of the court from the custody of which the process was obtained.

(3)   A party litigant—

   (a)   may borrow a process only—

      (i)   with leave of the sheriff; and

      (ii)   subject to such conditions as the sheriff may impose; or

   (b)   may inspect a process and obtain copies, where practicable, from the sheriff clerk.

(4)   The sheriff may, on the motion of any party, ordain any other party who has borrowed a part of process to return it within such time as the sheriff thinks fit.

## Failure to return parts of process

**11.4.**—(1)   Where a solicitor or party litigant has borrowed any part of process and fails to return it for any diet or hearing at which it is required, the sheriff may impose on such solicitor or party litigant a fine not exceeding £50, which shall be payable to the sheriff clerk; but an order imposing a fine may, on cause shown, be recalled by the sheriff.

(2)   An order made under this rule shall not be subject to appeal.

---

[1] As amended by the Act of Sederunt (Ordinary Cause and Summary Application Rules) Amendment (Miscellaneous) 2006 (SSI 2006/410) (effective August 18, 2006).

[2] Inserted by the Act of Sederunt (Ordinary Cause and Summary Application Rules) Amendment (Miscellaneous) 2006 (SSI 2006/410) (effective August 18, 2006).

[3] As inserted by the Act of Sederunt (Sheriff Court Rules) (Miscellaneous Amendments) (No.2) 2013 (SSI 2013/139) para.2 (effective June 3, 2013).

## Replacement of lost documents

**11.5.** Where any part of process is lost or destroyed, a copy of it, authenticated in such manner as the sheriff thinks fit, may be substituted for and shall, for the purposes of the cause to which the process relates, be treated as having the same force and effect as the original.

## Intimation of parts of process and adjustments

**11.6.**—[1](1) After a notice of intention to defend has been lodged, any party lodging a part of process or making an adjustment to his pleadings shall, at the same time, intimate such lodging or adjustment to every other party who has entered the process by delivering to every other party a copy of each part of process or adjustment, including, where practicable, copies of any documentary production.

(2) Unless otherwise provided in these Rules, the party required to give intimation under paragraph (1) shall deliver to every other party who has entered the process a copy of the part of process or adjustment or other document, as the case may be, by—

    (a)   any of the methods of service provided for in Chapter 5 (citation, service and intimation); or

    (b)   where intimation is to a party represented by a solicitor—

        (i)   personal delivery,

        (ii)   facsimile transmission,

        (iii)   first class ordinary post,

        (iv)   delivery to a document exchange,

    to that solicitor.

(3) Subject to paragraph (4), where intimation is given under—

    (a)   paragraph (2)(b)(i) or (ii), it shall be deemed to have been given—

        (i)   on the day of transmission or delivery where it is given before 5.00 p.m. on any day; or

        (ii)   on the day after transmission or delivery where it is given after 5.00 p.m. on any day; or

    (b)   paragraph (2)(b)(iii) or (iv), it shall be deemed to have been given on the day after posting or delivery.

(4) Where intimation is given or, but for this paragraph, would be deemed to be given on a Saturday, Sunday or public or court holiday, it shall be deemed to have been given on the next day on which the sheriff clerk's office is open for civil court business.

## Retention and disposal of parts of process by sheriff clerk

**11.7.**[2](1) Where any cause has been finally determined and the period for making an appeal has expired without an appeal having been made, the sheriff clerk shall—

    (a)   retain—

        (i)   the initial writ;

        (ii)   any closed record;

        (iii)   the interlocutor sheets;

        (iv)   any joint minute;

---

[1] As amended by SI 1996/2445 (effective November 1, 1996).

[2] As amended by the Act of Sederunt (Rules of the Court of Session, Sheriff Appeal Court Rules and Sheriff Court Rules Amendment) (Sheriff Appeal Court) 2015 (SSI 2015/419) r.5 (effective 1 January 2016).

(v)   any offer and acceptance of tender;

(vi)   any report from a person of skill;

(vii)   any affidavit; and

(viii)   any extended shorthand notes of the proof; and

(b)   dispose of all other parts of process (except productions) in such a manner as seems appropriate.

(2)   Where an appeal has been made on the final determination of the cause, the sheriff clerk shall exercise his duties mentioned in paragraph (1) after the final disposal of the appeal and any subsequent procedure.

## Uplifting of productions from process

**11.8.**—(1)[1] [2]   Where a party has lodged productions in a cause, that party must uplift the productions from process within the period specified in paragraph (1A).

(1A)   The period is within 14 days after—

(a)   the expiry of the period within which an appeal may be made following final determination of the cause, if no appeal is made; or

(b)   the date on which such an appeal is finally disposed of.

(2)   Where any production has not been uplifted as required by paragraph (1), the sheriff clerk shall intimate to—

(a)   the solicitor who lodged the production, or

(b)   where no solicitor is acting, the party himself or such other party as seems appropriate,

that if he fails to uplift the production within 28 days after the date of such intimation, it will be disposed of in such a manner as the sheriff directs.

Chapter 12

Interlocutors

## Signature of interlocutors by sheriff clerk

**12.1.**   In accordance with any directions given by the Sheriff Principal, any interlocutor other than a final interlocutor may be written and signed by the sheriff clerk and—

(a)   any interlocutor written and signed by a sheriff clerk shall be treated for all purposes as if it had been written and signed by the sheriff; and

(b)   any extract of such an interlocutor shall not be invalid by reason only of its being written and signed by a sheriff clerk.

## Further provisions in relation to interlocutors

**12.2.**—[3](1)   The sheriff may sign an interlocutor when outwith his or her sheriffdom.

(2)   At any time before extract, the sheriff may correct any clerical or incidental error in an interlocutor or note attached to it.

(3)   Paragraphs (4) and (5) apply in any cause other than—

(a)   an undefended family action within the meaning of rule 33.1(1); or

---

[1] As amended by the Act of Sederunt (Rules of the Court of Session, Sheriff Appeal Court Rules and Sheriff Court Rules Amendment) (Sheriff Appeal Court) 2015 (SSI 2015/419) r.5 (effective 1 January 2016).

[2] As substituted by the Act of Sederunt (Sheriff Appeal Court Rules 2015 and Sheriff Court Rules Amendment) (Miscellaneous) 2016 (SSI 2016/194) r.3 (effective 7 July 2016).

[3] As substituted by the Act of Sederunt (Sheriff Court Rules) (Miscellaneous Amendments) 2012 (SSI 2012/188) para.2 (effective August 1, 2012).

    (b)   an undefended civil partnership action within the meaning of rule 33A.1(1).

(4)  At the conclusion of any hearing in which evidence has been led, the sheriff shall either—

    (a)   pronounce an extempore judgment in accordance with rule 12.3; or

    (b)   reserve judgment in accordance with rule 12.4.

(5)  In circumstances other than those mentioned in paragraph (4), the sheriff may, and must when requested by a party, append to the interlocutor a note setting out the reasons for the decision.

(6)  A party must make a request under paragraph (5) in writing within 7 days of the date of the interlocutor.

(7)  Where a party requests a note of reasons other than in accordance with paragraph (6), the sheriff may provide such a note.

## Extempore judgments

**12.3.**—[1](1)  This rule applies where a sheriff pronounces an extempore judgment in accordance with rule 12.2(4)(a).

(2)  The sheriff must state briefly the grounds of his or her decision, including the reasons for his or her decision on any questions of fact or law or of admissibility of evidence.

(3)  The sheriff may, and must if requested to do so by a party, append to the interlocutor a note setting out the matters referred to in paragraph (2) and his or her findings in fact and law.

(4)  A party must make a request under paragraph (3) in writing within 7 days of the date of the extempore judgment.

(5)  Where a party requests a note of reasons other than in accordance with paragraph (4), the sheriff may provide such a note.

## Reserved judgments

**12.4.**—[2](1)  This rule applies where a sheriff reserves judgment in accordance with rule 12.2(4)(b).

(2)  The sheriff must give to the sheriff clerk—

    (a)   an interlocutor giving effect to the sheriff's decision and incorporating findings in fact and law; and

    (b)   a note stating briefly the grounds of his or her decision, including the reasons for his or her decision on any questions of fact or law or of admissibility of evidence.

(3)  The date of the interlocutor is the date on which it is received by the sheriff clerk.

---

[1] As inserted by the Act of Sederunt (Sheriff Court Rules) (Miscellaneous Amendments) 2012 (SSI 2012/188) para.2 (effective August 1, 2012).

[2] As inserted by the Act of Sederunt (Sheriff Court Rules) (Miscellaneous Amendments) 2012 (SSI 2012/188) para.2 (effective August 1, 2012).

(4)   The sheriff clerk must forthwith send a copy of the documents mentioned in paragraph (2) to each party.

## Chapter 13

## Party Minuter Procedure

*Annotations to Chapters 13 to 18 by Sheriff Iain Peebles.*

### Person claiming title and interest to enter process as defender

**13.1.**—(1)   A person who has not been called as a defender or third party may apply by minute for leave to enter a process as a party minuter and to lodge defences.

(2)   A minute under paragraph (1) shall specify—

(a)   the applicant's title and interest to enter the process; and

(b)   the grounds of the defence he proposes to state.

(3)   Subject to paragraph (4), after hearing the applicant and any party, the sheriff may—

(a)   if he is satisfied that the applicant has shown title and interest to enter the process, grant the applicant leave to enter the process as a party minuter and to lodge defences; and

(b)   make such order as to expenses or otherwise as he thinks fit.

(4)[1]   Where an application under paragraph (1) is made after the closing of the record or in a personal injuries action subject to personal injuries procedure after the date upon which the record is required to be lodged, the sheriff shall only grant leave under paragraph (3) if he is satisfied as to the reason why earlier application was not made.

### Procedure following leave to enter process

**13.2.**—(1)[2]   Where a party minuter lodges answers, the sheriff clerk shall fix a date and time under rule 9.2 for a hearing under rule 9.12 (Options Hearing) as if the party minuter had lodged a notice of intention to defend and the period of notice had expired on the date for lodging defences.

(2)   At the Options Hearing, or at any time thereafter, the sheriff may grant such decree or other order as he thinks fit.

(3)   A decree or other order against the party minuter shall have effect and be extractable in the same way as a decree or other order against a defender.

(4)[3]   Paragraphs (1), (2) and (3) shall not apply to a personal injuries action which is subject to personal injuries procedure.

(5)[4]   Where the sheriff grants an application under rule 13.1 in a personal injuries action which is subject to personal injuries procedure, the sheriff may make such further order as he thinks fit.

GENERAL NOTE

The procedure set out in this rule is appropriate where a person believes he has title and interest to defend an action but he has not been called as a defender or introduced as a third party by a defender using third party procedure. This rule allows a minute to be lodged setting forth their title, interest and proposed ground of defence.

---

[1] As amended by the Act of Sederunt (Ordinary Cause Rules Amendment) (Personal Injuries Actions) 2009 (SSI 2009/285) r.2 (effective November 2, 2009).
[2] As amended by SI 1996/2445 (effective November 1, 1996).
[3] As inserted by the Act of Sederunt (Ordinary Cause Rules Amendment) (Personal Injuries Actions) 2009 (SSI 2009/285) r.2 (effective November 2, 2009).
[4] As inserted by the Act of Sederunt (Ordinary Cause Rules Amendment) (Personal Injuries Actions) 2009 (SSI 2009/285) r.2 (effective November 2, 2009).

It is a matter of discretion for the court whether a person who establishes title and interest should be granted leave to enter the process in terms of this Rule of Court. If allowed to enter the process, defences are lodged in the usual form.

It may not be appropriate to allow the party to be sisted where no defence which has a reasonable chance of success has been stated (see: *Glasgow Corporation v Regent Oil Company Ltd* , 1971 S.L.T. (Sh.Ct) 61 per Sheriff Principal Sir Allan Walker at 62). It is important that a reasonably full statement of the proposed defence is set forth in the minute. For examples of situations where it was held not to be appropriate to grant see: *Laing's Sewing Machine Company v Norrie & Sons* , 1877 5 R. 29 and *Aberdeen Grit Company Ltd v The Corporation of the City of Aberdeen* , 1948 S.L.T. (N.) 44 (although the latter case may have been decided on a question of title and interest).

*"after closing of the record".*

before leave is granted to enter the process the court must in addition be satisfied that there is a proper reason why an earlier application was not made.

*"procedure following leave to enter".*

broadly follows that set out in Chapter 9.

<h1 style="text-align:center">Chapter 13A[1]</h1>

<h2 style="text-align:center">Interventions by the Commission for Equality and Human Rights</h2>

## Interpretation

**13A.1.** In this Chapter "the CEHR" means the Commission for Equality and Human Rights.

## Interventions by the CEHR

**13A.2.**—(1) The CEHR may apply to the sheriff for leave to intervene in any cause in accordance with this Chapter.

(2) This Chapter is without prejudice to any other entitlement of the CEHR by virtue of having title and interest in relation to the subject matter of any proceedings by virtue of section 30(2) of the Equality Act 2006 or any other enactment to seek to be sisted as a party in those proceedings.

(3) Nothing in this Chapter shall affect the power of the sheriff to make such other direction as he considers appropriate in the interests of justice.

(4) Any decision of the sheriff in proceedings under this Chapter shall be final and not subject to appeal.

## Applications to intervene

**13A.3.**—(1) An application for leave to intervene shall be by way of minute of intervention in Form O7A and the CEHR shall—

    (a) send a copy of it to all the parties; and

    (b) lodge it in process, certifying that subparagraph (a) has been complied with.

(2) A minute of intervention shall set out briefly—

    (a) the CEHR's reasons for believing that the proceedings are relevant to a matter in connection with which the CEHR has a function;

    (b) the issue in the proceedings which the CEHR wishes to address; and

    (c) the propositions to be advanced by the CEHR and the CEHR's reasons for believing that they are relevant to the proceedings and that they will assist the sheriff.

(3) The sheriff may—

    (a) refuse leave without a hearing;

---

[1] As inserted by the Act of Sederunt (Sheriff Court Rules) (Miscellaneous Amendments) 2008 (SSI 2008/223) r.4(2) (effective July 1, 2008).

    (b)   grant leave without a hearing unless a hearing is requested under paragraph (4);

    (c)   refuse or grant leave after such a hearing.

  (4)  A hearing, at which the applicant and the parties may address the court on the matters referred to in paragraph (6)(c), may be held if, within 14 days of the minute of intervention being lodged, any of the parties lodges a request for a hearing.

  (5)  Any diet in pursuance of paragraph (4) shall be fixed by the sheriff clerk who shall give written intimation of the diet to the CEHR and all the parties.

  (6)  The sheriff may grant leave only if satisfied that—

    (a)   the proceedings are relevant to a matter in connection with which the CEHR has a function;

    (b)   the propositions to be advanced by the CEHR are relevant to the proceedings and are likely to assist him; and

    (c)   the intervention will not unduly delay or otherwise prejudice the rights of the parties, including their potential liability for expenses.

  (7)  In granting leave the sheriff may impose such terms and conditions as he considers desirable in the interests of justice, including making provision in respect of any additional expenses incurred by the parties as a result of the intervention.

  (8)  The sheriff clerk shall give written intimation of a grant or refusal of leave to the CEHR and all the parties.

### Form of intervention

**13A.4.**—(1)  An intervention shall be by way of a written submission which (including any appendices) shall not exceed 5000 words.

  (2)  The CEHR shall lodge the submission and send a copy of it to all the parties by such time as the sheriff may direct.

  (3)  The sheriff may in exceptional circumstances—

    (a)   allow a longer written submission to be made;

    (b)   direct that an oral submission is to be made.

  (4)  Any diet in pursuance of paragraph (3)(b) shall be fixed by the sheriff clerk who shall give written intimation of the diet to the CEHR and all the parties.

Chapter 13B[1]

Interventions by the Scottish Commission for Human Rights

### Interpretation

**13B.1.**  In this Chapter—

    "the Act of 2006" means the Scottish Commission for Human Rights Act 2006; and

    "the SCHR" means the Scottish Commission for Human Rights.

### Application to intervene

**13B.2.**—(1)  An application for leave to intervene under section 14(2)(a) of the Act of 2006 shall be by way of minute of intervention in Form O7B and the SCHR shall—

    (a)   send a copy of it to all the parties; and

    (b)   lodge it in process, certifying that subparagraph (a) has been complied with.

---

[1] As inserted by the Act of Sederunt (Sheriff Court Rules) (Miscellaneous Amendments) 2008 (SSI 2008/223) r.4(2) (effective July 1, 2008).

(2)  In granting leave the sheriff may impose such terms and conditions as he considers desirable in the interests of justice, including making provision in respect of any additional expenses incurred by the parties as a result of the intervention.

(3)  The sheriff clerk shall give written intimation of a grant or refusal of leave to the SCHR and all the parties.

(4)  Any decision of the sheriff in proceedings under this Chapter shall be final and not subject to appeal.

**Invitation to intervene**

**13B.3.**—(1)  An invitation to intervene under section 14(2)(b) of the Act of 2006 shall be in Form O7C and the sheriff clerk shall send a copy of it to the SCHR and all the parties.

(2)  An invitation under paragraph (1) shall be accompanied by—

  (a)  a copy of the pleadings in the proceedings; and

  (b)  such other documents relating to those proceedings as the sheriff thinks relevant.

(3)  In issuing an invitation under section 14(2)(b) of the Act of 2006, the sheriff may impose such terms and conditions as he considers desirable in the interests of justice, including making provision in respect of any additional expenses incurred by the parties as a result of the intervention.

**Form of intervention**

**13B.4.**—(1)  An intervention shall be by way of a written submission which (including any appendices) shall not exceed 5000 words.

(2)  The SCHR shall lodge the submission and send a copy of it to all the parties by such time as the sheriff may direct.

(3)  The sheriff may in exceptional circumstances—

  (a)  allow a longer written submission to be made;

  (b)  direct that an oral submission is to be made.

(4)  Any diet in pursuance of paragraph (3)(b) shall be fixed by the sheriff clerk who shall give written intimation of the diet to the SCHR and all the parties.

Chapter 14

Applications by Minute

**Application of this Chapter**

**14.1.**—(1)  Where an application may be made by minute, the form of the minute and the procedure to be adopted shall, unless otherwise provided in these Rules, be in accordance with this Chapter.

(2)[1]  This Chapter shall not apply to—

  (a)  a minute of amendment;

  (b)  a minute of abandonment; or

  (c)  a joint minute.

GENERAL NOTE

The procedure set out in this rule is appropriate where a party is applying to the court for a decision on matters which cannot be dealt with by motion, and require a crave, supporting averments and plea-in-law.

---

[1] As amended by SI 1996/2445 (effective November 1, 1996).

## Form of minute

**14.2.** A minute to which this Chapter applies shall contain—

(a) a crave;

(b) where appropriate, a condescendence in the form of a statement of facts supporting the crave; and

(c) where appropriate, pleas-in-law.

"FORM OF MINUTES"

In all essential matters a minute will be in the same form as an Initial Writ.

## Lodging of minutes

**14.3.**—[1](1) Before intimating any minute, the minuter shall lodge the minute in process.

(2) On the lodging of a minute, and any document under rule 21.1(1)(b) (lodging documents founded on or adopted), the sheriff—

(a) may make an order for answers to be lodged;

(b) may order intimation of the minute without making an order for answers; or

(c) where he considers it appropriate for the expeditious disposal of the minute or for any other specified reason, may fix a hearing.

(3) Any answers ordered to be lodged under paragraph (2)(a) shall, unless otherwise ordered by the sheriff, be lodged within 14 days after the date of intimation of the minute.

(4) Where the sheriff fixes a hearing under paragraph (2)(c), the interlocutor fixing that hearing shall specify whether—

(a) answers are to be lodged;

(b) the sheriff will hear evidence at that hearing; and

(c) the sheriff will allow evidence by affidavit.

(5) Any answers or affidavit evidence ordered to be lodged under paragraph (4) shall be lodged within such time as shall be specified in the interlocutor of the sheriff.

(6) The following rules shall not apply to any hearing fixed under paragraph (2)(c):—

rule 14.7 (opposition where no order for answers made),

rule 14.8 (hearing of minutes where no opposition or no answers lodged),

rule 14.10 (notice of opposition or answers lodged).

(7) The sheriff clerk shall forthwith return the minute to the minuter with any interlocutor pronounced by the sheriff.

*"Lodging of Minutes"* After the lodging of the minute in process, depending on the nature of the decision sought and the whole circumstances as set out in the minute, the sheriff will make one of three orders regarding further procedure. If a hearing is fixed by the sheriff at this stage the interlocutor fixing this will further state (a) if evidence is to be heard at the hearing and (b) if evidence will be allowed in the form of affidavits. The normal reason for fixing a hearing at this stage is urgency in having the matter dealt with.

## Intimation of minutes

**14.4.**—[2](1) The party lodging a minute shall, on receipt from the sheriff clerk of the minute, intimate to every other party including any person referred to in rule 14.13(1)—

---

[1] Substituted by SI 1996/2445 (effective November 1, 1996).
[2] Inserted by SI 1996/2445 (effective November 1, 1996).

(a) a notice in Form G7A, G7B or G7C, as the case may be, by any of the methods provided for in rule 14.5 (methods of intimation); and

(b) a copy of—

    (i) the minute;

    (ii) any interlocutor; and

    (iii) any document referred to in the minute.

(2) The sheriff may, on cause shown, dispense with intimation.

*"Intimation of Minutes"* Intimation only occurs following the sheriff pronouncing an interlocutor in terms of 14.3(2).

## Methods of intimation

**14.5.**—[1](1) Intimation of a minute may be given by—

(a) any of the methods of service provided for in Chapter 5 (citation, service and intimation); or

(b) where intimation is to a party represented by a solicitor, by—

    (i) personal delivery,

    (ii) facsimile transmission,

    (iii) first class ordinary post, or

    (iv) delivery to a document exchange, to that solicitor.

(2) Where intimation is given—

(a) under paragraph (1)(b)(i) or (ii), it shall be deemed to have been given—

    (i) on the day of transmission or delivery where it is given before 5.00 p.m. on any day; or

    (ii) on the day after transmission or delivery where it is given after 5.00 p.m. on any day; or

(b) under paragraph 1(b)(iii) or (iv), it shall be deemed to have been given on the day after the date of posting or delivery.

*"Method of Intimation"* The methods of intimation are the same as in respect to motions.

## Return of minute with evidence of intimation

**14.6.**[2] Where intimation of any minute has been given, the minute and a certificate of intimation in Form G8 shall be returned to the sheriff clerk within 5 days after the date of intimation.

## Opposition where no order for answers made

**14.7.**—[3](1) Where a party seeks to oppose a minute lodged under rule 14.3 (lodging of minutes) in which no order for answers has been made under paragraph (2)(a) of that rule, that party shall, within 14 days after the date of intimation of the minute to him—

(a) complete a notice of opposition in Form G9;

(b) lodge the notice with the sheriff clerk; and

(c) intimate a copy of that notice to every other party.

(2) Rule 14.5 (methods of intimation) and rule 14.6 (return of minute with evidence of intimation) shall apply to intimation of opposition to a minute under paragraph (1)(c) of this rule as they apply to intimation of a minute.

(3) The sheriff may, on cause shown, reduce or dispense with the period for lodging the notice mentioned in paragraph (1)(b).

---

[1] Inserted by SI 1996/2445 (effective November 1, 1996).

[2] Inserted by SI 1996/2445 (effective November 1, 1996).

[3] Inserted by SI 1996/2445 (effective November 1, 1996).

The procedure to be followed where a minute is opposed and the sheriff has pronounced an interlocutor in terms of paragraph 2(a) of the Rule is as set out in 14.7.

## Hearing of minutes where no opposition or no answers lodged

**14.8.**—[1](1)  Where no notice of opposition is lodged or where no answers have been lodged to the minute within the time allowed, the minute shall be determined by the sheriff in chambers without the attendance of parties, unless the sheriff otherwise directs.

(2)  Where the sheriff requires to hear a party on a minute, the sheriff clerk shall—

(a)  fix a date, time and place for the party to be heard; and

(b)  inform that party—

(i)  of that date, time and place; and

(ii)  of the reasons for the sheriff wishing to hear him.

In the same way as with an unopposed motion an unopposed minute may be determined by the sheriff without the necessity of parties attending. As with an unopposed motion, if the sheriff believes it necessary he may order the attendance of parties to hear from them in relation to the minute.

## Intimation of interlocutor

**14.9.**[2]  Where a minute has been determined in accordance with rule 14.8 (hearing of minutes where no opposition or no answers lodged), the sheriff clerk shall intimate the interlocutor determining that minute to the parties forthwith.

## Notice of opposition or answers lodged

**14.10.**—[3](1)  Where a notice of opposition has, or answers have, been lodged to the minute, the sheriff clerk shall—

(a)  assign a date, time and place for a hearing on the first suitable court day after the date of the lodging of the notice of opposition or answers, as the case may be; and

(b)  intimate that date, time and place to the parties.

(2)  The interlocutor fixing a hearing under paragraph (1) shall specify whether the sheriff will hear evidence at the hearing or receive evidence by affidavit.

*"Notice of Opposition or Answers Lodged"*. If a hearing is fixed and a notice of opposition or answers are lodged then, as with a hearing ordered in terms of paragraph 2(c), the sheriff will specify whether evidence will be heard and if so whether affidavit evidence will be allowed. If answers have been lodged, this interlocutor will normally also allow an adjustment period. Usually adjustment will be allowed until 2 weeks before the date of the hearing. The interlocutor may also direct the lodging of a record, however, the lodging thereof is not mandatory in terms of this rule. If a case proceeds to a hearing in which evidence is to be led the procedure will be the same as at a proof.

## Orders under section 11 of the Children (Scotland) Act 1995

**14.10A.**—[4](1)  This rule applies where a notice of opposition or answers are lodged in respect of a minute including a crave for an order under section 11 of the Children (Scotland) Act 1995 (court orders relating to parental responsibilities etc.).

(2)  The sheriff, having regard to the measures referred to in Chapter 33AA (expeditious resolution of certain causes), may make such orders as the sheriff considers appropriate to ensure the expeditious resolution of the issues in dispute.

---

[1] Inserted by SI 1996/2445 (effective November 1, 1996).
[2] Inserted by SI 1996/2445 (effective November 1, 1996).
[3] Inserted by SI 1996/2445 (effective November 1, 1996).
[4] As inserted by the Act of Sederunt (Sheriff Court Rules)(Miscellaneous Amendments) (No.2) 2013 (SI 2013/139) para.2 (effective June 3, 2013).

**Procedure for hearing**

**14.11.**—[1](1) A certified copy of the interlocutor assigning a hearing under this Chapter and requiring evidence to be led shall be sufficient warrant to a sheriff officer to cite a witness on behalf of a party.

(2) At the hearing, the sheriff shall hear parties on the minute and any answers lodged, and may determine the minute or may appoint such further procedure as he considers necessary.

**Consent to minute**

**14.12.**[2] Subject to paragraph (2) of rule 14.8 (hearing of minutes where no opposition or no answers lodged), where all parties to the action indicate to the sheriff, by endorsement of the minute or otherwise in writing, their intention to consent to the minute, the sheriff may forthwith determine the minute in chambers without the appearance of parties.

**Procedure following grant of minute**

**14.13.**—[3](1) Where the minute includes a crave seeking leave—
- (a) for a person—
  - (i) to be sisted as a party to the action, or
  - (ii) to appear in the proceedings, or
- (b) for the cause to be transferred against the representatives of a party who has died or is under a legal incapacity,

the sheriff, on granting the minute, may order a hearing under rule 9.12 (Options Hearing) to be fixed or may appoint such further procedure as he thinks fit.

(2) Where an Options Hearing is ordered under paragraph (1), the sheriff clerk shall—
- (a) fix a date and time for such hearing, which date, unless the sheriff otherwise directs, shall be on the first suitable court day occurring not sooner than 10 weeks after the date of the interlocutor of the sheriff ordering such hearing be fixed;
- (b) forthwith intimate to the parties in Form G5—
  - (i) where appropriate, the last date for lodging defences;
  - (ii) where appropriate, the last date for adjustment; and
  - (iii) the date of the Options Hearing; and
- (c) prepare and sign an interlocutor recording those dates.

(3) For the purpose of fixing the date for the Options Hearing referred to in paragraph (1), the date of granting the minute shall be deemed to be the date of expiry of the period of notice.

GENERAL NOTE

"*Expenses*". If expenses are sought the sheriff will deal with the issue in accordance with the general rules in respect of the awarding of expenses.

---

[1] Inserted by SI 1996/2445 (effective November 1, 1996).
[2] Inserted by SI 1996/2445 (effective November 1, 1996).
[3] Inserted by SI 1996/2445 (effective November 1, 1996).

## Chapter 15[1]

## Motions

### Application of this Chapter

**15.A1.**[2](1)  This Chapter applies to any cause other than a cause to which Chapter 15A applies.

### Lodging of motions

**15.1.**—(1)  A motion may be made—

(a)  orally with leave of the court during any hearing of a cause; or

(b)  by lodging a written motion in Form G6.

(2)  Subject to paragraph (3), a written motion shall be lodged with the sheriff clerk within 5 days after the date of intimation of the motion required by rule 15.2 (intimation of motions) with—

(a)  a certificate of intimation in Form G8; and

(b)  so far as practicable any document referred to in the written motion and not already lodged in process.

(3)  Where the period for lodging opposition to the motion is varied under rule 15.2(4) (variation of and dispensing with period of intimation) to a period of 5 days or less, the written motion and certificate to be lodged in terms of paragraph (2) shall be lodged no later than the day on which the period for lodging opposition expires.

GENERAL NOTE

A motion is the means by which the court is requested to make an order either procedural or substantive in the course of a depending action.

"*Orally with Leave of the Court*". The vast majority of motions are made by lodging a written motion. However, it is competent to make an oral motion at the bar. Such motions most frequently occur in the course of a debate or proof when a party seeks leave to amend. Motions made during the course of a hearing may only be made with the leave of the court. The court will normally only allow such a motion to be made where there is firstly a good reason why a written motion was not lodged and secondly where there is no prejudice to the other party. Given the issue of prejudice to the other party it is often only with the consent of the other party that such a motion is allowed to be made. Where allowed to be made at the bar, such motions are often continued by the court in order to allow the other party time to prepare a reply and by this means the issue of possible prejudice to the other party is obviated.

### Intimation of motions

**15.2.**—(1)  Subject to paragraphs (4) and (7), a party intending to lodge a motion in accordance with rule 15.1(1)(b) (lodging written motion) shall intimate the motion in Form G7, and a copy of any document referred to in the motion, to every other party.

(2)  Intimation of a motion may be given by—

(a)  any of the methods of service provided for in Chapter 5 (citation, service and intimation); or

(b)  where intimation is to a party represented by a solicitor, by—

(i)  personal delivery,

(ii)  facsimile transmission,

(iii)  first class ordinary post, or

(iv)  delivery to a document exchange, to that solicitor.

---

[1]  Substituted by SI 1996/2445 (effective November 1, 1996).

[2]  As amended by the Act of Sederunt (Rules of the Court of Session 1994 and Sheriff Court Rules Amendment) (No. 2) (Personal Injury and Remits) 2015 (SSI 2015/227) para.8 (effective September 22, 2015).

(3) Where intimation is given—

    (a)    under paragraph (2)(b)(i) or (ii), it shall be deemed to have been given—

        (i)    on the day of transmission or delivery where it is given before 5.00 p.m. on any day; or

        (ii)    on the day after transmission or delivery where it is given after 5.00 p.m. on any day; or

    (b)    under paragraph (2)(b)(iii) or (iv), it shall be deemed to have been given on the day after posting or delivery.

(4) The sheriff may, on the application of a party intending to lodge a written motion, vary the period of 7 days specified in rule 15.3(1)(c) for lodging opposition to the motion or dispense with intimation.

(5) An application under paragraph (4) shall be made in the written motion, giving reasons for such variation or dispensation.

(6) Where the sheriff varies the period within which notice of opposition is to be lodged under rule 15.3(1)(c), the form of intimation required under rule 15.2(1) (intimation of motion in Form G7) shall state the date by which such notice requires to be lodged.

(7) A joint motion by all parties lodged in Form G6 need not be intimated.

"*Copy of any Document Referred to in the Motion*". Such a copy shall be intimated to every party and where practicable lodged in court.

"*Intimation of Motion and Intimation of Opposition to a Motion*". The method and timing of the intimation is the same in relation to both (see: 15.2(2) and (3)).

"*Intimation of Motion*". Intimation is in accordance with Chapter 5 except where the other party is represented by a solicitor where the forms of intimation are considerably widened.

"*Vary the Period for Lodging Opposition...or Dispense with Intimation*". Where such variation or dispensation is sought it should be sought in the written motion and must be supported by reasons. It should be noted that although lengthening of the period for lodging opposition is competent this is very rarely sought. Where shortening of the period is sought the usual reason given is urgency in having the matter dealt with by the court. The test as to whether the court will grant such shortening will be whether it is in the interests of justice to grant it, i.e. whether on balance the need for the matter being dealt with urgently outweighs any prejudice to the other party in shortening the period for lodging opposition.

As regards dispensing with intimation, this will only be granted on the basis of the most cogent of reasons. In terms of 15.5(7) where intimation has been dispensed with, the sheriff shall make such order as he thinks fit for intimation of his determination on those parties to whom intimation was dispensed with.

**Opposition to motions**

**15.3.**—(1) Where a party seeks to oppose a motion made in accordance with rule 15.1(1)(b) (written motion), he shall—

    (a)    complete a notice of opposition in Form G9;

    (b)    intimate a copy of that notice to every other party; and

    (c)    lodge the notice with the sheriff clerk within 7 days after the date of intimation of the motion or such other period as the sheriff may have determined under rule 15.2(6).

(2) Paragraphs (2) and (3) of rule 15.2 (methods and time of intimation of motions) shall apply to the intimation of opposition to a motion under paragraph (1)(b) of this rule as they apply to intimation under that rule.

**Consent to motions**

**15.4.** Where a party consents to a written motion, he shall endorse the motion, or give notice to the sheriff clerk in writing, of his consent.

**Hearing of motions**

**15.5.**—(1) Subject to paragraph (2), where no notice of opposition is lodged with the sheriff clerk within the period specified in rule 15.3(1)(c), or ordered by virtue of rule 15.2(4), the motion shall be determined by the sheriff in chambers without the appearance of parties, unless the sheriff otherwise directs.

(2) In accordance with any directions given by the sheriff principal, the sheriff clerk may determine any motion other than a motion which seeks a final interlocutor.

(3) Where the sheriff clerk considers that a motion dealt with by him under paragraph (2) should not be granted, he shall refer that motion to the sheriff who shall deal with it in accordance with paragraph (1).

(4) Where the sheriff requires to hear a party on a motion which is not opposed, the sheriff clerk shall—

(a)  fix a date, time and place for the party to be heard, and

(b)  inform that party—

(i)  of that date, time and place; and

(ii)  of the reasons for the sheriff wishing to hear him.

(5) Where a notice of opposition is lodged in accordance with rule 15.3(1), the sheriff clerk shall—

(a)  assign a date, time and place, on the first suitable court day after the lodging of the notice of opposition, for the motion to be heard; and

(b)  intimate that date, time and place to the parties.

(6) Where a motion has been determined under paragraph (1) or (2), the sheriff clerk shall intimate the interlocutor determining that motion to all parties forthwith.

(7) Where the sheriff, under paragraph (4) of rule 15.2, dispenses with intimation required by paragraph (1) of that rule, he shall make such order as he thinks fit for intimation of his determination of the motion to every party to the action in respect of whom intimation has been so dispensed with.

(8) Subject to paragraph (4), where all parties consent to a written motion, the sheriff may determine the motion in chambers without the appearance of parties.

(9) Subject to paragraph (4) where a joint motion of all parties in Form G6 is lodged with the sheriff clerk, the sheriff may determine the motion in chambers without the appearance of parties.

*"Hearing of Motions"*. Unlike in the Court of Session all unopposed motions may be granted without a hearing at which the appearance of counsel, solicitor or party litigant is necessary.

A sheriff principal may by direction delegate to the sheriff clerk the determination of any motions other than those which seek a final interlocutor. In practice the sheriffs principal have exercised this power in the same way and the list of motions which may be determined by the sheriff clerk is the same in each Sheriffdom. The motions which may be dealt with by the sheriff clerk are all minor and procedural.

An unopposed motion may be put out by a sheriff for a hearing. The sheriff will also give reasons for so ordering. Such a hearing may be procedural in nature or relate to the substance of the motion.

*Lengthy Hearings*. Where parties believe that an opposed motion is likely to require a lengthy hearing it is good practice to advise the sheriff clerk of the likelihood in order that necessary practical arrangements can be made for the hearing thereof.

**Motions to sist**

**15.6.**—[1](1)  Where a motion to sist is made, either orally or in writing in accordance with rule 15.1(1)(a) or (by—

    (a)   the reason for the sist shall be stated by the party seeking the sist; and

    (b)   that reason shall be recorded in the interlocutor.

(2)  Where a cause has been sisted, the sheriff may, after giving parties an opportunity to be heard, recall the sist.

"*Expenses*". Often the issue of expenses is not raised at the stage which the motion is dealt with by the court. If the issue is raised then the sheriff will deal with it in accordance with the general rules in respect of the awarding of expenses.

**Dismissal of action due to delay**

**15.7.**—[2](1)  Any party to an action may, while that action is depending before the court, apply by written motion for the court to dismiss the action due to inordinate and inexcusable delay by another party or another party's agent in progressing the action, resulting in unfairness.

(2)  A motion under paragraph (1) shall—

    (a)[3]  include a statement of the grounds on which it is proposed that the motion should be allowed; and

    (b)   be lodged in accordance with rule 15.1.

(3)  A notice of opposition to the motion in Form G9 shall include a statement of the grounds of opposition to the motion.

(4)  In determining an application made under this rule, the court may dismiss the action if it appears to the court that—

    (a)   there has been an inordinate and inexcusable delay on the part of any party or any party's agent in progressing the action; and

    (b)   such delay results in unfairness specific to the factual circumstances, including the procedural circumstances, of that action.

(5)  In determining whether or not to dismiss an action under paragraph (4), the court shall take account of the procedural consequences, both for the parties and for the work of the court, of allowing the action to proceed.

Chapter 15A[4]

Motions Intimated and Lodged by Email

**Application of this Chapter**

**15A.1.**  This Chapter applies—

---

[1] Inserted by SSI 2000/239 (effective October 2, 2000).

[2] As inserted by the Act of Sederunt (Sheriff Court Rules) (Miscellaneous Amendments) 2009 (SSI 2009/294) r.14 (effective October 1, 2009).

[3] As amended by the Act of Sederunt (Sheriff Court Rules) (Miscellaneous Amendments) 2010 (SSI 2010/279) r.7(1) (effective July 29, 2010).

[4] As inserted by the Act of Sederunt (Rules of the Court of Session 1994 and Sheriff Court Rules Amendment) (No.2) (Personal Injury and Remits) 2015 (SSI 2015/227) para.8 (effective September 22, 2015).

(a)   to a personal injuries action within the meaning of Part A1 of Chapter 36 proceeding in the all-Scotland sheriff court;

(b)   where each party to such an action has provided to the sheriff clerk an email address for the purpose of transacting motion business.

## Interpretation of this Chapter

**15A.1A.**[1](1)   In this Chapter—

"court day" means a day on which the sheriff clerk's office is open for civil court business;

"court day 1" means the court day on which a motion is treated as being intimated under rule 15A.4;

"court day 3" means the second court day after court day 1;

"court day 4" means the third court day after court day 1;

"lodging party" means the party lodging the motion;

"receiving party" means a party receiving the intimation of the motion from the lodging party; and

"transacting motion business" means—

     (a)   intimating and lodging motions;

     (b)   receiving intimation of motions;

     (c)   intimating consent or opposition to motions;

     (d)   receiving intimation of or opposition to motions.

(2)   In this Chapter, a reference to—

(a)   the address of a party is a reference to the email address of—

     (i)   that party's solicitor; or

     (ii)   that party,

included in the list maintained under rule 15A.2(4);

(b)   the address of the court is a reference to the email address of the court included in that list under rule 15A.2(5).

## Provision of email addresses to sheriff clerk

**15A.2.**—(1)   A solicitor representing a party in an action of the sort mentioned in rule 15A.1(a) must provide to the sheriff clerk an email address for the purpose of transacting motion business.

(2)   A solicitor who does not have suitable facilities for transacting motion business by email may make a declaration in writing to that effect, which must be—

(a)   sent to the sheriff clerk; and

(b)   intimated to each of the other parties to the cause.

(3)   A party to an action of the sort mentioned in rule 15A.1(a) who is not represented by a solicitor may provide to the sheriff clerk an email address for the purpose of transacting motion business.

(4)   The sheriff clerk must maintain a list of the email addresses provided for the purpose of transacting motion business, which must be published in up to date form on the website of the Scottish Courts and Tribunals Service.

(5)   The sheriff clerk must also include on that list an email address of the court for the purpose of lodging motions.

---

[1] As re-numbered by the Sheriff Court Rules Amendment) (No.2) (Personal Injury and Remits) 2015 (SSI 2015/227) para.8 (effective 22 September 2015), as amended by the Act of Sederunt (Ordinary Cause Rules 1993 Amendment and Miscellaneous Amendments) 2015 (SSI 2015/296) r.4(2) (effective 22 September 2015).

**Making of motions**

15A.3.   A motion may be made—
(a)   orally with leave of the court during any hearing; or
(b)   by lodging it in accordance with this Chapter.

**Intimation of motions by email**

15A.4.—(1)   Where—
(a)   a defender has lodged a notice of intention to defend under rule 9.1;
(b)   a party has lodged a minute or answers; or
(c)   provision is made in these Rules for the intimation of a motion to a party in accordance with this Part,
the lodging party must give intimation of his or her intention to lodge the motion, and of the terms of the motion, to every such party by sending an email in Form G6A (form of motion by email) to the addresses of every party.

(2)   The requirement under paragraph (1) to give intimation of a motion to a party by email does not apply where that party—
(a)   having lodged a notice of intention to defend, fails to lodge defences within the period for lodging those defences;
(b)   has not lodged answers within the period of notice for lodging those answers; or
(c)   has withdrawn or is deemed to have withdrawn the defences, minute or answers, as the case may be.

(3)   A motion intimated under this rule must be intimated not later than 5 p.m. on a court day.

**Opposition to motions by email**

15A.5.—(1)   A receiving party must intimate any opposition to a motion by sending an email in Form G9A (form of opposition to motion by email) to the address of the lodging party.

(2)   Any opposition to a motion must be intimated to the lodging party not later than 5 p.m. on court day 3.

(3)   Late opposition to a motion must be sent to the address of the court and may only be allowed with the leave of the court, on cause shown.

**Consent to motions by email**

15A.6.   Where a receiving party seeks to consent to a motion, that party may do so by sending an email confirming the consent to the address of the lodging party.

**Lodging unopposed motions by email**

15A.7.—(1)   This rule applies where no opposition to a motion has been intimated.

(2)   The motion must be lodged by the lodging party not later than 12.30 p.m. on court day 4 by sending an email in Form G6A headed "Unopposed motion" to the address of the court.

(3)   A motion lodged under paragraph (2) is to be determined by the court by 5 p.m. on court day 4.

(4)   Where for any reason it is not possible for a motion lodged under paragraph (2) to be determined by 5 p.m. on court day 4, the sheriff clerk must advise the parties or their solicitors of that fact and give reasons.

### Lodging opposed motions by email

**15A.8.**—(1) This rule applies where opposition to a motion has been intimated.

(2) The motion must be lodged by the lodging party not later than 12.30 p.m. on court day 4 by—

(a) sending an email in Form G6A headed "Opposed motion", to the address of the court;

(b) attaching to that email the opposition in Form G9A intimated by the receiving party to the lodging party.

(3) Where a motion is lodged under paragraph (2), the sheriff clerk must advise parties of the date on which the motion will be heard, which will be on the first suitable court day after court day 4.

### Issuing of interlocutor by email

**15A.9.** Where the court pronounces an interlocutor determining a motion, the sheriff clerk must email a copy of the interlocutor to the addresses of the lodging party and every receiving party.

### Other periods of intimation etc. under these Rules

**15A.10.**—(1) Where a provision of these Rules, other than Chapter 15 (motions), provides for a period of intimation of—

(a) a motion;

(b) opposition to a motion; or

(c) consent to a motion,

other than the period mentioned in this Chapter, that period will apply instead of the period mentioned in this Chapter.

(2) Paragraph (1) applies whether or not the intimation period mentioned elsewhere in these Rules is referred to by a specific number of days.

(3) Where—

(a) every receiving party in a cause consents to a shorter period of intimation; or

(b) the court shortens the period of intimation,

the motion may be lodged by the lodging party, or heard or otherwise determined by the court at an earlier time and date than that which is specified in this Part.

### Motions to sist

**15A.11.**—(1) Where a motion to sist is made—

(a) the reason for the sist must be stated by the party seeking the sist; and

(b) that reason must be recorded in the interlocutor.

(2) Where a cause has been sisted, the sheriff may, after giving parties an opportunity to be heard, recall the sist.

### Dismissal of action due to delay

**15A.12.**—(1) Any party to an action may, while that action is depending before the court, apply by motion for the court to dismiss the action due to inordinate and inexcusable delay by another party or another party's solicitor in progressing the action, resulting in unfairness.

(2) A motion under paragraph (1) must—

(a) include a statement of the grounds on which it is proposed that the motion should be allowed; and

(b) be lodged in accordance with rule 15A.3(b) (lodging of motions).

(3)   A notice of opposition to the motion in Form G9 (form of notice of opposition to motion or minute) or Form G9A (form of opposition to motion by email) must include a statement of the grounds of opposition to the motion.

(4)   In determining an application made under this rule, the sheriff may dismiss the action if it appears to the sheriff that—

(a)   there has been an inordinate and inexcusable delay on the part of any party or any party's solicitor in progressing the action; and

(b)   such delay results in unfairness specific to the factual circumstances, including the procedural circumstances, of that action.

(5)   In determining whether or not to dismiss an action under paragraph (4), the sheriff must take account of the procedural consequences, both for the parties and for the work of the court, of allowing the action to proceed.

## Chapter 16

### Decrees by Default

**Application of this Chapter**

**16.1.**[1]   This Chapter applies to any cause other than—

(a)   an action to which rule 33.37 (decree by default in family action) applies;

(aa)[2]   an action to which rule 33A.37 (decree by default in a civil partnership action) applies;

(b)   an action of multiplepoinding;

(c)   a cause under the Presumption of Death (Scotland) Act 1977; or

(d)   a commercial action within the meaning of Chapter 40.

**Decrees where party in default**

**16.2.**—(1)   In a cause to which this Chapter applies, where a party fails—

(a)   to lodge, or intimate the lodging of, any production or part of process within the period required under a provision in these Rules or an order of the sheriff,

(b)   to implement an order of the sheriff within a specified period,

(c)   to appear or be represented at any diet, or

(d)[3]   otherwise to comply with any requirement imposed upon that party by these Rules;

that party shall be in default.

(2)   Where a party is in default the sheriff may, as the case may be—

(a)   grant decree as craved with expenses;

(b)   grant decree of absolvitor with expenses;

(c)   dismiss the cause with expenses; or

(d)   make such other order as he thinks fit to secure the expeditious progress of the cause.

(3)   Where no party appears at a diet, the sheriff may dismiss the cause.

(4)   In this rule, "diet" includes—

(a)   a hearing under rule 9.12 (Options Hearing);

(b)   a hearing under rule 10.6 (Procedural Hearing);

(c)   a proof or proof before answer; and

---

[1] As amended by SSI 2001/8 (effective March 1, 2001).

[2] Inserted by Act of Sederunt (Ordinary Cause Rules) Amendment (Family Law (Scotland) Act 2006 etc.) 2006 (SSI 2006/207) (effective May 4, 2006).

[3] Inserted by the Act of Sederunt (Ordinary Cause and Summary Application Rules) Amendment (Miscellaneous) 2006 (SSI 2006/410) (effective August 18, 2006).

(d)   a debate.

## Prorogation of time where party in default

**16.3.**   In an action to which this Chapter applies, the sheriff may, on cause shown, prorogate the time for lodging any production or part of process or for giving intimation or for implementing any order.

GENERAL NOTE.

The purpose of the rule is to provide a discretionary remedy to the court in the event that a party to a defended action (being one in which a notice to defend has been lodged) prevents its proper progress by a failure to act in any of the ways specified in the rule.

NATURE OF DECREE.

A decree by default is (a) a final judgment and (b) if granted after the lodging of defences, and if other than a decree of dismissal, is a decree *in foro* founding a plea of res judicata. If granted prior to the lodging of defences it will not found a plea of res judicata (see: *Esso Petroleum Company Ltd v Law* , 1956, S.C. 33). A decree by default may be obtained prior to the lodging of defences in the event that defences are not lodged timeously (see: OCR 9.6(1)); namely, on the failure to comply with the foregoing rule.

It is a matter for the discretion of the court whether it is appropriate to grant absolvitor or dismissal. In considering whether to grant *absolvitor* or dismissal it is suggested that the court has to consider the issue of whether a decree of *absolvitor* is proportionate to the default and thus in all the circumstances in the interests of justice (see further below).

*Where the pursuer is in default* decree of *absolvitor* would normally be pronounced. However, in the case of *Group 4 Total Security v Jaymarke Developments Ltd* , 1995 S.C.L.R. 303 where a closed record was lodged late the court held it appropriate to grant only decree of dismissal, thus leaving it open for the action to be re-raised.

*Where the defender is in default*, the decree normally granted is that craved for.

"*Where no party appears at a diet*" the appropriate decree is a decree of dismissal with a finding of no expenses due to or by either party (pronounced on the basis of want of insistence).

DISCRETION.

In the exercise of discretion whether to grant decree by default, it is for the court in exercising said discretion to see that the interests of justice are met. The court should have regard to the following broad guidelines laid down by the Inner House in considering the interests of justice.

(a)   The court should have regard to whether there is a proper claim or defence. See *McKelvie v Scottish Steel Scaffolding* , 1938 S.C. 278 per Lord Moncrieffe at 281:

> "I would be most reluctant, in any case in which prima facie there appeared to be a proper defence put forward to allow decree to pass against the defender without investigation of that defence. Even if carelessness on the part of the defender or others for whom he had been responsible had delayed the course of the procedure of the action, I should, in such a case, always be willing to entertain an application of relief."

(b)   The court should have regard to whether the default has arisen as a result of the behaviour of the party to the action or his agent. If the default is due to his agent this should not normally result in decree by default. The appropriate finding would be an adverse award of expenses, and perhaps an adverse award of expenses against the agent personally.

(c)   The court should have regard to the seriousness of the default.

"PROROGATION OF TIME WHERE PARTY IN DEFAULT".

The court is given the specific power to prorogate. Cause must be shown and again the court will apply the test of what is in the interests of justice.

Apart from the specific power of prorogation in the rule the court may also be moved to exercise the dispensing power in OCR 2.1.(1).

Generally, if a party fails to appear at a calling of a case, the court will be slow to grant decree unless it can be satisfied that there is likely to be no acceptable reason for the failure (see: *Canmore Housing Association v Scott* , 2003 G.W.D. 9-243). No matter how nominally or informally a party is represented at a diet it is not appropriate for the court to grant decree by default (see: *Samson v Fielding* , 2003 S.L.T. (Sh. Ct) 48).

*Solicitor withdraws from acting.* in these circumstances the court must fix a peremptory diet (OCR 24.2(1)).

*Appeal* against decree by default can be made without leave. (See: *GAS Construction Co Ltd v Schrader* , 1992 S.L.T. 528). Appeal against refusal of a decree by default is only competent with the leave of the court.

## Chapter 17

## Summary Decrees

### Application of this Chapter

**17.1.** This Chapter applies to any action other than—
  (a)  a family action within the meaning of rule 33.1(1);
 (aa)[1] a civil partnership action within the meaning of rule 33A.1(1);
 (ab)[2] an action of proving the tenor;
  (b)  an action of multiplepoinding; or
  (c)  an action under the Presumption of Death (Scotland) Act 1977.

### Applications for summary decree

**17.2.**—[3,4](1)  Subject to paragraphs (2) to (4), a party to an action may, at any time after defences have been lodged, apply by motion for summary decree in accordance with rule 15.1(1)(b) (lodging of motions) or rule 15A.7(lodging unopposed motions by email) or rule 15A.8 (lodging opposed motions by email) as the case may be.

(2)  An application may only be made on the grounds that—
  (a)  an opposing party's case (or any part of it) has no real prospect of success; and
  (b)  there exists no other compelling reason why summary decree should not be granted at that stage.

(3)  The party enrolling the motion may request the sheriff—
  (a)  to grant decree in terms of all or any of the craves of the initial writ or counterclaim;
  (b)  to dismiss a cause or to absolve any party from any crave directed against him or her;
  (c)  to pronounce an interlocutor sustaining or repelling any plea-in-law; or
  (d)  to dispose of the whole or part of the subject-matter of the cause.

(4)  The sheriff may—
  (a)  grant the motion in whole or in part, if satisfied that the conditions in subparagraph (2) are met,
  (b)  ordain any party, or a partner, director, officer or office-bearer of any party—
    (i)  to produce any relevant document or article; or
    (ii)  to lodge an affidavit in support of any assertion of fact made in the pleadings or at the hearing of the motion.

(5)  Notwithstanding the refusal of all or part of a motion for summary decree, a subsequent motion may be made where there has been a change in circumstances.

---

[1] Inserted by Act of Sederunt (Ordinary Cause Rules) Amendment (Family Law (Scotland) Act 2006 etc.) 2006 (SSI 2006/207) r.2 (effective May 4, 2006).

[2] As inserted by the Act of Sederunt (Ordinary Cause Rules 1993 Amendment and Miscellaneous Amendments) 2015 (SSI 2015/296) para.2(2) (effective 21 September 2015).

[3] As substituted by the Act of Sederunt (Sheriff Court Rules) (Miscellaneous Amendments) 2012 (SSI 2012/188) para.3 (effective August 1, 2012).

[4] As amended by the Act of Sederunt (Rules of the Court of Session 1994 and Sheriff Court Rules Amendment) (No. 2) (Personal Injury and Remits) 2015 (SSI 2015/227) para.8 (effective September 22, 2015).

General Note

The rule may flow from comments made by Lord Stewart in *Ellon Castle Estates Company Ltd v MacDonald* , 1975 S.L.T. (News) 66. Although this case considerably predates the rule it is frequently founded upon as setting forth a definition of the type of defences the rule is intended to strike at.

The purpose of the introduction of this rule of court was summarised by Lord McDonald in an unreported decision of March 26, 1985: *McAlinden v Bearsden & Milngavie District Council* as follows:

"I have no doubt it is intended to deal with the regrettable situation where there is no valid stateable defence but procedural technicalities are founded upon to delay prompt settlement of an unanswerable claim."

In his judgment, in *McAlinden v Bearsden & Milngavie District Council* supra, Lord McDonald further stated—

"It (the summary decree motion) is not in my view intended to provide an opportunity on the motion roll for legal debate appropriate to the procedure roll."

This opinion has been followed in a number of cases (see example: *Mitchell v H A T Contracting Services Ltd (No. 2)* 1993 S.L.T. 734; and *Rankin v Reid* , 1987 S.L.T. 352). Thus a summary decree motion is not the appropriate forum for a decision on relevancy and if such an issue arises in the course of such a motion it should be sent to debate. However, Sheriff Principal Nicholson, Q.C., held in *Matthews v SLAB & Henderson* , 1995 S.C.L.R. 184 that where the sole issue in the course of the summary decree motion was whether there was a legal basis for the defence then it is not inappropriate for a sheriff to approach that issue in a manner which is not entirely different from that which would be appropriate at a debate. See: also *Royal Bank of Scotland Ltd v Dinwoodie* , 1987 S.L.T. 82 and *McKays Stores Ltd v City Wall (Holdings) Ltd* , 1989 S.L.T. 835 at 836E per Lord McCluskey "The test which I have to apply at this stage: I have to ask myself if the question of law which is raised admits of a clear and obvious answer". If the answer to that question is yes then the matter can be appropriately dealt with by way of a summary decree motion.

It should not, however, be thought that a summary decree motion is a narrower procedure than a debate. Rather as Lord Caplan stated in *Frimobar v Mobile Technical Plant (International) Ltd* , 1990 S.L.T. 180 at 181L "A hearing in a summary decree motion is more far reaching (than a debate) because the rules of court specifically admit material extraneous to the pleadings such as affidavits or productions. Thus the court is concerned not only to test the relevancy of the defence but the authenticity of the defence."

*"at any time after a defender has lodged defences".*

A motion for summary decree may be moved at any time up to final decree. Such motions are due to their nature most commonly enrolled shortly after the lodging of defences.

*"no defence to the action".*

In considering whether no defence is disclosed the court should have regard to the pleadings before it at the time of the motion. Although, in exceptional cases, the court may have regard to a minute of amendment presented but not yet part of the pleadings (see: *Robinson v Thomson* , 1987 S.L.T. 120). The court is further entitled to have regard to documents extraneous to the pleadings which have been lodged together with the history of the case and any relevant background information (see: *Spink & Son Ltd v McColl* , 1992 S.L.T. 470).

What the court should have regard to is the substance of the defence and not the manner in which it is pled. The issue for the court is to decide whether there is a genuine issue to try raised by the defences. The court is not confined to merely considering the narrow issue of relevancy (see: *Frimobar UK Ltd v Mobile Tech Plant (International) Ltd* supra). In considering the defence the court should consider whether by adjustment or minute of amendment a case can be improved to enable a genuine defence to be stated. In that event summary decree should not be pronounced.

Before the court can properly grant a summary decree it must be satisfied that no defence is disclosed. The test should be applied at the time that the motion is made (see: *Frimobar* supra). The standard of satisfaction has been defined by the court as being one of more than probability but less than complete certainty (see: *Watson-Towers Ltd v McPhail* , 1986 S.L.T. 617) or as put by Lord Prosser in *P and M Sinclair v The Bamber Gray Partnership* , 1987 S.C. 203 at 206 near certainty was required in order to fulfil the test.

*Personal Injury Actions.*

Generally courts have been slow to grant summary decrees in personal injury actions. It has been made clear that the putting forward of such a motion merely on the basis that the defender has lodged skeletal defences would not of itself be sufficient to obtain a summary decree (see: *McManus v Speirs Dick & Smith Ltd* , 1989 S.L.T. 806 per Lord Caplan at 807L). However, summary decree has been granted (see *Campbell v Golding* , 1992 S.L.T. 889) where the pursuer was able to found on an extract conviction relative to the defender. In *Struthers v British Alcan Rolled Products Ltd* , 1995 S.L.T. 142 summary decree was granted where the pursuer was able to found on a report lodged by the defenders indicating fault on their part.

*Order to produce a document or lodge an affidavit.*

The court may order the production of a document or the lodging of an affidavit which it considers may be of assistance in deciding the issue of whether there is a genuine defence.

It has been held that the court is entitled on the basis of evidence contained in an affidavit to hold itself satisfied that a certain state of fact exists although a denial of that state of facts is contained within the defences. (See: *Ingram Coal Co. v Nugent* , 1991 S.L.T. 603).

*"Change of circumstances" giving rise to a subsequent motion.*

Such a change of circumstances may arise from, for example, on an alteration in the pleadings; the lodging of certain documents in process; and the production of an affidavit.

*Appeal.*

If as a result of a summary decree motion a final judgment is pronounced (see: s.27 of the 1907 Act) then such decree is appealable without leave. Otherwise any other decision made in the course of a motion for summary decree with the exception of an interlocutor making an order *ad factum praestandum*, for example the lodging of a document requires leave to appeal.

*Counterclaim.*

The above points are equally applicable where an application for summary decree is made by a defender in terms of a counterclaim.

## Chapter 18

## Amendment of Pleadings

### Alteration of sum sued for

**18.1.**—(1)[1]  In a cause in which all other parties have lodged defences or answers, the pursuer may, before the closing of the record, alter any sum sued for by amending the crave of the initial writ, and any record.

(2)   The pursuer shall forthwith intimate any such amendment in writing to every other party.

### Powers of sheriff to allow amendment

**18.2.**—(1)   The sheriff may, at any time before final judgment, allow an amendment mentioned in paragraph (2).

(2)   Paragraph (1) applies to the following amendments:—

   (a)   an amendment of the initial writ which may be necessary for the purpose of determining the real question in controversy between the parties, notwithstanding that in consequence of such amendment—

      (i)   the sum sued for is increased or restricted after the closing of the record; or

      (ii)   a different remedy from that originally craved is sought;

   (b)   an amendment which may be necessary—

      (i)   to correct or supplement the designation of a party to the cause;

      (ii)   to enable a party who has sued or has been sued in his own right to sue or be sued in a representative capacity;

      (iii)   to enable a party who has sued or has been sued in a representative capacity to sue or be sued in his own right or in a different representative capacity;

      (iv)   to add the name of an additional pursuer or person whose concurrence is necessary;

      (v)   where the cause has been commenced or presented in the name of the wrong person, or it is doubtful whether it has been commenced

---

[1] As amended by SI 1996/2445 (effective November 1, 1996).

or presented in the name of the right person, to allow any other person to be sisted in substitution for, or in addition to, the original person; or

(vi)     to direct a crave against a third party brought into an action under Chapter 20 (third party procedure);

(c)     an amendment of a condescendence, defences, answers, pleas-in-law or other pleadings which may be necessary for determining the real question in controversy between the parties; and

(d)     where it appears that all parties having an interest have not been called or that the cause has been directed against the wrong person, an amendment inserting in the initial writ an additional or substitute party and directing existing or additional craves, averments and pleas-in-law against that party.

GENERAL NOTE.

Before this rule amendment procedure in the Sheriff Court was governed by Rules 79 and 80 of Schedule 1 to the 1970 Act which were in wholly different terms from Rule 18.2. Cases decided in terms of the old Sheriff Court Rules are no longer of relevance.

Rule 18 is now in broadly similar terms to Rule 24 in the Court of Session and cases decided in terms of said latter rule are accordingly of relevance.

The power to allow amendment given by this rule is a wide one. However, amendment cannot cure fundamental nullity (see: *Rutherford v Vertue* , 1993 S.C.L.R. 886).

*Test as to allowing of Minute of amendment.*

In terms of para.8.2(2)(a) and (c) the test as to whether a minute of amendment should be allowed is a two-part one.

*"necessary for...determining the real question in controversy":*

Firstly, is the minute of amendment necessary to determine the real question in controversy between the parties.

Secondly, should the court in the exercise of its discretion allow the minute of amendment? In other words, is it in the interests of justice to allow the minute of amendment? (See: *Thomson v Glasgow Corporation* , 1962 S.C. (HL) 36 per Thomson LJC at 51).

The decision as to whether to allow a minute of amendment is a matter for the discretion of the court, even when the amendment required to determine the real question in controversy is radical in nature and even if presented outwith the triennium (see: *Sellars v IMI Yorkshire Imperial Ltd* , 1986 S.L.T. 629).

In terms of the first test the court must consider inter alia:

1.     Is the minute of amendment relevant?
2.     Does the minute of amendment cure or at least to a material extent cure the identified defect or defects in the party's case?

Turning to the second part of the test, in seeking to apply the test of whether it is fair and in the interests of justice to allow the minute of amendment the court will have regard to inter alia the following broad factors—

1.     The whole procedural history of the case.
2.     The extent to which the amendment seeks to alter the case already pled.
3.     The procedural stage at which the amendment is sought.
4.     The extent and nature of the prejudice to the other party by the allowance of the amendment.
5.     The extent to which such prejudice can be ameliorated/obviated by the awarding of expenses against the party seeking to amend or by the attachment of any other conditions to the granting of the minute of amendment. The most common condition attached is the discharge of a diet of proof in order to allow the party who is required to answer the minute of amendment to prepare to meet the amendment.

*Stage in Procedure when minute of Amendment is Presented*

*General Rule. "before final Judgment".*

A minute of amendment may be competently moved at any time before final judgment.

It can be broadly stated that the later in an action leave is sought the more likely it is that prejudice to the other side will not be capable of amelioration by an award of expenses or otherwise.

*Specific Stages at Which Leave to Amend May be Sought*

(a) Where leave to amend is sought at or before a diet of debate it will often be allowed as it is unlikely that at that stage any prejudice to the other party will be of such a nature or extent that it cannot properly be compensated by an appropriate award of expenses. Where leave to amend is sought at the commencement of or during the course of a debate then it will be necessary for the party seeking leave to be in a position to satisfy the court that he can or will be able to answer the points set forth in the Rule 22 Note which it is accepted require to be answered.

(b) Where leave to amend is sought sufficiently prior to the proof not to require any adjournment it is likely to be allowed. On the other hand, if amendment is sought so close to the diet of proof as to require a discharge in order to allow investigation by the other side then leave to amend is more likely to be refused on the basis that it is not in the interests of justice that the other side should lose their diet of proof (see: *Dryburgh v NCB* 1962 S.C. 485 at 492 per Lord Guthrie). It will be of particular importance in persuading the court that leave should be allowed at this stage that there is some very good reason why the minute of amendment comes at such a late stage in the case.

(c) Where minute of amendment is tendered in the course of proof. In considering whether leave should be granted at this stage of a case, the court will consider a number of factors:
   (i) whether it has been presented at the first opportunity (see: *Cameron v Lanarkshire Health Board* , 1997 S.L.T. 1040 at 1043D to Eper Lord Gill and *Rafferty v Weir* , 1966 S.L.T. (News) 23).
   (ii) whether there is a good explanation as to why the minute of amendment is presented at such a late stage.
   (iii) prejudice to the other party.
   At this stage it is often difficult to see how an award of expenses or any other condition could compensate for the prejudice which has arisen to the other side by the late stage at which leave to amend is being sought. However, it should be borne in mind in relation to the issue of countering any prejudice to the other party that witnesses can be recalled.
   *Circumstances requiring an amendment during the course of a proof.* If it is sought to advance a ground not covered by the record (see: *Gunn v John McAdam & Son* , 1949 S.C. 31) then a minute of amendment is required.
   A ground is not covered by record where it can be described as being other than a "variation, modification or development" of the case on record. (See Thompson LJC in *Burns v Dixon's Ironworks Ltd* , 1961 S.C. 102 at 107).
   Such a motion to seek leave to amend will almost always arise on an objection of no record being made by the other side. Should the other side fail to object timeously to a line of evidence for which there is in fact no record and there should have been then amendment is not required (see: *McGlone v BRB* , 1966 S.C. (HL) 1).

(d) Where a minute of amendment is presented after proof. Such a minute of amendment although competent would only be granted in the rarest of situations given the almost inevitable material prejudice to the other side by allowing it. An example of where such a minute of amendment has been allowed is *Moyes v Burntisland Shipping Company* , 1952 S.L.T. 417. Here a minute of amendment was allowed following a jury trial. In that case the circumstances were described as exceptional and in order to deal to some extent with the prejudice caused by the lateness of the minute of amendment a proof before answer was ordered rather than a further jury trial.

(e) Where amendment is sought after the marking of an appeal. Frequently such amendment is allowed by the party which has lost at debate and then appeals. The considerations as to whether such an amendment should be allowed are broadly similar to those which are relevant where leave to amend is sought shortly before or at a diet of debate. However, following upon a hearing at which evidence has been led the granting of leave to appeal at this stage will be extremely rare. The factors referred to at (c) will again apply, however, with even more force.

(f) Where amendment is sought after expiry of the time limit. The court will not, in general, allow a pursuer by amendment to substitute the right defender for the wrong defender, or to cure a radical incompetence in his action, or to change the basis of his case if he only seeks to make such amendments after the expiry of a time limit which would have prevented him at that stage from raising fresh proceedings: see *Pompa's Trustees v The Magistrates of Edinburgh* , 1942 S.C. 119 at 125 per Cooper LJC.

The question which most frequently arises is what amounts to changing the basis of the case. Lord President Cooper in *McPhail v Lanarkshire County Council* , 1951 S.C. 301 at 309 elaborated on what he had said in *Pompa's Trustees v The Magistrates of Edinburgh supra* and gives the clearest statement of what amounts to the changing of the basis of the case:

I think the pursuer may well claim, not to have offered a new but only to have presented the old case but from a new angle, not to have changed the foundation of his action but only to have made certain alterations to the superstructure.

The appropriate time to consider the issue of time bar/prescription where it is raised in answer to the presentation of a minute of amendment is when the motion to allow the record to be amended is being heard (see: *Greenhorn v Smart* , 1979 S.C. 427 per Lord Cameron at 432 and *Stewart v Highlands & Islands Development Board* , 1991 S.L.T. 787).

The courts will not allow a new pursuer to be added by amendment post expiry of the relevant period of time bar or prescriptive period (see *MacLean v BRB* , 1966 S.L.T. 39).

"the sum sued for is increased:" Such amendment can be competently made following the expiry of a time limit in terms of the law of prescription or time bar (see *Mackie v Glasgow Corporation* , 1924 S.L.T. 510).

"a different remedy from that originally craved is sought:" A fundamental change in the form of the action is not competent see e.g. *Sleigh v City of Edinburgh District Council* , 1988 S.L.T. 253, in which a motion for leave to amend a petition for interdict to a petition for judicial review was refused under reference to Lord Cooper's opinion in *Pompa's Trustees supra.*

## Applications to amend

**18.3.**—(1)  A party seeking to amend shall lodge a minute of amendment in process setting out his proposed amendment and, at the same time, lodge a motion—

(a)  to allow the minute of amendment to be received; and

(b)  to allow—

  (i)  amendment in terms of the minute of amendment and, where appropriate, to grant an order under rule 18.5(1)(a) (service of amendment for additional or substitute party); or

  (ii)  where the minute of amendment may require to be answered, any other person to lodge answers within a specified period.

(2)  Where the sheriff has pronounced an interlocutor allowing a minute of amendment to be received and answered, he may allow a period of adjustment of the minute of amendment and answers and, on so doing, shall fix a date for parties to be heard on the minute of amendment and answers as adjusted.

(3)[1]  Any adjustment to any minute of amendment or answers shall be exchanged between parties and not lodged in process.

(4)[2]  Parties shall be responsible for maintaining a record of adjustment made and the date of their intimation.

(5)[3]  No adjustments shall be permitted after the period of adjustment allowed, except with leave of the sheriff.

(6)[4]  Each party shall, no later than 2 days before the hearing fixed in terms of paragraph (2), lodge in process a copy of their minute of amendment or answers with all adjustments made thereto in italic or bold type, or underlined.

"to add the name of an additional pursuer." The courts will allow this even when the pursuers title has been defective during the course of the action (see: *Donaghy v Rollo* , 1964 S.C. 278). A minute of sist is not required (see: Macphail, Sheriff Court Practice para. 10.09).

"Lodge a motion." The procedure as set out in OCR 15 should be followed.

"shall fix a date for parties to be heard on the minute of amendment." If there is opposition to the minute of amendment this is the appropriate stage for opposition to be made to the minute of amendment. Broadly, the only exception to this would be if the lodging of the minute of amendment due to the stage at which it is lodged gives rise to the issue of possible discharge of a proof or a debate. In such circumstances it would be appropriate to lodge opposition to the motion to have the minute of amendment received. The motion made at the hearing in terms of 18.3(2) for the record to be amended in terms of the minute of amendment and answers (if necessary as adjusted) is made orally as to do it by written motion would require the whole of OCR 15 to be followed.

"Each party shall no later than 2 days before the hearing—lodge in process a copy of their minute of amendment or answers with all adjustments made thereto in italics." It is important that this rule is complied with in that non compliance results in the court being unable to prepare for and conduct the hearing properly as in terms of 18.3(3) no copy of adjustments is lodged in court when adjustments are exchanged.

"Form of Minute of Amendment." It should begin with the instance and be followed by a preamble.

... for the pursuer/defender craved and hereby craves leave of the court to amend the initial writ/defence or to open the closed record and to amend the same as follows—

Thereafter in numbered paragraphs the amendments should be set out.

---

[1] Inserted by SSI 2000/239 (effective October 2, 2000).
[2] Inserted by SSI 2000/239 (effective October 2, 2000).
[3] Inserted by SSI 2000/239 (effective October 2, 2000).
[4] Inserted by SSI 2000/239 (effective October 2, 2000).

At the end IN RESPECT WHEREOF should appear.

"Form of Answers:" It should begin with the instance and be followed by a preamble—

... for the pursuer/defender craved and hereby craves leave of the court to answer the minute of amendment number...of process as follows—

Thereafter in numbered paragraphs the answers should be set out.

At the end IN RESPECT WHEREOF should appear.

## Applications for diligence on amendment

**18.4.**—(1)  Where a minute of amendment is lodged by a pursuer under rule 18.2(2)(d) (all parties not, or wrong person, called), he may apply by motion for warrant to use any form of diligence which could be used on the dependence of a separate action.

(2)  A copy certified by the sheriff clerk of the interlocutor granting warrant for diligence on the dependence applied for under paragraph (1) shall be sufficient authority for the execution of that diligence.

## Service of amended pleadings

**18.5.**—(1)[1]  Where an amendment under rule 18.2(2)(b)(iv), (v) or (vi) (additional or substitute defenders added by amendment) or rule 18.2(2)(d) (all parties not, or wrong person, called) has been made—

    (a)   the sheriff shall order that a copy of the initial writ or record, as the case may be, as so amended be served by the party who made the amendment on that additional or substitute party with—

        (i)[2]  in a cause in which a time to pay direction under the Debtors (Scotland) Act 1987 or a time order under the Consumer Credit Act 1974 may be applied for, a notice in Form 08 specifying the date by which a notice of intention must be lodged in process, a notice in Form 03 and a notice of intention to defend in Form 07; or

        (ii)  in any other cause, a notice in Form 09 specifying the date by which a notice of intention to defend must be lodged in process and a notice of intention to defend in Form 07; and

    (b)   the party who made the amendment shall lodge in process—

        (i)  a copy of the initial writ or record as amended;

        (ii)  a copy of the notice sent in Form 08 or Form 09; and

        (iii)  a certificate of service.

(2)  When paragraph (1) has been complied with, the cause as so amended shall proceed in every respect as if that party had originally been made a party to the cause.

(3)  Where a notice of intention to defend is lodged by virtue of paragraph (1)(a), the sheriff clerk shall fix a date for a hearing under rule 9.12 (Options Hearing).

GENERAL NOTE

Where in terms of the minute of amendment the parties to the action are intended to be altered then service of the writ or record as amended will be ordered. Service will require to conform to OCR 5.

---

[1] As amended by SI 1996/2445 (effective November 1, 1996).

[2] As amended by the Act of Sederunt (Ordinary Cause, Summary Application, Summary Cause and Small Claim Rules) Amendment (Miscellaneous) 2007 (SSI 2007/6), para.2(9) (effective January 29, 2007).

## Expenses and conditions of amendment

**18.6.** The sheriff shall find the party making an amendment liable in the expenses occasioned by the amendment unless it is shown that it is just and equitable that the expenses occasioned by the amendment should be otherwise dealt with, and may attach such other conditions as he thinks fit.

General Note

This rule specifically directs that the party amending will be found liable in the expenses occasioned by the amendment, unless it is just and equitable, to make any other type of award. The most common instance of where a party amending will not be found liable in expenses is where the other party adjusted shortly before the closing of the record not allowing adjustments in answer to be made timeously and thus requiring a minute of amendment to deal with these adjustments.

*expenses occasioned by the amendment*

will include the expenses of preparing answers (see: *Campbell v Henderson*, 1949 S.C. 172). Such awards of expenses may also cover more than merely the cost of preparing answers. If the lodging of the minute of amendment has resulted in either the procedure which has gone before in its entirety or to some specific prior stage for eg. the closing of the record being rendered worthless then the party amending may be found liable for either the whole of the procedure or to that specific stage (see: *Campbell v Henderson supra*). Further, where the lodging of a minute of amendment has resulted in the discharge of a debate or proof the party amending is likely to be found liable for the costs of the discharge (see e.g. *Mackenzie v Mackenzie*, 1951 S.C. 163 at 165–166).

## Effect of amendment on diligence

**18.7.** Where an amendment has been allowed, the amendment—

(a) shall not validate diligence used on the dependence of a cause so as to prejudice the rights of creditors of the party against whom the diligence has been executed who are interested in defeating such diligence; and

(b) shall preclude any objection to such diligence stated by a party or any person by virtue of a title acquired or in right of a debt contracted by him subsequent to the execution of such diligence.

## Preliminary pleas inserted on amendment

**18.8.**—(1) Where a party seeks to add a preliminary plea by amendment or answers to an amendment, or by adjustment thereto, a note of the basis for the plea shall be lodged at the same time as the minute, answers or adjustment, as the case may be.

(2) If a party fails to comply with paragraph (1), that party shall be deemed to be no longer insisting on the preliminary plea and the plea shall be repelled by the sheriff.

If the minute of amendment or answers thereto seeks to add a preliminary plea, a note of the basis of that plea must be lodged at the same time as the minute, answers or adjustments thereto which introduces the plea (OCR 18.8(1))

"Appeal." Leave to appeal is required both in relation to a grant and refusal of a motion for leave to amend.

## Chapter 19

## Counterclaims

*Annotations to Chapters 19 to 29 by Simon Di Rollo, Q.C.*

### Counterclaims

**19.1.**—(1)[1] In any action other than a family action within the meaning of rule 33.1(1), a civil partnership action within the meaning of rule 33A.1(1) or an action of multiplepoinding, a defender may counterclaim against a pursuer—

    (a) where the counterclaim might have been made in a separate action in which it would not have been necessary to call as defender any person other than the pursuer; and

    (b) in respect of any matter—

        (i) forming part, or arising out of the grounds, of the action by the pursuer;

        (ii) the decision of which is necessary for the determination of the question in controversy between the parties; or

        (iii) which, if the pursuer had been a person not otherwise subject to the jurisdiction of the court, might have been the subject-matter of an action against that pursuer in which jurisdiction would have arisen by reconvention.

  (2) A counterclaim shall be made in the defences—

    (a) when the defences are lodged or during the period for adjustment;

    (b) by amendment at any other stage, with the leave of the sheriff and subject to such conditions, if any, as to expenses or otherwise as the sheriff thinks fit.

  (3) Defences which include a counterclaim shall commence with a crave setting out the counterclaim in such form as, if the counterclaim had been made in a separate action, would have been appropriate in the initial writ in that separate action and shall include—

    (a) answers to the condescendence of the initial writ as required by rule 9.6(2) (form of defences);

    (b) a statement of facts in numbered paragraphs setting out the facts on which the counterclaim is founded, incorporating by reference, if necessary, any matter contained in the defences; and

    (c) appropriate pleas-in-law.

GENERAL NOTE

The Ordinary Cause Rules 1993 made several important changes to sheriff court counterclaim procedure. Care is required in relation to earlier sheriff court decisions made under the old rules. The terms of the sheriff court rule are now practically identical to the current Court of Session rule (see RCS 1994, Chapter 25). The language of the latter is in similar terms to the earlier Court of Session rule. The older Court of Session cases remain of value.

The purpose of the counterclaim procedure is to allow the defender to obtain a decree (apart from absolvitor or dismissal) against the pursuer where he has a claim against him which is connected with the grounds of the pursuer's action. It is expedient to permit the parties to resolve the whole of their dispute in one process. Family actions have their own discrete rules (see Chapter 33) and are excluded from Chapter 19 as are, for obvious reasons, actions of multiplepoinding. In all other actions under the Ordinary Cause Rules a counterclaim is competent under this chapter. Provided the requirements of the rules are

---

[1] As amended by Act of Sederunt (Ordinary Cause Rules) Amendment (Family Law (Scotland) ct 2006 etc.) 2006 (SSI 2006/207) r.2 (effective May 4, 2006).

otherwise satisfied, it is competent to counterclaim for interdict (*Mclean v Marwhirn Developments Ltd*, 1976 S.L.T. (Notes) 47) or delivery (*Borthwick v Dean Warwick Ltd*, 1985 S.L.T. 269) and presumably in an appropriate case for other types of non-pecuniary decree.

A counterclaim is often (but not exclusively) used in response to an action for payment of the contract price where the defender seeks damages for breach of contract, or in the converse situation. It is important not to confuse two questions. The first question is whether in an action for debt it is relevant to plead in defence that a debt is due by the pursuer to the defender. The answer to that question is a matter of the substantive law (see Wilson, *Debt* (2nd ed., 1991), Chap.13 and McBryde, *Contract* (2nd ed., 2001), pp.499–501). For a detailed and comprehensive review of the authorities on the substantive law see *Inveresk Plc v Tullis Russell Papermakers Ltd*, 2010 S.L.T. 941; 2010 SC (UKSC) 106. The second question is in an action what types of claim can form the basis of a counterclaim under the rule in this chapter? That is a question to be answered by the terms of this rule. In this context if the defender seeks to withhold the price on the ground of the pursuer's breach of contract then it may not be necessary to lodge a counterclaim (see Macphail, *Sheriff Court Practice* (2nd ed., 1998), p.390 footnote 37), but he still requires to give fair notice in his defences of the precise basis upon which payment is withheld and to make adequate relevant averments (including specification of the amount of the damage) to permit the equitable doctrine of retention (see *Inveresk Plc* (above) at paras [60] to [107]) to be operated.

OCR, r.19.1(1)(a), (b)(i), (ii) and (iii) define the scope of the connection required between the pursuer's action and the defender's response which permit the latter to lodge a counterclaim.

## RULE 19.1(1)(A)

First, it is essential that the counterclaim could have been brought by the same defender as a separate action against the same pursuer without having to call any other party as defender (*Tods Murray W.S. v Arakin Ltd*, 2001 S.C. 840, IH).

## RULE 19.1(1)(B)(I) OR (II) OR (III)

Secondly, the subject matter of the counterclaim must either (i) form part of the pursuer's action, or (ii) arise out of its grounds, or (iii) be a matter the decision of which is necessary for the determination of the question in controversy between the parties, or (iv) arise from the common law principle of reconvention (in so far as that has not been swept away by the Civil Jurisdiction and Judgements Act 1982).

## RULE 19.1(1)(B)(I) — "FORM PART OF THE PURSUER'S ACTION", OR "ARISE OUT OF ITS GROUNDS"

In the contractual context when a contract is one and indivisible, a counterclaim arising out of one item can be competently pursued in answer to a claim for payment on the whole contract. Often there is a series of transactions between the parties with each transaction or group representing a separate contract. In that event if the pursuer sues upon one contract the defender's counterclaim has to relate to that contract in order to be said to form part of the pursuer's action or arise out of its grounds (see *JW Chafer (Scotland) Ltd v Hope*, 1963 S.L.T. (Notes) 11). Nevertheless, the defender may be able to bring himself within rule 19.1(1)(b)(ii).

## RULE 19.1(1)(B)(II) — "NECESSARY FOR THE DETERMINATION OF THE QUESTION IN CONTROVERSY BETWEEN THE PARTIES"

This permits a counterclaim to be maintained even though the defender is not allowed under the substantive law of contract to retain a sum in defence to the pursuer's claim for payment. In *Fulton Clyde Ltd v JF McCallum & Co. Ltd*, 1960 S.C. 78; 1960 S.L.T. 253 the pursuer sought payment of the price of goods delivered. The defenders did not dispute that the goods had been delivered or the contract price. They sought to retain the price in respect of a failure to deliver goods on an earlier occasion. It was held that the earlier failure in delivery was a separate contract and so the defender was not entitled to retain the contract price in respect of the later delivery. Decree was granted for the sum sought by the pursuer. However, the court allowed the counterclaim to proceed on the basis that the questions in controversy between the parties on the whole pleadings included whether the defender was entitled to damages for breach of contract due to the failure to make an earlier delivery (see also *Borthwick v Dean Warwick Ltd*, 1985 S.L.T. 269 where the court considered that on the pleadings it could not be said that the counterclaim did not arise out of the same contract).

## RULE 19.1(1)(B)(III)

This only applies where the common law doctrine of reconvention can be invoked. Reconvention is a common law equitable doctrine that permits a pursuer who raises an action against the defender to be counterclaimed against where he would not otherwise be subject to the jurisdiction of the court. The basic principles involved are illustrated in *Thompson v Whitehead* (1862) 24 D. 331, and for a modern example where it was held to apply, see e.g. *MacKenzie v Macleod's Executor*, 1988 S.L.T. 207, OH. In the sheriff court the doctrine had statutory sanction by virtue of section 6(h) of the Sheriff Courts (Scotland) Act 1907 which provided that the sheriff had jurisdiction "where the party sued is the pursuer in any action pending within [his] jurisdiction against the party suing". Section 20 of the Civil Jurisdiction and Judgements Act 1982 provides that section 6 of the 1907 Act ceases to have effect to the extent that it determines jurisdiction in relation to any matter to which Schedule 8 applies. Paragraph 2(15)(c) of Schedule 8 to the 1982 Act provides that there is jurisdiction on a counterclaim arising from the same contract or facts on which the original claim was based, in the court in which the original claim is pending. The common law doctrine of reconvention can only be invoked in relation to those matters in Schedule 9 of the 1982 Act (see Anton, *Private International Law* (3rd ed., 2011), paras 8.331 and 8.332).

RULE 19.1(2)(A) AND (B)

Leave is required to lodge a counterclaim after the record has closed. Before that stage is reached, provided the counterclaim meets the requirement of the rules, there is no discretion to it being included in the defences.

RULE 19.1(3)

This prescribes how to set out the defences and counterclaim and should be followed in every case. The order is crave, answers to each article of condescendence, pleas-in-law relating to the answers, statement of facts and pleas in law relating to the statement of facts.

## Warrants for diligence on counterclaims

**19.2.**[1](1)   A defender who makes a counterclaim may apply for a warrant for interim diligence which would have been permitted had the warrant been sought in an initial writ in a separate action.

(2)–(4)   *[Repealed by the Act of Sederunt (Sheriff Court Rules) (Miscellaneous Amendments) 2009 (SSI 2009/294) r.10 (effective October 1, 2009).]*

GENERAL NOTE

See OCR 1993 Chapter 6 Interim Diligence. The law is codified in the Debtors (Scotland) Act 1987 ss.15A to 15N.

## Form of record where counterclaim lodged

**19.2A.**[2]   Where, under rule 9.10 (open record), 9.11 (record for Options Hearing), 10.4 (open record), or 10.5 (closed record), a record requires to be lodged in an action in which a counterclaim is included in the defences, the pleadings of the parties shall be set out in the record in the following order:—

    (a)   the crave of the initial writ;

    (b)   the condescendence and answers relating to the initial writ;

    (c)   the pleas-in-law of the parties relating to the crave of the initial writ;

    (d)   the crave of the counterclaim;

    (e)   the statement of facts and answers relating to the counterclaim; and

    (f)   the pleas-in-law of the parties relating to the counterclaim.

GENERAL NOTE

This rule helpfully provides the correct format of the record where there is a counterclaim, and should be followed in every case.

## Effect of abandonment of cause

**19.3.**—(1)   The right of a pursuer to abandon a cause under rule 23.1 shall not be affected by a counterclaim; and any expenses for which the pursuer is found liable as a condition of, or in consequence of, such abandonment shall not include the expenses of the counterclaim.

(2)   Notwithstanding abandonment by the pursuer, a defender may insist in his counterclaim; and the proceedings in the counterclaim shall continue in dependence as if the counterclaim were a separate action.

GENERAL NOTE

The counterclaim, once it is born, has an existence independent of the principal action. It can proceed in conjunction with the principal action or on its own should that be abandoned.

---

[1] As amended by the Act of Sederunt (Sheriff Court Rules) (Miscellaneous Amendments) 2009 (SSI 2009/294) r.10 (effective October 1, 2009).

[2] Inserted by SI 1996/2445 (effective November 1, 1996).

## Disposal of counterclaims

**19.4.** The sheriff may—

(a) deal with a counterclaim as if it had been stated in a separate action;

(b) regulate the procedure in relation to the counterclaim as he thinks fit; and

(c) grant decree for the counterclaim in whole or in part or for the difference between it and the sum sued for by the pursuer.

GENERAL NOTE

Usually the counterclaim will be subject to the same procedure as the main action but there is scope for having separate enquires or debates. The parties should make it clear what procedure they desire in relation to both the principal action and the counterclaim and any interlocutor should be specific to each in relation to any procedure to take place. The court has the same powers in relation to the disposal of the counterclaim as it does with regard to the principal action.

Chapter 20

Third Party Procedure

## Applications for third party notice

**20.1.**—(1) Where, in an action, a defender claims that—

(a) he has in respect of the subject-matter of the action a right of contribution, relief or indemnity against any person who is not a party to the action, or

(b) a person whom the pursuer is not bound to call as a defender should be made a party to the action along with the defender in respect that such person is—

    (i) solely liable, or jointly or jointly and severally liable with the defender, to the pursuer in respect of the subject-matter of the action, or

    (ii) liable to the defender in respect of a claim arising from or in connection with the liability, if any, of the defender to the pursuer,

he may apply by motion for an order for service of a third party notice upon that other person in Form O10 for the purpose of convening that other person as a third party to the action.

(2)[1] Where—

(a) a pursuer against whom a counterclaim has been made, or

(b) a third party convened in the action,

seeks, in relation to the claim against him, to make against a person who is not a party, a claim mentioned in paragraph (1) as a claim which could be made by a defender against a third party, he shall apply by motion for an order for service of a third party notice in Form O10 in the same manner as a defender under that paragraph; and rules 20.2 to 20.6 shall, with the necessary modifications, apply to such a claim as they apply in relation to such a claim by a defender.

GENERAL NOTE

Like the counterclaim procedure (see Chapter 19) the purpose of the third party procedure is to permit matters arising out of a dispute to be resolved in one process. Where a defender considers that responsibility for the pursuer's claim lies ultimately in whole or in part with another person, he may introduce that person into the action as a third party. The procedure is available when a defender claims: (1) a right of contribution, relief or indemnity against a third party; or (2) that the third party is either solely liable or jointly or jointly and severally liable with him to the pursuer. Again like counterclaim procedure the rule is purely procedural (see *National Coal Board v Knight Bros* , 1972 S.L.T. (Notes) 24, OH; *R and Watson Ltd v David Traill & Sons Ltd* , 1972 S.L.T. (Notes) 38). The terms "contribution, relief or indemnity" in the rule are to be interpreted in a broad way and it is not essential that any separate action against the third party would be put into any particular pigeon-hole (see, e.g. *Nicol Homeworld Contractors Ltd v Charles Gray Builders Ltd* , 1986 S.L.T. 317, OH). Thereafter the rights of the parties must be

---

[1] As amended by SI 1996/2445 (effective November 1, 1996).

worked out under reference to the substantive law. A pursuer in a counterclaim may also lodge a third party notice. A third party may counterclaim against a defender or lodge a further third party notice himself. In that event the further third party is referred to as "second third party".

Application to lodge a third party notice is made by motion for an order for service of a notice in Form O10. The notice requires specification of the basis upon which the third party is to be convened to the action, but the terms of any such notice do not prevent the defender from altering the pleadings against the third party from one of joint liability to sole fault or vice versa (*Beedie v Norrie* , 1966 S.C. 207; 1966 S.L.T. 295).

## Averments where order for service of third party notice sought

**20.2.**—(1)  Where a defender intends to apply by motion for an order for service of a third party notice before the closing of the record, he shall, before lodging the motion, set out in his defences, by adjustment to those defences, or in a separate statement of facts annexed to those defences—

  (a)   averments setting out the grounds on which he maintains that the proposed third party is liable to him by contribution, relief or indemnity or should be made a party to the action; and

  (b)   appropriate pleas-in-law.

(2)  Where a defender applies by motion for an order for service of a third party notice after the closing of the record, he shall, on lodging the motion, lodge a minute of amendment containing—

  (a)   averments setting out the grounds on which he maintains that the proposed third party is liable to him by contribution, relief or indemnity or should be made a party to the action, and

  (b)   appropriate pleas-in-law,

unless those grounds and pleas-in-law have been set out in the defences in the closed record.

(3)  A motion for an order for service of a third party notice shall be lodged before the commencement of the hearing of the merits of the cause.

GENERAL NOTE

*Rule 20.2(3)*

Until the commencement of the hearing on the merits it is entirely a matter for the discretion of the court whether a motion to introduce a third party is granted or not. The length of time that a case has been in dependence, the inevitable delay caused by allowing a motion and the requirement to discharge a proof may each be important factors weighing against allowing a motion to allow an order for service of a third party notice being granted. It is not competent to lodge a third party notice after the commencement of the hearing on the merits.

## Warrants for diligence on third party notice

**20.3.**[1](1)  A defender who applies for an order for service of a third party notice may apply for—

  (a)   a warrant for arrestment to found jurisdiction;

  (b)   a warrant for interim diligence,

which would have been permitted had the warrant been sought in an initial writ in a separate action.

(2)  Averments in support of the application for a warrant under paragraph (1)(a) shall be included in the defences or the separate statement of facts referred to in rule 20.2(1).

(3)  An application for a warrant under paragraph (1)(a) shall be made by motion—

---

[1]  As amended by the Act of Sederunt (Sheriff Court Rules) (Miscellaneous Amendments) 2009 (SSI 2009/294) r.10 (effective October 1, 2009).

(a)  at the time of applying for the third party notice; or

(b)  if not applied for at that time, at any stage of the cause thereafter.

(4)  A certified copy of the interlocutor granting warrant for diligence applied for under paragraph (2) shall be sufficient authority for execution of the diligence.

GENERAL NOTE

A warrant for diligence may be sought (see generally OCR 1993 Chapter 6 Interim Diligence). The law is codified in the Debtors (Scotland) Act 1987 ss.15A to 15N) but an explanation for seeking it has to be made expressly in the pleadings.

## Service on third party

**20.4.**—(1)  A third party notice shall be served on the third party within 14 days after the date of the interlocutor allowing service of that notice.

(2)  Where service of a third party notice has not been made within the period specified in paragraph (1), the order for service of it shall cease to have effect; and no service of the notice may be made unless a further order for service of it has been applied for and granted.

(3)[1]  There shall be served with a third party notice—

(a)  a copy of the pleadings (including any adjustments and amendments); and

(b)  where the pleadings have not been amended in accordance with the minute of amendment referred to in rule 20.2, a copy of that minute.

(4)  A copy of the third party notice, with a certificate of service attached to it, shall be lodged in process by the defender.

GENERAL NOTE

*Rule 20.4(1), (2)*

It is essential to serve the third party notice within 14 days of the order for service. This prevents a defender from delaying bringing in the third party once an order for service has been made. If service is not effective during that period the defender must return to court and obtain a fresh order.

*Rule 20.4(3)*

The pleadings served with the third party notice must contain the averments anent the basis of the claim made by the defender against the third party.

## Answers to third party notice

**20.5.**—(1)  An order for service of a third party notice shall specify 28 days, or such other period as the sheriff on cause shown may specify, as the period within which the third party may lodge answers.

(2)  Answers for a third party shall be headed "Answers for [E.F.], Third Party in the action at the instance of [A.B.], Pursuer against [C.D.], Defender" and shall include—

(a)  answers to the averments of the defender against him in the form of numbered paragraphs corresponding to the numbered articles of the condescendence annexed to the summons and incorporating, if the third party so wishes, answers to the averments of the pursuer; or

(b)  where a separate statement of facts has been lodged by the defender under rule 20.2(1), answers to the statement of facts in the form of numbered paragraphs corresponding to the numbered paragraphs of the statement of facts; and

(c)  appropriate pleas-in-law.

---

[1]  As amended by SSI 2003/26, r.2 (effective from January 24, 2003).

General Note

It is important that the answers for the third party are organised in such a way so as to make clear the response in relation to the pursuer's averments and thereafter the defenders averments. The answers should be headed "Answers to condescendence and answers to averments for the defender". The third party is entitled to be heard in relation to the pursuer's claim against the defender, including any plea to the relevancy or other preliminary plea.

## Consequences of failure to amend pleadings

**20.5A.**[1]  Where the pleadings have not been amended in accordance with the minute of amendment referred to in rule 20.2, no motion for a finding, order or decree against a third party may be enrolled by the defender unless, at or before the date on which he enrols the motion, he enrols a motion to amend the pleadings in accordance with that minute.

## Procedure following answers

**20.6.**—(1)  Where a third party lodges answers, the sheriff clerk shall fix a date and time under rule 9.2 for a hearing under rule 9.12 (Options Hearing) as if the third party had lodged a notice of intention to defend and the period of notice had expired on the date for lodging answers.

(2)  At the Options Hearing, or at any time thereafter, the sheriff may grant such decree or other order as he thinks fit.

(3)  A decree or other order against the third party shall have effect and be extractable in the same way as a decree or other order against a defender.

General Note

A final date for adjustment should be specified. The pursuer and the defender may require to adjust their pleadings in the light of the answers for the third party. The pursuer requires to consider whether or not to adopt the defender's case against the third party and/or whether or not to adopt the third party's case against the defender. If the pursuer wishes to adopt a case against the third party he requires to insert a crave for decree against the third party (which he must do by amendment) and to insert an appropriate plea in law. In any such amendment for the pursuer it is competent (but not essential) to redesign the third party as a second defender. The original defender may develop his case against the third party beyond what is stated as the ground of action in the third party notice.

Rule 20.6(2)

This rule is expressed in exceedingly wide terms and at first sight appears to permit the sheriff to deal with the merits of the whole case at the options hearing. It is thought, however, that the intention is to permit as much flexibility as possible in regulating further procedure as between all of the parties. It is possible to have separate debates or proofs depending on whether there are separate issues between the parties that may be advantageously resolved at different stages.

Chapter 21

Documents Founded on or Adopted in Pleadings

## Lodging documents founded on or adopted

**21.1.**—(1)  Subject to any other provision in these Rules, any document founded on by a party, or adopted as incorporated, in his pleadings shall, so far as in his possession or within his control, be lodged in process as a production by him—

(a)[2]  when founded on or adopted in an initial writ, at the time of returning the initial writ under rule 9.3 or, in the case of a personal injuries action raised under Part AI of Chapter 36, when the initial writ is presented for warranting in accordance with rule 5.1;

---

[1] As inserted by SSI 2003/26 r.2 (effective January 24, 2003).

[2] As amended by the Act of Sederunt (Ordinary Cause Rules Amendment) (Personal Injuries Actions) 2009 (SSI 2009/285) r.2 (effective November 2, 2009).

(b) when founded on or adopted in a minute, defences, counterclaim or answers, at the time of lodging that part of process; and

(c) when founded on or adopted in an adjustment to any pleadings, at the time when such adjustment is intimated to any other party.

(2) Paragraph (1) shall be without prejudice to any power of the sheriff to order the production of any document or grant a commission and diligence for recovery of it.

General Note

A document founded upon (by reference to it) or incorporated in the pleadings (by the use of a form of words expressly incorporating it) must be lodged. It is the original that must be lodged. A document is founded on if it is a document that forms the basis at least to some extent of the action. Typically, a contract, lease, title deed, will or invoice is apt to form the basis of an action. A document is incorporated in the pleadings if that is expressly stated, the traditional form of words being "The [the title of the document] is held as repeated herein *brevitatis causa*". A more modern form is "The [document] is held as incorporated here in full". Documents that contain assertions of fact or expressions of opinion from witnesses in relation to the issues in the case (such as expert reports or medical reports) should not under any circumstances be founded on in pleadings, nor should such items be incorporated in the pleadings. The pleader should extract from such documents the material required to make specific averments based on that material. Otherwise difficulties can arise (see e.g. *Reid v Shetland Sea Ferries* , 1999 S.C.C.R. 735). At a debate on relevancy or specification the court can only look at the pleadings. If the document has been incorporated then the document forms part of the pleadings and the court may have regard to it. If it has not been incorporated then even if the document is referred to and founded upon the court may not consider the document (although it must have regard to such parts of it as actually form part of the pleadings).

By virtue of OCR, rule 1.2(1), "document" has the meaning assigned to it in section 9 of the Civil Evidence (Scotland) Act 1988 (i.e. it includes maps, plans, graphs or drawings, photographs, discs, film, negatives, tapes, sound tracks or other devices from which sounds or other data or visual images are recorded so as to be capable (with or without the aid of some other equipment) of being reproduced).

A party may be penalised in expenses if there has been any wasted procedure through failure to lodge a document founded upon or incorporated.

*Rule 21.1(2)*

The sheriff has residuary power (presumably on the motion of a party or ex propio motu) to order production of a document at any stage of the cause (see Macphail, *Sheriff Court Practice* (3rd ed.), para.15.48).

## Consequences of failure to lodge documents founded on or adopted

**21.2.** Where a party fails to lodge a document in accordance with rule 21.1(1), he may be found liable in the expenses of any order for production or recovery of it obtained by any other party.

General Note

This is without prejudice to other sanctions available to secure compliance with OCR.

## Objection to documents founded on

**21.3.**—(1) Where a deed or writing is founded on by a party, any objection to it by any other party may be stated and maintained by exception without its being reduced.

(2) Where an objection is stated under paragraph (1) and an action of reduction would otherwise have been competent, the sheriff may order the party stating the objection to find caution or give such other security as he thinks fit.

(3)[1] An objection may not be stated by exception if the sheriff considers that the objection would be more conveniently disposed of in a separate action of reduction.

---

[1] As inserted by the Act of Sederunt (Ordinary Cause Rules Amendment) (Proving the Tenor and Reduction) 2015 (SSI 2015/176) para.2 (effective May 25, 2015).

GENERAL NOTE

A document that has a patent defect that renders it void or *ipso jure* null (such as a document that is executed without the necessary statutory solemnities or is unstamped) will simply not be given effect in any proceedings. If a defect is not of that type or there is room for doubt then the document has to be set aside by reduction. An action of reduction is not competent in the sheriff court but it is competent in certain circumstances to state an objection *ope exceptionis*. If a deed or writing (not decree) founded upon by a party in a sheriff court action is objected to then that objection may be stated and maintained, i.e. insisted upon (see Macphail, *Sheriff Court Practice* (3rd ed.), paras 12.66 to 12.72). Fair notice of the objection is required by averments and a plea in law.

## Chapter 22

## Preliminary Pleas

### Note of basis of preliminary plea

**22.1.**—(1)  A party intending to insist on a preliminary plea shall, not later than 3 days before the Options Hearing under rule 9.12 or the Procedural Hearing under rule 10.6—

(a)  lodge in process a note of the basis for the plea; and

(b)  intimate a copy of it to every other party.

(2)[1]  Where the Options Hearing is continued under rule 9.12(5) and a preliminary plea is added by adjustment, a party intending to insist on that plea shall, not later than 3 days before the date of the Options Hearing so continued—

(a)  lodge in process a note of the basis for the plea; and

(b)  intimate a copy of it to every other party.

(3)  If a party fails to comply with paragraph (1) or (2), he shall be deemed to be no longer insisting on the preliminary plea; and the plea shall be repelled by the sheriff at the Options Hearing or Procedural Hearing.

(4)[2]  At any proof before answer or debate, parties may on cause shown raise matters in addition to those set out in the note mentioned in paragraph (1) or (2).

(5)[3]  Where a note of the basis of a preliminary plea has been lodged under paragraph (1), and the Options Hearing is continued under rule 9.12(5), unless the basis of the plea has changed following further adjustment, it shall not be necessary for a party who is insisting on the plea to lodge a further note before the Options Hearing so continued.

GENERAL NOTE

*Rule 22.1(1)*

One of the most useful innovations of OCR 1993 was the removal of the automatic right to debate together with the requirement to provide notice of the basis of a preliminary plea. At the options hearing the court requires to make an informed decision as to further procedure. To do that in addition to studying the pleadings the sheriff must have a clear indication of the basis upon which any preliminary plea is stated. Accordingly any party that has a preliminary plea must lodge a note under this rule three days before the hearing. Failure to comply means that the preliminary plea must be repelled at the options hearing (or continued options hearing)—although it may just be possible in certain circumstances to invoke the dispensing power under OCR, rule 2.1 (see *Colvin v Montgomery Preservations Ltd* , 1995 S.L.T. (Sh. Ct) 14—that case involved sending the case for additional procedure in terms of Chapter 10 and was an early decision (less latitude might be shown now)). See also *Humphrey v Royal Sun Alliance Plc* , 2005 S.L.T. (Sh. Ct) 31.

---

[1] As inserted by the Act of Sederunt (Sheriff Court Ordinary Cause Rules Amendment) (Miscellaneous) 1996 (SI 1996/2445) (effective November 1, 1996).

[2] As amended by the Act of Sederunt (Sheriff Court Ordinary Cause Rules Amendment) (Miscellaneous) 2000 (SSI 2000/239) (effective October 2, 2000).

[3] As inserted by the Act of Sederunt (Sheriff Court Ordinary Cause Rules Amendment) (Miscellaneous) 1996 (SI 1996/2445) (effective November 1, 1996).

*Rule 22.1(2)*

Where a preliminary plea is added by adjustment between an options hearing and a continued options hearing a note of the basis of the plea must be lodged failing which it will be repelled. Likewise, where a preliminary plea is added by amendment (or answers thereto) it is necessary to lodge a note of argument failing which the plea must be repelled (see OCR, rule 18.8) (cf. *Sutherland v Duncan* , 1996 S.L.T. 428—another early case and where the sheriff's exercise of the dispensing power was not interfered with on appeal).

*Rule 22.1(4)*

On cause shown it is competent to make an argument in support of a preliminary plea not foreshadowed in the rule 22 note but if the argument is new, separate or distinct from the note of the basis of the plea as intimated it might, if successful, result in a penalty in expenses at least to some extent. On the other hand it is not competent to attempt at debate or by amendment to introduce a new or different plea (in relation to the same pleadings that have already been considered at the options hearing) or to reintroduce a plea that has been repelled already (see *George Martin (Builders) Ltd v Jamal* , 2001 S.L.T. (Sh. Ct) 119; see also *Bell v John Davidson (Pipes)* , 1995 S.L.T. (Sh. Ct) 15).

## Chapter 23

## Abandonment

## Abandonment of causes

**23.1.**—(1)  A pursuer may abandon a cause at any time before decree of absolvitor or dismissal by lodging a minute of abandonment and—

(a)  consenting to decree of absolvitor; or

(b)  seeking decree of dismissal.

(2)[1]  The sheriff shall not grant decree of dismissal under paragraph (1)(b) unless full judicial expenses have been paid to the defender, and any third party against whom the pursuer has directed any crave, within 28 days after the date of taxation.

(3)  If the pursuer fails to pay the expenses referred to in paragraph (2) to the party to whom they are due within the period specified in that paragraph, that party shall be entitled to decree of absolvitor with expenses.

GENERAL NOTE

A pursuer has a right to abandon an action against one or more defenders without reserving the ability to raise a fresh action against the same defender in respect of the same subject matter. Such abandonment without reservation will result in decree of absolvitor being pronounced in favour of the defender who will have the benefit of the plea of res judicata should the same pursuer raise the same action against him. The minute is in the following terms "[Name of Solicitor] for the pursuer stated and hereby stated to the court that the pursuer abandons the cause and consents to decree of absolvitor in terms of rule 23.2(1)(a) of the Ordinary Cause Rules". It is usual for the minute also to concede expenses, although this is not a prerequisite. The pursuer should enrol a motion to abandon in terms of the minute (*Walker v Walker* , 1995 S.C.L.R. 187). If the minute is silent as to expenses the defender should oppose the motion to abandon *quaod* the matter of expenses. Expenses as taxed will ordinarily be pronounced in favour of the defender unless, for example, the defender has wrongly misled the pursuer into raising an action against him in which case the pursuer may be able to persuade the court to award him expenses despite the abandonment.

The pursuer may want to reserve the right to raise a fresh action. To achieve that he must ensure that the court pronounces dismissal as opposed to absolvitor, and to do that he must comply with the peremptory terms of the rule. The court will not grant dismissal unless full judicial expenses are paid to the defender within 28 days of the date of taxation. The procedure is for a motion to be lodged for dismissal together with a minute stating "[Name of Solicitor] for the pursuer stated and hereby states to the court that the pursuer abandons the cause and seeks decree of dismissal in terms of rule 23.1(1)(b) of the Ordinary Cause Rules". The court allows the minute to be received, appoints the defender to lodge an account of expenses (within such period as the court may specify) and remits the same when lodged to the auditor of court to tax and to report. The pursuer has 28 days from the date of taxation in order to pay the account if he seeks dismissal as opposed to absolvitor. If he pays he should lodge the receipt in process together with a motion for dismissal in respect that the expenses as taxed due to the defender have been paid (or consigned) and the court then pronounces an interlocutor allowing the pursuer to abandon the cause and dismisses the action. If the expenses are not paid within the 28-day period the defender can enrol for absolvitor with expenses (see *VP Packaging Ltd v The ADF Partnership* , 2002 S.L.T. 1224; see

---

[1] As amended by SSI 2003/26, reg. 2 (effective from January 24, 2003).

also *Anderson v Hardie* , 1997 S.L.T. (Sh. Ct) 70), but the court still has a discretion to allow a pursuer to withdraw a minute of abandonment at any time before the final decree disposing of the action (subject to such conditions as to expenses as seem appropriate (see *Lee v Pollock's Trustees* (1906) F. 857)). Rule 23.1 makes no provision for the situation where parties agree on the amount of expenses without the account being taxed, and if that is done it has been held that the pursuer may be presumed to have abandoned any right to ask for dismissal in terms of the rule (see *VP Packaging* (above) but for a contrary view see *Beattie v The Royal Bank of Scotland Plc* , 2003 S.L.T. 564 which suggests that the dispensing power may be used in these circumstances).

## Application of abandonment to counterclaims

**23.2.** Rule 23.1 shall, with the necessary modifications, apply to the abandonment by a defender of his counterclaim as it applies to the abandonment of a cause.

### Chapter 24

### Withdrawal of Solicitors

## Intimation of withdrawal to court

**24.1.**—(1)[1] Subject to paragraph (3), where a solicitor withdraws from acting on behalf of a party, he shall intimate his withdrawal by letter to the sheriff clerk and to every other party.

(2)[2] The sheriff clerk shall forthwith lodge such letter in process.

(3)[3] Where a solicitor withdraws from acting on behalf of a party in open court and in the presence of the other parties to the action or their representatives, paragraph (1) shall not apply.

GENERAL NOTE

An agent is entitled to withdraw from acting without asking for leave from the court but must intimate the withdrawal by letter to the sheriff clerk and every other party. The agent also has a duty to furnish the agents for the other parties with the address of his former client, if it is known to him (see *Sime, Sullivan & Dickson's Trustee v Adam* , 1908 S.C. 32). Of course, notwithstanding the requirements of this rule the court still has discretion to pronounce decree by default if a party is unrepresented at a diet (see Chapter 16 and for an example see *Munro & Miller (Pakistan) Ltd v Wyvern Structures Ltd* , 1997 S.C. 1).

## Intimation to party whose solicitor has withdrawn

**24.2.**—(1)[4] Subject to paragraph (1A), the sheriff shall, of his own motion, or on the motion of any other party, pronounce an interlocutor ordaining the party whose solicitor has withdrawn from acting to appear or be represented at a specified diet fixed by the sheriff to state whether or not he intends to proceed, under certification that if he fails to do so the sheriff may grant decree or make such other order or finding as he thinks fit.

(1A)[5] Where any previously fixed diet is to occur within 14 days from the date when the sheriff first considers the solicitor's withdrawal, the sheriff may either—

    (a) pronounce an interlocutor in accordance with paragraph (1);
       or

    (b) consider the matter at the previously fixed diet.

---

[1] As amended by the Act of Sederunt (Sheriff Court Ordinary Cause Rules Amendment) (Miscellaneous) 2000 (SSI 2000/239) (effective October 2, 2000).

[2] As amended by the Act of Sederunt (Sheriff Court Ordinary Cause Rules Amendment) (Miscellaneous) 2000 (SSI 2000/239) (effective October 2, 2000).

[3] Inserted by the Act of Sederunt (Sheriff Court Ordinary Cause Rules Amendment) (Miscellaneous) 2000 (SSI 2000/239) (effective October 2, 2000).

[4] As amended by the Act of Sederunt (Sheriff Court Ordinary Cause Rules Amendment) (Miscellaneous) 2000 (SSI 2000/239) (effective October 2, 2000).

[5] Inserted by the Act of Sederunt (Sheriff Court Ordinary Cause Rules Amendment) (Miscellaneous) 2000 (SSI 2000/239) (effective October 2, 2000).

(2)   The diet fixed in the interlocutor under paragraph (1) shall not be less than 14 days after the date of the interlocutor unless the sheriff otherwise orders.

(3)   The party who has lodged the motion under paragraph (1), or any other party appointed by the sheriff, shall forthwith serve on the party whose solicitor has withdrawn a copy of the interlocutor and a notice in Form G10; and a certificate of service shall be lodged in process.

GENERAL NOTE

It is very important that the requirements of intimation, notice and certification are complied with to ensure the peremptory nature of the diet at which the now unrepresented party is required to appear.

## Consequences of failure to intimate intention to proceed

**24.3.**   Where a party on whom a notice and interlocutor has been served under rule 24.2(2) fails to appear or be represented at a diet fixed under rule 24.2(1) and to state his intention as required by that paragraph, the sheriff may grant decree or make such other order or finding as he thinks fit.

GENERAL NOTE

If the requirements of intimation, notice and certification are followed then, ordinarily, decree will be pronounced (see, e.g. *Connelly v Lanarkshire Health Board* , 1999 S.C. 364). The decree could be *de plano* in favour of a pursuer or dismissal in favour of a defender. It is competent to pronounce absolvitor in favour of a defender but generally the court will pronounce decree of dismissal. The decree is a decree *in foro*. If the requirements are followed then appeal though competent is unlikely to succeed (see *Connelly*).

## Chapter 25

## Minutes of Sist and Transference

# Minutes of sist

**25.1.**   Where a party dies or comes under legal incapacity while a cause is depending, any person claiming to represent that party or his estate may apply by minute to be sisted as a party to the cause.

GENERAL NOTE

Death of a party suspends all procedure in the cause at whatever stage it is at (including appeal) and any further procedure is inept unless the representatives of the deceased sist themselves to the cause, or the action is transferred (by amendment) against such representatives. Where a party becomes bankrupt during the dependence of the action the trustee has power (section 39(2)(b) of the Bankruptcy (Scotland) Act 1985) to carry it on (or continue to defend it) and if he so wishes he should sist himself as a party. By so doing he renders himself liable to the opposite party in the whole expenses of the action. If the trustee declines to sist himself as a party then the bankrupt, if he continues to have title to sue, may continue the action. If the bankrupt is a pursuer the court (if asked) will ordain him to find caution but not if he is a defender (see *William Dow (Potatoes) Ltd v Dow* , 2001 S.L.T. (Sh. Ct) 37). Where a party becomes insane the cause should be sisted so that a guardian may be appointed. Once appointed the guardian is entitled to sist himself as a party. If the guardian fails to sist himself as a party then the other party may apply for and obtain decree and expenses against the incapax (provided of course that proper intimation is made to the guardian).

In the case of corporate bodies, if a company is struck from the register under s.1000 of the Companies Act 2006 during the dependence of the action, the action should be sisted to allow an application to restore it to the register (see *Steans Fashions Ltd v General Assurance Society* [1995] B.C.C. 510—a decision of the English Court of Appeal). If a defender company goes into liquidation during the dependence of the action the permission of the court (in the liquidation process) is required to continue the proceedings against it (see section 130(2) of the Insolvency Act 1986). If the company is a pursuer then the liquidator has power to carry it on (see section 169(2) of the Insolvency Act 1986) and if he wishes to do so he should sist himself as a party to the action. In the case of a company in administration it is essential to obtain the permission of the administrator or the court (in the administration process) to continue proceedings against the company (see s.8 of the Insolvency Act 1988; Schedule B1 para.43(b)). It is unnecessary for an administrator or receiver to sist himself as a party to the action but the instance should be amended to narrate the position.

## Minutes of transference

**25.2.**[1]  Where a party dies or comes under legal incapacity while a cause is depending and the provisions of rule 25.1 are not invoked, any other party may apply by minute to have the cause transferred in favour of or against, as the case may be, any person who represents that party or his estate.

GENERAL NOTE

If the representatives of a deceased or incapax do not sist themselves to the cause, then any other party may apply by minute of transference to have it transferred in favour of or against the person who represents the estate. Decree *cognitionis causa tantum* should be sought so as to constitute the debt against a deceased's estate. If no one comes to represent a pursuer then decree of absolvitor may be obtained.

## Chapter 26

## Transfer and Remit of Causes

## Transfer to another sheriff court

**26.1.**—(1)[2]  The sheriff may, on cause shown, transfer any cause to another sheriff court.

(2)  Subject to paragraph (4), where a cause in which there are two or more defenders has been brought in the sheriff court of the residence or place of business of one of them, the sheriff may transfer the cause to any other sheriff court which has jurisdiction over any of the defenders.

(3)  Subject to paragraph (4), where a plea of no jurisdiction is sustained, the sheriff may transfer the cause to the sheriff court before which it appears to him the cause ought to have been brought.

(4)  The sheriff shall not transfer a cause to another sheriff court under paragraph (2) or (3) except—

    (a)  on the motion of a party; and

    (b)  where he considers it expedient to do so having regard to the convenience of the parties and their witnesses.

(5)  On making an order under paragraph (1), (2) or (3), the sheriff—

    (a)  shall state his reasons for doing so in the interlocutor; and

    (b)  may make the order on such conditions as to expenses or otherwise as he thinks fit.

(6)  The court to which a cause is transferred under paragraph (1), (2) or (3) shall accept the cause.

(7)  A transferred cause shall proceed in all respects as if it had been originally brought in the court to which it is transferred.

(8)  *[Repealed by the Act of Sederunt (Rules of the Court of Session, Sheriff Appeal Court Rules and Sheriff Court Rules Amendment) (Sheriff Appeal Court) 2015 (SSI 2015/419) r.5 (effective 1 January 2016).]*

GENERAL NOTE

The convenience of the parties and witnesses is the paramount consideration determining whether to transfer a cause from one sheriff court to another. The ability of the court to transfer rather than dismiss an action where it has no jurisdiction is based on expediency (see *Wilson v Ferguson* , 1957 S.L.T. (Sh.

---

[1] As amended by the Act of Sederunt (Sheriff Court Ordinary Cause Rules Amendment) (Miscellaneous) 1996 (SI 1996/2445) (effective November 1, 1996).

[2] As amended by the Act of Sederunt (Rules of the Court of Session 1994 and Sheriff Court Rules Amendment) (No. 2) (Personal Injury and Remits) 2015 (SSI 2015/227) para.7 (effective 22 September 2015).

Ct) 52). It is necessary that either the transferring court or the court to which the cause is transferred otherwise has jurisdiction over the defender. It is essential that the sheriff sets out the reasons for the transfer in the interlocutor.

## Remit and transfer of summary cause proceedings to all-Scotland sheriff court

**26.1A.**[1](1)   This rule applies where the sheriff directs that a summary cause is to be treated as an ordinary cause and, at the same time, makes an order transferring the action to the all-Scotland sheriff court.

(2)   The pursuer must lodge an initial writ and intimate it to every other party within 14 days of the date of the order.

(3)   The defender must lodge defences within 28 days after the date of the order.

(4)   Following the making of a direction and order mentioned in paragraph (1), the action is to be treated as a personal injuries action within the meaning of Part A1 of Chapter 36.

## Remit to the Court of Session: proceedings to which section 39 of the 2014 Act does not apply

**26.2.**[2](1)   An application under section 92(2) of the 2014 Act (remit of cases to the Court of Session) is to be made by motion.

(2)   Within 4 days after the sheriff has pronounced an interlocutor remitting a cause to the Court of Session under section 92(2), the sheriff clerk must—

(a)   send written notice of the remit to each party;

(b)   certify on the interlocutor sheet that subparagraph (a) has been complied with;

(c)   transmit the process to the Deputy Principal Clerk of Session.

(3)   Failure by a sheriff clerk to comply with paragraph (2)(a) or (b) does not affect the validity of a remit.

GENERAL NOTE

The general power to remit to the Court of Session is contained in section 37(1)(b) of the Sheriff Courts (Scotland) Act 1971, which provides:

"In the case of any ordinary cause brought in the sheriff court the sheriff—

(b)   may, subject to section 7 of the Sheriff Courts (Scotland) Act 1907, on the motion of any of the parties to the cause, if he is of the opinion that the *importance or difficulty* of the cause make it appropriate to do so, remit the cause to the Court of Session."

*"Importance or difficulty"*

The leading case is the five judge decision in *Mullan v Anderson* , 1993 S.L.T. 835. Despite the divergence of opinions it is submitted that there should not be much difficulty in practice in recognising a case that is suitable to be remitted to the Court of Session. In assessing the matter, the sheriff has a wide discretion and should consider the importance of the cause to the parties and weigh up the procedural implications as well as the expense and delay involved. He should also consider the public interest. In *Mullan* it was clearly appropriate that an allegation of murder be tried in the Supreme Court. In the personal injury field it is insufficient merely to assert that the claim is a substantial one to justify a remit (see *Butler v Thom* , 1982 S.L.T. (Sh. Ct) 57) but other considerations may justify a remit—see *Gallagher v Birse* , 2003 S.C.L.R. 623.

A decision to remit or not to remit may be appealed to the Court of Session without leave (see section 37(3)(b) of the Sheriff Courts (Scotland) Act 1971).

---

[1] As inserted by the Act of Sederunt (Rules of the Court of Session 1994 and Sheriff Court Rules Amendment) (No. 2) (Personal Injury and Remits) 2015 (SSI 2015/227) para.7 (effective September 22, 2015).

[2] As substituted by the Act of Sederunt (Rules of the Court of Session 1994 and Sheriff Court Rules Amendment) (No. 2) (Personal Injury and Remits) 2015 (SSI 2015/227) para.7 (effective September 22, 2015).

Section 37 of the Sheriff Courts (Scotland) Act 1971 also contains specific powers to remit in family actions and there are specific provisions under section 1 of the Presumption of Death (Scotland) Act 1977 and section 44 of the Crown Proceedings Act 1947.

If a remit is granted, the Sheriff Clerk must send the process to the Court of Session within four days. Once the process is received by him the Deputy Principal Clerk of Session writes the date of receipt on the interlocutor sheet and intimates that date to each party. Within 14 days after such intimation the party on whose motion the remit was made, or if the cause was remitted by the sheriff at his own instance, the pursuer makes up and lodges a process incorporating the sheriff court process in the General Department and makes a motion for such further procedure as he desires and thereafter the cause proceeds as though it had been initiated in the Court of Session (see RCS 1994, rr.32.3 and 32.4).

The other party is entitled to insist on the remit (RCS 1994, r.32.6), but if neither party enrols for further procedure the remit will be deemed to have been abandoned and the cause transmitted back to the sheriff clerk (RCS 1994, r.32.7).

The Court of Session also has power in terms of section 33 of the Court of Session Act to order transmission of a sheriff court process to it on the ground of contingency (see RCS 1994, r.32.2).

Once a cause is before the Court of Session it is incompetent (see *Baird v Scottish Motor Traction Co* , 1948 S.C. 526) to remit it back to the sheriff to consider questions relating to expenses (such as certification of the cause as suitable for the employment of counsel). There is no reason why such matters cannot be dealt with before a remit is granted. But if they have not been, then it is a matter for the Auditor of the Court of Session upon taxation to consider such issues relating to expenses relative to the whole action.

## Remit to the Court of Session: proceedings to which section 39 of the 2014 Act applies

**26.2A.**[1](1)   An application under section 92(4) of the 2014 Act (request for remit to the Court of Session) is to be made by motion.

(2)   The decision of a sheriff on an application made under section 92(4) is to be recorded in an interlocutor, and a note of the sheriff's reasons for that decision must be appended to that interlocutor.

(3)   Following receipt of an interlocutor from the Court of Session allowing the proceedings to be remitted the sheriff must issue an interlocutor remitting the proceedings under section 92(6).

(4)   Within 4 days after the sheriff has pronounced an interlocutor remitting a cause to the Court of Session under section 92(6), the sheriff clerk must—

(a)   send written notice of the remit to each party;

(b)   certify on the interlocutor sheet that subparagraph (a) has been complied with;

(c)   transmit the process to the Deputy Principal Clerk of Session.

(5)   Failure by a sheriff clerk to comply with paragraph (4)(a) or (b) does not affect the validity of a remit.

## Remit to the Court of Session: remits under other enactments

**26.2B.**[2](1)   This rule applies where the sheriff has pronounced an interlocutor remitting a cause to the Court of Session under an enactment other than section 92 of the 2014 Act.

(2)   Within 4 days after the sheriff has pronounced that interlocutor, the sheriff clerk must—

(a)   send written notice of the remit to each party;

(b)   certify on the interlocutor sheet that subparagraph (a) has been complied with;

(c)   transmit the process to the Deputy Principal Clerk of Session.

---

[1] As inserted by the Act of Sederunt (Rules of the Court of Session 1994 and Sheriff Court Rules Amendment) (No. 2) (Personal Injury and Remits) 2015 (SSI 2015/227) para.7 (effective September 22, 2015).

[2] As inserted by the Act of Sederunt (Rules of the Court of Session 1994 and Sheriff Court Rules Amendment) (No. 2) (Personal Injury and Remits) 2015 (SSI 2015/227) para.7 (effective September 22, 2015).

(3) Failure by a sheriff clerk to comply with paragraph (2)(a) or (b) does not affect the validity of a remit.

## Remit from Court of Session

**26.3.**[1] On receipt of the process in an action which has been remitted from the Court of Session under section 93 of the 2014 Act (remit of cases from the Court of Session), the sheriff clerk shall—

(a) record the date of receipt on the interlocutor sheet;

(b) fix a hearing to determine further procedure on the first court day occurring not earlier than 14 days after the date of receipt of the process; and

(c) forthwith send written notice of the date of the hearing fixed under sub-paragraph (b) to each party.

GENERAL NOTE

The provision under section 14 of the Law Reform (Miscellaneous Provisions) (Scotland) Act 1985 (to allow the Court of Session to remit a cause to the sheriff, "where, in the opinion of the court the nature of the action makes it appropriate to do") was not introduced to effect a general redistribution of work between the courts but to meet the needs of particular cases (see *McIntosh v British Railways Board (No.1)* , 1990 S.L.T. 637 (see also *Gribb v Gribb* , 1993 S.L.T. 178). The power to remit should be exercised on grounds particular to the case concerned (see *Bell v Chief Constable of Strathclyde* , 2011 S.L.T. 244). For an example where a remit was granted see *Colin McKay v Lloyd's TSB Mortgages Ltd* , 2005 S.C.L.R. 547.

## Chapter 27

## Caution and Security

## Application of this Chapter

**27.1.** This Chapter applies to—

(a) any cause in which the sheriff has power to order a person to find caution or give other security; and

(b) security for expenses ordered to be given by the election court or the sheriff under section 136(2)(i) of the Representation of the People Act 1983 in an election petition.

GENERAL NOTE

Caution or other security (usually but not necessarily consignation) may be ordered as a condition of recall of arrestment on the dependence. It may also be sought as an alternative to sisting a mandatary where the other party is not resident in an EU country (see *Deiter Rossmeier v Mounthooly Transport* , 2000 S.L.T. 208). Moreover, the court has power to order that a party find caution or consign a sum as security for expenses and/or the sum sought. There are certain particular provisions where caution consignation may be ordered, such as under OCR r.21.3(2) or section 100 of the Bills of Exchange Act 1882. Apart from these, the court has a general power within its discretion to make an order. In relation to natural persons, however, the court will generally not order that caution or security be found unless the party is an undischarged bankrupt, is a nominal pursuer or there are exceptional circumstances justifying an order. Being poor is not of itself a sufficient reason to require caution or security to be found since that would deprive a large section of the community of access to the court (see *Stevenson v Midlothian D.C.* , 1983 S.C. (H.L.) 50 and *McTear's Exr v Imperial Tobacco Ltd* , 1997 S.L.T. 530). If the case is patently without merit then an order may be granted, but such a situation is rare since agents have a professional duty not to prosecute or defend unstateable cases. Defenders are not generally required to find caution, nevertheless the terms of the defence will be scrutinised with care (and a defender with a counter claim falls to be treated in the same way as a pursuer: see *William Dow (Potatoes) Ltd v Dow* , 2001 S.L.T. (Sh Ct) 37). Limited companies as pursuers are required to find security under s.726(2) of the Companies Act 1985 (this is still in force; see Companies Act 2006 (Consequential Amendments Transitional Provisions and Savings) Order 2009 (SI 2009/1941)) if it appears by credible testimony that there is reason to believe that the company will be unable to pay the defender's expenses if successful in his defence. Absence of trading and the failure to comply with the requirements to lodge accounts or annual returns are relevant.

---

[1] As amended by the Act of Sederunt (Rules of the Court of Session 1994 and Sheriff Court Rules Amendment) (No. 2) (Personal Injury and Remits) 2015 (SSI 2015/227) para.7 (effective September 22, 2015).

## Form of applications

**27.2.**—(1)   An application for an order for caution or other security or for variation or recall of such an order, shall be made by motion.

(2)   The grounds on which such an application is made shall be set out in the motion.

General Note

It is important to provide detail in the motion as to the reason for seeking security and any supporting documents should be lodged.

## Orders

**27.3.**   Subject to section 726(2) of the Companies Act 1985 (expenses by certain limited companies), an order to find caution or give other security shall specify the period within which such caution is to be found or such security given.

General Note

Section 726(2) of the Companies Act 1985 permits the action to be sisted pending the finding of security, but the court is also entitled to impose a time limit within which caution should be found in relation to which failure to comply would amount to default. At common law it is competent to ordain a defender company to find caution. A defender company with a counterclaim falls to be treated in the same way as a pursuer under section 726(2): see *William Dow (Potatoes) Ltd v Dow* , 2001 S.L.T. (Sh Ct) 37.

## Methods of finding caution or giving security

**27.4.**—(1)   A person ordered—

(a)   to find caution, shall do so by obtaining a bond of caution; or

(b)   to consign a sum of money into court, shall do so by consignation under the Sheriff Court Consignations (Scotland) Act 1893 in the name of the sheriff clerk.

(2)   The sheriff may approve a method of security other than one mentioned in paragraph (1), including a combination of two or more methods of security.

(3)   Subject to paragraph (4), any document by which an order to find caution or give other security is satisfied shall be lodged in process.

(4)   Where the sheriff approves a security in the form of a deposit of a sum of money in the joint names of the agents of parties, a copy of the deposit receipt, and not the principal, shall be lodged in process.

(5)   Any document lodged in process, by which an order to find caution or give other security is satisfied, shall not be borrowed from process.

General Note

Joint deposit receipt is another form of security.

## Cautioners and guarantors[1]

**27.5.**[2]   A bond of caution or other security shall be given only by a person who is an "authorised person" within the meaning of section 31 of the Financial Services and Markets Act 2000.

General Note

See *Greens Annotated Rules of the Court of Session* (W.Green, 2002) and the annotation to RCS 1994, r.33.5.

---

[1] As substituted by the Act of Sederunt (Sheriff Court Ordinary Cause Rules Amendment) (Miscellaneous) 1996 (SI 1996/2445) r.3(31) (effective November 1, 1996).

[2] As amended by the Act of Sederunt (Ordinary Cause Rules) Amendment (Caution and Security) 2005 (SSI 2005/20) r.2(2) (effective February 1, 2005).

## Form of bonds of caution and other securities

**27.6.**—(1)  A bond of caution shall oblige the cautioner, his heirs and executors to make payment of the sums for which he has become cautioner to the party to whom he is bound, as validly and in the same manner as the party, his heirs and successors, for whom he is cautioner, are obliged.

(2)[1]  A bond of caution or other security document given by a person shall state whether that person is an "authorised person" within the meaning of section 31 of the Financial Services and Markets Act 2000.

## Sufficiency of caution or security and objections

**27.7.**—(1)  The sheriff clerk shall satisfy himself that any bond of caution, or other document lodged in process under rule 27.4(3), is in proper form.

(2)  A party who is dissatisfied with the sufficiency or form of the caution or other security offered in obedience to an order of the court may apply by motion for an order under rule 27.9 (failure to find caution or give security).

General Note

Clearly it is in the interest of the party in whose favour the order has been granted to satisfy himself that the security is in proper form.

## Insolvency or death of cautioner or guarantor

**27.8.**  Where caution has been found by bond of caution or security has been given by guarantee and the cautioner or guarantor, as the case may be—
- (a)  becomes apparently insolvent within the meaning assigned by section 7 of the Bankruptcy (Scotland) Act 1985 (constitution of apparent insolvency),
- (b)  calls a meeting of his creditors to consider the state of his affairs,
- (c)  dies unrepresented, or
- (d)  is a company and—
    - (i)[2]  an administration, bank administration or building society special administration order or a winding up, bank insolvency or building society insolvency order has been made, or a resolution for a voluntary winding up has been passed, with respect to it,
    - (ii)  a receiver of all or any part of its undertaking has been appointed, or
    - (iii)  a voluntary arrangement (within the meaning assigned by section 1(1) of the Insolvency Act 1986) has been approved under Part I of that Act,

    the party entitled to benefit from the caution or guarantee may apply by motion for a new security or further security to be given.

## Failure to find caution or give security

**27.9.**  Where a party fails to find caution or give other security (in this rule referred to as "the party in default") any other party may apply by motion—
- (a)  where he party in default is a pursuer, for decree of absolvitor; or
- (b)  where the party in default is a defender or a third party, for decree by default or for such other finding or order as the sheriff thinks fit.

---

[1] As amended by the Act of Sederunt (Ordinary Cause Rules) Amendment (Caution and Security) 2005 (SSI 2005/20) r.2(3) (effective February 1, 2005).
[2] As substituted by the Act of Sederunt (Sheriff Court Rules) (Miscellaneous Amendments) 2009 (SSI 2009/294) r.16 (effective October 1, 2009).

GENERAL NOTE

See Chapter 16. A decree whether absolvitor or by default is in foro and is res judicata between the parties. A successful motion to award caution cannot be appealed without leave (see sections 27 and 28 of the Sheriff Courts (Scotland) Act 1907), but a decree of absolvitor or default can be and the earlier interlocutor ganting security will be opened up as a result: see *McCue v Scottish Daily Record and Sunday Mail*, 1998 S.C. 811.

## Chapter 28

## Recovery of Evidence

### *Application and interpretation of this Chapter*

**28.1.**—(1) This Chapter applies to the recovery of any evidence in a cause depending before the sheriff.

(2) In this Chapter, "the Act of 1972" means the Administration of Justice (Scotland) Act 1972.

GENERAL NOTE

An application for recovery under Chapter 28 refers to a cause depending before the sheriff. Before the commencement of an action, the court may grant applications to recover documents, inspect and preserve property, etc. (under the Administration of Justice (Scotland) Act 1972 (as amended)). Such applications require to be brought by summary application (see Act of Sederunt (Summary Applications, Statutory Applications and Appeals etc. Rules) 1999 (SI 1999/929) (reproduced at page D 488) and Part I, rules 3.1.1 and 3.1.2 (page D 513)).

## Applications for commission and diligence for recovery of documents or for orders under section 1 of the Act of 1972

**28.2.**—(1) An application by a party for—

(a) a commission and diligence for the recovery of a document, or

(b) an order under section 1 of the Act of 1972,

shall be made by motion.

(2) At the time of lodging a motion under paragraph (1), a specification of—

(a) the document or other property sought to be inspected, photographed, preserved, taken into custody, detained, produced, recovered, sampled or experimented with or upon, as the case may be, or

(b) the matter in respect of which information is sought as to the identity of a person who might be a witness or a defender,

shall be lodged in process.

(3)[1] A copy of the specification lodged under paragraph (2) and the motion made under paragraph (1) shall be intimated by the applicant to—

(a) every other party;

(b) in respect of an application under section 1(1) of the Act of 1972, any third party haver; and

(c)[2] where necessary—

(i) the Advocate General for Scotland (in a case where the document or other property sought is in the possession of either a public authority exercising functions in relation to reserved matters within the meaning of Schedule 5 to the Scotland Act 1998, or a cross-border public authority within the meaning of section 88(5) of that Act); or

(ii) the Lord Advocate (in any other case),

---

[1] As substituted by SI 1996/2445 (effective November 1, 1996).

[2] As substituted by the Act of Sederunt (Ordinary Cause, Summary Application, Summary Cause and Small Claim Rules) Amendment (Miscellaneous) 2007 (SSI 2007/6) r.2(10) (effective January 29, 2007).

and, if there is any doubt, both.

(4)   Where the sheriff grants a motion under paragraph (1) in whole or in part, he may order the applicant to find such caution or give such other security as he thinks fit.

(5)   The Advocate General for Scotland or the Lord Advocate or both, as appropriate, may appear at the hearing of any motion under paragraph (1).

GENERAL NOTE

*Rule 28.2(1)(a)*

The common law process whereby evidence can be recovered and preserved for use in an action is termed commission and diligence. The commission is the written authority of the court to a person (normally a solicitor in practice at the sheriff court where the order is granted) to take the evidence of the witness (or haver) as to the existence or whereabouts of the document; and the diligence is the warrant to cite such witnesses or haver to appear before the commissioner.

*Rule 28.2(1)(b)*

Apart from the power to order recovery and inspection before the action is raised, the Administration of Justice (Scotland) Act 1972 also augments the common law powers of the court to order inspection, photographing, preservation, custody and detention of documents and other property which is property as to which any question may relevantly arise in any existing civil proceedings before that court. Section 1A of the 1972 Act also gives power to the court to require any person to disclose such information as he has as to the identity of witnesses to the proceedings. The general rule that a litigant will not normally be permitted to recover or inspect property until after the closing of the record is thus modified, and cases, such as *Boyle v Glasgow Royal Infirmary and Associated Hospitals Board of Management* , 1969 S.C. 72, decided before this provision came into force, require to be read in the light of it. The judicial climate and the background culture has altered significantly not least because of the passing into law of the Freedom of Information (Scotland) Act 2002 and there is now no reason why there should be any difference between the test for recovery before and after the closing of the record (cf. *Moore v Greater Glasgow Health Board* , 1978 S.C. 123—it is unthinkable now that an application of the type made in *Moore* could be opposed successfully).

Whether the application for recovery is at common law or under the statute it must satisfy the test of relevancy. A call is relevant if it is designed to recover documents or items which would permit a party to make more detailed or specific averments that are already in the pleadings (including responding to the other side's pleadings). Further a call is relevant if it is designed to recover a document the purpose of which is to prove an averment. Fishing (that is, looking for documents in the hope that material will be obtained to make a case not yet pled) is not permitted.

*Rule 28.2(2)*

The application is made by motion (see Chapter 15) and at the same time a specification of document(s) or, as the case may be, specification of property or matter requires to be lodged in process. If the application is made before the options hearing the pleadings as adjusted to date should be lodged in process (see OCR, rule 9.4).

*"Specification"*

A specification is in the form of written calls specifying precisely the document or items sought. There are two types of call. The first is a named description of the document or item. This is appropriate where the document or item is known to exist or at least to have been in existence and can be readily identified by a verbal description. The second type seeks a range of documents which may contain an entry relevant to the case. There is a tendency for practitioners to favour the second type of call. Nevertheless it is advantageous, wherever possible, to use the first type since that minimises the work of the haver in locating the particular document sought and thereafter of the commissioner in excerpting from the documents produced to him the relevant entries falling within the terms of the call. It is not necessary in any specification to identify the name of the haver, but it is helpful to all concerned if it is frequently done. Of course, frequently the haver is unknown and a series of diets of commission require to take place before the document or item is traced to any person.

*"Intimated"*

It is necessary to intimate the motion to every other party and to the Lord Advocate and/or the Advocate General where what is sought is in the possession of the Crown. Intimation to the Lord Advocate of an application to recover medical records is not necessary; see e.g. Practice Note No.2 of 2006 for Grampian, Highland and Islands (all the other Sherrifdoms have issued practice notes). It is also now necessary to intimate to the haver where what is sought is an order under section 1 of the Administration of Justice (Scotland) Act 1972. It is important therefore that the applicant is clear which of the court's powers is being invoked.

In the case of documents held by the Scottish Government, United Kingdom government departments or other public authorities an objection may be raised that recovery would be contrary to public policy. In that event the court, while accepting a statement to the effect that production would be contrary to the public interest, has to decide whether nevertheless justice requires that the order be granted in the interests of the individual party (*Glasgow Corporation v Central Land Board* , 1956 S.C. (H.L.) 1; *Rogers v Orr* , 1939 S.C. 492; *AB v Glasgow West of Scotland Blood Transfusion Service* , 1993 S.L.T. 36). The objection is frequently taken to protect information gathered by the Police, the Crown Office and Procurator Fiscal service. Whether the objection (which may be at the instance of a party or the haver or both) is successful depends upon the circumstances of the case, the nature of the application and the document sought to be recovered. (See generally, Walker, *Evidence* (3rd ed.), pp.193–198).

It is also the case that by virtue of art.8 of ECHR the Court may require the motion to other persons who may be affected; see *M v A Scottish Local Authority* , 2012 S.L.T. 6.

### Optional procedure before executing commission and diligence

**28.3.**—[1](1)  Subject to rule 28.3A (optional procedure where there is a party litigant), this rule applies where a party has obtained a commission and diligence for the recovery of a document on an application made under rule 28.2(1)(a).

(2)  Such a party may, at any time before executing the commission and diligence against a haver, serve on the haver an order in Form G11 (in this rule referred to as "the order").

(3)  The order and a copy of the specification referred to in rule 28.2(2), as approved by the sheriff, must be served on the haver or his known agent and must be complied with by the haver in the manner and within the period specified in the order.

(4)  Not later than the day after the date on which the order, and any document recovered, is received from a haver by the party who obtained the order, that party—

    (a)  must give written intimation of that fact in Form G11A to the sheriff clerk and every other party; and

    (b)  must—

        (i)  if the document has been sent by post, send a written receipt for the document in Form G11B to the haver; or

        (ii)  if the document has been delivered by hand, give a written receipt in Form G11B to the person delivering the document.

(5)  Where the party who has recovered any such document does not lodge it in process within 14 days of receipt of it, that party must—

    (a)  give written intimation to every party that that party may borrow, inspect or copy the document within 14 days after the date of that intimation; and

    (b)  in so doing, identify the document.

(6)  Where a party who has obtained any document under paragraph (5) wishes to lodge the document in process, that party must—

    (a)  lodge the document within 14 days after receipt of it; and

    (b)  at the same time, send a written receipt for the document in Form G11C to the party who obtained the order.

(7)  Where—

    (a)  no party wishes to lodge or borrow any such document under paragraph (5), the document is to be returned to the haver by the party who obtained the order within 14 days after the expiry of the period specified in paragraph (5)(a); or

    (b)  any such document has been uplifted by another party under paragraph (5)

---

[1] As substituted by the Act of Sederunt (Rules of the Court of Session, Ordinary Cause Rules and Summary Cause Rules Amendment) (Miscellaneous) 2014 (SSI 2014/152) r.3 (effective July 7, 2014).

and that party does not wish to lodge it in process, the document shall be returned to the haver by that party within 21 days after the date of receipt of it by him.

(8) Any such document lodged in process is to be returned to the haver by the party lodging it within 14 days after the expiry of any period allowed for appeal or, where an appeal has been marked, from the disposal of any such appeal.

(9) If any party fails to return any such document as provided for in paragraph (7) or (8), the haver may apply by motion (whether or not the cause is in dependence) for an order that the document be returned to him and for the expenses occasioned by that motion.

(10) The party holding any such document (being the party who last issued a receipt for it) is responsible for its safekeeping during the period that the document is in his custody or control.

(11) If the party who served the order is not satisfied that—

(a) full compliance has been made with the order, or

(b) adequate reasons for non-compliance have been given,

he may execute the commission and diligence under rule 28.4.

(12) Where an extract from a book of any description (whether the extract is certified or not) is produced under the order, the sheriff may, on the motion of the party who served the order, direct that that party may inspect the book and take copies of any entries falling with the specification.

(13) Where any question of confidentiality arises in relation to a book directed to be inspected under paragraph (12), the inspection shall be made, and any copies shall be taken, at the sight of the commissioner appointed in the interlocutor granting the commission and diligence.

(14) The sheriff may, on cause shown, order the production of any book (not being a banker's book or book of public record) containing entries falling under a specification, notwithstanding the production of a certified extract from that book.

GENERAL NOTE

The vast majority of commissions proceed under the optional procedure and a diet of commission is not required. The procedure is designed to ensure that all documents falling within the terms of the calls of the specification are produced to the sheriff clerk so that all parties are aware of all of the documents recovered, giving all parties an opportunity of lodging them in process and in the event that they are not lodged ensuring their safe return to the haver. A demand for production (within seven days) in Form G11 (or "order") is served on the haver or his known solicitor together with the specification as approved by the court. The haver produces to the sheriff clerk the certificate appended to the Form G11 together with all documents in his possession falling within the specification. The haver certifies (1) that he has produced all documents in his possession sought under the specification; (2) a list of any other documents that are believed to be in the hands of other named persons; and (3) that there are no other documents falling within the terms of the calls of the specification. No later than the day after the order and documents are produced, the sheriff clerk intimates the returned Form G11 and any document to each party. The party seeking the documents may or may not choose to uplift them from the sheriff clerk within seven days. If he does not then the sheriff clerk must inform every other party of this to enable it to uplift the documents. If a party uplifts the document but decides not to lodge it, the document must be returned to the sheriff clerk within 14 days. The sheriff clerk must intimate the return to all parties and after 14 days of that intimation return the document to the haver.

## Optional procedure where there is a party litigant

**28.3A.**—[1](1) This rule applies where any of the parties to the action is a party litigant.

---

[1] As inserted by the Act of Sederunt (Rules of the Court of Session, Ordinary Cause Rules and Summary Cause Rules Amendment) (Miscellaneous) 2014 (SSI 2014/152) r.3 (effective July 7, 2014).

(2)  The party who has obtained a commission and diligence for the recovery of a document on an application under rule 28.2(1)(a) may, at any time before executing it against a haver, serve on the haver an order in Form G11D (in this rule referred to as "the order").

(3)  The order and a copy of the specification referred to in rule 28.2(2), as approved by the sheriff, must be served on the haver or his known agent and must be complied with by the haver in the manner and within the period specified in the order.

(4)  Not later than the day after the date on which the order, and any document recovered, is received from a haver by the sheriff clerk, the sheriff clerk shall give written intimation of that fact to each party.

(5)  No party, other than the party who served the order, may uplift any such document until after the expiry of 7 days after the date of intimation under paragraph (4).

(6)  Where the party who served the order fails to uplift any such document within 7 days after the date of intimation under paragraph (4), the sheriff clerk must give written intimation of that failure to every other party.

(7)  Where no party has uplifted any such document within 14 days after the date of intimation under paragraph (6), the sheriff clerk must return it to the haver.

(8)  Where a party who has uplifted any such document does not wish to lodge it, he must return it to the sheriff clerk who must—

  (a)   give written intimation of the return of the document to every other party; and

  (b)   if no other party uplifts the document within 14 days after the date of intimation, return it to the haver.

(9)[1]  Any such document lodged in process is to be returned to the haver by the party lodging it within 14 days after the expiry of any period allowed for appeal or, where an appeal has been made, from the disposal of any such appeal.

(10)  If any party fails to return any such document as provided for in paragraph (8) or (9), the haver may apply by motion (whether or not the cause is in dependence) for an order that the document be returned to him and for the expenses occasioned by that motion.

(11)  The party holding any such document (being the party who last issued a receipt for it) is responsible for its safekeeping during the period that the document is in his custody or control.

(12)  If the party who served the order is not satisfied that—

  (a)   full compliance has been made with the order, or

  (b)   adequate reasons for non-compliance have been given,

he may execute the commission and diligence under rule 28.4.

(13)  Where an extract from a book of any description (whether the extract is certified or not) is produced under the order, the sheriff may, on the motion of the party who served the order, direct that that party shall be allowed to inspect the book and take copies of any entries falling within the specification.

---

[1] As amended by the Act of Sederunt (Rules of the Court of Session, Sheriff Appeal Court Rules and Sheriff Court Rules Amendment) (Sheriff Appeal Court) 2015 (SSI 2015/419) r.5 (effective 1 January 2016).

(14) Where any question of confidentiality arises in relation to a book directed to be inspected under paragraph (13), the inspection shall be made, and any copies shall be taken, at the sight of the commissioner appointed in the interlocutor granting the commission and diligence.

(15) The sheriff may, on cause shown, order the production of any book (not being a banker's book or book of public record) containing entries falling under a specification, notwithstanding the production of a certified extract from that book.

## Execution of commission and diligence for recovery of documents

**28.4.**—(1) The party who seeks to execute a commission and diligence for recovery of a document obtained under rule 28.2(1)(a) shall—

    (a)   provide the commissioner with a copy of the specification, a copy of the pleadings (including any adjustments and amendments) and a certified copy of the interlocutor of his appointment; and

    (b)   instruct the clerk and any shorthand writer considered necessary by the commissioner or any party; and

    (c)   be responsible for the fees of the commissioner and his clerk, and of any shorthand writer.

(2) The Commissioner shall, in consultation with the parties, fix a diet for the execution of the commission.

(3) The interlocutor granting such a commission and diligence shall be sufficient authority for citing a haver to appear before the commissioner.

(4)[1] A citation in Form G13 shall be served on the haver with a copy of the specification and, where necessary for a proper understanding of the specification, a copy of the pleadings (including any adjustments and amendments) and the party citing the haver shall lodge a certificate of citation in Form G12.

(5) The parties and the haver shall be entitled to be represented by a solicitor or person having a right of audience before the sheriff at the execution of the commission.

(6)[2] At the commission, the commissioner shall—

    (a)   administer the oath de fideli administratione to any clerk and any shorthand writer appointed for the commission; and

    (b)   administer to the haver the oath in Form G14, or, where the haver elects to affirm, the affirmation in Form G15.

(7) The report of the execution of the commission and diligence, any document recovered and an inventory of that document, shall be sent by the commissioner to the sheriff clerk.

(8) Not later than the day after the date on which such a report, document and inventory, if any, are received by the sheriff clerk, he shall intimate to the parties that he has received them.

(9) No party, other than the party who served the order, may uplift such a document until after the expiry of 7 days after the date of intimation under paragraph (8).

(10) Where the party who served the order fails to uplift such a document within 7 days after the date of intimation under paragraph (8), the sheriff clerk shall intimate that failure to every other party.

(11) Where no party has uplifted such a document within 14 days after the date of intimation under paragraph (10), the sheriff clerk shall return it to the haver.

---

[1] As amended by SI 1996/2445 (effective November 1, 1996).
[2] As amended by SI 1996/2445 (effective November 1, 1996).

(12) Where a party who has uplifted such a document does not wish to lodge it, he shall return it to the sheriff clerk who shall—

    (a) intimate the return of the document to every other party; and

    (b) if no other party uplifts the document within 14 days of the date of intimation, return it to the haver.

GENERAL NOTE

This rule provides the standard procedure to be followed where a party decides not to use the optional procedure or is not satisfied that there has been full compliance with the G11 order or that adequate reasons for non-compliance have been given. The commissioner may or may not have been appointed in the original interlocutor allowing the commission and diligence. If he has not been appointed then it is necessary to ask the sheriff to make an appointment before the commission can proceed. As well as the commissioner it is necessary to instruct the clerk and any shorthand writer. It is not essential to instruct a shorthand writer, but it is very unwise to proceed without one. Normally the clerk to the commission is the shorthand writer who takes the oath *de fideli administratione* "to faithfully discharge the duties of clerk and shorthand writer at this commission". The haver is cited to the diet of commission by the party seeking to recover the documents. Failure to obtemper a citation is dealt with in the same way as with any witness citation (see OCR, rules 28.15 and 29.10). If the haver is not a natural person a responsible official or representative should be cited. Usually the organisation will identify a suitable person, if not then the managing director or chief executive of the organisation may require to be cited. At a commission the haver is placed on oath but the questions that may be asked is very limited (see JA Maclaren, *Court of Session Practice* (1916), 1079). Legitimate questions are (1) whether the witness has the document or item; (2) whether he has had the document or item at any time; (3) whether he has disposed of it; (4) whether he knows or suspects where it is or has been; (5) whether he is aware of whether anyone else has had, has or has disposed of the document or item; (6) whether the document or item has been destroyed and, if so, when by whom, why and how; and (7) any question designed to ascertain the whereabouts of the document or item or facilitate its recovery. It is illegitimate to use the commission to inquire into the merits of the cause and any such question clearly having that purpose as opposed to a legitimate purpose should simply be disallowed by the commissioner. The haver's representative and any other party (if they have decided to attend) may ask questions to clarify any ambiguities in relation to the answers given to the restricted permissible questions but again must not stray into the merits of the cause.

The clerk will prepare the report which will include a transcript of the proceedings together with an inventory of the documents recovered. These items are transmitted to the sheriff clerk and may be uplifted and lodged, failing which, returned to the haver.

## Execution of orders for production or recovery of documents or other property under section 1(1) of the Act of 1972

**28.5.**—(1) An order under section 1(1) of the Act of 1972 for the production or recovery of a document or other property shall grant a commission and diligence for the production or recovery of that document or other property.

(2) Rules 28.3 (optional procedure before executing commission and diligence) and 28.4 (execution of commission and diligence for recovery of documents) shall apply to an order to which paragraph (1) applies as they apply to a commission and diligence for the recovery of a document.

GENERAL NOTE

This rules makes it clear that an order for production or recovery of documents or other items under the 1972 Act is for a commission and diligence and that the optional procedure and standard procedure apply mutatis mutandis.

## Execution of orders for inspection etc. of documents or other property under section 1(1) of the Act of 1972

**28.6.**—(1) An order under section 1(1) of the Act of 1972 for the inspection or photographing of a document or other property, the taking of samples or the carrying out of any experiment thereon or therewith, shall authorise and appoint a specified person to photograph, inspect, take samples of, or carry out any experiment on or with, any such document or other property, as the case may be, subject to such conditions, if any, as the sheriff thinks fit.

(2) A certified copy of the interlocutor granting such an order shall be sufficient authority for the person specified to execute the order.

(3)  When such an order is executed, the party who obtained the order shall serve on the haver a copy of the interlocutor granting it, a copy of the specification and, where necessary for a proper understanding of the specification, a copy of the pleadings (including any adjustments and amendments).

GENERAL NOTE

Rules 28.6 and 28.7 make specific provision where what is sought is inspection or preservation or documents or other property in terms of the 1972 Act as opposed to production and recovery.

## Execution of orders for preservation etc. of documents or other property under section 1(1) of the Act of 1972

**28.7.**—[1](1)  An order under section 1(1) of the Act of 1972 for the preservation, custody and detention of a document or other property shall grant a commission and diligence for the detention and custody of that document or other property.

(2)  The party who has obtained an order under paragraph (1) shall—

    (a)  provide the commissioner with a copy of the specification, a copy of the pleadings (including any adjustments and amendments) and a certified copy of the interlocutor of his appointment;

    (b)  be responsible for the fees of the commissioner and his clerk; and

    (c)  serve a copy of the order on the haver.

(3)  The report of the execution of the commission and diligence, any document or other property taken by the commissioner and an inventory of such property, shall be sent by the commissioner to the sheriff clerk for the further order of the sheriff.

## Confidentiality

**28.8.**—[2](1)  Where confidentiality is claimed for any evidence sought to be recovered under any of the following rules, such evidence shall, where practicable, be enclosed in a sealed packet:—

28.3 (optional procedure before executing commission and diligence),

[3]rule 28.3A (optional procedure where there is a party litigant),

28.4 (execution of commission and diligence for recovery of documents),

28.5 (execution of orders for production or recovery of documents or other property under section 1(1) of the Act of 1972),

28.7 (execution of orders for preservation etc. of documents or other property under section 1(1) of the Act of 1972).

(2)  A motion to have such a sealed packet opened up or such recovery allowed may be lodged by—

    (a)  the party who obtained the commission and diligence; or

    (b)[4]  any other party after the date of intimation under rule 28.3(5), 28.3A(8) or 28.4(10).

(3)  In addition to complying with rule 15.2 (intimation of motions) or rule 15A.4 (intimation of motions by email), the party lodging such a motion shall intimate the terms of the motion to the haver by post by the first class recorded delivery service.

(4)  The person claiming confidentiality may oppose a motion made under paragraph (2).

---

[1] As amended by SI 1996/2445 (effective November 1, 1996).

[2] As amended by SI 1996/2445 (effective November 1, 1996).

[3] As amended by the Act of Sederunt (Rules of the Court of Session, Ordinary Cause Rules and Summary Cause Rules Amendment) (Miscellaneous) 2014 (SSI 2014/152) r.3 (effective July 7, 2014).

[4] As amended by the Act of Sederunt (Rules of the Court of Session and Sheriff Court Rules Amendment) (Miscellaneous) 2014 (SSI 2014/201) r.3 (effective August 1, 2014).

GENERAL NOTE

Confidentiality can be claimed at the stage when a commission and diligence is sought and if success-ful will prevent the application being granted. Confidentiality can be claimed where the document (1) is a communication between a party and his solicitor (but the client that can plead or waive confidentiality and where the subject matter of the dispute involves an examination of the comunings between the client and agent there is no confidentiality (see *Micosta SA v Shetland Islands Council*, 1983 S.L.T. 483); (2) came into existence *post litam motam* (that is to say, material that a party has made in preparing his case but not otherwise; see *Komori v Tayside Health Board*, 2010 S.L.T. 387)—the full rigour of the *post litam motam* rule has been undermined by OCR, rule 9A.2 (entitlement to inspection and recovery of documents to be put in evidence at proof) and OCR, rule 36.17C (requirement to lodge medical reports to be relied on the action); (3) is a communication between a party or agents in an attempt to negotiate set-tlement; and (4) where art.8 of ECHR may be engaged see *M v A Scottish Local Authority*, 2012 S.L.T. 6. Where a party or the court has reason to anticipate that an issue of confidentiality may arise it is sensible to intimate the motion for a commission and diligence to the haver so that the issue may be dealt with at that stage. If confidentiality is claimed before the commission and diligence is granted the court may require all documents falling within the terms of the call to be produced to it so that it can determine the issue and it may (if there is a lot of material to be examined) appoint a commissioner for that purpose. Where a commissioner is appointed it remains for the court to determine whether or not any material identified by him as potentially confidential should be produced to the party seeking the recovery.

Frequently the first time that a haver will be in a position to claim confidentiality will be at a stage after he has been ordered to produce the documents or item. In that event the documents or item should, where practicable, be produced in a sealed packet. A motion is then made to open up the sealed packet which motion may be opposed by the haver.

## Warrants for production of original documents from public records

**28.9.**—(1) Where a party seeks to obtain from the keeper of any public record production of the original of any register or deed in his custody for the purposes of a cause, he shall apply to the sheriff by motion.

(2) Intimation of a motion under paragraph (1) shall be given to the keeper of the public record concerned at least 7 days before the motion is lodged.

(3) In relation to a public record kept by the Keeper of the Registers of Scotland or the Keeper of the Records of Scotland, where it appears to the sheriff that it is necessary for the ends of justice that a motion under this rule should be granted, he shall pronounce an interlocutor containing a certificate to that effect; and the party applying for production may apply by letter (enclosing a copy of the interlocutor duly certified by the sheriff clerk), addressed to the Deputy Principal Clerk of Session, for an order from the Court of Session authorising the Keeper of the Registers or the Keeper of the Records, as the case may be, to exhibit the original of any register or deed to the sheriff.

(4) The Deputy Principal Clerk of Session shall submit the application sent to him under paragraph (3) to the Lord Ordinary in chambers who, if satisfied, shall grant a warrant for production or exhibition of the original register or deed sought.

(5) A certified copy of the warrant granted under paragraph (4) shall be served on the keeper of the public record concerned.

(6) The expense of the production or exhibition of such an original register or deed shall be met, in the first instance, by the party who applied by motion under paragraph (1).

GENERAL NOTE

It may sometimes be necessary to obtain the original public record (for instance a coloured plan an-nexed to a deed, although any extract should also be in colour). If it is, then this rule provides the procedure. Normally an official extract of public record will suffice, and such a document is admissible (see Walkers, *Evidence* (1st ed.), para.227). Another approach is provided by s.6 of the Civil Evidence (Scotland) Act 1988.

## Commissions for examination of witnesses

**28.10.**—(1)[1]  This rule applies to a commission—

(a)  to take the evidence of a witness who—

    (i)  is resident beyond the jurisdiction of the court;

    (ii)  although resident within the jurisdiction of the court, resides at some place remote from that court; or

    (iii)  by reason of age, infirmity or sickness, is unable to attend the diet of proof;

(b)  in respect of the evidence of a witness which is in danger of being lost, to take the evidence to *lie in retentis*; or

(c)  on special cause shown, to take evidence of a witness on a ground other than one mentioned in sub-paragraph (a) or (b).

(2)  An application by a party for a commission to examine a witness shall be made by motion; and that party shall specify in the motion the name and address of at least one proposed commissioner for approval and appointment by the sheriff.

(2A)[2]  A motion under paragraph (2) may include an application for authority to record the proceedings before the commissioner by video recorder.

(3)  The interlocutor granting such a commission shall be sufficient authority for citing the witness to appear before the commissioner.

(4)[3]  At the commission, the commissioner shall—

(a)  administer the oath *de fideli administratione* to any clerk and any shorthand writer appointed for the commission; and

(b)  administer to the witness the oath in Form G14, or where the witness elects to affirm, the affirmation in Form G15.

(5)  Where a commission is granted for the examination of a witness, the commission shall proceed without interrogatories unless, on cause shown, the sheriff otherwise directs.

GENERAL NOTE

The recovery of evidence for use in an action is termed commission and diligence. The commission is the written authority of the court to the person appointed commissioner (either a solicitor or advocate but there is no reason why the Sheriff hearing the proof should not appoint himself commissioner) to take the evidence of the witness and the diligence is the warrant to cite the witness to appear before the commissioner.

A commission to take the evidence of a witness may be granted where a party wishes evidence that is in danger of being lost (through death or serious illness or prolonged absence abroad) to be taken to *lie in retentis* pending a proof or where the witness is unable to attend through age or infirmity or sickness or is resident beyond the jurisdiction or because of a special cause (such as holiday or important professional commitments). There has been an increased willingness to use the procedure so as not to cause disproportionate inconvenience to witnesses.

## Commissions on interrogatories

**28.11.**—(1)  Where interrogatories have not been dispensed with, the party who obtained the commission to examine a witness under rule 28.10 shall lodge draft interrogatories in process.

(2)  Any other party may lodge cross-interrogatories.

(3)  The interrogatories and any cross-interrogatories, when adjusted, shall be extended and returned to the sheriff clerk for approval and the settlement of any dispute as to their contents by the sheriff.

---

[1] As amended by SI 1996/2445 (effective November 1, 1996).

[2] As inserted by the Act of Sederunt (Sheriff Court Rules) (Miscellaneous Amendments) 2008 (SSI 2008/223) para.11 (effective July 1, 2008).

[3] As amended by SI 1996/2445 (effective November 1, 1996).

(4) The party who has obtained the commission shall—

   (a) provide the commissioner with a copy of the pleadings (including any adjustments and amendments), the approved interrogatories and any cross-interrogatories and a certified copy of the interlocutor of his appointment;

   (b) instruct the clerk; and

   (c) be responsible, in the first instance, for the fee of the commissioner and his clerk.

(5) The commissioner shall, in consultation with the parties, fix a diet for the execution of the commission to examine the witness.

(6) The executed interrogatories, any document produced by the witness and an inventory of that document, shall be sent by the commissioner to the sheriff clerk.

(7) Not later than the day after the date on which the executed interrogatories, any document and an inventory of that document, are received by the sheriff clerk, he shall intimate to each party that he has received them.

(8) The party who obtained the commission to examine the witness shall lodge in process—

   (a) the report of the commission; and

   (b) the executed interrogatories and any cross-interrogatories.

GENERAL NOTE

Unless dispensed with a commission proceeds upon interrogatories, that is a series of approved questions in writing for the witness to answer. This procedure is derived from the Court of Session where it was often used in divorce cases where the subject matter was exceedingly straightforward. Interrogatories are not ideal for anything but the simplest of cases. The exception is now the rule so that interrogatories are almost always dispensed with. See OCR r.28.10(5).

## Commissions without interrogatories

**28.12.**—(1) Where interrogatories have been dispensed with, the party who has obtained a commission to examine a witness under rule 28.10 shall—

   (a) provide the commissioner with a copy of the pleadings (including any adjustments and amendments) and a certified copy of the interlocutor of his appointment;

   (b) fix a diet for the execution of the commission in consultation with the commissioner and every other party;

   (c) instruct the clerk and any shorthand writer; and

   (d)[1] be responsible in the first instance for the fees of the commissioner, his clerk and any shorthand writer.

(2) All parties shall be entitled to be present and represented at the execution of the commission.

(3) The report of the execution of the commission, any document produced by the witness and an inventory of that document, shall be sent by the commissioner to the sheriff clerk.

(4) Not later than the day after the date on which such a report, any document and an inventory of that document are received by the sheriff clerk, he shall intimate to each party that he has received them.

(5) The party who obtained the commission to examine the witness shall lodge the report in process.

---

[1] As amended by the Act of Sederunt (Ordinary Cause, Summary Application, Summary Cause and Small Claim Rules) Amendment (Vulnerable Witnesses (Scotland) Act 2004) 2007, r.2(7) (effective November 1, 2007).

The standard commission takes place without interrogatories. The party whose commission it is fixes the diet and should also instruct a shorthand writer who will act as clerk. A shorthand writer is not compulsory but it is unwise to proceed without one. The commissioner should place the shorthand writer ("I do swear that I will faithfully discharge the duties of clerk and shorthand writer to this commission. So help me God") and witness ("I swear by almighty God that I will tell the truth, the whole truth and nothing but the truth") on oath. If the witness affirms then it is "I solemnly, sincerely and truly declare and affirm that I will tell the truth, the whole truth and nothing but the truth". Productions to be put to the witness should be borrowed from process in advance for that purpose. A commission can take place at any location. The party whose commission it is examines the witness and cross-examination and reexamination follows in the usual way. Objections to questions or to the line of evidence are normally dealt with by allowing the evidence to be heard subject to competency and relevancy. The evidence thus heard should be noted on a paper apart so that it is easily identifiable for determination as to its admissibility by the sheriff due course. Once the commission has been completed, a written transcript and report will be made up by the clerk (and shorthand writer) and signed by him and the commissioner. The report of the commission must be lodged in process.

## Evidence taken on commission

**28.13.—**(1)  Subject to the following paragraphs of this rule and to all questions of relevancy and admissibility, evidence taken on commission under rule 28.11 or 28.12 may be used as evidence at any proof of the cause.

(2)  Any party may object to the use of such evidence at a proof; and the objection shall be determined by the sheriff.

(3)  Such evidence shall not be used at a proof if the witness becomes available to attend the diet of proof.

(4)  A party may use such evidence in accordance with the preceding paragraphs of this rule notwithstanding that it was obtained at the instance of another party.

If the evidence is to be relied upon it must be tendered before the party relying upon it closes its case. Any of the parties may do so. Although there is no modern reported decision there seems no reason in principle why a witness who gives evidence at a proof having made a statement at a commission may not be examined as to consistencies or cross examined as to inconsistencies (see section 3 of the Civil Evidence (Scotland) Act 1988; cf. *Forrests v Low's Trs*, 1907 S.C. 1240).

## Letters of request

**28.14.—**[1](1)  Subject to paragraph (7), this rule applies to an application for a letter of request to a court or tribunal outside Scotland to obtain evidence of the kind specified in paragraph (2), being evidence obtainable within the jurisdiction of that court or tribunal, for the purposes of a cause depending before the sheriff.

(2)[2]  An application to which paragraph (1) applies may be made in relation to a request—

(a)  for the examination of a witness,

(b)  for the inspection, photographing, preservation, custody, detention, production or recovery of, or the taking of samples of, or the carrying out of any experiment on or with, a document or other property, as the case may be,

(c)  for the medical examination of any person,

(d)  for the taking and testing of samples of blood from any person, or

(e)  for any other order for obtaining evidence,

for which an order could be obtained from the sheriff.

(3)  Such an application shall be made by minute in Form G16 together with a proposed letter of request in Form G17.

---

[1] As amended by the Act of Sederunt (Taking of Evidence in the European Community) 2003 (SSI 2003/601).

[2] As amended by SI 1996/2445 (effective November 1, 1996).

(4)[1]  It shall be a condition of granting a letter of request that any solicitor for the applicant, or a party litigant, as the case may be, shall be personally liable, in the first instance, for the whole expenses which may become due and payable in respect of the letter of request to the court or tribunal obtaining the evidence and to any witness who may be examined for the purpose; and he shall consign into court such sum in respect of such expenses as the sheriff thinks fit.

(5)  Unless the court or tribunal to which a letter of request is addressed is a court or tribunal in a country or territory—

(a)  where English is an official language, or

(b)  in relation to which the sheriff clerk certifies that no translation is required,

then the applicant shall, before the issue of the letter of request, lodge in process a translation of that letter and any interrogatories and cross-interrogatories into the official language of that court or tribunal.

(6)[2]  The letter of request when issued; any interrogatories and cross-interrogatories adjusted as required by rule 28.11 and the translations (if any), shall be forwarded by the sheriff clerk to the Scottish Ministers or to such person and in such manner as the sheriff may direct.

(7)  This rule does not apply to any request for the taking of evidence under Council Regulation (EC) No. 1206/2001 of 28th May 2001 on cooperation between the courts of the Member States in the taking of evidence in civil or commercial matters.

GENERAL NOTE

There is no power to enforce the attendance of witnesses who are furth of Scotland but an application may be made to apply for evidence to be taken on commission or by letter of request. A commission still relies on co-operation of the witness outwith the jurisdiction. A letter of request enables the foreign court or tribunal to compel the witness to give evidence. In relation to witnesses in other parts of the United Kingdom, the sheriff appoints a commissioner to take the evidence and the attendance of that witness at a commission is compelled by the High Court in England and Wales and Northern Ireland (see Evidence (Proceedings in Other Jurisdictions) Act 1975, ss.1–4). Witnesses beyond the United Kingdom require to be considered under reference to the Hague Convention on the Taking of Evidence Abroad in Civil or Commercial Matters, March 18, 1970. OCR r.28.14 is for all practical purposes identical to the rule in the equivalent rule in the Court of Session (see *Greens Annotated Rules of the Court of Session* (W.Green, 2002), pp.C250–C253).

## Taking of evidence in the European Community

**28.14A.**—[3](1)  This rule applies to any request—

(a)  for the competent court of another Member State to take evidence under Article 1.1(a) of the Council Regulation; or

(b)  that the court shall take evidence directly in another Member State under Article 1.1(b) of the Council Regulation.

(2)  An application for a request under paragraph (1) shall be made by minute in Form G16, together with the proposed request in form A or I (as the case may be) in the Annex to the Council Regulation.

(3)  In this rule, "the Council Regulation" means Council Regulation (EC) No. 1206/2001 of 28th May 2001 on cooperation between the courts of the Member States in the taking of evidence in civil or commercial matters.

---

[1] As amended by SI 1996/2445 (effective November 1, 1996).

[2] As substituted by the Act of Sederunt (Sheriff Court Rules) (Miscellaneous Amendments) 2011 (SSI 2011/193) r.8 (effective April 4, 2011).

[3] As amended by the Act of Sederunt (Taking of Evidence in the European Community) 2003 (SSI 2003/601).

**Citation of witnesses and havers**

**28.15.** The following rules shall apply to the citation of a witness or haver to a commission under this Chapter as they apply to the citation of a witness for a proof:—
rule 29.7 (citation of witnesses) except paragraph 4,
rule 29.9 (second diligence against a witness,
rule 29.10 (failure of witness to attend).

General Note

A witness is cited for a commission as he would be for a proof and his attendance may likewise be enforced.

Chapter 28A[1]

Pre-Proof Hearing

**Pre-proof hearing**

**28A.1.**—(1)[2]   Subject to paragraph (1A) the appointment of a cause to a proof or proof before answer or thereafter on the motion of any party or of his own motion, the sheriff may appoint the cause to a pre-proof hearing.

(1A)[3]   Where Chapter 33AA applies, the sheriff will fix a pre-proof hearing at the case management hearing.

(2)   It shall be the duty of the parties to provide the sheriff with sufficient information to enable him to conduct the hearing as provided for in this rule.

(3)   At a pre-proof hearing the sheriff shall ascertain, so far as is reasonably practicable, whether the cause is likely to proceed to proof on the date fixed for that purpose and, in particular—

(a)   the state of preparation of the parties; and

(b)[4][5]   the extent to which the parties have complied with their duties under rules 9A.2, 9A.3, 29.11 and 29.15 and any orders made by the sheriff under rules 9.12(3)(a), (b), (d), or (e) or 10.6(3)(a) or (b) or Chapter 33AA; and

(c)[6]   consider any child witness notice or vulnerable witness application that has been lodged where no order has been made, or ascertain whether there is or is likely to be a vulnerable witness within the meaning of section 11(1) of the 2004 Act who is to give evidence at any proof or hearing and whether any order under section 12(1) of the Act of 2004 requires to be made.

(4)   At a pre-proof hearing the sheriff may—

(a)   discharge the proof or proof before answer and fix a new date for such proof or proof before answer;

---

[1] Inserted by the Act of Sederunt (Ordinary Cause and Summary Application Rules) Amendment (Miscellaneous) 2006 (SSI 2006/410) (effective August 18, 2006).

[2] As inserted by the Act of Sederunt (Sheriff Court Rules)(Miscellaneous Amendments) (No.2) 2013 (SI 2013/139) para.2 (effective June 3, 2013).

[3] As inserted by the Act of Sederunt (Sheriff Court Rules)(Miscellaneous Amendments) (No.2) 2013 (SI 2013/139) para.2 (effective June 3, 2013).

[4] As amended by the Act of Sederunt (Ordinary Cause, Summary Application, Summary Cause and Small Claim Rules) Amendment (Vulnerable Witnesses (Scotland) Act 2004) 2007, r.2(6)(a) (effective November 1, 2007).

[5] As amended by the Act of Sederunt (Sheriff Court Rules)(Miscellaneous Amendments) (No.2) 2013 (SI 2013/139) para.2 (effective June 3, 2013).

[6] As inserted by the Act of Sederunt (Ordinary Cause, Summary Application, Summary Cause and Small Claim Rules) Amendment (Vulnerable Witnesses (Scotland) Act 2004) 2007, r.2(6)(b) (effective November 1, 2007).

(b)    adjourn the pre-proof hearing; or

(c)    make such other order as he thinks fit to secure the expeditious progress of the cause.

(5)    For the purposes of rules 16.2 (decrees where party in default), 33.37 (decree by default in family action) and 33A.37 (decree by default in civil partnership action), a pre-proof hearing shall be a diet in accordance with those rules.

GENERAL NOTE

This is a particularly useful rule designed to allow effective management of court resources. The Sheriff is directed to find out whether parties are in a position to proceed and to check that they have complied with their obligations under the rules. There is sufficient flexibility to allow, if so advised, for the scope of the proof to be confined or restricted if appropriate.

## Chapter 29

## Proof

### Reference to oath

**29.1.**—(1)    Where a party intends to refer any matter to the oath of his opponent he shall lodge a motion to that effect.

(2)    If a party fails to appear at the diet for taking his deposition on the reference to his oath, the sheriff may hold him as confessed and grant decree accordingly.

GENERAL NOTE

The procedure is described in Walker's *Evidence*, Chapter 25. The Requirements of Writing (Scotland) Act 1995 has rendered the procedure of reference to oath of no practical importance although it remains theoretically possible that it could still be used in relation to events prior to the coming into force of that Act (see e.g. *McEleveen v McQuiilan's Executors* , 1997 S.L.T. (Sh Ct) 46.

### Remit to person of skill

**29.2.**—(1)    The sheriff may, on a motion by any party or on a joint motion, remit to any person of skill, or other person, to report on any matter of fact.

(2)    Where a remit under paragraph (1) is made by joint motion or of consent of all parties, the report of such person shall be final and conclusive with respect to the subject-matter of the remit.

(3)    Where a remit under paragraph (1) is made—

(a)    on the motion of one of the parties, the expenses of its execution shall, in the first instance, be met by that party; and

(b)    on a joint motion or of consent of all parties, the expenses shall, in the first instance, be met by the parties equally, unless the sheriff otherwise orders.

GENERAL NOTE

There are no modern reported examples of the use of this procedure but there may well be cases where it could be usefully employed, particularly now that many issues of disputed fact are spoken to by experts. Perhaps if the sheriff were able to remit to a man of skill *ex proprio motu* the procedure would be used more often. The rule does not prevent a remit being made before the record has closed but it is normally better to know what the parties' final position is in relation to the dispute before a remit is made as it offends against OCR r.29.17.

### Written statements

**29.3.**[1]    Where a statement in a document is admissible under section 2(1)(b) of the Civil Evidence (Scotland) Act 1988, any party who wishes to have that statement received in evidence shall—

(a)    docquet that document as follows:—

---

[1]    As inserted by the Act of Sederunt (Ordinary Cause, Summary Application and Small Claim Rules) Amendment (Miscellaneous) 2004 (SSI 2004/197) (effective May 21, 2004), para.2(11).

"(*Place and date*)

This document contains a statement admissible under section 2(1)(b) of the Civil Evidence (Scotland) Act 1988.

(*Signed*)

(*Designation and address*)";

(b)  lodge that document in process; and

(c)  provide all other parties with a copy of that document.

GENERAL NOTE

Rule 29.3 addresses a *lacuna* in the Ordinary Cause Rules by providing for receiving into evidence written statements.

## Renouncing probation

**29.4.**—[1](1)  Where, at any time, the parties seek to renounce probation, they shall lodge in process a joint minute to that effect with or without a statement of admitted facts and any productions.

(2)  On the lodging of a joint minute under paragraph (1), the sheriff may make such order as he thinks fit to secure the expeditious progress of the cause.

GENERAL NOTE

Once a joint minute is lodged renouncing probation, both parties are contractually barred from leading evidence. Any attempt to amend is likely to be refused. The renunciation of probation is rare but does happen from time to time where parties are in agreement as to the material facts. If necessary a separate statement of agreed facts can be lodged. The diet of proof may be converted into a diet of debate.

## Orders for proof

**29.5.**  Where proof is necessary in any cause, the sheriff shall fix a date for taking the proof and may limit the mode of proof.

GENERAL NOTE

In terms of OCR r.9.12(3), a proof will be ordered at the options hearing; but if after additional procedure, debate or amendment a proof is required, then this rule authorises that to be done at any procedural hearing or debate. This rule is also without prejudice to OCR r.28A(4).

The interlocutor allowing proof should make it clear whose averments are admitted to probation, and if any averments are not the subject of proof that should also be made clear. If the proof is a preliminary proof then the subject matter of the proof should be specified precisely in the interlocutor. Where there is a counter-claim the interlocutor should indicate whether the averments in the counterclaim are admitted to probation.

Proof by writ or oath has been abolished (see section 11 of the Requirements of Writing (Scotland) Act 1995) so the mode of proof will not be limited; but this is subject to section 14(3) which provides that the 1995 Act does not apply to anything done before the commencement of that Act.

## Hearing parts of proof separately

**29.6.**—(1)[2]  In any cause, the sheriff may—

(a)  of his own motion, or

(b)  on the motion of any party,

order that proof on liability or any specified issue be heard separately from proof on the question of the amount for which decree may be pronounced and determine the order in which the proofs shall be heard.

(2)  The sheriff shall pronounce such interlocutor as he thinks fit at the conclusion of the first proof of any cause ordered to be heard in separate parts under paragraph (1).

---

[1]  As amended by the Act of Sederunt (Ordinary Cause and Summary Application Rules) Amendment (Miscellaneous) 2006 (SI 2006/410) (effective August 18, 2006).

[2]  As amended by SI 1996/2445 (effective November 1, 1996).

GENERAL NOTE

This rule is designed to allow a certain amount of flexibility and to avoid wasted procedure.

The obvious examples are preliminary proof on the question of limitation or prescription and separation of proof on liability and quantum. Whether to split a proof is a matter for the discretion of the sheriff in the circumstances of any particular case. See also OCR r.28A(4).

## Citation of witnesses

**29.7.**—(1)  A witness shall be cited for a proof—

(a)  by registered post or the first class recorded delivery service by the solicitor for the party on whose behalf he is cited; or

(b)  by a sheriff officer—

    (i)  personally;

    (ii)  by a citation being left with a resident at the person's dwelling place or an employee at his place of business;

    (iii)  by depositing it in that person's dwelling place or place of business;

    (iv)  by affixing it to the door of that person's dwelling place or place of business; or

    (v)  by registered post or the first class recorded delivery service.

(2)  Where service is executed under paragraph (1)(b)(iii) or (iv), the sheriff officer shall, as soon as possible after such service, send, by ordinary post to the address at which he thinks it most likely that the person may be found, a letter containing a copy of the citation.

(3)  A certified copy of the interlocutor allowing a proof shall be sufficient warrant to a sheriff officer to cite a witness on behalf of a party.

(4)  A witness shall be cited on a period of notice of 7 days in Form G13 and the party citing the witness shall lodge a certificate of citation in Form G12.

(5)  A solicitor who cites a witness shall be personally liable for his fees and expenses.

(6)  In the event of a solicitor intimating to a witness that his citation is cancelled, the solicitor shall advise him that the cancellation is not to affect any other citation which he may have received from another party.

GENERAL NOTE

This rule is without prejudice to OCR r.9A.3 (exchange of list of witnesses). It is not necessary to cite a witness to lead him in evidence as the purpose of citation is to compel attendance, but it is wise to cite any witness that it is intended to call. The methods of citation are similar to the citation of parties. As soon as a proof is allowed the witnesses should be informed of its date and they should be cited with as much notice as possible. The seven-day period in the rule is a minimum period of notice. Parties should communicate with each other in order to minimise the inconvenience to witnesses. Fees of witnesses are set out in Act of Sederunt (Fees of Witnesses and Shorthand Writers in the Sheriff Court) 1992.

## Citation of witnesses by party litigants

**29.8.**—(1)  Where a party to a cause is a party litigant, he shall—

(a)  not later than 4 weeks before the diet of proof, apply to the sheriff by motion to fix caution in such sum as the sheriff considers reasonable having regard to the number of witnesses he proposes to cite and the period for which they may be required to attend court; and

(b)  before instructing a sheriff officer to cite a witness, find caution for such expenses as can reasonably be anticipated to be incurred by the witness in answering the citation.

(2)  A party litigant who does not intend to cite all the witnesses referred to in his application under paragraph (1)(a), may apply by motion for variation of the amount of caution.

General Note

The sheriff clerk has a duty to assist party litigants to comply with the requirements of this rule.

## Second diligence against a witness

**29.9.**—(1)   The sheriff may, on the motion of a party, grant a second diligence to compel the attendance of a witness under pain of arrest and imprisonment until caution can be found for his due attendance.

(2)   The warrant for a second diligence shall be effective without endorsation and the expenses of such a motion and diligence may be decerned for against the witness.

General Note

Where there is reason to think in advance of the proof that a witness will not attend, then a motion for second diligence to compel attendance may be made. The procedure is described in Maclaren *Court of Session Practice*, pp.343–344. The letters are issued by the sheriff clerk in the name of the sheriff principal and addressed to the sheriff officer, requiring him to apprehend the witness and imprison him within a named prison. Once caution is found the witness must be released. The appropriate sum as a penalty should now be £250 and the sheriff should fix the amount of caution. Letters of second diligence will not be granted unless the witness is essential, there has been effective citation failing which a clear attempt to evade it and that there is a real risk that the witness will not attend.

## Failure of witness to attend

**29.10.**—(1)   Where a witness fails to answer a citation after having been duly cited, the sheriff may, on the motion of a party and on production of a certificate of citation, grant warrant for the apprehension of the witness and for bringing him to court; and the expenses of such a motion and apprehension may be decerned for against the witness.

(2)   Where a witness duly cited and after having demanded and been paid his travelling expenses, fails to attend a diet, either before the sheriff or before a commissioner, the sheriff may—

(a)   ordain the witness to forfeit and pay a penalty not exceeding £250 unless a reasonable excuse be offered and sustained; and

(b)   grant decree for that penalty in favour of the party on whose behalf the witness was cited.

General Note

Decree for the penalty is enforceable by civil diligence.

## Lodging productions

**29.11.**—(1)[1,2]   Where a proof has been allowed, all productions and affidavits which are intended to be used at the proof shall be lodged in process not later than 28 days before the diet of proof.

(2)   A production which is not lodged in accordance with paragraph (1) shall not be used or put in evidence at a proof unless—

(a)   by consent of parties; or

(b)   with leave of the sheriff on cause shown and on such conditions, if any, as to expenses or otherwise as the sheriff thinks fit.

General Note

This rule is without prejudice to OCR r.9A.2 (inspection and recovery of documents); OCR r.21.1 (lodging of documents founded on or adopted); or OCR r.36.17C (lodging of medical reports in actions of damages). It is not necessary to lodge under this rule a document used (usually in cross-examination) only to test the credibility of a witness (see *Paterson & Sons v Kit Coffee Co. Ltd* (1908) 16 S.L.T. 180)

---

[1]   As amended by SSI 2000/239 (effective October 2, 2000).

[2]   As amended by the Act of Sederunt (Ordinary Cause and Summary Application Rules) Amendment (Miscellaneous) 2006 (SSI 2006/410) (effective August 18, 2006).

whether or not the witness is a party (Macphail, *Sheriff Court Practice* (2nd ed.), para.16.25, and see *Robertson v Anderson* , May 15, 2001 Unreported, OH Lord Carloway paras [64] to [68].

## Copy productions

**29.12.**—(1)[1]  A copy of every documentary production, marked with the appropriate number of process of the principal production, shall be lodged for the use of the sheriff at a proof not later than 48 hours before the diet of proof.

(2)  Each copy production consisting of more than one sheet shall be securely fastened together by the party lodging it.

GENERAL NOTE

Copy productions should be legible and have the same page numbers as the principal.

## Returning borrowed parts of process and productions before proof

**29.13.**  All parts of process and productions which have been borrowed shall be returned to process before 12.30 pm on the day preceding the diet of proof.

GENERAL NOTE

This rule is without prejudice to OCR rr.11.3, 11.4 and 11.5. Failure to return a borrowed production may result in liability for expenses if any procedure is wasted.

## Notices to admit and notices of non-admission

**29.14.**—(1)[2]  At any time after the record has closed, a party may intimate to any other party a notice or notices calling on him to admit for the purposes of that cause only—

    (a)    such facts relating to an issue averred in the pleadings as may be specified in the notice;

    (b)    that a particular document lodged in process and specified in the notice is—

        (i)    an original and properly authenticated document; or

        (ii)    a true copy of an original and properly authenticated document.

(2)  Where a party on whom a notice is intimated under paragraph (1)—

    (a)    does not admit a fact specified in the notice, or

    (b)    does not admit, or seeks to challenge, the authenticity of a document specified in the notice,

he shall, within 21 days after the date of intimation of the notice under paragraph (1), intimate a notice of non-admission to the party intimating the notice to him under paragraph (1) stating that he does not admit the fact or document specified.

(3)  A party who fails to intimate a notice of non-admission under paragraph (2) shall be deemed to have admitted the fact or document specified in the notice intimated to him under paragraph (1); and such fact or document may be used in evidence at a proof if otherwise admissible in evidence, unless the sheriff, on special cause shown, otherwise directs.

(4)  [Repealed by the Act of Sederunt (Sheriff Court Rules) (Miscellaneous Amendments) (No.2) 2008 (SSI 2008/365) para.4 (effective December 1, 2008).]

(5)  The party serving a notice under paragraph (1) or (2) shall lodge a copy of it in process.

(6)  A deemed admission under paragraph (3) shall not be used against the party by whom it was deemed to be made other than in the cause for the purpose for

---

[1] As amended by SSI 2000/239 (effective October 2, 2000).
[2] As amended by SSI 2000/239 (effective October 2, 2000).

which it was deemed to be made or in favour of any person other than the party by whom the notice was given under paragraph (1).

(7)[1] The sheriff may, at any time, allow a party to amend or withdraw an admission made by him on such conditions, if any, as he thinks fit.

(8)[2] A party may, at any time, withdraw in whole or in part a notice of non admission by intimating a notice of withdrawal.

GENERAL NOTE

The record is supposed to be the place where parties identify with precision what is truly in dispute between them. Each fact averred requires to be carefully considered by the other party and if appropriate admitted. Frequently the parties respond with a general denial which covers at least some averments that are not in dispute. The whole system of written pleading proceeds on trust that parties will honestly answer averments by an opponent on matters within their knowledge and a party must admit averments that he knows to be true. Unfortunately for one reason or another parties do not always live up to these expectations. Furthermore, it is often the case that facts even not strictly speaking within the knowledge of the other party should be identified as not being in dispute. Sometimes there are facts (and there may well be documents) that are not necessarily the subject of averment but which may be relevant to the proof of a parties case that can be usefully identified as being capable of agreement. This rule provides a mechanism apart from the written pleadings whereby a party can call upon the other to admit certain facts including the originality or authenticity of a document. A failure to respond results in a deemed admission and a response that turns out to be unjustified ought to result at the very least in liability in expenses for any unnecessary procedure. Admissions can be withdrawn and departed from on special cause being shown.

## Instruction of shorthand writer

**29.15.** Where a shorthand writer is to record evidence at a proof, the responsibility for instructing a shorthand writer shall lie with the pursuer.

GENERAL NOTE

Failure to instruct the shorthand writer means that the proof cannot proceed unless recording of the evidence by mechanical means is available or recording is dispensed with under r.29.18. Another option may be to seek to have the cause treated as a summary cause (under section 37(1)(a) of the Sheriff Courts (Scotland) Act 1971) but that will restrict any decree accordingly.

## Administration of oath or affirmation to witnesses

**29.16.** The sheriff shall administer the oath to a witness in Form G14 or, where the witness elects to affirm, the affirmation in Form G15.

GENERAL NOTE

"I swear by Almighty God that I will tell the truth, the whole truth and nothing but the truth"

"I solemnly sincerely and truly declare and affirm that I will tell the truth, the whole truth and nothing but the truth"

Children under 12 do not have the oath administered but are admonished to tell the truth. Between these ages whether to administer the oath is at the discretion of the Sheriff. The oath (or affirmation) should be administered where the child is 14 or over. It is unlawful to ask questions of a witness before he gives evidence intended to establish that he does not understand the duty to give truthful evidence or the difference between truth and lies (see Vulnerable Witnesses (Scotland) Act 2004 s.24).

## Proof to be taken continuously

**29.17.** A proof shall be taken continuously so far as possible; but the sheriff may adjourn the diet from time to time.

GENERAL NOTE

It is important that proof should proceed continuously so as to save time and expense and any adjournment for any period should be arranged with this rule in mind.

---

[1] Inserted by SSI 2000/239 (effective October 2, 2000).
[2] Inserted by SSI 2000/239 (effective October 2, 2000).

### Recording of evidence

**29.18.**—[1](1)[2]  Evidence in a cause shall be recorded by—

(a)   a shorthand writer, to whom the oath *de fideli administratione* in connection with the sheriff court service generally shall have been administered, or

(b)   tape recording or other mechanical means approved by the court, unless the parties, by agreement and with the approval of the sheriff, dispense with the recording of evidence.

(2)  Where a shorthand writer is employed to record evidence, he shall, in the first instance, be paid by the parties equally.

(3)  Where evidence is recorded by tape recording or other mechanical means, any fee payable shall, in the first instance, be paid by the parties equally.

(4)  The solicitors for the parties shall be personally liable for the fees payable under paragraph (2) or (3), and the sheriff may make an order directing payment to be made.

(5)  The record of the evidence at a proof shall include—

(a)   any objection taken to a question or to the line of evidence;

(b)   any submission made in relation to such an objection; and

(c)   the ruling of the court in relation to the objection and submission.

(6)  A transcript of the record of the evidence shall be made only on the direction of the sheriff; and the cost shall, in the first instance, be borne—

(a)   in an undefended cause, by the solicitor for the pursuer; and

(b)   in a defended cause, by the solicitors for the parties in equal proportions.

(7)  The transcript of the record of the evidence provided for the use of the court shall be certified as a faithful record of the evidence by—

(a)   the shorthand writer who recorded the evidence; or

(b)   where the evidence was recorded by tape recording or other mechanical means, by the person who transcribed the record.

(8)  The sheriff may make such alterations to the transcript of the record of the evidence as appear to him to be necessary after hearing the parties; and, where such alterations are made, the sheriff shall authenticate the alterations.

(9)  Where a transcript of the record of the evidence has been made for the use of the sheriff, copies of it may be obtained by any party from the person who transcribed the record on payment of his fee.

(10)  Except with leave of the sheriff, the transcript of the record of the evidence may be borrowed from process only for the purpose of enabling a party to consider whether to appeal against the interlocutor of the sheriff on the proof.

(11)  Where a transcript of the record of the evidence is required for the purpose of an appeal but has not been directed to be transcribed under paragraph (6), the appellant—

(a)   may request such a transcript from the shorthand writer or as the case may be, the cost of the transcript being borne by the solicitor for the appellant in the first instance; and

(b)   shall lodge the transcript in process; and copies of it may be obtained by any party from the shorthand writer or as the case may be, on payment of his fee.

---

[1] As amended by SI 1996/2445 (effective November 1, 1996).
[2] As amended by SI 1996/2445 (effective November 1, 1996).

(12)  Where the recording of evidence has been dispensed with under paragraph (1), the sheriff, if called upon to do so, shall—

(a)  in the case of an objection to—

(i)  the admissibility of evidence on the ground of confidentiality, or

(ii)  the production of a document on any ground,

note the terms in writing of such objections and his decision on the objection; and

(b)  in the case of any other objection, record, in the note to his interlocutor disposing of the merits of the cause, the terms of the objection and his decision on the objection.

(13)  This rule shall, with the necessary modifications, apply to the recording of evidence at a commission as it applies to the recording of evidence at a proof.

GENERAL NOTE

In the sheriff court the principal method of recording evidence remains the shorthand writer. It may seem curious that this superior form of recording the evidence should be retained in the ordinary sheriff court when it has disappeared from the Court of Session, High Court of Justiciary and solemn sheriff court procedure. Only in the ordinary sheriff court did (do) the parties pay for the shorthand writer. Further, if there was no shorthand writer then the clerk would have to remain in the court room to operate the tape recording equipment. This would have manning implications, particularly in the smaller courts.

*Rule 29.18(5)*

Parties themselves should keep a note of these matters as it is necessary to ask the sheriff to deal with reserved matters at the hearing on evidence. One of the advantages of a shorthand writer is that one can always ask for a note of these matters before they disappear at the end of the evidence.

*Rule 29.18(8)*

If the sheriff considers that the transcript is inaccurate he may correct it after hearing the parties and he may hear the witness again (see e.g. *Wilson v MacQueen* , 1925 S.L.T. (Sh Ct) 130.

## Rulings on admissibility of evidence: leave to appeal

**29.19.**[1]**(1)**  This rule applies where a party or any other person objects to—

(a)  the admissibility of oral or documentary evidence on the ground of confidentiality;

(b)  the production of a document on any ground.

(2)  An application for leave to appeal against the decision of the sheriff on the objection must be made immediately.

GENERAL NOTE

This is the only competent method of review as to the admissibility of evidence or production of a document during a proof. It would only be in exceptional circumstances that a sheriff would grant leave under this rule as any decision on admissibility can also be challenged following the final interlocutor (see section 27 of the Sheriff Courts (Scotland) Act 1907). Appeal from the sheriff principal also requires leave in terms of section 28 of the Sheriff Courts (Scotland) Act 1907.

## Parties to be heard at close of proof

**29.20.**  At the close of the proof, or at an adjourned diet if for any reason the sheriff has postponed the hearing, the sheriff shall hear parties on the evidence and thereafter shall pronounce judgment with the least possible delay.

GENERAL NOTE

Parties should tell the court in precise terms what order they require. They should bear in mind that in terms of OCR r.12.2(3)(a) the sheriff is required to make findings in fact and law. Accordingly, parties

---

[1] As substituted by the Act of Sederunt (Rules of the Court of Session, Sheriff Appeal Court Rules and Sheriff Court Rules Amendment) (Sheriff Appeal Court) 2015 (SSI 2015/419) r.5 (effective 1 January 2016).

should indicate what pleas-in-law are to be sustained and repelled and under reference to the pleadings, what averments of fact have been proved. Care should be taken to concentrate on findings necessary to resolve the issues (see *B v G*, 2012 S.L.T. 840 at para.48). If objection has been taken to evidence and the evidence allowed to be heard subject to competency and relevancy, then the party who has taken the objection should indicate whether he insists on the objection and if so justify such a position. Interest, the remuneration of witnesses attending but not called, the expenses of skilled witnesses and certification of the cause as suitable for the employment of counsel should be addressed at this stage. The question of expenses and any motion relating to modification or enhancement is normally better left until the outcome of the case is known.

## Chapter 30

## Decrees, Extracts and Execution

### Interpretation of this Chapter

**30.1.** In this Chapter, "decree" includes any judgment, deliverance, interlocutor, act, order, finding or authority which may be extracted.

### Taxes on funds under control of the court

**30.2.**—(1) Subject to paragraph (2), in a cause in which money has been consigned into court under the Sheriff Court Consignations (Scotland) Act 1893, no decree, warrant or order for payment to any person shall be granted until there has been lodged with the sheriff clerk a certificate by an authorised officer of the Inland Revenue stating that all taxes or duties payable to the Commissioners of Inland Revenue have been paid or satisfied.

(2) In an action of multiplepoinding, it shall not be necessary for the grant of a decree, warrant or order for payment under paragraph (1) that all of the taxes or duties payable on the estate of a deceased claimant have been paid or satisfied.

### Decrees for payment in foreign currency

**30.3.**—(1) Where decree has been granted for payment of a sum of money in a foreign currency or the sterling equivalent, a party requesting extract of the decree shall do so by minute endorsed on or annexed to the initial writ stating the rate of exchange prevailing on the date of the decree sought to be extracted or the date, or within 3 days before the date, on which the extract is ordered, and the sterling equivalent at that rate for the principal sum and interest decerned for.

(2) A certificate in Form G18, from the Bank of England or a bank which is an institution authorised under the Banking Act 1987 certifying the rate of exchange and the sterling equivalent shall be lodged with the minute requesting extract of the decree.

(3) The extract decree issued by the sheriff clerk shall mention any certificate referred to in paragraph (2).

### When decrees extractable

**30.4.**—(1)[1] Subject to the following paragraphs:—
  (a) subject to sub-paragraph (c), a decree in absence may be extracted after the expiry of 14 days from the date of decree;
  (b) subject to sub-paragraph (c), any decree pronounced in a defended cause may be extracted at any time after whichever is the later of the following:—
     (i) the expiry of the period within which an application for leave to appeal may be made and no such application has been made;

---

[1] As amended by SI 1996/2445 (effective November 1, 1996).

(ii) the date on which leave to appeal has been refused and there is no right of appeal from such refusal;

(iii)[1] the expiry of the period within which an appeal may be made and no appeal has been made; or

(iv) the date on which an appeal has been finally disposed of; and

(c) where, the sheriff has, in pronouncing decree, reserved any question of expenses, extract of that decree may be issued only after the expiry of 14 days from the date of the interlocutor disposing of the question of expenses unless the sheriff otherwise directs.

(2) The sheriff may, on cause shown, grant a motion to allow extract to be applied for and issued earlier than a date referred to in paragraph (1).

(3) In relation to a decree referred to in paragraph (1)(b) or (c), paragraph (2) shall not apply unless—

(a) the motion under that paragraph is made in the presence of parties; or

(b) the sheriff is satisfied that proper intimation of the motion has been made in writing to every party not present at the hearing of the motion.

(4) Nothing in this rule shall affect the power of the sheriff to supersede extract.

### Extract of certain awards notwithstanding appeal

**30.5.**[2] The sheriff clerk may issue an extract of an order under section 11 of the Children (Scotland) Act 1995 or in respect of aliment notwithstanding that an appeal has been made against an interlocutor containing such an award unless an order under rule 31.5 (appeals in connection with orders under section 11 of the Children (Scotland) Act 1995 or aliment) has been made excusing obedience to or implement of that interlocutor.

### Form of extract decree

**30.6.**—(1) The extract of a decree mentioned in Appendix 2 shall be in the appropriate form for that decree in Appendix 2.

(2) In the case of a decree not mentioned in Appendix 2, the extract of the decree shall be modelled on a form in that Appendix with such variation as circumstances may require.

### Form of warrant for execution

**30.7.** An extract of a decree on which execution may proceed shall include a warrant for execution in the following terms:— "This extract is warrant for all lawful execution hereon.".

### Date of decree in extract

**30.8.**—(1)[3] Where the Sheriff Appeal Court has adhered to the decision of the sheriff following an appeal, the date to be inserted in the extract decree as the date of decree shall be the date of the decision of the Sheriff Appeal Court.

---

[1] As amended by the Act of Sederunt (Rules of the Court of Session, Sheriff Appeal Court Rules and Sheriff Court Rules Amendment) (Sheriff Appeal Court) 2015 (SSI 2015/419) r.5 (effective 1 January 2016).

[2] As substituted by the Act of Sederunt (Sheriff Court Rules) (Miscellaneous Amendments) (No.2) 2010 (SSI 2010/416) r.6 (effective January 1, 2011).

[3] As amended by the Act of Sederunt (Rules of the Court of Session, Sheriff Appeal Court Rules and Sheriff Court Rules Amendment) (Sheriff Appeal Court) 2015 (SSI 2015/419) r.5 (effective 1 January 2016).

(2)   Where a decree has more than one date it shall not be necessary to specify in an extract what was done on each date.

### Service of charge where address of defender not known

**30.9.**—(1)   Where the address of a defender is not known to the pursuer, a charge shall be deemed to have been served on the defender if it is—

- (a)   served on the sheriff clerk of the sheriff court district where the defender's last known address is located; and
- (b)   displayed by the sheriff clerk on the walls of court for the period of the charge.

(2)   On receipt of such a charge, the sheriff clerk shall display it on the walls of court and it shall remain displayed for the period of the charge.

(3)   The period specified in the charge shall run from the first date on which it was displayed on the walls of court.

(4)   On the expiry of the period of charge, the sheriff clerk shall endorse a certificate on the charge certifying that it has been displayed in accordance with this rule and shall thereafter return it to the sheriff officer by whom service was executed.

### Expenses

**30.10.**[1]   A party who—

- (a)   is or has been represented by a person authorised under any enactment to conduct proceedings in the sheriff court; and
- (b)   would have been found entitled to expenses if he had been represented by a solicitor or an advocate,

may be awarded any expenses or outlays to which a party litigant may be found entitled under the Litigants in Person (Costs and Expenses) Act 1975 or any enactment under that Act.

Chapter 31

Appeals

### Time limit for appeal

**31.1.**   [Repealed by the Act of Sederunt (Rules of the Court of Session, Sheriff Appeal Court Rules and Sheriff Court Rules Amendment) (Sheriff Appeal Court) 2015 (SSI 2015/419) r.5 (effective 1 January 2016).]

### Applications for leave to appeal

**31.2.**—(1)   Where leave to appeal is required, applications for leave to appeal against an interlocutor of a sheriff shall be made within 7 days after the date of the interlocutor against which it is sought to appeal unless the interlocutor has been extracted following a motion under rule 30.4(2) (early extract).

(2)   [Repealed by the Act of Sederunt (Rules of the Court of Session, Sheriff Appeal Court Rules and Sheriff Court Rules Amendment) (Sheriff Appeal Court) 2015 (SSI 2015/419) r.5 (effective 1 January 2016).]

(3)[2]   An application for leave to appeal from a decision in relation to—

---

[1] As inserted by the Act of Sederunt (Ordinary Cause, Summary Application, Summary Cause and Small Claim Rules) Amendment (Miscellaneous) 2007 (SSI 2007/6), para.2(11) (effective January 29, 2007).

[2] As substituted by the Act of Sederunt (Ordinary Cause, Summary Application, Summary Cause and Small Claim Rules) Amendment (Miscellaneous) 2007 (SSI 2007/6), para.2(12) (effective January 29, 2007).

(a)    a time to pay direction under section 1 of the Debtors (Scotland) Act 1987;

(b)    the recall or restriction of an arrestment made under section 3(4) of that Act; or

(c)    a time order under section 129 of the Consumer Credit Act 1974,

shall specify the question of law on which the appeal is made.

### Appeals in connection with interim diligence

**31.2A.**   *[Repealed by the Act of Sederunt (Rules of the Court of Session, Sheriff Appeal Court Rules and Sheriff Court Rules Amendment) (Sheriff Appeal Court) 2015 (SSI 2015/419) r.5 (effective 1 January 2016).]*

### Form of appeal to Court of Session

**31.3.**   *[Repealed by the Act of Sederunt (Rules of the Court of Session, Sheriff Appeal Court Rules and Sheriff Court Rules Amendment) (Sheriff Appeal Court) 2015 (SSI 2015/419) r.5 (effective 1 January 2016).]*

### Form of appeal to the sheriff principal

**31.4.**   *[Repealed by the Act of Sederunt (Rules of the Court of Session, Sheriff Appeal Court Rules and Sheriff Court Rules Amendment) (Sheriff Appeal Court) 2015 (SSI 2015/419) r.5 (effective 1 January 2016).]*

### Transmission of process and notice to parties

**31.5.**   *[Repealed by the Act of Sederunt (Rules of the Court of Session, Sheriff Appeal Court Rules and Sheriff Court Rules Amendment) (Sheriff Appeal Court) 2015 (SSI 2015/419) r.5 (effective 1 January 2016).]*

### Record of pleadings etc.

**31.6**   *[Repealed by the Act of Sederunt (Rules of the Court of Session, Sheriff Appeal Court Rules and Sheriff Court Rules Amendment) (Sheriff Appeal Court) 2015 (SSI 2015/419) r.5 (effective 1 January 2016).]*

### Determination of appeal

**31.7.**   *[Repealed by the Act of Sederunt (Rules of the Court of Session, Sheriff Appeal Court Rules and Sheriff Court Rules Amendment) (Sheriff Appeal Court) 2015 (SSI 2015/419) r.5 (effective 1 January 2016).]*

### Fixing of Options Hearing or making other order following appeal

**31.8.**   *[Repealed by the Act of Sederunt (Rules of the Court of Session, Sheriff Appeal Court Rules and Sheriff Court Rules Amendment) (Sheriff Appeal Court) 2015 (SSI 2015/419) r.5 (effective 1 January 2016).]*

### Appeals in connection with orders under section 11 of the Children (Scotland) Act 1995 or aliment

**31.9.**[2]   Where an appeal is marked against an interlocutor making an order under section 11 of the Children (Scotland) Act 1995 (court orders relating to parental responsibilities etc.) or in respect of aliment, the marking of that appeal shall not excuse obedience to or implement of that order unless by order of the sheriff or the Sheriff Appeal Court.

---

[1] Inserted by SI 1996/2445 (effective November 1, 1996).

[2] As amended by the Act of Sederunt (Rules of the Court of Session, Sheriff Appeal Court Rules and Sheriff Court Rules Amendment) (Sheriff Appeal Court) 2015 (SSI 2015/419) r.5 (effective 1 January 2016).

### Interim possession etc. pending appeal

**31.10.**—[1,2](1)  Notwithstanding an appeal, the sheriff from whose decision an appeal has been taken shall have power—

(a)  to regulate all matters relating to interim possession;

(b)  to make any order for the preservation of any property to which the action relates or for its sale if perishable;

(c)  to make provision for the preservation of evidence; or

(d)  to make any interim order which a due regard to the interests of the parties may require.

(2)  An order made under paragraph (1) may be reviewed by the Sheriff Appeal Court.

### Abandonment of appeal

**31.11.**[3]

[Repealed by the Act of Sederunt (Rules of the Court of Session, Sheriff Appeal Court Rules and Sheriff Court Rules Amendment) (Sheriff Appeal Court) 2015 (SSI 2015/419) r.5 (effective 1 January 2016).]

Chapter 32

Taxation of Expenses

### Taxation before decree for expenses

**32.1.**  Expenses allowed in any cause, whether in absence or *in foro contentioso*, unless modified at a fixed amount, shall be taxed before decree is granted for them.

### Order to lodge account of expenses

**32.1A.**[4]  A party found liable in expenses may from 4 months after the date of the interlocutor finding him so liable apply by motion for an order ordaining the party entitled to expenses to lodge an account of those expenses in process.

### Decree for expenses in name of solicitor

**32.2.**  The sheriff may allow a decree for expenses to be extracted in the name of the solicitor who conducted the cause.

### Procedure for taxation

**32.3.**—(1)  Where an account of expenses awarded in a cause is lodged for taxation, the account and process shall be transmitted by the sheriff clerk to the auditor of court.

(2)  The auditor of court shall—

(a)  assign a diet of taxation not earlier than 7 days from the date he receives the account from the sheriff clerk; and

(b)  intimate that diet forthwith to the party who lodged the account.

(3)  The party who lodged the account of expenses shall, on receiving intimation from the auditor of court under paragraph (2)—

---

[1] Former rule 31.6 renumbered by SI 1996/2445 (effective November 1, 1996).

[2] As amended by the Act of Sederunt (Rules of the Court of Session, Sheriff Appeal Court Rules and Sheriff Court Rules Amendment) (Sheriff Appeal Court) 2015 (SSI 2015/419) r.5 (effective 1 January 2016).

[3] Former rule 31.7 renumbered by SI 1996/2445 (effective November 1, 1996).

[4] Inserted by the Act of Sederunt (Ordinary Cause, Summary Application and Small Claim Rules) Amendment (Miscellaneous) 2004 (SSI 2004/197) (effective May 21, 2004), para.2(12).

(a)   send a copy of the account, and

(b)   intimate the date, time and place of the diet of taxation,

to every other party.

(4)  After the account has been taxed, the auditor of court shall transmit the process with the account and his report to the sheriff clerk.

(5)  Where the auditor of court has reserved consideration of the account at the date of the taxation, he shall intimate his decision to the parties who attended the taxation.

(6)  Where no objections are lodged under rule 32.4 (objections to auditor's report), the sheriff may grant decree for the expenses as taxed.

### Objections to auditor's report

**32.4.**—(1)  A party may lodge a note of objections to an account as taxed only where he attended the diet of taxation.

(2)  Such a note shall be lodged within 7 days after—

(a)   the diet of taxation; or

(b)   where the auditor of court reserved consideration of the account under paragraph (5) of rule 32.3, the date on which the auditor of court intimates his decision under that paragraph.

(3)  The sheriff shall dispose of the objection in a summary manner, with or without answers.

Chapter 32A[1]

Live Links

**32A.1.**—(1)  On cause shown, a party may apply by motion for authority for the whole or part of—

(a)   the evidence of a witness or the party to be given; or

(b)   a submission to be made,

through a live link.

(2)  In paragraph (1)—

"witness" means a person who has been or may be cited to appear before the court as a witness, except a vulnerable witness within the meaning of section 11(1) of the Act of 2004;

"submission" means any oral submission which would otherwise be made to the court by the party or his representative in person including an oral submission in support of a motion; and

"live link" means a live television link or such other arrangement as may be specified in the motion by which the witness, party or representative, as the

---

[1] As inserted by the Act of Sederunt (Ordinary Cause, Summary Application, Summary Cause and Small Claim Rules) Amendment (Miscellaneous) 2007 (SSI 2007/6) r.2(12) (effective January 29, 2007).

case may be, is able to be seen and heard in the proceedings or heard in the proceedings and is able to see and hear or hear the proceedings while at a place which is outside the courtroom.

## SPECIAL PROVISIONS IN RELATION TO PARTICULAR CAUSES

### Chapter 33

### Family Actions

#### Part I – General Provisions

**Interpretation of this Chapter**

**33.1.**—[1](1)  In this Chapter, "family action" means—

(a)  an action of divorce;

(b)  an action of separation;

(c)  an action of declarator of legitimacy;

(d)  an action of declarator of illegitimacy;

(e)  an action of declarator of parentage;

(f)  an action of declarator of non-parentage;

(g)  an action of declarator of legitimation;

(h)  an action or application for, or in respect of, an order under section 11 of the Children (Scotland) Act 1995 (court orders relating to parental responsibilities etc.), except—

    (i)  an application for the appointment of a judicial factor mentioned in section 11(2)(g) of the Act of 1995 to which Part I of the Act of Sederunt (Judicial Factors Rules) 1992 applies;

    (ii)  *[Repealed by the Act of Sederunt (Sheriff Court Rules) (Miscellaneous Amendments) 2011 (SSI 2011/193) r.13 (effective April 4, 2011).]*

(i)  an action of affiliation and aliment;

(j)  an action of, or application for or in respect of, aliment;

(k)  an action or application for financial provision after a divorce or annulment in an overseas country within the meaning of Part IV of the Matrimonial and Family Proceedings Act 1984;

(l)  an action or application for an order under the Act of 1981;

(m)  an application for the variation or recall of an order mentioned in section 8(1) of the Law Reform (Miscellaneous Provisions) (Scotland) Act 1966.

(n)[2]  an action of declarator of marriage;

(o)[3]  an action of declarator of nullity of marriage.

(p)[4]  an action for declarator of recognition, or non-recognition, of a relevant foreign decree within the meaning of section 7(9) of the Domicile and Matrimonial Proceedings Act 1973.

(q)[5]  an application under section 28 or 29 of the Act of 2006 (financial provision for former co-habitants).

---

[1] As amended by SI 1996/2167 (effective November 1, 1996).

[2] Inserted or substituted by Act of Sederunt (Ordinary Cause Rules) Amendment (Family Law (Scotland) Act 2006 etc.) 2006 (SSI 2006/207) (effective May 4, 2006).

[3] Inserted or substituted by Act of Sederunt (Ordinary Cause Rules) Amendment (Family Law (Scotland) Act 2006 etc.) 2006 (SSI 2006/207) (effective May 4, 2006).

[4] As inserted by the Act of Sederunt (Sheriff Court Rules) (Miscellaneous Amendments) (No.2) 2010 (SSI 2010/416) r.8 (effective January 1, 2011).

[5] As inserted by the Act of Sederunt (Sheriff Court Rules) (Miscellaneous Amendments) 2012 (SSI 2012/188) para.5 (effective August 1, 2012).

(r)[1]  an action for declarator of recognition, or non-recognition, of a relevant foreign decree within the meaning of paragraph 1 of Schedule 1B to the Domicile and Matrimonial Proceedings Act 1973, or of a judgment to which paragraph 2(1)(b) of that Schedule refers.

(2)  In this Chapter, unless the context otherwise requires—

"the Act of 1975" means the Children Act 1975;

"the Act of 1976" means the Divorce (Scotland) Act 1976;

"the Act of 1981" means the Matrimonial Homes (Family Protection) (Scotland) Act 1981;

"the Act of 1985" means the Family Law (Scotland) Act 1985;

"the Act of 1995" means the Children (Scotland) Act 1995;

"the Act of 2006" means the Family Law (Scotland) Act 2006;

"contact order" has the meaning assigned in section 11(2)(d) of the Act of 1995;

"full gender recognition certificate" and "interim gender recognition certificate" mean the certificates issued as such under section 4 or 5 of the Gender Recognition Act 2004;[2]

"Gender Recognition Panel" is to be construed in accordance with Schedule 1 to the Gender Recognition Act 2004;

"local authority" means a council constituted under section 2 of the Local Government etc. (Scotland) Act 1994;

"mental disorder" has the meaning assigned in section 328 of the Mental Health (Care and Treatment) (Scotland) Act 2003;[3]

"order for financial provision" means, except in Part VII of this Chapter (financial provision after overseas divorce or annulment), an order mentioned in section 8(1) of the Act of 1985;

"parental responsibilities" has the meaning assigned in section 1(3) of the Act 1995;

"parental rights" has the meaning assigned in section 2(4) of the Act of 1995;

"residence order" has the meaning assigned in section 11(2)(c) of the Act of 1995;

"section 11 order" means an order under section 11 of the Act of 1995.

(3)  For the purposes of rules 33.2 (averments in actions of divorce or separation about other proceedings) and 33.3 (averments where section 11 order sought) and, in relation to proceedings in another jurisdiction, Schedule 3 to the Domicile and Matrimonial Proceedings Act 1973 (sisting of consistorial actions in Scotland), proceedings are continuing at any time after they have commenced and before they are finally disposed of.

## Averments in certain family actions about other proceedings[4]

**33.2.**—[5](1)[6]  This rule applies to an action of divorce, separation, declarator of marriage or declarator of nullity of marriage.

---

[1] As inserted by the Act of Sederunt (Rules of the Court of Session and Sheriff Court Rules Amendment No.2) (Marriage and Civil Partnership (Scotland) Act 2014) 2014 (SSI 2014/302) para.5 (effective December 16, 2014).

[2] Inserted by the Act of Sederunt (Ordinary Cause Rules) Amendment (Gender Recognition Act 2004) 2005 (SSI 2005/189) (effective April 4, 2005).

[3] Inserted or substituted by Act of Sederunt (Ordinary Cause Rules) Amendment (Family Law (Scotland) Act 2006 etc.) 2006 (SSI 2006/207) (effective May 4, 2006).

[4] As amended by Act of Sederunt (Ordinary Cause Rules) Amendment (Family Law (Scotland) Act 2006 etc.) 2006 (SSI 2006/207) (effective May 4, 2006).

[5] As amended by Act of Sederunt (Ordinary Cause Rules) Amendment (European Matrimonial and Parental Responsibility Jurisdiction and Judgments) 2001 (SSI 2001/144) (effective April 2, 2001).

[6] As amended by Act of Sederunt (Ordinary Cause Rules) Amendment (Family Law (Scotland) Act 2006 etc.) 2006 (SSI 2006/207) (effective May 4, 2006).

(2) In an action to which this rule applies, the pursuer shall state in the condescendence of the initial writ—

   (a)  whether to his knowledge any proceedings are continuing in Scotland or in any other country in respect of the marriage to which the initial writ relates or are capable of affecting its validity or subsistence; and

   (b)  where such proceedings are continuing—

       (i)  the court, tribunal or authority before which the proceedings have been commenced;

       (ii)  the date of commencement;

       (iii)  the names of the parties;

       (iv)  the date, or expected date of any proof (or its equivalent) in the proceedings; and

       (v)[1,2]  such other facts as may be relevant to the question of whether or not the action before the sheriff should be sisted under Schedule 3 to the Domicile and Matrimonial Proceedings Act 1973 or Council Regulation (E.C.) No. 2201/2003 of 27th November 2003 concerning jurisdiction and the recognition and enforcement of judgments in matrimonial matters and matters of parental responsibility for the 1996 Convention on Jurisdiction, Applicable Law, Recognition, Enforcement and Co-operation in Respect of Parental Responsibility and Measures for the Protection of Children, signed at the Hague on 19th October 1996.

(3) Where—

   (a)  such proceedings are continuing;

   (b)  the action before the sheriff is defended; and

   (c)  either—

       (i)  the initial writ does not contain the statement referred to in paragraph (2)(a), or

       (ii)  the particulars mentioned in paragraph (2)(b) as set out in the initial writ are incomplete or incorrect,

any defences or minute, as the case may be, lodged by any person to the action shall include that statement and, where appropriate, the further or correct particulars mentioned in paragraph (2)(b).

**Averments where section 11 order sought**

33.3.—[3](1) A party to a family action, who makes an application in that action for a section 11 order in respect of a child shall include in his pleadings—

   (a)[4]  where that action is an action of divorce, separation or declarator of nullity of marriage, averments giving particulars of any other proceedings known to him, whether in Scotland or elsewhere and whether concluded or not, which relate to the child in respect of whom the section 11 order is sought;

   (b)  in any other family action—

---

[1] As amended by Act of Sederunt (Ordinary Cause Rules) Amendment (Family Law (Scotland) Act 2006 etc.) 2006 (SSI 2006/207) (effective May 4, 2006).

[2] As amended by the Act of Sederunt (Sheriff Court Rules) (Miscellaneous Amendments) (No.2) 2012 (SSI 2012/221) para.3 (effective August 1, 2012).

[3] As amended by SI 1996/2167 (effective November 1, 1996) and SI 1996/2445 (effective November 1, 1996) (clerical error).

[4] As amended by Act of Sederunt (Ordinary Cause Rules) Amendment (Family Law (Scotland) Act 2006 etc.) 2006 (SSI 2006/207) (effective May 4, 2006).

(i) the averments mentioned in paragraph (a); and

(ii) averments giving particulars of any proceedings known to him which are continuing, whether in Scotland or elsewhere, and which relate to the marriage of the parents of that child.

(c)[1] where the party seeks an order such as is mentioned in any of paragraphs (a) to (e) of subsection (2) of that section, an averment that no permanence order (as defined in section 80(2) of the Adoption and Children (Scotland) Act 2007) is in force in respect of the child.

(2) Where such other proceedings are continuing or have taken place and the averments of the applicant for such a section 11 order—

(a) do not contain particulars of the other proceedings, or

(b) contain particulars which are incomplete or incorrect,

any defences or minute, as the case may be, lodged by any party to the family action shall include such particulars or such further or correct particulars as are known to him.

(3) In paragraph (1)(b)(ii), "child" includes a child of the family within the meaning assigned in section 42(4) of the Family Law Act 1986.

### Averments where identity or address of person not known

**33.4.** In a family action, where the identity or address of any person referred to in rule 33.7 as a person in respect of whom a warrant for intimation requires to be applied for is not known and cannot reasonably be ascertained, the party required to apply for the warrant shall include in his pleadings an averment of that fact and averments setting out what steps have been taken to ascertain the identity or address, as the case may be, of that person.

### Averments about maintenance orders

**33.5.** In a family action in which an order for aliment or periodical allowance is sought, or is sought to be varied or recalled, by any party, the pleadings of that party shall contain an averment stating whether and, if so, when and by whom, a maintenance order (within the meaning of section 106 of the Debtors (Scotland) Act 1987) has been granted in favour of or against that party or of any other person in respect of whom the order is sought.

### Averments where aliment or financial provision sought

**33.6.**—[2](1) In this rule—

"the Act of 1991" means the Child Support Act 1991;

"child" has the meaning assigned in section 55 of the Act of 1991;

"crave relating to aliment" means—

(a) for the purposes of paragraph (2), a crave for decree of aliment in relation to a child or for recall or variation of such a decree; and

(b) for the purposes of paragraph (3), a crave for decree of aliment in relation to a child or for recall or variation of such a decree or for the variation or termination of an agreement on aliment in relation to a child;

---

[1] As inserted by the Act of Sederunt (Sheriff Court Rules Amendment) (Adoption and Children (Scotland) Act 2007) 2009 (SSI 2009/284) (effective September 28, 2009).

[2] As amended by the Act of Sederunt (Ordinary Cause, Summary Application, Summary Cause and Small Claim Rules) Amendment (Miscellaneous) 2003 (SSI 2003/26) r.2(8) (effective January 24, 2003).

"maintenance calculation" has the meaning assigned in section 54 of the Act of 1991.

(2) A family action containing a crave relating to aliment and to which section 8(6), (7), (8) or (10) of the Act of 1991 (top up maintenance orders) applies shall—

    (a)   include averments stating, where appropriate—

        (i)   that a maintenance calculation under section 11 of that Act (maintenance calculations) is in force;

        (ii)   the date of the maintenance calculation;

        (iii)   the amount and frequency of periodical payments of child support maintenance fixed by the maintenance calculation; and

        (iv)   the grounds on which the sheriff retains jurisdiction under section 8(6), (7), (8) or (10) of that Act; and

    (b)   unless the sheriff on cause shown otherwise directs, be accompanied by any document issued by the Secretary of State to the party intimating the making of the maintenance calculation referred to in sub-paragraph (a).

(3) A family action containing a crave relating to aliment, and to which section 8(6), (7), (8) or (10) of the Act of 1991 does not apply, shall include averments stating—

    (a)   that the habitual residence of the absent parent, person with care or qualifying child, within the meaning of section 3 of that Act, is furth of the United Kingdom;

    (b)   that the child is not a child within the meaning of section 55 of that Act; or

    (c)   where the action is lodged for warranting before 7th April 1997, the grounds on which the sheriff retains jurisdiction.

(4) In an action for declarator of non-parentage or illegitimacy—

    (a)   the initial writ shall include an article of condescendence stating whether the pursuer previously has been alleged to be the parent in an application for a maintenance calculation under section 4, 6 or 7 of the Act of 1991 (applications for maintenance calculation); and

    (b)   where an allegation of paternity has been made against the pursuer, the Secretary of State shall be named as a defender in the action.

(5) A family action involving parties in respect of whom a decision has been made in any application, review or appeal under the Act of 1991 relating to any child of those parties, shall—

    (a)   include averments stating that such a decision has been made and giving details of that decision; and

    (b)   unless the sheriff on cause shown otherwise directs, be accompanied by any document issued by the Secretary of State to the parties intimating that decision.

### Averments where divorce sought on ground of issue of interim gender recognition certificate

**33.6ZA.**—[1](1) This rule applies to an action of divorce in which divorce is sought on the ground that an interim gender recognition certificate has been issued to either party.

(2) In an action to which this rule applies, the pursuer shall state in the condescendence of the initial writ—

---

[1] As inserted by the Act of Sederunt (Rules of the Court of Session and Sheriff Court Rules Amendment No.2) (Marriage and Civil Partnership (Scotland) Act 2014) 2014 (SSI 2014/302) para.5 (effective December 16, 2014).

(a) where the pursuer is the party to whom the interim gender recognition certificate was issued, whether or not the Gender Recognition Panel has issued a full gender recognition certificate to the pursuer, and

(b) where the defender is the party to whom the interim gender recognition certificate was issued, whether—

    (i) since the issue of the interim gender recognition certificate, the pursuer has made a statutory declaration consenting to the marriage continuing, and

    (ii) the Gender Recognition Panel has given the pursuer notice of the issue of a full gender recognition certificate to the defender.

### Application by survivor for provision on intestacy

**33.6A.**—[1](1) In an action for an order under section 29(2) of the Act of 2006 (application by survivor for provision on intestacy), the pursuer shall call the deceased's executor as a defender.

(2) An application under section 29(9) of the Act of 2006 for variation of the date or method of payment of the capital sum shall be made by minute in the process of the action to which the application relates.

(3) Words and expressions used in this rule shall have the same meaning as in section 29 of the Act of 2006.

### Warrants and forms for intimation

**33.7.**—[2](1) Subject to paragraphs (5) and (7), in the initial writ in a family action, the pursuer shall include a crave for a warrant for intimation—

(a) in an action where the address of the defender is not known to the pursuer and cannot reasonably be ascertained, to—

    (i)[3,4] every person who is a child of the family (as defined in section 12(4)(a) of the Act of 1995) who has reached the age of 16 years; and

    (ii) one of the next-of-kin of the defender who has reached that age, unless the address of such a person is not known to the pursuer and cannot reasonably be ascertained, and a notice of intimation in Form F1 shall be attached to the copy of the initial writ intimated to any such person;

(b)[5] in an action of divorce where the pursuer alleges that the defender has committed adultery with another person, to that person, unless—

    (i) that person is not named in the initial writ and, if the adultery is relied on for the purposes of section 1(2)(a) of the Act of 1976 (irretrievable breakdown of marriage by reason of adultery), the initial writ contains an averment that his or her identity is not known to the pursuer and cannot reasonably be ascertained; or

    (ii) the pursuer alleges that the defender has been guilty of rape upon or incest with, that named person,

---

[1] As inserted by the Act of Sederunt (Sheriff Court Rules) (Miscellaneous Amendments) 2012 (SSI 2012/188) para.5 (effective August 1, 2012).

[2] As amended by SI 1996/2167 (effective November 1, 1996) and SI 1996/2445 (effective November 1, 1996).

[3] As amended by the Act of Sederunt (Sheriff Court Rules) (Miscellaneous Amendments) 2012 (SSI 2012/188) para.5 (effective August 1, 2012).

[4] As amended by the Act of Sederunt (Sheriff Court Rules) (Miscellaneous Amendments) (No.2) 2012 (SSI 2012/221) para.3 (effective August 1, 2012).

[5] As amended by the Act of Sederunt (Sheriff Court Rules) (Miscellaneous Amendments) 2012 (SSI 2012/188) para.5 (effective August 1, 2012).

and a notice of intimation in Form F2 shall be attached to the copy of the initial writ intimated to any such person;

(c) in an action where the defender is a person who is suffering from a mental disorder, to—

    (i)[1] those persons mentioned in sub-paragraph (a)(i) and (ii), unless the address of such person is not known to the pursuer and cannot reasonably be ascertained;

    (ii) the curator bonis to the defender, if one has been appointed,

and a notice of intimation in Form F3 shall be attached to the copy of the initial writ intimated to any such person;

    (iii)[2] any person holding the office of guardian or continuing or welfare attorney to the defender under or by virtue of the Adults with Incapacity (Scotland) Act 2000,

(d) in an action relating to a marriage which was entered into under a law which permits polygamy where—

    (i) one of the decrees specified in section 2(2) of the Matrimonial Proceedings (Polygamous Marriages) Act 1972 is sought; and

    (ii) either party to the marriage in question has any spouse additional to the other party,

to any such additional spouse, and a notice of intimation in Form F4 shall be attached to the initial writ intimated to any such person;

(e)[3] in an action of divorce, separation or declarator of nullity of marriage where the sheriff may make a section 11 order in respect of a child—

    (i) who is in the care of a local authority, to that authority and a notice of intimation in Form F5 shall be attached to the initial writ intimated to that authority;

    (ii) who, being a child of one party to the marriage, has been accepted as a child of the family by the other party to the marriage and who is liable to be maintained by a third party, to that third party, and a notice of intimation in Form F5 shall be attached to the initial writ intimated to that third party; or

    (iii) in respect of whom a third party in fact exercises care and control, to that third party, and a notice of intimation in Form F6 shall be attached to the initial writ intimated to that third party;

(f) in an action where the pursuer craves a section 11 order, to any parent or guardian of the child who is not a party to the action, and a notice of intimation in Form F7 shall be attached to the initial writ intimated to any such parent or guardian;

(g) *[Repealed by the Act of Sederunt (Sheriff Court Rules) (Miscellaneous Amendments) (No.2) 2010 (SSI 2010/416) r.7 (effective January 1, 2011).]*

(h) in an action which includes a crave for a section 11 order, to the child to whom such an order would relate if not a party to the action, and a notice of intimation in Form F9 shall be intimated to that child;

(i) in an action where the pursuer makes an application for an order under section 8(1)(aa) of the Act of 1985 (transfer of property) and—

---

[1] As amended by Act of Sederunt (Ordinary Cause Rules) Amendment (Family Law (Scotland) Act 2006 etc.) 2006 (SSI 2006/207) r.2 (effective May 4, 2006).

[2] Inserted or substituted by Act of Sederunt (Ordinary Cause Rules) Amendment (Family Law (Scotland) Act 2006 etc.) 2006 (SSI 2006/207) r.2 (effective May 4, 2006).

[3] As amended by Act of Sederunt (Ordinary Cause Rules) Amendment (Family Law (Scotland) Act 2006 etc.) 2006 (SSI 2006/207) r.2 (effective May 4, 2006).

       (i)   the consent of a third party to such a transfer is necessary by virtue of an obligation, enactment or rule of law, or

       (ii)  the property is subject to a security,

to the third party or creditor, as the case may be, and a notice of intimation in Form F10 shall be attached to the initial writ intimated to any such person;

(j)  in an action where the pursuer makes an application for an order under section 18 of the Act of 1985 (which relates to avoidance transactions), to—

       (i)   any third party in whose favour the transfer of, or transaction involving, the property is to be or was made, and

       (ii)  any other person having an interest in the transfer of, or transaction involving, the property,

and a notice of intimation in Form F11 shall be attached to the initial writ intimated to any such person;

(k)  in an action where the pursuer makes an application for an order under the Act of 1981—

       (i)   where he is a non-entitled partner and the entitled partner has a spouse, to that spouse; or

       (ii)  where the application is under section 2(1)(e), 2(4)(a), 3(1), 3(2), 4, 7, 13 or 18 of that Act, and the entitled spouse or entitled partner is a tenant or occupies the matrimonial home by permission of a third party, to the landlord or the third party, as the case may be,

and a notice of intimation in Form F12 shall be attached to the initial writ intimated to any such person;

(l)  in an action where the pursuer makes an application for an order under section 8(1)(ba) of the Act of 1985 (orders under section 12A of the Act of 1985 for pension lump sum), to the person responsible for the pension arrangement, and a notice of intimation in Form F12A shall be attached to the initial writ intimated to any such person;

(m)[1]  in an action where a pursuer makes an application for an order under section 8(1)(baa) of the Act of 1985 (pension sharing orders), to the person responsible for the pension arrangement and a notice of intimation in Form F12B shall be attached to the initial writ intimated to any such person;

(n)[2]  in an action where a pursuer makes an application for an order under section 8(1)(bab) of the Act of 1985 (pension compensation sharing order), to the Board of the Pension Protection Fund, and a notice of intimation in Form F12C shall be attached to the initial writ intimated to that Board; and

(o)[3]  in an action where a pursuer makes an application for an order under section 8(1)(bb) of the Act of 1985 (an order under section 12B(2) of the Act of 1985 for pension compensation), to the Board of the Pension Protection Fund and a notice of intimation in Form F12D shall be attached to the initial writ intimated to that Board.

---

[1] Inserted by the Act of Sederunt (Ordinary Cause Rules) Amendment (No.2) (Pension Sharing on Divorce etc.) 2000 (SSI 2000/408) r.2(2)(b)(ii).

[2] As inserted by the Act of Sederunt (Sheriff Court Rules) (Miscellaneous Amendments) 2011 (SSI 2011/193) r.15 (effective April 6, 2011).

[3] As inserted by the Act of Sederunt (Sheriff Court Rules) (Miscellaneous Amendments) 2011 (SSI 2011/193) r.15 (effective April 6, 2011).

(p)[1]   in an action where a pursuer makes an application for an order under section 29(2) of the Act of 2006 (application by survivor for provision on intestacy) to any person having an interest in the deceased's net estate, and a notice of intimation in Form F12E shall be attached to the initial writ intimated to any such person.

(2)[2]   Expressions used in—

(a)   paragraph (1)(k) which are also used in the Act of 1981; and

(b)   paragraph (1)(p) which are also used in section 29 of the Act of 2006,

shall have the same meanings as in that Act or section, as the case may be.

(3)   A notice of intimation under paragraph (1) shall be on a period of notice of 21 days unless the sheriff otherwise orders; but the sheriff shall not order a period of notice of less than 2 days.

(4)   *[Repealed by the Act of Sederunt (Sheriff Court Rules) (Miscellaneous Amendments) (No.2) 2010 (SSI 2010/416) r.7 (effective January 1, 2011).]*

(5)[3, 4]   Where the address of a person mentioned in paragraph (1)(b), (d), (e), (f), (h), (i), (j), (k), (l), (m) or (p) is not known and cannot reasonably be ascertained, the pursuer shall include a crave in the initial writ to dispense with intimation; and the sheriff may grant that crave or make such other order as he thinks fit.

(6)   Where the identity or address of a person to whom intimation of a family action is required becomes known during the course of the action, the party who would have been required to insert a warrant for intimation to that person shall lodge a motion for a warrant for intimation to that person or to dispense with such intimation.

(7)   Where a pursuer considers that to order intimation to a child under paragraph (1)(h) is inappropriate, he shall—

(a)   include a crave in the initial writ to dispense with intimation to that child, and

(b)   include in the initial writ averments setting out the reasons why such intimation is inappropriate;

and the sheriff may dispense with such intimation or make such other order as he thinks fit.

### Intimation where alleged association[5]

**33.8.**—(1)[6]   In a family action where the pursuer founds upon an association between the defender and another named person, the pursuer shall, immediately after the expiry of the period of notice, lodge a motion for an order for intimation to that person or to dispense with such intimation.

(2)   In determining a motion under paragraph (1), the sheriff may—

(a)   make such order for intimation as he thinks fit; or

(b)   dispense with intimation; and

---

[1] As inserted by the Act of Sederunt (Sheriff Court Rules) (Miscellaneous Amendments) 2012 (SSI 2012/188) para.5 (effective August 1, 2012).

[2] As substituted by the Act of Sederunt (Sheriff Court Rules) (Miscellaneous Amendments) 2012 (SSI 2012/188) para.5 (effective August 1, 2012).

[3] As amended by Act of Sederunt (Ordinary Cause Rules) Amendment (Family Law (Scotland) Act 2006 etc.) 2006 (SSI 2006/207) r.2 (effective May 4, 2006).

[4] As amended by the Act of Sederunt (Sheriff Court Rules) (Miscellaneous Amendments) 2012 (SSI 2012/188) para.5 (effective August 1, 2012).

[5] As amended by Act of Sederunt (Ordinary Cause Rules) Amendment (Family Law (Scotland) Act 2006 etc.) 2006 (SSI 2006/207) r.2 (effective May 4, 2006).

[6] As amended by Act of Sederunt (Ordinary Cause Rules) Amendment (Family Law (Scotland) Act 2006 etc.) 2006 (SSI 2006/207) r.2 (effective May 4, 2006).

(c)    where he dispenses with intimation, order that the name of that person be deleted from the condescendence of the initial writ.

(3)   Where intimation is ordered under paragraph (2), a copy of the initial writ and an intimation in Form F13 shall be intimated to the named person.

(4)[1]  In paragraph (1), "association" means sodomy, incest or any homosexual relationship.

## Productions in action of divorce or where a section 11 order or order for financial provision may be made

**33.9.**[2,3]  Unless the sheriff otherwise directs—

(a)[4]   in an action of divorce or declarator of nullity of marriage, a warrant for citation shall not be granted without there being produced with the initial writ an extract of the relevant entry in the register of marriages or an equivalent document; and

(b)   in an action which includes a crave for a section 11 order, a warrant for citation shall not be granted without there being produced with the initial writ an extract of the relevant entry in the register of births or an equivalent document.

(c)[5]   in an action which includes a crave for an order for financial provision, the pursuer must lodge a completed Form F13A signed by the pursuer with the initial writ or minute of amendment as the case may be.

## Productions in action of divorce on ground of issue of interim gender recognition certificate

**33.9A.**—[6](1)  This rule applies where, in an action of divorce, the ground on which decree of divorce may be granted is that an interim gender recognition certificate has, after the date of the marriage, been issued to either party to the marriage.

(2)   Unless the sheriff otherwise directs, a warrant for citation shall not be granted without there being produced with the initial writ—

(a)   where the pursuer is the subject of the interim gender recognition certificate, the interim gender recognition certificate or, failing that, a certified copy of the interim gender recognition certificate; or

(b)   where the pursuer is the spouse of the person who is the subject of the interim gender recognition certificate, a certified copy of the interim gender recognition certificate.

(3)   For the purposes of this rule, a certified copy of an interim gender recognition certificate shall be a copy of that certificate sealed with the seal of the Gender Recognition Panels and certified to be a true copy by an officer authorised by the President of Gender Recognition Panels.

---

[1] As amended by Act of Sederunt (Ordinary Cause Rules) Amendment (Family Law (Scotland) Act 2006 etc.) 2006 (SSI 2006/207) r.2 (effective May 4, 2006).

[2] As amended by Act of Sederunt (Family Proceedings in the Sheriff Court) 1996 (SI 1996/2167) (effective November 1, 1996).

[3] As amended by the Act of Sederunt (Sheriff Court Rules) (Miscellaneous Amendments) 2012 (SSI 2012/188) para.4 (effective August 1, 2012).

[4] As amended by Act of Sederunt (Ordinary Cause Rules) Amendment (Family Law (Scotland) Act 2006 etc.) 2006 (SSI 2006/207) (effective May 4, 2006).

[5] As amended by the Act of Sederunt (Sheriff Court Rules) (Miscellaneous Amendments) 2012 (SSI 2012/188) para.4 (effective August 1, 2012).

[6] Inserted by the Act of Sederunt (Ordinary Cause Rules) Amendment (Gender Recognition Act 2004) 2005 (SSI 2005/189) r.2 (effective April 4, 2005).

## Application for corrected gender recognition certificate

**33.9B.**[1]  An application for a corrected gender recognition certificate under section 6 of the Gender Recognition Act 2004 by—

(a)   the person to whom a full gender recognition certificate has been issued; or

(b)   the Secretary of State,

shall be made by minute in the process of the action pursuant to which the full gender recognition certificate was issued.

## Warrant of citation

**33.10.**  The warrant of citation in a family action shall be in Form F14.

## Form of citation and certificate

**33.11.**—(1)   Subject to rule 5.6 (service where address of person is not known), citation of a defender shall be in Form F15, which shall be attached to a copy of the initial writ and warrant of citation and shall have appended to it a notice of intention to defend in Form F26.

(2)   The certificate of citation shall be in Form F16 which shall be attached to the initial writ.

## Intimation to local authority

**33.12.**—[2](1)   In any family action where the pursuer craves a residence order in respect of a child, the sheriff may, if the sheriff thinks fit, order intimation to the local authority in which area the pursuer resides; and such intimation shall be in Form F8.

(2)   Where an order for intimation is made under paragraph (1), intimation to that local authority shall be given within 7 days after the date on which an order for intimation has been made.

## Service in cases of mental disorder of defender

**33.13.**—(1)   In a family action where the defender suffers or appears to suffer from mental disorder and is resident in a hospital or other similar institution, citation shall be executed by registered post or the first class recorded delivery service addressed to the medical officer in charge of that hospital or institution; and there shall be included with the copy of the initial writ—

(a)   a citation in Form F15;

(b)   any notice required by rule 33.14(1);

(c)   a request in Form F17;

(d)   a form of certificate in Form F18 requesting the medical officer to—

　　(i)   deliver and explain the initial writ, citation and any notice or form of notice of consent required under rule 33.14(1) personally to the defender; or

　　(ii)   certify that such delivery or explanation would be dangerous to the health or mental condition of the defender; and

(e)   a stamped envelope addressed for return of that certificate to the pursuer or his solicitor, if he has one.

---

[1] Inserted by the Act of Sederunt (Ordinary Cause Rules) Amendment (Gender Recognition Act 2004) 2005 (SSI 2005/189) r.2 (effective April 4, 2005).

[2] As substituted by the Act of Sederunt (Sheriff Court Rules) (Miscellaneous Amendments) (No.2) 2010 (SSI 2010/416) r.7 (effective January 1, 2011).

(2)  The medical officer referred to in paragraph (1) shall send the certificate in Form F18 duly completed to the pursuer or his solicitor, as the case may be.

(3)  The certificate mentioned in paragraph (2) shall be attached to the certificate of citation.

(4)  Where such a certificate bears that the initial writ has not been delivered to the defender, the sheriff may, at any time before decree—

(a)  order such further medical inquiry, and

(b)  make such order for further service or intimation,

as he thinks fit.

### Notices in certain actions of divorce or separation

**33.14.**—(1)  In the following actions of divorce or separation there shall be attached to the copy of the initial writ served on the defender—

(a)[1]  in an action relying on section 1(2)(d) of the Act of 1976 (no cohabitation for one year with consent of defender to decree)—

(i)  which is an action of divorce, a notice in Form F19 and a notice of consent in Form F20;

(ii)  which is an action of separation, a notice in Form F21 and a form of notice of consent in Form F22;

(b)[2]  in an action relying on section 1(2)(e) of the Act of 1976 (no cohabitation for two years)—

(i)  which is an action of divorce, a notice in Form F23;

(ii)  which is an action of separation, a notice in Form F24.

(c)[3]  in an action relying on section 1(1)(b) of the Act of 1976 (grounds for divorce: interim gender recognition certificate), a notice in Form F24A

(2)[4]  The certificate of citation of an initial writ in an action mentioned in paragraph (1) shall state which notice or form mentioned in paragraph (1) has been attached to the initial writ.

### Orders for intimation

**33.15.**—(1)  In any family action, the sheriff may, at any time—

(a)  subject to paragraph (2), order intimation to be made on such person as he thinks fit;

(b)  postpone intimation, where he considers that such postponement is appropriate and, in that case, the sheriff shall make such order in respect of postponement of intimation as he thinks fit; or

(c)  dispense with intimation, where he considers that such dispensation is appropriate.

(2)  Where the sheriff is considering whether to make a section 11 order by virtue of section 12 of the Act of 1995 (restrictions on decrees for divorce, separation or annulment affecting children), he shall, subject to paragraph (1)(c) and without prejudice to paragraph (1)(b) of this rule, order intimation in Form F9 to the child to whom the section 11 order would relate unless—

(a)  intimation has been given to the child under rule 33.7(1)(h); or

---

[1] As amended by Act of Sederunt (Ordinary Cause Rules) Amendment (Family Law (Scotland) Act 2006 etc.) 2006 (SSI 2006/207) r.2 (effective May 4, 2006).

[2] As amended by Act of Sederunt (Ordinary Cause Rules) Amendment (Family Law (Scotland) Act 2006 etc.) 2006 (SSI 2006/207) r.2 (effective May 4, 2006).

[3] Inserted or substituted by Act of Sederunt (Ordinary Cause Rules) Amendment (Family Law (Scotland) Act 2006 etc.) 2006 (SSI 2006/207) r.2 (effective May 4, 2006).

[4] As amended by SI 1996/2445 (effective November 1, 1996).

(b) the sheriff considers that the child is not of sufficient age or maturity to express his views.

(3) Where a party makes a crave or averment in a family action which, had it been made in an initial writ, would have required a warrant for intimation under rule 33.7, that party shall include a crave in his writ for a warrant for intimation or to dispense with such intimation; and rule 33.7 shall, with the necessary modifications, apply to a crave for a warrant under this paragraph as it applies to a crave for a warrant under that rule.

### Appointment of curators ad litem to defenders

**33.16.**—(1)[1,2] This rule applies to a family action where it appears to the court that the defender is suffering from a mental disorder.

(2) In an action to which this rule applies, the sheriff shall—

(a) appoint a curator ad litem to the defender;

(b)[3] where the facts set out in section 1(2)(d) of the Act of 1976 (no cohabitation for one year with consent of defender to decree) are relied on—

    (i) make an order for intimation of the ground of the action to the Mental Welfare Commission for Scotland; and

    (ii) include in such an order a requirement that the Commission sends to the sheriff clerk a report indicating whether in its opinion the defender is capable of deciding whether or not to give consent to the granting of decree.

(3)[4] Within 7 days after the appointment of a curator ad litem under paragraph (2)(a), the pursuer shall send to him—

(a) a copy of the initial writ and any defences (including any adjustments and amendments) lodged; and

(b) a copy of any notice in Form G5 sent to him by the sheriff clerk.

(4) On receipt of a report required under paragraph (2)(b)(ii), the sheriff clerk shall—

(a) lodge the report in process; and

(b) intimate that this has been done to—

    (i) the pursuer;

    (ii) the solicitor for the defender, if known; and

    (iii) the curator ad litem.

(5) The curator ad litem shall lodge in process one of the writs mentioned in paragraph (6)—

(a) within 14 days after the report required under paragraph (2)(b)(ii) has been lodged in process; or

(b) where no such report is required, within 21 days after the date of his appointment under paragraph (2)(a).

(6) The writs referred to in paragraph (5) are—

(a) a notice of intention to defend;

(b) defences to the action;

---

[1] As amended by Act of Sederunt (Ordinary Cause Rules) Amendment (Family Law (Scotland) Act 2006 etc.) 2006 (SSI 2006/207) r.2 (effective May 4, 2006).

[2] As amended by the Act of Sederunt (Sheriff Court Rules) (Miscellaneous Amendments) 2012 (SSI 2012/188) para.5 (effective August 1, 2012).

[3] As amended by Act of Sederunt (Ordinary Cause Rules) Amendment (Family Law (Scotland) Act 2006 etc.) 2006 (SSI 2006/207) r.2 (effective May 4, 2006).

[4] As amended by SI 1996/2445 (effective November 1, 1996).

    (c)   a minute adopting defences already lodged; and

    (d)   a minute stating that the curator ad litem does not intend to lodge defences.

(7)  Notwithstanding that he has lodged a minute stating that he does not intend to lodge defences, a curator ad litem may appear at any stage of the action to protect the interests of the defender.

(8)  If, at any time, it appears to the curator ad litem that the defender is not suffering from mental disorder, he may report that fact to the court and seek his own discharge.

(9)  The pursuer shall be responsible, in the first instance, for payment of the fees and outlays of the curator ad litem incurred during the period from his appointment until—

    (a)   he lodges a minute stating that he does not intend to lodge defences;

    (b)   he decides to instruct the lodging of defences or a minute adopting defences already lodged; or

    (c)   being satisfied after investigation that the defender is not suffering from mental disorder, he is discharged.

### Applications for sist

**33.17.**  An application for a sist, or the recall of a sist, under Schedule 3 to the Domicile and Matrimonial Proceedings Act 1973 shall be made by written motion.

### Notices of consent to divorce or separation

**33.18.**—(1)[1]  Where, in an action of divorce or separation in which the facts in section 1(2)(d) of the Act of 1976 (no cohabitation for one year with consent of defender to decree) are relied on, the defender wishes to consent to the grant of decree of divorce or separation he shall do so by giving notice in writing in Form F20 (divorce) or Form F22 (separation), as the case may be, to the sheriff clerk.

(2)  The evidence of one witness shall be sufficient for the purpose of establishing that the signature on a notice of consent under paragraph (1) is that of the defender.

(3)  In an action of divorce or separation where the initial writ includes, for the purposes of section 1(2)(d) of the Act of 1976, an averment that the defender consents to the grant of decree, the defender may give notice by letter sent to the sheriff clerk stating that he has not so consented or that he withdraws any consent which he has already given.

(4)  On receipt of a letter under paragraph (3), the sheriff clerk shall intimate the terms of the letter to the pursuer.

(5)  On receipt of any intimation under paragraph (4), the pursuer may, within 14 days after the date of the intimation, if none of the other facts mentioned in section 1(2) of the Act of 1976 is averred in the initial writ, lodge a motion for the action to be sisted.

(6)  If no such motion is lodged, the pursuer shall be deemed to have abandoned the action and the action shall be dismissed.

(7)  If a motion under paragraph (5) is granted and the sist is not recalled or renewed within a period of 6 months from the date of the interlocutor granting the sist, the pursuer shall be deemed to have abandoned the action and the action shall be dismissed.

---

[1] As amended by Act of Sederunt (Ordinary Cause Rules) Amendment (Family Law (Scotland) Act 2006 etc.) 2006 (SSI 2006/207) r.2 (effective May 4, 2006).

## Procedure in respect of children

**33.19.**—[1](1)  In a family action, in relation to any matter affecting a child, where that child has—

    (a)   returned to the sheriff clerk Form F9, or

    (b)   otherwise indicated to the court a wish to express views on a matter affecting him,

the sheriff shall not grant any order unless an opportunity has been given for the views of that child to be obtained or heard.

(2)  Where a child has indicated his wish to express his views, the sheriff shall order such steps to be taken as he considers appropriate to ascertain the views of that child.

(3)  The sheriff shall not grant an order in a family action, in relation to any matter affecting a child who has indicated his wish to express his views, unless due weight has been given by the sheriff to the views expressed by that child, having due regard to his age and maturity.

## Recording of views of the child

**33.20**—[2](1)  This rule applies where a child expresses a view on a matter affecting him whether expressed personally to the sheriff or to a person appointed by the sheriff for that purpose or provided by the child in writing.

(2)  The sheriff, or the person appointed by the sheriff, shall record the views of the child in writing; and the sheriff may direct that such views, and any written views, given by a child shall—

    (a)   be sealed in an envelope marked "Views of the child—confidential";

    (b)   be kept in the court process without being recorded in the inventory of process;

    (c)   be available to a sheriff only;

    (d)   not be opened by any person other than a sheriff; and

    (e)   not form a borrowable part of the process.

## Child welfare reporters

**33.21.**—[3](1)  At any stage of a family action the sheriff may, in relation to any matter affecting a child, appoint a person (referred to in this rule as a "child welfare reporter")—

    (a)   to seek the views of the child and to report any views expressed by the child to the court; or

    (b)   to undertake enquiries and to report to the court.

(2)  A child welfare reporter may only be appointed under paragraph (1)(b) where the sheriff is satisfied that the appointment—

    (a)   is in the best interests of the child; and

    (b)   will promote the effective and expeditious determination of an issue in relation to the child.

(3)  An interlocutor appointing a child welfare reporter must—

    (a)   specify a date by which the report is to be submitted to the court;

    (b)   include a direction as to the fees and outlays of the child welfare reporter;

---

[1] As substituted by SI 1996/2167 (effective November 1, 1996).

[2] As substituted by SI 1996/2167 (effective November 1, 1996).

[3] As substituted by the Act of Sederunt (Rules of the Court of Session 1994 and Ordinary Cause Rules 1993 Amendment) (Child Welfare Reporters) 2015 (SSI 2015/312) para.4 (effective 26 October 2015).

(c) where the appointment is under paragraph (1)(a), specify the issues in respect of which the child's views are to be sought; and

(d) where the appointment is under paragraph (1)(b), specify the enquiries to be undertaken, and the issues requiring to be addressed in the report.

(4) An interlocutor complies with subparagraph (c) or (d) of paragraph (3) if the issues or, as the case may be the enquiries, referred to in that subparagraph are specified in an annex to the interlocutor in Form F44.

(5) Where the sheriff has appointed a child welfare reporter with a view to the report being considered at an assigned hearing, the date specified in accordance with paragraph (3)(a) must be a date no less than three clear days before that hearing, excluding any day on which the sheriff clerk's office is not open for civil court business, unless cause exists for specifying a later date.

(6) On appointing a child welfare reporter the sheriff may also—

(a) make such further order as may be required to facilitate the discharge of the child welfare reporter's functions;

(b) direct that a party to the proceedings is to be responsible for providing the child welfare reporter with copies of such documents lodged in the process as may be specified; and

(c) give the child welfare reporter directions.

(7) The direction referred to in paragraph (3)(b) must assign liability for payment of the child welfare reporter's fees and outlays in the first instance, and require that liability to be borne—

(a) in equal shares by—

(i) the pursuer,

(ii) any defender who has lodged a notice of intention to defend, and

(iii) any minuter who has been granted leave to enter the process; or

(b) by one or more parties to the proceedings on such other basis as may be justified on cause shown.

(8) On the granting of an interlocutor appointing a child welfare reporter the sheriff clerk must—

(a) give the child welfare reporter—

(i) a certified copy of the interlocutor, and

(ii) sufficient information to enable the child welfare reporter to contact the solicitor for each party to the proceedings, or any party not represented by a solicitor; and

(b) intimate the name and address of the child welfare reporter to any local authority to which intimation of the proceedings has been made.

(9) A child welfare reporter appointed under this rule must—

(a) where the appointment is under paragraph (1)(a)—

(i) seek the child's views on the specified issues, and

(ii) prepare a report for the court reporting any such views;

(b) where the appointment is under paragraph (1)(b)—

(i) undertake the specified enquiries, and

(ii) prepare a report for the court having regard to the specified issues;

(c) send the report to the sheriff clerk by the date specified; and

(d) unless otherwise directed, send a copy of the report to each party to the proceedings by that date.

(10) A child welfare reporter may—

(a) apply to the sheriff clerk to be given further directions by the sheriff;

(b)    bring to the attention of the sheriff clerk any impediment to the performance of any function arising under this rule.

(11)   Where a child welfare reporter acts as referred to in paragraph (10), the sheriff may, having heard parties, make any order or direction that could competently have been made under paragraph (6).

## Appointment of local authority to report on a child

**33.21A.**—[1](1)   This rule applies where the sheriff appoints a local authority to investigate and report to the court on the circumstances of a child and on the proposed arrangements for the care and upbringing of the child.

(2)   The following provisions of rule 33.21 apply as if the reference to the child welfare reporter was a reference to the local authority appointed by the sheriff—

    (a)    paragraph (3)(a) and (b);
    (b)    paragraph (6)(a) and (b);
    (c)    paragraph (7); and
    (d)    paragraph (8).

(3)   On completion of the report referred to in paragraph (1), the local authority must—

    (a)    send the report to the sheriff clerk; and
    (b)    unless otherwise directed by the sheriff, send a copy of the report to each party to the proceedings.

## Referral to family mediation

**33.22.**[2]   In any family action in which an order in relation to parental responsibilities or parental rights is in issue, the sheriff may, at any stage of the action, where he considers it appropriate to do so, refer that issue to a mediator accredited to a specified family mediation organisation.

## Child Welfare Hearing

**33.22A.**—[3](1)   Where—

    (a)    on the lodging of a notice of intention to defend in a family action in which the initial writ seeks or includes a crave for a section 11 order, a defender wishes to oppose any such crave or order, or seeks the same order as that craved by the pursuer,
    (b)    on the lodging of a notice of intention to defend in a family action, the defender seeks a section 11 order which is not craved by the pursuer, or
    (c)    in any other circumstances in a family action, the sheriff considers that a Child Welfare Hearing should be fixed and makes an order (whether at his own instance or on the motion of a party) that such a hearing shall be fixed,

the sheriff clerk shall fix a date and time for a Child Welfare Hearing on the first suitable court date occurring not sooner than 21 days after the lodging of such notice of intention to defend, unless the sheriff directs the hearing to be held on an earlier date.

---

[1] As inserted by the Act of Sederunt (Rules of the Court of Session 1994 and Ordinary Cause Rules 1993 Amendment) (Child Welfare Reporters) 2015 (SSI 2015/312) para.4 (effective 26 October 2015).

[2] As substituted by SI 1996/2167 (effective November 1, 1996).

[3] As inserted by the Act of Sederunt (Family Proceedings in the Sheriff Court) 1996 (SI 1996/2167) (effective November 1, 1996).

(2) On fixing the date for the Child Welfare Hearing, the sheriff clerk shall intimate the date of the Child Welfare Hearing to the parties in Form F41.

(3) The fixing of the date of the Child Welfare Hearing shall not affect the right of a party to make any other application to the court whether by motion or otherwise.

(4)[1] At the Child Welfare Hearing (which may be held in private), the sheriff shall seek to secure the expeditious resolution of disputes in relation to the child by ascertaining from the parties the matters in dispute and any information relevant to that dispute, and may—

    (a) order such steps to be taken, make such order, if any, or order further procedure, as he thinks fit, and

    (b) ascertain whether there is or is likely to be a vulnerable witness within the meaning of section 11(1) of the Act of 2004 who is to give evidence at any proof or hearing and whether any order under section 12(1) of the Act of 2004 requires to be made.

(5) All parties (including a child who has indicated his wish to attend) shall, except on cause shown, attend the Child Welfare Hearing personally.

(6) It shall be the duty of the parties to provide the sheriff with sufficient information to enable him to conduct the Child Welfare Hearing.

### Applications for orders to disclose whereabouts of children

**33.23.**—(1) An application for an order under section 33(1) of the Family Law Act 1986 (which relates to the disclosure of the whereabouts of a child) shall be made by motion.

(2) Where the sheriff makes an order under section 33(1) of the Family Law Act 1986, he may ordain the person against whom the order has been made to appear before him or to lodge an affidavit.

### Applications in relation to removal of children

**33.24.**—[2](1) An application for leave under section 51(1) of the Act of 1975 (authority to remove a child from the care and possession of the applicant for a residence order) or for an order under section 35(3) of the Family Law Act 1986 (application for interdict or interim interdict prohibiting removal of child from jurisdiction) shall be made—

    (a) by a party to the action, by motion; or

    (b) by a person who is not a party to the action, by minute.

(2) An application under section 35(3) of the Family Law Act 1986 need not be served or intimated.

(3) An application under section 23(2) of the Child Abduction and Custody Act 1985 (declarator that removal of child from United Kingdom was unlawful) shall be made—

    (a) in an action depending before the sheriff—

        (i) by a party, in the initial writ, defences or minute, as the case may be, or by motion; or

        (ii) by any other person, by minute; or

---

[1] As substituted by the Act of Sederunt (Ordinary Cause, Summary Application, Summary Cause and Small Claim Rules) Amendment (Vulnerable Witnesses (Scotland) Act 2004) 2007 (SSI 2007/463) r.2(9) (effective November 1, 2007).

[2] As amended by Act of Sederunt (Family Proceedings in the Sheriff Court) 1996 (SI 1996/2167) (effective November 1, 1996).

(b)  after final decree, by minute in the process of the action to which the application relates.

### Intimation to local authority before supervised contact order

**33.25.**[1]  Where the sheriff, at his own instance or on the motion of a party, is considering making a contact order or an interim contact order subject to supervision by the social work department of a local authority, he shall ordain the party moving for such an order to intimate to the Chief Executive of that local authority (where not already a party to the action and represented at the hearing at which the issue arises)—

(a)  the terms of any relevant motion;

(b)  the intention of the sheriff to order that the contact order be supervised by the social work department of that local authority; and

(c)  that the local authority shall, within such period as the sheriff has determined—

(i)  notify the sheriff clerk whether it intends to make representations to the sheriff; and

(ii)[2]  where it intends to make representations in writing, do so within that period.

### Joint minutes

**33.26.**[3]  Where any parties have reached agreement in relation to—

(a)  a section 11 order,

(b)  aliment for a child,

(c)  an order for financial provision, or

(d)[4]  an order under section 28 or 29 of the Act of 2006

a joint minute may be entered into expressing that agreement; and, subject to rule 33.19(3) (no order before views of child expressed), the sheriff may grant decree in respect of those parts of the joint minute in relation to which he could otherwise make an order, whether or not such a decree would include a matter for which there was no crave.

### Affidavits

**33.27.**  The sheriff may accept evidence by affidavit at any hearing for an order or interim order.

### Applications for postponement of decree under section 3A of the Act of 1976

**33.27A.**[5]  An application under section 3A(1) (application for postponement of decree where impediment to religious marriage exists) or section 3A(4) (application

---

[1]  As amended by the Act of Sederunt (Family Proceedings in the Sheriff Court) (Marriage and Civil Partnership 1996 (SI 1996/2167) (effective November 1, 1996).

[2]  As amended by Act of Sederunt (Ordinary Cause Rules) Amendment (Family Law (Scotland) Act 2006 etc.) 2006 (SSI 2006/207) r.2 (effective May 4, 2006).

[3]  As amended by Act of Sederunt (Family Proceedings in the Sheriff Court) 1996 (SI 1996/2167) (effective November 1, 1996).

[4]  As inserted by the Act of Sederunt (Sheriff Court Rules) (Miscellaneous Amendments) 2012 (SSI 2012/188) para.5 (effective August 1, 2012).

[5]  Substituted by Act of Sederunt (Ordinary Cause Rules) Amendment (Family Law (Scotland) Act 2006 etc.) 2006 (SSI 2006/207) r.2 (effective May 4, 2006) and amended by the Act of Sederunt (Ordinary Cause, Summary Application, Summary Cause and Small Claim Rules) Amendment (Miscellaneous) 2007 (SSI 2007/6) r.2(14) (effective February 26, 2007).

for recall of postponement) of the Act of 1976 shall be made by minute in the process of the action to which the application relates.

## Part II – Undefended Family Actions

### Evidence in certain undefended family actions

**33.28.**—[1](1)  This rule—

(a)  subject to sub-paragraph (b), applies to all family actions in which no notice of intention to defend has been lodged, other than a family action—

  (i)  for a section 11 order or for aliment;
  (ii)  of affiliation and aliment;
  (iii)  for financial provision after an overseas divorce or annulment within the meaning of Part IV of the Matrimonial and Family Proceedings Act 1984; or
  (iv)  for an order under the Act of 1981;
  (v)[2]  for declarator of recognition, or non-recognition, of a relevant foreign decree within the meaning of section 7(9) of the Domicile and Matrimonial Proceedings Act 1973;
  (vi)[3]  for an order under section 28 or 29 of the Act of 2006;
  (vii)[4]  for declarator of recognition, or non-recognition, of a relevant foreign decree within the meaning of paragraph 1 of Schedule 1B to the Domicile and Matrimonial Proceedings Act 1973, or of a judgment to which paragraph 2(1)(b) of that Schedule refers.

(b)  applies to a family action in which a curator ad litem has been appointed under rule 33.16 where the curator ad litem to the defender has lodged a minute intimating that he does not intend to lodge defences;

(c)  applies to any family action which proceeds at any stage as undefended where the sheriff so directs;

(d)  applies to the merits of a family action which is undefended on the merits where the sheriff so directs, notwithstanding that the action is defended on an ancillary matter.

(2)  Unless the sheriff otherwise directs, evidence shall be given by affidavits.

(3)  Unless the sheriff otherwise directs, evidence relating to the welfare of a child shall be given by affidavit, at least one affidavit being emitted by a person other than a parent or party to the action.

(4)  Evidence in the form of a written statement bearing to be the professional opinion of a duly qualified medical practitioner, which has been signed by him and lodged in process, shall be admissible in place of parole evidence by him.

### Procedure for decree in actions under rule 33.28

**33.29.**—(1)  In an action to which rule 33.28 (evidence in certain undefended family actions) applies, the pursuer shall at any time after the expiry of the period for lodging a notice of intention to defend—

---

[1] As amended by Act of Sederunt (Family Proceedings in the Sheriff Court) 1996 (SI 1996/2167) (effective November 1, 1996).

[2] As inserted by the Act of Sederunt (Sheriff Court Rules) (Miscellaneous Amendments) (No.2) 2010 (SSI 2010/416) r.8 (effective January 1, 2011).

[3] As inserted by the Act of Sederunt (Sheriff Court Rules) (Miscellaneous Amendments) 2012 (SSI 2012/188) para.5 (effective August 1, 2012).

[4] As inserted by the Act of Sederunt (Rules of the Court of Session and Sheriff Court Rules Amendment No.2) (Marriage and Civil Partnership (Scotland) Act 2014) 2014 (SSI 2014/302) r.5 (effective December 16, 2014).

(a)   lodge in process the affidavit evidence; and

(b)   endorse a minute in Form F27 on the initial writ.

(2)  The sheriff may, at any time after the pursuer has complied with paragraph (1), without requiring the appearance of parties—

(a)   grant decree in terms of the motion for decree; or

(b)   remit the cause for such further procedure, if any, including proof by parole evidence, as the sheriff thinks fit.

## Extracts of undefended decree

**33.30.**[1]  In an action to which rule 33.28 (evidence in certain undefended family actions) applies, the sheriff clerk shall, after the expiry of 14 days after the grant of decree under rule 33.29 (procedure for decree in cases under rule 33.28), issue to the pursuer and the defender an extract decree.

## Procedure in undefended family action for section 11 order

**33.31.**—[2](1)  Where no notice of intention to defend has been lodged in a family action for a section 11 order, any proceedings in the cause shall be dealt with by the sheriff in chambers.

(2)  In an action to which paragraph (1) applies, decree may be pronounced after such inquiry as the sheriff thinks fit.

## No recording of evidence

**33.32.**  It shall not be necessary to record the evidence in any proof in a family action which is not defended.

## Disapplication of Chapter 15

**33.33.**[3]  Other than rule 15.1(1), Chapter 15 (motions) shall not apply to a family action in which no notice of intention to defend has been lodged, or to a family action in so far as it proceeds as undefended.

## Late appearance and application for recall by defenders

**33.33A.**—[4](1)[56]  In a cause mentioned in rule 33.1(a) to (h) or (n) to (q), the sheriff may, at any stage of the action before the granting of final decree, make an order with such conditions, if any, as he thinks fit—

(a)   directing that a defender who has not lodged a notice of intention to defend be treated as if he had lodged such a notice and the period of notice had expired on the date on which the order was made; or

(b)   allowing a defender who has not lodged a notice of intention to defend to appear and be heard at a diet of proof although he has not lodged defences, but he shall not, in that event, be allowed to lead evidence without the pursuer's consent.

---

[1] As amended by Act of Sederunt (Ordinary Cause Rules) Amendment (Family Law (Scotland) Act 2006 etc.) 2006 (SSI 2006/207) r.2 (effective May 4, 2006).

[2] As amended by Act of Sederunt (Family Proceedings in the Sheriff Court) 1996 (SI 1996/2167) (effective November 1, 1996).

[3] As amended by SI 1996/2445 (effective November 1, 1996).

[4] As inserted by the Act of Sederunt (Sheriff Court Rules) (Miscellaneous Amendments) 2008 (SSI 2008/223) r.2(2) (effective July 1, 2008).

[5] As amended by the Act of Sederunt (Sheriff Court Rules) (Miscellaneous Amendments) (No.2) 2010 (SSI 2010/416) r.8 (effective January 1, 2011).

[6] As amended by the Act of Sederunt (Sheriff Court Rules) (Miscellaneous Amendments) 2012 (SSI 2012/188) para.5 (effective August 1, 2012).

(2) Where the sheriff makes an order under paragraph (1), the pursuer may recall a witness already examined or lead other evidence whether or not he closed his proof before that order was made.

(3) Where no order under paragraph (1) has been sought by a defender who has not lodged a notice of intention to defend and decree is granted against him, the sheriff may, on an application made within 14 days of the date of the decree, and with such conditions, if any, as he thinks fit, make an order recalling the decree.

(4) Where the sheriff makes an order under paragraph (3), the cause shall thereafter proceed as if the defender had lodged a notice of intention to defend and the period of notice had expired on the date on which the decree was recalled.

(5) An application under paragraph (1) or (3) shall be made by note setting out the proposed defence and explaining the defender's failure to appear.

(6) An application under paragraph (1) or (3) shall not affect any right of appeal the defender may otherwise have.

(7) A note lodged in an application under paragraph (1) or (3) shall be served on the pursuer and any other party.

Part III – Defended Family Actions

### Notice of intention to defend and defences etc.[1]

**33.34.**—[2](1) This rule applies where the defender in a family action seeks—

   (a)   to oppose any crave in the initial writ;

   (b)   to make a claim for—

         (i)   aliment;

         (ii)   an order for financial provision within the meaning of section 8(3) of the Act of 1985;

         (iii)   a section 11 order;

         (iv)[3]   an order for financial provision under section 28 or 29 of the Family Law (Scotland) Act 2006; or

   (c)   an order—

         (i)   under section 16(1)(b) or (3) of the Act of 1985 (setting aside or varying agreement as to financial provision);

         (ii)   under section 18 of the Act of 1985 (which relates to avoidance transactions); or

         (iii)   under the Act of 1981; or

   (d)   to challenge the jurisdiction of the court.

(2) In an action to which this rule applies, the defender shall—

   (a)   lodge a notice of intention to defend in Form F26 before the expiry of the period of notice; and

   (b)   make any claim or seek any order referred to in paragraph (1), as the case may be, in those defences by setting out in his defences—

         (i)   craves;

         (ii)   averments in the answers to the condescendence in support of those craves; and

         (iii)   appropriate pleas-in-law.

---

[1] As amended by the Act of Sederunt (Sheriff Court Rules) (Miscellaneous Amendments) 2012 (SSI 2012/188) para.5 (effective August 1, 2012).

[2] As amended by Act of Sederunt (Family Proceedings in the Sheriff Court) 1996 (SI 1996/2167) (effective November 1, 1996).

[3] As inserted by the Act of Sederunt (Sheriff Court Rules) (Miscellaneous Amendments) 2012 (SSI 2012/188) para.4,5 (effective August 1, 2012).

(3) Where a defender intends to make an application for a section 11 order which, had it been made in an initial writ, would have required a warrant for intimation under rule 33.7, the defender shall include a crave in his notice of intention to defend for a warrant for intimation or to dispense with such intimation; and rule 33.7 shall, with the necessary modifications, apply to a crave for a warrant under this paragraph as it applies to a crave for a warrant under that rule.

(4)[1,2] Where a defender opposes a crave for an order for financial provision or makes a claim in accordance with paragraph (1)(b)(ii), the defender must lodge a completed Form F13A signed by the defender with the defences, minute of amendment or answers as the case may be.

### Abandonment by pursuer

**33.35.** Notwithstanding abandonment by a pursuer, the court may allow a defender to pursue an order or claim sought in his defences; and the proceedings in relation to that order or claim shall continue in dependence as if a separate cause.

### Attendance of parties at Options Hearing

**33.36.** All parties shall, except on cause shown, attend personally the hearing under rule 9.12 (Options Hearing).

### Decree by default

**33.37.**—(1)[3] In a family action in which the defender has lodged a notice of intention to defend, where a party fails—
    (a)   to lodge, or intimate the lodging of, any production or part of process,
    (b)   to implement an order of the sheriff within a specified period,
    (c)   to appear or be represented at any diet, or
    (d)[4]  otherwise to comply with any requirement imposed upon that party by these Rules;
that party shall be in default.

(2)[5] Where a party is in default under paragraph (1), the sheriff may—
    (a)[6]  where the family action is one mentioned in rule 33.1(a) to (h) or (n) to (p) allow the cause to proceed as undefended under Part II of this Chapter; or
    (b)[7]  where the family action is one mentioned in rule 33.1(1)(i) to (m) or (q), grant decree as craved; or
    (c)   grant decree of absolvitor; or
    (d)   dismiss the family action or any claim made or order sought; or

---

[1] As inserted by the Act of Sederunt (Sheriff Court Rules) (Miscellaneous Amendments) 2012 (SSI 2012/188) para.4,5 (effective August 1, 2012).

[2] As amended by the Act of Sederunt (Sheriff Court Rules) (Miscellaneous Amendments) (No.2) 2012 (SSI 2012/221) para.2 (effective July 31, 2012).

[3] As amended by Act of Sederunt (Sheriff Court Ordinary Cause Rules Amendment) (Miscellaneous) 1996 (SI 1996/2445) (effective November 1, 1996) (clerical error).

[4] As inserted by the Act of Sederunt (Ordinary Cause and Summary Application Rules) Amendment (Miscellaneous) 2006 (SSI 2006/410) (effective August 18, 2006).

[5] As amended by Act of Sederunt (Ordinary Cause Rules) Amendment (Family Law (Scotland) Act 2006 etc.) 2006, para.2 (SSI 2006/207) (effective May 4, 2006) and the Act of Sederunt (Ordinary Cause and Summary Application Rules) Amendment (Miscellaneous) 2006 (SSI 2006/410) (effective August 18, 2006).

[6] As amended by the Act of Sederunt (Sheriff Court Rules) (Miscellaneous Amendments) (No.2) 2010 (SSI 2010/416) r.8 (effective January 1, 2011).

[7] As amended by the Act of Sederunt (Sheriff Court Rules) (Miscellaneous Amendments) 2012 (SSI 2012/188) para.5 (effective August 1, 2012).

(da)  make such other order as he thinks fit to secure the expeditious progress of the cause; and

(e)  award expenses.

(3)  Where no party appears at a diet in a family action, the sheriff may dismiss that action.

(4)  In a family action, the sheriff may, on cause shown, prorogate the time for lodging any production or part of process, or for intimating or implementing any order.

Part IV – Applications and Orders Relating to Children in Certain Actions

## Application and interpretation of this Part

**33.38.**[1,2]  This Part applies to an action of divorce, separation or declarator of nullity of marriage.

## Applications in actions to which this Part applies

**33.39.**—[3](1)  An application for an order mentioned in paragraph (2) shall be made—

(a)  by a crave in the initial writ or defences, as the case may be, in an action to which this Part applies; or

(b)  where the application is made by a person other than the pursuer or defender, by minute in that action.

(2)  The orders referred to in paragraph (1) are—

(a)  an order for a section 11 order; and

(b)  an order for aliment for a child.

**33.40.**  [Repealed by the Act of Sederunt (Family Proceedings in the Sheriff Court) 1996 (SI 1996/2167) (effective November 1, 1996).]

**33.41.**  [Repealed by the Act of Sederunt (Family Proceedings in the Sheriff Court) 1996 (SI 1996/2167) (effective November 1, 1996).]

**33.42.**  [Repealed by the Act of Sederunt (Family Proceedings in the Sheriff Court) 1996 (SI 1996/2167) (effective November 1, 1996).]

## Applications in depending actions by motion

**33.43.**[4]  An application by a party in an action depending before the court to which this Part applies for, or for variation of, an order for—

(a)  interim aliment for a child under the age of 18, or

(b)  a residence order or a contact order,

shall be made by motion.

---

[1]  As amended by Act of Sederunt (Family Proceedings in the Sheriff Court) 1996 (SI 1996/2167) (effective November 1, 1996).

[2]  As amended by Act of Sederunt (Ordinary Cause Rules) Amendment (Family Law (Scotland) Act 2006 etc.) 2006, para.2 (SSI 2006/207) (effective May 4, 2006).

[3]  As amended by Act of Sederunt (Family Proceedings in the Sheriff Court) 1996 (SI 1996/2167) (effective November 1, 1996).

[4]  As amended by Act of Sederunt (Family Proceedings in the Sheriff Court) 1996 (SI 1996/2167) (effective November 1, 1996).

### Applications after decree relating to a section 11 order

**33.44.**—[1](1)[2]  An application after final decree for, or for the variation or recall of, a section 11 order or in relation to the enforcement of such an order shall be made by minute in the process of the action to which the application relates.

(2)  Where a minute has been lodged under paragraph (1), any party may apply by motion for any interim order which may be made pending the determination of the application.

### Applications after decree relating to aliment

**33.45.**—(1)  An application after final decree for, or for the variation or recall of, an order for aliment for a child shall be made by minute in the process of the action to which the application relates.

(2)  Where a minute has been lodged under paragraph (1), any party may lodge a motion for any interim order which may be made pending the determination of the application.

### Applications after decree by persons over 18 years for aliment

**33.46.**—(1)  A person—

(a)  to whom an obligation of aliment is owed under section 1 of the Act of 1985,

(b)  in whose favour an order for aliment while under the age of 18 years was made in an action to which this Part applies, and

(c)  who seeks, after attaining that age, an order for aliment against the person in that action against whom the order for aliment in his favour was made,

shall apply by minute in the process of that action.

(2)  An application for interim aliment pending the determination of an application under paragraph (1) shall be made by motion.

(3)  Where a decree has been pronounced in an application under paragraph (1) or (2), any application for variation or recall of any such decree shall be made by minute in the process of the action to which the application relates.

Part V – Orders Relating to Financial Provision

### Application and interpretation of this Part

**33.47.**—(1)  This Part applies to an action of divorce.

(2)  In this Part, "incidental order" has the meaning assigned in section 14(2) of the Act of 1985.

### Applications in actions to which this Part applies

**33.48.**—(1)  An application for an order mentioned in paragraph (2) shall be made—

(a)  by a crave in the initial writ or defences, as the case may be, in an action to which this Part applies; or

(b)  where the application is made by a person other than the pursuer or defender, by minute in that action.

(2)  The orders referred to in paragraph (1) are—

---

[1] As amended by Act of Sederunt (Family Proceedings in the Sheriff Court) 1996 (SI 1996/2167) (effective November 1, 1996).
[2] As amended by SSI 2000/239 (effective October 2, 2000).

(a)   an order for financial provision within the meaning of section 8(3) of the Act of 1985;

(b)   an order under section 16(1)(b) or (3) of the Act of 1985 (setting aside or varying agreement as to financial provision);

(c)   an order under section 18 of the Act of 1985 (which relates to avoidance transactions); and

(d)   an order under section 13 of the Act of 1981 (transfer or vesting of tenancy).

### Applications in depending actions relating to incidental orders

**33.49.**—(1)   In an action depending before the sheriff to which this Part applies—

(a)   the pursuer, notwithstanding rules 33.34(2) (application by defender for order for financial provision) and 33.48(1)(a) (application for order for financial provision in initial writ or defences), may apply by motion for an incidental order; and

(b)   the sheriff shall not be bound to determine such a motion if he considers that the application should properly be by a crave in the initial writ or defences, as the case may be.

(2)   In an action depending before the sheriff to which this Part applies, an application under section 14(4) of the Act of 1985 for the variation or recall of an incidental order shall be made by minute in the process of the action to which the application relates.

### Applications relating to interim aliment

**33.50.**   An application for, or for the variation or recall of, an order for interim aliment for the pursuer or the defender shall be made by motion.

### Applications relating to orders for financial provision

**33.51.**—(1)   An application—

(a)   after final decree under any of the following provisions of the Act of 1985—

    (i)   section 8(1) for periodical allowance,

    (ii)   section 12(1)(b) (payment of capital sum or transfer of property),

    (iii)   section 12(4) (variation of date or method of payment of capital sum or date of transfer of property), or

    (iv)   section 13(4) (variation, recall, backdating or conversion of periodical allowance), or

    (v)[1]   section 14(1) (incidental orders), or

(b)   after the grant or refusal of an application under—

    (i)   section 8(1) or 14(3) for an incidental order, or

    (ii)   section 14(4) (variation or recall of incidental order),

shall be made by minute in the process of the action to which the application relates.

(2)   Where a minute is lodged under paragraph (1), any party may lodge a motion for any interim order which may be made pending the determination of the application.

---

[1] As inserted by the Act of Sederunt (Sheriff Court Rules) (Miscellaneous Amendments) (No.3) 2011 (SSI 2011/386) para.2 (effective November 28, 2011).

(3)[1] An application under—

    (a)   paragraph (5) of section 12A of the Act of 1985 (recall or variation of order in respect of a pension lump sum),

    (b)   paragraph (7) of that section (variation of order in respect of pension lump sum to substitute trustees or managers),

    (ba)[2]   section 12B(4) of the Act of 1985 (recall or variation of a capital sum order), or

    (c)   section 28(10) or 48(9) of the Welfare Reform and Pensions Act 1999,

shall be made by minute in the process of the action to which the application relates.

### Pension Protection Fund notification

**33.51A.**—[3](1)  In this rule—

"assessment period" shall be construed in accordance with section 132 of the Pensions Act 2004;

"pension arrangement" shall be construed in accordance with the definition in section 27 of the Act of 1985; and

"valuation summary" shall be construed in accordance with the definition in Schedule 2 to the Pension Protection Fund (Provision of Information) Regulations 2005.

(2)  This rule applies where a party at any stage in the proceedings applies for an order under section 8 or section 16 of the Act of 1985.

(3)  Where the party against whom an order referred to in paragraph (2) is sought has received notification in compliance with the Pension Protection Fund (Provision of Information) Regulations 2005 or does so after the order is sought—

    (a)   that there is an assessment period in relation to his pension arrangement; or

    (b)   that the Board of the Pension Protection Fund has assumed responsibility for all or part of his pension arrangement,

    he shall comply with paragraph (4).

(4)  The party shall—

    (a)   lodge the notification; and

    (b)   obtain and lodge as soon as reasonably practicable thereafter–

        (i)   a valuation summary; and

        (ii)   a forecast of his compensation entitlement.

(5)  Subject to paragraph (6), the notification referred to in paragraph (4)(a) requires to be lodged—

    (a)   where the notification is received before the order is sought, within 7 days of the order being sought;

    (b)   where the notification is received after the order is sought, within 7 days of receiving the notification.

(6)  Where an order is sought against the defender before the defences are lodged, and the notification is received before that step occurs, the notification shall be lodged with the defences.

---

[1] As inserted by SI 1996/2445 (effective November 1, 1996) and as amended by the Act of Sederunt (Ordinary Cause, Summary Application, Summary Cause and Small Claim Rules) Amendment (Miscellaneous) 2003 (SSI 2003/26), para.2(9) (effective January 24, 2003).

[2] As inserted by the Act of Sederunt (Sheriff Court Rules) (Miscellaneous Amendments) 2011 (SSI 2011/193) r.15 (effective April 6, 2011).

[3] As inserted by the Act of Sederunt (Sheriff Court Rules) (Miscellaneous Amendments) 2008 (SSI 2008/223) para.3(2) (effective July 1, 2008).

(7) At the same time as lodging documents under paragraph (4), copies shall be sent to the other party to the proceedings.

**Applications after decree relating to agreements and avoidance transactions**

**33.52.** An application for an order—

(a) under section 16(1)(a) or (3) of the Act of 1985 (setting aside or varying agreement as to financial provision), or

(b) under section 18 of the Act of 1985 (which relates to avoidance transactions),

made after final decree shall be made by minute in the process of the action to which the application relates.

Part VI – Applications Relating to Avoidance Transactions

**Form of applications**

**33.53.**—(1) An application for an order under section 18 of the Act of 1985 (which relates to avoidance transactions) by a party to an action shall be made by including in the initial writ, defences or minute, as the case may be, appropriate craves, averments and pleas-in-law.

(2) An application for an order under section 18 of the Act of 1985 after final decree in an action, shall be made by minute in the process of the action to which the application relates.

Part VII – Financial Provision after Overseas Divorce or Annulment

**Interpretation of this Part**

**33.54.** In this Part—

"the Act of 1984" means the Matrimonial and Family Proceedings Act 1984;

"order for financial provision" has the meaning assigned in section 30(1) of the Act of 1984;

"overseas country" has the meaning assigned in section 30(1) of the Act of 1984.

**Applications for financial provision after overseas divorce or annulment**

**33.55.**—[1](1) An application under section 28 of the Act of 1984 for an order for financial provision after a divorce or annulment in an overseas country shall be made by initial writ.

(2) An application for an order in an action to which paragraph (1) applies made before final decree under—

(a) section 13 of the Act of 1981 (transfer of tenancy of matrimonial home),

(b) section 29(4) of the Act of 1984 for interim periodical allowance, or

(c) section 14(4) of the Act of 1985 (variation or recall of incidental order),

shall be made by motion.

(3) An application for an order in an action to which paragraph (1) applies made after final decree under—

(a) section 12(4) of the Act of 1985 (variation of date or method of payment of capital sum or date of transfer of property),

(b) section 13(4) of the Act of 1985 (variation, recall, backdating or conversion of periodical allowance), or

(c) section 14(4) of the Act of 1985 (variation or recall of incidental order),

---

[1] Heading amended by SI 1996/2445 (effective November 1, 1996).

shall be made by minute in the process of the action to which the application relates.

(4)[1] An application under—

(a) paragraph (5) of section 12A of the Act of 1985 (recall or variation of order in respect of a pension lump sum), or

(b) paragraph (7) of that section (variation of order in respect of pension lump sum to substitute trustees or managers),

shall be made by minute in the process of the action to which the application relates.

(5) Where a minute has been lodged under paragraph (3), any party may apply by motion for an interim order pending the determination of the application.

<h3 style="text-align:center">Part VIII – Actions of Aliment</h3>

### Interpretation of this Part

**33.56.** In this Part, "action of aliment" means a claim for aliment under section 2(1) of the Act of 1985.

### Undefended actions of aliment

**33.57.**—(1) Where a motion for decree in absence under Chapter 7 (undefended causes) is lodged in an action of aliment, the pursuer shall, on lodging the motion, lodge all documentary evidence of the means of the parties available to him in support of the amount of aliment sought.

(2) Where the sheriff requires the appearance of parties, the sheriff clerk shall fix a hearing.

### Applications relating to aliment

**33.58.**—(1) An application for, or for variation of, an order for interim aliment in a depending action of aliment shall be made by motion.

(2) An application after final decree for the variation or recall of an order for aliment in an action of aliment shall be made by minute in the process of the action to which the application relates.

(3) A person—

(a) to whom an obligation of aliment is owed under section 1 of the Act of 1985,

(b) in whose favour an order for aliment while under the age of 18 years was made in an action of aliment, or

(c) who seeks, after attaining that age, an order for aliment against the person in that action against whom the order for aliment in his favour was made,

shall apply by minute in the process of that action.

(4) An application for interim aliment pending the determination of an application under paragraph (2) or (3) shall be made by motion.

(5) Where a decree has been pronounced in an application under paragraph (2) or (3), any application for variation or recall of any such decree shall be made by minute in the process of the action to which the application relates.

### Applications relating to agreements on aliment

**33.59.**—[2](1) Subject to paragraph (2) and rule 33A.53, an application under section 7(2) of the Act of 1985 (variation or termination of agreement on aliment) shall be made by summary application.

---

[1] Inserted by SI 1996/2445 (effective November 1, 1996).

[2] As amended by Act of Sederunt (Ordinary Cause Rules) Amendment (Family Law (Scotland) Act 2006 etc.) 2006, para.2 (SSI 2006/207) (effective May 4, 2006).

(2)   In a family action in which a crave for aliment may be made, an application under section 7(2) of the Act of 1985 shall be made by a crave in the initial writ or in defences, as the case may be.

Part IX – Applications for Orders under Section II of the Children (Scotland) Act 1995

## Application of this Part

**33.60.**[12]   This Part applies to an application for a section 11 order in a family action other than in an action of divorce, separation or declarator of nullity of marriage.

## Form of applications

**33.61.**[3]   Subject to any other provision in this Chapter, an application for a section 11 order shall be made—

(a)   by an action for a section 11 order;

(b)   by a crave in the initial writ or defences, as the case may be, in any other family action to which this Part applies; or

(c)   where the application is made by a person other than a party to an action mentioned in paragraph (a) or (b), by minute in that action.

## Defenders in action for a section 11 order

**33.62.**[4]   In an action for a section 11 order, the pursuer shall call as a defender—

(a)   the parents or other parent of the child in respect of whom the order is sought;

(b)   any guardian of the child;

(c)   any person who has treated the child as a child of his family;

(d)   any person who in fact exercises care or control in respect of the child; and

(e)   *[Repealed by SSI 2000/239 (effective October 2, 2000).]*

## Applications relating to interim orders in depending actions

**33.63.**[5, 6]   An application, in an action depending before the sheriff to which this Part applies, for, or for the variation or recall of, an interim residence order or an interim contact order shall be made—

(a)   by a party to the action, by motion; or

(b)   by a person who is not a party to the action, by minute.

**33.64.**   [Repealed by SI 1996/2167 (effective November 1, 1996).]

---

[1] Substituted by SI 1996/2167 (effective November 1, 1996).

[2] As amended by Act of Sederunt (Ordinary Cause Rules) Amendment (Family Law (Scotland) Act 2006 etc.) 2006, para.2 (SSI 2006/207) (effective May 4, 2006).

[3] As amended by Act of Sederunt (Family Proceedings in the Sheriff Court) 1996 (SI 1996/2167) (effective November 1, 1996).

[4] Substituted by SI 1996/2167 (effective November 1, 1996). Clerical error corrected by SI 1996/2445 (effective November 1, 1996).

[5] As amended by Act of Sederunt (Family Proceedings in the Sheriff Court) 1996 (SI 1996/2167) (effective November 1, 1996).

[6] As amended by Act of Sederunt (Ordinary Cause Rules) Amendment (Family Law (Scotland) Act 2006 etc.) 2006, para.2 (SSI 2006/207) (effective May 4, 2006).

**Applications after decree**

**33.65.**—[1](1)  An application after final decree for variation or recall of a section 11 order shall be made by minute in the process of the action to which the application relates.

(2)  Where a minute has been lodged under paragraph (1), any party may apply by motion for an interim order pending the determination of the application.

**Application for leave**

**33.65A.**—[2](1)  Where leave of the court is required under section 11(3)(aa) of the Act of 1995 for the making of an application for a contact order under that section, the applicant must lodge along with the initial writ a written application in the form of a letter addressed to the sheriff clerk stating—

    (a)  the grounds on which leave is sought;

    (b)  whether or not the applicant has applied for legal aid.

(2)  Where the applicant has applied for legal aid he must also lodge along with the initial writ written confirmation from the Scottish Legal Aid Board that it has determined, under regulation 7(2)(b) of the Civil Legal Aid (Scotland) Regulations 2002, that notification of the application should be dispensed with or postponed pending the making by the sheriff of an order for intimation under paragraph (4)(b).

(3)  Subject to paragraph (4)(b), an application under paragraph (1) shall not be served or intimated to any party.

(4)  The sheriff shall consider an application under paragraph (1) without hearing the applicant and may—

    (a)  refuse the application and pronounce an interlocutor accordingly; or

    (b)  if he is minded to grant the application order the applicant—

        (i)  to intimate the application to such persons as the sheriff considers appropriate; and

        (ii)  to lodge a certificate of intimation in, as near as may be, Form G8.

(5)  If any person who receives intimation of an application under paragraph (4)(b) wishes to be heard he shall notify the sheriff clerk in writing within 14 days of receipt of intimation of the application.

(6)  On receipt of any notification under paragraph (5) the sheriff clerk shall fix a hearing and intimate the date of the hearing to the parties.

(7)  Where an application under paragraph (1) is granted, a copy of the sheriffs interlocutor must be served on the defender along with the warrant of citation.

Part X – Actions under the Matrimonial Homes (Family Protection) (Scotland) Act 1981

**Interpretation of this Part**

**33.66.**  Unless the context otherwise requires, words and expressions used in this Part which are also used in the Act of 1981 have the same meaning as in that Act.

**Form of applications**

**33.67.**—(1)  Subject to any other provision in this Chapter, an application for an order under the Act of 1981 shall be made—

---

[1] As amended by Act of Sederunt (Family Proceedings in the Sheriff Court) 1996 (SI 1996/2167) (effective November 1, 1996).

[2] As inserted by the Act of Sederunt (Sheriff Court Rules Amendment) (Adoption and Children (Scotland) Act 2007) 2009 (SSI 2009/284) (effective September 28, 2009).

    (a)   by an action for such an order;

    (b)   by a crave in the initial writ or in defences, as the case may be, in any other family action; or

    (c)   where the application is made by a person other than a party to any action mentioned in paragraph (a) or (b), by minute in that action.

    (2)[1]  An application under section 7(1) (dispensing with consent of non-entitled spouse to a dealing) or section 11 (application in relation to attachment) shall, unless made in a depending family action, be made by summary application.

## Defenders

**33.68.**  The applicant for an order under the Act of 1981 shall call as a defender—

    (a)   where he is seeking an order as a spouse, the other spouse;

    (b)[2]  where he is a third party making an application under section 7(1) dispensing with consent of non-entitled spouse to a dealing), or 8(1) (payment from non-entitled spouse in respect of loan), of the Act of 1981, both spouses;

    (c)   where the application is made under section 18 of the Act of 1981 (occupancy rights of cohabiting couples), or is one to which that section applies, the other partner; and

    (d)[3]  where the application is made under section 18A of the Act of 1981 (application for domestic interdict), the other partner.

## Applications by motion

**33.69.**—(1)  An application under any of the following provisions of the Act of 1981 shall be made by motion in the process of the depending action to which the application relates:—

    (a)   section 3(4) (interim order for regulation of rights of occupancy, etc.);

    (b)   section 4(6) (interim order suspending occupancy rights);

    (c)   section 7(1) (dispensing with consent of non-entitled spouse to a dealing);

    (d)   [Omitted by Act of Sederunt (Ordinary Cause Rules) Amendment (Family Law (Scotland) Act 2006 etc.) 2006, para.2 (SSI 2006/207) (effective May 4, 2006).]; and

    (e)   the proviso to section 18(1) (extension of period of occupancy rights).

    (2)  Intimation of a motion under paragraph (1) shall be given—

    (a)   to the other spouse or partner, as the case may be;

    (b)   where the motion is under paragraph (1)(a), (b) or (e) and the entitled spouse or partner is a tenant or occupies the matrimonial home by the permission of a third party, to the landlord or third party, as the case may be; and

    (c)   to any other person to whom intimation of the application was or is to be made by virtue of rule 33.7(1)(k) (warrant for intimation to certain persons in actions for orders under the Act of 1981) or 33.15 (order for intimation by sheriff).

---

[1] As amended by the Act of Sederunt (Debt Arrangement and Attachment (Scotland) Act 2002) 2002 (SSI 2002/560), art.4, Sch.3 (effective December 30, 2002).

[2] As amended by Act of Sederunt (Ordinary Cause Rules) Amendment (Family Law (Scotland) Act 2006 etc.) 2006, para.2 (SSI 2006/207) (effective May 4, 2006).

[3] Inserted by Act of Sederunt (Ordinary Cause Rules) Amendment (Family Law (Scotland) Act 2006 etc.) 2006, para.2 (SSI 2006/207) (effective May 4, 2006).

## Applications by minute

**33.70.**—(1)  An application for an order under—

    (a)  section 5 of the Act of 1981 (variation and recall of orders regulating oc cupancy rights and of exclusion order), or

    (b)  [Omitted by Act of Sederunt (Ordinary Cause Rules) Amendment (Family Law (Scotland) Act 2006 etc.) 2006, para.2 (SSI 2006/207) (effective May 4, 2006).]

shall be made by minute.

    (2)  A minute under paragraph (1) shall be intimated—

    (a)  to the other spouse or partner, as the case may be;

    (b)  where the entitled spouse or partner is a tenant or occupies the matrimonial home by the permission of a third party, to the landlord or third party, as the case may be; and

    (c)  to any other person to whom intimation of the application was or is to be made by virtue of rule 33.7(1)(k) (warrant for intimation to certain person in actions for orders under the Act of 1981) or 33.15 (order for intimation by sheriff).

## Sist of actions to enforce occupancy rights

**33.71.**  Unless the sheriff otherwise directs, the sist of an action by virtue of sec tion 7(4) of the Act of 1981 (where action raised by non-entitled spouse to enforce occupancy rights) shall apply only to such part of the action as relates to the enforce ment of occupancy rights by a non-entitled spouse.

## Certificates of delivery of documents to chief constable

**33.72.**  [Omitted by Act of Sederunt (Ordinary Cause Rules) Amendment (Family Law (Scotland) Act 2006 etc.) 2006, para.2 (SSI 2006/207) (effective May 4, 2006).]

### Part XI – Simplified Divorce Applications

## Application and interpretation of this Part

**33.73.**—(1)[1]  This Part applies to an application for divorce by a party to a mar riage made in the manner prescribed in rule 33.74 (form of applications) if, but only if—

    (a)  that party relies on the facts set out in section 1(2)(d) (no cohabitation for one year with consent of defender to decree), or section 1(2)(e) (no cohabitation for two years), or section 1(1)(b) (issue of interim gender recognition certificate) of the Act of 1976;

    (b)  in an application under section 1(2)(d) of the Act of 1976, the other party consents to decree of divorce being granted;

    (c)  no other proceedings are pending in any court which could have the effect of bringing the marriage to an end;

    (d)  there are no children of the marriage under the age of 16 years;

    (e)  neither party to the marriage applies for an order for financial provision on divorce;

    (f)  neither party to the marriage suffers from mental disorder; and

---

[1] As amended by Act of Sederunt (Ordinary Cause Rules) Amendment (Family Law (Scotland) Act 2006 etc.) 2006, para.2 (SSI 2006/207) (effective May 4, 2006).

(g)[1]    neither party to the marriage applies for postponement of decree under section 3A of the Act of 1976 (postponement of decree where impediment to religious marriage exists).

(2)    If an application ceases to be one to which this Part applies at any time before final decree, it shall be deemed to be abandoned and shall be dismissed.

(3)    In this Part "simplified divorce application" means an application mentioned in paragraph (1).

## Form of applications

**33.74.**—[2](1)[3]    A simplified divorce application in which the facts set out in section 1(2)(d) of the Act of 1976 (no cohabitation for one year with consent of defender to decree) are relied on shall be made in Form F31 and shall only be of effect if—

(a)    it is signed by the applicant; and

(b)    the form of consent in Part 2 of Form F31 is signed by the party to the marriage giving consent.

(2)    A simplified divorce application in which the facts set out in section 1(2)(e) of the Act of 1976 (no cohabitation for two years) are relied on shall be made in Form F33 and shall only be of effect if it is signed by the applicant.

(3)[4]    A simplified divorce application in which the facts set out in section 1(1)(b) of the Act of 1976 (grounds of divorce: interim gender recognition certificate) are relied on shall be made in Form F33A and shall only be of effect if signed by the applicant.

## Lodging of applications

**33.75.**[5]    The applicant shall send a simplified divorce application to the sheriff clerk with—

(a)    an extract or certified copy of the marriage certificate;

(b)    the appropriate fee; and

(c)[6]    in an application under section 1(1)(b) of the Act of 1976 (grounds of divorce: interim gender recognition certificate), the interim gender recognition certificate or a certified copy within the meaning of rule 33.9A(3).

## Citation and intimation

**33.76.**—(1)    This rule is subject to rule 33.77 (citation where address not known).

(2)    It shall be the duty of the sheriff clerk to cite any person or intimate any document in connection with a simplified divorce application.

(3)    The form of citation—

---

[1] Inserted by Act of Sederunt (Ordinary Cause Rules) Amendment (Family Law (Scotland) Act 2006 etc.) 2006, para.2 (SSI 2006/207) (effective May 4, 2006) and substituted by the Act of Sederunt (Ordinary Cause, Summary Application, Summary Cause and Small Claim Rules) Amendment (Miscellaneous) 2007 (SSI 2007/6), para.2(15) (effective February 26, 2007).

[2] —As amended by Act of Sederunt (Ordinary Cause Rules) Amendment (Family Law (Scotland) Act 2006 etc.) 2006, para.2 (SSI 2006/207) (effective May 4, 2006).

[3] As amended by Act of Sederunt (Sheriff Court Ordinary Cause Rules Amendment) (Miscellaneous) 1996 (SI 1996/2445) (effective November 1, 1996) (clerical error).

[4] Inserted by Act of Sederunt (Ordinary Cause Rules) Amendment (Family Law (Scotland) Act 2006 etc.) 2006, para.2 (SSI 2006/207) (effective May 4, 2006).

[5] As amended by Act of Sederunt (Ordinary Cause Rules) Amendment (Family Law (Scotland) Act 2006 etc.) 2006, para.2 (SSI 2006/207) (effective May 4, 2006).

[6] Inserted by Act of Sederunt (Ordinary Cause Rules) Amendment (Family Law (Scotland) Act 2006 etc.) 2006, para.2 (SSI 2006/207) (effective May 4, 2006).

(a)[1]  in an application relying on the facts in section 1(2)(d) of the Act of 1976 shall be in Form F34;

(b)  in an application relying on the facts in section 1(2)(e) of the Act of 1976 shall be in Form F35; and

(c)[2]  in an application relying on the facts in section 1(1)(b) of the Act of 1976 shall be in Form F35A.

(4)[3]  The citation or intimation required by paragraph (2) shall be made—

(a)  by the sheriff clerk by registered post or the first class recorded delivery service in accordance with rule 5.3 (postal service or intimation);

(b)[4]  on payment of an additional fee, by a sheriff officer in accordance with rule 5.4(1) to (4) (service within Scotland by sheriff officer); or

(c)  where necessary, by the sheriff clerk in accordance with rule 5.5 (service on persons furth of Scotland).

(5)[5]  Where citation or intimation is made in accordance with paragraph (4)(c), the translation into an official language of the country in which service is to be executed required by rule 5.5(6) shall be provided by the party lodging the simplified divorce application.

**Citation where address not known**

**33.77.**—(1)[6]  In a simplified divorce application in which the facts in section 1(2)(e) of the Act of 1976 (no cohabitation for two years) or section 1(1)(b) of the Act of 1976 (grounds of divorce: issue of interim gender recognition certificate) are relied on and the address of the other party to the marriage is not known and cannot reasonably be ascertained—

(a)  citation shall be executed by displaying a copy of the application and a notice in Form F36 on the walls of court on a period of notice of 21 days; and

(b)  intimation shall be made to—

(i)  every child of the marriage between the parties who has reached the age of 16 years, and

(ii)  one of the next of kin of the other party to the marriage who has reached that age, unless the address of such person is not known and cannot reasonably be ascertained.

(2)  Intimation to a person referred to in paragraph (1)(b) shall be given by intimating a copy of the application and a notice of intimation in Form F37.

**Opposition to applications**

**33.78.**—(1)  Any person on whom service or intimation of a simplified divorce application has been made may give notice by letter sent to the sheriff clerk that he challenges the jurisdiction of the court or opposes the grant of decree of divorce and giving the reasons for his opposition to the application.

---

[1] As amended by Act of Sederunt (Ordinary Cause Rules) Amendment (Family Law (Scotland) Act 2006 etc.) 2006, para.2 (SSI 2006/207) (effective May 4, 2006).

[2] Inserted by Act of Sederunt (Ordinary Cause Rules) Amendment (Family Law (Scotland) Act 2006 etc.) 2006, para.2 (SSI 2006/207) (effective May 4, 2006).

[3] Substituted by SSI 2000/239 (effective October 2, 2000).

[4] As substituted by the Act of Sederunt (Sheriff Court Rules) (Miscellaneous Amendments) 2010 (SSI 2010/279) r.2 (effective July 29, 2010).

[5] Inserted by SSI 2000/239 (effective October 2, 2000).

[6] As amended by Act of Sederunt (Ordinary Cause Rules) Amendment (Family Law (Scotland) Act 2006 etc.) 2006, para.2 (SSI 2006/207) (effective May 4, 2006).

(2) Where opposition to a simplified divorce application is made under paragraph (1), the sheriff shall dismiss the application unless he is satisfied that the reasons given for the opposition are frivolous.

(3) The sheriff clerk shall intimate the decision under paragraph (2) to the applicant and the respondent.

(4) The sending of a letter under paragraph (1) shall not imply acceptance of the jurisdiction of the court.

## Evidence

**33.79.** Parole evidence shall not be given in a simplified divorce application.

## Decree

**33.80.**—(1) The sheriff may grant decree in terms of the simplified divorce application on the expiry of the period of notice if such application has been properly served provided that, when the application has been served in a country to which the Hague Convention on the Service Abroad of Judicial and Extra-Judicial Documents in Civil and Commercial Matters dated November 15, 1965 applies, decree shall not be granted until it is established to the satisfaction of the sheriff that the requirements of Article 15 of that Convention have been complied with.

(2) The sheriff clerk shall, not sooner than 14 days after the granting of decree in terms of paragraph (1), issue to each party to the marriage an extract of the decree of divorce in Form F38.

## Appeals

**33.81.**[1](1) Any appeal against an interlocutor granting decree of divorce under rule 33.80 (decree) may be made, within 14 days after the date of decree, by sending a letter to the court giving reasons for the appeal.

(2) Within 4 days after receiving an appeal, the sheriff clerk must transmit to the Clerk of the Sheriff Appeal Court—

(a) the appeal;
(b) all documents and productions in the simplified divorce application.

(3) On receipt of the appeal, the Clerk of the Sheriff Appeal Court is to fix a hearing and intimate the date, time and place of that hearing to the parties.

## Applications after decree

**33.82.** Any application to the court after decree of divorce has been granted in a simplified divorce application which could have been made if it had been made in an action of divorce shall be made by minute.

### Part XII – Variation of Court of Session Decrees

## Application and interpretation of this Part

**33.83.**—(1) This Part applies to an application to the sheriff for variation or recall of any order to which section 8 of the Act of 1966 (variation of certain Court of Session orders) applies.

(2) In this Part, the "Act of 1966" means the Law Reform (Miscellaneous Provisions) (Scotland) Act 1966.

---

[1] As amended by the Act of Sederunt (Rules of the Court of Session, Sheriff Appeal Court Rules and Sheriff Court Rules Amendment) (Sheriff Appeal Court) 2015 (SSI 2015/419) r.5 (effective 1 January 2016).

## Form of application and intimation to Court of Session

**33.84.**—(1)  An application to which this Part applies shall be made by initial writ.

(2)  In such an application there shall be lodged with the initial writ a copy of the interlocutor, certified by a clerk of the Court of Session, which it is sought to vary.

(3)  Before lodging the initial writ, a copy of the initial writ certified by the pursuer or his solicitor shall be lodged, or sent by first class recorded delivery post to the Deputy Principal Clerk of Session to be lodged in the process of the cause in the Court of Session in which the original order was made.

(4)  The pursuer or his solicitor shall attach a certificate to the initial writ stating that paragraph (3) has been complied with.

(5)[1]  The sheriff may, on cause shown, prorogate the time for lodging the certified copy of the interlocutor required under paragraph (2).

## Defended actions

**33.85.**—(1)  Where a notice of intention to defend has been lodged and no request is made under rule 33.87 (remit of application to Court of Session), the pursuer shall within 14 days after the date of the lodging of a notice of intention to defend or within such other period as the sheriff may order, lodge in process the following documents (or copies) from the process in the cause in the Court of Session in which the original order was made:—

    (a)  the pleadings;

    (b)  the interlocutor sheets;

    (c)  any opinion of the court; and

    (d)  any productions on which he seeks to found.

(2)  The sheriff may, on the joint motion of parties made at any time after the lodging of the documents mentioned in paragraph (1)—

    (a)  dispense with proof;

    (b)  whether defences have been lodged or not, hear the parties; and

    (c)  thereafter, grant decree or otherwise dispose of the cause as he thinks fit.

## Transmission of process to Court of Session

**33.86.**—(1)[2]  Where decree has been granted or the cause otherwise disposed of—

    (a)  and the period for making an appeal has elapsed without an appeal being made, or

    (b)  after the determination of the cause on any appeal,

the sheriff clerk shall transmit to the Court of Session the sheriff court process and the documents from the process of the cause in the Court of Session which have been lodged in the sheriff court process.

(2)  A sheriff court process transmitted under paragraph (1) shall form part of the process of the cause in the Court of Session in which the original order was made.

---

[1] As amended by Act of Sederunt (Sheriff Court Ordinary Cause Rules Amendment) (Miscellaneous) 1996 (SI 1996/2445) (effective November 1, 1996) (clerical error).

[2] As amended by the Act of Sederunt (Rules of the Court of Session, Sheriff Appeal Court Rules and Sheriff Court Rules Amendment) (Sheriff Appeal Court) 2015 (SSI 2015/419) r.5 (effective 1 January 2016).

### Remit of application to Court of Session

**33.87.**—(1)  A request for a remit to the Court of Session under section 8(3) of the Act of 1966 shall be made by motion.

(2)  The sheriff shall, in respect of any such motion, order that the cause be remitted to the Court of Session; and, within 4 days after the date of such order, the sheriff clerk shall transmit the whole sheriff court process to the Court of Session.

(3)  A cause remitted to the Court of Session under paragraph (2) shall form part of the process of the cause in the Court of Session in which the original order was made.

Part XIII – Child Support Act 1991

### Interpretation of this Part

**33.88.**[1]  In this Part—

"the Act of 1991" means the Child Support Act 1991;

"child" has the meaning assigned in section 55 of the Act of 1991;

"maintenance calculation" has the meaning assigned in section 54 of the Act of 1991.

### Restriction of expenses

**33.89.**  Where the Secretary of State is named as a defender in an action for declarator of non-parentage or illegitimacy, and the Secretary of State does not defend the action, no expenses shall be awarded against the Secretary of State.

### Effect of maintenance calculations

**33.90.**—(1)[2]  The sheriff clerk shall, on receiving notification that a maintenance calculation has been made, cancelled or has ceased to have effect so as to affect an order of a kind prescribed for the purposes of section 10 of the Act of 1991, endorse on the interlocutor sheet relating to that order a certificate, in Form F39 or F40, as the case may be.

### Effect of maintenance calculations on extracts relating to aliment

**33.91.**—(1)[3]  Where an order relating to aliment is affected by a maintenance calculation, any extract of that order issued by the sheriff clerk shall be endorsed with the following certificate:—

"A maintenance calculation having been made under the Child Support Act 1991 on (*insert date*), this order, in so far as it relates to the making or securing of periodical payments to or for the benefit of (*insert name(s) of child/children*), ceases to have effect from (*insert date 2 days after the date on which the maintenance calculation was made*)."

(2)  Where an order relating to aliment has ceased to have effect on the making of a maintenance calculation, and that maintenance calculation is later cancelled or ceases to have effect, any extract of that order issued by the sheriff clerk shall be

---

[1] As amended by SI 1996/2445 (effective November 1, 1996) and the Act of Sederunt (Ordinary Cause, Summary Application, Summary Cause and Small Claim Rules) Amendment (Miscellaneous) 2003 (SSI 2003/26), para.2(10) (effective January 24, 2003).

[2] As amended by the Act of Sederunt (Ordinary Cause, Summary Application, Summary Cause and Small Claim Rules) Amendment (Miscellaneous) 2003 (SSI 2003/26), para.2(11) (effective January 24, 2003).

[3] As amended by the Act of Sederunt (Ordinary Cause, Summary Application, Summary Cause and Small Claim Rules) Amendment (Miscellaneous) 2003 (SSI 2003/26), para.2(12) (effective January 24, 2003).

endorsed also with the following certificate:—

"The jurisdiction of the child support officer under the Child Support Act 1991 having terminated on (*insert date*), this order, in so far as it relates to (*insert name(s) of child/children*), again shall have effect as from (*insert date of termination of child support officer's jurisdiction*).".

### Applications to recall or vary an interdict

**33.91A.**[1] An application under section 32L(11)(b) of the Act of 1991 (orders preventing avoidance) for the variation or recall of an order for interdict is to be made by minute in the process of the action to which the application relates.

#### Part XIV – Referrals to Principal Reporter

**33.92.–33.94.** [*Repealed by the Act of Sederunt (Children's Hearings (Scotland) Act 2011) (Miscellaneous Amendments) 2013 (SI 2013/172) para.5 (effective June 24, 2013).*]

#### Part XV – Management of Money Payable to Children

**33.95.** Where the sheriff has made an order under section 13 of the Act of 1995 (awards of damages to children), an application by a person for an order by virtue of section 11(1)(d) of that Act (administration of child's property) may be made in the process of the cause in which the order under section 13 of that Act was made.

#### Part XVI[2] – Action of Declarator of Recognition or Non-recognition of a Foreign Decree

### Action of declarator in relation to certain foreign decrees

**33.96.**—(1)[3] This rule applies to an action for declarator of recognition, or non-recognition, of—

    (a)  a decree of divorce, nullity or separation granted outwith a member state of the European Union;

    (b)  a decree of divorce, nullity of separation in respect of a same sex marriage when granted in a member state of the European Union.

(2)  In an action to which this rule applies, the pursuer shall state in the condescendence of the initial writ—

    (a)  the court, tribunal or other authority which granted the decree;

    (b)  the date of the decree of divorce, annulment or separation to which the action relates;

    (c)  the date and place of the marriage to which the decree of divorce, nullity or separation relates;

    (d)  the basis on which the court has jurisdiction to entertain the action;

    (e)  whether to the pursuer's knowledge any other proceedings whether in Scotland or in any other country are continuing in respect of the marriage to which the action relates or are capable of affecting its validity or subsistence; and

    (f)  where such proceedings are continuing—

---

[1] As inserted by the Act of Sederunt (Ordinary Cause Rules) Amendment (Child Maintenance and Other Payments Act 2008) 2010 (SSI 2010/120) r.2 (effective April 6, 2010).

[2] As inserted by the Act of Sederunt (Sheriff Court Rules) (Miscellaneous Amendments) (No.2) 2010 (SSI 2010/416) r.8 (effective January 1, 2011).

[3] As amended by the Act of Sederunt (Rules of the Court of Session and Sheriff Court Rules Amendment No.2) (Marriage and Civil Partnership (Scotland) Act 2014) 2014 (SSI 2014/302) r.5 (effective December 16, 2014).

(i) the court, tribunal or authority before which the proceedings have been commenced;

(ii) the date of commencement;

(iii) the names of the parties; and

(iv) the date, or expected date of any proof (or its equivalent), in the proceedings.

(3) Where—

(a) such proceedings are continuing;

(b) the action before the sheriff is defended; and

(c) either—

(i) the initial writ does not contain the statement referred to in paragraph (2)(e), or

(ii) the particulars mentioned in paragraph (2)(f) as set out in the initial writ are incomplete or incorrect,

any defences or minute, as the case may be, lodged by any person to the action shall include that statement and, where appropriate, the further or correct particulars mentioned in paragraph (2)(f).

(4) Unless the sheriff otherwise directs, a declarator of recognition, or non-recognition, of a decree under this rule shall not be granted without there being produced with the initial writ—

(a) the decree in question or a certified copy of the decree;

(b) the marriage extract or equivalent document to which the action relates.

(5) Where a document produced under paragraph (4)(a) or (b) is not in English it shall, unless the sheriff otherwise directs, be accompanied by a translation certified by a notary public or authenticated by affidavit.

(6) For the purposes of this rule, proceedings are continuing at any time after they have commenced and before they are finally disposed of.

Chapter 33A[1]

Civil Partnership Actions

Part I – General Provisions

**Interpretation of this Chapter**

**33A.1.**—(1) In this Chapter, "civil partnership action" means—

(a) an action of dissolution of civil partnership;

(b) an action of separation of civil partners;

(c) an action or application for an order under Chapter 3 or Chapter 4 of Part 3 of the Act of 2004;

(d) an application for a declarator or other order under section 127 of the Act of 2004;

(e) an action or application for financial provision after overseas proceedings as provided for in Schedule 11 to the Act of 2004;

(f)[2] an action for declarator of nullity of civil partnership.

(2) In this Chapter, unless the context otherwise requires—

"the Act of 1985" means the Family Law (Scotland) Act 1985;

"the Act of 1995" means the Children (Scotland) Act 1995;

---

[1] Inserted by Act of Sederunt (Ordinary Cause Rules) Amendment (Civil Partnership Act 2004) 2005 (SSI 2005/638), para.2 (effective December 8, 2005).

[2] Inserted by Act of Sederunt (Ordinary Cause Rules) Amendment (Family Law (Scotland) Act 2006 etc.) 2006, para.2 (SSI 2006/207) (effective May 4, 2006).

"the Act of 2004" means the Civil Partnership Act 2004;

"civil partnership" has the meaning assigned in section 1(1) of the Act of 2004;

"contact order" has the meaning assigned in section 11(2)(d) of the Act of 1995;

"Gender Recognition Panel" is to be construed in accordance with Schedule 1 to the Gender Recognition Act 2004;

"interim gender recognition certificate" means the certificate issued under section 4 of the Gender Recognition Act 2004;

"local authority" means a council constituted under section 2 of the Local Government etc. (Scotland) Act 1994;

"mental disorder" has the meaning assigned in section 328 of the Mental Health (Care and Treatment) (Scotland) Act 2003;

"order for financial provision" means, except in Part VII of this Chapter (financial provision after overseas proceedings as provided for in Schedule 11 to the Act of 2004), an order mentioned in section 8(1) of the Act of 1985;

"parental responsibilities" has the meaning assigned in section 1(3) of the Act of 1995;

"parental rights" has the meaning assigned in section 2(4) of the Act of 1995;

"relevant interdict" has the meaning assigned in section 113(2) of the Act of 2004;

"residence order" has the meaning assigned in section 11(2)(c) of the Act of 1995;

"section 11 order" means an order under section 11 of the Act of 1995.

(3) For the purposes of rules 33A.2 (averments in actions of dissolution of civil partnership or separation of civil partners about other proceedings) and 33A.3 (averments where section 11 order sought) and, in relation to proceedings in another jurisdiction, Part XIII of this Chapter (sisting of civil partnership actions in Scotland), proceedings are continuing at any time after they have commenced and before they are finally disposed of.

### Averments in certain civil partnership actions about other proceedings[1]

**33A.2.**—(1)[2] This rule applies to an action of dissolution or declarator of nullity of civil partnership or separation of civil partners.

(2) In an action to which this rule applies, the pursuer shall state in the condescendence of the initial writ—

    (a) whether to his knowledge any proceedings are continuing in Scotland or in any other country in respect of the civil partnership to which the initial writ relates or are capable of affecting its validity or subsistence; and

    (b) where such proceedings are continuing—

        (i) the court, tribunal or authority before which the proceedings have been commenced;

        (ii) the date of commencement;

        (iii) the names of the parties;

        (iv) the date, or expected date of any proof (or its equivalent) in the proceedings; and

        (v) such other facts as may be relevant to the question of whether or

---

[1] As amended by Act of Sederunt (Ordinary Cause Rules) Amendment (Family Law (Scotland) Act 2006 etc.) 2006, para.2 (SSI 2006/207) (effective May 4, 2006).

[2] As amended by Act of Sederunt (Ordinary Cause Rules) Amendment (Family Law (Scotland) Act 2006 etc.) 2006, para.2 (SSI 2006/207) (effective May 4, 2006).

not the action before the sheriff should be sisted under Part XIII of this Chapter.

(3) Where—

    (a)   such proceedings are continuing;

    (b)   the action before the sheriff is defended; and

    (c)   either—

        (i)   the initial writ does not contain the statement referred to in paragraph (2)(a); or

        (ii)   the particulars mentioned in paragraph (2)(b) as set out in the initial writ are incomplete or incorrect,

any defences or minute, as the case may be, lodged by any person to the action shall include that statement and, where appropriate, the further or correct particulars mentioned in paragraph (2)(b).

### Averments where section 11 order sought

**33A.3.**—(1) A party to a civil partnership action who makes an application in that action for a section 11 order in respect of a child shall include in his pleadings—

    (a)[1]   where that action is an action of dissolution or declarator of nullity of civil partnership or separation of civil partners, averments giving particulars of any other proceedings known to him, whether in Scotland or elsewhere and whether concluded or not, which relate to the child in respect of whom the section 11 order is sought;

    (b)   (b) in any other civil partnership action—

        (i)   the averments mentioned in paragraph (a); and

        (ii)   averments giving particulars of any proceedings known to him which are continuing, whether in Scotland or elsewhere, and which relate to the civil partnership of either of the parents of that child.

    (c)[2]   where the party seeks an order such as is mentioned in any of paragraphs (a) to (e) of subsection (2) of that section, an averment that no permanence order (as defined in section 80(2) of the Adoption and Children (Scotland) Act 2007) is in force in respect of the child.

(2) Where such other proceedings are continuing or have taken place and the averments of the applicant for such a section 11 order—

    (a)   do not contain particulars of the other proceedings, or

    (b)   contain particulars which are incomplete or incorrect,

any defences or minute, as the case may be, lodged by any party to the civil partnership action shall include such particulars or such further or correct particulars as are known to him.

(3) In paragraph 1(b)(ii), "child" includes a child of the family within the meaning assigned in section 101(7) of the Act of 2004.

### Averments where identity or address of person not known

**33A.4.** In a civil partnership action, where the identity or address of any person referred to in rule 33A.7 as a person in respect of whom a warrant for intimation requires to be applied for is not known and cannot reasonably be ascertained, the

---

[1] As amended by Act of Sederunt (Ordinary Cause Rules) Amendment (Family Law (Scotland) Act 2006 etc.) 2006, para.2 (SSI 2006/207) (effective May 4, 2006).

[2] As inserted by the Act of Sederunt (Sheriff Court Rules Amendment) (Adoption and Children (Scotland) Act 2007) 2009 (SSI 2009/284) (effective September 28, 2009).

party required to apply for the warrant shall include in his pleadings an averment of that fact and averments setting out what steps have been taken to ascertain the identity or address, as the case may be, of that person.

### Averments about maintenance orders

**33A.5.** In a civil partnership action in which an order for aliment or periodical allowance is sought, or is sought to be varied or recalled, by any party, the pleadings of that party shall contain an averment stating whether and, if so, when and by whom, a maintenance order (within the meaning of section 106 of the Debtors (Scotland) Act 1987) has been granted in favour of or against that party or of any other person in respect of whom the order is sought.

### Averments where aliment or financial provision sought

**33A.6.**—(1) In this rule—

"the Act of 1991" means the Child Support Act 1991;
"child" has the meaning assigned in section 55 of the Act of 1991;
"crave relating to aliment" means—

    (a) for the purposes of paragraph (2), a crave for decree of aliment in relation to a child or for recall or variation of such a decree; and

    (b) for the purposes of paragraph (3), a crave for decree of aliment in relation to a child or for recall or variation of such a decree or for the variation or termination of an agreement on aliment in relation to a child;

"maintenance calculation" has the meaning assigned in section 54 of the Act of 1991.

(2) A civil partnership action containing a crave relating to aliment and to which section 8(6), (7), (8), or (10) of the Act of 1991 (top up maintenance orders) applies shall—

    (a) include averments stating, where appropriate—

        (i) that a maintenance calculation under section 11 of that Act (maintenance calculations) is in force;

        (ii) the date of the maintenance calculation;

        (iii) the amount and frequency of periodical payments of child support maintenance fixed by the maintenance calculation; and

        (iv) the grounds on which the sheriff retains jurisdiction under section 8(6), (7), (8) or (10) of that Act; and

    (b) unless the sheriff on cause shown otherwise directs, be accompanied by any document issued by the Secretary of State to the party intimating the making of the maintenance calculation referred to in sub paragraph (a).

(3) A civil partnership action containing a crave relating to aliment, and to which section 8(6), (7), (8) or (10) of the Act of 1991 does not apply, shall include averments stating—

    (a) that the habitual residence of the absent parent, person with care of qualifying child, within the meaning of section 3 of that Act, is further of the United Kingdom; or

    (b) that the child is not a child within the meaning of section 55 of that Act.

(4) A civil partnership action involving parties in respect of whom a decision has been made in any application, review or appeal under the Act of 1991 relating to any child of those parties, shall—

(a) include averments stating that such a decision has been made and giving details of that decision; and

(b) unless the sheriff on cause shown otherwise directs, be accompanied by any document issued by the Secretary of State to the parties intimating that decision.

### Warrants and forms for intimation

**33A.7.**—(1) Subject to paragraphs (5) and (7), in the initial writ in a civil partnership action, the pursuer shall include a crave for a warrant for intimation—

(a) in an action where the address of the defender is not known to the pursuer and cannot reasonably be ascertained, to—

    (i) every person who was a child of the family (within the meaning of section 101(7) of the Act of 2004) and who has reached the age of 16 years, and

    (ii) one of the next of kin of the defender who has reached that age,

unless the address of such a person is not known to the pursuer and cannot reasonably be ascertained, and a notice of intimation in Form CP1 shall be attached to the copy of the initial writ intimated to any such person;

(b) in an action where the defender is a person who is suffering from a mental disorder, to—

    (i) those persons mentioned in sub paragraph (a)(i) and (ii), unless the address of such person is not known to the pursuer and cannot reasonably be ascertained; and

    (ii) any person who holds the office of guardian, or continuing or welfare attorney to the defender under or by virtue of the Adults with Incapacity (Scotland) Act 2000,

and a notice of intimation in Form CP2 shall be attached to the copy of the initial writ intimated to any such person;

(c)[1] in an action of dissolution or declarator of nullity of civil partnership or separation of civil partners where the sheriff may make a section 11 order in respect of a child—

    (i) who is in the care of a local authority, to that authority and a notice of intimation in Form CP3 shall be attached to the initial writ intimated to that authority;

    (ii) who, being a child of one party to the civil partnership, has been accepted as a child of the family by the other party to the civil partnership and who is liable to be maintained by a third party, to that third party, and a notice of intimation in Form CP3 shall be attached to the initial writ intimated to that third party; or

    (iii) in respect of whom a third party in fact exercises care or control, to that third party, and a notice of intimation in Form CP4 shall be attached to the initial writ intimated to that third party;

(d) in an action where the pursuer craves a section 11 order, to any parent or guardian of the child who is not a party to the action, and a notice of intimation in Form CP5 shall be attached to the initial writ intimated to any such parent or guardian;

(e) *[Repealed by the Act of Sederunt (Sheriff Court Rules) (Miscellaneous Amendments) (No.2) 2010 (SSI 2010/416) r.7 (effective January 1, 2011).]*

---

[1] As amended by Act of Sederunt (Ordinary Cause Rules) Amendment (Family Law (Scotland) Act 2006 etc.) 2006, para.2 (SSI 2006/207) (effective May 4, 2006).

(f) in an action which includes a crave for a section 11 order, to the child to whom such an order would relate if not a party to the action, and a notice of intimation in Form CP7 shall be intimated to that child;

(g) in an action where the pursuer makes an application for an order under section 8(aa) of the Act of 1985 (transfer of property) and—

    (i) the consent of a third party to such a transfer is necessary by virtue of an obligation, enactment or rule of law, or

    (ii) the property is subject to a security,

to the third party or creditor, as the case may be, and a notice of intimation in Form CP8 shall be attached to the initial writ intimated to any such person;

(h) in an action where the pursuer makes an application for an order under section 18 of the Act of 1985 (which relates to avoidance transactions), to—

    (i) any third party in whose favour the transfer of, or transaction involving, the property is to be or was made, and

    (ii) any other person having an interest in the transfer of, or transaction involving, the property,

and a notice of intimation in Form CP9 shall be attached to the initial writ intimated to any such person;

(i) in an action where the pursuer makes an application for an order under Chapter 3 of Part 3 of the Act of 2004, where the application is under section 102(e), 102(4)(a), 103(1), 103(2), 104, 107 or 112 of that Act, and the entitled civil partner is a tenant or occupies the family home by permission of a third party, to the landlord or the third party, as the case may be and a notice of intimation in Form CP10 shall be attached to the initial writ intimated to any such person;

(j) in an action where the pursuer makes an application for an order under section 8(ba) of the Act of 1985 (orders under section 12A of the Act of 1985 for pension lump sum), to the person responsible for the pension arrangement, and a notice of intimation in Form CP11 shall be attached to the initial writ intimated to any such person;

(k) in an action where a pursuer makes an application for an order under section 8(baa) of the Act of 1985 (pension sharing orders), to the person responsible for the pension arrangement and a notice of intimation in Form CP12 shall be attached to the initial writ intimated to any such person.

(l)[1] in an action where a pursuer makes an application for an order under section 8(1)(bab) of the Act of 1985 (pension compensation sharing order), to the Board of the Pension Protection Fund, and a notice of intimation in Form CP12A shall be attached to the initial writ intimated to that Board; and

(m)[2] in an action where a pursuer makes an application for an order under section 8(1)(bb) of the Act of 1985 (an order under section 12B(2) of the Act of 1985 for pension compensation), to the Board of the Pension Protection Fund and a notice of intimation in Form CP12B shall be attached to the initial writ intimated to that Board.

---

[1] As inserted by the Act of Sederunt (Sheriff Court Rules) (Miscellaneous Amendments) 2011 (SSI 2011/193) r.15 (effective April 6, 2011).

[2] As inserted by the Act of Sederunt (Sheriff Court Rules) (Miscellaneous Amendments) 2011 (SSI 2011/193) r.15 (effective April 6, 2011).

(2) Expressions used in paragraph (1)(i) which are also used in Chapter 3 of Part 3 of the Act of 2004 have the same meaning as in that Chapter.

(3) A notice of intimation under paragraph (1) shall be on a period of notice of 21 days unless the sheriff otherwise orders; but the sheriff shall not order a period of notice of less than 2 days.

(4) *[Repealed by the Act of Sederunt (Sheriff Court Rules) (Miscellaneous Amendments) (No.2) 2010 (SSI 2010/416) r.7 (effective January 1, 2011).]*

(5) Where the address of a person mentioned in paragraph (1)(c), (d), (f), (g), (h), (i), (j) or (k) is not known and cannot reasonably be ascertained, the pursuer shall include a crave in the initial writ to dispense with intimation; and the sheriff may grant that crave or make such other order as he thinks fit.

(6) Where the identity or address of a person to whom intimation of a civil partnership action is required becomes known during the course of the action, the party who would have been required to insert a warrant for intimation to that person shall lodge a motion for a warrant for intimation to that person or to dispense with such intimation.

(7) Where a pursuer considers that to order intimation to a child under paragraph (1)(f) is inappropriate, he shall—

(a) include a crave in the initial writ to dispense with intimation to that child; and

(b) include in the initial writ averments setting out the reasons why such intimation is inappropriate;

and the sheriff may dispense with such intimation or make such other order as he thinks fit.

### Intimation where alleged association

**33A.8.**—(1) In a civil partnership action where the pursuer founds upon an alleged association between the defender and another named person, the pursuer shall, immediately after the expiry of the period of notice, lodge a motion for an order for intimation to that person or to dispense with such intimation.

(2) In determining a motion under paragraph (1), the sheriff may—

(a) make such order for intimation as he thinks fit; or

(b) dispense with intimation; and

(c) where he dispenses with intimation, order that the name of that person be deleted from the condescendence of the initial writ.

(3) Where intimation is ordered under paragraph (2), a copy of the initial writ and an intimation in Form CP13 shall be intimated to the named person.

(4) In paragraph (1), "association" means sodomy, incest, or any homosexual or heterosexual relationship.

### Productions in action of dissolution of civil partnership or where a section 11 order or order for financial provision may be made[1]

**33A.9.**—(1) This rule applies unless the sheriff directs otherwise.

(2)[2] In an action of dissolution or declarator of nullity of civil partnership, a warrant for citation shall not be granted without there being produced with the initial writ—

---

[1] As amended by the Act of Sederunt (Sheriff Court Rules) (Miscellaneous Amendments) 2012 (SSI 2012/188) para.4 (effective August 1, 2012).

[2] As amended by Act of Sederunt (Ordinary Cause Rules) Amendment (Family Law (Scotland) Act 2006 etc.) 2006, para.2 (SSI 2006/207) (effective May 4, 2006).

(a) an extract of the relevant entry in the civil partnership register or an equivalent document; and

(b) where the ground of action is that an interim gender recognition certificate has, after the date of registration of the civil partnership, been issued to either of the civil partners—

    (i) where the pursuer is the subject of the interim gender recognition certificate, the interim gender recognition certificate or, failing that, a certified copy of the interim gender recognition certificate; or

    (ii) where the defender is the subject of the interim gender recognition certificate, a certified copy of the interim gender recognition certificate.

(3) In a civil partnership action which includes a crave for a section 11 order, warrant for citation shall not be granted without there being produced with the initial writ an extract of the relevant entry in the register of births or an equivalent document.

(4) For the purposes of this rule, a certified copy of an interim gender recognition certificate shall be a copy of that certificate sealed with the seal of the Gender Recognition Panels and certified to be a true copy by an officer authorised by the President of Gender Recognition Panels.

(5)[1] In a civil partnership action which includes a crave for an order for financial provision, the pursuer must lodge a completed Form CP13A signed by the pursuer with the initial writ or minute of amendment as the case may be.

### Warrant of citation

**33A.10.** The warrant of citation in a civil partnership action shall be in Form CP14.

### Form of citation and certificate

**33A.11.**—(1) Subject to rule 5.6 (service where address of person is not known) citation of a defender shall be in Form CP15, which shall be attached to a copy of the initial writ and warrant of citation and shall have appended to it a notice of intention to defend in Form CP16.

(2) The certificate of citation shall be in Form CP17 which shall be attached to the initial writ.

### Intimation to local authority

**33A.12.**—(1) In any civil partnership action where the pursuer craves a residence order in respect of a child, the sheriff may, if the sheriff thinks fit, order intimation to the local authority in which area the pursuer resides; and such intimation shall be in Form CP6.

(2) Where an order for intimation is made under paragraph (1), intimation to that local authority shall be given within 7 days after the date on which an order for intimation has been made.

### Service in cases of mental disorder of defender

**33A.13.**—(1) In a civil partnership action where the defender suffers or appears to suffer from mental disorder and is resident in a hospital or other similar institu-

---

[1] As inserted by the Act of Sederunt (Sheriff Court Rules) (Miscellaneous Amendments) 2012 (SSI 2012/188) para.4 (effective August 1, 2012).

tion, citation shall be executed by registered post or the first class recorded delivery service addressed to the medical officer in charge of that hospital or institution; and there shall be included with the copy of the initial writ—

    (a)   a citation in Form CP15;

    (b)   any notice required by rule 33A.14(1);

    (c)   a request in Form CP18;

    (d)   a form of certificate in Form CP19 requesting the medical officer to—

        (i)   deliver and explain the initial writ, citation and any notice or form of notice of consent required under rule 33A.14(1) personally to the defender; or

        (ii)   certify that such delivery or explanation would be dangerous to the health or mental condition of the defender; and

    (e)   a stamped envelope addressed for return of that certificate to the pursuer or his solicitor, if he has one.

(2)   The medical officer referred to in paragraph (1) shall send the certificate in Form CP19 duly completed to the pursuer or his solicitor, as the case may be.

(3)   The certificate mentioned in paragraph (2) shall be attached to the certificate of citation.

(4)   Where such a certificate bears that the initial writ has not been delivered to the defender, the sheriff may, at any time before decree—

    (a)   order such further medical inquiry, and

    (b)   make such order for further service or intimation,

as he thinks fit.

### Notices in certain actions of dissolution of civil partnership or separation of civil partners

**33A.14.**—(1)  In the following actions of dissolution of civil partnership or separation of civil partners there shall be attached to the copy of the initial writ served on the defender—

    (a)[1]   in an action relying on section 117(3)(c) of the Act of 2004 (no cohabitation for one year with consent of defender to decree)—

        (i)   which is an action of dissolution of civil partnership, a notice in Form CP20 and a notice of consent in Form CP21;

        (ii)   which is an action of separation of civil partners, a notice in Form CP22 and a form of notice of consent in Form CP23;

    (b)[2]   in an action relying on section 117(3)(d) of the Act of 2004 (no cohabitation for two years)—

        (i)   which is an action of dissolution of civil partnership, a notice in Form CP24;

        (ii)   which is an action of separation of civil partners, a notice in Form CP25.

    (c)[3]   in an action relying on section 117(2)(b) of the Act of 2004 (grounds of dissolution: interim gender recognition certificate), a notice in Form CP25A.

---

[1] As amended by Act of Sederunt (Ordinary Cause Rules) Amendment (Family Law (Scotland) Act 2006 etc.) 2006, para.2 (SSI 2006/207) (effective May 4, 2006).
[2] As amended by Act of Sederunt (Ordinary Cause Rules) Amendment (Family Law (Scotland) Act 2006 etc.) 2006, para.2 (SSI 2006/207) (effective May 4, 2006).
[3] Inserted by Act of Sederunt (Ordinary Cause Rules) Amendment (Family Law (Scotland) Act 2006 etc.) 2006, para.2 (SSI 2006/207) (effective May 4, 2006).

(2) The certificate of citation of an initial writ in an action mentioned i paragraph (1) shall state which notice or form mentioned in paragraph (1) has bee attached to the initial writ.

**Orders for intimation**

**33A.15.**—(1) In any civil partnership action, the sheriff may, at any time—

   (a)  subject to paragraph (2), order intimation to be made on such person as h thinks fit;

   (b)  postpone intimation, where he considers that such postponement is ap propriate and, in that case, the sheriff shall make such order in respect o postponement of intimation as he thinks fit; or

   (c)  dispense with intimation, where he considers that such dispensation i appropriate.

(2) Where the sheriff is considering whether to make a section 11 order by virtu of section 12 of the Act of 1995 (restrictions on decrees for dissolution of civi partnership, separation or annulment affecting children), he shall, subject t paragraph (1)(c) and without prejudice to paragraph (1)(b) of this rule, order intima tion in Form CP7 to the child to whom the section 11 order would relate unless—

   (a)  intimation has been given to the child under rule 33A.7(1)(f); or

   (b)  the sheriff considers that the child is not of sufficient age or maturity t express his views.

(3) Where a party makes a crave or averment in a civil partnership action which had it been made in an initial writ, would have required a warrant for intimatio under rule 33.7, that party shall include a crave in his writ for a warrant for intima tion or to dispense with such intimation; and rule 33A.7 shall, with the necessar modifications, apply to a crave for a warrant under this paragraph as it applies to crave for a warrant under that rule.

**Appointment of curators ad litem to defenders**

**33A.16.**—(1)[1, 2] This rule applies to a civil partnership action where it appears t the court that the defender is suffering from a mental disorder.

(2) In an action to which this rule applies, the sheriff shall—

   (a)  appoint a curator ad litem to the defender;

   (b)[3]  where the facts set out in section 117(3)(c) of the Act of 2004 (no cohabita tion for one year with consent of defender to decree) are relied on—

      (i)  make an order for intimation of the ground of the action to th Mental Welfare Commission for Scotland; and

      (ii)  include in such an order a requirement that the Commission send to the sheriff clerk a report indicating whether in its opinion th defender is capable of deciding whether or not to give consent t the granting of decree.

(3) Within 7 days after the appointment of a curator ad litem under paragraph (2)(a), the pursuer shall send to him—

   (a)  a copy of the initial writ and any defences (including any adjustments and amendments) lodged; and

---

[1] As amended by Act of Sederunt (Ordinary Cause Rules) Amendment (Family Law (Scotland) Ac 2006 etc.) 2006, para.2 (SSI 2006/207) (effective May 4, 2006).

[2] As amended by the Act of Sederunt (Sheriff Court Rules) (Miscellaneous Amendments) 2012 (SS 2012/188) para.6 (effective August 1, 2012).

[3] As amended by Act of Sederunt (Ordinary Cause Rules) Amendment (Family Law (Scotland) Ac 2006 etc.) 2006, para.2 (SSI 2006/207) (effective May 4, 2006).

    (b)   a copy of any notice in Form G5 sent to him by the sheriff clerk.

(4) On receipt of a report required under paragraph (2)(b)(ii), the sheriff clerk shall—

    (a)   lodge the report in process; and

    (b)   intimate that this has been done to—

        (i)   the pursuer;

        (ii)   the solicitor for the defender, if known; and

        (iii)   the curator ad litem.

(5) The curator ad litem shall lodge in process one of the writs mentioned in paragraph (6)—

    (a)   within 14 days after the report required under paragraph (2)(b)(ii) has been lodged in process; or

    (b)   where no such report is required, within 21 days after the date of his appointment under paragraph (2)(a).

(6) The writs referred to in paragraph (5) are—

    (a)   a notice of intention to defend;

    (b)   defences to the action;

    (c)   a minute adopting defences already lodged; and

    (d)   a minute stating that the curator ad litem does not intend to lodge defences.

(7) Notwithstanding that he has lodged a minute stating that he does not intend to lodge defences, a curator ad litem may appear at any stage of the action to protect the interests of the defender.

(8) If, at any time, it appears to the curator ad litem that the defender is not suffering from mental disorder, he may report that fact to the court and seek his own discharge.

(9) The pursuer shall be responsible, in the first instance, for payment of the fees and outlays of the curator ad litem incurred during the period from his appointment until—

    (a)   he lodges a minute stating that he does not intend to lodge defences;

    (b)   he decides to instruct the lodging of defences or a minute adopting defences already lodged; or

    (c)   being satisfied after investigation that the defender is not suffering from mental disorder, he is discharged.

### Applications for sist

**33A.17.** An application for a sist, or the recall of a sist, under Part XIII of this Chapter shall be made by written motion.

### Notices of consent to dissolution of civil partnership or separation of civil partners

**33A.18.**—(1)[1] Where, in an action of dissolution of civil partnership or separation of civil partners in which the facts in section 117(3)(c) of the Act of 2004 (no cohabitation for one year with consent of defender to decree) are relied on, the defender wishes to consent to the grant of decree of dissolution of civil partnership or separation of civil partners he shall do so by giving notice in writing in Form CP21 (dissolution) or Form CP23 (separation), as the case may be, to the sheriff clerk.

---

[1] As amended by Act of Sederunt (Ordinary Cause Rules) Amendment (Family Law (Scotland) Act 2006 etc.) 2006, para.2 (SSI 2006/207) (effective May 4, 2006).

(2)  The evidence of one witness shall be sufficient for the purpose of establishing that the signature on a notice of consent under paragraph (1) is that of the defender.

(3)  In an action of dissolution of civil partnership or separation of civil partners where the initial writ includes, for the purposes of section 117(3)(c) of the Act of 2004, an averment that the defender consents to the grant of decree, the defender may give notice by letter sent to the sheriff clerk stating that he has not so consented or that he withdraws any consent which he has already given.

(4)  On receipt of a letter under paragraph (3), the sheriff clerk shall intimate the terms of the letter to the pursuer.

(5)  On receipt of any intimation under paragraph (4), the pursuer may, within 14 days after the date of the intimation, if none of the other facts mentioned in section 117(3) of the Act of 2004 is averred in the initial writ, lodge a motion for the action to be sisted.

(6)  If no such motion is lodged, the pursuer shall be deemed to have abandoned the action and the action shall be dismissed.

(7)  If a motion under paragraph (5) is granted and the sist is not recalled or renewed within a period of 6 months from the date of the interlocutor granting the sist, the pursuer shall be deemed to have abandoned the action and the action shall be dismissed.

### Procedure in respect of children

**33A.19.**—(1)  In a civil partnership action, in relation to any matter affecting a child, where that child has—

    (a)   returned to the sheriff clerk Form CP7, or

    (b)   otherwise indicated to the court a wish to express views on a matter affecting him, the sheriff shall not grant any order unless an opportunity has been given for the views of that child to be obtained or heard.

(2)  Where a child has indicated his wish to express his views, the sheriff shall order such steps to be taken as he considers appropriate to ascertain the views of that child.

(3)  The sheriff shall not grant an order in a civil partnership action, in relation to any matter affecting a child who has indicated his wish to express his views, unless due weight has been given by the sheriff to the views expressed by that child, having due regard to his age and maturity.

### Recording of views of the child

**33A.20.**—(1)  This rule applies where a child expresses a view on a matter affecting him whether expressed personally to the sheriff or to a person appointed by the sheriff for that purpose or provided by the child in writing.

(2)  The sheriff, or the person appointed by the sheriff, shall record the views of the child in writing; and the sheriff may direct that such views, and any written views, given by a child shall—

    (a)   be sealed in an envelope marked "Views of the child confidential";

    (b)   be kept in the court process without being recorded in the inventory of process;

    (c)   be available to a sheriff only;

    (d)   not be opened by any person other than a sheriff; and

    (e)   not form a borrowable part of the process.

## Child welfare reporters

**33A.21.**[1](1)   At any stage of a civil partnership action the sheriff may, in relation to any matter affecting a child, appoint a person (referred to in this rule as a "child welfare reporter")—

   (a)   to seek the views of the child and to report any views expressed by the child to the court; or

   (b)   to undertake enquiries and to report to the court.

(2)   A child welfare reporter may only be appointed under paragraph (1)(b) where the sheriff is satisfied that the appointment—

   (a)   is in the best interests of the child; and

   (b)   will promote the effective and expeditious determination of an issue in relation to the child.

(3)   An interlocutor appointing a child welfare reporter must—

   (a)   specify a date by which the report is to be submitted to the court;

   (b)   include a direction as to the fees and outlays of the child welfare reporter;

   (c)   where the appointment is under paragraph (1)(a), specify the issues in respect of which the child's views are to be sought; and

   (d)   where the appointment is under paragraph (1)(b), specify the enquiries to be undertaken, and the issues requiring to be addressed in the report.

(4)   An interlocutor complies with subparagraph (c) or (d) of paragraph (3) if the issues or, as the case may be the enquiries, referred to in that subparagraph are specified in an annex to the interlocutor in Form CP38.

(5)   Where the sheriff has appointed a child welfare reporter with a view to the report being considered at an assigned hearing, the date specified in accordance with paragraph (3)(a) must be a date no less than three clear days before that hearing, excluding any day on which the sheriff clerk's office is not open for civil court business, unless cause exists for specifying a later date.

(6)[2]   On appointing a child welfare reporter the sheriff may also—

   (a)   make such further order as may be required to facilitate the discharge of the child welfare reporter's functions;

   (b)   direct that a party to the proceedings is to be responsible for providing the child welfare reporter with copies of such documents lodged in the process as may be specified; and

   (c)   give the child welfare reporter directions.

(7)   The direction referred to in paragraph (3)(b) must assign liability for payment of the child welfare reporter's fees and outlays in the first instance, and require that liability to be borne—

   (a)   in equal shares by—

      (i)   the pursuer,

      (ii)   any defender who has lodged a notice of intention to defend, and

      (iii)   any minuter who has been granted leave to enter the process; or

   (b)   by one or more parties to the proceedings on such other basis as may be justified on cause shown.

(8)   On the granting of an interlocutor appointing a child welfare reporter the sheriff clerk must—

---

[1] As substituted by the Act of Sederunt (Rules of the Court of Session 1994 and Sheriff Court Rules Amendment) (Miscellaneous) 2016 (SSI 2016/102) r.3 (effective 21 March 2016).
[2] As amended by the Act of Sederunt (Sheriff Appeal Court Rules 2015 and Sheriff Court Rules Amendment) (Miscellaneous) 2016 (SSI 2016/194) r.3 (effective 7 July 2016).

(a) give the child welfare reporter—
    (i) a certified copy of the interlocutor, and
    (ii) sufficient information to enable the child welfare reporter t
    contact the solicitor for each party to the proceedings, or any part
    not represented by a solicitor; and

(b) intimate the name and address of the child welfare reporter to any loca
authority to which intimation of the proceedings has been made.

(9) A child welfare reporter appointed under this rule must—
  (a) where the appointment is under paragraph (1)(a)—
    (i) seek the child's views on the specified issues, and
    (ii) prepare a report for the court reporting any such views;
  (b) where the appointment is under paragraph (1)(b)—
    (i) undertake the specified enquiries, and
    (ii) prepare a report for the court having regard to the specified issues
  (c) send the report to the sheriff clerk by the date specified; and
  (d) unless otherwise directed, send a copy of the report to each party to the
  proceedings by that date.

(10) A child welfare reporter may—
  (a) apply to the sheriff clerk to be given further directions by the sheriff;
  (b) bring to the attention of the sheriff clerk any impediment to the perfor
  mance of any function arising under this rule.

(11) Where a child welfare reporter acts as referred to in paragraph (10), th
sheriff may, having heard parties, make any order or direction that could competentl
have been made under paragraph (6).

## Appointment of local authority to report on a child

**33A.21A.**[1](1) This rule applies where, in a civil partnership action, the sherif
appoints a local authority to investigate and report to the court on the circumstance
of a child and on the proposed arrangements for the care and upbringing of a child.

(2) The following provisions of rule 33A.21 apply as if the reference to the chil
welfare reporter was a reference to the local authority appointed by the sheriff—
  (a) paragraph (3)(a) and (b);
  (b) paragraph (6)(a) and (b);
  (c) paragraph (7); and
  (d) paragraph (8).

(3) On completion of the report referred to in paragraph (1), the local authority
must—

  (a) send the report to the sheriff clerk; and
  (b) unless otherwise directed by the sheriff, send a copy of the report to each
  party to the proceedings.

## Referral to family mediation

**33A.22.** In any civil partnership action in which an order in relation to parenta
responsibilities or parental rights is in issue, the sheriff may, at any stage of the action, where he considers it appropriate to do so, refer that issue to a mediator accredited to a specified family mediation organisation.

---

[1] As inserted by the Act of Sederunt (Rules of the Court of Session 1994 and Sheriff Court Rules
Amendment) (Miscellaneous) 2016 (SSI 2016/102) r.3 (effective 21 March 2016).

## Child Welfare Hearing

**33A.23.**—(1) Where—

(a) on the lodging of a notice of intention to defend in a civil partnership action in which the initial writ seeks or includes a crave for a section 11 order, a defender wishes to oppose any such crave or order, or seeks the same order as that craved by the pursuer,

(b) on the lodging of a notice of intention to defend in a civil partnership action, the defender seeks a section 11 order which is not craved by the pursuer, or

(c) in any other circumstances in a civil partnership action, the sheriff considers that a Child Welfare Hearing should be fixed and makes an order (whether at his own instance or on the motion of a party) that such a hearing shall be fixed,

the sheriff clerk shall fix a date and time for a Child Welfare Hearing on the first suitable court date occurring not sooner than 21 days after the lodging of such notice of intention to defend, unless the sheriff directs the hearing to be held on an earlier date.

(2) On fixing the date for the Child Welfare Hearing, the sheriff clerk shall intimate the date of the Child Welfare Hearing to the parties in Form CP26.

(3) The fixing of the date of the Child Welfare Hearing shall not affect the right of a party to make any other application to the court whether by motion or otherwise.

(4)[1] At the Child Welfare Hearing (which may be held in private), the sheriff shall seek to secure the expeditious resolution of disputes in relation to the child by ascertaining from the parties the matters in dispute and any information relevant to that dispute, and may—

(a) order such steps to be taken, make such order, if any, or order further procedure, as he thinks fit, and

(b) ascertain whether there is or is likely to be a vulnerable witness within the meaning of section 11(1) of the Act of 2004 who is to give evidence at any proof or hearing and whether any order under section 12(1) of the Act of 2004 requires to be made.

(5) All parties (including a child who has indicated his wish to attend) shall, except on cause shown, attend the Child Welfare Hearing personally.

(6) It shall be the duty of the parties to provide the sheriff with sufficient information to enable him to conduct the Child Welfare Hearing.

## Applications for orders to disclose whereabouts of children

**33A.24.**—(1) An application in a civil partnership action for an order under section 33(1) of the Family Law Act 1986 (which relates to the disclosure of the whereabouts of a child) shall be made by motion.

(2) Where the sheriff makes an order under section 33(1) of the Family Law Act 1986, he may ordain the person against whom the order has been made to appear before him or to lodge an affidavit.

## Applications in relation to removal of children

**33A.25.**—(1) An application in a civil partnership action for leave under section 51(1) of the Children Act 1975 (authority to remove a child from the care and pos-

---

[1] As substituted by the Act of Sederunt (Ordinary Cause, Summary Application, Summary Cause and Small Claim Rules) Amendment (Vulnerable Witnesses (Scotland) Act 2004) 2007, r.2(10) (effective November 1, 2007).

session of the applicant for a residence order) or for an order under section 35(3) of the Family Law Act 1986 (application for interdict or interim interdict prohibiting removal of child from jurisdiction) shall be made—

    (a)  by a party to the action, by motion; or

    (b)  by a person who is not a party to the action, by minute.

  (2)  An application under section 35(3) of the Family Law Act 1986 need not be served or intimated.

  (3)  An application in a civil partnership action under section 23(2) of the Child Abduction and Custody Act 1985 (declarator that removal of child from United Kingdom was unlawful) shall be made—

    (a)  in an action depending before the sheriff—

        (i)  by a party, in the initial writ, defences or minute, as the case may be, or by motion; or

        (ii)  by any other person, by minute; or

    (b)  after final decree, by minute in the process of the action to which the application relates.

### Intimation to local authority before supervised contact order

**33A.26.**  Where in a civil partnership action the sheriff, at his own instance or on the motion of a party, is considering making a contact order or an interim contact order subject to supervision by the social work department of a local authority, he shall ordain the party moving for such an order to intimate to the chief executive of that local authority (where not already a party to the action and represented at the hearing at which the issue arises)—

    (a)  the terms of any relevant motion;

    (b)  the intention of the sheriff to order that the contact order be supervised by the social work department of that local authority; and

    (c)  that the local authority shall, within such period as the sheriff has determined—

        (i)  notify the sheriff clerk whether it intends to make representations to the sheriff; and

        (ii)  where it intends to make representations in writing, do so within that period.

### Joint minutes

**33A.27.**  Where any parties in a civil partnership action have reached agreement in relation to—

    (a)  a section 11 order;

    (b)  aliment for a child; or

    (c)  an order for financial provision,

a joint minute may be entered into expressing that agreement; and, subject to rule 33A.19(3) (no order before views of child expressed), the sheriff may grant decree in respect of those parts of the joint minute in relation to which he could otherwise make an order, whether or not such a decree would include a matter for which there was no crave.

**Affidavits**

**33A.28.** The sheriff in a civil partnership action may accept evidence by affidavit at any hearing for an order or interim order.

Part II – Undefended Civil Partnership Actions

## Evidence in certain undefended civil partnership actions

**33A.29.**—(1)  This rule—

(a)  subject to sub paragraph (b), applies to all civil partnership actions in which no notice of intention to defend has been lodged, other than a civil partnership action—

(i)  for financial provision after overseas proceedings as provided for in Schedule 11 to the Act of 2004; or

(ii)  for an order under Chapter 3 or Chapter 4 of Part 3 or section 127 of the Act of 2004;

(b)  applies to a civil partnership action in which a curator ad litem has been appointed under rule 33A.16 where the curator ad litem to the defender has lodged a minute intimating that he does not intend to lodge defences;

(c)  applies to any civil partnership action which proceeds at any stage as undefended where the sheriff so directs;

(d)  applies to the merits of a civil partnership action which is undefended on the merits where the sheriff so directs, notwithstanding that the action is defended on an ancillary matter.

(2)  Unless the sheriff otherwise directs, evidence shall be given by affidavits.

(3)  Unless the sheriff otherwise directs, evidence relating to the welfare of a child shall be given by affidavit, at least one affidavit being emitted by a person other than a parent or party to the action.

(4)  Evidence in the form of a written statement bearing to be the professional opinion of a duly qualified medical practitioner, which has been signed by him and lodged in process, shall be admissible in place of parole evidence by him.

## Procedure for decree in actions under rule 33A.29

**33A.30.**—(1)  In an action to which rule 33A.29 (evidence in certain undefended civil partnership actions) applies, the pursuer shall at any time after the expiry of the period for lodging a notice of intention to defend—

(a)  lodge in process the affidavit evidence; and

(b)  endorse a minute in Form CP27 on the initial writ.

(2)  The sheriff may, at any time after the pursuer has complied with paragraph (1), without requiring the appearance of parties—

(a)  grant decree in terms of the motion for decree; or

(b)  remit the cause for such further procedure, if any, including proof by parole evidence, as the sheriff thinks fit.

## Extracts of undefended decree

**33A.31**  In an action to which rule 33A.29 (evidence in certain undefended civil partnership actions) applies, the sheriff clerk shall, after the expiry of 14 days after the grant of decree under rule 33A.30 (procedure for decree in actions under rule 33A.29), issue to the pursuer and the defender an extract decree.

## No recording of evidence

**33A.32.**  It shall not be necessary to record the evidence in any proof in a civil partnership action which is not defended.

**Disapplication of Chapter 15**

**33A.33.** Other than rule 15.1(1), Chapter 15 (motions) shall not apply to a civil partnership action in which no notice of intention to defend has been lodged, or to a civil partnership action in so far as it proceeds as undefended.

**Late appearance and application for recall by defenders**

**33A.33A.**—[1](1) In a cause mentioned in rule 33A.1(a), (b) or (f), the sheriff may, at any stage of the action before the granting of final decree, make an order with such conditions, if any, as he thinks fit—

    (a)   directing that a defender who has not lodged a notice of intention to defend be treated as if he had lodged such a notice and the period of notice had expired on the date on which the order was made; or

    (b)   allowing a defender who has not lodged a notice of intention to defend to appear and be heard at a diet of proof although he has not lodged defences but he shall not, in that event, be allowed to lead evidence without the pursuer's consent.

    (2)   Where the sheriff makes an order under paragraph (1), the pursuer may recall a witness already examined or lead other evidence whether or not he closed his proof before that order was made.

    (3)   Where no order under paragraph (1) has been sought by a defender who has not lodged a notice of intention to defend and decree is granted against him, the sheriff may, on an application made within 14 days of the date of the decree, and with such conditions, if any, as he thinks fit, make an order recalling the decree.

    (4)   Where the sheriff makes an order under paragraph (3), the cause shall thereafter proceed as if the defender had lodged a notice of intention to defend and the period of notice had expired on the date on which the decree was recalled.

    (5)   An application under paragraph (1) or (3) shall be made by note setting out the proposed defence and explaining the defender's failure to appear.

    (6)   An application under paragraph (1) or (3) shall not affect any right of appeal the defender may otherwise have.

    (7)   A note lodged in an application under paragraph (1) or (3) shall be served on the pursuer and any other party.

Part III – Defended Civil Partnership Actions

**Notice of intention to defend and defences[2]**

**33A.34.**—(1) This rule applies where the defender in a civil partnership action seeks—

    (a)   to oppose any crave in the initial writ;

    (b)   to make a claim for—

        (i)   aliment;

        (ii)   an order for financial provision within the meaning of section 8(3) of the Act of 1985; or

        (iii)   a section 11 order; or

    (c)   an order—

---

[1] As inserted by the Act of Sederunt (Sheriff Court Rules) (Miscellaneous Amendments) 2008 (SSI 2008/223) para.2(3) (effective July 1, 2008).
[2] As inserted by the Act of Sederunt (Sheriff Court Rules) (Miscellaneous Amendments) 2012 (SSI 2012/188) para.4 (effective August 1, 2012).

     (i)   under section 16(1)(b) or (3) of the Act of 1985 (setting aside or varying agreement as to financial provision);

    (ii)   under section 18 of the Act of 1985 (which relates to avoidance transactions); or

   (iii)   under Chapter 3 or Chapter 4 of Part 3 or section 127 of the Act of 2004; or

  (d)   to challenge the jurisdiction of the court.

  (2)  In an action to which this rule applies, the defender shall—

  (a)   lodge a notice of intention to defend in Form CP16 before the expiry of the period of notice; and

  (b)   make any claim or seek any order referred to in paragraph (1), as the case may be, in those defences by setting out in his defences—

     (i)   craves;

    (ii)   averments in the answers to the condescendence in support of those craves; and

   (iii)   appropriate pleas-in-law.

  (3)  Where a defender intends to make an application for a section 11 order which, had it been made in an initial writ, would have required a warrant for intimation under rule 33A.7, the defender shall include a crave in his notice of intention to defend for a warrant for intimation or to dispense with such intimation; and rule 33A.7 shall, with the necessary modifications, apply to a crave for a warrant under this paragraph as it applies to a crave for a warrant under that rule.

  (4)[1,2]  Where a defender opposes a crave for an order for financial provision or makes a claim in accordance with paragraph (1)(b)(ii), the defender must lodge a completed Form CP13A signed by the defender with the defences, minute of amendment or answers as the case may be.

## Abandonment by pursuer

**33A.35.**  Notwithstanding abandonment by a pursuer of a civil partnership action, the court may allow a defender to pursue an order or claim sought in his defences; and the proceedings in relation to that order or claim shall continue in dependence as if a separate cause.

## Attendance of parties at Options Hearing

**33A.36.**  All parties to a civil partnership action shall, except on cause shown, attend personally the hearing under rule 9.12 (Options Hearing).

## Decree by default

**33A.37.**—(1)  In a civil partnership action in which the defender has lodged a notice of intention to defend, where a party fails—

  (a)   to lodge, or intimate the lodging of, any production or part of process;

  (b)   to implement an order of the sheriff within a specified period; or

  (c)   to appear or be represented at any diet,

that party shall be in default.

  (2)  Where a party is in default under paragraph (1), the sheriff may—

---

[1] As inserted by the Act of Sederunt (Sheriff Court Rules) (Miscellaneous Amendments) 2012 (SSI 2012/188) para.4 (effective August 1, 2012).

[2] As amended by the Act of Sederunt (Sheriff Court Rules) (Miscellaneous Amendments) (No.2) 2012 (SSI 2012/221) para.2 (effective July 31, 2012).

(a)[1] where the civil partnership action is one mentioned in rule 33A.1(1)(a)
(b) or (f) allow that action to proceed as undefended under Part II of this
Chapter; or

(b) where the civil partnership action is one mentioned in rule 33A.1(1)(c) to
(e), grant decree as craved; or

(c) grant decree of absolvitor; or

(d) dismiss the civil partnership action or any claim made or order sought
and

(e) award expenses.

(3) Where no party appears at a diet in a civil partnership action, the sheriff may
dismiss that action.

(4) In a civil partnership action, the sheriff may, on cause shown, prorogate the
time for lodging any production or part of process, or for intimating or implementing any order.

Part IV – Applications And Orders Relating To Children In Certain Actions

**Application and interpretation of this Part**

**33A.38.**[2] This Part applies to an action of dissolution or declarator of nullity of
civil partnership or separation of civil partners.

**Applications in actions to which this Part applies**

**33A.39.**—(1) An application for an order mentioned in paragraph (2) shall be
made—

(a) by a crave in the initial writ or defences, as the case may be, in an action
to which this Part applies; or

(b) where the application is made by a person other than the pursuer or
defender, by minute in that action.

(2) The orders referred to in paragraph (1) are:—

(a) an order for a section 11 order; and

(b) an order for aliment for a child.

**Applications in depending actions by motion**

**33A.40.** An application by a party in an action depending before the court to
which this Part applies for, or for variation of, an order for—

(a) interim aliment for a child under the age of 18; or

(b) a residence order or a contact order,

shall be made by motion.

**Applications after decree relating to a section 11 order**

**33A.41.**—(1) An application after final decree for, or for the variation or recall
of, a section 11 order or in relation to the enforcement of such an order shall be
made by minute in the process of the action to which the application relates.

(2) Where a minute has been lodged under paragraph (1), any party may apply
by motion for any interim order which may be made pending the determination of
the application.

---

[1] As amended by Act of Sederunt (Ordinary Cause Rules) Amendment (Family Law (Scotland) Act
2006 etc.) 2006, para.2 (SSI 2006/207) (effective May 4, 2006).
[2] As amended by Act of Sederunt (Ordinary Cause Rules) Amendment (Family Law (Scotland) Act
2006 etc.) 2006, para.2 (SSI 2006/207) (effective May 4, 2006).

### Applications after decree relating to aliment

**33A.42.**—(1)  An application after final decree for, or for the variation or recall of, an order for aliment for a child shall be made by minute in the process of the action to which the application relates.

(2)  Where a minute has been lodged under paragraph (1), any party may lodge a motion for any interim order which may be made pending the determination of the application.

### Applications after decree by persons over 18 years for aliment

**33A.43**—(1)  A person—

(a)  to whom an obligation of aliment is owed under section 1 of the Act of 1985;

(b)  in whose favour an order for aliment while under the age of 18 years was made in an action to which this Part applies, and

(c)  who seeks, after attaining that age, an order for aliment against the person in that action against whom the order for aliment in his favour was made,

shall apply by minute in the process of that action.

(2)  An application for interim aliment pending the determination of an application under paragraph (1) shall be made by motion.

(3)  Where a decree has been pronounced in an application under paragraph (1) or (2), any application for variation or recall of any such decree shall be made by minute in the process of the action to which the application relates.

Part V – Orders Relating To Financial Provisions

### Application and interpretation of this Part

**33A.44.**—[1](1)  This Part applies to an action of dissolution or declarator of nullity of civil partnership.

(2)  In this Part, "incidental order" has the meaning assigned in section 14(2) of the Act of 1985.

### Applications in actions to which this Part applies

**33A.45.**—(1)  An application for an order mentioned in paragraph (2) shall be made—

(a)  by a crave in the initial writ or defences, as the case may be, in an action to which this Part applies; or

(b)  where the application is made by a person other than the pursuer or defender, by minute in that action.

(2)  The orders referred to in paragraph (1) are:—

(a)  an order for financial provision within the meaning of section 8(3) of the Act of 1985;

(b)  an order under section 16(1)(b) or (3) of the Act of 1985 (setting aside or varying agreement as to financial provision);

(c)  an order under section 18 of the Act of 1985 (which relates to avoidance transactions); and

(d)  an order under section 112 of the Act of 2004 (transfer of tenancy).

---

[1] As amended by Act of Sederunt (Ordinary Cause Rules) Amendment (Family Law (Scotland) Act 2006 etc.) 2006, para.2 (SSI 2006/207) (effective May 4, 2006).

### Applications in depending actions relating to incidental orders

**33A.46.**—(1)  In an action depending before the sheriff to which this Part applies—

(a)    the pursuer or defender, notwithstanding rules 33A.34(2) (application by defender for order for financial provision) and 33A.45(1)(a) (application for order for financial provision in initial writ or defences), may apply by motion for an incidental order; and

(b)    the sheriff shall not be bound to determine such a motion if he considers that the application should properly be by a crave in the initial writ or defences, as the case may be.

(2)   In an action depending before the sheriff to which this Part applies, an application under section 14(4) of the Act of 1985 for the variation or recall of an incidental order shall be made by minute in the process of the action to which the application relates.

### Applications relating to interim aliment

**33A.47.**   An application for, or for the variation or recall of, an order for interim aliment for the pursuer or defender shall be made by motion.

### Applications relating to orders for financial provision

**33A.48.**—(1)   An application—

(a)    after final decree under any of the following provisions of the Act of 1985—

    (i)    section 8(1) for periodical allowance;

    (ii)   section 12(1)(b) (payment of capital sum or transfer of property);

    (iii)  section 12(4) (variation of date or method of payment of capital sum or date of transfer of property); or

    (iv)   section 13(4) (variation, recall, backdating or conversion of periodical allowance); or

    (v)[1]   section 14(1) (incidental orders), or

(b)    after the grant or refusal of an application under—

    (i)    section 8(1) or 14(3) for an incidental order; or

    (ii)   section 14(4) (variation or recall of incidental order),

shall be made by minute in the process of the action to which the application relates.

(2)   Where a minute is lodged under paragraph (1), any party may lodge a motion for any interim order which may be made pending the determination of the application.

(3)   An application under—

(a)    paragraph (5) of section 12A of the Act of 1985 (recall or variation of order in respect of a pension lump sum);

(b)    paragraph (7) of that section (variation of order in respect of pension lump sum to substitute trustees or managers);

(ba)[2]   section 12B(4) of the Act of 1985 (recall or variation of a capital sum order); or

(c)    section 28(10) or 48(9) of the Welfare Reform and Pensions Act 1999,

shall be made by minute in the process of the action to which the application relates.

---

[1] As inserted by the Act of Sederunt (Sheriff Court Rules) (Miscellaneous Amendments) (No.3) 2011 (SSI 2011/386) para.2 (effective November 28, 2011).

[2] As inserted by the Act of Sederunt (Sheriff Court Rules) (Miscellaneous Amendments) 2011 (SSI 2011/193) r.15 (effective April 6, 2011).

**Pension Protection Fund notification**

**33A.48A.**—[1](1)  In this rule—

"assessment period" shall be construed in accordance with section 132 of the Pensions Act 2004;

"pension arrangement" shall be construed in accordance with the definition in section 27 of the Act of 1985; and

"valuation summary" shall be construed in accordance with the definition in Schedule 2 to the Pension Protection Fund (Provision of Information) Regulations 2005.

(2)  This rule applies where a party at any stage in the proceedings applies for an order under section 8 or section 16 of the Act of 1985.

(3)  Where the party against whom an order referred to in paragraph (2) is sought has received notification in compliance with the Pension Protection Fund (Provision of Information) Regulations 2005 or does so after the order is sought—

(a)  that there is an assessment period in relation to his pension arrangement; or

(b)  that the Board of the Pension Protection Fund has assumed responsibility for all or part of his pension arrangement, he shall comply with paragraph (4).

(4)  The party shall—

(a)  lodge the notification; and

(b)  obtain and lodge as soon as reasonably practicable thereafter—

(i)  a valuation summary; and

(ii)  a forecast of his compensation entitlement.

(5)  Subject to paragraph (6), the notification referred to in paragraph (4)(a) requires to be lodged—

(a)  where the notification is received before the order is sought, within 7 days of the order being sought;

(b)  where the notification is received after the order is sought, within 7 days of receiving the notification.

(6)  Where an order is sought against the defender before the defences are lodged, and the notification is received before that step occurs, the notification shall be lodged with the defences.

(7)  At the same time as lodging documents under paragraph (4), copies shall be sent to the other party to the proceedings.

**Applications after decree relating to agreements and avoidance transactions**

**33A.49.**  An application for an order—

(a)  under section 16(1)(a) or (3) of the Act of 1985 (setting aside or varying agreements as to financial provision), or

(b)  under section 18 of the Act of 1985 (which relates to avoidance transac-

---

[1] As inserted by the Act of Sederunt (Sheriff Court Rules) (Miscellaneous Amendments) 2008 (SSI 2008/223) r.3(3) (effective July 1, 2008).

tions), made after final decree shall be made by minute in the process of the action to which the application relates.

Part VI – Applications Relating To Avoidance Transactions

## Form of applications

**33A.50.**—(1) An application for an order under section 18 of the Act of 198 (which relates to avoidance transactions) by a party to a civil partnership action shall be made by including in the initial writ, defences or minute, as the case ma be, appropriate craves, averments and pleas in law.

(2) An application for an order under section 18 of the Act of 1985 after fina decree in a civil partnership action shall be made by minute in the process of the action to which the application relates.

Part VII – Financial Provision After Overseas Proceedings

## Interpretation of this Part

**33A.51.** In this Part—

"order for financial provision" has the meaning assigned in paragraph 4 of Schedule 11 to the Act of 2004;
"overseas proceedings" has the meaning assigned in paragraph 1(1)(a) of Schedule 11 to the Act of 2004.

## Applications for financial provision after overseas proceedings

**33A.52.**—(1) An application under paragraph 2(1) of Schedule 11 to the Act of 2004 for an order for financial provision after overseas proceedings shall be made by initial writ.

(2) An application for an order in an action to which paragraph (1) applies made before final decree under—

(a) section 112 of the Act of 2004 (transfer of tenancy of family home);
(b) paragraph 3(4) of Schedule 11 to the Act of 2004 for interim periodical allowance; or
(c) section 14(4) of the Act of 1985 (variation or recall of incidental order) shall be made by motion.

(3) An application for an order in an action to which paragraph (1) applies made after final decree under—

(a) section 12(4) of the Act of 1985 (variation of date or method of payment of capital sum or date of transfer of property);
(b) section 13(4) of the Act of 1985 (variation, recall, backdating or conversion of periodical allowance); or
(c) section 14(4) of the Act of 1985 (variation or recall of incidental order), shall be made by minute in the process of the action to which it relates.

(4) An application under—

(a) paragraph (5) of section 12A of the Act of 1985 (recall or variation of order in respect of a pension lump sum); or
(b) paragraph (7) of that section (variation of order in respect of pension lump sum to substitute trustees or managers),

shall be made by minute in the process of the action to which the application relates

(5)   Where a minute has been lodged under paragraph (3), any party may apply by motion for an interim order pending the determination of the application.

## Part VIII – Actions In Respect Of Aliment

### Applications relating to agreements on aliment

**33A.53.**   In a civil partnership action in which a crave for aliment may be made, an application under section 7(2) of the Act of 1985 shall be made by a crave in the initial writ or in defences, as the case may be.

## Part IX – Applications For Orders Under Section it Of The Children (Scotland) Act 1995

### Application of this Part

**33A.54**[1]   This Part applies to an application for a section 11 order in a civil partnership action other than in an action of dissolution or declarator of nullity of civil partnership or separation of civil partners.

### Form of applications

**33A.55.**   Subject to any other provision in this Chapter, an application for a section 11 order shall be made—

(a)   by a crave in the initial writ or defences, as the case may be, in a civil partnership action to which this Part applies; or

(b)   where the application is made by a person other than a party to an action mentioned in paragraph (a), by minute in that action.

### Applications relating to interim orders in depending actions

**33A.56.**   An application, in an action depending before the sheriff to which this Part applies, for, or for the variation or recall of, an interim residence order or an interim contact order shall be made—

(a)   by a party to the action, by motion; or

(b)   by a person who is not a party to the action, by minute.

### Applications after decree

**33A.57.**—(1)   An application after final decree for variation or recall of a section 11 order shall be made by minute in the process of the action to which the application relates.

(2)   Where a minute has been lodged under paragraph (1), any party may apply by motion for an interim order pending the determination of the application.

### Application for leave

**33A.57A.**—[2](1)   Where leave of the court is required under section 11(3)(aa) of the Act of 1995 for the making of an application for a contact order under that section, the applicant must lodge along with the initial writ a written application in the form of a letter addressed to the sheriff clerk stating—

(a)   the grounds of which leave is sought; and

(b)   whether or not the applicant has applied for legal aid.

---

[1] As amended by Act of Sederunt (Ordinary Cause Rules) Amendment (Family Law (Scotland) Act 2006 etc.) 2006, para.2 (SSI 2006/207) (effective May 4, 2006).

[2] As inserted by the Act of Sederunt (Sheriff Court Rules Amendment) (Adoption and Children (Scotland) Act 2007) 2009 (SSI 2009/284) (effective September 28, 2009).

(2)   Where the applicant has applied for legal aid he must also lodge along with the initial writ written confirmation from the Scottish Legal Aid Board that it ha determined, under regulation 7(2)(b) of the Civil Legal Aid (Scotland) Regulation 2002, that notification of the application for legal aid should be dispensed with or postponed pending the making by the sheriff of an order for intimation under paragraph (4)(b).

(3)   Subject to paragraph (4)(b) an application under paragraph (1) shall not be served or intimated to any party.

(4)   The sheriff shall consider an application under paragraph (1) without hearing the applicant and may—

    (a)   refuse the application and pronounce an interlocutor accordingly; or

    (b)   if he is minded to grant the application order the applicant—

        (i)   to intimate the application to such persons as the sheriff considers appropriate; and

        (ii)   to lodge a certificate of intimation in, as near as may be, Form G8.

(5)   If any person who receives intimation of an application under paragraph (4)(b) wishes to be heard he shall notify the sheriff clerk in writing within 14 days of receipt of intimation of the application.

(6)   On receipt of any notification under paragraph (5) the sheriff clerk shall fix a hearing and intimate the date of the hearing to the parties.

(7)   Where an application under paragraph (1) is granted, a copy of the sheriff's interlocutor must be served on the defender along with the warrant of citation.

## Part X – Actions Relating To Occupancy Rights And Tenancies

### Application of this Part

**33A.58.**   This Part applies to an action or application for an order under Chapter 3 or Chapter 4 of Part 3 or section 127 of the Act of 2004.

### Interpretation of this Part

**33A.59.**   Unless the context otherwise requires, words and expressions used in this Part which are also used in Chapter 3 or Chapter 4 of Part 3 of the Act of 2004 have the same meaning as in Chapter 3 or Chapter 4, as the case may be.

### Form of application

**33A.60.**—(1)   Subject to any other provision in this Chapter, an application for an order under this Part shall be made—

    (a)   by an action for such an order;

    (b)   by a crave in the initial writ or defences, as the case may be, in any other civil partnership action;

    (c)   where the application is made by a person other than a party to any action mentioned in paragraph (a) or (b), by minute in that action.

(2)   An application under section 107(1) (dispensation with civil partner's consent to dealing) or section 127 (application in relation to attachment) of the Act of 2004 shall, unless made in a depending civil partnership action, be made by summary application.

### Defenders

**33A.61.**   The applicant for an order under this Part shall call as a defender—

    (a)   where he is seeking an order as a civil partner, the other civil partner; and

    (b)   where he is a third party making an application under section 107(1) (dispensation with civil partner's consent to dealing), or 108(1) (payment from non-entitled civil partner in respect of loan) of the Act of 2004, both civil partners.

## Applications by motion

**33A.62.**—(1) An application under any of the following provisions of the Act of 2004 shall be made by motion in the process of the depending action to which the application relates—

(a) section 103(4) (interim order for regulation of rights of occupancy, etc.);

(b) section 104(6) (interim order suspending occupancy rights);

(c) section 107(1) (dispensation with civil partner's consent to dealing); and

(d) *[Omitted by Act of Sederunt (Ordinary Cause Rules) Amendment (Family Law (Scotland) Act 2006 etc.) 2006, para.2 (SSI 2006/207) (effective May 4, 2006).]*

(2) Intimation of a motion under paragraph (1) shall be given—

(a) to the other civil partner;

(b) where the motion is under paragraph (1)(a) or (b) and the entitled civil partner is a tenant or occupies the family home by the permission of a third party, to the landlord or third party, as the case may be; and

(c) to any other person to whom intimation of the application was or is to be made by virtue of rule 33A.7(1)(i) (warrant for intimation to certain persons in actions for orders under Chapter 3 of Part 3 of the Act of 2004) or rule 33A.15 (order for intimation by sheriff).

## Applications by minute

**33A.63.**—(1) An application for an order under section 105 of the Act of 2004 (variation and recall of orders made under section 103 or section 104 of the Act of 2004) shall be made by minute.

(2) A minute under paragraph (1) shall be intimated—

(a) to the other civil partner;

(b) where the entitled civil partner is a tenant or occupies the family home by the permission of a third party, to the landlord or third party, as the case may be; and

(c) to any other person to whom intimation of the application was or is to be made by virtue of rule 33A.7(1)(i) (warrant for intimation to certain persons in actions for orders under Chapter 3 of Part 3 of the Act of 2004) or rule 33A.15 (order for intimation by sheriff).

## Sist of actions to enforce occupancy rights

**33A.64.** Unless the sheriff otherwise directs, the sist of an action by virtue of section 107(4) of the Act of 2004 (where action raised by non entitled civil partner to enforce occupancy rights) shall apply only to such part of the action as relates to the enforcement of occupancy rights by a non entitled civil partner.

**Certificates of delivery of documents to chief constable**

**33A.65.** *[Omitted by Act of Sederunt (Ordinary Cause Rules) Amendment (Family Law (Scotland) Act 2006 etc.) 2006, para.2 (SSI 2006/207) (effective May 4 2006).]*

Part XI – Simplified Dissolution Of Civil Partnership Applications

**Application and interpretation of this Part**

**33A.66.**—(1)   This Part applies to an application for dissolution of civil partnership by a party to a civil partnership made in the manner prescribed in rule 33A.67 (form of applications) if, but only if—

(a)[1]   that party relies on the facts set out in section 117(3)(c) (no cohabitation for one year with consent of defender to decree), section 117(3)(d) (no cohabitation for two years), or section 117(2)(b) (issue of interim gender recognition certificate) of the Act of 2004;

(b)   in an application under section 117(3)(c) of the Act of 2004, the other party consents to decree of dissolution of civil partnership being granted;

(c)   no other proceedings are pending in any court which could have the effect of bringing the civil partnership to an end;

(d)[2]   there is no child of the family (as defined in section 12(4)(b) of the Act of 1995) under the age of 16 years;

(e)   neither party to the civil partnership applies for an order for financial provision on dissolution of civil partnership; and

(f)   neither party to the civil partnership suffers from mental disorder.

(2)   If an application ceases to be one to which this Part applies at any time before final decree, it shall be deemed to be abandoned and shall be dismissed.

(3)   In this Part "simplified dissolution of civil partnership application" means an application mentioned in paragraph (1).

**Form of applications**

**33A.67.**—(1)   A simplified dissolution of civil partnership application in which the facts set out in section 117(3)(c) of the Act of 2004 (no cohabitation for two years with consent of defender to decree) are relied on shall be made in Form CP29 and shall only be of effect if—

(a)   it is signed by the applicant; and

(b)   the form of consent in Part 2 of Form CP29 is signed by the party to the civil partnership giving consent.

(2)   A simplified dissolution of civil partnership application in which the facts set out in section 117(3)(d) of the Act of 2004 (no cohabitation for five years) are relied on shall be made in Form CP30 and shall only be of effect if it is signed by the applicant.

(3)   A simplified dissolution of civil partnership application in which the facts set out in section 117(2)(b) of the Act of 2004 (issue of interim gender recognition certificate) are relied on shall be made in Form CP31 and shall only be of effect if it is signed by the applicant.

---

[1] As amended by Act of Sederunt (Ordinary Cause Rules) Amendment (Family Law (Scotland) Act 2006 etc.) 2006, para.2 (SSI 2006/207) (effective May 4, 2006).
[2] As amended by the Act of Sederunt (Sheriff Court Rules) (Miscellaneous Amendments) 2012 (SSI 2012/188) para.9 (effective August 1, 2012).

## Lodging of applications

**33A.68.** The applicant shall send a simplified dissolution of civil partnership application to the sheriff clerk with—

(a) an extract or certified copy of the civil partnership certificate;

(b) the appropriate fee; and

(c) in an application under section 117(2)(b) of the Act of 2004, the interim gender recognition certificate or a certified copy, within the meaning of rule 33A.9(4).

## Citation and intimation

**33A.69.**—(1) This rule is subject to rule 33A.70 (citation where address not known).

(2) It shall be the duty of the sheriff clerk to cite any person or intimate any document in connection with a simplified dissolution of civil partnership application.

(3) The form of citation—

(a) in an application relying on the facts in section 117(3)(c) of the Act of 2004 shall be in Form CP32;

(b) in an application relying on the facts in section 117(3)(d) of the Act of 2004 shall be in Form CP33; and

(c) in an application relying on the facts in section 117(2)(b) of the Act of 2004 shall be in Form CP34.

(4) The citation or intimation required by paragraph (2) shall be made—

(a) by the sheriff clerk by registered post or the first class recorded delivery service in accordance with rule 5.3 (postal service or intimation);

(b)[1] on payment of an additional fee, by a sheriff officer in accordance with rule 5.4(1) to (4) (service within Scotland by sheriff officer); or

(c) where necessary, by the sheriff clerk in accordance with rule 5.5 (service on persons furth of Scotland).

(5) Where citation or intimation is made in accordance with paragraph (4)(c), the translation into an official language of the country in which service is to be executed required by rule 5.5(6) shall be provided by the party lodging the simplified dissolution of civil partnership application.

## Citation where address not known

**33A.70.**—(1)[2] In a simplified dissolution of civil partnership application in which the facts in section 117(3)(d) (no cohabitation for two years) or section 117(2)(b) (issue of interim gender recognition certificate) of the Act of 2004 are relied on and the address of the other party to the civil partnership is not known and cannot reasonably be ascertained—

(a) citation shall be executed by displaying a copy of the application and a notice in Form CP35 on the walls of court on a period of notice of 21 days; and

(b) intimation shall be made to—

---

[1] As substituted by the Act of Sederunt (Sheriff Court Rules) (Miscellaneous Amendments) 2010 (SSI 2010/279) r.3 (effective July 29, 2010).

[2] As amended by Act of Sederunt (Ordinary Cause Rules) Amendment (Family Law (Scotland) Act 2006 etc.) 2006, para.2 (SSI 2006/207) (effective May 4, 2006).

(i)[1] every person who was a child of the family (within the meaning of section 101(7) of the Act of 2004) who has reached the age of 16 years, and

(ii) one of the next of kin of the other party to the civil partnership who has reached that age, unless the address of such person is not known and cannot reasonably be ascertained.

(2) Intimation to a person referred to in paragraph (1)(b) shall be given by intimating a copy of the application and a notice of intimation in Form CP36.

### Opposition to applications

**33A.71.**—(1) Any person on whom service or intimation of a simplified dissolution of civil partnership application has been made may give notice by letter sent to the sheriff clerk that he challenges the jurisdiction of the court or opposes the grant of decree of dissolution of civil partnership and giving the reasons for his opposition to the application.

(2) Where opposition to a simplified dissolution of civil partnership application is made under paragraph (1), the sheriff shall dismiss the application unless he is satisfied that the reasons given for the opposition are frivolous.

(3) The sheriff clerk shall intimate the decision under paragraph (2) to the applicant and the respondent.

(4) The sending of a letter under paragraph (1) shall not imply acceptance of the jurisdiction of the court.

### Evidence

**33A.72.** Parole evidence shall not be given in a simplified dissolution of civil partnership application.

### Decree

**33A.73.**—(1) The sheriff may grant decree in terms of the simplified dissolution of civil partnership application on the expiry of the period of notice if such application has been properly served provided that, when the application has been served in a country to which the Hague Convention on the Service Abroad of Judicial and Extra Judicial Documents in Civil or Commercial Matters dated 15 November 1965 applies, decree shall not be granted until it is established to the satisfaction of the sheriff that the requirements of article 15 of that Convention have been complied with.

(2) The sheriff clerk shall, not sooner than 14 days after the granting of decree in terms of paragraph (1), issue to each party to the civil partnership an extract of the decree of dissolution of civil partnership in Form CP37.

### Appeals

**33A.74.**[2](1) Any appeal against an interlocutor granting decree of dissolution of civil partnership under rule 33A.73 (decree) may be made, within 14 days after the date of decree, by sending a letter to the court giving reasons for the appeal.

(2) Within 4 days after receiving an appeal, the sheriff clerk must transmit to the Clerk of the Sheriff Appeal Court—

---

[1] As amended by the Act of Sederunt (Sheriff Court Rules) (Miscellaneous Amendments) 2012 (SSI 2012/188) para.9 (effective August 1, 2012).

[2] As amended by the Act of Sederunt (Rules of the Court of Session, Sheriff Appeal Court Rules and Sheriff Court Rules Amendment) (Sheriff Appeal Court) 2015 (SSI 2015/419) r.5 (effective 1 January 2016).

(a) the appeal;

(b) all documents and productions in the simplified dissolution of civil partnership application.

(3) On receipt of the appeal, the Clerk of the Sheriff Appeal Court is to fix a hearing and intimate the date, time and place of that hearing to the parties.

**Applications after decree**

**33A.75.** Any application to the court after decree of dissolution of civil partnership has been granted in a simplified dissolution of civil partnership application which could have been made if it had been made in an action of dissolution of civil partnership shall be made by minute.

Part XII – Referrals To Principal Reporter

**33A.76.–33A.78.** *[Repealed by the Act of Sederunt (Children's Hearings (Scotland) Act 2011) (Miscellaneous Amendments) 2013 (SI 2013/172) para.5 (effective June 24, 2013).]*

Part XIII – Sisting Of Civil Partnership Actions

**Application and interpretation of this Part**

**33A.79.**—(1) This Part applies to any action for—
dissolution of civil partnership;
separation of civil partners.

(2) In this Part—

"another jurisdiction" means any country outside Scotland.

"related jurisdiction" means any of the following countries, namely, England and Wales, Northern Ireland, Jersey, Guernsey and the Isle of Man (the reference to Guernsey being treated as including Alderney and Sark).

(3) For the purposes of this Part—

(a) neither the taking of evidence on commission nor a separate proof relating to any preliminary plea shall be regarded as part of the proof in the action; and

(b) an action is continuing if it is pending and not sisted.

(4) Any reference in this Part to proceedings in another jurisdiction is to proceedings in a court or before an administrative authority of that jurisdiction.

**Duty to furnish particulars of concurrent proceedings**

**33A.80.** While any action to which this Part applies is pending in a sheriff court and proof in that action has not begun, it shall be the duty of the pursuer, and of any other person who has entered appearance in the action, to furnish, in such manner and to such persons and on such occasions as may be prescribed, such particulars as may be so prescribed of any proceedings which—

(a) he knows to be continuing in another jurisdiction; and

(b) are in respect of that civil partnership or capable of affecting its validity.

**Mandatory sists**

**33A.81.** Where before the beginning of the proof in any action for dissolution of civil partnership it appears to the sheriff on the application of a party to the civil partnership—

(a) that in respect of the same civil partnership proceedings for dissolution or nullity of civil partnership are continuing in a related jurisdiction; and

(b) that the parties to the civil partnership have resided together after the civil partnership was formed or treated as having been formed within the meaning of section 1(1) of the Act of 2004; and

   (c)   that the place where they resided together when the action was begun or if they did not then reside together, where they last resided together before the date on which that action was begun is in that jurisdiction; and

   (d)   that either of the said parties was habitually resident in that jurisdiction throughout the year ending with the date on which they last resided together before the date on which that action was begun;

it shall be the duty of the sheriff, subject to rule 33A.83(2) below, to sist the action before him.

## Discretionary sists

**33A.82.**—(1)  Where before the beginning of the proof in any action to which this Part applies, it appears to the sheriff—

   (a)   that any other proceedings in respect of the civil partnership in question or capable of affecting its validity are continuing in another jurisdiction, and

   (b)   that the balance of fairness (including convenience) as between the parties to the civil partnership is such that it is appropriate for those other proceedings to be disposed of before further steps are taken in the action,

the sheriff may then if he thinks fit sist that action.

(2)  In considering the balance of fairness and convenience for the purposes of paragraph (1)(b), the sheriff shall have regard to all factors appearing to be relevant including the convenience of witnesses and any delay or expense which may result from the proceedings being sisted, or not being sisted.

(3)  Paragraph (1) is without prejudice to the duty imposed by rule 33A.81 above.

(4)  If, at any time after the beginning of the proof in any action to which this Part applies, the sheriff is satisfied that a person has failed to perform the duty imposed on him in respect of the action and any such other proceedings as aforesaid by rule 33A.80, paragraph (1) shall have effect in relation to that action and to the other proceedings as if the words "before the beginning of the proof" were omitted but no action in respect of the failure of a person to perform such a duty shall be competent.

## Recall of sists

**33A.83.**—(1)  Where an action is sisted in pursuance of rule 33A.81 or 33A.82 the sheriff may if he thinks fit, on the application of a party to the action, recall the sist if it appears to him that the other proceedings by reference to which the action was sisted are sisted or concluded or that a party to those other proceedings has delayed unreasonably in prosecuting those other proceedings.

(2)  Where an action has been sisted in pursuance of rule 33A.82 by reference to some other proceedings, and the sheriff recalls the sist in pursuance of the preceding paragraph, the sheriff shall not again sist the action in pursuance of the said rule 33A.82.

## Orders in sisted actions

**33A.84.**—(1)  The provisions of paragraphs (2) and (3) shall apply where an action to which this Part applies is sisted by reference to proceedings in a related jurisdiction for any of those remedies; and in this rule—

    "the other proceedings", in relation to any sisted action, means the proceedings in another jurisdiction by reference to which the action was sisted;

    "relevant order" means an interim order relating to aliment or children; and "sisted" means sisted in pursuance of this Part.

(2)   Where an action such as is mentioned in paragraph (1) is sisted, then, without prejudice to the effect of the sist apart from this paragraph—

(a)   the sheriff shall not have power to make a relevant order in connection with the sisted action except in pursuance of sub paragraph (c); and

(b)   subject to the said sub paragraph (c), any relevant order made in connection with the sisted action shall (unless the sist or the relevant order has been previously recalled) cease to have effect on the expiration of the period of three months beginning with the date on which the sist comes into operation; but

(c)   if the sheriff considers that as a matter of necessity and urgency it is necessary during or after that period to make a relevant order in connection with the sisted action or to extend or further extend the duration of a relevant order made in connection with the sisted action, the sheriff may do so, and the order shall not cease to have effect by virtue of sub paragraph (b).

(3)   Where any action such as is mentioned in paragraph (1) is sisted and at the time when the sist comes into operation, an order is in force, or at a subsequent time an order comes into force, being an order made in connection with the other proceedings and providing for any of the following matters, namely periodical payments for a party to the civil partnership in question, periodical payments for a child, the arrangements to be made as to with whom a child is to live, contact with a child, and any other matter relating to parental responsibilities or parental rights, then, as from the time when the sist comes into operation (in a case where the order is in force at that time) or (in any other case) on the coming into force of the order—

(a)   any relevant order made in connection with the sisted action shall cease to have effect in so far as it makes for a civil partner or child any provision for any of the said matters as respects which the same or different provision for that civil partner or child is made by the other order; and

(b)   the sheriff shall not have power in connection with the sisted action to make a relevant order containing for a civil partner or child provision for any of the matters aforesaid as respects which any provision for that civil partner or child is made by the other order.

(4)   Nothing in this paragraph affects any power of a sheriff—

(a)   to vary or recall a relevant order in so far as the order is for the time being in force; or

(b)   to enforce a relevant order as respects any period when it is or was in force; or

(c)   to make a relevant order in connection with an action which was, but is no longer, sisted.

### Chapter 33AA[1]

### Expeditious Resolution of Certain Causes

## Application of Chapter

**33AA.1.**   This Chapter applies where a cause is proceeding to proof or proof before answer in respect of a crave for an order under section 11 of the Children (Scotland) Act 1995 (court orders relating to parental responsibilities etc.).

---

[1] As inserted by the Act of Sederunt (Sheriff Court Rules)(Miscellaneous Amendments) (No.2) 2013 (SI 2013/139) para.2 (effective June 3, 2013).

## Fixing date for Case Management Hearing

**33AA.2.**—(1)  The sheriff shall fix a date for a case management hearing—

    (a)  at the Options Hearing in accordance with rule 9.12(3)(f);

    (b)  at the Procedural Hearing in accordance with rule 10.6(3)(f);

    (c)  on the motion of any party; or

    (d)  on the sheriff's own motion.

(2)  Except on cause shown, the date and time to be fixed under paragraph (1) shall be not less than 14 days and not more than 28 days after the interlocutor appointing the cause to a proof or proof before answer.

## Pre-hearing conference

**33AA.3.**—(1)  In advance of the case management hearing the parties shall hold a prehearing conference, at which parties must—

    (a)  discuss settlement of the action;

    (b)  agree, so far as is possible, the matters which are not in dispute between them;

    (c)  discuss the information referred to in rule 33AA.4(1).

(2)  Prior to the case management hearing the pursuer shall lodge with the court a joint minute of the pre-hearing conference or explain to the sheriff why such a minute has not been lodged.

(3)  If a party is not present during the pre-hearing conference, that party's representative must be able to contact the party during the conference, and be in full possession of all relevant facts.

## Case Management Hearing

**33AA.4.**—(1)  At the case management hearing the parties must provide the sheriff with sufficient information to enable the sheriff to ascertain—

    (a)  the nature of the issues in dispute, including any questions of admissibility of evidence or any other legal issues;

    (b)  the state of the pleadings and whether amendment will be required;

    (c)  the state of preparation of the parties;

    (d)  the scope for agreement of facts, questions of law and matters of evidence;

    (e)  the scope for use of affidavits and other documents in place of oral evidence;

    (f)  the scope for joint instruction of a single expert;

    (g)  the number and availability of witnesses;

    (h)  the nature of productions;

    (i)  whether sanction is sought for the employment of counsel;

    (j)  the reasonable estimate of time needed by each party for examination-in-chief, cross-examination and submissions.

(2)  Subject to paragraph (4), at the case management hearing the sheriff will fix—

    (a)  a diet for proof or a proof before answer;

    (b)  a pre-proof hearing in accordance with Chapter 28A.

(3)  The diet fixed under paragraph (2)(a)—

    (a)  shall be assigned for the appropriate number of days for resolution of the issues with reference to the information provided under paragraph (1) and subject to paragraph (4);

    (b)  may only be extended or varied on exceptional cause shown and subject to such orders (including awards of expenses) as the sheriff considers appropriate.

(4) The sheriff may make such orders as thought fit to ensure compliance with this rule and the expeditious resolution of the issues in dispute, including—

(a) restricting the issues for proof;

(b) excluding specified documents, reports and/or witnesses from proof;

(c) fixing other hearings and awarding expenses.

(5) A case management hearing may, on cause shown, be continued to a further case management hearing.

(6) For the purposes of rules 16.2 (decrees where party in default), 33.37 (decree by default in family action) and 33A.37 (decree by default in civil partnership action), a case management hearing shall be a diet in accordance with those rules.

Chapter 33B

Financial Provision For Former Cohabitants

## Interpretation of this Chapter

**33B.** *[Omitted by the Act of Sederunt (Sheriff Court Rules) (Miscellaneous Amendments) 2012 (SSI 2012/188) para.7 (effective August 1, 2012).]*

Chapter 33C[1]

Referrals to Principal Reporter

## Application and interpretation of this Part

**33C.1.**—(1) In this Chapter—

"2011 Act" means the Children's Hearings (Scotland) Act 2011;

"relevant proceedings" means those proceedings referred to in section 62(5)(a) to (j) and (m) of the 2011 Act, ;

"section 62 statement" has the meaning given in section 62(4) of the 2011 Act;

"Principal Reporter" is the person referred to in section 14 of the 2011 Act or any person carrying out the functions of the Principal Reporter by virtue of paragraph 10(1) of schedule 3 to that Act.

(2) This Chapter applies where a sheriff, in relevant proceedings, makes a referral to the Principal Reporter under section 62(2) of the 2011 Act ("a referral").

## Intimation to Principal Reporter

**33C.2.** Where a referral is made, there shall be attached to the interlocutor a section 62 statement, which shall be intimated forthwith by the sheriff clerk to the Principal Reporter.

## Intimation of decision by Principal Reporter

**33C.3.**—(1) Where a referral is made and the Principal Reporter considers that it is necessary for a compulsory supervision order to be made in respect of the child and arranges a children's hearing under section 69(2) of the 2011 Act, the Principal Reporter shall intimate to the court which issued the section 62 statement the matters referred to in paragraph (2).

(2) The matters referred to in paragraph (1) are—

(a) the decision to arrange such a hearing;

---

[1] As inserted by the Act of Sederunt (Children's Hearings (Scotland) Act 2011) (Miscellaneous Amendments) 2013 (SI 2013/172) para.5 (effective June 24, 2013).

(b) where no appeal is made against the decision of that children's hearing prior to the period for appeal expiring, the outcome of the children's hearing; and

(c) where such an appeal has been made, that an appeal has been made and once determined, the outcome of that appeal.

(3) Where a referral has been made and the Principal Reporter determines that—

(a) none of the section 67 grounds apply in relation to the child; or

(b) it is not necessary for a compulsory supervision order to be made in respect of the child the Principal Reporter shall intimate that decision to the court which issued the section 62 statement.

Chapter 34

Actions Relating to Heritable Property

Part I – Sequestration for Rent

# [Revoked by the Act of Sederunt (Sheriff Court Rules Amendment) (Diligence) 2008 (SSI 2008/121) r.2(1)(a) (effective April 1, 2008).]

Part II – Removing

**Action of removing where fixed term of removal**

**34.5.**—(1) Subject to section 21 of the Agricultural Holdings (Scotland) Act 1991 (notice to quit and notice of intention to quit)—

(a) where the tenant has bound himself to remove by writing, dated and signed—

    (i) within 12 months after the term of removal; or

    (ii) where there is more than one ish, after the ish first in date to remove;

an action of removing may be raised at any time; and

(b) where the tenant has not bound himself, an action of removing may be raised at any time, but—

    (i) in the case of a lease of lands exceeding two acres in extent for three years and upwards, an interval of not less than one year nor more than two years shall elapse between the date of notice of removal and the term of removal first in date;

    (ii) in the case of a lease of lands exceeding two acres in extent, whether written or verbal, held from year to year or under tacit relocation, or for any other period less than three years, an interval of not less than six months shall elapse between the date of notice of removal and the term of removal first in date; and

    (iii) in the case of a house let with or without land attached not exceeding two acres in extent, as also of land not exceeding two acres in extent without houses, as also of mills, fishings, shootings, and all other heritable subjects excepting land exceeding two acres in extent, and let for a year or more, 40 days at least shall elapse between the date of notice of removal and the term of removal first in date.

(2) In any defended action of removing the sheriff may order the defender to find caution for violent profits.

(3) In an action for declarator of irritancy and removing by a superior against a vassal, the pursuer shall call as parties the last entered vassal and such heritable

creditors and holders of postponed ground burdens as are disclosed by a search for 20 years before the raising of the action, and the expense of the search shall form part of the pursuer's expenses of process.

### Form of notice of removal

**34.6.**—(1)[1]  A notice under the following sections of the Sheriff Courts (Scotland) Act 1907 shall be in Form H2:—

    (a)   section 34 (notice in writing to remove where lands exceeding two acres held on probative lease),

    (b)   section 35 (letter of removal where tenant in possession of lands exceeding two acres), and

    (c)   section 36 (notice of removal where lands exceeding two acres occupied by tenant without written lease).

    (2)   A letter of removal shall be in Form H3.

### Form of notice under section 37 of the Act of 1907

**34.7.**[2]  A notice under section 37 of the Sheriff Courts (Scotland) Act 1907 (notice of termination of tenancy) shall be in Form H4.

### Giving notice of removal

**34.8**—[3](1)  A notice under section 34, 35, 36, 37 or 38 of the Sheriff Courts (Scotland) Act 1907 (which relate to notices of removal) may be given by—

    (a)   a sheriff officer

    (b)   the person entitled to give such notice, or

    (c)   the solicitor or factor of such person,

posting the notice by registered post or the first class recorded delivery service at any post office within the United Kingdom in time for it to be delivered at the address on the notice before the last date on which by law such notice must be given, addressed to the person entitled to receive such notice, and bearing the address of that person at the time, if known, or, if not known, to the last known address of that person.

    (2)   A sheriff officer may also give notice under a section of the Sheriff Courts (Scotland) Act 1907 mentioned in paragraph (1) in any manner in which he may serve an initial writ; and, accordingly, rule 5.4 (service within Scotland by sheriff officer) shall, with the necessary modifications, apply to the giving of notice under this paragraph as it applies to service of an initial writ.

### Evidence of notice to remove

**34.9.**—(1)  A certificate of the sending of notice under rule 34.8 dated and endorsed on the lease or an extract of it, or on the letter of removal, signed by the sheriff officer or the person sending the notice, his solicitor or factor, or an acknowledgement of the notice endorsed on the lease or an extract of it, or on the letter of removal, by the party in possession or his agent, shall be sufficient evidence that notice has been given.

    (2)   Where there is no lease, a certificate of the sending of such notice shall be endorsed on a copy of the notice or letter of removal.

---

[1] As amended by SI 1996/2445 (effective November 1, 1996).
[2] As amended by SI 1996/2445 (effective November 1, 1996).
[3] As amended by SI 1996/2445 (effective November 1, 1996).

## Disposal of applications under Part II of the Conveyancing and Feudal Reform (Scotland) Act 1970 for non-residential purposes

**34.10.**—[1](1)  This rule applies to an application or counter-application made by virtue of paragraph 3(2)(a) of the Act of Sederunt (Sheriff Court Rules) (Enforcement of Securities over Heritable Property) 2010.

(2)  An interlocutor of the sheriff disposing of an application or counter-application is final and not subject to appeal except as to a question of title or as to any other remedy granted.

### Service on unnamed occupiers

**34.11.**—[2](1)  Subject to paragraph (2), this rule applies only to a crave for removing in an action of removing against a person or persons in possession of heritable property without right or title to possess the property.

(2)  This rule shall not apply with respect to a person who has or had a title or other right to occupy the heritable property and who has been in continuous occupation since that title or right is alleged to have come to an end.

(3)  Where this rule applies, the pursuer may apply by motion to shorten or dispense with the period of notice or other period of time in these Rules relating to the conduct of the action or the extracting of any decree.

(4)  Where the name of a person in occupation of the heritable property is not known and cannot reasonably be ascertained, the pursuer shall call that person as a defender by naming him as an "occupier".

(5)  Where the name of a person in occupation of the heritable property is not known and cannot reasonably be ascertained, the initial writ shall be served (whether or not it is also served on a named person), unless the court otherwise directs, by a sheriff officer—

> (a)  affixing a copy of the initial writ and a citation in Form H5 addressed to "the occupiers" to the main door or other conspicuous part of the premises and if practicable, depositing a copy of each of those documents in the premises; or

> (b)  in the case of land only, inserting stakes in the ground at conspicuous parts of the occupied land to each of which is attached a sealed transparent envelope containing a copy of the initial writ and a citation in Form H5 addressed to "the occupiers".

### Applications under the Mortgage Rights (Scotland) Act 2001

**34.12.**  *[Repealed by the Act of Sederunt (Sheriff Court Rules) (Enforcement of Securities over Heritable Property) 2010 (SSI 2010/324) para.2 (effective September 30, 2010).]*

## Chapter 35

## Actions of Multiplepoinding

*Annotations to Chapter 35 are by Tim Edward, Partner, Maclay Murray and Spens W.S.*

GENERAL NOTE

An action of multiplepoinding is used where any number of parties have claims on money or an item of property, whether heritable or moveable, which is held by another party. The purpose of the action is

---

[1]  As substituted by the Act of Sederunt (Sheriff Court Rules) (Enforcement of Securities over Heritable Property) 2010 (SSI 2010/324) para.3 (effective September 30, 2010).

[2]  Inserted by the Act of Sederunt (Sheriff Court Ordinary Cause Rules Amendment) (Miscellaneous) 2000 (SSI 2000/239) (effective October 2, 2000).

to decide which claimant is entitled to the property or in what proportions it should be divided between claimants. It also enables the holder of the property to part with it in a legally authorised manner. The subject of the action is known as the "fund *in medio*".

Originally, an action of multiplepoinding was competent only where there was double distress, where two or more arrestments of the fund had been lodged in the hands of the holder, but this rule has gradually been relaxed, and multiplepoindings are now competent wherever there are competing claims to one fund.

The court is generally more liberal towards the competency of a claim by the holder of the fund *in medio* than by a claimant, on the principle that the holder cannot raise a direct action, and should not be bound to remain a holder until the day of his death, or until the competing parties settle their claims. A holder has often been held entitled to bring a multiplepoinding even where a claim is obviously bad, since otherwise he would be liable to have to defend an unfounded action by that claimant.

An action of multiplepoinding may involve a succession of separate actions to determine (i) objections to the raising of the action, (ii) the extent and identity of the fund *in medio*, and (iii) the claims of the respective claimants in a competition on that fund.

*Jurisdiction*

This is regulated by Schedule 8 to the Civil Jurisdiction and Judgments Act 1982 as substituted by SI 2001/3929, Sch.2, para.7. Rule 2(i) of that act, which refers to "proceedings which are brought to assert, declare or determine proprietary or possessory rights, …in or over moveable property, or to obtain authority to dispose of moveable property", is deemed wide enough to include actions of multiplepoinding (Anton and Beaumont, *Civil Jurisdiction in Scotland*, 1995, para.10.42(2)). In such proceedings, the courts where the property is situated have jurisdiction. If the fund *in medio* consists of or includes immoveable property situated in Scotland, rule 5(1)(a) of Sch.8 to the C.J.J.A 1982 confers jurisdiction on the Sheriff Court of the place where it is situated, even if the defender's domicile is outwith the UK (rule 2(h)(ii)). Also, if any one of the defenders in an action of multiplepoinding is domiciled in Scotland, then the Sheriff Court of the place where that defender is domiciled has jurisdiction. (CJJA 1982, Sch.8, rule 2(o)(i)).

## Application of this Chapter

**35.1.**—(1)  This Chapter applies to an action of multiplepoinding.

## Application of Chapters 9 and 10

**35.2.**  Chapter 10 (additional procedure) and the following rules in Chapter 9 (standard procedure in defended causes) shall not apply to an action of multiplepoinding:—

rule 9.1 (notice of intention to defend),

rule 9.2 (fixing date for Options Hearing),

rule 9.4 (lodging of pleadings before Options Hearing),

rule 9.8 (adjustment of pleadings),

rule 9.9 (effect of sist on adjustment),

rule 9.10 (open record),

rule 9.11 (record for Options Hearing),

rule 9.12 (Options Hearing),

rule 9.15 (applications for time to pay directions).

An action of multiplepoinding has its own procedure, to which many general rules governing ordinary causes do not apply. Rule 35.2 lists these rules; they include the rule on notices of intention to defend and the rules on Options Hearings and related procedure.

## Parties

**35.3.**—(1)  An action of multiplepoinding may be brought by any person holding, or having an interest in, or claim on, the fund *in medio*, in his own name.

(2)  The pursuer shall call as defenders to such an action—

(a)  all persons so far as known to him as having an interest in the fund *in medio*; and

(b)  where he is not the holder of the fund, the holder of that fund.

The pursuer is the person who raises the action, whether he is the holder of the fund, or someone with an interest in or a claim on the fund. It is raised in his own name. If the holder of the fund raises the action he is known as the "pursuer and real raiser". Any other party raising the action is known as the 'pursuer and nominal raiser'. If the pursuer is not the holder of the fund, he must call the holder as a defender, and must also call as a defender any person whom he knows to have an interest in the fund. If there are heirs and beneficiaries whose identities are not known, the Lord Advocate should be called as representing the Crown as *ultimus haeres*.

Where the pursuer is the holder, the crave will be in the form:

"(1) To find that the Pursuer is the holder of [specific description of fund *in medio*], which is claimed by the defenders, and that he is only liable in once and single payment thereof and is entitled on payment, or consignation, to be exonerated thereof, and to obtain payment of his expenses;

(2) To grant decree in favour of the party or parties who shall be found to have the best right to the fund *in medio*."

"FUND IN MEDIO"

This is the property in dispute in an action of multiplepoinding. There must be a fund *in medio*; an action is incompetent if there is no debt which the holder is obliged to pay to someone. Therefore, it is incompetent to raise an action of multiplepoinding in respect of a right to future rents (*Pentland v Royal Exchange Assce. Co.* (1830) 9 S. 164), or a fund only in expectation (*Provan v Provan* (1840) 2 D. 298) or not yet received (*Anderson v Cameron's Trs* (1844) 17 Sc.Jur. 42). However, the amount or value of the fund need not be definitely ascertained, so long as there is a fund (*Highland Railway Co. v British Linen Co.* (1901) 38 S.L.R. 584).

The fund can consist of heritable property (e.g. *Edinburgh Merchant Maiden's Hospital v Greig's Exrs* (1902) 10 S.L.T. 317; *Boyd's Trs v Boyd* (1906) 13 S.L.T. 878) or moveable property (including right to title deeds: *Baillie v Baillie* (1830) 8 S. 318), or a combination of both heritable and moveable property (*Logan v Byres* (1895) 2 S.L.T. 445).

In the course of a multiplepoinding action the court may have to decide whether the property in dispute falls under the category of heritable or moveable property, for example where rights of succession to that property require to be determined: *Cowan v Cowan* (1887) 14 R. 670.

The fund *in medio* should include only what is in dispute and no other property: *McNab v Waddell* (1894) 21 R. 827; *MacGillvray's Trs v Dallas* (1905) 7 F. 733. If other property is included, then the court may dismiss the action as incompetent (as in *McNab*), or allow the holder to amend the condescendence of the fund (*MacGillvray's Trs*). If, before the conclusion of the action of multiplepoinding, the holder loses title to property in the fund *in medio*, (i.e. by reduction of that title in a separate action), that property to which the holder no longer has title should be excluded from the condescendence of the fund: *Dunn's Trs v Barstow* (1870) 9 M. 281.

"DEFENDERS"

There must be at least two parties called as defenders, otherwise the action must be a direct action and not a multiplepoinding. (See note to rule 35.8.)

"HAVING AN INTEREST IN"

The purpose of an action of multiplepoinding is to dispose of all competing claims to the fund *in medio* and free the holder from any future responsibility towards possible claimants, so all persons who are believed to have some claim on the fund must be called as defenders. Persons not called may be allowed to lodge a claim at a later stage than they would be in most ordinary cause actions: *Morgan v Morris* (1856) 18 D. 797; aff'd. sub. nom. *Young v Morris* (1858) 20 D. (HL)12. Hence the provision for advertisement at rule 35.7.

## Condescendence of fund in medio

**35.4.**—(1) Where the pursuer is the holder of the fund *in medio*, he shall include a detailed statement of the fund in the condescendence in the initial writ.

(2) Where the pursuer is not the holder of the fund *in medio*, the holder shall before the expiry of the period of notice—

(a) lodge in process—

(i) a condescendence of the fund *in medio*, stating any claim or lien which he may profess to have on that fund;

(ii) a list of all persons known to him as having an interest in the fund; and

(b) intimate a copy of the condescendence and list to any other party.

There must be a condescendence: *Carmichael v Todd* (1853) 15 D. 473. It is essential that the court be able to establish the extent of the fund *in medio*, otherwise it cannot go on to assess the various claims upon the fund. The condescendence should specify the grounds on which each defender is called, and state the facts which justify the raising of the action.

Where a party's case is founded on a document, that document must be produced and specifically described, either by quoting its critical provisions in the averments, or expressly incorporating the document and holding its provisions as repeated in the averments by reference *brevitatis causa*.

"DETAILED STATEMENT OF THE FUND"

It should be sufficient to identify the property comprising the fund.

"INITIAL WRIT"

This is in Form G1 in Appendix 1 to the Ordinary Cause Rules.

"WHERE THE PURSUER IS NOT THE HOLDER..."

In this case the holder must lodge in process a statement of the property comprising the fund *in medio*, and state any claim or lien which he himself has on the fund as well as a list of all the persons he knows to have an interest in the fund. His failure to state his own claim at this point may not bar the claim, if the claim is stateable by way of retention or compensation, when objections to the condescendence of the fund *in medio* are determined: *Ramsay's JF v British Linen Bank*, 1912 S.C. 206, 208. Trustees holding a fund for administration are obliged to lodge a claim, as trustees, for the whole fund for the purpose of administration: *Hall's Trs v McDonald* (1892)19 R. 567, 577 per Lord Kinnear.

"PERIOD OF NOTICE"

This is determined by reference to rule 3.6.

"INTIMATE"

For methods, see rule 5.3.

## Warrant of citation in multiplepoindings

**35.5.—** The warrant of citation of the initial writ in an action of multiplepoinding shall be in Form M1.

"WARRANT OF CITATION"

The writ is served on all defenders, including, where the pursuer is not the holder of the fund in medio, the holder of that fund. The warrant of citation is in the Form M1 in Appendix 1 to the Rules. The defender is ordained to intimate if he or she intends to lodge (a) defences challenging the jurisdiction of the court or the competence of the action; (b) objections to the condescendence of the fund in medio; or (c) a claim on the fund; or any combination of these.

## Citation

**35.6.—**(1) Subject to rule 5.6 (service where address of person is not known), citation of any person in an action of multiplepoinding shall be in Form M2 which shall be attached to a copy of the initial writ and warrant of citation and shall have appended to it a notice of appearance in Form M4.

(2) The certificate of citation shall be in Form M3 and shall be attached to the initial writ.

"RULE 5.6"

This rule provides for service upon a person whose address is unknown by the publication of an advertisement in a specified newspaper circulating in the area of the last known address of that person, or by displaying on the walls of court a copy of the instance and crave of the initial writ, the warrant of citation, and a notice in Form G4.

"NOTICE OF APPEARANCE"

See rule 35.8.

## Advertisement

**35.7.** The sheriff may make an order for advertisement of the action in such newspapers as he thinks fit.

Intimation of the raising of an action of multiplepoinding ensures that all persons entitled to make a claim have an opportunity to do so. Lord Neaves described it as "an essential prerequisite to any judgement in [a] competition": *Connell v Ferguson* (1861) 23 D. 683, at 687.

Further, rule 35.16 states that the sheriff may at any time during the action, either *ex proprio motu* or on the motion of any party, order further service on any person, or advertisement or further advertisement of the action.

## Lodging of notice of appearance

**35.8.** Where a party intends to lodge—

    (a)   defences to challenge the jurisdiction of the court or the competency of the action,

    (b)   objections to the condescendence of the fund *in medio*, or

    (c)   a claim on the fund,

he shall, before the expiry of the period of notice, lodge a notice of appearance in Form M4.

"DEFENCES TO CHALLENGE THE JURISDICTION... OR THE COMPETENCY..."

N.B. rule 35.12(2): defences must be disposed of before any further procedure in the action, unless the sheriff directs otherwise.

A party may wish to lodge defences on grounds such as lack of jurisdiction (see General Note at rule 35.1), or forum non conveniens (e.g. *Provan v Provan* (1840) 2 D. 298).

Also, an action of multiplepoinding is incompetent in a situation where a direct action is available to the claimant. Greater latitude is allowed, however, where the action is raised by the holder of the fund rather than a claimant. The holder of the fund 'is entitled to be relieved by means of an action of multiplepoinding ... and accordingly it is sufficient justification of the institution of the action, and is the criterion of its competency, that the claims intimated make it impossible for the depositary to pay to one of the parties without running the risk of an action at the instance of the other.': *Winchester v Blakey* (1890) 17 R. 1046, 1050 per Lord MacLaren. Accordingly, it is enough to show that there are competing claims which the holder of the fund is unable to meet. So, for example, actions of multiplepoinding which would otherwise have been dismissed as incompetent, because they raised an issue between two claimants which would have been triable by direct action, were nonetheless allowed when raised by the holders: *Royal Bank of Scotland v Price* (1893) 20 R. 290; *Commercial Bank of Scotland v Muir* (1897 ) 25 R. 219.

An action of multiplepoinding should not be used by trustees, executors, or those who hold property on behalf of others simply as a means of dealing with disputes over the property, if there is no genuine double distress. For example, an action of multiplepoinding raised by trustees was held to be incompetent where the only dispute was between a beneficiary and a creditor on the estate (*Glen's Trs v Miller* , 1911 S.C. 1178; cf. *Ogilvy's Trs v Chevallier* (1874)1 R. 693 (where a multiplepoinding by testamentary trustees was only reluctantly allowed where the only dispute was between the sole beneficiary and her creditor)) or where a solicitor was called upon to pay over the confirmed estate to the confirmed executor and another party claimed a right to those funds (*Adam Cochran & Co. v Conn* , 1989 S.L.T. (Sh. Ct.) 27).

Executors and trustees should not resort to a multiplepoinding to obtain exoneration and discharge where there is no difficulty obtaining this by the usual means (*Mackenzie's Trs v Gray* (1895) 2 S.L.T. 422); however, it is competent for those holding monies in a fiduciary capacity, such as executors and trustees, to raise an action of multiplepoinding in order to obtain exoneration and discharge if those who have the power to grant this refuse to do so (*Fraser's Exr v Wallace's Trs* (1893) 20 R. 374, 379 per Lord Maclaren), or where they are otherwise unable to grant sufficient exoneration (*Davidson v Ewen* (1895) 3 S.L.T. 162), or where, because of doubts as to the meaning of testamentary bequests it is unclear who is entitled to the fund and able to give valid discharge (*McClement's Trs v Lord Advocate* , 1949 S.L.T. (Notes) 59).

A judicial factor cannot obtain his exoneration and discharge through an action of multiplepoinding; he is appointed by the court in the exercise of its nobile officium and must likewise be discharged through the exercise of those powers: *Campbell v Grant* (1869) 7 M. 227, 233 per Lord Deas.

"OBJECTIONS TO THE CONDESCENDENCE OF THE FUND"

A party may wish to lodge objections to the existence or composition of the fund *in medio*. In *Provan v Provan* (1840) 23 D. 298, the Lord Ordinary himself raised an objection to the competency of the action on the ground that there was no fund *in medio*. A common objection is that there is some property which should be excluded from the condescendence of the fund: e.g. *Walker's Trs v Walker* (1878) 5 R. 678; *Donaldson's Trs v Beattie* 1914 1 S.L.T. 170. However, objections that the fund in medio includes property which is clearly not in dispute, appear to be treated rather as defences challenging the competency of the action itself, and dealt with at the initial stage of disposal of defences under rule 35.12(2): eg *McNab v Waddell* (1894) 21 R. 827. Likewise, an objection that the pursuer is not entitled to the fund is not an objection to the competency of the action, but one which affects the merits: *Greenshields' Trs v Greenshields* , 1915 2 S.L.T. 189.

"CLAIM ON THE FUND"

This is a short sentence in which the claimant claims to be ranked and preferred to the fund *in medio*, or to a particular portion of that fund. A holder's claim may include a right of retention or compensation.

In some circumstances, a claimant has what is known as a "riding claim", where he is ranked on the fund in medio by virtue of his debtor's claim in the multiplepoinding. However, that debtor's claim must be a direct one, and not a riding claim itself: *Gill's Trs v Patrick* (1889) 16 R. 403. A riding claim must be constituted (*Royal Bank of Scotland v Stevenson* (1849) 12 D. 250) and liquid (*Home's Trs v Ralston's Trs.* (1833) 12 S. 727; *Wilson v Young* (1851) 13 D. 1366). The riding claim must be lodged before decree for payment is pronounced in favour of the original claimant (i.e. the debtor): *Anglo-Foreign Banking Co.* (1879) 16 S.L.R. 731. There are no reported decisions to confirm it, but it would appear to be competent for more than one riding claim to be ranked on a principal claim, leading to a separate competition in respect of those riding claims on the principal claimant's share of the fund: Thomson & Middleton, *Manual of Court of Session Practice*, p.124.

"PERIOD OF NOTICE"

This is determined by reference to rule 3.6.

"NOTICE OF APPEARANCE"

The party lodging notice of appearance must specify in the notice the purpose of his intended appearance. The notice, in Form M4, is signed by the party or his solicitor. It is improper for parties with conflicting interests to be represented by the same firm of solicitors: *Dunlop's Trs v Farquharson* , 1956 S.L.T. 16.

If no notice of appearance is lodged, the sheriff may decide to order advertisement, or further advertisement, of the action, in accordance with rule 35.16.

## Fixing date for first hearing

**35.9.** Where a notice of appearance, or a condescendence on the fund *in medio* and list under rule 35.4(2)(a) has been lodged, the sheriff clerk shall—

    (a)    fix a date and time for the first hearing, which date shall be the first suitable court day occurring not sooner than 4 weeks after the expiry of the period of notice;

    (b)    on fixing the date for the first hearing forthwith intimate that date in Form M5 to each party; and

    (c)    prepare and sign an interlocutor recording the date of the first hearing.

"INTIMATE"

For methods, see rule 5.3.

"INTERLOCUTOR"

For rules relating to interlocutors, see rule 12.1.

## Hearings

**35.10.**—(1) The sheriff shall conduct the first, and any subsequent hearing, with a view to securing the expeditious progress of the cause by ascertaining from parties the matters in dispute.

(2)[1] The parties shall provide the sheriff with sufficient information to enable him to—

    (a)    conduct the hearing as provided for in this Chapter,

    (b)    consider any child witness notice or vulnerable witness application that has been lodged where no order has been made, or

    (c)    ascertain whether there is or is likely to be a vulnerable witness within the

---

[1] As substituted by the Act of Sederunt (Ordinary Cause, Summary Application, Summary Cause and Small Claim Rules) Amendment (Vulnerable Witnesses (Scotland) Act 2004) 2007, r.2(11) (effective November 1, 2007).

meaning of section 11(1) of the Act of 2004 who is to give evidence at any proof or hearing and whether any order under section 12(1) of the Act of 2004 requires to be made.

(3)   At the first, or any subsequent hearing, the sheriff shall fix a period within which defences, objections or claims shall be lodged, and appoint a date for a second hearing.

(4)   Where the list lodged under rule 35.4(2)(a) contains any person who is not a party to the action, the sheriff shall order—

    (a)   the initial writ to be amended to add that person as a defender;

    (b)   service of the pleadings so amended to be made on that person, with a citation in Form M6; and

    (c)   intimation to that person of any condescendence of the fund *in medio* lodged by a holder of the fund who is not the pursuer.

(5)   Where a person to whom service has been made under paragraph (4) lodges a notice of appearance under rule 35.8, the sheriff clerk shall intimate to him in Form M5 the date of the next hearing fixed in the action.

GENERAL NOTE

Rule 35.10 focuses on the need for efficiency throughout the course of an action of multiplepoinding, so that the case may be disposed of as quickly and satisfactorily as possible. These provisions are similar to the rules for the conduct of options hearings and procedural hearings in other ordinary causes. (See for example OCR rules 9.12(1), (2) and 10.6(1), (2).)

## Lodging defences, objections and claims

**35.11.**—(1)   Defences, objections and claims by a party shall be lodged with the sheriff clerk in a single document under separate headings.

(2)   Each claimant shall lodge with his claim any documents founded on in his claim, so far as they are within his custody or power.

"A SINGLE DOCUMENT"

This is the equivalent of lodging defences in a normal ordinary cause action. Each party must lodge a single document which, under separate headings, deals with defences, objections and claims. Where a party wishes to state defences to the competency of the action, he lodges defences in the usual form, with any objections or claim by the defender following the pleas-in-law under separate headings.

If a party does not wish to lodge defences to the competency of the action, but wishes to lodge objections, his writ is headed: "OBJECTIONS/for/A.B. [*designed*]/to/Condescendence of the fund *in medio*/in/Action of Multiplepoinding/[*names and designations of parties as in the instance*]." Objections are specifically stated in numbered paragraphs and are followed by appropriate pleas-in-law.

If a party simply wishes to lodge a claim, it is headed: "CONDESCENDENCE AND CLAIM/for/A.B. [*designed*], Claimant/in/Action of Multiplepoinding [etc., *as above*]."

A claim consists of a condescendence, claim, and pleas-in-law. The condescendence is headed "Condescendence" and sets out in numbered paragraphs the facts on which the claimant bases his claim. The claim is headed "Claim" and must set out specifically what is claimed. This is an essential part of the writ: *Connell v Ferguson* (1861) 23 D. 683, per Lord Neaves at 686. In a riding claim, the claimant is described as a riding claimant.

The plea in the pleas-in-law is that the claimant is entitled to be ranked and preferred to the fund *in medio* in terms of his claim.

"DOCUMENTS"

When a document is founded upon or adopted in defences, objections, or claims, it must, so far as in the possession or within the control of the party founding upon it or adopting it, be lodged in process by that party. If the document is not produced, it cannot be considered by the court: *Hayes v Robinson*, 1984 S.L.T. 300, per Lord Ross at 301. Under rule 21.1, the sheriff has power to order the production of any document or grant a commission and diligence for recovery of it.

## Disposal of defences

**35.12.**—(1)   Where defences have been lodged, the sheriff may order the initial writ and defences to be adjusted and thereafter close the record and regulate further procedure.

(2)   Unless the sheriff otherwise directs, defences shall be disposed of before any further procedure in the action.

The rules set out consecutive procedural stages by which defences, objections and claims are successively disposed of. Unless the sheriff otherwise directs, defences challenging the jurisdiction or competency of an action are dealt with first, before any further procedure. After defences have been lodged, the sheriff may order the initial writ and defences to be adjusted. He then closes the record and regulates further procedure, usually by appointing parties to debate. If the sheriff sustains the objections to jurisdiction or to the competency of the action, the case comes to an end here. If he rejects them, the case will continue to a new hearing at which further procedure will be determined.

### Objections to fund in medio

**35.13.**—(1)   Where objections to the fund *in medio* have been lodged, the sheriff may, after disposal of any defences, order the condescendence of the fund and objections to be adjusted, and thereafter close the record and regulate further procedure.

(2)   If no objections to the fund *in medio* have been lodged, or if objections have been lodged and disposed of, the sheriff may, on the motion of the holder of the fund, and without ordering intimation to any party approve the condescendence of the fund and find the holder liable only in one single payment.

*"objections to the fund in medio"*

Objections to the condescendence of the fund are dealt with next, after disposal of defences. The sheriff may order the condescendence and objections to be adjusted, after which he again closes the record and regulates further procedure. He will usually order a debate or proof, and then dispose of objections and fix a further hearing. The interlocutor disposing of the objections may be appealed without leave: *Walker's Trs v Walker* (1878) 5 R. 678; *Harris School Board v Davidson* (1881) 9 R. 371.

*"approve the condescendence of the fund"*

This is a final interlocutor, which, again, may be appealed without leave: *Harris School Board v Davidson* (1881) 9 R. 371.

The court's approval of the fund is essential, as the interlocutor determines the amount for which the holder is liable to account.

*"find the holder liable only in one single payment"*

This is a judicial determination that the action is competent.

(The motion in respect of this finding and the approval of the condescendence may be made at an earlier hearing on objections, so that the interlocutor disposing of objections may at the same time approve the condescendence and find the holder liable in one single payment.)

The purpose of this finding, once the objections (if any) are disposed of and the fund is approved, is to enable the holder to make payment (usually by consigning the fund into court) and effectively drop out of the action; that is, unless the holder also wishes to assert a claim on the fund.

### Preliminary pleas in multiplepoindings

**35.14.**—(1)   A party intending to insist on a preliminary plea shall, not later than 3 days before any hearing to determine further procedure following the lodging of defences, objections or claims, lodge with the sheriff clerk a note of the basis of the plea.

(2)   Where a party fails to comply with the provisions of paragraph (1), he shall be deemed to be no longer insisting on the plea and the plea shall be repelled by the sheriff at the hearing referred to in paragraph (1).

(3)   If satisfied that there is a preliminary matter of law which justifies a debate, the sheriff shall, after having heard parties and considered the note lodged under this rule, appoint the action to debate.

The provisions relating to preliminary pleas in actions of multiplepoinding are similar to those for other ordinary causes (cf. rule 22.1).

## Consignation of the fund and discharge of holder

**35.15.**—(1) At any time after the condescendence of the fund *in medio* has been approved, the sheriff may order the whole or any part of the fund to be sold and the proceeds of the sale consigned into court.

(2) After such consignation the holder of the fund *in medio* may apply for his exoneration and discharge.

(3) The sheriff may allow the holder of the fund *in medio*, on his exoneration and discharge, his expenses out of the fund as a first charge on the fund.

"CONSIGNATION OF THE FUND"

The amount consigned is the balance in the hands of the holder after deduction of the holder's taxed expenses (if any).

Unlike the 1983 Ordinary Cause Rules, the current rules make no specific provision for consignation into court where no sale takes place. However, consignation is still probably the appropriate step to take even where there is no sale.

The form of the fund, or part of it, may make consignation difficult. There may be a problem if the fund *in medio* consists of a bulky or valuable object which the parties do not wish to be sold. The only way for the sheriff clerk to keep such an object would be to arrange for it to be commercially stored, incurring costs which may significantly reduce the value of the fund *in medio*. In this situation, therefore, the court may ask the holder to retain it, or ask the parties to agree an arrangement for its safekeeping pending the outcome of the action.

For procedure where the fund *in medio* consists of or includes a heritable security, see *Currie's Trs v. Bothwell*, 1954 S.L.T. (Sh. Ct.) 87.

"EXONERATION AND DISCHARGE"

This allows the holder of the fund *in medio* legally to dispose of the property of which he has been in possession, and free him from the possibility of any future claims by any person: see e.g. *Farquhar v. Farquhar* (1896) 13 R. 596. This will be the end of his involvement in the action.

"HIS EXPENSES OUT OF THE FUND"

If the holder of the fund *in medio* is not the pursuer, he will be entitled to the expenses of the condescendence of the fund out of that fund. If the holder is the pursuer and the action was justified, he will usually be entitled to expenses out of the fund. However, if trustees raise an action of multiplepoinding which is subsequently found to be unjustified, they may be found personally liable in expenses: *MacKenzie's Trs v. Sutherland* (1894) 22 R. 233; *Paterson's Trs v. Paterson* (1897) 7 S.L.T. 134; cf. *Gens Trs v. Miller*, 1911 S.C. 1178.

In practice, the steps laid out in rules 35.13(2), and 35.15(2) and (3) are normally combined in a single interlocutor, in which the sheriff: (1) holds the fund *in medio* to be correctly stated in the initial writ or other pleading at the sum therein specified; (2) finds the holder liable in one single payment; (3) finds the holder entitled to payment of his expenses out of the fund *in medio* and allows an account of those expenses to be given in and remits the account, when lodged, to the auditor of court to tax and to report; (4) ordains the holder to lodge the fund *in medio*, with his expenses deducted, in the hands of the sheriff clerk; and (5) upon consignation being made exoners and discharges him of the fund *in medio* and of his whole actings and intromissions therewith. Once this has been done, the holder has no further involvement in the action.

Where the holder is to retain possession of the fund in the circumstances outlined above (in the notes for "*consignation of the fund*"), he cannot yet be exonered and discharged, but he may not wish to be further involved in the litigation. In this situation, the sheriff approves the condescendence of the fund, finds the holder liable only in one single payment, finds him entitled to expenses and has these taxed and approved. Thereafter the holder takes no part in the proceedings. The final interlocutor, as well as ranking and preferring the claimants, ordains delivery on payment of the holder's expenses, and on delivery being made exoners and discharges the holder.

## Further service or advertisement

**35.16.** The sheriff may at any time, of his own motion or on the motion of any party, order further service on any person or advertisement.

"FURTHER SERVICE ON ANY PERSON OR ADVERTISEMENT"

See under "*advertisement*" at notes for rule 35.7.

## Ranking of claims

**35.17.**—(1)  After disposal of any defences, and approval of the condescendence of the fund *in medio*, the sheriff may, where there is no competition on the fund, rank and prefer the claimants and grant decree in terms of that ranking.

(2)  Where there is competition on the fund, the sheriff may order claims to be adjusted and thereafter close the record and regulate further procedure.

"NO COMPETITION"

If there is no competition, the parties may agree in a joint minute to a ranking of their respective claims, though it is not necessary to do this. The sheriff grants decree, and directs the sheriff clerk to make payment to the claimants out of the consigned fund on the lodging of any necessary clearance certificate, and to require receipts. A decree of ranking and preference may be granted without proof (*Union Bank v. Grade* (1887) 25 S.L.R. 61), although the court may refuse to grant the decree, even where there is no competition, if it appears ex facie of a claimant's claim that he has no right to that part of the fund which he claims: *Clark's Exr v. Clark* , 1953 S.L.T. (Notes) 58.

Once a decree of ranking and preference has been pronounced, it can only be brought under review by a person called as defender in the multiplepoinding, by an action of reduction (*Stodart v. Bell* (1860) 22 D. 1092, 1093 per Lord Cowan); and where payment has been made, the only remedy is an action against the party who has received payment, the holder of the fund being no longer liable (*Geikie v. Morris* (1858) 3 Macq. 353).

The rule that payment must not be made until any necessary clearance certificate has been lodged (see rule 30.2(1)) must be strictly observed: *Simpson's Trs v. Fox* , 1954 S.L.T. (Notes) 12. If any payments are made out of the fund before all government duties have been paid, the court may not grant the holder of the fund exoneration and discharge: *Simpson's Trs v. Fox* , 1954 S.L.T. (Notes) 12. (But note the exception to this rule, at rule 30.2(2), which applies only to multiplepoindings: decree may be granted even though not all of the taxes or duties payable on the estate of a deceased claimant have yet been paid or satisfied.)

It is essential that the interlocutor disposing of an action of multiplepoinding be clearly expressed. Likewise, any joint minute should specify in detail the steps which the court is asked to take when pronouncing decree. In particular, the agreement contained in the joint minute should: (1) ensure that the total fund will be disposed of, and that provision will be made for such matters as the assignation of life policies or the delivery of goods; (2) wherever possible, specify the payments to be made in precise figures or in specific fractions of the total, rather than by reference to any formula; (3) deal clearly with any accrued interest; and (4) deal with expenses.

"COMPETITION"

A competition arises where the claims amount to more than the value of the fund, or where the claims are competing in respect of a particular part of the fund. The sheriff may order claims to be adjusted and then close the record and regulate further procedure. Here, as at any earlier closings of the record, the case may be heard by debate (provided that a note of the basis of the preliminary plea has been lodged as set out in rule 35.14), or by proof if there is a dispute as to fact. In the interlocutor disposing of the competition, the sheriff will rank and prefer the successful claimant or claimants and repel the claims of the unsuccessful. If the interlocutor deals with expenses it may be appealed without leave by the unsuccessful claimant (*Glasgow Corporation v. General Accident Fire and Life Assurance Corporation Ltd* , 1914 S.C. 835). The sheriff may make an order for payment in the same interlocutor, or he may delay dealing with this, in which case the interlocutor will make findings in fact and in law determining the principles on which division of the fund is to proceed, and grant leave to appeal.

The interlocutor ordering payment or transference of the fund in medio to the successful claimants protects the holder, after payment or transference, from any further claims at the instance of any person (Stair, IV, xvi, 3; Erskine, IV, iii, 23). It constitutes res judicata as against all the parties in the process: *McCaig v. Maitland* (1887) 14 R. 295; *Elder's Trs v. Elder* (1895) 22 R. 505.

## Remit to reporter

**35.18.**—(1)  Where several claims have been lodged, the sheriff may remit to a reporter to prepare a scheme of division and report.

(2)  The expenses of such remit, when approved by the sheriff, shall be made a charge on the fund, to be deducted before division.

"REPORTER"

In practice, it is rarely necessary for the sheriff to remit to a reporter. If he does, the scheme prepared by the reporter will show the amounts which the decree of ranking and preference determines to be payable to each of the successful claimants.

## Chapter 36

## Actions of Damages

Part AI[1] – Special Procedure for Actions for, or Arising from Personal Injuries

*Application and interpretation*

### Application and interpretation of this Part

**36.A1.**—(1)  This Part applies to a personal injuries action.

(2)  In this Part—

"personal injuries action" means an action of damages for, or arising from, personal injuries or death of a person from personal injuries; and

"personal injuries procedure" means the procedure established by rules 36.G1 to 36.L1.

(3)  In the definition of "personal injuries action", "personal injuries" includes any disease or impairment, whether physical or mental.

*Raising a personal injuries action*

### Form of initial writ

**36.B1.**—(1)  Subject to rule 36.C1, the initial writ in a personal injuries action shall be in Form P11 and there shall be annexed to it a brief statement containing—

(a)  averments in numbered paragraphs relating only to those facts necessary to establish the claim;

(b)  the names of every medical practitioner from whom, and every hospital or other institution in which, the pursuer or, in an action in respect of the death of a person,

the deceased received treatment for the personal injuries.

(2)  An initial writ may include—

(a)  warrants for intimation so far as permitted under these Rules, and

(b)  a specification of documents in Form PI2.

### Actions based on clinical negligence

**36.C1.**[2](1)  This rule applies to a personal injuries action based on alleged clinical negligence.

(2)  Where a pursuer intends to make an application under paragraph (3) to have the cause appointed to the procedure in Chapter 36A (case management of certain personal injuries actions), the pursuer must—

(a)  present the initial writ for warranting in Form G1 (form of initial writ); and

(b)  include in the initial writ a draft interlocutor in Form PI4 (form of interlocutor appointing the cause to the procedure in Chapter 36A).

---

[1] As inserted by the Act of Sederunt (Ordinary Cause Rules Amendment) (Personal Injuries Actions) 2009 (SSI 2009/285) r.2 (effective November 2, 2009).

[2] As substituted by the Act of Sederunt (Rules of the Court of Session 1994 and Sheriff Court Rules Amendment) (No. 2) (Personal Injury and Remits) 2015 (SSI 2015/227) para.8 (effective September 22, 2015).

(3)  At the same time as an initial writ which includes a draft interlocutor in Form PI4 is presented for warranting, the pursuer must lodge a written application in the form of a letter addressed to the sheriff clerk to have the cause appointed to the procedure in Chapter 36A.

(4)  On the making of an application under paragraph (3), the initial writ will be placed before a sheriff in chambers and in the absence of the parties.

(5)  On consideration of the initial writ in accordance with paragraph (4), the sheriff may—

    (a)  after considering the likely complexity of the action and being satisfied that the efficient determination of the action would be served by doing so, appoint the cause to the procedure in Chapter 36A by signing the draft interlocutor in the initial writ; or

    (b)  fix a hearing.

(6)  The sheriff clerk must notify the parties of the date and time of any hearing under paragraph (5)(b).

(7)  At a hearing under paragraph (5)(b), the sheriff may—

    (a)  refuse the application; or

    (b)  after considering the likely complexity of the action and being satisfied that the efficient determination of the action would be served by doing so, appoint the cause to the procedure in Chapter 36A by signing the draft interlocutor in the initial writ.

(8)  Where the sheriff appoints the cause to the procedure in Chapter 36A under paragraph (5)(a) or (7)(b)—

    (a)  the sheriff or, as the case may be, the sheriff clerk must sign a warrant in accordance with rule 5.1 (signature of warrants);

    (b)  the cause will proceed in accordance with Chapter 36A rather than in accordance with personal injuries procedure.

(9)  In this rule—

    "clinical negligence" means a breach of duty of care by a health care professional in connection with that person's diagnosis or the care and treatment of any person, by act or omission, while the health care professional was acting in a professional capacity;

    "health care professional" includes—

    (a)  a registered medical practitioner;

    (b)  a registered nurse; or

    (c)  any other member of a profession regulated by a body mentioned in section 25(3) (the Professional Standards Authority for Health and Social Care) of the National Health Service Reform and Health Care Professions Act 2002.

## Inspection and recovery of documents

**36.D1.**—(1)  This rule applies where the initial writ in a personal injuries action contains a specification of documents by virtue of rule 36.B1(2)(b).

(2)  On the granting of a warrant for citation, an order granting commission and diligence for the production and recovery of the documents mentioned in the specification shall be deemed to have been granted and the sheriff clerk shall certify Form PI2 to that effect by attaching thereto a docquet in Form PI3.

(3)  An order which is deemed to have been made under paragraph (2) shall be treated for all purposes as an interlocutor granting commission and diligence signed by the sheriff.

(4) The pursuer may serve an order under paragraph (2) and the provisions of Chapter 28 (recovery of evidence) shall thereafter apply, subject to any necessary modifications, as if the order were an order obtained on an application under rule 28.2 (applications for commission and diligence for recovery of documents etc.).

(5) Nothing in this rule shall affect the right of a party to apply under rule 28.2 for a commission and diligence for recovery of documents or for an order under section 1 of the Administration of Justice (Scotland) Act 1972 in respect of any document or other property whether or not mentioned in the specification annexed to the initial writ.

*Personal injuries action: application of other rules and withdrawal from personal injuries procedure*

## Application of other rules

**36.E1.**[1](1)  A defended personal injuries action will, instead of proceeding in accordance with Chapter 9 (standard procedure in defended causes), proceed in accordance with personal injuries procedure.

(2) But paragraph (1) does not apply to a personal injuries action following its appointment to the procedure in Chapter 36A under rule 36.C1, 36.F1 or 36A.1.

(3) Paragraphs (4) to (17) apply to a personal injuries action proceeding in accordance with personal injuries procedure but cease to apply when an action is appointed to the procedure in Chapter 36A.

(4) Despite paragraph (1), the following rules of Chapter 9 apply—
   (a) rule 9.1 (notice of intention to defend);
   (b) rule 9.3 (return of initial writ);
   (c) rule 9.5 (process folder);
   (d) rule 9.6 (defences); and
   (e) rule 9.7 (implied admissions).

(5) But the defences shall not include a note of pleas-in-law.

(6) In the application of rule 18.3(1) (applications to amend), a minute of amendment lodged in process must include, where appropriate, confirmation as to whether any warrants are sought under rule 36.B1(2)(a) (warrants for intimation) or whether a specification of documents is sought under rule 36.B1(2)(b) (specification of documents).

(7) In the application of rule 18.5(1)(a) (service of amended pleadings), the sheriff must order any timetable issued in terms of rule 36.G1 to be served together with a copy of the initial writ or record.

(8) Rule 18.5(3) (fixing of hearing following service of amended pleadings and lodging of notice of intention to defend) does not apply.

(9) In the application of rule 19.1 (counterclaims) a counterclaim may also include—
   (a) warrants for intimation so far as permitted under these Rules; and
   (b) a specification of documents in Form PI2.

(10) In rule 19.4 (disposal of counterclaims), paragraph (b) shall not apply.

(11) In the application of rule 20.4(3) (service on third party), any timetable already issued in terms of rule 36.G1 must also be served with a third party notice.

(12) In the application of rule 20.6 (procedure following answers)—

---

[1] As substituted by the Act of Sederunt (Rules of the Court of Session 1994 and Sheriff Court Rules Amendment) (No. 2) (Personal Injury and Remits) 2015 (SSI 2015/227) para.8 (effective September 22, 2015).

(a)  paragraphs (1) and (2) do not apply; and

(b)  where a third party lodges answers, any timetable already issued under rule 36.G1 applies to the third party.

(13)  Chapters 22 (preliminary pleas) and 28A (pre-proof hearing) do not apply.

(14)  Rule 29.11 does not apply.

(15)  References elsewhere in these Rules to the condescendence of an initial writ or to the articles of the condescendence are to be construed as references to the statement required under rule 36.B1(1) and the numbered paragraphs of that statement.

(16)  References elsewhere in these Rules to pleas-in-law, an open record, a closed record or a record for an Options Hearing are to be ignored.

(17)  References elsewhere in these Rules to any action carried out before or after the closing of the record are to be construed as references to that action being carried out before, or as the case may be, after, the date fixed for completion of adjustment under rule 36.G1(1A)(c).

### Disapplication of personal injuries procedure

**36.F1.**[1](1)  Any party to a personal injuries action proceeding in accordance with personal injuries procedure may, within 28 days of the lodging of defences (or, where there is more than one defender the first lodging of defences), by motion apply to have the action withdrawn from personal injuries procedure and appointed to the procedure in Chapter 36A.

(2)  No motion under paragraph (1) shall be granted unless the sheriff is satisfied that there are exceptional reasons for not following personal injuries procedure.

(3)  In determining whether there are exceptional reasons justifying the granting of a motion made under paragraph (1), the sheriff shall have regard to—

(a)  the likely need for detailed pleadings;

(b)  the length of time required for preparation of the action; and

(c)  any other relevant circumstances.

(4)  Where the sheriff appoints the cause to the procedure in Chapter 36A under paragraph (1)—

(a)  the pursuer must within 14 days lodge a revised initial writ in Form G1 (form of initial writ);

(b)  the defender must adjust the defences so as to comply with rule 9.6(2) (defences); and

(c)  the cause will proceed in accordance with Chapter 36A, rather than in accordance with personal injuries procedure.

*Personal injuries procedure*

### Allocation of diets and timetables

**36.G1.**—[2],[3](1)  The sheriff clerk shall, on the lodging of defences in the action or, where there is more than one defender, the first lodging of defences—

---

[1] As amended by the Act of Sederunt (Rules of the Court of Session 1994 and Sheriff Court Rules Amendment) (No. 2) (Personal Injury and Remits) 2015 (SSI 2015/227) para.8 (effective September 22, 2015).

[2] As amended by the Act of Sederunt (Sheriff Court Rules) (Miscellaneous Amendments) 2010 (SSI 2010/279) para.4 (effective July 29, 2010).

[3] As amended by the Act of Sederunt (Rules of the Court of Session 1994 and Sheriff Court Rules Amendment) (No. 2) (Personal Injury and Remits) 2015 (SSI 2015/227) para.8 (effective September 22, 2015).

    (a)   allocate a diet of proof of the action, which shall be no earlier than 4 months (unless the sheriff on cause shown directs an earlier diet to be fixed) and no later than 9 months from the date of the first lodging of defences; and

    (b)   issue a timetable stating—

        (i)   the date of the diet mentioned in subparagraph (a); and

        (ii)   the dates no later than which the procedural steps mentioned in paragraph (1A) are to take place.

(1A)   Those procedural steps are—

    (a)   application for a third party notice under rule 20.1;

    (b)[1]  the pursuer serving a commission for recovery of documents under rule 36.D1;

    (c)   the parties adjusting their pleadings;

    (d)   the pursuer lodging a statement of valuation of claim in process;

    (e)   the pursuer lodging a record;

    (f)   the defender (and any third party to the action) lodging a statement of valuation of claim in process;

    (g)   the parties each lodging in process a list of witnesses together with any productions upon which they wish to rely; and

    (h)   the pursuer lodging in process the minute of the pre-trial meeting.

(1B)  The dates mentioned in paragraph (1)(b)(ii) are to be calculated by reference to periods specified in Appendix 3, which, with the exception of the period specified in rule 36.K1(2), the sheriff principal may vary for his sheriffdom or for any court within his sheriffdom.;

(2)  A timetable issued under paragraph (1)(b) shall be in Form PI5 and shall be treated for all purposes as an interlocutor signed by the sheriff; and so far as the timetable is inconsistent with any provision in these Rules which relates to a matter to which the timetable relates, the timetable shall prevail.

(3)[2]  Where a party fails to comply with any requirement of a timetable other than that referred to in rule 36.K1(3), the sheriff clerk may fix a date and time for the parties to be heard by the sheriff.

(4)  The pursuer shall lodge a certified copy of the record, which shall consist of the pleadings of the parties, in process by the date specified in the timetable and shall at the same time send one copy to the defender and any other parties.

(5)  The pursuer shall, on lodging the certified copy of the record as required by paragraph (4), apply by motion to the sheriff, craving the court—

    (a)   to allow to parties a preliminary proof on specified matters;

    (b)   to allow a proof; or

    (ba)  to allow a jury trial;

    (c)   to make some other specified order.

(6)  The motion lodged under paragraph (5) must specify the anticipated length of the preliminary proof, proof, or jury trial, as the case may be.

(7)  In the event that any party proposes to crave the court to make any order other than an order allowing a proof under paragraph (5)(b) or a jury trial under paragraph (5)(ba), that party shall, on making or opposing (as the case may be) the

---

[1] As amended by the Act of Sederunt (Sheriff Court Rules) (Miscellaneous Amendments) (No.3) 2011 (SSI 2011/386) para.4 (effective November 28, 2011).

[2] As amended by the Act of Sederunt (Rules of the Court of Session and Sheriff Court Rules Amendment) (Miscellaneous) 2014 (SSI 2014/201) para.3 (effective July 7, 2014).

pursuer's motion, specify the order to be sought and give full notice in the motion or the notice of opposition thereto of the grounds thereof.

(8) *[As repealed by Act of Sederunt (Rules of the Court of Session, Ordinary Cause Rules and Summary Cause Rules Amendment) (Miscellaneous) 2014 (SSI 2014/152) para.3 (effective July 7, 2014).]*

(8A) A party who seeks to rely on the evidence of a person not on his or her list lodged in accordance with paragraph (1A)(g) must, if any other party objects to such evidence being admitted, seek leave of the sheriff to admit that evidence whether it is to be given orally or not; and such leave may be granted on such conditions, if any, as the sheriff thinks fit.

(8B) The list of witnesses intimated in accordance with paragraph (1A)(g) must include the name, occupation (where known) and address of each intended witness and indicate whether the witness is considered to be a vulnerable witness within the meaning of section 11(1) of the Act of 2004 and whether any child witness notice or vulnerable witness application has been lodged in respect of that witness.

(9) A production which is not lodged in accordance with paragraph (1A)(g) shall not be used or put in evidence at proof unless—

    (a) by consent of parties; or

    (b) with the leave of the sheriff on cause shown and on such conditions, if any, as to expenses or otherwise as the court thinks fit.

(10) In a cause which is one of a number of causes arising out of the same cause of action, the sheriff may—

    (a) on the motion of a party to that cause; and

    (b) after hearing parties to all those causes,

appoint that cause or any part of those causes to be the leading cause and to sist the other causes pending the determination of the leading cause.

(11) In this rule, "pursuer" includes additional pursuer or minuter as the case may be.

### Applications for sist or for variation of timetable

**36.H1.**—[1](1) The action may be sisted or the timetable varied by the sheriff on an application by any party to the action by motion.

(2) An application under paragraph (1)—

    (a) shall be placed before the sheriff; and

    (b)[2] shall be granted only on cause shown.

(3) Any sist of an action in terms of this rule shall be for a specific period.

(4) Where the timetable issued under rule 36.G1 is varied under this rule, the sheriff clerk shall issue a revised timetable in Form PI5.

(5) A revised timetable issued under paragraph (4) shall have effect as if it were a timetable issued under rule 36.G1 and any reference in this Part to any action being taken in accordance with the timetable shall be construed as a reference to its being taken in accordance with the timetable as varied under this rule.

### Statements of valuation of claim

**36.J1.**—[1](1) Each party to the action shall make a statement of valuation of claim in Form PI6.

---

[1] As amended by the Act of Sederunt (Sheriff Court Rules) (Miscellaneous Amendments) 2010 (SSI 2010/279) para.4 (effective July 29, 2010).

[2] As amended by the Act of Sederunt (Rules of the Court of Session and Sheriff Court Rules Amendment) (Miscellaneous) 2014 (SSI 2014/201) para.3 (effective July 7, 2014).

(2) A statement of valuation of claim (which shall include a list of supporting documents) shall be lodged in process.

(3) Each party shall, on lodging a statement of valuation of claim—

    (a) intimate the list of documents included in the statement of valuation of claim to every other party; and

    (b) lodge each of those documents.

(4) Nothing in paragraph (3) shall affect—

    (a) the law relating to, or the right of a party to object to, the recovery of a document on the ground of privilege or confidentiality; or

    (b) the right of a party to apply under rule 28.2 for a commission and diligence for recovery of documents or an order under section 1 of the Administration of Justice (Scotland) Act 1972.

(5) Without prejudice to paragraph (2) of rule 36.L1, where a party has failed to lodge a statement of valuation of claim in accordance with a timetable issued under rule 36.G1, the sheriff may, at any hearing under paragraph (3) of that rule—

    (a) where the party in default is the pursuer, dismiss the action; or

    (b) where the party in default is the defender, grant decree against the defender for an amount not exceeding the pursuer's valuation.

**Pre-trial meetings**

**36.K1.**[1](1) For the purposes of this rule, a pre-trial meeting is a meeting between the parties to—

    (a) discuss settlement of the action; and

    (b) agree, so far as is possible, the matters which are not in dispute between them.

(2) A pre-trial meeting must—

    (a) be held not later than four weeks before the date assigned for the proof or trial; and

    (b) be attended by parties—

        (i) in person; or

        (ii) by means of video-conference facilities.

(3) Subject to any variation of the timetable in terms of rule 36.H1 (applications for sist or variation of timetable), a joint minute of a pre-trial meeting, made in Form PI7 (minute of pre-trial meeting), must be lodged in process by the pursuer not later than three weeks before the date assigned for proof or trial.

(4) Where a joint minute in Form PI7 has not been lodged in accordance with paragraph (3) and by the date specified in the timetable the sheriff clerk must fix a date and time for the parties to be heard by the sheriff.

(5) If a party is not in attendance during the pre-trial meeting, the representative of such party must have access to the party or another person who has authority to commit the party in settlement of the action.

**Incidental hearings**

**36.L1.**—(1) Where the sheriff clerk fixes a date and time for a hearing under paragraph (3) or (8) of rule 36.G1 or paragraph (3) of rule 36.K1 he shall—

    (a) fix a date not less than seven days after the date of the notice referred to in subparagraph (b);

---

[1] As substituted by the Act of Sederunt (Rules of the Court of Session 1994 and Sheriff Court Rules Amendment) (No. 2) (Personal Injury and Remits) 2015 (SSI 2015/227) para.8 (effective September 22, 2015).

    (b)   give notice to the parties to the action—
         (i)   of the date and time of the hearing; and
        (ii)   requiring the party in default to lodge in process a written explanation as to why the timetable has not been complied with and to intimate a copy to all other parties, not less than two clear working days before the date of the hearing.

(2)   At the hearing, the sheriff—
    (a)   shall consider any explanation provided by the party in default;
    (b)   may award expenses against that party; and
    (c)   may make any other appropriate order, including decree of dismissal.

Part I – Intimation to Connected Persons in Certain Actions of Damages

### Application and interpretation of this Part

**36.1.**—[1](1)  This Part applies to an action of damages in which, following the death of any person from personal injuries, damages are claimed—
    (a)   in respect of the injuries from which the deceased died; or
    (b)   in respect of the death of the deceased.

(2)   In this Part—

"connected person" means a person, not being a party to the action, who has title to sue the defender in respect of the personal injuries from which the deceased died or in respect of his death;

### Averments

**36.2.**  In an action to which this Part applies, the pursuer shall aver in the condescendence, as the case may be—
    (a)   that there are no connected persons;
    (b)   that there are connected persons, being the persons specified in the crave for intimation;
    (c)   that there are connected persons in respect of whom intimation should be dispensed with on the ground that—
         (i)   the names or whereabouts of such persons are not known to, and cannot reasonably be ascertained by, the pursuer; or
        (ii)   such persons are unlikely to be awarded more than £200 each.

### Warrants for intimation

**36.3.**—(1)  Where the pursuer makes averments under rule 36.2(b) (existence of connected persons), he shall include a crave in the initial writ for intimation to any person who is believed to have title to sue the defender in an action in respect of the death of the deceased or the personal injuries from which the deceased died.

(2)  A notice of intimation in Form D1 shall be attached to the copy of the initial writ where intimation is given on a warrant under paragraph (1).

### Applications to dispense with intimation

**36.4.**—(1)  Where the pursuer makes averments under rule 36.2(c) (dispensing with intimation to connected persons), he shall apply by crave in the initial writ for an order to dispense with intimation.

---

[1] As amended by the Act of Sederunt (Sheriff Court Rules) (Miscellaneous Amendments) (No.2) 2011 (SSI 2011/289) para.2 (effective July 7, 2011).

(2)   In determining an application under paragraph (1), the sheriff shall have regard to—
   (a)   the desirability of avoiding a multiplicity of actions; and
   (b)   the expense, inconvenience or difficulty likely to be involved in taking steps to ascertain the name or whereabouts of the connected person.

(3)   Where the sheriff is not satisfied that intimation to a connected person should be dispensed with, he may—
   (a)   order intimation to a connected person whose name and whereabouts are known;
   (b)   order the pursuer to take such further steps as he may specify in the interlocutor to ascertain the name or whereabouts of any connected person; and
   (c)   order advertisement in such manner, place and at such times as he may specify in the interlocutor.

**Subsequent disclosure of connected persons**

**36.5.**   Where the name or whereabouts of a person, in respect of whom the sheriff has dispensed with intimation on a ground specified in rule 36.2(c) (dispensing with intimation to connected persons), subsequently becomes known to the pursuer, the pursuer shall apply to the sheriff by motion for a warrant for intimation to such a person; and such intimation shall be made in accordance with rule 36.3(2).

**Connected persons entering process**

**36.6.**—(1)   A connected person may apply by minute craving leave to be sisted as an additional pursuer to the action.

(2)   Such a minute shall also crave leave of the sheriff to adopt the existing grounds of action, and to amend the craves, condescendence and pleas-in-law.

(3)   The period within which answers to a minute under this rule may be lodged shall be 14 days from the date of intimation of the minute.

(4)[1]   Rule 14.13 (procedure following grant of minute) shall not apply to a minute to which this rule applies.

**Failure to enter process**

**36.7.**   Where a connected person to whom intimation is made in accordance with this Part—
   (a)   does not apply to be sisted as an additional pursuer to the action,
   (b)   subsequently raises a separate action against the same defender in respect of the same personal injuries or death, and
   (c)   would, apart from this rule, be awarded the expenses or part of the expenses of that action,
he shall not be awarded those expenses except on cause shown.

Part II – Interim Payments of Damages

**Application and interpretation of this Part**

**36.8.**—(1)   This Part applies to an action of damages for personal injuries or the death of a person in consequence of personal injuries.

(2)   In this Part—

---

[1] As substituted by the Act of Sederunt (Sheriff Court Ordinary Cause Rules Amendment) (Miscellaneous) 1996 (SI 1996/2445) r.3 (effective November 1, 1996).

"defender" includes a third party against whom the pursuer has a crave for damages;

"personal injuries" includes any disease or impairment of a physical or mental condition.

## Applications for interim payment of damages

**36.9.**—(1)  In an action to which this Part applies, a pursuer may, at any time after defences have been lodged, apply by motion for an order for interim payment of damages to him by the defender or, where there are two or more of them, by any one or more of them.

(2)  The pursuer shall intimate a motion under paragraph (1) to every other party on a period of notice of 14 days.

(3)  On a motion under paragraph (1), the sheriff may, if satisfied that—

(a)  the defender has admitted liability to the pursuer in the action, or

(b)  if the action proceeded to proof, the pursuer would succeed in the action on the question of liability without any substantial finding of contributory negligence on his part, or on the part of any person in respect of whose injury or death the claim of the pursuer arises, and would obtain decree for damages against any defender,

ordain that defender to make an interim payment to the pursuer of such amount as the sheriff thinks fit, not exceeding a reasonable proportion of the damages which, in the opinion of the sheriff, are likely to be recovered by the pursuer.

(4)  Any such payment may be ordered to be made in one lump sum or otherwise as the sheriff thinks fit.

(5)[1]  No order shall be made against a defender under this rule unless it appears to the sheriff that the defender is—

(a)  a person who is insured in respect of the claim of the pursuer;

(b)  a public authority;

(c)  a person whose means and resources are such as to enable him to make the interim payment; or

(d)  the person's liability will be met by—

(i)  an insurer under section 151 of the Road Traffic Act 1988; or

(ii)  an insurer acting under the Motor Insurers Bureau Agreement, or the Motor Insurers Bureau where it is acting itself.

(6)  Notwithstanding the grant or refusal of a motion for an interim payment, a subsequent motion may be made where there has been a change of circumstances.

(7)  Subject to Part IV (management of damages payable to persons under legal disability) an interim payment shall be paid to the pursuer unless the sheriff otherwise directs.

(8)  This rule shall, with the necessary modifications, apply to a counterclaim for damages for personal injuries made by a defender as it applies to an action in which the pursuer may apply for an order for interim payment of damages.

## Adjustment on final decree

**36.10.**  Where a defender has made an interim payment under rule 36.9, the sheriff may, when final decree is pronounced, make such order with respect to the interim payment as he thinks fit to give effect to the final liability of that defender to the pursuer; and in particular may order—

---

[1] Amended by the Act of Sederunt (Ordinary Cause, Summary Application and Small Claim Rules) Amendment (Miscellaneous) 2004 (SSI 2004/197) (effective May 21, 2004), para.2(13).

    (a)   repayment by the pursuer of any sum by which the interim payment exceeds the amount which that defender is liable to pay to the pursuer; or

    (b)   payment by any other defender or a third party, of any part of the interim payment which the defender who made it is entitled to recover from him by way of contribution or indemnity or in respect of any remedy or relief relating to, or connected with, the claim of the pursuer.

Part III – Provisional Damages for Personal Injuries

### Application and interpretation of this Part

**36.11.**—(1)  This Part applies to an action of damages for personal injuries.

(2)  In this Part—

"the Act of 1982" means the Administration of Justice Act 1982;

"further damages" means the damages referred to in section 12(4)(b) of the Act of 1982;

"provisional damages" means the damages referred to in section 12(4)(a) of the Act of 1982.

### Applications for provisional damages

**36.12.**  An application under section 12(2)(a) of the Act of 1982 for provisional damages for personal injuries shall be made by including in the initial writ—

    (a)   a crave for provisional damages;

    (b)   averments in the condescendence supporting the crave, including averments—

        (i)   that there is a risk that, at some definite or indefinite time in the future, the pursuer will, as a result of the act or omission which gave rise to the cause of action, develop some serious disease or suffer some serious deterioration of his physical or mental condition; and

        (ii)   that the defender was, at the time of the act or omission which gave rise to the cause of action, a public authority, public corporation or insured or otherwise indemnified in respect of the claim; and

    (c)   an appropriate plea-in-law.

### Applications for further damages

**36.13.**—(1)  An application for further damages by a pursuer in respect of whom an order under section 12(2)(b) of the Act of 1982 has been made shall be made by minute in the process of the action to which it relates and shall include—

    (a)   a crave for further damages;

    (b)   averments in the statement of facts supporting that crave; and

    (c)   appropriate pleas-in-law.

(2)  On lodging such a minute in process, the pursuer shall apply by motion for warrant to serve the minute on—

    (a)   every other party; and

    (b)   where such other party is insured or otherwise indemnified, his insurer or indemnifier, if known to the pursuer.

(3)  Any such party, insurer or indemnifier may lodge answers to such a minute in process within 28 days after the date of service on him.

(4) Where answers have been lodged under paragraph (3), the sheriff may, on the motion of any party, make such further order as to procedure as he thinks fit.

Part IV – Management of Damages Payable to Persons under Legal Disability

### Orders for payment and management of money

**36.14.**—(1)[1]  In an action of damages in which a sum of money becomes payable, by virtue of a decree or an extra-judicial settlement, to or for the benefit of a person under legal disability (other than a person under the age of 18 years), the sheriff shall make such order regarding the payment and management of that sum for the benefit of that person as he thinks fit.

(2) An order under paragraph (1) shall be made on the granting of decree for payment or of absolvitor.

### Methods of management

**36.15.** In making an order under rule 36.14(1), the sheriff may—

(a) appoint a judicial factor to apply, invest or otherwise deal with the money for the benefit of the person under legal disability;

(b) order the money to be paid to—

    (i)  the Accountant of Court, or

    (ii)  the guardian of the person under legal disability,

as trustee, to be applied, invested or otherwise dealt with and administered under the directions of the sheriff for the benefit of the person under legal disability;

(c) order the money to be paid to the sheriff clerk of the sheriff court district in which the person under legal disability resides, to be applied, invested or otherwise dealt with and administered, under the directions of the sheriff of that district, for the benefit of the person under legal disability; or

(d) order the money to be paid directly to the person under legal disability.

### Subsequent orders

**36.16.**—(1)  Where the sheriff has made an order under rule 36.14(1), any person having an interest may apply for an appointment or order under rule 36.15, or any other order for the payment or management of the money, by minute in the process of the cause to which the application relates.

(2) An application for directions under rule 36.15(b) or (c) may be made by any person having an interest by minute in the process of the cause to which the application relates.

### Management of money paid to sheriff clerk

**36.17.**—(1)  A receipt in Form D2 by the sheriff clerk shall be a sufficient discharge in respect of the amount paid to him under this Part.

(2) The sheriff clerk shall, at the request of any competent court, accept custody of any sum of money in an action of damages ordered to be paid to, applied, invested or otherwise dealt with by him, for the benefit of a person under legal disability.

(3) Any money paid to the sheriff clerk under this Part shall be paid out, applied, invested or otherwise dealt with by the sheriff clerk only after such intimation, service and enquiry as the sheriff may order.

---

[1] As amended by S.I. 1996 No. 2167 (effective November 1, 1996).

(4) Any sum of money invested by the sheriff clerk under this Part shall be invested in a manner in which trustees are authorised to invest by virtue of the Trustee Investments Act 1961.

## Part IV A[1] – Productions in Certain Actions of Damages

**36.17A.-36.17C** [*Omitted by the Act of Sederunt (Rules of the Court of Session 1994 and Sheriff Court Rules Amendment) (No.2) (Personal Injury and Remits) 2015 (SSI 2015/227) r.8 (effective September 22, 2015).*]

### Averments of medical treatment

**36.17B.** The condescendence of the initial writ in an action to which this Part applies shall include averments naming—

    (a)   every general medical practitioner or general medical practice from whom; and

    (b)   every hospital or other institution in which,

the pursuer or, in an action in respect of the death of a person, the deceased received treatment for the injuries sustained, or disease suffered, by him.

### Lodging of medical reports

**36.17C.**—(1)  In an action to which this Part applies, the pursuer shall lodge as productions, with the initial writ when it is presented for warranting in accordance with rule 5.1, all medical reports on which he intends, or intends to reserve the right, to rely in the action.

(2)  Where no medical report is lodged as required by paragraph (1), the defender may apply by motion for an order specifying a period within which such a report shall be lodged in process.

## Part V – Sex Discrimination Act 1975

### Causes under section 66 of the Act of 1975

**36.18.** [*Omitted by the Act of Sederunt (Ordinary Cause, Summary Application, Summary Cause and Small Claim Rules) Amendment (Equality Act 2006 etc.) 2006 (SSI 2006/509) (effective November 3, 2006).*]

## Part VI[2] – Mesothelioma Actions: Special Provisions

### Mesothelioma actions: special provisions

**36.19.**—(1)As amended by the Act of Sederunt (Sheriff Court Rules) (Miscellaneous Amendments) (No.2) 2011 (SSI 2011/289) para.2 (effective July 7, 2011). This Part applies where liability to a relative of the pursuer may arise under section 5 of the Damages (Scotland) Act 2011 (discharge of liability to pay damages: exception for mesothelioma).

(2)  On settlement of the pursuer's claim, the pursuer may apply by motion for all or any of the following—

    (a)   a sist for a specified period;

    (b)   discharge of any diet;

    (c)   where the action is one to which the personal injuries procedure in Part A1 of this Chapter applies, variation of the timetable issued under rule 36.G1.

---

[1] As inserted by the Act of Sederunt (Sheriff Court Ordinary Cause Rules Amendment) (Miscellaneous) 2000 (SSI 2000/239) (effective October 2, 2000).

[2] As inserted by the Act of Sederunt (Ordinary Cause Rules Amendment) (Personal Injuries Actions) 2009 (SSI 2009/285) r.2 (effective November 2, 2009).

(3)   Paragraphs (4) to (7) apply where a motion under paragraph (2) has been granted.

(4)   As soon as reasonably practicable after the death of the pursuer, any agent who immediately prior to the death was instructed in a cause by the deceased pursuer shall notify the court of the death.

(5)   The notification under paragraph (4) shall be by letter to the sheriff clerk and shall be accompanied by a certified copy of the death certificate relative to the deceased pursuer.

(6)   A relative of the deceased may apply by motion for the recall of the sist and for an order for further procedure.

(7)   On expiration of the period of any sist pronounced on a motion under paragraph (2), the sheriff clerk may fix a date and time for the parties to be heard by the sheriff.

## Chapter 36A[1]

### Case Management of Certain Personal Injuries Actions

**Application and interpretation of this Chapter**

**36A.1**—(1)   This Chapter applies to actions appointed to the procedure in this Chapter by virtue of rule 36.C1 (actions based on clinical negligence), rule 36.F1 (disapplication of personal injuries procedure), or under paragraph (2).

(2)   The sheriff may, after considering the likely complexity of an action and being satisfied that the efficient determination of the action would be served by doing so, appoint an action to which Chapter 36 applies (including actions relating to catastrophic injuries) to the procedure in this Chapter, rather than personal injuries procedure.

(3)   Any party to an action may apply by motion to have the action withdrawn from the procedure in this Chapter.

(4)   No motion under paragraph (3) will be granted unless the court is satisfied that there are exceptional reasons for not following the procedure in this Chapter.

(5)   These Rules apply to an action to which this Chapter applies, subject to the following modifications—

   (a)   Chapters 9, 9A, 10, 22 and 28A do not apply;

   (b)   despite subparagraph (a), the following rules of Chapter 9 apply—

      (i)   rule 9.1 (notice of intention to defend);

      (ii)   rule 9.3 (return of initial writ);

      (iii)   rule 9.5 (process folder);

      (iv)   rule 9.6 (defences);

      (v)   rule 9.7 (implied admissions);

   (c)   in the application of rule 18.3(1) (applications to amend), a minute of amendment lodged in process must include, where appropriate, confirmation as to whether any warrants are sought under rule 36.B1(2)(a) (warrants for intimation) or whether a specification of documents is sought under rule 36.B1(2)(b) (specification of documents);

   (d)   rule 18.5(3) (fixing of hearing following service of amended pleadings and lodging of notice of intention to defend) does not apply;

---

[1] As inserted by the Act of Sederunt (Rules of the Court of Session 1994 and Sheriff Court Rules Amendment) (No.2) (Personal Injury and Remits) 2015 (SSI 2015/227) para.8 (effective September 22, 2015).

(e) in the application of rule 19.1 (counterclaims) a counterclaim may also include—

    (i) warrants for intimation so far as permitted under these Rules; and

    (ii) a specification of documents in Form PI2;

(f) in rule 19.4 (disposal of counterclaims), paragraph (b) does not apply;

(g) in the application of rule 20.6 (procedure following answers)—

    (i) paragraphs (1) and (2) do not apply; and

    (ii) where a third party lodges answers, any timetable already fixed under rule 36A.9(5)(b) will apply to the third party;

(h) rule 29.11 does not apply;

(i) references elsewhere in these Rules to an Options Hearing are to be ignored; and

(j) references elsewhere in these Rules to any action carried out before or after the closing of the record will be construed as references to that action being carried out before, or as the case may be, after, the closing of the record under rule 36A.7.

(6) In this Chapter—

"personal injuries", "personal injuries action" and "personal injuries procedure" have the meanings given in rule 36.A1;

"witness statement" means a written statement containing a factual account conveying the evidence of the witness;

"proof" includes jury trial where an action is proceeding in the all Scotland sheriff court, and references to an action being sent to proof are to be construed as including the allowing of a jury trial in the action.

### Form of initial writ

**36A.2** Where the sheriff appoints an action to the procedure in this Chapter under rule 36A.1(2)—

(a) the pursuer must within 14 days thereof lodge a revised initial writ in Form G1 (form of initial writ); and

(b) the defender must thereafter adjust the defences so as to comply with rule 9.6(2) (defences).

### Averments of medical treatment

**36A.3.** The condescendence of the initial writ in an action to which this Chapter applies must include averments naming—

(a) every general medical practitioner or general medical practice from whom; and

(b) every hospital or other institution in which,

the pursuer or, in an action in respect of the death of a person, the deceased received treatment for the injuries sustained, or disease suffered.

### Making up open record

**36A.4.**—(1) The pursuer must lodge a copy of the pleadings in the form of an open record within the timescale in paragraph (2), (3) or (4), as the case may be.

(2) As regards an action appointed to this Chapter under rule 36.C1 (actions based on clinical negligence), the open record must be lodged within 14 days after the date on which defences are lodged under rule 9.6.

(3) As regards an action appointed to this Chapter under rule 36.F1 (disapplication of personal injuries procedure), the open record must be lodged within 14 days after the date on which defences are adjusted in accordance with rule 36.F1(4)(b).

(4)   As regards an action appointed to this Chapter under rule 36A.1 (actions withdrawn from Chapter 36 by sheriff), the open record must be lodged—

    (a)   where the action is appointed to this Chapter before the lodging of defences, within 14 days after the date on which defences are lodged under rule 9.6; or

    (b)   where the action is appointed to this Chapter following the lodging of defences, within 14 days after the date on which defences are adjusted in accordance with rule 36A.2(b).

## Period for adjustment

**36A.5.**—(1)   Where, under rule 36.C1 (actions based on clinical negligence), 36.F1 (disapplication of personal injuries procedure), or 36A.1 (actions withdrawn from Chapter 36 by sheriff), the sheriff orders that a cause will proceed in accordance with this Chapter, the sheriff must continue the cause for adjustment for a period of 8 weeks, which will commence the day after the lodging of the open record under rule 36A.4.

(2)   Paragraphs (2) and (3) of rule 9.8 (exchange and record of adjustments) apply to a cause in which a period for adjustment under paragraph (1) of this rule has been allowed as they apply to the period for adjustment under that rule.

## Variation of adjustment period

**36A.6.**—(1)   At any time before the expiry of the period for adjustment the sheriff may close the record if parties, of consent or jointly, lodge a motion seeking such an order.

(2)   The sheriff may, if satisfied that there is sufficient reason for doing so, extend the period for adjustment for such period as the sheriff thinks fit, if any party—

    (a)   lodges a motion seeking such an order; and

    (b)   lodges a copy of the record adjusted to the date of lodging of the motion.

(3)   A motion lodged under paragraph (2) must set out—

    (a)   the reasons for seeking an extension of the period for adjustment; and

    (b)   the period for adjustment sought.

## Closing record

**36A.7.**—(1)   On the expiry of the period for adjustment, the record closes.

(2)   Following the closing of the record, the sheriff clerk must, without the attendance of parties—

    (a)   prepare and sign an interlocutor recording the closing of the record and fixing the date of the Procedural Hearing under rule 36A.9, which date must be on the first suitable court day occurring not sooner than 21 days after the closing of the record; and

    (b)   intimate the date of the hearing to each party.

(3)   The pursuer must, no later than 7 days before the Procedural Hearing fixed under paragraph (2)—

    (a)   send a copy of the closed record to the defender and to every other party; and

    (b)   lodge a certified copy of the closed record in process.

(4)   The closed record is to consist only of the pleadings of the parties and any adjustments and amendments to them.

## Lodging of written statements

**36A.8.** Each party must, no later than 7 days before the Procedural Hearing fixed under rule 36A.7(2) lodge in process and send to every other party a written statement containing proposals for further procedure which must state—

    (a)   whether the party is seeking to have the action appointed to debate or to have the action sent to proof;

    (b)   where it is sought to have the action appointed to debate—

        (i)   the legal argument on which any preliminary plea should be sustained or repelled; and

        (ii)   the principal authorities (including statutory provisions) on which the argument is founded;

    (c)   where it is sought to have the action appointed to proof—

        (i)   the issues for proof;

        (ii)   the names, occupations (where known) and addresses of the witnesses who are intended to be called to give evidence, including the matters to which each witness is expected to speak and the time estimated for each witness;

        (iii)   whether any such witness is considered to be a vulnerable witness within the meaning of section 11(1) of the Act of 2004 and whether any child witness notice under section 12(2) of that Act or vulnerable witness application under section 12(6) of that Act has been, or is to be, lodged in respect of that witness;

        (iv)   the progress made in preparing and exchanging the reports of any skilled persons;

        (v)   the progress made in obtaining and exchanging records, particularly medical records;

        (vi)   the progress made in taking and exchanging witness statements;

        (vii)   the time estimated for proof and how that estimate was arrived at;

        (viii)   any other progress that has been made, is to be made, or could be made in advance of the proof;

        (ix)   whether an application has been or is to be made under rule 36B.2 (applications for jury trial).

## Procedural Hearing

**36A.9.**—(1) At the Procedural Hearing, the sheriff, after considering the written statements lodged by the parties under rule 36A.8 and hearing from the parties, is to determine whether the action should be appointed to debate or sent to proof on the whole or any part of the action.

(2) Before determining whether the action should be appointed to debate the sheriff is to hear from the parties with a view to ascertaining whether agreement can be reached on the points of law in contention.

(3) Where the action is appointed to debate, the sheriff may order that written arguments on any question of law are to be submitted.

(4) Before determining whether the action should be sent to proof, the sheriff is to hear from parties with a view to ascertaining—

    (a)   the matters in dispute between the parties;

    (b)   the readiness of parties to proceed to proof; and

    (c)   without prejudice to the generality of subparagraphs (a) and (b)—

        (i)   whether reports of skilled persons have been exchanged;

        (ii)   the nature and extent of the dispute between skilled persons;

    (iii)    whether there are facts that can be agreed between parties, upon which skilled persons can comment;

    (iv)[1]    the extent to which agreement can be reached between the parties on the relevant literature upon which skilled persons intend to rely;

    (v)    whether there has been a meeting between skilled persons, or whether such a meeting would be useful;

    (vi)    whether a proof on a particular issue would allow scope for the matter to be resolved;

    (vii)    whether witness statements have been exchanged;

    (viii)    whether any party is experiencing difficulties in obtaining precognition facilities;

    (ix)    whether all relevant records have been recovered and whether there is an agreed bundle of medical records;

    (x)    whether there is a relevant case that is supported by evidence of skilled persons;

    (xi)    if there is no evidence of skilled persons to support a relevant case, whether such evidence is necessary;

    (xii)    whether there is a relevant defence to any or all of the cases supported by evidence of skilled persons;

    (xiii)    if there is no evidence of skilled persons to support a relevant defence, whether such evidence is necessary;

    (xiv)    whether causation of some or all of the injuries is the main area of dispute and, if so, what the position of the respective skilled person is;

    (xv)    whether valuations have been, or could be, exchanged;

    (xvi)    if valuations have been exchanged showing a significant disparity, whether parties should be asked to provide an explanation for such disparity;

    (xvii)    whether a joint minute has been considered;

    (xviii)    whether any of the heads of damage can be agreed;

    (ixx)    whether any orders would facilitate the resolution of the case or the narrowing of the scope of the dispute;

    (xx)    whether a pre-trial meeting should be fixed;

    (xxi)    whether amendment, other than updating, is anticipated; and

    (xxii)    the time required for proof.

(5)  Where the action is sent to proof the sheriff must—

  (a)    fix a date for the hearing of the proof;

  (b)    fix a pre-proof timetable in accordance with rule 36A.10.

(6)  The sheriff may fix a further Procedural Hearing—

  (a)    on the motion of any party;

  (b)    on the sheriff's own initiative.

(7)  A further hearing under paragraph (6) may be fixed—

  (a)    at the Procedural Hearing or at any time thereafter;

  (b)    whether or not the action has been appointed to debate or sent to proof.

---

[1] As amended by the Act of Sederunt (Rules of the Court of Session 1994 and Sheriff Court Rules Amendment) (No.2) (Personal Injury and Remits) 2015 (SI 2015/227) r.8, as amended by the Act of Sederunt (Ordinary Cause Rules 1993 Amendment and Miscellaneous Amendments) 2015 (SSI 2015/296) r.4(3) (effective 1 January 2016).

**Pre-proof timetable**

**36A.10.**—(1) The pre-proof timetable mentioned in rule 36A.9(5)(b) must contain provision for the following—

(a) no later than 24 weeks before the proof—

(i) a date for a pre-proof hearing;

(ii) the last date for the lodging of a draft valuation and vouchings by the pursuer;

(b) no later than 20 weeks before the proof, the last date for the lodging of a draft valuation and vouchings by the defender;

(c) no later than 16 weeks before the proof, the last date for the lodging of witness lists and productions, including a paginated joint bundle of medical reports, by the parties;

(d) no later than 12 weeks before the proof, the last date for a pre-trial meeting;

(e) no later than 8 weeks before the proof, a date for a further pre-proof hearing.

(2) Rule 36.K1(1), (2)(b) and (5) applies to a pre-trial meeting held under this Chapter as it applies to a pre-trial meeting held under Chapter 36.

(3) Prior to the pre-proof hearing mentioned in subparagraph (1)(e)—

(a) the pursuer must lodge in process a joint minute of the pre-trial meeting in Form PI7 (minute of pre-trial meeting);

(b) the parties must lodge in process any other joint minutes.

(4) At any time the sheriff may, at the sheriff's own instance or on the motion of a party—

(a) fix a pre-proof hearing;

(b) vary the pre-proof timetable,

where the sheriff considers that the efficient determination of the action would be served by doing so.

**Power of sheriff to make orders**

**36A.11.**—(1) Following the fixing of a hearing under rule 36A.9(6) or 36A.10(4)(a), or the variation of the pre-proof timetable under rule 36A.10(4)(b), the sheriff may make such orders as the sheriff thinks necessary to secure the efficient determination of the action

(2) In particular, the sheriff may make orders to resolve any matters arising or outstanding from the written statements lodged by the parties under rule 36A.8 or the pre-proof timetable fixed under rule 36A.9(5)(b).

Chapter 36B[1]

Jury Trials

**Application and interpretation of this Chapter**

**36B.1.**—(1) This Chapter applies where a personal injuries action is—

(a) proceeding in the all-Scotland sheriff court; and

(b) an interlocutor has been issued allowing a jury trial—

(i) following an application under rule 36.G1 (allocation of diets and timetables); or

---

[1] As inserted by the Act of Sederunt (Rules of the Court of Session 1994 and Sheriff Court Rules Amendment) (No.2) (Personal Injury and Remits) 2015 (SSI 2015/227) para.8 (effective September 22, 2015).

(ii)   under rule 36A.9 (procedural hearing).

(2)   For the purposes of this Chapter, references in other provisions of these Rules to proof are to be construed as including jury trial.

(3)   In this Chapter—

(a)   the "issue" or "issues" for jury trial means the question or questions to be put to the jury within the meaning of section 63 of the 2014 Act;

(b)   "personal injuries action" has the meaning given in rule 36.A1.

## Applications for jury trial

**36B.2.**—(1)   Within 14 days after the date of an interlocutor allowing a jury trial, the pursuer must lodge in process the proposed issue for jury trial and a copy of it for the use of the court.

(2)   Where the pursuer fails to lodge a proposed issue—

(a)   the pursuer is held to have departed from the right to jury trial unless—

(i)   the court, on cause shown, otherwise orders; or

(ii)   another party lodges a proposed issue under paragraph (3);

(b)   any other party may apply by motion for a proof.

(3)   Where a pursuer fails to lodge a proposed issue, any other party may, within 7 days after the expiry of the period specified in paragraph (1), lodge in process a proposed issue for jury trial and a copy of it.

(4)   Where a proposed issue has been lodged under paragraph (1) or (3), any other party may, within 7 days after the date on which the proposed issue has been lodged, lodge in process a proposed counter-issue and a copy of it for the use of the court.

(5)   A proposed counter-issue may include any question of fact which is made the subject of a specific averment on record or is relevant to the party's pleas-in-law notwithstanding that it does not in terms meet the proposed issue.

(6)   The party lodging a proposed issue must, on the day after the date on which the period for lodging a proposed counter-issue expires, apply by motion for approval of the proposed issue.

(7)   Any party who has lodged a proposed counter-issue under paragraph (4) must, within 7 days after the lodging of a motion for approval of a proposed issue under paragraph (6), apply by motion for approval of the proposed counter-issue.

(8)   Where a motion for approval of a proposed counter-issue has been lodged, the motion for approval of a proposed issue will be heard at the same time as that motion.

(9)   The sheriff, on granting a motion for approval of a proposed issue or proposed counter-issue, must specify in an interlocutor the approved issues to be put to the jury.

## Citation of jurors

**36B.3.**—(1)   The interlocutor of a sheriff issued under rule 36B.2(9) is sufficient authority for the sheriff clerk to summon persons to attend as jurors at the diet for jury trial in accordance with this rule.

(2)   Where an interlocutor is issued under rule 36B.2(9)—

(a)   a list of not less than 36 jurors is to be prepared of an equal number of men and women from the lists of potential jurors maintained for the sheriff court district of Edinburgh in accordance with section 3 of the Jurors (Scotland) Act 1825; and

(b)   the sheriff clerk is to summon those persons to attend as jurors at the diet for jury trial.

(3)   A citation of a person to attend as a juror is to be in Form G13A (form of citation of juror) and is to be executed by post.

### Ineligibility for, and excusal from, jury service

**36B.4.**—(1)   A person summoned to serve on a jury may, as soon as possible after receipt of Form G13A, apply to the sheriff clerk to be released from the citation by completing and returning that Form.

(2)   The sheriff clerk may, if satisfied that—

(a)   there are good and sufficient grounds for excusal; or

(b)   the person is ineligible for jury service,

grant the application.

(3)   The sheriff to preside at the jury trial may, at any time before the jury is empanelled, excuse any person summoned to attend as a juror from attendance if satisfied that there are good and sufficient grounds for doing so.

### Application of certain rules relating to proofs

**36B.5.**—(1)   Chapter 29 of these Rules applies to an action in which issues have been approved for jury trial as they apply to an action in which a proof has been allowed.

(2)   Despite paragraph (1), the following rules of Chapter 29 do not apply—

(a)   rule 29.4 (renouncing probation);

(b)   rule 29.5 (orders for proof);

(c)   rule 29.6 (hearing parts of proof separately);

(d)   rule 29.11 (lodging productions);

(e)   rule 29.15 (instruction of shorthand writer).

### Failure of party to appear at jury trial

**36B.6.**   Where a party does not appear at the diet for jury trial, then—

(a)   if the party appearing is the pursuer or the party on whom the burden of proof lies, that party will be entitled to lead evidence, and go to the jury for a verdict;

(b)   if the party appearing is the defender or the party on whom the burden of proof does not lie, that party will be entitled to obtain a verdict in that party's favour without leading evidence.

### Administration of oath or affirmation to jurors

**36B.7.**—(1)   Subject to paragraph (2), the sheriff clerk must administer the oath collectively to the jury in Form PI8 (form of oath for jurors).

(2)   Where a juror elects to affirm, the sheriff clerk will administer the affirmation to that juror in Form PI9 (form of affirmation for jurors).

### Exceptions to sheriff's charge

**36B.8.**—(1)   Where a party seeks to take exception to a direction on a point of law given by the sheriff in the sheriff's charge to the jury or to request the sheriff to give a direction differing from or supplementary to the directions in the charge, that party must, immediately on the conclusion of the charge, so intimate to the sheriff, who will hear the parties in the absence of the jury.

(2)   The party dissatisfied with the charge to the jury must formulate in writing the exception taken or the direction sought; and the exception or direction, as the case may be, and the sheriff's decision on it, must be recorded in a note of exception under the direction of the sheriff and is to be certified by the sheriff.

(3)   After the note of exception has been certified, the sheriff may give such further or other directions to the jury in open court as the sheriff thinks fit before the jury considers its verdict.

## Further questions for jury

**36B.9.**—(1)   The sheriff may, after the evidence has been led, submit to the jury such further questions as the sheriff thinks fit.

(2)   Any such questions must be specified by the sheriff in an interlocutor and submitted to the jury in writing along with the issue and any counter-issue.

## Application of verdicts

**36B.10.**   Any party may, after the expiry of 7 days after the date on which the verdict was returned in accordance with section 68 of the 2014 Act, apply by motion to apply the verdict, grant decree in accordance with it and make any award in relation to expenses.

## Recording of proceedings at jury trial

**36B.11.**—(1)   Subject to any other provisions in these Rules, proceedings at a jury trial must be recorded by—

   (a)   a shorthand writer to whom the oath *de fideli administratione* in connection with the sheriff court service generally has been administered; or

   (b)   tape recording or other mechanical means approved by the court.

(2)   In paragraph (1), "the proceedings" means the whole proceedings including, without prejudice to that generality—

   (a)   discussions—

        (i)   with respect to any challenge of a juror; and

        (ii)   on any question arising in the course of the trial;

   (b)   the decision of the sheriff on any matter referred to in subparagraph (a);

   (c)   the evidence led at the trial;

   (d)   the sheriff's charge to the jury;

   (e)   the speeches of counsel or solicitors;

   (f)   the verdict of the jury; and

   (g)   any request for a direction to be given under rule 36B.8, any hearing in relation to such a request and any direction so given.

(3)   A transcript of the record of proceedings will be made only on the direction of the court and the cost must, in the first instance, be borne by the solicitors for the parties in equal proportions.

(4)   Any transcript so made must be certified as a faithful record of proceedings—

   (a)   where the recording was under paragraph (1)(a), by whoever recorded the proceedings; and

   (b)   where it was under paragraph (1)(b), by whoever transcribed the record.

(5)   The sheriff may make such alterations to the transcript as appear to the sheriff to be necessary after hearing the parties and, where such alterations are made, the sheriff must authenticate the alterations.

(6)   Where a transcript has been so made for the use of the court, copies of it may be obtained by any party from the transcriber on payment of the transcriber's fee.

(7)   Except with leave of the court, the transcript may be borrowed from process only for the purpose of enabling a party to consider whether to appeal against the interlocutor of the sheriff applying the verdict of the jury or whether to apply for a new trial.

(8)   Where a transcript is required for a purpose mentioned in paragraph (7) but has not been directed to be transcribed under paragraph (3), a party—

(a)   may request such a transcript from the shorthand writer, or as the case may be, from a person who might have transcribed the recording had there been such a direction, the cost of the requested transcript being borne by the solicitor for the requester in the first instance; and

(b)   must lodge the transcript in process;

and copies of it may be obtained by any party from the transcriber on payment of the transcriber's fee.

## Chapter 37

### Causes under the Presumption of Death (Scotland) Act 1977

**Interpretation of this Chapter**

**37.1.**   In this Chapter—

"the Act of 1977" means the Presumption of Death (Scotland) Act 1977;
"action of declarator" means an action under section 1(1) of the Act of 1977;
"missing person" has the meaning assigned in section 1(1) of the Act of 1977.

**Parties to, and service and intimation of, actions of declarator**

**37.2.**—(1)[1,2]   In an action of declarator—

(a)   the missing person shall be named as the defender;

(b)   subject to paragraph (2), service on that person shall be executed by advertisement in such newspaper or other publication as the sheriff thinks fit of such facts relating to the missing person and set out in the initial writ as the sheriff may specify; and

(c)   the period of notice shall be 21 days from the date of publication of the advertisement unless the sheriff otherwise directs.

(2)[3]   The advertisement mentioned in paragraph (1) shall be in Form P1.

(3)   Subject to paragraph (5), in an action of declarator, the pursuer shall include a crave for a warrant for intimation to—

(a)   the missing person's—

(i)   spouse, and

(ii)   children, or, if he has no children, his nearest relative known to the pursuer,

(b)   any person, including any insurance company, who so far as known to the pursuer has an interest in the action, and

(c)   the Lord Advocate,

in the following terms:— "For intimation to (*name and address*) as [husband or wife, child *or* nearest relative] [a person having an interest in the presumed death] of (*name and last known address of the missing person*) and to the Lord Advocate.".

(4)[4]   A notice of intimation in Form P2 shall be attached to the copy of the initial writ where intimation is given on a warrant under paragraph (3).

---

[1] As amended by the Act of Sederunt (Sheriff Court Ordinary Cause Rules Amendment) (Miscellaneous) 1996 (SI 1996/2445) (effective November 1, 1996) (clerical error).

[2] Substituted by the Act of Sederunt (Sheriff Court Ordinary Cause Rules Amendment) (Miscellaneous) 2000 (SSI 2000/239) (effective October 2, 2000).

[3] Substituted by the Act of Sederunt (Sheriff Court Ordinary Cause Rules Amendment) (Miscellaneous) 2000 (SSI 2000/239) (effective October 2, 2000).

[4] As amended by the Act of Sederunt (Sheriff Court Ordinary Cause Rules Amendment) (Miscellaneous) 2000 (SSI 2000/239) (effective October 2, 2000).

(5) The sheriff may, on the motion of the pursuer, dispense with intimation on a person mentioned in paragraph (3)(a) or (b).

(6) An application by minute under section 1(5) of the Act of 1977 (person interested in seeking determination or appointment not sought by pursuer) shall contain a crave for the determination or appointment sought, averments in the answers to the condescendence in support of that crave and an appropriate plea-in-law.

(7) On lodging a minute under paragraph (6), the minuter shall—

    (a)    send a copy of the minute by registered post or the first class recorded delivery service to each person to whom intimation of the action has been made under paragraph (2); and

    (b)    lodge in process the Post Office receipt or certificate of posting of that minute.

### Further advertisement

**37.3.** Where no minute has been lodged indicating knowledge of the present whereabouts of the missing person, at any time before the determination of the action, the sheriff may, of his own motion or on the motion of a party, make such order for further advertisement as he thinks fit.

### Applications for proof

**37.4.**—(1) In an action of declarator where no minute has been lodged, the pursuer shall, after such further advertisement as may be ordered under rule 37.3, apply to the sheriff by motion for an order for proof.

(2) A proof ordered under paragraph (1) shall be by affidavit evidence unless the sheriff otherwise directs.

### Applications for variation or recall of decree

**37.5.**—(1) An application under section 4(1) of the Act of 1977 (variation or recall of decree) shall be made by minute in the process of the action to which it relates.

(2) On the lodging of such a minute, the sheriff shall make an order—

    (a)    for service on the missing person, where his whereabouts have become known;

    (b)    for intimation to those persons mentioned in rule 37.2(3) or to dispense with intimation to a person mentioned in rule 37.2(3)(a) or (b); and

    (c)    for any answers to the minute to be lodged in process within such period as the sheriff thinks fit.

(3) An application under section 4(3) of the Act of 1977 (person interested seeking determination or appointment not sought by applicant for variation order) shall be made by lodging answers containing a crave for the determination or appointment sought.

(4) A person lodging answers containing a crave under paragraph (3) shall, as well as sending a copy of the answers to the minuter—

    (a)    send a copy of the answers by registered post or the first class recorded delivery service to each person on whom service or intimation of the minute was ordered; and

    (b)    lodge in process the Post Office receipt or certificate of posting of those answers.

## Appointment of judicial factors

**37.6.**—(1) The Act of Sederunt (Judicial Factors Rules) 1992 shall apply to an application for the appointment of a judicial factor under section 2(2)(c) or section 4(2) of the Act of 1977 as it applies to a petition for the appointment of a judicial factor.

(2) In the application of rule 37.5 (applications for variation or recall of decree) to an application under section 4(1) of the Act of 1977 in a cause in which variation or recall of the appointment of a judicial factor is sought, for reference to a minute there shall be substituted references to a note.

### Chapter 38

### European Court

## Interpretation of this Chapter

**38.1.**—(1) In this Chapter—

"appeal" includes an application for leave to appeal;

"the European Court" means the Court of Justice of the European Communities;

"reference" means a reference to the European Court for

    (a)[1,2] a preliminary ruling under Article 267 of the Treaty on the Functioning of the European Union, Article 150 of the Euratom Treaty or Article 41 of the E.C.S.C. Treaty; or

    (b) a ruling on the interpretation of the Conventions, as defined in section 1(1) of the Civil Jurisdiction and Judgments Act 1982, under Article 3 of Schedule 2 to that Act.

(2)[3] The expressions "Euratom Treaty" and "E.C.S.C. Treaty" have the meanings assigned respectively in Schedule 1 to the European Communities Act 1972.

(3)[4] In paragraph (1), "the Treaty on the Functioning of the European Union" means the treaty referred to in section 1(2)(s) of the European Communities Act 1972.

## Applications for reference

**38.2.**—(1) A reference may be made by the sheriff of his own motion or on the motion of a party.

(2) *[Repealed by SSI 2000/239 (effective October 2, 2000).]*

## Preparation of case for reference

**38.3.**—(1) Where the sheriff decides that a reference shall be made, he shall continue the cause for that purpose and, within 4 weeks after the date of that continuation, draft a reference.

---

[1] As amended by the Act of Sederunt (Sheriff Court Ordinary Cause Rules Amendment) (Miscellaneous) 2000 (SSI 2000/239) (effective October 2, 2000).

[2] As amended by the Act of Sederunt (Sheriff Court Rules) (Miscellaneous Amendments) (No.3) 2012 (SSI 2012/271) para.6 (effective November 1, 2012).

[3] As amended by the Act of Sederunt (Sheriff Court Rules) (Miscellaneous Amendments) (No.3) 2012 (SSI 2012/271) para.6 (effective November 1, 2012).

[4] As inserted by the Act of Sederunt (Sheriff Court Rules) (Miscellaneous Amendments) (No.3) 2012 (SSI 2012/271) para.6 (effective November 1, 2012).

(1A)[1]  Except in so far as the sheriff may otherwise direct, a reference shall be prepared in accordance with Form E1, having regard to the guidance set out in the Notes for Guidance issued by the Court of Justice of the European Communities.

(2)  On the reference being drafted, the sheriff clerk shall send a copy to each party.

(3)  Within 4 weeks after the date on which copies of the draft have been sent to parties, each party may—

    (a)  lodge with the sheriff clerk, and

    (b)  send to every other party,

a note of any adjustments he seeks to have made in the draft reference.

(4)  Within 14 days after the date on which any such note of adjustments may be lodged, the sheriff, after considering any such adjustments, shall make and sign the reference.

(5)  The sheriff clerk shall forthwith intimate the making of the reference to each party.

### Sist of cause

**38.4.**—(1)  Subject to paragraph (2), on a reference being made, the cause shall, unless the sheriff when making such a reference otherwise orders, be sisted until the European Court has given a preliminary ruling on the question referred to it.

(2)  The sheriff may recall a sist made under paragraph (1) for the purpose of making an interim order which a due regard to the interests of the parties may require.

### Transmission of reference

**38.5.**—(1)  Subject to paragraph (2), a copy of the reference, certified by the sheriff clerk, shall be transmitted by the sheriff clerk to the Registrar of the European Court.

(2)  Unless the sheriff otherwise directs, a copy of the reference shall not be sent to the Registrar of the European Court where an appeal against the making of the reference is pending.

(3)  For the purpose of paragraph (2), an appeal shall be treated as pending—

    (a)  until the expiry of the time for making that appeal; or

    (b)  where an appeal has been made, until that appeal has been determined.

### Chapter 39[2]

### Provisions in Relation to Curators Ad Litem

### Fees and outlays of curators ad litem in respect of children

**39.1.**—(1)  This rule applies to any civil proceedings whether or not the child is a party to the action.

(2)  In an action where the sheriff appoints a curator ad litem to a child, the pursuer shall in the first instance, unless the court otherwise directs, be responsible for the fees and outlays of the curator ad litem incurred during the period from his appointment until the occurrence of any of the following events:

    (a)  he lodges a minute stating that he does not intend to lodge defences or to enter the process;

---

[1] Inserted by the Act of Sederunt (Sheriff Court Ordinary Cause Rules Amendment) (Miscellaneous) 2000 (S.S.I 2000 No. 239) (effective October 2, 2000).

[2] Inserted by the Act of Sederunt (Sheriff Court Ordinary Cause Rules Amendment) (Miscellaneous) 2000 (SSI 2000/239) (effective October 2, 2000).

(b)  he decides to instruct the lodging of defences or a minute adopting defences already lodged; or(c) the discharge, before the occurrence of the events mentioned in sub paragraphs (a) and (b), of the curator.

## Chapter 40[1]

## Commercial Actions

*Annotations by Sheriff James Taylor*

GENERAL NOTE

In 1994 new rules were introduced to the Court of Session governing commercial actions (RCS, Chapter 47). These were deemed to be a success and provided litigants with a more efficient means of resolving commercial disputes. It was sometimes referred to as a "fast track" procedure but this could be misleading. Undoubtedly some actions can be decided with a minimum of procedure, such as a dispute which turns on the interpretation of a contract, thus rendering the description appropriate. However, it was accepted that there are some actions which require a reasonable amount of time for the appropriate experts to be instructed and report and notice be given to the opponent. The advantage of using Chapter 47 procedure was that there was case management from the bench. This resulted in an efficient procedure.

Sheriff Principal Bowen, Q.C., the sheriff principal of Glasgow and Strathkelvin, decided in 1999 to introduce a similar procedure to Glasgow Sheriff Court. Four sheriffs were designated as commercial sheriffs. There were however no rules equivalent to Chapter 47. One of the essential features of Chapter 47 is the preliminary hearing which must take place before the assigned judge within 14 days of defences being lodged. Under the Ordinary Cause Rules of the sheriff court a case would not come before a sheriff until the options hearing. The options hearing requires to be fixed not sooner than 10 weeks after the expiry of the period of notice (OCR, r.9.2). If the advantages of Chapter 47 procedure were to be replicated, the case would need to call before then. To overcome this difficulty the Civil Department of the Sheriff Clerk's Office identified cases which appeared to fit the description of a commercial action using the same definition as in the Practice Note for Commercial Actions in the Court of Session (No. 12 of 1994). After defences had been lodged the solicitors in the case were invited to attend a preliminary hearing. At this hearing the issues in the case were identified and a procedure agreed for resolving the issues. At first, approximately 50 per cent of the cases in which invitations were extended had preliminary hearings, but as the procedure became more familiar that rose to over 90 per cent. Due to the lack of rules the procedure required to be agreed. There was no sanction if one of the parties did not comply. This problem was resolved with the introduction of Chapter 40 to the Ordinary Cause Rules (Act of Sederunt (Ordinary Cause Rules) Amendment (Commercial Actions) 2001 (SSI 2001/8)).

## Application and interpretation of this Chapter

**40.1.**—(1)  This Chapter applies to a commercial action.

(2)  In this Chapter—

(a)  "commercial action" means—an action arising out of, or concerned with, any transaction or dispute of a commercial or business nature including, but not limited to, actions relating to—

(i)  the construction of a commercial document;

(ii)  the sale or hire purchase of goods;

(iii)  the export or import of merchandise;

(iv)  the carriage of goods by land, air or sea;

(v)  insurance;

(vi)  banking;

(vii)  the provision of services;

(viii)  a building, engineering or construction contract; or

(ix)  a commercial lease; and

(b)  "commercial action" does not include an action in relation to consumer credit transactions.

(3)  A commercial action may be raised only in a sheriff court where the Sheriff Principal for the sheriffdom has directed that the procedure should be available.

---

[1] Inserted by the Act of Sederunt (Ordinary Cause Rules) Amendment (Commercial Actions) 2001 (SSI 2001/8).

GENERAL NOTE

Before advantage can be taken of this chapter the sheriff principal must direct that these rules will apply to the particular court in the sheriffdom in which the action is raised. The only courts in which there is such a direction are Glasgow, Jedburgh, Selkirk and Duns Sheriff Courts. Jedburgh, Selkirk and Duns are included because the sheriff presently appointed to these courts was one of the original commercial sheriffs in Glasgow.

The definition of a commercial action closely follows the definition under Chapter 47 procedure in the Court of Session.

*"The provision of services"*

The minor differences between the two definitions are that where the Court of Session definition refers to "the provision of financial services", the equivalent description in Chapter 40 is "the provision of services". The sheriff court definition can thus be seen to be broader. The Court of Session definition also refers specifically to actions relating to "mercantile agency" and "mercantile usage or a custom of trade". There is no equivalent in Chapter 40.

*"Arising out of, or concerned with, any transaction or dispute of a commercial or business nature"*

The differences between the Court of Session and Ordinary Cause Rules are of no significance since the examples in both sets of rules are not limiting and the overarching criteria is the same in both, namely that the action should arise out of, or be concerned with, a commercial or business dispute. This phrase is intended to be of broad scope and is habile to include an action by a trustee in sequestration for declarator of vesting of acquirenda, where the issue was one of insolvency and not of succession: *Rankin's Trs v HC Somerville & Russell*, 1999 S.C. 166.

*"Does not include an action in relation to consumer credit transactions"*

This exclusion is self-explanatory.

## Proceedings before a nominated sheriff

**40.2.** All proceedings in a commercial action shall be brought before—

(a) a sheriff of the sheriffdom nominated by the Sheriff Principal; or

(b) where a nominated sheriff is not available, any other sheriff of the sheriffdom.

GENERAL NOTE

The working party, which consulted before the introduction of Chapter 47 procedures to the Court of Session, recognised a demand for a forum where commercial disputes could be resolved before a judge who had commercial experience. To reflect this expression, there requires to be in the sheriff court where the procedures are available, a sheriff or sheriffs designated by the sheriff principal to deal with commercial business. As a backstop, where a designated commercial sheriff is unavailable another sheriff can deal with proceedings in a commercial action. There are currently three designated commercial sheriffs in Glasgow and one in Jedburgh, Selkirk and Duns.

## Procedure in commercial actions

**40.3.**—(1) In a commercial action the sheriff may make such order as he thinks fit for the progress of the case in so far as not inconsistent with the provisions in this Chapter.

(2) Where any hearing is continued, the reason for such continuation shall be recorded in the interlocutor.

GENERAL NOTE

*"May make such order as he thinks fit"*

The intent of the rules is that the sheriff, counsel and solicitors who may be involved in the action should not be constrained by rules of procedure in dealing efficiently with a case. Thus it is deemed that an order is competent unless it is inconsistent with the commercial rules. A specific enabling power is not necessary.

## Election of procedure for commercial actions

**40.4.** The pursuer may elect to adopt the procedure in this Chapter by bringing an action in Form G1A.

General Note

In order to distinguish a commercial action from an ordinary action, all that is required is for the pursuer's solicitor to type the words "Commercial Action" above the words "Initial Writ" in the instance of the initial writ. Thus the pursuer has the right to elect for Chapter 40 procedure. The defender is protected, should the election be inappropriate, by the terms of rule 40.6(1). To facilitate communication, Glasgow Sheriff Court request that the initial writ, notice of intention to defend and defences should have marked on them the name of the individual solicitor dealing with the case and that individual's telephone number and e-mail address.

## Transfer of action to be a commercial action

**40.5.**—(1)  In an action within the meaning of rule 40.1(2) in which the pursuer has not made an election under rule 40.4, any party may apply by motion at any time to have the action appointed to be a commercial action.

(2)  An interlocutor granted under paragraph (1) shall include a direction as to further procedure.

General Note

If the pursuer does not elect for the action to be dealt with as a commercial action at the time when the action is raised, it is still open to the pursuer, or any other party, once the action has been warranted, to move that these rules should apply.

Since these rules are applicable in Glasgow, Jedburgh, Selkirk and Duns Sheriff Courts only, there have been motions made in other courts, where the rules are not available, for particular cases to be remitted to one of the four courts. These have usually involved the defender prorogating the jurisdiction of one of the four courts. Glasgow is prepared to accept such remits, but the Borders Courts are not.

## Appointment of a commercial action as an ordinary cause

**40.6.**—(1)  At any time before, or at the Case Management Conference, the sheriff shall appoint a commercial action to proceed as an ordinary cause—

(a)  on the motion of a party where—

(i)  detailed pleadings are required to enable justice to be done between the parties; or

(ii)  any other circumstances warrant such an order being made; or

(b)  on the joint motion of parties.

(2)  If a motion to appoint a commercial action to proceed as an ordinary action is refused, no subsequent motion to appoint the action to proceed as an ordinary cause shall be considered except on a material change of circumstances.

(3)  Where the sheriff orders that a commercial action shall proceed as an ordinary cause the interlocutor granting such shall prescribe—

(a)  a period of adjustment, if appropriate; and

(b)  the date, time and place for any options hearing fixed.

(4)  In determining what order to make in deciding that a commercial action proceed as an ordinary cause the sheriff shall have regard to the periods prescribed in rule 9.2.

General Note

This rule provides for an action being remitted from the commercial roll to the ordinary roll on the motion of any party or on joint motion.

*"Detailed pleadings are required"*

The only guidance as to when such a motion should be considered, apart from the generality that "circumstances warrant such", is if detailed pleadings are required. It is submitted that this is a strange provision. Several of the commercial actions raised under these rules have involved detailed pleading. There is nothing in the rules which makes the rules unsuitable to regulate actions where detailed pleading is required. No motion to have the case remitted to the ordinary roll has succeeded when reliance has been placed on this specific provision only.

The rule does not give the sheriff power *ex proprio motu* to remit the case to the ordinary role. This was originally the case under Chapter 47 procedure in the Court of Session. That was remedied in the Court of Session by para.2(7) of SSI 2000/66, which gives the commercial judge power, *ex proprio motu*, to remit the case to the ordinary roll.

In the event that a motion to remit to the ordinary roll is successful, the interlocutor shall allow a period of adjustment, if appropriate. If the reason for the motion succeeding is that detailed pleadings are required, it would be consistent for there to be a further period allowed for adjustment. One might expect a subsequent motion to seek that the action be dealt with in terms of Chapter 10.

## Special requirements for initial writ in a commercial action

**40.7.**—(1) Where the construction of a document is the only matter in dispute no pleadings or pleas-in-law require to be included in the initial writ.

(2) There shall be appended to an initial writ in Form G1A a list of the documents founded on or adopted as incorporated in the initial writ.

GENERAL NOTE

This provision enables a pursuer who considers that the construction of a document will resolve a dispute to put that clearly in focus in the initial writ. There will still require to be a crave in which it would be open to a pursuer to seek declarator that the provisions of the document in question, properly understood, have a particular meaning. There could still be a secondary crave dealing with the consequences in the event of declarator being granted, e.g. a crave for payment or specific implement. Averments will still be required to establish jurisdiction. It would be appropriate, although not necessary, in such circumstances to set out in outline in the condescendence, the argument to be deployed by the pursuer in submitting that the document should be said to have the construction for which he contends. It might even be thought appropriate to cite any authorities said to support the desired construction.

*"List of the documents founded on"*

Rule 40.7(2) reflects the provisions of rule 47.3(3) of the Court of Session Rules. It would be good practice to send to the defender's solicitor a copy of the documents founded upon as soon as a notice of intention to defend the action is intimated if these have not been served with the initial writ. This will enable the issues to be more easily identified at the case management conference. Absent any specific order of the Court in terms of rule 40.12, all productions will require to be lodged not later than 14 days before the diet of proof (rule 29.11(1)).

## Notice of Intention to Defend

**40.8.**—(1) Where the defender intends to—

(a)   challenge the jurisdiction of the court;

(b)   state a defence; or

(c)   make a counterclaim,

he shall, before the expiry of the period of notice lodge with the sheriff clerk a notice of intention to defend in Form O7 and shall, at the same time, send a copy to the pursuer.

(2) The lodging of a notice of intention to defend shall not imply acceptance of the jurisdiction of the court.

GENERAL NOTE

A defender who wishes to defend a commercial action requires to lodge a notice of intention to defend in the same way and within the same period of notice as he would were the action an ordinary action. As for ordinary actions, the rules specifically provide that the defender can lodge a notice of intention to defend and still challenge the jurisdiction of the court to hear the case.

## Defences

**40.9.**—(1) Where a notice of intention to defend has been lodged, the defender shall lodge defences within 7 days after the expiry of the period of notice.

(2) There shall be appended to the defences a list of the documents founded on or adopted as incorporated in the defences.

(3) Subject to the requirement that each article of condescendence in the initial writ need not be admitted or denied, defences shall be in the form of answers that allow the extent of the dispute to be identified and shall have appended a note of the pleas in law of the defender.

In a commercial action the defender has only seven days from the expiry of the period of notice in which to lodge defences as opposed to 14 days in an ordinary action (rule 9.6(1)). Unlike an ordinary action there will be no intimation from the sheriff clerk specifying the date by which defences require to be lodged. As a pursuer has to append a list of documents to the initial writ, so a defender has to append a list of the documents upon which he founds, or which have been incorporated into the pleadings, to the defences. It is considered good practice for the documents to be lodged in process before the first case management conference. The defences should contain the name of the solicitor dealing with the case together with the telephone number and e-mail address.

*"Each article of condescendence in the initial writ need not be admitted or denied".*

The defences do not require to be in traditional form where the defender repeats *ad longum* which of the pursuer's averments are admitted. It has never been good practice to adopt such an approach with regard to denials. It would appear therefore that the reference to each article of condescendence not requiring to be denied is meant to convey that a defender will no longer be deemed to have admitted a fact which is subject to an averment by the pursuer and which is within the defender's knowledge but which is not covered by a general denial.

*"Answers that allow the extent of the dispute to be identified"*

The guiding principle is always whether fair notice is given to the other side to enable them to know the case which they require to meet and to be able to properly prepare for proof. The means of achieving that can take a number of forms. Lengthy narrative is discouraged. Parties regularly use spreadsheets or schedules to set out their position with regard to particular issues. The sheriffs welcome this. It is a cardinal feature of commercial actions that parties make full and frank disclosure. Some guidance as to the degree of specification required can be found in *Kaur v Singh* , 1998 S.C. 233 at 237C, per Lord Hamilton, and *Johnston v WH Brown Construction (Dundee) Ltd* , 2000 S.L.T. 223.

*"Shall have appended a note of the pleas-in-law"*

It is worth noting that the defences require that there be pleas-in-law appended to them. There is no dispensation for defences as there is with an initial writ when the only matter in dispute is the construction of a document as one finds in rule 40.7(1).

## Fixing date for Case Management Conference

**40.10.**—(1)  On the lodging of defences, the sheriff clerk shall fix a date and time for a Case Management Conference, which date shall be on the first suitable court day occurring not sooner than 14 days, nor later than 28 days after the date of expiry of the period of notice.

(2)  On fixing the date for the Case Management Conference, the sheriff clerk shall—

    (a)  forthwith intimate to the parties the date and time of the Case Management Conference; and

    (b)  prepare and sign an interlocutor recording that information.

(3)  The fixing of the date of the Case Management Conference shall not affect the right of a party to make application by motion, to the court.

On defences being lodged the process is normally placed before one of the commercial sheriffs who will decide whether the first case management conference will be conducted in court, chambers, or, in Glasgow, by conference call. The majority of case management conferences in Glasgow Sheriff Court are now dealt with by conference call which the sheriff initiates. The introduction of conference call facilities was in response to the profession and litigants being concerned by the inefficiency of having to travel to court and wait for their case to call. If a solicitor does not wish to make use of the conference call facility, he or she is entitled to request a traditional hearing. The date of the case management conference, which must not be sooner than 14 days after the period of notice nor later than 28 days after its expiry, is then intimated to the parties. In Glasgow Sheriff Court this intimation informs the parties of the date and time for the case management conference, whether it will be in court or chambers or whether it can proceed by conference call, the identity of the commercial sheriff allocated to the case and the e-mail address for that particular sheriff. Wherever possible that sheriff will deal with all hearings in the case.

It is important that the solicitor with responsibility for the case is available for the case management conference and it is not uncommon for the initial date and time to be altered to suit solicitors' diaries.

The rules make it clear that the fixing of a case management conference will not preclude a party from enrolling a motion. Very often the motion will be dealt with at the case management conference but where there is a degree of urgency the motion can usually be accommodated in advance of that date.

### Applications for summary decree in a commercial action

**40.11.** *[Repealed by the Act of Sederunt (Sheriff Court Rules) (Miscellaneous Amendments) 2012 (SSI 2012/188) r.3(3) (effective August 1, 2012: repeal has effect subject to savings specified in SSI 2012/188 r.15).]*

GENERAL NOTE

In an ordinary action should a pursuer, or counterclaiming defender, enrol a motion for summary decree, notice of opposition must be given within seven days (rule 15.3(1)(c)). That period is shortened to 48 hours in a commercial action.

### Case Management Conference

**40.12.**—(1) At the Case Management Conference in a commercial action the sheriff shall seek to secure the expeditious resolution of the action.

(2) Parties shall be prepared to provide such information as the sheriff may require to determine—

(a) whether, and to what extent, further specification of the claim and defences is required; and

(b) the orders to make to ensure the expeditious resolution of the action; and

(c)[1] whether there is or is likely to be a vulnerable witness within the meaning of section 11(1) of the Act of 2004 who is to give evidence at any proof or hearing, consider any child witness notice or vulnerable witness application that has been lodged where no order has been made and consider whether any order under section 12(1) of the Act of 2004 requires to be made.

(3) The orders the sheriff may make in terms of paragraph 2(b) may include but shall not be limited to—

(a) the lodging of written pleadings by any party to the action which may be restricted to particular issues;

(b) the lodging of a statement of facts by any party which may be restricted to particular issues;

(c) allowing an amendment by a party to his pleadings;

(d) disclosure of the identity of witnesses and the existence and nature of documents relating to the action or authority to recover documents either generally or specifically;

(e) the lodging of documents constituting, evidencing or relating to the subject matter of the action or any invoices, correspondence or similar documents;

(f) the exchanging of lists of witnesses;

(g) the lodging of reports of skilled persons or witness statements;

(h) the lodging of affidavits concerned with any of the issues in the action;

(i) the lodging of notes of arguments setting out the basis of any preliminary plea;

(j) fixing a debate or proof, with or without any further preliminary procedure, to determine the action or any particular aspect thereof;

(k) the lodging of joint minutes of admission or agreement;

---

[1] As inserted by the Act of Sederunt (Ordinary Cause, Summary Application, Summary Cause and Small Claim Rules) Amendment (Vulnerable Witnesses (Scotland) Act 2004) 2007, r.2(12) (effective November 1, 2007).

(l)   recording admissions made on the basis of information produced; or

(m)   any order which the sheriff thinks will result in the speedy resolution of the action (including the use of alternative dispute resolution), or requiring the attendance of parties in person at any subsequent hearing.

(4)  In making any order in terms of paragraph (3) the sheriff may fix a period within which such order shall be complied with.

(5)  The sheriff may continue the Case Management Conference to a specified date where he considers it necessary to do so—

(a)   to allow any order made in terms of paragraph (3) to be complied with; or

(b)   to advance the possibility of resolution of the action.

(6)  Where the sheriff makes an order in terms of paragraph (3) he may ordain the pursuer to—

(a)   make up a record; and

(b)   lodge that record in process,

within such period as he thinks fit.

GENERAL NOTE

The Ordinary Cause Rules did not follow the Court of Session model and avoided having both a preliminary and procedural hearing. Instead there is a case management conference which serves the purpose of both. If the action involves the interpretation of a contract it can be sent straight to a debate. The only further procedure in such a case might be the preparation of notes of argument and lists of authorities. Otherwise the purpose of the case management conference is to identify the issues and agree upon a framework for their resolution. For example, it is quite common to restrict the first stage to identifying the contractual terms regulating the relationship between the parties, should these be in issue. Sometimes liability is determined first leaving quantum for a later stage. Further factual information may well be required to properly identify the issues. The case management conference can be continued for this purpose. There is often a time frame agreed within which the information is to be obtained and exchanged.

*Form of the case management conference*

In Glasgow Sheriff Court the case management conference will often be conducted by telephone conference call which is initiated by the sheriff. If there is a hearing, wigs and gowns are not worn and parties remain seated. It is intended that the hearing be conducted as a business meeting. One of the advantages of conference calls is that the principal solicitor is able to conduct the hearing regardless of where his office is located. Conference call facilities are not presently available in the Borders Courts. If the principal solicitor is unable to appear at the case management conference, it is vital that the solicitor instructed to appear is properly briefed and able to contribute fully to the discussion.

*Written pleadings*

Although written pleadings remain the most common vehicle for focusing issues, spreadsheets, schedules and similar forms are increasingly used. Intimation of pleadings, etc. is usually given in electronic form both between solicitors and to the sheriff. If there are issues with regard to a lack of specification, these are normally discussed and resolved at a case management conference and should not thereafter be the focus for a debate. Any adjustment to the initial writ and defences should be achieved by red lining, striking out or similar. The court will not welcome receipt of a traditional "note of adjustment".

*Recovery and disclosure of documents*

The procedures in Chapter 28 for recovery of evidence are still available to the parties. However, recourse to this provision is not usually required when the documents, the production of which is sought, are in the hands of the parties to the litigation. It is normally agreed that such documents should be produced and the timescale for achieving this.

*Exchange of lists of witnesses*

Unlike Chapter 47 procedure in the Court of Session, lists of witnesses are not normally required in advance of proof being allowed. However, parties are required to know how many witnesses they will be leading in evidence in order that the appropriate number of days can be allowed for the proof. A list of witnesses is normally required at least 28 days before the diet of proof.

*Reports of skilled persons and witness statements*

If parties have retained expert witnesses it is customary for their reports to be lodged and exchanged before proof is allowed. If this is not done voluntarily it is unlikely that a party will be able to resist a motion that their expert's report should be lodged as a production. Little recourse is made to the production of witness statements.

*Affidavits*

As for witness statements, parties are not usually put to the expense of preparing affidavits. The exception to this is when there is a motion for summary decree. On such occasions the commercial sheriff may require that an affidavit be produced, usually by the defender, covering a particularly critical averment.

*Notes of argument*

If there has been a full discussion of the basis of a preliminary plea at a case management conference, the lodging of a note of argument might be dispensed with. However, it is more than likely that the commercial sheriff will require a note of argument in advance of the debate being allowed. Although there is no specific provision in the rules for producing a note on further procedure, this is sometimes ordered at the same time as is the note of argument. The two documents then assist the sheriff in deciding whether there should be some form of enquiry into the facts or whether the case should go to debate. In advance of any debate the commercial sheriff will normally require that lists of authorities be exchanged. The commercial sheriff is not obliged to send a case to debate only because one of the parties has tabled a preliminary plea.

*"Speedy resolution"*

Perhaps this is an unfortunate expression as it might give the impression that thoroughness and fairness will be sacrificed at the altar of speed. A more balanced expression might be "efficient resolution".

*Record*

It should be noted that unless ordained so to do the pursuer does not require to lodge a record. The initial writ and defences, as these have been adjusted, are often sufficient for the purposes of the commercial sheriff and the parties.

## Lodging of productions

**40.13** Prior to any proof or other hearing at which the documents listed in terms of rules 40.7(2) and 40.9(2) are to be referred to parties shall, in addition to lodging the productions in terms of rule 21.1, prepare, for the use of the sheriff, a working bundle in which the documents are arranged chronologically or in another appropriate order.

General Note

This rule reflects the terms of para.14 of Court of Session Practice Note No. 12 of 1994. In practice it is not always insisted upon by the commercial sheriff. In advance of the hearing solicitors should ascertain from the sheriff if the terms of this rule can be dispensed with.

## Hearing for further procedure

**40.14.** At any time before final judgement, the sheriff may—

(a) of his own motion or on the motion of any party, fix a hearing for further procedure; and

(b) make such other order as he thinks fit.

General Note

The main thrust of Chapter 40 rules is that the commercial sheriff should be involved in managing all procedural aspects of the case. This rule enables the sheriff to put a case out for a by order hearing at any time before final judgment when the sheriff would, in any event, be functus. It is sometimes used by the sheriff to convene a pre-proof hearing to ascertain how preparations for the proof are proceeding and if there is likely to be a settlement. It is also used after there has been a debate or preliminary proof to discuss what further procedure there should be once the decision on the debate or preliminary point is known.

## Failure to comply with rule or order of sheriff

**40.15** Any failure by a party to comply timeously with a provision in this Chapter or any order made by the sheriff in a commercial action shall entitle the sheriff, of his own motion—

    (a)   to refuse to extend any period for compliance with a provision in these Rules or an order of the court;

    (b)   to dismiss the action or counterclaim, as the case may be, in whole or in part;

    (c)   to grant decree in respect of all or any of the craves of the initial writ or counterclaim, as the case may be; or

    (d)   to make an award of expenses,

as he thinks fit.

GENERAL NOTE

This rule provides the commercial sheriff with the necessary sanctions to attain the aim of achieving an efficient determination of commercial actions.

## Determination of action

**40.16.** It shall be open to the sheriff, at the end of any hearing, to restrict any interlocutor to a finding.

GENERAL NOTE

This provision may be thought to dispense with the requirement to make findings in fact at the conclusion of a diet of proof or proof before answer. Such dispensation would be consistent with the stated desire to achieve a speedy decision.

## Parts of Process

**40.17.** All parts of process lodged in a commercial action shall be clearly marked "Commercial Action".

GENERAL NOTE

Not only should the initial writ bear the expression "Commercial Action" but all steps in the process should also be so distinguished.

Chapter 41[1]

Protection from Abuse (Scotland) Act 2001

## Interpretation

**41.1.**—(1) In this Chapter a section referred to by number means the section so numbered in the Protection from Abuse (Scotland) Act 2001.

(2) Words and expressions used in this Chapter which are also used in the Protection from Abuse (Scotland) Act 2001 have the same meaning as in that Act.

## Attachment of power of arrest to interdict

**41.2.**—[2](1) An application under section 1(1) (application for attachment of power of arrest to interdict)—

    (a)   shall be made in the crave in the initial writ, defences or counterclaim in which the interdict to which it relates is applied for, or, if made after the

---

[1] Inserted by the Act of Sederunt (Ordinary Cause Rules) Amendment (Applications under the Protection from Abuse (Scotland) Act 2001) 2002 (SSI 2002/128), para.2.

[2] As amended by the Act of Sederunt (Ordinary Cause, Summary Application, Summary Cause and Small Claim Rules) Amendment (Miscellaneous) 2003 (SSI 2003/26), para.2(13) (effective January 24, 2003).

application for interdict, by motion in the process of the action in which the interdict was sought, or by minute, with answers if appropriate, should the sheriff so order; and

(b)  shall be intimated to the person against whom the interdict is sought or was obtained.

(2)[1]  Where the sheriff attaches a power of arrest under section 1(2) or (1A) (order attaching power of arrest) the following documents shall be served along with the power of arrest in accordance with section 2(1) (documents to be served along with power of arrest)—

(a)  a copy of the application for interdict;

(b)  a copy of the interlocutor granting interdict; and

(c)  where the application to attach the power of arrest was made after the interdict was granted, a copy of the certificate of service of the interdict.

(3)  After the power of arrest has been served, the following documents shall be delivered by the person who obtained the power to the chief constable in accordance with section 3(1) (notification to police)—

(a)  a copy of the application for interdict;

(b)  a copy of the interlocutor granting interdict;

(c)  a copy of the certificate of service of the interdict; and

(d)  where the application to attach the power of arrest was made after the interdict was granted—

  (i)  a copy of the application for the power of arrest;

  (ii)  a copy of the interlocutor granting it; and

  (iii)  a copy of the certificate of service of the power of arrest and the documents that required to be served along with it in accordance with section 2(1).

(e)[2]  where a determination has previously been made in respect of such interdict under section 3(1) of the Domestic Abuse (Scotland) Act 2011, a copy of the interlocutor in Form DA1.

## Extension or recall of power of arrest

**41.3.**—(1)  An application under either of the following provisions shall be made by minute in the process of the action in which the power of arrest was attached—

(a)  section 2(3) (extension of duration of power of arrest);

(b)  section 2(7) (recall of power of arrest).

(2)  Where the sheriff extends the duration of, or recalls, a power of arrest, the person who obtained the extension or recall must deliver a copy of the interlocutor granting the extension or recall in accordance with section 3(1).

## Documents to be delivered to chief constable in relation to recall or variation of interdict

**41.4.**  Where an interdict to which a power of arrest has been attached under section 1(2) is varied or recalled, the person who obtained the variation or recall must deliver a copy of the interlocutor varying or recalling the interdict in accordance with section 3(1).

---

[1] As amended by Act of Sederunt (Ordinary Cause Rules) Amendment (Family Law (Scotland) Act 2006 etc.) 2006, para.2 (SSI 2006/207) (effective May 4, 2006).

[2] As inserted by the Act of Sederunt (Sheriff Court Rules) (Miscellaneous Amendments) (No.2) 2011 (SSI 2011/289) para.2 (effective July 20, 2011).

### Certificate of delivery of documents to chief constable

**41.5.** Where a person is in any circumstances required to comply with section 3(1) he shall, after such compliance, lodge in process a certificate of delivery in Form PA1.

### Chapter 41A[1]

### Domestic Abuse (Scotland) Act 2011

### Interpretation and application of this Chapter

**41A.1.**—(1) In this Chapter—

"the 2011 Act" means the Domestic Abuse (Scotland) Act 2011;
"interdict" includes interim interdict.

(2) This Chapter applies to an application for a determination under section 3(1) of the 2011 Act that an interdict is a domestic abuse interdict.

### Applications for a determination that an interdict is a domestic abuse interdict

**41A.2.**—(1) An application made before the interdict is obtained must be made by crave in the initial writ, defences or counterclaim in which the interdict is sought.

(2) An application made after the interdict is obtained must be made by minute.

(3) Where a determination is made under section 3(1) of the 2011 Act, the interlocutor shall be in Form DA1.

(4) In pursuance of section 3(4) of the 2011 Act, the applicant must serve a copy of the interlocutor in Form DA1 on the person against whom the interdict has been granted and lodge in process a certificate of service in Form DA2.

(5) Where a determination is recalled under section 3(5)(b) of the 2011 Act, the interlocutor shall be in Form DA3.

(6) Paragraph (7) applies where, in respect of the same interdict—

    (a)   a power of arrest under section 1 of the Protection from Abuse (Scotland) Act 2001 is in effect; and

    (b)   a determination under section 3(1) of the 2011 Act is made.

(7)[2] Where a determination is made or where such determination is recalled, the sheriff must appoint a person to send forthwith to the chief constable of the Police Service of Scotland a copy of—

    (a)   the interlocutor in Form DA1 and the certificate of service in Form DA2; or

    (b)   the interlocutor in Form DA3,

as the case may be.

---

[1] As inserted by the Act of Sederunt (Sheriff Court Rules) (Miscellaneous Amendments) (No.2) 2011 (SSI 2011/289) para.5 (effective July 20, 2011).

[2] As amended by the Act of Sederunt (Sheriff Court Rules)(Miscellaneous Amendments) 2013 (SSI 2013/135) para.4 (effective May 27, 2013).

(8)[1]  Where a person is required by virtue of this Chapter to send documents to the chief constable, such person must, after each such compliance, lodge in process a certificate of sending in Form DA4.

## Chapter 42[2]

## Competition Appeal Tribunal

### Interpretation

**42.1.**  In this Chapter—

"the 1998 Act" means the Competition Act 1998; and
"the Tribunal" means the Competition Appeal Tribunal established by section 12 of the Enterprise Act 2002.

### Transfer of proceedings to the Tribunal

**42.2.**—(1)[3]  Where proceedings (or any part of them) relate to an infringement issue, within the meaning of section 16(6) of the Enterprise Act 2002, the sheriff may make an order transferring those proceedings (or that part of them) to the Tribunal—

(a)  of the sheriff's own accord, or

(b)  on the motion of a party.

(1A)[4]  Where the sheriff orders that such proceedings (or any part of them) are transferred to the Tribunal, the sheriff may make such orders as the sheriff thinks fit to allow the Tribunal to determine the issue.

(2)  Where the sheriff orders that such proceedings (or any part of them) are transferred to the Tribunal, the sheriff clerk shall, within 7 days from the date of such order—

(a)  transmit the process (or the appropriate part) to the clerk of the Tribunal;

(b)  notify each party to the proceedings in writing of the transmission under sub paragraph (a); and

(c)  certify, by making an appropriate entry on the interlocutor sheet, that he has made all notifications required under sub paragraph (b).

(3)  Transmission of the process under paragraph (2)(a) shall be valid notwithstanding any failure by the sheriff clerk to comply with paragraph (2)(b) and (c).

## Chapter 43[5]

## Causes Relating to Articles 101 and 102 of the Treaty Establishing the European Community

### Intimation of actions to the Office of Fair Trading

**43.1**—(1)  In this rule—

---

[1] As amended by the Act of Sederunt (Sheriff Court Rules)(Miscellaneous Amendments) 2013 (SSI 2013/135) para.4 (effective May 27, 2013).

[2] Inserted by the Act of Sederunt (Ordinary Cause Rules) Amendment (Competition Appeal Tribunal) 2004 (SSI 2004/350), para.2 (effective August 20, 2004).

[3] As substituted by the Act of Sederunt (Sheriff Court Rules Amendment) (Miscellaneous) 2015 (SSI 2015/424) para.2 (effective 1 February 2016).

[4] As inserted by the Act of Sederunt (Sheriff Court Rules Amendment) (Miscellaneous) 2015 (SSI 2015/424) para.2 (effective 1 February 2016).

[5] Inserted by Act of Sederunt (Ordinary Cause Rules) Amendment (Causes Relating to Articles 81 and 82 of the Treaty Establishing the European Community) 2006 (SSI 2006/293) (effective June 16, 2006) and amended by the Act of Sederunt (Sheriff Court Rules) (Miscellaneous Amendments) (No.3) 2012 (SSI 2012/271) para.6 (effective November 1, 2012).

"the Treaty" means Treaty on the Functioning of the European Union, as referred to in section 1(2)(s) of the European Communities Act 1972; and "the OFT" means the Office of Fair Trading.

(2) In an action where an issue under Article 101 or 102 of the Treaty is raised—

    (a)  by the pursuer in the initial writ;

    (b)  by the defender in the defences;

    (c)  by any party in the pleadings;

intimation of the action shall be given to the OFT by the party raising the issue by a notice of intimation in Form OFT1.

(3) The initial writ, defences or pleadings in which the issue under Article 81 or 82 of the Treaty is raised shall include a crave for warrant for intimation to the OFT.

(4) A certified copy of an interlocutor granting a warrant under paragraph (3) shall be sufficient authority for the party to intimate by notice in Form OFT1.

(5) A notice of intimation under paragraph (2) shall be on a period of notice of 21 days unless the sheriff otherwise orders; but the sheriff shall not order a period of notice of less than 2 days.

(6) There shall be attached to the notice of intimation—

    (a)  a copy of the initial writ, defences or pleadings (including any adjustments and amendments), as the case may be;

    (b)  a copy of the interlocutor allowing intimation of the notice; and

    (c)  where the pleadings have not been amended in accordance with any minute of amendment, a copy of that minute.

Chapter 44[1]

The Equality Act 2010

## Interpretation and application

**44.1.**—[2](1) In this Chapter—

"the Commission" means the Commis sion for Equality and Human Rights; and

"the 2010 Act" means the Equality Act 2010.

(2) This Chapter applies to claims made by virtue of section 114(1) of the 2010 Act including a claim for damages.

## Intimation to Commission

**44.2.**[3] The pursuer shall send a copy of the initial writ to the Commission by registered or recorded delivery post.

## Assessor

**44.3.**—(1) The sheriff may, of his own motion or on the motion of any party, appoint an assessor.

(2) The assessor shall be a person who the sheriff considers has special qualifications to be of assistance in determining the cause.

---

[1] As inserted by the Act of Sederunt (Ordinary Cause, Summary Application, Summary Cause and Small Claim Rules) Amendment (Equality Act 2006 etc.) 2006 (SSI 2006/509), (effective November 3, 2006). Chapter title amended by the Act of Sederunt (Sheriff Court Rules) (Equality Act 2010) 2010 (SSI 2010/340) para.2 (effective October 1, 2010).

[2] As substituted by the Act of Sederunt (Sheriff Court Rules) (Equality Act 2010) 2010 (SSI 2010/340) para.2 (effective October 1, 2010).

[3] As inserted by the Act of Sederunt (Sheriff Court Rules) (Miscellaneous Amendments) 2008 (SSI 2008/223) para.4(3)(b) (effective July 1, 2008).

**Taxation of Commission expenses**

**44.4.** *[Omitted by the Act of Sederunt (Sheriff Court Rules) (Miscellaneous Amendments) 2008 (SSI 2008/223) para.4(3)(c) (effective July 1, 2008).]*

**National security**

**44.5.**—[1](1)  Where, on a motion under paragraph (3) or of the sheriff's own motion, the sheriff considers it expedient in the interests of national security, the sheriff may—

    (a)   exclude from all or part of the proceedings—

        (i)   the pursuer;

        (ii)   the pursuer's representatives;

        (iii)   any assessors;

    (b)   permit a pursuer or representative who has been excluded to make a statement to the court before the commencement of the proceedings or the part of the proceedings, from which he or she is excluded;

    (c)   take steps to keep secret all or part of the reasons for his or her decision in the proceedings.

    (2)  The sheriff clerk shall, on the making of an order under paragraph (1) excluding the pursuer or the pursuer's representatives, notify the Advocate General for Scotland of that order.

    (3)  A party may apply by motion for an order under paragraph (1).

    (4)  The steps referred to in paragraph (1)(c) may include the following—

    (a)   directions to the sheriff clerk; and

    (b)   orders requiring any person appointed to represent the interests of the pursuer in proceedings from which the pursuer or the pursuer's representatives are excluded not to communicate (directly or indirectly) with any persons (including the excluded pursuer)—

        (i)   on any matter discussed or referred to;

        (ii)   with regard to any material disclosed,

during or with reference to any part of the proceedings from which the pursuer or the pursuer's representatives are excluded.

    (5)  Where the sheriff has made an order under paragraph (4)(b), the person appointed to represent the interests of the pursuer may apply by motion for authority to seek instructions from or otherwise communicate with an excluded person.

**Transfer to Employment Tribunal**

**44.6.**—[2](1)  On transferring proceedings to an employment tribunal under section 140(2) of the 2010 Act, the sheriff—

    (a)   shall state his or her reasons for doing so in the interlocutor; and

    (b)   may make the order on such conditions as to expenses or otherwise as he or she thinks fit.

    (2)  The sheriff clerk must, within 7 days from the date of such order—

    (a)   transmit the process to the Secretary of the Employment Tribunals (Scotland);

    (b)   notify each party to the proceedings in writing of the transmission under subparagraph (a); and

---

[1] As substituted by the Act of Sederunt (Sheriff Court Rules) (Equality Act 2010) 2010 (SSI 2010/340) para.2 (effective October 1, 2010).

[2] As inserted by the Act of Sederunt (Sheriff Court Rules) (Equality Act 2010) 2010 (SSI 2010/340) para.2 (effective October 1, 2010).

(c) certify, by making an appropriate entry on the interlocutor sheet, that he or she has made all notifications required under subparagraph (b).

(3) Transmission of the process under paragraph (2)(a) will be valid notwithstanding any failure by the sheriff clerk to comply with paragraph (2)(b) and (c).

## Transfer from Employment Tribunal

**44.7.**—[1](1) On receipt of the documentation in proceedings which have been remitted from an employment tribunal under section 140(3) of the 2010 Act, the sheriff clerk must—

(a) record the date of receipt on the first page of the documentation;

(b) fix a hearing to determine further procedure not less than 14 days after the date of receipt of the process; and

(c) forthwith send written notice of the date of the hearing fixed under subparagraph (b) to each party.

(2) At the hearing fixed under paragraph (1)(b) the sheriff may make such order as he or she thinks fit to secure so far as practicable that the cause thereafter proceeds in accordance with these Rules.

Chapter 45[2]

Vulnerable Witnesses (Scotland) Act 2004

## Interpretation

**45.1.** In this Chapter—

"child witness notice" has the meaning given in section 12(2) of the Act of 2004;

"review application" means an application for review of arrangements for vulnerable witnesses pursuant to section 13 of the Act of 2004;

"vulnerable witness application" has the meaning given in section 12(6) of the Act of 2004.

## Child Witness Notice

**45.2.** A child witness notice lodged in accordance with section 12(2) of the Act of 2004 shall be in Form G19.

## Vulnerable Witness Application

**45.3.** A vulnerable witness application lodged in accordance with section 12(6) of the Act of 2004 shall be in Form G20.

## Intimation

**45.4.**—(1) The party lodging a child witness notice or vulnerable witness application shall intimate a copy of the child witness notice or vulnerable witness application to all the other parties to the proceedings and complete a certificate of intimation.

(2) A certificate of intimation referred to in paragraph (1) shall be in Form G21 and shall be lodged with the child witness notice or vulnerable witness application.

---

[1] As inserted by the Act of Sederunt (Sheriff Court Rules) (Equality Act 2010) 2010 (SSI 2010/340) para.2 (effective October 1, 2010).

[2] As inserted by the Act of Sederunt (Ordinary Cause, Summary Application, Summary Cause and Small Claim Rules) Amendment (Vulnerable Witnesses (Scotland) Act 2004) 2007, r.2(13) (effective November 1, 2007).

**Procedure on lodging child witness notice or vulnerable witness application**

**45.5.**—(1)  On receipt of a child witness notice or vulnerable witness application, the sheriff may—

    (a)  make an order under section 12(1) or (6) of the Act of 2004 without holding a hearing;

    (b)  require further information from any of the parties before making any further order;

    (c)  fix a date for a hearing of the child witness notice or vulnerable witness application.

(2)  The sheriff may, subject to any statutory time limits, make an order altering the date of the proof or other hearing at which the child or vulnerable witness is to give evidence and make such provision for intimation of such alteration to all parties concerned as he deems appropriate.

(3)  An order fixing a hearing for a child witness notice or vulnerable witness application shall be intimated by the sheriff clerk—

    (a)  on the day the order is made; and

    (b)  in such manner as may be prescribed by the sheriff,

to all parties to the proceedings and such other persons as are named in the order where such parties or persons are not present at the time the order is made.

**Review of arrangements for vulnerable witnesses**

**45.6.**—(1)  A review application shall be in Form G22.

(2)  Where the review application is made orally, the sheriff may dispense with the requirements of paragraph (1).

**Intimation of review application**

**45.7.**—(1)  Where a review application is lodged, the applicant shall intimate a copy of the review application to all other parties to the proceedings and complete a certificate of intimation.

(2)  A certificate of intimation referred to in paragraph (1) shall be in Form G23 and shall be lodged together with the review application.

**Procedure on lodging a review application**

**45.8.**—(1)  On receipt of a review application, the sheriff may—

    (a)  if he is satisfied that he may properly do so, make an order under section 13(2) of the Act of 2004 without holding a hearing or, if he is not so satisfied, make such an order after giving the parties an opportunity to be heard;

    (b)  require of any of the parties further information before making any further order;

    (c)  fix a date for a hearing of the review application.

(2)  The sheriff may, subject to any statutory time limits, make an order altering the date of the proof or other hearing at which the child or vulnerable witness is to give evidence and make such provision for intimation of such alteration to all parties concerned as he deems appropriate.

(3)  An order fixing a hearing for a review application shall be intimated by the sheriff clerk—

    (a)  on the day the order is made; and

    (b)  in such manner as may be prescribed by the sheriff,

to all parties to the proceedings and such other persons as are named in the order where such parties or persons are not present at the time the order is made.

**Determination of special measures**

**45.9.** When making an order under section 12(1) or (6) or 13(2) of the Act of 2004 the sheriff may, in light thereof, make such further orders as he deems appropriate in all the circumstances.

**Intimation of an order under section 12(1) or (6) or 13(2)**

**45.10.** An order under section 12(1) or (6) or 13(2) of the Act of 2004 shall be intimated by the sheriff clerk—

    (a)   on the day the order is made; and

    (b)   in such manner as may be prescribed by the sheriff,

to all parties to the proceedings and such other persons as are named in the order where such parties or persons are not present at the time the order is made.

**Taking of evidence by commissioner**

**45.11.**—(1) An interlocutor authorising the special measure of taking evidence by a commissioner shall be sufficient authority for the citing the witness to appear before the commissioner.

    (2)   At the commission the commissioner shall—

    (a)   administer the oath *de fideli administratione* to any clerk appointed for the commission; and

    (b)   administer to the witness the oath in Form G14, or where the witness elects to affirm, the affirmation in Form G15.

    (3)   The commission shall proceed without interrogatories unless, on cause shown, the sheriff otherwise directs.

**Commission on interrogatories**

**45.12.**—(1) Where interrogatories have not been dispensed with, the party citing or intending to cite the vulnerable witness shall lodge draft interrogatories in process.

    (2)   Any other party may lodge cross-interrogatories.

    (3)   The interrogatories and cross-interrogatories, when adjusted, shall be extended and returned to the sheriff clerk for approval and the settlement of any dispute as to their contents by the sheriff.

    (4)   The party who cited the vulnerable witness shall—

    (a)   provide the commissioner with a copy of the pleadings (including any adjustments and amendments), the approved interrogatories and any cross-interrogatories and a certified copy of the interlocutor of his appointment;

    (b)   instruct the clerk; and

    (c)   be responsible in the first instance for the fee of the commissioner and his clerk.

    (5)   The commissioner shall, in consultation with the parties, fix a diet for the execution of the commission to examine the witness.

**Commission without interrogatories**

**45.13.** Where interrogatories have been dispensed with, the party citing or intending to cite the vulnerable witness shall—

    (a)   provide the commissioner with a copy of the pleadings (including any adjustments and amendments) and a certified copy of the interlocutor of his appointment;

    (b)   fix a diet for the execution of the commission in consultation with the commissioner and every other party;

(c)   instruct the clerk; and

(d)   be responsible in the first instance for the fees of the commissioner and his clerk.

### Lodging of video record and documents

**45.14.**—(1)   Where evidence is taken on commission pursuant to an order made under section 12(1) or (6) or 13(2) of the Act of 2004 the commissioner shall lodge the video record of the commission and relevant documents with the sheriff clerk.

(2)   On the video record and any documents being lodged the sheriff clerk shall—

(a)   note—

(i)   the documents lodged;

(ii)   by whom they were lodged; and

(iii)   the date on which they were lodged, and

(b)   intimate what he has noted to all parties concerned.

### Custody of video record and documents

**45.15.**—(1)   The video record and documents referred to in rule 45.14 shall, subject to paragraph (2), be kept in the custody of the sheriff clerk.

(2)   Where the video record of the evidence of a witness is in the custody of the sheriff clerk under this rule and where intimation has been given to that effect under rule 45.14(2), the name and address of that witness and the record of his evidence shall be treated as being in the knowledge of the parties; and no party shall be required, notwithstanding any enactment to the contrary—

(a)   to include the name of that witness in any list of witnesses; or

(b)   to include the record of his evidence in any list of productions.

### Application for leave for party to be present at the commission

**45.16.**   An application for leave for a party to be present in the room where the commission proceedings are taking place shall be by motion..

(1)   In Appendix 1—

(a)   for Form G13 there shall be substituted the form set out in Part 1 of Schedule 1 to this Act of Sederunt; and

(b)   after Form G18 there shall be inserted the forms set out in Part 2 of Schedule 1 to this Act of Sederunt.

### Chapter 46[1]

### Companies Act 2006

### Leave to raise derivative proceedings

**46.1.**—(1)   Where leave of the court is required under section 266(1) (derivative proceedings: requirement for leave and notice) of the Companies Act 2006 (the "2006 Act"), the applicant must lodge, along with the initial writ, a written application in the form of a letter addressed to the sheriff clerk stating the grounds on which leave is sought.

(2)   Subject to paragraph (4), an application under paragraph (1) is not to be served on, or intimated to, any party.

(3)   The application is to be placed before the sheriff, who shall consider it for the purposes of section 266(3) of the 2006 Act without hearing the applicant.

---

[1] As inserted by the Act of Sederunt (Sheriff Court Rules) (Miscellaneous Amendments) 2010 (SSI 2010/279) r.5 (effective July 29, 2010).

(4)   Service under section 266(4)(a) of the 2006 Act may be given by any of the methods provided for in Chapter 5 (citation, service and intimation) and a certificate of service must be lodged.

(5)   If the company wishes to be heard it must, within 21 days after the date of service of the application, lodge written submissions setting out its position in relation to the application.

(6)   Subject to section 266(4)(b) of the 2006 Act, the next stage in the proceedings is a hearing at which the applicant and the company may be heard.

(7)   The sheriff clerk is to fix the hearing and intimate its date to the applicant and the company.

(8)   Where an application under paragraph (1) is granted, a copy of the sheriff's interlocutor must be served on the defender along with the warrant of citation.

## Application to continue proceedings as derivative proceedings

**46.2.**   An application under section 267(2) (application to continue proceedings as derivative proceedings) of the 2006 Act is to be in the form of a minute and Chapter 14 (applications by minute) applies with the necessary modifications.

Chapter 47[1]

Actions of Division and Sale and Orders for Division and/or Sale of Property

## Remit to reporter to examine heritable property

**47.1.**—(1)   In an action of division and sale of heritable property, the sheriff may, in accordance with paragraph (2), remit to a reporter to examine the property and to report to the sheriff—

(a)   whether the property is capable of division in a manner equitable to the interests of the *pro indiviso* proprietors and, if so, how such division may be effected; and

(b)   in the event that the property is to be sold—

(i)   whether the property should be sold as a whole or in lots and, if in lots, what those lots should be;

(ii)   whether the property should be exposed for sale by public roup or private bargain;

(iii)   whether the sale should be subject to any upset or minimum price and, if so, the amount;

(iv)   the manner and extent to which the property should be advertised for sale; and

(v)   any other matter which the reporter considers pertinent to a sale of the property.

(2)   A remit under paragraph (1) shall be made—

(a)   where the action is undefended, on the motion of the pursuer at any time after the expiry of the period of notice;

(b)   where the action is defended—

(i)   at the options hearing, on the motion of any party to the action;

(ii)   on the sheriff finding, after a debate or proof, that the pursuer is entitled to bring and insist in the action of division and sale; or

(iii)   at such other time as the sheriff thinks fit.

---

[1] As inserted by the Act of Sederunt (Sheriff Court Rules) (Miscellaneous Amendments) (No.3) 2011 (SSI 2011/386) para.2 (effective November 28, 2011).

(3) On completion of a report made under paragraph (1), the reporter shall send the report, with a copy for each party, to the sheriff clerk.

(4) On receipt of such report, the sheriff clerk must—

    (a) lodge the report in process; and

    (b) give written intimation to each party that this has been done and that parties may uplift a copy of the report from the process.

(5) After the lodging of such a report, any party may apply by motion for further procedure or for approval of the report.

(6) At the hearing of a motion under paragraph (5), the sheriff may—

    (a) in the event of a challenge to any part of the report, order parties to state their objections to the report and answers to such objections and lodge them within such period as the sheriff thinks fit; or

    (b) in the absence of such challenge, order that the property be divided or sold, as the case may be, in accordance with the recommendations of the reporter, subject to such modification, if any, as the sheriff thinks fit.

(7) Where, in accordance with paragraph (6)(a), the lodging of objections and answers has been ordered, the sheriff clerk will fix a date and time for the parties to be heard by the sheriff; and the sheriff may make such order for further procedure as he or she thinks fit.

### Division and/or sale of property

**47.2.**—(1) Where the sheriff orders the division and/or sale of property, heritable or otherwise, the sheriff shall direct that the division and/or sale, as the case may be, shall be conducted under the oversight and direction of the sheriff clerk or any other fit person whom the sheriff may appoint for that purpose.

(2) The sheriff clerk or person appointed under paragraph (1), as the case may be, may report any matter of difficulty arising in the course of the division and/or sale to the sheriff.

(3) At a hearing on a report made under paragraph (2), the sheriff may give such directions as the sheriff thinks fit, including authority to the sheriff clerk to sign, on behalf of any proprietor, a disposition of his or her interest in the property.

(4) On the conclusion of a sale of property—

    (a) the proceeds of the sale, under deduction of the expenses of the sale, shall be consigned into court; and

    (b) the sheriff clerk or the person appointed under paragraph (1), as the case may be, shall lodge in process a report of the sale and a proposed scheme of division of the proceeds of sale.

(5) At the hearing of a motion for approval of a report of the sale of property lodged under paragraph (4) and the proposed scheme of division, the sheriff may—

    (a) approve the report and scheme of division, and direct that payment of the proceeds of sale be made in terms of the report;

    (b) deal with any question as to the expenses of process or of sale; and

(c)   make such other order as the sheriff thinks fit.

Chapter 48[1] [2]

Reporting Restrictions

**Interpretation and application of this Chapter**

**48.1.**(1)   This Chapter applies to orders which restrict the reporting of proceedings.

(2)   In this Chapter, *"interested person"* means a person—

(a)   who has asked to see any order made by the sheriff which restricts the reporting of proceedings, including an interim order; and

(b)   whose name is included on a list kept by the Lord President for the purposes of this Chapter.

**Interim orders: notification to interested persons**

**48.2.**—(1)   Where the sheriff is considering making an order, the sheriff may make an interim order.

(2)   Where the sheriff makes an interim order, the sheriff clerk shall immediately send a copy of the interim order to any interested person.

(3)   The sheriff shall specify in the interim order why the sheriff is considering making an order.

**Interim orders: representations**

**48.3.**—(1)   Paragraph (2) applies where the sheriff has made an interim order.

(2)   An interested person who would be directly affected by the making of an order shall have an opportunity to make representations to the sheriff before an order is made.

(3)   Representations shall—

(a)   be made by letter addressed to the sheriff clerk;

(b)   where an urgent hearing is sought, include reasons explaining why an urgent hearing is necessary;

(c)   be lodged no later than 2 days after the interim order is sent to interested persons in accordance with rule 48.2(2).

(4)   Where the period for lodging representations expires on a Saturday, Sunday, or public or court holiday, it shall be deemed to expire on the next day on which the sheriff clerk's office is open for civil court business.

(5)   On representations being made—

(a)   the sheriff shall appoint a date and time for a hearing—

(i)   on the first suitable court day thereafter; or

(ii)   where the sheriff is satisfied that an urgent hearing is necessary, at such earlier date and time as the sheriff may determine;

(b)   the sheriff clerk shall—

(i)   notify the date and time of the hearing to the parties to the proceedings and the person who has made representations; and

(ii)   send a copy of the representations to the parties to the proceedings.

---

[1] As inserted by the Act of Sederunt (Sheriff Court Rules) (Miscellaneous Amendments) (No.3) 2011 (SSI 2011/386) para.3 (effective November 28, 2011).

[2] As substituted by the Act of Sederunt (Rules of the Court of Session and Sheriff Court Rules Amendment No. 3) (Reporting Restrictions) 2015 (SSI 2015/85) para.3 (effective April 1, 2015).

(6)   Where no interested person makes representations in accordance with rule 48.3(2), the sheriff clerk shall put the interim order before the sheriff in chambers in order that the sheriff may resume consideration as to whether to make an order.

(7)   Where the sheriff, having resumed consideration under rule 48.3(6), makes no order, the sheriff shall recall the interim order.

(8)   Where the sheriff recalls an interim order, the sheriff clerk shall immediately notify any interested person.

### Notification of reporting restrictions

**48.4.**—(1)   Where the court makes an order, the sheriff clerk shall immediately—

(a)   send a copy of the order to any interested person;

(b)   arrange for the publication of the making of the order on the Scottish Court Service website.

### Applications for variation or revocation

**48.5.**—(1)   A person aggrieved by an order may apply to the sheriff for its variation or revocation.

(2)   An application shall be made by letter addressed to the sheriff clerk.

(3)   On an application being made—

(a)   the sheriff shall appoint the application for a hearing;

(b)   the sheriff clerk shall—

(i)   notify the date and time of the hearing to the parties to the proceedings and the applicant;

(ii)   send a copy of the application to the parties to the proceedings.

(4)   The hearing shall, so far as reasonably practicable, be before the sheriff who made the order.

Chapter 49[1]

Admiralty Actions

### Interpretation of this Chapter

**49.1.**   In this Chapter—

"Admiralty action" means an action having a crave appropriate for the enforcement of a claim to which section 47(2) of the Administration of Justice Act 1956 applies;

"ship" has the meaning assigned in section 48(f) of that Act.

### Forms of action

**49.2.**—(1)   An Admiralty action against the owners or demise charterers of, or other parties interested in, a ship or the owners of the cargo may be brought—

(a)   in rem, where the crave of the initial writ is directed to recovery in respect of a maritime lien against the ship or cargo or the proceeds of it as sold under order of the sheriff or where arrestment in rem may be made under section 47(3) of the Administration of Justice Act 1956;

(b)   in personam, where the crave of the initial writ is directed to a decree against the defender; or

(c)   both in rem and in personam, where sub-paragraphs (a) and (b) apply.

---

[1] As inserted by the Act of Sederunt (Sheriff Court Rules) (Miscellaneous Amendments) 2012 (SSI 2012/188) para.10 (effective August 1, 2012).

(2) When bringing an Admiralty action, the pursuer shall use Form G1 (initial writ) and insert the words "Admiralty Action in rem", "Admiralty Action in personam" or "Admiralty Action in rem and in personam", as the case may be, immediately below where the Sheriffdom and court are designed, above the instance.

### Actions in rem

49.3.—(1) In an Admiralty action in rem—
- (a) where the owners or demise charterers of, or other parties interested in, the ship or the owners of the cargo against which the action is directed are known to the pursuer, they shall be called as defenders by name;
- (b) where such owners or demise charterers or other parties are unknown to the pursuer—
    - (i) the pursuer may call them as defenders as "the owners of or parties interested in the ship (*name and identify by its port of registry*) or the owners of the cargo"; and
    - (ii) the master, if known, shall also be called as a defender representing the owners or demise charterers.

(2) In an Admiralty action in rem, the ship or cargo shall be arrested in rem and a warrant for such arrestment may include warrant to dismantle where craved in the initial writ.

### Actions in personam

49.4.—(1) In an Admiralty action in personam directed against the owners or demise charterers, or other parties, interested in a ship, or the owners of cargo, the defenders shall, if known to the pursuer, be called as defenders by name.

(2) In such an action, where—
- (a) the vessel is not a British ship, and
- (b) the names of the owners or demise charterers are not known to the pursuer, the master of the ship may be called as the defender representing the owners or demise charterers.

(3) In an action to which paragraph (2) applies, any warrant to arrest to found jurisdiction shall be executed against the master of the ship in his or her representative capacity.

(4) In an action to which paragraph (2) applies, any decree shall be pronounced against the master in his or her representative capacity.

(5) A decree in an Admiralty action in personam may be pronounced against an owner or demise charterer of, or other party interested in, the ship or the owner of the cargo only where that owner or demise charterer or other party interested, as the case may be, has been called or added as a defender.

### Sale of ship or cargo

49.5.—(1) This rule shall not apply to the sale of a cargo arrested on the dependence of an Admiralty action in personam.

(2) Where, in an Admiralty action or an action of declarator and sale of a ship—
- (a) the sheriff makes a finding that the pursuer has a claim which falls to be satisfied out of an arrested ship or cargo, or
- (b) a decree for a sum of money has been granted in an action in which a ship has been arrested on the dependence,
the pursuer may apply by motion for an order for the sale of that ship or a share in it, or the cargo, as the case may be, by public auction or private bargain.

(3)   Before making such an order, the sheriff shall remit to a reporter for the purpose of obtaining—

(a)   an inventory of,

(b)   a valuation and recommendation upset price for, and

(c)   any recommendation as to the appropriate advertisement for the sale of, the ship, share or cargo.

(4)   Where a remit is made under paragraph (3), the pursuer shall instruct the reporter within 14 days after the date of the interlocutor making the remit and be responsible, in the first instance, for payment of his or her fee.

(5)   On completion of a report following a remit under paragraph (3), the reporter shall send the report and a copy for each party to the sheriff clerk.

(6)   On receipt of such a report, the sheriff clerk shall—

(a)   give written intimation to each party of receipt of the report;

(b)   request the pursuer to show to him or her a discharge in respect of the fee for which the pursuer is responsible under paragraph (4); and

(c)   after sight of such a discharge—

(i)   lodge the report in process;

(ii)   give written intimation to each party that this has been done and that he or she may uplift a copy of the report from process; and

(iii)   cause the action to call for a procedural hearing.

(7)   Where the sheriff orders the sale of a ship, share or cargo, the conduct of the sale, including any advertisement of it, shall be under the direction of the sheriff clerk.

(8)   Where such a sale is the sale of a ship or a share in it, the interlocutor ordering the sale shall include a declaration that the right to transfer the ship or share to the purchaser is vested in the sheriff clerk.

(9)   Where, in such a sale, no offer to purchase the ship, share or cargo, as the case may be, has reached the upset price, the pursuer may apply by motion for authority to expose such ship, share or cargo for sale at a reduced upset price.

(10)   The proceeds of such a sale shall be consigned into court, under deduction of all dues to the date the sheriff adjudges the ship, share or cargo to belong to the purchaser under paragraph (11)(a), payable to Her Majesty's Revenue and Customs or to the port or harbour authority within the jurisdiction of which the ship or cargo lies and in respect of which such port or harbour authority has statutory power to detain the ship or cargo.

(11)   On consignation being made under paragraph (10), the sheriff shall—

(a)   adjudge the ship, share or cargo, as the case may be, declaring the same to belong to the purchaser, freed and disburdened of all bonds, mortgages, liens, rights of retention and other incumbrances affecting it and ordering such ship, share or cargo to be delivered to the purchaser on production of a certified copy of the interlocutor pronounced under this subparagraph; and

(b)   order such intimation and advertisement, if any, for claims on the consigned fund as the sheriff thinks fit.

(12)   The sheriff shall, after such hearing or inquiry as the sheriff thinks fit—

(a)   determine all questions of expenses;

(b)   rank and prefer any claimants in order of preference; and

(c)   make such other order, if any, as the sheriff thinks fit.

## Ship collisions and preliminary acts

**49.6.**—(1) Subject to rule 49.7 (applications to dispense with preliminary acts), this rule applies to an Admiralty action of damages arising out of a collision between ships at sea.

(2) An action to which this rule applies may be brought in rem, in personam or in rem and in personam.

(3) An initial writ in such an action shall not contain a condescendence or pleas-in-law.

(4) Where such an action is brought in personam, the crave of the initial writ shall contain sufficient detail to enable the defender to identify the date and place of and the ships involved in the collision.

(5) Where a notice of intention to defend has been lodged Rule 9.2 shall, subject to paragraph 11 of this rule, not apply.

(6) Within 7 days after the expiry of the period of notice, the pursuer shall lodge in process a sealed envelope containing—

    (a) a preliminary act in Form 49.6; and

    (b) a brief condescendence and appropriate pleas-in-law.

(7) Within 28 days after the preliminary act for the pursuer has been lodged under paragraph (6), the defender shall lodge in process a sealed envelope containing a preliminary act in Form 49.6.

(8) A party who lodges a preliminary act under paragraph (6) or (7) shall not send a copy of it to any other party.

(9) On the lodging of a preliminary act by the defender under paragraph (7) the sheriff clerk shall—

    (a) open both sealed envelopes;

    (b) mark the contents of those envelopes with appropriate numbers of process; and

    (c) give written intimation to each party that subparagraphs (a) and (b) have been complied with.

(10) On receipt of the written intimation under paragraph (9)(c), the pursuer and defender shall exchange copies of the contents of their respective envelopes.

(11) Within 7 days after the sealed envelopes have been opened up under paragraph (9), the sheriff clerk shall fix a date and time for an Options Hearing and send parties Form G5 in terms of Rule 9.2.

(12) When the pursuer lodges a record in terms of Rule 9.11 he or she shall do so with a copy of each of the preliminary acts appended to it.

(13) No amendment, adjustment or alteration may be made to a preliminary act except by order of the sheriff.

## Applications to dispense with preliminary acts

**49.7.**—(1) Within 7 days after the expiry of the period of notice, any party may apply for an order to dispense with preliminary acts in an action to which rule 49.6 applies.

(2) An application under paragraph (1) shall be made by minute craving the sheriff to dispense with preliminary acts and setting out the grounds on which the application is made.

(3) Before lodging such a minute in process, the party making the application shall intimate a copy of the minute, and the date on which it will be lodged, to every other party.

(4)   Any other party may lodge in process answers to such a minute within 14 days after such a minute has been lodged.

(5)   After the expiry of the period mentioned in paragraph (4), the sheriff may, on the motion of any party, after such further procedure, if any, as the sheriff thinks fit, dispense with preliminary acts.

(6)   Where the sheriff dispenses with preliminary acts, the pursuer shall lodge a condescendence with appropriate pleas-in-law within such period as the sheriff thinks fit; and the action shall thereafter proceed in the same way as an ordinary action.

(7)   Where the sheriff refuses to dispense with preliminary acts, the sheriff shall ordain a party or parties, as the case may be, to lodge preliminary acts under rule 49.6 within such period as the sheriff thinks fit.

(8)   An interlocutor dispensing or refusing to dispense with preliminary acts shall be final and not subject to review.

### Ship collision and salvage actions

**49.8.**—(1)   Without prejudice to rule 29.11 (lodging productions), in an Admiralty action arising out of a collision between ships at sea or salvage, the parties shall—

   (a)   within 4 days after the interlocutor allowing proof,

   (b)   within 4 days before the taking of evidence on commission, or

   (c)   on or before such other date as the sheriff, on special cause shown, shall determine,

lodge in process the documents, if any, mentioned in paragraph (2).

(2)   The documents to be lodged under paragraph (1) are—

   (a)   the log books, including scrap log books, of the ships concerned;

   (b)   all *de recenti* written reports in connection with the collision or salvage, as the case may be, by the masters or mates of the vessels concerned to their respective owners; and

   (c)   reports of any surveys of the ship in respect of which damage or salvage is claimed.

### Arrestment of ships and arrestment in rem of cargo on board ship

**49.9.**—(1)   An arrestment of a ship in rem or on the dependence, or an arrestment in rem of cargo on board ship, may be executed on any day by a sheriff officer who shall affix the schedule of arrestment—

   (a)   to the mainmast of the ship;

   (b)   to the single mast of the ship; or

   (c)   where there is no mast, to some prominent part of the ship.

(2)   In the execution of an arrestment of a ship on the dependence, the sheriff officer shall, in addition to complying with paragraph (1), mark the initials "ER" above the place where the schedule of arrestment is fixed.

(3)   On executing an arrestment under paragraph (1), the sheriff officer shall deliver a copy of the schedule of arrestment and a copy of the certificate of execution of it to the master of the ship, or other person on board in charge of the ship or cargo, as the case may be, as representing the owners or demise charterers of, or parties interested in, the ship or the owners of the cargo, as the case may be.

(4)   Where the schedule of arrestment and the copy of the certificate of execution of it cannot be delivered as required under paragraph (3)—

   (a)   the certificate of execution shall state that fact; and

   (b)   either—

      (i)   the arrestment shall be executed by serving it on the harbour master of the port where the ship lies; or

     (ii)   where there is no harbour master, or the ship is not in a harbour, the pursuer shall enrol a motion for such further order as to intimation and advertisement, if any, as may be necessary.

(5)  A copy of the schedule of arrestment and a copy of the certificate of execution of it shall be delivered by the sheriff officer to the harbour master, if any, of any port where the ship lies.

## Arrestment of cargo

**49.10.**—(1)  An arrestment of cargo on board a ship shall be executed by a sheriff officer who shall serve the schedule of arrestment on—

    (a)   the master of the ship;

    (b)   any other person in charge of the ship or cargo; or

    (c)   other proper arrestee.

(2)  Where the schedule of arrestment cannot be executed in accordance with paragraph (1), the arrestment may be executed as provided for in rule 49.9(4) and (5).

## Forms for diligence in admiralty actions

**49.11.**—(1)  In the execution of diligence in an Admiralty action, the following forms shall be used—

    (a)   in the case of—

        (i)   an arrestment to found jurisdiction (other than the arrestment of a ship), a schedule in Form 49.11-A and a certificate of execution in Form 49.11-E;

       (ii)   an arrestment of a ship to found jurisdiction, a schedule in Form 49.11-AA and a certificate of execution in Form 49.11-F;

    (b)   subject to subparagraph (e), in the case of an arrestment on the dependence, a schedule in Form G4B and a certificate of execution in Form 49.11-E;

    (c)   in the case of an arrestment in rem of a ship, cargo or other maritime *res* to enforce a maritime hypothec or lien, a schedule in Form 49.11-B and a certificate of execution in Form 49.11-G;

    (d)   in the case of an arrestment in rem of a ship to enforce a non-pecuniary claim, a schedule in Form 49.11-C and a certificate of execution in Form 49.11-G;

    (e)   in the case of an arrestment on the dependence of—

        (i)   a cargo on board a ship, a schedule in Form G4B;

       (ii)   a ship, a schedule in Form 49.11-D,

and a certificate of execution in Form 49.11-H.

(2)  Where two or more of the arrestments mentioned in paragraph (1)(a), (b) and (c) are to be executed, they may be combined in one schedule of arrestment.

## Movement of arrested property

**49.12.**(1)  Any person who has an interest in a ship or cargo which is the subject of an arrestment under this Chapter may apply by motion for a warrant authorising the movement of the ship or cargo.

(2)  Where the sheriff grants a warrant sought under paragraph (1), the sheriff may make such further order as the sheriff thinks fit to give effect to that warrant.

**Arrestment before service**

**49.13.** Before the service of an Admiralty action, where it is craved in the initial writ, the pursuer may apply by motion for warrant for arrestment of any of the types of arrestment mentioned in this Chapter.

Chapter 50[1]

Lodging Audio or Audio-visual Recordings of Children

**Interpretation**

**50.1.** In this Chapter "child" is a person under the age of 16 on the date of commencement of the proceedings and "children" shall be construed accordingly.

**Lodging an audio or audio-visual recording of a child**

**50.2.**—(1) Where a party seeks to lodge an audio or audio-visual recording of a child as a production, such party must—

    (a)   ensure that the recording is in a format that can be heard or viewed by means of equipment available in court;

    (b)   place the recording together with a copy of the relevant inventory of productions in a sealed envelope marked with—

        (i)   the names of the parties to the court action;

        (ii)   the case reference number;

        (iii)   (where available) the date and time of commencement and of termination of the recording; and

        (iv)   "recording of a child - confidential".

(2) The sealed envelope must be lodged with the sheriff clerk.

(3) In the remainder of this Chapter a "recording of a child" means any such recording lodged under this rule.

**Separate inventory of productions**

**50.3.**—(1) On each occasion that a recording of a child is lodged, a separate inventory of productions shall be lodged in process.

(2) The sheriff clerk will mark the date of receipt and the number of process on the sealed envelope containing a recording of a child.

**Custody of a recording of a child**

**50.4.**—(1) A recording of a child—

    (a)   must be kept in the safe custody of the sheriff clerk;

    (b)   subject to rule 50.5, will not form a borrowable part of the process.

(2) The seal of the envelope containing a recording of a child shall be broken only with the authority of the sheriff and on such conditions as the sheriff thinks fit (which conditions may relate to listening to or viewing the recording).

**Access to a recording of a child**

**50.5.**—(1) A party may lodge a written motion to gain access to and listen to or view a recording of a child.

(2) The sheriff may refuse a motion or grant it on such conditions as the sheriff thinks fit, including—

---

[1] As inserted by the Act of Sederunt (Sheriff Court Rules) (Miscellaneous Amendments) (No.3) 2012 (SSI 2012/271) para.2 (effective November 1, 2012).

(a) allowing only such persons as the sheriff may specify to listen to or view the recording;

(b) specifying the location where such listening or viewing is to take place;

(c) specifying the date and time when such listening or viewing is to take place;

(d) allowing a copy of the recording to be made (in the same or different format) and arrangements for the safe-keeping and disposal of such copy;

(e) arrangements for the return of the recording and re-sealing the envelope.

(3)[1] An application for leave to appeal against the decision of the sheriff on that motion must be made immediately.

### Incidental appeal against rulings on access to a recording of a child

**50.6.** *[Repealed by the Act of Sederunt (Rules of the Court of Session, Sheriff Appeal Court Rules and Sheriff Court Rules Amendment) (Sheriff Appeal Court) 2015 (SSI 2015/419) r.5 (effective 1 January 2016).]*

### Exceptions

**50.7.**—(1) The sheriff may, on the application of a party and on cause shown, disapply the provisions of this Chapter.

(2) An application under paragraph (1) shall be made—

(a) at the time of presenting the recording for lodging;

(b) by letter addressed to the sheriff clerk stating the grounds on which the application is made.

### Application of other rules

**50.8.**—(1) The following rules do not apply to a recording of a child—

(a) rule 9A.2(2) (inspection of documents);

(b) rule 11.6(1) (intimation of parts of process and adjustments), in so far as it would otherwise require a party to deliver a copy of a recording of a child to every other party;

(c) rule 29.12(1) (copy productions).

Chapter 51[2]

Land Registration Etc.

### Interpretation of this Chapter

**51.1.** In this Chapter—

"the 2012 Act" means the Land Registration etc. (Scotland) Act 2012;
"plot of land" has the meaning given by section 3(4) and (5) of the 2012 Act;
"proprietor" has the meaning given by section 113(1) of the 2012 Act.

### Applications under Part 6 of the 2012 Act

**51.2.**—(1) An application under section 67(2) (warrant to place a caveat) of the 2012 Act shall be made by motion.

(2) The motion shall—

---

[1] As inserted by the Act of Sederunt (Rules of the Court of Session, Sheriff Appeal Court Rules and Sheriff Court Rules Amendment) (Sheriff Appeal Court) 2015 (SSI 2015/419) r.5 (effective 1 January 2016).

[2] As inserted by the Act of Sederunt (Rules of the Court of Session and Sheriff Court Rules Amendment No.2) (Miscellaneous) 2014 (SSI 2014/291) r.3 (effective December 8, 2014).

(a)  identify, by reference to section 67(1) of the 2012 Act, the type of civil proceedings constituted by the action;

(b)  in respect of each plot of land, contain—

    (i)  a description of the registered plot of land;

    (ii)  the title number; and

    (iii)  the name and address of the proprietor;

(c)  where the caveat is to apply only to part of a plot of land, be accompanied by a plan indicating the part so affected.

(3)  An application under the following provisions of the 2012 Act shall be made by motion—

(a)  section 69(1) (renewal of caveat);

(b)  section 70(1) (restriction of caveat);

(c)  section 71(1) (recall of caveat).

### Form of orders under Part 6 of the 2012 Act

**51.3.**—(1)  An order under section 67(3) or 69(2) of the 2012 Act shall be in Form 51.3-A.

(2)  An order under section 70(2) of the 2012 Act shall be in Form 51.3-B.

(3)  An order under section 71(2) of the 2012 Act shall be in Form 51.3-C.

### Effect of warrant to place or renew caveat

**51.4.**  A certified copy of an order in Form 51.3-A may be registered in the Register of Inhibitions and Adjudications.

### Form of order for rectification of a document

**51.5.**  An order for rectification under section 8 of the Law Reform (Miscellaneous Provisions) (Scotland) Act 1985 in respect of a document which has been registered in the Land Register of Scotland shall be in Form 51.5.

Chapter 52[1]

Mutual Recognition of Protection Measures in Civil Matters

### Interpretation

**52.1.**  In this Chapter—

"Article 5 certificate" means a certificate issued under Article 5 of the Regulation;

"Article 14 certificate" means a certificate issued under Article 14 of the Regulation;

"person causing the risk" has the meaning given by Article 3(3) of the Regulation;

"protected person" has the meaning given by Article 3(2) of the Regulation;

"protection measure" has the meaning given by Article 3(1) of the Regulation;

"registered post service" has the meaning given by section 125(1) of the Postal Services Act 2000;

"the Regulation" means Regulation (EU) No. 606/2013 of the European Parliament and of the Council of 12 June 2013 on mutual recognition of protection measures in civil matters.

---

[1] As inserted by the Act of Sederunt (Rules of the Court of Session and Sheriff Court Rules Amendment No.3) (Mutual Recognition of Protection Measures) 2014 (SSI 2014/371) para.3 (effective January 11, 2015).

**Form of application for Article 5 certificate**

**52.2.** An application for the issue of an Article 5 certificate shall be made by lodging Form 52.2 in process.

**Issue of Article 5 certificate**

**52.3.** The sheriff shall issue an Article 5 certificate where—
(a) the order in respect of which the certificate is sought is a protection measure;
(b) the person applying for the certificate is a protected person in respect of the protection measure;
(c) the first condition specified in rule 52.4 is satisfied; and
(d) the second condition specified in rule 52.4 is satisfied, if the protection measure is an interim interdict.

**Conditions for issue of Article 5 certificate**

**52.4.**—(1) The first condition is that—
(a) at the hearing when the interlocutor granting the protection measure was pronounced, the person causing the risk was—
   (i) personally present in court; or
   (ii) represented by a solicitor or an advocate; or
(b) the interlocutor granting the protection measure has been intimated to the person causing the risk.

(2) The second condition is that either paragraph (3) or (4) applies.

(3) This paragraph applies where—
(a) the writ seeking interdict was intimated to the person causing the risk before interim interdict was granted;
(b) interim interdict was granted pursuant to a motion intimated on the person causing the risk; and
(c) the person causing the risk had a sufficient opportunity to oppose the motion, whether or not he or she did so.

(4) This paragraph applies where the sheriff is satisfied that the person causing the risk has had a sufficient opportunity to apply for recall of the interim interdict.

(5) Where the sheriff requires to be satisfied that any writ, motion or interlocutor has been intimated for the purposes of this rule, it is for the person on whose behalf intimation has been given to lodge in process a certificate of intimation if such a certificate is not already in process.

**Notice of issue of Article 5 certificate**

**52.5.**—(1) Where the sheriff issues an Article 5 certificate, the sheriff clerk shall—
(a) give the protected person—
   (i) the certificate, and
   (ii) a certified copy of the interlocutor granting the protection measure; and
(b) give the person causing the risk notice of the issue of the certificate in accordance with paragraphs (2) to (4).

(2) Where the address of the person causing the risk is known, notice shall be given by sending that person—
(a) a notice in Form 52.5-A,
(b) a copy of the certificate; and
(c) a copy of the interlocutor granting the protection measure.

(3)   Where the address of the person causing the risk is outwith the United Kingdom, the sheriff clerk shall send the documents mentioned in paragraph (2) by a registered post service.

(4)   Where the address of the person causing the risk is not known, notice shall be given by displaying on the walls of court a notice in Form 52.5-B.

(5)   In this rule, "Article 5 certificate" includes a rectified Article 5 certificate issued under Article 9(1)(a) of the Regulation.

**Effect of variation of order**

**52.6.**   Where the order in respect of which a certificate under Article 5 of the Regulation is sought has been varied prior to the issue of the certificate—

    (a)   the reference to the order in rule 52.3(a) is to the order as so varied; and

    (b)   the references to the interlocutor in rule 52.5 include a reference to any interlocutor varying the order.

**Application for rectification or withdrawal of Article 5 certificate**

**52.7.**—(1)   An application to the sheriff under Article 9 of the Regulation for rectification or withdrawal of an Article 5 certificate shall be made by lodging Form 52.7 in process.

(2)   The sheriff may determine an application without a hearing unless the sheriff considers that a hearing is required.

**Issue of Article 14 certificate**

**52.8.**—(1)   An application for the issue of an Article 14 certificate shall be made by letter addressed to the sheriff clerk.

(2)   Where the sheriff issues an Article 14 certificate, the sheriff clerk shall send the certificate to the party on whose application the certificate was issued.

Chapter 53[1]

Proving the Tenor

**Application of this Chapter**

**53.1.**   This Chapter applies to an action of proving the tenor.

**Parties**

**53.2.**(1)   The pursuer must call as a defender every person who (so far as known to the pursuer) has an interest in the document to be proved.

(2)   Where only the pursuer has such an interest, the pursuer must call the Lord Advocate as a defender, as representing the public interest.

**Supporting evidence**

**53.3.**   When lodging an initial writ, the pursuer must lodge in process supporting documentary evidence of the tenor of the document to be proved, so far as in the possession or control of the pursuer.

**Undefended actions**

**53.4.**—(1)   This rule applies where no notice of intention to defend has been lodged.

(2)   Evidence is to be given by affidavit unless the sheriff otherwise directs.

---

[1] As inserted by the Act of Sederunt (Ordinary Cause Rules Amendment) (Proving the Tenor and Reduction) 2015 (SSI 2015/176) para.2 (effective May 25, 2015).

(3) The pursuer may apply for decree by minute in Form 53.4.

(4) The sheriff may, on consideration of that minute, supporting documentary evidence and affidavits, without requiring appearance—

(a) grant decree in terms of the minute; or

(b) remit the cause for further procedure (including proof by parole evidence).

Chapter 54[1]

Reduction

### Application of this Chapter

**54.1.** This Chapter applies to an action of reduction.

### Craves for suspension and interdict

**54.2.**(1) This rule applies to an action that seeks to reduce a document upon which real or personal diligence may proceed.

(2) The pursuer may include in the initial writ, in relation to that diligence, craves for suspension and interdict.

### Production: objection by defender

**54.3.**(1) This rule applies where a defender objects to satisfying a crave for production of a document sought to be reduced.

(2) The defender must state in the defences—

(a) the grounds of objection; and

(b) any defence on the merits of the action.

(3) The defender is not required to satisfy a crave for production at the time of lodging defences.

(4) Where the sheriff repels or reserves an objection to satisfying a crave for production, the defender must be ordered to satisfy that crave within such period as the sheriff thinks fit.

(5) Where the defender, following that order, lodges in process any document, a motion to hold production satisfied (or satisfied in respect of the document lodged) must also be made.

(6) Where the defender does not comply with that order, the pursuer may make a motion for decree by default.

### Production: no objection by defender

**54.4.**—(1) This rule applies where a defender does not state an objection to satisfying a crave for production of a document sought to be reduced.

(2) The defender must, when lodging defences—

(a) lodge in process any such document in the defender's possession or control; and

(b) make a motion to hold production satisfied (or satisfied in respect of the document lodged).

(3) If the defender does not do so, the pursuer may make a motion for decree by default.

---

[1] As inserted by the Act of Sederunt (Ordinary Cause Rules Amendment) (Proving the Tenor and Reduction) 2015 (SSI 2015/176) para.2 (effective May 25, 2015).

## Production: no objection by defender

**54.5.**—(1)  This rule applies where the pursuer has possession or control of a document in respect of which reduction is craved.

(2)  The pursuer must lodge that document in process with the initial writ.

(3)  The sheriff may, at any stage, order the pursuer to satisfy a crave for production of a document sought to be reduced.

(4)  Where the pursuer does not comply with that order, the defender may make a motion for dismissal.

(5)  When lodging a document under subparagraph (2) or (3), the pursuer must make a motion to hold production satisfied (or satisfied in respect of the document lodged).

## Production: joint minute for reduction

**54.6.**—(1)  This rule applies where—
  (a)  a crave for production has not been satisfied, and
  (b)  parties enter into a joint minute in terms of which the decree of reduction is to be pronounced.

(2)  The document to be reduced must be lodged in process with the joint minute.

(3)  The terms of the joint minute must be sufficient to enable the sheriff to hold the crave for production satisfied.

## Production: satisfaction by a copy

**54.7.**—  The sheriff may, with the consent of the parties, hold production to be satisfied by a copy of the document sought to be reduced.

**Appendix 1**

**FORMS**

**Rule 1.4**

**FORM 1A.2**[1]

Rule 1A.2(2)(b)

Statement by prospective lay representative for Pursuer/Defender*

Case Ref. No.:

in the cause

SHERIFFDOM OF (*insert name of sheriffdom*)

AT (*insert place of sheriff court*)

[A.B.], (*insert designation and address*), Pursuer

against

[C.D.], (*insert designation and address*), Defender

Court ref. no:

| | |
|---|---|
| Name and address of prospective lay representative who requests to make oral submissions on behalf of party litigant: | |
| Identify hearing(s) in respect of which permission for lay representation is sought: | |
| The prospective lay representative declares that: | |
| (a) | I have no financial interest in the outcome of the case or I have the following financial interest in it:* |

---

[1] As inserted by the Act of Sederunt (Sheriff Court Rules) (Lay Representation) 2013 (SSI 2013/91) r.2 (effective April 4, 2013).

| (b) | I am not receiving remuneration or other reward directly or indirectly from the litigant for my assistance and will not receive directly or indirectly such remuneration or other reward from the litigant. |
|-----|---|
| (c) | I accept that documents and information are provided to me by the litigant on a confidential basis and I undertake to keep them confidential. |
| (d) | I have no previous convictions *or* I have the following convictions: (list convictions)* |
| (e) | I have not been declared a vexatious litigant under the Vexatious Actions (Scotland) Act 1898 *or* I was declared a vexatious litigant under the Vexatious Actions (Scotland) Act 1898 on [insert date].* |

*(Signed)*
[Name of prospective lay representative]
[Date]

*(Insert Place/Date)*
The Sheriff grants/refuses* the application.

*[Signed]*
Sheriff Clerk
[Date]

*(*delete as appropriate)*

## FORM G1
Form of initial writ

Rule 3.1(1)(a)

### INITIAL WRIT

SHERIFFDOM OF (*insert name of sheriffdom*)
AT (*insert place of sheriff court*)
[A.B.] (*design and state any special capacity in which the pursuer is suing*). Pursuer.

### Against

[C.D.] (*design and state any special capacity in which the defender is being sued*). Defender.

The Pursuer craves the court (*here state the specific decree, warrant or order sought*).

### CONDESCENDENCE
(*State in numbered paragraphs the facts which form the ground of action*)
### PLEAS-IN-LAW
(*State in numbered sentences*)

Signed
[A.B.], Pursuer.
or [X.Y.], Solicitor for the pursuer (*state designation and business address*)

### ¹FORM G1A
Form of initial writ in a commercial action

Rule 3.1(1)(b) and 40.4
SHERIFFDOM OF (*insert name of sheriffdom*)
AT (*insert place of sheriff court*)

---

¹ Inserted by the Act of Sederunt (Ordinary Cause Rules) Amendment (Commercial Actions) Rules 2001 (SSI 2001/8) (effective March 1, 2001).

## COMMERCIAL ACTION

[A.B.] (*design and state any special capacity in which the pursuer is being sued*). Pursuer.

### Against

[C.D.] (*design and state any special capacity in which the defender is being sued*). Defender.

[A.B.] for the Pursuer craves the court (*specify the orders sought*)

## CONDESCENDENCE

(*provide the following, in numbered paragraphs—*

*information sufficient to identify the transaction or dispute from which the action arises; a summary of the circumstances which have resulted in the action being raised; and details setting out the grounds on which the action proceeds.*)

*Note: Where damages are sought, the claim may be summarised in the pleadings— in the form of a statement of damages; or*

*by lodging with the initial writ a schedule detailing the claim.*

## PLEAS-IN-LAW

(*state in numbered sentences*)

Signed

[A.B.], Pursuer

*or* [X.Y.], Solicitor for the Pursuer (*state designation and business address*)

## FORM G2

Rule 4.2(1)

[*Omitted by* Act of Sederunt (Sheriff Court Caveat Rules) 2006 (SI 2006/198), *effective April 28, 2006*]

## FORM G3

### Form of advertisement

Rule 5.6(1)(a)

NOTICE TO [C.D.]............... Court ref. no...........

An action has been raised in..........Sheriff Court by [A.B.], Pursuer, calling as a Defender [C.D.] whose last known address was (*insert last known address of defender*). If [C.D.] wishes to defend the action [*where notice is given in a family action add*: or make any claim or seek any order] he [*or* she] should immediately contact the sheriff clerk at (*insert address*) from whom the service copy initial writ may be obtained. If he [*or* she] fails to do so decree may be granted against him [*or* her].

Signed

[X.Y.], (*add designation and business address*)

Solicitor for the pursuer *or* [P.Q.], (*add business address*)

Sheriff officer

## FORM G4

### Form of notice for walls of court

Rule 5.6(1)(b)

NOTICE TO [C.D.]............... Court ref. no...........

An action has been raised in..........Sheriff Court by [A.B.], Pursuer, calling as a Defender [C.D.] whose last known address was (*insert last known address of defender*). If [C.D.] wishes to defend the action [*where notice is to be given in a family action add*: or make any claim or seek any order] he [*or* she] should immediately contact the sheriff clerk at (*insert address*) from whom the service copy initial writ may be obtained. If he [*or* she] fails to do so decree may be granted against him [*or* her].

Date (*insert date*)...............(*Signed*)

Sheriff clerk (depute)

Telephone no. (*insert telephone number of sheriff clerk's office*)
¹**FORM G4A**

Rule 6.A2(2)

Statement to accompany application for interim diligence

DEBTORS (SCOTLAND) ACT 1987 Section 15D [or DEBT ARRANGEMENT
AND ATTACHMENT (SCOTLAND) ACT 2002 Section 9C]

Sheriff Court..........

In the Cause (Cause Reference No.)

[A.B.] (*designation and address*)

Pursuer

against

[C.D.] (*designation and address*)

Defender

Statement

1. The applicant is the pursuer [*or* defender] in the action by [A.B] (*design*)
   against [C.D.] (*design*).
2. [The following persons have an interest (*specify names and addresses*)].
3. The applicant is [*or* is not] seeking the grant under section 15E(1) of the
   1987 Act of warrant for diligence [*or* section 9D(1) of the 2002 Act of
   interim attachment] in advance of a hearing on the application.
4. [*Here provide such other information as may he prescribed by regulations
   made by the Scottish Ministers under* section 15D(2)(d) of the 1987 Act or
   9C(2)(d) of the 2002 Act]

(*Signed*)

Solicitor [*or* Agent] for A.B. [*or* C.D.]

(include full designation)

²**FORM G4B**

Rule 6.A8

Form of schedule of arrestment on the dependence
*Schedule of Arrestment On the Dependence*

Date: (*date of execution*)

Time: (*time arrestment executed*)

To: (*name and address of arrestee*)

IN HER MAJESTY'S NAME AND AUTHORITY AND IN NAME AND
AUTHORITY OF THE SHERIFF, I, (*name*), Sheriff Officer, by virtue of:

- an initial writ containing warrant which has been granted for arrestment on
  the dependence of the action at the instance of (*name and address of pursuer*)
  against (*name and address of defender*) and dated (*date*);
- a counterclaim containing a warrant which has been granted for arrestment
  on the dependence of the claim by (*name and address of creditor*) against
  (*name and address of debtor*) and dated (*date of warrant*);
- an order of the Sheriff at (*place*) dated (*date of order*) granting warrant [for
  arrestment on the dependence of the action raised at the instance of (*name
  and address of pursuer*) against (*name and address of defender*)] [*or* for arrestment on the dependence of the claim in the counterclaim [*or* third party

---

¹ As inserted by the Act of Sederunt (Sheriff Court Rules Amendment) (Diligence) (SSI 2008/121)
r.5(7) (effective April 1, 2008).
² As inserted by the Act of Sederunt (Sheriff Court Rules Amendment) (Diligence) 2008 (SSI 2008/
121) r.5(7) (effective April 1, 2008) and substituted by the Act of Sederunt (Sheriff Court Rules
Amendment) (Diligence) 2009 (SSI 2009/107) (effective April 22, 2009).

notice] by (*name and address of creditor*) against (*name and address or debtor*)],
arrest in your hands (i) the sum of (*amount*), in excess of the Protected Minimum Balance, where applicable (*see Note 1*), more or less, due by you to (*defender's name*) [*or name and address of common debtor if common debtor is not the defender*] or to any other person on his [*or* her] [*or* its] [*or* their] behalf; and (ii) all moveable things in your hands belonging or pertaining to the said (*name of common debtor*), to remain in your hands under arrestment until they are made forthcoming to (*name of pursuer*) [*or name and address of creditor if he is not the pursuer*] or until further order of the court.

This I do in the presence of (*name, occupation and address of witness*).

(*Signed*)
Sheriff Officer
(*Address*)

NOTE

1. This Schedule arrests in your hands (i) funds due by you to (*name of common debtor*) and (ii) goods or other moveables held by you for him. **You should not pay any funds to him or hand over any goods or other moveables to him without taking legal advice.**

2. This Schedule may be used to arrest a ship or cargo. If it is, you should consult your legal adviser about the effect of it.

3. The Protected Minimum Balance is the sum referred to in section 73F(4) of the Debtors (Scotland) Act 1987. This sum is currently set at [*insert current sum*]. The Protected Minimum Balance applies where the arrestment attaches funds standing to the credit of a debtor in an account held by a bank or other financial institution and the debtor is an individual. The Protected Minimum Balance does not apply where the account is held in the name of a company, a limited liability partnership, a partnership or an unincorporated association or where the account is operated by the debtor as a trading account.

4. Under section 73G of the Debtors (Scotland) Act 1987 you must also, within the period of 3 weeks beginning with the day on which the arrestment is executed, disclose to the creditor the nature and value of the funds and/or moveable property which have been attached. This disclosure must be in the form set out in Schedule 8 to the Diligence (Scotland) Regulations 2009. Failure to comply may lead to a financial penalty under section 73G of the Debtors (Scotland) Act 1987 and may also be dealt with as a contempt of court. You must, at the same time, send a copy of the disclosure to the debtor and to any person known to you who owns (or claims to own) attached property and to any person to whom attached funds are (or are claimed to be due), solely or in common with the debtor.

**IF YOU WISH FURTHER ADVICE CONTACT ANY CITIZENS ADVICE BUREAU/LOCAL ADVICE CENTRE/SHERIFF CLERK OR SOLICITOR**

¹FORM G4C

Form of certificate of execution of arrestment on the dependence

Rule 6.A8

CERTIFICATE OF EXECUTION

---

¹ As inserted by the Act of Sederunt (Sheriff Court Rules Amendment) (Diligence) 2008 (SSI 2008/121) r.5(7) (effective April 1, 2008) and substituted by the Act of Sederunt (Sheriff Court Rules Amendment) (Diligence) 2009 (SSI 2009/107) (effective April 22, 2009).

I, (*name*), Sheriff Officer, certify that I executed an arrestment on the dependence, by virtue of an interlocutor of the Sheriff at (*place*) on (*date*) obtained at the instance of (*name and address of party arresting*) against (*name and address of defender*) on (name of arrestee)—

*   by delivering the schedule of arrestment to (*name of arrestee or other person*) at (*place*) personally on (*date*).

*   by leaving the schedule of arrestment with (*name and occupation of person with whom left*) at (*place*) on (*date*) [and by posting a copy of the schedule to the arrestee by registered post or first class recorded delivery to the address specified on the receipt annexed to this certificate].

*   by depositing the schedule of arrestment in (*place*) on (*date*). (*Specify that enquiry made and reasonable grounds exist for believing that the person on whom service is to be made resides at the place but is not available*) [and by posting a copy of the schedule to the arrestee by registered post or first class recorded delivery to the address specified on the receipt annexed to this certificate].

*   by affixing the schedule of arrestment to the door at (*place*) on (*date*). (*Specify that enquiry-made and that reasonable grounds exist for believing that the person on whom service is to be made resides at the place but is not available*) [and by posting a copy of the schedule to the arrestee by registered post or first class recorded delivery to the address specified on the receipt annexed to this certificate].

*   by leaving the schedule of arrestment with (*name and occupation of person with whom left*) at (*place of business*) on (*date*) [and by posting a copy of the schedule to the arrestee by registered post or first class recorded delivery to the address specified on the receipt annexed to this certificate].

*   by depositing the schedule of arrestment at (*place of business*) on (*date*). (*Specify that enquiry made and that reasonable grounds exist for believing that the person on whom service is to be made carries on business at that place*) [and by posting a copy of the schedule to the arrestee by registered post or first class recorded delivery to the address specified on the receipt annexed to this certificate].

*   by affixing the schedule of arrestment to the door at (*place of business*) on (*date*). (*Specify that enquiry made and that reasonable grounds exist for believing that the person on whom service is to be made carries on business at that place.*) [and by posting a copy of the schedule to the arrestee by registered post or first class recorded delivery to the address specified on the receipt annexed to this certificate].

*   by leaving the schedule of arrestment at (*registered office*) on (*date*), in the hands of (*name of person*) [and by posting a copy of the schedule to the arrestee by registered post or first class recorded delivery to the address specified on the receipt annexed to this certificate].

*   by depositing the schedule of arrestment at (*registered office*) on (*date*) [and by posting a copy of the schedule to the arrestee by registered post or first class recorded delivery to the address specified on the receipt annexed to this certificate].

*   by affixing the schedule of arrestment to the door at (*registered office*) on (*date*) [and by posting a copy of the schedule to the arrestee by registered post or first class recorded delivery to the address specified on the receipt annexed to this certificate].

I did this in the presence of (*name, occupation and address of witness*).

(Signed)

Sheriff Officer
*(Address)*
*(Signed)*
*(Witness)*

\*Delete where not applicable

**NOTE**

**A copy of the Schedule of arrestment on the dependence is to be attached to this certificate.**

**[1]FORM G5**

Form of intimation of Options Hearing

Rules 9.2(2)(a) and 33.16(3)(b)

Sheriff Court (insert address and telephone number)............... Court ref. no..........

[A.B.] (design) Pursuer against [C.D.] (*design*) Defender

You are given notice that in this action:—

| | |
|---|---|
| (insert date) | is the last day for lodging defences; |
| (insert date) | is the last day for making adjustments to the writ or defences; |
| (insert date, time and place) | is the date, time and place for the Options Hearing. |

Date (insert date)............... (Signed)..........

Sheriff clerk (depute)

NOTE:

If you fail to comply with the terms of this notice or with any of the rules 9.3, 9.4, 9.6, 9.10 and 9.11 of the Standard Procedure of the Ordinary Cause Rules of the Sheriff Court or, where applicable, rule 33.37 (decree by default in a family action), decree by default may be granted in terms of rule 16.2(2) of those Rules.

NOTE TO BE ADDED WHERE PARTY UNREPRESENTED

**Note**

**IF YOU ARE UNCERTAIN WHAT ACTION TO TAKE** you should consult a solicitor. You may be eligible for legal aid depending on your income, and you can get information from any Citizens Advice Bureau or other advice agency.

**FORM G6**

Form of motion

Rule 15.1(1)(b)

SHERIFFDOM OF (*insert name of sheriffdom*)............... Court ref. no..........

AT (*insert place of sheriff court*)

MOTION FOR THE PURSUER [or DEFENDER]

in the cause

[A.B.] (*insert designation and address*)

Pursuer

against

[C.D.] (*insert designation and address*)

Defender

[1] As amended by S.I. 1996 No. 2445 (effective November 1, 1996)

The (*insert description of party*) moves the court to (*insert details of motion and, where appropriate, the reason (s) for seeking the order*).

List the documents or parts of process lodged with the motion:—

(*Insert description of document or name part of process*)

Date (insert date)............... (Signed)..........

Party (insert name and description of party)
or Solicitor for party (insert designation and business address)

## FORM G6A[1]
Form of motion by email

Rule 15A.4(1)

## SHERIFFDOM OF LOTHIAN AND BORDERS
## AT EDINBURGH
## IN THE ALL-SCOTLAND SHERIFF COURT
### Unopposed [ *or* Opposed] motion

**To: (email address of the court)**

1. Case name:..........
2. Court ref number:..........
3. Is the case in court in the next 7 days?..........
4. Solicitors or party lodging motion:..........
(a) Reference:..........
(b) Telephone number:..........
(c) Email address:..........
5. Lodging motion on behalf of:..........
6. Motion (in brief terms):..........
7. Submissions in support of motion (if required):..........
8. Date of lodging of motion:..........
9. Intimation made to:..........
(a) Provided email address(es):..........
(b) Additional email address(es) of fee-earner or other person(s) dealing with the case on behalf of a receiving party (if applicable):..........
10. Date intimations sent:..........
11. Opposition must be intimated to opponent not later than 5 p.m. on:..........
12. Is motion opposed or unopposed?..........
13. Has consent to the motion been provided?..........
14. Document(s) intimated and lodged with motion:..........

**EXPLANATORY NOTE TO BE ADDED WHERE RECEIVING PARTY IS NOT**

**LEGALLY REPRESENTED OPPOSITION TO THE MOTION MAY BE MADE by completing Form G9A (Form of opposition to motion by email) and intimating it to the party intending to lodge the motion (insert email address) on or before the last date for intimating opposition (see paragraph 11 above).**

**IN THE EVENT OF A FORM OF OPPOSITION BEING INTIMATED, the party intending to lodge the motion will lodge an opposed motion and the sheriff clerk will assign a date, time and place for hearing parties on the motion. Intimation of this hearing will be sent to parties by the sheriff clerk.**

**IF NO NOTICE OF OPPOSITION IS LODGED, OR IF CONSENT TO THE MOTION IS INTIMATED TO THE PARTY INTENDING TO LODGE THE MOTION, the motion will be considered without the attendance of parties.**

---

[1] As inserted by the Act of Sederunt (Rules of the Court of Session 1994 and Sheriff Court Rules Amendment) (No.2) (Personal Injury and Remits) 2015 (SSI 2015/227) para.8 (effective September 22, 2015).

**IF YOU ARE UNCERTAIN WHAT ACTION TO TAKE you should consult a solicitor. You may also obtain advice from a Citizens Advice Bureau or other advice agency.**

## ¹FORM G7

Form of intimation of motion

Rule 15.2(1) Cause Rules 1993

SHERIFFDOM OF (insert name of sheriffdom)............... Court ref. no...........

AT (insert place of sheriff court)

in the cause

[A.B.] (insert name and address)

Pursuer

against

[C.D.] (insert name and address)

Defender

| LAST DATE FOR LODGING NOTICE OF OPPOSITION: |
| --- |

APPLICATION IS MADE BY MOTION FOR THE ORDER(S) SOUGHT IN THE ATTACHED FORM (attach a copy of the motion in Form G6)

* A copy of the document(s) or part(s) of process referred to in Form G6 is/are attached.

OPPOSITION TO THE MOTION MAY BE MADE by completing Form G9 (notice of opposition to motion) and lodging it with the sheriff clerk at (insert address) on or before the last date for lodging notice of opposition. A copy of the notice of opposition must be sent immediately to any other party in the action.

IN THE EVENT OF A NOTICE OF OPPOSITION BEING LODGED the sheriff clerk will assign a date, time and place for hearing parties on the motion. Intimation of this hearing will be sent to parties by the sheriff clerk.

IF NO NOTICE OF OPPOSITION IS LODGED, the motion may be considered by the sheriff without the attendance of parties.

Date (*insert date*)................... (*Signed*)

Pursuer (*or as the case may be*)

[*or* Solicitor for pursuer [*or as the case may be*]

(*insert name and business address*)]

Explanatory Note to Be Added Where Party to Whom Intimation is Made is Not Legally Represented

**IF YOU ARE UNCERTAIN WHAT ACTION TO TAKE you should consult a solicitor. You may also obtain advice from a Citizens Advice Bureau or other advice agency.**

NOTE: If YOU intend to oppose the motion you must appear or be represented on the date of the hearing. If you return Form G9 (notice of opposition to motion) and then fail to attend or be represented at the court hearing, the court may consider the motion in your absence and may grant the order(s) sought.

* Delete if not applicable

## ²FORM G7A

Form of intimation of minute (answers lodged)

Rule 14.4(1)(a)

---

¹ Substituted by S.I. 1996 No. 2445 (effective November 1, 1996).
² Inserted by S.I. 1996 No. 2445 (effective November 1, 1996).

SHERIFFDOM OF (insert name of sheriffdom).............. Court ref. no.
AT (*insert place of sheriff court*)

in the cause
[A.B.] (*insert name and address*)

Pursuer

against
[C.D.] (insert name and address)

Defender

---

| LAST DATE FOR LODGING ANSWERS: |
| --- |

APPLICATION IS MADE BY MOTION FOR THE ORDER(S) SOUGHT IN THE MINUTE ATTACHED (attach a copy of minute and interlocutor)

* A copy of the document(s) or part(s) of process referred to in the minute is/are attached.

IN THE EVENT OF ANSWERS BEING LODGED the sheriff clerk will assign a date, time and place for hearing parties on the minute and answers. Intimation of this hearing will be sent to parties by the sheriff clerk.

IF NO ANSWERS ARE LODGED, the motion may be considered by the sheriff without the attendance of parties.

Date (insert date).............. (Signed)

Pursuer (or as the case may be)

[or Solicitor for pursuer [or as the case may he]
(Add name and business address)]

Explanatory Note to Be Added Where Party to Whom Intimation is Made is Not Legally Represented

---

**IF YOU ARE UNCERTAIN WHAT ACTION TO TAKE** you should consult a solicitor. You may also obtain advice from a Citizens Advice Bureau or other advice agency.

---

NOTE: If you intend to oppose the minute you must appear or be represented on the date of the hearing. If you return Form G9 (notice of opposition to minute) and then fail to attend or be represented at the court hearing, the court may consider the minute in your absence and may grant the order(s) sought.

---

* Delete if not applicable
[1]**FORM G7B**
Form of intimation of minute (no order for answers or no hearing fixed)
Rule 14.4(1)(a)
SHERIFFDOM OF (insert name of sheriffdom).............. Court ref. no.
AT (*insert place of sheriff court*)

in the cause
[A.B.] (*insert name and address*)

Pursuer

against

[C.D.] (*insert name and address*)

Defender

---

| LAST DATE FOR LODGING NOTICE OF OPPOSITION: |
| --- |

---

[1] Inserted by S.I. 1996 No. 2445 (effective November 1, 1996).

APPLICATION IS MADE BY MINUTE FOR THE ORDER(S) SOUGHT IN THE MINUTE ATTACHED (*attach a copy of minute and interlocutor*)

* A copy of the document(s) or part(s) of process referred to in the minute is/are attached.

OPPOSITION TO THE MOTION MAY BE MADE by completing Form G9 (notice of opposition to motion) and lodging it with the sheriff clerk at (*insert address*) on or before the last date for lodging notice of opposition. A copy of the notice of opposition must be sent immediately to any other party in the action.

IN THE EVENT OF A NOTICE OF OPPOSITION BEING LODGED the sheriff clerk will

assign a date, time and place for hearing parties on the minute. Intimation of this hearing will be sent to parties by the sheriff clerk.

IF NO NOTICE OF OPPOSITION IS LODGED, the minute may be considered by the sheriff without the attendance of parties.

Date (*insert date*)...............(*Signed*)

Pursuer (or as the case may be)

[or Solicitor for pursuer [or as the case may be]

(Add name and business address)]

Explanatory Note to Be Added Where Party to Whom Intimation is Made is Not Legally Represented

---

**IF YOU ARE UNCERTAIN WHAT ACTION TO TAKE** you should consult a solicitor. You may also obtain advice from a Citizens Advice Bureau or other advice agency.

---

NOTE: If YOU intend to oppose the minute you must appear or be represented on the date of the hearing. If you return Form G9 (notice of opposition to minute) and then fail to attend or be represented at the court hearing, the court may consider the motion in your absence and may grant the order(s) sought.

---

* Delete if not applicable

**[1]FORM G7C**

Form of intimation of minute (hearing fixed)

Rule 14.4(1)(a)

SHERIFFDOM OF (*insert name of sheriffdom*)............... Court ref. no.

AT (*insert place of sheriff court*)

in the cause

[A.B.] (*insert name and address*)

Pursuer

against
[C.D.] (*insert name and address*)

Defender

---

DATE AND TIME FOR HEARING MINUTE:

---

*DATE FOR LODGING ANSWERS OR AFFIDAVIT EVIDENCE:

---

APPLICATION IS MADE FOR THE ORDER(S) SOUGHT IN THE MINUTE ATTACHED (*attach a copy of minute and interlocutor*)

---

[1] Inserted by SI 1996/2445 (effective November 1, 1996).

\* A copy of the document(s) or part(s) of process referred to in the minute is/are attached.

IF YOU WISH TO OPPOSE THE MINUTE OR MAKE ANY REPRESENTATIONS you must attend or be represented at (insert name and address of court) on the date and time referred to above.

\* If an order has been made for you to lodge answers or affidavit evidence these must be lodged with the sheriff clerk (insert address) on or before the above date.

IF YOU FAIL TO ATTEND OR BE REPRESENTED the minute may be determined in your absence.

Date (*insert date*)............... (*Signed*)

Pursuer (*or as the case may be*)

[*or* Solicitor for pursuer [*or as the case may be*]

(*Add name and business address*)]

Explanatory Note to Be Added Where Party to Whom Intimation is Made is Not Legally Represented

**IF YOU ARE UNCERTAIN WHAT ACTION TO TAKE** you should consult a solicitor. You may also obtain advice from a Citizens Advice Bureau or other advice agency.

NOTE: If you intend to oppose the minute you must appear or be represented on the date of the hearing. If you return Form G9 (notice of opposition to minute) and then fail to attend or be represented at the court hearing, the court may consider the minute in your absence and may grant the order(s) sought.

\* Delete if not applicable

Rules 14.6 and 15.1(2)

### [1]FORM G8
Form of certificate of intimation of motion or minute
CERTIFICATE OF INTIMATION OF MOTION [*or* MINUTE]

I certify that intimation of the motion [*or* minute] was made to (*insert names of parties or solicitors for the parties, as appropriate*) by (*insert method of intimation; where intimation is by facsimile transmission, insert fax number to which Intimation sent*) on (*insert date of intimation*).

Date (*insert date*)

(*Signed*)

Solicitor [*or* Sheriff Officer]

(*Add name and business address*)

Rules 14.7(1)(a) and 15.3(1)(a)

### [2]FORM G9
Form of notice of opposition to motion or minute
NOTICE OF OPPOSITION TO MOTION [*or* MINUTE]
SHERIFFDOM OF (*insert name of sheriffdom*)

Court ref. no.:

AT (*insert place of sheriff court*)

in the cause

[A.B.] (*insert name and address*)

Pursuer

against

[C.D.] (*insert name and address*)

Defender

---

[1] Substituted by SI 1996/2445 (effective November 1, 1996).
[2] Substituted by SI 1996/2445 (effective November 1, 1996).

Notice of opposition to motion [*or* minute] given by (*insert name of party opposing motion*) to (*insert names of all other parties, or solicitors for the parties, to the action*) by (*insert method of intimation; where intimation is made by facsimile transmission, Insert fax number to which notice of opposition sent*) on (*insert date of intimation*).

Date (*insert date*)

(*Signed*)

Pursuer (*or as the case may be*)

(*insert name and address of party*)
[*or* Solicitor for Pursuer [*or as the case may be*]
(*Add name and business address*)]
Rule 24.2(3)

## FORM G9A[1]
### Form of opposition to motion by email
Rule 15A.5(1)

### SHERIFFDOM OF LOTHIAN AND BORDERS
### AT EDINBURGH
### IN THE ALL-SCOTLAND SHERIFF COURT
### TO BE INTIMATED TO THE PARTY INTENDING TO LODGE THE MOTION

1. Case name:..........
2. Court ref number:..........
3. Date of intimation of motion:..........
4. Date of intimation of opposition to motion:..........
5. Solicitors or party opposing motion:..........
(a) Reference:..........
(b) Telephone number:..........
(c) Email address:..........
6. Opposing motion on behalf of:..........
7. Grounds of opposition:..........
8. Estimated duration of hearing:..........

### [2]FORM G10
Form of intimation to a party whose solicitor has withdrawn
SHERIFFDOM OF (*insert name of sheriffdom*) AT (*insert place of sheriff court*)
in the cause
[A.B.] (*insert designation*)

Pursuer

against

[C.D.] (*insert designation*)

Defender

Court ref. no.

The court has been informed that your solicitors have ceased to act for you.

As a result the sheriff has ordered that you appear or be represented on (insert date and time) within the Sheriff Court at the above address. A copy of the order is attached.

When you appear you will be asked by the sheriff to state whether you intend to proceed with your action [or defences or answers].

---

[1] As inserted by the Act of Sederunt (Rules of the Court of Session 1994 and Sheriff Court Rules Amendment) (No.2) (Personal Injury and Remits) 2015 (SSI 2015/227) para.8 (effective September 22, 2015).

[2] As amended by SI 1996/2445 (effective November 1, 1996).

**NOTE:**

**IF YOU ARE UNCERTAIN WHAT ACTION TO TAKE** you should consult a solicitor. You may also obtain advice from a Citizens Advice Bureau or other advice agency.

Rule 28.3(1)

### FORM G11[1]

Rule 28.3(2)

**Form of notice in optional procedure for commission and diligence**

Court ref. no: (*insert court reference number*)

SHERIFFDOM OF (*insert name of sheriffdom*)

AT (*insert place of sheriff court*)

*in the cause*

[A.B.], (*insert name and address*), Pursuer

against

[C.D.], (*insert name and address*), Defender

To: (*insert name and address of party or parties or named third party haver, from whom the documents are sought to be recovered*).

1. You are hereby required to produce to the agent for the Pursuer or as the case may be, (*insert name and address of agents*) within seven days of the service on you of this Order—

   (a)   this Order which must be produced intact;

   (b)   the certificate below duly dated and signed by you; and

   (c)   all documents in your possession falling within the enclosed specification and a list or inventory of such documents signed by you relating to this Order and your certificate.

2. Subject to note (1) below, you may produce these documents either by sending them by registered post or by the first class recorded delivery, or by hand to the address above.

Date: (*insert date on which service was*   (*Signed*) ..........
*executed. N.B. Rule 5.3(2) relating to
postal service or intimation.*)

                            Solicitor for party (*add designation and business address of the solicitor for the party in whose favour commission and diligence has been granted*)

### NOTES

1. If you claim that any of the documents produced by you are **confidential**, you must still produce such documents but may place them in a separate sealed packet by themselves, marked "confidential". In that event, they should NOT be sent to the address above. They must be hand delivered or sent by registered post or by the first class recorded delivery service or registered postal packet to the sheriff clerk at (*insert name and address of sheriff court*).

2. The document will be considered by the parties to the action and they may or may not be lodged in the court process. A written receipt will be given or sent to you

---

[1] As substituted by the Act of Sederunt (Rules of the Court of Session, Ordinary Cause Rules and Summary Cause Rules Amendment) (Miscellaneous) 2014 (SSI 2014/152) Sch.1 para.1 (effective July 7, 2014).

by the party recovering the documents, who may thereafter allow them to be inspected by the other parties. The party in whose possession the documents are will be responsible for their safekeeping.

3. Parties are obliged by rules of court to return the documents to you when their purpose with the documents is finished. If they do not do so, you will be entitled to apply to the court, under rule 28.3(9) of the Ordinary Cause Rules, for an order to have this done and you may apply for an award of the expenses incurred in doing so. Further information about this can be obtained from the sheriff clerk's office at (*insert name and address of sheriff court*).

### Certificate

I hereby certify with reference to the above order of the sheriff at (*insert name of sheriff court*) in the cause (*insert court reference number*) and the enclosed specification of documents, served on me and marked respectively X and Y:—

1. That the documents which are produced and which are listed in the enclosed inventory signed by me and marked Z, are all documents in my possession falling within the specification.

*or*

That I have no documents in my possession falling within the specification.

2. That, to the best of my knowledge and belief, there are in existence other documents falling within the specification, but not in my possession. These documents are as follows:—

(*describe them by reference to the descriptions of documents in the specification*).

They were last seen by me on or about (*date*), at (*place*), in the hands of (*insert name and address of the person*).

*or*

That I know of the existence of no documents in the possession of any person, other than myself, which fall within the specification.

(*Insert date*) ..........        (*Signed*) ..........
                                  (*Name and address*) ..........

### FORM G11A[1]

Rule 28.3(4)(a)

**Form of intimation to the sheriff clerk and other parties of documents recovered under optional procedure**

Court ref. no: (*insert court reference number*)
SHERIFFDOM OF (*insert name of sheriffdom*)
AT (*insert place of sheriff court*)
*in the cause*
[A.B.], (*insert name and address*), Pursuer
against
[C.D.], (*insert name and address*), Defender

The undernoted document[s] was [were] recovered from (*insert name and address of haver*) on (*insert date of receipt*) under order of the sheriff at (*insert name of sheriff court*) dated (*insert date of interlocutor authorising commission and diligence*) in so far as it relates to the specification of documents No. .......... of Process.

Document[s] received:— (*identify each document*).

---

[1] As inserted by the Act of Sederunt (Rules of the Court of Session, Ordinary Cause Rules and Summary Cause Rules Amendment) (Miscellaneous) 2014 (SSI 2014/152) Sch.1 para.1 (effective July 7, 2014).

Date: .........                     (*Signed*) .........
                                    Solicitor for party (*add designation and
                                    business address of the solicitor for the
                                    party in whose favour commission and
                                    diligence has been granted*)

## FORM G11B[1]

Rule 28.3(4)(b)

**Form of receipt to haver for documents recovered under optional procedure**

Court ref. no: (*insert court reference number*)

SHERIFFDOM OF (*insert name of sheriffdom*)

AT (*insert place of sheriff court*)

*in the cause*

[A.B.], (*insert name and address*), Pursuer

against

[C.D.], (*insert name and address*), Defender

The document[s] noted below, being recovered by order of the sheriff at (*insert name of sheriff court*) dated (*insert date of interlocutor authorising commission and diligence*) in so far as it relates to the specification of documents No ......... of Process, have been recovered from (*insert name and address of haver*).

Document[s] received:— (*identify each document*)

Date: .........                     (*Signed*) .........
                                    Solicitor for party (*add designation and
                                    business address of the solicitor for the
                                    party in whose favour commission and
                                    diligence has been granted*)

## FORM G11C[2]

Rule 28.3(6)(b)

**Form of receipt from party other than party who originally recovered documents under optional procedure**

Court ref. no: (*insert court reference number*)

SHERIFFDOM OF (*insert name of sheriffdom*)

AT (*insert place of sheriff court*)

*in the cause*

[A.B.], (*insert name and address*), Pursuer

against

[C.D.], (*insert name and address*), Defender

I acknowledge receipt of the undernoted document[s] received from you and recovered under order of the sheriff at (*insert name of sheriff court*) dated (*insert date of interlocutor authorising commission and diligence*).

Document[s] received:— (*identify each document*)

Date: .........                     (*Signed*) .........

---

[1] As inserted by the Act of Sederunt (Rules of the Court of Session, Ordinary Cause Rules and Summary Cause Rules Amendment) (Miscellaneous) 2014 (SSI 2014/152) Sch.1 para.1 (effective July 7, 2014).

[2] As inserted by the Act of Sederunt (Rules of the Court of Session, Ordinary Cause Rules and Summary Cause Rules Amendment) (Miscellaneous) 2014 (SSI 2014/152) Sch.1 para.1 (effective July 7, 2014).

Solicitor for party (*add designation and business address of the solicitor for the party receiving documents*)

## FORM G11D[1]

Rule 28.3A(2)

**Form of notice in optional procedure for commission and diligence in party litigant cases**

Court ref. no: (*insert court reference number*)

SHERIFFDOM OF (*insert name of sheriffdom*)

AT (*insert place of sheriff court*)

*in the cause*

[A.B.], (*insert name and address*), Pursuer

against

[C.D.], (*insert name and address*), Defender

To: (*insert name and address of party or parties or named third party haver, from whom the documents are sought to be recovered*).

1. You are hereby required to produce to the sheriff clerk at (*insert name and address of sheriff court*) within seven days of the date of service on you of this Order—

   (a)   this Order which must be produced intact;

   (b)   the certificate below duly dated and signed by you; and

   (c)   all documents in your possession falling within the enclosed specification and a list or inventory of such documents signed by you relating to this Order and your certificate.

2. You may produce these documents either by lodging them at the sheriff clerk's office at (*insert name and address of sheriff court*) or by sending them by registered post or by the first class recorded delivery service, addressed to the sheriff clerk at (*insert name and address of sheriff court*).

Date: (*insert date on which service was executed. N.B. Rule 5.3(2) relating to postal service or intimation.*)     (*Signature, name and address of party in whose favour commission and diligence has been granted*)

### NOTES

1. If you claim that any of the documents produced by you are **confidential**, you must still produce such documents but may place them in a separate sealed packet by themselves, marked "confidential".

2. The documents will be considered by the parties to the action and they may or may not be lodged in the court process. If they are not so lodged they will be returned to you by the sheriff clerk. The party in whose possession the documents are will be responsible for their safekeeping.

3. Parties are obliged by rules of court to return the documents to you when their purpose with the documents is finished. If they do not do so, you will be entitled to apply to the court, under rule 28.3A(10) of the Ordinary Cause Rules, for an order to have this done and you may apply for an award of the expenses incurred in doing so. Further information about this can be obtained from the sheriff clerk's office at (*insert name and address of sheriff court*).

### Certificate

---

[1] As inserted by the Act of Sederunt (Rules of the Court of Session, Ordinary Cause Rules and Summary Cause Rules Amendment) (Miscellaneous) 2014 (SSI 2014/152) Sch.1 para.1 (effective July 7, 2014).

I hereby certify with reference to the above order of the sheriff at (*insert name of sheriff court*) in the cause (*insert court reference number*) and the enclosed specification of documents, served on me and marked respectively X and Y:—

1. That the documents which are produced and which are listed in the enclosed inventory signed by me and marked Z, are all documents in my possession falling within the specification.

*or*

That I have no documents in my possession falling within the specification.

2. That, to the best of my knowledge and belief, there are in existence other documents falling within the specification, but not in my possession. These documents are as follows:—

(*describe them by reference to the descriptions of documents in the specification*).

They were last seen by me on or about (*date*), at (*place*), in the hands of (*insert name and address of the person*).

*or*

That I know of the existence of no documents in the possession of any person, other than myself, which fall within the specification.

(*Insert date*) ..........                          (*Signed*) ..........

                                                   (*Name and address*) ..........

## NOTES

1. If you claim that any of the documents produced by you are **confidential**, you must still produce such documents but may place them in a separate sealed packet by themselves, marked "confidential".

2. The documents will be considered by the parties to the action and they may or may not be lodged in the court process. If they are not so lodged they will be returned to you by the sheriff clerk. The party in whose possession the documents are will be responsible for their safekeeping.

3. Parties are obliged by rules of court to return the documents to you when their purpose with the documents is finished. If they do not do so, you will be entitled to apply to the court, under rule 28.3A(10) of the Ordinary Cause Rules, for an order to have this done and you may apply for an award of the expenses incurred in doing so. Further information about this can be obtained from the sheriff clerk's office at (*insert name and address of sheriff court*).

### Certificate

I hereby certify with reference to the above order of the sheriff at (*insert name of sheriff court*) in the cause (*insert court reference number*) and the enclosed specification of documents, served on me and marked respectively X and Y:—

1. That the documents which are produced and which are listed in the enclosed inventory signed by me and marked Z, are all documents in my possession falling within the specification.

*or*

That I have no documents in my possession falling within the specification.

2. That, to the best of my knowledge and belief, there are in existence other documents falling within the specification, but not in my possession. These documents are as follows:—

(*describe them by reference to the descriptions of documents in the specification*).

They were last seen by me on or about (*date*), at (*place*), in the hands of (*insert name and address of the person*).

*or*

That I know of the existence of no documents in the possession of any person, other than myself, which fall within the specification.

*(Insert date)* ..........        *(Signed)* ..........

                                  *(Name and address)* ..........

Rules 28.4(4) and 29.7(4)

## FORM G12
### Form of certificate of citation of witness or haver

I certify that on *(insert date of citation)*.......... I duly cited [K.L.], *(design)* to attend at *(insert name of sheriff court)* Sheriff Court on *(insert date)* at *(insert time)* as a witness for the pursuer [*or* defender] in the action at the instance of [A.B.] *(design)*, Pursuer, against [C.D.] *(design)*, Defender, [and I required him [*or* her] to bring with him [*or* her] *(specify documents)*]. This I did by *(state mode of citation)*.

Date (insert date)

                                  *(Signed)*

                           [P.Q.], Sheriff officer;

           *or* [X.Y.], *(add designation and business address)*

               Solicitor for the pursuer [*or* defender]

## ¹FORM G13
### Form of citation of witness or haver

Rule 28.4(4) and 29.7(4)

                                    *(date)*

Citation

SHERIFFDOM OF *(insert name of sheriffdom)*

AT *(insert place of sheriff court)*

To [A.B.] *(design)*

*(Name)* who is pursuing/defending a case against *(name)* [or is a *(specify)*) in the case of *(name)* against *(name)* has asked you to be a witness. You must attend the above sheriff court on *(insert date)* at *(insert time)* for that purpose, [and to bring with you *(specify documents)*].

If you would like to know more about being a witness

are a child under the age of 16

think you may be a vulnerable witness within the meaning of section 11(1) of the Vulnerable Witnesses (Scotland) Act 2004 (that is someone the court considers may be less able to give their evidence due to mental disorder or fear or distress connected to giving your evidence at the court hearings)

you should contact *(specify the solicitor acting for the party or the litigant citing the witness)* for further information.

If you are a vulnerable witness (including a child under the age of 16), then you should be able to use a special measure (such measures include the use of a screen, a live TV link or a supporter, or a commissioner) to help you give evidence.

*Expenses*

You may claim back money which you have to spend and any earnings you have lost within certain specified limits, because you have to come to court on the above date. These may be paid to you if you claim within specified time limits. Claims should be made to the person who has asked you to attend court. Proof of any loss of earnings should be given to that person.

If you wish your travelling expenses to be paid before you go to court, you should apply for payment to the person who has asked you to attend court.

---

¹ As substituted by SSI 2007/463 (effective November 1, 2007).

*Failure to attend*

*It is very important that you attend court and you should note that failure to do so may result in a warrant being granted for your arrest. In addition, if you fail to attend without any good reason, having requested and been paid your travelling expenses, you may be ordered to pay a penalty not exceeding £250.*

If you have any questions about anything in this citation, please contact (*specify the solicitor acting for the party or the party litigant citing the witness*) for further information.

Signed

[P.Q.], Sheriff Officer,

or [X.Y.], (*add designation and business address*)

Solicitor for the pursuer [*or defender*] [*or specify*]

Rules 28.4(6)(b), 28.10(4)(b) and 29.16

## FORM G13A[1]
### Form of citation of juror

Rule 36B.3

## SHERIFFDOM OF LOTHIAN AND BORDERS
## AT EDINBURGH
## IN THE ALL-SCOTLAND SHERIFF COURT
## JUROR'S CITATION

*Citation Number:*..........     *Date:*..........

*To:*..........     *Time:*..........

*Place:*..........

*Name of case:*..........

**You are cited to attend personally on the date and at the time and place stated above, and on such succeeding days as may be necessary to serve, if required, as a juror. If you fail to attend, you will be liable to the penalty prescribed by law.**

***Sheriff Clerk Depute***

*Please read the enclosed leaflets carefully BEFORE attending court for selection.*

*Expenses: Claims for loss of earnings and/or expenses should be made at the end of your jury service. You will be provided with an envelope for return of the completed form, and payment will be made by cheque to your home address, seven to ten days from receipt of the claim.*

### YOU MUST BRING THIS CITATION WITH YOU TO COURT

*If you wish to apply for exemption or excusal from jury service, please complete this form and return it as soon as possible to:* **Sheriff Clerk, Edinburgh Sheriff Court, 27 Chambers Street, Edinburgh EH1 1LB.**

**DECLARATION:** *Please state why you are applying for exemption or excusal from jury service:*

[ ] **Age:**     I am .......... years of age. My date of birth is ..........

[ ] **Occupation:**     I am employed as .......... and therefore statutorily exempt from service.

---

[1] As inserted by the Act of Sederunt (Rules of the Court of Session 1994 and Sheriff Court Rules Amendment) (No.2) (Personal Injury and Remits) 2015 (SSI 2015/227) para.8 (effective September 22, 2015).

**[ ] Medical Condition:**   I am medically unfit for jury service and enclose a medical certificate from my doctor.

**[ ] Special Reason:**       ...............

**N.B.** *Should you be **excused** from jury service on this occasion, a further juror's citation may be sent out to you within twelve months.*

**I declare that the foregoing information is correct and acknowledge that I may be asked for proof of any statement made above.**

Signature ..........                    Date ..........

*If you have any queries telephone* **0131 225 2525.** *Please quote citation number and date of attendance.*

   ***Unfortunately there are no facilities for car parking at or near the court.***

## CLAIMING FOR TRAVELLING/FINANCIAL LOSS

If you wish to claim for travelling/financial loss, you must read the guidance sheet enclosed and complete this form carefully and accurately. If you are claiming loss of earnings/benefit or childminding/adult dependant carer allowance you must get your employer/the carer to complete the certificate that is enclosed and return it with this claim form. If it is not enclosed then payment cannot be made. Please note: the allowances are meant to compensate you for your out-of-pocket expenses and loss of earnings or benefit. They are not meant to compensate your partner or spouse. There is a maximum amount which can be claimed. The rate is fixed by Scottish Ministers, and is reviewed every year.

**There is no scope for any juror to be paid more than these maximum amounts. Receipts or tickets must be attached, otherwise we will be unable to pay your claim.**

| | OFFICIAL USE ONLY *(delete as applicable) | | |
|---|---|---|---|
| | Allowed | No. of days | Total |
| TRAVELLING<br>By public transport<br> (a) Say whether rail, bus &c<br>  ..........<br>  ..........<br> (b) Daily return fare £<br>  ..........<br>  ..........<br>  ..........<br>In own car, &c<br> (a) Car, m/cycle &c ..........<br>  Engine capacity ..........*c.c.*<br> (b) Daily mileage (round trip) | £ .......... p | | £ .......... p |

| | OFFICIAL USE ONLY *(delete as applicable) | | |
|---|---|---|---|
| | Allowed | No. of days | Total |
| .......... .......... (c) Could you have travelled by public transport? *YES/NO If YES, indicate how much time was saved by using your own vehicle. SUBSISTENCE On the days on which the court has NOT provided meals for you, have you necessarily incurred expenses on subsistence? *YES/NO **If YES, give number of hours, including travelling time you were away from your home or place of business.** (If you attended Court on more than one day, show the number of hours for each day) .......... .......... .......... LOSS OF EARNINGS (only refundable if certified above) Will you suffer any loss of earnings as a result of your attendance for jury service? *YES/NO If YES, please state (a) your occupation .......... .......... .......... (b) daily or hourly rate | | | |

| | OFFICIAL USE ONLY *(delete as applicable) | | |
|---|---|---|---|
| | Allowed | No. of days | Total |
| (or equivalent) £ .......... | | | |
| (c) number of days and half-days lost .......... .......... | | | |
| Have you paid any person to act as a substitute for you during your attendance for jury service (*e.g.* at your place of employment, or to look after your children or a dependent adult &c)? *YES/NO If YES, please state | | | |
| (a) capacity in which paid substitute employed .......... | | | |
| (b) his/her daily or hourly rate £ .......... .......... | | | |
| (c) number of days and half-days paid substitute employed .......... .......... .......... .......... | | | |
| I DECLARE that to the best of my knowledge and belief the particulars in the foregoing claim are correct | | | |
| TOTALS | | | |

| | OFFICIAL USE ONLY *(delete as applicable) | | |
|---|---|---|---|
| | Allowed | No. of days | Total |
| .......... .......... Signature of Claimant | | | |

### FORM G14
Form of oath for witness

The witness to raise his right hand and repeat after the sheriff [*or* commissioner]: "I swear by Almighty God that I will tell the truth, the whole truth and nothing but the truth".

Rules 28.4(6)(b), 28.10(4)(b) and 29.16

### FORM G15
Form of affirmation for witness

The witness to repeat after the sheriff [*or* commissioner]: "I solemnly, sincerely and truly declare and affirm that I will tell the truth, the whole truth and nothing but the truth".

### ¹FORM G16

Rules 28.14(3) and 28.14A(2)

Form of minute for [letter of request] [taking of evidence in the European Community]*

SHERIFFDOM OF (*insert name of sheriffdom*)

AT (*insert place of sheriff court*)

MINUTE FOR PURSUER [DEFENDER]*

in the cause

[A.B.] (*insert designation and address*)

Pursuer

against

[C.D.] (*insert designation and addres*)

Defender

Court ref. no.

The Minuter states that the evidence specified in the attached [letter of request] [Form A] [Form I]* is required for the purpose of these proceedings and craves the court to issue [a letter of request] [that Form]* to (*specify in the case of a letter of request the central or other appropriate authority of the country or territory in which the evidence is to he obtained, and in the case of Form A or I the applicable court, tribunal, central body or competent authority*) to obtain the evidence specified.

Date (*insert date*)

Signed

(*insert designation and address*)

* *delete as applicable*

### FORM G17

Rule 28.14(3)

Form of letter of request

---

¹ As substituted by the Act of Sederunt (Taking of Evidence in the European Community) 2003 (SSI 2003/601).

**Letter of Request**

1. Sender (insert name and address)

2. Central authority of the requested state (insert name and address)

3. Person to whom the executed request is to (insert name and address)
be returned

4. The undersigned applicant has the honour
to submit the following request:

5. a. Requesting judicial authority (insert name and address)

b. To the competent authority (insert name of requested state)

6. Names and addresses of the parties and
their representatives

a. Pursuer

b. Defender

c. Other parties

7. Nature and purpose of the proceedings
and summary of facts

8. Evidence to be obtained or other judicial
act to be performed

(Items to be completed where applicable)

9. Identity and address of any person to be
examined

10. Questions to be put to the persons to be (or see attached list)
examined or statement of the subject-matter
about which they are to be examined

11. Documents or other property to be in- (specify whether it is to he produced,
spected copied, valued, etc.)

12. Any requirement that the evidence be (in the event that the evidence can-
given on oath or affirmation and any special not be taken in the manner reform to be used quested, specify whether it is to be
taken in such manner as provided by
local law for the formal taking of
evidence)

13. Special methods or procedure to be followed

14. Request for notification of the time and
place for the execution of the request and
identity and address of any person to be notified

15. Request for attendance or participation
of judicial personnel of the requesting authority at the execution of the letter of request

16. Specification of privilege or duty to
refuse to give evidence under the law of the
state of origin

17. The fees and expenses (costs) incurred (insert name and address)
will be borne by

(Items to be included in all letters of request)

**Letter of Request**

18. Date of request

19. Signature and seal of the requesting authority

## FORM G18

Rule 30.3(2)

Form of certificate of rate of exchange

Certificate of Rate of Exchange

I (insert designation and address) certify that the rates current in London for the purchase of (state the unit of currency in which the decree is expressed) on (insert date) was (state rate of exchange) to the £ sterling and at this rate the sum of (state the amount of the sum in the decree) amounts to (insert sterling equivalent).

Date (Insert date)

Signed

For and on behalf of the bank manager or other official

## [1]FORM G19

Form of child witness notice

Rule 45.2

VULNERABLE WITNESSES (SCOTLAND) ACT 2004 Section 12

Received the day of 20

(Date of receipt of this notice)

..........(signed)

Sheriff Clerk

Child Witness Notice

Sheriff Court...........

..........20..........

Court Ref. No.

1. The applicant is the pursuer [or defender] in the action by [A.B.] (design) against [C.D.] (design).

2. The applicant has cited [or intends to cite] [E.F.] (date of birth) as a witness.

3. [E.F.] is a child witnesses under section 11 of the Vulnerable Witnesses (Scotland) Act 2004 [and was under the age of sixteen on the date of the commencement of proceedings].

4. The applicant considers that the following special measure[s] is [are] the most appropriate for the purpose of taking the evidence of [E.F.][or that [E.F.] should give evidence without the benefit of any special measure]:—

(delete as appropriate and specify any special measure(s) sought).

5. [(a) The reason[s] this [these] special measure[s] is [are] considered the most appropriate is [are] as follows:—

(here specify the reason(s) for the special measure(s) sought)].

OR

[(b) The reason[s] it is considered that [E.F.] should give evidence without the benefit of any special measure is [are]:—

(here explain why it is felt that no special measures are required)].

6. [E.F.] and the parent[s] of [or person[s] with parental responsibility for] [E.F.] has [have] expressed the following view[s] on the special measure[s] that is [are]

---

[1] As inserted by the Act of Sederunt (Ordinary Cause, Summary Application, Summary Cause and Small Claim Rules) Amendment (Vulnerable Witnesses (Scotland) Act 2004) 2007 (SSI 2007/463) (effective November 1, 2007).

considered most appropriate [or [the appropriateness of [E.F.] giving evidence without the benefit of any special measure]:—
(delete as appropriate and set out the views(s) expressed and how they were obtained)
7. Other information considered relevant to this application is as follows:—
(here set out any other information relevant to the child witness notice).
8. The applicant asks the court to —
(a) consider this child witness notice;
(b) make an order authorising the special measure[s] sought; or
(c) make an order authorising the giving of evidence by [E.F.] without the benefit of special measures.
(delete as appropriate)

(Signed)
[A.B. or CD]
[or Legal representative of A.B. [or C.D.]] (include full designation)
NOTE: This form should be suitably adapted where section 16 of the Act of 2004 applies.

### ¹FORM G20
Form of vulnerable witness application

Rule 45.3

VULNERABLE WITNESSES (SCOTLAND) ACT 2004 Section 12

Received the..........day of..........20..........
*(Date of receipt of this notice)*
..........*(signed)*
Sheriff Clerk

VULNERABLE WITNESS APPLICATION

Sheriff Court....................

..........20..........

Court Ref. No.

1. The applicant is the pursuer [*or* defender] in the action by [A.B] *(design)* against [C.D.] *(design)*.
2. The applicant has cited [*or* intends to cite] [E.F.] *(date of birth)* as a witness.
3. The applicant considers that [E.F.] is a vulnerable witness under section 11(1)(b) of the Vulnerable Witnesses (Scotland) Act 2004 for the following reasons:—
(*here specify reasons witness is considered to be a vulnerable witness*).
4. The applicant considers that the following special measure[s] is [are] the most appropriate for the purpose of taking the evidence of [E.F.]:—
(*specify any special measure(s) sought*).
5. The reason[s] this [these] special measure[s] is [are] considered the most appropriate is [are] as follows:—
(*here specify the reason(s) for the special measures(s) sought*).
6. [E.F.] has expressed the following view[s] on the special measure[s] that is [are] considered most appropriate:—
(*set out the views expressed and how they were obtained*).
7. Other information considered relevant to this application is as follows:—
(*here set out any other information relevant to the vulnerable witness application*).
8. The applicant asks the court to—

---

¹ As inserted by the Act of Sederunt (Ordinary Cause, Summary Application, Summary Cause and Small Claim Rules) Amendment (Vulnerable Witnesses (Scotland) Act 2004) 2007 (SSI 2007/463) (effective November 1, 2007).

(a)   consider this vulnerable witness application;

(b)   make an order authorising the special measure[s] sought.

...............(*Signed*)

[A.B. *or* C.D.]

[*or* Legal representative of A.B. [*or* C.D.]] (*include full designation*)

*NOTE: This form should be suitably adapted where* section 16 of the Act of 2004 *applies.*

### ¹FORM G21
#### Form of certificate of intimation

Rule 45.4(1)

VULNERABLE WITNESSES (SCOTLAND) ACT 2004 Section 12

CERTIFICATE OF INTIMATION

Sheriff Court..........

..........20..........

Court Ref. No.

I certify that intimation of the child witness notice [*or* vulnerable witness application] relating to (*insert name of witness*) was made to (*insert names of parties or solicitors for parties, as appropriate*) by (*insert method of intimation; where intimation is by facsimile transmission, insert fax number to which intimation sent*) on (*insert dale of intimation*).

Date:..........

..........(*Signed*)

Solicitor [*or* Sheriff Officer]

(*include full business designation*)

### ²FORM G22
#### Form of application for review

Rule 45.6

VULNERABLE WITNESSES (SCOTLAND) ACT 2004 Section 13

Received the..........day of..........20..........

(*date of receipt of this notice*)

...............(*signed*)

Sheriff Clerk

APPLICATION FOR REVIEW OF ARRANGEMENTS FOR VULNERABLE WITNESS

Sheriff Court...............

..........20..........

Court Ref. No.

1. The applicant is the pursuer [*or* defender] in the action by [A.B.] (*design*) against [C.D.] (*design*).

2. A proof [*or* hearing] is fixed for (*date*) at (*time*).

3. [E.F.] is a witness who is to give evidence at, or for the purposes of, the proof [*or* hearing ]. [E.F.] is a child witness [*or* vulnerable witness] under section 11 of the Vulnerable Witnesses (Scotland) Act 2004.

4. The current arrangements for taking the evidence of [E.F.] are (*here specify current arrangements*).

---

¹ As inserted by the Act of Sederunt (Ordinary Cause, Summary Application, Summary Cause and Small Claim Rules) Amendment (Vulnerable Witnesses (Scotland) Act 2004) 2007 (SSI 2007/463) (effective November 1, 2007).

² As inserted by the Act of Sederunt (Ordinary Cause, Summary Application, Summary Cause and Small Claim Rules) Amendment (Vulnerable Witnesses (Scotland) Act 2004) 2007 (SSI 2007/463) (effective November 1, 2007).

5. The current arrangements should be reviewed as (*here specify reasons for review*).

6. [E.F.] [and the parent[s] of [*or* person[s] with parental responsibility for] [E.F.]] has [have] expressed the following view[s] on [the special measure[s] that is [are] considered most appropriate] [*or* the appropriateness of [E.F.] giving evidence without the benefit of any special measure]:—

(*delete as appropriate and set out the view(s) expressed and how they were obtained*).

7. The applicant seeks (here specify the order sought).

(*Signed*)

[A.B. *or* C.D.]

[*or* Legal representative of A.B. [*or* C.D.]] (*include full designation*)

*NOTE: This form should be suitably adapted where* section 16 of the Act of 2004 *applies.*

### ¹FORM G23
Form of certificate of intimation

Rule 45.7(2)

VULNERABLE WITNESSES (SCOTLAND) ACT 2004 Section 13
CERTIFICATE OF INTIMATION

Sheriff Court.........

.........20.........

Court Ref. No.

I certify that intimation of the review application relating to (*insert name of witness*) was made to (*insert names of parties or solicitors for parties, as appropriate*) by (*insert method of intimation; where intimation is by facsimile transmission, insert fax number to which intimation sent*) on (*insert date of intimation*).

Date:.........

(*Signed*)

Solicitor [*or* Sheriff Officer]

(*include full business designation*)

### FORM O1                Rule 3.3(1)

Form of warrant of citation

(*Insert place and date*) Grants warrant to cite the defender (*insert name and address*) by serving upon him [*or* her] a copy of the writ and warrant on a period of notice of (*insert period of notice*) days, and ordains him [*or* her], if he [*or* she] intends to defend the action or make any claim, to lodge a notice of intention to defend with the sheriff clerk at (*insert place of sheriff court*) within the said period of notice after such service [and grants warrant to arrest on the dependence].

[Meantime grants interim interdict; *or* grants warrant to arrest to found jurisdiction; *or* sequestrates and grants warrant to inventory; *or otherwise, as the case may be*.]

Signed

Sheriff [*or* sheriff clerk]

---

¹ As inserted by the Act of Sederunt (Ordinary Cause, Summary Application, Summary Cause and Small Claim Rules) Amendment (Vulnerable Witnesses (Scotland) Act 2004) 2007 (SSI 2007/463) (effective November 1, 2007).

## [1]FORM O2        Rule 3.3(2)

Form of warrant of citation where time to pay direction or time order may be applied for

(*Insert place and date*) Grants warrant to cite the defender (*insert name and address*) by serving a copy of the writ and warrant, with Form O3, on a period of notice of (*insert period of notice*) days and ordains him [*or* her] if he [*or* she]—

(a) intends to defend the action or make any claim, to lodge a notice of intention to defend; or

(b) admits the claim and intends to apply for a time to pay direction [*or* time order] [and apply for recall or restriction of an arrestment] to lodge the appropriate part of Form O3 duly completed;

with the sheriff clerk at (*insert place of sheriff court*) within the said period of notice after such service [and grants warrant to arrest on the dependence].

[Meantime grants interim interdict, or grants warrant to arrest to found jurisdiction; *or* sequestrates and grants warrant to inventory; *or otherwise, as the case may be*.]

Signed<br>Sheriff [or sheriff clerk]

## FORM O2A

Form of warrant in an action to which rule 3.2(3) applies

[*Repealed by the* Act of Sederunt (Sheriff Court Rules) (Enforcement of Securities over Heritable Property) 2010 (SSI 2010/324) para.2 *(effective September 30, 2010)*.]

## [2] [3]FORM O3

Form of notice to be served on defender in ordinary action where time to pay direction or time order may be applied for

Rule 3.3(3), 7.3(2) and 18.5(1)(a)

### ACTION RAISED BY

..........PURSUER..........DEFENDER

AT...............SHERIFF COURT

(Including address)

COURT REF. NO.

DATE OF EXPIRY OF

PERIOD OF NOTICE

**THIS SECTION MUST BE COMPLETED BY THE PURSUER BEFORE SERVICE**

(1) Time to pay directions

The Debtors (Scotland) Act 1987 gives you the right to apply to the court for a "time to pay direction" which is an order permitting you to pay any sum of money you are ordered to pay to the pursuer (which may include interest and court expenses) either by way of instalments or deferred lump sum. A deferred lump sum means that you must pay all the amount at one time within a period specified by the court.

---

[1] As amended by the Act of Sederunt (Ordinary Cause, Summary Application, Summary Cause and Small Claim Rules) Amendment (Miscellaneous) 2007 (SSI 2007/6), para.2(16) (effective January 29, 2007).

[2] As amended by SSI 2007/6 (effective January 29, 2007) and substituted by the Act of Sederunt (Sheriff Court Rules) (Miscellaneous Amendments) 2009 (SSI 2009/294) r.2 (effective December 1, 2009).

[3] As amended by the Act of Sederunt (Sheriff Court Rules) (Miscellaneous Amendments) 2011 (SSI 2011/193) r.9 (effective April 4, 2011).

When making a time to pay direction the court may recall or restrict an arrestment made on your property by the pursuer in connection with the action or debt (for example, your bank account may have been frozen).

(2) Time Orders

The Consumer Credit Act 1974 allows you to apply to the court for a "time order" during a court action, to ask the court to give you more time to pay a loan agreement. **A time order is similar to a time to pay direction, but can only be applied for where the court action is about a credit agreement regulated by the Consumer Credit Act.** The court has power to grant a time order in respect of a regulated agreement to reschedule payment of the sum owed. This means that a time order can change:

- the amount you have to pay each month
- how long the loan will last
- in some cases, the interest rate payable

A time order can also stop the creditor taking away any item bought by you on hire purchase or conditional sale under the regulated agreement, so long as you continue to pay the instalments agreed.

### HOW TO APPLY FOR A TIME TO PAY DIRECTION OR TIME ORDER WHERE YOU ADMIT THE CLAIM AND YOU DO NOT WANT TO DEFEND THE ACTION

1. The appropriate application forms are attached to this notice. If you want to make an application you should lodge the completed application with the sheriff clerk at the above address before the expiry of the period of notice, the date of which is given above. No court fee is payable when lodging the application.

2. Before completing the application please read carefully the notes on how to complete the application. In the event of difficulty you may contact the court's civil department at the address above or any sheriff clerk's office, solicitor, Citizens Advice Bureau or other advice agency. Written guidance can also be obtained from the Scottish Court Service website (www.scotcourts.gov.uk).

NOTE

Where this form is being served on a defender along with Form O9 (notice to additional defender) the reference to "date of expiry of period of notice" should be amended to "date for lodging of defences or an application for a time to pay direction or time order" and the reference to "before the expiry of the period of notice" should be amended to "on or before the date for lodging of defences or an application for a time to pay direction or time order".

### WHAT WILL HAPPEN NEXT

If the pursuer objects to your application, a hearing will be fixed and the court will advise you in writing of the date and time.

If the pursuer does not object to your application, a copy of the court order for payment (called an extract decree) will be served on you by the pursuer's solicitor advising when instalment payments should commence or deferred payment be made.

Court ref. no.

### APPLICATION FOR A TIME TO PAY DIRECTION UNDER THE
DEBTORS (SCOTLAND) ACT 1987

**\*PART A**

By

**\*(This section must be completed by pursuer before service)**

DEFENDER
**In an action raised by**
PURSUER

### HOW TO COMPLETE THE APPLICATION

PLEASE WRITE IN INK USING BLOCK CAPITALS

**PART A** of the application will have been completed in advance by the pursuer and gives details of the pursuer and you as the defender.

**PART B** If you wish to apply to pay by instalments enter the amount and tick the appropriate box at B3(1). If you wish to apply to pay the full sum due in one deferred payment enter the period of deferment you propose at B3(2).

**PART C** Give full details of your financial position in the space provided.

**PART D** If you wish the court, when making the time to pay direction, to recall or restrict an arrestment made in connection with the action, enter the appropriate details about what has been arrested and the place and date of the arrestment at D5, and attach the schedule of arrestment or copy.

Sign the application where indicated. Retain the copy initial writ and the form of notice which accompanied this application form as you may need them at a later stage. You should ensure that your application arrives at the court before the expiry of the period of notice.

**Part B**

1. The applicant is a defender in the action brought by the above named pursuer.
2. The defender admits the claim and applies to the court for a time to pay direction.
3. The defender applies

(1) To pay by instalments of £

(Tick one box only)

EACH WEEK          FORTNIGHT                    MONTH

OR

(2) To pay the sum ordered in one payment within

WEEKS/MONTHS

Please state in this box why you say a time to pay direction should be made. In doing so, please consider the Note below.

**NOTE**

**Under the** 1987 Act **, the court is required to make a time to pay direction if satisfied that it is reasonable in the circumstances to do so, and having regard in particular to the following matters—**

**The nature of and reasons for the debt in relation to which decree is granted or the order is sought**

**Any action taken by the creditor to assist the debtor in paying the debt**

**The debtor's financial position**

**The reasonableness of any proposal by the debtor to pay that debt**

**The reasonableness of any refusal or objection by the creditor to any proposal or offer by the debtor to pay the debt.**

PART C

4. **Defender's financial position**

I am employed /self employed / unemployed

| My net income is: | weekly, fort-nightly    or monthly | My outgoings are: | weekly, fort-nightly    or monthly |
|---|---|---|---|
| Wages | £ | Mortgage/rent | £ |
| State benefits | £ | Council tax | £ |
| Tax credits | £ | Gas/electricity etc | £ |

| My net income is: | weekly, fort-nightly or monthly | My outgoings are: | weekly, fort-nightly or monthly |
|---|---|---|---|
| Other | £ | Food | £ |
| | | Credit and loans | £ |
| | | Phone | £ |
| | | Other | £ |
| Total | £ | Total | £ |

People who rely on your income (e.g. spouse/civil partner/partner/children) — how many

Here list all assets (if any) e.g. value of house; amounts in bank or building society accounts; shares or other investments:

Here list any outstanding debts:

**Part D**

5. The defender seeks to recall or restrict an arrestment of which the details are as follows (*please state, and attach the schedule of arrestment or copy*).

6. This application is made under sections 1(1) and 2(3) of the Debtors (Scotland) Act 1987.

Therefore the defender asks the court

*to make a time to pay direction

*to recall the above arrestment

*to restrict the above arrestment (*in which case state restriction wanted*)

Date (*insert date*)

Signed

Defender

Court ref. no.

## APPLICATION FOR A TIME ORDER UNDER THE CONSUMER CREDIT ACT 1974

**\*PART A**

By

**\*(This section must be completed by pursuer before service)**

DEFENDER

**In an action raised by**

PURSUER

## HOW TO COMPLETE THE APPLICATION
### PLEASE WRITE IN INK USING BLOCK CAPITALS

**PART A** of the application will have been completed in advance by the pursuer and gives details of the pursuer and you as the defender.

**PART B** If you wish to apply to pay by instalments enter the amount and tick the appropriate box at B3. If you wish the court to make any additional orders, please give details at B4. Please give details of the regulated agreement at B5.

**PART C** Give full details of your financial position in the space provided.

Sign the application where indicated. Retain the copy initial writ and the form of notice which accompanied this application form as you may need them at a later stage. You should ensure that your application arrives at the court before the expiry of the period of notice.

**Part B**

1. The Applicant is a defender in the action brought by the above named pursuer.

**I/WE WISH TO APPLY FOR A TIME ORDER under the** Consumer Credit Act 1974

**2. Details of order(s) sought**

The defender wishes to apply for a time order under section 129 of the Consumer Credit Act 1974

The defender wishes to apply for an order in terms of section..........of the Consumer Credit Act 1974

**3. Proposals for payment**

I admit the claim and apply to pay the arrears and future instalments as follows:

By instalments of £ .......... per *week/fortnight/month

No time to pay direction or time to pay order has been made in relation to this debt.

**4. Additional orders sought**

The following additional order(s) is (are) sought: (*specify*)

The order(s) sought in addition to the time order is (are) sought for the following reasons:

**5. Details of regulated agreement**

(*Please attach a copy of the agreement if you have retained it and insert details of the agreement where known*)

(a)  Date of agreement
(b)  Reference number of agreement
(c)  Names and addresses of other parties to agreement
(d)  Name and address of person (if any) who acted as surety (guarantor) to the agreement
(e)  Place where agreement signed (e.g. the shop where agreement signed, including name and address)
(f)  Details of payment arrangements
     i.   The agreement is to pay instalments of £..........per week/month
     ii.   The unpaid balance is £........../ I do not know the amount of arrears
     iii.   I am £..........in arrears / I do not know the amount of arrears

**Part C**

4. Defender's financial position

I am employed /self employed / unemployed

| My net income is: | weekly, fortnightly or monthly | My outgoings are: | weekly, fortnightly or monthly |
| --- | --- | --- | --- |
| Wages | £ | Mortgage/rent | £ |
| State benefits | £ | Council tax | £ |
| Tax credits | £ | Gas/electricity etc | £ |
| Other | £ | Food | £ |
| Credit and loans | £ | Phone | £ |
| | | Other | £ |
| Total | £ | Total | £ |

People who rely on your income (e.g. spouse/civil partner/partner/children) — how many

Here list all assets (if any) e.g. value of house; amounts in bank or building society accounts; shares or other investments:

Here list any outstanding debts:

Therefore the defender asks the court to make a time order

Date...............Signed..........

...............Defender..........

310

Rule 7.3(4)                         [1]**FORM O3A**

Form of pursuer's response objecting to application for time to pay direction or time order

**Court ref no:**

SHERIFFDOM OF (*insert name of sheriffdom*)
AT (*insert place of sheriff court*)
PURSUER'S RESPONSE OBJECTING TO APPLICATION FOR TIME TO PAY
DIRECTION OR TIME ORDER
in the cause
[A.B.], (*insert designation and address*), Pursuer
against
[C.D.], (*insert designation and address*), Defender

1. The pursuer received a copy application for a time to pay direction or time order lodged by the defender on (*date*).

2. The pursuer does not accept the offer.

3. The debt is (*please specify the nature of the debt*).

4. The debt was incurred on (*specify date*) and the pursuer has contacted the defender in relation to the debt on (*specify date(s)*).

*5. The contractual payments were (*specify amount*).

*6. (*Specify any action taken by the pursuer to assist the defender to pay the debt*).

*7. The defender has made payment(s) towards the debt of (*specify amount(s)*) on (*specify date(s)*).

*8. The debtor has made offers to pay (*specify amount(s)*) on (*specify date(s)*) which offer(s) was [were] accepted [*or* rejected] and (*specify amount*) was paid on (*specify date(s)*).

9. (*Here set out any information you consider relevant to the court's determination of the application*).

* delete as appropriate

Minute for decree

(*Signed*)
Pursuer *or* Solicitor for pursuer
(*Date*)

Rule 5.2(1)                    [2][3]**FORM O4**

Form of Citation

CITATION
SHERIFFDOM OF (*insert name of Sheriffdom*)
AT (*insert place of sheriff court*)
[A.B.], (*insert designation and address*), Pursuer, against [C.D.], (*insert designation and address*), Defender

**Court Ref No:**

(*Insert place and date*). You [C.D.], are hereby served with this copy writ and warrant, with Form 07 (notice of intention to defend).

---

[1] As inserted by Act of Sederunt (Sheriff Court Rules) (Miscellaneous Amendments) 2009 (SSI 2009/294) r.2 (effective December 1, 2009).

[2] As substituted by the Act of Sederunt (Sheriff Court Ordinary Cause Rules Amendment) (Miscellaneous) 2000 (SSI 2000/239) (effective October 2, 2000).

[3] As amended by the Act of Sederunt (Sheriff Court Rules) (Miscellaneous Amendments) (No.2) 2008 (SSI 2008/365) para.2 (effective December 1, 2008).

**Form O7** is served on you for use should you wish to intimate an intention to defend this action.

*IF YOU WISH TO DEFEND THIS ACTION* you should consult a solicitor with a view to lodging a notice of intention to defend (Form 07). The notice of intention to defend, together with the court fee of £ (*insert amount*) must be lodged with the Sheriff Clerk at the above address within 21 days (*or insert the appropriate period of notice*) of (*insert the date on which service was executed NB. Rule 5.3(2) relating to postal service*).

**A copy of any notice of intention to defend should be sent to the Solicitor for the pursuer at the same time as your notice of intention to defend is lodged with the Sheriff Clerk.**

**IF THE WORDS "COMMERCIAL ACTION" APPEAR AT THE HEAD OF THIS INITIAL WRIT** then you should note that this action is a commercial action governed by Chapter 40 of the Ordinary Cause Rules 1993. You should also note in particular that if you lodge a notice of intention to defend you must then lodge defences within 7 days of the expiry of the period of notice. You will receive no further notification of this requirement from the court.

**IF YOU ARE UNCERTAIN WHAT ACTION TO TAKE** you should consult a solicitor. You may be eligible for legal aid depending on your income, and you can get information about legal aid from a solicitor. You may also obtain advice from any Citizens' Advice Bureau or other advice agency.

**PLEASE NOTE THAT IF YOU DO NOTHING IN ANSWER TO THIS DOCUMENT** the court may regard you as admitting the claim made against you and the pursuer may obtain decree against you in your absence.

Signed

[P.Q.], Sheriff Officer

*or* [X.Y.] (*add designation and business address*)

Solicitor for the Pursuer

Rule 5.2(2)　　　　　　　　　　　　　[1] [2]**FORM O5**

Form of citation where time to pay direction or time order may be applied for

CITATION

SHERIFFDOM OF (*insert name of Sheriffdom*)

AT (*insert place of Sheriff Court*)

[A.B.], (*insert designation and address*) Pursuer against [C.D.], (*insert designation and address*) Defender

Court Ref No:

(*insert place and date*). You [C.D.], are hereby served with this copy writ and warrant, together with the following forms—

Form 03 (application for time to pay direction or time order); and

Form 07 (notice of intention to defend).

---

[1] As substituted by the Act of Sederunt (Sheriff Court Ordinary Cause Rules Amendment) (Miscellaneous) 2000 (SSI 2000/239) (effective October 2, 2000) and amended by the Act of Sederunt (Ordinary Cause, Summary Application, Summary Cause and Small Claim Rules) Amendment (Miscellaneous) 2007 (SSI 2007/6), para.2(16) (effective January 29, 2007).

[2] As amended by the Act of Sederunt (Sheriff Court Rules) (Miscellaneous Amendments) (No.2) 2008 (SSI 2008/365) para.2 (effective December 1, 2008).

**Form 03** is served on you because it is considered that you may be entitled to apply for a time to pay direction or time order [and for the recall or restriction of an arrestment used on the dependence of the action or in security of the debt referred to in the copy writ]. See Form 03 for further details.

**IF YOU ADMIT THE CLAIM AND WISH TO APPLY FOR A TIME TO PAY DIRECTION OR TIME ORDER**, you must complete Form 03 and return it to the Sheriff Clerk at (*insert address*) within 21 days (*or insert the appropriate period of notice*) of (*insert the date on which service was executed. NB* Rule 5.3 (2) *relating to postal service*).

**IF YOU ADMIT THE CLAIM AND WISH TO AVOID A COURT ORDER BEING MADE AGAINST YOU**, the whole sum claimed including interest and any expense due should be paid to the pursuer or his solicitor in good time before the expiry of the period of notice.

**Form 07** is served on you for use should you wish to intimate an intention to defend the action.

**IF YOU WISH TO DEFEND THIS ACTION** you should consult a solicitor with a view to lodging a notice of intention to defend (Form 07). The notice of intention to defend, together with the court fee of £ (*insert amount*) must be lodged with the Sheriff Clerk at the above address within 21 days (*or insert the appropriate period of notice*) of (*insert the date on which service was executed. NB* Rule 5.3(2) *relating to postal service*).

**A copy of any notice of intention to defend should be sent to the Solicitor for the pursuer at the same time as your notice of intention to defend is lodged with the Sheriff Clerk.**

**IF THE WORDS "COMMERCIAL ACTION" APPEAR AT THE HEAD OF THIS INITIAL WRIT** then you should note that this action is a commercial action governed by Chapter 40 of the Ordinary Cause Rules 1993. You should also note in particular that if you lodge a notice of intention to defend you must then lodge defences within 7 days of the expiry of the period of notice. You will receive no further notification of this requirement from the court.

**IF YOU ARE UNCERTAIN WHAT ACTION TO TAKE** you should consult a solicitor. You may be eligible for legal aid depending on your income, and you can get information about legal aid from a solicitor. You may also obtain advice from any Citizens' Advice Bureau or other advice agency.

**PLEASE NOTE THAT IF YOU DO NOTHING IN ANSWER TO THIS DOCUMENT** the court may regard you as admitting the claim made against you and the pursuer may obtain decree against you in your absence.

Signed

[P.Q.], Sheriff Officer
*or* [X.Y.] (*add designation and business address*)
Solicitor for the Pursuer

**FORM 05A**
Form of citation in an action to which rule 3.2(3) applies

[*Repealed by the* Act of Sederunt (Sheriff Court Rules) (Enforcement of Securities over Heritable Property) 2010 (SSI 2010/324) para.2 *(effective September 30. 2010).*]

Rule 5.2(3)                                   ¹**FORM O6**
                    Form of certificate of citation
                      CERTIFICATE OF CITATION
(*Insert place and date*) I, hereby certify that upon the day of I duly cited [C.D.], Defender, to answer to the foregoing writ. This I did by (*state method of service; if by officer and not by post, add*: in presence of [L.M.], (*insert designation*), witness hereto with me subscribing; *and where service executed by post state whether by registered post or the first class recorded delivery service*).

(*In actions in which a time to pay direction may be applied for, state whether Form O2 and Form O3 were sent in accordance with* rule 3.3).

Signed
[P.Q.], Sheriff officer
[L.M.], witness
*or* [X.Y.]. (*add designation and business address*)
Solicitor for the pursuer

Rules 5.2(1) and 9.1(1)                       ²**FORM O7**
                 Form of notice of intention to defend
                 **NOTICE OF INTENTION TO DEFEND**

*PART A            in an action raised at        Sheriff Court
Court Ref No

(Insert name and business address of solicitor for the Pursuer)

                                                 **Pursuer**

             Solicitor for the pur-
                       suer
                                                 **Defender**
*(**This section to be completed by the
Pursuer before service**)
DATE    OF                DATE OF EXPIRY OF PERIOD OF NOTICE:
SERVICE:

Part B
**(This section to be completed by the defender or defender's solicitors, and both parts of this form to be returned to the Sheriff Clerk (insert address of**

---

¹ As substituted by the Act of Sederunt (Amendment of Ordinary Cause Rules and Summary Applications, Statutory Applications and Appeals etc. Rules) (Applications under the Mortgage Rights (Scotland) Act 2001) 2002 (SSI 2002 No.7), para.2(6) and amended by the Act of Sederunt (Sheriff Court Rules) (Enforcement of Securities over Heritable Property) 2010 (SSI 2010/324) para.2 (effective September 30, 2010).
² As substituted by the Act of Sederunt (Sheriff Court Ordinary Cause Rules Amendment) (Miscellaneous) 2000 (SSI 2000/239) (effective October 2, 2000).

**Sheriff Clerk) on or before the date of expiry of the period of notice referred to in PART A above. At the same time a copy of the form should be sent to the Solicitor for the Pursuer).**

(*Insert place and date*)

[C.D.], (*insert designation and address*), Defender, intends to defend the action raised by [A.B.], (*insert designation and address*), Pursuer, against him (and others).

Signed

[C.D.], Defender

*or* [X.Y.], (*add designation and business address*)

Solicitor for the defender

Paragraph 4(4)

## ¹FORM O7A

Rule 13A.3(1)

Form of minute of intervention by the Commission for Equality and Human Rights

SHERIFFDOM OF (*insert name of sheriffdom*)

Court ref. no.

AT (*insert place of sheriff court*)

Application for Leave to Intervene by the Commission for Equality And Human Rights

in the cause

[A.B.] (*designation and address*), Pursuer

against

[C.D.] (*designation and address*), Defender

[*Here set out briefly:*

(a)  the Commission's reasons for believing that the proceedings are relevant to a matter in connection with which the Commission has a function;

(b)  the issue in the proceedings which the Commission wishes to address; and

(c)  the propositions to be advanced by the Commission and the Commission's reasons for believing that they are relevant to the proceedings and that they will assist the court.]

## ²FORM O7B

Rule 13B.2(1)

Form of minute of intervention by the Scottish Commission for Human Rights

SHERIFFDOM OF (*insert name of sheriffdom*)

Court ref. no.

AT (*insert place of sheriff court*)

APPLICATION FOR LEAVE TO INTERVENE BY THE SCOTTISH COMMISSION FOR HUMAN RIGHTS

in the cause

[A.B.] (*designation and address*), Pursuer

against

[C.D.] (*designation and address*), Defender

[*Here set out briefly:*

(a)  the issue in the proceedings which the Commission intends to address;

(b)  a summary of the submission the Commission intends to make.]

---

¹ As inserted by the Act of Sederunt (Sheriff Court Rules) (Miscellaneous Amendments) 2008 (SSI 2008/223) para.4(4) (effective July 1, 2008).

² As inserted by the Act of Sederunt (Sheriff Court Rules) (Miscellaneous Amendments) 2008 (SSI 2008/223) para.4(4) (effective July 1, 2008).

¹**FORM O7C**

Rule 13B.3(1)

Invitation to the Scottish Commission for Human Rights to intervene

SHERIFFDOM OF *(insert name of sheriffdom)*

Court ref. no.

AT *(insert place of sheriff court)*

INVITATION TO THE SCOTTISH COMMISSION FOR HUMAN RIGHTS TO INTERVENE

in the cause

[A.B.] *(designation and address)*, Pursuer

against

[C.D.] *(designation and address)*, Defender

[*Here set out briefly:*

(a)   the facts, procedural history and issues in the proceedings;

(b)   the issue in the proceedings on which the court seeks a submission.]

²**FORM 08**

Rule 18.5(1)(a)(i)

Form of notice to additional or substitute defender where time to pay direction or time order may be applied for

SHERIFFDOM OF *(insert name of sheriffdom)*

AT *(insert place of sheriff court)*

To [E.F.] *(insert designation and address of additional* [or *substitute*] *defender)*

Court ref. no.

You [E.F.] are given notice that in this action in which [A.B.] is the pursuer and [C.D.] is the defender, your name has, by order of the court dated *(insert date of court order)* been added [or substituted] as a defender to the said action; and the action, originally against [C.D.] is now [or also] directed against you.

Enclosed with this notice are the following documents—

Copies of the [*insert as appropriate*, pleadings as adjusted *or* closed record];

Form 03 (application for a time to pay direction or time order); and

Form 07 (notice of intention to defend).

**Form 03** is served on you because it is considered that you may be entitled to apply for a time to pay direction or time order [and for the recall or restriction of an arrestment used on the dependence of the action or in security of the debt referred to in the copy writ]. See Form 03 for further details.

**IF YOU ADMIT THE CLAIM AND WISH TO APPLY FOR A TIME TO PAY DIRECTION OR TIME ORDER,** you must complete Form 03 and return it to the sheriff clerk at *(insert address)* within 21 days *(or insert the appropriate period of notice)* of *(Insert the date on which service was executed. N.B. Rule 5.3(2) relating to postal citation)*.

**IF YOU ADMIT THE CLAIM AND WISH TO AVOID A COURT ORDER BEING MADE AGAINST YOU,** the whole sum claimed including interest and any expenses due should be paid to the pursuer or his solicitor in good time before the expiry of the period of notice.

**Form 07** is served on you for use should you wish to intimate an intention to defend the action.

---

¹ As inserted by the Act of Sederunt (Sheriff Court Rules) (Miscellaneous Amendments) 2008 (SSI 2008/223) para.4(4) (effective July 1, 2008).

² As amended by the Act of Sederunt (Ordinary Cause, Summary Application, Summary Cause and Small Claim Rules) Amendment (Miscellaneous) 2007 (SSI 2007/6) para.2(16) (effective January 29, 2007).

**IF YOU WISH TO DEFEND THIS ACTION** you should consult a solicitor with a view to lodging a notice of intention to defend (Form 07). The notice of intention to defend, together with the court fee of £ (*insert amount*) must be lodged with the sheriff clerk at the above address within 21 days (*or insert the appropriate period of notice*) of (*insert the date on which service was executed. N.B. See Rule 5.3(2) relating to postal service*).

**IF YOU ARE UNCERTAIN WHAT ACTION TO TAKE** you should consult a solicitor. You may be eligible for legal aid depending on your income, and you can get information about legal aid from a solicitor. You may also obtain advice from any Citizens Advice Bureau or other advice agency.

**PLEASE NOTE THAT IF YOU DO NOTHING IN ANSWER TO THIS DOCUMENT** the court may regard you as admitting the claim made against you and the pursuer may obtain decree against you in your absence.

Signed

[P.Q.], Sheriff officer

*or* [X.Y.] (*add designation and business address*)

Solicitor for the pursuer [or defender]

### FORM O9

Rule 18.5(1)(a)(ii)

Form of notice to additional or substitute defender

SHERIFFDOM OF (*insert name of sheriffdom*)

AT (*insert place of sheriff court*)

To [E.F.] (*insert designation and address of additional* [or *substitute*] defender)

Court ref. no.

You [E.F.] are given notice that in this action in which [A.B.] is the pursuer and [C.D.] is the defender, your name has, by order of the court dated (*insert date of court order*) been added [*or* substituted] as a defender to the said action; and the action, originally against the said [C.D.] is now [*or* also] directed against you.

Enclosed with this notice are the following documents—

Copies of the [*insert as appropriate* pleadings as adjusted *or* closed record]; and

Form 07 (notice of intention to defend).

**Form 07** is served on you for use should you wish to intimate an intention to defend the action.

**IF YOU WISH TO DEFEND THIS ACTION** you should consult a solicitor with a view to lodging a notice of intention to defend (Form 07). The notice of intention to defend, together with the court fee of £ (insert amount) must be lodged with the sheriff clerk at the above address with 28 days (*or insert the appropriate period of notice*) of (*insert the date on which service was executed. N.B. Rule 5.3(2) relating to postal service*).

**IF YOU ARE UNDERTAIN WHAT ACTION TO TAKE** you should consult a solicitor. You may be eligible for legal aid depending on your income, and you can get information about legal aid from a solicitor. You may also obtain advice from any Citizens Advice Bureau or other advice agency.

**PLEASE NOTE THAT IF YOU DO NOTHING IN ANSWER TO THIS DOCUMENT** the court may regard you as admitting the claim made against you and the pursuer may obtain decree against you in your absence.

Signed

[P.Q.], Sheriff officer

*or* [X.Y.] (*add designation and business address*)

Solicitor for the pursuer [or defender]

## ¹FORM O10

Rule 20.1

### Form of third party notice

SHERIFFDOM OF (*insert name of sheriffdom*)

Court ref. no.

AT (*insert place of sheriff court*)...............

### THIRD PARTY NOTICE
in the cause

[A.B.], (*insert designation and address*), Pursuer

against

[C.D.], (*insert designation and address*), Defender

To [E.F.]

You are given notice by [C.D.] of an order granted by Sheriff (*insert name of sheriff*) in this action in which [A.B.] is the pursuer and [C.D.] the defender. In the action the pursuer claims against the defender the sum of £ as damages in respect of (*insert brief account of the circumstances of the claim*) as more fully appears in the [*insert as appropriate*, pleadings as adjusted *or* amended *or* closed record] enclosed.

*The defender admits [*or* denies] liability to the pursuer but claims that, if he [*or* she] is liable to the pursuer, you are liable to relieve him [*or* her] wholly [*or* partially] of his [*or* her] liability because (*set forth contract or other right of contribution, relief, or indemnity*) as more fully appears from the defences lodged by him [*or* her] in the action,

or

*Delete appropriate.* as *The defender denies liability for the injury claimed to have been suffered by the pursuer and maintains that liability, if any, to the pursuer rests solely on you [along with (*insert names of any other person whom defender maintains is liable to him [or her] by way of contribution, relief or indemnity*)] as more fully appears from the defences lodged by him [*or* her] in the action.

or

*The defender denies liability for the injury said to have been suffered by the pursuer but maintains that if there is any liability he [*or* she] shares that with you, as more fully appears from the defences lodged by him [*or* her] in the action.

or

*The defender admits liability in part for the injury suffered by the pursuer but disputes the amount of damages and maintains that liability falls to be shared by you, as more fully appears from the defences lodged by him [*or* her] in the action.

or

*The defender admits liability in part for the injury suffered by the pursuer and for the damages claimed but maintains that liability falls to be shared by you, as more fully appears from the defences lodged by him [*or* her] in the action.

---

¹ As amended by SI 1996/2445 (effective November 1,1996) (clerical error).

or

*(*Otherwise as the case may be*)

IF YOU WISH TO resist either the claim of the pursuer against the defender, or the claim of the defender against you, you must lodge answers with the sheriff clerk at the above address within 28 days of (*insert the date on which service was executed. N.B.* Rule 5.3(2) *relating to postal service*). You must also pay the court fee of £ (*insert amount*).

Date (*insert date*)...............(*Signed*)

Solicitor for the defender.

Rule 31.4(1)

## FORM A1

*[Repealed by the Act of Sederunt (Rules of the Court of Session, Sheriff Appeal Court Rules and Sheriff Court Rules Amendment) (Sheriff Appeal Court) 2015 (SSI 2015/419) r.5 (effective 1 January 2016).]*

Rule 33.7(1)(a)

## FORM F1

Form of intimation to children and next-of-kin in an action of divorce or separation where the defender's address is not known

Court ref. no.

To (*insert name and address as in warrant*)

You are given NOTICE that an action of divorce [*or* separation] has been raised against (*insert name*) your (*insert relationship, e.g. father, mother, brother or other relative as the case may be*). If you know of his [*or* her] present address, you are requested to inform the sheriff clerk (*insert address of sheriff clerk*) in writing immediately. If you wish to appear as a party you must lodge a minute with the sheriff clerk for leave to do so. Your minute must be lodged within 21 days of (*insert date on which intimation was given. N.B.* Rule 5.3(2) *relating to postal service or intimation*).

Date (*insert date*)

(*Signed*)

Solicitor for the pursuer (*add designation and business address*)

**NOTE**

If you decide to lodge a minute it may be in your best interest to consult a solicitor. The minute should be lodged with the sheriff clerk together with the appropriate fee of (*insert amount*) and a copy of this intimation.

**IF YOU ARE UNCERTAIN WHAT ACTION TO TAKE** you should consult a solicitor. You may be entitled to legal aid depending on your financial circumstances, and you can get information about legal aid from a solicitor. You may also obtain advice from any Citizens Advice Bureau or other advice agency.

Rule 33.7(1)(b)

## FORM F2

Form of intimation to alleged adulterer in action of divorce or separation

To (*insert name and address as in warrant*)

Court ref. no.

You are given NOTICE that in this action, you are alleged to have committed adultery. A copy of the initial writ is attached. If you wish to dispute the truth of the allegation made against you, you must lodge a minute with the sheriff clerk (*insert address of sheriff clerk*) for leave to appear as a party. Your minute must be lodged within 21 days of (*insert date on which intimation was given. N.B.* Rule 5.3(2) *relating to postal service or intimation*).

Date (*insert date*)

(*Signed*)

Solicitor for the pursuer

**NOTE**

If you decide to lodge a minute it may be in your best interest to consult a solicitor. The minute should be lodged with the sheriff clerk together with the appropriate fee of (*insert amount*) and a copy of this intimation.

**IF YOU ARE UNCERTAIN WHAT ACTION TO TAKE** you should consult a solicitor. You may be entitled to legal aid depending on your financial circumstances, and you can get information about legal aid from a solicitor. You may also obtain advice from any Citizens Advice Bureau or other advice agency.

Rule 33.7(1)(c)

## FORM F3

Form of intimation to children, next-of-kin and *curator bonis* in an action of divorce or separation where the defender suffers from a mental disorder

To (*insert name and address as in warrant*)

Court ref. no.

You are given NOTICE that an action of divorce [*or* separation] has been raised against (*insert name and designation*) your (*insert relationship, e.g. father, mother, brother or other relative, or ward, as the case may be*). A copy of the initial writ is enclosed. If you wish to appear as a party, you must lodge a minute with the sheriff clerk (*insert address of sheriff clerk*), for leave to do so. Your minute must be lodged within 21 days of (*insert date on which intimation was given. N.B.* Rule 5.3(2) *relating to postal service or intimation*).

Date (*insert date*)

(*Signed*)

Solicitor for the pursuer (*insert designation and business address*)

**NOTE**

If you decide to lodge a minute it may be in your best interest to consult a solicitor. The minute should be lodged with the sheriff clerk together with the appropriate fee of (*insert amount*) and a copy of this intimation.

**IF YOU ARE UNCERTAIN WHAT ACTION TO TAKE** you should consult a solicitor. You may be entitled to legal aid depending on your financial circumstances, and you can get information about legal aid from a solicitor. You may also obtain advice from any Citizens Advice Bureau or other advice agency.

**IF YOU ARE UNCERTAIN WHAT ACTION TO TAKE** you should consult a solicitor. You may be entitled to legal aid depending on your financial circumstances, and you can get information about legal aid from a solicitor. You may also obtain advice from any Citizens Advice Bureau or other advice agency.

Rule 33.7(1)(d)

## FORM F4

Form of intimation to additional spouse of either party in proceedings relating to a polygamous marriage

To (*name and address as in warrant*)

Court ref. no.

You are given NOTICE that this action for divorce [*or* separation], involves (*insert name and designation*) your spouse. A copy of the initial writ is attached. If you wish to appear as a party, you must lodge a minute with the sheriff clerk (*insert address of sheriff clerk*) for leave to do so. Your minute must be lodged within 21 days of (*insert date on which intimation was given. N.B.* Rule 5.3(2) *relating to postal service or intimation*).

Date (*insert date*)

(*Signed*)

Solicitor for the pursuer

**NOTE**

If you decide to lodge a minute it may be in your best interest to consult a solicitor. The minute should be lodged with the sheriff clerk together with the appropriate fee of (*insert amount*) and a copy of this intimation.

**IF YOU ARE UNCERTAIN WHAT ACTION TO TAKE** you should consult a solicitor. You may be entitled to legal aid depending on your financial circumstances, and you can get information about legal aid from a solicitor. You may also obtain advice from any Citizens Advice Bureau or other advice agency.

Rule 33.7(1)(e)(i) and (ii)

### ¹FORM F5

Form of intimation to a local authority or third party who may be liable to maintain a child

To (*insert name and address as in warrant*)

Court ref. no.

YOU ARE GIVEN NOTICE that in this action, the court may make an order under section 11 of the Children (Scotland) Act 1995 in respect of (*insert name and address*), a child in your care [or liable to be maintained by you]. A copy of the initial writ is attached. If you wish to appear as a party, you must lodge a minute with the sheriff clerk (*insert address of sheriff clerk*) for leave to do so. Your minute must be lodged within 21 days of (*insert date on which intimation was given. N.B. Rule 5.3(2) relating to postal service or intimation*).

Date (*insert date*)

(*Signed*)

Solicitor for the pursuer

**NOTE**

If you decide to lodge a minute it may be in your best interests to consult a solicitor. The minute should be lodged with the sheriff clerk together with the appropriate fee of (*insert amount*) and a copy of this intimation.

**IF YOU ARE UNCERTAIN WHAT ACTION TO TAKE** you should consult a solicitor. You may be entitled to legal aid depending on your financial circumstances, and you can get information about legal aid from a solicitor. You may also obtain advice from any Citizens Advice Bureau or other advice agency.

Rule 33.7(1)(e)(iii)

### ²FORM F6

Form of intimation to person who in fact exercises care or control of a child

To (*insert name and address as in warrant*)

Court ref. no.

YOU ARE GIVEN NOTICE that in this action, the court may make an order under section 11 of the Children (Scotland) Act 1995 in respect of (*insert name and address*) a child at present in your care or control. A copy of the initial writ is attached. If you wish to appear as a party, you must lodge a minute with the sheriff clerk (*insert address of sheriff clerk*) for leave to do so. Your minute must be lodged within 21 days of (*insert date on which intimation was given. N.B. Rule 5.3(2) relating to postal service or intimation*).

Date (*insert date*)...............(*Signed*)

Solicitor for the pursuer

**NOTE**

---

[1] Substituted by SI 1996/216 (effective November 1, 1996).
[2] Substituted by SI 1996/2167 (effective November 1, 1996).

If you decide to lodge a minute it may be in your best interests to consult a solicitor. The minute should be lodged with the sheriff clerk together with the appropriate fee of (*insert amount*) and a copy of this intimation.

**IF YOU ARE UNCERTAIN WHAT ACTION TO TAKE** you should consult a solicitor. You may be entitled to legal aid depending on your financial circumstances, and you can get information about legal aid from a solicitor. You may also obtain advice from any Citizens Advice Bureau or other advice agency.

Rule 33.7(1)(f)

[1]**FORM F7**

Form of notice to parent or guardian in action for a section 11 order in respect of a child

1. YOU ARE GIVEN NOTICE that in this action, the pursuer is applying for an order under section 11 of the Children (Scotland) Act 1995 in respect of the child (*insert name of child*). A copy of the initial writ is served on you and is attached to this notice.

2. If you wish to oppose this action, or oppose the granting of any order applied for by the pursuer in respect of the child, you must lodge a notice of intention to defend (Form F26). See Form F26 attached for further details.

Date (*insert date*)

(*Signed*)

Pursuer

*or* Solicitor for the pursuer (*add designation and business address*)

**NOTE: IF YOU ARE UNCERTAIN WHAT ACTION TO TAKE** you should consult a solicitor. You may be entitled to legal aid depending on your financial circumstances, and you can get information about legal aid from a solicitor. You may also obtain advice from any Citizens Advice Bureau or other advice agency.

Rules 33.7(1)(g), 33.7(4) and 33.12(2) and (3)

[2]**FORM F8**

Form of notice to local authority

To (insert name and address)

Court ref. no.

1. YOU ARE GIVEN NOTICE that in an action in the Sheriff Court at (*insert address*) the pursuer has applied for a residence order in respect of the child (*insert name of child*). A copy of the initial writ is enclosed.

2. If you wish to oppose this action, or oppose the granting of any order applied for by the pursuer in respect of the child, you must lodge a notice of intention to defend (Form F26). See Form F26 attached for further details.

Date (*insert date*)

(*Signed*)

Solicitor for the pursuer (*add designation and business address*)

Rule 33.7(1)(h)

[3]**FORM F9**

Form of intimation in an action which includes a crave for a section 11 order

PART A

Court ref. No.

---

[1] Substituted by S.I. 1996 No. 2167 (effective November 1, 1996).

[2] Substituted by SI 1996/2167 (effective November 1, 1996) and SSI 2010/416 (effective January 1, 2011).

[3] Substituted by SI 1996/2167 (effective November 1, 1996) and amended by SSI 2003/26 (effective January 24, 2003).

> This part must be completed by the Pursuer's solicitor in language a child is capable of understanding.

To (1)

The Sheriff (the person who has to decide about your future) has been asked by (2).........to decide:—

  (a)  (3) and (4)

  (b)  (5)

  (c)  (6)

If you want to tell the Sheriff what you think about the things your (2).......... has asked the Sheriff to decide about your future you should complete Part B of this form and send it to the Sheriff Clerk at (7) by (8)........... An envelope which does not need a postage stamp is enclosed for you to use to return the form.

**IF YOU DO NOT UNDERSTAND THIS FORM OR IF YOU WANT HELP TO COMPLETE IT you may get help from a SOLICITOR or contact the SCOTTISH CHILD LAW CENTRE ON the FREE ADVICE TELEPHONE LINE ON 0800 328 8970.**

If you return the form it will be given to the Sheriff. The Sheriff may wish to speak with you and may ask you to come and see him or her.

Notes for Completion

| | |
|---|---|
| (1) Insert name and address of child. | (2) Insert relationship to the child of party making the application to court. |
| (3) Insert appropriate wording for residence order sought. | (4) Insert address. |
| (5) Insert appropriate wording for contact order sought. | (6) Insert appropriate wording for any other order sought. |
| (7) Insert address of sheriff clerk. | (8) Insert the date occurring 21 days after the date on which intimation is given. N.B. Rule 5.3(2) relating to intimation and service. |
| (9) Insert court reference number. | (10) Insert name and address of parties to the action. |

Part B

<u>IF YOU WISH THE SHERIFF TO KNOW YOUR VIEWS ABOUT YOUR FUTURE YOU SHOULD COMPLETE THIS PART OF THE FORM</u>

To the Sheriff Clerk, (7)

Court Ref. No. (9)

(10)................................................

QUESTION (1): DO YOU WISH THE SHERIFF TO KNOW WHAT YOUR VIEWS ARE ABOUT YOUR FUTURE?

(PLEASE TICK BOX)

| | |
|---:|---|
| Yes | |
| No | |

If you have ticked YES please also answer Question (2) *or* (3)

QUESTION (2): WOULD YOU LIKE A FRIEND, RELATIVE OR OTHER PERSON TO TELL THE SHERIFF YOUR VIEWS ABOUT YOUR FUTURE?

(PLEASE TICK BOX)

| | Yes | |
|---|---|---|
| | No | |

If you have ticked YES please write the name and address of the person you wish to tell the Sheriff your views in Box (A) below. You should also tell that person what your views are about your future.

| | | |
|---|---|---|
| BOX A: | (NAME)........................................ | |
| | (ADDRESS)...................................... | |
| | ................................. | |
| | Is this A person:— friend? ☐ | A rela- ☐ tive? |
| | A teacher? ☐ | Other? ☐ |

OR

QUESTION (3): WOULD YOU LIKE TO WRITE TO THE SHERIFF AND TELL HIM WHAT YOUR VIEWS ARE ABOUT YOUR FUTURE?

(PLEASE TICK BOX)

| | Yes | |
|---|---|---|
| | No | |

If you decide that you wish to write to the Sheriff you can write what your views are about your future in Box (B) below or on a separate piece of paper. If you decide to write your views on a separate piece of paper you should send it along with this form to the Sheriff Clerk in the envelope provided.

| | |
|---|---|
| BOX B: | WHAT I HAVE TO SAY ABOUT MY FUTURE:— |
| | |

NAME: ......................................

ADDRESS: ......................................

DATE: ......................................

Rule 33.7(1)(a)

**FORM F10**

Form of intimation to creditor in application for order for the transfer of property under section 8 of the Family Law (Scotland) Act 1985

To (*insert name and address as in warrant*)

Court ref. no.

You are given NOTICE that in this action an order is sought for the transfer of property (*specify the order*), over which you hold a security. A copy of the initial writ is attached. If you wish to appear as a party, you must lodge a minute with the sheriff clerk (*insert address of sheriff clerk*) for leave to do so. Your minute must be lodged within 21 days of (*insert date on which intimation was given. N.B.* Rule 5.3(2) *relating to postal service or intimation*).

Date (*insert date*)

(*Signed*)

Solicitor for the pursuer

**NOTE**

324

If you decide to lodge a minute it may be in your best interests to consult a solicitor. The minute should be lodged with the sheriff clerk together with the appropriate fee of (*insert amount*) and a copy of this intimation.

**IF YOU ARE UNCERTAIN WHAT ACTION TO TAKE** you should consult a solicitor. You may be entitled to legal aid depending on your financial circumstances, and you can get information about legal aid from a solicitor. You may also obtain advice from any Citizens Advice Bureau or other advice agency.

Rule 33.7(1)(j)

## FORM F11

Form of intimation in an action where the pursuer makes an application for an order under section 18 of the Family Law (Scotland) Act 1985

To (*insert name and address as in warrant*)

Court ref. no.

You are given NOTICE that in this action, the pursuer craves the court to make an order under section 18 of the Family Law (Scotland) Act 1985. A copy of the initial writ is attached. If you wish to appear as a party, you must lodge a minute with the sheriff clerk (*insert address of sheriff clerk*) for leave to do so. Your minute must be lodged within 21 days of (*insert date on which intimation was given. N.B. Rule 5.3(2) relating to postal service or intimation*).

Date (*insert date*)
(*Signed*)
Solicitor for the pursuer

**NOTE**

If you decide to lodge a minute it may be in your best interests to consult a solicitor. The minute should be lodged with the sheriff clerk together with the appropriate fee of (*insert amount*) and a copy of this intimation.

**IF YOU ARE UNCERTAIN WHAT ACTION TO TAKE** you should consult a solicitor. You may be entitled to legal aid depending on your financial circumstances, and you can get information about legal aid from a solicitor. You may also obtain advice from any Citizens Advice Bureau or other advice agency.

Rule 33.7(1)(k)

## FORM F12

Form of intimation in an action where a non-entitled pursuer makes an application for an order under the Matrimonial Homes (Family Protection) (Scotland) Act 1981

To (*insert name and address as in warrant*)

Court ref. no.

You are given NOTICE that in this action, the pursuer craves the court to make an order under section (*insert the section under which the order(s) is sought*) of the Matrimonial Homes (Family Protection) (Scotland) Act 1981. A copy of the initial writ is attached. If you wish to appear as a party, you must may lodge a minute with the sheriff clerk (*insert address of sheriff clerk*) for leave to do so. Your minute must be lodged within 21 days of (*insert date on which intimation was given. N.B. Rule 5.3(2) relating to postal service or intimation*).

Date (*insert date*)

(*Signed*)
Solicitor for the pursuer

**NOTE**

If you decide to lodge a minute it may be in your best interests to consult a solicitor. The minute should be lodged with the sheriff clerk together with the appropriate fee of (*insert amount*) and a copy of this intimation.

**IF YOU ARE UNCERTAIN WHAT ACTION TO TAKE** you should consult a solicitor. You may be entitled to legal aid depending on your financial circumstances, and you can get information about legal aid from a solicitor. You may also obtain advice from any Citizens Advice Bureau or other advice agency.

Rule 33.7(1)(1)

[1]**FORM F12A**

Form of intimation to person responsible for pension arrangement in relation to order for payment in respect of pension lump sum under section 12A of the Family Law (Scotland) Act 1985

To (*insert name and address as in warrant*)

Court ref. no.

You are given NOTICE that in this action the pursuer has applied for an order under section 8 of the Family Law (Scotland) Act 1985 for a capital sum in circumstances where the matrimonial property includes rights in a pension scheme under which a lump sum is payable. The relevant pension scheme is (*give brief details, including number, if known*). If you wish to apply to appear as a party, you must lodge a minute with the sheriff clerk (*insert address of sheriff clerk*) for leave to do so. Your minute must be lodged within 21 days of (*insert date on which intimation was given. N.B.* rule 5.3(2) *relating to postal service or intimation.*)

Date (*insert date*)

(*Signed*)

Solicitor for the pursuer

(*add designation and business address*)

**NOTE**

If you decide to lodge a minute it may be in your best interests to consult a solicitor. The minute should be lodged with the sheriff clerk together with the appropriate fee of (*insert amount*) and a copy of this intimation.

**IF YOU ARE UNCERTAIN WHAT ACTION TO TAKE** you should consult a solicitor. You may be entitled to legal aid depending on your financial circumstances, and you can get information about legal aid from a solicitor. You may also obtain advice from any Citizens Advice Bureau or other advice agency.

Rule 33.7(1)(m)

[2]**FORM F12B**

Form of intimation to person responsible for the pension arrangement in relation to pension sharing order under section 8(1)(baa) of the Family Law (Scotland) Act 1985.

Court ref. no.

To (*insert name and address as in warrant*)

You are given NOTICE that in this action the pursuer has applied under section 8 of the Family Law (Scotland) Act 1985 for a pension sharing order in circumstances where the matrimonial property includes rights in a pension scheme. The relevant pension scheme is (give brief details, including number, if known). If you wish to apply to appear as a party, you must lodge a minute with the sheriff clerk (insert address of sheriff clerk) for leave to do so. Your minute must be lodged within 21 days of (*insert date on which intimation was given, N.B.* rule 5.3(2) *relating to postal service or intimation.*)

---

[1] Inserted by S.I. 1996 No. 2445 (effective November 1, 1996) and amended by the Act of Sederunt (Ordinary Cause Rules) Amendment (No.2)(Pension Sharing on Divorce etc.) 2000 (S.S.I. 2000 No. 408) para. 2(3)(a).

[2] Inserted by the Act of Sederunt (Ordinary Cause Rules) Amendment (No.2)(Pension Sharing on Divorce etc.) 2000 (S.S.I. 2000 No. 408) para. 2(3)(b).

Date (*insert date*)

(*Signed*)
Solicitor for the pursuer
(*add designation and business address*)

**NOTE**

If you decide to lodge a minute it may be in your best interests to consult a solicitor. The minute should be lodged with the sheriff clerk together with the appropriate fee of (insert amount) and a copy of this intimation.

**IF YOU ARE UNCERTAIN WHAT ACTION TO TAKE** you should consult a solicitor. You may be entitled to legal aid depending on your financial circumstances, and you can get information about legal aid from a solicitor. You may also obtain advice from any Citizens Advice Bureau or other advice agency.

Rule 33.7(1)(n)

### [1]**FORM F12C**

Form of intimation to Board of the Pension Protection Fund in relation to pension compensation sharing order under section 8(1)(bab) of the Family Law (Scotland) Act 1985

Court ref. no.

To (*insert name and address as in warrant*)

You are given NOTICE that in this action the pursuer has applied under section 8(1)(bab) of the Family Law (Scotland) Act 1985 for a pension compensation sharing order in circumstances where the matrimonial property includes rights to Pension Protection Fund compensation. The relevant pension arrangement is (*give brief details, including number, if known*). If you wish to appear as a party, you must lodge a minute with the sheriff clerk (*insert address of sheriff clerk*), for leave to do so. Your minute must be lodged within 21 days of (*insert date on which intimation was given. N.B.* Rule 5.3(2) *relating to postal service or intimation*).

Date (*insert date*)

(*Signed*)
Solicitor for the pursuer
(*insert designation and business address*)

Rule 33.7(1)(o)

### [2]**FORM F12D**

Form of intimation to Board of the Pension Protection Fund in relation to an order under section 12B(2) of the Family Law (Scotland) Act 1985

Court ref. no.

To (*insert name and address as in warrant*)

You are given NOTICE that in this action the pursuer has applied under section 8(1)(bb) of the Family Law (Scotland) Act 1985 for an order under section 12B(2) of the Act in circumstances where the matrimonial property includes rights to Pension Protection Fund compensation. The relevant pension arrangement is (*give brief details, including number, if known*). If you wish to appear as a party, you must lodge a minute with the sheriff clerk (*insert address of sheriff clerk*), for leave to do so. Your minute must be lodged within 21 days of (*insert date on which intimation was given. N.B.* Rule 5.3(2) *relating to postal service or intimation*).

Date (*insert date*)

(*Signed*)

---

[1] As inserted by the Act of Sederunt (Sheriff Court Rules) (Miscellaneous Amendments) 2011 (SSI 2011/193) r.15 (effective April 6, 2011).

[2] As inserted by the Act of Sederunt (Sheriff Court Rules) (Miscellaneous Amendments) 2011 (SSI 2011/193) r.15 (effective April 6, 2011).

Solicitor for the pursuer
(*insert designation and business address*)

Rule 33.7(1)(p)                    [1][2]**FORM F12E**

Form of intimation of application for financial provision on intestacy under section 29(2) of the Family Law (Scotland) Act 2006

To: (insert name and address as in war-   Court ref no.
rant)

You are given NOTICE that the pursuer has applied for an order for financial provision on intestacy under section 29(2) of the Family Law (Scotland) Act 2006. A copy of the initial writ is attached. If you wish to appear as a party, you must lodge a minute with the sheriff clerk (*insert address of sheriff clerk*) for leave to do so. Your minute must be lodged within 21 days of (*insert date on which intimation is given. N.B.* rule 5.3(2) *relating to postal service or intimation*).

Date (insert date)                         (signed)

Solicitor for the pursuer

---

**NOTE**

If you decide to lodge a minute it may be in your best interests to consult a solicitor. The minute should be lodged with the sheriff clerk together with the appropriate fee of (*insert amount*) and a copy of this intimation.

---

**IF YOU ARE UNCERTAIN WHAT ACTION TO TAKE** you should consult a solicitor.

You may be entitled to legal aid depending on your financial circumstances, and you can get information about legal aid from a solicitor. You may also obtain advice from any Citizens Advice Bureau or other advice agency.

---

Rule 33.8(3)                         **FORM F13**

Form of intimation to person with whom an improper association is alleged to have occurred

To (*insert name and address as in war-*   Court ref. no.
*rant*)

You are given NOTICE that in this action, the defender is alleged to have had an improper association with you. A copy of the initial writ is attached. If you wish to dispute the truth of the allegation made against you, you must lodge a minute with the sheriff clerk (*insert address of sheriff clerk*) for leave to appear as a party. Your minute must be lodged within 21 days of (*insert date on which intimation was given. N.B.* Rule 5.3(2) *relating to postal service or intimation*).

Date (*insert date*)                       (*Signed*)

Solicitor for the pursuer

---

[1] Inserted by Act of Sederunt (Ordinary Cause Rules) Amendment (Family Law (Scotland) Act 2006 etc.) 2006, para.2 (SSI 2006/207) (effective May 4, 2006).

[2] As amended and renumbered by the Act of Sederunt (Sheriff Court Rules) (Miscellaneous Amendments) 2012 (SSI 2012/188) para.8 (effective August 1, 2012).

> **NOTE**
> If you decide to lodge a minute it may be in your best interests to consult a solicitor. The minute should be lodged with the sheriff clerk together with the appropriate fee of (*insert amount*) and a copy of this intimation.

> **IF YOU ARE UNCERTAIN WHAT ACTION TO TAKE** you should consult a solicitor.
> You may be entitled to legal aid depending on your financial circumstances, and you can get information about legal aid from a solicitor. You may also obtain advice from any Citizens Advice Bureau or other advice agency.

Rules 33.9(c) and 33.34(4)

¹**FORM F13A**

Form of statement of matrimonial property in the cause
SHERIFFDOM OF (*insert name of sheriffdom*)
AT (*insert place of sheriff court*)
[A.B.], (*insert designation and address*, Pursuer against
[C.D..], (*insert designation and address*, Defender
Court ref. no:

| |
|---|
| **The [Pursuer] [Defender]rsquo;s\* financial position at ( *insert date* ), being the relevant date as defined in** section 10(3) of the Family Law (Scotland) Act 1985 |
| Here list all assets owned by you, including assets which are jointly owned (if any) e.g. bank or building society accounts; shares or other investments; houses; land; pension entitlement; and life policies: |
| Here list your outstanding debts including joint debts with the other party: |
| Date (*insert date*) |
| I certify that this information is correct to the best of my knowledge and belief. |
| (*Signed*) |
| [Pursuer][Defender]\* |

(\*delete as applicable)

Rule 33.10                **FORM F14**

Form of warrant of citation in family action

(*Insert place and date*)

Grants warrant to cite the defender (*insert name and address of defender*) by serving upon him [*or* her] a copy of the writ and warrant upon a period of notice of (*insert period of notice*) days, and ordains the defender to lodge a notice of intention to defend with the sheriff clerk at (*insert address of sheriff court*) if he [*or* she] wishes to:

  (a)   challenge the jurisdiction of the court;
  (b)   oppose any claim made or order sought;
  (c)   make any claim or seek any order.

[Meantime grants interim interdict, *or* warrant to arrest on the dependence].

---

¹ As inserted by the Act of Sederunt (Sheriff Court Rules) (Miscellaneous Amendments) 2012 (SSI 2012/188) para.4 (effective August 1, 2012).

Rules 33.11(1) and 33.13(1)(a)     **FORM F15**

Form of citation in family action
  CITATION
  SHERIFFDOM OF (*insert name of sheriffdom*)
  AT (*insert place of sheriff court*)
  [A.B.], (*insert designation and address*), Pursuer, against [C.D.], (*insert designation and address*), Defender.

(*Insert place and date*)     Court ref. no.

You [C.D.], are hereby served with this copy writ and warrant, with Form F26 (notice of intention to defend) [and (*insert details of any other form of notice served, e.g. any of the forms served in accordance with* rule 33.14.)].

---

**Form F26** is served on you for use should you wish to intimate an intention to defend the action.

**IF YOU WISH TO—**
  (a)   challenge the jurisdiction of the court;
  (b)   oppose any claim made or order sought;
  (c)   make any claim or seek any order; or
  (d)   seek any order;

you should consult a solicitor with a view to lodging a notice of intention to defend (Form F26). The notice of intention to defend, together with the court fee of £ (*insert amount*) must be lodged with the sheriff clerk at the above address within 21 days (*or insert appropriate period of notice*) of (*insert the date on which service was executed. N.B.* Rule 5.3(2) *relating to postal service or intimation*).

---

**IF YOU ARE UNCERTAIN WHAT ACTION TO TAKE** you should consult a solicitor. You may be entitled to legal aid depending on your financial circumstances, and you can get information about legal aid from a solicitor. You may also obtain advice from any Citizens Advice Bureau or other advice agency. **PLEASE NOTE THAT IF YOU DO NOTHING IN ANSWER TO THIS DOCUMENT** the court may regard you as admitting the claim made against you and the pursuer may obtain decree against you in your absence.

---

Signed
[P.Q.], Sheriff officer
*or*
[X.Y.], (*add designation and business address*)
Solicitor for the pursuer

Rule 33.11(2)     **FORM F16**

Form of certificate of citation in family action
CERTIFICATE OF CITATION

(*Insert place and date*) I, .......... hereby certify that upon the .......... day of .......... I duly cited [C.D.], Defender, to answer to the foregoing writ. This I did by (*state method of service; if by officer and not by post, add*: in presence of [L.M.], (*insert designation*), witness hereto with me subscribing; *and* (*insert details of any forms of intimation or notice sent including details of the person to whom intimation sent and the method of service*).

Signed

[P.Q.], Sheriff officer

[L.M.], witness

*or*

[X.Y.] (*add designation and business address*)

Solicitor for the pursuer

## FORM F17

Rule 33.13(1)(c)

Form of request to medical officer of hospital or similar institution

To (*insert name and address of medical officer*)

In terms of rule 33.13(1)(c) of the Ordinary Cause Rules of the Sheriff Court a copy of the initial writ at the instance of (*insert name and address of pursuer*), Pursuer, against (*insert name and address of defender*), Defender, is enclosed and you are requested to

    (a)   deliver it personally to (*insert name of defender*), and

    (b)   explain the contents to him or her,

unless you are satisfied that such delivery or explanation would be dangerous to his or her health or mental condition. You are further requested to complete and return to me in the enclosed stamped addressed envelope the certificate appended hereto, making necessary deletions.

Date (*insert date*)

(*Signed*)

Solicitor for the pursuer (*add designation and business address*)

## FORM F18

Rules 33.13(1)(d) and 33.13(2)

Form of certificate by medical officer of hospital or similar institution

Court ref. no.

I (*insert name and designation*) certify that I have received a copy initial writ in an action of (*type of family action to be inserted by the party requesting service*) at the instance of (*insert name and designation*), Pursuer, against (*insert name and designation*), Defender, and that

    * I have on the.......... day of.......... personally delivered a copy thereof to the said defender who is under my care at (*insert address*) and I have explained the contents or purport thereof to him or her, *or*

    * I have not delivered a copy thereof to the said defender who is under my care at (*insert address*) and I have not explained the contents or purport thereof to him or her because (*state reasons*).

Date (*insert date*)

(*Signed*)

Medical officer (*add designation and address*)

* Delete as appropriate.

## ¹FORM F19

Rule 33.14(1)(a)(i)

Form of notice to defender where it is stated that defender consents to the granting of decree of divorce

YOU ARE GIVEN NOTICE that the copy initial writ served on you with this notice states that you consent to the grant of decree of divorce.

1. If you do so consent the consequences for you are that:—

²(a)   provided the pursuer establishes the fact that he [or she] has not cohabited

---

¹ Substituted by SI 1996/2167 (effective November 1, 1996).

² As amended by Act of Sederunt (Ordinary Cause Rules) Amendment (Family Law (Scotland) Act 2006 etc.) 2006, para.2 (SSI 2006/207) (effective May 4, 2006).

with you at any time during a continuous period of one year after the date of your marriage and immediately preceding the bringing of this action and that you consent, a decree of divorce will be granted;

(b)   on the grant of a decree of divorce you may lose your rights of succession to the pursuer's estate; and

(c)   decree of divorce will end the marriage thereby affecting any right to such pension as may depend on the marriage continuing, or, on your being left a widow the state widow's pension will not be payable to you when the pursuer dies.

Apart from these, there may be other consequences for you depending upon your particular circumstances.

2. You are entitled, whether or not you consent to the grant of decree of divorce in this action, to apply to the sheriff in this action—

(a)   to make financial or other provision for you under the Family Law (Scotland) Act 1985;

(b)   for an order under section 11 of the Children (Scotland) Act 1995 in respect of any child of the marriage, or any child accepted as such, who is under 16 years of age; or

(c)   for any other competent order.

3. IF YOU WISH TO APPLY FOR ANY OF THE ABOVE ORDERS you should consult a solicitor with a view to lodging a notice of intention to defend (Form F26).

4. If, after consideration, you wish to consent to the grant of decree of divorce in this action, you should complete and sign the attached notice of consent (Form F20) and send it to the sheriff clerk at the sheriff court referred to in the initial writ within 21 days of (*insert the date on which service was executed. N.B.* Rule 5.3(2) *relating to postal service*).

5. If at a later stage, you wish to withdraw your consent to decree being granted against you in this action, you must inform the sheriff clerk immediately in writing.

Date (*insert date*)

*(Signed)*

Solicitor for the pursuer (*add designation and business address*)

**FORM F20**

Rules 33.14(1)(a)(i) and 33.18(1)

Form of notice of consent in actions of divorce under section 1(2)(d) of the Divorce (Scotland) Act 1976

Court ref. no.

[A.B.], (*insert designation and address*), Pursuer, against [C.D.], (*insert designation and address*), Defender.

I (*full name and address of the defender to be inserted by pursuer or pursuer's solicitor before sending notice*) have received a copy of the initial writ in the action against me at the instance of (*full name and address of pursuer to be inserted by pursuer or pursuer's solicitor before sending notice*). I understand that it states that I consent to the grant of decree of divorce in this action. I have considered the consequences for me mentioned in the notice (Form F19) sent to me with this notice. I consent to the grant of decree of divorce in this action.

Date (*insert date*)

*(Signed)*
Defender

¹ ²**FORM F21**

---

¹ Substituted by SI 1996/2167 (effective November 1, 1996).

Rule 33.14(1)(a)(ii)

Form of notice to defender where it is stated that defender consents to the granting of decree of separation

YOU ARE GIVEN NOTICE that the copy initial writ served on you with this notice states that you consent to the grant of decree of separation.

1. If you do so consent the consequences for you are that—

[1](a) provided the pursuer establishes the fact that he [or she] has not cohabited with you at any time during a continuous period of one year after the date of your marriage and immediately preceding the bringing of this action and that you consent, a decree of separation will be granted;

(b) on the grant of a decree of separation you will be obliged to live apart from the pursuer but the marriage will continue to subsist; you will continue to have a legal obligation to support your spouse and children;

Apart from these, there may be other consequences for you depending upon your particular circumstances.

2. You are entitled, whether or not you consent to the grant of decree of separation in this action, to apply to the sheriff in this action—

(a) to make financial or other provision for you under the Family Law (Scotland) Act 1985;

(b) for an order under Section 11 of the Children (Scotland) Act 1995 in respect of any child of the marriage, or any child accepted as such, who is under 16 years of age; or

(c) for any other competent order.

3. IF YOU WISH TO APPLY FOR ANY OF THE ABOVE ORDERS you should consult a solicitor with a view to lodging a notice of intention to defend (Form F26).

4. If, after consideration, you wish to consent to the grant of decree of separation in this action, you should complete and sign the attached notice of consent (Form F22) and send it to the sheriff clerk at the sheriff court referred to in the initial writ and other papers within 21 days of (*insert the date on which service was executed. N.B. Rule 5.3(2) relating to postal service or intimation*).

5. If at a later stage you wish to withdraw your consent to decree being granted against you in this action, you must inform the sheriff clerk immediately in writing.

Date (*insert date*)

(*Signed*)

Solicitor for the pursuer (*add designation and business address*)

**FORM F22**

Rules 33.14(1)(a)(ii) and 33.18(1)

Form of notice of consent in actions of separation under section 1 (2)(d) of the Divorce (Scotland) Act 1976

Court ref. no.

---

[2] As amended by Act of Sederunt (Rules of the Court of Session and Sheriff Court Rules Amendment No. 2) (Marriage and Civil Partnership (Scotland) Act 2014) 2014 (SSI 2014/302) r.6 (effective December 16, 2014).

[1] As amended by Act of Sederunt (Ordinary Cause Rules) Amendment (Family Law (Scotland) Act 2006 etc.) 2006, para.2 (SSI 2006/207) (effective May 4, 2006).

[A.B.], (*insert designation and address*), Pursuer against [C.D.], (*insert designation and address*), Defender.

I (*full name and address of the defender to be inserted by pursuer or pursuer's solicitor before sending notice*) confirm that I have received a copy of the initial writ in the action against me at the instance of (*full name and address of pursuer to be Inserted by pursuer or pursuer's solicitor before sending notice*). I understand that it states that I consent to the grant of decree of separation in this action. I have considered the consequences for me mentioned in the notice (Form F21) sent together with this notice. I consent to the grant of decree of separation in this action.

Date (*insert date*)

(*Signed*)

Defender

## ¹FORM F23

Rule 33.14(1)(b)(i)

²Form of notice to defender in an action of divorce where it is stated there has been two years' non-cohabitation

YOU ARE GIVEN NOTICE that—

³1.    The copy initial writ served on you with this notice states that there has been no cohabitation between you and the pursuer at any time during a continuous period of two years after the date of the marriage and immediately preceding the commencement of this action. If the pursuer establishes this as a fact and the sheriff is satisfied that the marriage has broken down irretrievably, a decree will be granted.

2.    Decree of divorce will end the marriage thereby affecting any right to such pension as may depend on the marriage continuing, or, on your being left a widow the state widow's pension will not be payable to you when the pursuer dies. You may also lose your rights of succession to the pursuer's estate.

⁴3.    You are entitled, whether or not you dispute that there has been no such cohabitation during that two year period, to apply to the sheriff in this action—

      (a)   to make financial or other provision for you under the Family Law (Scotland) Act 1985;

      (b)   for an order under section 11 of the Children (Scotland) Act 1995 in respect of any child of the marriage, or any child accepted as such, who is under 16 years of age; or

      (c)   for any other competent order.

4.    IF YOU WISH TO APPLY FOR ANY OF THE ABOVE ORDERS you should consult a solicitor with a view to lodging a notice of intention to defend (Form F26).

Date (*insert date*)

(*Signed*)

Solicitor for the pursuer (*add designation and business address*)

**NOTE**

---

[1] Substituted by SI 1996/2167 (effective November 1, 1996).

[2] As amended by Act of Sederunt (Ordinary Cause Rules) Amendment (Family Law (Scotland) Act 2006 etc.) 2006, para.2 (SSI 2006/207) (effective May 4, 2006).

[3] As amended by Act of Sederunt (Ordinary Cause Rules) Amendment (Family Law (Scotland) Act 2006 etc.) 2006, para.2 (SSI 2006/207) (effective May 4, 2006).

[4] As amended by Act of Sederunt (Ordinary Cause Rules) Amendment (Family Law (Scotland) Act 2006 etc.) 2006, para.2 (SSI 2006/207) (effective May 4, 2006).

[1] [2]**FORM F24**

Rule 33.14(1)(b)(ii)

[3]Form of notice to defender in an action of separation where it is stated there has been two years' non-cohabitation

YOU ARE GIVEN NOTICE that—

[4]1.  The copy initial writ served on you together with this notice states that there has been no cohabitation between you and the pursuer at any time during a continuous period of two years after the date of the marriage and immediately preceding the commencement of this action and that if the pursuer establishes this as a fact, and the sheriff is satisfied that there are grounds justifying decree of separation, a decree will be granted.

2.  On the granting of decree of separation you will be obliged to live apart from the pursuer but the marriage will continue to subsist. You will continue to have a legal obligation to support your spouse and children.

[5]3.  You are entitled, whether or not you dispute that there has been no such cohabitation during that two year period, to apply to the sheriff in this action—

    (a)  to make provision under the Family Law (Scotland) Act 1985;

    (b)  for an order under section 11 of the Children (Scotland) Act 1995 in respect of any child of the marriage, or any child accepted as such, who is under 16 years of age; or

    (c)  for any other competent order.

4.  **IF YOU WISH TO APPLY FOR ANY OF THE ABOVE ORDERS** you should consult a solicitor with a view to lodging a notice of intention to defend (Form F26).

Date (*insert date*)

*(Signed)*

Solicitor for the pursuer (*add designation and business address*)

[6] [7]**FORM F24A**

Rule 33.14(1)(c)

Form of notice to defender in action of divorce where an interim gender recognition certificate has been issued

YOU ARE GIVEN NOTICE that—

1.  The copy initial writ served on you together with this notice states that an interim gender recognition certificate has been issued to you [or the pursuer]. If the pursuer establishes this as a matter of fact, and that the Gender Recognition Panel has not issued a full gender recognition certificate, decree will be granted.

---

[1] Substituted by SI 1996/2167 (effective November 1, 1996).

[2] As amended by Act of Sederunt (Rules of the Court of Session and Sheriff Court Rules Amendment No.2) (Marriage and Civil Partnership (Scotland) Act 2014) 2014 (SSI 2014/302) para.6 (effective December 16, 2014).

[3] As amended by Act of Sederunt (Ordinary Cause Rules) Amendment (Family Law (Scotland) Act 2006 etc.) 2006, para.2 (SSI 2006/207) (effective May 4, 2006).

[4] As amended by Act of Sederunt (Ordinary Cause Rules) Amendment (Family Law (Scotland) Act 2006 etc.) 2006, para.2 (SSI 2006/207) (effective May 4, 2006).

[5] As amended by Act of Sederunt (Ordinary Cause Rules) Amendment (Family Law (Scotland) Act 2006 etc.) 2006, para.2 (SSI 2006/207) (effective May 4, 2006).

[6] Inserted by Act of Sederunt (Ordinary Cause Rules) Amendment (Family Law (Scotland) Act 2006 etc.) 2006, para.2 (SSI 2006/207) (effective May 4, 2006).

[7] As amended by Act of Sederunt (Rules of the Court of Session and Sheriff Court Rules Amendment No. 2) (Marriage and Civil Partnership (Scotland) Act 2014) 2014 (SSI 2014/302) r.6 (effective December 16, 2014).

2. Decree of divorce will end the marriage thereby affecting any right to such pension as may depend on the marriage continuing, or, on your being left a widow the state widow's pension will not be payable to you when the pursuer dies. You may also lose your rights of succession to the pursuer's estate.

3. If the pursuer is entitled to a decree of divorce, you are nevertheless entitled to apply to the sheriff in this action—

    (a) to make financial or other provision for you under the Family Law (Scotland) Act 1985;

    (b) for an order under section 11 of the Children (Scotland) Act 1995 in respect of any child of the marriage, or any child accepted as such, who is under 16 years of age; or

    (c) for any competent order.

4. IF YOU WISH TO APPLY FOR ANY OF THE ABOVE ORDERS you should consult a solicitor with a view to lodging a notice of intention to defend (Form F26).

Date (*insert date*)

*(Signed)*

Solicitor for the pursuer (*add designation and business address*)

### FORM F25

[Removed by SI 1996/2167 (effective November 1, 1996).]

### ¹FORM F26

Rules 33.11(1) and 33.34(2)(a)

Form of notice of intention to defend in family action

### NOTICE OF INTENTION TO DEFEND

### PART A

| PART A (This section to be completed by the pursuer's solicitor before service.) [Insert name and business address of solicitor for the pursuer] | Court ref. No. In an action brought in Sheriff Court | Date of expiry of period of notice |
|---|---|---|
| | Pursuer | |
| | Defender Date of service: | |

### PART B

**(This section to be completed by the defender or defender's solicitor, and both parts of the form to be returned to the Sheriff Clerk at the above Sheriff Court on or before the date of expiry of the period of notice referred to in Part A above.)**

(*Insert place and date*)

[C.D.] (Insert designation and address), Defender, intends to

(a) challenge the jurisdiction of the court;

(b) oppose a crave in the initial writ;

(c) make a claim;

(d) seek an order;

---

¹ Substituted by Act of Sederunt (Ordinary Cause, Summary Application, Summary Cause and Small Claim Rules) Amendment (Miscellaneous) 2005 (SSI 2005/648), para.2 (effective January 2, 2006).

in the action against him [or her] raised by [A.B.], (insert designation and address), Pursuer.

## PART C

**(This section to be completed by the defender or the defender's solicitor where an order under section 11 of the Children (Scotland) Act 1995 in respect of a child is opposed by the defender).**

DO YOU WISH TO OPPOSE THE MAKING OF ANY ORDER CRAVED BY THE PURSUER IN RESPECT OF A CHILD?

YES/NO*

*delete as appropriate

If you answered YES to the above question, please state here the order(s) which you wish to oppose and the reasons why the court should not make such order(s).

## PART D

**(This section to be completed by the defender or the defender's solicitor where an order under section 11 of the Children (Scotland) Act 1995 in respect of a child is sought by the defender).**

DO YOU WISH THE COURT TO MAKE ANY ORDER UNDER SECTION 11 OF THE CHILDREN (SCOTLAND) ACT 1995 IN RESPECT OF A CHILD?

YES/NO*

*delete as appropriate

If you answered YES to the above question, please state here the order(s) which you wish the court to make and the reasons why the court should make such order(s).

## PART E

IF YOU HAVE COMPLETED PART D OF THIS FORM YOU MUST IN-CLUDE EITHER CRAVE (1) OR (2) BELOW (*delete as appropriate)

(1)   * Warrant for intimation of notice in terms of Form F9 on the child(ren) (insert full name(s) and date (s) of birth) is sought.

(2)   * I seek to dispense with intimation on the child(ren) (insert full name(s) and date(s) of birth) for the following reasons:—

Signed

[C.D.] Defender [or [X.Y.] (add designation and business address) Solicitor for Defender]

## FORM F27

**Rule 33.29(1)(b)**

Form of minute for decree in family action to which rule 33.28 applies

(*Insert name of solicitor for the pursuer*) having considered the evidence contained in the affidavits and the other documents all as specified in the schedule hereto, and being satisfied that upon the evidence a motion for decree (in terms of the crave of the initial writ) [*or in such restricted terms as may be appropriate*] may properly be made, moves the court accordingly.

In respect whereof

Signed

Solicitor for the Pursuer (*add designation and business address*)

Schedule

(*Number and specify documents considered*)

## FORM F28

**Rules 33.40(c) and 33.64(1)(c)**

Form of notice of intimation to local authority or third party to whom care of a child is to be given

To (*name and address as in warrant*)

Court ref. no.

You are given NOTICE that in this action, the sheriff proposes to commit to your care the child (*insert name and address*). A copy of the initial writ is attached. If you wish to appear as a party, you must lodge a minute with the sheriff clerk (*insert address of sheriff clerk*) for leave to do so. Your minute must be lodged within 21 days of (*insert date on which intimation was given. N.B.* Rule 53(2) *relating to postal service or intimation*).

Date (*insert date*)

(*Signed*)

Solicitor for the pursuer

**NOTE**

If you decide to lodge a minute it may be in your best interest to consult a solicitor. The minute should be lodged with the sheriff clerk together with the appropriate fee of (*insert amount*) and a copy of this intimation.

**IF YOU ARE UNCERTAIN WHAT ACTION TO TAKE** you should consult a solicitor. You may be entitled to legal aid depending on your financial circumstances, and you can get information about legal aid from a solicitor. You may also obtain advice from any Citizens Advice Bureau or other advice agency.

## FORM F29

**Rules 33.41 and 33.64(2)**

Form of notice of intimation to local authority of supervision order

[A.B.], (*insert designation and address*), Pursuer, against [C.D.], (*Insert designation and address*), Defender.

To (*insert name and address of local authority*)

Court ref. no.

You are given NOTICE that on (*insert date*) in the Sheriff Court at (*insert place*) the sheriff made a supervision order under section 12 of the Matrimonial Proceedings (Children) Act 1958 [*or* section 1 l(1)(b) of the Guardianship Act 1973] placing the child (*insert name and address of child*) under your supervision. A certified copy of the sheriffs interlocutor is attached.

Date (*Insert date*)

(*Signed*)

Sheriff clerk (depute)

## FORM F30

**Rules 33.72(1) and 33.72(2)**

[*Omitted by Act of Sederunt (Ordinary Cause Rules) Amendment (Family Law (Scotland) Act 2006 etc.) 2006, para.2 (SSI 2006/207) (effective May 4, 2006).*]

[1] [2] [3] [4]**FORM F31**

**Rule 33.74(1)**

Form of simplified divorce application under section 1(2)(d) of the Divorce (Scotland) Act 1976

Sheriff Clerk

---

[1] As amended by SI 1996/2445 (effective November 1, 1996) and the Act of Sederunt (Ordinary Cause Rules) Amendment (Form of Simplified Divorce Application) 2003 (SSI 2003/ 25), para.2(2)(a) (effective January 31, 2003).

[2] As amended by Act of Sederunt (Ordinary Cause Rules) Amendment (Family Law (Scotland) Act 2006 etc.) 2006, para.2 (SSI 2006/207) (effective May 4, 2006).

[3] As amended by the Act of Sederunt (Ordinary Cause, Summary Application, Summary Cause and Small Claim Rules) Amendment (Miscellaneous) 2007 (SSI 2007/6), para.2(16)(f) (effective February 26, 2007).

[4] As amended by Act of Sederunt (Rules of the Court of Session and Sheriff Court Rules Amendment No.2) (Marriage and Civil Partnership (Scotland) Act 2014) 2014 (SSI 2014/302) r.6 (effective December 16, 2014).

Sheriff Court House

....................

....................

(Telephone) ...............

## APPLICATION FOR DIVORCE WITH CONSENT OF OTHER PARTY TO THE MARRIAGE (SPOUSES HAVING LIVED APART FOR AT LEAST ONE YEAR)

Before completing this form, you should have read the leaflet entitled "Do it yourself Divorce", which explains the circumstances in which a divorce may be sought by this method. If simplified procedure appears to suit your circumstances, you may use this form to apply for divorce. Below you will find directions designed to assist you with your application. Please follow them carefully. In the event of difficulty, you may contact any sheriff clerk's office or Citizens Advice Bureau.

### Directions for making application

WRITE IN INK, USING BLOCK CAPITALS

| | |
|---|---|
| Application (Part 1) | 1. Complete and sign Part 1 of the form (pages 3–7), paying particular attention to the notes opposite each section. |
| Consent of spouses (Part 2) | 2. When you have completed Part 1 of the form, attach the (blue) instruction sheet SP3 to it and send both documents to your spouse for completion of (Part 2) the consent at (page 9). |

**NOTE:** If your spouse does NOT complete and sign the form of consent, your application cannot proceed further under the simplified procedure. In that event, if you still wish to obtain a divorce, you should consult a solicitor.

| | |
|---|---|
| Affidavit (Part 3) | 3. When the application has been returned to you with the consent (Part 2) duly completed and signed, you should take the form to a Justice of the Peace, Notary Public, Commissioner for Oaths or other duly authorised person so that your affidavit at Part 3 (page 10) may be completed and sworn. |
| Returning completed application form to court | 4. When directions 1–3 above have been complied with, your application is now ready to be sent to the sheriff clerk at the above address. With it you must enclose: |

    (i)   your marriage certificate (the document headed "Extract of an entry in a Register of Marriages", which will be returned to you in due course), and

    (ii)  either a cheque or postal order in respect of the court fee, crossed and made payable to "the Scottish Court Service" or a completed fee exemption form,

or a completed form SP15, claiming exemption from the court fee.

5. Receipt of your application will be promptly acknowledged. Should you wish to withdraw the application for any reason, please contact the sheriff clerk immediately.

## PART 1

### WRITE IN INK, USING BLOCK CAPITALS

1. NAME AND ADDRESS OF APPLICANT

Surname ...............

Other name(s) in full ...............

....................

Present address ...............
...................
Daytime telephone number (if any)
...................
2. NAME AND ADDRESS OF SPOUSE
Surname ...............
Other name(s) in full ...............
...................
Present address ...............
...................
Daytime telephone number (if any) ...............
3. JURISDICTION
Please indicate with a tick (✔) in the appropriate box or boxes which of the following apply:
PART A

| | | |
|---|---|---|
| (i) | My spouse and I are habitually resident in Scotland | ☐ |
| (ii) | My spouse and I were last habitually resident in Scotland, and one of us still resides there | ☐ |
| (iii) | My spouse is habitually resident in Scotland | ☐ |
| (iv) | I am habitually resident in Scotland having resided there for at least a year immediately before this application was made | ☐ |
| (v) | I am habitually resident in Scotland having resided there for at least six months immediately before this application was made and am domiciled in Scotland | ☐ |
| (vi) | My spouse and I are domiciled in Scotland | ☐ |

**If you have ticked one or more of the boxes in Part A, you should go direct to Part C. You should only complete Part B if you have not ticked any boxes in Part A**
PART B

| | | |
|---|---|---|
| (i) | I am domiciled in Scotland | ☐ |
| (ii) | My spouse is domiciled in Scotland | ☐ |

AND

| | | |
|---|---|---|
| (iii) | No court of a Contracting State has jurisdiction under the Council Regulation (E.C.) No. 2201/2003 of 27th November 2003 concerning jurisdiction and the recognition and enforcement of judgments in matrimonial matters and in matters of Parental Responsibility (O.J. No L.338, 23.12.2003, p.1) | ☐ |

PART C

| | | |
|---|---|---|
| (i) | I have lived at the address shown above for at least 40 days immediately before the date I signed this application | ☐ |
| (ii) | My spouse has lived at the address shown above for at least 40 days immediately before the date I signed this application | ☐ |

(iii)     I lived at the address shown above for a period of at least 40 days ending not more than 40 days before the date I signed this application and have no known residence in Scotland at that date ☐

(iv)     My spouse lived at the address shown above for a period of at least 40 days ending not more than 40 days before the date I signed this application and has no known residence in Scotland at that date ☐

## 4. DETAILS OF PRESENT MARRIAGE

Place of Marriage............... (Registration District)

Date of Marriage: Day .......... month .......... year ..........

### 5. Period of Separation

(i)     Please the date on which you ceased to live with your spouse. (If more than 1 year, just give the month and year)

     Day .......... Month .......... Year ..........

(ii)    Have you lived with your spouse since that date?    *[YES/NO]

(iii)   If yes, for how long in total did you live together before finally separating again?

               .............. months

## 6. RECONCILIATION

Is there any reasonable prospect of reconciliation with your spouse?    *[YES/NO]

Do you consider that the marriage has broken down ir-retrievably?    *[YES/NO]

## 7. CONSENT

Does your spouse consent to a divorce being granted?    *[YES/NO]

## 8. MENTAL DISORDER

Does your spouse have any mental disorder (whether mental illness, personality disorder or learning disability)?..........(if yes, give details)    *[YES/NO]

## 9. CHILDREN

Are there any children of the marriage under the age of 16?    *[YES/NO]

## 10. OTHER COURT ACTIONS

Are you aware of any court actions currently proceeding in any    *[YES/NO]

country (including Scotland) which may affect your marriage?..........(If yes, give details)    *Delete as appropriate

## 11. DECLARATION AND REQUEST FOR DIVORCE

I confirm that the facts stated in paragraphs 1–10 above apply to my marriage.

I do NOT ask the sheriff to make any financial provision in connection with this application.

I do NOT ask the court to postpone the grant of decree under section 3A of the Divorce (Scotland) Act 1976.

I request the sheriff to grant decree of divorce from my spouse.

Date .......... Signature of applicant's spouse ...............

**IMPORTANT**

Part 1 MUST be completed, signed and dated before sending the application form to your spouse.

## PART 2
### NOTICE TO CONSENTING SPOUSE
*(Insert name and address of consenting spouse)*

CONSENT TO APPLICATION FOR DIVORCE (SPOUSES HAVING LIVED APART FOR AT LEAST ONE YEAR)

In Part 1 of the enclosed application form your spouse is applying for divorce on the ground that the marriage has broken down irretrievably because you and he [*or* she] have lived apart for at least one year and you consent to the divorce being granted.

Such consent must be given formally in writing at Part 2 of the application form. BEFORE completing that part, you are requested to read it over carefully so that you understand the effect of consenting to divorce. Thereafter if you wish to consent—

(a) check the details given by the Applicant at Part 1 of the form to ensure that they are correct to the best of your knowledge;

(b) complete Part 2 (Consent by Applicant's spouse to divorce) by entering your name and address at the appropriate place and adding your signature and the date; and

(c) return the whole application form to your spouse at the address given in Part 1.

Once your husband or wife has completed the remainder of the form and has submitted it to the court, a copy of the whole application (including your consent) will later be served upon you formally by the sheriff clerk.

In the event of the divorce being granted, you will automatically be sent a copy of the extract decree. (Should you change your address before receiving the copy extract decree, please notify the sheriff clerk immediately.)

If you do NOT wish to consent please return the application form, with Part 2 uncompleted, to your spouse and advise him or her of your decision.

The sheriff will NOT grant a divorce on this application if Part 2 of the form is not completed by you.

Sheriff clerk (depute)
Sheriff Court (*insert address*)

CONSENT BY APPLICANT'S SPOUSE TO DIVORCE

NOTE: Before completing this part of the form, please read the notes opposite (page 8)

I, ...................

*(Insert full name, in BLOCK letters, of Applicant's spouse)*
residing at

...................

*(Insert address, also in BLOCK letters)*

...................

...................

HEREBY STATE THAT

(a) I have read Part 1 of this application;

(b) the Applicant has lived apart from me for a continuous period of one year immediately preceding the date of the application (paragraph 11 of Part 1);

(c)   I do not ask the sheriff to make any financial provision for me including—
    (i)   the payment by the Applicant of a periodical allowance (i.e. a regular payment of money weekly or monthly, etc. for maintenance);
    (ii)  the payment by the Applicant of a capital sum (i.e. a lump sum payment);

(d)   I understand that divorce may result in the loss to me of property rights;

(e)   I do not ask the court to postpone the grant of decree under section 3A of the Divorce (Scotland) Act 1976; and

(f)   I CONSENT TO DECREE OF DIVORCE BEING GRANTED IN RESPECT OF THIS APPLICATION.

Date .......... Signature ...............

NOTE: You may withdraw your consent, even after giving it, at any time before divorce is granted by the sheriff. Should you wish to do so, please contact the sheriff clerk immediately.

## PART 3

APPLICANT'S AFFIDAVIT

To be completed by the Applicant only after Parts 1 and 2 have been signed and dated.

**I**, (*insert Applicant's full name*) ...............
residing at (*insert Applicant's present home address*) ..........
....................
....................

SWEAR that to the best of my knowledge and belief:
(1)   the facts stated in Part 1 of this Application are true; and
(2)   the signature in Part 2 of this Application is that of my spouse.
Signature of Applicant...............

To be completed by Justice of the Peace, Notary Public or Commissioner for Oaths

SWORN at (insert place) ...............
this .......... day of ..........19.......... before me (*insert full name*) ............... (*insert full address*)...............
....................

....................

Signature ...............
*Justice of the Peace/Notary Public/Commissioner for Oaths
*Delete as appropriate

### [1]FORM F32
### [2 3 4 5]FORM F33

Rule 33.74(2)

---

[1] Repealed by SI 1996/2445 (effective November 1, 1996).

[2] As amended by SI 1996/2445 (effective November 1, 1996) and the Act of Sederunt (Ordinary Cause Rules) Amendment (Form of Simplified Divorce Application) 2003 (SSI 2003/ 25), para.2(2)(b) (effective January 31, 2003).

[3] As amended by Act of Sederunt (Ordinary Cause Rules) Amendment (Family Law (Scotland) Act 2006 etc.) 2006, para.2 (SSI 2006/207) (effective May 4, 2006).

Form of simplified divorce application under section 1(2)(e) of the Divorce (Scotland) Act 1976

Sheriff Clerk

Sheriff Court House

....................

....................

(Telephone)..............

APPLICATION FOR DIVORCE (SPOUSES HAVING LIVED APART FOR AT LEAST TWO YEARS)

Before completing this form, you should have read the leaflet entitled "Do it yourself Divorce", which explains the circumstances in which a divorce may be sought by this method. If the simplified procedure appears to suit your circumstances, you may use this form to apply for divorce.

Below you will find directions to assist you with your application. Please follow them carefully. In the event of difficulty, you may contact any sheriff clerk's office or Citizens Advice Bureau.

### Directions for making application

WRITE IN INK, USING BLOCK CAPITALS

Application (Part 1)

1. Complete and sign Part 1 of the form (pages 3-7), paying particular attention to the notes opposite each section.

Affidavits (Part 2)

2. When you have completed Part 1, you should take the form to a Justice of the Peace, Notary Public, Commissioner for Oaths or other duly authorised person in order that your affidavit in Part 2 (page 8) may be completed and sworn.

Returning completed application form to court

3. When directions 1 and 2 above have been complied with, your is now ready to be sent to the sheriff clerk at the above address. With it you application must enclose:

(i)  your marriage certificate (the document headed "Extract of an entry in a Register of Marriages", which will be returned to you in due course). Check the notes on page 2 to see if you need to obtain a letter from the General Register Office stating that there is no record of your spouse having divorced you, and

(ii)  either a cheque or postal order in respect of the court fee, crossed and made out to "the Scottish Court Service" or a completed fee exemption form.

4. Receipt of your application will be promptly acknowledged. Should you wish to withdraw the application for any reason, please contact the sheriff clerk immediately.

## PART 1

### WRITE IN INK, USING BLOCK CAPITALS

---

[4] As amended by the Act of Sederunt (Ordinary Cause, Summary Application, Summary Cause and Small Claim Rules) Amendment (Miscellaneous) 2007 (SSI 2007/6), para.2(16)(g) (effective February 26, 2007).

[5] As amended by Act of Sederunt (Rules of the Court of Session and Sheriff Court Rules Amendment No. 2) (Marriage and Civil Partnership (Scotland) Act 2014) 2014 (SSI 2014/302) para.6 (effective December 16, 2014).

1. NAME AND ADDRESS OF APPLICANT

Surname ...............

Other name(s) in full ...............

Present address ...............

....................

Daytime telephone number (if any) ...............

2. NAME OF SPOUSE

Surname ...............

Other name(s) in full ...............

3. ADDRESS OF SPOUSE (if the address of your spouse is not known, please enter "not known" in this paragraph and proceed to paragraph 4)

Present address ...............

....................

....................

Daytime telephone (if any) ...............

4. Only complete this paragraph if you do not know the present address of your spouse

NEXT-OF-KIN

Name ...............

Address ...............

....................

....................

Relationship to your spouse ...............

CHILDREN OF THE MARRIAGE

Names     and  Addresses
dates of birth

....................          ....................

                  ....................

....................          ....................

                  ....................

....................          ....................

                  ....................

If insufficient space is available to list all the children of the marriage, please continue on a separate sheet and attach to this form.

5. JURISDICTION

Please indicate with a tick ( ✔ ) in the appropriate box or boxes which of the following apply:

PART A

(i)     My spouse and I are habitually resident in Scotland          ☐

(ii)    My spouse and I were last habitually resident in Scotland, ☐
        and one of us still resides there

(iii)    My spouse is habitually resident in Scotland ☐

(iv)    I am habitually resident in Scotland having resided there ☐ for at least a year immediately before this application was made

(v)    I am habitually resident in Scotland having resided there ☐ for at least six months immediately before this application was made and am domiciled in Scotland

(vi)    My spouse and I are domiciled in Scotland ☐

**If you have ticked one or more of the boxes in Part A, you should go direct to Part C. You should only complete Part B if you have not ticked any boxes in Part A**

   PART B

(i)    I am domiciled in Scotland ☐

(ii)    My spouse is domiciled in Scotland ☐

AND

(iii)    No court of a Contracting State has jurisdiction under the ☐ Council Regulation (E.C.) No. 2201/2003 of 27th November 2003 concerning jurisdiction and the recognition and enforcement of judgments in matrimonial matters and in matters of Parental Responsibility (O.J. No L.338, 23.12.2003, p.1)

PART C

(i)    I have lived at the address shown above for at least 40 days ☐ immediately before the date I signed this application

(ii)    My spouse has lived at the address shown above for at least ☐ 40 days immediately before the date I signed this application

(iii)    I lived at the address shown above for a period of at least 40 ☐ days ending not more than 40 days before the date I signed this application and have no known residence in Scotland at that date

(iv)    My spouse lived at the address shown above for a period of ☐ at least 40 days ending not more than 40 days before the date I signed this application and has no known residence in Scotland at that date

6. DETAILS OF PRESENT MARRIAGE
   Place of Marriage ............... (Registration District)
   Date of Marriage: Day .......... month .......... year ..........
7. PERIOD OF SEPARATION

(i)    Please state the date on which you ceased to live with your spouse. (If more than 2 years, just give the month and year) Day .......... Month .......... Year ..........

(ii)    Have you lived with your spouse since that date?   *[YES/NO]

(iii)    If yes, for how long in total did you live together before finally separating again?

.............. months

## 8. RECONCILIATION

Is there any reasonable prospect of reconciliation with your  *[YES/NO]
spouse?

Do you consider that the marriage has broken down irretriev-  *[YES/NO]
ably?

## 9. MENTAL DISORDER

Does your spouse have any mental disorder (whether mental ill-  *[YES/NO]
ness, personality disorder or learning disability)?..........(If yes,
give details)

## 10. CHILDREN

Are there any children of the marriage under the age of 16?      *[YES/NO]

## 11. Other Court Actions

Are you aware of any court actions currently proceeding in any  *[YES/NO]
country (including Scotland) which may affect your marriage?
(If yes, give details)

*Delete as ap-
propriate

## 12. DECLARATION AND REQUEST FOR DIVORCE

I confirm that the facts stated in paragraphs 1–12 above apply to my marriage.

I do NOT ask the sheriff to make any financial provision in connection with this
application.

I do NOT ask the court to postpone the grant of decree under section 3A of the
Divorce (Scotland) Act 1976.

I request the sheriff to grant decree of divorce from my spouse.

Date ..............

Signature of Applicant ..............

## PART 2

APPLICANT'S AFFIDAVIT

(To be completed by the Applicant only after Part 1 has been signed and dated.)

I, (*insert full name*) ..............

residing at (*insert present home address*) ..........

...................

SWEAR that to the best of my knowledge and belief the facts stated in Part 1 of
this Application are true.

Signature of Applicant ..............

SWORN at (*insert place*)

To be com-
pleted by Jus-
tice of the
Peace, Notary
Public or Com-
missioner for
Oaths

this .......... day of .......... 19......... before me (*insert full
name*) .............. of (insert full address) ..............

...................

...................

Signature ...............
*Justice of the Peace/Notary Public/Commissioner for Oaths
*Delete as appropriate

¹ ² ³**FORM F33A**

**Rule 33.74(1)(3)**

Form of simplified divorce application under section 1(1)(b) of the Divorce (Scotland) Act 1976

Sheriff Clerk
Sheriff Court House

...................
...................

(Telephone) ...............

APPLICATION FOR DIVORCE (INTERIM GENDER RECOGNITION CERTIFICATE ISSUED TO ONE OF THE PARTIES AFTER THE MARRIAGE

Before completing this form, you should have read the leaflet entitled "Do it yourself Divorce", which explains the circumstances in which a divorce may be sought by this method. If the simplified procedure appears to suit your circumstances, you may use this form to apply for divorce. Below you will find directions designed to assist you with your application. Please follow them carefully. In the event of difficulty, you may contact any sheriff clerk's office or Citizen's Advice Bureau.

**Directions for making application**

WRITE IN INK, USING BLOCK CAPITALS

| | |
|---|---|
| Application (Part 1) | 1. Complete and sign Part 1 of the form (pages 3-7), paying particular attention to the notes opposite each section. |
| Affidavits (Part 2) | 2. When you have completed Part 1, you should take the form to a Justice of the Peace, Notary Public, Commissioner for Oaths or other duly authorised person so that your affidavit at Part 2 (page 8) may be completed and sworn. |
| Returning completed application form to court | 3. When directions 1-2 above have been complied with, your application is now ready to be sent to the sheriff clerk at the above address. With it you must enclose: |

    (i)    your marriage certificate (the document headed "Extract of an entry in a Register of Marriages, which will be returned to you in due course). Check the notes on page 2 to see if you also need to obtain a letter from the General Register Office stating that there is no record that your spouse has divorced you, and,

    (ii)    either a cheque or postal order in respect of the court fee, crossed and made payable to "Scottish Court Service or a completed fee exemption form, and

---

¹ Inserted by Act of Sederunt (Ordinary Cause Rules) Amendment (Family Law (Scotland) Act 2006 etc.) 2006, para.2 (SSI 2006/207) (effective May 4, 2006).

² As amended by the Act of Sederunt (Ordinary Cause, Summary Application, Summary Cause and Small Claim Rules) Amendment (Miscellaneous) 2007 (SSI 2007/6), para.2(16)(h) (effective February 26, 2007).

³ As amended by Act of Sederunt (Rules of the Court of Session and Sheriff Court Rules Amendment No. 2) (Marriage and Civil Partnership (Scotland) Act 2014) 2014 (SSI 2014/302) para.6 (effective December 16, 2014).

    (iii)    the interim gender recognition certificate or a copy sealed with the seal of the Gender Recognition Panels and certified to be a true copy by an officer authorised by the President of Gender Recognition Panels.

4. Receipt of your application will be promptly acknowledged. Should you wish to withdraw the application for any reason, please contact the sheriff clerk immediately.

Part 1

**WRITE IN INK, USING BLOCK CAPITALS**

1. NAME AND ADDRESS OF APPLICANT

Surname...............

Other name(s) in full...............

...............

Present address...............

........................

Daytime telephone number (if any)...............

2. NAME OF SPOUSE

Surname...............

Other name(s) in full...............

3. ADDRESS OF SPOUSE (if the address of your spouse is not known, please enter "not known" in this paragraph and proceed to paragraph 4)

Present address...............

....................

....................

Daytime telephone (if any)...............

4. Only complete this paragraph if you do not know the present address of your spouse

NEXT-OF-KIN

Name...............

Address...............

....................

....................

Relationship to your spouse...............

CHILDREN OF THE MARRIAGE

| **Names and dates of birth** | **Addresses** |
|---|---|
| ............... | ............... |
| | ............... |
| ............... | ............... |
| | ............... |
| ............... | ............... |
| | ............... |

If insufficient space is available to list all the children of the marriage, please continue on a separate sheet and attach to this form.

5. JURISDICTION

Please indicate with a tick (✔) in the appropriate box or boxes which of the following apply:

PART A

(i)   My spouse and I are habitually resident in Scotland ☐

(ii)  My spouse and I were last habitually resident in Scotland, and one ☐
of us still resides there

(iii) My spouse is habitually resident in Scotland ☐

(iv)  I am habitually resident in Scotland having resided there for at least ☐
a year immediately before this application was made

(v)   I am habitually resident in Scotland having resided there for at least ☐
six months immediately before this application was made and am
domiciled in Scotland

(vi)  My spouse and I are domiciled in Scotland ☐

**If you have ticked one or more of the boxes in Part A, you should go direct to
Part C. You should only complete Part B if you have not ticked any boxes in
Part A**

Part B

| | | |
|---|---|---|
| (i) | I am domiciled in Scotland | ☐ |
| (ii) | My spouse is domiciled in Scotland | ☐ |

AND

| | | |
|---|---|---|
| (iii) | No court of a Contracting State has jurisdiction under Council Regulation (E.C.) No. 2201/2003 of 27th November 2003 concerning jurisdiction and the recognition and enforcement of judgments in matrimonial matters and matters of parental responsibility (O.J. No. L. 338, 23.12.2003, p.1.) | ☐ |

Part C

| | | |
|---|---|---|
| (i) | I have lived at the address shown above for at least 40 days immediately before the date I signed this application | ☐ |
| (ii) | My spouse has lived at the address shown above for at least 40 days immediately before the date I signed this application | ☐ |
| (iii) | I lived at the address shown above for a period of at least 40 days | ☐ |

ending not more than
40 days before the date
I signed this application
and have no known
residence in Scotland at
that date

(iv)                    My spouse lived at the ☐
address shown above
for a period of at least
40 days ending not
more than 40 days be-
fore the date I signed
this application and has
no known residence in
Scotland at that date

## 6. DETAILS OF PRESENT MARRIAGE

Place of Marriage.......... (Registration District)

Date of Marriage: Day.......... month.......... year..........

## 7. DETAILS OF ISSUE OF INTERIM GENDER RECOGNITION CERTIFI-CATE

(i) Please state whether the interim gender recognition certificate has been issued to you or your spouse

(ii) Please state the date the interim gender recognition certificate was issued Day.......... Month.......... Year..........

Please answer the following question only if the interim gender recognition certificate was issued to you—

(iii) Has the Gender Recognition Panel issued you with a full  *[YES/NO] gender recognition certificate?

Please answer the following question only if the interim gender recognition certificate was issued to your spouse—

(iv) Since the date referred to in question (ii), have you made a  *[YES/NO] statutory declaration consenting to the marriage continuing?

## 8. MENTAL DISORDER

Does your spouse have any mental disorder (whether mental ill-  *[YES/NO] ness, personality disorder or learning disability)? (If yes, give details)

## 9. CHILDREN

Are there any children of the marriage under the age of 16?      *[YES/NO]

## 10. OTHER COURT ACTIONS

Are you aware of any court actions currently proceeding in any country  *[YES/NO] (including Scotland) which may affect your marriage? (If yes, give details)

                                                * Delete as appropriate

## 11. DECLARATION AND REQUEST FOR DIVORCE

I confirm that the facts stated in paragraphs 1–10 above apply to my marriage.

I do NOT ask the sheriff to make any financial provision in connection with this application.

I do NOT ask the court to postpone the grant of decree under section 3A of the Divorce (Scotland) Act 1976.

I request the sheriff to grant decree of divorce from my spouse.

Date............... Signature of Applicant...............

PART 2

APPLICANT'S AFFIDAVIT

To be completed by the Applicant only after Part 1 has been signed and dated.

I, (*Insert Applicant's full name*)...............

residing at (insert Applicant's present home address)...............

...................

...................

SWEAR that to the best of my knowledge and belief the facts stated in Part 1 of this Application are true.

Signature of Applicant....................

To be completed by Jus-  SWORN at (*insert place*)............... this.......... day
tice of the Peace, Notary  of.......... 20.......... before   me   (*insert   full*
Public or Commissioner  *name*)...............of (*insert full address*)....................
for Oaths

Signature...............

*Justice of the Peace/Notary Public/Commissioner for Oaths

*Delete as appropriate

### [1] [2] [3]FORM F34

**Rule 33.76(3)(a)**

Form of citation in application relying on the facts in section 1(2)(d) of the Divorce (Scotland) Act 1976

(*Insert name and address of non-applicant spouse*)

APPLICATION FOR DIVORCE (SPOUSES HAVING LIVED APART FOR AT LEAST ONE YEAR WITH CONSENT OF OTHER PARTY)

Your spouse has applied to the sheriff for divorce on the ground that the marriage has broken down irretrievably because you and he or she have lived apart for a period of at least one year and you consent to divorce being granted.

A copy of the application is hereby served upon you.

1. Please note:

(a)   that the sheriff may not make financial provision under this procedure and that your spouse is making no claim for—

     (i)   the payment by you of a periodical allowance (i.e. a regular payment of money weekly or monthly, etc. for maintenance);

     (ii)  the payment by you of a capital sum (i.e. a lump sum payment);

---

[1] As amended by Act of Sederunt (Ordinary Cause Rules) Amendment (Family Law (Scotland) Act 2006 etc.) 2006, para.2 (SSI 2006/207) (effective May 4, 2006).

[2] As amended by the Act of Sederunt (Ordinary Cause, Summary Application, Summary Cause and Small Claim Rules) Amendment (Miscellaneous) 2007 (SSI 2007/6), para.2(16)(i) (effective February 26, 2007).

[3] As amended by Act of Sederunt (Rules of the Court of Session and Sheriff Court Rules Amendment No. 2) (Marriage and Civil Partnership (Scotland) Act 2014) 2014 (SSI 2014/302) para.6 (effective December 16, 2014).

(b)   that no application may be made under this procedure for postponement of decree under section 3A of the Divorce (Scotland) Act 1976 (postponement of decree where impediment to religious marriage exists).

2. Divorce may result in the loss to you of property rights (e.g. the right to succeed to the Applicant's estate on his or her death) or the right, where appropriate, to a widow's pension.

3. If you wish to oppose the granting of a divorce, you should put your reasons in writing and send your letter to the address shown below. Your letter must reach the sheriff clerk before (insert date).

4. In the event of the divorce being granted, you will be sent a copy of the extract decree. Should you change your address before receiving the copy extract decree, please notify the sheriff clerk immediately.

Signed

Sheriff clerk (depute)

(*insert address and telephone number of the sheriff clerk*) *or* Sheriff officer

NOTE: If you wish to exercise your right to make a claim for financial provision, or if you wish to apply for postponement of decree under section 3A of the Divorce (Scotland) Act 1976 (postponement of decree where impediment to religious marriage exists), you should immediately advise the sheriff clerk that you oppose the application for that reason, and thereafter consult a solicitor.

[1] [2] [3]FORM F35

**Rule 33.76(3)(b)**

Form of citation in application relying on the facts in section 1 (2)(e) of the Divorce (Scotland) Act 1976

(*Insert name and address of non-applicant spouse*)

APPLICATION FOR DIVORCE (SPOUSES HAVING LIVED APART FOR AT LEAST TWO YEARS)

Your spouse has applied to the sheriff for divorce on the ground that the marriage has broken down irretrievably because you and he or she have lived apart for a period of at least two years.

A copy of the application is hereby served upon you.

1. Please note:

(a)   that the sheriff may not make financial provision under this procedure and that your spouse is making no claim for—

     (i)   the payment by you of a periodical allowance (i.e. a regular payment of money weekly or monthly, etc., for maintenance);

    (ii)   the payment by you of a capital sum (i.e. a lump sum payment);

(b)   that no application may be made under this procedure for postponement of decree under section 3A of the Divorce (Scotland) Act 1976 (postponement of decree where impediment to religious marriage exists).

2. Divorce may result in the loss to you of property rights (e.g. the right to succeed to the Applicant's estate on his or her death) or the right, where appropriate, to a widow's pension.

---

[1] As amended by Act of Sederunt (Ordinary Cause Rules) Amendment (Family Law (Scotland) Act 2006 etc.) 2006, para.2 (SSI 2006/207) (effective May 4, 2006).

[2] As amended by the Act of Sederunt (Ordinary Cause, Summary Application, Summary Cause and Small Claim Rules) Amendment (Miscellaneous) 2007 (SSI 2007/6), para.2(16)G) (effective February 26, 2007).

[3] As amended by Act of Sederunt (Rules of the Court of Session and Sheriff Court Rules Amendment No. 2) (Marriage and Civil Partnership (Scotland) Act 2014) 2014 (SSI 2014/302) para.6 (effective December 16, 2014).

3. If you wish to oppose the granting of a divorce, you should put your reasons in writing and send your letter to the address shown below. Your letter must reach the sheriff clerk before (*insert date*).

4. In the event of the divorce being granted, you will be sent a copy of the extract decree. Should you change your address before receiving the copy extract decree, please notify the sheriff clerk immediately.

Signed..........<br>Sheriff clerk (depute)

(*insert the address and telephone* number of the sheriff court)
*or* Sheriff officer

NOTE: If you wish to exercise your right to make a claim for financial provision, or if you wish to apply for postponement of decree under section 3A of the Divorce (Scotland) Act 1976 (postponement of decree where impediment to religious marriage exists), you should immediately advise the sheriff clerk that you oppose the application for that reason, and thereafter consult a solicitor.

[1] [2]FORM 35A

Rule 33.76(3)(c)

Form of citation in application on grounds under section 1(1)(b) of the Divorce (Scotland) Act 1976

(*Insert name and address of non-applicant spouse*)

APPLICATION FOR DIVORCE (INTERIM GENDER RECOGNITION CERTIFICATE ISSUED TO ONE OF THE PARTIES AFTER THE MARRIAGE)

Your spouse has applied to the sheriff for divorce on the ground that an interim gender recognition certificate has been issued to you or your spouse after your marriage.

A copy of the application is hereby served upon you.

1. Please note that the sheriff may not make financial provision under this procedure and that your spouse is making no claim for—

   (a)   the payment by you of a periodical allowance (i.e. a regular payment of money weekly or monthly, etc. for maintenance);

   (b)   the payment by you of a capital sum (i.e. a lump sum payment).

2. Divorce may result in the loss to you of property rights (e.g. the right to succeed to the Applicant's estate on his or her death) or the right, where appropriate, to a pension.

2A. Please note that no application may be made under this procedure for postponement of decree under section 3A of the Divorce (Scotland) Act 1976 (postponement of decree where impediment to religious marriage exists).

3. If you wish to oppose the granting of a decree of divorce, you should put your reasons in writing and send your letter to the address shown below. Your letter must reach the sheriff clerk before (*insert date*).

4. In the event of the decree of divorce being granted, you will be sent a copy of the extract decree. Should you change your address before receiving the copy extract decree, please notify the sheriff clerk immediately.

(*Signed*)

Sheriff clerk (depute) (*insert address and telephone number of the sheriff clerk*) [*or* Sheriff officer]

---

[1] As inserted by Act of Sederunt (Ordinary Cause Rules) Amendment (Family Law (Scotland) Act 2006 etc.) 2006, para.2 (SSI 2006/207) (effective May 4, 2006).

[2] As amended by the Act of Sederunt (Ordinary Cause, Summary Application, Summary Cause and Small Claim Rules) Amendment (Miscellaneous) 2007 (SSI 2007/6), para.2(16)(k) (effective February 26, 2007).

NOTE: If you wish to exercise your right to make a claim for financial provision, or if you wish to apply for postponement of decree under section 3A of the Divorce (Scotland) Act 1976 (postponement of decree where impediment to religious marriage exists), you should immediately advise the sheriff clerk that you oppose the application for that reason, and thereafter consult a solicitor.

## FORM F36

**Rule 33.77(1)(a)**

Form of intimation of simplified divorce application for display on the walls of court

Court ref. no.

An application for divorce has been made in this sheriff court by [A.B.], (*insert designation and address*), Applicant, naming [C.D.], (*insert designation and address*) as Respondent.

If [C.D.] wishes to oppose the granting of decree of divorce he [*or* she] should immediately contact the sheriff clerk from whom he [*or* she] may obtain a copy of the application.

Date (*insert date*)

Signed
Sheriff clerk (depute)

## FORM F37

**Rule 33.77(2)**

Form of intimation to children and next-of-kin in simplified divorce application

To (*insert name and address*)

Court ref. no.

You are hereby given NOTICE that an application for divorce has been made against (*insert name of respondent*) your (*insert relationship e.g. father, mother, brother or other relative as the case may be*). A copy of this application is attached.

If you know of his or her present address, you are requested to inform the sheriff clerk (*insert address of sheriff clerk*) in writing immediately. You may also, if you wish, oppose the granting of decree of divorce by sending a letter to the court giving your reasons for your opposition to the application. Your letter must be sent to the sheriff clerk within 21 days of (*insert date on which intimation was given. N.B.* Rule 53(2) *relating to postal service or intimation*).

Date (*insert date*)

Signed
Sheriff clerk (depute)

**NOTE**

**IF YOU ARE UNCERTAIN WHAT ACTION TO TAKE** you should consult a solicitor. You may be entitled to legal aid depending on your financial circumstances, and you can get information about legal aid from a solicitor. You may also obtain advice from any Citizens Advice Bureau or other advice agency.

Rule 33.80(2)

## FORM F38

Form of extract decree of divorce in simplified divorce application

At (*insert place and date*)

in an action in the Sheriff Court of the Sheriffdom of (*insert name of sheriffdom*) at (*insert place of sheriff court*)

at the instance of [A.B.], (*insert full name of applicant*), Applicant,

against (*insert full name of respondent*), Respondent,

who were married at (*insert place*) on (*insert date*),

the sheriff pronounced decree divorcing the Respondent from the Applicant.

Extracted at (*insert place and date*)

by me, sheriff clerk of the Sheriffdom of (*insert name of sheriffdom*).

Signed<br>Sheriff clerk (depute)

Rule 33.90

## FORM F39

Form of certificate relating to the making of a maintenance assessment under the Child Support Act 1991

Sheriff Court (*insert address*)

Date (*insert date*)

I certify that notification has been received from the Secretary of State under section 10 of the Child Support Act 1991 of the making of a maintenance assessment under that Act which supersedes the decree or order granted on (*insert date*) in relation to aliment for (*insert the name(s) of child(ren)*) with effect from (*insert date*).

Signed<br>Sheriff clerk (depute)

Rule 33.90

## FORM F40

Form of certificate relating to the cancellation or ceasing to have effect of a maintenance assessment under the Child Support Act 1991

Sheriff Court (*insert address*) Date (*insert date*)

I certify that notification has been received from the Secretary of State under section 10 of the Child Support Act 1991 that the maintenance assessment made on (*insert date*) has been cancelled [*or* ceased to have effect] on (*insert date*).

Signed<br>Sheriff clerk (depute)

Rule 33.22A(2)

### [1]FORM F41

Form of intimation to parties of a Child Welfare Hearing

Sheriff Court (*insert address and telephone number*)

Court Ref No:

In the action [A.B.], (*design*), Pursuer against [C.D.], (*design*), Defender

YOU ARE GIVEN NOTICE that a Child Welfare Hearing has been fixed for (*insert time*) on (*insert date*) at (*insert place*).

Date (*insert date*)

Signed...............<br>Sheriff Clerk (Depute)

**NOTE**

**Please note that in terms of** Rule 33.22A(5) **parties to the action must attend personally**

\* *IF YOU ARE UNCERTAIN WHAT ACTION TO TAKE* you should consult a solicitor. You may be eligible for legal aid depending on your financial circumstances, and you can get information about legal aid from a solicitor. You may also obtain information from any Citizens' Advice Bureau or other advice agency.

\* This section to be deleted where service is to be made on a solicitor.

Rule 33.27A(1)

### [2]FORM F42

---

[1] Substituted by SSI 2000/239 (effective October 2, 2000).

[2] Omitted by the Act of Sederunt (Rules of the Court of Session 1994 and Ordinary Cause Rules 1993 Amendment) (Child Welfare Reporters) 2015 (SSI 2015/312) para.4 (effective 26 October 2015)

**¹FORM F43**

## ²FORM F44

## Form F44

**Rule 33.21(4)**

Form of annex to interlocutor appointing a child welfare reporter

☐   Appointment of Child Welfare Reporter under rule 33.21(1)(a).

   Where this box is ticked the Child Welfare Reporter is required to seek the views of the child [or children] on the issue(s) specified in Part 1 below.

☐   Appointment of Child Welfare Reporter under rule 33.21(1)(b).

   Where this box is ticked the Child Welfare Reporter is required to carry out the enquiries specified in Part 2 below, and to address the issue(s) specified in Part 3 below.

PART 1

| |
|---|
| Issue(s) in respect of which views of the child [or children] are to be sought [*specify*] |

PART 2

Enquiries to be undertaken—

☐   Seek views of child

☐   Visit home of [*specify*]

☐   Visit nursery / school / child minder / other [*specify*]

☐   Interview mother / father

---

¹ Omitted by the Act of Sederunt (Rules of the Court of Session 1994 and Ordinary Cause Rules 1993 Amendment) (Child Welfare Reporters) 2015 (SSI 2015/312) para.4 (effective 26 October 2015)

² As inserted by the Act of Sederunt (Rules of the Court of Session 1994 and Ordinary Cause Rules 1993 Amendment) (Child Welfare Reporters) 2015 (SSI 2015/312) para.4 (effective 26 October 2015).

☐    Interview other family members [*specify*]

☐    Interview child minder / nanny

☐    Interview teacher / head teacher

☐    Interview child's health visitor / GP / other health professional [*specify*]

☐    Interview a party's GP / other health professional [*specify*]

☐    Interview social worker [*specify*]

☐    Interview domestic abuse case worker [*specify*]

☐    Interview other persons [*specify*]

☐    Obtain criminal conviction certificate under section 112 of the Police Act 1997 in respect of [*specify party*]

☐    Observe contact [*specify*]

☐    Observe child in home environment pre/post contact [*specify*]

☐    Obtain record of parties' attendance from contact centre

☐    Other [*specify*]

PART 3

| Issues to be addressed in report [*specify*] |
| --- |
|  |

## ¹FORM CP1

Rule 33A.7(1)(a)

Form of intimation to children and next-of-kin in an action of dissolution of civil partnership or separation of civil partners where defender's address is not known

Court ref. no.

To (*insert name and address as in warrant*)

You are given NOTICE that an action of dissolution of a civil partnership [or separation of civil partners] has been raised against (*insert name*) your (*insert relationship, e.g. father, mother, brother or other relative as the case may be*). If you know of his [or her] present address, you are requested to inform the sheriff

---

¹ Inserted by Act of Sederunt (Ordinary Cause Rules) Amendment (Civil Partnership Act 2004) 2005 (SSI 2005/638), para.3 (effective December 8, 2005).

clerk (*insert address of sheriff clerk*) in writing immediately. If you wish to appear as a party you must lodge a minute with the sheriff clerk for leave to do so. Your minute must be lodged within 21 days of (*insert date on which intimation was given. N.B. Rule 5.3(2) relating to postal service or intimation*).

Date (*insert date*)

(*Signed*)

Solicitor for the pursuer

(*insert designation and business address*)

**NOTE**

If you decide to lodge a minute it may be in your best interests to consult a solicitor. The minute should be lodged with the sheriff clerk together with the appropriate fee of (*insert amount*) and a copy of this intimation.

**IF YOU ARE UNCERTAIN WHAT ACTION TO TAKE** you should consult a solicitor. You may be entitled to legal aid depending on your financial circumstances, and you can get information about legal aid from a solicitor. You may also obtain advice from any Citizens Advice Bureau or other advice agency.

[1]**FORM CP2**

Rule 33A.7(1)(b)

Form of intimation to children, next-of-kin, guardian and attorney in action of dissolution of civil partnership or separation of civil partners where defender suffers from a mental disorder

Court ref. no.

To (*insert name and address as in warrant*)

You are given NOTICE that an action of dissolution of a civil partnership [*or* separation of civil partners] has been raised against (*insert name*) your (*insert relationship, e.g. father, mother, brother or other relative, ward or granter of a power of attorney as the case may be*). A copy of the initial writ is enclosed. If you wish to appear as a party, you must lodge a minute with the sheriff clerk (*insert address of sheriff clerk*), for leave to do so. Your minute must be lodged within 21 days of (*insert date on which intimation was given. N.B. Rule 5.3(2) relating to postal service or intimation*).

Date (*insert date*)

(*Signed*)

Solicitor for the pursuer

(*insert designation and business address*)

**NOTE**

If you decide to lodge a minute it may be in your best interests to consult a solicitor. The minute should be lodged with the sheriff clerk together with the appropriate fee of (*insert amount*) and a copy of this intimation.

**IF YOU ARE UNCERTAIN WHAT ACTION TO TAKE** you should consult a solicitor. You may be entitled to legal aid depending on your financial circumstances, and you can get information about legal aid from a solicitor. You may also obtain advice from any Citizens Advice Bureau or other advice agency.

[2]**FORM CP3**

Rule 33A.7(1)(c)(i) and (ii)

Form of intimation to a local authority or third party who may be liable to maintain a child in a civil partnership action

---

[1] Inserted by Act of Sederunt (Ordinary Cause Rules) Amendment (Civil Partnership Act 2004) 2005 (SSI 2005/638), para.3 (effective December 8, 2005).

[2] Inserted by Act of Sederunt (Ordinary Cause Rules) Amendment (Civil Partnership Act 2004) 2005 (SSI 2005/638), para.3 (effective December 8, 2005).

Court ref. no.

To (*insert name and address as in warrant*)

YOU ARE GIVEN NOTICE that in this action, the court may make an order under section 11 of the Children (Scotland) Act 1995 in respect of (*insert name and address*), a child in your care *[or liable to be maintained by you]*. A copy of the initial writ is attached. If you wish to appear as a party, you must lodge a minute with the sheriff clerk (*insert address of sheriff clerk*), for leave to do so. Your minute must be lodged within 21 days of (*insert date on which intimation was given. N.B. Rule 5.3(2) relating to postal service or intimation*).

Date (*insert date*)

(*Signed*)
Solicitor for the pursuer
(*insert designation and business address*)

**NOTE**

If you decide to lodge a minute it may be in your best interests to consult a solicitor. The minute should be lodged with the sheriff clerk together with the appropriate fee of (*insert amount*) and a copy of this intimation.

**IF YOU ARE UNCERTAIN WHAT ACTION TO TAKE** you should consult a solicitor. You may be entitled to legal aid depending on your financial circumstances, and you can get information about legal aid from a solicitor. You may also obtain advice from any Citizens

### [1]FORM CP4

Rule 33A.7(1)(c)(iii)

Form of intimation to person who in fact exercises care or control of a child in a civil partnership action

Court ref. no.

To (*insert name and address as in warrant*)

YOU ARE GIVEN NOTICE that in this action, the court may make an order under section 11 of the Children (Scotland) Act 1995 in respect of (*insert name and address*), a child at present in your care or control. A copy of the initial writ is attached. If you wish to appear as a party, you must lodge a minute with the sheriff clerk (*insert address of sheriff clerk*), for leave to do so. Your minute must be lodged within 21 days of (*insert date on which Intimation was given. N.B. Rule 5.3(2) relating to postal service or intimation*).

Date (*insert date*)

(*Signed*)
Solicitor for the pursuer
(*insert designation and business address*)

**NOTE**

If you decide to lodge a minute it may be in your best interests to consult a solicitor. The minute should be lodged with the sheriff clerk together with the appropriate fee of (*insert amount*) and a copy of this intimation.

**IF YOU ARE UNCERTAIN WHAT ACTION TO TAKE** you should consult a solicitor. You may be entitled to legal aid depending on your financial circumstances, and you can get information about legal aid from a solicitor. You may also obtain advice from any Citizens Advice Bureau or other advice agency.

### [2]FORM CP5

---

[1] Inserted by Act of Sederunt (Ordinary Cause Rules) Amendment (Civil Partnership Act 2004) 2005 (SSI 2005/638), para.3 (effective December 8, 2005).

[2] Inserted by Act of Sederunt (Ordinary Cause Rules) Amendment (Civil Partnership Act 2004) 2005 (SSI 2005/638), para.3 (effective December 8, 2005).

Rule 33A.7(1)(d)

Form of notice to parent or guardian in a civil partnership action which includes a crave for a section 11 order in respect of a child

Court ref. no.

1. YOU ARE GIVEN NOTICE that in this action, the pursuer is applying for an order under section 11 of the Children (Scotland) Act 1995 in respect of the child (*insert name of child*). A copy of the initial writ is served on you and is attached to this notice.

2. If you wish to oppose this action, or oppose the granting of any order applied for by the pursuer in respect of the child, you must lodge a notice of intention to defend (Form CP16). See Form CP16 attached for further details.

Date (*insert date*)

(*Signed*)

Pursuer

[*or* Solicitor for the pursuer]

(*insert designation and business address*)

**NOTE: IF YOU ARE UNCERTAIN WHAT ACTION TO TAKE** you should consult a solicitor. You may be entitled to legal aid depending on your financial circumstances, and you can get information about legal aid from a solicitor. You may also obtain advice from any Citizens Advice Bureau or other advice agency.

### [1]FORM CP6

Rule 33A.7(1)(e), 33A.7(4) and 33A.12(2) and (3)

Form of notice to local authority

Court ref. no.

To (*insert name and address*)

1. YOU ARE GIVEN NOTICE that in an action in the Sheriff Court at (*insert address*) the pursuer has applied for a residence order in respect of the child (*insert name of child*). A copy of the initial writ is enclosed.

2. If you wish to oppose this action, or oppose the granting of any order applied for by the pursuer in respect of the child, you must lodge a notice of intention to defend (Form CP16). See Form CP16 attached for further details.

Date (*insert date*)

(*Signed*)

Solicitor for the pursuer

(*insert designation and business address*)

### [2]FORM CP7

Rule 33A.7(1)(f), 33A.15(2) and 33A.19(1)(a)

Form of intimation in a civil partnership action which includes a crave for a section 11 order

Court ref. no.

Part A

This part must be completed by the Pursuer's solicitor in language a child is capable of understanding.

To (1)

---

[1] Inserted by Act of Sederunt (Ordinary Cause Rules) Amendment (Civil Partnership Act 2004) 2005 (SSI 2005/638), para.3 (effective December 8, 2005) and substituted by the Act of Sederunt (Sheriff Court Rules) (Miscellaneous Amendments) (No.2) 2010 (SSI 2010/416) r.7 (effective January 1, 2011).

[2] Inserted by Act of Sederunt (Ordinary Cause Rules) Amendment (Civil Partnership Act 2004) 2005 (SSI 2005/638), para.3 (effective December 8, 2005).

The Sheriff (the person who has to decide about your future) has been asked by (2) to decide:—

(a) (3) and (4)

(b) (5)

(c) (6)

If you want to tell the Sheriff what you think about the things your (2) .......... has asked the Sheriff to decide about your future you should complete Part B of this form and send it to the Sheriff Clerk at (7) by (8) .......... . An envelope which does not need a postage stamp is enclosed for you to use to return the form.

**IF YOU DO NOT UNDERSTAND THIS FORM OR IF YOU WANT HELP TO COMPLETE IT you may get help from a SOLICITOR or contact the SCOTTISH CHILD LAW CENTRE on the FREE ADVICE TELEPHONE LINE ON 0800 328 8970.**

If you return the form it will be given to the Sheriff. The Sheriff may wish to speak with you and ask you to come and see him or her.

## NOTES FOR COMPLETION

| | |
|---|---|
| (1) Insert name and address of child | (2) Insert relationship to the child of party making the application to court. |
| (3) Insert appropriate wording for residence | (4) Insert address |
| (5) Insert appropriate wording for contact order sought. | (6) Insert appropriate wording for any other order sought. |
| (7) Insert address of sheriff clerk. | (8) Insert the date occurring 21 days after the date on which intimation is given. N.B. Rule 5.3(2) relating to intimation and service. |
| (9) Insert court reference number. | (10) Insert name and address of parties to the action. |

PART B

IF YOU WISH THE SHERIFF TO KNOW YOUR VIEWS ABOUT YOUR FUTURE YOU SHOULD COMPLETE THIS PART OF THE FORM

To the Sheriff Clerk, (7)

Court Ref. No. (9)

(10)....................

QUESTION (1): DO YOU WISH THE SHERIFF TO KNOW WHAT YOUR VIEWS ARE ABOUT YOUR FUTURE?

(PLEASE TICK BOX)

| | |
|---|---|
| Yes | |
| No | |

If you have ticked YES please also answer Question (2) *or* (3)

QUESTION (2): WOULD YOU LIKE A FRIEND, RELATIVE OR OTHER PERSON TO TELL THE SHERIFF YOUR VIEWS ABOUT YOUR FUTURE?

(PLEASE TICK BOX)

| Yes | |
|-----|---|
| No | |

If you have ticked YES please write the name and address of the person you wish to tell the Sheriff your views in Box (A) below. You should also tell that person what your views are about your future.

BOX A:     (NAME).............................

          (ADDRESS).............................
          ....................

          Is this      A                ☐        A               ☐
          person:      friend?                   rela-
                                                  tive?

                       A                ☐        Other?          ☐
                       teacher?

OR
    QUESTION (3): WOULD YOU LIKE TO WRITE TO THE SHERIFF AND TELL HIM WHAT YOUR VIEWS ARE ABOUT YOUR FUTURE?

                                                        (PLEASE TICK BOX)

| Yes | |
|-----|---|
| No | |

If you decide that you wish to write to the Sheriff you can write what your views are about your future in Box (B) below or on a separate piece of paper. If you decide to write your views on a separate piece of paper you should send it along with this form to the Sheriff Clerk in the envelope provided.

    BOX B: WHAT I HAVE TO SAY ABOUT MY FUTURE:-
    NAME: ...................
    ADDRESS: ....................
    DATE: ...................

### [1]FORM CP8

Rule 33A.7(1)(g)
    Form of intimation to creditor in application for order for the transfer of property under section 8 of the Family Law (Scotland) Act 1985 in a civil partnership action

                                                        Court ref. no.

    To (*insert name and address as in warrant*)
    You are given NOTICE that in this action, an order is sought for the transfer of property (*specify the order*), over which you hold a security. A copy of the initial writ is attached. If you wish to appear as a party, you must lodge a minute with the

---

[1] Inserted by Act of Sederunt (Ordinary Cause Rules) Amendment (Civil Partnership Act 2004) 2005 (SSI 2005/638), para.3 (effective December 8, 2005).

sheriff clerk (*insert address of sheriff clerk*), for leave to do so. Your minute must be lodged within 21 days of (*insert date on which intimation was given. N.B. Rule 5.3(2) relating to postal service or intimation*).

Date (*insert date*)

(*Signed*)
Solicitor for the pursuer
(*insert designation and business address*)

**NOTE**

If you decide to lodge a minute it may be in your best interests to consult a solicitor. The minute should be lodged with the sheriff clerk together with the appropriate fee of (*insert amount*) and a copy of this intimation.

**IF YOU ARE UNCERTAIN WHAT ACTION TO TAKE** you should consult a solicitor. You may be entitled to legal aid depending on your financial circumstances, and you can get information about legal aid from a solicitor. You may also obtain advice from any Citizens Advice Bureau or other advice agency.

### [1]**FORM CP9**

Rule 33A.7(1)(h)

Form of intimation in a civil partnership action where the pursuer makes an application for an order under section 18 of the Family Law (Scotland) Act 1985

Court ref. no.

To (*insert name and address as in warrant*)

You are given NOTICE that in this action, the pursuer craves the court to make an order under section 18 of the Family Law (Scotland) Act 1985. A copy of the initial writ is attached. If you wish to appear as a party, you must lodge a minute with the sheriff clerk (*insert address of sheriff clerk*), for leave to do so. Your minute must be lodged within 21 days of (*insert date on which intimation was given. N.B. Rule 5.3(2) relating to postal service or intimation*).

Date (*insert date*)

(*Signed*)
Solicitor for the pursuer
(*insert designation and business address*)

**NOTE**

If you decide to lodge a minute it may be in your best interests to consult a solicitor. The minute should be lodged with the sheriff clerk together with the appropriate fee of (*insert amount*) and a copy of this intimation.

**IF YOU ARE UNCERTAIN WHAT ACTION TO TAKE** you should consult a solicitor. You may be entitled to legal aid depending on your financial circumstances, and you can get information about legal aid from a solicitor. You may also obtain advice from any Citizens Advice Bureau or other advice agency.

### [2]**FORM CP10**

Rule 33A.7(1)(i)

Form of intimation in an action where an application is made under Chapter 3 of Part 3 of the Civil Partnership Act 2004

Court ref. no

To (*insert name and address as in warrant*)

You are given NOTICE that in this action the pursuer craves the court to make an order under Section (*insert the section under which the order(s) is sought*) of

---

[1] Inserted by Act of Sederunt (Ordinary Cause Rules) Amendment (Civil Partnership Act 2004) 2005 (SSI 2005/638), para.3 (effective December 8, 2005).

[2] Inserted by Act of Sederunt (Ordinary Cause Rules) Amendment (Civil Partnership Act 2004) 2005 (SSI 2005/638), para.3 (effective December 8, 2005).

Chapter 3 of Part 3 of the Civil Partnership Act 2004. A copy of the initial writ is attached. If you wish to appear as a party, you must lodge a minute with the sheriff clerk (*insert address of sheriff clerk*), for leave to do so. Your minute must be lodged within 21 days of (*insert date on which intimation was given. N.B. Rule 5.3(2) relating to postal service or intimation*).

Date (*insert date*)

(*Signed*)

Solicitor for the pursuer

(*insert designation and business address*)

**NOTE**

If you decide to lodge a minute it may be in your best interests to consult a solicitor. The minute should be lodged with the sheriff clerk together with the appropriate fee of (*insert amount*) and a copy of this intimation.

**IF YOU ARE UNCERTAIN WHAT ACTION TO TAKE** you should consult a solicitor. You may be entitled to legal aid depending on your financial circumstances, and you can get information about legal aid from a solicitor. You may also obtain advice from any Citizens Advice Bureau or other advice agency.

### [1]FORM CP11

Rule 33A.7(1)(j)

Form of intimation to person responsible for pension arrangement in relation to an order for payment in respect of pension lump sum under section 12A of the Family Law (Scotland) Act 1985 in a civil partnership action

Court ref. no.

To (*insert name and address as in warrant*)

You are given NOTICE that in this action, the pursuer has applied for an order under section 8 of the Family Law (Scotland) Act 1985 for a capital sum in circumstances where the family property includes rights in a pension arrangement under which a lump sum is payable. The relevant pension arrangement is (*give brief details, including number, if known*). If you wish to appear as a party, you must lodge a minute with the sheriff clerk (*insert address of sheriff clerk*), for leave to do so. Your minute must be lodged within 21 days of (*insert date on which intimation was given. N.B. Rule 5.3(2) relating to postal service or intimation*).

Date (*insert date*)

(*Signed*)

Solicitor for the pursuer

(*insert designation and business address*)

**NOTE**

If you decide to lodge a minute it may be in your best interests to consult a solicitor. The minute should be lodged with the sheriff clerk together with the appropriate fee of (*insert amount*) and a copy of this intimation.

**IF YOU ARE UNCERTAIN WHAT ACTION TO TAKE** you should consult a solicitor. You may be entitled to legal aid depending on your financial circumstances, and you can get information about legal aid from a solicitor. You may also obtain advice from any Citizens Advice Bureau or other advice agency.

### [2]FORM CP12

Rule 33A.7(1)(k)

---

[1] Inserted by Act of Sederunt (Ordinary Cause Rules) Amendment (Civil Partnership Act 2004) 2005 (SSI 2005/638), para.3 (effective December 8, 2005).

[2] Inserted by Act of Sederunt (Ordinary Cause Rules) Amendment (Civil Partnership Act 2004) 2005 (SSI 2005/638), para.3 (effective December 8, 2005).

Form of intimation to person responsible for pension arrangement in relation to pension sharing order under section 8(1)(baa) of the Family Law (Scotland) Act 1985 in a civil partnership action

Court ref. no.

To (*insert name and address as in warrant*)

You are given NOTICE that in this action, the pursuer has applied under section 8 of the Family Law (Scotland) Act 1985 for a pension sharing order in circumstances where the family property includes rights in a pension arrangement. The relevant pension arrangement is (*give brief details, including number, if known*). If you wish to appear as a party, you must lodge a minute with the sheriff clerk (*insert address of sheriff clerk*), for leave to do so. Your minute must be lodged within 21 days of (*insert date on which intimation was given. N.B. Rule 5.3(2) relating to postal service or intimation*).

Date (*insert date*)

(*Signed*)

Solicitor for the pursuer

(*insert designation and business address*)

**NOTE**

If you decide to lodge a minute it may be in your best interests to consult a solicitor. The minute should be lodged with the sheriff clerk together with the appropriate fee of (*insert amount*) and a copy of this intimation.

**IF YOU ARE UNCERTAIN WHAT ACTION TO TAKE** you should consult a solicitor. You may be entitled to legal aid depending on your financial circumstances, and you can get information about legal aid from a solicitor. You may also obtain advice from any Citizens Advice Bureau or other advice agency.

### [1]FORM CP12A

Rule 33A.7(1)(l)

Form of intimation to Board of the Pension Protection Fund in relation to pension compensation sharing order under section 8(1)(bab) of the Family Law (Scotland) Act 1985 in a civil partnership action

Court ref. no.

To (*insert name and address as in warrant*)

You arc given NOTICE that in this action the pursuer has applied under section 8(1)(bab) of the Family Law (Scotland) Act 1985 for a pension compensation sharing order in circumstances where the family property includes rights to Pension Protection Fund compensation. The relevant pension arrangement is (*give brief details, including number, if known*). If you wish to appear as a party, you must lodge a minute with the sheriff clerk (*insert address of sheriff clerk*), for leave to do so. Your minute must be lodged within 21 days of (*insert date on which intimation was given. N.B. Rule 5.3(2) relating to postal service or intimation*).

Date (*insert date*)

(*Signed*)

Solicitor for the pursuer

(*insert designation and business address*)

### [2]FORM CP12B

Rule 33.7(1)(m)

---

[1] As inserted by the Act of Sederunt (Sheriff Court Rules) (Miscellaneous Amendments) 2011 (SSI 2011/193) r.15 (effective April 6, 2011).

[2] As inserted by the Act of Sederunt (Sheriff Court Rules) (Miscellaneous Amendments) 2011 (SSI 2011/193) r.15 (effective April 6, 2011).

Form of intimation to Board of the Pension Protection Fund in relation to an order under section 12B(2) of the Family Law (Scotland) Act 1985 in a civil partnership action

Court ref. no.

To (*insert name and address as in warrant*)

You arc given NOTICE that in this action the pursuer has applied under section 8(1)(bb) of the Family Law (Scotland) Act 1985 for an order under section 12B(2) of the Act in circumstances where the family property includes rights to Pension Protection Fund compensation. The relevant pension arrangement is (*give brief details, including number, if known*). If you wish to appear as a party, you must lodge a minute with the sheriff clerk (*insert address of sheriff clerk*), for leave to do so. Your minute must be lodged within 21 days of (*insert date on which intimation was given. N.B. Rule 5.3(2) relating to postal service or intimation*).

Date (*insert date*)

(*Signed*)
Solicitor for the pursuer
(*insert designation and business address*)

### ¹FORM CP13

Rule 33A.8(3)

Form of intimation to person with whom an association is alleged to have occurred in a civil partnership action

Court ref. no.

To (*insert name and address as in warrant*)

You are given NOTICE that in this action, the defender is alleged to have had an association with you. A copy of the initial writ is attached. If you wish to dispute the truth of the allegation made against you, you must lodge a minute with the sheriff clerk (*insert address of sheriff clerk*), for leave to appear as a party. Your minute must be lodged within 21 days of (*insert date on which intimation was given. N.B. Rule 5.3(2) relating to postal service or intimation*).

Date (*insert date*)

(*Signed*)
Solicitor for the pursuer
(*insert designation and business address*)

**NOTE**

If you decide to lodge a minute it may be in your best interests to consult a solicitor. The minute should be lodged with the sheriff clerk together with the appropriate fee of (*insert amount*) and a copy of this intimation.

**IF YOU ARE UNCERTAIN WHAT ACTION TO TAKE** you should consult a solicitor. You may be entitled to legal aid depending on your financial circumstances, and you can get information about legal aid from a solicitor. You may also obtain advice from any Citizens Advice Bureau or other advice agency.

Rules 33A.9(5) and 33A.34(4)    ²**FORM CP13A**

Form of statement of civil partnership property in the cause
SHERIFFDOM OF (*insert name of sheriffdom*)
AT (*insert place of sheriff court*)
[A.B.], (*insert designation and address*, Pursuer against

---

¹ Inserted by Act of Sederunt (Ordinary Cause Rules) Amendment (Civil Partnership Act 2004) 2005 (SSI 2005/638), para.3(effective December 8, 2005).

² As inserted by the Act of Sederunt (Sheriff Court Rules) (Miscellaneous Amendments) 2012 (SSI 2012/188) para.4 (effective August 1, 2012).

[C.D..], (*insert designation and address*, Defender Court ref. no:

| |
|---|
| **The [Pursuer] [Defender]'s\* financial position at ( *insert date* ), being the relevant date as defined in** section 10(3) of the Family Law (Scotland) Act 1985 |
| Here list all assets owned by you, including assets which are jointly owned (if any) e.g. bank or building society accounts; shares or other investments; houses; land; pension entitlement; and life policies: |
| |
| Here list your outstanding debts including joint debts with the other party: |
| |
| Date (*insert date*) |
| I certify that this information is correct to the best of my knowledge and belief. (*Signed*) |
| [Pursuer][Defender]\* |

(\*delete as applicable)

Rule 33A.10                 ¹**FORM CP14**

Form of warrant of citation in a civil partnership action

Court ref. no.

(*Insert place and date*)

Grants warrant to cite the defender (*insert name and address of defender*) by serving upon him [*or* her] a copy of the writ and warrant upon a period of notice of (*insert period of notice*) days, and ordains the defender to lodge a notice of intention to defend with the sheriff clerk at (*insert address of sheriff court*), if he [*or* she] wishes to:

   (a)    challenge the jurisdiction of the court;

   (b)    oppose any claim made or order sought;

   (c)    make any claim or seek any order.

[Meantime grants interim interdict, or warrant to arrest on the dependence].

Rule 33A.11(1) and 33A.13(1)(a)      ²**FORM CP15**

Form of citation in a civil partnership action

CITATION

SHERIFFDOM OF (*insert name of sheriffdom*)

AT (*insert place of sheriff court*)

[A.B.], (*insert designation and address*), Pursuer, against [C.D.], (*insert designation and address*), Defender.

(*Insert place and date*)

Court ref. no.

You [C.D.], are hereby served with this copy writ and warrant, with Form CP16 (notice of intention to defend) [and (*insert details of any other form of notice served, e.g. any of the forms served in accordance with* rule 33A.14.)].

Form CP16 is served on you for use should you wish to intimate an intention to defend the action.

**IF YOU WISH TO—**

---

¹ Inserted by Act of Sederunt (Ordinary Cause Rules) Amendment (Civil Partnership Act 2004) 2005 (SSI 2005/638), para.3 (effective December 8, 2005).

² Inserted by Act of Sederunt (Ordinary Cause Rules) Amendment (Civil Partnership Act 2004) 2005 (SSI 2005/638), para.3 (effective December 8, 2005).

    (a)   challenge the jurisdiction of the court;

    (b)   oppose any claim made or order sought;

    (c)   make any claim; or

    (d)   seek any order;

you should consult a solicitor with a view to lodging a notice of intention to defend (Form CP16). The notice of intention to defend, together with the court fee of £ (*insert amount*) must be lodged with the sheriff clerk at the above address within 21 days (*or insert appropriate period of notice*) of (*insert the date on which service was executed. N.B.* Rule 5.3(2) *relating to postal service or intimation*).

    **IF YOU ARE UNCERTAIN WHAT ACTION TO TAKE** you should consult a solicitor. You may be entitled to legal aid depending on your financial circumstances, and you can get information about legal aid from a solicitor. You may also obtain advice from any Citizens Advice Bureau or other advice agency.

    **PLEASE NOTE THAT IF YOU DO NOTHING IN ANSWER TO THIS DOCUMENT** the court may regard you as admitting the claim made against you and the pursuer may obtain decree against you in your absence.

(*Signed*)

[P.Q.], Sheriff officer

[*or*

[X.Y.], (*insert designation and business address*)

Solicitor for the pursuer]

Rules 33A.11(1) and 33A.34(2)(a)    ¹**FORM CP16**

Form of notice of intention to defend in a civil partnership action

**Notice of Intention to Defend**

**Part A**

| PART A | Court ref. No. | Date of expiry of period of notice |
|---|---|---|
| (This section to be completed by the pursuer's solicitor before service.) | | |
| | In an action brought in Sheriff Court | |
| [*Insert name and business address of solicitor for the pursuer*] | Pursuer | |
| | Defender | |
| | Date of service | |

**Part B**

**(This section to be completed by the defender or defender's solicitor, and both parts of the form to be returned to the Sheriff Clerk at the above Sheriff Court on or before the date of expiry of the period of notice referred to in Part A above.)**

    (*Insert place and date*)

    [C.D.] (*Insert designation and address*), Defender, intends to

    (a)   challenge the jurisdiction of the court;

---

¹ Inserted by Act of Sederunt (Ordinary Cause Rules) Amendment (Civil Partnership Act 2004) 2005 (SSI 2005/638), para.3 (effective December 8, 2005).

(b)  oppose a crave in the initial writ;

(c)  make a claim;

(d)  seek an order;

in the action against him [*or* her] raised by [A.B.], (*insert designation and address*), Pursuer.

## Part C

**(This section to be completed by the defender or the defender's solicitor where an order under** section 11 of the Children (Scotland) Act 1995 **in respect of a child is opposed by the defender).**

DO YOU WISH TO OPPOSE THE MAKING OF ANY ORDER CRAVED BY THE PURSUER IN RESPECT OF A CHILD?

YES/NO*

*delete as appropriate

If you answered YES to the above question, please state here the order(s) which you wish to oppose and the reasons why the court should not make such order(s).

## Part D

**(This section to be completed by the defender or the defender's solicitor where an order under** section 11 of the Children (Scotland) Act 1995 **in respect of a child is sought by the defender).**

DO YOU WISH THE COURT TO MAKE ANY ORDER UNDER SECTION 11 OF THE CHILDREN (SCOTLAND) ACT 1995 IN RESPECT OF A CHILD?

YES/NO*

*delete as appropriate

If you answered YES to the above question, please state here the order(s) which you wish the court to make and the reasons why the court should make such order(s).

## Part E

IF YOU HAVE COMPLETED PART D OF THIS FORM YOU MUST IN-CLUDE EITHER CRAVE (1) OR (2) BELOW (*delete as appropriate)

(1)  * Warrant for intimation of notice in terms of Form CP7 on the child(ren) (*insert full name(s) and date(s) of birth*) is sought.

(2)  * I seek to dispense with intimation on the child(ren) (*insert full name(s) and date(s) of birth*) for the following reasons:—

Signed

[C.D.] Defender [or [X.Y.]

(*add designation and business address*)

Solicitor for Defender]

Rule 33A.11(2)                    ¹**FORM CP17**

Form of certificate of citation in a civil partnership action

Certificate of Citation

(*Insert place and date*) I,.......... hereby certify that upon the.......... day of.......... I duly cited [C.D.], Defender, to answer to the foregoing writ. This I did by (*state method of service; if by-officer and not by post, add*: in the presence of [L.M.], (*insert designation*), witness hereto with me subscribing; *and insert details of any forms of intimation or notice sent including details of the person to whom intimation sent and the method of service*).

(*Signed*)

[P.Q.], Sheriff officer

---

¹ Inserted by Act of Sederunt (Ordinary Cause Rules) Amendment (Civil Partnership Act 2004) 2005 (SSI 2005/638), para.3 (effective December 8, 2005).

[L.M.], witness
[*or*
[X.Y.] (*add designation and business address*)
Solicitor for the pursuer]

Rule 33A.13(1)(c)      [1]**FORM CP18**

Form of request to medical officer of hospital or similar institution in a civil partnership action

To (*insert name and address of medical officer*)

In terms of rule 33A.13(1)(c) of the Ordinary Cause Rulesof the Sheriff Court a copy of the initial writ at the instance of (*insert name and address of pursuer*), Pursuer, against (*insert name and address of defender*), Defender, is enclosed and you are requested to

(a)   deliver it personally to (*insert name of defender*), and

(b)   explain the contents to him or her,

unless you are satisfied that such delivery or explanation would be dangerous to his or her health or mental condition. You are further requested to complete and return to me in the enclosed stamped addressed envelope the certificate appended hereto, making necessary deletions.

Date (insert date)..........      (*Signed*)..........
                                    Solicitor for the pursuer
                                    (*insert designation and business address*)

Rule 33A.13(1)(d) and 33A.13(2)      [2]**FORM CP19**

Form of certificate by medical officer of hospital or similar institution in a civil partnership action

                                    Court ref. no.

I (*insert name and designation*) certify that I have received a copy initial writ in an action of (*type of civil partnership action to be inserted by the party requesting service*) at the instance of (*insert name and designation*), Pursuer, against (*insert name and designation*), Defender, and that

* I have on the.......... day of.......... personally delivered a copy thereof to the said defender who is under my care at (*insert address*) and I have explained the contents or purport thereof to him or her, *or*

* I have not delivered a copy thereof to the said defender who is under my care at (*insert address*) and I have not explained the contents thereof to him or her because (*state reasons*).

Date (*insert date*)

                                         (*Signed*)

Medical officer (*add designation and address*)

* Delete as appropriate.

Rule 33A.14(1)(a)(i)      [3]**FORM CP20**

[1] Inserted by Act of Sederunt (Ordinary Cause Rules) Amendment (Civil Partnership Act 2004) 2005 (SSI 2005/638), para.3 (effective December 8, 2005).

[2] Inserted by Act of Sederunt (Ordinary Cause Rules) Amendment (Civil Partnership Act 2004) 2005 (SSI 2005/638), para.3 (effective December 8, 2005).

[3] Inserted by Act of Sederunt (Ordinary Cause Rules) Amendment (Civil Partnership Act 2004) 2005 (SSI 2005/638), para.3 (effective December 8, 2005).

Form of notice to defender where it is stated that defender consents to granting decree of dissolution of a civil partnership

YOU ARE GIVEN NOTICE that the copy initial writ served on you with this notice states that you consent to the grant of decree of dissolution of your civil partnership.

1. If you do so consent the consequences for you are that—
    [1](a) provided the pursuer establishes the fact that he [*or* she] has not cohabited with you at any time during a continuous period of one year after the date of registration of your civil partnership and immediately preceding the bringing of this action and that you consent, a decree of dissolution of your civil partnership will be granted;
    (b) on the grant of a decree of dissolution of your civil partnership you may lose your rights of succession to the pursuer's estate; and
    (c) decree of dissolution will end your civil partnership thereby affecting any right to such pension as may depend on the civil partnership continuing, or, your right to any state pension that may have been payable to you on the death of your civil partner.

Apart from these, there may be other consequences for you depending upon your particular circumstances.

2. You are entitled, whether or not you consent to the grant of decree of dissolution of your civil partnership, to apply to the sheriff in this action—
    (a) to make financial or other provision for you under the Family Law (Scotland) Act 1985;
    (b) for an order under section 11 of the Children (Scotland) Act 1995 in respect of any child of the family within the meaning of section 101(7) of the Civil Partnership Act 2004; or
    (c) for any other competent order.

3. IF YOU WISH TO APPLY FOR ANY OF THE ABOVE ORDERS you should consult a solicitor with a view to lodging a notice of intention to defend (Form CP16).

4. If, after consideration, you wish to consent to the grant of decree of dissolution of your civil partnership in this action, you should complete and sign the attached notice of consent (Form CP21) and send it to the sheriff clerk at the sheriff court referred to in the initial writ within 21 days of (*insert the date on which service was executed N.B. Rule 5.3(2) relating to postal service*).

5. If, at a later stage, you wish to withdraw your consent to decree being granted against you in this action, you must inform the sheriff clerk immediately in writing.

Date (*insert date*)

(*Signed*)
Solicitor for the pursuer
(*insert designation and business address*)

Rules 33A.14(1)(a)(i) and 33A.18(1)        [2]**FORM CP21**

Form of notice of consent in actions of dissolution of a civil partnership under section 117(3)(c) of the Civil Partnership Act 2004

---

[1] As amended by Act of Sederunt (Ordinary Cause Rules) Amendment (Family Law (Scotland) Act 2006 etc.) 2006, para.2 (SSI 2006/207) (effective May 4, 2006).

[2] Inserted by Act of Sederunt (Ordinary Cause Rules) Amendment (Civil Partnership Act 2004) 2005 (SSI 2005/638), para.3 (effective December 8, 2005).

Court ref. no.

[A.B.], (*insert designation and address*), Pursuer, against [C.D.], (*insert designation and address*), Defender.

I, (*full name and address of the defender to be inserted by pursuer or pursuer's solicitor before sending notice*) have received a copy of the initial writ in the action against me at the instance of (*full name and address of pursuer to be inserted by pursuer or pursuer's solicitor before sending notice*). I understand that it states that I consent to the grant of decree of dissolution of the civil partnership in this action. I have considered the consequences for me mentioned in the notice (Form CP20) sent to me with this notice. I consent to the grant of decree of dissolution of the civil partnership in this action.

Date (insert date).........

(Signed)

Defender

Rule 33A.14(1)(a)(ii)                           [1]**FORM CP22**

Form of notice to defender where it is stated that defender consents to the granting of decree of separation of civil partners

YOU ARE GIVEN NOTICE that the copy initial writ served on you with this notice states that you consent to the grant of decree of separation of you and your civil partner.

1.  If you do so consent the consequences for you are that—

    [2](a)  provided the pursuer establishes the fact that he [*or* she] has not cohabited with you at any time during a continuous period of one year after the date of registration of your civil partnership and immediately preceding the bringing of this action and that you consent, a decree of separation of civil partners will be granted;

    (b)  on the grant of a decree of separation of civil partners you will be obliged to live apart from the pursuer but the civil partnership will continue to subsist; you will continue to have a legal obligation to support your civil partner and any child of the family within the meaning of section 101(7) of the Civil Partnership Act 2004; and

Apart from these, there may be other consequences for you depending upon your particular circumstances.

2.  You are entitled, whether or not you consent to the grant of decree of separation of civil partners, to apply to the sheriff in this action—

    (a)  to make financial or other provision for you under the Family Law (Scotland) Act 1985;

    (b)  for an order under section 11 of the Children (Scotland) Act 1995 in respect of any child of the family within the meaning of section 101(7) of the Civil Partnership Act 2004; or

    (c)  for any other competent order.

3.  IF YOU WISH TO APPLY FOR ANY OF THE ABOVE ORDERS you should consult a solicitor with a view to lodging a notice of intention to defend (Form CP16).

4.  If, after consideration, you wish to consent to the grant of decree of separa-

---

[1] Inserted by Act of Sederunt (Ordinary Cause Rules) Amendment (Civil Partnership Act 2004) 2005 (SSI 2005/638), para.3 (effective December 8, 2005).

[2] As amended by Act of Sederunt (Ordinary Cause Rules) Amendment (Family Law (Scotland) Act 2006 etc.) 2006, para.2 (SSI 2006/207) (effective May 4, 2006).

tion of civil partners in this action, you should complete and sign the attached notice of consent (Form CP23) and send it to the sheriff clerk at the sheriff court referred to in the initial writ and other papers within 21 days of (*insert the date on which service was executed. N.B.* Rule 5.3(2) *relating to postal service or intimation*).

5. If, at a later stage, you wish to withdraw your consent to decree being granted against you in this action, you must inform the sheriff clerk immediately in writing.

Date (*insert date*)

(*Signed*)

Solicitor for the pursuer (*add designation and business address*)

Rules 33A.14(1)(a)(ii) and 33A.18(1)      [1]**FORM CP23**

Form of notice of consent in actions of separation of civil partners under section 120 of the Civil Partnership Act 2004

Court ref. no

[A.B.], (*insert designation and address*), Pursuer against [C.D.], (*insert designation and address*), Defender.

I, (*full name and address of the defender to be inserted by pursuer or pursuer's solicitor before sending notice*) confirm that I have received a copy of the initial writ in the action against me at the instance of (*full name and address of pursuer to be inserted by pursuer or pursuer's solicitor before sending notice*). I understand that it states that I consent to the grant of decree of separation of civil partners in this action. I have considered the consequences for me mentioned in the notice (Form CP22) sent together with this notice. I consent to the grant of decree of separation of civil partners in this action.

Date (*insert date*)

(*Signed*)
Defender

Rule 33A.14(1)(b)(i)                [2][3]**FORM CP24**

Form of notice to defender in an action for dissolution of a civil partnership where it is stated there has been two years' non-cohabitation

YOU ARE GIVEN NOTICE that—

1. The copy initial writ served on you with this notice states that there has been no cohabitation between you and the pursuer at any time during a continuous period of two years after the date of registration of the civil partnership and immediately preceding the commencement of this action. If the pursuer establishes this as a fact and the sheriff is satisfied that the civil partnership has broken down irretrievably, a decree will be granted.

2. Decree of dissolution will end the civil partnership thereby affecting any right to such pension as may depend on the civil partnership continuing or your right to any state pension that may have been payable to you on the

---

[1] Inserted by Act of Sederunt (Ordinary Cause Rules) Amendment (Civil Partnership Act 2004) 2005 (SSI 2005/638), para.3 (effective December 8, 2005).

[2] Inserted by Act of Sederunt (Ordinary Cause Rules) Amendment (Civil Partnership Act 2004) 2005 (SSI 2005/638), para.3 (effective December 8, 2005).

[3] As amended by Act of Sederunt (Ordinary Cause Rules) Amendment (Family Law (Scotland) Act 2006 etc.) 2006, para.2 (SSI 2006/207) (effective May 4, 2006).

death of your civil partner. You may also lose your rights of succession to the pursuer's estate.

3. You are entitled, whether or not you dispute that there has been no such cohabitation during that five year period, to apply to the sheriff in this action—

    (a) to make financial or other provision for you under the Family Law (Scotland) Act

    (b) for an order under section 11 of the Children (Scotland) Act 1995 in respect of any child of the family within the meaning of section 101(7) of the Civil Partnership Act 2004; or

    (c) for any other competent order.

4. IF YOU WISH TO APPLY FOR ANY OF THE ABOVE ORDERS you should consult a solicitor with a view to lodging a notice of intention to defend (Form CP16).

Date (*insert date*)

                                                        (*Signed*)

        Solicitor for the pursuer (*add designation and business address*)

## Rule 33A.14(1)(b)(ii)        [1][2]FORM CP25

Form of notice to defender in an action for separation of civil partners where it is stated there has been two years' non-cohabitation

YOU ARE GIVEN NOTICE that—

1. The copy initial writ served on you with this notice states that there has been no cohabitation between you and the pursuer at any time during a continuous period of five years after the date of registration of the civil partnership and immediately preceding the commencement of this action. If the pursuer establishes this as a fact and the sheriff is satisfied that there are grounds justifying a decree of separation of civil partners, a decree will be granted.

2. On the granting of decree of separation you will be obliged to live apart from the pursuer but the civil partnership will continue to subsist. You will continue to have a legal obligation to support your civil partner and any child of the family within the meaning of section 101(7) of the Civil Partnership Act 2004.

3. You are entitled, whether or not you dispute that there has been no such cohabitation during that two year period, to apply to the sheriff in this action—

    (a) to make provision under the Family Law (Scotland) Act 1985;

    (b) for an order under section 11 of the Children (Scotland) Act 1995 in respect of any child of the family within the meaning of section 101(7) of the Civil Partnership Act 2004; or

    (c) for any other competent order.

4. IF YOU WISH TO APPLY FOR ANY OF THE ABOVE ORDERS you should consult a solicitor with a view to lodging a notice of intention to defend (Form CP16).

Date (*insert date*)

                                                        (*Signed*)

---

[1] Inserted by Act of Sederunt (Ordinary Cause Rules) Amendment (Civil Partnership Act 2004) 2005 (SSI 2005/638), para.3 (effective December 8, 2005).

[2] As amended by Act of Sederunt (Ordinary Cause Rules) Amendment (Family Law (Scotland) Act 2006 etc.) 2006, para.2 (SSI 2006/207) (effective May 4, 2006).

Solicitor for the pursuer (*add designation and business address*)

**Rule 33A.14(1)(c)**                    [1]**FORM CP25A**

Form of notice to defender in action of dissolution of civil partnership where an interim gender recognition certificate has been issued

YOU ARE GIVEN NOTICE that—

1.  The copy initial writ served on you together with this notice states that an interim gender recognition certificate has been issued to you [*or* the pursuer]. If the pursuer establishes this as a fact, decree will be granted.

2.  Decree of dissolution will end the civil partnership thereby affecting any right to such pension as may depend on the civil partnership continuing or your right to any state pension that may have been payable to you on the death of your civil partner. You may also lose your rights of succession to the pursuer's estate.

3.  If the pursuer is entitled to decree of dissolution you are nevertheless entitled to apply to the sheriff in this action—

    (a)  to make financial or other provision for you under the Family Law (Scotland) Act 1985;

    (b)  for an order under section 11 of the Children (Scotland) Act 1995 in respect of any child of the family within the meaning of section 101(7) of the Civil Partnership Act 2004; or

    (c)  for any other competent order.

4.  IF YOU WISH TO APPLY FOR ANY OF THE ABOVE ORDERS you should consult a solicitor with a view to lodging a notice of intention to defend (Form CP16).

Date (*insert date*)                     (*Signed*)

Solicitor for the pursuer (*add designation and business address*)

Rule 33A.23(2)                    [2]**FORM CP26**

Form of intimation to parties of a Child Welfare Hearing in a civil partnership action

Sheriff court (*insert address and telephone number*).......... Court ref. no.

In this action [A.B.], (*design*), Pursuer, against [C.D.] (*design*), Defender

YOU ARE GIVEN NOTICE that a Child Welfare Hearing has been fixed for (*insert time*) on (*insert date*) at (*insert place*).

Date (*insert date*)                     Signed....................

Sheriff Clerk (Depute)

**Rule 33A.30(1)(b)**                    [3]**FORM CP27**

Form of minute for decree in a civil partnership action to which rule 33A.29 applies

---

[1] Inserted by Act of Sederunt (Ordinary Cause Rules) Amendment (Family Law (Scotland) Act 2006 etc.) 2006, para.2 (SSI 2006/207) (effective May 4, 2006).

[2] Inserted by Act of Sederunt (Ordinary Cause Rules) Amendment (Civil Partnership Act 2004) 2005 (SSI 2005/638), para.3 (effective December 8, 2005).

[3] Inserted by Act of Sederunt (Ordinary Cause Rules) Amendment (Civil Partnership Act 2004) 2005 (SSI 2005/638), para.3 (effective December 8, 2005).

(*Insert name of solicitor for the pursuer*) having considered the evidence contained in the affidavits and the other documents all as specified in the schedule hereto, and being satisfied that upon the evidence a motion for decree (in terms of the crave of initial writ) [*or in such restricted terms as may he appropriate*] may be properly be made, moves the court accordingly.

In respect whereof<br>Signed

Solicitor for the Pursuer (*add designation and business address*)<br>Schedule

(*Number and specify documents considered*)

### Rules 33A.65(1) and 33A.65(2)     [1] [2]FORM CP28

Form of certificate of delivery of documents to chief constable in a civil partnership action

[*Omitted by* Act of Sederunt (Ordinary Cause Rules) Amendment (Family Law (Scotland) Act 2006 etc.) 2006, para.2 (SSI 2006/207) (*effective May 4, 2006).*]

### Rule 33A.67(1)     [3] [4]FORM CP29

Form of simplified dissolution of civil partnership application under section 117(3)(c) of the Civil Partnership Act 2004

Sheriff Clerk

Sheriff Court House

..............

..............

(Telephone)..............

APPLICATION FOR DISSOLUTION OF A CIVIL PARTNERSHIP WITH CONSENT OF OTHER PARTY TO THE CIVIL PARTNERSHIP (CIVIL PARTNERS HAVING LIVED APART FOR AT LEAST ONE YEAR)

Before completing this form, you should have read the leaflet entitled "Do it yourself Dissolution", which explains the circumstances in which a dissolution of a civil partnership may be sought by this method. If the simplified procedure appears to suit your circumstances, you may use this form to apply for dissolution of your civil partnership. Below you will find directions designed to assist you with your application. Please follow them carefully. In the event of difficulty, you may contact any sheriff clerk's office or Citizen Advice Bureau.

**Directions for making application**

Write In Ink, Using Block Capitals

| | |
|---|---|
| Application (Part 1) | 1. Complete and sign Part 1 of the form (pages 3-7), paying particular attention to the notes opposite each section. |
| Consent of civil partner (Part 2) | 2. When you have completed Part 1 of the form, attach the (blue) instruction |

---

[1] Inserted by Act of Sederunt (Ordinary Cause Rules) Amendment (Civil Partnership Act 2004) 2005 (SSI 2005/638), para.3 (effective December 8, 2005).

[2] As amended by Act of Sederunt (Ordinary Cause Rules) Amendment (Family Law (Scotland) Act 2006 etc.) 2006, para.2 (SSI 2006/207) (effective May 4, 2006).

[3] Inserted by Act of SEderunt (Ordinary Cause Rules) Amendment (Civil Partnership Act 2004) 2005 (SSI 2005/638), para.3 (effective December 8, 2005),

[4] As amended by Act of Sederunt (Ordinary Cause Rules) Amendment (Family Law (Scotland) Act 2006 etc.) 2006, para.2 (SSI 2006/207) (effective May 4, 2006).

civil partner sheet SP3 to it and send both documents to your for completion of the consent at Part 2 (page 9).

**NOTE:** If your civil partner does **NOT** complete and sign the form of consent, your application cannot proceed further under the simplified procedure. In that event, if you still wish to obtain a dissolution of your civil partnership, you should consult a solicitor.

Affidavit (Part 3)

3. When the application has been returned to you with the consent (Part 2) duly completed and signed, you should take the form to a Justice of the Peace, Notary Public, Commissioner for Oaths or other duly authorised person so that your affidavit at Part 3 (page 10) may be completed and sworn.

Returning completed application form to court

4. When directions 1–3 above have been complied with, your application is now ready to be sent to the sheriff clerk at the above address. With it you must enclose:

(i) an extract of the registration of your civil partnership in the civil partnership register (the document headed "Extract of an entry in the Register of Civil Partnerships", which will be returned to you in due course), or an equivalent document, and

(ii) either a cheque or postal order in respect of the court fee, crossed and made payable to "the Scottish Court Service",

or a completed form SP15, claiming exemption from the court fee.

5. Receipt of your application will be promptly acknowledged. Should you wish to withdraw the application for any reason, please contact the sheriff clerk immediately.

## PART 1
### WRITE IN INK, USING BLOCK CAPITALS
1. NAME AND ADDRESS OF APPLICANT
Surname ...............
Other name(s) in full ...............
...................
Present address ...................
...................
Daytime telephone number (if any) ...............
2. NAME AND ADDRESS OF CIVIL PARTNER

Surname ...............
Other name(s) in full ...............
....................
Present address ...............
....................
Daytime telephone number (if any) ...............

3. JURISDICTION Please indicate with a tick () in the appropriate box or boxes which of the following apply:

PART A

(i)     My civil partner and I are habitually resident in Scotland ☐
(ii)    My civil partner and I were last habitually resident in ☐
        Scotland, and one of us still resides there
(iii)   My civil partner is habitually resident in Scotland ☐
(iv)    I am habitually resident in Scotland having resided there ☐
        for at least a year immediately before this application
        was made
(v)     I am habitually resident in Scotland having resided there ☐
        for at least six months immediately before this applica-
        tion was made and am domiciled in Scotland

**If you have ticked one or more of the boxes in Part A, you should go direct to Part C. You should only complete Part B if you have not ticked any of the boxes in Part A**

PART B

(i)     I am domiciled in Scotland ☐
(ii)    My civil partner is domiciled in Scotland ☐
(iii)   No court has, or is recognised as having, jurisdiction ☐
        under regulations made under section 219 of the Civil
        Partnership Act 2004

PART C

(i)     I have lived at the address shown above for at least 40 ☐
        days immediately before the date I signed this applica-
        tion
(ii)    My civil partner has lived at the address shown above ☐
        for at least 40 days immediately before the date I signed
        this application
(iii)   I lived at the address shown above for a period of at ☐
        least 40 days ending not more than 40 days before the
        date I signed this application and have no known
        residence in Scotland at that date
(iv)    My civil partner lived at the address shown above for a ☐
        period of at least 40 days ending not more than 40 days
        before the date I signed this application and has no
        known residence in Scotland at that date

4. DETAILS OF PRESENT CIVIL PARTNERSHIP
Place of Registration of Civil Partnership...............(Registration District)
Date of Registration of Civil Partnership: Day..........month..........year..........
5. PERIOD OF SEPARATION

(i)     Please state the date on which you ceased to live with your civil partner. (If more than 1 year, just give the month and year)

Day..........Month..........Year..........

(ii)     Have you lived with your civil partner since that date?     *[YES/NO]

(iii)     If yes, for how long in total did you live together before finally separating again?

..........months

## 6. RECONCILIATION

Is there any reasonable prospect of reconciliation with your civil   *[YES/NO] partner?

Do you consider that the civil partnership has broken down ir-   *[YES/NO] retrievably?

## 7. CONSENT

Does your civil partner consent to a dissolution of the civil   *[YES/NO] be-
partnership granted?     ing

## 8. MENTAL DISORDER

Does your civil partner have any mental disorder (whether   *[YES/NO]
mental illness, personality disorder or learning disability)?

Is your civil partner suffering from any mental disorder     *[YES/NO]
(whether illness or handicap)?(If yes, give details)

## 9. CHILDREN

Are there any children of the family under the age of 16?     *[YES/NO]

## 10. Other Court Actions

Are you aware of any court actions currently proceeding in any   *[YES/NO]
country (including Scotland) which may affect your civil partnership?

(If yes, give details)

* Delete as appropriate

## 11. REQUEST FOR DISSOLUTION OF THE CIVIL PARTNERSHIP AND DISCLAIMER OF FINANCIAL PROVISION

I confirm that the facts stated in paragraphs 1–10 above apply to my civil partnership.

I do NOT ask the sheriff to make any financial provision in connection with this application.

I request the sheriff to grant decree of dissolution of my civil partnership.

Date ..........         Signature of Applicant ..............

## IMPORTANT

Part 1 MUST be completed, signed and dated before sending the application form to your civil partner.

Part 2

Notice to Consenting Civil Partner

*(Insert name and address of consenting civil partner)*

CONSENT TO APPLICATION FOR DISSOLUTION OF A CIVIL PARTNER-
SHIP (CIVIL PARTNERS HAVING LIVED APART FOR AT LEAST ONE
YEAR)

In Part 1 of the enclosed application form your civil partner is applying for dissolution of your civil partnership on the ground the civil partnership has broken
down irretrievably because you and he [or she] have lived apart for at least one year
and you consent to the dissolution being granted.

Such consent must be given formally in writing at Part 2 of the application form.
BEFORE completing that part, you are requested to read it over carefully so that
you understand the effect of consenting to the dissolution of the civil partnership.
Thereafter if you wish to consent—

(a) check the details given by the Applicant at Part 1 of the form to ensure that
they are correct to the best of your knowledge;

(b) complete Part 2 (Consent by Applicant's civil partner to dissolution) by
entering your name and address at the appropriate place and adding your
signature and the date; and

(c) return the whole application form to your civil partner at the address given
in Part 1.

Once your civil partner has completed the remainder of the form and has submitted
it to the court, a copy of the whole application (including your consent) will later be
served upon you formally by the sheriff clerk.

In the event of the dissolution of the civil partnership being granted, you will
automatically be sent a copy of the extract decree. (Should you change your address
before receiving the copy extract decree, please notify the sheriff clerk immediately.)

If you do NOT wish to consent please return the application form, with Part 2
uncompleted, to your civil partner and advise him or her of your decision.

The sheriff will NOT grant a dissolution of your civil partnership on this application if Part 2 of the form is not completed by you.

CONSENT BY APPLICANT'S CIVIL PARTNER TO DISSOLUTION OF
CIVIL PARTNERSHIP

NOTE: Before completing this part of the form, please read the notes opposite
(page 8)

I, ....................

*(Insert full name, in BLOCK letters, of Applicant's civil partner)*

residing at ....................

....................

....................

*(Insert address, also in BLOCK letters)*

HEREBY STATE THAT

(a) I have read Part 1 of this application;

(b) the Applicant has lived apart from me for a continuous period of one year
immediately preceding the date of the application (paragraph 11 of Part 1);

(c) I do not ask the sheriff to make any financial provision for me including—

(i) the payment by the Applicant of a periodical allowance (i.e. a regular
payment of money weekly or monthly, etc. for maintenance);

(ii) the payment by the Applicant of a capital sum (i.e. a lump sum
payment);

(d) I understand that dissolution of my civil partnership may result in the loss to
me of property rights; and

(e) I CONSENT TO DECREE OF DISSOLUTION BEING GRANTED IN
RESPECT OF THIS APPLICATION

381

Date .........        Signature ..............

NOTE: You may withdraw your consent, even after giving it, at any time before the dissolution of the civil partnership is granted by the sheriff. Should you wish to do so, please contact the sheriff clerk immediately.

Part 3

APPLICANT'S AFFIDAVIT

To be completed by the Applicant only after Parts 1 and 2 have been signed and dated.

I, (*Insert Applicant's full name*) ...................

residing at (*insert Applicant's present home address*) ..............

...................

...................

SWEAR that to the best of my knowledge and belief:

(1)    the facts stated in Part 1 of this Application are true; and

(2)    the signature in Part 2 of this Application is that of my civil partner.

Signature of Applicant ....................

                        SWORN at (*insert place*) ..............

To be com-  this..........day of..........20..........
pleted by Jus-
tice of the
Peace,
Notary Public   before me (*insert full name*) ..............
or Commis-
sioner for
Oaths         (*insert full address*) ...................

                 ...................

                 ...................

                 Signature ...................

                 *Justice of the Peace/ Notary Public/Commissioner for Oaths

                 * Delete as appropriate

**Rule 33A.67(2)**

[1] [2]**FORM CP30**

Form of simplified dissolution of civil partnership application under section 117(3)(d) of the Civil Partnership Act 2004

Sheriff Clerk

Sheriff Court House

..............

..............

(Telephone)..............

APPLICATION FOR DISSOLUTION OF A CIVIL PARTNERSHIP (CIVIL PARTNERS HAVING LIVED APART FOR AT LEAST TWO YEARS)

---

[1] Inserted by Act of Sederunt (Ordinary Cause Rules) Amendment (Civil Partnership Act 2004) 2005 (SSI 2005/638), para.3 (effective December 8, 2005).

[2] As amended by Act of Sederunt (Ordinary Cause Rules) Amendment (Family Law (Scotland) Act 2006 etc.) 2006, para.2 (SSI 2006/207) (effective May 4, 2006).

Before completing this form, you should have read the leaflet entitled "Do it yourself Dissolution", which explains the circumstances in which a dissolution of a civil partnership may be sought by this method. If the simplified procedure appears to suit your circumstances, you may use this form to apply for dissolution of your civil partnership. Below you will find directions designed to assist you with your application. Please follow them carefully. In the event of difficulty, you may contact any sheriff clerk's office or Citizen Advice Bureau.

**Directions for making application**

WRITE IN INK, USING BLOCK CAPITALS

| | |
|---|---|
| Application (Part 1) | 1. Complete and sign Part 1 of the form (pages 3–7), paying particular attention to the notes opposite each section. |
| Affidavits (Part 2) | 2. When you have completed Part 1, you should take the form to a Justice of the Peace, Notary Public, Commissioner for Oaths or other duly authorised person so that your affidavit at Part 2 (page 8) may be completed and sworn. |
| Returning completed application form to court | 3. When directions 1–2 above have been complied with, your application now ready to be sent to the sheriff clerk at the above address. With it you must enclose: |

(i) an extract of the registration of your civil partnership in the civil partnership register (the document headed "Extract of an entry in the Register of Civil Partnerships", which will be returned to you in due course), or an equivalent document. Check the notes on page 2 to see if you need to obtain a letter from the General Register Office stating that there is no record of your civil partner having dissolved the civil partnership, and

(ii) either a cheque or postal order in respect of the court fee, crossed and made payable to "the Scottish Court Service",

or a completed fee exemption form.

4. Receipt of your application will be promptly acknowledged. Should you wish to withdraw the application for any reason, please contact the sheriff clerk immediately.

PART 1

WRITE IN INK, USING BLOCK CAPITALS

1. NAME AND ADDRESS OF APPLICANT

Surname ...............

Other name(s) in full...............

....................

Present address...............

....................

Daytime telephone number (if any)...............

2. NAME OF CIVIL PARTNER

Surname ...............

Other name(s) in full ...............

3. ADDRESS OF CIVIL PARTNER (If the address of your civil partner is not known, please enter "not known" in this paragraph and proceed to paragraph 4)

Present address ...............

....................

....................

Daytime telephone number (if any) ...............

4. Only complete this paragraph if you do not know the present address of your civil partner

NEXT-OF-KIN Name...............

Address ...................

....................

....................

Relationship to your civil partner ...............

CHILDREN OF THE FAMILY

| **Names and dates of birth** | **Addresses** |
| --- | --- |
| ............... | ............... |
| | ............... |
| ............... | ............... |
| | ............... |

If insufficient space is available to list all the children of the family, please continue on a separate sheet and attach to this form.

5. JURISDICTION

Please indicate with a tick () in the appropriate box or boxes which of the following apply:

PART A

(i)     My civil partner and I are habitually resident in Scotland  ☐

(ii)    My civil partner and I were last habitually resident in ☐
        Scotland, and one of us still resides there

(iii)   My civil partner is habitually resident in Scotland      ☐

(iv)    I am habitually resident in Scotland having resided there ☐
        for at least a year immediately before this application
        was made

(v)     I am habitually resident in Scotland having resided there ☐
        for at least six months immediately before this applica-
        tion was made and am domiciled in Scotland

**If you have ticked one or more of the boxes in Part A, you should go direct to Part C. You should only complete Part B if you have not ticked any of the boxes in Part A.**

PART B

(i)     I am domiciled in Scotland                               ☐

(ii)    My civil partner is domiciled in Scotland               ☐

(iii)   No court has, or is recognised as having, jurisdiction  ☐
        under regulations made under section 219 of the Civil
        Partnership Act 2004

PART C

(i)     I have lived at the address shown above for at least 40 ☐
        days immediately before the date I signed this applica-
        tion

(ii)    My civil partner has lived at the address shown above   ☐
        for at least 40 days immediately before the date I signed
        this application

(iii)   I lived at the address shown above for a period of at   ☐

384

least 40 days ending not more than 40 days before the date I signed this application and have no known residence in Scotland at that date

(iv)    My civil partner lived at the address shown above for a ☐ period of at least 40 days ending not more than 40 days before the date I signed this application and has no known residence in Scotland at that date

## 6. DETAILS OF PRESENT CIVIL PARTNERSHIP

Place of Registration of Civil Partnership...............(Registration District)

Date of Registration of Civil Partnership: Day.........month..........year..............

## 7. PERIOD OF SEPARATION

(i)    Please state the date on which you ceased to live with your civil partner. (If more than 2 years, just give the month and year)
Day..........Month..........Year..........

(ii)    Have you lived with your civil partner since that date?    *[YES/NO]

(iii)    If yes, for how long in total did you live together before finally separating again?

..........months

## 8. RECONCILIATION

Is there any reasonable prospect of reconciliation with your civil  *[YES/NO] partner?

Do you consider that the civil partnership has broken down ir-  *[YES/NO] retrievably?

## 9. MENTAL DISORDER

Does your civil partner have any mental disorder (whether  *[YES/NO] mental illness, personality disorder or learning disability)?
(If yes, give details)

## 10. CHILDREN

Are there any children of the family under the age of 16?    *[YES/NO]

## 11. OTHER COURT ACTIONS

Are you aware of any court actions currently proceeding in any  *[YES/NO] country (including Scotland) which may affect your civil partner-ship?

(If yes, give details)    * Delete as ap-propriate

## 12. DECLARATION AND REQUEST FOR DISSOLUTION OF THE CIVIL PARTNERSHIP

I confirm that the facts stated in paragraphs 1–11 above apply to my civil partnership.

I do NOT ask the sheriff to make any financial provision in connection with this application.

I request the sheriff to grant decree of dissolution of my civil partnership.

Date............... Signature of Applicant...............

PART 2

APPLICANT'S AFFIDAVIT

To be completed by the Applicant only after Part 1 has been signed and dated.

I, (*Insert Applicant's full name*) ....................

residing at (*insert Applicant's present home address*) ...............

....................

....................

SWEAR that to the best of my knowledge and belief the facts stated in Part 1 of this Application are true.

Signature of Applicant....................

SWORN at (*insert place*)....................

To be completed by Justice of the Peace,

this..........day of..........20 ..........

Notary Public or Commissioner for

before me (*insert full name*)...............

Oaths

(*insert full address*)...............

....................

....................

Signature....................

*Justice of the Peace/ Notary Public/Commissioner for Oaths

* Delete as appropriate

Rule 33A.67(3)

[1] [2]**FORM CP31**

Form of simplified dissolution of a civil partnership application on grounds under section 117(2)(b) of the Civil Partnership Act 2004

Sheriff Clerk

Sheriff Court House

....................

....................

(Telephone) ....................

APPLICATION FOR DISSOLUTION OF A CIVIL PARTNERSHIP (INTERIM GENDER RECOGNITION CERTIFICATE ISSUED TO ONE OF THE CIVIL PARTNERS AFTER REGISTRATION OF THE CIVIL PARTNERSHIP)

Before completing this form, you should have read the leaflet entitled "Do it yourself Dissolution", which explains the circumstances in which a dissolution of a civil partnership may be sought by this method. If the simplified procedure appears to suit your circumstances, you may use this form to apply for dissolution of your civil partnership. Below you will find directions designed to assist you with your application. Please follow them carefully. In the event of difficulty, you may contact any sheriff clerk's office or Citizen Advice Bureau.

**Directions for making application**

WRITE IN INK, USING BLOCK CAPITALS

---

[1] Inserted by Act of Sederunt (Ordinary Cause Rules) Amendment (Civil Partnership Act 2004) 2005 (SSI 2005/638), para.3 (effective December 8, 2005).

[2] As amended by Act of Sederunt (Ordinary Cause Rules) Amendment (Family Law (Scotland) Act 2006 etc.) 2006, para.2 (SSI 2006/207) (effective May 4, 2006).

Application
(Part 1)

1. Complete and sign Part 1 of the form (pages 3–7), paying particular attention to the notes opposite each section

Affidavits (Part 2)

2. When you have completed Part 1, you should take the form to a Justice of the Peace, Notary Public, Commissioner for Oaths or other duly authorised person so that your affidavit at Part 2 (page 8) may be completed and sworn.

Returning Completed Application form to court

3. When directions 1–2 above have been complied with, your application is now ready to be sent to the sheriff clerk at the above address. With it you must enclose: form to court

(i) an extract of the registration of your civil partnership in the civil partnership register (the document headed "Extract of an entry in the Register of Civil Partnerships", which will be returned to you in due course), or an equivalent document. Check the notes on page 2 to see if you need to obtain a letter from the General Register Office stating that there is no record of your civil partner having dissolved the civil partnership,

(ii) either a cheque or postal order in respect of the court fee, crossed and made payable to "the Scottish Court Service" or a completed fee exemption form, and

(iii) the interim gender recognition certificate or a copy sealed with the seal of the Gender Recognition Panels and certified to be a true copy by an officer authorised by the President of Gender Recognition Panels.

4. Receipt of your application will be promptly acknowledged. Should you wish to withdraw the application for any reason, please contact the sheriff clerk immediately.

## PART 1
### WRITE IN INK, USING BLOCK CAPITALS
1. NAME AND ADDRESS OF APPLICANT

Surname ....................

Other name(s) in full ....................

....................

Present address ....................

....................

Daytime telephone number (if any) ....................

2. NAME OF CIVIL PARTNER

Surname ....................

Other name(s) in full ....................

3. ADDRESS OF CIVIL PARTNER (If the address of your civil partner is not known, please enter "not known" in this paragraph and proceed to paragraph 4)

Present address ....................

....................

....................

Daytime telephone number (if any) ....................

4. Only complete this paragraph if you do not know the present address of your civil partner

NEXT-OF-KIN

Name ....................

Address ....................

....................
....................
Relationship to your civil partner ..........
CHILDREN OF THE FAMILY

Names and dates of birth                    Addresses

..........                                         ..........

                                               ..........

..........                                         ..........

                                               ..........

If insufficient space is available to list all the children of the family, please continue on a separate sheet and attach to this form.

5. JURISDICTION

Please indicate with a tick () in the appropriate box or boxes which of the following apply:

PART A

(i)      My civil partner and I are habitually resident in Scotland ☐

(ii)     My civil partner and I were last habitually resident in ☐ Scotland, and one of us still resides there

(iii)    My civil partner is habitually resident in Scotland ☐

(iv)    I am habitually resident in Scotland having resided there ☐ for at least a year immediately before this application was made

(v)     I am habitually resident in Scotland having resided there ☐ for at least six months immediately before this application was made and am domiciled in Scotland

If you have ticked one or more of the boxes in Part A, you should go direct to Part C. You should only complete Part B if you have not ticked any of the boxes in Part A

PART B

(i)      I am domiciled in Scotland ☐

(ii)     My civil partner is domiciled in Scotland ☐

(iii)    No court has, or is recognised as having, jurisdiction ☐ under regulations made under section 219 of the Civil Partnership Act 2004

PART C

(i)      I have lived at the address shown above for at least 40 ☐ days immediately before the date I signed this application

(ii)     My civil partner has lived at the address shown above ☐ for at least 40 days immediately before the date I signed this application

(iii)    I lived at the address shown above for a period of at ☐ least 40 days ending not more than 40 days before the date I signed this application and have no known residence in Scotland at that date

(iv)    My civil partner lived at the address shown above for a ☐ period of at least 40 days ending not more than 40 days before the date I signed this application and has no known residence in Scotland at that date

## 6. DETAILS OF PRESENT CIVIL PARTNERSHIP

Place of Registration of Civil Partnership ..............(Registration District)

Date of Registration of Civil Partnership: Day..........month..........year..........

## 7. DETAILS OF ISSUE OF INTERIM GENDER RECOGNITION CERTIFI-CATE

(i)    Please state whether the interim gender recognition certificate has been issued to you or your civil partner

(ii)    Please state the date the interim gender recognition certificate was issued Day..........Month...........Year..........

## 8. MENTAL DISORDER

Does your civil partner have any mental disorder (whether    *[YES/NO] mental illness, personality disorder or learning disability)?

(If yes, give details)

9. CHILDREN Are there any children of the family under the    *[YES/NO] age of 16?

## 10. OTHER COURT ACTIONS

Are you aware of any court actions currently proceeding in any    *[YES/NO] country (including Scotland) which may affect your civil partner-ship?

(If yes, give details)    * Delete as appropriate

## 11. DECLARATION AND REQUEST FOR DISSOLUTION OF THE CIVIL PARTNERSHIP

I confirm that the facts stated in paragraphs 1-10 above apply to my civil partnership.

I do NOT ask the sheriff to make any financial provision in connection with this application.

I request the sheriff to grant decree of dissolution of my civil partnership.

Date.......... Signature of Applicant................

### PART 2

APPLICANT'S AFFIDAVIT

To be completed by the Applicant only after Part 1 has been signed and dated.

I, (*Insert Applicant's full name*) ...............

residing at (*insert Applicant's present home address*) ..........

....................

....................

SWEAR that to the best of my knowledge and belief the facts stated in Part 1 of this Application are true.

Signature of Applicant    ...............

    SWORN at (*insert place*) ...............

To be completed by Jus-    this..........day of..........20 ..........
tice of the Peace,

SHERIFF COURTS (SCOTLAND) ACT 1907

Notary Public or Com- before me (*insert full name*) ...............
missioner for

Oaths                  (*insert full address*) ...............

.....................

.....................

Signature ...............

*Justice of the Peace/ Notary Public/Commissioner for Oaths

* Delete as appropriate

**Rule 33A.69(3)(a)**

<sup>1 2</sup>**FORM CP32**

Form of citation in application relying on facts in section 117(3)(c) of the Civil Partnership Act 2004

(*Insert name and address of non-applicant civil partner*)

APPLICATION FOR DISSOLUTION OF A CIVIL PARTNERSHIP (CIVIL PARTNERS HAVING LIVED APART FOR AT LEAST ONE YEAR WITH THE CONSENT OF THE OTHER CIVIL PARTNER)

Your civil partner has applied to the sheriff for dissolution of your civil partnership on the ground that the civil partnership has broken down irretrievably because you and he or she have lived apart for a period of at least one year and you consent to decree of dissolution being granted.

A copy of the application is hereby served upon you.

1. Please note that the sheriff may not make financial provision under this procedure and that your civil partner is making no claim for—

(a)   the payment by you of a periodical allowance (i.e. a regular payment of money weekly or monthly, etc. for maintenance);

(b)   the payment by you of a capital sum (i.e. a lump sum payment).

2. Dissolution of your civil partnership may result in the loss to you of property rights (e.g. the right to succeed to the Applicant's estate on his or her death) or the right, where appropriate, to a pension.

3. If you wish to oppose the granting of a decree of dissolution of your civil partnership, you should put your reasons in writing and send your letter to the address shown below. Your letter must reach the sheriff clerk before (*insert date*).

4. In the event of the decree of dissolution of your civil partnership being granted, you will be sent a copy of the extract decree. Should you change your address before receiving the copy extract decree, please notify the sheriff clerk immediately.

Signed

Sheriff clerk (depute)

(*insert address and telephone number of the sheriff clerk*)

[*or* Sheriff officer]

NOTE: If you wish to exercise your right to make a claim for financial provision you should immediately advise the sheriff clerk that you oppose the application for that reason, and thereafter consult a solicitor.

**Rule 33A.69(3)(b)**

---

<sup>1</sup> Inserted by Act of Sederunt (Ordinary Cause Rules) Amendment (Civil Partnership Act 2004) 2005 (SSI 2005/638), para.3 (effective December 8, 2005).

<sup>2</sup> As amended by Act of Sederunt (Ordinary Cause Rules) Amendment (Family Law (Scotland) Act 2006 etc.) 2006, para.2 (SSI 2006/207) (effective May 4, 2006).

¹ ²**FORM CP33**

Form of citation in application relying on facts in section 117(3)(d) of the Civil Partnership Act 2004

(*Insert name and address of non-applicant civil partner*)

APPLICATION FOR DISSOLUTION OF A CIVIL PARTNERSHIP (CIVIL PARTNERS HAVING LIVED APART FOR AT LEAST TWO YEARS)

Your civil partner has applied to the sheriff for dissolution of your civil partnership on the ground that the civil partnership has broken down irretrievably because you and he or she have lived apart for a period of at least two years.

A copy of the application is hereby served upon you.

1. Please note:

(a) that the sheriff may not make financial provision under this procedure and that your civil partner is making no claim for—

(i) the payment by you of a periodical allowance (i.e. a regular payment of money weekly or monthly, etc. for maintenance);

(ii) the payment by you of a capital sum (i.e. a lump sum payment);

(b) *[Omitted by Act of Sederunt (Ordinary Cause Rules) Amendment (Family Law (Scotland) Act 2006 etc.) 2006, para.2 (SSI 2006/207) (effective May 4, 2006).]*

2. Dissolution of your civil partnership may result in the loss to you of property rights (e.g. the right to succeed to the Applicant's estate on his or her death) or the right, where appropriate, to a pension.

3. If you wish to oppose the granting of a decree of dissolution of your civil partnership, you should put your reasons in writing and send your letter to the address shown below. Your letter must reach the sheriff clerk before (*insert date*).

4. In the event of the decree of dissolution of your civil partnership being granted, you will be sent a copy of the extract decree. Should you change your address before receiving the copy extract decree, please notify the sheriff clerk immediately.

Signed

Sheriff clerk (depute)

(*insert address and telephone number of the sheriff clerk*)

[*or* Sheriff officer]

NOTE: If you wish to exercise your right to make a claim for financial provision you should immediately advise the sheriff clerk that you oppose the application for that reason, and thereafter consult a solicitor.

**Rule 33A.69(3)(c)**

³FORM CP34

Form of citation in application on grounds under section 117(2)(b) of the Civil Partnership Act 2004

(*Insert name and address of non-applicant civil partner*)

APPLICATION FOR DISSOLUTION OF A CIVIL PARTNERSHIP (INTERIM GENDER RECOGNITION CERTIFICATE ISSUED TO ONE OF THE CIVIL PARTNERS AFTER THE REGISTRATION OF THE CIVIL PARTNERSHIP)

Your civil partner has applied to the sheriff for dissolution of your civil partnership on the ground that an interim gender recognition certificate has been issued to you or your civil partner after your civil partnership was registered.

A copy of the application is hereby served upon you.

---

¹ Inserted by Act of Sederunt (Ordinary Cause Rules) Amendment (Civil Partnership Act 2004) 2005 (SSI 2005/638), para.3 (effective December 8, 2005).

² As amended by Act of Sederunt (Ordinary Cause Rules) Amendment (Family Law (Scotland) Act 2006 etc.) 2006, para.2 (SSI 2006/207) (effective May 4, 2006).

³ Inserted by Act of Sederunt (Ordinary Cause Rules) Amendment (Civil Partnership Act 2004) 2005 (SSI 2005/638), para.3 (effective December 8, 2005).

1. Please note that the sheriff may not make financial provision under this procedure and that your civil partner is making no claim for—
   (a) the payment by you of a periodical allowance (i.e. a regular payment of money weekly or monthly, etc. for maintenance);
   (b) the payment by you of a capital sum (i.e. a lump sum payment).

2. Dissolution of your civil partnership may result in the loss to you of property rights (e.g. the right to succeed to the Applicant's estate on his or her death) or the right, where appropriate, to a pension.

3. If you wish to oppose the granting of a decree of dissolution of your civil partnership, you should put your reasons in writing and send your letter to the address shown below. Your letter must reach the sheriff clerk before (*insert date*).

4. In the event of the decree of dissolution of your civil partnership being granted, you will be sent a copy of the extract decree. Should you change your address before receiving the copy extract decree, please notify the sheriff clerk immediately.

Signed

Sheriff clerk (depute)

(*insert address and telephone number of the sheriff clerk*)

[*or* Sheriff officer]

NOTE: If you wish to exercise your right to make a claim for financial provision you should immediately advise the sheriff clerk that you oppose the application for that reason, and thereafter consult a solicitor.

Rule 33A.70(1)(a)

### [1]FORM CP35

Form of intimation of simplified dissolution of a civil partnership application for display on the walls of court

Court ref. no.

An application for dissolution of a civil partnership has been made in this sheriff court by [A.B.], (*insert designation and address*), Applicant, naming [C.D.], (*insert designation and address*) as Respondent.

If [C.D.] wishes to oppose the granting of decree of dissolution of the civil partnership he [*or* she] should immediately contact the sheriff clerk from whom he [*or* she] may obtain a copy of the application.

Date (*insert date*)

Signed

Sheriff clerk (depute)

Rule 33A.70(2)

### [2]FORM CP36

Form of intimation to children of the family and next-of-kin in a simplified dissolution of a civil partnership application

Court ref. no.

To (*insert name and address*)

You are hereby given NOTICE that an application for dissolution of a civil partnership has been made against (*insert name of respondent*) your (*insert relationship e.g. father, mother, brother or other relative as the case may be*). A copy of this application is attached.

If you know of his or her present address, you are requested to inform the sheriff clerk (*insert address of sheriff clerk*) in writing immediately. You may also, if you

---

[1] Inserted by Act of Sederunt (Ordinary Cause Rules) Amendment (Civil Partnership Act 2004) 2005 (SSI 2005/638), para.3 (effective December 8, 2005).
[2] Inserted by Act of Sederunt (Ordinary Cause Rules) Amendment (Civil Partnership Act 2004) 2005 (SSI 2005/638), para.3 (effective December 8, 2005).

wish, oppose the granting of the decree of dissolution by sending a letter to the court giving your reasons for your opposition to the application. Your letter must be sent to the sheriff clerk within 21 days of (*insert date on which intimation was given. N.B.* Rule 5.3(2) *relating to postal service or intimation*).

Date (*insert date*)

Signed

Sheriff clerk (depute)

**IF YOU ARE UNCERTAIN WHAT ACTION TO TAKE** you should consult a solicitor. You may be entitled to legal aid depending on your financial circumstances, and you can get information about legal aid from a solicitor. You may also obtain advice from any Citizens Advice Bureau or other advice agency.

Rule 33A.73(2)

### [1]FORM CP37

Form of extract decree of dissolution of a civil partnership in an application for a simplified dissolution of a civil partnership

At (*insert place and date*)

in an action in the Sheriff Court of the Sheriffdom of (*insert name of sheriffdom*) at (*insert place of sheriff court*)

at the instance of (*insert full name of applicant*), Applicant,

against (*insert full name of respondent*), Respondent,

whose civil partnership was registered at (*insert place*) on (*insert date*),

the sheriff pronounced decree dissolving the civil partnership of the Applicant and the Respondent.

Extracted at (*insert place and date*)

by me, sheriff clerk of the Sheriffdom of (*insert name of sheriffdom*).

Signed

Sheriff clerk (depute)

Form CP38[2]

Rule 33A.21(4)

Form of annex to interlocutor appointing a child welfare reporter

☐ Appointment of Child Welfare Reporter under rule 33A.21(1)(a).

Where this box is ticked the Child Welfare Reporter is required to seek the views of the child [or children] on the issue(s) specified in Part 1 below.

☐ Appointment of Child Welfare Reporter under rule 33A.21(1)(b).

Where this box is ticked the Child Welfare Reporter is required to carry out the enquiries specified in Part 2 below, and to address the issue(s) specified in Part 3 below.

PART 1

Issue(s) in respect of which views of the child [or children] are to be sought [*specify*]

---

[1] Inserted by Act of Sederunt (Ordinary Cause Rules) Amendment (Civil Partnership Act 2004) 2005 (SSI 2005/638), para.3 (effective December 8, 2005).

[2] As inserted by the Act of Sederunt (Rules of the Court of Session 1994 and Sheriff Court Rules Amendment) (Miscellaneous) 2016 (SSI 2016/102) para.3 (effective 21 March 2016).

[empty bordered box]

**PART 2**

Enquiries to be undertaken—

- ☐ Seek views of child
- ☐ Visit home of *[specify]*
- ☐ Visit nursery / school / child minder / other *[specify]*
- ☐ Interview mother / father
- ☐ Interview other family members *[specify]*
- ☐ Interview child minder / nanny
- ☐ Interview teacher / head teacher
- ☐ Interview child's health visitor / GP / other health professional *[specify]*
- ☐ Interview a party's GP / other health professional *[specify]*
- ☐ Interview social worker *[specify]*
- ☐ Interview domestic abuse case worker *[specify]*
- ☐ Interview other persons *[specify]*
- ☐ Obtain criminal conviction certificate under section 112 of the Police Act 1997 in respect of *[specify party]*
- ☐ Observe contact *[specify]*
- ☐ Observe child in home environment pre/post contact *[specify]*
- ☐ Obtain record of parties' attendance from contact centre
- ☐ Other *[specify]*

**PART 3**

Issues to be addressed in report *[specify]*

[empty bordered box]

Rule 34.1(2)

### [1]FORM H1

Form of notice informing defender of right to apply for certain orders under the Debtors (Scotland) Act 1987 on sequestration for rent

---

[1] Revoked by the Act of Sederunt (Sheriff Court Rules Amendment) (Diligence) 2008 (SSI 2008/121) r.2(1)(a) (effective April 1, 2008).

Rule 34.6(1)

## FORM H2
### Form of notice of removal

To (*insert name, designation, and address of party in possession*). You are required to remove from (*describe subjects*) at the term of (*or if different terms, state them and the subjects to which they apply*), in terms of lease (*describe it*) [or in terms of your letter of removal dated (*insert date*)] [or otherwise as the case may be].

Date (*insert date*)         Signed

(*add designation and address*)

Rule 34.6(2)

## FORM H3
### Form of letter of removal

To (*insert name and designation of addressee*)

(*Insert place and date*) I am to remove from (*state subjects by usual name or short description sufficient for identification*) at the term of (*insert term and date*)

          [K.L.] (*add designation and address*).

(*If not holograph, to be attested thus—*

        [M.N.] (*add designation and address*), witness.)

Rule 34.7

## FORM H4
Form of notice of removal under section 37 of the 1907 Act

NOTICE OF REMOVAL UNDER SECTION 37 OF THE SHERIFF COURTS (SCOTLAND) ACT 1907

To (*insert designation and address*).

You are required to remove from (*insert description of heritable subjects, land, ground, etc.*) at the term of [Whitsunday or Martinmas], (*insert date*)

Date (*insert date*)         Signed

(*add designation and address*)

## [1]FORM H5

Rule 34.11(4)

Form of citation of unnamed occupiers

CITATION

SHERIFFDOM OF (*insert name of sheriffdom*)

AT (*insert place of sheriff court*)

[A.B.] (*insert designation and address*)

Pursuer

against

The Occupier[s] of (*address*)

Defender

An action has been brought in the above Sheriff Court by [A.B.]. [A.B.] calls as a defender the occupier[s] of the property at (*insert address*). If the occupier[s] [or any of them] wish[es] to challenge the jurisdiction of the court or to defend the action, he [or she [or it] [or they]] should contact the sheriff clerk at (*insert address of sheriff court*) immediately and in any event by (*date on which period of notice expires*).

        Signed

---

[1] Inserted by SSI 2000/239 (effective October 2, 2000).

Sheriff [or Sheriff Clerk]

## FORM M1

Rule 35.5

Form of warrant of citation in an action of multiplepoinding

(*Insert place and date*) Grants warrant to cite the defender (*insert name and address*) by serving a copy of the writ and warrant upon a period of notice of (*insert period of notice*) days, and ordains him [*or* her], if he [*or* she] intends to lodge:—

(a) defences challenging the jurisdiction of the court or the competence of the action; or

(b) objections to the condescendence on the fund *in medio*; or

(c) a claim on the fund;

to lodge a notice of appearance with the sheriff clerk at (*insert name and address of sheriff court*) within the said period of notice after such service [and grants warrant to arrest on the dependence].

[*Where the holder of the fund in medio is a defender, insert:* Appoints the holder of the fund in medio to

(a) lodge with the sheriff clerk at (*insert place of sheriff court*) within the said period of notice after such service

(i)   a detailed condescendence on the fund in medio; and

(ii)   a list of parties having an interest in the fund; and

(b) intimate to all parties to the action a copy of the condescendence and list.]

## FORM M2

Rule 35.6(1)

Form of citation in an action of multiplepoinding

Citation

SHERIFFDOM OF (*insert name of sheriffdom*) ............... Court ref. no. ..........

AT (*insert place of sheriff court*) ...............

[A.B.]. (*insert designation and address*). Pursuer, against [C.D.], (*insert designation and address*). Defender.

(*Insert place and date*) You [C.D.] arc hereby served with this copy writ and warrant, together with Form M4 (notice of appearance).

[*Where the defender is the holder of the fund in medio. insert the following paragraph*:— As holder of the fund in medio you must lodge with the sheriff clerk at the above address within (*insert period of notice*) days of (insert date on which service was executed. N. B. Rule 5.3(2) relating to postal service)—

(a) a detailed condescendence on the fund in medio: and

(b) a list of parties having an interest in the fund.

You must at the same time intimate to all other parties to the action a copy of

(a) the detailed condescendence on the fund; and

(b) the list of parties having an interest in the fund.]

---

**Form M4** is served on you for use should you wish to intimate that you intend to lodge:—

(a) defences challenging the jurisdiction of the court or the competence of the action; or

(b) objections to the condescendence on the fund in medio: or

(c) a claim on the fund.

**IF YOU WISH TO APPEAR IN THIS ACTION** you should consult a solicitor with a view to lodgng a notice of appearnce (Form M4). The notice of appearance, together with the court fee of £(*insert amount*) must be lodged with the sheriff clerk at the above address within (*insert the appropriat period of notice*) days of

---

> (*insert the date on which service was executed. N. B.* Rule 5.3(2) **relating to postal service**).

**IF YOU ARE UNCERTAIN WHAT ACTION TO TAKE** you should consult a solicitor. You may be eligible for legal aid depending on your income. You can get information about legal aid from a solicitor. You may also obtain advice from any Citizens Advice Bureau or other advice agency.

**PLEASE NOTE THAT IF YOU DO NOTHING IN ANSWER TO THIS DOCUMENT** the court may regard you as having no interest in the fund in medio and will proceed accordingly.

Signed

[P.O.], Sheriff officer,

*or* [X.Y.] (*add designation and business address*)

Solicitor for the pursuer

## FORM M3

Rule 35.6(2)

Form of certificate of citation in an action of multiplepoinding

Certificate of Citation

(*Insert place and date*) I,.......... hereby certify that upon the..........day of..........

I duly cited [C.D.]. Defender, to answer to the foregoing writ. This I did by (*state method of service; if by officer and not by post, add:* in presence of [L.M.], (*insert designation*), witness hereto with me subscribing *and where service is executed by post state whether made by registered post of the first class recorded delivery service*):

Signed

[P.O.]. Sheriff officer [L.M.], witness

*or* [X.Y.] (*add designation and business address*)

Solicitor for the pursuer

## FORM M4

Rules 35.6(1) and 35.8

Form of notice of appearance in an action of multiplepoinding

NOTICE OF APPEARANCE (MULTIPLEPOINDING)

*PART A Court Ref. No.

(Insert name and business address of solicitor for the pursuer)

In an action raised at Sheriff Court

Pursuer

Solicitor for the pursuer

Defender

*(This part to be completed by the pursuer before service)

DATE OF SERVICE: DATE OF EXPIRY OF PERIOD OF NOTICE:

....................

*PART B

* **(This section to be completed by the defender or the defender's solicitor and both parts of this form returned to the sheriff clerk at (insert address of sheriff clerk) on or before the expiry of the period of notice referred to in PART A above)**

(*Insert place and date*)

[C.D.] (design), Defender, intends to lodge:

<table>
<tr><td></td><td>☐</td><td>defences challenging the jurisdiction of the court or the competence of the action.</td></tr>
<tr><td>Tick the appropriate box(es)</td><td>☐</td><td>objections to the condescendence on the fund *in medio*</td></tr>
<tr><td></td><td>☐</td><td>a claim on the fund *in medio*.</td></tr>
</table>

Signed

[C.D.] Defender,

*or* [X.Y.] (*add designation and business address*)

Solicitor for the defender

## FORM M5

Rules 35.9(b) and 35.10(5)

Form of intimation of first hearing in an action of multiplepoinding

SHERIFFDOM OF (*insert name of sheriffdom*)............... Court ref. no. ..........

AT (*insert place of sheriff court*)

[A.B.] (*insert designation and address*). Pursuer, against [C.D.] (*insert designation and address*), Defender.

You are given notice that in this action of multiplepoinding

| |
|---|
| *Insert date, time and place)* |

is the date, time and place for the first hearing.

Date (*Insert date*)

Signed

Sheriff clerk (dispute)

**Note**

If the pursuer fails to return the writ in terms of rule 9.3 of the Ordinary Cause Rules of the Sheriff Court or any party fails to comply with the terms of this notice or to provide the sheriff at the hearing with sufficient information to enable it to be conducted it in terms of rule 35.10 of these rules, the sheriff may make such order or finding against that party so failing as he thinks fit.

NOTE TO BE ADDED WHERE PARTY UNREPRESENTED

**Note**

**IF YOU ARE UNCERTAIN WHAT ACTION TO TAKE** you should consult a solicitor. You may be eligible for legal aid depending on your income. You can get information about legal aid from a solicitor. You may also obtain advice from any Citizens Advice Bureau or other advice agency.

## FORM M6

Rule 35.10(4)(b)

Form of citation of person having an interest in the fund in an action of multiplepoinding

CITATION

SHERIFFDOM OF (*insert name of sheriffdom*)...............Court ref. no. AT (*insert place of sheriff court*)

[A.B.], (*insert designation and address*), Pursuer, against [C.D.], (*insert designation and address*), Defender.

(*Insert place and date*) In the above action the court has been advised that you (*insert name and address*) have an interest in (*insert details of the fund in medio*). You are hereby served with a copy of the pleadings in this action, together with Form M4 (notice of appearance).

Form M4 is served on you for use should you wish to intimate that you intend to lodge:

(a) defences challenging the jurisdiction of the court or the competence of the action; or

(b) objections to the condescendence on the fund *in medio*; or

(c) a claim on the fund.

**IF YOU WISH TO APPEAR IN THIS ACTION** you should consult a solicitor with a view to lodging a notice of appearance (Form M4). The notice of appearance, together with the court fee of £ (insert amount) must be lodged with the sheriff clerk at the above address within.......... days of (*insert date on which service was executed N.B.* Rule 5.3(2) *relating to postal service*).

NOTE:

**IF YOU ARE UNCERTAIN WHAT ACTION TO TAKE** you should consult a solicitor. You may be eligible for legal aid depending on your income. You can get information about legal aid from a solicitor. You may also obtain advice from any Citizens Advice Bureau or other advice agency.

*PLEASE NOTE THAT IF YOU DO NOTHING IN ANSWER TO THIS DOCU-MENT* the court may regard you as having no interest in the fund *in medio* and will proceed accordingly.

Signed

[P.Q.], Sheriff officer,

*or* [X.Y.] (*add designation and business address*)

**FORM PI1**[1]

**Form of initial writ in a personal injuries action**

Rules 3.1(1) and 36.B1(1)

INITIAL WRIT

(Personal Injuries Action)

SHERIFFDOM OF (*insert name of sheriffdom*)

AT (*insert place of sheriff court; if appropriate, state that the action is for determination in the all-Scotland sheriff court at Edinburgh*)

[A.B.] (*design and state any special capacity in which pursuer is suing*), Pursuer

against

[C.D.] (*design and state any special capacity in which defender is being sued*), Defender

The pursuer craves the court to grant decree—

(a) for payment by the defender to the pursuer of the sum of (*amount of sum in words and figures*);

(b) (*enter only if a claim for provisional damages is sought in terms of* rule 36.12) for payment by the defender to the pursuer of (*enter amount in words and figures*) of provisional damages; and

(c) for the expenses of the action.

STATEMENT OF CLAIM

1. The pursuer is (*state designation, address, National Insurance Number (where applicable), occupation and date of birth of pursuer*). (*In an action*

---

[1] As substituted by the Act of Sederunt (Rules of the Court of Session 1994 and Sheriff Court Rules Amendment) (No.2) (Personal Injury and Remits) 2015 (SSI 2015/227) para.8 (effective September 22, 2015).

*arising out of the death of a relative state designation of the deceased and relation to the pursuer).*

2. The defender is (*state designation, address and occupation of the defender*).
3. The court has jurisdiction to hear this claim against the defender because (*state briefly ground of jurisdiction; if the action is raised in the all-Scotland sheriff court, state whether the action is for determination in the exercise of the sheriff's all-Scotland jurisdiction or the sheriff's local jurisdiction*).
4. (*State briefly the facts necessary to establish the claim*).
5. (*State briefly the personal injuries suffered and the heads of claim. Give names and addresses of medical practitioners and hospitals or other institutions in which the person injured received treatment*).
6. (*State whether claim based on fault at common law or breach of statutory duty. If breach of statutory duty, state provision of enactment*).

(*Signed*)

[A.B.], Pursuer

or [X.Y.], Solicitor for the pursuer (*insert designation and business address*)

¹**FORM PI2**

Rule 36.B1

Form of order of court for recovery of documents in personal injuries action

Court ref. no.

SHERIFFDOM OF (*insert name of sheriffdom*)

AT (*insert place of sheriff court*)

SPECIFICATION OF DOCUMENTS

*in the cause*

[A.B.] (*designation and address*), Pursuer against

[C.D.] (*designation and address*), Defender

Date: (*date of posting or other method of service*)

To: (*name and address of party or parties from whom the following documents are sought to be recovered*)

You are hereby required to produce to the agent for the pursuer within seven days of the service on you of this Order:

[*Insert such of the following calls as are required*].

1. All books, medical records, reports, charts, X-rays, notes and other documents of (*specify the name of each medical practitioner or general practitioner practice named in initial writ in accordance with* rule 36.B1 (1)(b)), and relating to the pursuer [*or, as the case may be, the deceased*] from (*insert date*), in order that excerpts may be taken therefrom at the sight of the Commissioner of all entries showing or tending to show the nature, extent and cause of the pursuer's [*or, as the case may be, the deceased's*] injuries when he attended his doctor on or after (*specify date*) and the treatment received by him since that date.

2. All books, medical records, reports, charts, X-rays, notes and other documents of (*specify, in separate calls, the name of each hospital or other institution named in initial writ in accordance with* rule 36.B1 (1)(b)), and relating to the pursuer [*or, as the case may be, the deceased*] from (*insert date*), in order that excerpts may be taken therefrom at the sight of the Commissioner of all entries showing or tending to show the nature, extent and cause of the pursuer's [*or, as the case may be, the deceased's*] injuries when

---

¹ As inserted by the Act of Sederunt (Ordinary Cause Rules Amendment) (Personal Injuries Actions) 2009 (SSI 2009/285) r.2 (effective November 2, 2009).

he was admitted to that institution on or about (*specify date*), the treatment received by him since that date and his certificate of discharge, if any.

3. The medical records and capability assessments held by the defender's occupational health department relating to the pursuer [*or, as the case may be, the deceased*], except insofar as prepared for or in contemplation of litigation, in order that excerpts may be taken therefrom at the sight of the Commissioner of all entries showing or tending to show the nature and extent of any injuries, symptoms and conditions from which the pursuer [*or, as the case may he, the deceased*] was suffering and the nature of any assessment and diagnosis made thereof on or subsequent to (*specify date*).

4. All wage books, cash books, wage sheets, computer records and other earnings information relating to the pursuer [*or, as the case may he, the deceased*] (N.I. number (*specify number*)) held by or on behalf of (*specify employer*), for the period (*specify dates commencing not earlier than 26 weeks prior to the date of the accident or the first date of relevant absence, as the case may be*) in order that excerpts may be taken therefrom at the sight of the Commissioner of all entries showing or tending to show—

   (a) the pursuer's [*or, as the case may be, the deceased's*] earnings, both gross and net of income tax and employee National Insurance Contributions, over the said period;

   (b) the period or periods of the pursuer's [*or, as the case may be, the deceased's*] absence from employment over the said period and the reason for absence;

   (c) details of any increases in the rate paid over the period (*specify dates*) and the dates on which any such increases took effect;

   (d) the effective date of, the reasons for and the terms (including any terms relative to any pension entitlement) of the termination of the pursuer's [*or, as the case may be, the deceased's*] employment;

   (e) the nature and extent of contributions (if any) to any occupational pension scheme made by the pursuer [*or, as the case may be, the deceased*] and his employer;

   (f) the pursuer's present entitlement (if any) to any occupational pension and the manner in which said entitlement is calculated.

5. All accident reports, memoranda or other written communications made to the defender or anyone on his behalf by an employee of the defender who was present at or about the time at which the pursuer [*or, as the case may be, the deceased*] sustained the injuries in respect of which the initial writ in this cause was issued and relevant to the matters contained in the statement of claim.

6. Any assessment current at the time of the accident referred to in the initial writ or at the time of the circumstances referred to in the initial writ giving rise to the cause of action (as the case may be) undertaken by or on behalf of the defender for the purpose of regulation 3 of the Management of Health and Safety at Work Regulations 1992 and subsequently regulation 3 of the Management of Health and Safety at Work Regulations 1999 [*or (specify the regulations or other legislative provision under which the risk assessment is required)*] in order that excerpts may be taken therefrom at the sight of the Commissioner of all entries relating to the risks posed to workers [*or (specify the matters set out in the statement of claim to which the risk assessment relates)*].

7. Failing principals, drafts, copies or duplicates of the above or any of them.

(Signature, name and business address of the agent for the pursuer)

*NOTES:*

1.  The documents recovered will be considered by the parties to the action and they may or may not be lodged in the court process. A written receipt will be given or sent to you by the pursuer, who may thereafter allow them to be inspected by the other parties. The party in whose possession the documents are will be responsible for their safekeeping.

2.  Payment may be made, within certain limits, in respect of claims for outlays incurred in relation to the production of documents. Claims should be made in writing to the person who has obtained an order that you produce the documents.

3.  If you claim that any of the documents produced by you is **confidential** you must still produce such documents but may place them in a separate sealed packet by themselves, marked "CONFIDENTIAL". In that event they must be delivered or sent by post to the sheriff clerk. Any party who wishes to open the sealed packet must apply to the sheriff by motion. A party who makes such an application must intimate the motion to you.

4.  Subject to paragraph 3 above, you may produce these documents by sending them by registered post or by the first class recorded delivery service or registered postal packet, or by hand to (*name and address of the agent for the pursuer*).

### CERTIFICATE

(*Date*)

I hereby certify with reference to the above order in the cause (*cause reference number*) and the enclosed specification of documents, served on me and marked respectively X and Y—

1.  That the documents which are produced and which are listed in the enclosed inventory signed by me and marked Z, are all the documents in my possession falling within the specification. OR That I have no documents in my possession falling within the specification.

2.  That, to the best of my knowledge and belief, there are in existence other documents falling within the specification, but not in my possession. These documents are as follows: (*describe them by reference to the descriptions of documents in the specification*). They were last seen by me on or about (*date*), at (*place*), in the hands of (*name and address of the person*). OR That I know of the existence of no documents in the possession of any person, other than me, which fall within the specification.

(*Signed*)

(*Name and address*)

### ¹FORM PI3

Rule 36.D1

Form of docquet for deemed grant of recovery of documents in a personal injuries action

Court (*insert court*)

Date (*insert date*)

Commission and diligence for the production and recovery of the documents called for in this specification of documents is deemed to have been granted.

(*Signed*)

---

¹ As inserted by the Act of Sederunt (Ordinary Cause Rules Amendment) (Personal Injuries Actions) 2009 (SSI 2009/285) r.2 (effective November 2, 2009).

Sheriff Clerk (depute)

# FORM PI4[1]

**Form of interlocutor appointing the cause to the procedure in** Chapter 36A

Rule 36.C1

(To be inserted on the first page of the initial writ, above the crave(s)

**Appointment of cause to** Chapter 36A

The sheriff, having considered the application of the pursuer [, having heard parties [or parties's solicitors] thereon], and being satisfied, considering the likely complexity of the action, that the efficient determination of the action would be served by doing so, appoints the cause to the procedure in Chapter 36A.

(*Signed*)

Sheriff

(*date*)

## [2] [3]FORM PI5

**Rule 36.G1**

Form of timetable

TIMETABLE

Court ref. no.

In the cause [A.B.], Pursuer

Against

[C.D.], Defender

This timetable has effect as if it were an interlocutor of the sheriff

1. The diet allocated for the proof in this action will begin on (*date*). Subject to any variation under rule 36.H1, this order requires the parties to undertake the conduct of this action within the periods specified in paragraphs 2 to 9 below.
2. Any motion under rule 20.1 (third party notice) shall be made by (*date*).
3. Where the pursuer has obtained a commission and diligence for the recovery of documents by virtue of rule 36.D1, the pursuer shall serve an order under rule 28.3 not later than (*date*).
4. The pursuer shall lodge a statement of valuation of claim under rule 36.J1 not later than (*date*).
5. For the purposes of rule 36.G1, the adjustment period shall end on (*date*).
6. The pursuer shall lodge a record not later than (*date*).
7. The defender and any third party convened in the action shall lodge a statement of valuation of claim under rule 36.J1 not later than (*date*).
8. Not later than (*date*) parties shall lodge lists of witnesses and productions.
9. Not later than (*date*) the pursuer shall lodge a pre-proof minute under rule 36.K1.

### [4]FORM PI6

Rule 36.J1

Form of statement of valuation of claim

---

[1] As substituted by the Act of Sederunt (Rules of the Court of Session 1994 and Sheriff Court Rules Amendment) (No.2) (Personal Injury and Remits) 2015 (SSI 2015/227) para.8 (effective September 22, 2015).

[2] As inserted by the Act of Sederunt (Ordinary Cause Rules Amendment) (Personal Injuries Actions) 2009 (SSI 2009/285) r.2 (effective November 2, 2009).

[3] As amended by the Act of Sederunt (Rules of the Court of Session 1994 and Sheriff Court Rules Amendment) (No.2) (Personal Injury and Remits) 2015 (SSI 2015/227) para.8 (effective September 22, 2015).

[4] As inserted by the Act of Sederunt (Ordinary Cause Rules Amendment) (Personal Injuries Actions) 2009 (SSI 2009/285) r.2 (effective November 2, 2009).

| Head of claim | Components | Valuation |
|---|---|---|
| Solatium | Past | £x |
| | Future | £x |
| Interest on past solatium | Percentage applied to past solatium (state percentage rate) | £x |
| Past wage loss | Date from which wage loss claimed: (date) | £x |
| | Date to which wage loss claimed: (date) | |
| | Rate of net wage loss (per week, per month or per annum) | |
| Interest on past wage loss | Percentage applied to pas wage loss: (state percentage rate) | £x |
| Future wage loss | Multiplier: (state multiplier) | £x |
| | Multiplicand: (state multiplicand and show how calculated) | |
| | Discount factor applied (if appropriate): (state factor) | |
| | Or specify any other method of calculation | |
| Past services | Date from which services claimed: (date) | £x |
| | Date to which services claimed: (date) | |
| | Nature of services:(..........) | |
| | Person by whom services provided: (..........) | |
| | Hours per week services provided: (..........) | |
| | Net hourly rate claimed: (..........) | |
| | Total amount claimed: (..........) | |
| | Interest | |
| Future loss of capacity to provide personal service | Multiplier: (insert multiplier) | £x |
| | Multiplicand: (insert multiplicand, showing how calculated) | |

| Head of claim | Components | Valuation |
|---|---|---|
| Needs and other expenses | One off | £x |
| | Multiplier: (insert multiplier) | |
| | Multiplicand: (insert multiplicand) | |
| | Interest | |
| Any other heads as appropriate (specify) | | |

**FORM PI7**[1]
### Form of minute of pre-trial meeting
Rules 36.K1 and 36A.10(3)

SHERIFFDOM OF (*insert sheriffdom*) AT (*insert place*)
JOINT MINUTE OF PRE-TRIAL MEETING
in the cause
[A.B.], Pursuer
against
[C.D.], Defender

[E.F] for the pursuer and [G.H.] for the defender hereby state to the court:

1. That the pre-trial meeting was held in this case at (*place*) [*or* by video conference] on (*date*).
2. That the following persons were present— (*state names and designations of persons attending meeting*)
3. That the following persons were available to provide instructions by telephone— (*state names and designations of persons available to provide instructions by telephone*)
4. That the persons participating in the meeting discussed settlement of the action.
5. That the following questions were addressed—

**Section 1**

| | | Yes | No |
|---|---|---|---|
| 1. | Is the diet of proof or trial still required? | | |
| 2. | If the answer to question 1 is "yes", does the defender admit liability? (If "no", complete section 2) If yes, does the defender plead contributory negligence? If yes, is the degree of contributory negligence agreed? If yes, state % degree of fault attributed to the pursuer. | | |

---

[1] As substituted by the Act of Sederunt (Rules of the Court of Session 1994 and Sheriff Court Rules Amendment) (No.2) (Personal Injury and Remits) 2015 (SSI 2015/227) para.8 (effective September 22, 2015).

| | | Yes | No |
|---|---|---|---|
| 3. | If the answer to question 1 is "yes", is the quantum of damages agreed? (If "no", complete section 3). | | |

## Section 2
*(To be inserted only if the proof or trial is still required)*

It is estimated that the hearing will last *(insert number of days)*.

N.B. *If the estimate differs from the number of days previously allocated for the proof or trial then this should be brought to the attention of the sheriff clerk. This may affect prioritisation of the case.*

During the course of the pre-trial meeting, the pursuer called on the defender to agree certain facts, questions of law and matters of evidence.

Those calls, and the defender's responses, are as follows—

| Call | Response | |
|---|---|---|
| | Admitted | Denied |
| 1. | | |
| 2. | | |
| 3. | | |
| 4. | | |

During the course of the pre-trial meeting, the defender called on the pursuer to agree certain facts, questions of law and matters of evidence.

Those calls, and the pursuer's responses, are as follows—

| Call | Response | |
|---|---|---|
| | Admitted | Denied |
| 1. | | |
| 2. | | |
| 3. | | |
| 4. | | |

## Section 3
Quantum of damages

Please indicate where agreement has been reached on an element of damages.

| Head of claim | Components | Not agreed | Agreed at |
|---|---|---|---|
| Solatium | Past | | |
| | Future | | |
| Interest on past solatium | Percentage applied to past solatium (state percentage) | | |
| Past wage loss | Date from which wage loss claimed | | |
| | Date to which wage loss claimed | | |
| | Rate of net wage loss (per week, per month or per annum) | | |

| Head of claim | Components | Not agreed | Agreed at |
|---|---|---|---|
| Interest on past wage loss | | | |
| Future wage loss | Multiplier | | |
| | Multiplicand (showing how calculated) | | |
| Past necessary services | Date from which services claimed | | |
| | Date to which services claimed | | |
| | Hour per week services provided | | |
| | Net hourly rate claimed | | |
| Past personal services | Date from which services claimed | | |
| | Date to which services claimed | | |
| | Hour per week services provided | | |
| | Net hourly rate claimed | | |
| Interest on past services | | | |
| Future necessary services | Multiplier | | |
| | Multiplicand (showing how calculated) | | |
| Future personal services | Multiplier | | |
| | Multiplicand (showing how calculated) | | |
| Needs and other expenses | One off | | |
| | Multiplier | | |
| | Multiplicand (showing how calculated) | | |
| Any other heads as appropriate (*specify*) | | | |

*(Signed by each party/his or her solicitor)*

**FORM PI8**[1]

**Form of oath for jurors**

Rule 36B.7(1)

The jurors are to raise their right hands and the sheriff clerk will ask them—

"Do you swear by Almighty God that you will well and truly try the issue and give a true verdict according to the evidence?"

---

[1] As inserted by the Act of Sederunt (Rules of the Court of Session 1994 and Sheriff Court Rules Amendment) (No.2) (Personal Injury and Remits) 2015 (SSI 2015/227) para.8 (effective September 22, 2015).

The jurors must reply:

"I do".

## FORM PI9[1]
### Form of affirmation for jurors
Rule 36B.7(2)

The jurors must repeat after the sheriff clerk—

"I solemnly, sincerely and truly declare and affirm that I will well and truly try the issue and give a true verdict according to the evidence".

## FORM D1

Rule 36.3(2)

Form of intimation to connected person in damages action

SHERIFFDOM OF (*insert name of sheriffdom*) ............... Court ref.no. ..........

AT (*insert place of sheriff court*) ...............

You are given NOTICE that an action has been raised in the above sheriff court by (*insert name and designation of pursuer*) against (*insert name and designation of defender*). A copy of the initial writ is attached.

It is believed that you may have a title or interest to sue the said (*insert name of defender*) in an action based upon [the injuries from which the late (*insert name and designation*) died] [or the death of the late (*insert name and designation*)]. You may therefore be entitled to enter this action as an additional pursuer. If you wish to do so, you may apply by lodging a minute with the sheriff clerk at the above address to be sisted as an additional pursuer within (*insert the appropriate period of notice*) days of (*insert the date on which service was executed N.B. Rule 5.3(2) relating to postal service*).

Signed...............

Solicitor for the pursuer..........

---

NOTE

The minute must be lodged with the sheriff clerk with the court fee of (*insert amount*) and a motion seeking leave for the minute to be received and for answers to be lodged. When lodging the minute you must present to the sheriff clerk a copy of the initial writ and this intimation.

---

IF YOU ARE UNCERTAIN WHAT ACTION TO TAKE you should consult a solicitor. You may be eligible for legal aid depending on your income, and you can obtain information about legal aid from any solicitor. You may also obtain advice from any Citizens Advice Bureau or other advice agency.

---

## FORM D2

Rule 36.17(1)

Form of receipt for payment into court
RECEIPT

In the Sheriff Court of (*insert name of sheriffdom*) at (*insert place of sheriff court*) in the cause, (*state names of parties or other appropriate description*) [A.B.] (*insert designation*) has this day paid into court the sum of (*insert sum concerned*) being a

---

[1] As inserted by the Act of Sederunt (Rules of the Court of Session 1994 and Sheriff Court Rules Amendment) (No.2) (Personal Injury and Remits) 2015 (SSI 2015/227) para.8 (effective September 22, 2015).

payment into court in terms of rule 36.14 of the Ordinary Cause Rules of the Sheriff Court of money which in an action of damages, has become payable to a person under legal disability.

[*If the payment is made under* rule 36.15(c) *add*: [the custody of which money has been accepted at the request of (*insert name of court making request*).]

Date (*insert date*)...............Signed

Sheriff clerk (depute)

## ¹FORM P1

Rule 37.2(2)

Form of advertisement in an action of declarator under section 1(1) of the Presumption of Death (Scotland) Act 1977

(insert such facts relating to the missing person as set out in the initial writ as the sheriff may specify).

Sheriff Court (*insert address*)...............Court ref. no. ..........

An action has been raised in (*insert name of sheriff court*) by [A.B.], Pursuer, to declare that [C.D.], Defender, whose last known address was (*insert last known address of [C.D.]*) is dead.

Any person wishing to defend the action must apply to do so by (*insert date, being [21] days after the date of the advertisement*) by lodging a minute seeking to be sisted a a party to the action with the sheriff clerk at the above address.

A copy of the initial writ may be obtained from the sheriff clerk at the above address.

Date (*insert date*)...............Signed...............

[X.Y.] (*add designation and business address*) Solicitor for the pursuer *or* [P.Q.] Sheriff officer

## FORM P2

Rule 37.2(4)

Form of intimation to missing person's spouse and children or nearest known relative

To (*insert name and address as in warrant*)...............Court ref. no. ..........

You are given notice that in this action the pursuer craves the court to declare that (*insert the name and last known address of missing person*) is dead. A copy of the initial writ is enclosed.

If you wish to appear as a party, and make an application under section 1 (5) of the Presumption of Death (Scotland) Act 1977 craving the court to make any determination or appointment not sought by the pursuer, you must lodge a minute with the sheriff clerk at (*insert address of sheriff clerk*).

Your minute must be lodged within [..........] days of (*insert the date on which intimation was given N.B. Rule 5.3(2) relating to postal service or intimation*).

Date (*insert date*)...............Signed..........

Solicitor for the pursuer<br>(add designation and business address)

---

NOTE

The minute must be lodged with the sheriff clerk with the court fee of (*insert amount*) and a motion seeking leave for the minute to be received and for answers to be lodged. When lodging the minute you must present to the sheriff clerk a copy of the initial writ and this intimation.

---

¹ As amended by the Act of Sederunt (Sheriff Court Ordinary Cause Rules Amendment) (Miscellaneous) 2000 (SSI 2000/239) (effective October 2, 2000).

> **IF YOU ARE UNCERTAIN WHAT ACTION TO TAKE** you should consult a solicitor. You may be eligible for legal aid depending on your income, and you can obtain information about legal aid from any solicitor. You may also obtain advice from any Citizens Advice Bureau or other advice agency.

## ¹FORM E1

Rule 38.3(1A)

### Form of reference to the European Court

REQUEST
for
PRELIMINARY RULING
of
THE COURT OF JUSTICE OF THE EUROPEAN COMMUNITIES
from

THE SHERIFFDOM OF *insert name of sheriffdom*) at (*insert place of court*)
in the cause

[A.B.] (*insert designation and address*), Pursuer

against

[C.D.] (*insert designation and address*), Defender

[Here set out a clear and succinct statement of the case giving rise to the request for the ruling of the European Court in order to enable the European Court to consider and understand the issues of Community law raised and to enable governments of Member States and other interested parties to submit observations. The statement of the case should include:

(a)  particulars of the parties;
(b)  the history of the dispute between the parties;
(c)  the history of the proceedings;
(d)  the relevant facts as agreed by the parties or found by the court or, failing such agreement or finding, the contentions of the parties on such facts;
(e)  the nature of the issues of law and fact between the parties;
(f)  the Scots law, so far as relevant;
(g)  the Treaty provisions or other acts, instruments or rules of Community law concerned; and
(h)  an explanation of why the reference is being made.]

The preliminary ruling of the Court of Justice of the European Communities is accordingly requested on the following questions:

1, 2, etc. [Here set out the question on which the ruling is sought, identifying the Treaty provisions or other acts, instruments or rules of Community law concerned.] Dated the day of 20 .

**Rule 41.5**

## FORM PA1² ³

Form of certificate of delivery of documents to chief constable

---

¹ As substituted by the Act of Sederunt (Sheriff Court Ordinary Cause Rules Amendment) (Miscellaneous) 2000 (SSI 2000/239) (effective October 2, 2000).
² As inserted by the Act of Sederunt (Ordinary Cause Rules) (Applications under the Protection from Abuse (Scotland) Act 2001) 2002 (SSI 2002/128), para. 2(3) and Sched.
³ As amended by the Act of Sederunt (Sheriff Court Rules)(Miscellaneous Amendments) 2013 (SSI 2013/135) para.4 (effective May 27, 2013).

*(Insert place and date)* I, hereby certify that upon the day of I duly delivered to the chief constable of the Police Service of Scotland *(insert details of the documents delivered)*. This I did by *(state method of delivery)*.

Signed
Solicitor/sheriff officer
*(add designation and business address)*

**Rule 41A.2(3)**

**FORM DA1**[1][2]

Form of interlocutor for a determination of a domestic abuse interdict

Court ref no.

SHERIFFDOM OF *(insert name of sheriffdom)*

AT *(insert place of sheriff court)*

[A.B.], *(insert designation and address)*, Pursuer

against

[C.D.], *(insert designation and address)*, Defender

*(Date)*

The sheriff, in pursuance of section 3(1) of the Domestic Abuse (Scotland) Act 2011, makes a determination that the [interim*] interdict dated *(insert date)* [and to which a power of arrest was attached by interlocutor dated *(insert date)*\*] is a domestic abuse interdict. [The sheriff appoints *(insert name of person)*] to send forthwith a copy of this interlocutor and a copy of the certificate of service in Form DA2 to the chief constable of the Police Service of Scotland].

*(\*delete as appropriate)*

*(Sheriff)*..........

**Rule 41A.2(4)**

[3]**FORM DA2**

Form of certificate of service

Court ref no.

SHERIFFDOM OF (insert name of sheriffdom)*(insert name of sheriffdom)*

AT *(insert place of sheriff court)*

[A.B.], *(insert designation and address)*, Pursuer

against

[C.D.], *(insert designation and address)*, Defender

*(Insert place and date)*

I hereby certify that on *(insert date)* I duly served on *(insert name and address of person subject to the interdict)* a copy of Form DA1. This I did by *(state method of service)*.

*(Signed)*
(Solicitor/sheriff officer)
*(add designation and business address)*

**Rule 41A.2(5)**

[4][5]**FORM DA3**

---

[1] As inserted by the Act of Sederunt (Sheriff Court Rules) (Miscellaneous Amendments) (No.2) 2011 (SSI 2011/289) para.5 (effective July 20, 2011).

[2] As amended by the Act of Sederunt (Sheriff Court Rules)(Miscellaneous Amendments) 2013 (SSI 2013/135) para.4 (effective May 27, 2013).

[3] As inserted by the Act of Sederunt (Sheriff Court Rules) (Miscellaneous Amendments) (No.2) 2011 (SSI 2011/289) para.5 (effective July 20, 2011).

[4] As inserted by the Act of Sederunt (Sheriff Court Rules) (Miscellaneous Amendments) (No.2) 2011 (SSI 2011/289) para.5 (effective July 20, 2011).

[5] As amended by the Act of Sederunt (Sheriff Court Rules)(Miscellaneous Amendments) 2013 (SSI 2013/135) para.4 (effective May 27, 2013).

Form of interlocutor for recall of a determination of a domestic abuse interdict

Court ref n

SHERIFFDOM OF *(insert name of sheriffdom)*
AT *(insert place of sheriff court)*
[A.B.], *(insert designation and address)*, Pursuer
against
[C.D.], *(insert designation and address)*, Defender
(Date)

The sheriff, in pursuance of section 3(5)(b) of the Domestic Abuse (Scotland) A
2011, recalls the determination that the [interim*] interdict dated *(insert date)* is
domestic abuse interdict. [The sheriff appoints *(insert name of person)*] to se
forthwith a copy of this interlocutor to the chief constable of the Police Service
Scotland]. *(*delete as appropriate)*

*(Sheri*

## FORM DA4[1] [2]
**Rule 41A.2(8)**

Form of certificate of sending documents to the chief constable

Court ref n

SHERIFFDOM OF *(insert name of sheriffdom)*
AT *(insert place of sheriff court)*
[A.B.], *(insert designation and address)*, Pursuer
against
[C.D.], *(insert designation and address)*, Defender
*(Insert place and date)*

I hereby certify that on *(insert date)* I duly sent to the chief constable of the Polic
Service of Scotland a copy of [the interlocutor in Form DA1 and the certificate
service in Form DA2*] [the interlocutor in Form DA3*]. This I did by *(state metho
of sending)*. *delete as appropriate)*

*(Signe*
*(Solicitor/sheriff office*
*(add designation and business addres*

## [3]FORM OFT1
**Rule 43.1(2)**

Form of notice of intimation to the Office of Fair Trading
Date: *(date of posting or other method of intimation)*
To: The Office of Fair Trading
TAKE NOTICE

*(Name and address of pursuer or defender)* has brought an action against [*or* ha
defended an action brought by] *(name and address of defender or pursuer)*. The ac
tion raises an issue under Article 101 or 102 of the Treaty on the Functioning of th
European Union. A copy of the initial writ is [*or* pleadings and interlocutor allowin
intimation are] attached.

If you wish to submit written observations to the court, these should be addresse
to the sheriff clerk *(insert address of sheriff clerk)* and must be lodged within 2

---

[1] As inserted by the Act of Sederunt (Sheriff Court Rules) (Miscellaneous Amendments) (No.2) 201
(SSI 2011/289) para.5 (effective July 20, 2011).
[2] As amended by the Act of Sederunt (Sheriff Court Rules)(Miscellaneous Amendments) 2013 (SS
2013/135) para.4 (effective May 27, 2013).
[3] As inserted by Act of Sederunt (Ordinary Cause Rules) Amendment (Causes Relating to Articles 8
and 82 of the Treaty Establishing the European Community) 2006 (SSI 2006/293) (effective June 1
2006) and amended by the Act of Sederunt (Sheriff Court Rules) (Miscellaneous Amendment
(No.3) 2012 (SSI 2012/271) para.6 (effective November 1, 2012).

days of (*insert date on which intimation was given. N.B.* rule 5.3(2) *relating to postal service or intimation*).

If you wish to submit oral observations to the court, you must lodge a minute with the sheriff clerk (*insert address of sheriff clerk*) for leave to do so. Your minute must be lodged within 21 days of (*insert date on which intimation was given. N.B.* rule 5.3(2) *relating to postal service or intimation*).

Date (*insert date*)..........(*Signed*)

Solicitor for pursuer/defender

## FORM 49.6

**Rule 49.6(6)** and (7)

Form of preliminary act in ship collision action

In the action in which ............... is Pursuer

.......... and ..........

............... is Defender

Preliminary Act

for

Pursuer [*or* Defender]

Court Ref. No:..............

(1) (*State the names of the vessels which came into collision, their ports or registry, and the names of their masters.*)

(2) (*State the date and time of the collision.*)

(3) (*State the place of the collision.*)

(4) (*State the direction and force of the wind.*)

(5) (*State the state of the weather.*)

(6) (*State the state, direction and force of the tidal or other current.*)

(7) (*State the magnetic course steered and speed through the water of the vessel when the other vessel was first seen or immediately before any measures were taken with reference to her presence, whichever was the earlier.*)

(8) (*State the lights (if any) carried by the vessel.*)

(9) (*State the distance and bearing of the other vessel if and when her echo was first observed by radar.*)

(10) (*State the distance, bearing and approximate heading of the other vessel when first seen.*)

(11) (*State what light or combination of lights (if any) of the other vessel when first seen.*)

(12) (*State what other lights or combinations of lights (if any) of the other vessel were subsequently seen, before the collision, and when.*)

(13) (*State what alterations (if any) were made to the course and speed of the vessel after the earlier of the two times referred to in paragraph (7) up to the time of the collision, and when, and what measures (if any), other than alterations of course and speed, were taken to avoid the collision and when.*)

(14) (*State the parts of each vessel which first came into contact and the approximate angle between the two vessels at the moment of contact.*)

(15) (*State what sound signals (if any) were given, and when.*)

(16) (*State what sound signals (if any) were heard from the other vessel and when.*)

(*Signed by solicitor or Agent*)
(*Name*)

---

[1] As inserted by the Act of Sederunt (Sheriff Court Rules) (Miscellaneous Amendments) 2012 (SSI 2012/188) para.10 (effective August 1, 2012).

(*Address*)

(*Telephone number*)

(*Date*)

### [1]FORM 49.11-A

Rule 49.11(1)(a)(i)

Form of schedule of arrestment of found jurisdiction

Court:...............

Court Ref. No:..............

### SCHEDULE OF ARRESTMENT TO FOUND JURISDICTION

Date: (*date of execution*)

Time: (*time arrestment executed*)

To: (*name and address of arrestee*)

I, (*name*), Sheriff Officer, by virtue of an interlocutor of the Sheriff at (*place*) on (*date*) containing a warrant for arrestment to found jurisdiction, at the instance of (*name and address of pursuer*) against (*name and address of defender*), arrest to found jurisdiction against (*name of defender*) in your hands: (i) the sum of (*amount*), more or less, due by you to (*name of defender*) or to any other person on his [*or* her] [*or* its] [*or* their] behalf; and (ii) all moveable subjects in your hands and belonging or pertaining to (*name of defender*).

This I do in the presence of (*name, occupation and address of witness*).

(*Signed*)

Sheriff Officer

(*Address*)

### NOTE

(*Do not use this note where arrestment to found jurisdiction is combined with arrestment on the dependence in one schedule.*)

(The name, address and twenty-four hour contact telephone number of the agent for the party on whose behalf the arrestment was executed are to be inserted here.)

(*Name of agent*)

(*Address*)

(*Telephone number*)

### [2]FORM 49.11-AA

Rule 49.11(1)(a)(ii)

Form of schedule of arrestment of ship to found jurisdiction

Court:...............

Court Ref. No:..............

### SCHEDULE OF ARRESTMENT OF SHIP TO FOUND JURISDICTION

Date: (*date of execution*)

Time: (*time arrestment executed*)

I, (*name*), Sheriff Officer, by virtue of an interlocutor of the Sheriff at (*place*) on (*date*) containing a warrant for arrestment to found jurisdiction, at the instance of (*name and address of pursuer*) against (*name and address of defender*), arrest to found jurisdiction against (*name of defender*) the ship (*name*) presently lying in (*describe location*) and belonging to the defender.

This I do in the presence of (*name, occupation and address of witness*).

(*Signed*)

Sheriff Officer

---

[1] As inserted by the Act of Sederunt (Sheriff Court Rules) (Miscellaneous Amendments) 2012 (SSI 2012/188) para.10 (effective August 1, 2012).

[2] As inserted by the Act of Sederunt (Sheriff Court Rules) (Miscellaneous Amendments) 2012 (SSI 2012/188) para.10 (effective August 1, 2012).

*(Address)*

**NOTE**

You should consult your legal adviser about the effect of this arrestment.

(The name, address and twenty-four hour contact telephone number of the agent for the party on whose behalf the arrestment was executed are to be inserted here.)

*(Name of agent)*
*(Address)*
*(Telephone number)*

### [1]FORM 49.11-B

Rule 49.11(1)(c)

Form of schedule of arrestment in rem of ship, cargo or other maritime res to enforce maritime hypothec or lien

Court:...............

Court Ref. No:...............

SCHEDULE OF ARRESTMENT IN REM IN ADMIRALTY ACTION IN REM

Date: *(date of execution)*

Time: *(time arrestment executed)*

I, *(name)*, Sheriff Officer, by virtue of an interlocutor of the Sheriff at *(place)* on *(date)* containing a warrant for arrestment in rem of the ship *(name of ship)* [*or* cargo *(describe)*] [*or other maritime res (describe)*] in an Admiralty action in rem at the instance of *(name and address of pursuer)* against *(name and address of defender)*, arrest the ship *(name)* presently lying in *(describe current location e.g. the port of X)* with her float, boats, furniture, appurtenances and apparelling [*or* cargo] [*or other maritime res*] *(describe location)*], to remain in that *(specify more precisely if required)* under arrestment in rem until they are sold or until this arrestment is recalled or other order of the sheriff.

This I do in the presence of *(name, occupation and address of witness)*.

*(Signed)*
Sheriff Officer
*(Address)*

**NOTE**

You should consult your legal adviser about the effect of this arrestment.

(The name, address and twenty-four hour contact telephone number of the agent for the party on whose behalf the arrestment was executed are to be inserted here.)

*(Name of agent)*
*(Address)*
*(Telephone number)*

### [2]FORM 49.11-C

Rule 49.11(1)(d)

Form of schedule of arrestment in rem of ship to enforce non-pecuniary claim

Court:...............

Court Ref. No:...............

SCHEDULE OF ARRESTMENT IN REM OF SHIP UNDER THE ADMINISTRATION OF JUSTICE ACT 1956, SECTION 47(3)(b)

Date: *(date of execution)*

Time: *(time arrestment executed)*

I, *(name)*, Sheriff Officer, by virtue of —

---

[1] As inserted by the Act of Sederunt (Sheriff Court Rules) (Miscellaneous Amendments) 2012 (SSI 2012/188) para.10 (effective August 1, 2012).

[2] As inserted by the Act of Sederunt (Sheriff Court Rules) (Miscellaneous Amendments) 2012 (SSI 2012/188) para.10 (effective August 1, 2012).

*an interlocutor of the Sheriff at (*place*) on (*date*) granting warrant for arrestme in rem under section 47(3)(b) of the Administration of Justice Act 1956 of the sh (*name of ship*) in an action,

*an interlocutor of the Sheriff at (*place*) on (*date*) containing a warrant for arres ment in rem under section 47(3)(b) of the Administration of Justice Act 1956 of th ship (*name of ship*), at the instance of (*name and address of pursuer*) against (*nam and address of defender*), arrest the ship [*or* vessel*] (*name*) presently lying i (*describe current location e.g. the port of X*) with her float, boats, furniture, aj purtenances and apparelling to remain in that (*specify more precisely if require* under arrestment in rem until this arrestment is recalled or other order of the sheri

This I do in the presence of (*name, occupation and address of witness*).

(*Signee*
Sheriff Offic
(*Addres*

## NOTE

You should consult your legal adviser about the effect of this arrestment.

(The name, address and twenty-four hour contact telephone number of the age for the party on whose behalf the arrestment was executed are to be inserted here.)

(*Name of agen*
(*Addres*
(*Telephone numbe*

* Delete where not applicable.

**FORM 49.11-D**

Rule 49.11(1)(e)(ii)
Court:..............
Court Ref. No:...............

Form of schedule of arrestment of ship on the dependence
Court: (*date of execution*)
Time: (*time arrestment executed*)
I, (*name*), Sheriff Officer, by virtue of —

*an interlocutor of the Sheriff at (*place*) on (*date*) granting warrant for arrestme on the dependence of the action at the instance of (*name and address of pursue against (*name and address of defender*),

*a counterclaim containing a warrant which has been granted for arrestment c the dependence of the claim by (*name and address of creditor*) against (*name an address of debtor*) and dated (*date of warrant*),

*an interlocutor dated (*date*) granting warrant [for arrestment on the dependen of the action raised at the instance of (*name and address of pursuer*) against (*nam and address of defender*)] [*or* for arrestment on the dependence of the claim in th counterclaim [*or* third party notice] by (*name and address of creditor*) against (*nam and address of debtor*) [*or* to arrest in the cause of (*name and address of petitione against (*name and address of respondent*)].

arrest the ship (*name of ship*) presently lying in (*describe current location e.g. th port of X*) to remain in that (*more precisely if required*) under arrestment on th dependence of the action [*or* claim] until further interlocutor of the sheriff.

This I do in the presence of (*name, occupation and address of witness*).

(*Signee*
Sheriff Offic

---

[1] As inserted by the Act of Sederunt (Sheriff Court Rules) (Miscellaneous Amendments) 2012 (S 2012/188) para.10 (effective August 1, 2012).

(Address)

## NOTE

You should consult your legal adviser about the effect of this arrestment.

(The name, address and twenty-four hour contact telephone number of the agent for the party on whose behalf the arrestment was executed are to be inserted here.)

(Name of agent)
(Address)
(Telephone number)

\* Delete where not applicable.

### ¹FORM 49.11-E

Rule 49.11(1)(a)(i) and (b)

Form of certificate of execution of arrestment

### CERTIFICATE OF EXECUTION

I, (*name*), Sheriff Officer, certify that I executed (*specify the kind of arrestment, whether on the dependence of an action, counterclaim or third party notice, whether on the authority of an interlocutor (specify), or in execution of a decree (specify)*), [obtained] at the instance of (*name and address of party arresting*) against (*name and address of common debtor*) on (*name of person on whom executed*)—

\* by leaving the schedule of [arrestment] with (*name of defender or other person*] at (*place*) on (*date*).

\* by leaving the schedule of [arrestment] with (*name and occupation of person with whom left*) at (*place*) on (*date*). (*Specify that enquiry made and that reasonable grounds exist for believing that the person on whom service is to be made resides at the place but is not available.*)

\* by depositing the schedule of [arrestment] in (*place*) on (*date*). (*Specify that enquiry made and that reasonable grounds exist for believing that the person on whom service is to be made resides at the place but is not available.*)

\* by leaving the schedule of [arrestment] with (*name and occupation of person with whom left*) at (*place of business*) on (*date*). (*Specify that enquiry made and that reasonable grounds exist for believing that the person on whom service is to be made carries on business at the place.*)

\* by depositing the schedule of [arrestment] at (*place of business*) on (*date*). (*Specify that enquiry made and that reasonable grounds exist for believing that the person on whom service is to be made carries on business at that place.*)

\* by leaving the schedule of [arrestment] with (*registered office or place of business*) on (*date*), in the hands of (*name of person*).

\* by leaving [*or depositing*] the schedule of [arrestment] at (*registered office, official address or place of business*) on (*date*) in such a way that it was likely to come to the attention of (*name of defender or other person on whom served*). (*Specify how left.*)

\* by leaving the schedule of [arrestment] with (*name and occupation of person with whom left*) at the office of the sheriff clerk at (*place*) on (*date*) and sending a copy of the schedule by first class post (*defender's last known address*) on (*date*).

I did this in the presence of (*name, occupation and address of witness*).

(Signed)
Sheriff Officer
(Address)
(Signed)

---

¹ As inserted by the Act of Sederunt (Sheriff Court Rules) (Miscellaneous Amendments) 2012 (SSI 2012/188) para.10 (effective August 1, 2012).

Witness

*Delete where not applicable.

### ¹FORM 49.11-F

Rule 49.11(1)(a)(ii)

Form of certificate of arrestment of ship to found jurisdiction

CERTIFICATE OF EXECUTION OF ARRESTMENT OF SHIP TO FOUND JURISDICTION

I, *(name)*, Sheriff Officer, certify that I, by virtue of an interlocutor of the Sheriff at *(place)* on *(date)* containing a warrant for arrestment to found jurisdiction, executed an arrestment of the ship *(name)* at the instance of *(name and address of pursuer)* against *(name and address of defender)* by affixing the schedule of arrestment to the mainmast *[or as the case may be]* of the ship *(name)* and marked the initials ER above that affixed schedule at *(place)* on *(date)*.

I did this in the presence of *(name, occupation and address of witness)*.

*(Signed)*
Sheriff Officer
*(Address)*
*(Signed)*
Witness

### ²FORM 49.11-G

Rule 49.11(1)(c) and (d)

Form of certificate of execution of arrestment of ship or cargo in rem

CERTIFICATE OF EXECUTION OF ARRESTMENT OF SHIP *[OR* CARGO] IN REM

I, *(name)*, Sheriff Officer, certify that I executed an arrestment in rem of the ship *[or* vessel] *(name)* *[or* cargo *(describe)]* by virtue of an interlocutor of the Sheriff at *(place)* on *(date)* at the instance of *(name and address of pursuer)* against *(name and address of defender)* by affixing the schedule of arrestment to the mainmast *[or as the case may be]* of the ship *[or* vessel] *[or in the case of cargo landed or transhipped* on *(name)* as custodian for the time being of the cargo *[or* as harbourmaster of the harbour where the cargo lies]] *[and delivering a copy of the schedule of arrestment and of this certificate to *(name)* the master of the ship *[or as the case may be]* at *(place)* on *(date)*.

I did this in the presence of *(name, occupation and address of witness)*.

*(Signed)*
Sheriff Officer
*(Address)*
*(Signed)*
Witness

### ³FORM 49.11-H

Rule 49.11(1)(e)

Form of certificate of execution of arrestment of ship or cargo on the dependence

CERTIFICATE OF EXECUTION OF ARRESTMENT OF SHIP *[OR* CARGO] ON THE DEPENDENCE

---

[1] As inserted by the Act of Sederunt (Sheriff Court Rules) (Miscellaneous Amendments) 2012 (SSI 2012/188) para.10 (effective August 1, 2012).

[2] As inserted by the Act of Sederunt (Sheriff Court Rules) (Miscellaneous Amendments) 2012 (SSI 2012/188) para.10 (effective August 1, 2012).

[3] As inserted by the Act of Sederunt (Sheriff Court Rules) (Miscellaneous Amendments) 2012 (SSI 2012/188) para.10 (effective August 1, 2012).

I, (*name*), Sheriff Officer, certify that I executed an arrestment on the dependence of the ship [*or* vessel] (*name*) [*or* cargo (*describe*)] by virtue of an interlocutor of the Sheriff at (*place*) on (*date*) at the instance of (*name and address of pursuer*) against (*name and address of defender*) by affixing the schedule of arrestment to the mainmast [*or as the case may be*] of the ship [*or* vessel] (*name*) and marked the initials ER above the same [*or* by (*state method of service*)] at (*place*) on (*date*).

I did this in the presence of (*name, occupation and address of witness*).

(*Signed*)
Sheriff Officer
(*Address*)
(*Signed*)
Witness

Rule 51.3(1)

### [1]FORM 51.3-A
#### Form of warrant to place [or renew] a caveat under
Court reference no. (*insert reference*)

SHERIFFDOM OF (*insert name of sheriffdom*)
AT (*insert place of sheriff court*)
WARRANT TO PLACE [*or* RENEW] CAVEAT
in the cause
[A.B.] (*designation and address*)
Pursuer

Against
[C.D.] (*designation and address*)
Defender

Date: (*date of interlocutor*)
To the Keeper of the Registers of Scotland

**THE SHERIFF**, having considered the application of the pursuer [*or* defender] and being satisfied as to the matters mentioned in section 67(4) [*or* 69(3)] of the Land Registration etc. (Scotland) Act 2012,

**GRANTS** warrant to place [*or* renew] a caveat on the title sheet of the plot of land—

(a)   at (*state description of the plot(s) of land*);
(b)   registered under title number (*state title number(s)*);
(c)   registered in the name of (*state name and address of proprietor*).

(*Signed*)

NOTE: append a copy of any plan of the plot(s) of land lodged in accordance with rule 51.2(2)(c).

Rule 51.3(2)

### [2]FORM 51.3-B
#### Form of order restricting a caveat under section 70(2) of the Land Registration etc. (Scotland) Act 2012
Court reference no. (*insert reference*)

SHERIFFDOM OF (*insert name of sheriffdom*)
AT (*insert place of sheriff court*)
ORDER RESTRICTING A CAVEAT
in the cause

---

[1] As inserted by the Act of Sederunt (Rules of the Court of Session and Sheriff Court Rules Amendment No.2) (Miscellaneous) 2014 (SSI 2014/291) para.3 (effective December 8, 2014).

[2] As inserted by the Act of Sederunt (Rules of the Court of Session and Sheriff Court Rules Amendment No.2) (Miscellaneous) 2014 (SSI 2014/291) para.3 (effective December 8, 2014).

[A.B.] (*designation and address*)

Pursue

against

[C.D.] (*designation and address*)

Defende

Date: (*date of interlocutor*)

To the Keeper of the Registers of Scotland

**THE SHERIFF**, having considered the application of the pursuer [*or* defender
being satisfied—

 (a) as to the matters mentioned in section 70(3) of the Land Registration etc
   (Scotland) Act 2012; and

 (b) that it is reasonable in all the circumstances to do so,

**ORDERS** that the caveat on the title sheet of the plot of land:

 (a) at (*state description of the plot(s) of land*);

 (b) registered under title number (*state title number(s)*);

 (c) registered in the name of (*state name and address of proprietor*),

be restricted as follows:

(*specify nature and extent of restriction*)

(*Signea*

Rule 51.3(3)

## ¹FORM 51.3-C

### Form of order recalling a caveat under section 71(2) of the Land Registration etc. (Scotland) Act 2012

Court reference no. (*insert reference*

SHERIFFDOM OF (*insert name of sheriffdom*)

AT (*insert place of sheriff court*)

ORDER RECALLING A CAVEAT

in the cause

[A.B.] (*designation and address*)

Pursue

against

[C.D.] (*designation and address*)

Defende

Date: (*date of interlocutor*)

To the Keeper of the Registers of Scotland

**THE SHERIFF**, having considered the application of the pursuer [*or* defender
and no longer being satisfied as to the matters mentioned in section 71(3) of the
Land Registration etc.(Scotland) Act 2012,

**ORDERS** that the caveat on the title sheet of the plot of land—

 (a) at (*state description of the plot(s) of land*);

 (b) registered under title number (*state title number(s)*);

 (c) registered in the name of (*state name and address of proprietor*),

be recalled.

(*Signed*

Rule 51.5

## ²FORM 51.5

---

¹ As inserted by the Act of Sederunt (Rules of the Court of Session and Sheriff Court Rules Amend
ment No.2) (Miscellaneous) 2014 (SSI 2014/291) para. 3 (effective December 8, 2014).
² As inserted by the Act of Sederunt (Rules of the Court of Session and Sheriff Court Rules Amendment No.2) (Miscellaneous) 2014 (SSI 2014/291) para.3 (effective December 8, 2014).

**Form of order for rectification of a document to which** section 8A of the Law Reform (Miscellaneous Provisions) (Scotland) Act 1985 **applies**

SHERIFFDOM OF (*insert name of sheriffdom*)

AT (*insert place of sheriff court*)

ORDER FOR RECTIFICATION OF A DOCUMENT UNDER SECTION 8 OF THE LAW REFORM (MISCELLANEOUS PROVISIONS) (SCOTLAND) ACT 1985

*[Date]*

The sheriff, on the motion of the pursuer, orders the rectification of *[insert type of deed, parties to the deed and date of registration in the Land Register of Scotland]* registered in the Land Register of Scotland under title number *[state title number and, if applicable, lease title number]* to the extent of *[insert details of the rectification including, if applicable, a statement in terms of section 8(3A) of the Law Reform (Miscellaneous Provisions) (Scotland) Act 1985 (i.e. statement of consent)]*.

**FORM 52.2**

Rule 52.2

APPLICATION FOR A CERTIFICATE UNDER ARTICLE 5 OF REGULATION (EU) NO. 606/2013 OF THE EUROPEAN PARLIAMENT AND OF THE COUNCIL OF 12TH JUNE 2013 ON MUTUAL RECOGNITION OF PROTECTION MEASURES IN CIVIL MATTERS

Sheriff Court ..........

Court Ref. No. ..........

1. The applicant is the pursuer *[or* defender] in the action by [A.B.] (*design*) against [C.D.] (*design*).

2. The applicant's date of birth is (*insert date of birth*).

3. The applicant's place of birth is (*insert place of birth*).

4. The address of the applicant to be used for notification purposes is (*insert address – the address given, which may be disclosed to the person against whom the protection measures was granted, must be an address to which any notification to the applicant can be sent*).

5. The application relates to an order granted on (*insert date of order granting protection measure*) in which (*insert name of person against whom protection measure was granted*) was prohibited from (*insert short description of prohibitions imposed*).

6. The date of birth of the person against whom the order was granted is (*insert date of birth or "not known"*).

7. The place of birth of the person against whom the order was granted is (*insert place of birth or "not known"*).

8. The address of the person against whom the order was granted is (*insert address or "not known"*).

9. The applicant asks the court to issue a certificate pursuant to Article 5(1) of Regulation (EU) No. 606/2013 of the European Parliament and of the Council of 12th June 2013 on mutual recognition of protection measures in civil matters in relation to the order referred to in paragraph 5.

Date (*insert date*)

(*Signed*)

[A.B. *or* C.D.]

*[or* Solicitor for Applicant]

---

[1] As inserted by the Act of Sederunt (Rules of the Court of Session and Sheriff Court Rules Amendment No.3) (Mutual Recognition of Protection Measures) 2014 (SSI 2014/371) para.3 (effective January 11, 2015).

*(add designation and business address)*

**FORM 52.5-A[1]**

Rule 52.5(2)(a)

NOTICE OF ISSUE OF CERTIFICATE UNDER ARTICLE 5 OF REGULATION (EU) NO. 606/2013 OF THE EUROPEAN PARLIAMENT AND OF THE COUNCIL OF 12TH JUNE 2013 ON MUTUAL RECOGNITION OF PROTECTION MEASURES IN CIVIL MATTERS

Sheriff Court .........

Court Ref. No. ..........

Date: *(insert date of posting or other method of intimation)*

To: *(insert name and address of person causing the risk)*

A certificate has been issued to *(insert name of party to whom certificate was issued)* in accordance with Article 5(1) of Regulation (EU) No. 606/2013 of the European Parliament and of the Council of 12th June 2013 on mutual recognition of protection measures in civil matters. The certificate relates to an order granted by the sheriff on *(insert date of interlocutor containing protection measure)*. A copy of the certificate and a copy of the order accompany this notice.

As a result of the issue of the certificate, *(insert name of person to whom certificate was issued)* can invoke the order in other Member States of the European Union.

If you consider that the certificate was wrongly issued, or that the certificate does not accurately reflect the terms of the order, you can apply to have the certificate withdrawn, or for the issue of a rectified certificate, by lodging an application in Form 52.7 with the sheriff clerk at the address below.

*(Signed)*
Sheriff Clerk
*(insert address and telephone number)*

**FORM 52.5-B[2]**

Rule 52.5(4)

NOTICE FOR WALLS OF COURT OF ISSUE OF CERTIFICATE UNDER ARTICLE 5 OF REGULATION (EU) NO. 606/2013 OF THE EUROPEAN PARLIAMENT AND OF THE COUNCIL OF 12TH JUNE 2013 ON MUTUAL RECOGNITION OF PROTECTION MEASURES IN CIVIL MATTERS

Sheriff Court .........

Court Ref. No. ..........

Date: *(insert date)*

To: *(insert name and address of person causing the risk)*

A certificate has been issued to *(insert name of party to whom certificate was issued)* in accordance with Article 5(1) of Regulation (EU) No. 606/2013 of the European Parliament and of the Council of 12th June 2013 on mutual recognition of protection measures in civil matters. The certificate relates to an order granted by the sheriff on *(insert date of interlocutor containing protection measure)* against *(insert name of person causing the risk)*, whose last known address was *(insert last known address of person causing the risk)*.

---

[1] As inserted by the Act of Sederunt (Rules of the Court of Session and Sheriff Court Rules Amendment No.3) (Mutual Recognition of Protection Measures) 2014 (SSI 2014/371) para.3 (effective January 11, 2015).

[2] As inserted by the Act of Sederunt (Rules of the Court of Session and Sheriff Court Rules Amendment No.3) (Mutual Recognition of Protection Measures) 2014 (SSI 2014/371) para.3 (effective January 11, 2015).

As a result of the issue of the certificate, (*insert name of person to whom certificate was issued*) can invoke the order in other Member States of the European Union.

If (*insert name of person causing the risk*) wishes to obtain a copy of the certificate and the order, that person should immediately contact the sheriff clerk at the address below.

If (*insert name of person causing the risk*) considers that the certificate was wrongly issued, or that the certificate does not accurately reflect the terms of the order, that person can apply to have the certificate withdrawn, or for the issue of a rectified certificate, by lodging an application in Form 52.7 with the sheriff clerk at the address below.

(*Signed*)
Sheriff Clerk
(*insert address and telephone number*)

## FORM 52.7[1]

Rule 52.7(1)

### APPLICATION FOR RECTIFICATION OR WITHDRAWAL OF A CERTIFICATE ISSUED UNDER ARTICLE 5 OF REGULATION (EU) NO. 606/2013 OF THE EUROPEAN PARLIAMENT AND OF THE COUNCIL OF 12TH JUNE 2013 ON MUTUAL RECOGNITION OF PROTECTION MEASURES IN CIVIL MATTERS

Sheriff Court ..........
Court Ref. No. ..........

1. The applicant is the defender [*or* pursuer] in the action by [A.B.] (*design*) against [C.D.] (*design*).
2. On the application of the pursuer [*or* defender], the sheriff has issued a certificate in accordance with Article 5(1) of Regulation (EU) No. 606/2013 of the European Parliament and of the Council of 12th June on mutual recognition of protection measures in civil matters.
3. The certificate relates to an order granted by the sheriff on (*insert date of interlocutor containing protection measure*).
4. The applicant considers that the certificate does not accurately reflect the terms of the order because: (*here specify nature of discrepancy*).

[*or* 4. The applicant considers that the certificate was wrongly issued because: (*here specify the reason the certificate was wrongly issued*).]

5. The applicant asks the court to issue a rectified certificate [*or* to withdraw the certificate].

Date (*insert date*)

(*Signed*)
[A.B. *or* C.D.]
[*or* Solicitor for Applicant]
(*add designation and business address*)

## FORM 53.4[2]

Rule 53.4(3)
SHERIFFDOM OF (*sheriffdom*) AT (*place*)
FORM OF MINUTE FOR DECREE

---

[1] As inserted by the Act of Sederunt (Rules of the Court of Session and Sheriff Court Rules Amendment No.3) (Mutual Recognition of Protection Measures) 2014 (SSI 2014/371) para.3 (effective January 11, 2015).
[2] As inserted by the Act of Sederunt (Ordinary Cause Rules Amendment) (Proving the Tenor and Reduction) 2015 (SSI 2015/176) (effective May 25, 2015).

in

## UNDEFENDED ACTION OF PROVING THE TENOR

(*insert name of solicitor for the pursuer*), having considered the evidence contained in the affidavits and the other documents as specified in the schedule and being satisfied that on this evidence a motion for decree (in terms of the crave of the initial writ) [*or in such restricted terms as may be appropriate*] may properly be made, moves the court accordingly.

In respect whereof

Signed

Solicitor for the Pursuer (*add designation and business address*)

SCHEDULE

(*numbered list of documents*)

## APPENDIX 2

Rule 30.6(1)

## FORMS FOR EXTRACT DECREES

### FORM 1

Form of extract decree for payment

## EXTRACT DECREE FOR PAYMENT

| | |
|---|---|
| Sheriff Court | Court ref. no. |
| Date of decree | * In absence |
| Pursuer(s) | Defender(s) |

The sheriff granted decree against the .......... for payment to the .......... of the undernoted sums.

Sum decerned for £ .......... with interest at .......... per cent a year from .......... until payment and expenses against the .......... of £ ..........

* A time to pay direction was made under section 1(1) of the Debtors (Scotland) Act 1987.

* The amount is payable by instalments of £ .......... per .......... commencing within .......... of intimation of this extract decree.

* The amount is payable by lump sum within .......... of intimation of this extract decree.

This extract is warrant for all lawful execution hereon.

Date ............... Sheriff clerk (depute)

* Delete as appropriate.

### FORM 2

Form of extract decree ad factum praestandum

## EXTRACT DECREE *AD FACTUM PRAESTANDUM*

| | |
|---|---|
| Sheriff Court | Court ref. no. |
| Date of decree | * In absence |
| Pursuer(s) | Defender(s) |

The sheriff ordained the defender(s)...............and granted decree against the......... for payment of expenses of £...........

This extract is warrant for all lawful execution hereon.

Date

Sheriff clerk (depute)

* Delete as appropriate.

### FORM 3

Form of extract decree of removing

## EXTRACT DECREE OF REMOVING

424

Sheriff Court

Date of decree

Pursuer(s)

Court ref. no.

* In absence

Defender(s)

The sheriff ordained the defender(s) to remove* himself/herself/themselves and his/her/their sub-tenants, dependents and others, and all effects from the premises at the undernoted address and to leave those premises vacant** [and that after a charge of.......... days].

In the event that the defender(s) fail(s) to remove the sheriff granted warrant to sheriff officers to eject the defender(s), sub-tenants, dependents and others, with all effects, from those premises so as to leave them vacant.

The Sheriff granted decree against the.......... for payment of expenses of £...........

Full address of premises:—

This extract is warrant for all lawful execution hereon.

Date

Sheriff clerk (depute)

** Delete as appropriate.

** Delete if period of charge is not specified in the decree.

## FORM 4
Form of extract decree of declarator
### EXTRACT DECREE OF DECLARATOR

Sheriff Court

Date of decree

Pursuer(s)

Court ref. no.

* In absence

Defender(s)

The sheriff found and declared that...............and granted decree against the...............for payment of expenses of £...........

This extract is warrant for all lawful execution hereon.

Date

Sheriff clerk (depute)

* Delete as appropriate.

## FORM 5
Form of extract decree of forthcoming
### EXTRACT DECREE OF FURTHCOMING

Sheriff Court

Date of decree

Date of original decree

Pursuer(s)

Court ref. no.

* In absence

Defender(s)/Arrestee(s)

Common Debtor(s)

The sheriff granted against the arrestee(s) for payment of the undernoted sums.

Sum decerned for £.......... or such other sum(s) as may be owing by the arrestee(s) to the common debtor(s) by virtue of the original decree dated above in favour of the pursuer(s) against the common debtor(s).

Expenses of £.......... * payable out of the arrested fund / payable by the common debtor(s).

This extract is warrant for all lawful execution hereon.

Date

Sheriff clerk (depute)

* Delete as appropriate.

## FORM 6

Form of extract decree of absolvitor
## EXTRACT DECREE OF ABSOLVITOR

Sheriff Court            Court ref. no.

Date of first warrant      Date of decree

Pursuer(s)               Defender(s)

*(Insert the nature of crave(s) in the above action)*

The sheriff absolved.............. the defender(s) and granted decree against the......... for payment of expenses of £...........

This extract is warrant for all lawful execution hereon.

Date

Sheriff clerk (depute

## FORM 7
Form of extract decree of dismissal
## EXTRACT DECREE OF DISMISSAL

Sheriff Court            Court ref. no.

Date of first warrant      Date of decree

Pursuer(s)               Defender(s)

The sheriff dismissed the action against the.............. defender(s) and granted decree against the.............. for payment of expenses of £...........

* This extract is warrant for all lawful execution hereon.

Date

Sheriff clerk (depute

* Delete as appropriate.

## FORM 8
[Repealed by the Act of Sederunt (Sheriff Court Ordinary Cause Rules Amendment) (Miscellaneous) 1996 (S.I. 1996 No. 2445) (effective November 1, 1996).]

## FORM 9
Form of extract decree
## EXTRACT DECREE

Sheriff Court            Court ref. no.

Date of decree          *In absence

Pursuer(s)               Defender(s)

The sheriff and granted decree against the.............. for payment of expenses of £...........

This extract is warrant for all lawful execution hereon.

Date

Sheriff clerk (depute)

*Delete as appropriate.

## ¹FORM 10
Form of extract decree of divorce
## EXTRACT DECREE OF DIVORCE

Sheriff Court            Court Ref No

Date of Decree         *In absence

---

[1] As substituted by the Act of Sederunt (Sheriff Court Ordinary Cause Rules Amendment) (Miscellaneous) 2000 (S.S.I. 2000 No. 239)(effective October 2, 2000).

Pursuer                                    Defender

Date of parties marriage...............Place of parties marriage

The sheriff granted decree

(1) divorcing the defender from the Pursuer;

*(2) ordering that the following child(ren):

..........Full name(s)...............Date(s) of birth

Reside with the *pursuer/defender and finding the *pursuer/defender entitled to be in contact with the following child(ren): as follows:

All in terms of the Children (Scotland) Act 1995.

*(3) ordaining payment

*(a)   by the to the of a periodical allowance of £ per

*(b)   by the.......... to the.......... of a capital sum of £

*(c)   by the.......... to the.......... of £ per.......... as aliment for each child until that child attains years of age, said sum payable in advance and beginning at the date of this decree with interest thereon at the rate of per cent a year until payment;

*(d)   by the.......... to the.......... of £ of expenses;

*(4) finding the.......... liable to the.......... in expenses as the same may be subsequently taxed.

This extract is warrant for all lawful execution hereon.

Date: *(insert date)*

Sheriff Clerk (depute)

* Delete as appropriate.

## FORM 11

Form of extract decree of separation and aliment

### EXTRACT DECREE OF SEPARATION AND ALIMENT

Sheriff Court                              Court Ref No

Date of Decree                            *In absence

Pursuer                                    Defender

The sheriff found and declared that the pursuer is entitled to live separately from the defender from the date of decree and for all time thereafter.

The Sheriff ordered that the following child(ren):

..........Full name(s)...............Date(s) of birth

Reside with the *pursuer/defender

And found the *pursuer/defender entitled to be in contact with the following child(ren):

as follows:

All in terms of the Children (Scotland) Act 1995.

* The sheriff ordained payment by the .......... to the .......... of £.......... per .......... as aliment for the .........., said sum payable in advance and beginning at the date of this decree with interest thereon at .......... per cent a year until payment.

* The sheriff ordained payment by the .......... to the .......... of £.......... per .......... as aliment for each child, until that child attains .......... years of age, said sum payable in advance and beginning at the date of this decree with interest thereon at .......... per cent a year until payment; and granted decree against the .......... for payment of £..........

---

[1] As substituted by the Act of Sederunt (Sheriff Court Ordinary Cause Rules Amendment) (Miscellaneous) 2000 (S.S.I. 2000 No. 239)(effective October 2, 2000).

This extract is warrant for all lawful execution hereon.

Date: *(insert date)*

Sheriff Clerk (Depute) *Delete as appropriate.

[1]**FORM 12**

Form of extract decree: Residence Order/Contact Order and aliment

EXTRACT DECREE OF RESIDENCE ORDER/CONTACT ORDER AND ALIMENT

Sheriff Court          Court Ref No

Date of Decree       *In absence

Pursuer             Defender

The Sheriff granted decree against the *pursuer/defender.

The Sheriff ordered that the following child(ren):

..........Full name(s)...............Date(s) of birth

reside with the *pursuer/defender and found the *pursuer/defender entitled to be in contact with the following child(ren):

as follows:

All in terms of the Children (Scotland) Act 1995.

*The sheriff ordained payment by the .......... to the of £.......... per .......... as aliment for each child, until that child attains .......... years of age, said sum payable in advance and beginning at the date of this decree with interest thereon at .......... per cent a year until payment;

and granted decree with interest thereon at per cent a year until payment;and granted decree against the for payment of expenses of £...........

This extract is warrant for all lawful execution hereon.

Date: *(insert date)*

Sheriff Clerk (Depute)

* Delete as appropriate.

**Rule 36.G1(1B)**

[2]**APPENDIX 3**

### Schedule of Timetable Under Personal Injuries Procedure

| Steps referred to under rule 36.G1 (1A) | Period of time within which action must be carried out* |
|---|---|
| Application for a third party notice under rule 20.1 (rule 36.G1 (1A)(a)) | Not later than 28 days after defences have been lodged |
| Pursuer executing a commission for recovery of documents under rule 36.D1 (rule 36.G1(1A)(b)) | Not later than 28 days after defences have been lodged |
| Parties adjusting their pleadings (rule 36.G1(1A)(c)) | Not later than 8 weeks after defences have been lodged |

[1] As substituted by the Act of Sederunt (Sheriff Court Ordinary Cause Rules Amendment) (Miscellaneous) 2000 (S.S.I. 2000 No. 239)(effective October 2, 2000).

[2] As substituted by the Act of Sederunt (Sheriff Court Rules) (Miscellaneous Amendments) 2010 (SSI 2010/279) Sch.1 App.001 para.1 (effective July 29, 2010) and amended by the Act of Sederunt (Sheriff Court Rules) (Miscellaneous Amendments) (No.3) 2011 (SSI 2011/386) para.5 (effective November 28, 2011).

| Steps referred to under rule 36.G1 (1A) | Period of time within which action must be carried out* |
|---|---|
| Pursuer lodging a statement of valuation of claim in process (rule 36.G1(1A)(d)) | Not later than 8 weeks after defences have been lodged |
| Pursuer lodging a record (rule 36.G1(1A)(e)) | Not later than 10 weeks after defences have been lodged |
| Defender (and any third party to the action) lodging a statement of valuation of claim in process (rule 36.G1(1A)(f)) | Not later than 12 weeks after defences have been lodged |
| Parties lodging in process a list of witnesses together with any productions upon which they wish to rely (rule 36.G1(1A)(g)) | Not later than 8 weeks before the date assigned for the proof |
| Pursuer lodging in process the minute of the pre-proof conference (rule 36.G1(1A)(h)) | Not later than 21 days before the date assigned for the proof |
| *NOTE: Where there is more than one defender in an action, references in the above table to defences having been lodged should be read as references to the first lodging of defences. | |

# SHERIFF COURTS (CIVIL JURISDICTION AND PROCEDURE) (SCOTLAND) ACT 1963

## (1963 c. 22)

An Act to increase the amount by reference to which actions are classified as summary causes in the sheriff court in Scotland; to increase the amount by reference to which the small debt jurisdiction of the sheriff is limited; to amend the law with regard to the bringing of actions between spouses for interim aliment of small amounts in the sheriff's small debt court and with regard to the jurisdiction of the sheriff in such actions brought as aforesaid; and for purposes connected with the matters aforesaid.

[10th July 1963]

**1, 2.**　*[Repealed by the Sheriff Courts (Scotland) Act 1971, Sched. 2.]*

### Actions for aliment of small amounts

**3.**—(1)[1]　An action under section 2 of the Family Law (Scotland) Act 1985 for aliment only (whether or not expenses are also sought) may be brought before the sheriff as a summary cause if the aliment claimed in the action does not exceed—

    (a)　in respect of a child under the age of 18 years, the sum of £35 per week; and

    (b)　in any other case, the sum of £70 per week;

and any provision in any enactment limiting the jurisdiction of the sheriff in a summary cause by reference to any amount, or limiting the period for which a decree granted by him shall have effect, shall not apply in relation to such an action.

(2)　*[Repealed by the Civil Jurisdiction and Judgments Act 1982, Sched. 14.]*

(3)[2]　The Secretary of State may by order vary the amounts prescribed in paragraphs (a) and (b) of subsection (1) above.

(4)　The power to make an order under subsection (3) above shall be exercisable by statutory instrument subject to annulment in pursuance of a resolution of either House of Parliament and shall include power to vary or revoke any order made there under.

### Citation, construction and commencement

**4.**—(1)　This Act may be cited as the Sheriff Courts (Civil Jurisdiction and Procedure) (Scotland) Act 1963.

(2)　In this Act the expression "the principal Act" means the Sheriff Courts (Scotland) Act 1907, as amended by any other enactment, and the principal Act and this Act shall be construed together as one.

(3)　This Act shall come into operation on 1st October 1963.

---

[1] Substituted by the Family Law (Scotland) Act 1985, s.23.
[2] As amended by SI 1999 No. 678, Art. 2, Sched. (effective May 19, 1999).

An Act to increase the amount up to which claims may be made in respect of maintenance in the sheriff court in Scotland; to increase the amount by which the small debt jurisdiction of the sheriff is limited; to amend the law with regard to the bringing of actions for aliment in respect of the maintenance of children.

...

**Accounts for alimentary sums amounts**

**8.**—(1) An action under section 2 of the Family Law (Scotland) Act 1985 for aliment may, whether or not expenses are also sought, may be raised in..., the sheriff as scheduled...

...

**432**

# SHERIFF COURTS (SCOTLAND) ACT 1971

## (1971 c. 58)

An Act to amend the law with respect to sheriff courts in Scotland, and for purposes connected therewith.

[27th July 1971]

PART I – CONSTITUTION, ORGANISATION AND ADMINISTRATION

*General duty of the Secretary of State*

## Secretary of State to be responsible for organisation and administration of sheriff courts

**1.** *[Repealed by the Judiciary and Courts (Scotland) Act 2008 (asp 6) Pt 3 s.48 (effective April 1, 2010 subject to transitional provisions and savings specified in SSI 2010/39 art.6).]*

*Sheriffdoms*

## Power of Secretary of State to alter sheriffdoms

**2.**—(1) [1]

(2) [2]

(2A) [3]

(2B) [4]

(3) [5]

(4) [6]

(5) [7]

*Sheriff court districts and places where sheriff courts are to be held*

## Sheriff court districts and places where sheriff courts are to be held

**3.**—(1) [8]

(2) [9]

---

[1] Repealed by the Courts Reform (Scotland) Act 2014 (asp 18) Sch.5 Pt 1 para.6 (effective 1 April 2015; as to transitional provisions and savings see SSI 2015/77).
[2] Repealed by the Courts Reform (Scotland) Act 2014 (asp 18) Sch.5 Pt 1 para.6 (effective 1 April 2015; as to transitional provisions and savings see SSI 2015/77).
[3] Repealed by the Courts Reform (Scotland) Act 2014 (asp 18) Sch.5 Pt 1 para.6 (effective 1 April 2015; as to transitional provisions and savings see SSI 2015/77).
[4] Repealed by the Courts Reform (Scotland) Act 2014 (asp 18) Sch.5 Pt 1 para.6 (effective 1 April 2015; as to transitional provisions and savings see SSI 2015/77).
[5] Repealed by the Courts Reform (Scotland) Act 2014 (Consequential Provisions and Modifications) Order 2015 (SI 2015/700) art.2(3) (effective 1 April 2015).
[6] Repealed by the Courts Reform (Scotland) Act 2014 (asp 18) Sch.5 Pt 1 para.6 (effective 1 April 2015; as to transitional provisions and savings see SSI 2015/77).
[7] Repealed by the Courts Reform (Scotland) Act 2014 (asp 18) Sch.5 Pt 1 para.6 (effective 1 April 2015; as to transitional provisions and savings see SSI 2015/77).
[8] Repealed by the Courts Reform (Scotland) Act 2014 (asp 18) Sch.5 Pt 1 para.6 (effective 1 April 2015; as to transitional provisions and savings see SSI 2015/77).
[9] Repealed by the Courts Reform (Scotland) Act 2014 (asp 18) Sch.5 Pt 1 para.6 (effective 1 April 2015; as to transitional provisions and savings see SSI 2015/77).

(2A) [1]

(2B) [2]

(3) [3]

(4) [4]

(5) [5]

(5A) [6]

(6) [7]

**4.–30.** [8]

## PART III – CIVIL JURISDICTION, PROCEDURE AND APPEALS

### Civil Jurisdiction

## Upper limit to privative jurisdiction of sheriff court to be £5,000

**31.** [9]

**32.–34.** [10]

### Summary causes

**Summary causes**

**35.**[11](1)    The definition of "summary cause" contained in paragraph (i) of section 3 of the Sheriff Courts (Scotland) Act 1907 shall cease to have effect, and for the purposes of the procedure and practice in civil proceedings in the sheriff court there shall be a form of process, to be known as a "summary cause", which shall be used for the purposes of all civil proceedings brought in that court, being proceedings of one or other of the following descriptions, namely—

    (a)[12]    actions for payment of money not exceeding £5000 in amount (exclusive of interest and expenses);

---

[1] Repealed by the Courts Reform (Scotland) Act 2014 (asp 18) Sch.5 Pt 1 para.6 (effective 1 April 2015; as to transitional provisions and savings see SSI 2015/77).

[2] Repealed by the Courts Reform (Scotland) Act 2014 (asp 18) Sch.5 Pt 1 para.6 (effective 1 April 2015; as to transitional provisions and savings see SSI 2015/77).

[3] Repealed by the Courts Reform (Scotland) Act 2014 (asp 18) Sch.5 Pt 1 para.6 (effective 1 April 2015; as to transitional provisions and savings see SSI 2015/77).

[4] Repealed by the Courts Reform (Scotland) Act 2014 (Consequential Provisions and Modifications) Order 2015 (SI 2015/700) art.2(3) (effective 1 April 2015).

[5] Repealed by the Courts Reform (Scotland) Act 2014 (asp 18) Sch.5 Pt 1 para.6 (effective 1 April 2015; as to transitional provisions and savings see SSI 2015/77).

[6] Repealed by the Courts Reform (Scotland) Act 2014 (asp 18) Sch.5 Pt 1 para.6 (effective 1 April 2015; as to transitional provisions and savings see SSI 2015/77).

[7] Repealed by the Courts Reform (Scotland) Act 2014 (asp 18) Sch.5 Pt 1 para.6 (effective 1 April 2015; as to transitional provisions and savings see SSI 2015/77).

[8] Repealed by the Courts Reform (Scotland) Act 2014 (asp 18) Sch.5 Pt 1 para.6 (effective 1 April 2015; as to transitional provisions and savings see SSI 2015/77).

[9] Repealed by the Courts Reform (Scotland) Act 2014 (asp 18) Sch.5 Pt 1 para.6 (effective 1 April 2015; as to transitional provisions and savings see SSI 2015/77).

[10] Repealed by the Courts Reform (Scotland) Act 2014 (asp 18) Sch.5 Pt 1 para.6 (effective 1 April 2015; as to transitional provisions and savings see SSI 2015/77).

[11] Prospectively repealed by the Courts Reform (Scotland) Act 2014 (asp 18) Sch.5 Pt 1 para.6 (date to be appointed).

[12] Figure substituted by the Sheriff Courts (Scotland) Act 1971 (Privative Jurisdiction and Summary Cause) Order 2007 (SSI 2007/507) art.3 (effective January 14, 2008: substitution has effect subject to savings specified in SSI 2007/507 art.4)

(b)[1][2]   actions of multiple poinding, actions of furthcoming, where the value of the fund in medio , or the value of the arrested fund or subject, as the case may be, does not exceed £5000 (exclusive of interest and expenses);

(c)[3]   actions ad factum praestandum and actions for the recovery of possession of heritable or moveable property, other than actions in which there is claimed in addition, or as an alternative, to a decree ad factum praestandum or for such recovery, as the case may be, a decree for payment of money exceeding £5000 in amount (exclusive of interest and expenses);

(d)   proceedings which, according to the law and practice existing immediately before the commencement of this Act, might competently be brought in the sheriff's small debt court or were required to be conducted and disposed of in the summary manner in which proceedings were conducted and disposed of under the Small Debt Acts;

and any reference in the following provisions of this Act, or in any other enactment (whether passed or made before or after the commencement of this Act) relating to civil procedure in the sheriff court, to a summary cause shall be construed as a reference to a summary cause within the meaning of this subsection.

(1A)[4]   For the avoidance of doubt it is hereby declared that nothing in subsection (1) above shall prevent the Court of Session from making different rules of procedure and practice in relation to different descriptions of summary cause proceedings.

(2)[5][6]   There shall be a form of summary cause process, to be known as a "small claim", which shall be used for the purposes of such descriptions of summary cause proceedings as are prescribed by the Secretary of State by order.

(3)[7]   No enactment or rule of law relating to admissibility or corroboration of evidence before a court of law shall be binding in a small claim.

(4)[8]   An order under subsection (2) above shall be by statutory instrument but shall not be made unless a draft of it has been approved by a resolution of each House of Parliament.

## Procedure in summary causes

**36.**[9](1)[10]

---

[1] As amended by the Bankruptcy and Diligence etc. (Scotland) Act 2007 (asp 3) Sch.6(1) para.1 (effective April 1, 2008: as SSI 2008/115).

[2] Figure substituted by the Sheriff Courts (Scotland) Act 1971 (Privative Jurisdiction and Summary Cause) Order 2007 (SSI 2007/507) art.3 (effective January 14, 2008: substitution has effect subject to savings specified in SSI 2007/507 art.4)

[3] Figure substituted by the Sheriff Courts (Scotland) Act 1971 (Privative Jurisdiction and Summary Cause) Order 2007 (SSI 2007/507) art.3 (effective January 14, 2008: substitution has effect subject to savings specified in SSI 2007/507 art.4)

[4] As inserted by the Law Reform (Miscellaneous Provisions) (Scotland) Act 1985 (c.73), Sch.2, para.14, with effect from December 30, 1985.

[5] New subss (2)–(4) substituted for subs. (2) by the Law Reform (Miscellaneous Provisions) (Scotland) Act 1985 (c.73), s.18(1).

[6] As amended by SI 1999/678, art.2, Sch.(effective May 19, 1999).

[7] New subss (2)–(4) substituted for subs. (2) by the Law Reform (Miscellaneous Provisions) (Scotland) Act 1985 (c.73), s.18(1).

[8] New subss (2)–(4) substituted for subs. (2) by the Law Reform (Miscellaneous Provisions) (Scotland) Act 1985 (c.73), s.18(1).

[9] Prospectively repealed by the Courts Reform (Scotland) Act 2014 (asp 18) Sch.5 Pt 1 para.6 (date to be appointed).

[10] Repealed by the Courts Reform (Scotland) Act 2014 (asp 18) Sch.5 Pt 1 para.6 (effective April 1, 2015; as to transitional provisions and savings see SSI 2015/77).

(2)   A summary cause shall be commenced by a summons in, or as nearly as is practicable in, such form as may be prescribed by rules under the said section 32.

(3)[1]   The evidence, if any, given in a summary cause shall not be recorded.

(4)   *[Repealed by the Debtors (Scotland) Act 1987 (c.18), Sch.8.]*

## Further provisions as to small claims

**36A.**[2][3]   Where the pursuer in a small claim is not—

   (a)   a partnership or a body corporate; or

   (b)   acting in a representative capacity,

he may require the sheriff clerk to effect service of the summons on his behalf.

## Expenses in small claims

**36B.**—[4,5](1)[6]   No award of expenses shall be made in a small claim in which the value of the claim does not exceed such sum as the Secretary of State shall prescribe by order.

(2)[7]   Any expenses which the sheriff may award in any other small claim shall not exceed such sum as the Secretary of State shall prescribe by order.

(3)   Subsections (1) and (2) above do not apply to a party to a small claim—

   (a)   who being a defender—

      (i)   has not stated a defence; or

      (ii)   having stated a defence, has not proceeded with it; or

      (iii)   having stated and proceeded with a defence, has not acted in good faith as to its merits; or

   (b)   on whose part there has been unreasonable conduct in relation to the proceedings or the claim;

nor do they apply in relation to an appeal to the sheriff principal.

(4)   An order under this section shall be by statutory instrument but shall not be made unless a draft of it has been approved by a resolution of each House of Parliament.

## Remits

**37.**—[8,9](1)[10]   In the case of any ordinary cause brought in the sheriff court the sheriff—

   (a)   shall at any stage, on the joint motion of the parties to the cause, direct that the cause be treated as a summary cause, and in that case the cause shall be treated for all purposes (including appeal) as a summary cause and shall proceed accordingly;

---

[1] Excluded by the Maintenance Orders (Reciprocal Enforcement) Act 1972 (c.18), s.4(4)(b).

[2] As inserted by the Law Reform (Miscellaneous Provisions) (Scotland) Act 1985 (c.73), s.18(2).

[3] Prospectively repealed by the Courts Reform (Scotland) Act 2014 (asp 18) Sch.5 Pt 1 para.6 (date to be appointed).

[4] As inserted by the Law Reform (Miscellaneous Provisions) (Scotland) Act 1985 (c.73), s.18(2).

[5] Prospectively repealed by the Courts Reform (Scotland) Act 2014 (asp 18) Sch.5 Pt 1 para.6 (date to be appointed).

[6] As amended by SI 1999/678, art.2, Sch. (effective May 19, 1999).

[7] As amended by SI 1999/678, art.2, Sch. (effective May 19, 1999).

[8] As inserted by the Agricultural Holdings (Scotland) Act 2003 (asp 11), Pt 7, s.86(1).

[9] Prospectively repealed by the Courts Reform (Scotland) Act 2014 (asp 18) Sch.5 Pt 1 para.6 (date to be appointed).

[10] As amended by the Law Reform (Miscellaneous Provisions) (Scotland) Act 1980 (c.55), s.16(a). See the Land Tenure Reform (Scotland) Act 1974 (c.38), s.9(6).

(b) [1]

(2) In the case of any summary cause, the sheriff at any stage—

(a) shall, on the joint motion of the parties to the cause, and

(b) may, on the motion of any of the parties to the cause, if he is of the opinion that the importance or difficulty of the cause makes it appropriate to do so,

direct that the cause be treated as an ordinary cause, and in that case the cause shall be treated for all purposes (including appeal) as an ordinary cause and shall proceed accordingly:

Provided that a direction under this subsection may, in the case of an action for the recovery of possession of heritable or moveable property, be given by the sheriff of his own accord.

(2A) [2]

(2B)[3] In the case of any small claim the sheriff at any stage—

(a) may, if he is of the opinion that a difficult question of law or a question of fact of exceptional complexity is involved, of his own accord or on the motion of any party to the small claim;

(b) shall, on the joint motion of the parties to the small claim,

direct that the small claim be treated as a summary cause (not being a small claim) or ordinary cause, and in that case the small claim shall be treated for all purposes (including appeal) as a summary cause (not being a small claim) or ordinary cause as the case may be.

(2C)[4] In the case of any cause which is not a small claim by reason only of any monetary limit applicable to a small claim or to summary causes, the sheriff at any stage shall, on the joint motion of the parties to the cause, direct that the cause be treated as a small claim and in that case the cause shall be treated for all purposes (including appeal) as a small claim and shall proceed accordingly.

(2D) [5]

(3)[6] A decision—

(a) to remit, or not to remit, under subsection (2A), (2B) or (2C) above; or

(b) to make, or not to make, a direction by virtue of paragraph (b) of, or the proviso to, subsection (2) above,

shall not be subject to review; but from a decision to remit, or not to remit, under subsection (1)(b) above an appeal shall lie to the Court of Session.

(4) In this section "sheriff" includes a sheriff principal.

**Appeal in summary causes**

**38.**[7] [8] In the case of—

---

[1] Repealed by the Courts Reform (Scotland) Act 2014 (asp 18) Sch.5 Pt 1 para.6 (effective 22 September 2015; as SSI 2015/247).

[2] Repealed by the Courts Reform (Scotland) Act 2014 (asp 18) Sch.5 Pt 1 para.6 (effective 22 September 2015; as SSI 2015/247).

[3] Added by the Law Reform (Miscellaneous Provisions) (Scotland) Act 1988, s.18(3).

[4] Added by the Law Reform (Miscellaneous Provisions) (Scotland) Act 1988, s.18(3).

[5] Repealed by the Courts Reform (Scotland) Act 2014 (asp 18) Sch.5 Pt 1 para.6 (effective 22 September 2015; as SSI 2015/247).

[6] As substituted by the Law Reform (Miscellaneous Provisions) (Scotland) Act 1980 (c.55), s.16(c). As amended by the Law Reform (Miscellaneous Provisions) (Scotland) Act 1985 (c.73), s.18(3)(b).

[7] As amended by the Law Reform (Miscellaneous Provisions) (Scotland) Act 1985 (c.73), s.18(4). Excluded by the Debtors (Scotland) Act 1987 (c.18), s.103(1).

[8] Prospectively repealed by the Courts Reform (Scotland) Act 2014 (asp 18) Sch.5 Pt 1 para.6 (date to be appointed).

(a) any summary cause an appeal shall lie to the sheriff principal on any point of law from the final judgment of the sheriff; and

(b) any summary cause other than a small claim an appeal shall lie to the Court of Session on any point of law from the final judgment of the sheriff principal, if the sheriff principal certifies the cause as suitable for such an appeal,

but save as aforesaid an interlocutor of the sheriff or the sheriff principal in any such cause shall not be subject to review.

*Miscellaneous and supplemental*

**39, 40.** *[Repealed by the Law Reform (Miscellaneous Provisions) (Scotland) Act 1980 (c.55), Sch.3.]*

**41.–42.** [1]

PART IV – MISCELLANEOUS AND GENERAL

[2]

**Interpretation**

**45.—** [3]

[4]

SCHEDULES

SCHEDULE 1

MINOR AND CONSEQUENTIAL AMENDMENT OF ENACTMENTS

*General*

[5]

SCHEDULE 2

REPEAL OF ENACTMENTS

[6]

---

[1] Repealed by the Courts Reform (Scotland) Act 2014 (asp 18) Sch.5 Pt 1 para.6 (effective April 1, 2015; as to transitional provisions and savings see SSI 2015/77).

[2] Repealed by the Courts Reform (Scotland) Act 2014 (asp 18) Sch.5 Pt 1 para.6 (effective April 1, 2015; as to transitional provisions and savings see SSI 2015/77).

[3] Repealed by the Courts Reform (Scotland) Act 2014 (asp 18) Sch.5 Pt 1 para.6 (effective April 1, 2015; as to transitional provisions and savings see SSI 2015/77).

[4] Repealed by the Courts Reform (Scotland) Act 2014 (asp 18) Sch.5 Pt 1 para.6 (effective April 1, 2015; as to transitional provisions and savings see SSI 2015/77).

[5] [Repealed by the Courts Reform (Scotland) Act 2014 (asp 18) Sch.5 Pt 1 para.6 (effective April 1, 2015; as to transitional provisions and savings see SSI 2015/77).]

[6] [Repealed by the Courts Reform (Scotland) Act 2014 (asp 18) Sch.5 Pt 1 para.6 (effective April 1, 2015; as to transitional provisions and savings see SSI 2015/77).]

# DISTRICT COURTS (SCOTLAND) ACT 1975

(1975 c. 20)

*[Repealed by the Justice of the Peace Courts (Sheriffdom of South Strathclyde, Dumfries and Galloway) etc. Order 2009 (SSI 2009/332) art.7 (effective February 22, 2010).]*

# FATAL ACCIDENTS AND SUDDEN DEATHS INQUIRY (SCOTLAND) ACT 1976

## (1976 c.14)

An Act to make provision for Scotland for the holding of public inquiries in respect of fatal accidents, deaths of persons in legal custody, sudden, suspicious and unexplained deaths and deaths occurring in circumstances giving rise to serious public concern.[1]

[April 13, 1976.]

## Investigation of death and application for public inquiry

1.—(1) Subject to the provisions of any enactment specified in Schedule 1 to this Act and subsection (2) below, where—

    (a)    in the case of a death to which this paragraph applies—

        (i)    it appears that the death has resulted from an accident occurring in Scotland while the person who has died, being an employee, was in the course of his employment or, being an employer or self-employed person, was engaged in his occupation as such; or

        (ii)    the person who has died was, at the time of his death, in legal custody; or

    (b)    it appears to the Lord Advocate to be expedient in the public interest in the case of a death to which this paragraph applies that an inquiry under this Act should be held into the circumstances of the death on the ground that it was sudden, suspicious or unexplained, or has occurred in circumstances such as to give rise to serious public concern,

the procurator fiscal for the district with which the circumstances of the death appear to be most closely connected shall investigate those circumstances and apply to the sheriff for the holding of an inquiry under this Act into those circumstances.

(2) Paragraph (a) of subsection (1) above applies to a death occurring in Scotland after the commencement of this Act (other than such a death in a case where criminal proceedings have been concluded against any person in respect of the death or any accident from which the death resulted, and the Lord Advocate is satisfied that the circumstances of the death have been sufficiently established in the course of such proceedings), and paragraph (b) of that subsection applies to a death occurring there at any time after the date three years before such commencement.

(3) An application under subsection (1) above—

    (a)    shall be made to the sheriff with whose sheriffdom the circumstances of the death appear to be most closely connected;

    (b)    shall narrate briefly the circumstances of the death so far as known to the procurator fiscal;

    (c)    may, if it appears that more deaths than one have occurred as a result of the same accident or in the same or similar circumstances, relate to both or all such deaths.

(4) For the purposes of subsection (1)(a)(ii) above, a person is in legal custody if—

    (a)    he is detained in, or is subject to detention in, a prison, remand centre,

---

[1] See the Anatomy Act 1984 (c.14), s.4(6).

detention centre, borstal institution, or young offenders institution, all within the meaning of the Prisons (Scotland) Act 1952; or

(b) he is detained in a police station, police cell, or other similar place; or

(ba)[1] he is detained in, or is subject to detention in, service custody premises (within the meaning of section 300 of the Armed Forces Act 2006);

(c) he is being taken—

    (i)[2] to any of the places specified in paragraphs (a) and (b) and (ba) of this subsection to be detained therein; or

    (ii) from any such place in which immediately before such taking he was detained.

### Death of service personnel abroad

**1A.**—[3](1) Subsection (4) applies where—

(a) the Lord Advocate is notified under section 12(4) or (5) of the Coroners and Justice Act 2009 in relation to a death,

(b) the death is within subsection (2) or (3), and

(c) the Lord Advocate—

    (i) decides that it would be appropriate in the public interest for an inquiry under this Act to be held into the circumstances of the death, and

    (ii) does not reverse that decision.

(2) A death is within this subsection if the person who has died was, at the time of the death, in legal custody (as construed by reference to section 1(4)).

(3) A death is within this subsection if it appears to the Lord Advocate that the death—

(a) was sudden, suspicious or unexplained, or

(b) occurred in circumstances such as to give rise to serious public concern.

(4) The procurator fiscal for the appropriate district must—

(a) investigate the circumstances of the death, and

(b) apply to the sheriff for the holding of an inquiry under this Act into those circumstances.

(5) But subsection (4) does not extend to a death within subsection (2) if the Lord Advocate is satisfied that the circumstances of the death have been sufficiently established in the course of any criminal proceedings against any person in respect of the death.

(6) An application under subsection (4)(b)—

(a) is to be made to the sheriff of the appropriate sheriffdom,

(b) must narrate briefly the circumstances of the death so far as known to the procurator fiscal,

(c) may relate to more than one death if the deaths occurred in the same or similar circumstances.

(7) It is for the Lord Advocate to determine the appropriate district and appropriate sheriffdom for the purposes of subsections (4) and (6)(a).

---

[1] As inserted by the Armed Forces Act 2006 (c.52) Sch.16 para.72 (effective October 31, 2009).

[2] As substituted by the Armed Forces Act 2006 (c.52) Sch.16 para.72 (effective October 31, 2009).

[3] As inserted by the Coroners and Justice Act 2009 (c.25) Pt 1 c.7 s.50(2) (effective September 24, 2012).

## Citation of witnesses for precognition

**2.**—(1)[1]  The procurator fiscal may, for the purpose of carrying out his investigation under section 1(1) or 1A(4) of this Act, cite witnesses for precognition by him, and this section shall be sufficient warrant for such citation.

(2)  If any witness cited under subsection (1) above—

    (a)  fails without reasonable excuse and after receiving reasonable notice to attend for precognition by the procurator fiscal at the time and place mentioned in the citation served on him; or

    (b)  refuses when so cited to give information within his knowledge regarding any matter relevant to the investigation in relation to which such precognition is taken,

the procurator fiscal may apply to the sheriff for an order requiring the witness to attend for such precognition or to give such information at a time and place specified in the order; and the sheriff shall, if he considers it expedient to do so, make such an order.

(3)[2]  If the witness fails to comply with the order of the sheriff under subsection (2) above, he shall be liable to be summarily punished forthwith by a fine not exceeding level 3 on the standard scale or by imprisonment for any period not exceeding 20 days.

## Holding of public inquiry

**3.**—(1)[3]  On an application under section 1 or 1A of this Act being made to him, the sheriff shall make an order—

    (a)  fixing a time and place for the holding by him of an inquiry under this Act (hereafter in this Act referred to as "the inquiry"), which shall be as soon thereafter as is reasonably practicable in such courthouse or other premises as appear to him to be appropriate, having regard to the apparent circumstances of the death; and

    (b)  granting warrant to cite witnesses and havers to attend at the inquiry at the instance of the procurator fiscal or of any person who may be entitled by virtue of this Act to appear at the inquiry.

(2)  On the making of an order under subsection (1) above, the procurator fiscal shall—

    (a)  intimate the holding of the inquiry and the time and place fixed for it to the wife or husband or the nearest known relative and, in a case where the inquiry is being held in respect of such a death as is referred to in section 1(1)(a)(i) of this Act, to the employer, if any, of the person whose death is the subject of the inquiry, and to such other person or class of persons as may be prescribed in rules made under section 7(1)(g) of this Act; and

    (b)  give public notice of the holding of the inquiry and of the time and place fixed for it.

---

[1] As inserted by the Coroners and Justice Act 2009 (c.25) Pt 1 c.7 s.50(3) (effective September 24, 2012).

[2] As amended by the Criminal Procedure (Consequential Provisions) (Scotland) Act 1995 (c.40) Sch.4, para. 10.

[3] As inserted by the Coroners and Justice Act 2009 (c.25) Pt 1 c.7 s.50(4) (effective September 24, 2012).

(3)[1]  Where an application under section 1 or 1A of this Act relates to more than one death, the order made under subsection (1) above shall so relate; and in this Act references to a death shall include references to both or all deaths or to each death as the case may require, and in subsection (2)(a) above the reference to the person whose death is the subject of the inquiry shall include a reference to each person whose death is the subject of the inquiry.

## Conduct of public inquiry

**4.**—(1)  At the inquiry, it shall be the duty of the procurator fiscal to adduce evidence with regard to the circumstances of the death which is the subject of the inquiry.

(2)  The wife or husband, or the nearest known relative, and, in a case where the inquiry is being held in respect of such a death as is referred to in section 1(1)(a)(i) of this Act, the employer, if any, of the person whose death is the subject of the inquiry, an inspector appointed under section 19 of the Health and Safety at Work etc. Act 1974 and any other person who the sheriff is satisfied has an interest in the inquiry may appear and adduce evidence at the inquiry.

(3)  Subject to subsection (4) below, the inquiry shall be open to the public.

(4)  Where a person under the age of 17 is in any way involved in the inquiry, the sheriff may, at his own instance or on an application made to him by any party to the inquiry, make an order providing that—

    (a)  no report of the inquiry which is made in a newspaper or other publication or a sound or television broadcast shall reveal the name, address or school, or include any particulars calculated to lead to the identification of that person;

    (b)  no picture relating to the inquiry which is or includes a picture of that person shall be published in any newspaper or other publication or televised broadcast.

(5)[2]  Any person who contravenes an order made under subsection (4) above shall be guilty of an offence and shall be liable on summary conviction to a fine not exceeding level 4 on the standard scale in respect of each offence.

(6)  The sheriff may, either at his own instance or at the request of the procurator fiscal or of any party who may be entitled by virtue of this Act to appear at the inquiry, summon any person having special knowledge and being willing to do so, to act as an assessor at the inquiry.

(7)  Subject to the provisions of this Act and any rules made under section 7 of this Act, the rules of evidence, the procedure and the powers of the sheriff to deal with contempt of court and to enforce the attendance of witnesses at the inquiry shall be as nearly as possible those applicable in an ordinary civil cause brought before the sheriff sitting alone.

## Criminal proceedings and compellability of witnesses

**5.**—(1)  The examination of a witness or haver at the inquiry shall not be a bar to criminal proceedings being taken against him.

(2)  No witness at the inquiry shall be compellable to answer any question tending to show that he is guilty of any crime or offence.

---

[1] As inserted by the Coroners and Justice Act 2009 (c.25) Pt 1 c.7 s.50(4) (effective September 24, 2012).

[2] As amended by virtue of the Criminal Procedure (Scotland) Act 1975 (c.21), ss.289F and 289G.

## Sheriffs determination, etc.

**6.**—(1) At the conclusion of the evidence and any submissions thereon, or as soon as possible thereafter, the sheriff shall make a determination setting out the following circumstances of the death so far as they have been established to his satisfaction—

(a) where and when the death and any accident resulting in the death took place;

(b) the cause or causes of such death and any accident resulting in the death;

(c) the reasonable precautions, if any, whereby the death and any accident resulting in the death might have been avoided;

(d) the defects, if any, in any system of working which contributed to the death or any accident resulting in the death; and

(e) any other facts which are relevant to the circumstances of the death.

(2) The sheriff shall be entitled to be satisfied that any circumstances referred to in subsection (1) above have been established by evidence, notwithstanding that that evidence is not corroborated.

(3) The determination of the sheriff shall not be admissible in evidence or be founded on in any judicial proceedings, of whatever nature, arising out of the death or out of any accident from which the death resulted.

(4) On the conclusion of the inquiry

(a) the sheriff clerk shall send to the Lord Advocate a copy of the determination of the sheriff and, on a request being made to him, send to any Minister or Government Department or to the Health and Safety Commission, a copy of

    (i)[1] the application made under section 1 or 1A of this Act;

    (ii) the transcript of the evidence;

    (iii) any report or documentary production used in the inquiry;

    (iv) the determination of the sheriff, and

(b) the procurator fiscal shall send to the Registrar General of Births, Deaths and Marriages for Scotland the name and last known address of the person who has died and the date, place and cause of his death.

(5) Upon payment of such fee as may be prescribed in rules made under paragraph (i) of section 7(1) of this Act, any person—

(a) may obtain a copy of the determination of the sheriff;

(b) who has an interest in the inquiry may, within such period as may be prescribed in rules made under paragraph (j) of the said section 7(1), obtain a copy of the transcript of the evidence,

from the sheriff clerk.

## Rules

**7.**—(1)[2] The Secretary of State may, by rules, provide in relation to inquiries under this Act—

(a) as to the form of any document to be used in or for the purposes of such inquiries;

(b) for the representation, on such conditions as may be specified in the rules, of any person who is entitled by virtue of this Act to appear at the inquiry;

---

[1] As amended by the Coroners and Justice Act 2009 (c.25) Pt 1 c.7 s.50(5) (effective September 24, 2012).

[2] As amended by SI 1999/678, Art.2, Sch. (effective May 19, 1999).

(c) for the authorisation by the sheriff of the taking and holding in safe custody of anything which it may be considered necessary to produce;

(d) for the inspection by the sheriff or any person authorised by him of any land, premises, article, or other thing;

(e) that written statements and reports may, on such conditions as may be specified in the rules, be admissible in lieu of parole evidence;

(f) as to the duties, remuneration and other conditions of appointment of any assessor summoned under section 4 of this Act, and for keeping of lists of persons willing to act as such;

(g) as to intimation of the holding of the inquiry;

(h) as to the payment of fees to solicitors and expenses to witnesses and havers;

(i) as to the payment of a fee by a person obtaining a copy of the determination of the sheriff or a copy of the transcript of the evidence;

(j) as to the period within which a person entitled may obtain a copy of the transcript of the evidence at the inquiry;

(k) as to such other matters relating to procedure as the Lord Advocate thinks appropriate.

(2) The power to make rules conferred by any provision of this Act shall be exercisable by statutory instrument.

(3) Rules made by the Lord Advocate under this Act may contain such incidental, consequential and supplemental provisions as appear to him to be necessary or proper for bringing the rules into operation and giving full effect thereto.

## Minor and consequential amendments and repeals

**8.** [Not reprinted.]

## Application to continental shelf

**9.**[1] For the purposes of this Act a death or any accident from which death has resulted which has occurred—

(a) in connection with any activity falling within subsection (2) of section 23 of the Oil and Gas (Enterprise) Act 1982; and

(b) in that area, or any part of that area, in respect of which it is provided by Order in Council under subsection (1) of that section that questions arising out of acts or omissions taking place therein shall be determined in accordance with the law in force in Scotland,

shall be taken to have occurred in Scotland.

## Interpretation, transitional, citation, commencement and extent

**10.**—(1) Any reference in this Act to any other enactment shall be construed as a reference to that enactment as amended by or under any other enactment including this Act.

(2)–(3) *[Repealed by the Statute Law (Repeals) Act 1989 (c.43), Sch.1, Pt I.]*

(4) This Act may be cited as the Fatal Accidents and Sudden Deaths Inquiry (Scotland) Act 1976.

(5) *[Repealed by the Statute Law (Repeals) Act 1989 (c.43), Sch.1, Pt I.]*

---

[1] As amended by the Oil and Gas (Enterprise) Act 1982 (c.23), Sch.3, para.34 and substituted by the Petroleum Act 1998 (c.17), Sch.4 para.9 (effective February 15, 1999).

(6)   This Act, other than subsections (4) and (5) of section 4 and section 9 of this Act, extends to Scotland only.

## VULNERABLE WITNESSES (SCOTLAND) ACT 2004

### Vulnerable Witnesses (Scotland) Act 2004

((ASP 3))

[April 14, 2004]

### PART 2 CIVIL PROCEEDINGS

*Evidence of children and other vulnerable witnesses: special measures*

11. Interpretation of this Part
12. Orders authorising the use of special measures for vulnerable witnesses
13. Review of arrangements for vulnerable witnesses
14. Procedure in connection with orders under sections 12 and 13
15. Vulnerable witnesses: supplementary provision
16. Party to proceedings as a vulnerable witness
17. Crown application and saving provision
18. The special measures
19. Taking of evidence by a commissioner
20. Live television link
21. Screens
22. Supporters

*Establishment of grounds of referral to children's hearings: restrictions on evidence*

23. Establishment of grounds of referral to children's hearings: restrictions on evidence

### PART 3 MISCELLANEOUS AND GENERAL

*Abolition of the competence test*

24. Abolition of the competence test for witnesses in criminal and civil proceedings

### PART 2 – CIVIL PROCEEDINGS

*Evidence of children and other vulnerable witnesses: special measures*

**Interpretation of this Part**

**11.**—(1)[1]  For the purposes of this Part of this Act, a person who is giving or is to give evidence in or for the purposes of any civil proceedings is a vulnerable witness if—

(a) the person is under the age of 18 on the date of commencement of the proceedings (such a vulnerable witness being referred to in this Part as a "child witness"),

(b) where the person is not a child witness, there is a significant risk that the quality of the evidence to be given by the person will be diminished by reason of—

    (i) mental disorder (within the meaning of section 328 of the Mental Health (Care and Treatment) (Scotland) Act 2003 (asp 13)), or

    (ii) fear or distress in connection with giving evidence in the proceedings; or

---

[1] As amended by the Victims and Witnesses (Scotland) Act 2014 (asp 1) s.22 (effective 1 September 2015; as to transitional provisions see SSI 2015/200 art.5).

    (c)    the person is of such description or is a witness in such proceedings as the Scottish Ministers may by order subject to the affirmative procedure prescribe.

(2)   In considering whether a person is a vulnerable witness by virtue of subsection (1)(b) above, the court must take into account—

    (a)    the nature and circumstances of the alleged matter to which the proceedings relate,

    (b)    the nature of the evidence which the person is likely to give,

    (c)    the relationship (if any) between the person and any party to the proceedings,

    (d)    the person's age and maturity,

    (e)    any behaviour towards the person on the part of—

        (i)    any party to the proceedings,

        (ii)    members of the family or associates of any such party,

        (iii)   any other person who is likely to be a party to the proceedings or a witness in the proceedings, and

    (f)    such other matters, including—

        (i)    the social and cultural background and ethnic origins of the person,

        (ii)    the person's sexual orientation,

        (iii)   the domestic and employment circumstances of the person,

        (iv)   any religious beliefs or political opinions of the person, and

        (v)    any physical disability or other physical impairment which the person has,

as appear to the court to be relevant.

(3)   For the purposes of subsection (1)(a) above, proceedings are taken to have commenced when the petition, summons, initial writ or other document initiating the proceedings is served, and, where the document is served on more than one person, the proceedings shall be taken to have commenced when the document is served on the first person on whom it is served.

(4)   In subsection (1)(b), the reference to the quality of evidence is to its quality in terms of completeness, coherence and accuracy.

(5)[1]   In this Part

"the 2011 Act" means the Children's Hearings (Scotland) Act 2011 (asp 1),

"child witness notice" has the meaning given in section 12(2),

"civil proceedings" includes, in addition to such proceedings in any of the ordinary courts of law, relevant proceedings,

"court" is to be construed in accordance with the meaning of "civil proceedings",

"relevant proceedings" means proceedings under Part 10 of the 2011 Act (other than section 98 or 99),

"special measure" means any of the special measures set out in, or prescribed under, section 18,

"vulnerable witness application" has the meaning given in section 12(6)(a).

## Orders authorising the use of special measures for vulnerable witnesses

**12.**—(1)   Where a child witness is to give evidence in or for the purposes of any civil proceedings, the court must, before the proof or other hearing at which the

---

[1] As amended by the Children's Hearings (Scotland) Act 2011 (asp 1) Pt 17 s.176 (effective June 24, 2013).

child is to give evidence, make an order—

    (a)   authorising the use of such special measure or measures as the court considers to be the most appropriate for the purpose of taking the child witness's evidence, or

    (b)   that the child witness is to give evidence without the benefit of any special measure.

(2)   The party citing or intending to cite a child witness must lodge with the court a notice (referred to in this Part as a "child witness notice")—

    (a)   specifying the special measure or measures which the party considers to be the most appropriate for the purpose of taking the child witness's evidence, or

    (b)   if the party considers that the child witness should give evidence without the benefit of any special measure, stating that fact,

and the court must have regard to the child witness notice in making an order under subsection (1) above.

(3)   If a child witness notice specifies any of the following special measures, namely—

    (a)   the use of a live television link in accordance with section 20 where the place from which the child witness is to give evidence by means of the link is another part of the court building in which the court-room is located,

    (b)   the use of a screen in accordance with section 21, or

    (c)   the use of a supporter in accordance with section 22 in conjunction with either of the special measures referred to in paragraphs (a) and (b) above,

that special measure is, for the purposes of subsection (1)(a) above, to be taken to be the most appropriate for the purposes of taking the child witness's evidence.

(4)   The court may make an order under subsection (1)(b) above only if satisfied—

    (a)   that the child witness has expressed a wish to give evidence without the benefit of any special measure and that it is appropriate for the child witness so to give evidence, or

    (b)   that—

        (i)   the use of any special measure for the purpose of taking the evidence of the child witness would give rise to a significant risk of prejudice to the fairness of the proceedings or otherwise to the interests of justice, and

        (ii)   that risk significantly outweighs any risk of prejudice to the interests of the child witness if the order is made.

(5)   Subsection (6) below applies in relation to a person other than a child witness who is to give evidence in or for the purpose of any civil proceedings (referred to in this section as "the witness").

(6)   The court may—

    (a)   on an application (referred to in this Part as a "vulnerable witness application") made to it by the party citing or intending to cite the witness, and

    (b)   if satisfied that the witness is a vulnerable witness,

make an order authorising the use of such special measure or measures as the court considers most appropriate for the purpose of taking the witness's evidence.

(7)   In deciding whether to make an order under subsection (6) above, the court must—

    (a)   have regard to—

        (i)   the possible effect on the witness if required to give evidence without the benefit of any special measure, and

(ii)   whether it is likely that the witness would be better able to give evidence with the benefit of a special measure, and

(b)   take into account the matters specified in section 11(2)(a) to (f).

(8)[1]   In the case of relevant proceedings, the child witness notice or vulnerable witness application—

(a)   must be lodged or made before the commencement of the hearing at which the child or, as the case may be, vulnerable witness is to give evidence,

(b)   on cause shown, may be lodged or made after the commencement of that hearing.

## Review of arrangements for vulnerable witnesses

**13.**—(1)   In any civil proceedings in which a person who is giving or is to give evidence (referred to in this section as "the witness") appears to the court to be a vulnerable witness, the court may at any stage in the proceedings (whether before or after the commencement of the proof or other hearing at which the witness is giving or is to give evidence or before or after the witness has begun to give evidence)—

(a)   on the application of the party citing or intending to cite the witness, or

(b)   of its own motion,

review the current arrangements for taking the witness's evidence and make an order under subsection (2) below.

(2)   The order which may be made under this subsection is—

(a)   where the current arrangements for taking the witness's evidence include the use of a special measure or combination of special measures authorised by an order under section 12 or under this subsection (referred to as the "earlier order"), an order varying or revoking the earlier order, or

(b)   where the current arrangements for taking the witness's evidence do not include any special measure, an order authorising the use of such special measure or measures as the court considers most appropriate for the purpose of taking the witness's evidence.

(3)   An order under subsection (2)(a) above varying an earlier order may—

(a)   add to or substitute for any special measure authorised by the earlier order such other special measure as the court considers most appropriate for the purpose of taking the witness's evidence, or

(b)   where the earlier order authorises the use of a combination of special measures for that purpose, delete any of the special measures so authorised.

(4)   The court may make an order under subsection (2)(a) above revoking an earlier order only if satisfied that—

(a)   the witness has expressed a wish to give or, as the case may be, continue to give evidence without the benefit of any special measure and that it is appropriate for the witness so to give evidence, or

(b)   that—

(i)   the use, or continued use, of the special measure for the purpose of taking the witness's evidence would give rise to a significant risk of prejudice to the fairness of the proceedings or otherwise to the interests of justice, and

---

[1] As inserted by the Children's Hearings (Scotland) Act 2011 (asp 1) Pt 17 s.176 (effective June 24, 2013).

(ii) that risk significantly outweighs any risk of prejudice to the interests of the witness if the order is made.

(5) Subsection (7) of section 12 applies to the making of an order under subsection (2)(b) of this section as it applies to the making of an order under subsection (6) of that section but as if the references to the witness were to the witness within the meaning of this section.

(6) In this section, "current arrangements" means the arrangements in place at the time the review under this section is begun.

**Procedure in connection with orders under sections 12 and 13**

**14.**—(1) In section 5 (power to regulate procedure etc. in the Court of Session by act of sederunt) of the Court of Session Act 1988 (c. 36), after paragraph (d) there is inserted—

> "(da) to regulate the procedure to be followed in proceedings in the Court in connection with the making of orders under sections 12(1) and (6) and 13(2) of the Vulnerable Witnesses (Scotland) Act 2004 (asp 3) ("the 2004 Act");
>
> (db) to regulate, so far as not regulated by the 2004 Act, the use in any proceedings in the Court of any special measures authorised by virtue of that Act to be used;".

(2) In section 32(1) (power of Court of Session to regulate civil procedure in the sheriff court) of the Sheriff Courts (Scotland) Act 1971 (c. 58), after paragraph (e) there is inserted—

> "(ea) regulating the procedure to be followed in connection with the making of orders under sections 12(1) and (6) and 13(2) of the Vulnerable Witnesses (Scotland) Act 2004 (asp 3) ("the 2004 Act");
>
> (eb) regulating, so far as not regulated by the 2004 Act, the use of special measures authorised by virtue of that Act to be used;".

**Vulnerable witnesses: supplementary provision**

**15.**—(1) Subsection (2) below applies where—

(a) a party is considering for the purposes of a child witness notice or a vulnerable witness application which of the special measures is or are the most appropriate for the purpose of taking the evidence of the person to whom the notice or application relates, or

(b) the court is making an order under section 12(1) or (6) or 13(2).

(2) The party or, as the case may be, the court must—

(a) have regard to the best interests of the witness, and

(b) take account of any views expressed by—

(i) the witness (having regard, where the witness is a child witness, to the witness's age and maturity), and

(ii) where the witness is a child witness, the witness's parent.

(3) For the purposes of subsection (2)(b) above, where the witness is a child witness—

(a) the witness is to be presumed to be of sufficient age and maturity to form a view if aged 12 or older, and

(b) in the event that any views expressed by the witness are inconsistent with any views expressed by the witness's parent, the views of the witness are to be given greater weight.

(4) In this section—

"parent", in relation to a child witness, means any person having parental responsibilities within the meaning of section 1(3) of the Children (Scotland) Act 1995 (c. 36) in relation to the child witness,
"the witness" means—
    (a)  in the case referred to in subsection (1)(a) above, the person to whom the child witness notice or vulnerable witness application relates,
    (b)  in the case referred to in subsection (1)(b) above, the person to whom the order would relate.

## Party to proceedings as a vulnerable witness

**16.—**  Where a child witness or other person who is giving or is to give evidence in or for the purposes of any civil proceedings (referred to in this section as "the witness") is a party to the proceedings—
    (a)  sections 12 and 13 have effect in relation to the witness as if references in those sections to the party citing or intending to cite the witness were references to the witness, and
    (b)  section 15 has effect in relation to the witness as if—
        (i)  in subsection (1), paragraph (a) were omitted, and
        (ii)  in subsection (2), the words "The party or, as the case may be," were omitted.

## Relevant proceedings: Principal Reporter's power to act for party to proceedings

**16A.—**[1](1)  Subsection (2) applies where a child witness or other person who is giving or is to give evidence in or for the purposes of relevant proceedings (referred to in this section as "the party") is a party to the proceedings.
    (2)  The Principal Reporter may, on the party's behalf—
    (a)  lodge a child witness notice under section 12(2),
    (b)  make a vulnerable witness application for an order under section 12(6),
    (c)  make an application under section 13(1)(a) for review of the current arrangements for taking a witness's evidence.

## Crown application and saving provision

**17.—**(1)  Sections 11 to 15 of this Act apply to the Crown.
    (2)  Nothing in section 12 or 13 of this Act affects any power or duty which a court has otherwise than by virtue of those sections to make or authorise any special arrangements for taking the evidence of any person in any civil proceedings.

## The special measures

**18.—**(1)  The special measures which may be authorised to be used by virtue of section 12 or 13 of this Act for the purpose of taking the evidence of a vulnerable witness are—
    (a)  taking of evidence by a commissioner in accordance with section 19,
    (b)  use of a live television link in accordance with section 20,
    (c)  use of screen in accordance with section 21,

---

[1] As inserted by the Children's Hearings (Scotland) Act 2011 (asp 1) Pt 17 s.176 (effective June 24, 2013).

(d)   use of a supporter in accordance with section 22, and

(e)   such other measures as the Scottish Ministers may, by order made by statutory instrument, prescribe.

(2)   An order under subsection (1)(e) above is not to be made unless a draft of the statutory instrument containing the order has been laid before and approved by a resolution of the Scottish Parliament.

### Taking of evidence by a commissioner

**19.**—(1)   Where the special measure to be used is taking of evidence by a commissioner, the court must appoint a commissioner to take the evidence of the vulnerable witness in respect of whom the special measure is to be used.

(2)   Proceedings before a commissioner appointed under subsection (1) above must be recorded by video recorder.

(3)   A party to the proceedings—

(a)   must not, except by leave of the court, be present in the room where such proceedings are taking place, but

(b)   is entitled by such means as seem suitable to the court to watch and hear the proceedings.

(4)   The recording of the proceedings made in pursuance of subsection (2) above is to be received in evidence without being sworn to by witnesses.

### Live television link

**20.**—(1)   Where the special measure to be used is a live television link, the court must make such arrangements as seem to it appropriate for the vulnerable witness in respect of whom the special measure is to be used to give evidence by means of such a link.

(2)   Where—

(a)   the live television link is to be used in proceedings in a sheriff court, but

(b)   that court lacks accommodation or equipment necessary for the purpose of receiving such a link,

the sheriff may by order transfer the proceedings to any sheriff court in the same sheriffdom which has such accommodation or equipment available.

(3)   An order may be made under subsection (2) above—

(a)   at any stage in the proceedings (whether before or after the commencement of the proof or other hearing at which the vulnerable witness is to give evidence), or

(b)   in relation to a part of the proceedings.

### Screens

**21.**—(1)   Where the special measure to be used is a screen, the screen must be used to conceal the parties to the proceedings from the sight of the vulnerable witness in respect of whom the special measure is to be used.

(2)   However, the court must make arrangements to ensure that the parties are able to watch and hear the vulnerable witness giving evidence.

(3)   Subsections (2) and (3) of section 20 apply for the purposes of use of a screen under this section as they apply for the purposes of use of a live television link under that section but as if—

(a)   references to the live television link were references to the screen, and

(b)   the reference to receiving such a link were a reference to the use of a screen.

**Supporters**

**22.**—(1)   Where the special measure to be used is a supporter, another person ("the supporter") nominated by or on behalf of the vulnerable witness in respect of whom the special measure is to be used may be present alongside the witness for the purpose of providing support whilst the witness is giving evidence.

(2)   Where the person nominated as the supporter is to give evidence in the proceedings, that person may not act as the supporter at any time before giving evidence.

(3)   The supporter must not prompt or otherwise seek to influence the vulnerable witness in the course of giving evidence.

**Giving evidence in chief in the form of a prior statement**

**22A.**—[1](1)   This section applies to proceedings in relation to—
- (a)   an application made by virtue of section 93 or 94 of the 2011 Act to determine whether the ground mentioned in section 67(2)(j) of that Act is established, or
- (b)   an application under section 110 of that Act for review of a finding that the ground mentioned in section 67(2)(j) of that Act is established.

(2)   The special measures which may be authorised by virtue of section 12 or 13 for the purpose of taking the evidence of a vulnerable witness at a hearing to consider such an application include (in addition to those listed in section 18(1)) the giving of evidence in chief in the form of a prior statement in accordance with subsections (3) to (10).

(3)   Where that special measure is to be used, a statement made by the vulnerable witness (a "prior statement") may be lodged in evidence for the purposes of this section by or on behalf of the party citing the vulnerable witness.

(4)   A prior statement is admissible as the witness's evidence in chief, or as part of the witness's evidence in chief, without the witness being required to adopt or otherwise speak to the statement in giving evidence.

(5)   A prior statement is admissible as evidence of any matter stated in it of which direct oral evidence by the vulnerable witness would be admissible if given at the hearing.

(6)   A prior statement is admissible under this section only if—
- (a)   it is contained in a document, and
- (b)   at the time the statement was made, the vulnerable witness would have been a competent witness for the purposes of the hearing.

(7)   Subsection (6) does not apply to a prior statement—
- (a)   contained in a precognition on oath, or
- (b)   made in other proceedings (whether criminal or civil and whether taking place in the United Kingdom or elsewhere).

(8)   A prior statement of a type mentioned in subsection (7) is not admissible for the purposes of this section unless it is authenticated in such manner as may be prescribed by regulations made by statutory instrument by the Scottish Ministers.

(9)   This section does not affect the admissibility of any statement made by any person which is admissible otherwise than by virtue of this section.

(10)   In this section—

---

[1] As inserted by the Children's Hearings (Scotland) Act 2011 (asp 1) Pt 17 s.176 (effective June 24, 2013).

"document" has the meaning given by section 262(3) of the Criminal Procedure (Scotland) Act 1995 (c.46),

"statement"—

    (a)   includes—

        (i)   any representation, however made or expressed, of fact or opinion, and

        (ii)   any part of a statement, but

    (b)   does not include a statement in a precognition other than a precognition on oath.

(11)   For the purposes of this section, a statement is contained in a document where the person who makes it—

    (a)   makes the statement in the document personally,

    (b)   makes a statement which is, with or without the person's knowledge, embodied in a document by whatever means or by any person who has direct personal knowledge of the making of the statement, or

    (c)   approves a document as embodying the statement.

(12)   A statutory instrument containing regulations under subsection (8) is subject to annulment in pursuance of a resolution of the Scottish Parliament.

## Establishment of grounds of referral to children's hearings: restrictions on evidence

**23.**   *[As repealed by the Children's Hearings (Scotland) Act 2011 (asp 1) Sch.6 para.1 (effective June 24, 2013).]*

PART 3 – MISCELLANEOUS AND GENERAL

*Abolition of the competence test*

## Abolition of the competence test for witnesses in criminal and civil proceedings

**24.**—(1)   The evidence of any person called as a witness (referred to in this section as "the witness") in criminal or civil proceedings is not inadmissible solely because the witness does not understand—

    (a)   the nature of the duty of a witness to give truthful evidence, or

    (b)   the difference between truth and lies.

(2)   Accordingly, the court must not, at any time before the witness gives evidence, take any step intended to establish whether the witness understands those matters.

# COURTS REFORM (SCOTLAND) ACT 2014

## (2014 ASP 18)

## CONTENTS

Section

### PART 1 SHERIFF COURTS

Chapter 1 Sheriffdoms, sheriff court districts and sheriff courts

1    Sheriffdoms, sheriff court districts and sheriff courts
2    Power to alter sheriffdoms, sheriff court districts and sheriff courts

Chapter 2 Judiciary of the sheriffdoms

*Permanent and full-time judiciary*

3    Sheriffs principal
4    Sheriffs
5    Summary sheriffs

*Temporary and part-time judiciary*

6    Temporary sheriff principal
7    Temporary sheriff principal: further provision
8    Part-time sheriffs
9    Reappointment of part-time sheriffs
10    Part-time summary sheriffs
11    Reappointment of part-time summary sheriffs

*Re-employment of former holders of certain judicial offices*

12    Re-employment of former judicial office holders
13    Re-employment of former judicial office holders: further provision

*Qualification and disqualification*

14    Qualification for appointment
15    Disqualification from practice, etc.

*Remuneration and expenses*

16    Remuneration
17    Expenses

*Leave of absence*

18    Leave of absence

*Residence*

19    Place of residence

*Cessation of appointment*

20    Cessation of appointment of judicial officers

*Fitness for office*

21    Tribunal to consider fitness for office
22    Tribunal investigations: suspension from office
23    Further provision about tribunals
24    Tribunal report
25    Removal from office

*Honorary sheriffs*

26    Abolition of the office of honorary sheriff

Chapter 3 Organisation of business

*Sheriff principal's general responsibilities*

27    Sheriff principal's responsibility for efficient disposal of business in sheriff courts

28    Sheriff principal's power to fix sittings of sheriff courts

29    Lord President's power to exercise functions under sections 27 and 28

*Deployment of judiciary*

30    Power to authorise a sheriff principal to act in another sheriffdom

31    Power to direct a sheriff or summary sheriff to act in another sheriffdom

32    Power to re-allocate sheriffs principal, sheriffs and summary sheriffs between sheriffdoms

33    Allocation of sheriffs and summary sheriffs to sheriff court districts

*Judicial specialisation*

34    Determination of categories of case for purposes of judicial specialisation

35    Designation of specialist judiciary

36    Allocation of business to specialist judiciary

37    Saving for existing powers to provide for judicial specialisation

Chapter 4 Competence and jurisdiction

*Sheriffs: civil competence and jurisdiction*

38    Jurisdiction and competence of sheriffs

39    Exclusive competence

40    Territorial jurisdiction

41    Power to confer all-Scotland jurisdiction for specified cases

42    All-Scotland jurisdiction: further provision

43    Jurisdiction over persons, etc.

*Summary sheriffs: civil and criminal competence and jurisdiction*

44    Summary sheriff: civil competence and jurisdiction

45    Summary sheriff: criminal competence and jurisdiction

Part 2 The Sheriff Appeal Court

Chapter 1 Establishment and role

46    The Sheriff Appeal Court

47    Jurisdiction and competence

48    Status of decisions of the Sheriff Appeal Court in precedent

Chapter 2 Appeal Sheriffs

49    Sheriffs principal to be Appeal Sheriffs

50    Appointment of sheriffs as Appeal Sheriffs

51    Re-employment of former Appeal Sheriffs

52    Expenses

53    Temporary provision

Chapter 3 Organisation of business

*President and Vice President*

54    President and Vice President of the Sheriff Appeal Court

55    President and Vice President: incapacity and suspension

*Disposal of business*

56    President's responsibility for efficient disposal of business

*Sittings*

57    Sittings of the Sheriff Appeal Court

58    Rehearing of pending case by a larger Court

Chapter 4 Administration

*Clerks*

59    Clerk of the Sheriff Appeal Court

60   Deputy Clerks of the Sheriff Appeal Court
61   Clerk and Deputy Clerks: further provision

*Records*

62   Records of the Sheriff Appeal Court

PART 3 CIVIL PROCEDURE

Chapter 1 Sheriff court

*Civil jury trials*

63   Civil jury trials in an all-Scotland sheriff court
64   Selection of the jury
65   Application to allow the jury to view property
66   Discharge or death of juror during trial
67   Trial to proceed despite objection to opinion and direction of the sheriff
68   Return of verdict
69   Application for new trial
70   Restrictions on granting a new trial
71   Verdict subject to opinion of the Sheriff Appeal Court

*Simple procedure*

72   Simple procedure
73   Proceedings in an all-Scotland sheriff court
74   Proceedings for aliment of small amounts under simple procedure
75   Rule-making: matters to be taken into consideration
76   Service of documents
77   Evidence in simple procedure cases
78   Transfer of cases to simple procedure
79   Proceedings in an all-Scotland sheriff court: transfer to simple procedure
80   Transfer of cases from simple procedure
81   Expenses in simple procedure cases
82   Appeals from simple procedure cases
83   Transitional provision: summary causes

*Interdicts and other orders: effect outside sheriffdom*

84   Interdicts having effect in more than one sheriffdom
85   Proceedings for breach of an extended interdict
86   Power to enable sheriff to make orders having effect outside sheriffdom

*Execution of deeds relating to heritage*

87   Power of sheriff to order sheriff clerk to execute deed relating to heritage

*Interim orders*

88   Interim orders

Chapter 2 Court of Session

89   Judicial review
90   Interim orders
91   Warrants for ejection

Chapter 3 Remit of cases between courts

92   Remit of cases to the Court of Session
93   Remit of cases from the Court of Session
94   Remit of cases to the Scottish Land Court

Chapter 4 Lay representation for non-natural persons

95   Key defined terms
96   Lay representation in simple procedure cases

| | |
|---|---|
| 97 | Lay representation in other proceedings |
| 98 | Lay representation: supplementary provision |

Chapter 5 Jury service

| | |
|---|---|
| 99 | Jury service |

Chapter 6 Vexatious proceedings

| | |
|---|---|
| 100 | Vexatious litigation orders |
| 101 | Vexatious litigation orders: further provision |
| 102 | Power to make orders in relation to vexatious behaviour |

PART 4 PROCEDURE AND FEES

*Procedure*

| | |
|---|---|
| 103 | Power to regulate procedure etc. in the Court of Session |
| 104 | Power to regulate procedure etc. in the sheriff court and the Sheriff Appeal Court |

*Fees of solicitors etc.*

| | |
|---|---|
| 105 | Power to regulate fees in the Court of Session |
| 106 | Power to regulate fees in the sheriff court and the Sheriff Appeal Court |

*Court fees*

| | |
|---|---|
| 107 | Power to provide for fees for SCTS, court clerks and other officers |

*Sanction for counsel*

| | |
|---|---|
| 108 | Sanction for counsel in the sheriff court and Sheriff Appeal Court |

PART 5 CIVIL APPEALS

*Appeals to the Sheriff Appeal Court*

| | |
|---|---|
| 109 | Abolition of appeal from a sheriff to the sheriff principal |
| 110 | Appeal from a sheriff to the Sheriff Appeal Court |
| 111 | Sheriff Appeal Court's powers of disposal in appeals |
| 112 | Remit of appeal from the Sheriff Appeal Court to the Court of Session |

*Appeals to the Court of Session*

| | |
|---|---|
| 113 | Appeal from the Sheriff Appeal Court to the Court of Session |
| 114 | Appeal from the sheriff principal to the Court of Session |
| 115 | Appeals: granting of leave or permission and assessment of grounds of appeal |

*Effect of appeal*

| | |
|---|---|
| 116 | Effect of appeal |

*Appeals to the Supreme Court*

| | |
|---|---|
| 117 | Appeals to the Supreme Court |

PART 6 CRIMINAL APPEALS

*Appeals from summary criminal proceedings*

| | |
|---|---|
| 118 | Appeals to the Sheriff Appeal Court from summary criminal proceedings |
| 119 | Appeals from the Sheriff Appeal Court to the High Court |
| 120 | Power to refer points of law for the opinion of the High Court |
| 121 | References by the Scottish Criminal Cases Review Commission |

*Bail appeals*

| | |
|---|---|
| 122 | Bail appeals |

PART 7 JUDGES OF THE COURT OF SESSION

| | |
|---|---|
| 123 | Appointment of Court of Session judges, etc. |
| 124 | Payment of salaries of Court of Session judges |
| 125 | Expenses |

Part 8 Scottish Land Court

126    Scottish Land Court: remuneration and expenses

Part 9 Justice of the Peace Courts

127    Establishing, relocating and disestablishing justice of the peace courts
128    Abolition of the office of stipendiary magistrate
129    Summary sheriffs to sit in justice of the peace courts

Part 10 The Scottish Courts and Tribunals Service

130    The Scottish Courts and Tribunals Service

Part 11 The Judicial Appointments Board for Scotland

131    Assistants to the Judicial Appointments Board for Scotland

Part 12 General

132    Modifications of enactments
133    Subordinate legislation
134    References to "sheriff"
135    Definition of "family proceedings"
136    Interpretation
137    Ancillary provision
138    Commencement
139    Short title
Schedule 1 —Civil proceedings, etc. in relation to which summary sheriff has competence
Schedule 2—Appeal Sheriffs: temporary provision
Schedule 3 —[*Not reproduced.*]
Schedule 4 —[*Not reproduced.*]
Schedule 5 —[*Not reproduced.*]

An Act of the Scottish Parliament to make provision about the sheriff courts; to establish a Sheriff Appeal Court; to make provision about civil court procedure; to make provision about appeals in civil proceedings; to make provision about appeals in criminal proceedings; to make provision about judges of the Court of Session; to make provision about the Scottish Land Court; to make provision about justice of the peace courts; to rename the Scottish Court Service and give it functions in relation to tribunals; to provide for assistants to the Judicial Appointments Board for Scotland; and for connected purposes.

**The Bill for this Act of the Scottish Parliament was passed by the Parliament on 7th October 2014 and received Royal Assent on 10th November 2014**

Part 1 – Sheriff courts

Chapter 1 – Sheriffdoms, sheriff court districts and sheriff courts

**Sheriffdoms, sheriff court districts and sheriff courts**

**1.**—(1)    For the purposes of the administration of justice, Scotland is to be divided into areas, each to be known as a "sheriffdom".

(2)    A sheriffdom is to comprise one or more areas, each to be known as a "sheriff court district".

(3)    Within each sheriff court district a place is to be designated at which the judiciary of the sheriffdom are to sit and hold court for the purpose of exercising their judicial functions; and such sittings are to be known as a "sheriff court".

(4)   The sheriffdoms and sheriff court districts existing immediately before the date on which this section comes into force are to continue to exist on and after that date, and are accordingly the first sheriffdoms and sheriff court districts for the purposes of subsections (1) and (2).

(5)   On and after the date on which this section comes into force, sheriff courts are to continue to be held at the places at which they were held immediately before that date, and accordingly those places are the first places designated for the holding of sheriff courts for the purposes of subsection (3).

(6)   Subsections (4) and (5) are subject to an order under section 2.

### Power to alter sheriffdoms, sheriff court districts and sheriff courts

**2.**—(1)   The Scottish Ministers may, following submission of a proposal under subsection (2), by order do any of the following—

(a)   alter the boundaries of sheriffdoms or sheriff court districts,

(b)   abolish sheriffdoms or sheriff court districts,

(c)   form new sheriffdoms or sheriff court districts,

(d)   provide that sheriff courts are to be held, or to cease being held, at any place specified in the order.

(2)   The Scottish Courts and Tribunals Service may, with the agreement of the Lord President of the Court of Session, submit a proposal to the Scottish Ministers for the making of an order under subsection (1).

(3)   Before submitting a proposal to the Scottish Ministers, the Scottish Courts and Tribunals Service must consult such persons as it considers appropriate.

(4)   If, following submission of a proposal, the Scottish Ministers decide to make an order, they must have regard to the proposal in deciding what provision to make in the order.

(5)   The Scottish Ministers may make an order under subsection (1) only with the consent of—

(a)   the Lord President, and

(b)   the Scottish Courts and Tribunals Service.

(6)   An order under subsection (1) may—

(a)   abolish any office in consequence of any provision made under subsection (1),

(b)   modify any enactment (including this Act).

### Chapter 2 – Judiciary of the sheriffdoms

*Permanent and full-time judiciary*

### Sheriffs principal

**3.**—(1)   For each sheriffdom, there is to continue to be a judicial officer to be known as the "sheriff principal" of the sheriffdom.

(2)   It is for Her Majesty to appoint an individual to the office of sheriff principal.

(3)   The First Minister may, under section 95(4) of the Scotland Act 1998, recommend to Her Majesty the appointment of an individual to the office of sheriff principal only if the individual is qualified for appointment (see section 14).

(4)   Subsection (3) does not affect the operation of section 11 of the Judiciary and Courts (Scotland) Act 2008 (recommendation by the Judicial Appointments Board for Scotland).

(5)    In addition to the jurisdiction and powers that attach specifically to the office of sheriff principal, the sheriff principal of a sheriffdom may also exercise in the sheriffdom the jurisdiction and powers that attach to the office of sheriff.

(6)    Subsection (5) is subject to any provision, express or implied, to the contrary in any other enactment.

## Sheriffs

**4.**—(1)    For each sheriffdom, there are to continue to be judicial officers each to be known as a "sheriff" of the sheriffdom.

(2)    It is for Her Majesty to appoint an individual to the office of sheriff.

(3)    The First Minister may, under section 95(4) of the Scotland Act 1998, recommend to Her Majesty the appointment of an individual to the office of sheriff only if the individual is qualified for appointment (see section 14).

(4)    Subsection (3) does not affect the operation of section 11 of the Judiciary and Courts (Scotland) Act 2008 (recommendation by the Judicial Appointments Board for Scotland).

## Summary sheriffs

**5.**—(1)    For each sheriffdom, there are to be judicial officers each to be known as a "summary sheriff" of the sheriffdom.

(2)    It is for Her Majesty to appoint an individual to the office of summary sheriff.

(3)    Her Majesty may appoint an individual only if the individual has been recommended for appointment by the First Minister.

(4)    The First Minister may recommend to Her Majesty the appointment of an individual only if the individual is qualified for appointment (see section 14).

(5)    Before making a recommendation under subsection (3), the First Minister must consult the Lord President of the Court of Session.

(6)    Subsection (4) does not affect the operation of section 11 of the Judiciary and Courts (Scotland) Act 2008 (recommendation by the Judicial Appointments Board for Scotland).

*Temporary and part-time judiciary*

## Temporary sheriff principal

**6.**—(1)    Subsection (2) applies where, in relation to a sheriffdom—

(a)    a vacancy occurs in the office of sheriff principal,

(b)    the Lord President of the Court of Session believes that the sheriff principal is unable to perform all or some of the functions of the office, or

(c)    the sheriff principal rules that he or she is precluded from performing all or some of those functions.

(2)    If the Lord President so requests, the Scottish Ministers must appoint—

(a)    a person holding the office of sheriff (whether of the same or another sheriffdom), or

(b)    a qualifying former sheriff principal (whether of the same or another sheriffdom),

to act as sheriff principal of the sheriffdom.

(3)    A "qualifying former sheriff principal" is an individual who—

(a)    ceased to hold that office other than by virtue of an order under section 25, and

(b)    has not reached the age of 75.

(4)   The appointment may be made for the purposes of the exercise of—

(a)   all of the sheriff principal's functions, or

(b)   only those functions that the sheriff principal is unable to perform or is precluded from performing.

(5)   An individual appointed under subsection (2) is to be known as a "temporary sheriff principal".

(6)   The Lord President may request the appointment of a temporary sheriff principal for a sheriffdom in the circumstances specified in subsection (1)(a) only if the Lord President considers such an appointment to be necessary or expedient in order to avoid a delay in the administration of justice in the sheriffdom.

**Temporary sheriff principal: further provision**

7.—(1)   Subject to subsection (3), an individual's appointment as a temporary sheriff principal lasts until recalled under subsection (2).

(2)   The Scottish Ministers must, if requested to do so by the Lord President of the Court of Session, recall the appointment of a temporary sheriff principal.

(3)   A sheriff's appointment as a temporary sheriff principal ceases if the sheriff—

(a)   ceases to hold office as sheriff, or

(b)   is suspended from office as sheriff.

(4)   Subject to section 6(4)(b), a temporary sheriff principal of a sheriffdom may exercise the jurisdiction and powers that attach to the office of sheriff principal of the sheriffdom, and does not need a commission for that purpose.

(5)   The appointment of a sheriff as a temporary sheriff principal does not affect the sheriff's appointment as sheriff.

(6)   Where a sheriff of one sheriffdom ("sheriffdom A") is appointed as temporary sheriff principal of another sheriffdom ("sheriffdom B")—

(a)   the sheriff must not, while remaining temporary sheriff principal of sheriffdom B, act in the capacity of sheriff of sheriffdom A, but

(b)   in addition to the jurisdiction and powers that attach specifically to the office of sheriff principal, the sheriff, by virtue of the appointment as temporary sheriff principal of sheriffdom B, may also exercise in that sheriffdom the jurisdiction and powers that attach to the office of sheriff of that sheriffdom.

**Part-time sheriffs**

8.—(1)   The Scottish Ministers may appoint individuals to act as sheriffs; and individuals so appointed are to be known as "part-time sheriffs".

(2)   The Scottish Ministers may appoint an individual only if—

(a)   the individual is qualified for appointment (see section 14), and

(b)   the Scottish Ministers have consulted the Lord President of the Court of Session before making the appointment.

(3)   Subject to section 20, an appointment as a part-time sheriff lasts for 5 years.

(4)   A part-time sheriff may exercise the jurisdiction and powers that attach to the office of sheriff in every sheriffdom, and does not need a commission for that purpose.

(5)   A part-time sheriff is subject to such instructions, arrangements and other provisions as may be made under this Act by the sheriff principal of the sheriffdom in which the parttime sheriff is for the time being sitting.

(6)   In carrying out their functions under this Act, sheriffs principal must together have regard to the desirability of securing that every part-time sheriff—

    (a)   is given the opportunity of sitting on not fewer than 20 days in each successive period of 12 months beginning with the day of the part-time sheriff's appointment, and

    (b)   does not sit for more than 100 days in each such successive period.

### Reappointment of part-time sheriffs

**9.**—(1)   A part-time sheriff whose appointment comes to an end by virtue of the expiry of the 5 year period mentioned in section 8(3) is to be reappointed unless—

    (a)   the part-time sheriff declines reappointment,

    (b)   a sheriff principal has made a recommendation to the Scottish Ministers against the reappointment, or

    (c)   the part-time sheriff has sat for fewer than 50 days in total in that 5 year period.

(2)   Section 8 (apart from subsection (2)) applies to a reappointment under subsection (1) as it applies to an appointment.

(3)   A part-time sheriff whose appointment comes to an end by resignation under section 20 may be reappointed.

(4)   Section 8 applies to a reappointment under subsection (3) as it applies to an appointment.

### Part-time summary sheriffs

**10.**—(1)   The Scottish Ministers may appoint individuals to act as summary sheriffs; and individuals so appointed are to be known as "part-time summary sheriffs".

(2)   The Scottish Ministers may appoint an individual only if—

    (a)   the individual is qualified for appointment (see section 14), and

    (b)   the Scottish Ministers have consulted the Lord President of the Court of Session before making the appointment.

(3)   Subject to section 20, an appointment as a part-time summary sheriff lasts for 5 years.

(4)   A part-time summary sheriff may exercise the jurisdiction and powers that attach to the office of summary sheriff in every sheriffdom, and does not need a commission for that purpose.

(5)   A part-time summary sheriff is subject to such instructions, arrangements and other provisions as may be made under this Act by the sheriff principal of the sheriffdom in which the part-time summary sheriff is for the time being sitting.

(6)   In carrying out their functions under this Act, sheriffs principal must together have regard to the desirability of securing that every part-time summary sheriff—

    (a)   is given the opportunity of sitting on not fewer than 20 days in each successive period of 12 months beginning with the day of the part-time summary sheriff's appointment, and

    (b)   does not sit for more than 100 days in each such successive period.

### Reappointment of part-time summary sheriffs

**11.**—(1)   A part-time summary sheriff whose appointment comes to an end by virtue of the expiry of the 5 year period mentioned in section 10(3) is to be reappointed unless—

    (a)   the part-time summary sheriff declines reappointment,

(b) a sheriff principal has made a recommendation to the Scottish Ministers against the reappointment, or

(c) the part-time summary sheriff has sat for fewer than 50 days in total in that 5 year period.

(2) Section 10 (apart from subsection (2)) applies to a reappointment under subsection (1) as it applies to an appointment.

(3) A part-time summary sheriff whose appointment comes to an end by resignation under section 20 may be reappointed.

(4) Section 10 applies to a reappointment under subsection (3) as it applies to an appointment.

*Re-employment of former holders of certain judicial offices*

### Re-employment of former judicial office holders

12.—(1) A sheriff principal of a sheriffdom may appoint—

(a) a qualifying former sheriff principal to act as a sheriff of the sheriffdom,

(b) a qualifying former sheriff to act as such a sheriff,

(c) a qualifying former part-time sheriff to act as such a sheriff,

(d) a qualifying former summary sheriff to act as a summary sheriff of the sheriffdom,

(e) a qualifying former part-time summary sheriff to act as such a summary sheriff.

(2) An individual appointed to act as mentioned in any of paragraphs (a) to (e) of subsection (1) may so act only during such periods or on such occasions as the sheriff principal may determine.

(3) A sheriff principal may make an appointment under subsection (1) only if it appears to the sheriff principal to be expedient as a temporary measure in order to facilitate the disposal of business in the sheriff courts of the sheriffdom.

(4) A "qualifying former sheriff principal" is an individual who—

(a) ceased to hold that office other than by virtue of an order under section 25, and

(b) has not reached the age of 75.

(5) A "qualifying former sheriff" is an individual who—

(a) ceased to hold that office other than—

(i) by virtue of an order under section 25, or

(ii) by being appointed as a sheriff principal, and

(b) has not reached the age of 75.

(6) A "qualifying former part-time sheriff" is an individual who—

(a) ceased to hold that office other than—

(i) by virtue of removal under section 25,

(ii) by virtue of not being reappointed to the office on either of the grounds mentioned in section 9(1)(b) and (c), or

(iii) by being appointed as a sheriff principal, and

(b) has not reached the age of 75.

(7) A "qualifying former summary sheriff" is an individual who—

(a) ceased to hold that office other than—

(i) by virtue of an order under section 25, or

(ii) by being appointed as a sheriff, and

(b) has not reached the age of 75.

(8) A "qualifying former part-time summary sheriff" is an individual who—

(a)   ceased to hold that office other than—

  (i)   by virtue of removal under section 25,

  (ii)   by virtue of not being reappointed to the office on either of the grounds mentioned in section 11(1)(b) and (c), or

  (iii)   by being appointed as a sheriff, and

(b)   has not reached the age of 75.

## Re-employment of former judicial office holders: further provision

**13.**—(1)   Subject to subsection (4), an individual's appointment under section 12(1) lasts until the sheriff principal by whom the individual was appointed (or a successor to that sheriff principal) recalls the individual's appointment.

(2)   An individual appointed under section 12(1) to act as a sheriff of a sheriffdom may exercise in the sheriffdom the jurisdiction and powers that attach to the office of sheriff, and does not need a commission for that purpose.

(3)   An individual appointed under section 12(1) to act as a summary sheriff of a sheriffdom may exercise in the sheriffdom the jurisdiction and powers that attach to the office of summary sheriff, and does not need a commission for that purpose.

(4)   An individual's appointment under section 12(1) ceases when the individual reaches the age of 75.

(5)   Despite the ending (whether by virtue of subsection (4) or otherwise) of an individual's appointment under section 12(1)—

(a)   the individual may continue to deal with, give judgment in or deal with an ancillary matter relating to, a case begun before the individual while acting under that appointment,

(b)   so far as necessary for that purpose, and for the purpose of any subsequent proceedings arising out of the case or matter, the individual is to be treated as acting or, as the case may be, having acted under that appointment.

*Qualification and disqualification*

## Qualification for appointment

**14.**—(1)   An individual is qualified for appointment to a judicial office mentioned in subsection (2) if the individual—

(a)   immediately before the appointment, held any other judicial office specified in that subsection, or

(b)   at the time of appointment—

  (i)   is legally qualified, and

  (ii)   has been so qualified throughout the period of 10 years immediately preceding the appointment.

(2)   The judicial offices are—

(a)   sheriff principal,

(b)   sheriff,

(c)   summary sheriff,

(d)   part-time sheriff,

(e)   part-time summary sheriff.

(3)   For the purposes of subsection (1), an individual is legally qualified if the individual is a solicitor or an advocate.

**Disqualification from practice, etc.**

**15.**—(1)  An individual holding a judicial office mentioned in subsection (2) must not, for so long as the individual holds the office—

(a)  engage, whether directly or indirectly, in practice as a solicitor or advocate or in any other business,

(b)  be in partnership with, or employed by, a person so engaged, or

(c)  act as agent for a person so engaged.

(2)  The judicial offices are—

(a)  sheriff principal,

(b)  sheriff,

(c)  summary sheriff.

(3)  A part-time sheriff, or a part-time summary sheriff, who is a solicitor in practice must not carry out any function as a part-time sheriff or, as the case may be, a part-time summary sheriff in a sheriff court district in which his or her place of business as such solicitor is situated.

*Remuneration and expenses*

**Remuneration**

**16.**—(1)  Each sheriff principal and sheriff is to be paid such salary as the Treasury may determine.

(2)  Such salary is to be paid quarterly or otherwise in every year, as the Treasury may determine.

(3)  Each summary sheriff is to be paid such remuneration as the Scottish Ministers may determine.

(4)  The Scottish Ministers may determine different amounts of remuneration for—

(a)  different summary sheriffs, or

(b)  different descriptions of summary sheriff.

(5)  Each judicial officer mentioned in subsection (7) is to be paid such remuneration as the Scottish Ministers may determine.

(6)  The Scottish Ministers may determine different amounts of remuneration for—

(a)  different judicial officers mentioned in subsection (7), or

(b)  different descriptions of such judicial officers.

(7)  The judicial officers are—

(a)  a part-time sheriff,

(b)  a part-time summary sheriff,

(c)  an individual appointed to act as a sheriff or summary sheriff under section 12(1).

(8)  Subsection (9) applies in relation to—

(a)  a sheriff principal of a sheriffdom authorised under section 30 to perform the functions of a sheriff principal in another sheriffdom, and

(b)  a sheriff of a sheriffdom ("sheriffdom A") directed under section 31 to perform the functions of sheriff in another sheriffdom in addition to sheriffdom A.

(9)  The sheriff principal or sheriff is to be paid, in respect of the additional functions, such remuneration as appears to the Secretary of State, with the consent of the Treasury, to be reasonable in all the circumstances.

(10)   Subsection (11) applies in relation to a summary sheriff of a sheriffdom ("sheriffdom B") directed under section 31 to perform the functions of a summary sheriff in another sheriffdom in addition to sheriffdom B.

(11)   The summary sheriff is to be paid, in respect of the additional functions, such remuneration as appears to the Scottish Ministers to be reasonable in all the circumstances.

(12)   Salaries and remuneration under subsections (1) to (11) are to be paid by the Scottish Courts and Tribunals Service.

(13)   Sums required by the Scottish Courts and Tribunals Service for the payment of a salary under subsection (1) or remuneration under subsection (3) are charged on the Scottish Consolidated Fund.

## Expenses

**17.**—(1)   The Scottish Courts and Tribunals Service may pay to a judicial officer mentioned in subsection (3) such sums as it may determine in respect of expenses reasonably incurred by the officer in the performance of, or in connection with, the officer's duties.

(2)   The Scottish Courts and Tribunals Service may—

   (a)   determine the circumstances in which such sums may be paid, and

   (b)   determine different circumstances for—

      (i)   different judicial officers, or

      (ii)   different descriptions of judicial officers.

(3)   The judicial officers are—

   (a)   a sheriff principal,

   (b)   a sheriff,

   (c)   a summary sheriff,

   (d)   a temporary sheriff principal,

   (e)   a part-time sheriff,

   (f)   a part-time summary sheriff,

   (g)   individuals appointed to act as a sheriff or summary sheriff under section 12(1).

*Leave of absence*

## Leave of absence

**18.**—(1)   The Lord President of the Court of Session may, for any sheriff principal or temporary sheriff principal, approve leave of absence for recreational or other purposes.

(2)   The sheriff principal of a sheriffdom may, for any sheriff or summary sheriff of the sheriffdom, approve leave of absence for recreational or other purposes.

(3)   The amount of leave for recreational purposes approved under this section for any sheriff principal, temporary sheriff principal, sheriff or summary sheriff must not exceed 7 weeks in any year.

(4)   That limit may be exceeded in any case with the permission of the Lord President.

(5)   The Lord President may grant permission under subsection (4) only if there are special reasons in the particular case that justify exceeding the limit.

(6)   The Lord President may delegate to a judge of the Court of Session a function conferred on the Lord President by this section.

(7)   In subsections (1) and (2), the references to leave of absence for purposes other than recreational purposes include (but are not limited to) references to sick leave, compassionate leave and study leave.

*Residence*

**Place of residence**

19.—(1)   The Lord President of the Court of Session may require a judicial officer mentioned in subsection (2) to reside ordinarily at such place as the Lord President may specify.

(2)   The judicial officers are—

    (a)   a sheriff principal,

    (b)   a sheriff,

    (c)   a summary sheriff.

*Cessation of appointment*

**Cessation of appointment of judicial officers**

20.—(1)   A judicial officer mentioned in subsection (3) may resign at any time by giving notice to that effect to the Scottish Ministers.

(2)   An individual's appointment as such a judicial officer ends—

    (a)   when the individual resigns in accordance with subsection (1),

    (b)   when the individual retires from office,

    (c)   if the individual is removed from office as such under section 25, or

    (d)   if the individual is appointed as another such judicial officer.

(3)   The judicial officers are—

    (a)   a sheriff principal,

    (b)   a sheriff,

    (c)   a summary sheriff,

    (d)   a part-time sheriff,

    (e)   a part-time summary sheriff.

*Fitness for office*

**Tribunal to consider fitness for office**

21.—(1)   The First Minister must, if requested to do so by the Lord President of the Court of Session, constitute a tribunal to investigate and report on whether an individual holding a judicial office mentioned in subsection (3) is unfit to hold the office by reason of inability, neglect of duty or misbehaviour.

(2)   Subject to subsection (1), the First Minister may, in such circumstances as the First Minister thinks fit and after consulting the Lord President, constitute such a tribunal.

(3)   The judicial offices are—

    (a)   sheriff principal,

    (b)   sheriff,

    (c)   summary sheriff,

    (d)   part-time sheriff, and

    (e)   part-time summary sheriff.

(4)   A tribunal constituted under this section is to consist of—

(a)   one individual who is a qualifying member of the Judicial Committee of the Privy Council,

(b)   one individual who holds the relevant judicial office,

(c)   one individual who is, and has been for at least 10 years—

    (i)   an advocate, or

    (ii)   a solicitor, and

(d)   one individual who—

    (i)   is not and never has been a qualifying member of the Judicial Committee of the Privy Council,

    (ii)   does not hold and never has held a judicial office mentioned in subsection (3), and

    (iii)   is not and never has been an advocate or solicitor.

(5)   In subsection (4)—

"a qualifying member of the Judicial Committee of the Privy Council" means someone who is a member of that Committee by virtue of section 1(2)(a) of the Judicial Committee Act 1833 (that is, someone who holds or has held high judicial office),

"the relevant judicial office" means—

    (a)   in respect of an investigation into whether an individual is fit to hold the office of sheriff principal, that office,

    (b)   in respect of an investigation into whether an individual is fit to hold the office of sheriff or part-time sheriff, the office of sheriff,

    (c)   in respect of an investigation into whether an individual is fit to hold the office of summary sheriff or part-time summary sheriff, the office of summary sheriff.

(6)   It is for the First Minister, with the agreement of the Lord President, to select persons to be members of a tribunal constituted under this section.

(7)   The person who is an individual mentioned in subsection (4)(a) is to chair the tribunal and has a casting vote.

### Tribunal investigations: suspension from office

**22.**—(1)   Subsection (2) applies where the Lord President of the Court of Session has requested that the First Minister constitute a tribunal under section 21.

(2)   The Lord President may, at any time before the tribunal reports to the First Minister, suspend from office the individual who is, or is to be, the subject of the tribunal's investigation.

(3)   Such a suspension lasts until the Lord President orders otherwise.

(4)   A tribunal constituted under section 21 may, at any time before the tribunal reports to the First Minister, recommend in writing to the First Minister that the individual who is the subject of the tribunal's investigation be suspended from office.

(5)   On receiving such a recommendation, the First Minister may suspend the individual from office.

(6)   Such a suspension lasts until the First Minister orders otherwise.

(7)   Suspension of an individual from the office of sheriff principal, sheriff or summary sheriff under this section does not affect any remuneration payable to, or in respect of, the individual in respect of the period of suspension.

### Further provision about tribunals

**23.**—(1)   A tribunal constituted under section 21 may require any person—

(a)  to attend its proceedings for the purpose of giving evidence,

(b)  to produce documents in the person's custody or under the person's control.

(2)  A person on whom such a requirement is imposed is not obliged—

(a)  to answer any question which the person would be entitled to refuse to answer in a court in Scotland,

(b)  to produce any document which the person would be entitled to refuse to produce in such a court.

(3)  Subsection (4) applies where a person on whom a requirement has been imposed under subsection (1)—

(a)  refuses or fails, without reasonable excuse, to comply with the requirement,

(b)  refuses or fails, without reasonable excuse, to answer any question while attending the tribunal proceedings to give evidence,

(c)  deliberately alters, conceals or destroys any document that the person is required to produce.

(4)  The Court of Session may, on an application made to it by the tribunal—

(a)  make such order for enforcing compliance as it sees fit, or

(b)  deal with the matter as if it were a contempt of the Court.

(5)  The Court of Session may by act of sederunt make provision as to the procedure to be followed by and before a tribunal constituted under section 21.

(6)  The Scottish Ministers—

(a)  must pay such expenses as they consider are reasonably required to be incurred to enable a tribunal constituted under section 21 to carry out its functions, and

(b)  may pay such remuneration to, and such expenses of, the members of such a tribunal as they think fit.

## Tribunal report

**24.**—(1)  The report of a tribunal constituted under section 21 must—

(a)  be in writing,

(b)  contain reasons for its conclusion, and

(c)  be submitted to the First Minister.

(2)  The First Minister must lay the report before the Scottish Parliament.

## Removal from office

**25.**—(1)  The First Minister may remove an individual from the office of sheriff principal, sheriff, part-time sheriff, summary sheriff or part-time summary sheriff—

(a)  if a tribunal constituted under section 21 reports to the First Minister that the individual is unfit to hold that office by reason of inability, neglect of duty or misbehaviour, and

(b)  only after the First Minister has laid the report before the Scottish Parliament under section 24(2).

(2)  The First Minister may remove a sheriff principal, sheriff or summary sheriff under subsection (1) only by order.

(3)  Such an order is subject to the negative procedure.

*Honorary sheriffs*

## Abolition of the office of honorary sheriff

**26.** The office of honorary sheriff is abolished.

## Chapter 3 – Organisation of business

*Sheriff principal's general responsibilities*

## Sheriff principal's responsibility for efficient disposal of business in sheriff courts

**27.**—(1) The sheriff principal of a sheriffdom is responsible for ensuring the efficient disposal of business in the sheriff courts of the sheriffdom.

(2) The sheriff principal must make such arrangements as appear necessary or expedient for the purpose of carrying out the responsibility imposed by subsection (1).

(3) In particular, the sheriff principal may—

(a) provide for the allocation of business among the judiciary of the sheriffdom,

(b) make special provision of a temporary nature for the disposal of any business by any member of the judiciary of the sheriffdom in addition to or in place of that member's own duties.

(4) If, in carrying out the responsibility imposed by subsection (1), the sheriff principal gives a direction of an administrative character to a person mentioned in subsection (5), the person must comply with the direction.

(5) Those persons are—

(a) any other member of the judiciary of the sheriffdom,

(b) a member of the staff of the Scottish Courts and Tribunals Service.

(6) Nothing in subsections (1) to (4) enables a member of the judiciary of the sheriffdom to dispose of any business which that member could not otherwise competently dispose of in the exercise of the jurisdiction and powers that attach to the member's office.

(7) Subsections (1) to (4) are subject to section 2(2)(a) and (3) of the Judiciary and Courts (Scotland) Act 2008 (the Head of the Scottish Judiciary's responsibility for efficient disposal of business in the Scottish courts).

## Sheriff principal's power to fix sittings of sheriff courts

**28.**—(1) The sheriff principal of a sheriffdom may by order prescribe—

(a) the number of sittings of sheriff courts to be held at each place designated for the holding of sheriff courts in the sheriffdom,

(b) the days on which, and the times at which, those sittings are to be held, and

(c) the descriptions of business to be disposed of at those sittings.

(2) The sheriff principal must publish notice of the matters prescribed by an order under subsection (1) in such manner as the sheriff principal thinks appropriate in order to bring those matters to the attention of persons having an interest in them.

(3) Subsection (1) is subject to section 2(2)(a) and (3) of the Judiciary and Courts (Scotland) Act 2008.

### Lord President's power to exercise functions under sections 27 and 28

**29.**—(1)   Subsection (2) applies where in any case the Lord President of the Court of Session considers that the exercise by the sheriff principal of a sheriffdom of a function under section 27 or 28—

    (a)   is prejudicial to the efficient disposal of business in the sheriff courts of the sheriffdom,

    (b)   is prejudicial to the efficient organisation or administration of those courts, or

    (c)   is otherwise against the interest of the public.

    (2)   The Lord President may in that case—

    (a)   rescind the sheriff principal's exercise of the function, and

    (b)   exercise the function.

    (3)   Subsections (1) and (2) apply in relation to a failure to exercise a function mentioned in subsection (1) as they apply to the exercise of such a function, but as if paragraph (a) of subsection (2) were omitted.

    (4)   The exercise of a function by the Lord President by virtue of subsection (2)(b) is to be treated as if it were the exercise of the function by the sheriff principal.

*Deployment of judiciary*

### Power to authorise a sheriff principal to act in another sheriffdom

**30.**—(1)   Subsection (2) applies where, in relation to a sheriffdom ("sheriffdom A")—

    (a)   a vacancy occurs in the office of sheriff principal,

    (b)   the Lord President of the Court of Session believes that the sheriff principal is unable to perform all or some of the functions of the office, or

    (c)   the sheriff principal rules that he or she is precluded from performing all or some of those functions.

    (2)   The Lord President may authorise the sheriff principal of another sheriffdom ("sheriffdom B") to perform the functions of sheriff principal in sheriffdom A (in addition to sheriffdom B) until the Lord President decides otherwise.

    (3)   The authorisation may be made for the purpose of the performance of—

    (a)   all of the functions of the sheriff principal of sheriffdom A, or

    (b)   only those functions that that sheriff principal is unable to perform or is precluded from performing.

    (4)   The Lord President may make an authorisation in the circumstances specified in subsection (1)(a) only if the Lord President considers such an authorisation to be necessary or expedient in order to avoid a delay in the administration of justice in sheriffdom A.

    (5)   A sheriff principal authorised under this section to perform the functions of sheriff principal in another sheriffdom may exercise the jurisdiction and powers that attach to the office of sheriff principal in the other sheriffdom and does not need a commission for that purpose.

    (6)   References in this section to the sheriff principal of a sheriffdom include references to any temporary sheriff principal of the sheriffdom.

## Power to direct a sheriff or summary sheriff to act in another sheriffdom

**31.**—(1) The Lord President of the Court of Session may direct a sheriff or summary sheriff of a sheriffdom ("sheriffdom A") to perform the functions of sheriff or, as the case may be, summary sheriff in another sheriffdom ("sheriffdom B") until the Lord President decides otherwise.

(2) The direction may require the sheriff or summary sheriff to perform the functions in sheriffdom B either in addition to or instead of performing the functions in sheriffdom A.

(3) The Lord President may at any time give a further direction to the sheriff or summary sheriff directing the sheriff or, as the case may be, summary sheriff to perform the functions of sheriff or, as the case may be, summary sheriff in another sheriffdom until the Lord President decides otherwise.

(4) Where a further direction is given under subsection (3) requiring functions to be carried out in another sheriffdom, the direction may require the sheriff or summary sheriff to perform the functions in that other sheriffdom in addition to or instead of performing the functions—

    (a) in sheriffdom A, or

    (b) in any other sheriffdom by virtue of—

        (i) a direction under subsection (1), or

        (ii) a further direction under subsection (3).

(5) A sheriff or summary sheriff directed under this section to perform the functions of sheriff or summary sheriff in another sheriffdom may exercise the jurisdiction and powers that attach to the office of sheriff or, as the case may be, summary sheriff in the other sheriffdom and does not need a commission for that purpose.

## Power to re-allocate sheriffs principal, sheriffs and summary sheriffs between sheriffdoms

**32.**—(1) The Lord President of the Court of Session may direct that—

    (a) the sheriff principal of a sheriffdom is to cease to be the sheriff principal of that sheriffdom and is instead to be sheriff principal of such other sheriffdom as is specified in the direction,

    (b) a sheriff of a sheriffdom is to cease to be a sheriff of that sheriffdom and is instead to be a sheriff of such other sheriffdom as is specified in the direction,

    (c) a summary sheriff of a sheriffdom is to cease to be a summary sheriff of that sheriffdom and is instead to be a summary sheriff of such other sheriffdom as is specified in the direction.

(2) A direction under subsection (1) takes effect on such date as is specified in the direction.

(3) The reference in subsection (1) to the sheriff principal, a sheriff or summary sheriff of a sheriffdom is to one—

    (a) appointed for the sheriffdom, or

    (b) who is the sheriff principal, a sheriff or, as the case may be, summary sheriff of the sheriffdom by virtue of a previous direction under subsection (1).

(4) A sheriff principal, sheriff or summary sheriff directed under subsection (1) to be the sheriff principal, a sheriff or summary sheriff of another sheriffdom may exercise the jurisdiction and powers that attach to the office of sheriff principal, sheriff or, as the case may be, summary sheriff in the other sheriffdom and does not need a commission for that purpose.

**Allocation of sheriffs and summary sheriffs to sheriff court districts**

33.—(1)   On the appointment of a sheriff or summary sheriff of a sheriffdom, the Lord President of the Court of Session must give the sheriff or summary sheriff a direction designating the sheriff court district or districts in which the sheriff or summary sheriff is to sit and perform the functions of sheriff or, as the case may be, summary sheriff.

(2)   The Lord President may at any time give a further direction to the sheriff or summary sheriff designating a different sheriff court district in which the sheriff or summary sheriff is to sit and perform the functions of sheriff or, as the case may be, summary sheriff.

(3)   A direction given to a sheriff or summary sheriff of a sheriffdom under this section is subject to any direction given under section 27 to the sheriff or summary sheriff by the sheriff principal of the sheriffdom for the purpose of giving effect to special provision made under subsection (3)(b) of that section.

(4)   Subsection (1) applies in the case where a direction under section 32(1) is made in relation to a sheriff or summary sheriff as it applies in the case where a sheriff or, as the case may be, summary sheriff is appointed.

*Judicial specialisation*

**Determination of categories of case for purposes of judicial specialisation**

34.—(1)   The Lord President of the Court of Session may, by direction, determine categories of sheriff court case that the Lord President considers to be suited to being dealt with by judicial officers that specialise in the category of case.

(2)   The Lord President may determine categories of case under subsection (1) by reference to subject matter, value or such other criteria as the Lord President considers appropriate.

(3)   The Lord President may issue different directions under subsection (1) in relation to different types of judicial officer.

(4)   The Lord President may vary or revoke any direction made under subsection (1).

(5)   In this section—

   "judicial officer" means—
      (a)   a sheriff,
      (b)   a summary sheriff,
      (c)   a part-time sheriff,
      (d)   a part-time summary sheriff,
   "sheriff court case" means any type of proceedings (whether civil or criminal) that may competently be brought in the sheriff court.

**Designation of specialist judiciary**

35.—(1)   This section applies where the Lord President of the Court of Session has made a direction under section 34.

(2)   The sheriff principal of a sheriffdom may—
      (a)   in relation to any category of case determined in the direction that may competently be dealt with by a sheriff, designate one or more sheriffs of the sheriffdom as specialists in that category of case,
      (b)   in relation to any category of case determined in the direction that may

competently be dealt with by a summary sheriff, designate one or more summary sheriffs of the sheriffdom as specialists in that category of case.

(3)   The sheriff principal may designate the same sheriff or summary sheriff in relation to more than one category of case determined in the direction.

(4)   The sheriff principal of a sheriffdom may at any time withdraw a designation made (whether by that sheriff principal or another) under subsection (2) in relation to any sheriff, or summary sheriff, of the sheriffdom.

(5)   The Lord President may—

(a)   in relation to any category of case determined in the direction that may competently be dealt with by a part-time sheriff, designate one or more part-time sheriffs as specialists in that category,

(b)   in relation to any category of case determined in the direction that may competently be dealt with by a part-time summary sheriff, designate one or more part-time summary sheriffs as specialists in that category.

(6)   The Lord President may at any time withdraw a designation made under subsection (5).

(7)   The designation of a sheriff, summary sheriff, part-time sheriff or part-time summary sheriff (a "designated judicial officer") under this section does not affect—

(a)   the designated judicial officer's competence to deal with any category of case other than the one in relation to which the designation is made, or

(b)   the competence of any other sheriff, summary sheriff, part-time sheriff or parttime summary sheriff to deal with the category of case in relation to which the designation is made.

### Allocation of business to specialist judiciary

**36.**—(1)   Subsection (2) applies where the Lord President of the Court of Session or the sheriff principal of a sheriffdom is exercising any function relating to the allocation of business among the judiciary of a sheriffdom.

(2)   The Lord President or, as the case may be, the sheriff principal must have regard to the desirability of ensuring that cases falling within a category determined under section 34 are dealt with by sheriffs, summary sheriffs, part-time sheriffs or, as the case may be, part-time summary sheriffs designated under section 35 as specialists in that category of case.

### Saving for existing powers to provide for judicial specialisation

**37.**   Sections 34 to 36 do not affect any power that the Lord President of the Court of Session has apart from those sections to provide for judicial specialisation in the sheriff courts.

Chapter 4 – Competence and jurisdiction

Sheriffs: civil competence and jurisdiction

### Jurisdiction and competence of sheriffs

**38.**—(1)   A sheriff continues to have the jurisdiction and competence that attached to the office of sheriff in relation to civil proceedings immediately before this section comes into force.

(2)   Without limiting that generality, a sheriff has competence as respects proceedings for or in relation to—

(a)   declarator,

    (b)   aliment or separation,

    (c)   recovery of maintenance arising out of an application under section 31(1) of the Maintenance Orders (Reciprocal Enforcement) Act 1972,

    (d)   divorce,

    (e)   division of commonty and division, or division and sale, of common property,

    (f)   questions of heritable right or title, including declarator of irritancy and removing,

    (g)   reduction, other than reduction of a decree of any court,

    (h)   proving the tenor,

    (i)   suspension of charges or threatened charges upon decrees of court granted by a sheriff or upon decrees of registration proceeding upon bonds, bills, contracts or other obligations registered in the books of a sheriff court or the Books of Council and Session,

    (j)   all civil maritime proceedings formerly competent in the High Court of Admiralty in Scotland.

(3)   For the purpose of subsection (2)(e), the Division of Commonties Act 1695 has effect as if it conferred the same competence on a sheriff as it confers on the Court of Session.

## Exclusive competence

**39.**—(1)   This section applies to any civil proceedings—

    (a)   which a sheriff has competence to deal with, and

    (b)   in which—

        (i)   one or more orders of value are sought, and

        (ii)   the aggregate total value of all such orders sought, exclusive of interest and expenses, does not exceed £100,000.

(2)   The proceedings may be brought only in the sheriff court and may not be brought in any other court.

(3)   This section does not apply to family proceedings unless the only order sought in the proceedings is an order for payment of aliment.

(4)   Subsection (2) is subject to section 92(7) (remit of cases in exceptional circumstances to the Court of Session).

(5)   The Scottish Ministers may by order substitute another sum for the sum for the time being specified in subsection (1)(b)(ii).

(6)   For the purposes of this Act, an order is an order of value if it is—

    (a)   an order for payment of money, or

    (b)   an order determining rights in relation to property.

(7)   Provision may be made by the Court of Session by act of sederunt for determining, for the purposes of this Act—

    (a)   the value of an order,

    (b)   the aggregate total value of all the orders of value sought in any proceedings.

(8)   An act of sederunt under subsection (7) may make different provision for different purposes.

## Territorial jurisdiction

**40.**—(1)   This section applies for the purpose of determining the territorial extent of the jurisdiction of a sheriff of a sheriffdom in relation to matters other than criminal matters.

(2) The sheriff's jurisdiction extends throughout the sheriffdom and includes all of the following so far as located in or adjoining the sheriffdom—

(a) navigable rivers,

(b) ports,

(c) harbours,

(d) creeks,

(e) shores,

(f) anchoring grounds.

(3) Where two sheriffdoms are separated by a river, firth or estuary, the sheriffs of each sheriffdom on either side have concurrent jurisdiction over the intervening space occupied by the water.

(4) This section does not affect any other enactment or rule of law that has effect for the purpose of determining the territorial extent of the jurisdiction of a sheriff of a sheriffdom, whether generally or in relation to a particular case or description of case.

(5) This section is subject to an order under section 41(1).

### Power to confer all-Scotland jurisdiction for specified cases

**41.**—(1) The Scottish Ministers may by order provide that the jurisdiction of a sheriff of a specified sheriffdom sitting at a specified sheriff court extends territorially throughout Scotland for the purposes of dealing with specified types of civil proceedings.

(2) In subsection (1), "specified" means specified in an order under that subsection.

(3) An order under subsection (1) may be made only with the consent of the Lord President of the Court of Session.

(4) An order under subsection (1) does not affect—

(a) in relation to the sheriffdom specified in the order, the jurisdiction or competence of a sheriff of any other sheriffdom to deal with proceedings of the type specified in the order, or

(b) in relation to the sheriff court specified in the order, the jurisdiction or competence of a sheriff sitting at any other sheriff court to deal with such proceedings.

(5) This section does not apply in relation to proceedings under the Children's Hearings (Scotland) Act 2011.

### All-Scotland jurisdiction: further provision

**42.**—(1) This section applies in relation to a sheriff sitting at a sheriff court specified in an order under section 41(1) (referred to in this section as a "specified sheriff court").

(2) The sheriff's all-Scotland jurisdiction is concurrent with, and alternative to, the sheriff's local jurisdiction.

(3) The sheriff's "all-Scotland jurisdiction" is the extended jurisdiction in relation to specified proceedings that the sheriff has by virtue of the order under section 41(1).

(4) The sheriff's "local jurisdiction" is the jurisdiction that the sheriff would have in relation to specified proceedings apart from the order under section 41(1).

(5) A party bringing specified proceedings in the specified sheriff court must indicate, at the time the proceedings are brought, whether they are for determination in the exercise of a sheriff's all-Scotland jurisdiction or a sheriff's local jurisdiction.

(6)   Subsection (5) does not affect any power that a sheriff has to decline jurisdiction in any case.

(7)   In this Act, references to an "all-Scotland sheriff court" are references to a specified sheriff court so far as the court is constituted by a sheriff sitting in the exercise of the sheriff's all-Scotland jurisdiction.

(8)   For the purposes of any provision of this Act, or any other enactment, relating to the transfer or remit of proceedings between courts, a specified sheriff court is, when constituted as an all-Scotland sheriff court, taken to be a separate sheriff court from the court as constituted by a sheriff sitting in the exercise of the sheriff's local jurisdiction.

(9)   In this section, "specified proceedings" means, in relation to a specified sheriff court, civil proceedings of a type that are specified in relation to that court in the order under section 41(1).

### Jurisdiction over persons, etc.

**43.**—(1)   Subsection (2) applies for the purpose of determining the jurisdiction of a sheriff in relation to any civil proceedings that may competently be dealt with by a sheriff.

(2)   The proceedings may be brought before the sheriff of a particular sheriffdom if—

   (a)   the defender (or, where there is more than one defender, one of them) resides in the sheriffdom,

   (b)   the defender (or, where there is more than one defender, one of them) formerly resided in the sheriffdom for at least 40 days and the defender—
      (i)   has ceased to reside there for fewer than 40 days, and
      (ii)   has no known residence in Scotland,

   (c)   the defender—
      (i)   carries on business in the sheriffdom,
      (ii)   has a place of business in the sheriffdom, and
      (iii)   is cited in the sheriffdom, either personally or at the place of business,

   (d)   where the defender is not otherwise subject to the jurisdiction of any court in Scotland, there has been arrested in the sheriffdom—
      (i)   a ship or vessel of which the defender is an owner or part-owner, demise charterer or master, or
      (ii)   goods, debts, money or other moveable property belonging to the defender,

   (e)   any property of which the defender is (either individually or as trustee) the owner, part-owner, tenant or joint tenant is located in the sheriffdom and the proceedings relate to such property or to the defender's interest in it,

   (f)   in proceedings for interdict, the alleged wrong is being committed or threatened to be committed in the sheriffdom,

   (g)   in proceedings relating to a contract—
      (i)   the place of execution or performance of the contract is located in the sheriffdom, and
      (ii)   the defender is personally cited in the sheriffdom,

   (h)   in actions of furthcoming or multiplepoinding—
      (i)   the fund or property that is the subject of the proceedings is located in the sheriffdom, or
      (ii)   the sheriff otherwise has jurisdiction over the arrestee or holder of

the fund or property that is the subject of the proceedings,

   (i)   the party sued is the pursuer in any proceedings pending in the sheriffdom against the party suing,

   (j)   where the proceedings are founded in delict, the delict was committed in the sheriffdom,

   (k)   the defender has prorogated the jurisdiction of the sheriff or courts of the sheriffdom.

(3)   Subsection (2) is subject to—

   (a)   section 8 of, and Schedule 1B to, the Domicile and Matrimonial Proceedings Act 1973,

   (b)   the Civil Jurisdiction and Judgments Act 1982,

   (c)   Chapter 3 of Part 1 of the Family Law Act 1986, and

   (d)   any other enactment or rule of law that applies for the purpose of determining the jurisdiction of a sheriff in relation to persons or subject-matter.

*Summary sheriffs: civil and criminal competence and jurisdiction*

## Summary sheriff: civil competence and jurisdiction

**44.**—(1)   A summary sheriff may, in relation to civil proceedings in the sheriff court, exercise the jurisdiction and powers that attach to the office of sheriff, but only in relation to the proceedings and other matters listed in schedule 1.

(2)   This section does not affect the jurisdiction and competence of a sheriff in relation to the proceedings and other matters listed in schedule 1.

(3)   The Scottish Ministers may by order modify schedule 1.

## Summary sheriff: criminal competence and jurisdiction

**45.**—(1)   A summary sheriff may, in relation to criminal investigations and proceedings (whether summary or solemn proceedings), exercise the jurisdiction and powers that attach to the office of sheriff.

(2)   Without limiting the generality of subsection (1), the jurisdiction and powers exercisable by a summary sheriff under that subsection include, in particular, those of a sheriff under the Criminal Procedure (Scotland) Act 1995 ("the 1995 Act").

(3)   Despite subsections (1) and (2), a summary sheriff does not have jurisdiction or power to do any of the following in solemn criminal proceedings—

   (a)   to preside at any of the following diets, other than for the purpose of adjourning the diet—

      (i)   a first diet,

      (ii)   a diet under section 76(1) of the 1995 Act,

      (iii)   a trial diet,

   (b)   to pass sentence on an offender, or make any other order or disposal in respect of the conviction of an offender of an offence,

   (c)   to review, vary, revoke or discharge any sentence or such other order or disposal.

(4)   This section does not affect the jurisdiction and competence of a sheriff in relation to any matter mentioned in subsection (1).

## Part 2 – The Sheriff Appeal Court

### Chapter 1 – Establishment and role

### The Sheriff Appeal Court

**46.**—(1)   There is established a court of law to be known as the Sheriff Appeal Court.

(2)   The Court consists of judges each to be known as an Appeal Sheriff.

### Jurisdiction and competence

**47.**—(1)   The Sheriff Appeal Court has jurisdiction and competence to hear and determine appeals to such extent as is provided by or under—

    (a)   this Act, or

    (b)   any other enactment.

(2)   The Court's jurisdiction and competence is exercisable by one or more of the Appeal Sheriffs at sittings of the Court.

(3)   The Court has all such powers as are, under the law of Scotland, inherently possessed by a court of law for the purposes of the discharge of its jurisdiction and competence and giving full effect to its decisions.

(4)   Subsection (3) is subject to any other provision of this Act or any other enactment that restricts or excludes any power of the Court in determining or disposing of an appeal.

### Status of decisions of the Sheriff Appeal Court in precedent

**48.**—(1)   A decision of the Sheriff Appeal Court on the interpretation or application of the law is binding—

    (a)   in proceedings before a sheriff anywhere in Scotland,

    (b)   in proceedings before a justice of the peace court anywhere in Scotland,

    (c)   in proceedings before the Sheriff Appeal Court, except in a case where the Court hearing the proceedings is constituted by a greater number of Appeal Sheriffs than those constituting the Court which made the decision.

(2)   In subsection (1)(a), the reference to proceedings before a sheriff includes, in the case of criminal proceedings, a reference to solemn proceedings before a sheriff and jury.

### Chapter 2 – Appeal Sheriffs

### Sheriffs principal to be Appeal Sheriffs

**49.**—(1)   Each person who holds office as a sheriff principal also holds office as an Appeal Sheriff by virtue of this subsection.

(2)   A person holding office as a sheriff principal ceases to hold office as an Appeal Sheriff if the person ceases to hold office as a sheriff principal.

(3)   If a person holding office as a sheriff principal is suspended from that office for any period, the person is also suspended from office as an Appeal Sheriff for the same period.

## Appointment of sheriffs as Appeal Sheriffs

**50.**—(1)   The Lord President of the Court of Session may appoint persons holding the office of sheriff to hold office also as Appeal Sheriffs.

(2)   The Lord President may appoint as many Appeal Sheriffs under subsection (1) as the Lord President considers necessary for the purposes of the Sheriff Appeal Court.

(3)   A person may be appointed under subsection (1) only if the individual has held office as a sheriff for at least 5 years.

(4)   The appointment of a sheriff as an Appeal Sheriff does not affect the sheriff's appointment as a sheriff and the sheriff may accordingly continue to act in that capacity.

(5)   A person holding office as an Appeal Sheriff under this section ceases to hold that office if the person ceases to hold office as a sheriff.

(6)   If a person holding office as an Appeal Sheriff under this section is suspended from the office of sheriff for any period, the person is also suspended from office as an Appeal Sheriff for the same period.

(7)   The Lord President may, with the consent of a majority of the sheriffs principal, remove a sheriff from office as an Appeal Sheriff.

(8)   Removal of a sheriff from the office of Appeal Sheriff under subsection (7) does not affect the sheriff's appointment as a sheriff.

## Re-employment of former Appeal Sheriffs

**51.**—(1)   The Lord President of the Court of Session may appoint a qualifying former Appeal Sheriff to act as an Appeal Sheriff during such periods or on such occasions as the Lord President may determine.

(2)   The Lord President may make such an appointment only if the appointment appears to the Lord President to be expedient as a temporary measure in order to facilitate the disposal of business in the Sheriff Appeal Court.

(3)   A "qualifying former Appeal Sheriff" is an individual who—

    (a)   ceased to hold that office other than by virtue of—

        (i)   an order under section 25 (as read with sections 49(2) and 50(5)), or

        (ii)   removal from office under section 50(7), and

    (b)   has not reached the age of 75.

(4)   An individual appointed under subsection (1) is to be treated for all purposes (other than for the purposes of section 50) as an Appeal Sheriff and may exercise the jurisdiction and powers that attach to the office of Appeal Sheriff.

(5)   An individual's appointment under subsection (1) ceases when the individual reaches the age of 75.

(6)   Despite the ending (whether by virtue of subsection (5) or otherwise) of an individual's appointment under subsection (1)—

    (a)   the individual may continue to deal with, give judgment in or deal with an ancillary matter relating to, a case begun before the individual while acting under that appointment,

    (b)   so far as necessary for that purpose, and for the purpose of any subsequent proceedings arising out of the case or matter, the individual is to be treated as acting or, as the case may be, having acted under that appointment.

(7)   An individual appointed under subsection (1) is to be paid such remuneration as the Scottish Ministers may determine.

(8)   The Scottish Ministers may determine different amounts of remuneration for—

    (a)   different individuals so appointed, or

    (b)   different descriptions of individuals so appointed.

(9)   Remuneration under subsection (7) is to be paid by the Scottish Courts and Tribunals Service.

## Expenses

**52.**—(1)   The Scottish Courts and Tribunals Service may pay to an Appeal Sheriff such sums as it may determine in respect of expenses reasonably incurred by the Appeal Sheriff in the performance of, or in connection with, the Appeal Sheriff's duties as such.

(2)   The Scottish Courts and Tribunals Service may—

    (a)   determine the circumstances in which such sums may be paid, and

    (b)   determine different circumstances for different Appeal Sheriffs.

## Temporary provision

**53.**   Schedule 2 (which makes further provision, for a temporary period, in relation to Appeal Sheriffs) has effect.

Chapter 3 – Organisation of business

President and Vice President

## President and Vice President of the Sheriff Appeal Court

**54.**—(1)   The Lord President of the Court of Session is to appoint, in accordance with this section—

    (a)   one of the sheriffs principal to be the President of the Sheriff Appeal Court, and

    (b)   another sheriff principal to be the Vice President of the Court.

(2)   A sheriff principal holds office as President or Vice President for such period as the Lord President may determine.

(3)   The President or Vice President may at any time resign office by giving notice in writing to the Lord President.

(4)   The Lord President may at any time remove a sheriff principal from office as President or Vice President.

(5)   If a person holding office as President or Vice President is suspended from office as a sheriff principal for any period, the person is also suspended from office as President or, as the case may be, Vice President for the same period.

## President and Vice President: incapacity and suspension

**55.**—(1)   Subsection (2) applies during any period when the President of the Sheriff Appeal Court—

    (a)   is unable (for any reason) to carry out the functions of the office, or

    (b)   is suspended from office.

(2)   During such a period—

    (a)   the functions of the President are to be carried out instead by the Vice President, and

(b) anything that falls to be done in relation to the President falls to be done instead in relation to the Vice President.

(3) Subsection (4) applies during any period when—

(a) subsection (2) would, but for subsection (4), apply, and

(b) the Vice President of the Sheriff Appeal Court—

    (i) is unable (for any reason) to carry out the functions of the President, or

    (ii) is suspended from office.

(4) During such a period, subsection (2) does not apply and, instead—

(a) the functions of the President are to be carried out instead by such sheriff principal (other than the President or Vice President) as the Lord President of the Court of Session may appoint to act in place of the President, and

(b) anything that falls to be done in relation to the President falls to be done instead in relation to that sheriff principal.

*Disposal of business*

## President's responsibility for efficient disposal of business

**56.**—(1) The President of the Sheriff Appeal Court is responsible for ensuring the efficient disposal of business in the Sheriff Appeal Court.

(2) The President must make such arrangements as appear necessary or expedient for the purpose of carrying out the responsibility imposed by subsection (1).

(3) In particular, the President may provide for the allocation of business among the Appeal Sheriffs.

(4) If, in carrying out the responsibility imposed by subsection (1), the President gives a direction of an administrative character to a person specified in subsection (5), the person must comply with the direction.

(5) Those persons are—

(a) an Appeal Sheriff,

(b) a member of the staff of the Scottish Courts and Tribunals Service.

(6) This section is subject to section 2(2)(a) and (2A) of the Judiciary and Courts (Scotland) Act 2008 (the Head of the Scottish Judiciary's responsibility for efficient disposal of business in the Scottish courts).

*Sittings*

## Sittings of the Sheriff Appeal Court

**57.**—(1) Sittings of the Sheriff Appeal Court may be held at any place in Scotland designated by virtue of this Act for the holding of sheriff courts.

(2) More than one sitting of the Court may take place at the same time, and at different places.

(3) The President of the Sheriff Appeal Court may by order prescribe—

(a) the number of sittings of the Court that are to be held at each place at which they may be held,

(b) the days on which, and the times at which, those sittings are to be held, and

(c) the descriptions of business to be disposed of at those sittings.

(4) The President must publish notice of the matters prescribed by an order under subsection (3) in such manner as the President thinks appropriate in order to bring those matters to the attention of persons having an interest in them.

(5) Subsection (3) is subject to section 2(2)(a) and (2A) of the Judiciary and Courts (Scotland) Act 2008.

## Rehearing of pending case by a larger Court

**58.**—(1) Subsection (2) applies where, in relation to any appeal pending before the Sheriff Appeal Court—

(a) the Appeal Sheriff or Appeal Sheriffs constituting the Court consider the appeal to be one of particular difficulty or importance, or

(b) where the Court is constituted by more than one Appeal Sheriff, they are equally divided on any matter, whether of fact or law.

(2) The Appeal Sheriff or Appeal Sheriffs may appoint the appeal to be reheard at another sitting of the Court constituted by such larger number of Appeal Sheriffs as may be necessary for the proper disposal of the appeal.

## Chapter 4 – Administration

### *Clerks*

## Clerk of the Sheriff Appeal Court

**59.**—(1) The Scottish Courts and Tribunals Service must appoint a person holding office as a sheriff clerk also to hold the office of Clerk of the Sheriff Appeal Court.

(2) A person's appointment as Clerk of the Sheriff Appeal Court does not affect the person's appointment as a sheriff clerk.

(3) A person holding office as Clerk of the Sheriff Appeal Court ceases to hold that office if the person ceases to hold office as a sheriff clerk.

(4) Otherwise, a person's appointment as Clerk of the Sheriff Appeal court—

(a) lasts for such period, and

(b) is on such other terms and conditions,

as the Scottish Courts and Tribunals Service may determine.

(5) In this section, "sheriff clerk" does not include sheriff clerk depute.

## Deputy Clerks of the Sheriff Appeal Court

**60.**—(1) The Scottish Courts and Tribunals Service may appoint individuals to be Deputy Clerks of the Sheriff Appeal Court.

(2) The number of Deputy Clerks is for the Scottish Courts and Tribunals Service to determine.

(3) An individual's appointment as Deputy Clerk—

(a) lasts for such period, and

(b) is on such other terms and conditions,

as the Scottish Courts and Tribunals Service may determine.

(4) An individual may hold office as a Deputy Clerk of the Sheriff Appeal Court at the same time as holding office as clerk, or deputy or assistant clerk, of another court.

## Clerk and Deputy Clerks: further provision

**61.**—(1) The Clerk and Deputy Clerks of the Sheriff Appeal Court are also members of staff of the Scottish Courts and Tribunals Service.

(2) Accordingly, a reference in any enactment to the staff of the Scottish Courts and Tribunals Service includes, except where the context requires otherwise, a reference to the Clerk and Deputy Clerks of the Sheriff Appeal Court.

(3) The Clerk of the Sheriff Appeal Court may, with the consent of the Scottish Courts and Tribunals Service, delegate the carrying out of any of the Clerk's functions to—

    (a) a Deputy Clerk of the Sheriff Appeal Court, or

    (b) any other member of staff of the Scottish Courts and Tribunals Service.

(4) Subsection (5) applies in relation to any period during which—

    (a) the office of Clerk of the Sheriff Appeal Court is vacant, or

    (b) the holder of that office is for any reason unable to carry out the functions of the office.

(5) The Scottish Courts and Tribunals Service may make arrangements for the functions of the Clerk of the Sheriff Appeal Court to be carried out during the period referred to in subsection (4) by—

    (a) a Deputy Clerk of the Sheriff Appeal Court, or

    (b) any other member of staff of the Scottish Courts and Tribunals Service.

(6) The Scottish Courts and Tribunals Service may give such instructions to the Clerk of the Sheriff Appeal Court, or a person carrying out the Clerk's functions under subsection (5), as it considers necessary for the purposes of this Act; and the Clerk or, as the case may be, such person must comply with any such instructions.

*Records*

**Records of the Sheriff Appeal Court**

62.—(1) A record of the Sheriff Appeal Court is authenticated by being signed by—

    (a) an Appeal Sheriff, or

    (b) the Clerk of the Court.

(2) A record authenticated in accordance with subsection (1), or a certified copy of such a record or of an extract of such a record, is sufficient evidence of the facts recorded in the record.

(3) The Sheriff Appeal Court may keep (and produce) records in electronic form.

(4) For the purposes of this section, a reference to a record or a copy of a record being signed or, as the case may be, certified, includes a reference to the record or copy being authenticated by means of—

    (a) an electronic signature, or

    (b) such other means of authentication as may be specified for that purpose by an act of sederunt under section 104(1).

(5) In this section—

    "certified copy" means a copy certified by the Clerk of the Sheriff Appeal Court as a true copy,

    "electronic signature" is to be construed in accordance with section 7(2) of the Electronic Communications Act 2000, but includes a version of an electronic signature which is reproduced on a paper document,

    "record" means any interlocutor, decree, minute or other document by which the proceedings and decisions of the Sheriff Appeal Court are recorded.

Part 3 – Civil procedure

Chapter 1 – Sheriff court

*Civil jury trials*

### Civil jury trials in an all-Scotland sheriff court

**63.**—(1) This section applies in relation to relevant proceedings in an all-Scotland sheriff court.

(2) If the proceedings are remitted to probation, they must be tried by jury unless—

   (a) the parties agree otherwise, or

   (b) special cause is shown.

(3) Facts or circumstances constitute special cause for the purposes of subsection (2)(b) only if they would constitute special cause for the purpose of section 9(b) of the Court of Session Act 1988 (allowing of proof by Lord Ordinary).

(4) The questions to be put to the jury are to be—

   (a) approved by the sheriff, and

   (b) specified by the sheriff in an interlocutor.

(5) The jury is to consist of 12 jurors.

(6) Proceedings which are to be tried by jury under this section are referred to in this Chapter as "jury proceedings".

(7) In this section, "relevant proceedings" means proceedings—

   (a) of a type specified in an order under section 41(1), and

   (b) which would be a jury action within the meaning of section 11 of the Court of Session Act 1988 if the same proceedings were (disregarding section 39)—

      (i) taken by an action in the Court of Session, and

      (ii) remitted to probation there.

### Selection of the jury

**64.**—(1) The jurors for the trial in jury proceedings are to be selected in open court by ballot.

(2) Each party to the proceedings may challenge the selection of any juror whose name is drawn in the ballot.

(3) A party may, under subsection (2), at any time during the selection of jurors—

   (a) challenge the selection of up to 4 jurors without having to give a reason, and

   (b) challenge the selection of any other juror, provided a reason for the challenge is stated.

### Application to allow the jury to view property

**65.**—(1) A party to jury proceedings may apply to the sheriff to allow the jury to view any heritable or moveable property relevant to the proceedings.

(2) Where an application is made under subsection (1), the sheriff may grant the application if the sheriff considers it proper and necessary for the jury to view the property.

### Discharge or death of juror during trial

**66.**—(1)  In jury proceedings, the sheriff may, in the course of the trial, discharge a member of the jury from further service on the jury if satisfied that the juror—

    (a)   is, by reason of illness, unable to continue to serve on the jury, or

    (b)   should, for any other reason, be discharged from further service on the jury.

    (2)   Subsections (3) and (4) apply where a member of the jury—

    (a)   is discharged under subsection (1), or

    (b)   dies.

    (3)   So long as there remain at least 10 members of the jury—

    (a)   the remaining members of the jury are in all respects deemed to constitute the jury for the purpose of the trial, and

    (b)   any verdict returned by the remaining members of the jury, whether unanimous or by majority, is to have the same force and effect as if it were a unanimous or, as the case may be, majority verdict of the whole number of the jury.

    (4)   If there remain fewer than 10 members of the jury, the sheriff must—

    (a)   discharge the jury, and

    (b)   order the proceedings to be tried by another jury.

### Trial to proceed despite objection to opinion and direction of the sheriff

**67.**—  In jury proceedings, despite any objection being taken in the course of the trial to the opinion and direction of the sheriff—

    (a)   the trial is to proceed, and

    (b)   the jury are to return their verdict and, where necessary, assess damages.

### Return of verdict

**68.**—(1)  In jury proceedings, the sheriff must, at the end of the sheriff's charge to the jury, direct the jury to select one of their members to speak for them when returning their verdict.

    (2)   The jury may at any time return a verdict by a simple majority of their members.

    (3)   Subsection (4) applies if the jury—

    (a)   have been enclosed for at least 3 hours, and

    (b)   at the end of that time are unable to agree a verdict or to return a verdict by majority.

    (4)   The sheriff may—

    (a)   discharge the jury without their having returned a verdict, and

    (b)   order the proceedings to be tried by another jury.

    (5)   When the verdict is returned, it is to be—

    (a)   declared orally in open court by the juror selected under subsection (1), and

    (b)   taken down in writing by the sheriff clerk before the jury is discharged.

    (6)   In jury proceedings containing a claim for damages, where the jury return a verdict for the pursuer, the jury must also assess the amount of damages.

    (7)   The verdict of the jury is final so far as relating to the facts found by the jury.

    (8)   Subsection (7) is subject to sections 69 and 71.

**Application for new trial**

**69.**—(1)  After the jury have returned their verdict in jury proceedings, any party to the proceedings may, on any ground specified in subsection (2), apply to the Sheriff Appeal Court for a new trial.

(2)  The grounds are—

    (a)  the sheriff misdirected the jury,

    (b)  undue admission or rejection of evidence,

    (c)  the verdict is contrary to the evidence,

    (d)  damages awarded are excessive or inadequate,

    (e)  new evidence or information has come to light since the trial,

    (f)  any other ground essential to the justice of the case.

(3)  On an application under subsection (1), the Sheriff Appeal Court may grant or refuse a new trial.

(4)  Subsection (3) is subject to section 70.

(5)  Where the Court grants a new trial—

    (a)  the verdict of the jury is set aside, and

    (b)  the proceedings are to be tried by another jury.

(6)  Subsection (7) applies where—

    (a)  an application is made under subsection (1) on the ground that the verdict is contrary to the evidence, and

    (b)  after hearing the parties, the Sheriff Appeal Court is of the opinion that—

        (i)  the ground is established, and

        (ii)  it has before it all the relevant evidence that could reasonably be expected to be obtained in relation to the proceedings.

(7)  The Court may, instead of granting a new trial—

    (a)  set aside the verdict of the jury, and

    (b)  enter judgment for the party unsuccessful at the trial.

(8)  In a case where the Court is constituted by more than one Appeal Sheriff, the opinion referred to in subsection (6)(b) must be the opinion of all of them.

**Restrictions on granting a new trial**

**70.**—(1)  Subsection (2) applies where—

    (a)  an application is made under section 69(1) on the ground of undue admission of evidence, and

    (b)  the Sheriff Appeal Court is of the opinion that exclusion of the evidence in question could not have led to a different verdict from the one actually returned.

(2)  The Court must refuse to grant a new trial.

(3)  Subsection (4) applies where—

    (a)  an application is made under section 69(1) on the ground of undue rejection of documentary evidence, and

    (b)  the Sheriff Appeal Court is of the opinion that the documents in question would not have affected the jury's verdict.

(4)  The Court must refuse to grant a new trial.

(5)  Subsection (6) applies where—

    (a)  an application is made under section 69(1), and

    (b)  the Sheriff Appeal Court is of the opinion that—

        (i)  the only ground for granting a new trial is that damages awarded are excessive or inadequate, and

      (ii)   a new trial is essential to the justice of the case.

(6)   The Court may grant a new trial restricted to the question of the amount of damages only.

(7)   On an application under section 69(1), where the Sheriff Appeal Court is constituted by more than one Appeal Sheriff—

    (a)   the Court may not grant a new trial except in conformity with the opinion of a majority of the Appeal Sheriffs hearing the application, and

    (b)   in the case of equal division, the Court must refuse to grant a new trial.

### Verdict subject to opinion of the Sheriff Appeal Court

**71.**—(1)   This section applies in relation to any jury proceedings in which the sheriff has directed the jury on any matter.

(2)   A party against whom the verdict of the jury is returned may apply to the Sheriff Appeal Court for the verdict instead to be entered in the party's favour.

(3)   On an application under subsection (2), the Court may—

    (a)   set aside the verdict and exercise either of the powers in subsections (4) and (6), or

    (b)   refuse the application.

(4)   Where the Court is of the opinion—

    (a)   that the sheriff's direction was erroneous, and

    (b)   that the party making the application was entitled to the verdict in whole or in part,

it may direct the verdict to be entered in that party's favour.

(5)   The Court may direct the verdict to be so entered—

    (a)   either in whole or in part, and

    (b)   either absolutely or on such terms as the Court thinks fit.

(6)   Where the Court is of the opinion that it is necessary to do so, it may order the proceedings to be tried by another jury.

*Simple procedure*

### Simple procedure

**72.**—(1)   For the purposes of the procedure and practice in civil proceedings in the sheriff court, there is to be a form of procedure to be known as "simple procedure".

(2)   Subject to the provisions of this Part, further provision about simple procedure is to be made by act of sederunt under section 104(1).

(3)   The following types of proceedings may only be brought subject to simple procedure (and no other types of proceedings may be so brought)—

    (a)   proceedings for payment of a sum of money not exceeding £5,000,

    (b)   actions of multiplepoinding where the value of the fund or property that is the subject of the action does not exceed £5,000,

    (c)   actions of furthcoming where the value of the arrested fund or subject does not exceed £5,000,

    (d)   actions ad factum praestandum, other than actions in which there is claimed, in addition or as an alternative to a decree ad factum praestandum, a decree for payment of a sum of money exceeding £5,000,

    (e)   proceedings for the recovery of possession of heritable property or moveable property, other than proceedings in which there is claimed, in addition or as an alternative to a decree for such recovery, a decree for payment of a sum of money exceeding £5,000.

(4) Subsection (3) is subject to sections 78 (transfer of cases to simple procedure), 80 (transfer of cases from simple procedure) and 83 (transitional provision: summary cause).

(5) Subsection (3)(a) is subject to sections 73 and 74.

(6) The calculation of a sum for the time being mentioned in subsection (3) is to be determined in accordance with provision made by the Court of Session by act of sederunt.

(7) An act of sederunt under subsection (6) may make different provision for different purposes.

(8) An act of sederunt under section 104(1) may make provision for the purposes of this Act for determining whether proceedings are of a type mentioned in subsection (3).

(9) Proceedings that—
  (a) are subject to simple procedure under subsection (3) or by virtue of any other enactment,
  (b) are brought subject to simple procedure under section 74, or
  (c) are continued subject to simple procedure by virtue of section 78 or 79,
are referred to in this Part as a "simple procedure case".

(10) Subsection (9) is subject to section 80.

(11) References in subsection (3) to a sum of money is to that amount exclusive of interest and expenses.

(12) The Scottish Ministers may by order substitute for any sum for the time being specified in this section a different sum.

### Proceedings in an all-Scotland sheriff court

**73.**—(1) Section 72(3), so far as requiring any relevant proceedings to be brought subject to simple procedure, does not apply to any such proceedings in an all-Scotland sheriff court, and no such proceedings may be brought or continued in such a court subject to simple procedure.

(2) Subsection (1) does not affect the application of section 72(3) in relation to any relevant proceedings brought in any other sheriff court.

(3) In this section, "relevant proceedings" means proceedings of a type mentioned in section 72(3)(a) so far as they are also of a type specified in an order under section 41(1).

### Proceedings for aliment of small amounts under simple procedure

**74.**—(1) Subsection (2) applies to a claim for aliment only (whether or not expenses are also sought) under section 2 of the Family Law (Scotland) Act 1985 (actions for aliment).

(2) The claim may be brought subject to simple procedure if the aliment claimed does not exceed—
  (a) in respect of a child under the age of 18 years, the sum of £100 per week, and
  (b) in any other case, the sum of £200 per week.

(3) A provision such as is mentioned in subsection (4) does not apply in relation to a claim brought subject to simple procedure under subsection (2).

(4) The provision referred to in subsection (3) is provision in any enactment—

(a) limiting the jurisdiction of a sheriff in a simple procedure case by reference to any amount, or

(b) limiting the period for which a decree granted by a sheriff is to have effect.

(5)  The Scottish Ministers may by order substitute for any sum for the time being mentioned in subsection (2) a different sum.

**Rule-making: matters to be taken into consideration**

**75.**  The power to make provision relating to simple procedure by act of sederunt under section 104(1) is to be exercised so far as possible with a view to ensuring that the sheriff before whom a simple procedure case is conducted—

(a) is able to identify the issues in dispute,

(b) may facilitate negotiation between or among the parties with a view to securing a settlement,

(c) may otherwise assist the parties in reaching a settlement,

(d) can adopt a procedure that is appropriate to and takes account of the particular circumstances of the case.

**Service of documents**

**76.**—(1)  An act of sederunt under section 104(1) may permit a party to a simple procedure case, in such circumstances as may be specified in the act, to require the sheriff clerk to effect service of any document relating to the case on behalf of the party.

(2)  In subsection (1)—

(a) the reference to a party to a simple procedure case includes a reference to a description of such a party as may be specified in an act of sederunt mentioned in that subsection,

(b) the reference to any document relating to the case includes a reference to a description of any such document as may be so specified.

**Evidence in simple procedure cases**

**77.**—(1)  Any enactment or rule of law that prevents evidence being led on grounds of admissibility before a court of law does not apply in simple procedure cases.

(2)  The evidence, if any, given in simple procedure cases is not to be recorded.

**Transfer of cases to simple procedure**

**78.**—(1)  This section applies to any civil proceedings in the sheriff court that are being conducted otherwise than as a simple procedure case.

(2)  The parties to the proceedings may, at any stage, make a joint application for the proceedings to continue subject to simple procedure if the proceedings are of a type that, if brought at the time when the application is made—

(a) would or could be brought subject to simple procedure by virtue of any enactment, or

(b) would or could be so brought but for the fact that a financial limit specified in section 72(3) or 74(2) is exceeded.

(3)  Where such a joint application is made, the sheriff must direct that the proceedings are to continue subject to simple procedure for all purposes (including appeal).

**Proceedings in an all-Scotland sheriff court: transfer to simple procedure**

**79.**—(1)  This section applies to any relevant proceedings in an all-Scotland sheriff court.

(2)  A party to the proceedings may, at any stage, make an application for the proceedings to continue subject to simple procedure in another sheriff court.

(3)  Where such an application is made, the sheriff may, on special cause shown—

(a)  direct that the proceedings are to continue subject to simple procedure for all purposes (including appeal), and

(b)  make an order transferring the proceedings to another sheriff court having jurisdiction in relation to the proceedings.

(4)  Where a sheriff makes a direction under section 78(3) in relation to proceedings to which this section applies, the sheriff must make an order transferring the proceedings to another sheriff court having jurisdiction in relation to the proceedings.

(5)  In this section, "relevant proceedings" has the same meaning as in section 73.

**Transfer of cases from simple procedure**

**80.**—(1)  A party to a simple procedure case may, at any stage, make an application for the case not to proceed subject to simple procedure.

(2)  Where such an application is made, the sheriff may direct that the proceedings are no longer subject to simple procedure.

(3)  Where a direction is made under subsection (2), the proceedings are to continue for all purposes (including appeal) subject to such procedure as would have been applicable to them had they not been subject to simple procedure.

**Expenses in simple procedure cases**

**81.**—(1)  The Scottish Ministers may by order provide that—

(a)  in such category of simple procedure cases as may be prescribed in the order, no award of expenses may be made,

(b)  in such other category of simple procedure cases as may be so prescribed, any expenses awarded may not exceed such sum as may be so prescribed.

(2)  The categories of simple procedure cases mentioned in subsection (1) may be prescribed by reference to—

(a)  the value of the claim in the cases,

(b)  the subject matter of the claim in the cases.

(3)  Categories may be prescribed subject to specified exceptions.

(4)  An order under subsection (1) does not apply—

(a)  to simple procedure cases such as those mentioned in subsection (5),

(b)  in relation to an appeal to the Sheriff Appeal Court from any decision in a simple procedure case, or

(c)  to a simple procedure case in respect of which a direction under subsection (7) is made.

(5)  The simple procedure cases referred to in subsection (4)(a) are those in which—

(a)  the defender—

(i)  has not stated a defence,

(ii)  having stated a defence, has not proceeded with it, or

> (iii) having stated and proceeded with a defence, has not acted in good faith as to its merits, or

(b) a party to the case has behaved unreasonably in relation to the case.

(6) Subsection (7) applies where the sheriff in a simple procedure case is of the opinion that a difficult question of law, or a question of fact of exceptional complexity, is involved.

(7) The sheriff may, at any stage, on the application of any party to the case, direct that an order under subsection (1) is not to apply in relation to the case.

### Appeals from simple procedure cases

**82.**—(1) An appeal may be taken to the Sheriff Appeal Court under section 110 on a point of law only against a decision of the sheriff constituting final judgment in a simple procedure case.

(2) Any other decision of the sheriff in such a case is not subject to review.

### Transitional provision: summary causes

**83.**—(1) Any reference, however expressed, in a pre-commencement enactment to proceedings being subject to summary cause procedure is, on and after the coming into force of this section, to be construed as a reference to proceedings being subject to simple procedure.

(2) Accordingly, any reference to proceedings being taken by way of summary cause is to be construed as a reference to proceedings being subject to simple procedure.

(3) In subsection (1), "pre-commencement enactment" means any enactment passed or made before this section comes into force.

*Interdicts and other orders: effect outside sheriffdom*

### Interdicts having effect in more than one sheriffdom

**84.**—(1) A sheriff has competence to grant an interdict having effect in relation to conduct at places outside the sheriff's sheriffdom as well as at places within the sheriff's sheriffdom.

(2) In this section, "interdict" includes "interim interdict".

### Proceedings for breach of an extended interdict

**85.**—(1) In this section, "extended interdict" means an interdict granted by a sheriff, by virtue of section 84(1), having effect in relation to conduct at places outside the sheriff's sheriffdom.

(2) Proceedings for breach of an extended interdict may be brought before a sheriff of the sheriffdom—

(a) in which the defender is domiciled,

(b) in which the interdict was granted,

(c) in which the alleged breach occurred.

(3) A sheriff before whom proceedings for breach of an extended interdict are brought may make an order transferring the proceedings to a sheriff of another sheriffdom (whether or not one mentioned in subsection (2)) if satisfied that it would be more appropriate for the proceedings to be dealt with by a sheriff of the other sheriffdom.

(4) A sheriff may make an order under subsection (3)—

(a)   on the application of a party to the proceedings, or

(b)   on the sheriff's own initiative.

(5)   Where an order is made under subsection (3), a sheriff of the sheriffdom to whom the proceedings are to be transferred has jurisdiction and competence to consider and determine the proceedings.

(6)   This section does not affect any power that a sheriff has to decline jurisdiction in any case.

## Power to enable sheriff to make orders having effect outside sheriffdom

86.—(1)   In this section, "relevant order" means an order—

(a)   which a sheriff has competence and jurisdiction to make in civil proceedings, but

(b)   which, apart from this section, the sheriff could make only so as to have effect or be enforceable within the sheriff's sheriffdom.

(2)   The Scottish Ministers may by order provide for a sheriff to have competence to make relevant orders having effect (and being capable of being enforced) outside the sheriff's sheriffdom as well as within that sheriffdom (referred to in this section as "extended competence").

(3)   An order under subsection (2) may—

(a)   make provision in relation to all relevant orders or in relation only to specified categories or descriptions of relevant order,

(b)   make different provision in relation to different categories or descriptions of relevant order,

(c)   provide for a sheriff to have extended competence only—

(i)   in such circumstances,

(ii)   in relation to such civil proceedings, or

(iii)   subject to such conditions,

as are specified in the order,

(d)   make provision about jurisdiction in relation to proceedings for relevant orders,

(e)   make provision for the transfer of proceedings for relevant orders between different sheriffdoms,

(f)   make provision about the enforcement of orders made in the exercise of extended competence (including provision about jurisdiction in relation to enforcement proceedings).

(4)   Subsection (3) does not affect the generality of section 133(1).

(5)   In subsection (1), "order"—

(a)   includes "interim order", but

(b)   does not include an interdict or an interim interdict.

*Execution of deeds relating to heritage*

## Power of sheriff to order sheriff clerk to execute deed relating to heritage

87.—(1)   This section applies where—

(a)   an action relating to heritable property is before a sheriff, or

(b)   it appears to a sheriff that an order under this section is necessary to implement a decree of a sheriff relating to heritable property.

(2)   The sheriff may make an order such as is mentioned in subsection (4)—

(a)   on an application by the grantee of any deed relating to the heritable property, and

  (b)  if satisfied as to the matters mentioned in subsection (3).

(3)  The matters are that the grantor of any deed relating to the heritable property—

  (a)  cannot be found,
  (b)  refuses to execute the deed,
  (c)  is unable, or otherwise fails, to execute the deed.

(4)  The order is one—

  (a)  dispensing with the execution of the deed by the grantor, and
  (b)  directing the sheriff clerk to execute the deed.

(5)  A deed executed by the sheriff clerk in accordance with a direction in an order under this section has the same force and effect as if it had been executed by the grantor.

(6)  In this section—

"grantor", in relation to a deed relating to the heritable property, means a person who is under an obligation to execute the deed,

"grantee" means the person to whom that obligation is owed.

*Interim orders*

**Interim orders**

**88.**—(1)  A sheriff may, on the application of a party to any civil proceedings before the sheriff, make—

  (a)  such interim order as the sheriff thinks fit in relation to—
    (i)  the possession of any heritable or movable property to which the proceedings relate,
    (ii)  the subject matter of the proceedings,
  (b)  an interim order ad factum praestandum.

(2)  Subsection (1) does not apply in relation to proceedings under the Children's Hearings (Scotland) Act 2011.

Chapter 2 – Court of Session

**Judicial review**

**89.**  After section 27 of the Court of Session Act 1988, insert—

*"Applications to the supervisory jurisdiction of the Court*

**Time limits**

**27A.**—(1)  An application to the supervisory jurisdiction of the Court must be made before the end of—

  (a)  the period of 3 months beginning with the date on which the grounds giving rise to the application first arise, or
  (b)  such longer period as the Court considers equitable having regard to all the circumstances.

(2)  Subsection (1) does not apply to an application to the supervisory jurisdiction of the Court which, by virtue of any enactment, is to be made before the end of a period ending before the period of 3 months mentioned in that subsection (however that first-ending period may be expressed).

### Requirement for permission

**27B.**—(1) No proceedings may be taken in respect of an application to the supervisory jurisdiction of the Court unless the Court has granted permission for the application to proceed.

(2) Subject to subsection (3), the Court may grant permission under subsection (1) for an application to proceed only if it is satisfied that—

    (a) the applicant can demonstrate a sufficient interest in the subject matter of the application, and

    (b) the application has a real prospect of success.

(3) Where the application relates to a decision of the Upper Tribunal for Scotland in an appeal from the First-tier Tribunal for Scotland under section 46 of the Tribunals (Scotland) Act 2014, the Court may grant permission under subsection (1) for the application to proceed only if it is satisfied that—

    (a) the applicant can demonstrate a sufficient interest in the subject matter of the application,

    (b) the application has a real prospect of success, and

    (c) either—

        (i) the application would raise an important point of principle or practice, or

        (ii) there is some other compelling reason for allowing the application to proceed.

(4) The Court may grant permission under subsection (1) for an application to proceed—

    (a) subject to such conditions as the Court thinks fit,

    (b) only on such of the grounds specified in the application as the Court thinks fit.

(5) The Court may decide whether or not to grant permission without an oral hearing having been held.

### Oral hearings where permission refused, etc.

**27C.**—(1) Subsection (2) applies where, in relation to an application to the supervisory jurisdiction of the Court—

    (a) the Court—

        (i) refuses permission under subsection 27B(1) for the application to proceed, or

        (ii) grants permission for the application to proceed subject to conditions or only on particular grounds, and

    (b) the Court decides to refuse permission, or grant permission as mentioned in paragraph (a)(ii), without an oral hearing having been held.

(2) The person making the application may, within the period of 7 days beginning with the day on which that decision is made, request a review of the decision at an oral hearing.

(3) A request under subsection (2) must be considered by a different Lord Ordinary from the one who refused permission or granted permission as mentioned in subsection (1)(a)(ii).

(4) Where a request under subsection (2) is granted, the oral hearing must be conducted before a different Lord Ordinary from the one who refused or so granted permission.

(5) At a review following a request under subsection (2), the Court must consider whether to grant permission for the application to proceed; and subsections (2), (3) and (4) of section 27B apply for that purpose.

(6) Section 28 does not apply—

    (a) where subsection (2) applies, or

    (b) in relation to the refusal of a request made under subsection (2).

### Appeals following oral hearings

**27D.**—(1) Subsection (2) applies where, after an oral hearing to determine whether or not to grant permission for an application to the supervisory jurisdiction of the Court to proceed, the Court—

    (a)  refuses permission for the application to proceed, or

    (b)  grants permission for the application to proceed subject to conditions or only on particular grounds.

(2) The person making the application may, within the period of 7 days beginning with the day on which the Court makes its decision, appeal under this section to the Inner House (but may not appeal under any other provision of this Act).

(3) In an appeal under subsection (2), the Inner House must consider whether to grant permission for the application to proceed; and subsections (2), (3) and (4) of section 27B apply for that purpose.

(4) In subsection (1), the reference to an oral hearing is to an oral hearing whether following a request under section 27C(2) or otherwise.".

## Interim orders

**90.** In section 47 of the Court of Session Act 1988 (interim interdict and other interim orders), after subsection (2) insert—

"(2A) The power under subsection (2) to make an order includes, in particular, power to make an order ad factum praestandum (including an interim order).".

## Warrants for ejection

**91.** After section 47 of the Court of Session Act 1988, insert—

#### Power to grant warrant for ejection

"**47A.** In any proceedings where the Court has competence to grant a decree of removing, it also has competence to grant a warrant for ejection.".

### Chapter 3 – Remit of cases between courts

## Remit of cases to the Court of Session

**92.**—(1) Subsection (2) applies to any civil proceedings before a sheriff that are—

    (a)  proceedings that the Court of Session also has competence and jurisdiction to deal with,

    (b)  not proceedings to which section 39 applies, and

    (c)  not subject to simple procedure.

(2) On the application of any of the parties to the proceedings, the sheriff may, at any stage, remit the proceedings to the Court of Session if the sheriff considers that the importance or difficulty of the proceedings makes it appropriate to do so.

(3) Subsection (4) applies to any civil proceedings before a sheriff that are—

    (a)  proceedings to which section 39 applies,

    (b)  proceedings that the Court of Session would (but for that section) also have competence and jurisdiction to deal with, and

    (c)  not subject to simple procedure.

(4)   On the application of any of the parties to the proceedings, the sheriff may, at any stage, request the Court of Session to allow the proceedings to be remitted to that Court if the sheriff considers that the importance or difficulty of the proceedings makes it appropriate to do so.

(5)   On receiving a request under subsection (4), the Court of Session may, on cause shown, allow the proceedings to be remitted to the Court.

(6)   If the Court of Session allows the proceedings to be remitted to that Court, the sheriff is to remit the proceedings to that Court.

(7)   Where the proceedings are remitted to the Court of Session under subsection (6), the proceedings may be dealt with and disposed of by that Court despite section 39(2).

## Remit of cases from the Court of Session

93.—(1)   Subsection (2) applies to any proceedings in the Court of Session if—

    (a)   they are proceedings that a sheriff also has competence and jurisdiction to deal with,

    (b)   they would be proceedings to which section 39 applies but for the fact that subsection (1)(b)(ii) of that section is not satisfied, and

    (c)   the Court considers, at any stage, that it is unlikely that the aggregate total value of all the orders of value granted in the proceedings, exclusive of interest and expenses, will be greater than the sum specified in that subsection.

(2)   The Court must remit the proceedings to an appropriate sheriff, unless the Court considers, on cause shown, that the proceedings should remain in the Court of Session.

(3)   In considering the matter in subsection (1)(c), the Court is to assume—

    (a)   that liability for the order sought is established, and

    (b)   that there will, where appropriate, be no deduction for contributory negligence.

(4)   Subsection (5) applies to any proceedings in the Court of Session if—

    (a)   they are proceedings that a sheriff also has competence and jurisdiction to deal with, but

    (b)   are not proceedings to which paragraph (b) or (c) of subsection (1) applies.

(5)   The Court may, at any stage, remit the proceedings to an appropriate sheriff if the Court considers that the nature of the proceedings makes it appropriate to do so.

(6)   The Court may remit proceedings under subsection (2) or (5)—

    (a)   on the application of any party to the proceedings, or

    (b)   on its own initiative.

(7)   In this section, "an appropriate sheriff" means, in relation to proceedings remitted from the Court of Session under this section, a sheriff having competence and jurisdiction to deal with the proceedings sitting at such sheriff court as the Court may, at the time of the remit, specify.

## Remit of cases to the Scottish Land Court

94.—(1)   Subsection (2) applies to any proceedings before a sheriff where the matter to which the proceedings relate could competently be determined by the Scottish Land Court under—

    (a)   the Agricultural Holdings (Scotland) Act 1991, or

(b)   the Agricultural Holdings (Scotland) Act 2003.

(2)   The sheriff may, at any stage, remit the proceedings to the Scottish Land Court if the sheriff considers that it is appropriate to do so.

(3)   The sheriff may remit proceedings under subsection (2)—

(a)   on the application of any party to the proceedings, or

(b)   on the sheriff's own initiative.

(4)   A decision of the sheriff to remit, or not to remit, the proceedings under subsection (2) is final and no appeal may be taken against it.

Chapter 4 – Lay representation for non-natural persons

## Key defined terms

**95.**—(1)   This section applies for the purposes of the interpretation of this Chapter.

(2)   "Non-natural person" means—

(a)   a company (whether incorporated in the United Kingdom or elsewhere),

(b)   a limited liability partnership,

(c)   any other partnership,

(d)   an unincorporated association of persons.

(3)   "Lay representative" means an individual who is not a legal representative.

(4)   "Legal representative" means—

(a)   a solicitor,

(b)   an advocate, or

(c)   a person having a right to conduct litigation, or a right of audience, by virtue of section 27 of the Law Reform (Miscellaneous Provisions) (Scotland) Act 1990.

(5)   An individual holds a relevant position with a non-natural person if the individual—

(a)   in the case of a company, is a director or secretary of the company,

(b)   in the case of a limited liability partnership, is a member of the partnership,

(c)   in the case of any other partnership, is a partner in the partnership,

(d)   in the case of an unincorporated association, is a member or office holder of the association.

(6)   For the purposes of section 96, an individual also holds a relevant position with a non-natural person if the individual is an employee of the non-natural person.

(7)   References to conducting proceedings are references to exercising, in relation to the proceedings, a function or right (including a right of audience) that a legal representative could exercise in the proceedings.

## Lay representation in simple procedure cases

**96.**—(1)   This section applies in any simple procedure case to which a non-natural person is a party.

(2)   A lay representative may conduct proceedings in the case on behalf of the non-natural person if—

(a)   the lay representative holds a relevant position with the non-natural person,

(b)   the responsibilities of the lay representative in that position do not consist wholly or mainly of conducting legal proceedings on behalf of the non-natural person or another person,

    (c)   the lay representative is authorised by the non-natural person to conduct the proceedings,

    (d)   the lay representative does not have a personal interest in the subject matter of the proceedings, and

    (e)   the lay representative is not the subject of an order such as is mentioned in section 98(2)(f).

(3)   In subsection (2)(d), "personal interest" means an interest other than one that anyone holding the position that the lay representative holds with the non-natural person would have.

(4)   Subsection (2) is subject to provision made by an act of sederunt under section 98.

## Lay representation in other proceedings

**97.**—(1)   This section applies in civil proceedings (other than a simple procedure case) to which a non-natural person is a party.

(2)   A lay representative may, if the court grants permission, conduct the proceedings on behalf of the non-natural person.

(3)   The court may grant permission if satisfied that—

    (a)   the non-natural person is unable to pay for the services of a legal representative to conduct the proceedings,

    (b)   the lay representative is a suitable person to conduct the proceedings, and

    (c)   it is in the interests of justice to grant permission.

(4)   For the purposes of subsection (3)(b), a lay representative is a suitable person to conduct the proceedings if—

    (a)   the lay representative holds a relevant position with the non-natural person,

    (b)   the responsibilities of the lay representative in that position do not consist wholly or mainly of conducting legal proceedings on behalf of the non-natural person or another person,

    (c)   the lay representative is authorised by the non-natural person to conduct the proceedings,

    (d)   the lay representative does not have a personal interest in the subject matter of the proceedings, and

    (e)   the lay representative is not the subject of an order such as is mentioned in section 98(2)(f).

(5)   In subsection (4)(d), "personal interest" means an interest other than one that anyone holding the position that the lay representative holds with the non-natural person would have.

(6)   For the purposes of subsection (3)(c), in deciding whether it is in the interests of justice to grant permission, the court must have regard, in particular, to—

    (a)   the non-natural person's prospects of success in the proceedings, and

    (b)   the likely complexity of the proceedings.

(7)   Subsection (2) is subject to provision made by an act of sederunt under section 98.

(8)   In this section—

    "civil proceedings" means civil proceedings in—

        (a)   the Court of Session,

        (b)   the Sheriff Appeal Court, or

        (c)   the sheriff court,

"the court", in the case of proceedings in the sheriff court, means the sheriff.

**Lay representation: supplementary provision**

98.—(1)   The Court of Session may, by act of sederunt, make further provision about—

    (a)   the granting of permission under section 97, and

    (b)   the conduct of proceedings by lay representatives by virtue of this Chapter.

(2)   Provision under subsection (1) may include, in particular, provision—

    (a)   about the procedure to be followed in considering applications for permission under section 97 (including provision for applications to be considered in chambers and without hearing the parties),

    (b)   regulating the conduct of lay representatives in exercising a function or right by virtue of this Chapter,

    (c)   about the authorisation of lay representatives for the purposes of this Chapter,

    (d)   imposing conditions on the exercise by lay representatives of a function or right by virtue of this Chapter or enabling the court to impose such conditions in particular cases,

    (e)   enabling the court, in particular cases, to withdraw a lay representative's right to exercise a function or right by virtue of this Chapter if the representative contravenes provision made by virtue of the act of sederunt,

    (f)   enabling the court to make an order preventing a lay representative from conducting any proceedings before any court on behalf of non-natural persons,

    (g)   enabling the court, in awarding expenses against a non-natural person in any case, to find a lay representative jointly and severally liable for the expenses.

(3)   An act of sederunt under subsection (1) may make different provision for different purposes.

(4)   In this section, "the court", in the case of proceedings in the sheriff court, means the sheriff.

Chapter 5 – Jury service

**Jury service**

99.—(1)   The Law Reform (Miscellaneous Provisions) (Scotland) Act 1980 is amended in accordance with this section.

(2)   In section 1 (qualification of jurors)—

    (a)   in subsection (1)—

       (i)   the words "to subsections (2) and (3) below and" are repealed, and

       (ii)   for paragraph (b) substitute—

           "(b)   is not less than 18 years of age;",

    (b)   subsections (1A), (2) and (3) are repealed,

    (c)   in subsection (5), the words "under subsection (2) or (3) above or" are repealed.

(3)   In section 1A (excusal of jurors in relation to criminal proceedings)—

    (a)   in each of subsections (1), (2) and (3), the words "in relation to criminal proceedings" are repealed,

505

    (b)   in subsection (3), for "(a)(iii)" substitute "(ab)",

    (c)   the title of the section becomes "**Excusal of jurors as of right**".

  (4)   In Part III of Schedule 1 (persons excusable from jury service as of right), in Group F, for paragraphs (a) and (aa) substitute—

> "(a)   persons who have served as a juror in the period of 5 years ending with the date on which the person is cited first to attend;
>
> (aa)   persons who have attended for jury service, but have not served as a juror, in the period of 2 years ending with the date on which the person is cited first to attend;
>
> (ab)   persons who have attained the age of 71;".

## Chapter 6 – Vexatious proceedings

### Vexatious litigation orders

**100.**—(1)   The Inner House may, on the application of the Lord Advocate, make a vexatious litigation order in relation to a person (a "vexatious litigant").

  (2)   A vexatious litigation order is an order which has either or both of the following effects—

    (a)   the vexatious litigant may institute civil proceedings only with the permission of a judge of the Outer House,

    (b)   the vexatious litigant may take a specified step in specified ongoing civil proceedings only with such permission.

  (3)   In subsection (2)(b)—

    (a)   "specified ongoing civil proceedings" means civil proceedings which—

        (i)   were instituted by the vexatious litigant before the order was made, and

        (ii)   are specified in the order,

    (b)   "specified step" means a step specified in the order.

  (4)   A vexatious litigation order has effect—

    (a)   during such period as is specified in the order, or

    (b)   if no period is so specified, indefinitely.

  (5)   In this section and section 101—

    (a)   "the Inner House" means the Inner House of the Court of Session,

    (b)   "the Outer House" means the Outer House of the Court of Session,

    (c)   "vexatious litigant" means, in relation to a vexatious litigation order, the person to whom the order relates,

    (d)   "vexatious litigation order" means an order made under subsection (1).

### Vexatious litigation orders: further provision

**101.**—(1)   The Inner House may make a vexatious litigation order in relation to a person only if satisfied that the person has habitually and persistently, without any reasonable ground for doing so—

    (a)   instituted vexatious civil proceedings, or

    (b)   made vexatious applications to the court in the course of civil proceedings (whether or not instituted by the person).

  (2)   For the purpose of subsection (1), it does not matter whether the proceedings—

    (a)   were instituted in Scotland or elsewhere,

    (b)   involved the same parties or different parties.

  (3)   A copy of a vexatious litigation order must be published in the Edinburgh Gazette.

(4) A judge of the Outer House may grant permission to a vexatious litigant to institute civil proceedings or, as the case may be, to take a step in such proceedings only if satisfied that there is a reasonable ground for the proceedings or the taking of the step.

(5) The decision of the judge to refuse to grant permission under subsection (4) is final.

(6) Subsection (7) applies in relation to civil proceedings instituted in any court by a vexatious litigant before the Inner House makes a vexatious litigation order in relation to the vexatious litigant.

(7) The court may make such order as it sees fit in consequence of the vexatious litigation order.

(8) In subsection (7), "the court" means—

    (a) the court which is dealing with the proceedings,

    (b) in the case of proceedings in the sheriff court, the sheriff.

### Power to make orders in relation to vexatious behaviour

**102.**—(1) The Scottish Ministers may by regulations confer on the Court of Session, a sheriff or the Sheriff Appeal Court the power to make an order of a kind mentioned in subsection (2) in relation to a person who has behaved in a vexatious manner in civil proceedings before the Court of Session, sheriff or, as the case may be, Sheriff Appeal Court.

(2) The order referred to in subsection (1) is an order that the person may do any of the following only with the permission of a court or a judge of any court—

    (a) take such a step in those proceedings as is specified in the order,

    (b) take such a step as is so specified in such other civil proceedings (whether or not those proceedings are before the Court of Session, sheriff or, as the case may be, Sheriff Appeal Court) as are so specified,

    (c) institute civil proceedings in such a court as is so specified.

(3) For the purpose of subsection (1), a person behaves in a vexatious manner in civil proceedings if the person—

    (a) institutes the proceedings and they are vexatious, or

    (b) makes a vexatious application in the course of the proceedings (whether or not they were instituted by the person).

(4) Regulations under subsection (1) may include provision for—

    (a) an order to be made on the application of a party to the proceedings or on the Court's or, as the case may be, sheriff's own initiative,

    (b) circumstances in which the Court or sheriff may make an order, and the requirements as to permission which may be imposed in an order in those circumstances,

    (c) the factors which the Court or sheriff may take into account in deciding whether to make an order (including the person's behaviour in other civil proceedings, whether in Scotland or elsewhere),

    (d) the courts in relation to which an order may have effect,

    (e) the maximum period for which an order may have effect,

    (f) the effect of an order in any other respects.

(5) The Scottish Ministers must consult the Lord President of the Court of Session before making regulations under subsection (1).

(6) Regulations under subsection (1)—

    (a) are subject to the negative procedure,

    (b) may make different provision for different purposes,

    (c)   may make incidental, supplemental, consequential, transitional, transitory or saving provision.

Part 4 – Procedure and fees

*Procedure*

## Power to regulate procedure etc. in the Court of Session

    **103.**—(1)   The Court of Session may by act of sederunt make provision for or about—

    (a)   the procedure and practice to be followed in proceedings in the Court,

    (b)   any matter incidental or ancillary to such proceedings.

    (2)   Without limiting that generality, the power in subsection (1) includes power to make provision for or about—

    (a)   execution or diligence following on such proceedings,

    (b)   avoiding the need for, or mitigating the length and complexity of, such proceedings, including—

        (i)   encouraging settlement of disputes and the use of alternative dispute resolution procedures,

        (ii)   action to be taken before such proceedings are brought by persons who will be party to the proceedings,

    (c)   other aspects of the conduct and management of such proceedings, including the use of technology,

    (d)   simplifying the language used in connection with such proceedings or matters incidental or ancillary to them,

    (e)   the form of any document to be used in connection with such proceedings, matters incidental or ancillary to them or matters specified in this subsection,

    (f)   appeals against a decision of the Court,

    (g)   applications that may be made to the Court,

    (h)   time limits in relation to proceedings mentioned in subsection (1), matters incidental or ancillary to them or matters specified in this subsection,

    (i)   the steps that the Court may take where there has been an abuse of process by a party to such proceedings,

    (j)   expenses that may be awarded to parties to such proceedings,

    (k)   other payments such parties may be required to make in respect of their conduct relating to such proceedings,

    (l)   the payment, investment or application of any sum of money awarded in such proceedings to or in respect of a person under a legal disability,

    (m)   the representation of parties to such proceedings, and others, including representation by persons who—

        (i)   are neither solicitors nor advocates, or

        (ii)   do not have the right to conduct litigation, or a right of audience, by virtue of section 27 of the Law Reform (Miscellaneous Provisions) (Scotland) Act 1990,

    (n)   the functions and rights of persons appointed by the Court in connection with such proceedings,

    (o)   witnesses and evidence, including modifying the rules of evidence as they apply to such proceedings,

    (p)   the quorum for a Division of the Inner House considering purely proce-

508

dural matters and, in the case of an extra Division, as to which judge is to preside and to sign any judgment or interlocutor pronounced by the extra Division,

(q) such other matters as the Court thinks necessary or appropriate for the purposes of carrying out or giving effect to the provisions of any enactment (including this Act) relating to such proceedings or matters incidental or ancillary to them.

(3) An act of sederunt under subsection (1) may make—

(a) incidental, supplemental, consequential, transitional, transitory or saving provision,

(b) provision amending, repealing or revoking any enactment (including any provision of this Act) relating to matters with respect to which an act of sederunt may be made,

(c) different provision for different purposes.

(4) This section is without prejudice to—

(a) any enactment that enables the Court to make rules (by act of sederunt or otherwise) regulating the practice and procedure to be followed in proceedings to which this section applies, or

(b) the inherent powers of the Court.

## Power to regulate procedure etc. in the sheriff court and the Sheriff Appeal Court

**104.**—(1) The Court of Session may by act of sederunt make provision for or about—

(a) the procedure and practice to be followed in civil proceedings in the sheriff court or in the Sheriff Appeal Court,

(b) any matter incidental or ancillary to such proceedings.

(2) Without limiting that generality, the power in subsection (1) includes power to make provision for or about—

(a) execution or diligence following on such proceedings,

(b) avoiding the need for, or mitigating the length and complexity of, such proceedings, including—

(i) encouraging settlement of disputes and the use of alternative dispute resolution procedures,

(ii) action to be taken before such proceedings are brought by persons who will be party to the proceedings,

(c) other aspects of the conduct and management of such proceedings, including the use of technology,

(d) simplifying the language used in connection with such proceedings or matters incidental or ancillary to them,

(e) the form of any document to be used in connection with such proceedings, matters incidental or ancillary to them or matters specified in this subsection,

(f) appeals against a decision of a sheriff or the Sheriff Appeal Court,

(g) applications that may be made to a sheriff or the Sheriff Appeal Court,

(h) time limits in relation to proceedings mentioned in subsection (1), matters incidental or ancillary to them or matters specified in this subsection,

(i) the steps that a sheriff or the Sheriff Appeal Court may take where there has been an abuse of process by a party to such proceedings,

(j) expenses that may be awarded to parties to such proceedings,

    (k)   other payments such parties may be required to make in respect of their conduct relating to such proceedings,

    (l)   the payment, investment or application of any sum of money awarded in such proceedings to or in respect of a person under a legal disability,

    (m)   the representation of parties to such proceedings, and others, including representation by persons who—

        (i)   are neither solicitors nor advocates, or

        (ii)   do not have the right to conduct litigation, or a right of audience, by virtue of section 27 of the Law Reform (Miscellaneous Provisions) (Scotland) Act 1990,

    (n)   the functions and rights of persons appointed by a sheriff or the Sheriff Appeal Court in connection with such proceedings,

    (o)   witnesses and evidence, including modifying the rules of evidence as they apply to such proceedings,

    (p)   the quorum for sittings of the Sheriff Appeal Court,

    (q)   determining which Appeal Sheriff is to preside at such sittings where the Court is constituted by more than one Appeal Sheriff,

    (r)   such other matters as the Court of Session thinks necessary or appropriate for the purposes of carrying out or giving effect to the provisions of any enactment (including this Act) relating to such proceedings or matters incidental or ancillary to them.

    (3)   Nothing in an act of sederunt under subsection (1) is to derogate from the provisions of sections 72 to 82 (simple procedure).

    (4)   An act of sederunt under subsection (1) may make—

    (a)   incidental, supplemental, consequential, transitional, transitory or saving provision,

    (b)   provision amending, repealing or revoking any enactment (including any provision of this Act) relating to matters with respect to which an act of sederunt under subsection (1) may be made,

    (c)   different provision for different purposes.

    (5)   Before making an act of sederunt under subsection (1) with respect to any matter, the Court of Session must—

    (a)   consult the Scottish Civil Justice Council, and

    (b)   take into consideration any views expressed by the Council with respect to that matter.

    (6)   Subsection (5) does not apply in relation to an act of sederunt that embodies, with or without modifications, draft rules submitted by the Scottish Civil Justice Council to the Court of Session.

    (7)   This section is without prejudice to—

    (a)   any enactment that enables the Court of Session to make rules (by act of sederunt or otherwise) regulating the practice and procedure to be followed in proceedings to which this section applies, or

    (b)   the inherent powers of a sheriff or the Sheriff Appeal Court.

*Fees of solicitors etc.*

**Power to regulate fees in the Court of Session**

    **105.**—(1)   The Court of Session may, in relation to any proceedings in the Court (including any execution or diligence following such proceedings), by act of sederunt make provision for or about the fees of—

    (a)   solicitors,

   (b)   messengers-at-arms,

   (c)   persons acting under the Execution of Diligence (Scotland) Act 1926,

   (d)   witnesses,

   (e)   shorthand writers,

   (f)   such other persons, or persons of such descriptions, as the Scottish Ministers may by order specify.

(2)   An act of sederunt under subsection (1) may not make any provision for or about the fees that the Scottish Ministers may regulate under or by virtue of section 33 of the Legal Aid (Scotland) Act 1986 (fees and outlays of solicitors and counsel).

(3)   An act of sederunt under subsection (1) and an order under subsection (1)(f) may make—

   (a)   incidental, supplemental, consequential, transitional, transitory or saving provision,

   (b)   different provision for different purposes.

(4)   Before making an order under subsection (1)(f), the Scottish Ministers must consult the Lord President of the Court of Session.

(5)   An act of sederunt under subsection (1) is subject to the negative procedure.

### Power to regulate fees in the sheriff court and the Sheriff Appeal Court

**106.**—(1)   The Court of Session may, in relation to civil proceedings in the sheriff court or the Sheriff Appeal Court (including any execution or diligence following such proceedings), by act of sederunt make provision for or about the fees of—

   (a)   solicitors,

   (b)   sheriff officers,

   (c)   persons acting under the Execution of Diligence (Scotland) Act 1926,

   (d)   witnesses,

   (e)   shorthand writers,

   (f)   such other persons, or persons of such descriptions, as the Scottish Ministers may by order specify.

(2)   An act of sederunt under subsection (1) may not make any provision for or about the fees that the Scottish Ministers may regulate under or by virtue of section 33 of the Legal Aid (Scotland) Act 1986 (fees and outlays of solicitors and counsel).

(3)   An act of sederunt under subsection (1) may make—

   (a)   incidental, supplemental, consequential, transitional, transitory or saving provision,

   (b)   different provision for different purposes.

(4)   Before making an order under subsection (1)(f), the Scottish Ministers must consult the Lord President of the Court of Session.

(5)   An act of sederunt under subsection (1) is subject to the negative procedure.

*Court fees*

### Power to provide for fees for SCTS, court clerks and other officers

**107.**—(1)   The Scottish Ministers may by order make provision for the charging of fees in respect of the carrying out of the functions of the Scottish Courts and Tribunals Service ("the SCTS") or a relevant officer in connection with—

   (a)   proceedings in the Scottish Courts, or

   (b)   any other matter dealt with by a relevant officer.

(2)   An order under subsection (1) may—

(a) in particular include provision—

    (i) specifying, or for determining, the amount of fees,

    (ii) specifying, or for determining, the persons or types of person who are to pay the fees,

    (iii) specifying the times when, places where and persons to whom the fees are to be paid,

    (iv) for exemptions from the requirement to pay fees,

    (v) for the remission of fees,

    (vi) for modification of fees,

(b) make different provision for different purposes or circumstances including, in particular, different provision for—

    (i) different Scottish Courts,

    (ii) different relevant officers,

    (iii) different proceedings or types of proceedings.

(3) In this section—

"relevant officer" means—

    (a) a clerk, deputy clerk or assistant clerk of any of the Scottish Courts,

    (b) the Accountant of Court,

    (c) the Auditor of the Court of Session,

    (d) the auditor of a sheriff court,

    (e) any other officer who is a member of the staff of the SCTS,

"Scottish Courts" means—

    (a) the Court of Session,

    (b) the High Court of Justiciary,

    (c) the court for hearing appeals under section 57(1)(b) of the Representation of the People Act 1983,

    (d) the election court in Scotland constituted under section 123 of that Act,

    (e) the Scottish Land Court,

    (f) the Lands Valuation Appeal Court,

    (g) the Sheriff Appeal Court,

    (h) sheriff courts,

    (i) justice of the peace courts.

(4) The Scottish Ministers may by order modify (either or both of) the definitions of "relevant officer" and "Scottish Courts" in subsection (3).

*Sanction for counsel*

### Sanction for counsel in the sheriff court and Sheriff Appeal Court

**108.**—(1) This section applies in civil proceedings in the sheriff court or the Sheriff Appeal Court where the court is deciding, for the purposes of any relevant expenses rule, whether to sanction the employment of counsel by a party for the purposes of the proceedings.

(2) The court must sanction the employment of counsel if the court considers, in all the circumstances of the case, that it is reasonable to do so.

(3) In considering that matter, the court must have regard to—

(a) whether the proceedings are such as to merit the employment of counsel, having particular regard to—

   (i)   the difficulty or complexity, or likely difficulty or complexity, of
        the proceedings,

   (ii)   the importance or value of any claim in the proceedings, and

(b)   the desirability of ensuring that no party gains an unfair advantage by
     virtue of the employment of counsel.

(4)   The court may have regard to such other matters as it considers appropriate.

(5)   References in this section to proceedings include references to any part or
aspect of the proceedings.

(6)   In this section—

   "counsel" means—

      (a)   an advocate,

      (b)   a solicitor having a right of audience in the Court of Session
           under section 25A of the Solicitors (Scotland) Act 1980,

   "court", in relation to proceedings in the sheriff court, means the sheriff,

   "relevant expenses rule" means, in relation to any proceedings mentioned in
     subsection (1), any provision of an act of sederunt requiring, or having the
     effect of requiring, that the employment of counsel by a party for the
     purposes of the proceedings be sanctioned by the court before the fees of
     counsel are allowable as expenses that may be awarded to the party.

(7)   This section is subject to an act of sederunt under section 104(1) or 106(1).

### PART 5 – CIVIL APPEALS

*Appeals to the Sheriff Appeal Court*

## Abolition of appeal from a sheriff to the sheriff principal

**109.**—(1)   No appeal may be taken to the sheriff principal against any decision
of a sheriff in civil proceedings.

(2)   Subsection (3) applies to any provision of any pre-commencement enactment that—

(a)   provides for an appeal to the sheriff principal from any decision of a sheriff
     in civil proceedings, or

(b)   restricts or excludes any such appeal.

(3)   The provision has effect as if for the reference to the sheriff principal there
were substituted a reference to the Sheriff Appeal Court.

(4)   In subsection (2), "pre-commencement enactment" means an enactment
passed or made before this section comes into force.

## Appeal from a sheriff to the Sheriff Appeal Court

**110.**—(1)   An appeal may be taken to the Sheriff Appeal Court, without the
need for permission, against—

(a)   a decision of a sheriff constituting final judgment in civil proceedings, or

(b)   any decision of a sheriff in civil proceedings—

      (i)   granting, refusing or recalling an interdict, whether interim or final,

      (ii)   granting interim decree for payment of money other than a decree
           for expenses,

      (iii)   making an order ad factum praestandum,

      (iv)   sisting an action,

      (v)   allowing, refusing or limiting the mode of proof, or

      (vi)   refusing a reponing note.

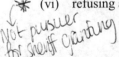

Not pusuer
for sheriff granting

(2)   An appeal may be taken to the Sheriff Appeal Court against any other decision of a sheriff in civil proceedings if the sheriff, on the sheriff's own initiative or on the application of any party to the proceedings, grants permission for the appeal.

(3)   In an appeal to the Sheriff Appeal Court, the Court may allow further proof.

(4)   This section does not affect any other right of appeal to the Sheriff Appeal Court under any other enactment.

(5)   This section does not affect any right of appeal against any decision of a sheriff to the Court of Session under any other enactment.

(6)   This section is subject to any provision of this or any other enactment that restricts or excludes a right of appeal from a sheriff to the Sheriff Appeal Court.

### Sheriff Appeal Court's powers of disposal in appeals

**111.**—(1)   In determining an appeal under section 110, the Court has power to—

(a)   grant such disposal as the Court sees fit, including by (in whole or in part)—

(i)   adhering to the decision that is subject to the appeal,

(ii)   recalling the decision,

(iii)   varying the decision,

(iv)   remitting the case back to the sheriff,

(v)   dismissing the appeal,

(b)   make such incidental or interim orders as may be necessary, and

(c)   determine any incidental or other issue that needs to be determined for the purpose of doing justice in the appeal.

(2)   Subsection (1)—

(a)   does not affect the generality of section 47(3), but

(b)   is subject to any other provision of this Act or any other enactment that restricts or excludes any power of the Court in determining or disposing of an appeal.

### Remit of appeal from the Sheriff Appeal Court to the Court of Session

**112.**—(1)   This section applies in relation to an appeal to the Sheriff Appeal Court against a decision of a sheriff in civil proceedings.

(2)   The Sheriff Appeal Court may—

(a)   on the application of a party to the appeal, and

(b)   if satisfied that the appeal raises a complex or novel point of law,

remit the appeal to the Court of Session.

(3)   Where an appeal is remitted to the Court of Session under subsection (2), the Court of Session may deal with and dispose of the appeal as if it had originally been made direct to that Court.

*Appeals to the Court of Session*

### Appeal from the Sheriff Appeal Court to the Court of Session

**113.**—(1)   An appeal may be taken to the Court of Session against a decision of the Sheriff Appeal Court constituting final judgment in civil proceedings, but only—

(a)   with the permission of the Sheriff Appeal Court, or

(b)   if that Court has refused permission, with the permission of the Court of Session.

(2)   The Sheriff Appeal Court or the Court of Session may grant permission under subsection (1) only if the Court considers that—

(a)   the appeal would raise an important point of principle or practice, or

(b)   there is some other compelling reason for the Court of Session to hear the appeal.

(3)   This section does not affect any other right of appeal against any decision of the Sheriff Appeal Court to the Court of Session under any other enactment.

(4)   This section is subject to any provision of any other enactment that restricts or excludes a right of appeal from the Sheriff Appeal Court to the Court of Session.

### Appeal from the sheriff principal to the Court of Session

**114.**—(1)   An appeal may be taken to the Court of Session against a decision of a sheriff principal constituting a final judgment in relevant civil proceedings.

(2)   This section does not affect any other right of appeal against any decision of a sheriff principal to the Court of Session under any other enactment.

(3)   This section is subject to any provision of any other enactment that restricts or excludes any right of appeal from a sheriff principal to the Court of Session.

(4)   In subsection (1), "relevant civil proceedings" means civil proceedings (other than an appeal) under an enactment that provides for the proceedings to be brought before a sheriff principal rather than a sheriff.

### Appeals: granting of leave or permission and assessment of grounds of appeal

**115.**   In the Court of Session Act 1988, after section 31 insert—

#### Power to provide for single judge of Inner House to determine leave or permission and assess grounds of appeal

"**31A**(1)   The Court may by act of sederunt provide for any applications to the Court for leave or permission to appeal to the Inner House to be determined by a single judge of the Inner House.

(2)   The Court may by act of sederunt provide for—

(a)   any appeal proceedings to be considered initially (and, where required, after leave or permission to appeal has been granted) by a single judge of the Inner House, and

(b)   for the single judge to decide, by reference to whether the grounds of appeal or any of them are arguable—

(i)   whether the appeal proceedings should be allowed to proceed in the Inner House, and

(ii)   if so, on which grounds.

(3)   An act of sederunt under subsection (1) or (2)—

(a)   must include provision—

(i)   about the procedure to be followed in the proceedings before the single judge, including provision for the parties to be heard before the judge makes a decision,

(ii)   for review, on the application of any party to the proceedings, of the decision of the single judge by a Division of the Inner House,

(iii)   about the grounds on which the decision may be so reviewed,

(iv)   about the procedure to be followed in such a review,

(v)   about the matters that may be considered in such a review and the powers available to the Division on disposing of the review, and

(b)   may make different provision in relation to different types of—

(i)   applications for leave or permission,

(ii)   appeal proceedings.

(4)   Subject to any provision made in an act of sederunt by virtue of subsection (3)(a)(ii) to (v), the decision of any single judge under an act of sederunt under subsection (1) or (2) is final.

(5)   Subsection (6) applies in appeal proceedings in which—

(a)   a single judge has granted leave or permission for the appeal by virtue of subsection (1), and

(b) the judge's decision is subject to review by a Division of the Inner House by virtue of subsection (3)(a)(ii).

(6) Where this subsection applies, the reference in subsection (2)(a) to leave or permission to appeal having been granted is a reference to its having been confirmed following review by the Division of the Inner House.

(7) In subsection (2)(a), "appeal proceedings" means proceedings on—

(a) a reclaiming application under section 28 (reclaiming against decisions of a Lord Ordinary),

(b) an application under section 29 (application for a new trial),

(c) an application under section 31 (application to overturn jury verdict),

(d) an appeal from the Sheriff Appeal Court under section 113 of the Courts Reform (Scotland) Act 2014,

(e) an appeal from a sheriff principal under section 114 of that Act,

(f) any other appeal taken to the Court (whether under an enactment or otherwise).".

*Effect of appeal*

## Effect of appeal

**116.**—(1) This section applies to—

(a) an appeal to the Sheriff Appeal Court under section 110 (including such an appeal remitted to the Court of Session under section 112), and

(b) an appeal to the Court of Session under section 113 or 114.

(2) In the appeal, all prior decisions in the proceedings (whether made at first instance or at any stage of appeal) are open to review.

(3) Any party to the proceedings may insist in the appeal even though the party is not the one who initiated the appeal.

(4) An appeal to which this section applies does not prevent the immediate execution of any of the following, which may continue to have effect despite the appeal until recalled—

(a) a warrant to take inventories,

(b) a warrant to place effects in custody for the interim,

(c) a warrant for interim preservation,

(d) an interim interdict.

*Appeals to the Supreme Court*

## Appeals to the Supreme Court

**117.** In the Court of Session Act 1988, for section 40 (appeals to the Supreme Court: appealable interlocutors) substitute—

### Appeals to the Supreme Court

"**40.**(1) An appeal may be taken to the Supreme Court against a decision of the Inner House mentioned in subsection (2), but only—

(a) with the permission of the Inner House, or

(b) if the Inner House has refused permission, with the permission of the Supreme Court.

(2) The decisions are—

(a) a decision constituting final judgment in any proceedings,

(b) a decision in an exchequer cause,

(c) a decision, on an application under section 29, to grant or refuse a new trial in any proceedings,

(d) any other decision in any proceedings if—

(i) there is a difference of opinion among the judges making the decision, or

    (ii) the decision is one sustaining a preliminary defence and dismissing the proceedings.

(3) An appeal may be taken to the Supreme Court against any other decision of the Inner House in any proceedings, but only with the permission of the Inner House.

(4) In an appeal against a decision mentioned in subsection (2)(c), the Supreme Court has the same powers as the Inner House had in relation to the application under section 29, including, in particular, the powers under sections 29(3) and 30(3).

(5) No appeal may be taken to the Supreme Court against any decision of a Lord Ordinary.

(6) But subsection (5) does not affect the operation of subsections (1) and (3) in relation to a decision of the Inner House in a review of a decision of a Lord Ordinary.

(7) In an appeal to the Supreme Court under this section against a decision of the Inner House in any proceedings, all prior decisions in the proceedings (whether made at first instance or at any stage of appeal) are open to review by the Supreme Court.

(8) This section is subject to—

  (a) sections 27(5) and 32(5),

  (b) any provision of any other enactment that restricts or excludes an appeal from the Court of Session to the Supreme Court.

(9) This section does not affect any right of appeal from the Court of Session to the Supreme Court that arises apart from this section.

(10) In this section—

"final judgment", in relation to any proceedings, means a decision which, by itself or taken along with prior decisions in the proceedings, disposes of the subject matter of the proceedings on its merits, even though judgment may not have been pronounced on every question raised or expenses found due may not have been modified, taxed or decerned for,

"preliminary defence", in relation to any proceedings, means a defence that does not relate to the merits of the proceedings.

**Permission for appeal under section 40**

40A.—(1) An application to the Inner House for permission to take an appeal under section 40(1) or (3) must be made—

  (a) within the period of 28 days beginning with the date of the decision against which the appeal is to be taken, or

  (b) within such longer period as the Inner House considers equitable having regard to all the circumstances.

(2) An application to the Supreme Court for permission to take an appeal under section 40(1) must be made—

  (a) within the period of 28 days beginning with the date on which the Inner House refuses permission for the appeal, or

  (b) within such longer period as the Supreme Court considers equitable having regard to all the circumstances.

(3) The Inner House or the Supreme Court may grant permission for an appeal under section 40(1) or (3) only if the Inner House or, as the case may be, the Supreme Court considers that the appeal raises an arguable point of law of general public importance which ought to be considered by the Supreme Court at that time.".

PART 6 – CRIMINAL APPEALS

*Appeals from summary criminal proceedings*

## Appeals to the Sheriff Appeal Court from summary criminal proceedings

118.—(1) There are transferred to and vested in the Sheriff Appeal Court all the powers and jurisdiction of the High Court of Justiciary (whether under an enactment or otherwise) so far as relating to appeals from courts of summary criminal jurisdiction.

(2)   Subsection (1) does not apply to the nobile officium of the High Court.

(3)   Schedule 3 (which modifies the Criminal Procedure (Scotland) Act 1995 in consequence of subsection (1)) has effect.

### Appeals from the Sheriff Appeal Court to the High Court

**119.**   In the Criminal Procedure (Scotland) Act 1995, after Part X (appeals from summary proceedings), insert—

"Part 10ZA – Appeals from Sheriff Appeal Court

#### Appeal from the Sheriff Appeal Court

**194ZB.**—(1)   An appeal on a point of law may be taken to the High Court against any decision of the Sheriff Appeal Court in criminal proceedings, but only with the permission of the High Court.

(2)   An appeal under subsection (1) may be taken by any party to the appeal in the Sheriff Appeal Court.

(3)   The High Court may give permission for an appeal under subsection (1) only if the Court considers that—

(a)   the appeal would raise an important point of principle or practice, or

(b)   there is some other compelling reason for the Court to hear the appeal.

(4)   An application for permission for an appeal under subsection (1) must be made before the end of the period of 14 days beginning with the day on which the decision of the Sheriff Appeal Court that would be the subject of the appeal was made.

(5)   The High Court may extend the period of 14 days mentioned in subsection (4) if satisfied that doing so is justified by exceptional circumstances.

#### Appeals: applications and procedure

**194ZC.**—(1)   An appeal under section 194ZB(1) is to be made by way of note of appeal.

(2)   A note of appeal must specify the point of law on which the appeal is being made.

(3)   For the purposes of considering and deciding an appeal under section 194ZB(1)—

(a)   three of the judges of the High Court are to constitute a quorum of the Court,

(b)   decisions are to be taken by a majority vote of the members of the Court sitting (including the presiding judge),

(c)   each judge sitting may pronounce a separate opinion.

#### Application for permission for appeal: determination by single judge

**194ZD.**—(1)   An application to the High Court for permission for an appeal under section 194ZB(1) is to be determined by a single judge of the High Court.

(2)   If the judge gives permission for the appeal, the judge may make comments in writing in relation to the appeal.

(3)   If the judge refuses permission for the appeal—

(a)   the judge must give reasons in writing for the refusal, and

(b)   where the appellant is on bail and the sentence imposed on the appellant on conviction is one of imprisonment, the judge must grant a warrant to apprehend and imprison the appellant.

(4)   A warrant under subsection (3)(b) does not take effect until the expiry of the period of 14 days mentioned in section 194ZE(1) (or, where that period is extended under section 194ZE(2) before the period being extended expires, until the expiry of the period as so extended) without an application for permission having been lodged by the appellant under section 194ZE(1).

### Further application for permission where single judge refuses permission

**194ZE.**—(1)   Where the judge refuses permission for the appeal under section 194ZD, the appellant may, within the period of 14 days beginning with the day on which intimation of the decision is given under section 194ZF(2), apply again to the High Court for permission for the appeal.

(2)   The High Court may extend the period of 14 days mentioned in subsection (1), or that period as extended under this subsection, whether or not the period to be extended has expired.

(3)   The High Court may extend a period under subsection (2) only if satisfied that doing so is justified by exceptional circumstances.

(4)   Three of the judges of the High Court are to constitute a quorum for the purposes of considering an application under subsection (1).

(5)   If the High Court gives permission for the appeal, the Court may make comments in writing in relation to the appeal.

(6)   If the High Court refuses permission for the appeal—

(a)   the Court must give reasons in writing for the refusal, and

(b)   where the appellant is on bail and the sentence imposed on the appellant on conviction is one of imprisonment, the Court must grant a warrant to apprehend and imprison the appellant.

### Applications for permission: further provision

**194ZF.**—(1)   An application for permission for an appeal under section 194ZB(1) is to be considered and determined (whether under section 194ZD or 194ZE)—

(a)   in chambers without the parties being present,

(b)   by reference to section 194ZB(3), and

(c)   on the basis of consideration of—

(i)   the note of appeal under section 194ZC(1), and

(ii)   such other document or information (if any) as may be specified by act of adjournal.

(2)   The Clerk of Justiciary must, as soon as possible, intimate to the appellant or the appellant's solicitor and to the Crown Agent—

(a)   a decision under section 194ZD or 194ZE determining the application for permission for an appeal, and

(b)   in the case of a refusal of permission for the appeal, the reasons for the decision.

### Restriction of grounds of appeal

**194ZG.**—(1)   Comments in writing made under section 194ZD(2) or 194ZE(5) may specify the arguable grounds of appeal (whether or not they were stated in the note of appeal) on the basis of which permission for the appeal was given.

(2)   Where the arguable grounds of appeal are specified under subsection (1), the appellant may not, except with the permission of the High Court on cause shown, found any aspect of the appeal on a ground of appeal stated in the application for permission but not specified under subsection (1).

(3)   An application by the appellant for permission under subsection (2) must—

    (a)  be made before the end of the period of 14 days beginning with the date of intimation under section 194ZF(2), and

    (b)  be intimated by the appellant to the Crown Agent before the end of that period.

(4)  The High Court may extend the period of 14 days mentioned in subsection (3) if satisfied that doing so is justified by exceptional circumstances.

(5)  The appellant may not, except with the permission of the High Court on cause shown, found any aspect of the appeal on a matter not stated in the note of appeal (or in a duly made amendment or addition to the note of appeal).

(6)  Subsection (5) does not apply in relation to a matter specified as an arguable ground of appeal under subsection (1).

## Disposal of appeals

**194ZH.**—(1)  In disposing of an appeal under section 194ZB(1), the High Court may—

    (a)  remit the case back to the Sheriff Appeal Court with its opinion and any direction as to further procedure in, or disposal of, the case, or

    (b)  exercise any power that the Sheriff Appeal Court could have exercised in relation to disposal of the appeal proceedings before that Court.

(2)  So far as necessary for the purposes or in consequence of the exercise of a power by the High Court by virtue of subsection (1)(b)—

    (a)  references in Part X to the Sheriff Appeal Court are to be read as including references to the High Court, and

    (b)  references in Part X to a verdict of or sentence passed by the inferior court are to be read as incuding references to a verdict of or sentence passed by the Sheriff Appeal Court in disposing of the appeal before it.

(3)  Subsections (1)(b) and (2) do not affect any power in relation to the consideration or disposal of appeals that the High Court has apart from those subsections.

## Procedure where appellant in custody

**194ZI.**—(1)  Section 177 (procedure where appellant in custody) applies in the case where a party making an appeal (other than an excepted appeal) under section 194ZB(1) is in custody as it applies in the case where an appellant making an application under section 176 is in custody.

(2)  In subsection (1), "excepted appeal" means an appeal against a decision of the Sheriff Appeal Court in—

    (a)  an appeal under section 32, or

    (b)  an appeal under section 177(3).

## Abandonment of appeal

**194ZJ.**  An appellant in an appeal under section 194ZB(1) may at any time abandon the appeal by minute to that effect—

    (a)  signed by the appellant or the appellant's solicitor,

    (b)  lodged with the Clerk of Justiciary, and

    (c)  intimated to the respondent or the respondent's solicitor.

## Finality of proceedings

**194ZK.**—(1)  Every interlocutor and sentence (including disposal or order) pronounced by the High Court in disposing of an appeal relating to summary proceedings is final and conclusive and not subject to review by any court whatsoever.

(2)   Subsection (1) is subject to—

    (a)   Part XA and section 288AA, and

    (b)   paragraph 13(a) of Schedule 6 to the Scotland Act 1998.

(3)   It is incompetent to stay or suspend any execution or diligence issuing from the High Court under this Part, except for the purposes of an appeal under—

    (a)   section 288AA, or

    (b)   paragraph 13(a) of Schedule 6 to the Scotland Act 1998.

### Computation of time

**194ZL.**   If any period of time specified in this Part expires on a Saturday, Sunday or court holiday prescribed for the relevant court, the period is extended to expire on the next day which is not a Saturday, Sunday or such a court holiday.".

## Power to refer points of law for the opinion of the High Court

**120.**   In the Criminal Procedure (Scotland) Act 1995, after section 175, insert—

**Power to refer points of law for the opinion of the High Court**

"**175A**(1)   In an appeal under this Part, the Sheriff Appeal Court may refer a point of law to the High Court for its opinion if it considers that the point is a complex or novel one.

(2)   The Sheriff Appeal Court may make a reference under subsection (1)—

    (a)   on the application of a party to the appeal proceedings, or

    (b)   on its own initiative.

(3)   On giving its opinion on a reference under subsection (1), the High Court may also give a direction as to further procedure in, or disposal of, the appeal.".

## References by the Scottish Criminal Cases Review Commission

**121.**—(1)   In the Criminal Procedure (Scotland) Act 1995, section 194B (references by the Commission) is amended in accordance with this section.

(2)   In subsection (1), after "High Court", in the first place where those words appear, insert "or the Sheriff Appeal Court".

(3)   After subsection (3), insert—

"(3A)   For the purposes of an appeal under Part X of this Act in a case referred to the High Court under subsection (1)—

    (a)   the High Court may exercise in the case all the powers and jurisdiction that the Sheriff Appeal Court would, had the case been an appeal to that Court, have had in relation to the case by virtue of section 118 of the Courts Reform (Scotland) Act 2014, and

    (b)   accordingly, Part X of this Act has effect in relation to the case subject to the following modifications—

        (i)   references to the Sheriff Appeal Court are to be read as references to the High Court,

        (ii)   references to an Appeal Sheriff are to be read as references to a judge of the High Court,

        (iii)   references to the Clerk of the Sheriff Appeal Court are to be read as reference to the Clerk of Justiciary.".

*Bail appeals*

## Bail appeals

**122.**—(1)   Section 32 of the Criminal Procedure (Scotland) Act 1995 (bail appeals) is amended in accordance with this section.

(2)   In each of subsections (1), (2), (3H)(a), (3I), (4), (5) and (7) for "High Court" substitute "appropriate Appeal Court".

(3)   For subsections (3D) and (3E) substitute—

"(3CA)   The clerk of the court from which the appeal is to be taken (unless that clerk is the Clerk of Justiciary) must—

(a)   send the notice of appeal without delay to the clerk of the appropriate Appeal Court, and

(b)   before the end of the day after the day of receipt of the notice of appeal, send the judge's report (if provided by then) to the clerk of the appropriate Appeal Court.".

(4)   In each of subsections (3F), (3G) and (10), for "Clerk of Justiciary" in each place it occurs substitute "clerk of the appropriate Appeal Court".

(5)   In subsection (3H)—

(a)   for "Where" substitute "In a case where the Sheriff Appeal Court is the appropriate Appeal Court, if", and

(b)   for "(3E)" substitute "(3CA)".

(6)   In each of subsections (4) and (5), for "Lord Commissioner of Justiciary" substitute "judge of the appropriate Appeal Court".

(7)   In subsection (7B)(a), for "High Court" substitute "the appropriate Appeal Court".

(8)   After subsection (10), insert—

"(11)   In this section—

"appropriate Appeal Court" means—

(a)   in the case of an appeal under this section against a bail decision of the High Court or a judge of the High Court, that Court,

(b)   in the case of an appeal under this section against a bail decision of the Sheriff Appeal Court, the High Court,

(c)   in the case of an appeal under this section against a bail decision of a sheriff (whether in solemn or summary proceedings) or a JP court, the Sheriff Appeal Court,

"judge of the appropriate Appeal Court" means—

(a)   in a case where the High Court is the appropriate Appeal Court, judge of that Court,

(b)   in a case where the Sheriff Appeal Court is the appropriate Appeal Court, Appeal Sheriff,

"the clerk of the appropriate Appeal Court" means—

(a)   in a case where the High Court is the appropriate Appeal Court, the Clerk of Justiciary,

(b)   in a case where the Sheriff Appeal Court is the appropriate Appeal Court, the Clerk of that Court.

(12)   In a case where the Sheriff Appeal Court is the appropriate Appeal Court, the references in subsections (3G)(b) and (10) to the Crown Agent are to be read as references to the prosecutor.".

## PART 7 – JUDGES OF THE COURT OF SESSION

### Appointment of Court of Session judges, etc.

**123.**   In the Judiciary and Courts (Scotland) Act 2008, for sections 21 to 23 substitute—

## Qualification of certain individuals for appointment as Court of Session judge

**20A.**—(1) An individual is qualified for appointment as a judge of the Court of Session if the individual—

    (a)  immediately before the appointment—

        (i)  held the office of sheriff principal or sheriff, and

        (ii)  had held office as either sheriff principal or sheriff throughout the period of 5 years immediately preceding the appointment, or

    (b)  at the time of appointment—

        (i)  is a solicitor having a right of audience in the Court of Session or the High Court of Justiciary under section 25A of the Solicitors (Scotland) Act 1980 (rights of audience), and

        (ii)  has been such a solicitor throughout the period of 5 years immediately preceding the appointment.

(2) Subsection (1) does not affect an individual's qualification for appointment as a judge of the Court of Session by virtue of article xix of the Union with England Act 1707.

## Temporary judges

**20B.**—(1) The Scottish Ministers may appoint an individual to act as a judge of the Court of Session; and an individual so appointed is to be known as a "temporary judge".

(2) An individual appointed under subsection (1) may also, by virtue of the appointment, act as a judge of the High Court of Justiciary.

(3) The Scottish Ministers may appoint an individual under subsection (1) only if—

    (a)  the individual is qualified for appointment as a judge of the Court of Session, and

    (b)  the Scottish Ministers have consulted the Lord President before making the appointment.

(4) Subject to section 20C, an appointment as a temporary judge lasts for 5 years.

(5) Subject to subsection (6), an individual appointed under subsection (1) is, while acting as a judge of the Court of Session or the High Court of Justiciary, to be treated for all purposes as a judge of that Court and may exercise the jurisdiction and powers that attach to that office.

(6) Such an individual is not to be treated as a judge of the Court of Session for the purposes of any enactment or rule of law relating to—

    (a)  the appointment, tenure of office, retirement, removal or disqualification of judges of that Court (including, without limiting that generality, any enactment or rule of law relating to the number of judges who may be appointed),

    (b)  the remuneration, allowances or pensions of such a judge.

(7) The appointment of an individual under subsection (1) does not affect—

    (a)  any appointment of the individual as a sheriff principal or sheriff, or

    (b)  the individual's continuing with any business or professional occupation not inconsistent with the individual acting as a judge.

## Reappointment of temporary judges

**20C.**—(1) A temporary judge whose appointment comes to an end by virtue of the expiry of the 5 year period mentioned in section 20B(4) is to be reappointed unless—

    (a)  the temporary judge declines reappointment,

    (b)  the Lord President has made a recommendation to the Scottish Ministers against the reappointment, or

    (c)  the temporary judge has sat for fewer than 50 days in total in that 5 year period.

(2) Section 20B (apart from subsection (3)) applies to a reappointment under subsection (1) as it applies to an appointment.

(3) A temporary judge whose appointment comes to an end by resignation under section 20D may be reappointed.

(4) Section 20B applies to a reappointment under subsection (3) as it applies to an appointment.

### Cessation of appointment of temporary judges

**20D.**—(1)   A temporary judge may resign at any time by giving notice to that effect to the Scottish Ministers.

(2)   An individual's appointment as a temporary judge ends—

(a)   when the individual resigns in accordance with subsection (1),

(b)   when the individual retires from office, or

(c)   if the individual is removed from office as such under section 39 (temporary judges: removal from office).

### Re-employment of former Court of Session and Supreme Court judges

**20E.**—(1)   The Lord President may appoint a qualifying former judge to act as a judge of the Court of Session.

(2)   An individual appointed under subsection (1) may also, by virtue of the appointment, act as a judge of the High Court of Justiciary.

(3)   An individual so appointed may act as a judge only during such periods or on such occasions as the Lord President may determine.

(4)   The Lord President may make an appointment under subsection (1) only if it appears to the Lord President to be expedient as a temporary measure in order to facilitate the disposal of business in the Court of Session or the High Court of Justiciary.

(5)   A "qualifying former judge" is an individual who—

(a)   has ceased to hold the office of—

(i)   judge of the Court of Session other than by virtue of section 95(6) of the Scotland Act 1998, or

(ii)   Justice of the Supreme Court or President or Deputy President of that Court and who, at the time of being appointed to the office in question, was eligible for appointment as a judge in the Court of Session, and

(b)   has not reached the age of 75.

### Re-employment of former judges: further provision

**20F.**—(1)   Subject to subsection (2), an individual's appointment under section 20E(1) lasts until recalled by the Lord President.

(2)   An individual's appointment under section 20E(1) ceases when the individual reaches the age of 75.

(3)   Despite the ending of an individual's appointment under section 20E(1)—

(a)   the individual may continue to deal with, give judgment in or deal with an ancillary matter relating to, a case begun before the individual while acting under that appointment,

(b)   so far as necessary for that purpose, and for the purpose of any subsequent proceedings arising out of the case or matter, the individual is to be treated as acting or, as the case may be, having acted under that appointment.

(4)   Subject to subsection (5), an individual appointed under section 20E(1) is, while acting as a judge of the Court of Session or the High Court of Justiciary, to be treated for all purposes as a judge of that Court and may exercise the jurisdiction and powers that attach to that office.

(5)   Such an individual is not to be treated as a judge of the Court of Session for the purposes of any enactment or rule of law relating to—

(a)   the appointment, tenure of office, retirement, removal or disqualification of judges of that Court (including, without limiting that generality, any enactment or rule of law relating to the number of judges who may be appointed),

(b)   the oaths to be taken by such judges,

(c)   the remuneration, allowances or pensions of such a judge.

### Remuneration and expenses of temporary and former judges

**20G.**—(1)   The Scottish Courts and Tribunals Service ("the SCTS") is to pay to an individual appointed under section 20B(1) or 20E(1) such remuneration as the Scottish Ministers may determine.

(2) The Scottish Ministers may determine different amounts of remuneration for—

    (a) different individuals so appointed, or

    (b) different descriptions of individuals so appointed.

(3) The SCTS may pay to an individual appointed under section 20B(1) or 20E(1) such sums as it may determine in respect of expenses reasonably incurred by the individual in the performance of, or in connection with, the individual's duties.

(4) The SCTS may—

    (a) determine the circumstances in which such sums may be paid, and

    (b) determine different circumstances for different individuals.".

## Payment of salaries of Court of Session judges

**124.**—(1) The salaries of judges of the Court of Session determined under section 9 of the Administration of Justice Act 1973 (judicial salaries) are to be paid by the Scottish Courts and Tribunals Service.

(2) Sums required by the Scottish Courts and Tribunals Service for the payment of such salaries are charged on the Scottish Consolidated Fund.

## Expenses

**125.**—(1) The Scottish Courts and Tribunals Service may pay to a Senator of the College of Justice such sums as it may determine in respect of expenses reasonably incurred by the Senator in the performance of, or in connection with, the Senator's duties.

(2) The Scottish Courts and Tribunals Service may—

(a) determine the circumstances in which sums may be paid, and

(b) determine different circumstances for—

    (i) different Senators,

    (ii) different descriptions of Senators,

    (iii) the different duties of Senators.

## PART 8 – SCOTTISH LAND COURT

### Scottish Land Court: remuneration and expenses

**126.**—(1) Schedule 1 to the Scottish Land Court Act 1993 (the Land Court) is amended in accordance with this section.

(2) For paragraph 3 substitute—

"**3**(1) The Scottish Courts and Tribunals Service ("the SCTS") is to pay to the Chairman of the Land Court such salary as the Treasury may determine.

(2) The SCTS is to pay to each of the other members of the Land Court such salary as the SCTS may determine.

(3) Sums required by the SCTS for the payment of a salary under this paragraph are charged on the Scottish Consolidated Fund.

**3A**(1) The SCTS may pay to a member of the Land Court such sums as it may determine in respect of expenses reasonably incurred by the member in the performance of, or in connection with, the member's duties.

(2) The SCTS may—

    (a) determine the circumstances in which sums may be paid, and

    (b) determine different circumstances for different members.".

(3) For paragraph 18 substitute—

"**18**(1) The Scottish Ministers are to pay to each of the following persons such remuneration as they may determine—

    (a) the principal clerk of the Land Court,

    (b) persons appointed or employed under paragraph 8 of this Schedule.

(2) The Scottish Courts and Tribunals Service ("the SCTS") is to pay to each of the following persons such remuneration as the SCTS may determine—

(a) persons nominated under paragraph 7A of this Schedule,

(b) persons appointed under paragraph 10 of this Schedule.

(3) The SCTS may pay to each of the following persons such sums as it may determine in respect of expenses reasonably incurred by the person in the performance of, or in connection with, the person's duties—

(a) persons nominated under paragraph 7A of this Schedule,

(b) persons appointed under paragraph 10 of this Schedule.

(4) The SCTS may—

(a) determine the circumstances in which sums may be paid, and

(b) determine different circumstances for different persons.

(5) Expenditure incurred by the Land Court in the performance of its functions may be paid by the Scottish Ministers.".

## PART 9 – JUSTICE OF THE PEACE COURTS

### Establishing, relocating and disestablishing justice of the peace courts

**127.**—(1) Section 59 of the Criminal Proceedings etc. (Reform) (Scotland) Act 2007 (establishing etc. JP courts) is amended in accordance with subsections (2) and (3).

(2) In each of subsections (2) and (6), after "may" insert ", following submission of a proposal under subsection (7),".

(3) For subsections (7) and (7A) substitute—

"(7) The Scottish Courts and Tribunals Service may, with the agreement of the Lord President, submit a proposal to the Scottish Ministers for the making of an order under subsection (2) or (6).

(7A) Before submitting a proposal to the Scottish Ministers, the Scottish Courts and Tribunals Service must consult such persons as it considers appropriate.

(7B) If, following submission of a proposal, the Scottish Ministers decide to make an order, they must have regard to the proposal in deciding what provision to make in the order.

(7C) The Scottish Ministers may make an order under subsection (2) or (6) only with the consent of—

(a) the Lord President, and

(b) the Scottish Courts and Tribunals Service.".

(4) In section 81(3)(a) of that Act (orders under the Act that are subject to affirmative procedure), after "56" insert ", 59(2) or (6)".

### Abolition of the office of stipendiary magistrate

**128.**—(1) The office of stipendiary magistrate is abolished.

(2) Subsection (3) applies to a person who, immediately before this section comes into force, holds office as a full-time stipendiary magistrate.

(3) The person is to be appointed, by virtue of this subsection, as a summary sheriff unless the person declines the appointment.

(4) Subsection (3) applies regardless of whether the person is qualified for appointment as a summary sheriff.

(5) Subsection (6) applies to a person who, immediately before this section comes into force, holds office as a part-time stipendiary magistrate.

(6) The person is to be appointed, by virtue of this subsection, as a part-time summary sheriff unless the person declines the appointment.

(7) Subsection (6) applies regardless of whether the person is qualified for appointment as a part-time summary sheriff.

(8) A person appointed—

(a) as a summary sheriff by virtue of subsection (3) is to be treated for all purposes as if appointed as such under section 5(2),

(b) as a part-time summary sheriff by virtue of subsection (6) is to be treated for all purposes as if appointed as such under section 10(1).

### Summary sheriffs to sit in justice of the peace courts

**129.** A summary sheriff of a sheriffdom may constitute, and exercise the jurisdiction and powers of, any justice of the peace court established for any sheriff court district in the sheriffdom.

#### PART 10 – THE SCOTTISH COURTS AND TRIBUNALS SERVICE

### The Scottish Courts and Tribunals Service

**130.**—(1) The Scottish Court Service is renamed and is to be known as the Scottish Courts and Tribunals Service ("the SCTS").

(2) After section 61 of the Judiciary and Courts (Scotland) Act 2008 insert—

#### Administrative support for the Scottish Tribunals and their members etc.

"**61A.**(1) The SCTS has the function of providing, or ensuring the provision of, the property, services, officers and other staff required for the purposes of—

    (a) the Scottish Tribunals,

    (b) the members of those Tribunals, and

    (c) such other tribunals (and their members) as the Scottish Ministers may by order specify.

(2) In carrying out that function, the SCTS must—

    (a) take account, in particular, of the needs of members of the public and those involved in proceedings in the tribunals, and

    (b) so far as practicable and appropriate, co-operate and co-ordinate activity with any other person having functions in relation to the administration of justice.

(3) In this Part, references to—

    (a) the Scottish Tribunals are to the First-tier Tribunal for Scotland and the Upper Tribunal for Scotland,

    (b) the members of the Scottish Tribunals are to be construed in accordance with the Tribunals (Scotland) Act 2014.".

(3) Schedule 4, which makes further provision in relation to the Scottish Courts and Tribunals Service, has effect.

(4) Any reference in any enactment to the Scottish Court Service is, unless the contrary intention appears, to be construed as a reference to the Scottish Courts and Tribunals Service.

#### PART 11 – THE JUDICIAL APPOINTMENTS BOARD FOR SCOTLAND

### Assistants to the Judicial Appointments Board for Scotland

**131.**—(1) In schedule 1 to the Judiciary and Courts (Scotland) Act 2008 (the Judicial Appointments Board for Scotland)—

    (a) after paragraph 13 insert—

*"Appointment of persons to assist the Board*

**13A.**(1) The Board may appoint persons (other than Board members) to assist the Board with the carrying out of its functions.

(2) The Board may appoint persons under sub-paragraph (1) as—

    (a) legal assistants, or

(b)   lay assistants.

(3)   A person may be appointed as a legal assistant if the person is a solicitor or advocate practising as such in Scotland.

(4)   A person may be appointed as a lay assistant if the person is eligible for appointment as a lay member of the Board.

(5)   It is for the Board to determine the number of persons who may be appointed under this paragraph.

(6)   A person who is disqualified from membership of the Board by virtue of paragraph 5 is also disqualified from being a legal assistant or a lay assistant.

(7)   Persons appointed under this paragraph are to be appointed for such period of not more than 3 years as the Board may determine.

(8)   At the end of a period of appointment, a person may be reappointed.

(9)   A person appointed under this paragraph may resign by giving notice in writing to the Board.

(10)   The Chairing Member may, by notice in writing, rescind a person's appointment under this paragraph if satisfied that the person—

(a)   has been convicted of any offence,

(b)   has become insolvent, or

(c)   is otherwise unfit to be a legal assistant or, as the case may be, a lay assistant or unable for any reason to discharge the functions of such an assistant.

(11)   Each person appointed under this paragraph is entitled to such fees and expenses, if any, as the Scottish Ministers may determine.

(12)   It is for the Scottish Ministers to pay those fees and expenses.

*Powers and conduct of persons appointed to assist the Board*

**13B.**(1)   A person appointed under paragraph 13A(1) as a legal assistant may, so far as authorised by the Board, do anything that a legal member of the Board may do, other than take part in a decision of the Board to recommend an individual for appointment.

(2)   A person appointed under paragraph 13A(1) as a lay assistant may, so far as authorised by the Board, do anything that a lay member of the Board may do, other than take part in a decision of the Board to recommend an individual for appointment.

(3)   The Board must issue (and may from time to time revise) a code of conduct for persons appointed under paragraph 13A(1).

(4)   Persons appointed under paragraph 13A(1) must have regard to the provisions of the code of conduct while assisting the Board in the carrying out of its functions.",

(b)   in paragraph 16A (proceedings relating to the Scottish Tribunals), after sub-paragraph (6) insert—

"(6A)   Sub-paragraph (6B) applies if—

(a)   the Board is exercising any function under this Act in connection with a position mentioned in section 10(2A),

(b)   the Board authorises a person appointed under paragraph 13A(1) to assist it in relation to any proceedings relating to the function, and

(c)   the person authorised to assist the Board in relation to the proceedings is a member of the Scottish Tribunals.

(6B)   The member of the Scottish Tribunals selected under sub-paragraph (3) may elect not to take part in the proceedings in respect of which the assistant is authorised to assist.".

(2)   In paragraph 10(1)(b) of schedule 9 to the Tribunals (Scotland) Act 2014, (transitional provision: making appointments), for "and (3)" substitute ", (3), (6A) and (6B)".

## Part 12 – General

### Modifications of enactments

**132.**   Schedule 5 makes minor modifications of enactments and modifications consequential on the provisions of this Act.

### Subordinate legislation

**133.**—(1)   Any power of the Scottish Ministers to make an order under this Act includes power to make—

(a)   different provision for different purposes or areas,

(b)   incidental, supplemental, consequential, transitional, transitory or saving provision.

(2)   The following orders are subject to the affirmative procedure—

(a)   an order under section 2(1), 39(5), 44(3), 72(12), 81(1), 107(4) or 135(2) or paragraph 3(5) of schedule 4, or

(b)   an order under section 137(1) containing provisions which add to, replace or omit any part of the text of an Act.

(3)   All other orders made by the Scottish Ministers under this Act are subject to negative procedure.

(4)   This section does not apply to an order under section 138(2).

### References to "sheriff"

**134.**—(1)   In this Act, references to a sheriff include references to any other member of the judiciary of a sheriffdom, so far as that member has the jurisdiction and competence that attaches to the office of sheriff.

(2)   So far as necessary for the purposes, or in consequence, of the exercise by a member of the judiciary of a sheriffdom other than a sheriff of the jurisdiction and competence of a sheriff, references in any other enactment to a sheriff are to be read as including references to any of the members of the judiciary of a sheriffdom.

(3)   Subsections (1) and (2) do not apply—

(a)   to references to the office of sheriff,

(b)   to any provision of this Act or any other enactment relating to—

(i)   the appointment, retirement, removal or disqualification of sheriffs,

(ii)   the tenure of office of, and oaths to be taken by, sheriffs,

(iii)   the remuneration, allowances or pensions of sheriffs,

(c)   where the context requires otherwise.

### Definition of "family proceedings"

**135.**—(1)   In this Act, "family proceedings" means proceedings for or in relation to—

(a)   divorce,

(b)   separation,

(c)   declarator of parentage,

(d)    declarator of non-parentage,

(e)    an order under section 11 of the Children (Scotland) Act 1995 (court orders relating to parental responsibilities, etc.) other than an application for the appointment of a judicial factor mentioned in subsection (2)(g) of that section to which Part 1 of the Act of Sederunt (Judicial Factors Rules) 1992 (S.I. 1992/272) applies,

(f)    aliment (including affiliation and aliment),

(g)    financial provision after a divorce or annulment in an overseas country within the meaning of Part 4 of the Matrimonial and Family Proceedings Act 1984 (financial provision in Scotland after overseas divorce, etc.),

(h)    an order under the Matrimonial Homes (Family Protection) (Scotland) Act 1981,

(i)    variation or recall of an order mentioned in section 8(1) of the Law Reform (Miscellaneous Provisions) (Scotland) Act 1966 (variation and recall by the sheriff of certain orders made by the Court of Session),

(j)    declarator of marriage,

(k)    declarator of nullity of marriage,

(l)    declarator of recognition, or non-recognition, of a relevant foreign decree within the meaning of section 7(9) of the Domicile and Matrimonial Proceedings Act 1973,

(m)    an order under section 28(2) (financial provision where cohabitation ends otherwise than by death) or section 29(2) (application by survivor cohabitant for provision on intestacy) of the Family Law (Scotland) Act 2006,

(n)    dissolution of civil partnership,

(o)    separation of civil partners,

(p)    declarator of nullity of civil partnership,

(q)    an order under Chapter 3 (occupancy rights and tenancies) or Chapter 4 (interdicts) of Part 3 of the Civil Partnership Act 2004,

(r)    a declarator or other order under section 127 of that Act (attachment),

(s)    financial provision after overseas proceedings as provided for in Schedule 11 to that Act (financial provision in Scotland after overseas proceedings).

(2)    The Scottish Ministers may by order modify subsection (1).

### Interpretation

**136.**—(1)    In this Act, unless the context requires otherwise—

"advocate" means a member of the Faculty of Advocates,

"all-Scotland sheriff court" is to be construed in accordance with section 42(7),

"civil proceedings" includes—

(a)    proceedings under the Children's Hearings (Scotland) Act 2011, and

(b)    proceedings for contempt of court where the contempt—

(i)    arises in, or in connection with, civil proceedings, or

(ii)    relates to an order made in civil proceedings,

"decision", in relation to a sheriff, judge or court, includes interlocutor, order or judgment,

"final judgment" means a decision which, by itself, or taken along with previous decisions, disposes of the subject matter of proceedings, even though judgment may not have been pronounced on every question raised or expenses found due may not have been modified, taxed or decerned for,

"sheriff clerk" includes sheriff clerk depute,

"solicitor" means a solicitor enrolled in the roll of solicitors kept under section 7 of the Solicitors (Scotland) Act 1980.

(2)   In this Act, references to the judiciary of a sheriffdom are, in relation to a sheriffdom, references to the following—

(a)   the sheriff principal of the sheriffdom,

(b)   any other sheriff principal so far as authorised under section 30 to perform the functions of the sheriff principal of the sheriffdom,

(c)   any temporary sheriff principal appointed for the sheriffdom,

(d)   the sheriffs and summary sheriffs of the sheriffdom,

(e)   any other sheriffs or summary sheriffs so far as directed under section 31 to perform the functions of sheriff or summary sheriff in the sheriffdom,

(f)   any part-time sheriffs and part-time summary sheriffs for the time being sitting in the sheriffdom,

(g)   any person appointed under section 12(1) to act as a sheriff or summary sheriff of the sheriffdom,

and references to a "member" of the judiciary of a sheriffdom are to be construed accordingly.

(3)   In this Act, references to proceedings in the sheriff court are references to proceedings before any member of the judiciary of a sheriffdom.

### Ancillary provision

**137.**—(1)  The Scottish Ministers may by order make such incidental, supplemental, consequential, transitional, transitory or saving provision as they consider necessary or expedient for the purposes of, in consequence of, or for giving full effect to, any provision of this Act.

(2)   An order under this section may modify any enactment (including this Act), instrument or document.

### Commencement

**138.**—(1)   This Part, other than sections 132 and 134(2), comes into force on the day after Royal Assent.

(2)   The remaining provisions of this Act come into force on such day as the Scottish Ministers may by order appoint.

(3)   An order under subsection (2) may include transitional, transitory or saving provision.

### Short title

**139.**   The short title of this Act is the Courts Reform (Scotland) Act 2014.

### SCHEDULE 1

Civil proceedings, etc. in relation to which summary sheriff has competence

**(introduced by section 44(1))**

*Family proceedings*

1   Family proceedings.

*Domestic abuse proceedings*

2   Proceedings for or in relation to—

   (a)   an action of harassment under section 8(2) of the Protection from Harassment Act 1997,

   (b)   an exclusion order under section 4(2) of the Matrimonial Homes (Family Protection) (Scotland) Act 1981,

   (c)   a matrimonial interdict (within the meaning of section 14 of that Act),

   (d)   a domestic interdict (within the meaning of section 18A of that Act),

   (e)   an exclusion order under section 104 of the Civil Partnership Act 2004,

   (f)   a relevant interdict (within the meaning of section 113 of that Act).

### Adoption proceedings

**3**  Proceedings for or in relation to—

   (a)   an adoption order within the meaning of section 28(1) of the Adoption and Children (Scotland) Act 2007,

   (b)   an order under section 59(1) of that Act (preliminary order where child to be adopted abroad),

   (c)   a permanence order under section 80(1) of that Act.

### Children's hearings proceedings

**4**  Proceedings under the Children's Hearings (Scotland) Act 2011.

### Forced marriage proceedings

**5**  Proceedings for or in relation to—

   (a)   a forced marriage protection order under section 1(1) of the Forced Marriage etc. (Protection and Jurisdiction) (Scotland) Act 2011,

   (b)   an interim forced marriage protection order under section 5(1) of that Act.

### Warrants and interim orders

**6**  The granting of—

   (a)   a warrant of citation (including such warrants where the address of the defender is unknown),

   (b)   an interim interdict,

   (c)   an order for the interim preservation of property,

   (d)   an order to recall an interim interdict.

### Diligence proceedings

**7**  Proceedings under—

   (a)   Part 1A of the Debtors (Scotland) Act 1987 (diligence on the dependence) (including proceedings to which that Part is applied by section 15N of that Act), other than proceedings in which there is claimed, in addition or as an alternative to a warrant, a decree for payment of a sum of money exceeding £5,000,

   (b)   Part III of that Act (diligence against earnings),

   (c)   Part 3A of that Act (arrestment and action of furthcoming),

   (d)   Part 8 of the Bankruptcy and Diligence etc. (Scotland) Act 2007 (attachment of money).

**8**  The receipt of a report of money attachment under section 182(1) of the Bankruptcy and Diligence etc. (Scotland) Act 2007.

**9**  The granting of authority to begin or continue execution of a decree for removing from heritable property under section 217(2) of the Bankruptcy and Diligence etc. (Scotland) Act 2007.

**10**  Proceedings for or in relation to—

   (a)   a warrant for the arrest of a ship on the dependence of an action or for the arrest of a ship in rem under section 47 of the Administration of Justice Act 1956, other than proceedings in which there is claimed, in addition or as an alternative to a warrant, a decree for payment of a sum of money exceeding £5,000,

(b)   an order for the sale of a ship arrested on the dependence of an action under section 47E of that Act, other than an order relating to a decree for payment of a sum of money exceeding £5,000.

### Extension of time to pay debts

11   Proceedings for or in relation to—

(a)   a time to pay direction under section 1 of the Debtors (Scotland) Act 1987,

(b)   a time to pay order under section 5 of that Act.

### Simple procedure

12   A simple procedure case within the meaning of section 72(9).

## SCHEDULE 2

### APPEAL SHERIFFS: TEMPORARY PROVISION

**(introduced by section 53)**

### The transitional period

1   In this schedule, "the transitional period" means the period of 3 years beginning with the day on which section 46 comes into force.

### Appointment of Senators of the College of Justice to act as Appeal Sheriffs

2(1)   The Lord President of the Court of Session may appoint persons holding the office of Senator of the College of Justice to act as Appeal Sheriffs for the transitional period.

(2)   The Lord President may appoint as many persons under sub-paragraph (1) as the Lord President considers necessary for the purposes of the Sheriff Appeal Court during the transitional period.

(3)   A person may be appointed under sub-paragraph (1) only if the person has held office as a Senator of the College of Justice for at least one year.

(4)   The appointment of a Senator of the College of Justice to act as an Appeal Sheriff does not affect the Senator's appointment as a Senator and the Senator may accordingly continue to act in that capacity.

(5)   A person appointed under sub-paragraph (1) is to be treated for all purposes (other than for the purposes of the enactments specified in sub-paragraph (6)) as an Appeal Sheriff and may exercise the jurisdiction and powers that attach to the office of Appeal Sheriff.

(6)   The enactments referred to in sub-paragraph (5) are—

(a)   sections 50 and 51,

(b)   section 304(2)(c)(zi) of the Criminal Procedure (Scotland) Act 1995.

### Tenure

3(1)   A person's appointment under paragraph 2(1) ceases—

(a)   if the person ceases to hold office as a Senator of the College of Justice,

(b)   on the expiry of the transitional period.

(2)   If a person appointed under paragraph 2(1) is suspended from office as a Senator of the College of Justice for any period, the person's appointment under paragraph 2(1) is also suspended for the same period.

(3) The Lord President may, after consulting the President of the Sheriff Appeal Court, recall a person's appointment under paragraph 2(1).

(4) The recall of a person's appointment under sub-paragraph (3) does not affect the person's appointment as a Senator of the College of Justice.

*Savings*

**4** Despite the ending by virtue of paragraph 3(1)(b) of a person's appointment under paragraph 2(1)—

(a) the person may continue to deal with, give judgment in or deal with an ancillary matter relating to, a case begun before the person while acting under that appointment,

(b) so far as necessary for that purpose, and for the purpose of any subsequent proceedings arising out of the case or matter, the person is to be treated as acting, or having acted, under that appointment.

## SCHEDULE 3

### TRANSFER OF SUMMARY CRIMINAL APPEAL JURISDICTION TO THE SHERIFF APPEAL COURT

**(introduced by section 118(3))**

*[Not reproduced.]*

## SCHEDULE 4

### THE SCOTTISH COURTS AND TRIBUNALS SERVICE

**(introduced by section 130(3))**

*[Not reproduced.]*

## SCHEDULE 5

### MODIFICATIONS OF ENACTMENTS

**(introduced by section 132)**

*[Not reproduced.]*

# SUMMARY SUSPENSION 1993

## (SI 1993/3128)

### *10 December 1993.*

The Lords of Council and Session, under and by virtue of the powers conferred on them by section 32 of the Sheriff Courts (Scotland) Act 1971 and of all other powers enabling them in that behalf, having approved, with modifications, draft rules submitted to them by the Sheriff Court Rules Council in accordance with section 34 of that Act, do hereby enact and declare:

### Citation and commencement

**1.**—(1)  This Act of Sederunt may be cited as the Act of Sederunt (Summary Suspension) 1993 and shall come into force on 1st January 1994.

(2)  This Act of Sederunt shall be inserted in the Books of Sederunt.

### Summary application for suspension of charge

**2.**[1]  Where a charge for payment has been executed on any decree to which section 38(2)(i) of the Courts Reform (Scotland) Act 2014 applies the person so charged may apply to the sheriff in the sheriff court having jurisdiction over him for suspension of such charge and diligence.

### Sist of diligence

**3.**—(1)  On sufficient caution being found or other security given for—

(a)  the sum charged for with interest and expenses, and

(b)  a further sum to be fixed by the sheriff in respect of expenses to be incurred in the suspension process.

the sheriff may sist diligence, order intimation and answers, and proceed to dispose of the cause in a summary manner.

(2)  The following rules of the Ordinary Cause Rules 1993 shall, with the necessary modifications, apply to an applicant under paragraph 2—

rule 27.4 (methods of finding caution or giving security)

rule 27.5 (cautioners and guarantors)

rule 27.6 (forms of bonds of caution and other securities)

rule 27.7 (sufficiency of caution or security and objections)

rule 27.8 (insolvency or death of cautioner or guarantor).

### Objections

**4.**[2]  Where objections are taken to the competency or regularity of suspension proceedings, the decision of the sheriff on such objections may be appealed to the Sheriff Appeal Court whose decision shall be final and not subject to appeal.

---

[1] As amended by the Act of Sederunt (Rules of the Court of Session, Sheriff Appeal Court Rules and Sheriff Court Rules Amendment) (Sheriff Appeal Court) 2015 (SSI 2015/419) r.6(2) (effective 1 January 2016).

[2] As amended by the Act of Sederunt (Rules of the Court of Session, Sheriff Appeal Court Rules and Sheriff Court Rules Amendment) (Sheriff Appeal Court) 2015 (SSI 2015/419) r.6(3) (effective 1 January 2016).

## Savings for proceedings arising out of causes already commenced

**5.** Nothing in this Act of Sederunt shall affect suspension proceedings arising out of causes commenced before the date of coming into force of this Act of Sederunt, which shall proceed according to the law and practice in force immediately before that date.

# CHILD CARE AND MAINTENANCE RULES 1997

## (SI 1997/291)

### *1 April 1997.*

### ARRANGEMENT OF RULES

#### Chapter 1: Preliminary

1.1. Citation and commencement.
1.2. Interpretation.
1.3. Affidavits.
1.4. Revocations and transitional provisions.

#### Chapter 2: Adoption of Children

##### PART I GENERAL

2.1. Interpretation.
2.2. Expenses.
2.3. Intimation to Principal Reporter.
2.4 Timetables under section 25A of the Act.

##### PART II APPLICATION FOR AN ORDER DECLARING A CHILD FREE FOR ADOPTION

2.5.– *[Repealed.]*
2.14.

##### PART III REVOCATION ORDERS, ETC.

2.15.– *[Repealed.]*
2.20.

##### PART IV ADOPTION ORDERS

2.21.– *[Repealed.]*
2.36.

##### PART IVA CONVENTION ADOPTION ORDERS

2.36A.– *[Repealed].*
2.36G.

##### PART V PARENTAL RESPONSIBILITIES ORDERS

2.37.– *[Repealed.]*
2.44.

##### PART VI HUMAN FERTILISATION AND EMBRYOLOGY

2.45. Interpretation.
2.46. Form of application and productions.
2.47. Confidentiality.
2.48. Agreements to parental order.
2.49. Orders for evidence.
2.50. Protection of identity of petitioners.
2.51. Appointment of reporting officer and curator ad litem.
2.52. Selection of reporting officer and curator ad litem.
2.53. Duties of reporting officer and curator ad litem.
2.54. Hearing.
2.55. Applications for return, removal or prohibition of removal of child.
2.56. Applications to amend, or revoke a direction in, a parental order.
2.57. Registration of certified copy interlocutor.
2.58. Extract of order.
2.59. Final procedure.

Chapter 3: Children's hearings, secure accommodation, etc.: application to the sheriff

PART I INTERPRETATION

3.1.    Interpretation.

PART II GENERAL RULES

*Procedure in Respect of Children*

3.2.    Application of rules 3.3 to 3.5A.
3.3.    Power to dispense with service on child.
3.3A.   Child to attend hearing.
3.4.    Service on child.
3.5.    Procedure for obtaining a child's view.
3.5A.   Confidentiality

*Safeguarders*

3.6.    Application.
3.7.    Appointment of safeguarder.
3.8.    Rights, powers and duties of safeguarder on appointment.
3.9     Representation of safeguarder.
3.10.   Provision where safeguarder intimates his intention not to become a party to the proceedings.

*Fixing of First Hearing*

3.11.   Assigning of diet for hearing.

*Service, Citation and Notice*

3.12.   Service and notice to persons named in application.
3.13.   Period of notice.
3.14.   Citation of witnesses, parties and persons having an interest.
3.15.   Modes of service.
3.16.   Persons who may effect service.
3.17.   Production of certificates of execution of service.
3.18.   Power to dispense with service.

*Miscellaneous*

3.19.   Expenses.
3.20.   Record of proceedings.
3.21.   Representation.
3.22.   Applications for evidence by live link.
3.23.   Orders and transfer of cases.
3.24.   Exclusion of certain enactments.

PART III CHILD ASSESSMENT ORDERS

3.25.   Interpretation.
3.26.   Form of application.
3.27.   Orders.
3.28.   Intimation.

PART IV CHILD PROTECTION ORDERS

3.29.   Interpretation.
3.30.   Form of application.
3.31.   Determination of application.
3.32.   Intimation of making of order.
3.33.   Application to vary or terminate a child protection order.

PART V EXCLUSION ORDERS

3.34.   Interpretation.

3.35.    Form of application.
3.36.    Hearing following interim order.
3.37.    Orders.
3.38.    Certificates of delivery of documents to chief constable.
3.39.    Power to make child protection order in an application for an exclusion order.
3.40.    Variation or recall of an exclusion order.

### PART VI WARRANT FOR FURTHER DETENTION OF A CHILD

3.41.–    *[Omitted.]*
3.43.

### PART VII PROCEDURE IN APPLICATIONS UNDER SECTION 65(7) OR (9) OF THE ACT

3.44.    Interpretation.
3.45.    Lodging of application, etc.
3.46.    Withdrawal of application.
3.46A.   Expeditions determination of application.
3.47.    Hearing on evidence.
3.48.    Amendment of the statement of grounds.
3.49.    Adjournment for inquiry, etc.
3.50.    Power of sheriff in making findings as to offences.
3.51.    Decision of sheriff.
3.52.    Signature of warrants.

### PART VIII PROCEDURE IN APPEALS TO THE SHERIFF AGAINST DECISIONS OF CHILDREN'S HEARINGS

3.53.    Form of appeal.
3.54.    Appointment and intimation of first diet.
3.55.    Answers.
3.56.    Procedure at hearing of appeal.
3.57.    Adjournment of appeals.
3.58.    Decision of sheriff in appeals.

### PART VIIIA APPLICATIONS FOR REVIEW BY LOCAL AUTHORITY

3.58A.   Review applications by local authority.
3.58B.   Hearing on application.

### PART VIIIB PROCEDURE IN APPEALS TO THE SHERIFF UNDER SECTION 44A OF THE CPSA 1995

3.58C.   Form of appeal.
3.58D.   Appointment and intimation of appeal hearing.
3.58E.   Procedure at hearing of appeal.
3.58F.   Adjournment or continuation of appeals.
3.58G.   Decision of sheriff in appeals.

### PART IX PROCEDURE IN APPEALS

3.59.    Appeals.
3.60.    Lodging of reports and statements with sheriff.
3.61.    Hearing.
3.61A.   Leave of the sheriff principal to appeal to the Court of Session.

### PART X APPLICATION FOR REVIEW OF GROUNDS DETERMINATION

3.62.    Application.
3.63.    Hearing on application.
3.64.    *[Omitted.]*

Part XA Orders under the Children's Hearings (Scotland) Act 2011

3.64A.    Interim compulsory supervision order.
3.64B    Compulsory supervision order.
3.64C.    Medical examination order.

Part XI Vulnerable Witnesses (Scotland) Act 2004

3.65.    Interpretation.
3.66.    Extent of application of this Part.

Chapter 4: Registration of Child Custody Orders

4.1.    Interpretation.
4.2.    Applications for registration of Part I order in another court.
4.3.    Transmission of application for registration.
4.4.    Notification of refusal of application.
4.5.    Retention of application and related documents.
4.6.    Cancellation or variation of registered Part I order.

Chapter 5: Maintenance Orders

Part I General

5.1.    Interpretation.
5.2.    Application.
5.3.    Prescribed officer.
5.4.    Maintenance Orders Register.
5.5.    Inspection.

Part II Outgoing Orders under the 1950 Act

5.6.    Commencement of proceedings.
5.7.    Application for registration.
5.8.    Transmission.
5.9.    Application to adduce evidence.
5.10.    Re-registration in the High Court.
5.11.    Transmission for re-registration.
5.12.    Discharge and variation.
5.13.    Cancellation of registration.

Part III Outgoing Orders under the 1972 Act

5.14.    Application for transmission of order for enforcement in a reciprocating country.
5.15.    Application for transmission of order for enforcement in the Republic of Ireland.
5.16.    Application for transmission of order to Hague Convention Country.
5.16A.    Application for transmission of order for enforcement in the USA.
5.17.    Service on defender in Hague Convention Country.
5.17A.    Service of notice of proceedings on payer residing in USA.
5.18.    Provisional order made with a view to transmission to a reciprocating country.
5.19.    Evidence adduced prior to confirmation of provisional order.
5.20.    Provisions in relation to intimation and entering appearance.
5.21.    Authentication of documents.
5.22.    Application under section 4 or 5 of the 1972 Act.
5.22A.    Representations or evidence by payer residing in the USA.
5.22B.    Application by payer residing in the USA for variation or revocation of order.
5.23.    Evidence.
5.23A.    Taking of evidence at request of a court in the USA.

5.23B.     Requests for taking of evidence by a court in the USA.

5.23C.     Communication with courts in the USA.

5.23D.     Disapplication of provisions where payer resides or has assets in the USA.

PART IV INCOMING ORDERS UNDER THE 1950 ACT

5.24.     Registration.

5.25.     Variation of rate of payment.

5.26.     Application to adduce evidence.

5.27.     Discharge and variation.

5.28.     Cancellation of registration.

PART V INCOMING ORDERS UNDER THE 1972 ACT

5.29.     Provisions in relation to intimation and entering appearance.

5.30.     Authentication of documents.

5.31.     Application under sections 9 and 20 of the 1972 Act.

5.32.     Information to be provided where payer has ceased to reside in Scotland.

5.33.     Evidence.

5.34.     Intimation of registration of, or of decision not to register, an order made in the Republic of Ireland.

5.35.     Application to set aside registration of, or to set aside decision not to register, an order made in the Republic of Ireland.

5.36.     Intimation of registration of, or refusal to register, an order made in a Hague Convention Country.

5.37.     Application to set aside registration of, or to set aside decision not to register, an order made in a Hague Convention Country.

5.37A.     Taking of evidence at the request of a court in the USA.

5.37B.     Communication with courts in the USA.

5.37C.     Disapplication of provisions in respect of orders made by courts in the USA.

PART VI INCOMING ORDERS UNDER THE 1982 ACT

5.38.     Applications under section 5 of the 1982 Act.

5.39.     Address of applicant's solicitor for service.

5.40.     Notice of determination of application.

5.41.     Appeal by party against whom enforcement is authorised.

5.42.     Appeal by applicant.

5.43.     Enforcement of registered order.

PART VII MAINTENANCE DECISIONS UNDER THE MAINTENANCE REGULATION

5.44.     Application for transmission of a Maintenance Decision to another Maintenance Regulation State

5.45.     Enforcement of a Maintenance Decision made by a court in a Maintenance Regulation State other than Denmark

PART VIII RECOGNITION AND ENFORCEMENT OF MAINTENANCE DECISIONS MADE BY COURTS IN DENMARK ETC.

5.46.     Recognition and enforcement of a Maintenance Decision made in Denmark etc.

5.47.     Intimation of registration of, or refusal to register, a Maintenance Decision made in Denmark etc.

5.48.     Application to set aside registration of, or to set aside decision not to register, a Maintenance Decision made in Denmark etc.

5.49     Sist of proceedings

Chapter 6: Applications under the Social Security Administration Act

6.1.     Interpretation.

6.2.      Applications under section 106 of the Act.
6.3.      Transfer of rights under section 107 of the Act.
6.4.      Notice to Secretary of State under section 108(5) of the Act.
6.5.      Notice to Secretary of State of making of maintenance order.
Schedule 1:   Forms.
Schedule 2:   Revocations.
Schedule 3:   Exclusion of Enactments.

The Lords of Council and Session, under and by virtue of the powers conferred on them by sections 17, 20, 22, 23, 24 and 28(1) of the Maintenance Orders Act 1950, sections 2(4)(c), 2A(1) and 21(1) of the Maintenance Orders Act 1958, section 32 of the Sheriff Courts (Scotland) Act 1971, section 59 of the Adoption (Scotland) Act 1978 (as modified and applied in relation to parental orders under section 30 of the Human Fertilisation and Embryology Act 1990 and applications for such orders by paragraph 15 of Schedule 1 to the Parental Orders (Human Fertilisation and Embryology) (Scotland) Regulations 1994, section 48 of the Civil Jurisdiction and Judgments Act 1982, sections 27(2), 28(1) and 42(1) of the Family Law Act 1986 and section 91 of the Children (Scotland) Act 1995 and of all other powers enabling them in that behalf, having approved, with modifications, draft rules submitted to them by the Sheriff Court Rules Council in accordance with section 34 of the Sheriff Courts (Scotland) Act 1971, do hereby enact and declare:

## CHAPTER 1

### PRELIMINARY

**Citation and commencement**

**1.1**—(1)   This Act of Sederunt may be cited as the Act of Sederunt (Child Care and Maintenance Rules) 1997 and shall come into force on 1st April 1997.

(2)   This Act of Sederunt shall be inserted in the Books of Sederunt.

**Interpretation**

**1.2**—(1)   In this Act of Sederunt, unless the context otherwise requires—

"Ordinary Cause Rules" means the First Schedule to the Sheriff Courts (Scotland) Act 1907;
"Principal Reporter" is the person referred to in section 14 of the Children's Hearings (Scotland) Act 2011 or any person carrying out the functions of the Principal Reporter by virtue of paragraph 10(1) of schedule 3 to that Act;[1]
"sheriff clerk" includes sheriff clerk depute.

(2)   Unless the context otherwise requires, any reference in this Act of Sederunt to a specified Chapter, Part or rule shall be construed as a reference to the Chapter, Part or rule bearing that number in this Act of Sederunt, and a reference to a specified paragraph, sub-paragraph or head shall be construed as a reference to the paragraph, sub-paragraph or head so numbered or lettered in the provision in which that reference occurs.

---

[1] As substituted by the Act of Sederunt (Children's Hearings (Scotland) Act 2011) (Miscellaneous Amendments) 2013 (SSI 2013/172) para.3 (effective June 24, 2013).

(3)   Any reference in this Act of Sederunt to a numbered Form shall be construed as a reference to the Form so numbered in Schedule 1 to this Act of Sederunt and includes a form substantially to the same effect with such variation as circumstances may require.

## Affidavits

**1.3**   An affidavit required in terms of any provision of this Act of Sederunt may be emitted—
- (a)   in the United Kingdom, before an notary public or any other competent authority;
- (b)   outwith the United Kingdom, before a British diplomatic or consular officer, or any person authorised to administer an oath or affirmation under the law of the place where the oath or affirmation is made.

## Revocations and transitional provisions

**1.4**—(1)   Subject to paragraphs (2) and (3), the Acts of Sederunt mentioned in column (1) of Schedule 2 to this Act of Sederunt are revoked to the extent specified in column (3) of that Schedule.

(2)   Nothing in paragraph (1) or in Chapter 2 shall affect any cause which has been commenced before 1st April 1997 and to which that Chapter would otherwise apply, and such a cause shall proceed according to the law and practice in force immediately before that date.

(3)   Nothing in paragraph (1) shall affect any cause to which paragraph 8(1) of Schedule 3 to the Children (Scotland) Act applies, and such a cause shall proceed according to the law and practice in force immediately before 1st April 1997.

## Vulnerable witnesses

**1.5.**—[1](1)   This rule shall apply to proceedings under these rules, except those proceedings to which the rules in Part XI of Chapter 3 apply.

(2)   At any hearing on an application under these rules, the sheriff shall ascertain whether there is or is likely to be a vulnerable witness who is to give evidence at or for the purposes of any proof or hearing, consider any child witness notice or vulnerable witness application that has been lodged where no order has been made under section 12(1) or (6) of the Vulnerable Witnesses (Scotland) Act 2004 and consider whether any order under section 12(1) of that Act requires to be made.

(3)   Except where the sheriff otherwise directs, where a vulnerable witness is to give evidence at or for the purposes of any proof or hearing in an application under these rules, any application in relation to the vulnerable witness or special measure that may be ordered shall be dealt with in accordance with the rules within Chapter 45 of the Ordinary Cause Rules.

(4)   In this rule, "vulnerable witness" means a witness within the meaning of section 11(1) of the Vulnerable Witnesses (Scotland) Act 2004.

---

[1] As inserted by the Act of Sederunt (Child Care and Maintenance Rules 1997) Amendment (Vulnerable Witnesses (Scotland) Act 2004) 2007, r.2 (effective November 1, 2007).

## Lodging audio or audio-visual recordings of children

**1.6.**—[1](1)  In this rule "child" is a person under the age of 16 on the date of commencement of the proceedings and "children" shall be construed accordingly.

(2)  Except where the sheriff otherwise directs, where a party seeks to lodge an audio or audio-visual recording of a child as a production in an application under this Act of Sederunt, this shall be done in accordance with and regulated by Chapter 50 of the Ordinary Cause Rules.

(3)  A party who has lodged a recording of a child shall—
- (a) within 28 days after the final determination of the application, where no subsequent appeal has been marked, or
- (b) within 28 days after the disposal of any appeal marked on the final determination of the application,

uplift the recording from process.

(4)  Where a recording has not been uplifted as required by paragraph (3), the sheriff clerk shall intimate to—
- (a) the solicitor who lodged the recording, or
- (b) where no solicitor is acting, the party or such other party as seems appropriate,

that if he or she fails to uplift the recording within 28 days after the date of such intimation, it will be disposed of in such a manner as the sheriff directs.

## CHAPTER 2

### ADOPTION OF CHILDREN

### Part I

### General

## Interpretation

**2.1**[2]  In this Chapter, unless the context otherwise requires—

"the Act" means the Adoption (Scotland) Act 1978;

"the 1995 Act" means the Children (Scotland) Act 1995;

"Her Majesty's Forces" means the regular forces as defined in section 374 of the Armed Forces Act 2006;[3]

"Registrar General" means the Registrar General of Births, Deaths and Marriages for Scotland.

## Expenses

**2.2**  The sheriff may make such an order with regard to the expenses, including the expenses of a reporting officer and a curator ad litem or any other person who at-

---

[1] As inserted by the Act of Sederunt (Sheriff Court Rules) (Miscellaneous Amendments) (No.3) 2012 (SSI 2012/271) para.4 (effective November 1, 2012).

[2] As amended by the Act of Sederunt (Child Care and Maintenance Rules 1997) (Amendment) (Adoption and Children Act 2002) 2006 (SI 2006/411) (effective August 18, 2006) and by the Act of Sederunt (Sheriff Court Rules Amendment) (Adoption and Children (Scotland) Act 2007) 2009 (SSI 2009/284) (effective September 28, 2009).

[3] As substituted by the Act of Sederunt (Sheriff Court Rules) (Miscellaneous Amendments) 2009 (SSI 2009/294) r.17 (effective October 1, 2009).

tended a hearing, of an application under this Chapter as he thinks fit and may modify such expenses or direct them to be taxed on such scale as he may determine.

## Intimation to Principal Reporter

**2.3** *[Repealed by the Act of Sederunt (Sheriff Court Rules Amendment) (Adoption and Children (Scotland) Act 2007) 2009 (SSI 2009/284) r.4(1)(a)(ii) (effective September 28, 2009: subject to savings and transitional provisions specified in SSI 2009/284 r.4(2) to (7)).]*

## Timetables under section 25A of the Act

**2.4** *[Repealed by the Act of Sederunt (Sheriff Court Rules Amendment) (Adoption and Children (Scotland) Act 2007) 2009 (SSI 2009/284) r.4(1)(a)(ii) (effective September 28, 2009: subject to savings and transitional provisions specified in SSI 2009/284 r.4(2) to (7)).]*

### Part II

## Application for an Order Declaring a Child Free for Adoption

*[Repealed by the Act of Sederunt (Sheriff Court Rules Amendment) (Adoption and Children (Scotland) Act 2007) 2009 (SSI 2009/284) r.4(1) (effective September 28, 2009: repeal has effect subject to savings and transitional provisions specified in SSI 2009/284 r.4(2)–(7)).]*

### Part III

## Revocation Orders, etc

*[Repealed by the Act of Sederunt (Sheriff Court Rules Amendment) (Adoption and Children (Scotland) Act 2007) 2009 (SSI 2009/284) r.4(1) (effective September 28, 2009: repeal has effect subject to savings and transitional provisions specified in SSI 2009/284 r.4(2)–(7)).]*

### Part IV

## Adoption Orders

*[Repealed by the Act of Sederunt (Sheriff Court Rules Amendment) (Adoption and Children (Scotland) Act 2007) 2009 (SSI 2009/284) r.4(1) (effective September 28, 2009: repeal has effect subject to savings and transitional provisions specified in SSI 2009/284 r.4(2)–(7)).]*

### Part IVA

## Convention Adoption Orders

*[Repealed by the Act of Sederunt (Sheriff Court Rules Amendment) (Adoption and Children (Scotland) Act 2007) 2009 (SSI 2009/284) r.4(1) (effective September 28, 2009: repeal has effect subject to savings and transitional provisions specified in SSI 2009/284 r.4(2)–(7)).]*

### Part V

## Parental Responsibilities Orders

*[Repealed by the Act of Sederunt (Sheriff Court Rules Amendment) (Adoption and Children (Scotland) Act 2007) 2009 (SSI 2009/284) r.4(1) (effective September 28, 2009: repeal has effect subject to savings and transitional provisions specified in SSI 2009/284 r.4(2)–(7)).]*

### Part VI[1]

## Human Fertilisation and Embryology

## Interpretation

**2.45.** In this Part—

"2007 Act" means the Adoption and Children (Scotland) Act 2007;

"2008 Act" means the Human Fertilisation and Embryology Act 2008;

"parental order" means an order under section 54 of the 2008 Act; and

"the Regulations" means the Human Fertilisation and Embryology (Parental Orders) Regulations 2010.

## Form of application and productions

**2.46.**—(1) An application for a parental order is to be made by petition in Form 22.

(2) The following documents must be lodged in process along with the petition—

(a) an extract or a certified copy of the entry in the Register of Births relating to the child who is the subject of the application;

(b) extracts or certified copies of any entries in the Register of Births relating to the birth of each of the petitioners;

(c) in the case of an application under section 54(2)(a) of the 2008 Act, an extract or a certified copy of the entry in the Register of Marriages relating to the marriage of the petitioners;

(d) in the case of an application under section 54(2)(b) of the 2008 Act, an extract or a certified copy of the entry in the Register of Civil Partnerships relating to the civil partnership of the petitioners; and

(e) any other document founded on by the petitioners in support of the terms of the petition.

## Confidentiality

**2.47.**—(1) Unless the sheriff otherwise directs, all documents lodged in process (including the reports by the curator ad litem and reporting officer) are to be available only to the sheriff, the curator ad litem, the reporting officer and the parties; and such documents must be treated as confidential by all persons involved in, or party to, the proceedings and by the sheriff clerk.

(2) The reporting officer and the curator ad litem—

(a) must treat all information obtained in the exercise of their duties as confidential; and

(b) must not disclose any such information to any person unless disclosure of such information is necessary for the purpose of their duties.

(3) This rule is subject to rule 2.53.

## Orders for evidence

**2.48.**—(1) The sheriff may, before determining the cause, order—

(a) production of further documents (including affidavits); or

(b) parole evidence.

(2) A party may apply by motion for the evidence of a person to be received in evidence by affidavit; and the sheriff may make such order as the sheriff thinks fit.

---

[1] As substituted by the Act of Sederunt (Child Care and Maintenance Rules) Amendment (Human Fertilisation and Embryology Act 2008) 2010 (SSI 2010/137) r.2(2) (effective April 6, 2010: substitution has effect subject to transitional provisions and savings as specified in SSI 2010/137 r.3).

## Protection of identity of petitioners

**2.49.**—(1)   Where persons who propose to apply for a parental order wish to prevent their identities being disclosed to any person whose agreement to the parental order is required, they may, before presenting the petition, apply by letter to the sheriff clerk for a serial number to be assigned to them for all purposes connected with the petition.

(2)   On receipt of an application under paragraph (1), the sheriff clerk must—
    (a)   assign a serial number to the applicants; and
    (b)   enter a note of the number opposite the name of the applicants in a register of serial numbers kept by the sheriff clerk.

(3)   The contents of the register of serial numbers and the names of the persons to whom each number relates must be treated as confidential by the sheriff clerk and must not be disclosed to any person other than the sheriff.

(4)   Where a serial number has been assigned under paragraph (2)(a), any form of agreement to a parental order under section 54(6) of the 2008 Act—
    (a)   must refer to the petitioners by means of the serial number assigned to them;
    (b)   must not contain the names and designation of the petitioners; and
    (c)   must specify the year in which and the court by which the serial number was assigned.

## Appointment of a curator ad litem and reporting officer

**2.50.**—(1)   The sheriff must on the lodging of a petition under rule 2.46, appoint a curator ad litem and reporting officer.

(2)   The same person may be appointed as curator ad litem and reporting officer in the same petition, if the sheriff considers that doing so is appropriate in the circumstances.

(3)   The sheriff may appoint a person who is not a member of a panel established under regulations made by virtue of section 101(1) of the 1995 Act to be curator ad litem or a reporting officer.

(4)   The sheriff may, on cause shown, appoint a reporting officer prior to the lodging of such a petition.

(5)   An application for an appointment under paragraph (4) is to be made by letter addressed to the sheriff clerk specifying the reasons for the appointment, and shall not require to be intimated to any other person.

(6)   The sheriff clerk must intimate the appointment of a curator ad litem and reporting officer under paragraph (1) or (4) to the petitioner and to the person or persons appointed.

(7)   Where the curator ad litem is not also the reporting officer, the sheriff may order the reporting officer to make available to the curator ad litem any report or information in relation to the child.

## Duties of reporting officer and curator ad litem

**2.51.**—(1)   The other duties of a reporting officer appointed under rule 2.50(1) prescribed for the purposes of section 108(1)(b) of the 2007 Act as modified and applied in relation to applications for parental orders by regulation 4 of, and Schedule 3, to the Regulations (rules: appointment of curators ad litem and reporting officers) are—
    (a)   to ascertain the whereabouts of all persons whose agreement to the making of a parental order in respect of the child is required;

(b) to ascertain whether there is any person other than those mentioned in the petition upon whom notice of the petition should be served;

(c) in the case of each person who is not a petitioner and whose agreement to the making of a parental order is required under section 54(6) of the 2008 Act—

    (i) to ascertain whether that person understands the effect of the parental order;

    (ii) to ascertain whether alternatives to a parental order have been discussed with that person;

    (iii) to confirm that that person understands that he or she may withdraw his or her agreement at any time before an order is made;

    (iv) to ascertain whether that person suffers or appears to suffer from a mental disorder within the meaning of section 328 of the Mental Health (Care and Treatment) (Scotland) Act 2003; and

(d) to ascertain whether the conditions in subsections (2) to (8) of section 54 of the 2008 Act have been satisfied;

(e) to draw to the attention of the court any matter which may be of assistance; and

(f) to report in writing on the matters mentioned in subparagraphs (a) to (e) to the sheriff within 4 weeks from the date of the interlocutor appointing the reporting officer, or within such other period as the sheriff in his or her discretion may allow.

(2)[1] A curator ad litem appointed under rule 2.50 must—

(a) have regard to safeguarding the interests of the child as his or her paramount duty;

(b) enquire, so far as he or she considers necessary, into the facts and circumstances stated in the petition;

(c) establish that the petitioners understand the nature and effect of a parental order and in particular that the making of the order will render them responsible for the maintenance and upbringing of the child;

(d) ascertain whether any money or other benefit which is prohibited by section 54(8) of the 2008 Act (prohibition on gift or receipt of money or other benefit) has been received or agreed upon;

(e) ascertain whether it may be in the interests of the welfare of the child that the sheriff should make the parental order subject to particular terms and conditions or require the petitioners to make special provision for the child and, if so, what provision;

(f) ascertain whether it would be better for the child that the court should make the order than it should not make the order;

(g) establish whether the proposed parental order is likely to safeguard and promote the welfare of the child throughout the child's life; and

(h) ascertain from the child whether he or she wishes to express a view and, where a child indicates his or her wish to express a view, ascertain that view.

---

[1] As substituted by the Act of Sederunt (Sheriff Court Rules) (Miscellaneous Amendments) 2010 (SSI 2010/279) r.7(4) (effective July 29, 2010).

(3)   Subject to paragraph (4), the curator ad litem must report in writing on the matters mentioned in paragraph (2) to the sheriff within 4 weeks from the date of the interlocutor appointing the curator, or within such other period as the sheriff in his or her discretion may allow.

(4)   Subject to any order made by the sheriff under rule 2.53(1), the views of the child ascertained in terms of paragraph (2)(h) may, if the curator ad litem considers appropriate, be conveyed to the sheriff orally.

(5)   The reporting officer must, on completion of his or her report in terms of paragraph (1), in addition send to the sheriff clerk—

(a)   a copy of his or her report for each party; and

(b)   any agreement for the purposes of section 54(6) of the 2008 Act.

(6)   The curator ad litem must, on completion of his or her report in terms of paragraph (3), in addition send a copy of it for each party to the sheriff clerk.

### Agreement

**2.52.**—(1)   The agreement of a person required by section 54(6) of the 2008 Act is to be in Form 23.

(2)[1]   The form of agreement mentioned in paragraph (1) must be witnessed—

(a)   where it is executed in Scotland, by the reporting officer appointed under rule 2.50;

(b)   where it is executed outwith Scotland but within the United Kingdom, by a justice of the peace or commissioner for oaths;

(c)   where it is executed outwith the United Kingdom—

(i)    if the person who executes the agreement is serving in Her Majesty's Forces, by an officer holding a commission in any of those forces; or

(ii)   in any other case, by a British diplomatic or consular official or any person authorised to administer an oath or affirmation under the law of the place where the agreement is executed.

### Procedure where child wishes to express a view

**2.53**—(1)   Where a child to whom section 54(11) of the 2008 Act applies indicates his or her wish to express a view, the sheriff, without prejudice to rule 2.51(2)(h)—

(a)   may order such procedural steps to be taken as the sheriff considers appropriate to ascertain the views of that child; and

(b)   must not make an order under this Part unless an opportunity has been given for the views of that child to be obtained or heard.

(2)   Where the views of a child, whether obtained under this rule or under rule 2.51(2)(h) have been recorded in writing, the sheriff may direct that such a written record is to—

(a)   be sealed in an envelope marked "Views of the child — confidential";

(b)   be available to a sheriff only;

(c)   not be opened by any person other than a sheriff; and

(d)   not form a borrowable part of the process.

---

[1] As substituted by the Act of Sederunt (Sheriff Court Rules) (Miscellaneous Amendments) 2010 (SSI 2010/279) r.7(4) (effective July 29, 2010).

## Hearing

**2.54**—(1)   On receipt of the reports referred to in rule 2.51, the sheriff must fix a hearing.

(2)   The sheriff may—

    (a)   order any person whose agreement is required to attend the hearing;

    (b)   order intimation of the date of the hearing to any person not mentioned in paragraph (3)(a), (b) or (c); and

    (c)   order the reporting officer or curator ad litem to perform additional duties to assist him or her in determining the petition.

(3)   The petitioners or, where a serial number has been assigned under rule 2.49, the sheriff clerk, must intimate the date of the hearing in Form 24 by registered post or recorded delivery letter to—

    (a)   every person whose whereabouts are known to them and whose agreement is required;

    (b)[1]   the reporting officer appointed under rule 2.50;

    (c)[2]   the curator ad litem appointed under rule 2.50; and

    (d)   any person on whom intimation has been ordered under paragraph (2)(b).

(4)   At the hearing—

    (a)   the petitioners, the reporting officer and the curator ad litem must, if required by the sheriff, appear and may be represented;

    (b)   any other person required by the sheriff to attend the hearing must appear and may be represented; and

    (c)   any other person to whom intimation was made under paragraph (3) (a) or (d) may appear or be represented.

## Applications under sections 22 and 24 of the 2007 Act

**2.55**—(1)   An application under section 22(3) (restrictions on removal: application for parental order pending), section 24(1) (return of child removed in breach of certain provisions) or section 24(2) (order directing person not to remove child) of the 2007 Act all as modified and applied in relation to applications for parental orders by regulation 4 of, and Schedule 3 to, the Regulations, is to be made by minute in the process of the petition for a parental order to which it relates.

(2)   A minute under paragraph (1) must include an appropriate crave and statement of facts.

(3)   On receipt of a minute under paragraph (1), the sheriff must—

    (a)   order a diet of hearing to be fixed; and

    (b)   ordain the minuter, or where a serial number has been assigned under rule 2.49, the sheriff clerk, to send a notice of such hearing in Form 25 together with a copy of the minute, by recorded delivery letter to the curator ad litem in the original petition, to any person who may have care and possession of the child and to such other persons as the sheriff considers appropriate.

---

[1] As substituted by the Act of Sederunt (Sheriff Court Rules) (Miscellaneous Amendments) 2010 (SSI 2010/279) r.7(4) (effective July 29, 2010).
[2] As substituted by the Act of Sederunt (Sheriff Court Rules) (Miscellaneous Amendments) 2010 (SSI 2010/279) r.7(4) (effective July 29, 2010).

## Amendment of parental order

**2.56**—(1)   An application under paragraph 7 of Schedule 1 to the 2007 Act, as modified and applied in relation to parental orders by regulation 4 of, and Schedule 3 to, the Regulations (amendment of orders and rectification of registers) is to be made by petition to the court which made the parental order.

(2)   The sheriff may order the petitioners to intimate the petition to such persons as the sheriff considers appropriate.

## Communication to the Registrar General

**2.57**   The communication to the Registrar General of a parental order required to be made by the sheriff clerk under paragraph 4(1) of Schedule 1 to the 2007 Act, as modified and applied in relation to parental orders by regulation 4 of, and Schedule 3 to, the Regulations (registration of parental orders), is to be made by sending a certified copy of the order to the Registrar General either by recorded delivery post in an envelope marked "Confidential", or by personal delivery by the sheriff clerk in a sealed enveloped marked "Confidential".

## Extract of order

**2.58**   An extract of a parental order must not be issued except by order of the court on an application to it—

    (a)   where there is a petition for the parental order depending before the court, by motion in that process; or

    (b)   where there is no such petition depending before the court, by petition.

## Final procedure

**2.59**—(1)   After the granting of a parental order the court process must, immediately upon the communication under rule 2.57 being made or, in the event of an extract of the order being issued under rule 2.58, immediately upon such issue, be sealed by the sheriff clerk in an envelope marked "Confidential".

(2)   The envelope referred to in paragraph (1) is not to be unsealed by the sheriff clerk or by any other person having control of the records of that or any court, and the process is not to be made accessible to any person for one hundred years after the date of the granting of the order except—

    (a)   to the person who is the subject of the parental order after he or she has reached the age of 16 years; and

    (b)   to a person on the granting of an application made by him or her to the sheriff setting forth the reason for which access to the process is required.

## Appeals

**2.60.**—(1)   Chapter 31 of the Ordinary Cause Rules is to apply, with any necessary modifications, to an appeal against an order of the sheriff under this Part as it applies to an appeal against an order of the sheriff under the Ordinary Cause Rules.

CHAPTER 3[1] [2]

---

[1] Rule 3.1 as amended by the Act of Sederunt (Children's Hearings (Scotland) Act 2011) (Miscellaneous Amendments) 2013 (SSI 2013/172) para.3 (effective June 24, 2013).

CHILDREN'S HEARINGS, SECURE ACCOMMODATION, ETC.: APPLICATION TO THE
SHERIFF

## Part I

## Interpretation

### Interpretation

**3.1**—[1](1)   In this Chapter, unless the context otherwise requires—

"1995 Act" means the Children (Scotland) Act 1995 and (except where the context otherwise requires) references to terms defined in that Act have the same meaning here as given there;

"2011 Act" means the Children's Hearings (Scotland) Act 2011 and (except where the context otherwise requires) references to terms defined in that Act have the same meaning here as given there;

"relevant person" means—

    (aa)   a person referred to in section 200(1) of the 2011 Act or

    (bb)   a person deemed a relevant person by virtue of section 81(3) or 160(4)(b) of the 2011 Act;

"service" includes citation, intimation or the giving of notice as required in terms of this Chapter.

(2)   In this Chapter any reference, however expressed, to disputed grounds shall be construed as a reference to a statement of grounds which forms the subject of an application under section 93(2)(a) or 94(2)(a) of the 2011 Act.

(3)   Except as otherwise provided, this Chapter applies to applications to the sheriff (including reviews and appeals) under the 1995 Act or the 2011 Act.

(4)   All hearings in respect of applications to the sheriff must be held in private.

## Part II

## General Rules

*Procedure in Respect of Children*

### Application of rules 3.3 to 3.5A

**3.2**—[2](1)   Rules 3.3 to 3.5 apply where a sheriff is coming to a decision about a matter relating to a child within the meaning of section 27 of the 2011 Act.

(2)   Rule 3.5A applies in the circumstances referred to in paragraph (1) and in respect of applications under Part V of this Chapter.

---

[2] Chapter 3 heading as substituted by the Act of Sederunt (Sheriff Court Rules Amendment) (Miscellaneous) 2015 (SSI 2015/424) para.3 (effective 1st February 2015).

[1] Rule 3.1 as amended by the Act of Sederunt (Children's Hearings (Scotland) Act 2011) (Miscellaneous Amendments) 2013 (SSI 2013/172) para.3 (effective June 24, 2013).

[2] As amended by the Act of Sederunt (Children's Hearings (Scotland) Act 2011) (Miscellaneous Amendments) 2013 (SSI 2013/172) para.3 (effective June 24, 2013).

## Power to dispense with service on child

**3.3**[1]  Where the sheriff is satisfied, so far as practicable and taking account of the age and maturity of the child, that it would be inappropriate to order service on the child, the sheriff may dispense with service on the child.

## Child to attend hearing

**3.3A**—[2](1)  This rule applies where an application is made to the sheriff under the 2011 Act, other than where section 103 or 112 of the 2011 Act applies.

(2)  A child must attend all hearings, unless the sheriff otherwise directs.

(3)  A child may attend a hearing even if the child is excused from doing so.

(4)  If the child is not excused from attending the hearing but does not attend the sheriff may grant a warrant to secure attendance in relation to the child.

(5)  Paragraph (6) applies if—

    (a)  the hearing of the application is to be continued to another day; and

    (b)  the sheriff is satisfied that there is reason to believe that the child will not attend on that day.

(6)  The sheriff may grant a warrant to secure attendance in relation to the child.

## Service on child

**3.4**—(1)  Subject to rule 3.3 and to paragraph (2), after the issue of the first order or warrant to cite, as the case may be, the applicant shall forthwith serve a copy of the application and first order or warrant to cite on the child, together with a notice or citation in—

    (a)  Form 26 in respect of an application for a child assessment order under Part III of this Chapter;

    (b)[3]  Form 27 in respect of an application to vary or terminate a child protection order in terms of rule 3.33;

    (c)  Form 28 in respect of an application for an exclusion order in terms of rules 3.34 to 3.39;

    (d)  Form 29 in respect of an application to vary or recall an exclusion order in terms of rule 3.40;

    (e)  *[Repealed by the Act of Sederunt (Children's Hearings (Scotland) Act 2011) (Miscellaneous Amendments) 2013 (SSI 2013/172) para.3 (effective June 24, 2013).]*

    (f)[4]  subject to subparagraph (g), in Form 31 in respect of an application under section 93(2)(a) or 94(2)(a) of the 2011 Act;

    (g)[5]  Form 31A in respect of an application under section 94(2)(a) of the 2011 Act where a procedural hearing has been fixed; and

---

[1] As substituted by the Act of Sederunt (Children's Hearings (Scotland) Act 2011) (Miscellaneous Amendments) 2013 (SSI 2013/172) para.3 (effective June 24, 2013).

[2] As substituted by the Act of Sederunt (Children's Hearings (Scotland) Act 2011) (Miscellaneous Amendments) 2013 (SSI 2013/172) para.3 (effective June 24, 2013).

[3] As amended by the Act of Sederunt (Children's Hearings (Scotland) Act 2011) (Miscellaneous Amendments) 2013 (SSI 2013/172) para.3 (effective June 24, 2013).

[4] As substituted by the Act of Sederunt (Children's Hearings (Scotland) Act 2011) (Miscellaneous Amendments) 2013 (SSI 2013/172) para.3 (effective June 24, 2013).

[5] As substituted by the Act of Sederunt (Children's Hearings (Scotland) Act 2011) (Miscellaneous Amendments) 2013 (SSI 2013/172) para.3 (effective June 24, 2013).

(h)[1]  Form 31B in respect of an application under section 110(2) of the 2011 Act.

(2)   The sheriff may, on application by the applicant or of his own motion, order that a specified part of the application is not served on the child.

### Procedure for obtaining a child's view

**3.5**—(1)[2]  Subject to section 27(3) of the 2011 Act, the sheriff—

(a)   may order such steps to be taken as he considers appropriate to ascertain the views of that child; and

(b)[3]   shall not come to a decision about a matter relating to a child within the meaning of section 27 of the 2011 Act unless an opportunity has been given for the views of that child to be obtained or heard.

(2)   Subject to any order made by the sheriff under paragraph (1)(a) and to any other method as the sheriff in his discretion may permit, the views of the child may be conveyed—

(a)   by the child orally or in writing;

(b)   by an advocate or solicitor acting on behalf of the child;

(c)   by any safeguarder; or

(ca)[4]   by any curator ad litem

(d)   by any other person (either orally or in writing), provided that the sheriff is satisfied that that person is a suitable representative and is duly authorised to represent the child.

(3)   Where the views of the child are conveyed orally to the sheriff, the sheriff shall record those views in writing.

(4)   The sheriff may direct that any written views given by a child, or any written record of those views, shall—

(a)   be sealed in an envelope marked "Views of the child—confidential";

(b)   be kept in the court process without being recorded in the inventory of process;

(c)   be available to a sheriff only;

(d)   not be opened by any person other than a sheriff, and

(e)   not form a borrowable part of the process.

### Confidentiality

**3.5A.**—[5](1)   Unless the sheriff otherwise directs, all documents lodged in process are to be available only to the sheriff, the reporter, the safeguarder, the curator ad litem and the parties; and such documents must be treated as confidential by all persons involved in, or party to, the proceedings and by the sheriff clerk.

(2)   The safeguarder and the curator ad litem must—

---

[1] As substituted by the Act of Sederunt (Children's Hearings (Scotland) Act 2011) (Miscellaneous Amendments) 2013 (SSI 2013/172) para.3 (effective June 24, 2013).

[2] As amended by the Act of Sederunt (Children's Hearings (Scotland) Act 2011) (Miscellaneous Amendments) 2013 (SSI 2013/172) para.3 (effective June 24, 2013).

[3] As substituted by the Act of Sederunt (Children's Hearings (Scotland) Act 2011) (Miscellaneous Amendments) 2013 (SSI 2013/172) para.3 (effective June 24, 2013).

[4] As inserted by the Act of Sederunt (Children's Hearings (Scotland) Act 2011) (Miscellaneous Amendments) 2013 (SSI 2013/172) para.3 (effective June 24, 2013).

[5] As inserted by the Act of Sederunt (Children's Hearings (Scotland) Act 2011) (Miscellaneous Amendments) 2013 (SSI 2013/172) para.3 (effective June 24, 2013).

(a) treat all information obtained in the exercise of their duties as confidential; and

(b) not disclose any such information to any person unless disclosure of such information is necessary for the purpose of their duties.

(3) This rule is subject to rule 3.5.

*Safeguarders*

## Application

**3.6**[1] Rules 3.7 to 3.9 apply, as regards a safeguarder, to all applications and proceedings to which this Chapter applies except for an application under section 37 of the Act for a child protection order.

## Appointment of safeguarder

**3.7**—(1)[2] Where a safeguarder has not been appointed for the child, the sheriff—

(a) shall, as soon as reasonably practicable after the lodging of an application or the commencing of any proceedings, consider whether it is necessary to appoint a safeguarder in the application or proceedings; and

(b) may at that stage, or at any later stage of the application or proceedings, appoint a safeguarder.

(2) [2] Where a sheriff appoints a safeguarder, the appointment and the reasons for it must be recorded in an interlocutor.

## Rights, powers and duties of safeguarder on appointment

**3.8** A safeguarder appointed in an application shall—

(a) have the powers and duties at common law of a curator ad litem in respect of the child;

(b) be entitled to receive from the Principal Reporter copies of the application, all of the productions in the proceedings and any papers which were before the children's hearing;

(c) subject to rule 3.5(1)(a), determine whether the child wishes to express his views in relation to the application and, if so, where the child so wishes to transmit his views to the sheriff;

(d) make such enquiries so far as relevant to the application as he considers appropriate; and

(e) without delay, and in any event before the hearing on the application, intimate in writing to the sheriff clerk whether or not he intends to become a party to the proceedings.

(f)[3] whether or not a party, be entitled to receive from the sheriff clerk all interlocutors subsequent to his or her appointment.

---

[1] As amended by the Act of Sederunt (Children's Hearings (Scotland) Act 2011) (Miscellaneous Amendments) 2013 (SSI 2013/172) para.3 (effective June 24, 2013).
[2] As amended by the Act of Sederunt (Children's Hearings (Scotland) Act 2011) (Miscellaneous Amendments) 2013 (SSI 2013/172) para.3 (effective June 24, 2013).
[3] As inserted by the Act of Sederunt (Children's Hearings (Scotland) Act 2011) (Miscellaneous Amendments) 2013 (SSI 2013/172) para.3 (effective June 24, 2013).

**Representation of safeguarder[1]**

**3.9**[2]  A safeguarder may appear personally in the proceedings or instruct an advocate or solicitor to appear on his behalf.

(2)   Where an advocate or a solicitor is appointed to act as a safeguarder, he shall not act also as advocate or solicitor for the child in the proceedings.

**Provision where safeguarder intimates his intention not to become a party to the proceedings**

**3.10**   *[Repealed by the Act of Sederunt (Children's Hearings (Scotland) Act 2011) (Miscellaneous Amendments) 2013 (SSI 2013/172) para.3 (effective June 24, 2013).]*

*Fixing of First Hearing*

**Assigning of diet for hearing**

**3.11**[3]   Except where otherwise provided in these Rules, after the lodging of any application the sheriff clerk shall forthwith assign a diet for the hearing of the application and shall issue a first order or a warrant to cite in Form 32, Form 32A or Form 33, as the case may be.

*Service, Citation and Notice*

**Service and notice to persons named in application**

**3.12**—(1)   Subject to the provisions of rule 3.4 (service on child), after the issue of the first order or warrant to cite, as the case may be, the applicant shall forthwith give notice of the application by serving a copy of the application and the first order or warrant to cite together with a notice or citation, as the case may be, on the persons named in the application or, as the case may be, a person who should receive notice of the application (subject to paragraph (2)) in—

    (a)   Form 34 in respect of an application for a child assessment order under Part III of this Chapter;

    (b)[4]   Form 35 in respect of an application to vary or terminate a child protection order in terms of rule 3.33;

    (c)   Form 36 in respect of an application for an exclusion order in terms of rules 3.34 to 3.39;

    (d)   Form 37 in respect of an application to vary or recall an exclusion order in terms of rule 3.40;

    (e)   *[Repealed by the Act of Sederunt (Children's Hearings (Scotland) Act 2011) (Miscellaneous Amendments) 2013 (SSI 2013/172) para.3 (effective June 24, 2013).]*

---

[1] As amended by the Act of Sederunt (Childrensquo;s Hearings (Scotland) Act 2011) (Miscellaneous Amendments) 2013 (SSI 2013/172) para.3 (effective June 24, 2013).

[2] As inserted by the Act of Sederunt (Children's Hearings (Scotland) Act 2011) (Miscellaneous Amendments) 2013 (SSI 2013/172) para.3 (effective June 24, 2013).

[3] As amended by the Act of Sederunt (Children's Hearings (Scotland) Act 2011) (Miscellaneous Amendments) 2013 (SSI 2013/172) para.3 (effective June 24, 2013).

[4] As amended by the Act of Sederunt (Children's Hearings (Scotland) Act 2011) (Miscellaneous Amendments) 2013 (SSI 2013/172) para.3 (effective June 24, 2013).

(f)[1]   subject to subparagraph (g), in Form 39 in respect of an application under section 93(2)(a) or 94(2)(a) of the 2011 Act made under Part VII of this Chapter; or

(g)[2]   in Form 39A where a procedural hearing has been fixed in respect of an application under section 94(2)(a) of the 2011 Act made under Part VII of this Chapter.

(2)[3]   Notice of the application shall be given in the case of a safeguarder or curator ad litem by serving a copy of the application and the first order or warrant to cite together with notice in Form 40.

### Period of notice

**3.13**—(1)   Subject to paragraph (2), citation or notice authorised or required by this Chapter shall be made not later than forty-eight hours, or in the case or postal citation seventy-two hours, before the date of the diet to which the citation or notice relates.

(2)   Paragraph (1) shall not apply in relation to citation or notice of the following applications or proceedings—

(a)[4]   an appeal referred to in section 157(1), 160(1), 161(1) or 162(3) of the 2011 Act;

(b)   a hearing in respect of an exclusion order where an interim order has been granted in terms of rule 3.36;

(c)[5]   a hearing on an application to vary or terminate a child protection order;

(d)   an application for a child assessment order,

in which cases the period of notice and the method of giving notice shall be as directed by the sheriff.

### Citation of witnesses, parties and persons having an interest

**3.14**—(1)   The following shall be warrants for citation of witnesses, parties and havers—

(a)[6]   the warrant for the hearing on evidence in an application;

(b)   an interlocutor fixing a diet for the continued hearing of an application; and

(c)   an interlocutor assigning a diet for a hearing of an appeal or application.

(2)   In an application or an appeal, witnesses or havers may be cited in Form 41.

(3)   The certificate of execution of citation of witnesses and havers shall be in Form 42.

---

[1] As substituted by the Act of Sederunt (Children's Hearings (Scotland) Act 2011) (Miscellaneous Amendments) 2013 (SSI 2013/172) para.3 (effective June 24, 2013).
[2] As substituted by the Act of Sederunt (Children's Hearings (Scotland) Act 2011) (Miscellaneous Amendments) 2013 (SSI 2013/172) para.3 (effective June 24, 2013).
[3] As amended by the Act of Sederunt (Children's Hearings (Scotland) Act 2011) (Miscellaneous Amendments) 2013 (SSI 2013/172) para.3 (effective June 24, 2013).
[4] As substituted by the Act of Sederunt (Children's Hearings (Scotland) Act 2011) (Miscellaneous Amendments) 2013 (SSI 2013/172) para.3 (effective June 24, 2013).
[5] As substituted by the Act of Sederunt (Children's Hearings (Scotland) Act 2011) (Miscellaneous Amendments) 2013 (SSI 2013/172) para.3 (effective June 24, 2013).
[6] As amended by the Act of Sederunt (Children's Hearings (Scotland) Act 2011) (Miscellaneous Amendments) 2013 (SSI 2013/172) para.3 (effective June 24, 2013).

**Modes of service**

**3.15**—(1)   Service authorised or required by this Chapter shall be made by any mode specified in paragraphs (2) and (3).

(2)   It shall be deemed legal service to or on any person if such service is—

    (a)   delivered to him personally;

    (b)   left for him at his dwelling-house or place of business with some person resident or employed therein;

    (c)   where it cannot be delivered to him personally and he has no known dwelling-house or place of business, left for him at any other place at which he may at the time be resident;

    (d)   where he is the master of, or a seaman or other person employed in, a vessel, left with a person on board or connected with the vessel;

    (e)   sent by first class recorded delivery post, or the nearest equivalent which the available postal service permits, to his dwelling-house or place of business, or if he has no known dwelling-house or place of business to any other place in which he may at the time be resident;

    (f)   where the person has the facility to receive facsimile or other electronic transmission, by such facsimile or other electronic transmission; or

    (g)   where the person has a numbered box at a document exchange, given by leaving at the document exchange.

(3)   Where service requires to be made and there is not sufficient time to employ any of the methods specified in paragraph (2), service shall be effected orally or in such other manner as the sheriff directs.

**Persons who may effect service**

**3.16.**—(1)   Subject to paragraphs (2) and (3), service shall be effected—

    (a)   in the case of any of the modes specified in rule 3.15(2), by a sheriff officer;

    (b)[1]   in the case of any of the modes specified in rule 3.15(2)(e) to (g), by a solicitor, the sheriff clerk, the Principal Reporter or an officer of the local authority; or

    (c)   in the case of any mode specified by the sheriff in terms of rule 3.15(3), by such person as the sheriff directs.

(2)   In relation to the citation of witnesses, parties and havers in terms of rule 3.14 or service of any application, "officer of the local authority" in paragraph (1)(b) includes any officer of a local authority authorised to conduct proceedings under these Rules in terms of rule 3.21 (representation).

(3)[2]   Where required by the sheriff, the sheriff clerk shall cite the Principal Reporter, the authors or compilers of any reports or statements and any other person whom the sheriff may wish to examine under section 155(5) of the 2011 Act (procedure in appeal to sheriff against decision of children's hearing).

**Production of certificates of execution of service**

**3.17.**—(1)   The production before the sheriff of—

    (a)   a certificate of execution of service in Form 43; and

---

[1] As amended by the Act of Sederunt (Children's Hearings (Scotland) Act 2011) (Miscellaneous Amendments) 2013 (SSI 2013/172) para.3 (effective June 24, 2013).

[2] As substituted by the Act of Sederunt (Children's Hearings (Scotland) Act 2011) (Miscellaneous Amendments) 2013 (SSI 2013/172) para.3 (effective June 24, 2013).

(b)[1]  additionally in the case of postal service, a post office receipt of the registered or recorded delivery letter,

shall be sufficient evidence that service was duly made.

(2)   It shall be sufficient to lodge the execution of service at the hearing, unless the sheriff otherwise directs or on cause shown.

### Power to dispense with service

**3.18.**   Subject to rule 3.3, the sheriff may, on cause shown, dispense with service on any person named.

*Miscellaneous*

### Expenses

**3.19.**   No expenses shall be awarded in any proceedings in which this Chapter applies.

### Record of proceedings

**3.20.**   Proceedings under this Chapter shall be conducted summarily.

### Representation

**3.21.**—(1)   In any proceedings any party may be represented by an advocate or a solicitor or, subject to paragraphs (2) and (3), other representative authorised by the party.

(2)   Such other representative must throughout the proceedings satisfy the sheriff that he is a suitable person to represent the party and that he is authorised to do so.

(3)   Such other representative may in representing a party do all such things for the preparation and conduct of the proceedings as may be done by an individual on his own behalf.

### Applications for evidence by live link

**3.22.**—[2](1)   On cause shown, a party may apply in the form prescribed in paragraph (3) for authority for the whole or part of—

(a)   the evidence of a witness or party; or

(b)   a submission,

to be made through a live link.

(2)   In paragraph (1)—

"witness" means a person who has been or may be cited to appear before the sheriff as a witness (including a witness who is outwith Scotland), except in circumstances where such witness is a vulnerable witness within the meaning of section 11(1) of the Vulnerable Witnesses (Scotland) Act 2004;

"submission" means any oral submission which would otherwise be made to the court by the party or such party's representative in person including an oral submission in support of an application;

---

[1] As amended by the Act of Sederunt (Children's Hearings (Scotland) Act 2011) (Miscellaneous Amendments) 2013 (SSI 2013/172) para.3 (effective June 24, 2013).

[2] As substituted by the Act of Sederunt (Children's Hearings (Scotland) Act 2011) (Miscellaneous Amendments) 2013 (SSI 2013/172) para.3 (effective June 24, 2013).

"live link" means a live television link or such other arrangement as may be specified in the application by which the witness, party or representative, as the case may be, is able to be seen and heard in the proceedings or heard in the proceedings and is able to see and hear or hear the proceedings while at a place which is outside the courtroom.

(3) An application under paragraph (1) shall be made—

    (a) in Form 44A in the case of a witness or party;

    (b) in Form 44B in the case of a submission.

(4) The application shall be lodged with the sheriff clerk prior to the hearing at which the witness is to give evidence or the submission is to be made (except on special cause shown).

(5) The sheriff shall—

    (a) order intimation of the application to be made to the other party or parties to the proceedings in such form as he or she prescribes; and

    (b) hear the application as soon as reasonably practicable.

### Orders and transfer of cases

**3.23.**—(1) The sheriff who hears an application under rule 3.22 shall, after hearing the parties and allowing such further procedure as the sheriff thinks fit, make an order granting or refusing the application.

(2) Where the sheriff grants the application, he may—

    (a) transfer the case to be heard in whole; or

    (b) hear the case himself or such part of it as he shall determine,

in another sheriff court in the same sheriffdom.

### Exclusion of certain enactments

**3.24.** The enactments specified in column (1) of Schedule 3 to this Act of Sederunt (being enactments relating to matters with respect to which this Chapter is made) shall not, to the extent specified in column (3) of that Schedule, apply to an application or appeal.

## Part III

## Child Assessment Orders

### Interpretation

**3.25.**[1] In this Part, "application" means an application for a child assessment order in terms of section 35(1) of the 2011 Act.

### Form of application

**3.26.** An application shall be made in Form 45.

### Orders

**3.27.**—(1) After hearing parties and allowing such further procedure as he thinks fit, the sheriff shall make an order granting or refusing the application.

---

[1] As amended by the Act of Sederunt (Children's Hearings (Scotland) Act 2011) (Miscellaneous Amendments) 2013 (SSI 2013/172) para.3 (effective June 24, 2013).

(2)   Where an order is made granting the application, that order shall be made in Form 46 and shall contain the information specified therein.

(3)[1]   Where the sheriff, in terms of section 36(3) of the 2011 Act, has decided to make a child protection order pursuant to an application, rules 3.31 to 3.33 shall apply.

## Intimation

**3.28.**   The local authority shall intimate the grant or refusal of an application to such persons, if any, as the sheriff directs.

Part IV

## Child Protection Orders

## Interpretation

**3.29**[2]   In this Part, "application" means, except in rule 3.33, an application for a child protection order in terms of section 37 of the 2011 Act.

## Form of application

**3.30**   An application made by a local authority shall be in Form 47 and an application made by any other person shall be in Form 48.

## Determination of application

**3.31**—(1)   On receipt of an application, the sheriff, having considered the grounds of the application and the supporting evidence, shall forthwith grant or refuse it.

(2)[3]   Where an order is granted, it shall be in Form 49 and it shall contain any directions made under section 40, 41 or 42 of the 2011 Act.

## Intimation of making of order

**3.32**   Where an order is granted, the applicant shall forthwith serve a copy of the order on—

    (a)   the child, along with a notice in Form 50;

    (b)[4]   the persons referred to in section 43(1)(a), (c), (d) and (e) of the 2011 Act, along with a notice in Form 51; and

    (c)   such other persons as the sheriff may direct and in such manner as he or she may direct.

---

[1] As amended by the Act of Sederunt (Children's Hearings (Scotland) Act 2011) (Miscellaneous Amendments) 2013 (SSI 2013/172) para.3 (effective June 24, 2013).

[2] As amended by the Act of Sederunt (Children's Hearings (Scotland) Act 2011) (Miscellaneous Amendments) 2013 (SSI 2013/172) para.3 (effective June 24, 2013).

[3] As amended by the Act of Sederunt (Children's Hearings (Scotland) Act 2011) (Miscellaneous Amendments) 2013 (SSI 2013/172) para.3 (effective June 24, 2013).

[4] As substituted by the Act of Sederunt (Children's Hearings (Scotland) Act 2011) (Miscellaneous Amendments) 2013 (SSI 2013/172) para.3 (effective June 24, 2013).

## Application to vary or terminate a child protection order

**3.33**—[1](1)   An application under section 48 of the 2011 Act for the variation or termination of a child protection order or a direction given under section 58 of the Act or such an order shall be made in Form 52.

(2)   A person applying under section 48 of the 2011 Act for the variation or termination of a child protection order shall require the lodge with his application a copy of that order.

(3)   Without prejudice to rule 3.5, any person on whom service is made under section 49 of the 2011 Act may appear or be represented at the hearing of the application.

(4)   The sheriff, after hearing parties and allowing such further procedure as he thinks fit, shall grant or refuse the application.

(5)   Where an order is made granting the application for variation, the order shall be in Form 53.

(6)   Where the sheriff so directs, intimation of the granting or refusing of an application shall be given by the applicant to such persons as the sheriff shall direct.

Part V

## Exclusion Orders

### Interpretation

**3.34**[2]   In this Part, "application" means, except in rule 3.40, an application by a local authority for an exclusion order in terms of sections 76 to 80 of the 1995 Act; and "ancillary order" and "interim order" shall be construed accordingly.

### Form of application

**3.35**   An application shall be made in Form 54.

### Hearing following interim order

**3.36**[3]   Where an interim order is granted under subsection (4) of section 76 of the 1995 Act, the hearing under subsection (5) of that section shall take place not later than 3 working days after the granting of the interim order.

### Orders

**3.37**—(1)   After hearing parties and allowing such further procedure as he thinks fit, the sheriff shall make an order granting or refusing the application.

(2)   Where the sheriff grants an order in terms of paragraph (1), it shall be in Form 55 and shall be served forthwith by the local authority on—

    (a)   the named person;

    (b)   the appropriate person;

---

[1] As amended by the Act of Sederunt (Children's Hearings (Scotland) Act 2011) (Miscellaneous Amendments) 2013 (SSI 2013/172) para.3 (effective June 24, 2013).

[2] As amended by the Act of Sederunt (Children's Hearings (Scotland) Act 2011) (Miscellaneous Amendments) 2013 (SSI 2013/172) para.3 (effective June 24, 2013).

[3] As amended by the Act of Sederunt (Children's Hearings (Scotland) Act 2011) (Miscellaneous Amendments) 2013 (SSI 2013/172) para.3 (effective June 24, 2013).

   (c)   the relevant child; and

   (d)   the Principal Reporter.

## Certificates of delivery of documents to chief constable

**3.38—**[1](1)   After the local authority have complied with section 78(4) of the 1955 Act, they shall forthwith lodge in process a certificate of delivery in Form 56.

(2)   After a person has complied with section 78(5) of the 1995 Act, he shall lodge in process a certificate of delivery in Form 56.

## Power to make child protection order in an application for an exclusion order

**3.39**[2]   Where the sheriff, in terms of section 76(8) of the 1995 Act, has decided to make a child protection order under Part 5 of the 2011 Act pursuant to an application, rules 3.31 to 3.33 shall apply.

## Variation or recall of an exclusion order

**3.40—**[3](1)   Any application for the variation or recall of an exclusion order and any warrant, interdict, order or direction granted or made under section 77 of the 1995 Act shall be in Form 57.

(2)   After hearing parties and allowing such further procedure as he thinks fit, the sheriff shall make an order granting or refusing the application.

(3)   Where an order is made granting the application for variation, that order shall be in Form 58.

(4)   Intimation of the granting or refusing of an application shall be given by the applicant to such persons as the sheriff shall direct.

## Part VI

## Warrant for Further Detention of a Child

**3.41–3.43**   *[Repealed by the Act of Sederunt (Children's Hearings (Scotland) Act 2011) (Miscellaneous Amendments) 2013 (SSI 2013/172) para.3 (effective June 24, 2013).]*

## Part VII

## Procedure in Applications under Section 93(2)(a) or 94(2)(a) of the 2011 Act[4]

## Interpretation

**3.44**[5]   In this Part, "application" means an application under section 93(2)(a) or 94(2)(a) of the 2011 Act.

---

[1] As amended by the Act of Sederunt (Children's Hearings (Scotland) Act 2011) (Miscellaneous Amendments) 2013 (SSI 2013/172) para.3 (effective June 24, 2013).
[2] As substituted by the Act of Sederunt (Children's Hearings (Scotland) Act 2011) (Miscellaneous Amendments) 2013 (SSI 2013/172) para.3 (effective June 24, 2013).
[3] As amended by the Act of Sederunt (Children's Hearings (Scotland) Act 2011) (Miscellaneous Amendments) 2013 (SSI 2013/172) para.3 (effective June 24, 2013).
[4] As amended by the Act of Sederunt (Children's Hearings (Scotland) Act 2011) (Miscellaneous Amendments) 2013 (SSI 2013/172) para.3 (effective June 24, 2013).
[5] As amended by the Act of Sederunt (Children's Hearings (Scotland) Act 2011) (Miscellaneous Amendments) 2013 (SSI 2013/172) para.3 (effective June 24, 2013).

**Lodging of application, etc.**

**3.45**—[1](1)   Within a period of 7 days beginning with the date on which the Principal Reporter was directed in terms of section 93(2)(a) or 94(2)(a) of the 2011 Act to make an application to the sheriff, the Principal Reporter shall lodge an application in Form 60 with the sheriff clerk of the sheriff court district in which the child is habitually resident.

(1A)   Paragraph (1) is subject to the terms of section 102(2) of the 2011 Act.

(1B)   The sheriff may, on cause shown, remit any application to another sheriff court.

(1C)   Not later than 28 days after the day on which the application is lodged the sheriff clerk shall fix a hearing on evidence as required under section 101(2) of the 2011 Act.

(2)   Where a safeguarder has been appointed by the chairman at the children's hearing, the Principal Reporter shall intimate such appointment to the sheriff clerk and shall lodge along with the application any report made by the safeguarder.

(3)   Paragraphs (4) to (7) apply where an application under paragraph (1) is made by virtue of section 94(2)(a) of the 2011 Act.

(4)   The sheriff may fix a procedural hearing to determine whether or not the section 67 grounds in the statement of grounds are accepted by each relevant person.

(5)   Such procedural hearing must take place before the expiry of the period of 7 days beginning with the day on which the application is lodged.

(6)   The sheriff shall appoint service and intimation of the procedural hearing as the sheriff thinks fit.

(7)   Subject to paragraph (9)(a) and (b), subsequent to the procedural hearing the sheriff may discharge the hearing on evidence and determine the application.

(8)   Where paragraph (7) applies the sheriff shall make such orders for intimation as the sheriff thinks fit.

(9)   Where—
   (a)   a relevant person does not accept the section 67 grounds in the statement of grounds at the procedural hearing;
   (b)   section 106(2)(a) or (b) of the 2011 Act applies; or
   (c)   the sheriff has not fixed a procedural hearing;
a hearing on evidence must take place in accordance with rule 3.47.

**Withdrawal of application**

**3.46**—[2](1)   At any stage of the proceedings before the application is determined the Principal Reporter may withdraw the application, either in whole or in part, by lodging a minute to that effect or by motion at the hearing.

(2)   The Principal Reporter shall intimate such withdrawal to—
   (a)   the child, except where service on the child had been dispensed with in terms of rule 3.3;
   (b)   any relevant person whose whereabouts are known to the Principal Reporter; and
   (c)   any safeguarder appointed by the sheriff and curator ad litem.

---

[1] As amended by the Act of Sederunt (Children's Hearings (Scotland) Act 2011) (Miscellaneous Amendments) 2013 (SSI 2013/172) para.3 (effective June 24, 2013).
[2] As amended by the Act of Sederunt (Children's Hearings (Scotland) Act 2011) (Miscellaneous Amendments) 2013 (SSI 2013/172) para.3 (effective June 24, 2013).

(3)   In the event of withdrawal in whole in terms of paragraph (1), the sheriff shall dismiss the application and discharge the referral.

## Expeditious determination of application

**3.46A**[1]   Prior to or at a hearing on evidence under rule 3.47 (or any adjournment or continuation thereof under rule 3.49), the sheriff may order parties to take such steps as the sheriff deems necessary to secure the expeditious determination of the application, including but not limited to—
- (a)   instructing a single expert;
- (b)   using affidavits;
- (c)   restricting the issues for proof;
- (d)   restricting witnesses;
- (e)   applying for evidence to be taken by live link in accordance with rule 3.22.

## Hearing on evidence

**3.47**—[2](A1)   If, at a hearing on evidence (or any adjournment or continuation thereof under rule 3.49), the section 67 grounds (or as they may be amended) are no longer in dispute, the sheriff may determine the application without hearing evidence.

(1)   In the case of every section 67 ground, the sheriff shall, in relation to any ground of referral which is in dispute, hear evidence tendered by or on behalf of the Principal Reporter, including evidence given pursuant to an application granted under rule 3.23.

(2)   At the close of the evidence led by the Principal Reporter in a case where it is disputed that the ground set out in section 67(2)(j) of the 2011 Act applies, the sheriff shall consider whether sufficient evidence has been led to establish that ground and shall give all the parties an opportunity to be heard on the question of sufficiency of evidence.

(3)   Where the sheriff is not satisfied that sufficient evidence has been led as mentioned in paragraph (2), he shall make a determination to that effect.

(4)   Paragraph (4A) applies where—
- (a)   paragraph (2) applies and the sheriff is satisfied that sufficient evidence has been led;
- (b)   any other section 67 ground is in dispute.

(4A)   The child, the relevant person and any safeguarder may give evidence and may, with the approval of the sheriff, call witnesses with regard to the ground in question.

(5)   Where the sheriff excuses the child from attending all or part of the hearing in accordance with section 103(3) of the 2011 Act, the following persons shall be permitted to remain during the absence of the child—
- (a)   any safeguarder appointed in relation to the child;
- (b)   any curator ad litem appointed in relation to the child;
- (c)   any relevant person;
- (d)   the child's representative.

---

[1] As amended by the Act of Sederunt (Children's Hearings (Scotland) Act 2011) (Miscellaneous Amendments) 2013 (SSI 2013/172) para.3 (effective June 24, 2013).
[2] As amended by the Act of Sederunt (Children's Hearings (Scotland) Act 2011) (Miscellaneous Amendments) 2013 (SSI 2013/172) para.3 (effective June 24, 2013).

(6)   Subject to paragraph (7), the sheriff may exclude any person, including the relevant person, while any child is giving evidence if the sheriff is satisfied that this is necessary in the interests of the child and that—

   (a)   he must do so in order to obtain the evidence of the child; or

   (b)   the presence of the person or persons in question is causing, or is likely to cause, significant distress to the child.

(7)   Where the relevant person is not legally represented at the hearing and has been excluded under paragraph (6), the sheriff shall inform that relevant person of the substance of any evidence given by the child and shall give that relevant person an opportunity to respond by leading evidence or otherwise.

(8)   Where evidence has been heard in part and a safeguarder thereafter becomes a party to proceedings, the sheriff may order the evidence to be reheard in whole or in part.

## Amendment of the statement of grounds

**3.48**[1]   The sheriff may at any time, on the application of any party or on his own motion, allow amendment of any statement of grounds.

## Adjournment for inquiry, etc.

**3.49**[2][3]   The sheriff on the motion of any party or on his own motion may continue the hearing fixed under rule 3.45(1C) in order to allow time for further inquiry into any application, in consequence of the amendment of any statement under rule 3.48, or for any other necessary cause, for such reasonable time as he may in the circumstances consider necessary.

## Power of sheriff in making findings as to offences

**3.50**[4]   Where in a statement of grounds it is alleged that an offence has been committed by or against any child, the sheriff may determine that any other offence established by the facts has been committed.

## Decision of sheriff

**3.51**—[5](1)   Subject to rule 3.47(3), the sheriff shall give his decision orally at the conclusion of the hearing.

(2)   The sheriff clerk shall forthwith send a copy of the interlocutor containing that decision to—

   (a)   the child, except where service on the child has been dispensed with in terms of rule 3.3;

   (b)   any relevant person whose whereabouts are known;

   (c)   any safeguarder and curator ad litem;

---

[1] As amended by the Act of Sederunt (Children's Hearings (Scotland) Act 2011) (Miscellaneous Amendments) 2013 (SSI 2013/172) para.3 (effective June 24, 2013).
[2] As amended by the Act of Sederunt (Children's Hearings (Scotland) Act 2011) (Miscellaneous Amendments) 2013 (SSI 2013/172) para.3 (effective June 24, 2013).
[3] As amended by the Act of Sederunt (Rules of the Court of Session and Sheriff Court Rules Amendment) (Miscellaneous) 2014 (SSI 2014/201) r.5(2) (effective August 1, 2014).
[4] As amended by the Act of Sederunt (Children's Hearings (Scotland) Act 2011) (Miscellaneous Amendments) 2013 (SSI 2013/172) para.3 (effective June 24, 2013).
[5] As amended by the Act of Sederunt (Children's Hearings (Scotland) Act 2011) (Miscellaneous Amendments) 2013 (SSI 2013/172) para.3 (effective June 24, 2013).

(d) the Principal Reporter; and

(e) such other persons as the sheriff may direct.

(3) The sheriff may, when giving his decision in terms of paragraph (1) or within 7 days thereafter, issue a note of the reasons for his decision and the sheriff clerk shall forthwith send a copy of such a note to the persons referred to in paragraph (2).

## Signature of warrants

**3.52**—[1](1) Subject to paragraph (3) a warrant granted under the 2011 Act may be signed by the sheriff or the sheriff clerk.

(2) A warrant signed by the sheriff clerk shall be treated for all purposes as if it had been signed by the sheriff.

(3) A warrant to secure attendance must be signed by the sheriff.

Part VIII[2]

## Procedure in Appeals to the Sheriff against Decisions of Children's Hearings

## Form of appeal

**3.53**—[3](1) This Part applies to appeals to the sheriff under sections 154(1), 160(1), 161(1) and 162(3) of the 2011 Act.

(1A) An appeal to the sheriff under the sections of the 2011 Act prescribed in paragraph (1B) must be—

(a) made in the form prescribed in paragraph (1B);

(b) accompanied by a copy of the decision complained of and any document relevant to it that was before the children's hearing; and

(c) lodged with the sheriff clerk of the sheriff court district in which the child is habitually resident or, on cause shown, such other court as the sheriff may direct.

(1B) The prescribed sections and form of appeal are—

(a) in the case of an appeal under section 154(1) (appeal to sheriff against decision of children's hearing), in Form 61;

(b) in the case of an appeal under section 160(1) (appeal to sheriff against relevant person determination), in Form 62;

(c) in the case of an appeal under section 161(1) (appeal to sheriff against decision affecting contact or permanence order), in Form 63;

(d) in the case of an appeal under section 162(3) (appeal to sheriff against decision to implement secure accommodation authorisation), in Form 63A.

(2) Subject to paragraph (3), the appeal shall be signed by the appellant or his representative.

(3) An appeal by a child may be signed on his behalf by any safeguarder.

(4) Where leave to appeal is required by virtue of section 159(2) of the 2011 Act, such application for leave shall be—

---

[1] As substituted by the Act of Sederunt (Children's Hearings (Scotland) Act 2011) (Miscellaneous Amendments) 2013 (SSI 2013/172) para.3 (effective June 24, 2013).

[2] As amended by the Act of Sederunt (Children's Hearings (Scotland) Act 2011) (Miscellaneous Amendments) 2013 (SSI 2013/172) para.3 (effective June 24, 2013).

[3] As amended by the Act of Sederunt (Children's Hearings (Scotland) Act 2011) (Miscellaneous Amendments) 2013 (SSI 2013/172) para.3 (effective June 24, 2013).

(a) made by letter addressed to the sheriff clerk setting out the grounds on which the application is made;

(b) accompanied by a copy of the decision referred to in section 159(2) of the 2011 Act;

(c) lodged with the sheriff clerk with the relevant form of appeal.

(5) On receipt of such application the sheriff clerk shall forthwith fix a hearing and intimate the application and the date of the hearing to the other parties to the proceedings.

(6) Where leave to appeal is granted, the appeal will proceed in accordance with rule 3.54.

**Appointment and intimation of first diet**

**3.54**—[1](1) On the lodging of the appeal, the sheriff clerk shall forthwith assign a date for the hearing and shall at the same time intimate to the appellant or his representative and, together with a copy of the appeal, to—

(a) the Principal Reporter;

(b) subject to the provisions of paragraph (4), the child (if not the appellant);

(c) any relevant person (if not the appellant);

(d) any safeguarder; and

(e) any other person the sheriff considers necessary, including those referred to in section 155(5)(c) and (e) of the 2011 Act.

(f) in the case of appeals under section 162(3), the chief social work officer of the relevant local authority for the child.

(2) The sheriff clerk shall endorse on the appeal a certificate of execution of intimation under paragraph (1).

(3) Intimation to a child in terms of paragraph (1)(b) shall be in Form 64.

(4) The sheriff may dispense with intimation to a child in terms of paragraph (1)(b) where he considers that such dispensation is appropriate.

(5) The date assigned for the hearing under paragraph (1) shall be within the time limits prescribed in, or by virtue of, the 2011 Act and in any event, no later than 28 days after the lodging of the appeal.

**Answers**

**3.55**—(1)[2] Subject to paragraph (1A), if any person on whom service of the appeal has been made wishes to lodge answers to the appeal, he or she must do so not later than 7 days before the diet fixed for the hearing of the appeal.

(1A)[3] Paragraph (1) does not apply to those appeals referred to in section 157(1), 160(1), 161(1) or 162(3) of the 2011 Act.

(2) Any person who has lodged answers shall forthwith intimate a copy thereof to any other person on whom service has been made under rule 3.54(1).

---

[1] As amended by the Act of Sederunt (Children's Hearings (Scotland) Act 2011) (Miscellaneous Amendments) 2013 (SSI 2013/172) para.3 (effective June 24, 2013).
[2] As substituted by the Act of Sederunt (Children's Hearings (Scotland) Act 2011) (Miscellaneous Amendments) 2013 (SSI 2013/172) para.3 (effective June 24, 2013).
[3] As substituted by the Act of Sederunt (Children's Hearings (Scotland) Act 2011) (Miscellaneous Amendments) 2013 (SSI 2013/172) para.3 (effective June 24, 2013).

## Procedure at hearing of appeal

**3.56**—[1](1)   Before proceeding to examine the Principal Reporter and the authors or compilers of any reports or statements, the sheriff shall hear the appellant or his representative and any party to the appeal.

(2)   On receipt of any further report required by the sheriff under or by virtue of the 2011 Act, the sheriff shall direct the Principal Reporter to send a copy of the report to every party to the appeal.

(3)   At any appeal the sheriff may hear evidence—

    (a)   where a ground of the appeal is an alleged irregularity in the conduct of a hearing, as to that irregularity;

    (b)   in any other circumstances where he considers it appropriate to do so.

(4)   Where the nature of the appeal or of any evidence is such that the sheriff is satisfied that it is in the interests of the child that he should not be present at any stage of the appeal, the sheriff may exclude the child from the hearing during that stage and, in that event, any safeguarder appointed and any relevant person or representative of the child shall be permitted to remain during the absence of the child.

(5)   Subject to paragraph (6), the sheriff may exclude any relevant person, or that person and any representative of his, or any such representative from any part or parts of the hearing for so long as he considers it is necessary in the interests of any child, where he is satisfied that—

    (a)   he must do so in order to obtain the views of the child in relation to the hearing; or

    (b)   the presence of the person or persons in question is causing, or is likely to cause, significant distress to the child.

(6)   Where any relevant person has been excluded under paragraph (5) the sheriff shall, after that exclusion has ended, explain to him the substance of what has taken place in his absence and shall give him an opportunity to respond to any evidence given by the child by leading evidence or otherwise.

(7)   Where an appeal has been heard in part and a safeguarder thereafter becomes a party to the appeal, the sheriff may order the hearing of the appeal to commence of new.

## Adjournment or continuaton of appeals

**3.57**—[2](1)   The sheriff may, on the motion of any party or on his own motion, adjourn or continue the hearing of the appeal for such reasonable time and for such purpose as may in the circumstances be appropriate.

(2)   In the event of such adjournment or continuation the sheriff may make such order as the sheriff deems necessary to secure the expeditious determination of the appeal.

---

[1] As amended by the Act of Sederunt (Children's Hearings (Scotland) Act 2011) (Miscellaneous Amendments) 2013 (SSI 2013/172) para.3 (effective June 24, 2013).

[2] As amended by the Act of Sederunt (Children's Hearings (Scotland) Act 2011) (Miscellaneous Amendments) 2013 (SSI 2013/172) para.3 (effective June 24, 2013).

## Decision of sheriff in appeals

**3.58**—[1](1)   The sheriff shall give his decision orally either at the conclusion of the appeal or on such day as he shall appoint, subject to the provisions of, or by virtue of, the 2011 Act.

(2)   The sheriff may issue a note of the reasons for his decision, and shall require to do so where he takes any of the steps referred to in section 156(2) or (3) of the 2011 Act.

(3)   Any note in terms of paragraph (2) shall be issued at the time the sheriff gives his decision or within 7 days thereafter.

(4)   The sheriff clerk shall forthwith send a copy of the interlocutor containing the decision of the sheriff, and where appropriate of the note referred to in paragraph (2), to the Principal Reporter, to the appellant (and to any child or the relevant person, if not the appellant), any safeguarder and such other persons as the sheriff may direct, and shall also return to the Principal Reporter any documents lodged with the sheriff clerk.

(5)   Where section 159 of the 2011 Act applies the sheriff clerk shall send a copy of the interlocutor containing the decision of the sheriff to the Scottish Legal Aid Board.

## Part VIIIA[2]

## Applications for Review by Local Authority

### Review applications by local authority

**3.58A**—[3](1)   This Part of Chapter 3 applies to applications to the sheriff for a review under section 166(2) of the 2011 Act.

(2)   An application shall be made in Form 64A and must contain—

   (a)   the name and address of the local authority;

   (b)   the name of the child in respect of whom the duty was imposed and the child's representative (if any);

   (c)   the name and address of any relevant person in relation to the child and such person's representative (if any);

   (d)   the name and address of any safeguarder;

   (e)   the name and address of any curator ad litem ;

   (f)   the name and address of any other party to the application;

   (g)   the name and address of any other local authority with an interest;

   (h)   the date and determination made and the place of the sheriff court which made the determination, or alternatively the date and decision made by the children's hearing;

     (i)   the grounds for the making of the application;

   (j)   any reports, affidavits and productions upon which the applicant intends to rely.

---

[1] As amended by the Act of Sederunt (Children's Hearings (Scotland) Act 2011) (Miscellaneous Amendments) 2013 (SSI 2013/172) para.3 (effective June 24, 2013).

[2] As inserted by the Act of Sederunt (Children's Hearings (Scotland) Act 2011) (Miscellaneous Amendments) 2013 (SSI 2013/172) para.3 (effective June 24, 2013).

[3] As inserted by the Act of Sederunt (Children's Hearings (Scotland) Act 2011) (Miscellaneous Amendments) 2013 (SSI 2013/172) para.3 (effective June 24, 2013).

**Hearing on application**

**3.58B**—[1](1)   After lodging the application in terms of rule 3.58A, the sheriff clerk shall assign a date for hearing the application and shall issue a warrant to cite in Form 64B, which shall require any party to lodge answers if so advised within such time as the sheriff shall appoint.

(2)   Subject to the provisions of rule 3.3 (power to dispense with service on child), after the issue of the warrant to cite, the applicant shall forthwith give notice of the application by serving a copy and the warrant on the persons referred to in rule 3.58A.

(3)   At the hearing the sheriff may determine the application or allow such further procedure as the sheriff thinks fit.

(4)   The provisions of rule 3.51 shall apply to any order made under this Part.

Part VIIIB[2]

**Procedure in Appeals to the Sheriff under Section 44A of the CPSA 1995**

**Form of Appeal**

**3.58C**—(1)   An appeal to the sheriff under section 44A of the CPSA 1995 must be—

 (a)   made in Form 64C;
 (b)   accompanied by a copy of the decision complained of and any document relevant to it that was taken into account by the local authority when making that decision;
 (c)   lodged with the sheriff clerk of the sheriff court district in which the child is habitually resident or, on cause shown, such other court as the sheriff may direct.

(2)   The appeal must be signed by the appellant or the appellant's representative.

**Appointment and intimation of appeal hearing**

**3.58D**—(1)   On the lodging of an appeal, the sheriff clerk must—

 (a)   assign a date for the hearing;
 (b)   intimate the date of the hearing to the appellant or the appellant's representative;
 (c)   intimate the date of the hearing, together with a copy of the appeal, to the persons specified in paragraph (2).

(2)   Those persons are—

 (a)   the child, unless the child is the appellant;
 (b)   the chief social work officer of the appropriate local authority;
 (c)   any relevant person, other than a relevant person who is the appellant;
 (d)   any other person that the sheriff considers necessary.

(3)   The sheriff clerk must endorse a certificate of execution on the appeal.

(4)   Where an appeal is intimated to a child, that intimation must be in Form 64D.

---

[1] As inserted by the Act of Sederunt (Children's Hearings (Scotland) Act 2011) (Miscellaneous Amendments) 2013 (SSI 2013/172) para.3 (effective June 24, 2013).
[2] As inserted by the Act of Sederunt (Sheriff Court Rules Amendment) (Miscellaneous) 2015 (SSI 2015/424) para.3 (effective 1st February 2015).

(5) The sheriff may dispense with intimation to a child if the sheriff considers it appropriate to do so.

## Procedure at hearing of appeal

**3.58E**—(1) At any appeal the sheriff may hear evidence where he or she considers it appropriate to do so.

(2) The sheriff must hear the appellant or the appellant's representative and any party to the appeal before examining—

    (a) the chief social work officer;

    (b) the authors or compilers of any reports or statements;

    (c) the Principal Reporter.

(3) Where the nature of the appeal or of any evidence is such that the sheriff is satisfied that it is in the interests of the child not to be present at any stage of the appeal, the sheriff may exclude the child from the hearing during that stage.

(4) Where the sheriff excludes a child, any relevant person or representative of the child will be permitted to remain during the child's absence.

(5) Where the sheriff is satisfied that—

    (a) it is necessary in order to obtain the views of the child in relation to the hearing; or

    (b) the presence of the person or persons in question is causing, or is likely to cause, significant distress to the child,

the sheriff may exclude the persons mentioned in paragraph (6) from the hearing for so long as the sheriff considers it necessary in the interests of the child.

(6) Those persons are—

    (a) a relevant person;

    (b) any representative of a relevant person.

(7) After the exclusion of any person under paragraph (5), the sheriff must—

    (a) explain the substance of what has taken place in that person's absence;

    (b) give that person an opportunity to respond to any evidence given by the child by leading evidence or otherwise.

## Adjournment or continuation of appeals

**3.58F**—(1) The sheriff may adjourn or continue the hearing of the appeal on the motion of any party or on the sheriff's own motion.

(2) Where the sheriff adjourns or continues a hearing, the sheriff may make any order that is necessary to secure the expeditious determination of the appeal.

## Decision of sheriff in appeals

**3.58G**—(1) The sheriff must give his or her decision orally, either at the conclusion of the appeal or on such day as the sheriff may appoint.

(2) The sheriff may issue a note of the reasons for his or her decision.

(3) Any note in terms of paragraph (2) must be issued at the time the sheriff's decision is given or within 7 days after the date of the decision.

(4) The sheriff clerk must immediately send to the persons mentioned in paragraph (5)—

    (a) a copy of the interlocutor containing the sheriff's decision;

    (b) where a note of reasons has been issued, a copy of that note.

(5) Those persons are—

    (a) the appellant;

    (b)   the child, unless the child is the appellant;

    (c)   any relevant person, other than a relevant person who is the appellant;

    (d)   any other person that the sheriff may direct.

(6)   The sheriff clerk must return to the Principal Reporter any documents that the Principal Reporter may have lodged with the sheriff clerk.

## Part IX

## Procedure in Appeals by Stated Case under Part 15 of the 2011 Act[1]

### Appeals

**3.59**—[2](A1)   This Part applies to appeals by stated case under section 163(1), 164(1), 165(1) and 167(1) of the 2011 Act.

(1)[3]   An application to the sheriff to state a case for the purposes of an appeal to the sheriff principal to which this Part applies shall specify the point of law upon which the appeal is to proceed or the procedural irregularity, as the case may be.

(2)[4]   The appellant shall, at the same time as lodging the application for a stated case, intimate the lodging of an appeal from the decision of the sheriff to—

    (a)   the Principal Reporter;

    (b)   the child (if not the appellant), except where service on the child has been dispensed with in terms of rule 3.3;

    (c)   any relevant person (if not the appellant);

    (d)   any safeguarder;

    (e)   any other party to proceedings.

(3)[5]   The sheriff shall, within 21 days of the lodging of the application for a stated case, issue a draft stated case—

    (a)   containing findings in fact and law or, where appropriate, a narrative of the proceedings before him;

    (b)   containing appropriate questions of law or setting out the procedural irregularity concerned; and

    (c)   containing a note stating the reasons for his decisions in law,

and the sheriff clerk shall send a copy of the draft stated case to the appellant and to parties referred to in paragraph (2).

(4)   Within 7 days of the issue of the draft stated case—

    (a)   the appellant or a party referred to in paragraph (2) may lodge with the sheriff clerk a note of any adjustments which he seeks to make;

    (b)   the appellant or such a party may state any point of law or procedural irregularity which he wishes to raise in the appeal; and

    (c)   the note of adjustment and, where appropriate, point of law or procedural irregularity shall be intimated to the appellant and the other such parties.

(5)   The sheriff may, on the motion of the appellant or a party referred to in paragraph (2) or of his own accord, and shall where he proposes to reject any

---

[1] As amended by the Act of Sederunt (Children's Hearings (Scotland) Act 2011) (Miscellaneous Amendments) 2013 (SSI 2013/172) para.3 (effective June 24, 2013).

[2] As amended by the Act of Sederunt (Children's Hearings (Scotland) Act 2011) (Miscellaneous Amendments) 2013 (SSI 2013/172) para.3 (effective June 24, 2013).

[3] As amended by SI 1998/2130, effective September 1, 1998.

[4] As amended by SI 1998/2130, effective September 1, 1998.

[5] As amended by SI 1998/2130, effective September 1, 1998.

proposed adjustment, allow a hearing on adjustments and may provide for such further procedure under this rule prior to the hearing of the appeal as he thinks fit.

(6)   The sheriff shall, within 14 days after—

    (a)   the latest date on which a note of adjustments has been or may be lodged; or

    (b)   where there has been a hearing on adjustments, that hearing,

and after considering such note and any representations made to him at the hearing, state and sign the case.

(7)   The stated case signed by the sheriff shall include—

    (a)   questions of law, framed by him, arising from the points of law stated by the parties and such other questions of law as he may consider appropriate;

    (b)   any adjustments, proposed under paragraph (4), which are rejected by him;

    (c)   a note of the procedural irregularity averred by the parties and any questions of law or other issue which he considers arise therefrom,

as the case may be.

(8)   *[Repealed by the Act of Sederunt (Sheriff Appeal Court Rules 2015 and Sheriff Court Rules Amendment) (Miscellaneous) 2016 (SSI 2016/194) para.4 (effective 7 July 2016).]*

(9)   In the hearing of an appeal, a party referred to in paragraph (2) shall not be allowed to raise questions of law or procedural irregularities of which notice has not been given except on cause shown and subject to such conditions as the sheriff principal may consider appropriate.

(10)   The sheriff may, on an application by any party or on his own motion, reduce any of the periods mentioned in paragraph (3), (4) or (6) to such period or periods as he considers reasonable.

(11)   Where the sheriff is temporarily absent from duty for any reason, the sheriff principal may extend any period specified in paragraph (3) or (6) for such period or periods as he considers reasonable.

## Lodging of reports and information in appeals

**3.60.**[1]   Where, in an appeal—

    (a)   it appears to the sheriff that any report or information lodged under section 155(2) of the 2011 Act is relevant to any issue which is likely to arise in the stated case; and

    (b)   the report or information has been returned to the Principal Reporter,

the sheriff may require the Principal Reporter to lodge the report or information with the sheriff clerk.

## Hearing

**3.61.**—(1)   The sheriff principal, on hearing the appeal, may either pronounce his decision or reserve judgment.

(2)   Where judgment is so reserved, the sheriff principal shall within 28 days give his decision in writing which shall be intimated by the sheriff clerk to the parties.

---

[1] As amended by the Act of Sederunt (Children's Hearings (Scotland) Act 2011) (Miscellaneous Amendments) 2013 (SSI 2013/172) para.3 (effective June 24, 2013).

## Leave of the sheriff principal to appeal to the Court of Session

**3.61A**—(1)  This rule applies to applications for leave to appeal under section 163(2), 164(2) or 165(2) of the 2011 Act.

(2)  An application shall be made by letter addressed to the sheriff clerk, which must—

(a)  state the point of law or procedural irregularity upon which the appeal is to proceed;

(b)  be lodged with the sheriff clerk before the expiry of the period of 7 days beginning with the day on which the determination or decision appealed against was made.

(3)  On receipt of such application the sheriff clerk shall—

(a)  forthwith fix a hearing which should take place no later than 14 days from the date of receipt of the application;

(b)  intimate the application and the date of the hearing to the other parties to the proceedings.

(4)  Where leave to appeal is granted, the appeal shall be lodged in accordance with the timescales prescribed in the relevant section of the 2011 Act.

Part X[1]

## Applications for Review of Grounds Determination

### Application

**3.62**—[2](1)  An application under section 110 of the 2011 Act for a review of a grounds determination made in terms of section 108 of the 2011 Act (determination that grounds for referral established) shall contain—

(a)  the name and address of the applicant and his or her representative (if any);

(b)  the name and address (if known) of the person who is the subject of the grounds determination (even if that person is no longer a child), if not the applicant;

(c)  the name and address of the safeguarder (if any);

(d)  the name and address of the curator ad litem (if any);

(e)  the name and address of any person who is, or was at the time the grounds determination was made, a relevant person in relation to the child, if not the applicant;

(f)  the date and grounds determination made and the place of the sheriff court which made the grounds determination;

(g)  the grounds for the making of the application;

(h)  specification of the nature of evidence in terms of section 111(3) of the 2011 Act not considered by the sheriff who made the grounds determination;

  (i)  the explanation for the failure to lead such evidence on the original application; and

(j)  any reports, affidavits and productions upon which the applicant intends to rely.

---

[1] As amended by the Act of Sederunt (Children's Hearings (Scotland) Act 2011) (Miscellaneous Amendments) 2013 (SSI 2013/172) para.3 (effective June 24, 2013).
[2] As substituted by the Act of Sederunt (Children's Hearings (Scotland) Act 2011) (Miscellaneous Amendments) 2013 (SSI 2013/172) para.3 (effective June 24, 2013).

(2)    Where the applicant does not wish to disclose the address or whereabouts of the child or any other person to persons receiving notice of the application, the applicant shall set out his or her reasons for this.

## Hearing on application

**3.63**—[1](1)    Where an application has been lodged in terms of rule 3.62, the sheriff clerk shall—

(a)    assign a diet for hearing the application;

(b)    issue a warrant to cite in Form 65 requiring the Principal Reporter to lodge answers if so advised within such time as the sheriff shall appoint.

(2)    Subject to the provisions of rule 3.4 (service on child), after the issue of the warrant to cite, the applicant shall forthwith give notice of the application by serving a copy and the warrant on the persons named in rule 3.62 and such other person as the sheriff directs.

(3)    After hearing parties and having considered the terms of section 111(3) of the 2011 Act and allowing such further procedure as the sheriff thinks fit to secure the expeditious determination of the application, the sheriff shall make an order as appropriate.

(4)    The provisions of rule 3.51 shall apply to any order made under paragraph (3).

## Hearing to consider the evidence

**3.64.**    *[Repealed by the Act of Sederunt (Children's Hearings (Scotland) Act 2011) (Miscellaneous Amendments) 2013 (SSI 2013/172) para.3 (effective June 24, 2013).]*

## Part XA[2]

## Orders under the Children's Hearings (Scotland) Act 2011

### Interim compulsory supervision order

**3.64A**—[3](1)    Where a sheriff makes an interim compulsory supervision order under section 100, 109 or 156(3)(d) of the 2011 Act, such order shall be in Form 65A and, subject to rule 3.3, shall be intimated forthwith to the child by the Principal Reporter in Form 65B.

(2)    An application for the extension or extension and variation of an interim compulsory supervision order shall be made to the sheriff in Form 65C.

(3)    An application for the further extension or further extension and variation of an interim compulsory supervision order shall be made to the sheriff in Form 65D.

(4)    Subject to rule 3.3, an application under paragraph (2) or (3) must be intimated forthwith by the applicant to the child and each relevant person and such other persons as the sheriff determines and in such manner as the sheriff determines.

---

[1] As amended by the Act of Sederunt (Children's Hearings (Scotland) Act 2011) (Miscellaneous Amendments) 2013 (SSI 2013/172) para.3 (effective June 24, 2013).

[2] As inserted by the Act of Sederunt (Children's Hearings (Scotland) Act 2011) (Miscellaneous Amendments) 2013 (SSI 2013/172) para.3 (effective June 24, 2013).

[3] As inserted by the Act of Sederunt (Children's Hearings (Scotland) Act 2011) (Miscellaneous Amendments) 2013 (SSI 2013/172) para.3 (effective June 24, 2013).

(5) Where the sheriff grants an application under paragraph (2) or (3), the interlocutor shall state the terms of such extension or extension and variation and subject to rule 3.3, shall be intimated forthwith to the child by the Principal Reporter in Form 65B.

(6) Subject to paragraphs (1) and (5), where the sheriff—

    (a) makes an interim compulsory supervision order under paragraph (1); or

    (b) grants an application under paragraph (2) or (3),

the Principal Reporter shall intimate the order forthwith to the implementation authority and to such other persons as the sheriff determines in Form 65E.

## Compulsory supervision order

**3.64B.**[1] Where a sheriff varies or continues a compulsory supervision order, the interlocutor shall state the terms of such variation or continuation and shall be intimated forthwith by the sheriff clerk to the parties and the relevant implementation authority.

## Medical examination order

**3.64C.**[2] Where a sheriff varies or continues a medical examination order, the interlocutor shall state the terms of such variation or continuation and shall be intimated forthwith by the sheriff clerk to the parties and the relevant local authority or establishment.

Part XI[3]

### Vulnerable Witnesses (Scotland) Act 2004

## Interpretation

**3.65.**[4] In this Part—

"the Act of 2004" means the Vulnerable Witnesses (Scotland) Act 2004;
"child witness notice" has the meaning given in section 12(2) of the Act of 2004;
"review application" means an application for review of arrangements for vulnerable witnesses pursuant to section 13 of the Act of 2004;
"vulnerable witness application" has the meaning given in section 12(6)(a) of the Act of 2004.[5]

## Extent of application of this Part

This Part of Chapter 3 shall apply to proceedings where—

---

[1] As inserted by the Act of Sederunt (Children's Hearings (Scotland) Act 2011) (Miscellaneous Amendments) 2013 (SSI 2013/172) para.3 (effective June 24, 2013).

[2] As inserted by the Act of Sederunt (Children's Hearings (Scotland) Act 2011) (Miscellaneous Amendments) 2013 (SSI 2013/172) para.3 (effective June 24, 2013).

[3] As inserted by the Act of Sederunt (Child Care and Maintenance Rules) Amendment (Vulnerable Witnesses (Scotland) Act 2004) 2005 (SSI 2005/190) r.2(3) (effective April 1, 2005).

[4] As amended by the Act of Sederunt (Children's Hearings (Scotland) Act 2011) (Miscellaneous Amendments) 2013 (SSI 2013/172) para.3 (effective June 24, 2013).

[5] As inserted by the Act of Sederunt (Child Care and Maintenance Rules) Amendment (Vulnerable Witnesses (Scotland) Act 2004) 2006 (SSI 2006/75) r.2(2) (effective April 1, 2006).

   (a)   an application is made to the sheriff under section 93(2)(a), 94(2)(a) or 110 of the 2011 Act;

   (b)   an appeal is made to the sheriff under Part 15 of the 2011 Act; or

   (c)   an appeal is made under section 44A of the CPSA 1995.

## Child Witness Notice

**3.67.**   A child witness notice lodged in accordance with section 12(2) of the Act of 2004 shall be in Form 75.

**3.68.**—[1](1)   The party lodging a child witness notice shall intimate a copy of the child witness notice to all other parties to the proceedings and to any safeguarder and complete a certificate of intimation.

(2)   A certificate of intimation referred to in this rule shall be in Form 76 and shall be lodged together with the child witness notice.

**3.69.**—(1)   On receipt of a child witness notice, a sheriff may—

   (a)   make an order under section 12(1) of the Act of 2004 without holding a hearing;

   (b)   require of any of the parties further information before making any further order;

   (c)   fix a date for a hearing of the child witness notice and grant warrant to cite witnesses and havers.

(2)   The sheriff may, subject to any statutory time limits, make an order altering the date of the proof or other hearing at which the child is to give evidence and make such provision for intimation of such alteration to all parties concerned as he deems appropriate.

(3)   An order fixing a hearing for a child witness notice shall be intimated by the sheriff clerk—

   (a)   on the day the order is made; and

   (b)   in such manner as may be prescribed by the sheriff,

to all parties to the proceedings and such other persons as are named in the order where such parties or persons are not present at the time the order is made.

**3.69A.**[2]   A vulnerable witness application made in accordance with section 12(6)(a) of the Act of 2004 shall be in Form 76A.

**3.69B.**—[3, 4](1)   The party making a vulnerable witness application shall intimate a copy of the vulnerable witness application to all other parties to the proceedings and to any safeguarder and complete a certificate of intimation.

(2)   A certificate of intimation referred to in this rule shall be in Form 76B and shall be lodged together with the vulnerable witness application.

**3.69C.**—[5](1)   On receipt of a vulnerable witness application a sheriff may—

---

[1] As amended by the Act of Sederunt (Children's Hearings (Scotland) Act 2011) (Miscellaneous Amendments) 2013 (SSI 2013/172) para.3 (effective June 24, 2013).

[2] As inserted by the Act of Sederunt (Child Care and Maintenance Rules) Amendment (Vulnerable Witnesses (Scotland) Act 2004) 2006 (SSI 2006/75) r.2(3) (effective April 1, 2006).

[3] As inserted by the Act of Sederunt (Child Care and Maintenance Rules) Amendment (Vulnerable Witnesses (Scotland) Act 2004) 2006 (SSI 2006/75) r.2(3) (effective April 1, 2006).

[4] As amended by the Act of Sederunt (Children's Hearings (Scotland) Act 2011) (Miscellaneous Amendments) 2013 (SSI 2013/172) para.3 (effective June 24, 2013).

[5] As inserted by the Act of Sederunt (Child Care and Maintenance Rules) Amendment (Vulnerable Witnesses (Scotland) Act 2004) 2006 (SSI 2006/75) r.2(3) (effective April 1, 2006).

    (a)   make an order under section 12(6) of the Act of 2004 without holding a hearing;

    (b)   require of any of the parties further information before making any further order; or

    (c)   fix a date for a hearing of the vulnerable witness application and grant warrant to cite witnesses and havers.

  (2)   The sheriff may, subject to any statutory time limits, make an order altering the date of the proof or other hearing at which the vulnerable witness is to give evidence and make such provision for intimation of such alteration to all parties concerned as he deems appropriate.

  (3)   An order fixing a hearing for a vulnerable witness application shall be intimated by the sheriff clerk—

    (a)   on the day the order is made; and

    (b)   in such manner as may be prescribed by the sheriff,

to all parties to the proceedings and such other persons as are named in the order where such parties or persons are not present at the time the order is made.

### Review of arrangements for vulnerable witnesses

  **3.70.**—(1)   A review application shall be in Form 77.

  (2)   Where the review application is made during the sheriff's hearing of the case, the sheriff may dispense with the requirements of paragraph (1).

  **3.71.**—[1](1)   Where a review application is in Form 77, the applicant shall intimate a copy of the review application to all other parties to the proceedings and to any safeguarder and complete a certificate of intimation.

  (2)   A certificate of intimation referred to in this rule shall be in Form 78 and shall be lodged together with the review application.

  **3.72.**—(1)   On receipt of a review application, a sheriff may—

    (a)   if he is satisfied that he may properly do so, make an order under section 13(2) of the Act of 2004 without holding a hearing or, if he is not so satisfied, make such an order after giving the parties an opportunity to be heard;

    (b)   require of any of the parties further information before making any further order;

    (c)   fix a date for a hearing of the review application and grant warrant to cite witnesses and havers.

  (2)[2]   The sheriff may, subject to any statutory time limits, make an order altering the date of the proof or other hearing at which the witness is to give evidence and make such provision for intimation of such alteration to all parties concerned as he deems appropriate.

  (3)   An order fixing a hearing for a review application shall be intimated by the sheriff clerk—

    (a)   on the day the order is made; and

    (b)   in such manner as may be prescribed by the sheriff,

to all parties to the proceedings and such other persons as are named in the order where such parties or persons are not present at the time the order is made.

---

[1] As amended by the Act of Sederunt (Children's Hearings (Scotland) Act 2011) (Miscellaneous Amendments) 2013 (SSI 2013/172) para.3 (effective June 24, 2013).

[2] As substituted by the Act of Sederunt (Child Care and Maintenance Rules) Amendment (Vulnerable Witnesses (Scotland) Act 2004) 2006 (SSI 2006/75) r.2(4) (effective April 1, 2006).

### Determination of special measures

**3.73.**[1] When making an order under section 12(1), 12(6) or 13(2) of the Act of 2004 a sheriff may, in light thereof, make such further orders as he deems appropriate in all the circumstances.

### Intimation of an order under section 12(1), 12(6) or 13(2)

**3.74.**[2] An order under section 12(1), 12(6) or 13(2) of the Act of 2004 shall be intimated by the sheriff clerk—
    (a)   on the day the order is made; and
    (b)   in such manner as may be prescribed by the sheriff,
to all parties to the proceedings and such other persons as are named in the order where such parties or persons are not present at the time the order is made.

### Lodging audio and audio-visual recordings and documents[3]

**3.75.**—[4](1)[5] Where evidence is taken on commission pursuant to an order made under section 12(1), 12(6) or 13(2) of the Act of 2004 the commissioner shall lodge any audio or audio-visual recording of the commission and relevant documents with the sheriff clerk.

(2)   On any audio or audio-visual recording and any documents being lodged the sheriff clerk shall—
    (a)   note—
        (i)   the documents lodged;
        (ii)   by whom they were lodged; and
        (iii)   the date on which they were lodged, and
    (b)   intimate what he has noted to all parties concerned.

### Custody of audio or audio-visual recordings and documents[6]

**3.76.**—[7](1)   The audio or audio-visual recording and documents referred to in rule 3.75 shall, subject to paragraph (2), be kept in the custody of the sheriff clerk.

(2)   Where the audio or audio-visual recording of the evidence of a witness is in the custody of the sheriff clerk under this rule and where intimation has been given to that effect under rule 3.75(2), the name and address of that witness and the record of his evidence shall be treated as being in the knowledge of the parties; and no party shall be required, notwithstanding any enactment to the contrary—
    (a)   to include the name of that witness in any list of witnesses; or
    (b)   to include the record of his evidence in any list of productions.

---

[1] As amended by the Act of Sederunt (Child Care and Maintenance Rules) Amendment (Vulnerable Witnesses (Scotland) Act 2004) 2006 (SSI 2006/75) r.2(5) (effective April 1, 2006).
[2] As amended by the Act of Sederunt (Child Care and Maintenance Rules) Amendment (Vulnerable Witnesses (Scotland) Act 2004) 2006 (SSI 2006/75) r.2(5) (effective April 1, 2006).
[3] As amended by the Act of Sederunt (Children's Hearings (Scotland) Act 2011) (Miscellaneous Amendments) 2013 (SSI 2013/172) para.3 (effective June 24, 2013).
[4] As amended by the Act of Sederunt (Children's Hearings (Scotland) Act 2011) (Miscellaneous Amendments) 2013 (SSI 2013/172) para.3 (effective June 24, 2013).
[5] As amended by the Act of Sederunt (Child Care and Maintenance Rules) Amendment (Vulnerable Witnesses (Scotland) Act 2004) 2006 (SSI 2006/75) r.2(5) (effective April 1, 2006).
[6] As amended by the Act of Sederunt (Children's Hearings (Scotland) Act 2011) (Miscellaneous Amendments) 2013 (SSI 2013/172) para.3 (effective June 24, 2013).
[7] As amended by the Act of Sederunt (Children's Hearings (Scotland) Act 2011) (Miscellaneous Amendments) 2013 (SSI 2013/172) para.3 (effective June 24, 2013).

Part XIA[1]

## Cases Involving Sexual Behaviour

### Interpretation and application of this Part

**3.76A**—[2](1)  This Part of Chapter 3 applies to proceedings where—
- (a)  an application is made to the sheriff under section 93(2)(a), 94(2)(a) or 110 of the 2011 Act or an appeal is made under Part 15 of the 2011 Act; and
- (b)  the section 67 ground involves sexual behaviour engaged in by any person.

(2)  In the case of relevant appeals the provisions of sections 173 to 175 of the 2011 Act shall be deemed to apply as they apply to applications.

(3)  The evidence referred to in section 173(2) of the 2011 Act may be in writing or take the form of an audio or audio-visual recording.

(4)  In this Part an "admission application" means an application to the sheriff for an order as to evidence pursuant to section 175(1) of the 2011 Act.

### Application for admission of restricted evidence

**3.77.**—(1)  An admission application shall be in Form 79.

(2)  Where an admission application is made during the sheriff's hearing of the case, the sheriff may dispense with the requirements of paragraph (1).

**3.78.**—[3](1)  Where an admission application is made under rule 3.77, the applicant shall intimate a copy of the admission application to all other parties to the proceedings and to any safeguarder and complete a certificate of intimation.

(2)  A certificate of intimation referred to in this rule shall be in Form 80 and shall be lodged together with the admission application.

**3.79.**—[4](1)  On receipt of an admission application, a sheriff may—
- (a)  grant the admission application in whole or in part;
- (b)  require of any of the parties further information before making any further order;
- (c)  fix a date for a hearing of the admission application and grant warrant to cite witnesses and havers.

(2)  The sheriff may, subject to any statutory time limits, make an order altering the date of the proof or other hearing to which the admission application relates and make such provision for intimation of such alteration to all parties concerned as he deems appropriate.

(3)  An order fixing a hearing for an admission application shall be intimated by the sheriff clerk—
- (a)  on the day the order is made; and
- (b)  in such manner as may be prescribed by the sheriff,

---

[1] As inserted by the Act of Sederunt (Children's Hearings (Scotland) Act 2011) (Miscellaneous Amendments) 2013 (SSI 2013/172) para.3 (effective June 24, 2013).

[2] As inserted by the Act of Sederunt (Children's Hearings (Scotland) Act 2011) (Miscellaneous Amendments) 2013 (SSI 2013/172) para.3 (effective June 24, 2013).

[3] As amended by the Act of Sederunt (Children's Hearings (Scotland) Act 2011) (Miscellaneous Amendments) 2013 (SSI 2013/172) para.3 (effective June 24, 2013).

[4] As inserted by the Act of Sederunt (Children's Hearings (Scotland) Act 2011) (Miscellaneous Amendments) 2013 (SSI 2013/172) para.3 (effective June 24, 2013).

to all parties to the proceedings and such other persons as are named in the order where such parties or persons are not present at the time the order is made.

**3.80.**—(1)  When making an order pursuant to rule 3.79(1)(a) a sheriff may, in light thereof, make such further orders as he deems appropriate in all the circumstances.

**3.81.**—(1)  An order made pursuant to rule 3.79(1)(a) shall be intimated by the sheriff clerk—

(a)   on the day the order is made; and

(b)   in such manner as may be prescribed by the sheriff,

to all parties to the proceedings and such other persons as are named in the order where such parties or persons are not present at the time the order is made.

### Lodging restricted evidence

**3.81A.**—[1](1)  Where the sheriff makes an order under section 175(1) or (c) of the 2011 Act, the applicant shall lodge any relevant recording and documents with the sheriff clerk.

(2)   On the recording and documents being lodged the sheriff clerk shall—

(a)   note—

(i)   the evidence lodged;

(ii)   by whom they were lodged;

(iii)   the date on which they were lodged; and

(b)   intimate what he or she has noted to all parties concerned.

(3)   The recording and documents referred to in paragraph (1) shall, subject to paragraph (4), be kept in the custody of the sheriff clerk.

(4)   Where the recording of the evidence of a witness is in the custody of the sheriff clerk under this rule and where intimation has been given to that effect under paragraph (2), the name and address of that witness and the record of his or her evidence shall be treated as being in the knowledge of the parties; and no party shall be required, notwithstanding any enactment to the contrary—

(a)   to include the name of that witness in any list of witnesses; or

(b)   to include the record of his or her evidence in any list of productions.

### CHAPTER 4

### REGISTRATION OF CHILD CUSTODY ORDERS

### Interpretation

**4.1.**   In this Chapter, unless the context otherwise requires—

"the Act" means the Family Law Act 1986;

"appropriate court" means the High Court in England and Wales or the High Court in Northern Ireland or, in relation to a specified dependent territory, the corresponding court of that territory, as the case may be;

"appropriate register" means the sheriff court book in which there is registered the action in which the Part I order was made;

---

[1] As inserted by the Act of Sederunt (Children's Hearings (Scotland) Act 2011) (Miscellaneous Amendments) 2013 (SSI 2013/172) para.3 (effective June 24, 2013).

"corresponding court", in relation to a specified dependent territory, means the corresponding court specified in relation to that territory in Schedule 3 to the Family Law Act 1986 (Dependent Territories) Order 1991;

"Part I order" has the meaning assigned to it by sections 1, 32 42(5) and 42(6) of the Act;

"proper officer" means the Secretary of the Principal Registry of the Family Division of the High Court in England and Wales or the Master (Care and Protection) of the High Court in Northern Ireland or, in relation to a specified dependent territory, the corresponding officer of the appropriate court in that territory, as the case may be; and

"specified dependent territory" means a territory specified in column 1 of Schedule 1 to the Family Law Act 1986 (Dependent Territories) Order 1991.

### Applications for registration of Part I order in another court

**4.2**—(1) An application under section 27 of the Act (registration) to register a Part I order made by a sheriff court in an appropriate court shall be made by letter to the sheriff clerk of the court in which the order was made.

(2) An application under paragraph (1) of this rule shall be accompanied by—
    (a) a copy of the letter of application;
    (b) an affidavit by the applicant;
    (c) a copy of that affidavit;
    (d) a certified copy of the interlocutor making the Part I order and any variation thereto which is still in force; and
    (e) any other document relevant to the application together with a copy of it.

(3) The affidavit required under this rule shall set out—
    (a) the name and address of the applicant and his right under the Part I order;
    (b) the name and date of birth of the child in respect of whom the Part I order was made, the present whereabouts or suspected whereabouts of the child and the name of any person with whom he is alleged to be;
    (c) the name and address of any other person who has an interest in the Part I order;
    (d) the appropriate court in which it is sought to register the Part I order;
    (e) whether the Part I order is in force;
    (f) whether the Part I order is already registered and, if so, where it is registered; and
    (g) details of any order known to the applicant which affects the child and is in force in the jurisdiction in which the Part I order is to be registered.

### Transmission of application for registration

**4.3**—(1) Unless it appears to the court that the Part I order is no longer in force, the sheriff clerk shall send the documents mentioned in section 27(3) of the Act to the proper officer of the court in which the Part I order is to be registered.

(2) For the purposes of section 27(3) of the Act the prescribed particulars of any variation of a Part I order which is in force shall be a certified copy of the interlocutor making any such variation.

(3) On sending an application under paragraph (1) of this rule, the sheriff clerk shall record the date and particulars of the application and the Part I order in the appropriate register.

(4)   On receiving notification from the appropriate court that the Part I order has been registered in that court under section 27(4) of the Act, the sheriff clerk shall record the date of registration in the appropriate register.

### Notification of refusal of application

**4.4**   Where the court refuses to send an application under rule 4.2 to the appropriate court on the ground that the Part I order is no longer in force, the sheriff clerk shall notify the applicant in writing of the court's decision.

### Retention of application and related documents

**4.5**   The sheriff clerk shall retain the letter of application under rule 4.2 together with any documents which accompanied it and which are not transmitted to the appropriate court under section 27(3) of the Act.

### Cancellation or variation of registered Part I order

**4.6**—(1)   Where the court revokes, recalls or varies a Part I order which it has made and which has been registered under section 27(4) of the Act, the sheriff clerk shall—

> (a)send a certified copy of the appropriate interlocutor to the proper officer of the court in which the Part I order is registered;
> (b)record the transmission of the certified copy in the appropriate register; and
> (c)record the revocation, recall or variation in the appropriate register.

(2)   On receiving notification from the court in which the Part I order is registered that the revocation, recall or variation has been recorded, the sheriff clerk shall record that fact in the appropriate register.

CHAPTER 5

MAINTENANCE ORDERS

Part I

**General**

### Interpretation

**5.1.**[1, 2, 3]   In this Chapter, unless the context otherwise requires—

"the 1950 Act" means the Maintenance Orders Act 1950;
"the 1958 Act" means the Maintenance Orders Act 1958;
"the 1972 Act" means the Maintenance Orders (Reciprocal Enforcement) Act 1972;
"the 1982 Act" means the Civil Jurisdiction and Judgments Act 1982;

---

[1] As amended by the Act of Sederunt (Child Care and Maintenance Rules) Amendment 2009 (SSI 2009/29) r.2(2) (effective March 2, 2009).
[2] As amended by the Act of Sederunt (Sheriff Court Rules) (Miscellaneous Amendments) (No.3) 2011 (SSI 2011/386) para.9 (effective November 28, 2011).
[3] As amended by the Act of Sederunt (Rules of the Court of Session and Sheriff Court Rules Amendment) (Miscellaneous) 2014 (SSI 2014/201) r.4 (effective August 1, 2014).

"2011 Regulations" means the Civil Jurisdiction and Judgments (Maintenance) Regulations 2011;

"2012 Regulations" means the International Recovery of Maintenance (Hague Convention 2007) (Scotland) Regulations 2012;

"clerk of court" means the clerk to the magistrates' court in England or Northern Ireland and, in relation to a county court in England or Northern Ireland, means the registrar of that court;

"clerk of the magistrates' court" means the clerk to the magistrates' court in England or Northern Ireland as the case may be;

"Contracting State" means a State bound by the Convention other than an EU Member State;

"the Convention" means the Convention on the International Recovery of Child Support and other forms of Family Maintenance done at The Hague on 23rd November 2007;

"Convention Maintenance Decision" means a decision, or part of a decision, to which Chapter V of the Convention applies by virtue of Article 19(1) made by—

    (a)   a court in a Contracting State; or

    (b)   a sheriff;

"Court in a Hague Convention Country" includes any judicial or administrative authority in a Hague Convention Country;

"Maintenance Decision" has the meaning given to "decision" by Article 2(1) of the Maintenance Regulation;

"Maintenance Regulation" means Council Regulation (EC) No 4/2009 of 18th December 2008 including as applied in relation to Denmark by virtue of the Agreement made on 19th October 2005 between the European Community and the Kingdom of Denmark;

"Maintenance Regulation State" in the application of any provision in relation to the Maintenance Regulation, refers to any of the Member States;

"order" includes decree;

"reciprocating country" has the meaning assigned to it by section 1 of the 1972 Act;

"the Registrar", in relation to the High Court in England, means the Senior Registrar of the principal Registry of the Family Division of the High Court in England; and

## Application

**5.2**—(1)   Part II of this Chapter shall have effect in relation to the registration in other parts of the United Kingdom of orders granted by the sheriff to which the 1950 and 1958 Acts apply and such orders are referred to in this Chapter as "outgoing orders under the 1950 Act".

(2)   Part III of this Chapter shall have effect in relation to the registration outwith the United Kingdom of orders to which the 1972 Act, or the 1972 Act as amended by any Order in Council made under Part III of the 1972 Act, applies and such orders are referred to as "outgoing orders under the 1972 Act".

(3)   Part IV of this Chapter shall have effect in relation to the registration in the sheriff court of orders made by courts in other parts of the United Kingdom to which the 1950 Act applies and such orders are referred to in this Chapter as "incoming orders under the 1950 Act".

(4)   Part V of this Chapter shall have effect in relation to the registration in the sheriff court of orders made by courts outwith the United Kingdom to which the

1972 Act, or the 1972 Act as amended by any Order in Council made under Part III of the 1972 Act, applies and such orders are referred to in this Chapter as "incoming orders under the 1972 Act".

(5)    Part VI of this Chapter shall have effect in relation to the registration in the sheriff court of orders made by courts outwith the United Kingdom to which the 1982 Act applies and such orders are referred to in this Chapter as "incoming orders under the 1982 Act".

(6)[1]    Part VII of this Chapter shall have effect in relation to a Maintenance Decision.

(7)[2]    Part VIII of this Chapter shall have effect only in relation to—

(a)    a Maintenance Decision made by a court in Denmark; and

(b)    a Maintenance Decision to which sections 2 and 3 of Chapter IV of the Maintenance Regulation apply by virtue of Article 75(2)(a) or (b) of that Regulation.

(8)[3]    Part IX of this Chapter shall have effect in relation to a Convention Maintenance Decision.

**Prescribed officer**

**5.3**—(1)    The sheriff clerk shall be—

(a)[4]    the prescribed officer for the purposes of the 1950, 1958 and 1972 Acts, the 1972 Act as amended by any Order in Council, the 1982 Act and the 2011 Regulations; and

(b)    the proper officer for the purposes of Schedules 6 and 7 to the 1982 Act (enforcement of UK judgments).

(2)    Unless otherwise provided, all communications which the prescribed officer is required to send to—

(a)    an addressee in the United Kingdom shall be sent by first class recorded delivery post; and

(b)    an addressee outwith the United Kingdom shall be sent by registered letter or the nearest equivalent which the available postal service permits.

**Maintenance Orders Register**

**5.4**—[5](1)[6]    The sheriff clerk shall maintain a Register called "the Maintenance Orders Register" for the purpose of the 1950, 1958 and 1972 Acts, the 1972 Act as amended by any Order in Council, the 1982 Act, the Maintenance Regulation and the 2012 Regulations, Part I of which shall relate to outgoing orders and Part II to incoming orders.

---

[1] As inserted by the Act of Sederunt (Sheriff Court Rules) (Miscellaneous Amendments) (No.3) 2011 (SSI 2011/386) para.9 (effective November 28, 2011).

[2] As inserted by the Act of Sederunt (Sheriff Court Rules) (Miscellaneous Amendments) (No.3) 2011 (SSI 2011/386) para.9 (effective November 28, 2011).

[3] As inserted by the Act of Sederunt (Rules of the Court of Session and Sheriff Court Rules Amendment) (Miscellaneous) 2014 (SSI 2014/201) r.4 (effective August 1, 2014).

[4] As amended by the Act of Sederunt (Sheriff Court Rules) (Miscellaneous Amendments) (No.3) 2011 (SSI 2011/386) para.9 (effective November 28, 2011).

[5] As amended by the Act of Sederunt (Sheriff Court Rules) (Miscellaneous Amendments) (No.3) 2011 (SSI 2011/386) para.9 (effective November 28, 2011).

[6] As amended by the Act of Sederunt (Rules of the Court of Session and Sheriff Court Rules Amendment) (Miscellaneous) 2014 (SSI 2014/201) r.4 (effective August 1, 2014).

(2)   The sheriff clerk shall make appropriate entries in the Maintenance Orders Register in respect of any action taken by him or notified to him in accordance with the relevant provisions, and shall keep in such manner as he considers appropriate any documents sent to him in connection with any such action.

(3)   Every entry registering a maintenance order shall specify the relevant provision including where appropriate any Order in Council under which the maintenance order in question is registered.

(4)   When a registered maintenance order is varied, revoked or cancelled, the sheriff clerk shall make an appropriate entry against the entry for the original order.

## Inspection

**5.5**—(1)   The sheriff clerk shall, on an application by—

(a)   any person entitled to, or liable to make, payments under an order in respect of which any entry has been made in the Maintenance Orders Register; or

(b)   a solicitor acting on behalf of any such person,

permit that person or his solicitor, as the case may be, to inspect any such entry and any document in his possession relating to that entry and to take copies of any such entry or document.

(2)   On an application by or on behalf of any other person, the sheriff clerk may, on being satisfied of that person's interest, grant that person or his solicitor permission to inspect or take copies of any such entry or document.

Part II

## Outgoing Orders under the 1950 Act

### Commencement of proceedings

**5.6**—(1)   Every writ by which proceedings are begun in a sheriff court having jurisdiction under or by virtue of Part I of the 1950 Act against a person residing in another part of the United Kingdom, and all parts of process (other than productions) lodged in any proceedings taken in a sheriff court under or by virtue of the 1950 Act or the 1958 Act, shall be headed "Maintenance Orders Act 1950" or as the case may be "Maintenance Orders Act 1958".

(2)   The warrant of citation upon any writ which by virtue of those Acts is to be served upon a person residing in another part of the United Kingdom shall proceed upon a period of notice of 21 days, and such warrant of citation may be signed by the sheriff clerk.

(3)   In connection with the service under section 15 of the 1950 Act (service of process) of a writ from a sheriff court the expressions "initial writ", "writ" and "summons" in the said section and in the forms contained in the Second Schedule to that Act shall include the warrant of citation relative thereto.

### Application for registration

**5.7**—(1)   An application for registration in a magistrates' court in England or Northern Ireland of an order granted by a sheriff court to which the 1950 Act applies shall be made by lodging with the sheriff clerk—

(a)   a letter of application;

(b)   an affidavit by the applicant;

(c)   a copy of that affidavit; and

(d)   a certified copy of the order.

(2)   An affidavit under this rule shall include—

(a)   the name and address of the person liable to make payments under the order;

(b)   details of any arrears due under the order and the date to which they are calculated;

(c)   the reason for the application; and

(d)   a statement that the order is not already registered under the 1950 Act.

## Transmission

**5.8**   On the grant of an application under rule 5.7, the sheriff clerk shall send to the clerk of the magistrates' court—

(a)   the affidavit of the applicant;

(b)   the certified copy of the order; and

(c)   a letter requesting registration of the order.

## Application to adduce evidence

**5.9**—(1)   An application to a sheriff court under section 22(5) of the 1950 Act to adduce evidence in connection with an order granted by that court and registered in a court in England or Northern Ireland shall be made by initial writ.

(2)   Any evidence adduced in pursuance of such an application shall be recorded in such manner as the sheriff shall direct and the record of evidence certified by the sheriff shall be the transcript or summary of the evidence adduced, and shall be signed by the deponent, together with any documentary productions referred to therein.

(3)   Where the sheriff clerk of a court in which an order was granted receives a transcript or summary of evidence connected with that order adduced, under section 22(5) of the 1950 Act, in the court where the order was registered, he shall lodge such transcript or summary in the process containing that order.

## Re-registration in the High Court

**5.10**—(1)   When an order has been registered in the magistrates' court, an application to the sheriff court for the re-registration of that order in the High Court in England under the 1958 Act shall be made by lodging with the sheriff clerk—

(a)   a letter of application;

(b)   an affidavit by the applicant;

(c)   a certified copy of that affidavit; and

(d)   a certified copy of the order.

(2)   An affidavit under this rule shall include—

(a)   the name and address of the person liable to make payments under the order;

(b)   details of any arrears due under the order and the date to which they are calculated;

(c)   the reason for the application;

(d)   the date and place of the original registration;

(e)   where the order has been re-registered, the date and place of the last re-registration and whether or not that has been cancelled, or where any of these facts is not known a statement to that effect; and

(f)   a declaration that no process remains in force for the enforcement of the registered order.

### Transmission for re-registration

**5.11** If an application under rule 5.10 is granted, the sheriff clerk shall send to the Registrar—
(a) the affidavit of the applicant; and
(b) a letter stating that the application has been granted and requesting him to take steps to have the order registered in the High Court.

### Discharge and variation

**5.12** Where an interlocutor is pronounced in the sheriff court varying or discharging an order registered under the 1950 Act or the 1958 Act, the sheriff clerk shall send to the clerk of the magistrates' court and, as the case may be, to the Registrar—
(a) a certified copy of the interlocutor; and
(b) a letter requesting the clerk of the magistrates' court and, as the case may be, the Registrar to take the appropriate action under those Acts, in accordance with the interlocutor, and to notify him of the result.

### Cancellation of registration

**5.13**—(1) An application under section 24(2) of the 1950 Act (cancellation of registration) in connection with an order granted by a sheriff court and registered in a court in England or Northern Ireland shall be made by lodging with the sheriff clerk an affidavit by the person liable to make payments under the order stating the facts on which the application is founded.

(2) Where it appears to the sheriff clerk that the applicant has ceased to reside in England or Northern Ireland, as the case may be, the sheriff clerk shall send notice to that effect to the clerk of the magistrates' court and the Registrar, as the case may be, of any court in which the order is registered.

### Part III

### Outgoing Orders under the 1972 Act

### Application for transmission of order for enforcement in a reciprocating country

**5.14**—(1) An application for the transmission of a maintenance order for enforcement in a reciprocating country shall be made by letter addressed to the sheriff clerk.

(2) There shall be lodged with any such application—
(a) a certified copy of the relevant order;
(b) a statement signed by the applicant or his solicitor of any arrears outstanding in respect of the order;
(c) a statement signed by the applicant or his solicitor giving such information as to the whereabouts of the payer as he possesses;
(d) a statement signed by the applicant or his solicitor giving such information as the applicant possesses for facilitating the identification of the payer;
(e) where available, a photograph of the payer.

## Application for transmission of order for enforcement in the Republic of Ireland

**5.15—** *[Repealed by the Act of Sederunt (Sheriff Court Rules) (Miscellaneous Amendments) (No.3) 2011 (SSI 2011/386) para.9 (effective November 28, 2011).]*

## Application for transmission of order to Hague Convention Country

**5.16—**(1)   An application for the transmission of a maintenance order to a Court in a Hague Convention Country for registration and enforcement shall be made by letter addressed to the sheriff clerk.

(2)   There shall be lodged with any such application—

    (a)   a certified copy of the relevant order;

    (b)   a statement signed by the applicant or his solicitor of any arrears outstanding in respect of that order;

    (c)   a statement signed by the applicant or his solicitor giving such information as to the whereabouts of the payer as he possesses;

    (d)   a statement signed by the applicant or his solicitor giving such information as the applicant possesses for facilitating the identification of the payer;

    (e)   where available, a photograph of the payer;

    (f)   a statement signed by the applicant or his solicitor which establishes that notice of the order was sent to the payer;

    (g)   if the payee received legal aid in the proceedings, a statement to that effect; and

    (h)   if the payer did not appear in the proceedings in which the maintenance order was made, the original or a certified true copy of a document which establishes that notice of the institution of the proceedings was served on the payer.

## Application for transmission of order for enforcement in the USA[1]

**5.16A.—**(1)   An application for the transmission of a maintenance order to the United States of America for enforcement shall be made by letter addressed to the sheriff clerk.

(2)   There shall be lodged with any such application—

    (a)   three certified copies of the maintenance order;

    (b)   a certificate of arrears signed by the applicant or his solicitor;

    (c)   a sworn statement signed by the payee—

        (i)   giving the address of the payee;

        (ii)   giving such information as is known as to the whereabouts of the payer; and

        (iii)   giving a description, so far as is known, of the nature and location of any assets of the payer available for execution; and

    (d)   a statement signed by the applicant giving such information as the applicant possesses for facilitating the identification of the payer including a photograph if available.

---

[1] As inserted by the Act of Sederunt (Child Care and Maintenance Rules) Amendment 2000 (SSI 2000/388) (effective November 20, 2000) and amended by the Act of Sederunt (Child Care and Maintenance Rules) Amendment 2009 (SSI 2009/29) r.2(3) and (4) (effective March 2, 2009).

## Service on defender in Hague Convention Country

**5.17** For the purposes of section 4(4) of the 1972 Act as applied in respect of a defender in a Hague Convention Country, service on such a defender shall be effected in accordance with the Ordinary Cause Rules.

## Service of notice of proceedings on payer residing in USA

**5.17A.**[1] Where service of a document is executed in accordance with section 5(4)(a) of the 1972 Act as applied to the United States of America, the Scottish Ministers shall obtain and lodge with the sheriff clerk a certificate by a person who is conversant with the law of the United States of America and who practises or who has practised law in that country or is a duly accredited representative of the Government of the United States of America, stating that the method of service employed is in accordance with the law of the place where service was executed.

## Provisional order made with a view to transmission to a reciprocating country

**5.18** A certificate signed by the sheriff clerk in terms of section 3(5)(c) of the 1972 Act (certificate of grounds), as read with section 4(6) thereof, shall also be signed by the sheriff.

## Evidence adduced prior to confirmation of provisional order

**5.19**—(1) Where under section 5(9) of the 1972 Act it appears to the sheriff that a provisional order ought not to have been made, the sheriff clerk shall send by first class recorded delivery a notice in Form 66 to the person on whose application the order was made.

(2) Where such a person wishes to make representations, he shall lodge with the sheriff clerk within 21 days of the date of posting of the notice a minute narrating the representations and the further evidence which he intends to adduce.

(3) On the expiry of the period of 21 days, the cause shall be enrolled before the sheriff who shall appoint a diet for the hearing of further evidence or make such other order as may be appropriate.

## Provisions in relation to intimation and entering appearance

**5.20**—(1) Where the 1972 Act provides that on intimation to a payee of the receipt by the court of a provisional order the payee is to enter appearance within a prescribed period, intimation shall be given in Form 67 and the period shall be—

(a) 21 days from the date of posting where the payee is resident in Europe; and

(b) 42 days from the date of posting where the payee is resident outside Europe.

(2) To enter appearance in terms of section 5(6) of the 1972 Act, the payee shall lodge an application—

(a) stating that he opposes confirmation of the order; and

(b) setting forth averments in answer to the case upon which the provisional order was made, supported by the appropriate pleas-in-law.

---

[1] As inserted by the Act of Sederunt (Child Care and Maintenance Rules) Amendment 2009 (SSI 2009/29) r.2(5) (effective March 2, 2009).

(3)   Where the payee enters appearance in terms of section 5(6) of the 1972 Act, the sheriff shall appoint a diet for the hearing of evidence or make such other order as may be appropriate to enable the court to proceed in accordance with the procedure and practice in ordinary civil proceedings in the sheriff court as if the application for the variation or revocation of the maintenance order had been made to it.

### Authentication of documents

**5.21**   Where the 1972 Act provides that a document is to be authenticated in a prescribed manner, it shall be authenticated by a certificate signed by the sheriff clerk declaring that the document is authentic.

### Application under section 4 or 5 of the 1972 Act

**5.22**[1]   An application for a provisional order under section 4 of the 1972 Act or an application under section 5 of that Act for variation or revocation of a maintenance order shall proceed as an ordinary cause in accordance with the terms of Chapter 33 (family actions) or 33A (civil partnership actions), as the case may be, of the Ordinary Cause Rules.

### Representations or evidence by payer residing in the USA

**5.22A.**—[2](1)   Where notices are provided in accordance with section 5(4) of the 1972 Act as applied to the United States of America, the sheriff clerk shall notify the recipients of the notices that if the payer wishes the court in Scotland to take into account any representations made by him or any evidence adduced by him or on his behalf, then such representations or evidence must be lodged with the sheriff clerk not later than 21 days before the date fixed for the hearing.

(2)   Where such representations are lodged, or such evidence is lodged, the sheriff clerk shall serve a copy of the representations or evidence—

  (a)   where the payee is represented by a solicitor, on that solicitor, by—
      (i)   personal delivery;
      (ii)   facsimile transmission;
      (iii)   first class ordinary post; or
      (iv)   delivery to a document exchange; and
  (b)   where the payee is not represented by a solicitor, on the payee, by any of the methods of service provided for in Chapter 5 of the Ordinary Cause Rules (citation, service and intimation).

### Application by payer residing in the USA for variation or revocation of order

**5.22B.**—[3](1)   Where an application is made in accordance with section 5(6) of the 1972 Act as applied to the United States of America, the sheriff clerk shall give notice of institution of the proceedings, including notice of the substance of the application, in accordance with subparagraph (2) or (3).

---

[1] As amended by the Act of Sederunt (Child Care and Maintenance Rules) Amendment 2009 (SSI 2009/29) r.2(6) (effective March 2, 2009).
[2] As inserted by the Act of Sederunt (Child Care and Maintenance Rules) Amendment 2009 (SSI 2009/29) r.2(7) (effective March 2, 2009).
[3] As inserted by the Act of Sederunt (Child Care and Maintenance Rules) Amendment 2009 (SSI 2009/29) r.2(7) (effective March 2, 2009).

(2)   Where the payee is represented by a solicitor, the document referred to in subparagraph (1) shall be served on that solicitor by—

    (a)   personal delivery;

    (b)   facsimile transmission;

    (c)   first class ordinary post; or

    (d)   delivery to a document exchange.

(3)   Where the payee is not represented by a solicitor, the document referred to in subparagraph (1) shall be served on the payee by any of the methods of service provided for in Chapter 5 of the Ordinary Cause Rules (citation, service and intimation).

### Evidence

**5.23**—(1)[1]   Where any request to take evidence is made by or on behalf of a court in terms of section 14 of the 1972 Act, or section 14 of the 1972 Act as amended by any Order in Council made under Part III of that Act, or by the Secretary of State in terms of section 38 thereof, such evidence shall be taken before a sheriff of the sheriffdom in which the witness resides and shall be—

    (a)   recorded by tape recording or other mechanical means approved by the court; or

    (b)   taken down by a shorthand writer, or where the sheriff so directs, by the sheriff,

and the extended notes of evidence certified by the sheriff shall be the notes of the evidence taken.

(2)   Where a provisional order is made under section 4 or 5 of the 1972 Act and evidence has been taken by a shorthand writer, the applicant or his solicitor shall provide the sheriff clerk with a copy of the extended notes of evidence.

### Taking of evidence at request of a court in the USA

**5.23A.**[2]   Where evidence is taken by a sheriff under section 14(1) of the 1972 Act as applied to the United States of America, rules 29.7 (citation of witnesses), 29.9 (second diligence against a witness) and 29.10 (failure of witness to attend) of the Ordinary Cause Rules shall apply in respect of the matters set out in those rules.

### Requests for the taking of evidence by a court in the USA

**5.23B.**[3]   An application made to a sheriff for the purposes of section 14(5) of the 1972 Act as applied to the United States of America shall follow as nearly as may be the procedure set out in rule 28.14 of the Ordinary Cause Rules (letters of request), subject to any modifications necessitated by that provision of the 1972 Act as so applied.

---

[1] As substituted by the Act of Sederunt (Child Care and Maintenance Rules) Amendment 2009 (SSI 2009/29) r.2(8) (effective March 2, 2009).

[2] As inserted by the Act of Sederunt (Child Care and Maintenance Rules) Amendment 2009 (SSI 2009/29) r.2(9) (effective March 2, 2009).

[3] As inserted by the Act of Sederunt (Child Care and Maintenance Rules) Amendment 2009 (SSI 2009/29) r.2(9) (effective March 2, 2009).

## Communication with courts in the USA

**5.23C.**[1]  In so far as applicable to outgoing orders under the 1972 Act to the United States of America, for the purposes of the provisions in Part I of the 1972 Act, the sheriff may communicate with a court or courts in the United States of America in such circumstances and in such manner as he thinks fit.

## Disapplication of provisions where payer resides or has assets in the USA

**5.23D.**[2]  In any case in which the payer under a maintenance order made by a court in Scotland is residing or has assets in the United States of America, none of the provisions in this Part shall apply except this rule and rules 5.16A, 5.17A, 5.21, 5.22, 5.22A, 5.22B, 5.23, 5.23A, 5.23B and 5.23C.

## Part IV

## Incoming Orders under the 1950 Act

### Registration

**5.24**—(1)  On receiving a certified copy of a maintenance order made by a court in England or Northern Ireland, the sheriff clerk shall—

   (a)   retain any certificate or affidavit sent with the certified copy of the order as to the amount of any arrears due under the order;

   (b)   endorse on the certified copy order a declaration in Form 68 and retain such certified copy order and declaration; and

   (c)   notify the clerk of the court which made the order that it has been registered.

(2)  The sheriff clerk may issue an extract of the order with the declaration thereon, and such extract shall have the same force and effect as, and may be enforced in all respects as if it was, an extract decree of the sheriff court in which the certified copy is registered.

### Variation of rate of payment

**5.25**  An application to a sheriff court under section 22(1) of the 1950 Act for variation of the rate of payment under a maintenance order made by a court in England or Northern Ireland and registered in that sheriff court shall be made by initial writ.

### Application to adduce evidence

**5.26**—(1)  An application to a sheriff court under section 22(5) of the 1950 Act to adduce evidence in connection with a maintenance order made by a court in England or Northern Ireland and registered in that sheriff court shall be made by initial writ.

---

[1] As inserted by the Act of Sederunt (Child Care and Maintenance Rules) Amendment 2009 (SSI 2009/29) r.2(9) (effective March 2, 2009).

[2] As inserted by the Act of Sederunt (Child Care and Maintenance Rules) Amendment 2009 (SSI 2009/29) r.2(9) (effective March 2, 2009).

(2)   Any evidence adduced in pursuance of such an application shall be recorded in such manner as the sheriff shall direct and the record of evidence certified by the sheriff shall be the transcript or summary of the evidence adduced.

(3)   Where the sheriff clerk of a court in which an order is registered receives a transcript or summary of evidence connected with that order adduced under section 22(5) of the 1950 Act in the court where that order was made, he shall lodge such transcript or summary in the process of any proceedings for variation of the order before the sheriff court.

## Discharge and variation

**5.27**—(1)   Where a maintenance order made by a court in England or Northern Ireland and registered under the 1950 Act in a sheriff court is varied by that sheriff court, the sheriff clerk shall give notice of the variation to the clerk of the court by which the order was made by sending him a certified copy of the interlocutor varying the order.

(2)   Where a maintenance order made by a court in England or Northern Ireland and registered in a sheriff court is discharged or varied by any court other than that sheriff court, the sheriff clerk shall on receipt of a certified copy of the order discharging or varying the registered order notify the clerk of the appropriate court that the discharge or variation has been entered in the Maintenance Orders Register.

(3)   Paragraphs (1)(a) and (b) and (2) of rule 5.24 shall apply to an order varying a registered order as they apply to the registered order.

## Cancellation of registration

**5.28**—(1)   An application under section 24(1) of the 1950 Act for the cancellation of the registration of a maintenance order made by a court in England or Northern Ireland and registered in a sheriff court shall be made by lodging with the sheriff clerk—

    (a)   an application for that purpose which shall state the date of the registration of the order; and

    (b)   a copy of the order the registration of which is sought to be cancelled.

(2)   Where under section 24(1) or (2) of the 1950 Act the sheriff clerk cancels the registration of a maintenance order, he shall—

    (a)   notify the clerk of the court by which the order was made; and

    (b)   notify the person liable to make payments under the order.

## Part V

## Incoming Orders under the 1972 Act

### Provisions in relation to intimation and entering appearance

**5.29**—(1)   Where the 1972 Act provides that on intimation to a payer of the receipt by the court of a provisional order the payer is to enter appearance within a prescribed period, intimation shall be given in Form 67 and the period shall be—

    (a)   21 days from the date of posting where the payer is resident in Europe; and

    (b)   42 days from the date of posting where the payer is resident outside Europe.

(2)   To enter appearance in terms of section 7(4) or 9(7) of the 1972 Act, the payer shall lodge an application—

(a) stating that he opposes confirmation of the order; and

(b) setting forth averments in answer to the case upon which the provisional order was made, supported by appropriate pleas-in-law.

(3) Where the payer enters appearance in terms of section 7(4) of the 1972 Act, the sheriff shall appoint a diet for the hearing of evidence or make such other order as may be appropriate to enable the court to proceed in accordance with the procedure and practice in ordinary civil proceedings in the sheriff court as if an application for a maintenance order against the payer had been made to it.

(4) Where the payer enters appearance in terms of section 9(7) of the 1972 Act, the sheriff shall appoint a diet for the hearing of evidence or make such other order as may be appropriate to enable the court to proceed in accordance with the procedure and practice in ordinary civil proceedings in the sheriff court as it an application for the variation of the maintenance order had been made to it.

### Authentication of documents

**5.30** Where the 1972 Act provides that a document is to be authenticated in a prescribed manner, it shall be authenticated by a certificate signed by the sheriff clerk declaring that the document is authentic.

### Application under sections 9 and 20 of the 1972 Act

**5.31**—(1) An application under section 9 of the 1972 Act (variation and revocation of maintenance orders) for variation or revocation of a maintenance order shall be brought as an ordinary cause.

(2) An application under section 20 of the 1972 Act (restriction on enforcement of arrears) for leave to enforce the payment of any arrears due under a maintenance order registered in Scotland shall be made by lodging a minute in the process.

### Information to be provided where payer has ceased to reside in Scotland

**5.32**—(1) Where the registration of an order is cancelled in the circumstances set out in section 10(2) of the 1972 Act, the payee or his solicitor shall provide the sheriff clerk so far as is possible with information to enable the sheriff clerk to prepare the certificate and statement referred to in section 10(7) of the 1972 Act.

(2) Where the sheriff clerk is required in terms of section 32(1) of the 1972 Act (transfer of orders) to send to the Secretary of State the related documents specified in section 32(8) of that Act, the payee or his solicitor shall provide the sheriff clerk so far as possible with information to enable the sheriff clerk to prepare the certificate and statement to be included among those documents.

### Evidence

**5.33** Where a provisional order is made under section 9 of the 1972 Act and evidence has been taken by a shorthand writer, the applicant or his solicitor shall provide the sheriff clerk with a copy of the extended notes of evidence.

### Intimation of registration of, or of decision not to register, an order made in the Republic of Ireland

**5.34** *[Repealed by the Act of Sederunt (Sheriff Court Rules) (Miscellaneous Amendments) (No.3) 2011 (SSI 2011/386) para.9 (effective November 28, 2011).]*

## Application to set aside registration of, or to set aside decision not to register, an order made in the Republic of Ireland

**5.35** *[Repealed by the Act of Sederunt (Sheriff Court Rules) (Miscellaneous Amendments) (No.3) 2011 (SSI 2011/386) para.9 (effective November 28, 2011).]*

## Intimation of registration of, or refusal to register, an order made in a Hague Convention Country

**5.36**—(1) Intimation of the registration of a maintenance order in terms of section 6 of the 1972 Act as applied to an order made in a Hague Convention Country shall be given by the sheriff clerk—

    (a)   to the payer, by sending an intimation in Form 72; and

    (b)   to the payee, by sending a notice in Form 70.

(2) Notice of a refusal to register a maintenance order on any of the grounds set out in section 6(5), (6) or (7) of the 1972 Act as applied to an order made in a Hague Convention Country shall be given by the sheriff clerk to the payee, by sending a notice in Form 71.

## Application to set aside registration of, or to set aside decision not to register, an order made in a Hague Convention Country

**5.37** Application to the court under section 6(9) or (12) of the 1972 Act as applied to an order made in a Hague Convention Country shall be made by summary application setting out the grounds of the application.

## Taking of evidence at the request of a court in the USA

**5.37A.**[1] Where evidence is taken under section 38(2) of the 1972 Act in consequence of a request made by a court in the United States of America under section 38(1) of that Act, rules 29.7 (citation of witnesses), 29.9 (second diligence against a witness) and 29.10 (failure of witness to attend) of the Ordinary Cause Rules shall apply in respect of the matters set out in those rules.

## Communication with courts in the USA

**5.37B.**[2] In so far as applicable to incoming orders under the 1972 Act from the United States of America, for the purposes of the provisions in Part I of the 1972 Act, the sheriff may communicate with a court or courts in the United States of America in such circumstances and in such manner as he thinks fit.

## Disapplication of provisions in respect of orders made by courts in the USA

**5.37C.**[3] In any case in which a maintenance order is made by a court in the United States of America which falls to be dealt with under sections 6 to 11 of the

---

[1] As inserted by the Act of Sederunt (Child Care and Maintenance Rules) Amendment 2009 (SSI 2009/29) r.2(10) (effective March 2, 2009).

[2] As inserted by the Act of Sederunt (Child Care and Maintenance Rules) Amendment 2009 (SSI 2009/29) r.2(10) (effective March 2, 2009).

[3] As inserted by the Act of Sederunt (Child Care and Maintenance Rules) Amendment 2009 (SSI 2009/29) r.2(10) (effective March 2, 2009).

1972 Act as those provisions are applied to the United States of America, none of the provisions in this Part shall apply except this rule and rules 5.30, 5.32, 5.37A and 5.37B.

## Part VI

### Incoming Orders under the 1982 Act

**Applications under section 5A of the 1982 Act**

**5.38**—[1](1) Applications under section 5A of the 1982 Act shall be in writing addressed to the Scottish Ministers, signed by the applicant, or a solicitor or professional person qualified to act in such matters in the Contracting State of origin on his behalf, and shall specify—

(a) an address within Scotland for service on the applicant;

(b) the usual and last known address of the person against whom judgment was granted;

(c) the place where the applicant seeks to enforce the judgment;

(d) whether at the date of the application the judgment has been satisfied in whole or in part;

(e) whether interest is recoverable under the judgment in accordance with the law of the country in which it was granted and, if so, the rate of interest and the date from which interest became due; and

(f) whether the time for bringing an appeal against the judgment has expired without an appeal having been brought or whether an appeal has been brought against the judgment and is pending or has been finally disposed of.

(2) An application under paragraph (1) shall be accompanied by—

(a) a copy of the judgment authenticated by the court which made the order;

(b) documents which establish that, according to the law of the country in which the judgment has been given, the judgment is enforceable and has been served;

(c) in the case of a judgment given in default, documents which establish that the party in default was served with the documents instituting the proceedings;

(d) where appropriate, a document showing that the applicant is in receipt of legal aid in the country in which the judgment was given; and

(e) where the judgment or any of the documents specified in sub-paragraphs (b) to (d) are in a language other than English, a translation into English certified by a person qualified to do so in one of the Contracting States.

(3) Where the applicant does not produce a document required under paragraph (2)(c) or (d), the sheriff clerk may—

(a) fix a time within which the document is to be produced;

(b) accept an equivalent document; or

(c) dispense with production of the document.

---

[1] Heading and section as amended by the Act of Sederunt (Child Care and Maintenance Rules) Amendment (No.2) 2009 (SSI 2009/449) r.2 (effective January 1, 2010) and the Act of Sederunt (Sheriff Court Rules) (Miscellaneous Amendments) (No.3) 2011 (SSI 2011/386) para.9 (effective November 28, 2011).

**Address of applicant's solicitor for service**

**5.39**    Where the sheriff clerk is informed by a solicitor practising in Scotland that he is acting on behalf of the applicant, the business address of the solicitor shall thereafter be treated as the address for service on the applicant.

**Notice of determination of application**

**5.40**    Immediately after determination of an application for the recognition or enforcement of an order, the sheriff clerk shall serve, in accordance with the Ordinary Cause Rules so far as not inconsistent with the terms of this Chapter, a notice in Form 73 on the applicant and on the person against whom enforcement is sought.

**Appeal by party against whom enforcement is authorised**

**5.41**—(1)    Where enforcement of a maintenance order is authorised to any extent, the party against whom enforcement is authorised may appeal by way of summary application to the sheriff against the decision of the sheriff clerk—

(a)    within one month from the date of service of the notice under rule 5.40; or

(b)    if the person against whom enforcement is sought is domiciled in a Contracting State other than the United Kingdom, within two months from the date of service of such notice.

(2)    The determination of the sheriff of such a summary application shall be subject to a final appeal on a point of law to the Inner House of the Court of Session in accordance with the Ordinary Cause Rules.

**Appeal by applicant**

**5.42**—(1)    Where the application for enforcement of a maintenance order is refused, the applicant may appeal by way of summary application to the sheriff within one month from the date of service of the notice under rule 5.40.

(2)    The determination of the sheriff of such a summary application shall be subject to a final appeal on a point of law to the Inner House of the Court of Session in accordance with the Ordinary Cause Rules.

**Enforcement of registered order**

**5.43**[1]    The applicant may obtain an extract of a registered order and proceed to arrest in execution, to intimate the order (for the purposes of section 54(1) of the Debtors (Scotland) Act 1987), to inhibit and to charge and attach thereon, but may not proceed to an action of furthcoming in respect of an arrestment, serve a current maintenance arrestment schedule, make application for a conjoined arrestment order, proceed to adjudication in respect of inhibition or auction in respect of an attachment until the time for appeal against the determination of the sheriff under rules 5.41 or 5.42 has elapsed and any appeal has been disposed of.

Part VII[2]

---

[1] As amended by SSI 2002/560, Sch.3, para.7.

[2] As inserted by the Act of Sederunt (Sheriff Court Rules) (Miscellaneous Amendments) (No.3) 2011 (SSI 2011/386) para.9 (effective November 28, 2011).

## Maintenance Decisions under the Maintenance Regulation

### Application for transmission of a Maintenance Decision to another Maintenance Regulation State

**5.44.**—(1) This rule applies to applications under Article 40 of the Maintenance Regulation to enforce a Maintenance Decision of a sheriff in another Maintenance Regulation State.

(2) On receipt of an application in the form of a letter, the sheriff clerk will provide the applicant with a certified copy of the Maintenance Decision and a completed extract from the decision in the form of Annex I or II to the Maintenance Regulation as the case may be.

(3) The letter must be addressed to the sheriff clerk and must include—

    (a) the name and National Insurance number (if known) of the parties to the proceedings;

    (b) the date, or approximate date, of the proceedings in which the Maintenance Decision was made and the nature of those proceedings;

    (c) the Maintenance Regulation State in which the application for recognition or enforcement has been made or is to be made; and

    (d) the postal address of the applicant.

### Enforcement of a Maintenance Decision made by a court in a Maintenance Regulation State other than Denmark

**5.45.** The "enforcing court" under paragraph 4(2) of Schedule 1 to the 2011 Regulations, means the sheriff court having jurisdiction in the matter in accordance with Schedule 8 to the 1982 Act.

## Part VIII[1]

## Recognition and Enforcement of Maintenance Decisions made by Courts in Denmark etc.

### Recognition and enforcement of a Maintenance Decision made in Denmark etc.

**5.46.** The "registering court" under paragraph 6(2) of Schedule 1 to the 2011 Regulations, means the sheriff court having jurisdiction in the matter in accordance with Schedule 8 to the 1982 Act.

### Intimation of registration of, or refusal to register, a Maintenance Decision made in Denmark etc.

**5.47.**—(1) Intimation of the registration of a Maintenance Decision in accordance with Article 31 of the Maintenance Regulation shall be given by the sheriff clerk—

    (a) to the payer, by sending an intimation in Form 73A; and

    (b) to the payee, by sending a notice in Form 73B.

(2) Notice of a refusal to register a Maintenance Decision shall be given by the sheriff clerk to the payee, by sending a notice in Form 73C.

---

[1] As inserted by the Act of Sederunt (Sheriff Court Rules) (Miscellaneous Amendments) (No.3) 2011 (SSI 2011/386) para.9 (effective November 28, 2011).

**Application to set aside registration of, or to set aside decision not to register, a Maintenance Decision made in Denmark etc.**

**5.48.** An application under Article 32 of the Maintenance Regulation shall be by summary application setting out the grounds of the application.

**Sist of proceedings**

**5.49.** An application under Article 35 of the Maintenance Regulation shall be made by motion.

Part IX

**Recognition and Enforcement of Convention Maintenance Decisions**

**Application for transmission of Convention Maintenance Decision to a Contracting State**

**5.50**—(1)   This rule applies to an application under Article 10(1) of the Convention to enforce a Convention Maintenance Decision of a sheriff in another Contracting State.

(2)   On receipt of an application in the form of a letter, the sheriff clerk must provide the applicant with a certified copy of the Convention Maintenance Decision.

(3)   The letter must be addressed to the sheriff clerk and must include—

    (a)   the name and National Insurance number (if known) of the parties to the proceedings;

    (b)   the date, or approximate date, of the proceedings in which the Convention Maintenance Decision was made and the nature of those proceedings;

    (c)   the Contracting State in which the application for recognition or enforcement has been made or is to be made; and

    (d)   the postal address of the applicant.

**Intimation of registration of, or refusal to register, a Convention Maintenance Decision**

**5.51**—(1)   Intimation of the registration of a Convention Maintenance Decision in accordance with Article 23 of the Convention shall be given by the sheriff clerk—

    (a)   to the payer, by sending an intimation in Form 73D; and

    (b)   to the payee, by sending a notice in Form 73E.

(2)   Notice of a refusal to register a Convention Maintenance Decision shall be given by the sheriff clerk to the payee, by sending a notice in Form 73F.

CHAPTER 6

APPLICATIONS UNDER THE SOCIAL SECURITY ADMINISTRATION ACT 1992

**Interpretation**

**6.1**   In this Chapter "the Act" means the Social Security Administration Act 1992 and, unless the context otherwise requires, expressions used in this Chapter which are also used in that Act shall have the meaning assigned to them by the Act.

## Applications under section 106 of the Act

**6.2**—(1)   An application to the sheriff under section 106(1) of the Act (recovery of expenditure on benefit from person liable for maintenance) shall be by summary application.

(2)   Where, in such an application, a sum is craved which represents or includes a personal allowance element, that element shall be identified in the application.

## Transfer of rights under section 107 of the Act

**6.3**—(1)   The sheriff clerk, on receiving notice from the Secretary of State of a transfer of rights to an order by virtue of section 107(3) or (8) of the Act, shall endorse on the interlocutor sheet a certificate in Form 74.

(2)   Where, following a transfer by virtue of section 107(3) or (8) of the Act, the dependent parent or the Secretary of State requests an extract of the order originally granted, the sheriff clerk shall issue an extract with a certified copy of the latest certificate referred to in paragraph (1) endorsed on it.

## Notice to Secretary of State under section 108(5) of the Act

**6.4**   The notice required to be given to the Secretary of State by the sheriff clerk under section 108(5) of the Act (notice of application to vary etc. a maintenance order), as read with regulation 3 of the Income Support (Liable Relatives) Regulations 1990, shall—

    (a)   be in writing;

    (b)   specify any date assigned for the hearing of the application;

    (c)   be accompanied by a copy of the application; and

    (d)   be sent by recorded delivery post.

## Notice to Secretary of State of making of maintenance order

**6.5**   Where an order granted by the sheriff in favour of the Secretary of State under section 106(2) of the Act has been transferred to the dependent parent in accordance with section 107(3) of the Act and a maintenance order is subsequently granted by the sheriff in favour of the dependent relative, the sheriff clerk shall forthwith notify the Secretary of State in writing and by recorded delivery post of the granting of the maintenance order.

SCHEDULE 1

**Rule 1.2(3)**

FORM 1

Rule 2.5(1)

APPLICATION FOR AN ORDER DECLARING A CHILD FREE FOR ADOPTION UNDER SECTION 18 OF THE ADOPTION (SCOTLAND) ACT 1978

[A.B. (address)], Petitioner

[or serial number where allocated]

For an order in relation to the child, CD.

([Full Name])...............

([Date of Birth])...............

[(Address or serial number where allocated]])...............

605

The Petitioner craves the court [(1)] to make an order declaring the child, CD., free for adoption; and (2) to dispense with the agreement [or consent] of......... on the ground that..............

The following documents are produced herewith:

a. An extract of the entry in the Register of Births, relating to the child;
b. *Consent of ([name and address]) to the making of this application;
c. *Consent by the child dated
d. *Adoption agency report dated

Signed .........
[designation].........
Date .........

*Delete as appropriate

## FORM 2

Rule 2.6(1)

### FORM OF PARENTAL AGREEMENT UNDER SECTION 18(1)(a) OF THE ADOPTION (SCOTLAND) ACT 1978

In the petition by (adoption agency, name and address)............... for an order declaring the child—...............(full name of child)..........free for adoption,..........

I, (name, address)............... confirm that I am the mother/father/guardian of the child. I fully understand that on the making of an order under section 18 of the Adoption (Scotland) Act 1978 any parental responsibility or right which I have at present relating to the child vests in the petitioners and that the effect of an adoption order will be to deprive me of these parental responsibilities or rights permanently. I freely agree generally and unconditionally to the making of an adoption order in relation to the child.

I have signed this agreement at (place of signing)............... on the.......... day of......... Nineteen hundred and ninety.......... years.

(Signature) ...............

This agreement was signed in the presence of:—...............

(Signature of reporting officer or other person authorised)...............

Full name...............

Address...............

## FORM 3

Rule 2.6(1)

### FORM OF PARENTAL CONSENT UNDER SECTION 18(2) OF THE ADOPTION (SCOTLAND) ACT 1978

In the petition by (adoption agency, name and address)............... for an order declaring the child—...............(full name of child)..........free for adoption,...............

I, (name, address)............... confirm that I am the mother/father/guardian of the child. I fully understand that on the making of an order under section 18 of the Adoption (Scotland) Act 1978 any parental responsibility or right which I have at present relating to the child vests in the petitioners and that the effect of an adoption order will be to extinguish these parental responsibilities or rights. I freely consent, generally and unconditionally to the making of an application to the court for an order declaring the child free for adoption.

I have signed this consent at [place].......... on the.......... day of.......... Nineteen hundred and ninety.......... years.

(Signature) ...............

This consent was signed in the presence of:—...............

(Signature of reporting officer or other person authorised) ...............

Full name...............

Address...............

*delete as appropriate.

FORM 4

Rules 2.6(1) and 2.23(1)

## FORM OF CONSENT UNDER SECTION 12(8) OR 18(8) OF THE ADOPTION (SCOTLAND) ACT 1978

in the

petition by

(Name and address).......... Petitioner..............

I, (full name of child) confirm that I understand the nature and effect of any order declaring me free for adoption/adoption order for which application is made. I hereby consent to the making of such an order in the petitioner's favour in respect of myself.

I have signed this consent at (place of signing).................... on the.......... day of.......... Nineteen hundred and.......... years.

(Signature)...............

This consent was signed in the presence of:—...............

(Signature of reporting officer or other person authorised) ...............

Full name...............

Address...............

FORM 5

Rules 2.10(1) and 2.13(3)

## DECLARATION UNDER SECTION 18(6) OR SECTION 19(4) OF THE ADOPTION (SCOTLAND) ACT 1978

In the petition by (adoption agency, name and address)............... for an order declaring the child [full name]............... free for adoption,..........

I/We,............... being the............... of the child hereby declare that I/we prefer not to be involved in future questions concerning the adoption of the child.

In witness whereof I/we have signed this declaration on the.......... day of.......... Nineteen hundred and ninety...........

Signature...............

Signature...............

Signed in the presence of...............

(Signature)...............

Full name...............

Designation.......... and Reporting Officer

Address...............

### FOR OFFICIAL USE ONLY

The foregoing declaration was received at the Sheriff Clerk's Office,..........

on.......... 19.........., and has been duly entered in the Adoption Register of that court.

Signature ..........

Sheriff Clerk Depute

FORM 6

Rule 2.10(5)

## WITHDRAWAL OF DECLARATION UNDER SECTION 18(6) OR SECTION 19(4) OF THE ADOPTION (SCOTLAND) ACT 1978

In the petition by (adoption agency, name and address).......... for an order declaring the child [full name]............... free for adoption,...............

I/We,............... being the (*insert relationship to the child*)............... of the child hereby withdraw the declaration dated (*insert date of declaration*) that I/we prefer not to be involved in future questions concerning the adoption of the child.

I/we have signed this withdrawal of declaration on the.......... day of.......... Nineteen hundred and ninety...........

Signature ...............
Signature ...............
.....................

FOR OFFICIAL USE ONLY

The foregoing withdrawal of declaration was received at the Sheriff Clerk's Office, on 19.........., and has been duly entered in the Adoption Register of that court and intimation of the withdrawal made to the Local Authority.

Signature ..........
Sheriff Clerk Depute

## FORM 7

Rules 2.11(2) and 2.28(3) and (4)

### FORM OF INTIMATION OF DIET OF HEARING UNDER SECTION 12 OR SECTION 18 OF THE ADOPTION (SCOTLAND) ACT 1978

To:...............

(Full name and address of person to whom this intimation is to be sent)..........

Notice is given that a hearing will take place at (Name of sheriff court) Sheriff Court (Full address of court) on.......... (date) at.......... (time) in relation to the child (full name of child as given in the birth certificate)

when the court will consider an application for an order declaring the child free for adoption [or an application for adoption of the child].

You do not need to attend this hearing if you do not wish to be heard by the court.

If you do not attend this hearing the court may make an order as noted above.

Signature ...............
Designation...............
Date...............

## FORM 8

Rule 2.15(1)

### APPLICATION TO REVOKE AN ORDER FREEING A CHILD FOR ADOPTION UNDER SECTION 20(1) OF THE ADOPTION (SCOTLAND) ACT 1978

MINUTE

by

.....................

[full name, address]
in relation to the child

.....................

[full name and date of birth]

The minuter craves the court to revoke the order declaring the child free for adoption on the ground that he/she wishes to resume parental responsibilities and rights and condescends as follows:

1. An order freeing the child for adoption was made on...........
2. More than 12 months have elapsed since the child was freed for adoption.
3. No adoption order has been made in respect of the child.
4. The child at present resides at.......... and does not have his home with a person with whom he had been placed for adoption.
5. The minuter makes the following proposals for the future well-being of the child:—

Signed ..........
[designation]
Date ..........

## FORM 9

Rule 2.19(1)

APPLICATION (FOR LEAVE OF COURT) TO PLACE CHILD FOR ADOPTION UNDER SECTION 20(2) OF THE ADOPTION (SCOTLAND) ACT 1978

MINUTE

by

....................

[full name, address]

in relation to the child

....................

[full name and date of birth]

residing at present at...............

The minuters crave leave of the court to place the child for adoption and condescend as follows:

a. An order in terms of section 18 of the Adoption (Scotland) Act 1978 declaring the child free for adoption was made by the court on.......... 19.........., in a petition by the minuters.

b. An application to revoke the aforesaid order was lodged on.......... 19..........,by and that application for revocation has not yet been determined by the court.

c. [Set out here the circumstances justifying the placing of the child]

Date ..........

Signature ..........

[designation]

FORM 10

Rule 2.20

FURTHER APPLICATION BY FORMER PARENT TO REVOKE AN ORDER FREEING A CHILD FOR ADOPTION UNDER SECTION 20(5) OF THE ADOPTION (SCOTLAND) ACT 1978

MINUTE

by

....................

[full name, address]

in relation to the child

....................

[full name and address] born on [date of birth]

The minuter craves leave of the court to make this further application on the ground that:—

[narrate the change in circumstances or other proper reason for application]..........

The minuter craves the court to revoke the order declaring the child free for adoption on the ground that he wishes to resume parental responsibilities and rights and condescends as follows:

a. An order freeing the child for adoption was made on..........

b. An application to the court to revoke the order was made on.........., but was refused on...........

c. More than 12 months have elapsed since the child was freed for adoption.

d. No adoption order has been made in respect of the child.

e. The child at present resides at .......... and does not have his home with a person with whom he has been placed for adoption.

f. The minuter makes the following proposals for the future well-being of the child:—

Date..........

Signature..........

[designation]

FORM 11

Rule 2.21(1)
PETITION FOR ADOPTION ORDER UNDER SECTION 12 OF THE ADOP-
TION (SCOTLAND) ACT 1978
PETITION OF

[A.B., full name]...............
[and (full name of spouse)...............
Maiden surname...............
Any previous married surname]...............
[Address]...............

For authority to adopt the child

[Full name of child as shown on birth certificate], born on...............
[Child's date of birth]...............
[Child's present address]...............

The petitioner(s) crave(s) the court [(1)] to make an adoption order in his/her/
their favour under section 12 of the Adoption (Scotland) Act 1978, in relation to the
child [; and to dispense with the agreement [or consent] of.......... on the ground
that.......... ] and condescends as follows:

1.[1]>

a.  The petitioner(s) is/are domiciled in.......... and reside(s) at.......... [or the
male/female petitioner is domiciled in.......... and both petitioners reside
at.......... ].

b.  The occupation(s) of the petitioner(s) is/are.......... .

c.  The petitioner(s) is/are married [or unmarried or widow or widower]. (If
married, state whether spouse resides with, or apart from, the petitioner.)

d.  The petitioner(s) is/are [respectively].......... [and].......... years of age.

e.  The petitioner(s) has/have resident with him/her/them the following persons,
namely..........

f.  The child was received into the home of the petitioners on (date).

g.  The child has continuously had his home with the petitioner(s) since the date
shown above.

h.  *Arrangements for placing the child in the care of the petitioner(s) were
made by (give full name and address of the agency or authority or person
making such arrangement) [*and therefore notification in terms of section
22(1) of the Adoption (Scotland) Act 1978 is not required].

i.  The petitioner(s) notified (give name of local authority notified) of his/their
intention to apply for an adoption order in relation to the child on (date).

j.  An order freeing the child for adoption was made at.......... Sheriff Court on
(date).......... [or an order declaring the child free for adoption has not been
made].

k.  No reward or payment has been given or received by the petitioner(s) for or
of in consideration of the adoption of the child or the giving of consent to the
making of an adoption order.

l.  *Each parent or guardian of the child has consented under section 20(1)
(advance consent to adoption: England and Wales) of the Adoption and
Children Act 2002 and has not withdrawn that consent.

m.  *By notice under section 20(4)(a) (notice that information about application
for adoption order not required: England and Wales) of the Adoption and

---

[1] As amended by the Act of Sederunt (Child Care and Maintenance Rules 1997) (Amendment) (Adoption and Children Act 2002) 2006 (SSI 2006/411) (effective August 18, 2006).

Children Act 2002 (*name of parent or guardian*) [and (*name of parent or guardian*] stated that he [or she or they] did not wish to be informed of any application for an adoption order and that statement has not been withdrawn.

n.  *The child has been placed for adoption by an adoption agency within the meaning of section 2(1) (adoption agencies in England and Wales) of the Adoption and Children Act 2002 with the petitioner(s) and the child was placed for adoption [*under section 19(1) (placing children with parental consent: England and Wales) of that Act with the consent of each parent or guardian and the consent of the mother was given when the child was at least six weeks old] [*under an order made under section 21(1) (placement orders: England and Wales) of that Act and the child was at least six weeks old when that order was made].

(*Delete as appropriate)

2.

a.  The child is.......... years of age, having been born on the.......... day of.......... 19.......... , at.......... in the County of..............

b.  The child is not and never has been married and is male/female.

c.  The child's natural mother is (full name and address).

d.  *The child's natural father is (full name and address).

e.  *Paternity of the child has not been admitted or established by decree of any court.

(*Delete either (d) or (e) as appropriate)

f.  The child is of British/or.......... nationality.

g.  The child is entitled to the following property, namely..........

h.  The child has the following tutors, curators or guardians. (Either give full names and addresses or delete the paragraph if it does not apply.)..........

3. .......... is/are liable to contribute to the support of the child.

4. The child has not been the subject of an adoption order or of a petition for an adoption order save that..............

5. The petitioner(s) is/are prepared to undertake, if any order is made on this petition, to make the said child the following provisions, namely—..............

6. There is lodged along with this application the following documents

(i)  extract birth certificate relating to the child

(ii)  extract marriage certificate relating to the petitioner(s)

(Note: this need be lodged only in the case of a joint application by spouses)

(iii)  medical certificate relating to the health of the male petitioner

(iv)  medical certificate relating to the health of the female petitioner

(Note: medical certificate need not be produced where either the petitioner or one of the joint petitioners is a parent of the child)

(v)  *agreement to the adoption by the child's natural mother

(vi)  *agreement to the adoption by the child's natural father

(vii)  *consent to the adoption by the child

(viii)  *consent to the adoption by the tutor or curator

(ix)  *extract of the order freeing the child for adoption

(x)  *acknowledgement by local authority of letter by petitioner(s) intimating intention to apply for adoption order

(xi)  *report by local authority in terms of section 22(2) of the Adoption (Scotland) Act 1978

(xii)  *report by the adoption agency in terms of section 23 of the Adoption (Scotland) Act 1978

(xiii)  *any other document not referred to above.

(*Delete as appropriate)

7.......... have taken part in the arrangements for placing the child in the care of the petitioner(s)—

The petitioner(s) crave(s) the court to dispense with intimation and to order notice of this petition to be served on such persons, if any, as the court may think proper, and thereafter, on resuming consideration hereon, to make an adoption order in favour of the petitioner(s) under section 12 of the Adoption (Scotland) Act 1978 on such terms and conditions (if any) as the court may think fit, and to direct the Registrar General for Scotland to make an entry regarding the adoption in the Adopted Children Register in the form prescribed by him, giving.......... as the forename(s), and the surname of the adopter(s) as the surname of.......... in the form; and further, upon proof to the satisfaction of the court in the course of the proceedings to follow hereon, that (name of child).......... was born on the.......... day of.......... in the year Nineteen hundred and.......... and is identical with the.......... to whom any entry numbered.......... and made on the.......... day of.......... in the year 19.........., in the Register of Births for the Registration District of.......... in the.......... relates, to direct the said Registrar General to cause such birth entry to be marked with the word "adopted" and to include the abovementioned date of birth in the entry recording the adoption in the manner indicated in the Schedule to the said Act.......... and to pronounce such other or further orders or directions upon such matters, including the expenses of this petition, as the court may think fit.

..............
Signature of male petitioner
..............
Signature of female petitioner
or
..............
Signature of solicitor with designation and address
..............
..............

FORM 12

Rule 2.21(1)

## PETITION FOR AN ORDER UNDER SECTION 49 OF THE ADOPTION (SCOTLAND) ACT 1978

PETITION OF..............
[A.B. full name]..............
[and (full name of spouse)..............
Maiden surname..............
Previous married surname]..............

For an order vesting in him/her/them the parental rights and responsibilities relating to the child..........

[Full name of child as shown on birth certificate], born on..............
[Child's date of birth]..............
[Child's present address]..............

1. The petitioner(s) crave(s) the court [(1)] to make an order under section 49 of the Adoption (Scotland) Act 1978 vesting in him/her/them the parental rights and responsibilities relating to the child [; and to dispense with the agreement [or consent] of.......... on the ground that..........] and condescends as follows:

   a.   The petitioner(s) is/are domiciled in..........and reside(s) at..........
   b.   The occupation(s) of the petitioner(s) is/are..............
   c.   The petitioner(s) is/are married [or unmarried or widow or widower]. (If married, state whether spouse resides with, or apart from, the petitioner)..........

   d.   The petitioner(s) is/are [respectively].......... [and].......... years of age
   e.   The petitioner(s) has/have resident with him/her/them the following persons, namely.........
   f.   The child was received into the home of the petitioners on (date)..........
   g.   The child has continuously had his home with the petitioner(s) since the date shown above
   h.   *Arrangements for placing the child in the care of the petitioner(s) were made by (give full name and address of agency or authority or person making such arrangements) and therefore notification in terms of section 22(1) of the Adoption (Scotland) Act 1978 is not required
   i.   *The petitioner(s) notified (give name of local authority notified) of his/her/their intention to apply for an adoption order in relation to the child on (date)..........

(*Delete as appropriate)

   j.   An order freeing the child for adoption was made at.......... Sheriff Court on (date) [or an order declaring the child free for adoption has not been made]..........
   k.   No reward or payment has been given or received by the petitioner(s) for or in consideration of the adoption fo the child or the giving of consent to the making of an adoption order

2.

   a.   The child is.......... years of age, having been born on the.......... day of 19.........., at.......... in the County of..............
   b.   The child is not and never has been married and is male/female
   c.   The child's natural mother is.............. (full name and address)
   d.   *The child's natural father is.............. (full name and address)

OR

   e.   *Paternity of the child has not been admitted or established by decree of any court

(*Delete either (d) or (e) as appropriate)

   f.   The child is of British/or.......... nationality
   g.   The child is entitled to the following property, namely..............
   h.   The child has the following tutors, curators or guardians. (Either give full names and addresses or delete the paragraph if it does not apply)

3. .......... is/are liable to contribute to the support of the child.

4. The child has not been the subject of an adoption order or of a petition for an adoption order save that..............

5. The petitioner(s) is/are prepared to undertake, if any order is made on this petition, to make for the said child the following provisions, namely:—..............

6. There is lodged along with this application the following documents—

   (i)   extract birth certificate relating to the child
   (ii)   extract marriage certificate relating to the petitioner(s)

(Note: this need be lodged only in the case of a joint application by spouses)

   (iii)   medical certificate relating to the health of the male petitioner
   (iv)   medical certificate relating to the health of the female petitioner

(Note: medical certificate need not be produced where either the petitioner or one of the joint petitioners is a parent of the child)

   (v)   *agreement to the adoption by the child's natural mother
   (vi)   *agreement to the adoption by the child's natural father
   (vii)   *consent to the adoption by the child
   (viii)   *consent to the adoption by the tutor or curator
   (ix)   *extract of the order freeing the child for adoption

(x) *acknowledgement by local authority of letter by petitioner(s) intimating intention to apply for adoption order

(xi) *report by local authority in terms of section 22(2) of the Adoption (Scotland) Act 1978

(xii) *report by the adoption agency in terms of section 23 of the Adoption (Scotland) Act 1978

(xiii) *an affidavit by.......... who is conversant with the law of adoption of.......... and has practised law as a.......... [or represents that country as (state capacity).......... in the United Kingdom]

(*Delete where appropriate)

7. .......... have taken part in the arrangements for placing the child in the care of the petitioner(s)—

The petitioner(s) crave(s) the court to dispense with intimation and to order notice of this petition to be served on such persons, if any, as the court may think proper, and thereafter, on resuming consideration hereon, to make an adoption order in favour of the petitioner(s) under the Adoption (Scotland) Act 1978 section 49, vesting in the petitioners the parental responsibilities and rights relating to (name of child) on such terms and conditions (if any) as the court may think fit, to authorise removal of the child for the purpose of adoption under the laws of..........; to find the petitioners entitled to the custody of the child pending such adoption and to direct the Registrar General for Scotland to make an entry regarding the order in the Adopted Children Register in the form prescribed by him, giving.......... as the forename(s), and the surname of the adopters as the surname of.......... in the form; and further, upon proof to the satisfaction of the court in the course of the proceedings to follow hereon, that the child.......... was born on the.......... day of.......... in the year Nineteen hundred and.......... and is identical with the.......... to whom any entry numbered.......... and made on the.......... day of.......... in the year 19.........., in the Register of Births for the Registration District of.......... in the.......... relates, to direct the said Registrar General to cause such birth entry to be marked with the words "proposed foreign adoption" and to include the abovementioned date of birth in the entry recording the order in the manner indicated in the Schedule to the said Act; and to pronounce such other or further orders or directions upon such matters, including the expenses of this petition, as the court may think fit.

..............
Signature of male petitioner or agent

..............
Signature of female petitioner or agent

or

..............
Signature of solicitor with designation and address

..............

## FORM 13

Rule 2.23(1)

## FORM OF PARENTAL AGREEMENT UNDER SECTION 16(1)(b)(i) OF THE ADOPTION (SCOTLAND) ACT 1978[1]

In the petition relating to the adoption of...............

(Insert the full name of the child as it is given in the birth certificate)

to which petition the court has assigned the serial number..........

---

[1] As amended by the Act of Sederunt (Child Care and Maintenance Rules 1997) (Amendment) (Adoption and Children Act 2002) 2006 (SSI 2006/411) (effective August 18, 2006).

I, (name and addess)...............
confirm that I am the mother/father/guardian of the child. I fully understand that the effect of the adoption order for which application has been made will be to deprive me permanently of all parental rights or responsibilities which I have at present over the child. I freely agree generally and unconditionally to the making of an adoption order in relation to the child.

I have signed this agreement at (place of signing)....................on the.......... day of......... Nineteen hundred and...............

This agreement was signed in the presence of:—....................(Signature of reporting officer)

...............
Full name of Reporting Officer

...............
Address

### FORM 14[1]

Rule 2.23(1)

## FORM OF PARENTAL AGREEMENT UNDER SECTION 15(1)(aa) AND 16(1)(b)(i) OF THE ADOPTION (SCOTLAND) ACT 1978

In the petition relating to the adoption of...............(Insert the full name of the child as it is given in the birth certificate)

I, (name and address)...............confirm that I am the mother/father/guardian of the child. I fully understand that the effect of the adoption order for which application has been made will be to share with the petitioner all parental responsibilities and rights which I have at present over the child. I freely agree generally and unconditionally to the making of an adoption order in relation to the child.

I have signed this agreement at (place of signing)...............on the.......... day of...............

This agreement was signed in the presence of:—...............(Signature of reporting officer)

...............
Full name of Reporting Officer

...............
Address

### FORM 15

Rule 2.36(3)

## FORM OF INTIMATION OF DIET OF HEARING UNDER SECTION 27, 28, 29 OR 30 OF THE ADOPTION (SCOTLAND) ACT 1978

Notice of hearing of minute in petition for authority to adopt..........(Full name of child as given in the birth certificate)

To:—....................(Full name and address of person to whom this intimation is to be sent)

Notice is hereby given that a hearing in the petition for authority to adopt the child, which hearing will be restricted to matters bearing upon the crave of the minute, a copy of which is attached hereto, will take place at (name of sheriff court).......... Sheriff Court (address) on.......... (date) at.......... (time) when you may appear and be heard personally or be represented by solicitor or counsel.

Signature ...............
Designation...............

---

[1] As amended by the Act of Sederunt (Child Care and Maintenance Rules 1997) (Amendment) (Adoption and Children Act 2002) 2006 (SSI 2006/411) (effective August 18, 2006).

Date...............

FORM 16

Rule 2.38(1)

APPLICATION FOR A PARENTAL RESPONSIBILITIES ORDER UNDER
SECTION 86 OF THE CHILDREN (SCOTLAND) ACT 1995

Case No...........

Date lodged..........

Application to Sheriff Court at...............for a Parental Responsibilities Order under section 86 of the Children (Scotland) Act 1995

1

| | |
|---|---|
| APPLICANT | *[insert name, address, telephone and fax numbers, and details of the capacity of the person making the application on behalf of the local authority, e.g. solicitor for local authority, social worker]* |
| CHILD | *[insert name, address, gender and date of birth exactly as given in birth certificate]* |
| RELEVANT PER-SON(S) | *[insert name, address and the basis for the person being a relevant person within the meaning of section 86(4) of the Act]* |
| REPORTING OF-FICER | *[insert name and address and details of appointment of Reporting Officer appointed prior to the application in terms of rules 2.7 or 2.25]* |
| ANY OTHER PER-SON WHO SHOULD RECEIVE NOTICE OF THE APPLICATION | *[insert name, address of person and provide details of their interest in the appication and/or child]* |

2. GROUNDS I OR MAKING APPLICATION

The Applicant asks the Court to make a Parental Responsibilities Order for the following reasons:— *[applicant to provide details of grounds for making the application]*

OTHER APPLICATIONS AND ORDERS WHICH AFFECT THE CHILD

*[insert details of any other applications or orders made which affect or are relevant to the child who is the subject of this application including any details of a supervision requirement of a Children's Hearing]*

3. REQUEST FOR ORDER

1. The applicants request the court to make a Parental Responsibilities Order transferring the appropriate parental rights and responsibilities to them.

2. The petitioners request the court to dispense with the agreement of

...................

...................

on the ground that ...............[in terms of section 86(2)(b)]

4. REPORTS/DOCUMENTARY EVIDENCE ETC.

*delete as appropriate

The following documents are produced with this petition:—

a) An extract of the entry in the Register of Births relating to the child

b) Agreement of relevant persons within the meaning of Section 86(4) of the Act

c) * Any other document founded upon by the petitioner in support of the terms of the petition

5. OTHER ORDERS

*In terms of section 88(3) of the Act the sheriff is requested to make the following is directions as to contact with the child by *[insert name and address of persons and his or her relationship with the child] [insert details of any directions sought as to contact with the child]*

*delete as appropriate

*[insert details of any other orders craved e.g. Crave for warrant for delivery of the child and warrant to open shut and lockfast places]*

## 6. DETAILS OF FIRST ORDER SOUGHT FROM SHERIFF

The applicant requests the sheriff to appoint a curator ad litem and a Reporting Officer to the child for the purpose of investigating and reporting to the court within 4 weeks and on receipt of the reports by the curator ad litem and reporting officer to fix a hearing

SIGNED ...............

DATE ...............

*[insert Name, Address, telephone, DX and Fax number]*...............

FORM 17

Rule 2.38(2)

## FORM OF AGREEMENT OF RELEVANT PERSON UNDER SECTION 86(2) OF THE CHILDREN (SCOTLAND) ACT 1995

In the application for a Parental Responsibilities Order in respect of...................*(Insert the full name of the child as it is given in the birth certificate)*

I, *(insert name and address)*...............confirm that I am the *mother/*father/ *person with parental rights. I fully understand that the effect of the Parental Responsibilities Order for which application has been made will be to transfer my parental rights and responsibilities to *(insert name and address of Local Authority)*.......... during such period as the Order remains in force. I freely, and with full understanding of what is involved, agree unconditionally to the making of a Parental Responsibilities Order in relation to the child.

.....................
*(Signature of relevant person)*

.....................
*(Signature of Reporting Officer)*

I have signed this agreement at *(place of signing)*...............on the.......... day of.......... 199...............

This agreement was signed in the presence of *(Full name and address of Reporting Officer)*..........

*delete as appropriate

YOU SHOULD GET ADVICE FROM A SOLICITOR OR LOCAL ADVICE AGENCY OR LAW CENTRE about the application and bout Legal Aid.

FORM 18

Rule 2.42(2)

## FORM OF INTIMATION OF DIET OF HEARING UNDER SECTION 86 OF THE CHILDREN (SCOTLAND) ACT 1995

To:...............*(Full name and address of person to whom this intimation is to be sent)*

Notice is given that a hearing will take place at *(Name of Sheriff Court)* Sheriff Court *(Full address of Sheriff Court)* on.......... *(date)* at.......... *(time)* in relation to the child *(full name of child as given in the birth certificate)*...............when the court will consider an application for a Parental Responsibilities Order in relation to the child.

Signature...............

Designation...............

Date................

WHAT YOU SHOULD DO

You need not attend this hearing if you do not wish to be heard by the court.

If you do not attend or are not represented at the hearing, the application may be determined in your absence.

YOU SHOULD GET ADVICE FROM A SOLICITOR OR LOCAL ADVICE AGENCY OR LAW CENTRE about the application and about Legal Aid.

## FORM 19

Rule 2.43(2)

## PARENTAL RESPONSIBILITIES ORDER UNDER SECTION 86 OF THE CHILDREN (SCOTLAND) ACT 1995

IN THE SHERIFF COURT

at ...............

on ...............

Case No

The sheriff orders tht all parental rights and responsibilities relating to the child *[insert name, address, gender and date of birth]* except any right to agree, or decline to agree—

(a) to the making of an application in relation to the child under section 18 (freeing for adoption) or 55 (adoption abroad) of the Adoption Act 1976, under section 18 or 49 of the Adoption (Scotland) Act 1978 or under Article 17, 18 or 57 of the Adoption (Northern Ireland) Order 1987 (corresponding provision for Scotland and Northern Ireland); or

(b) to the making of an Adoption Order are transferred to *[insert name and address of Local Authority]* during the period that the Parental Responsibilities Order remains in force.

*In terms of section 88 of the Act the sheriff makes the following directions as to contact with the child by *[insert name and address of person and his or her relationships with child]*—

*[insert details of any other orders granted e.g. Warrant for delivery of the child etc.]*

*delete as appropriate

...................

*For the purpose of enforcing this order warrant is granted for all lawful execution, including warrant to open shut and lockfast places.

...................

Signed .........

Sheriff of .......... at ..........

Date ..........

## FORM 20

Rule 2.44(6)

## FORM OF INTIMATION OF DIET OF HEARING UNDER SECTION 86(5) OF THE CHILDREN (SCOTLAND) ACT 1995

To: ...............

*(Full name and address of person to whom this intimation is to be sent)*

Notice is given that a hearing will take place at *(Name of Sheriff Court)* Sheriff Court *(Full address of Sheriff Court)* on ..........*(date)* at ..........*(time)* in relation to the child *(full name and date of birth of child as given in the birth certificate)*...................when the court will consider an application for *variation/discharge of the Parental Responsibilities Order in relation to the child dated *(insert date of Order)*. A copy of the minute for *variation/discharge is attached.

Signature ...............

Designation ...............
Date ...............
*delete as appropriate
WHAT YOU SHOULD DO
You need not attend this hearing if you do not wish to be heard by the court.

If you do not attend or are not represented at the hearing, the application may be determined in your absence.

YOU SHOULD GET ADVICE FROM A SOLICITOR OR LOCAL ADVICE AGENCY OR LAW CENTRE about the application and about Legal Aid

FORM 21

Rule 2.44(7)

FORM OF DISCHARGE OR VARIATION OF PARENTAL RESPONSIBILI-TIES ORDER UNDER SECTION 86(5) OF THE CHILDREN (SCOTLAND) ACT 1995

To: ...............
*(Full name and address of person to whom intimation of the order is to be sent)*
[N.B. See Rule 2.44(7)]

In the application for *variation/discharge of Parental Responsibilities Order in relation to the child...................*(full name and date of birth of child as given in the birth certificate)*

At *(Name of Sheriff Court)* on *(date of Order)*, the Sheriff

(1) Discharged the Parental Responsibilities Order dated *(insert date of original Order)*

*or*

(2) Varied the Parental Responsibilities Order dated *(insert date of original Order)* by *(insert details of variation)*

Signature ...............
Designation ...............
Date ...............
*delete as appropriate

FORM 22[1]

**Rule 2.46(1)**

FORM OF PETITION FOR PARENTAL ORDER UNDER SECTION 54 OF THE HUMAN FERTILISATION AND EMBRYOLOGY ACT 2008
SHERIFFDOM OF *(insert name of sheriffdom)*
AT *(insert place of sheriff court)*
PETITION
of
[A.B.] *(designation and address)**
and
[C.D.] *(designation and address)**
[*or serial number where one has been assigned]*

Petitioners

for
a parental order under section 54 of the Human Fertilisation and Embryology Act 2008
in respect of
[E.F.] *(name as in birth certificate)*

---

[1] As amended by the Act of Sederunt (Sheriff Court Rules) (Miscellaneous Amendments) 2012 (SSI 2012/188) r.13(2) (effective August 18, 2006).

The petitioners condescend as follows—

1. The petitioners are [married to each other] *or* [civil partners of each other] *or* [two persons who are living as partners in an enduring family relationship and are not within prohibited degrees of relationship in relation to each other], are domiciled in the [United Kingdom][Channel Islands]*or* [Isle of Man] and reside at (*state full address*).

2. The petitioners are respectively .......... and .......... years of age.

3. (*State name of child, the subject of the petition*) is [male] *or* [female] and is .......... [months] *or* [years] old having been born on .......... at ..........

4. [A court has not previously refused the petitioners' application for a parental order in respect of the child] *or* [A court has previously refused the petitioners' application for a parental order in respect of the child but the court directed that section 33(1) of the Adoption and Children (Scotland) Act 2007 as modified, should not apply] *or* [A court has previously refused the petitioners' application for a parental order in respect of the child but the petitioners aver that it is proper for the court to hear the application because .......... (*give full details*)].

5. The child is not and never has been married or a civil partner.

6. The child's home is with the petitioners.

7. The child was carried by a woman who is not one of the petitioners as the result of [the placing in her of an embryo] *or* [the placing in her of sperm and eggs] *or* [her artificial insemination].

8. The gametes of (*state which petitioner or if both state both petitioners*) were used to bring about the creation of the embryo of the child.

9. The child is not the subject of any other pending or completed court proceedings (*if the child is so subject give full details*).

[10. (*State full name and address of the other parent of the child*), who is [the father of the child by virtue of sections 35 or 36 of the Human Fertilisation and Embryology Act 2008] *or* [the other parent of the child by virtue of sections 42 or 43 of the Human Fertilisation and Embryology Act 2008] or [the other parent of the child by virtue of (*specify*)], where he or she is not one of the petitioners has freely and with full understanding of what is involved, agreed unconditionally to the making of the order sought.]

[[11.] (*State full name and address of the woman who carried the child*), is the woman who carried the child and has freely and with full understanding of what is involved, agreed unconditionally to the making of the order sought.]

[12.] No money or benefit, other than for expenses reasonably incurred, has been given or received by the petitioners for or in consideration of

    (a)   the making of the order sought;

    (b)   any agreement required for the making of the order sought;

    (c)   the handing over of the child to the petitioners, or

    (d)   the making of any arrangements with a view to the making of the order,

[other than (*state any money or other benefit given or received by authority of the court and specify such authority*)].

[[13.] [The father of the child by virtue of sections 35 or 36 of the Human Fertilisation and Embryology Act 2008] *or* [The other parent of the child by virtue of sections 42 or 43 of the Human Fertilisation and Embryology Act 2008] *or* [The other parent of the child by virtue of (*specify*)] [and] [or] [The woman who carried the child] [cannot be found (*state the efforts which have been made to find the person(s) concerned*)] *or* [is [*or are*] incapable of giving agreement by reason of (*state reasons*)].]

The petitioners crave the court—

1. To order notice of the petition to be intimated to such person or persons as the court thinks fit.

2. To appoint a reporting officer and a curator ad litem to the child and direct them to report.

[3. To dispense with the agreement of the other parent of the child [*and*] [*or*] [the woman who carried the child] [who cannot be found] *or* [who is [*or are*] incapable of giving agreement].]

[4.] On resuming consideration of this petition and the reports by the reporting officer and the curator ad litem, to make a parental order in their favour under section 54 of the Human Fertilisation and Embryology Act 2008 in respect of the child.

[5.] To direct the Registrar General for Scotland to make an entry regarding the parental order in the Parental Order Register in the form prescribed by him or her giving [*insert forename(s)*] as the forename(s) and [*insert surname*] as the surname of the child; and upon proof to the satisfaction of the court in the course of the proceedings to follow hereon, to find that the child was born on the [*insert date*] day of [*insert month*] in the year [*insert year*] and is identical with the child to whom an entry numbered [*insert entry number*] and made on the [*insert date*] day of [*insert month*] in the year [*insert year*], in the Register of Births for the registration district of [*insert district*] relates; and to direct the Registrar General for Scotland to cause such birth entry to be marked with the words "Parental Order" and to include the above mentioned date of birth in the entry recording the parental order in the manner indicated in that form.

[6.] To pronounce such other or further orders or directions upon such matters, including the expenses of this petition, as the court thinks fit.

[(*Signed*)

First Petitioner

(*Signed*)

Second petitioner]

or [(*Signed*)

Solicitor for petitioners]

(*Address*)

FORM 23[1]

**Rule 2.48(1)**

FORM OF AGREEMENT TO A PARENTAL ORDER UNDER SECTION 54(6) OF THE HUMAN FERTILISATION AND EMBRYOLOGY ACT 2008

In the petition applying for a parental order in relation to (*insert the full name of the child as it is given in the birth certificate*).

[*to which petition the court has assigned the serial number (*insert serial number*).] (*delete as appropriate*)

I, (*insert name and address*), confirm that I am [the woman who carried the child] *or* [the father of the child by virtue of sections 35 or 36 of the Human Fertilisation and Embryology Act 2008] *or* [the other parent of the child by virtue of sections 42 or 43 of the Human Fertilisation and Embryology Act 2008] *or* [the other parent of the child by virtue of (*specify*)]. I confirm that:—

(1) I fully understand that the effect of the making of a parental order in respect of the child will be to extinguish all the parental responsibilities and parental rights which I have at present in respect of the child.

---

[1] As amended by the Act of Sederunt (Child Care and Maintenance Rules) Amendment (Human Fertilisation and Embryology Act 2008) 2010 (SSI 2010/137) Sch.1 para.1 (effective April 6, 2010: substitution has effect subject to transitional provisions and savings as specified in SSI 2010/137 r.3

(2) I understand that the court cannot make a parental order in relation to the child without my agreement [and the agreement of [the woman who carried the child] *or* [the father of the child by virtue of sections 35 or 36 of the Human Fertilisation and Embryology Act 2008] *or* [the other parent of the child by virtue of sections 42 or 43 of the Human Fertilisation and Embryology Act 2008] *or* [the other parent of the child by virtue of (*specify*)], where he or she is not one of the petitioners] unless the court dispenses with agreement on the ground that the person concerned cannot be found or is incapable of giving agreement.

(3) I understand that when the hearing of the petition to determine the application for a parental order in relation to the child is heard, this document may be used as evidence of my agreement to the making of the order unless I inform the court that I no longer agree.

(4) I freely, and with full understanding of what is involved, agree unconditionally to the making of a parental order in relation to the child.

(5) I have not received or given any money or benefit, other than for expenses reasonably incurred, for or in consideration of—

(a)   the making of the parental order,

(b)   the execution of this agreement,

(c)   the handing over of the child to the petitioners, or

(d)   the making of any arrangements with a view to the making of a parental order,

[other than (*state any money or other benefit given or received by authority of the court and specify such authority*)].

I have signed this agreement at (*place of signing*) on the .......... day of .......... Two thousand and ..........

(*Signed by the [woman who carried the child] [father] or [other parent of the child]*)

This agreement was signed in the presence of:—

................

(*Signature of witness*)

................

[*Insert full name and address of witness*]

FORM 24[1]

**Rule 2.54(3)**

FORM OF INTIMATION OF DIET OF THE HEARING OF APPLICATION FOR A PARENTAL ORDER UNDER SECTION 54 OF THE HUMAN FERTILISATION AND EMBRYOLOGY ACT 2008

To: (*insert full name and address of person to whom this intimation is to be sent*)

You are given NOTICE that a hearing will take place at (*insert name and address of sheriff court*) on (*insert date*) at (*insert time*) in relation to the child (*insert full name of child as given in the birth certificate*)

when the court will consider an application for a parental order under section 54 of the Human Fertilisation and Embryology Act 2008 in respect of the child.

You are [not] obliged to attend the hearing [unless you wish to do so].

If you do not attend this hearing the court may make an order as noted above.

[While the petition is pending you must not, except with the leave of the court, remove the child from the care of the petitioners.]

---

[1] As substituted by the Act of Sederunt (Child Care and Maintenance Rules) Amendment (Human Fertilisation and Embryology Act 2008) 2010 (SSI 2010/137) Sch.1 para.1 (effective April 6, 2010: substitution has effect subject to transitional provisions and savings as specified in SSI 2010/137 r.3).

[The court has been requested to dispense with your agreement to the making of an order on the ground[s] that (*specify ground(s)*)].

Date (*insert date*)

[(*Signed*)
First petitioner
(*Signed*)
Second petitioner]
or [(*Signed*)
[*Solicitor for petitioners*] or [*sheriff clerk**]
(*Address*)]
*where serial number assigned

FORM 25[1]

Rule 2.55(3)(b)

## FORM OF INTIMATION OF DIET OF THE HEARING OF APPLICATION UNDER SECTIONS 22(1) OR 24 OF THE HUMAN FERTILISATION AND EMBRYOLOGY ACT 2008

To: (*insert full name and address of person to whom this intimation is to be sent*)

You are given NOTICE that a hearing will take place at (*insert name and address of sheriff court*) on (*insert date*) at (*insert time*) in relation to the child (*insert full name of child as given in the birth certificate*)

when the court will consider a minute of application under rule 2.55 of the Act of Sederunt (Child Care and Maintenance Rules) 1997 in respect of the child. A copy of the application is attached.

You do not need to attend this hearing if you do not wish to be heard by the court.

Date (*insert date*)

(*Signed*)
Minuter
or [(*Signed*)
[*Solicitor for minuter*] or [*sheriff clerk**]
(*Address*)]
*where serial number has been assigned

FORM 26[2]

**Rule 3.4(1)(a)**

## NOTICE TO CHILD OF APPLICATION FOR A CHILD ASSESSMENT ORDER UNDER SECTION 35 OF THE CHILDREN'S HEARINGS (SCOTLAND) ACT 2011

Court ref. no.:

Dear [*insert name by which child is known*]

I am writing to tell you that because there are worries about the way you are being treated the sheriff [the person who has to decide] is being asked to make a "Child Assessment Order" to make sure that you are being treated properly.

---

[1] As substituted by the Act of Sederunt (Child Care and Maintenance Rules) Amendment (Human Fertilisation and Embryology Act 2008) 2010 (SSI 2010/137) Sch.1 para.1 (effective April 6, 2010: substitution has effect subject to transitional provisions and savings as specified in SSI 2010/137 r.3

[2] As amended by the Act of Sederunt (Children's Hearings (Scotland) Act 2011) (Miscellaneous Amendments) 2013 (SSI 2013/172) para.4 (effective June 24, 2013).

The application to the sheriff has been made by *[insert in simple language the person making the application, the reason for making it and the order(s) sought]*. The sheriff would like to hear your views about what you would like to happen before making a decision.

You can tell the sheriff what you think by:

**Going to see the Sheriff**

The sheriff will consider what to do next on *[insert date, time and place of hearing]*.

You can take someone like a friend, parent, teacher or a social worker with you to see the sheriff to support you; or

You can ask a lawyer to come with you and tell the sheriff your views.

If you think you would like to go to see the sheriff it is usually best to talk it over with a lawyer.

**Not going to see the Sheriff**

You can fill in the attached form or write down your views on a separate sheet of paper and send them back in the enclosed stamped addressed envelope **before** the date on which the sheriff is to hear the application, which is at the end of this letter.

**REMEMBER**

That someone like a friend or teacher can help you to fill in the form or write down your views.

— If you return the form it will be given to the sheriff and, if he needs more information, he will ask the Sheriff Clerk who works with him to contact you about this.

**IMPORTANT NOTE**—You do not have to do any of these things if you would prefer not to; however, it is very important for you to understand that, if you do not do anything, the sheriff might make an order without knowing what your views are.

---

**If you are unsure about what to do you can get free legal advice from a Lawyer or Local Advice Agency or Law Centre about the application and about legal aid.**
**The Scottish Child Law Centre can refer you to specially trained lawyers who can help you.**
**They give advice on their free phone no (0800 328 8970) any time between 9.30 am and 4.00 pm Monday to Friday.**

---

**The hearing to consider the application will be held on [insert date] at [insert time], in [insert name of court] SHERIFF COURT, [insert address of court].**

You will see that, along with this letter, there is a copy of the application to the sheriff and the sheriff's order fixing the hearing. If you decide to get advice, or to be represented, make sure that you give your advisor a copy of the application, and the sheriff's order.

Signed Date ............... Date ..........

To the Sheriff Clerk

I would like the Sheriff to know what I have to say before he or she makes a decision.

**Write what you want to say here, or you can use a separate sheet of paper.**

...............

Name ...............

Address ...............

...............

...............

Court Reference Number ..........

(if you know it)

## FORM 27

Rule 3.4(1)(b)

## NOTICE TO CHILD OF APPLICATION TO VARY OR SET ASIDE CHILD PROTECTION ORDER UNDER SECTION 60 OF THE CHILDREN (SCOTLAND) ACT 1995

### CASE NUMBER

### KEEPING YOU SAFE

Dear *[insert name by which child is known]*

A Child Protection Order was made on .......... to keep you safe from harm.

The sheriff [the person who has to decide] made the order, which says that you are to continue to live at *[insert address]* at present.

Now the sheriff has been asked to have another look at your situation, *[insert in simple language the person making the application, the reason for making it and the order(s) sought]*. The sheriff would like to hear your views about what you would like to happen before making a decision.

You can tell the sheriff what you think by:—

**Going to see the Sheriff**

You can take someone like a friend, parent, a teacher or a social worker with you to see the sheriff to support you; or you can ask a lawyer to come with you and tell the sheriff your views.

**Not going to see the Sheriff**

You can fill in the attached form and send it back in the enclosed stamped addressed envelope before the hearing date which is at the end of this letter.

**REMEMBER**

That someone can help you to fill in the form.

If you return the form it will be given to the sheriff and, if he needs more information, he will ask the Sheriff Clerk who works with him to contact you about this.

**IMPORTANT NOTE**—You do not have to do any of these things if you would prefer not to; however, it is very important for you to understand that, if you do not do anything, the sheriff might make an order without knowing what your views are.

**If you are unsure about what to do you can get free legal advice from a Lawyer or Local Advice Agency or Law Centre about the application and about legal aid.**
**The Scottish Child Law Centre can refer you to specially trained lawyers who can help you.**
**They give advice on their free phone no (0800 317 500) any time between 9.00 am and 5.00 pm Monday to Friday.**

**The hearing to consider the application will be held on [insert date] at [insert time], in [insert name of court] SHERIFF COURT, [insert address of court].**

You will see that, along with this letter, there is a copy of the application to the sheriff, and the sheriff's order fixing the hearing. If you decide to get advice, or to ask someone to go to see the sheriff for you, make sure that you give your advisor a copy of the application, and the sheriff's order.

SIGNED ...............

DATE: ...............

To the Sheriff Clerk

I would like the Sheriff to know what I have to say before he or she makes a decision.

**Write what you want to say here, or you can use a separate sheet of paper.**

.....................

Name ...............

Address ...............

...............

...............

Court Reference Number ..........

(if you know it)

FORM 28[1]

Rule 3.4(1)(c)

## NOTICE TO CHILD OF APPLICATION FOR AN EXCLUSION ORDER UNDER SECTION 76 OF THE CHILDREN (SCOTLAND) ACT 1995

Court ref. no.:

### KEEPING YOU SAFE

Dear *[insert name by which child is known]*

I am writing to tell you that because there are worries about your safety the sheriff [the person who has to decide] has been asked to sort out some practical arrangements to make sure you can be kept safe. The sheriff is being asked to make an "Exclusion Order" to make sure that *[insert name of person]* does not come into the family home at *[insert address]*. You are to stay [at home/where you are]* at present.

*delete as appropriate

The application to the sheriff has been made by *[insert in simple language the person making the application, the reason for making it and the order(s) sought]*. The sheriff would like to hear your views about what you would like to happen before making a decision.

You can tell the sheriff what you think by:—

**Going to see the Sheriff**

You can take someone like a friend, parent, a teacher or a social worker with you to see the sheriff to support you; or you can ask a lawyer to come with you and tell the sheriff your views.

If you think you would like to go to see the sheriff it is usually best to talk it over with a lawyer.

**Not going to see the Sheriff**

You can fill in the attached form or write down your views on a separate sheet of paper and send them back in the enclosed stamped addressed envelope **before** the date on which the court is to hear the application, which is at the end of this letter.

**REMEMBER**

That someone like a friend or teacher can help you to fill in the form or write down your views.

If you return the form it will be given to the sheriff, and, if he needs more information, he will ask the Sheriff Clerk who works with him to contact you about this.

---

[1] As amended by the Act of Sederunt (Children's Hearings (Scotland) Act 2011) (Miscellaneous Amendments) 2013 (SSI 2013/172) para.4 (effective June 24, 2013).

**IMPORTANT NOTE**—You do not have to do any of these things if you would prefer not to; however, it is very important for you to understand that, if you do not do anything, the sheriff might make an order without knowing what your views are.

> **If you are unsure about what to do you can get free legal advice from a Lawyer or Local Advice Agency or Law Centre about the application and about legal aid.**
> **The Scottish Child Law Centre can refer you to specially trained lawyers who can help you.**
> **They give advice on their free phone no (0800 328 8970) any time between 9.30 am and 4.00 pm Monday to Friday.**

The hearing to consider the application will be held on [insert date] at [insert time], in [insert name of court] SHERIFF COURT, [insert address of court].

You will see that, along with this letter, there is a copy of the application to the sheriff and the sheriff's order fixing the hearing. If you decide to get advice, or to ask someone to go to see the sheriff for you, make sure that you give your advisor a copy of the application, and the sheriff's order.

SIGNED ............... DATE: ..........

To the Sheriff Clerk

I would like the Sheriff to know what I have to say before he or she makes a decision.

**Write what you want to say here, or you can use a separate sheet of paper.**

....................

Name ...............

Address ...............

...............

...............

Court Reference Number ..........

(if you know it)

FORM 29[1]

Rule 3.4(1)(d)

NOTICE TO CHILD OF APPLICATION TO VARY AN EXCLUSION ORDER UNDER SECTION 79(3) OF THE CHILDREN (SCOTLAND) ACT 1995

> Court ref. no.:

### CHANGING THE ARRANGEMENTS FOR KEEPING YOU SAFE

Dear *[insert name by which child is known]*

I am writing to tell you that the sheriff has been asked to look again at the arrangements that were made to make sure you can be kept safe. The sheriff is being asked to *[change or cancel]** the "Exclusion Order" he made on *[insert date]*. You are to stay *[at home/where you are]** at present.

*delete as appropriate

---

[1] As amended by the Act of Sederunt (Children's Hearings (Scotland) Act 2011) (Miscellaneous Amendments) 2013 (SSI 2013/172) para.4 (effective June 24, 2013).

The application to the sheriff has been made by *[insert in simple language the person making the application, the reason for making it and the order(s) sought]*. The sheriff would like to hear your views about what you would like to happen before making a decision.

You can tell the sheriff what you think in the same way that you did when the original order was made. If you told the sheriff your views last time you might want to do so again using the same method again. You can if you prefer use a different method to tell the sheriff this time.

Even if you did not tell anything to the sheriff last time he would like to hear your views.

You can tell the sheriff what you think by:—

**Going to see the Sheriff**

You can take someone like a friend, parent, a teacher or a social worker with you to see the sheriff to support you; or you can ask a lawyer to come with you and tell the sheriff your views.

If you think you would like to see the sheriff it is usually best to talk it over with a lawyer.

**Not going to see the Sheriff**

You can fill in the attached form or write down your views on a separate sheet of paper and send them back in the enclosed stamped addressed envelope **before** the date on which the sheriff is to hear the application, which is at the end of this letter.

**REMEMBER**

That someone like a friend or teacher can help you to fill in the form or write down your views.

If you return the form it will be given to the sheriff and, if he needs more information, he will ask the Sheriff Clerk who works with him to contact you about this.

**IMPORTANT NOTE**—You do not have to do any of these things if you would prefer not to; however, it is very important for you to understand that, if you do not do anything, the sheriff might make an order without knowing what your views are.

---

**If you are unsure about what to do you can get free legal advice from a Lawyer or Local Advice Agency or Law Centre The Scottish Child Law Centre can refer you to specially trained lawyers who can help you. They give advice on their free phone no (0800 328 8970) any time between 9.30 am and 4.00 pm Monday to Friday.**

---

**The hearing to consider the application will be held on [insert place] at [insert time], in [insert name] SHERIFF COURT, [insert address of sheriff].**

You will see that, along with this letter, there is a copy of the application to the sheriff, and the sheriff's order fixing the hearing. If you decide to get advice, or to ask someone to go to sheriff for you, make sure that you give your advisor a copy of the application, and the sheriff's order.

SIGNED........................ DATE:........

To the Sheriff Clerk

I would like the Sheriff to know what I have to say before he or she makes a decision.

**Write what you want to say here, or you can use a separate sheet of paper.**

.....................

Name ..............

Address ...............

...............

...............

Court Reference Number ..........

(if you know it)

FORM 30

Rule 3.4(1)(e)

NOTICE TO CHILD OF APPLICATION FOR A FURTHER DETENTION WARRANT UNDER SECTION 67 OF THE CHILDREN (SCOTLAND) ACT 1995

*[Repealed by the Act of Sederunt (Children's Hearings (Scotland) Act 2011) (Miscellaneous Amendments) 2013 (SSI 2013/172) para.4 (effective June 24, 2013).]*

FORM 31[1]

Rule 3.4(1)(f)

CITATION OF CHILD IN APPLICATION UNDER SECTION 93(2)(A) OR 94(2)(A) OF THECHILDREN'S HEARINGS (SCOTLAND) ACT 2011 (NO PROCEDURAL HEARING FIXED)

Court ref. no.:

Dear *[insert name by which child is known]*,

As you know at the Children's Hearing held on *[insert date]* not everyone agreed that the information given to you in the statement of grounds was correct. *[The information on the statement of grounds was not accepted by *[insert name of person who did not accept the grounds]*] or* [The hearing was satisfied that *you/*[insert name of relevant person]* *could not/did not understand the reasons why you were there]. This means that your case has been sent to a sheriff,who will decide whether the information given to you in the statement of grounds is correct.

**WHAT THE SHERIFF DOES:** A sheriff assists for lots of different reasons, but this time the purpose is to help the Children's Hearing. If the sheriff decides that the worries about you are justified the case will go back to the Children's Hearing who will decide what is to happen in your case.

**HEARING ON EVIDENCE:** The sheriff has set a date for a hearing on evidence. The hearing on evidence will take place on *[insert time and date of hearing]* at *[insert address of sheriff court]*.

[*You are required to attend court on that date *or* You are not required to attend court on that date, but you may wish to do so.]

At the hearing on evidence the sheriff will listen to the evidence in your case, and will make a decision. This decision is very important for you [*and it is necessary for you to attend the hearings to tell the sheriff about your circumstances and how you feel. You might be asked some questions. You can be represented by a solicitor or another person].

*[**IMPORTANT NOTE: IT IS VERY IMPORTANT THAT YOU ATTEND** on the date and time given. If an emergency arises and you cannot attend you must contact the sheriff clerk on (*insert telephone number*) or the Principal Reporter because it is possible, if you do not attend, you may be detained and kept in a safe place until a later date.]

*[The sheriff has said that you do not have to attend the hearing on *[insert date]* at *[insert time]* at *[insert name and address of sheriff court]*, but if you want to go along to hear what is said at the hearing then you can. If you do not want to go to court then you can still let the sheriff know what you think by filling in the attached form or you can write down what you want to say on a separate sheet of paper and send them back in the enclosed stamped addressed envelope before the date on

---

[1] As substituted by the Act of Sederunt (Children's Hearings (Scotland) Act 2011) (Miscellaneous Amendments) 2013 (SSI 2013/172) para.4 (effective June 24, 2013).

which the sheriff is to hear the application, which is at the end of this letter. Alternatively, you can ask a lawyer to go to the hearing to tell the sheriff your views.]

**If you are unsure about what to do you can get free legal advice from a Lawyer or Local Advice Agency or Law Centre about the application and about legal aid. The Scottish Child Law Centre can refer you to specially trained lawyers who can help you. They give advice on their free phone number (0800 328 8970) any time between 9.30am and 4.00pm Monday to Friday.**

You will see that, along with this letter, there is a copy of the application to the sheriff, and the sheriff's order fixing the hearing. If you decide to get advice, or to ask someone to go with you to see the sheriff, make sure that you give them a copy of the application and the sheriff's order.

.....................

(Signed)          (Date)

*(\*delete as appropriate)*

To the Sheriff Clerk:

**I would like the Sheriff to know what I have to say before he or she makes a decision** (write what you want to say here, or you can use a separate sheet of paper):

Your Name:

Your Address:

Court Reference Number (if you know it):

FORM 31A[1]

Rule 3.4(1)(g)

CITATION OF CHILD IN APPLICATION UNDER SECTION 94(2)(A) OF THE CHILDREN'S HEARINGS (SCOTLAND) ACT 2011 (PROCEDURAL HEARING FIXED)

Court ref. no.:

Dear *[insert name by which child is known]*,

As you know at the Children's Hearing held on *[insert date]* not everyone agreed that the information given to you in the statement of grounds was correct. The hearing was satisfied that you \*could not/did not understand the reasons why you were there. This means that your case has been sent to a sheriff, who will decide whether the information given to you in the statement of grounds is correct.

**WHAT THE SHERIFF DOES:** A sheriff assists for lots of different reasons, but this time the purpose is to help the Children's Hearing. If the sheriff decides that the worries about you are justified the case will go back to the Children's Hearing who will decide what is to happen in your case.

**PROCEDURAL HEARING:** The sheriff has arranged a procedural hearing to determine whether or not each relevant person (whose names are *[insert names of relevant persons]*) accepts that the information given to you in the statement of grounds is correct. The procedural hearing will take place on *[insert time and date of hearing]* at *[insert address of sheriff court]*. [\*You are required to attend court on that date or You are not required to attend court on that date, but you may wish to do so.] If, at the procedural hearing, all the relevant persons accept that that the information that has been given is correct then the sheriff may make a decision without

---

[1] As inserted by the Act of Sederunt (Children's Hearings (Scotland) Act 2011) (Miscellaneous Amendments) 2013 (SSI 2013/172) para.4 (effective June 24, 2013).

hearing evidence. You have the right though to ask the sheriff to hear evidence, even if all relevant persons accept that the information in the statement of grounds is correct.

**HEARING ON EVIDENCE:** The sheriff has also set a date for a hearing on evidence. Unless you receive notice that the sheriff has discharged the hearing on evidence, it will take place on [*insert time and date of hearing*] at [*insert address of sheriff court*]. [*You are required to attend court on that date *or* You are not required to attend court on that date, but you may wish to do so.]

At the hearing on evidence the sheriff will listen to the evidence in your case, and will make a decision. This decision is very important for you [*and it is necessary for you to attend the hearing to tell the sheriff about your circumstances and how you feel. You might be asked some questions. You can be represented by a solicitor or another person].

*[**IMPORTANT NOTE: IT IS VERY IMPORTANT THAT YOU ATTEND** on the dates and times given. If an emergency arises and you cannot attend you must contact the sheriff clerk on (*insert telephone number*) or the Principal Reporter because it is possible, if you do not attend, you may be detained and kept in a safe place until a later date.]

*[The sheriff has said that you do not have to attend the hearing on [*insert date*] at [*insert time*] at [*insert name and address of sheriff court*], but if you want to go along to hear what is said at the hearing then you can. If you do not want to go to court then you can still let the sheriff know what you think by filling in the attached form or you can write down what you want to say on a separate sheet of paper and send them back in the enclosed stamped addressed envelope before the date on which the sheriff is to hear the application, which is at the end of this letter. Alternatively, you can ask a lawyer to go to the hearing to tell the sheriff your views.]

**If you are unsure about what to do you can get free legal advice from a Lawyer or Local Advice Agency or Law Centre about the application and about legal aid. The Scottish Child Law Centre can refer you to specially trained lawyers who can help you. They give advice on their free phone number (0800 328 8970) any time between 9.30am and 4.00pm Monday to Friday.**

You will see that, along with this letter, there is a copy of the application to the sheriff, and the sheriff's order fixing the hearings. If you decide to get advice, or to ask someone to go with you to see the sheriff, make sure that you give them a copy of the application and the sheriff's order.

....................

(Signed)          (Date)

*(*delete as appropriate)*
To the Sheriff Clerk:
**I would like the Sheriff to know what I have to say before he or she makes a decision** (write what you want to say here, or you can use a separate sheet of paper):
Your Name:
Your Address:
Court Reference Number (if you know it):

FORM 31B[1]

---

[1] As inserted by the Act of Sederunt (Children's Hearings (Scotland) Act 2011) (Miscellaneous Amendments) 2013 (SSI 2013/172) para.4 (effective June 24, 2013).

Rule 3.4(1)(h)

## NOTICE TO CHILD OF APPLICATION FOR REVIEW OF GROUNDS DETERMINATION UNDER THE CHILDREN'S HEARINGS (SCOTLAND) ACT 2011

Court ref. no.:

Dear [insert name by which child is known],

I am writing to tell you that the sheriff has been asked to look again at the decision that [he or she]* made on [insert date], which found that [insert details in simple terms of the grounds determination]. You are to stay [at home/where you are]* at present.

The application to the sheriff has been made by [insert in simple language the person making the application]. That person thinks that before making the grounds determination the sheriff should have considered [insert in simple language the evidence that was not considered by the sheriff and why]. The sheriff would like to hear your views about what you would like to happen before making a decision.

*[So that you can tell the sheriff what you think, you need to go and see the sheriff on [insert date] at [insert time] at [insert name and address of sheriff court]. It is very important that you turn up on this date. You can take someone like a friend, parent, a teacher or a social worker with you to see the sheriff and to support you. Alternatively, you can ask a lawyer to come with you and tell the sheriff your views. If you think you would like to go to see the sheriff it is usually best to talk it over with a lawyer.] OR

*[The sheriff has said that you do not have to attend the hearing on [insert date] at [insert time] at [insert name and address of sheriff court], but if you want to go along to hear what is said at the hearing then you can. If you do not want to go to court then you can still let the sheriff know what you think by filling in the attached form or you can write down what you want to say on a separate sheet of paper and send them back in the enclosed stamped addressed envelope before the date on which the sheriff is to hear the application, which is at the end of this letter. Alternatively, you can ask a lawyer to go to the hearing to tell the sheriff your views.

**REMEMBER** that someone like a friend or teacher can help you to fill in the form or write down your views. If you return the form it will be given to the sheriff and, if the sheriff needs more information, he or she will ask the sheriff clerk who works with the sheriff to contact you about this.]

**If you are unsure about what to do you can get free legal advice from a Lawyer or Local Advice Agency or Law Centre. The Scottish Child Law Centre can refer you to specially trained lawyers who can help you. They give advice on their free phone number (0800 328 8970) any time between 9.30am and 4.00pm Monday to Friday.**

You will see that, along with this letter, there is a copy of the application to the sheriff, and the sheriff's order fixing the hearing. If you decide to get advice, or to ask someone to go with you to see the sheriff, make sure that you give them a copy of the application and the sheriff's order.

....................

(Signed)          (Date)

(*delete as appropriate)

To the Sheriff Clerk:

**I would like the Sheriff to know what I have to say before he or she makes a decision** (write what you want to say here, or you can use a separate sheet of paper):

Your Name:

Your Address:

Court Reference Number (if you know it):

## FORM 32[1]

Rule 3.11

### FORM OF FIRST ORDER UNDER THE CHILDREN (SCOTLAND) ACT 1995

Court ref. no.:

SECTION 76 (Application for Exclusion Order),

SECTION 79 (Application to vary or recall Exclusion Order) and

*[Place and date]*

The court assigns *[date]* at *[hour]* within the *[name court]* in chambers at *[place]* for the hearing of the application;

appoints the applicant forthwith to give notice of the application and hearing to the persons listed in PART I of the application by serving a copy of the application and this order together with notices in Forms *[insert form Nos.]*;

*dispenses with notice and service on *[insert name]* for the following reason(s) *[insert reason(s)]*.

[Note: *Insert details of any other order granted and in an application under* section 76 of the Children (Scotland) Act 1995 *for an exclusion order insert as appropriate*

Meantime grants an interim exclusion order; *or* interim interdict; *or otherwise as the case may be.]*

.............
*Sheriff or sheriff clerk

*delete as appropriate

## FORM 32A[2]

Rule 3.11

### FORM OF FIRST ORDER UNDER THE CHILDREN'S HEARINGS (SCOTLAND) ACT 2011

Court ref. no.:

Section 35 (Application for Child Assessment Order),

Section 48 (Application to vary or terminate a Child Protection Order)

[*Place and date*]

The court assigns [*date*] at [*hour*] within chambers at [*insert name and address of sheriff court*] for the hearing of the application;

appoints the applicant forthwith to give notice of the application and hearing to the persons listed in PART I of the application by serving a copy of the application and this order together with notices in Forms [*insert Form Numbers*];

*dispenses with notice and service on [*insert name*] for the following reason(s) [*insert reason(s)*].

[Note: *In the case of* section 48 *applications only, insert details of the* Child Protection Order.]

.............
(Sheriff or sheriff clerk)

(**delete as appropriate*)

---

[1] As amended by the Act of Sederunt (Children's Hearings (Scotland) Act 2011) (Miscellaneous Amendments) 2013 (SSI 2013/172) para.4 (effective June 24, 2013).

[2] As inserted by the Act of Sederunt (Children's Hearings (Scotland) Act 2011) (Miscellaneous Amendments) 2013 (SSI 2013/172) para.4 (effective June 24, 2013).

FORM 33[1]

Rule 3.11

## FORM OF WARRANT TO CITE CHILD AND TO GIVE NOTICE/INTIMATE TO RELEVANT PERSON(S) AND SAFEGUARDER IN APPLICATIONS UNDER SECTION 93(2)(a) or 94(2)(a) OF THE CHILDREN'S HEARINGS (SCOTLAND) ACT 2011

Court ref. no.:

*[Place and date]*

The court

1. Assigns *[date]* at *[hour]* within the *[name court]* in chambers at *[place]* for the hearing of the application;

*[and fixes a procedural hearing to take place on *[insert date]* at *[insert time]* within *[name court]* in chambers at *[place]*]*

2. Appoints the Principal Reporter forthwith

to cite AB *[name of child]*,

to give notice/intimate to BB *[insert name of relevant person or persons (within the meaning of Rule 3.1(1) )]* whose whereabouts are known and to [CD] (name and design) the safeguarder *[and [EF] (name and design) the curator *ad litem*],

by serving a copy of the application and relative statement of grounds of referral;

3. Grants warrant to cite witnesses and havers.

4. *Dispenses with notice and service on *[insert name]* for the following reason(s) *[insert reason(s)]*.

5. *Dispenses with the obligation to attend of *[insert name of child]* for the following reason(s) *[insert reason(s)]*.

..............

*Sheriff or Sheriff Clerk

*delete as appropriate

FORM 34[2]

Rule 3.12(1)(a)

## NOTICE OF APPLICATION FOR A CHILD ASSESSMENT ORDER TO A PERSON NAMED IN APPLICATION UNDER SECTION 35(1) OF THE CHILDREN'S HEARINGS (SCOTLAND) ACT 2011

Court ref. no.:

**Application to Sheriff Court at** *[insert name]*

for a Child Assessment Order under section 35 of the Children's hearings (Scotland) Act 2011

To *[insert name and address of person to whom notice is given]*.

...................

You are given notice that the court will hear this application—

*[applicant to insert details of the date, time and place for hearing the application]*

on..............

at..............

in..............

---

[1] As amended by the Act of Sederunt (Children's Hearings (Scotland) Act 2011) (Miscellaneous Amendments) 2013 (SSI 2013/172) para.4 (effective June 24, 2013).

[2] As amended by the Act of Sederunt (Children's Hearings (Scotland) Act 2011) (Miscellaneous Amendments) 2013 (SSI 2013/172) para.4 (effective June 24, 2013).

Along with this notice there is attached a copy of the application and the court's order fixing this hearing.

Signed ............... Date ..........

WHAT YOU SHOULD DO

YOU SHOULD ATTEND OR BE REPRESENTED AT THE HEARING.

If you do not attend in person you may instruct someone else to represent you.

**If you do not attend or are not represented at the hearing, the court may decide the case in your absence.**

YOU SHOULD OBTAIN ADVICE FROM A SOLICITOR OR LOCAL AD-VICE AGENCY OR LAW CENTRE. You may be entitled to legal aid. Advice about legal aid is available from any solicitor, advice agency or law centre.

FORM 35[1]

Rule 3.12(1)(b)

NOTICE OF APLICATION TO VARY OR TERMINATE CHILD PROTEC-TION ORDER TO PERSON NAMED IN APPLICATION UNDER SECTION 48 OF THE CHILDREN'S HEARINGS (SCOTLAND) ACT 2011

Court ref. no.:

**Application to Sheriff Court at** *[insert name]*...............

to vary or terminate a Child Protection Order under section 48 of the Children's Hearings (Scotland) Act 2011

To *(insert name and address)*...............

You are given notice that the court will hear this application—

*[applicant to insert details of the date, time and place for hearing the application]*

The application is to *(insert details of purpose application)*

on...............

at...............

in...............

Along with this notice there is attached a copy of the application and the court's order fixing this hearing.

Signed ............... Date ..........

WHAT YOU SHOULD DO

YOU SHOULD ATTEND OR BE REPRESENTED AT THE HEARING.

If you do not attend in person you may instruct someone else to represent you.

**If you do not attend or are not represented at the hearing, the court may decide the case in your absence.**

YOU SHOULD OBTAIN ADVICE FROM A SOLICITOR OR LOCAL AD-VICE AGENCY OR LAW CENTRE. You may be entitled to legal aid. Advice about legal aid is available from any solicitor, advice agency or law centre.

FORM 36[2]

Rule 3.12(1)(c)

NOTICE OF APPLICATION FOR AN EXCLUSION ORDER TO PERSON NAMED IN APPLICATION OR ANY OTHER PERSON UNDER SECTION 76 OF THE CHILDREN (SCOTLAND) ACT 1995

Court ref. no.:

**Application to Sheriff Court at** *(insert name)*

---

[1] As amended by the Act of Sederunt (Children's Hearings (Scotland) Act 2011) (Miscellaneous Amendments) 2013 (SSI 2013/172) para.4 (effective June 24, 2013).

[2] As amended by the Act of Sederunt (Children's Hearings (Scotland) Act 2011) (Miscellaneous Amendments) 2013 (SSI 2013/172) para.4 (effective June 24, 2013).

for an exclusion order under section 76 of the Children (Scotland) Act 1995 in respect of

*you/*[insert name and address of named person]*

*delete as appropriate

To *[insert name and address of person to whom notice is given].*

You are given notice that the court will hear this application—

*[applicant to insert details of the date, time and place for hearing the application]*

on...............

at...............

in...............

Along with this notice there is attached a copy of the application and the court's order fixing this hearing *which includes details of any interim orders granted.

Signed .......... Date ..........

WHAT YOU SHOULD DO

YOU SHOULD ATTEND OR BE REPRESENTED AT THE HEARING.

**If you do not attend or are not represented at the hearing, the court may decide the case in your absence.** If the order sought is to exclude you then the granting of the order will have an effect on a number of your rights including the suspending of any rights of occupancy you have.

Details of the orders sought are contained in the application form.

YOU SHOULD OBTAIN ADVICE FROM A SOLICITOR OR LOCAL ADVICE AGENCY OR LAW CENTRE. You may be entitled to legal aid. Advice about legal aid is available from any solicitor, advice agency or law centre.

*delete as appropriate

## FORM 37[1]

Rule 3.12(1)(d)

NOTICE OF APPLICATION TO VARY OR RECALL AN EXCLUSION ORDER TO PERSON NAMED IN APPLICATION OR ANY OTHER PERSON UNDER SECTION 79 OF THE CHILDREN (SCOTLAND) ACT 1995

Court ref. no.:

Application to Sheriff Court at **(insert name)**

to vary or recall* an exclusion order under section 79 of the Children (Scotland) Act 1995 in respect of *you/*[insert name and address of named person]*

*delete as appropriate

To *[insert name and address of person to whom notice is given]*

You are given notice that the court will hear this application—

*[applicant to insert details of the date, time and place for hearing the application]*

on...............

at...............

in...............

Along with this notice there is attached a copy of the application and the court's order fixing the hearing

Signed .......... Date ..........

WHAT YOU SHOULD DO

YOU SHOULD ATTEND OR BE REPRESENTED AT THE HEARING.

---

[1] As amended by the Act of Sederunt (Children's Hearings (Scotland) Act 2011) (Miscellaneous Amendments) 2013 (SSI 2013/172) para.4 (effective June 24, 2013).

**If you do not attend or are not represented at the hearing, the court may decide the case in your absence.** Details of the orders sought are contained in the application form.

YOU SHOULD OBTAIN ADVICE FROM A SOLICITOR OR LOCAL ADVICE AGENCY OR LAW CENTRE. You may be entitled to legal aid. Advice about legal aid is available from any solicitor, advice agency or law centre. If you instructed any person to represent you at the original hearing which granted the application you should consider bringing this application to their attention without delay.

FORM 38

Form 3.12(1)(e)

NOTICE OF APPLICATION FOR FURTHER DETENTION OF CHILD TO PERSON NAMED IN APPLICATION OR ANY OTHER PERSON UNDER SECTION 67 OF THE CHILDREN (SCOTLAND) ACT 1995

*[Repealed by the Act of Sederunt (Children's Hearings (Scotland) Act 2011) (Miscellaneous Amendments) 2013 (SSI 2013/172) para.4 (effective June 24, 2013).]*

FORM 39[1]

Rule 3.12(1)(f)

NOTICE TO RELEVANT PERSON IN APPLICATION UNDER SECTION 93(2)(a) or 94(2)(a) OF THE CHILDREN'S HEARINGS (SCOTLAND) ACT 2011 (NO PROCEDURAL HEARING)

Court ref. no.:

1. *[Place and Date]*

To *[name and address of relevant person (within the meaning of Rule 3.1(1) )]*

TAKE NOTICE that the court has received the application which accompanies this intimation.

2. **YOU MAY ATTEND COURT** for the hearing of the application as shown below.

3.  Place of Hearing:                          Sheriff Court ...............

                                                              Address ...............

                                                              ...............

                                                              ...............

                                                              ...............

     Date of hearing:                           ...............

     Time of hearing:                           ...............

                                                              ...............

(Signed)

Principal Reporter

WHAT YOU SHOULD DO

YOU SHOULD ATTEND OR BE REPRESENTED AT THE HEARING.

**If you do not attend or are not represented at the hearing, the court may decide the case in your absence.** Details of the orders sought are contained in the application form.

YOU SHOULD OBTAIN ADVICE FROM A SOLICITOR OR LOCAL ADVICE AGENCY OR LAW CENTRE. You may be entitled to legal aid. Advice about legal aid is available from any solicitor, advice agency or law centre.

---

[1] As amended by the Act of Sederunt (Children's Hearings (Scotland) Act 2011) (Miscellaneous Amendments) 2013 (SSI 2013/172) para.4 (effective June 24, 2013).

FORM 39A[1]

Rule 3.12(1)(g)

## NOTICE TO RELEVANT PERSON IN APPLICATION UNDER SECTION 94(2)(A) OF THE CHILDREN'S HEARINGS (SCOTLAND) ACT 2011 (PROCEDURAL HEARING FIXED)

Court ref. no.:

1. [*Insert place and date*]

To [*insert name and address of relevant person (within the meaning of* Rule 3.1(1)*)*]

TAKE NOTICE that the court has received the application which accompanies this intimation.

2. **PROCEDURAL HEARING:** The sheriff has fixed a procedural hearing to determine whether or not the section 67 grounds in the statement of grounds are accepted by each relevant person. The procedural hearing will take place on [*insert time and date of hearing*] at [*insert address of sheriff court*]. If you accept the grounds YOU SHOULD ATTEND OR BE REPRESENTED AT COURT ON THAT DATE so that you can tell the sheriff that you accept the section 67 grounds. If you do not attend the procedural hearing, then you should attend the hearing on evidence referred to in paragraph 3 below.

If, at the procedural hearing, all the relevant persons accept that that the information that has been given is correct then the sheriff may make a decision without hearing evidence. You have the right though to ask the sheriff to hear evidence, even if all other relevant persons accept that the information in the statement of grounds is correct.

3. A hearing on evidence has also been fixed. Unless you receive notice in accordance with rule 3.45(8) of the Act of Sederunt (Child Care and Maintenance Rules) 1997 that the sheriff has discharged that hearing, the hearing on evidence will take place on [*insert time and date of hearing*] at [*insert address of sheriff court*]. YOU SHOULD ATTEND COURT on that date for the hearing of the application.

(*signed*)

Principal Reporter

**WHAT YOU SHOULD DO:**

**YOU SHOULD ATTEND OR BE REPRESENTED AT THE HEARINGS.**

If you do not attend or are not represented at the hearings, the court may decide the case in your absence. Details of the orders sought are contained in the application form.

**YOU SHOULD OBTAIN ADVICE FROM A SOLICITOR OR LOCAL ADVICE AGENCY OR LAW CENTRE.** You may be entitled to legal aid. Advice about legal aid is available from any solicitor, advice agency or law centre.

FORM 40[2]

Rule 3.12(2)

## NOTICE TO SAFEGUARDER/CURATOR *AD LITEM IN* APPLICATION UNDER SECTION 93(2)(A) OR 94(2)(A) OF THE CHILDREN'S HEARINGS (SCOTLAND) ACT 2011

Court ref. no.:

1. [*Place and Date*]

To [*name and address of safeguarder and/or curator ad litem*]

---

[1] As inserted by the Act of Sederunt (Children's Hearings (Scotland) Act 2011) (Miscellaneous Amendments) 2013 (SSI 2013/172) para.4 (effective June 24, 2013).

[2] As amended by the Act of Sederunt (Children's Hearings (Scotland) Act 2011) (Miscellaneous Amendments) 2013 (SSI 2013/172) para.4 (effective June 24, 2013).

TAKE NOTICE that the court has received the application which accompanies this intimation.

2. A hearing of evidence in respect of the application has been fixed as follows:

Place of
Hearing:

Sheriff Court ...............

Address ...............

...............

...............

...............

Date of
hearing:

...............

Time of
hearing:

...............

...............

*(In addition, a procedural hearing has been fixed to take place on *[insert date]* at *[insert time]* within *[name court]* in chambers at *[place]*)

(Signed)
Principal Reporter

**PLEASE NOTE:**

Your attention is drawn to the provisions of rules 3.6 to 3.9 of the Act of Sederunt (Child Care and Maintenance Rules) 1997 which regulate the appointment and duties of safeguarders.

(**delete as appropriate*)

FORM 41[1]

Rule 3.14(2)

CITATION OF WITNESS OR HAVER UNDER THE CHILDREN'S HEARINGS (SCOTLAND) ACT 2011 OR THE CHILDREN (SCOTLAND) ACT 1995

Court ref. no.:

KL [address], you are required to attend at .......... Sheriff Court on .......... at .......... to give evidence in the hearing of [an application by the Principal Reporter] to the sheriff for a determination of whether the section 67 grounds in the case of *[insert name of child]* are established]

OR

[an appeal to the sheriff against a decision of a children's hearing in the case of [name of child]]

OR

[an application by *[insert name and address]* for [insert details of purpose of hearing]]

[You are required to bring with you [specify documents]].

**If you fail to attend without reasonable excuse having demanded and been paid your travelling expenses, warrant may be granted for your arrest.**

Signed PQ, Sheriff Officer;

---

[1] As amended by the Act of Sederunt (Children's Hearings (Scotland) Act 2011) (Miscellaneous Amendments) 2013 (SSI 2013/172) para.4 (effective June 24, 2013).

or

XY Solicitor/Sheriff Clerk/ Principal Reporter/Officer of the Local Authority
[address]

Note:

Within certain specified limits claims for necessary outlays and loss of earnings will be met.

Claims should be made to the person who has cited you to attend and proof of any loss of earnings should be given to that person. If you wish your travelling expenses to be paid prior to your attendance you should apply to the person who has cited you.

## FORM 42[1]

Rule 3.14(3)

### CERTIFICATE OF EXECUTION OF CITATION UNDER THE CHILDREN'S HEARINGS (SCOTLAND) ACT 2011 OR THE CHILDREN (SCOTLAND) ACT 1995

Court ref. no.:

1. [Place and Date]

I [Name and designation] hereby certify that on the above date, I duly...............
cited [full name of witness]

by

*posting, on [date] between the hours of (..........) and (..........) at the [place], a copy of [the foregoing application, warrant and] *citation/*intimation to *him/*her, in a *registered/*recorded delivery letter addressed as follows—[full name and address]

and the receipt for that letter accompanies this certificate.

*or by [set forth the mode of citation or intimation]

(signed, A B Principal Reporter)
C D Sheriff Officer
E F (Witness)
G H Solicitor

*delete as appropriate

### FORM 43[2]

Rule 3.17(3)

### *CERTIFICATE OF EXECUTION OF CITATION OF SERVICE UNDER THE CHILDREN'S HEARINGS (SCOTLAND) ACT 2011 OR THE CHILDREN (SCOTLAND) ACT 1995

Court ref. no.

1. *[Place, date]*

I *[Name and designation]* hereby certify that on the date shown above, I duly
*cited *[full name of child]*
*gave notice to *[full name of person]*
by

---

[1] As amended by the Act of Sederunt (Children's Hearings (Scotland) Act 2011) (Miscellaneous Amendments) 2013 (SSI 2013/172) para.4 (effective June 24, 2013).

[2] As amended by the Act of Sederunt (Children's Hearings (Scotland) Act 2011) (Miscellaneous Amendments) 2013 (SSI 2013/172) para.4 (effective June 24, 2013).

*posting, on *[date]* between the hours of [..........] and [..........] at the *[place]*, a copy of the foregoing application, warrant and *citation/*intimation to *him/*her, in a *registered/*recorded delivery letter addressed as follows—*[full name and address]*

and the receipt for that letter accompanies this certificate.

*or by *[set forth the mode of citation or intimation]*

[signed]

*Principal Reporter

or solicitor for applicant

[Officer of Local Authority/Sheriff clerk]

or Sheriff Officer

*[name and business address]*

and *[name and address of any witness]*

*Delete as appropriate

FORM 44A[1]

Rule 3.22(3)(a)

APPLICATION FOR AUTHORISATION OF THE GIVING OF EVIDENCE BY A WITNESS OR PARTY BY MEANS OF A LIVE LINK

Court ref. no.:

*[Insert name, address and designation of applicant*

*e.g. Principal Reporter/Parent/Safeguarder]*

in the case of

*[insert name of child]*

1. On *[insert date of application]* the Principal Reporter made an application to the sheriff to find whether the section 67 grounds [[*not accepted by the said *[insert name of child]* or *[insert name of relevant person(s) within the meaning of* Rule 3.1(1)]] or [*not understood by the said *[insert name of child]* are established] or [*as the case may be].

2. The court assigned *[insert date]* at *[insert time]* in chambers at *[insert name and address of sheriff court]* for the hearing of the application.

*3. That *[insert name and address of witness]* is a witness in the application.

4. That *[here state reasons for application]*.

5. *[Insert name of applicant]* therefore applies to the sheriff under Rule 3.22(1) of the Act of Sederunt (Child Care and Maintenance Rules) 1997 for an order that the evidence of the said *[insert name of witness]* shall be given by means of live link.

*[Signed]*

[*Principal Reporter /Parent/

Safeguarder etc. as appropriate]

[state designation, address and contact

numbers]

*(*delete as appropriate)*

---

[1] As inserted by the Act of Sederunt (Children's Hearings (Scotland) Act 2011) (Miscellaneous Amendments) 2013 (SSI 2013/172) para.4 (effective June 24, 2013).

FORM 44B[1]

Rule 3.22(3)(b)

## APPLICATION FOR AUTHORISATION OF THE MAKING OF A SUBMISSION BY MEANS OF A LIVE LINK

Court ref. no.:

*[Insert name, address and designation of applicant]*
*e.g. Principal Reporter/Parent/Safeguarder*
in the case of
*[insert name of child]*

1. On *[insert date of application]* the Principal Reporter made an application to the sheriff to find whether the section 67 grounds [[*not accepted by the said *[insert name of child]* or *[insert name of relevant person(s) within the meaning of* Rule 3.1(1)]] or [*not understood by the said *[insert name of child]* are established] or [*as the case may be].

2. The court assigned *[insert date]* at *[insert time]* in chambers at *[insert name and address of sheriff court]* for the hearing of the application.

3. That *[insert name and address of person]* wishes to make a submission in respect of the application.

4. That *[here state reasons for application]*.

5. The *[insert name of applicant]* therefore applies to the sheriff under Rule 3.22(1) of the Act of Sederunt (Child Care and Maintenance Rules) 1997 for an order that the submission of the said *[insert name]* shall be given by means of live link.

*[Signed]*
[*Principal
Reporter/Parent/Safeguarder
etc. as appropriate]
[state designation, address and
contact numbers]

*(*delete as appropriate)*


FORM 45[2]

Rule 3.26

## APPLICATION FOR A CHILD ASSESSMENT ORDER UNDER SECTION 35 OF THE CHILDREN'S HEARINGS (SCOTLAND) ACT 2011

Court ref. no.:
Date lodged..........

**Application to Sheriff Court at**

for a Child Assessment Order under section 35 of the Children's Hearings (Scotland) Act 2011

**PART 1. DETAILS OF APPLICANT AND OTHER PERSONS WHO THE APPLICANT BELIEVES SHOULD RECEIVE NOTICE OF THE APPLICATION**

APPLICANT          *[insert name, address, telephone, DX and fax numbers of local authority]*

---

[1] As inserted by the Act of Sederunt (Children's Hearings (Scotland) Act 2011) (Miscellaneous Amendments) 2013 (SSI 2013/172) para.4 (effective June 24, 2013).

[2] As amended by the Act of Sederunt (Children's Hearings (Scotland) Act 2011) (Miscellaneous Amendments) 2013 (SSI 2013/172) para.4 (effective June 24, 2013).

CHILD                    **[insert name, address, gender and date of birth]***

RELEVANT PER-            *[insert name, address and the basis for the person being*
SON(S)                   *a relevant person within the meaning of* Rule 3.1(1) *of*
                         *the Act]*

SAFEGUARDER             *[insert name, address, telephone, DX and fax numbers*
                        *(if known) of any safeguarder]*

THE PRINCIPAL RE-       *[insert address, telephone, DX and fax numbers]*
PORTER

ANY OTHER PER-          [For example, any person who is caring for the child at
SON WHO SHOULD          the time of the application being made: *insert name, ad-*
RECEIVE NOTICE OF       *dress and telephone number of person and provide*
THE APPLICATION         *details of their interest in the application and/or child]*
                        [The court may seek views from applicants in relation to
                        other persons on whom service should be made.]

**\*Note: Information to be provided in Part 3 where applicant does not wish to disclose the address or whereabouts of the child or any other person to persons receiving notice of the application.**

## PART 2. INFORMATION ABOUT THE APPLICATION AND ORDERS SOUGHT

GROUNDS FOR MAKING APPLICATION

*[applicant to provide details of grounds for making the application: including reasons why a Child Protection Order is not being sought]*

\*OTHER APPLICATIONS AND ORDERS WHICH AFFECT THE CHILD

*[insert details of any other applications or orders made which affect or are relevant to the child who is the subject of this application]*

REPORTS/DOCUMENTARY EVIDENCE ETC.

The following reports/documentary evidence is attached/will be produced\*—*[list any reports, statements or affidavits which are or will be produced at any subsequent hearing of the application]*

\*delete as appropriate

## PART 3. DETAILS OF THE ASSESSMENT AND ORDERS SOUGHT

ASSESSMENT

*[in terms of* section 35(2) *insert the following details of the assessment sought]*

a. The type of assessment is [provide details of the type of assessment that is sought including information on the child's health or development or the way in which the child has been or is being treated or neglected].

b. The assessment would begin on *[insert date] (which must be no later than 24 hours after the order is granted).*

c. The assessment will have effect for *[insert number of days]* from that date (*which must not exceed the maximum period of 3 days* ).

d. The person(s) to be authorised to carry out any assessment is/are *[insert name(s), designation and address]*

e. *[insert name and address]* would be required to produce the child to the authorised person and permit that person or any other authorised person to carry out an assessment in accordance with the order.

OTHER ORDERS

*[in terms of* section 35(3) *provide the following information about any other order sought]*

\*a. In terms of section 35(3)(b) an order is sought to permit the child to be taken to *[insert details of the place]* for the purpose of the assessment, and to authorise the child to be kept at that place or any other place for [*specify period*].

*b.    In terms of section 35(3)(c) the sheriff is requested to make the following directions as to contact with the child by [*insert name and address of person and his or her relationship with child*] while the child is in the aforementioned place

[*insert details of any directions sought as to contact with the child*]

   [*insert details and grounds for any order sought in relation*

   a)   *to non-disclosure of address or whereabouts of child; or*

   b)   *service of restricted documents on child.*]

*delete as appropriate

### PART 4. DETAILS OF FIRST ORDER SOUGHT FROM THE SHERIFF

The applicant requests the sheriff to:

a.   Fix a hearing.

*b.   Order service on the child, together with a notice in form 26* or order service of the following documents only [*insert details of documents to be served on child, e.g. notice in form 26 only*]

*c.   Order service of a copy of the application and the first order on the persons listed in Part 1 of this application, together with a notice in form 34.

*d.   Order that the address of [*insert name*] should not be disclosed in the application.

*e.   Dispense with service on the child or any other person for the following reasons [*insert details*].

*delete as appropriate

Signed .......... Date ..........

[name, designation and address

telephone, DX and fax numbers]

FORM 46[1]

Rule 3.27(2)

CHILD ASSESSMENT ORDER UNDER SECTION 35 OF THE CHILDREN'S HEARINGS (SCOTLAND) ACT 2011

Court ref. no.:

**IN THE SHERIFF COURT**

**at**..............

**on**..............

The sheriff orders that there shall be a [*insert details of assessment*] assessment of the child [*insert name, address, gender and date of birth*]

This order has effect from [ *insert time and date (to be no later than 24 hours after the order is granted)* ] until [ *insert time and date (not exceeding 3 days from time the order took effect)* ]

The person authorised to carry out the assessment is [*insert name, designation and address*]

\* The sheriff orders that [*insert name and address*] is required to produce the child to the authorised person and permit that person or any other authorised person to carry out the assessment in accordance with this order.

---

[1] As amended by the Act of Sederunt (Children's Hearings (Scotland) Act 2011) (Miscellaneous Amendments) 2013 (SSI 2013/172) para.4 (effective June 24, 2013).

In terms of section 35(3)(b) the sheriff permits the child to be taken to [ *insert details of the place* ] for the purpose of the assessment, and authorises the child to be kept at that place or any other place for [ *specify period* ].

\* In terms of section 35(3)(c) the sheriff makes the following directions as to contact with the child by *[insert name and address of person and his or her relationship with child]* while the child is in the aforementioned place—

*[insert details of any directions sought as to contact with the child]*

\*delete as appropriate

For the purpose of enforcing this order, warrant is granted to officers of law for all lawful execution, including-

(a) searching for and apprehending the child;

(b) taking the child to the authorised place;

(c) where (i) it is not reasonably practicable to take the child immediately to the authorised place; and (ii) the authorised place is not a place of safety, taking the child to and detaining the child in a place of safety for as short a period of time as is practicable;

(d) so far as necessary, by breaking open shut and lockfast places.

Signed ..........

Sheriff ..........

Time ..........

## FORM 47[1]

Rule 3.30

APPLICATION FOR A CHILD PROTECTION ORDER BY LOCAL AUTHORITY UNDER SECTION 37 OF THE CHILDREN'S HEARINGS (SCOTLAND) ACT 2011

Court ref. no.:

Date lodged ..........

**Application to Sheriff at**

for a Child Protection Order under section 37(1) of the Children's Hearings (Scotland) Act 2011

**PART 1. DETAILS OF APPLICANT AND OTHER PERSONS WHO THE APPLICANT BELIEVES SHOULD RECEIVE NOTICE OF THE APPLICATION**

| | |
|---|---|
| APPLICANT | *[insert name, address, telephone, DX and fax numbers of the local authority]* |
| CHILD | *[insert name, address, gender and date of birth]* |
| RELEVANT PERSON(S) | *[insert name, address and the basis for the person being a relevant person within the meaning of* section Rule 3.1(1) of the Act] |
| SAFEGUARDER | *[insert name, address, telephone, DX and fax numbers (if known) of any safeguarder]* |
| THE PRINCIPAL REPORTER | *[insert address, telephone, DX and fax numbers]* |
| ANY OTHER PERSON WHO SHOULD RECEIVE NOTICE OF THE APPLICATION | *[For example, any person who is caring for the child at the time of the application being made: insert name, address and telephone number of person and provide details of their interest in the application and/or child]* |

---

[1] As amended by the Act of Sederunt (Children's Hearings (Scotland) Act 2011) (Miscellaneous Amendments) 2013 (SSI 2013/172) para.4 (effective June 24, 2013).

**\*Note: Information to be provided in Part 3 where applicant does not wish to disclose the address or whereabouts of the child or any other person to persons receiving notice of the application.**

## PART 2. INFORMATION ABOUT THE APPLICATION AND ORDERS SOUGHT

GROUNDS FOR MAKING APPLICATION

*[applicant to provide details of grounds for making the application: see* section 38(2) and 39(2) of the Act]

OTHER APPLICATIONS AND ORDERS WHICH AFFECT THE CHILD

*[insert details of any other applications or orders made which affect or are relevant to the child who is the subject of this application]*

SUPPORTING EVIDENCE

The following supporting evidence is produced—

*[list reports, statements, affidavits or other evidence produced]*

## PART 3. DETAILS OF ORDER AND DIRECTION(S) SOUGHT

ORDER SOUGHT: The applicant requests the sheriff to make a Child Protection Order in respect of the child *[insert name]*

In terms of section 37 the applicant seeks an order to *[insert details of the order sought including details of the specified person (if appropriate)]*.

**\*DIRECTIONS IN RELATION TO THE EXERCISE OR FULFILMENT OF PARENTAL RESPONSIBILITIES OR PARENTAL RIGHTS**

In terms of section 42(1) the applicant seeks the following direction(s)—
*insert details of the direction(s) sought]*.

*ANY OTHER AUTHORISATION, REQUIREMENT OR DIRECTION(S) SOUGHT*

*[insert here details and grounds for any other authorisation, requirement or direction sought including—*

(a) *an information non-disclosure direction under* section 40;

(b) *a contact direction under* section 41.]

## PART 4. DETAILS OF ORDER SOUGHT

The applicant requests the sheriff to:

a. Make a child protection order in respect of the said child *[insert name of the child]* including any authorisation, requirement or direction set out in Part 3 of the application.

\*b. Order the applicant to forthwith serve a copy of the Child Protection Order *[and a copy of the application]* on,

    i. the child, together with a notice in form 50\* or orders service of the following documents only *[insert details of documents to be served on child, e.g. notice inform 50 only]*; and

    ii. the other persons listed in Part 1 of this application, together with a notice in form 51.

\*c. Order that the address of *[insert name]* should not be disclosed in the application.

\*d. Dispense with service on the child or any other person for the following reasons

*[insert details]*.

\*delete as appropriate

Signed .............. Date .........

[name, designation and address

telephone, DX and fax numbers]

FORM 48[1]

Rule 3.30

## APPLICATION FOR A CHILD PROTECTION ORDER BY ANY PERSON (OTHER THAN A LOCAL AUTHORITY) UNDER SECTION 37 OF THE CHILDREN'S HEARINGS (SCOTLAND) ACT 2011

Court ref. no.:

Date lodged.........

**Application to Sheriff at**

for a Child Protection Order under section 37(1) of the Children's Hearings (Scotland) Act 2011

### PART 1. DETAILS OF APPLICANT OR OTHER PERSONS WHO THE APPLICANT BELIEVES SHOULD RECEIVE NOTICE OF THE APPLICATION

APPLICANT
*[insert name and address, telephone, DX and fax numbers and capacity in which application is made]*

CHILD
*[insert name, address, gender and date of birth]*\*

RELEVANT PERSON(S)
*[insert name, address and the basis for the person being a relevant person within the meaning of Rule 3.1(1) of the Act]*

SAFEGUARDER
*[insert name, address, telephone, DX and fax numbers (if known) of any safeguarder]*

LOCAL AUTHORITY
*[insert and address, DX and telephone and fax numbers]*

THE PRINCIPAL REPORTER
*[insert address, telephone, DX and fax numbers]*

ANY OTHER PERSON WHO SHOULD RECEIVE NOTICE OF THE APPLICATION
*[For example, any person who is caring for the child at the time of the application being made: insert name and address of person and provide details of their interest in the application and/or child]*

**\*Note: Information to be provided in Part 3 where applicant does not wish to disclose the address or whereabouts of the child or any other person to persons receiving notice of the application.**

### PART 2. INFORMATION ABOUT THE APPLICATION AND ORDERS SOUGHT

GROUNDS FOR MAKING APPLICATION

*[applicant to provide details of grounds for making the application: see section 39(2) of the Act ]*

OTHER APPLICATIONS AND ORDERS WHICH AFFECT THE CHILD

*[insert details of any other applications or orders made which affect or are relevant to the child who is the subject of this application]*

SUPPORTING EVIDENCE

The following supporting evidence is produced—

*[list reports, statements, affidavits or other evidence produced]*

### PART 3. DETAILS OF ORDER AND DIRECTION SOUGHT ETC.

---

[1] As amended by the Act of Sederunt (Children's Hearings (Scotland) Act 2011) (Miscellaneous Amendments) 2013 (SSI 2013/172) para.4 (effective June 24, 2013).

ORDER SOUGHT: The applicant requests the sheriff to make a Child Protection Order in respect of the child *[insert name]*

In terms of section 37 the applicant seeks an order to

*[insert details of the order sought including details of the specified person (if appropriate)].*

*DIRECTIONS IN RELATION TO THE EXERCISE OR FULFILMENT OF PARENTAL RESPONSIBILITIES OR PARENTAL RIGHTS

In terms of section 42(1) the applicant seeks the following direction(s)—

*[insert details of the direction(s) sought].*

*ANY OTHER AUTHORISATION, REQUIREMENT OR DIRECTION(S) SOUGHT*

*[insert here details and grounds for any other authorisation, requirement or direction sought including—*

(a) *an information non-disclosure direction under section 40*;

(b) *a contact direction under section 41.]*

*delete as appropriate

### PART 4. DETAILS OF FIRST ORDER SOUGHT FROM THE SHERIFF

The applicant requests the sheriff to:

a. Make a child protection order in respect of the said child *[insert name of the child]* including any authorisation, requirement or direction set out in Part 3 of the application.

*b. Order the applicant to forthwith serve a copy of the Child Protection Order [and a copy of the application] on,

    i. the child, together with a notice in form 50* or orders service of the following documents only *[insert details of documents to be served on child, e.g. notice in form 50 only]*; and

    ii. the other persons listed in Part 1 of this application, together with a notice in form 51.

*c. Order that the address of *[insert name]* should not be disclosed in the application.

*d. Dispense with service on the child or any other person for the following reasons *[insert details].*

*delete as appropriate

Signed .......... Date ..........

[name, designation and address

telephone, DX and fax numbers]

FORM 49[1]

Rule 3.31(2)

CHILD PROTECTION ORDER UNDER SECTION 37 OF THE CHILDREN'S HEARINGS (SCOTLAND) ACT 2011

Court ref. no.:

**IN THE SHERIFF COURT**

**at**..........

**on**..........

In the application by *[insert name and address]* for a Child Protection Order/ Child Assessment Order *the sheriff makes a Child Protection Order in respect of the child *[insert name, address (unless an information non disclosure order made), gender and date of birth of the child]*

*The sheriff orders that *[insert name and address of person]* is required to produce the child to a specified person *[insert name and address of the specified person].*

---

[1] As amended by the Act of Sederunt (Children's Hearings (Scotland) Act 2011) (Miscellaneous Amendments) 2013 (SSI 2013/172) para.4 (effective June 24, 2013).

*The sheriff authorises the removal of the child by the specified person to *[insert details of the place] a place of safety and for the keeping of the child at that place.

*The sheriff authorises the prevention of the removal of the child from [insert details of the place].

*The sheriff authorises the carrying out (subject to section 186) of an assessment of—

(a)    the child's health or development, or

(b)    the way in which the child has been or is being treated or neglected.

DIRECTIONS

The Sheriff directs that—

(a)    *the location of any place of safety; and

(b)    *any other information [specify information]

must not be disclosed (directly or indirectly) to the following persons (specify person or class of persons)

(*delete as applicable)

*In terms of section 41 the sheriff gives the following directions to the applicant as to contact with the child—

[insert details of any directions]

*In terms of section 42 the sheriff gives the following directions as to the exercise or fulfilment of parental responsibilities or parental rights in repect of the child—

[insert details of any directions]

*delete as appropriate

For the purpose of enforcing this order, warrant is granted to officers of law for all lawful execution, including—

(a)    searching for and apprehending the child;

(b)    taking the child to the authorised place;

(c)    where (i) it is not reasonably practicable to take the child immediately to the authorised place; and (ii) the authorised place is not a place of safety, taking the child to and detaining the child in a place of safety for as short a period of time as is practicable;

(d)    so far as necessary, by breaking open shut and lockfast places.

Signed..........

Sheriff..........

Time..........

FORM 50[1]

Rule 3.32(a)

NOTICE OF CHILD PROTECTION ORDER TO CHILD IN TERMS OF SEC-
TION 37 OF THE CHILDREN'S HEARINGS (SCOTLAND) ACT 2011
ARRANGEMENTS TO KEEP YOU SAFE

Court ref. no.:

Dear [insert name by which child is known]

I am writing to tell you that because there were worries about your safety the court was asked to sort out some practical arrangements to make sure you are kept safe.

After hearing about your situation the court made an order, called a "Child Protection Order". That means that the court gave permission to [insert in simple language the order(s) and any directions granted and their effect on the child]

---

[1] As amended by the Act of Sederunt (Children's Hearings (Scotland) Act 2011) (Miscellaneous Amendments) 2013 (SSI 2013/172) para.4 (effective June 24, 2013).

If you are unhappy with this order or any authorisation, requirement or direction you can ask the court to change it. For example, you might want to ask the court to allow you *[insert an example e.g. to allow more contact with certain members of the family etc.]*

**Any change must be requested without delay**

If you want to do this you can ask the court which made the order to listen to you. You will need a lawyer to help you.

***Remember*** that if you do not agree with the order or any directions you must get advice **IMMEDIATELY.**

*In the meantime you must do what the order says.*

> **If you are unsure about what to do you can get free legal advice from a Lawyer or Local Advice Agency or Law Centre about the application and about legal aid.**
> **The Scottish Child Law Centre can refer you to specially trained lawyers who can help you.**
> **They give advice on their free phone no (0800 328 8970) any time between 9.30 am and 4.00 pm Monday to Friday.**

You will see that, along with this letter, there is [a copy of the application which was made to the court, and the order the court (delete if appropriate)] has made which affects you. If you decide to get advice, or to ask someone to go to court for you, make sure that you give your advisor a copy of the application, and the court's order.

Signed:............... Date: ...............

Time..........

FORM 51[1]

Rule 3.32(b)

**NOTICE OF CHILD PROTECTION ORDER TO A NAMED PERSON UNDER SECTION 37 OF THE CHILDREN'S HEARINGS (SCOTLAND) ACT 2011**

Court ref. no.:

**Notice of Child Protection Order made under section 37 of the Children's Hearings (Scotland) Act 2011 in the Sheriff Court at**

To *[insert name and address of person to whom notice is given].*

You are given notice of the making of a Child Protection Order in respect of the child *[insert name, address, gender and date of birth of child]* by the sheriff at *[name of sheriff court]* on *[date of order].*

Along with this notice there is attached a copy of the application and the order.

Signed .......... Date ..........

WHAT YOU SHOULD DO

**YOU MUST COMPLY WITH THE ORDER AND ANY AUTHORISA-TION, REQUIREMENT OR DIRECTION CONTAINED WITHIN IT. FAIL-URE TO COMPLY IS AN OFFENCE UNDER SECTION 59 OF THE CHIL-DREN'S HEARINGS (SCOTLAND) ACT 2011 AND COULD LEAD TO YOU BEING FINED.**

*YOU MAY WISH TO OBTAIN ADVICE FROM A SOLICITOR OR LOCAL ADVICE AGENCY OR LAW CENTRE. You may be entitled to legal aid. Advice about legal aid is available from any solicitor, advice agency or law centre.

---

[1] As amended by the Act of Sederunt (Children's Hearings (Scotland) Act 2011) (Miscellaneous Amendments) 2013 (SSI 2013/172) para.4 (effective June 24, 2013).

**\*You may be able to contest or vary the order, and in such circumstances you should obtain legal advice without delay.**

\*delete as appropriate

FORM 52[1]

Rule 3.33(1)

APPLICATION TO VARY OR TERMINATE A CHILD PROTECTION ORDER UNDER SECTION 48 OF THE CHILDREN'S HEARINGS (SCOTLAND) ACT 2011

Court ref. no.:

Date lodged.........

**Application to Sheriff at**

to vary or terminate a Child Protection Order under section 48 of the Children's Hearings (Scotland) Act 2011

**PART 1. DETAILS OF APPLICANT AND OTHER PERSONS WHO THE APPLICANT BELIEVES SHOULD RECEIVE NOTICE OF THE APPLICATION**

APPLICANT *[insert name, address, telephone, DX and fax numbers, and details of the capacity of the person making the application]*

CHILD *[insert name, address, gender and date of birth]\**

SAFEGUARDER **If not applicant** *[insert name, address, telephone, DX and fax numbers (if known) of any safeguarder]*

RELEVANT PERSON(S) **If not applicant** *[insert name, address and telephone number (if known) and the basis for the person being a relevant person within the meaning of section Rule 3.1(1) of the Act ]*

LOCAL AUTHORITY *[insert name, address, telephone, DX and fax numbers]*

THE PRINCIPAL REPORTER *[insert address, telephone, DX and fax numbers]*

ANY OTHER PERSON WHO SHOULD RECEIVE NOTICE OF THE APPLICATION *[For example, any person who is caring for the child at the time of the application being made any person who applied for the child protection order or any person specified in the order under section 37(2)(a) , unless the person is the applicant: insert name, address and telephone number of person and provide details of their interest in the application and/or child]*

**\*Note: Information to be provided in Part 3 where applicant does not wish to disclose the address or whereabouts of the child or any other person to persons receiving notice of the application.**

**PART 2. INFORMATION ABOUT THE APPLICATION AND ORDERS SOUGHT**

On *[date of order]* the Sheriff made a Child Protection Order in the following terms *[insert full details of order, including any authorisation, requirement or direction attaching to it]* *[Copy original order must be attached in terms of* Rule 3.33 *]*.

---

[1] As amended by the Act of Sederunt (Children's Hearings (Scotland) Act 2011) (Miscellaneous Amendments) 2013 (SSI 2013/172) para.4 (effective June 24, 2013).

OTHER APPLICATIONS AND ORDERS WHICH AFFECT THE CHILD

*[insert details of any other applications or orders made which affect or are relevant to the child who is the subject of this application]*

ORDER(S), INCLUDING ANY AUTHORISATION, REQUIREMENT OR DIRECTION THE VARIATION OR TERMINATION OF WHICH ARE SOUGHT

*[applicant to insert details of order now sought]*

GROUNDS FOR MAKING APPLICATION

*[applicant to provide details of grounds for seeking the variation or termination]*

SUPPORTING EVIDENCE

The following supporting evidence is produced—

*[list reports, statements, affidavits or other evidence produced]*

**PART 3. DETAILS OF ORDER SOUGHT AND ANY TERMS, CONDITIONS OR DIRECTIONS**

FIRST ORDER

The applicant requests the sheriff to:

a. Assign a hearing on the application.

*b. Order the applicant to forthwith serve a copy of the application together with the date of hearing on,

    i. The Principal Reporter

    ii. The Local Authority

    iii. The child, together with a notice in form 27; and

    iv. The other persons listed in part 1 of this application, together with a notice in form 35.

*c. Dispense with service on the child or any other person for the following reasons *[insert details]*.

And thereafter to *[enter details of what you want the sheriff to vary or terminate]*.

  *delete as appropriate

Signed ...............

Date ..........

[name, designation and address
telephone, DX and fax numbers}

FORM 53[1]

Rule 3.33(5)

VARIATION OR TERMINATION OF CHILD PROTECTION ORDER UNDER SECTION 48 OF THE CHILDREN'S HEARINGS (SCOTLAND) ACT 2011

Court ref. no.:

**IN THE SHERIFF COURT**
**at..........**
**on..........**

The sheriff makes the following order in the application by *[insert name and address]* to vary or terminate a Child Protection Order in respect of the child *[insert name, address (unless order made re non disclosure), gender and date of birth of the child]*

*[insert order granted in this application]*

AUTHORISATIONS, REQUIREMENTS AND DIRECTIONS IN FORCE UNDER CHILD PROTECTION ORDER AFTER VARIATION

*[insert name and address of person]* is ordered to produce the child to the specified person *[insert name and address of the specified person]*.

*the removal of the child by the specified person to * *[insert details of the place]* a place of safety and for the keeping of the child at that place is authorised.

---

[1] As amended by the Act of Sederunt (Children's Hearings (Scotland) Act 2011) (Miscellaneous Amendments) 2013 (SSI 2013/172) para.4 (effective June 24, 2013).

*the prevention of the removal of the child from *[insert details of the place]* is authorised.

*the carrying out (subject to section 186 of the Act) of an assessment of—

(a)  the child's health or development, or

(b)  the way in which the child has been or is being treated or neglected

is authorised.

DIRECTIONS

The Sheriff directs that—

(a)  *the location of any place of safety; and

(b)  *any other information *[specify information]*

must not be disclosed (directly or indirectly) to the following person or class of person *(specify person or class of person)*

(*delete as applicable)

*In terms of section 41 the sheriff gives the following directions to the applicant as to contact with the child—

*[insert details of any directions]*

*In terms of section 42 the sheriff gives the following directions as to the exercise or fulfilment of parental responsibilities or parental rights in respect of the child—

*[insert details of any directions]*

*delete as appropriate

For the purpose of enforcing this order, warrant is granted to officers of law for all lawful execution, including—

(a)  searching for and apprehending the child;

(b)  taking the child to the authorised place;

(c)  where (i) it is not reasonably practicable to take the child immediately to the authorised place; and (ii) the authorised place is not a place of safety, taking the child to and detaining the child in a place of safety for as short a period of time as is practicable;

(d)  so far as necessary, by breaking open shut and lockfast places.

Signed ..........

Sheriff ..........

Time..........


FORM 54[1]

Rule 3.35

APPLICATION FOR EXCLUSION ORDER BY LOCAL AUTHORITY UNDER SECTION 76 OF THE CHILDREN (SCOTLAND) ACT 1995

Court ref. no.:

**Application to Sheriff**                                     Date lodged..........

**at**

for an Exclusion Order under section 76(1) of the Children (Scotland) Act 1995

**PART 1. DETAILS OF APPLICANT AND OTHER PERSONS WHO THE APPLICANT BELIEVES SHOULD RECEIVE NOTICE OF THE AP-PLICATION**

---

[1] As amended by the Act of Sederunt (Children's Hearings (Scotland) Act 2011) (Miscellaneous Amendments) 2013 (SSI 2013/172) para.4 (effective June 24, 2013).

| APPLICANT | *[insert name and address, telephone, DX and fax numbers]* |
| CHILD | *[insert name, address, gender and date of birth]\** |
| THE NAMED PERSON | *[insert name and address of person to be excluded]* |
| SAFEGUARDER | *[insert name, address, telephone, DX and fax numbers (if known) of any safeguarder appointed by a children's hearing or court in respect of the child]* |
| RELEVANT PERSON(S) | *[insert name, address and the basis for the person being a relevant person within the meaning of Rule 3.1(1) of the Act]* |
| THE APPROPRIATE PERSON | *[insert name and address of person who is to have care of the child if the order is made]* |
| THE PRINCIPAL REPORTER | *[insert address, telephone, DX and fax numbers]* |
| ANY OTHER PERSON WHO SHOULD RECEIVE NOTICE OF THE APPLICATION | *[insert name, address and telephone number of person and provide details of their interest in the aplication and/or child]* |

\*Note: Information to be provided in Part 3 where applicant does not wish to disclose the address or whereabouts of the child or any other person to persons receiving notice of the application.

**PART 2. INFORMATION ABOUT THE APPLICATION AND ORDERS SOUGHT**

CONDITIONS FOR MAKING APPLICATION

*[applicant to provide details of grounds for making the application including the address of the family home and details of all persons resident there.]*

ANY OTHER RELEVANT APPLICATION OR ORDER WHICH AFFECTS THE CHILD

*[insert details of any other aplications or orders made which affect or are relevant to the child who is the subject of this application]*

SUPPORTING EVIDENCE

The following supporting evidence is produced—

*[list reports, statements, affidavits or other evidence produced]*

PROPOSALS BY THE LOCAL AUTHORITY FOR FINANCIAL OR OTHER SUPPORT FOR THE NAMED PERSON

*[insert details; Section 76(9) and (10) of the Act refer]*

**PART 3. DETAILS OF ORDER SOUGHT AND ANY TERMS, CONDITIONS OR DIRECTIONS**

ORDER SOUGHT: The applicant requests the sheriff to *[insert details of the order sought and any terms and conditions to be attached to the ordeer]* in respect of the child *[insert name]*

ANCILLARY OR INTERIM ORDERS SOUGHT

In terms of section 77(3) the following orders or interim orders are sought:

*[specify orders sought and provide information about the reasons for seeking order]*

TERMS AND CONDITIONS TO BE ATTACHED TO ORDER

In terms of section 77(7) the applicant seeks an order to:

*[insert details of the order sought].*

DIRECTIONS AS TO PRESERVATION OF NAMED PERSON'S PROPERTY

In terms of section 77(5) the applicant seeks the following direction:

*[insert details of the direction sought].*

In terms of section 78(1) a power of arrest is sought in relation to:

*[insert details of interdict and provide information about the reasons for seeking power of arrest]*

## PART 4. DETAILS OF FIRST ORDER SOUGHT FROM THE SHERIFF

The applicant requests the sheriff to:

  a.  Fix a hearing.

  b.  Order the applicant to forthwith serve a copy of the application on

      i.  the child, together with a notice in form 28;

      ii.  the named person, together with a notice in Form 36 and

      iii.  the persons listed in paragraph 1 of this application, together with a notice in form 36.

*c.  Dispense with service on the child or any other person for the following reasons *[insert details]*

*d.  Make an interim exclusion order excluding the named person from the child's family home in terms of part 2 *on the terms and conditions set out in part 3 above, and subject to the directions sought.

*e.  Grant the following ancillary order. *[specify order sought]*

*f.  Grant a power of arrest.

*delete as appropriate

Signed.................... Date..............

[name, designation and address

telephone, DX and fax numbers]


### FORM 55[1]

Rule 3.37(2)

### EXCLUSION ORDER UNDER SECTION 76 OF THE CHILDREN (SCOTLAND) ACT 1995

Court ref. no.:

## IN THE SHERIFF COURT

**at.........**

**on.........**

In the application by the Local Authority for an exclusion order in terms of section 76 of the Act the sheriff orders that *[insert name and address of named person]* shall be excluded from *[insert address of child's family home]* *forthwith/from *[insert date]* until *[insert date when order shall cease to have effect].*

*From the effective date the rights of occupancy of *[insert name]* from the said address are suspended.

*delete as appropriate

ANCILLARY ORDERS

In terms of section 77 the sheriff makes the following ancillary orders:

*[insert details of the orders granted and any terms and conditions or directions made by the sheriff or power of arrest attached to any interdict]*

For the purpose of enforcing this order warrant is granted for all lawful execution, including warrant to open shut and lockfast places.

Signed..............

Sheriff at.........

Time.........

---

[1] As amended by the Act of Sederunt (Children's Hearings (Scotland) Act 2011) (Miscellaneous Amendments) 2013 (SSI 2013/172) para.4 (effective June 24, 2013).

FORM 56[1] [2]

Rule 3.38(1) and (2)

## CERTIFICATE OF DELIVERY TO THE CHIEF CONSTABLE UNDER SECTION 78 OF THE CHILDREN (SCOTLAND) ACT 1995

Court ref. no.:

*[Insert place and date]*I,.......... hereby certify that upon the..........day of I duly delivered to the chief constable of the Police Service of Scotland (*insert details of the documents delivered*). This I did by (*state method of service*).

Signed..........

(name, designation and address)

(*add designation and business address*)

FORM 57[3]

Rule 3.40(1)

## APPLICATION TO VARY OR RECALL AN EXCLUSION ORDER UNDER SECTION 79(3) OF THE CHILDREN (SCOTLAND) ACT 1995

Court ref. no.:

Date lodged..........

**Application to Sheriff at**

to vary or recall an Exclusion Order under section 79(3) of the Children (Scotland) Act 1995

**PART 1. DETAILS OF A APPLICANT AND OTHER PERSONS WHO THE APPLICANT BELIEVES SHOULD RECEIVE NOTICE OF THE APPLICATION**

| | |
|---|---|
| APPLICANT | *[insert name, address, telephone, DX and fax numbers, and details of the capacity of the person making the application]* |
| CHILD | *[insert name, address, gender and date of birth]** |
| THE NAMED PERSON | **If not applicant** *[insert name and address of person excluded]* |
| SAFEGUARDER | *[insert name, address, telephone, DX and fax numbers (if known) of any safeguarder appointed by a children's hearing or court in respect of the child]* |
| APPROPRIATE PERSON(S) | **If not applicant** *[insert name, address and the basis for the person being an appropriate person within the meaning of section 76(2)(c) of the Act ]* |
| RELEVANT PERSON | *[insert name, address, and the basis for the person being a relevant person within the meaning of Rule 3.1(1) ]* |

---

[1] As amended by the Act of Sederunt (Sheriff Court Rules) (Miscellaneous Amendments) 2013 (SI 2013/135) para.5 (effective May 27, 2013).
[2] As amended by the Act of Sederunt (Children's Hearings (Scotland) Act 2011) (Miscellaneous Amendments) 2013 (SSI 2013/172) para.4 (effective June 24, 2013).
[3] As amended by the Act of Sederunt (Children's Hearings (Scotland) Act 2011) (Miscellaneous Amendments) 2013 (SSI 2013/172) para.4 (effective June 24, 2013).

THE PRINCIPAL REPORTER  *[insert address, telephone, DX and fax numbers]*
ANY OTHER PERSON WHO  *[insert name, address and telephone numbers of*
SHOULD RECEIVE NOTICE  *person and provide details of their interest in*
OF THE APPLICATION  *the application and/or child]*

***\*Note: Information to be provided in Part 3 where applicant does not wish to disclose the address or whereabouts of the child or any other person to persons receiving notice of the application***

PART2. INFORMATION ABOUT THE APPLICATION AND ORDERS SOUGHT

On *[date of order]* the sheriff made an exclusion order in the following terms *[insert full details of order and conditions attaching to it] [Copy original order to be attached].*

OTHER APPLICATIONS AND ORDERS WHICH AFFECT THE CHILD

*[insert details of any other applications or orders made which affect or are relevant to the child who is the subject of this application]*

SUPPORTING EVIDENCE

The following supporting evidence is produced—

*[list reports, statements, affidavits or other evidence including financial information produced]*

**PART 3. DETAILS OF ORDER SOUGHT AND ANY TERMS, CONDITIONS OR DIRECTIONS**

ORDER SOUGHT: The applicant requests the sheriff to *[insert details of the variation or recall sought and any terms and conditions to be attached to the order]* in respect of the child [insert name] *[insert here details and grounds for any order sought in relation*

  a)  *to non-disclosure of address or whereabouts of child; or*
  b)  *service of restricted documents on child.]*

**PART 4. DETAILS OF FIRST ORDER SOUGHT FROM THE SHERIFF**

The applicant requests the sheriff to:

  a.  Fix a hearing.
  *b.  Order the applicant to forthwith serve a copy of the application on
     i.  the Principal Reporter
     ii.  the Local Authority
     iii.  the named person, together with a notice in Form 37; and
     iv.  the child, together with a notice in form 29;
     v.  the persons listed in part 1 of this application, together with a notice in Form 37.
  *c.  Dispense with service on the child or any other person for the following reasons *[insert details]*
  *d.  Grant the following ancillary order, *[specify order sought]*
  *e.  Grant a power of arrest.
*delete as appropriate

Signed.................... Date...............
[name, designation and address
telephone, DX and fax numbers]

FORM 58[1]

Rule 3.40(3)

VARIATION OF EXCLUSION ORDER UNDER SECTION 79 OF THE CHILDREN (SCOTLAND) ACT 1995

---

[1] As amended by the Act of Sederunt (Children's Hearings (Scotland) Act 2011) (Miscellaneous Amendments) 2013 (SSI 2013/172) para.4 (effective June 24, 2013).

Court ref. no.:

**IN THE SHERIFF COURT**
**at..........**
**on..........**

The sheriff makes the following order in the application by *[insert name and address]* to vary or recall an exclusion order in respect of *[insert name and address of named person]* in relation to

*[insert address of child's family home]*
*[insert order granted in this application]*

TERMS AND CONDITIONS IN FORCE UNDER EXCLUSION ORDER
AFTER VARIATION

\* *[insert name and address of named person]* is excluded from *[insert address of child's family home]* from *[insert date]* until *[insert date when order shall cease to have effect]*.

\*from *[insert date]* the rights of occupancy of *[insert name]* from the said address are suspended.

\*the following ancillary orders are in force in terms of section 77:

*[insert details of any orders in force and any terms and conditions or directions made by the sheriff or power of arrest attached to any interdict]*

\*delete as appropriate

For the purpose of enforcing any of these orders warrant is granted for all lawful execution, including warrant to open shut and lockfast places.

Signed...............
Sheriff...............
Time...............

FORM 59

Rule 3.42

APPLICATION BY PRINCIPAL REPORTER FOR FURTHER DETENTION OF
CHILD UNDER SECTION 67 OF THE CHILDREN (SCOTLAND) ACT 1995
*[Repealed by the Act of Sederunt (Children's Hearings (Scotland) Act 2011) (Miscellaneous Amendments) 2013 (SSI 2013/172) para.4 (effective June 24, 2013).]*


FORM 60[1]

Rule 3.45(1)

FORM OF APPLICATION TO SHERIFF UNDER SECTION 93(2)(A) OR
94(2)(A) OF THE CHILDREN'S HEARINGS (SCOTLAND) ACT 2011

Court ref. no.:

SHERIFF COURT AT (*insert place of sheriff court*)

Application to sheriff under section \*93(2)(a) and/or 94(2)(a) of the Children's Hearings (Scotland) Act 2011

by

**The Principal Reporter**

in the case of

*[insert name of child]*

1. At *[insert location of children's hearing]* on *[insert date]* a children's hearing gave a direction to the Principal Reporter under section \*93(2)(a) and/or 94(2)(a) of the Children's Hearings (Scotland) Act 2011 in respect of *[insert name of child]*

---

[1] As substituted by the Act of Sederunt (Children's Hearings (Scotland) Act 2011) (Miscellaneous Amendments) 2013 (SSI 2013/172) para.4 (effective June 24, 2013).

2. *The hearing appointed [*insert name and designation*] as a safeguarder/no safeguarder was appointed.

3. *[An interim compulsory supervision order is in force in relation to the said [*insert name of child*], which [*insert details of what that order specifies*]] OR [No interim compulsory supervision order is in force in relation to the said [*insert name of child*]].

4. A copy of the statement of grounds by the Principal Reporter setting out the section 67 grounds of referral of the case of the said [*insert name of child*] to the children's hearing is attached [*together with the report(s) of the safeguarder].

5. (a) The said *[*insert name of child*] and/or *[*insert name and address and status of the relevant person or persons (within the meaning of* Rule 3.1(1) *)]* did not accept [*specify ground(s) not accepted*] of the statement of grounds.

(b) The *[children's hearing][grounds hearing] was satisfied that the said *[*insert name of child*] and/or *[*insert name and address and status of the relevant person or persons (within the meaning of* Rule 3.1(1) *)]* would not be capable of understanding or has not understood the explanation given in compliance with section 90(1) of the 2011 Act in relation to a section 67 ground.

6. The Principal Reporter applies to the sheriff to determine whether the section 67 ground(s) not accepted by the said *[*insert name of child*] or [*insert name of relevant person or persons (within the meaning of* Rule 3.1(1) *)]* are established.

7. The Principal Reporter intends to call the following witnesses (*specify names and roles of witnesses*):

*8. The Principal Reporter requests the sheriff to remove the obligation on the child to attend the hearing in view of [*insert reason*]. The Principal Reporter requests the sheriff to dispense with service on [*insert name of child*] on the basis that [*insert reason*].

(*Signed*)

(*name, designation and address, telephone number, [DX and fax numbers]*)

(*Date*)

[*Insert place and date*]

The sheriff—

1. Assigns [*insert date*] at [*insert time*] within chambers at [*insert name and place of court*] for the hearing of evidence in respect of the application.

*2. Appoints the Principal Reporter forthwith to serve a copy of the application and relative statement of grounds and this warrant on—

a. the child, *[together with a notice in [*Form 31 or Form 31A]] *or* [orders service of the following documents only [*insert details of documents to be served on child e.g. notice in Form 31/Form 31A only*]]; and

b. [*insert name of relevant person or persons (within the meaning of* Rule 3.1(1) *)]* together with a notice in Form 39 or Form 39A as the case may be.

c. any safeguarder [*insert name and designation*].

*3. Orders that the address of [*insert name*] should not be disclosed in the application.

*4. Dispenses with service on the child or any other person for the following reasons [*insert details*].

*5 Dispenses with the obligation on the child to attend the hearing in view of [*insert details*].

6. Grants warrant to cite witnesses and havers.

(*Signed*)

(Sheriff or Sheriff clerk)

*7-day hearing (where child unable to understand grounds)
[*Insert place and date*]

The sheriff assigns [*insert date*] at [*insert time*] within chambers at [*insert name and place of court*] for a procedural hearing in terms of section 106(4) of the 2011 Act and ordains parties to attend if so advised.

(*Signed*)
(Sheriff or Sheriff clerk)

(*\*delete as appropriate*)

FORM 61[1]

Rule 3.53(1B)(a)

APPEAL TO SHERIFF UNDER SECTION 154(1) OF THE CHILDREN'S HEARINGS (SCOTLAND) ACT 2011

Court ref. no.:

SHERIFF COURT AT (*insert place of sheriff court*)

Appeal under section 154(1) of the Children's Hearings (Scotland) Act 2011
by
[*insert names of child; and names and address of relevant person(s) and/or safeguarder (as appropriate)*]

Appellant

against

a decision of the children' hearing at [*state location of children's hearing*]

1. On [*insert date*] a children's hearing at [*insert location of children's hearing*] decided that [*insert details of relevant decision as referred to in section 154(3) of the Children's Hearings (Scotland) Act 2011*].

2. *[The children's hearing appointed [*insert name and address*] to act as safeguarder] *or* [No safeguarder has been appointed].

3. The following person(s) is/are* relevant persons [*insert name(s) and address(es) of relevant person(s) (within the meaning of Rule 3.1(1) )*].

4. The decision is not justified because [*state briefly the reasons why the decision is being appealed against*].

5. The said [*insert names of child, relevant person(s) (within the meaning of* Rule 3.1(1) *) or safeguarder (as appropriate)*] appeals to the sheriff against the decision.

(*Signed*)
*[Appellant(s)] *or* [Solicitor for Appellant(s) [*insert name and address*]]
[*Insert place and date*]

The sheriff assigns [*insert date*] at [*insert time*] within chambers at [*insert name and address of sheriff court*] for the hearing of the application;

The sheriff—

1. Appoints the sheriff clerk forthwith to intimate a copy of the application and this warrant to—

(a) the Principal Reporter;

*(b) the child together with a notice in Form 64;

*(c) [insert name of relevant person(s) (*within the meaning of* Rule 3.1(1) )];

*(d) [insert name of any safeguarder];

---

[1] As substituted by the Act of Sederunt (Children's Hearings (Scotland) Act 2011) (Miscellaneous Amendments) 2013 (SSI 2013/172) para.4 (effective June 24, 2013).

*(e) [insert names of any other person the sheriff thinks necessary].

*2. Dispenses with service on the child for the following reasons [insert details].

*3. Appoints answers to be lodged, if so advised, not later than [insert number of days] before the said diet.

4. Grants warrant to cite witnesses and havers.

(Signed)

(Sheriff or Sheriff clerk)

(Insert Place/Date)

Intimated this day by me in terms of Rule 3.54(1).

(Signed)

(Sheriff Clerk/Depute)

[Date]

(*delete as appropriate)


FORM 62[1]

Rule 3.53(1B)(b)

APPEAL TO SHERIFF UNDER SECTION 160(1) OF THE CHILDREN'S HEARINGS (SCOTLAND) ACT 2011

Court ref. no.:

SHERIFF COURT AT (insert place of sheriff court)

Appeal under section 160(1) of the Children's Hearings (Scotland) Act 2011

by

[insert name of child; and names and addresses of relevant person(s) and/or individual deemed not to be a relevant person (as appropriate)]

Appellant

against

a determination of a pre-hearing panel or children's hearing at [state location of pre-hearing panel/children's hearing]

1. On [insert date] the *[[pre-hearing panel] or [children's hearing]] at [insert location of children's hearing or pre-hearing panel] determined that [insert details of relevant person determination]. A copy of the relevant person determination is attached.

2. *[The [pre-hearing panel] or [children's hearing] appointed [insert name and address] to act as safeguarder] or [No safeguarder has been appointed].

3. The following person(s) is/are* relevant persons [insert name(s) and address(es) of relevant person(s) (within the meaning of Rule 3.1(1) )].

4. The determination is not justified because [state briefly the reasons why the determination is being appealed against].

5. The said [insert names of child, relevant person(s) (within the meaning of Rule 3.1(1) ) or individual deemed not to be a relevant person (as appropriate)] appeals to the sheriff against the determination.

(Signed)

*[Appellant(s)] or [Solicitor for Appellant(s) [insert name and address]]

[Insert place and date]

---

[1] As substituted by the Act of Sederunt (Children's Hearings (Scotland) Act 2011) (Miscellaneous Amendments) 2013 (SSI 2013/172) para.4 (effective June 24, 2013).

The sheriff assigns [*insert date*] at [*insert time*] within chambers at [*insert name and address of sheriff court*] for the hearing of the application;

The sheriff—

1. Appoints the sheriff clerk forthwith to intimate a copy of the application and this warrant to—

(a) the Principal Reporter;

*(b) the child together with a notice in Form 64;

*(c) [insert name of relevant person(s) (*within the meaning of* Rule 3.1(1) *)*];

*(d) [insert name of any safeguarder];

*(e) [insert names of any other person the sheriff thinks necessary].

*2. Dispenses with service on the child for the following reasons [*insert details*].

3. Grants warrant to cite witnesses and havers.

(*Signed*)
(Sheriff or Sheriff clerk)

Intimated this day by me in terms of Rule 3.54(1).

(*Signed*)
(Sheriff Clerk/Depute)
[Date]

(**delete as appropriate*)

FORM 63[1]

Rule 3.53(1B)(c)

### APPEAL TO SHERIFF UNDER SECTION 161(1) OF THE CHILDREN'S HEARINGS (SCOTLAND) ACT 2011

Court ref. no.:

SHERIFF COURT AT (*insert place of sheriff court*)

Appeal under section 161(1) of the Children's Hearings (Scotland) Act 2011

by

[*insert names and addresses of appellant within the meaning of* section 161(2) of the Children's Hearings (Scotland) Act 2011 *)*]

Appellant

against

a decision of the children's hearing at [*state location of children's hearing*]

1. On [*insert date*] the children's hearing at [*insert location of children's hearing*] decided that [*insert details of relevant decision as referred to in* section 161(3) of the Children's Hearings (Scotland) Act 2011]. A copy of the relevant decision is attached.

2. *[The children's hearing appointed [*insert name and address*] to act as safeguarder] *or* [No safeguarder has been appointed].

3. The following person(s) is/are* relevant persons [*insert name(s) and address(es) of relevant person(s) (within the meaning of* Rule 3.1(1) *)*].

4. The decision is not justified because [*state briefly the reasons why the decision is being appealed against*].

5. The said [*insert name of appellant*] appeals to the sheriff against the decision.

(*Signed*)
*[Appellant(s)] *or* [Solicitor for Appellant(s) [*insert name and address*]]

[*Insert place and date*]

---

[1] As substituted by the Act of Sederunt (Children's Hearings (Scotland) Act 2011) (Miscellaneous Amendments) 2013 (SSI 2013/172) para.4 (effective June 24, 2013).

The sheriff assigns [*insert date*] at [*insert time*] within chambers at [*insert name and address of sheriff court*] for the hearing of the application;

The sheriff—

1. Appoints the sheriff clerk forthwith to intimate a copy of the application and this warrant to—

(a) the Principal Reporter;

*(b) the child together with a notice in Form 64;

*(c) [insert name of relevant person(s) (*within the meaning of* Rule 3.1(1) *)*];

*(d) [insert name of any safeguarder];

*(e) [insert names of any other person the sheriff thinks necessary].

*2. Dispenses with service on the child for the following reasons [*insert details*].

3. Grants warrant to cite witnesses and havers.

(*Signed*)

(Sheriff or Sheriff clerk)

Intimated this day by me in terms of Rule 3.54(1).

(*Signed*)

(Sheriff Clerk/Depute)

[Date]

(*\*delete as appropriate*)

FORM 63A[1]

Rule 3.53(1B)(d)

APPEAL TO SHERIFF UNDER SECTION 162(3) OF THE CHILDREN'S HEARINGS (SCOTLAND) ACT 2011

Court ref. no.:

SHERIFF COURT AT (*insert place of sheriff court*)

Appeal under section 162(3) of the Children's Hearings (Scotland) Act 2011

by

[*insert name of child and/or name and address of relevant person(s)*]

Appellant

against

a decision of the chief social work officer at [*insert location of local authority*]

1. On [*insert date*], the chief social work officer at [*insert location of local authority*] decided that [*insert details of relevant decision as referred to in* section 162(4) of the Children's Hearings (Scotland) Act 2011]. A copy of the relevant decision is attached.

2. *[The children's hearing that made a relevant order or warrant in relation to the child appointed [*insert name and address*] to act as safeguarder] *or* [No safeguarder has been appointed].

3. The following person(s) is/are* relevant persons [*insert name(s) and address(es) of relevant person(s) (within the meaning of* Rule 3.1(1) *)*].

4. The decision is not justified because [*state briefly the reasons why the decision is being appealed against*].

5. The said [*insert name of child and/or relevant person(s)*] appeals to the sheriff against the decision.

[*Signed*]

*[Appellant(s)] *or* [Solicitor for Appellant(s) [*insert name and address*]]

---

[1] As inserted by the Act of Sederunt (Children's Hearings (Scotland) Act 2011) (Miscellaneous Amendments) 2013 (SSI 2013/172) para.4 (effective June 24, 2013).

*[Insert place and date]*

The sheriff assigns *[insert date]* at *[insert time]* within chambers at *[insert name and address of sheriff court]* for the hearing of the application;

The sheriff—

1. Appoints the sheriff clerk forthwith to intimate a copy of the application and this warrant to—

(a) the Principal Reporter;

*(b) the child together with a notice in Form 64;

*(c) [insert name of relevant person(s) *(within the meaning of Rule 3.1(1) )*];

*(d) [insert name of any safeguarder];

*(e) [insert names of any other person the sheriff thinks necessary];

(f) [insert name of the chief social work officer].

*2. Dispenses with service on the child for the following reason *[insert details]*.

3. Grants warrant to cite witnesses and havers.

[*Signed*]

[Sheriff or Sheriff clerk]

Intimated this day by me in terms of Rule 3.54(1).

[*Signed*]

[Sheriff Clerk/Depute]

[Date]

*(\*delete as appropriate)*

FORM 64[1]

Rule 3.54(3)

INTIMATION TO CHILD IN RESPECT OF APPEALS TO THE SHERIFF
UNDER THE CHILDREN'S HEARINGS (SCOTLAND) ACT 2011

Court ref. no.:

Dear *[insert name by which child is known]*,

As you know at the *Children's Hearing/pre-hearing panel held on *[insert date]* not everyone agreed with the decision that was made. Since the decision of the hearing to *[insert details of decision being appealed]* was not accepted by *[insert name of person(s) who did not accept the decision]* your case has been sent to a sheriff who will decide whether the decision made by the *Children's Hearing/pre-hearing panel is correct.

**WHAT THE SHERIFF DOES:** A sheriff assists for lots of different reasons, but this time the purpose is to help the *Children's Hearing/pre-hearing panel. If the sheriff decides that the decision should be reconsidered the case may go back to the *Children's Hearing/pre-hearing panel to think again what is to happen in your case.

**HEARING:** The sheriff has set a date for hearing your case. The hearing will take place on *[insert time and date of hearing]* at *[insert address of sheriff court]*. [*You are required to attend court on that date *or* You are not required to attend court on that date, but you may wish to do so.]

At the hearing the sheriff will listen to the evidence in your case, and will make a decision. This decision is very important for you [*and it is necessary for you to at-

---

[1] As substituted by the Act of Sederunt (Children's Hearings (Scotland) Act 2011) (Miscellaneous Amendments) 2013 (SSI 2013/172) para.4 (effective June 24, 2013).

tend the hearing to tell the sheriff about your circumstances and how you feel. You might be asked some questions. You can be represented by a solicitor or another person].

*[**IMPORTANT NOTE: IT IS VERY IMPORTANT THAT YOU ATTEND** on the date and time given. If an emergency arises and you cannot attend you must contact the sheriff clerk on (*insert telephone number*) or the Principal Reporter because it is possible, if you do not attend, you may be detained and kept in a safe place until a later date.]

*[The sheriff has said that you do not have to attend the hearing on [*insert date*] at [*insert time*] at [*insert name and address of sheriff court*], but if you want to go along to hear what is said at the hearing then you can. If you do not want to go to court then you can still let the sheriff know what you think by filling in the attached form or you can write down what you want to say on a separate sheet of paper and send them back in the enclosed stamped addressed envelope before the date on which the sheriff is to hear the application, which is at the end of this letter. Alternatively, you can ask a lawyer to go to the hearing to tell the sheriff your views.]

**If you are unsure about what to do you can get free legal advice from a Lawyer or Local Advice Agency or Law Centre about the application and about legal aid. The Scottish Child Law Centre can refer you to specially trained lawyers who can help you. They give advice on their free phone number (0800 328 8970) any time between 9.30am and 4.00pm Monday to Friday.**

You will see that, along with this letter, there is a copy of the application to the sheriff, and the sheriff's order fixing the hearing. If you decide to get advice, or to ask someone to go with you to see the sheriff, make sure that you give them a copy of the application and the sheriff's order.

..................              ..................

(Signed)                    (Date)

(**delete as appropriate*)

To the Sheriff Clerk:

**I would like the Sheriff to know what I have to say before he or she makes a decision** (write what you want to say here, or you can use a separate sheet of paper):

Your Name:

Your Address:

Court Reference Number (if you know it):

### FORM 64A[1]

Rule 3.58A(2)

FORM OF APPLICATION UNDER SECTION 166(2) OF THE CHILDREN'S HEARINGS (SCOTLAND) ACT 2011

Court ref. no.:

SHERIFF COURT AT (*insert place of sheriff court*)

Application to sheriff under section 166(2) of the Children's Hearings (Scotland) Act 2011 to review requirement imposed on local authority

by

[*insert name and address of local authority*]

Applicant

---

[1] As substituted by the Act of Sederunt (Children's Hearings (Scotland) Act 2011) (Miscellaneous Amendments) 2013 (SSI 2013/172) para.4 (effective June 24, 2013).

in the case of
[*insert name of child*]
PART 1: DETAILS OF PERSONS WHOM THE APPLICANT BELIEVES SHOULD RECEIVE NOTICE OF THE APPLICATION
THE NATIONAL
CONVENER
THE PRINCIPAL
REPORTER
CHILD [*insert name of child in respect of whom the duty was imposed and the child's representative (if any)*]
RELEVANT PERSON [*insert name and address of relevant person(s) (within the meaning of* Rule 3.1(1) *) and such person's representative(s) (if any)*]
SAFEGUARDER [*insert name and address of any safeguarder*]
CURATOR *AD LITEM* [*insert name and address of any curator ad litem*]
ANY OTHER PARTY [*insert name and address of any other party to the application*]
ANY OTHER
LOCAL AUTHORITY [*insert name and address of any other local authority with an interest*]
*Note: Information to be provided in Part 2 where applicant does not wish to disclose the address or whereabouts of the child or any other person to persons receiving notice of the application*
PART 2: INFORMATION ABOUT THE APPLICATION AND THE ORDERS SOUGHT
On [*insert date*], *[the sheriff at [*insert place*] made a determination in the following terms [*insert full details of order and conditions attaching to it*] OR [the children's hearing at [*insert place*] imposed a duty on the applicant local authority in respect of [*insert name of child*] in the following terms [*insert full details of order and conditions attaching to it*]. A copy of the relevant order is attached.
The applicant local authority is satisfied for the following reasons that it is not the relevant local authority for the child in respect of whom the duty has been imposed and requests the sheriff to review the decision or determination that imposed the duty on it: [*insert details of the basis on which such application is made*].
The following supporting evidence is produced (*insert details of the evidence produced in support of the application*)—
*[*Insert here details and grounds where applicant does not wish to disclose the address or whereabouts of any person to persons receiving notice of the application.*]
[*Signed*]
*[Solicitor for the local authority
[*insert name and address*]]
(*delete as appropriate)


FORM 64B[1]
Rule 3.58B(1)
APPLICATION UNDER SECTION 166(2) OF THE CHILDREN'S HEARINGS (SCOTLAND) ACT 2011:

---

[1] As substituted by the Act of Sederunt (Children's Hearings (Scotland) Act 2011) (Miscellaneous Amendments) 2013 (SSI 2013/172) para.4 (effective June 24, 2013). As inserted by the Act of Sederunt (Sheriff Court Rules Amendment) (Miscellaneous) 2015 (SSI 2015/424) para.3 (effective 1 February 2016).

## FORM OF WARRANT TO CITE

Court ref. no.:

*[Insert place and date]*

The sheriff—

1. Assigns *[insert date]* at *[insert time]* within chambers at *[insert name and address of sheriff court]* for the hearing of the application;

2. Appoints the Applicant forthwith to serve a copy of the application and this warrant to—

(a) the National Convener;

*(b) the Principal Reporter;

*(c) the child together with a notice in Form 64;

*(d) [insert name of relevant person(s) (*within the meaning of Rule 3.1(1) )*];

*(e) [insert name of any safeguarder];

*(f) [insert name of any curator *ad litem*];

*(g) [insert name of local authority(ies)];

*(h) [insert names of any other person the sheriff thinks necessary].

*3. Dispenses with service on the child for the following reason *[insert details]*.

4. Grants warrant to cite witnesses and havers.

5. Orders that answers must be lodged (if so advised) by *(insert date)*.

[Signed]

[Sheriff or Sheriff clerk]

(**delete as appropriate*)

## FORM 64C[1]

Rule 3.58C(1)(a)

### APPEAL TO SHERIFF UNDER SECTION 44A OF THE CRIMINAL PROCEDURE (SCOTLAND) ACT 1995

Court ref. no.

SHERIFF COURT AT (*insert place of sheriff court*)

Appeal under section 44A of the Criminal Procedure (Scotland) Act 1995

*[insert name of child and/or name and address of relevant person(s)]*

Appellant

against

a decision of the chief social work officer at *[insert location of local authority]*

1. On *[insert date]*, the chief social work officer at *[insert location of local authority]* decided that *[insert details of the decision to detain child in secure accommodation as referred to in section 44A of the Criminal Procedure (Scotland) Act 1995]*. A copy of the decision is attached.

2. The following person(s) is/are relevant persons *[insert name(s) and address(es) of relevant person(s) (within the meaning of section 44A of the Criminal Procedure (Scotland) Act 1995)]*.

3. The decision is not justified because *[state briefly the reasons why the decision is being appealed against]*.

4. The said *[insert name of child and/or relevant person(s)]* appeals to the sheriff against the decision.

[Signed]

[Appellant(s)]*or*[Solicitor for the Appellant(s)]

---

[1] As inserted by the Act of Sederunt (Sheriff Court Rules Amendment) (Miscellaneous) 2015 (SSI 2015/424) para.3 (effective 1 February 2016).

*[insert name and address]*

*[insert place and date]*

The sheriff assigns *[insert date]* at *[insert time]* within chambers at *[insert name and address of sheriff court]* for the hearing of the application;

The sheriff—

1. Appoints the sheriff clerk to immediately intimate a copy of the application and this warrant to—

*(a) the child together with a notice in Form 64D;

*(b) *[insert name of relevant person(s) (within the meaning of Rule 3.1(1))]*;

*(c) *[insert name of any other person the sheriff thinks necessary]*;

(d) *[insert the name of the chief social work officer]*.

2. Dispenses with service on the child for the following reason *[insert details]*.

3. Grants warrant to cite witnesses and havers.

*[Signed]*

[Sheriff or Sheriff Clerk]

Intimated this day by me in terms of Rule 3.58D.

*[Signed]*

[Sheriff Clerk/Depute]

[Date]

(*\*delete as appropriate*)

FORM 64D[1]

Rule 3.58D(4)

INTIMATION TO CHILD IN RESPECT OF APPEAL TO SHERIFF UNDER SECTION 44A OF THE CRIMINAL PROCEDURE (SCOTLAND) ACT 1995

Court ref. no.

Dear *[insert name by which child is known]*,

As you know, the chief social work officer at *[insert location of local authority]* decided that you *[insert details of the decision to place the child into secure accommodation]*. Not everyone agrees with that decision. Since it was not accepted by *[insert name of person(s) who have appealed the decision]*, your case has been sent to a sheriff who will decide whether the decision made by the chief social work officer is correct.

**WHAT THE SHERIFF DOES**: A sheriff assists for lots of different reasons, but this time the purpose is to decide if the chief social work officer made the right decision. If the sheriff decides that the chief social work officer did make the right decision, the decision will be confirmed. If the sheriff decides that the chief social work officer made the wrong decision, the chief social work officer will be told that you should be moved to a new place to stay, which is not secure accommodation.

**HEARING**: The sheriff has set a date for hearing your case. The hearing will take place on *[insert time and date of hearing]* at *[insert address of sheriff court]*. [*You must attend court on that date or You do not have to attend court on that date, but you can attend if you want to.]

At the hearing the sheriff will listen to the evidence in your case, and will make a decision. This decision is very important for you [*and it is necessary for you to attend the hearing to tell the sheriff about your circumstances and how you feel. You might be asked some questions. You can be represented by a solicitor or another person].

---

[1] As inserted by the Act of Sederunt (Sheriff Court Rules Amendment) (Miscellaneous) 2015 (SSI 2015/424) para.3 (effective 1 February 2016).

**\*[IMPORTANT NOTE: IT IS VERY IMPORTANT THAT YOU ATTEND** on the date and time given. If an emergency arises and you cannot attend you must contact the Sheriff Clerk on (*insert telephone number*) because it is possible, if you do not attend, that you may be detained and kept in a safe place until a later date.]

\*[The sheriff has said that you do not have to attend the hearing on *[insert date]* at *[insert time]* at *[insert name and address of sheriff court]*, but if you want to go along to hear what is said at the hearing, then you can. If you do not want to go to court, you can still let the sheriff know what you think by filling in the attached form or you can write down what you want to say on a separate sheet of paper and send it back in the enclosed addressed envelope before *[insert date]*, which is the date on which the sheriff will hear the appeal. If you would prefer, you can ask a lawyer to go to the hearing to tell the sheriff your views.]

**If you are unsure about what to do you can get free legal advice from a lawyer or local advice agency or law centre about the appeal and about legal aid. The Scottish Child Law Centre can refer you to specially trained lawyers who can help you. They give advice on their free phone number (0800 328 8970) any time between 9.30am and 4.00pm Monday to Friday.**

You will see that, along with this letter, there is a copy of the appeal to the sheriff and the sheriff's order fixing the hearing. If you decide to get advice, or to ask someone to go with you to see the sheriff, make sure that you give them a copy of the appeal and the sheriff's order.

(Signed)          (Date)

(\**delete as appropriate*)

To the Sheriff Clerk:

**I would like the sheriff to know what I have to say before he or she makes a decision** (*write what you want to say here, or you can use a separate piece of paper*):

Your name:

Your address:

Court reference number (if you know it):

FORM 65[1]

Rule 3.63(1)

APPLICATION UNDER SECTION 110 OF THE CHILDREN'S HEARINGS (SCOTLAND) ACT 2011: FORM OF WARRANT TO CITE PRINCIPAL REPORTER

Court ref. no.:

*[Place and date]*

The court

1. Assigns *[date]* at *[hour]* within the *[name court]* in chambers at *[place]* for the hearing of the application.

2. Appoints the Applicant to forthwith cite the Principal Reporter to lodge answers, if so advised, within *[enter period set by sheriff]*

3. Appoints the Applicant to forthwith intimate the application to

    i     BB\* *[insert name of relevant person or persons (within the meaning of Rule 3.1(1) (if not the Applicant))]* whose whereabouts are known and

    ii    [AB]\* (name and design) the safeguarded

   (iia)   [YZ] ( name and design ) any curator *ad litem*

    iii   [BC]\* (name and design) a party to the application,

by serving a copy of the application and this warrant upon *[each of]* \*them;

---

[1] As amended by the Act of Sederunt (Children's Hearings (Scotland) Act 2011) (Miscellaneous Amendments) 2013 (SSI 2013/172) para.4 (effective June 24, 2013).

(iv)   [CD]* *(insert name of child (if not the Applicant))*

4.   Grants warrant to cite witnesses and havers.

5.   *Dispenses with notice and service on *[insert name]* for the following reason(s) *[insert reason(s)]*.

..............

Sheriff Clerk

*delete as appropriate

FORM 65A[1, 2]

Rule 3.64A(1)

INTERIM COMPULSORY SUPERVISION ORDER UNDER THE CHILDREN'S HEARINGS (SCOTLAND) ACT 2011

Court ref. no.:

*[Insert place and date]*

In the application under *[specify relevant section of the Children's Hearings (Scotland) Act 2011*]* the sheriff—

1. Made an interim compulsory supervision order in relation to *[insert name of child]* because the sheriff was satisfied that *[insert details why the child's circumstances are such that it was necessary as a matter of urgency for the sheriff to make the order]*.

*2. Ordered that the interim compulsory supervision order includes the following measures—

*(a) a requirement that the child reside at *(insert address of specified place OR a place of safety away from the place where the child predominantly resides at (insert address of predominant residence))*;

*(b) a direction authorising the person who is in charge of the place specified in paragraph (a) to restrict the child's liberty to the extent that the person considers appropriate having regard to the measures included in this order;

*(c) a prohibition on the disclosure (whether directly or indirectly) of a place specified under paragraph (a);

*(d) a movement restriction in the following terms: *[insert relevant details, including details of the person designated under regulation 4(1) of the Children's Hearings (Scotland) Act 2011 (Movement Restriction Conditions) Regulations 2013]*;

*(e) a secure accommodation authorisation in the following terms: *[insert relevant details]*;

*(f) a requirement that the implementation authority arrange *(insert details of the specified medical or other examination of the child OR the specified medical or other treatment for the child]*;

*(g) a direction regulating contact between the child and *[insert name and address of specified person OR specify class of person]*;

*(h) a requirement that the child comply with *[specify any other condition]*;

*(i) a requirement that the implementation authority carry out the following duties in relation to the child: *(insert specified duties)*.

3. Specified that *[insert name and address of local authority]* (the implementation authority) is to be responsible for giving effect to the measures included in the order.

---

[1] As substituted by the Act of Sederunt (Children's Hearings (Scotland) Act 2011) (Miscellaneous Amendments) 2013 (SSI 2013/172) para.4 (effective June 24, 2013).

[2] As amended by the Act of Sederunt (Rules of the Court of Session and Sheriff Court Rules Amendment) (Miscellaneous) 2014 (SSI 2014/201) r.4 (effective August 1, 2014).

4. Specified that this order has effect until [*specify the relevant period*].

5. [Ordered the *[Principal Reporter to intimate this order to the child in Form 65B]] *or* [dispensed with intimation to the child].

6. Ordered the Principal Reporter to intimate this order to the implementation authority.

*7. Ordered the Principal Reporter to intimate this order to [*insert name of other persons*] in Form 65E.

[*Signed*]
[Sheriff clerk]

*(*delete as appropriate)*

For the purpose of enforcing this order warrant is granted to officers of law for all lawful execution, including—

(a) searching for and apprehending the child;

(b) taking the child to the authorised place;

(c) where (i) it is not reasonably practicable to take the child immediately to the authorised place; and (ii) the authorised place is not a place of safety, taking the child to and detaining the child in a place of safety for as short a period of time as is practicable;

(d) so far as necessary, by breaking open shut and lockfast places.

[*Signed*]
[Sheriff or Sheriff clerk]
Date & time ...............

FORM 65B[1]

Rule 3.64A

NOTICE TO CHILD OF AN INTERIM COMPULSORY SUPERVISION
ORDER UNDER THE CHILDREN'S HEARINGS (SCOTLAND) ACT 2011

Court ref. no.:

Dear [*insert name by which child is known*],

I am writing to let you know that because there are worries about your safety, the sheriff has made an order to keep you safe. This order is called an interim compulsory supervision order. It means that [*insert details in simple terms of what the order means for the child and refer to any previous order if appropriate*]. This is because the sheriff is concerned that [*insert the reason why the sheriff made the order*]. The interim compulsory supervision order will be in force until [*insert date — see section 86(3) of the Children's Hearings (Scotland) Act 2011*]. A copy of the order is attached.

**If you are unsure about what to do you can get free legal advice from a Lawyer or Local Advice Agency or Law Centre. The Scottish Child Law Centre can refer you to specially trained lawyers who can help you. They give advice on their free phone number (0800 328 8970) any time between 9.30am and 4.00pm Monday to Friday.**

*(Principal Reporter)*                    *(Date)*

FORM 65C[2]

Rule 3.64A(2)

---

[1] As substituted by the Act of Sederunt (Children's Hearings (Scotland) Act 2011) (Miscellaneous Amendments) 2013 (SSI 2013/172) para.4 (effective June 24, 2013).
[2] As substituted by the Act of Sederunt (Children's Hearings (Scotland) Act 2011) (Miscellaneous Amendments) 2013 (SSI 2013/172) para.4 (effective June 24, 2013).

APPLICATION TO EXTEND OR EXTEND AND VARY AN INTERIM COMPULSORY SUPERVISION ORDER UNDER THE CHILDREN'S HEARINGS (SCOTLAND) ACT 2011

Court ref. no.:

SHERIFF COURT AT (*insert place of sheriff court*)

Application to sheriff under [*insert relevant section*] of the Children's Hearings (Scotland) Act 2011 to [*extend *OR* extend and vary] an interim compulsory supervision order

by

**The Principal Reporter**

in the case of

[*insert name of child*]

PART 1: DETAILS OF PERSONS WHOM THE APPLICANT BELIEVES SHOULD RECEIVE NOTICE OF THE APPLICATION

CHILD                    [*insert name, gender and date of birth\**]

RELEVANT
PERSON                   [*insert name(s) and address(es) of relevant person(s) (within the meaning of Rule 3.1(1) )*]

SAFEGUARDER              [*insert name, address and telephone numbers (if known) of any safeguarder*]

IMPLEMENTA-
TION
AUTHORITY                [*insert name of local authority, if appropriate*]

ANY OTHER
PERSON                   [*insert name, address and telephone numbers (if known) of any other persons and provide details of their interest in the application*]

*Note: Information to be provided in Part 2 where applicant does not wish to disclose the address or whereabouts of the child or any other person to persons receiving notice of the application*

PART 2: INFORMATION ABOUT THE APPLICATION AND THE ORDERS SOUGHT

On [*insert date*], the children's hearing at [*insert place*] made an interim compulsory supervision order in respect of [*insert name and address of child*] in the following terms [*insert full details of order and conditions attaching to it*]. A copy of the relevant order is attached.

The applicant requests the sheriff to [*extend *OR* extend and vary] the order in the following terms: [*insert details of the extension or extension and variation sought*].

The following supporting evidence is produced (*insert details of the evidence produced in support of the application)*—

*[*Insert here details and grounds where applicant does not wish to disclose the address of any person to persons receiving notice of the application.*]

[*Signed*]

*[Principal Reporter] *or*

[Solicitor for Principal Reporter

[*insert name and address*]]

PART 3: FORM OF INTERLOCUTOR

[*Insert place and date*]

The sheriff—

1. Assigns [*insert date*] at [*insert time*] within chambers at [*insert name and address of sheriff court*] for the hearing of the application;

2. Appoints the Applicant forthwith to serve a copy of the application and this warrant to—

(a) the child;

(b) the other persons listed in Part 1 of this application.

*3. Dispenses with service on the child or any other person for the following reason [*insert details*].

4. Grants warrant to cite witnesses and havers.

5. Appoints answers to be lodged, if so advised, not later than [*insert number of days*] before the said diet.

[*Signed*]

[Sheriff clerk]

(*\*delete as appropriate*)

FORM 65D[1]

Rule 3.64A(3)

APPLICATION TO FURTHER EXTEND OR FURTHER EXTEND AND VARY AN INTERIM COMPULSORY SUPERVISION ORDER UNDER THE CHILDREN'S HEARINGS (SCOTLAND) ACT 2011

Court ref. no.:

SHERIFF COURT AT (*insert place of sheriff court*)

Application to sheriff under section 99 of the Children's Hearings (Scotland) Act 2011 to [*further extend *OR* further extend and vary] an interim compulsory supervision order

by

**The Principal Reporter**

in the case of

[*insert name of child*]

PART 1: DETAILS OF PERSONS WHOM THE APPLICANT BELIEVES SHOULD RECEIVE NOTICE OF THE APPLICATION

| | |
|---|---|
| CHILD | [*insert name, gender and date of birth\**] |
| RELEVANT PERSON | [*insert name(s) and address(es) of relevant person(s) (within the meaning of *Rule 3.1(1)*)*] |
| SAFEGUARDER | [*insert name, address and telephone numbers (if known) of any safeguarder*] |
| IMPLEMENTATION AUTHORITY | [*insert name of local authority, if appropriate*] |
| ANY OTHER PERSON | [*insert name, address and telephone numbers (if known) of any other persons and provide details of their interest in the application*] |

*\*Note: Information to be provided in Part 2 where applicant does not wish to disclose the address or whereabouts of the child or any other person to persons receiving notice of the application*

---

[1] As substituted by the Act of Sederunt (Children's Hearings (Scotland) Act 2011) (Miscellaneous Amendments) 2013 (SSI 2013/172) para.4 (effective June 24, 2013).

PART 2: INFORMATION ABOUT THE APPLICATION AND THE ORDERS SOUGHT

On [*insert date*], the children's hearing at [*insert place*] [\*extended *OR* extended and varied *OR* further extended *OR* further extended and varied] an interim compulsory supervision order in respect of [*insert name and address of child*] in the following terms [*insert full details of order and conditions attaching to it*]. A copy of the relevant order [as extended *OR* extended and varied *OR* further extended *OR* further extended and varied] is attached.

The applicant requests the sheriff to [\*further extend *OR* further extend and vary] the order in the following terms: [*insert details of the further extension or further extension and variation sought*].

The following supporting evidence is produced (*insert details of the evidence produced in support of the application*)—

\*[*Insert here details and grounds where applicant does not wish to disclose the address of any person to persons receiving notice of the application.*]

[*Signed*]
\*[Principal Reporter] *or*
[Solicitor for Principal Reporter
[*insert name and address*]]

PART 3: FORM OF INTERLOCUTOR

[*Insert place and date*]

The sheriff—

1. Assigns [*insert date*] at [*insert time*] within chambers at [*insert name and address of sheriff court*] for the hearing of the application;

2. Appoints the Applicant forthwith to serve a copy of the application and this warrant to—

(a) the child;

(b) the other persons listed in Part 1 of this application.

\*3. Dispenses with service on the child or any other person for the following reason [*insert details*].

4. Grants warrant to cite witnesses and havers.

5. Appoints answers to be lodged, if so advised, not later than [*insert number of days*] before the said diet.

[*Signed*]
[Sheriff clerk]

(\**delete as appropriate*)


FORM 65E[1]

Rule 3.64A(6)

NOTICE OF INTIMATION OF AN INTERIM COMPULSORY SUPERVISION ORDER UNDER THE CHILDREN'S HEARINGS (SCOTLAND) ACT 2011

Court ref. no.:

To [*insert name and address of person receiving intimation as required by the sheriff under* Rule 3.64A(6)]

I am writing to let you know that the sheriff has made an interim compulsory supervision order in respect of [*insert name of child*]. It means that [*insert details of what the order means for the child and the specified person (if appropriate) and*

---

[1] As substituted by the Act of Sederunt (Children's Hearings (Scotland) Act 2011) (Miscellaneous Amendments) 2013 (SSI 2013/172) para.4 (effective June 24, 2013).

*refer to any previous order if appropriate*]. This is because the sheriff is concerned that [*insert the reason why the sheriff made the order*]. The interim compulsory supervision order will be in force until [*insert date — see section 86(3) of the Children's Hearings (Scotland) Act 2011*]. A copy of the order is attached.

**\*[YOU SHOULD OBTAIN ADVICE FROM A SOLICITOR OR LOCAL ADVICE AGENCY OR LAW CENTRE.** You may be entitled to legal aid. Advice about legal aid is available from any solicitor, advice agency or law centre.]

(*Date*)                                           (*signed*)

                                                        Principal Reporter

(*\*delete as appropriate*)

### FORM 66                                    Rule 5.19(1)

(Place).......... (Date)...............
   AB (design)
   Intimation is hereby given that there has been received at (..........) Sheriff Court evidence relative to the provisional maintenance order made on your application on .........., as a result of which it appears that the provisional order ought not to have been made.
   *A copy of the document summarising that evidence taken by the [name of Court] in proceedings relating to the confirmation of the provisional order accompanies this intimation.

or

   *A copy of the note of that evidence taken at [name of Court] Sheriff Court accompanies this intimation.
   IF YOU WISH TO MAKE REPRESENTATIONS AND ADDUCE FURTHER EVIDENCE with respect to the evidence received you must lodge a minute narrating the representations and the further evidence you intend to adduce with the Sheriff Clerk at [name and address of Sheriff Court] within 21 days afer the date of this intimation.
   IF YOU DO NOTHING IN ANSWER TO THIS INTIMATION the Court may revoke the provisional maintenance order.

                                                        [Signed]
                                                        Sheriff Clerk

  *Delete as appropriate

### FORM 67                    Rules   5.20(1)   and
                                                5.29(1)

MAINTENANCE ORDERS (RECIPROCAL ENFORCEMENT) ACT 1972
(Place).......... (Date)...............
   AB (Design)
   Intimation is hereby given of the receipt at [name and address of Sheriff Court] of a provisional order made by [name of Court] at .......... on ...............
   A copy of the provisional order together with a summary of the evidence upon which the order was made [*and a statement of the grounds upon which the order might have been opposed] accompanies this intimation.
   IF YOU WISH TO OPPOSE THE ORDER, you must lodge an application with the Sheriff Clerk at [name and address of Sheriff Court] within 21/42* days after the date of this intimation and at the same time present this copy intimation.
   IF YOU DO NOTHING IN ANSWER TO THIS INTIMATION the order will be confirmed.

[Signed]
Sheriff Clerk

*Delete as appropriate

FORM 68           Rule 5.24(1)(b)

## FORM OF DECLARATION

I hereby declare that the foregoing certified copy of a maintenance order has been duly registered by me in Part II of the Maintenance Orders Register kept in this Court in terms of the Maintenance Orders Act 1950, and of Chapter 5 of the Act of Sederunt (Child Care and Maintenance Rules) 1997.

[Signed]
Sheriff Clerk Depute

FORM 69           Rule 5.34(1)(a)

## NOTICE OF REGISTRATION FOR ENFORCEMENT IN SCOTLAND OF A MAINTENANCE ORDER MADE IN THE REPUBLIC OF IRELAND

*[Repealed by the Act of Sederunt (Sheriff Court Rules) (Miscellaneous Amendments) (No.3) 2011 (SSI 2011/386) para.9 (effective November 28, 2011).]*

FORM 70[1]           Rules 5.34(1)(b) and 5.36(1)(b)

## NOTICE OF REGISTRATION FOR THE PURPOSES OF ENFORCEMENT IN SCOTLAND OF A MAINTENANCE ORDER MADE IN A HAGUE CONVENTION COUNTRY

(Place).......... (Date)..............

AB (Design)

Notice is hereby given of the registration in the Maintenance Order Register kept at [name and address of Sheriff Court] of a maintenance order made by [name and address of Court in Hague Convention Country] on [date of making order].

In terms of said maintenance order CD [design payer] is required to pay to you [narrate terms of order].

[Signed]
Sheriff Clerk

FORM 71[2]           Rules 5.34(2) and 5.36(2)

## NOTICE OF A DECISION NOT TO REGISTER, FOR THE PURPOSES OF THE ENFORCEMENT IN SCOTLAND, A MAINTENANCE ORDER MADE IN A HAGUE CONVENTION COUNTRY

(Place).......... (Date)..............

AB (Design)

Notice is hereby given that the maintenance order made by [name and address of Court in Hague Convention Country] on [date of making order] requiring CD (design) to pay to you [narrate terms of order] has NOT been registered in the Maintenance Orders Register kept at this Sheriff Court.

The Order has not been registered on the grounds that [narrate grounds].

---

[1] As amended by the Act of Sederunt (Sheriff Court Rules) (Miscellaneous Amendments) (No.3) 2011 (SSI 2011/386) para.9 (effective November 28, 2011).

[2] As amended by the Act of Sederunt (Sheriff Court Rules) (Miscellaneous Amendments) (No.3) 2011 (SSI 2011/386) para.9 (effective November 28, 2011).

You may within one calendar month from the date of this notice make application to this Sheriff Court to set aside the decision not to register the order by lodging at this Sheriff Court a summary application setting out the grounds of your application.

[Signed]
Sheriff Clerk

FORM 72[1]                                  Rule 5.36(1)(a)

## INTIMATION OF REGISTRATION FOR ENFORCEMENT IN SCOTLAND OF A MAINTENANCE ORDER MADE IN A HAGUE CONVENTION COUNTRY

(Place).......... (Date)...............
AB (Design)

Intimation is hereby given of the registration in the Maintenance Orders Register kept at [name and address of Sheriff Court] of a maintenance order made by [name and address of Court in Hague Convention Country] on [date of making order].

In terms of the said maintenance order you are required [narrate terms of order and payee].

You may within one calendar month from the date of this intimation make application to [name and address of Sheriff Court] to set aside the registration of the order by lodging with the Sheriff Clerk at [name and address of Sheriff Court] a summary application setting out the grounds of the application.

The grounds upon which application to set aside the registration may be made are

(a)  [name of Court in Hague Convention Country] did not have jurisdiction to make the order;

(b)  registration is manifestly contrary to public policy;

(c)  the order was obtained by fraud in connection with a matter of procedure;

(d)  proceedings between you and the payee under the mainenance order and having the same purpose are pending before a court in Scotland and those proceedings were the first to be instituted;

(e)  the order is incompatible with an order made in proceedings between you and the payee and having the same purpose either in the United Kingdom or in another country, provided that the latter order fulfils the conditions necessary for registration and enforcement;

(f)  you did not appear in the proceedings in the Hague Convention Country and you were not served in accordance with the institution of proceedings including notice of the substance of the claim in sufficient time, having regard to the circumstances, to enable you to defend the proceedings.

[Signed]
Sheriff Clerk

FORM 73[2]                                  Rule 5.40

## NOTICE OF DETERMINATION BY SHERIFF CLERK OF APPLICATION UNDER SECTION 5A OF THE CIVIL JURISDICTION AND JUDGMENTS ACT 1982

Sheriff Court (Address)
............... (Applicant) v. ............... (Respondent)

TAKE NOTICE that the application by [name and address], for the recognition and/or enforcement of a maintenance order granted by [state Court of Tribunal] on

---

[1] As amended by the Act of Sederunt (Sheriff Court Rules) (Miscellaneous Amendments) (No.3) 2011 (SSI 2011/386) para.9 (effective November 28, 2011).
[2] As amended by the Act of Sederunt (Sheriff Court Rules) (Miscellaneous Amendments) (No.3) 2011 (SSI 2011/386) para.9 (effective November 28, 2011).

the .......... day of ..........; has been *GRANTED/REFUSED (state reasons in brief for refusal); and has been registered in the Books of Court to the extent that (state the extent).

(Signed)
Sheriff Clerk
Date

NOTE:

1. If the application has been granted to any extent, the person against whom enforcement is sought may appeal against this decision within one month from the date of service of this Notice, unless he is domiciled in another Contracting State in which case he may appeal within two months from the date of service.

2. If the application has been refused or not granted in full the Applicant may appeal against the decision within one month from the date of service of this Notice.

3. A solicitor qualified in Scots law should be consulted for the purposes of any appeal.

*Delete as appropriate

Rule 5.47(1)(a)                    FORM 73A[1]

INTIMATION OF REGISTRATION FOR ENFORCEMENT IN SCOTLAND OF A MAINTENANCE DECISION MADE BY A COURT IN DENMARK ETC.

(*Insert place*) ...............
(*Insert date*) ..............

[A.B.], (*Design*)

Intimation is hereby given of the registration in the Maintenance Orders Register kept at [*insert name and address of sheriff court*] of a Maintenance Decision made by [*name and address of Court*] on [*insert date of making order*].

In terms of the said Maintenance Decision you are required [*narrate terms of order and payee*].

You may within [30 days] *or* [*where the party against whom enforcement is sought has his/her habitual residence outwith the United Kingdom*, 45 days] from the date of this intimation make an application to [*insert name and address of sheriff court*] to set aside the registration of the order by lodging with the sheriff clerk at [*insert name and address of sheriff court*] a summary application setting out the grounds of the application.

The grounds upon which an application to set aside the registration may be made are:

(a)  the court does not have jurisdiction;

(b)  such registration is manifestly contrary to public policy in any part of the United Kingdom. The test of public policy may not be applied to the rules relating to jurisdiction;

(c)  where the decision was given in default of appearance, if you were not served with the document which instituted the proceedings or with an equivalent document in sufficient time and in such a way as to enable you to arrange for your defence, unless you failed to commence proceedings to challenge the decision when it was possible for you to do so;

(d)  if the decision is irreconcilable with a Maintenance Decision given in a dispute between the same parties in Scotland or another part of the United Kingdom;

---

[1] As inserted by the Act of Sederunt (Sheriff Court Rules) (Miscellaneous Amendments) (No.3) 2011 (SSI 2011/386) para.9 (effective November 28, 2011).

(e) if the decision is irreconcilable with an earlier decision given in another Member Regulation State or in a third State in a dispute involving the same cause of action and between the same parties, provided that the earlier decision fulfils the conditions necessary for its recognition in Scotland or another part of the United Kingdom.

**Note: A Maintenance Decision which has the effect of modifying an earlier Maintenance Decision on the basis of changed circumstances shall not be considered an irreconcilable decision within the meaning of points (d) and (e).**

[Signed]
(Sheriff Clerk)

Rule 5.47(1)(b)                    FORM 73B[1]

NOTICE OF REGISTRATION FOR THE PURPOSES OF ENFORCEMENT IN SCOTLAND OF A MAINTENANCE DECISION MADE BY A COURT IN DENMARK ETC.

*(Insert place)*
*(Insert date)*
[A.B.], *(Design)*
Notice is hereby given of the registration in the Maintenance Orders Register kept at *[insert name and address of sheriff court]* of a Maintenance Decision made by *[insert name and address of Court]* on *[insert date of making order]*.

In terms of the said Maintenance Decision CD *[design payer]* is required to pay to you *[narrate terms of order]*.

[Signed]
(Sheriff Clerk)

Rule 5.47(2)                    FORM 73C[2]

NOTICE OF A DECISION NOT TO REGISTER, FOR THE PURPOSES OF THE ENFORCEMENT IN SCOTLAND, A MAINTENANCE DECISION MADE BY A COURT IN DENMARK ETC.

*(Insert place)*
*(Insert date)*
[A.B.], *(Design)*
Notice is hereby given that the Maintenance Decision made by *[insert name and address of Court]* on *[insert date of making order]* requiring CD *[design payer]* to pay to you *[narrate terms of order]* has NOT been registered in the Maintenance Orders Register kept at this Sheriff Court.

The Maintenance Decision has not been registered on the grounds that *[narrate grounds]*.

You may within 30 days from the date of this intimation make an application to *[insert name and address of sheriff court]* to set aside the decision not to register the order by lodging with the sheriff clerk at *[insert name and address of sheriff court]* a summary application setting out the grounds of the application.

[Signed]
(Sheriff Clerk)

---

[1] As inserted by the Act of Sederunt (Sheriff Court Rules) (Miscellaneous Amendments) (No.3) 2011 (SSI 2011/386) para.9 (effective November 28, 2011).
[2] As inserted by the Act of Sederunt (Sheriff Court Rules) (Miscellaneous Amendments) (No.3) 2011 (SSI 2011/386) para.9 (effective November 28, 2011).

FORM 73D[1]                                      Rule 5.51(1)(a)

**INTIMATION OF REGISTRATION FOR ENFORCEMENT IN SCOTLAND OF A CONVENTION MAINTENANCE DECISION**

(Place).......... (Date)...............

[A.B.], (Design)

Intimation is hereby given of the registration in the Maintenance Orders Register kept at [*insert name and address of sheriff court*] of a Convention Maintenance Decision made by [*name and address of Court*] on [*insert date of making order*].

In terms of the said Convention Maintenance Decision you are required [*narrate terms of order and payee*].

You may within [30 day] or [where the party against whom enforcement is sought has his/her habitual residence outwith the United Kingdom, 60 days] from the date of this intimation make an application to [insert name and address of sheriff court] to set aside the registration of the order by lodging with the sheriff clerk at [insert name and address of sheriff court] a summary application setting out the grounds of the application.

The grounds upon which an application to set aside the registration may be made are set out in Article 23(7) of the 2007 Hague Convention.

.......... (Signed)

(Sheriff Clerk)

FORM 73E[2]                                      Rule 5.51(1)(b)

**NOTICE OF REGISTRATION FOR THE PURPOSES OF ENFORCEMENT IN SCOTLAND OF A CONVENTION MAINTENANCE DECISION**

(Place).......... (Date)...............

[A.B.], (Design)

Notice is hereby given of the registration in the Maintenance Orders Register kept at [*insert name and address of sheriff court*] of a Convention Maintenance Decision made by [*name and address of Court*] on [*insert date of making order*].

In terms of the said Convention Maintenance Decision C.D. [design payer] is required to pay to you [*narrate terms of order*].

.......... (Signed)

(Sheriff Clerk)

FORM 73F[3]                                      Rule 5.52(2)

**NOTICE OF A DECISION NOT TO REGISTER, FOR THE PURPOSES OF ENFORCEMENT IN SCOTLAND, A CONVENTION MAINTENANCE DECISION**

(Place).......... (Date)...............

[A.B.], (Design)

Notice is hereby given that the Convention Maintenance Decision made by [insert name and address of Court] on [insert date of making order] requiring C.D. [design payer] to pay you [narrate terms of order] has NOT been registered in the Maintenance Orders Register kept at this Sheriff Court.

---

[1] As inserted by the Act of Sederunt (Rules of the Court of Session and Sheriff Court Rules Amendment) (Miscellaneous) 2014 (SSI 2014/201) Sch. (effective August 1, 2014).

[2] As inserted by the Act of Sederunt (Rules of the Court of Session and Sheriff Court Rules Amendment) (Miscellaneous) 2014 (SSI 2014/201) Sch. (effective August 1, 2014).

[3] As inserted by the Act of Sederunt (Rules of the Court of Session and Sheriff Court Rules Amendment) (Miscellaneous) 2014 (SSI 2014/201) Sch. (effective August 1, 2014).

The Convention Maintenance Decision has not been registered on the grounds that [narrate grounds].

You may within 30 days from the date of this intimation make an application to [insert name and address of sheriff court] to set aside the decision not to register the order by lodging with the sheriff clerk at [insert name and address of sheriff court] a summary application setting out the grounds of the application.

.......... (Signed)
(Sheriff Clerk)

FORM 74                    Rule 6.3(1)

### FORM OF CERTIFICATE OF A TRANSFER OF RIGHTS TO AN ORDER BY VIRTUE OF SECTION 107 OF THE SOCIAL SECURITY ADMINISTRATION ACT 1992

(Place).......... (Date)..............

I certify that notice has today been received from the Secretary of State under section 107 of the Social Security Administration Act 1992 of a transfer of rights under an order granted on (date) from (name and design) to (name and design) with effect from (date).

(Signed)<br>Sheriff Clerk [Depute]

FORM 75[1][2][3]                    Rule 3.67

CHILD WITNESS NOTICE<br>VULNERABLE WITNESSES (SCOTLAND) ACT 2004 Section 12

Received the ............... day of ............... 20.....
(Date of receipt of this notice)
.......... [signed]
Sheriff Clerk

**CHILD WITNESS NOTICE**

Sheriff Court ............... ............... 20.....

(Court Ref. No.)

1. [A.B.] (the Applicant) is a party to an [application under section [93(2)(a), 94(2)(a) *or* 110] of the Children's Hearings (Scotland) Act 2011] *or* [an appeal under Part 15 of the 2011 Act] *or* [an appeal under section 44A of the Criminal Procedure (Scotland) Act 1995]. [*State the nature of the interest of the party*].".

2. The applicant [has cited [or intends to cite]] [C.D.] (*date of birth*) as a witness.

3. [C.D.] is a child witness under section 11 of the Vulnerable Witnesses (Scotland) Act 2004 [and was under the age of eighteen on the date of the commencement of proceedings].

4. The applicant considers [that the following special measure[s] is [are] the most appropriate for the purpose of taking the evidence of [C.D.]] *or* [that [C.D.] should give evidence without the benefit of any special measure]:–

(*delete as appropriate and specify any special measure(s) sought*).

---

[1] As amended by the Act of Sederunt (Children's Hearings (Scotland) Act 2011) (Miscellaneous Amendments) 2013 (SSI 2013/172) para.4 (effective June 24, 2013).

[2] As amended by the amended by the Act of Sederunt (Rules of the Court of Session 1994 and Sheriff Court Rules Amendment) (No. 3) (Miscellaneous) 2015 (SSI 2015/283) r.4(2) (effective 1 September 2015).

[3] As amended by the Act of Sederunt (Sheriff Court Rules Amendment) (Miscellaneous) 2015 (SSI 2015/424) para.3 (effective 1st February 2015).

5. [(a) The reason[s] this [these] special measure[s] is [are] considered the most appropriate is [are] as follows:–

*(here specify reason(s) for the special measure(s) sought).*]

OR

[(b) The reason[s] it is considered that [C.D.] should give evidence without the benefit of any special measure is [are]–

*(here explain why it is felt that no special measures are required).*

6. [C.D.] [and the parent[s] of] *or* [person[s] with parental responsibility for] [C.D.]] have expressed the following view[s] on [the special measure[s] that is [are] considered most appropriate] *or* [the appropriateness of [C.D.] giving evidence without the benefit of any special measure]:–

*(delete as appropriate and set out the view(s) expressed and how they were obtained).*

7. Other information considered relevant to this application is as follows:–

*(here set out any other information relevant to the child witness notice).*

8. The applicant asks the court to–

(a)   consider this child witness notice;

(b)   make an order authorising the special measure[s] sought; *or*

(c)   make an order authorising the giving of evidence by [C.D.] without the benefit of special measures.

*(delete as appropriate)*

.......... (Signed)

[A.B.]

*or* [Legal representative of A.B.] *(include full designation)*

*NOTE: This form should be suitably adapted where* section 16 of the Act of 2004 applies.

FORM 76    Rule 3.68

CERTIFICATE OF INTIMATION

VULNERABLE WITNESSES (SCOTLAND) ACT 2004 Section 12

Sheriff Court ..................... .......... 20.....

(Court Ref. No.)

I certify that intimation of the child witness notice relating to [name of child] was made to *(insert names of parties or solicitors for parties, as appropriate)* by *(insert method of intimation; where intimation is by facsimile transmission, insert fax number to which intimation sent)* on *(insert date of intimation).*

Date: ...............

............... Signed

Solicitor [or Sheriff Officer]

*(include full business designation)*

FORM 76A[1][2][3]   Rule 3.67

VULNERABLE WITNESS APPLICATION

VULNERABLE WITNESSES (SCOTLAND) ACT 2004 Section 12

Received the ............... day of ............... 20.....

---

[1] As inserted by the Act of Sederunt (Child Care and Maintenance Rules) Amendment (Vulnerable Witnesses (Scotland) Act 2004) 2006 (SSI 2006/75) Sch.1 para.1 (effective April 1, 2006).

[2] As amended by the Act of Sederunt (Children's Hearings (Scotland) Act 2011) (Miscellaneous Amendments) 2013 (SSI 2013/172) para.4 (effective June 24, 2013).

[3] As amended by the Act of Sederunt (Sheriff Court Rules Amendment) (Miscellaneous) 2015 (SSI 2015/424) para.3 (effective 1st February 2015).

(Date of receipt of this notice)

........................ [signed]

Sheriff Clerk

## VULNERABLE WITNESS APPLICATION

Sheriff Court ................... ............... 20.....

(Court Ref. No.)

1. [A.B.] (the Applicant) is a party to an [application under section [93(2)(a), 94(2)(a) *or* 110] of the Children's Hearings (Scotland) Act 2011] *or* [an appeal under Part 15 of the 2011 Act] *or* [an appeal under section 44A of the Criminal Procedure (Scotland) Act 1995]. [*State the nature of the interest of the party*].

2. The applicant [has cited [or intends to cite]] [C.D.] (*date of birth*) as a witness.

3. The applicant considers that [C.D.] is a vulnerable witness under section 11(1)(b) of the Vulnerable Witnesses (Scotland) Act 2004 for the following reasons:– (*here specify reasons witness is considered to be a vulnerable witness*).

4. The applicant considers that the following special measure[s] is [are] the most appropriate for the purpose of taking the evidence of [C.D.]. (*specify any special measure(s) sought*)

5. The reason[s] this [these] special measure[s] is [are] considered the most appropriate is [are] as follows:– (*here specify reason(s) for the special measure(s) sought*).]

6. [C.D.] has expressed the following view[s] on [the special measure[s] that is [are] considered most appropriate]:– (*set out the views expressed and how they were obtained*).

7. Other information considered relevant to this application is as follows:– (*here set out any other information relevant to the vulnerable witness application*).

8. The applicant asks the court to–

(a)   consider this vulnerable witness application;

(b)   make an order authorising the special measure[s] sought.

.......... (Signed)

[A.B.]

*or* [Legal representative of A.B.] (*include full designation*)

*NOTE: This form should be suitably adapted where section 16 of the Act of 2004 applies.*

FORM 76B[1]          Rule 3.71(2)

## CERTIFICATE OF INTIMATION
## VULNERABLE WITNESSES (SCOTLAND) ACT 2004

Sheriff Court .............. .......... 20.....

(Court Ref. No.)

CERTIFICATE OF INTIMATION

I certify that intimation of the vulnerable witness application relating to [name of witness] was made to (*insert names of parties or solicitors for parties, as appropriate*) by (*insert method of intimation; where intimation is by facsimile transmission, insert fax number to which intimation sent*) on (*insert date of intimation*).

Date: ...............

.......... Signed

Solicitor [or Sheriff Officer]

(*include full business designation*)

---

[1] As inserted by the Act of Sederunt (Child Care and Maintenance Rules) Amendment (Vulnerable Witnesses (Scotland) Act 2004) 2006 (SSI 2006/75) Sch.1 para.1 (effective April 1, 2006).

FORM 77[1][2][3]          Rule 3.70

APPLICATION FOR REVIEW OF ARRANGEMENTS FOR VULNERABLE WITNESS

VULNERABLE WITNESSES (SCOTLAND) ACT 2004 SECTION 13

Received the ............... day of ............... 20.....

(Date of receipt of this notice)

............... [signed]

Sheriff Clerk

**APPLICATION FOR REVIEW OF ARRANGEMENTS FOR VULNER-ABLE WITNESS**

Sheriff Court ............... ............... 20.....

(Court Ref. No.)

1. [A.B.] (the Applicant) is a party to an [application under section [93(2)(a), 94(2)(a) *or* 110] of the Children's Hearings (Scotland) Act 2011] *or* [an appeal under Part 15 of the 2011 Act] *or* [an appeal under section 44A of the Criminal Procedure (Scotland) Act 1995]. [ *State the nature of the interest of the party* ].

2. A hearing is fixed for [(*date*)] at [(*time*)].

3. [C.D.] is a witness who is to give evidence at, or for the purposes of, the hearing. [C.D.] is a vulnerable witness under section 11 of the Vulnerable Witnesses (Scotland) Act 2004.

4. The current arrangements for taking the evidence of [C.D.] are (*here specify current arrangements*).

5. The current arrangements should be reviewed as (*here specify reasons for review*).

6. [C.D.] and [the parent[s] of] *or* [person[s] with parental responsibility for] [C.D.]] has [or have] expressed the following view[s] on [the special measure[s] that is [or are] considered most appropriate] *or* [the appropriateness of [C.D.] giving evidence without the benefit of any special measure]:–

(*delete as appropriate and set out the view(s) expressed and how they were obtained*).

7. The applicant seeks (*here specify the order sought*).

............... (Signed)

[A.B.]

[*or* Legal representative of A.B.] (*include full designation*)

*NOTE: This form should be suitably adapted where* section 16 of the Act of 2004 *applies.*

FORM 78          Rule 3.71(2)

CERTIFICATE OF INTIMATION

VULNERABLE WITNESSES (SCOTLAND) ACT 2004 SECTION 13

Sheriff Court ............... ............... 20.....

(Court Ref. No.)

CERTIFICATE OF INTIMATION

I certify that intimation of the review application relating to [name of witness] was made to (insert names of parties or solicitors for parties, as appropriate) by

---

[1] As amended by the Act of Sederunt (Child Care and Maintenance Rules) Amendment (Vulnerable Witnesses (Scotland) Act 2004) 2006 (SSI 2006/75) Sch.1 para.2 (effective April 1, 2006).

[2] As amended by the Act of Sederunt (Children's Hearings (Scotland) Act 2011) (Miscellaneous Amendments) 2013 (SSI 2013/172) para.4 (effective June 24, 2013).

[3] As amended by the Act of Sederunt (Sheriff Court Rules Amendment) (Miscellaneous) 2015 (SSI 2015/424) para.3 (effective 1st February 2015).

(insert method of intimation; where intimation is by facsimile transmission, insert fax number to which intimation sent) on (insert date of intimation).

Date ...............

............... Signed

Solicitor [or Sheriff Officer]

(*include full business designation*)

FORM 79[1]          Rule 3.77

APPLICATION TO SHERIFF FOR ORDER AS TO EVIDENCE UNDER SECTION 175 OF THE CHILDREN'S HEARINGS (SCOTLAND) ACT 2011

Received the ............... day of ............... 20.....

(Date of receipt of this notice)

.......... [signed]

Sheriff Clerk

**Application for admission of evidence or allowance of questioning**

Sheriff Court ............... ............... 20.....

(Court Ref. No.)

1. [A.B.] (the Applicant) is a party to an [application under section [93(2)(a), 94(2)(a) *or* 110] of the Children's Hearings (Scotland) Act 2011] *or* [an appeal under Part 15 of the 2011 Act] in relation to the child [C.D.]. [ *State the nature of the interest of the party* ].

2. A hearing is fixed for [(*date*)] at [(*time*)].

3. The applicant asks the court to admit, or allow questioning designed to elicit or enable to be taken by commissioner, evidence which shows or tends to show that [C.D.] or [other person]:

* is not of good character (whether in relation to sexual matters or otherwise);
* has, at any time, engaged in sexual behaviour not forming part of the subject matter of the statement of grounds;
* has, at any time (other than shortly before, at the same time as or shortly after the acts which form part of the subject-matter of the ground), engaged in behaviour (not being sexual behaviour), that might found an inference that the person is not credible or the person's evidence is not reliable;
* has, at any time, been subject to any condition or predisposition that might found the inference that the person is not credible or the person's evidence is not reliable.

4. The circumstances justifying this application are:

(*here set out these circumstances with particular reference to* section 175 of the 2011 Act).

.......... (Signed)

[A.B.]

*or* [Legal representative of A.B.] (*include full designation*)

(**delete as appropriate*)

FORM 80[2]          Rule 3.78

CERTIFICATE OF INTIMATION UNDER SECTION 175 OF THE CHILDREN'S HEARINGS (SCOTLAND) ACT 2011

Sheriff Court ............... .......... 20.....

---

[1] As amended by the Act of Sederunt (Children's Hearings (Scotland) Act 2011) (Miscellaneous Amendments) 2013 (SSI 2013/172) para.4 (effective June 24, 2013).

[2] As amended by the Act of Sederunt (Children's Hearings (Scotland) Act 2011) (Miscellaneous Amendments) 2013 (SSI 2013/172) para.4 (effective June 24, 2013).

(Court Ref. No.)

I certify that intimation of the application for [admission of evidence]/[allowance of questioning] was made to (*insert names of parties or solicitors for parties, as appropriate*) by (*insert method of intimation; where intimation is by facsimile transmission, insert fax number to which intimation sent* on (*insert date of intimation*).

Date ...............

............... Signed

Solicitor [or Sheriff Officer]

(*include full business designation*)

SCHEDULE 2

REVOCATIONS

**Rule 1.4(1)**

| (1)<br>**Act of Sederunt revoked** | (2)<br>**Reference** | (3)<br>**Extension of revocation** |
|---|---|---|
| Act of Sederunt (Social Work) (Sheriff Court Procedure Rules) 1971 | SI 1971/92 | The whole Act of Sederunt |
| Act of Sederunt (Social Work) (Sheriff Court Procedure Rules Amendment) 1972 | SI 1972/1671 | The whole Act of Sederunt |
| Act of Sederunt (Maintenance Orders (Reciprocal Enforcement) Act 1972 Rules) 1974 | SI 1974/939 | In rule 1(2) the words ""Sheriff Clerk" includes Sheriff Clerk depute"; in rule 2 the words from "and the provisions" to the end; in rule 3(1) the words "and the Sheriff Clerk shall be the "prescribed officer" for the Sheriff Court"; rule 3(1A) and Part III |
| Act of Sederunt (Maintenance Orders (Reciprocal Enforcement) Act 1972 Amendment Rules) 1975 | SI 1975/474 | The whole Act of Sederunt |
| Act of Sederunt (Reciprocal Enforcement of Maintenance Orders (Republic of Ireland) Order 1974 Rules) 1975 | SI 1975/475 | In rule 1(2) the words ""Sheriff Clerk" includes Sheriff Clerk Depute"; in rule 2 the words "and the provisions of Part III of this Act of Sederunt shall apply for the purposes of the Act to orders made by or registered in the Sheriff Court"; in rule 3(1) the words "and the Sheriff Clerk shall be the "prescribed |

| (1)<br>Act of Sederunt | (2)<br>Reference | (3)<br>Extension of revocation |
|---|---|---|
| **revoked** | | |
| | | officer" for the Sheriff Court"; and Part III |
| Act of Sederunt (Reciprocal Enforcement of Maintenance Orders) (Hague Convention Countries) 1980 | SI 1980/291 | In rule 2(1) the words " "Sheriff Clerk" includes the Sheriff Clerk Depute"; rule 3(2); rule 4(1)(b); in rule 4(2) the words "and the Sheriff Clerk"; and Part III |
| Act of Sederunt (Reciprocal Maintenance Orders (America)) Rules 1980 | SI 1980/423 | The whole Act of Sederunt |
| Act of Sederunt (Social Work) (Sheriff Court Procedure Rules Amendment) 1980 | SI 1980/1443 | The whole Act of Sederunt |
| Act of Sederunt (Maintenance Orders Acts, Rules) 1980 | SI 1980/1732 | The whole Act of Sederunt |
| Act of Sederunt (Adoption of Children) 1984 | SI 1984/1013 | The whole Act of Sederunt |
| Act of Sederunt (Social Work (Scotland) Act 1968) (Safe-guarders) 1985 | SI 1985/780 | The whole Act of Sederunt |
| Act of Sederunt (Social Work) (Sheriff Court Procedure Rules 1971) (Amendment) 1985 | SI 1985/781 | The whole Act of Sederunt |
| Act of Sederunt (Social Work) (Sheriff Court Procedure Rules 1971) (Amendment No. 2) 1985 | SI 1985/1976 | The whole Act of Sederunt |
| Act of Sederunt (Enforcement of Judgments under the Civil Jurisdiction and Judgments Act 1982) 1986 | SI 1986/1947 | Paragraph 6 and Form 6 |
| Act of Sederunt (Rules for the Registration of Custody Orders of the Sheriff Court) 1988 | SI 1988/613 | The whole Act of Sederunt |
| Act of Sederunt (Applications under the Social Security Act 1986) 1990 | SI 1990/2238 | The whole Act of Sederunt |
| Act of Sederunt (Rules for the Registration of Custody Orders of the Sheriff Court) (Amend-ment) 1991 | SI 1991/2205 | The whole Act of Sederunt |
| Act of Sederunt (Adoption of Children) (Amendment) 1992 | SI 1992/1076 | The whole Act of Sederunt |
| Act of Sederunt (Sheriff Court Parental Orders (Human Fertili-sation and Embryology) Rules) | SI 1994/2805 | The whole Act of Sederunt |

| (1)<br>Act of Sederunt<br>revoked<br>1994 | (2)<br>Reference | (3)<br>Extension of revocation |
|---|---|---|

## SCHEDULE 3[1]

### EXCLUSION OF ENACTMENTS

**Rule 3.24**

| Column (1)<br>Enactment excluded | Column (2)<br>Reference | Column (3)<br>Extent of exclusion |
|---|---|---|
| The Citation Act 1592 | 1592 c.59 (S. ) | The whole Act |
| The Citation Act 1686 | 1686 c.5 (S. ) | The whole Act |
| The Debtors (Scotland) Act 1838, section 32 (as applied by the Citation (Scotland) Act 1846) | 1838 c.114 | The words "and more than one witness shall not be required for service or execution thereof" |
| The Citation Amendment (Scotland) Act 1882 | 1882 c.77 | The whole Act |
| The Sheriff Courts (Scotland) Act 1907, section 39 and the First Schedule | 1907 c.51 | The whole section; the whole Schedule except rule 29.10 (failure of witness to attend) and Chapter 45 (Vulnerable Witnesses (Scotland) Act 2004) and Chapter 50 (lodging recordings of children) |

---

[1] As amended by the Act of Sederunt (Child Care and Maintenance Rules 1997) Amendment (Vulnerable Witnesses (Scotland) Act 2004) 2007, r.2(3) (effective November 1, 2007) and by the Act of Sederunt (Sheriff Court Rules) (Miscellaneous Amendments) (No.3) 2012 (SSI 2012/271) para.4 (effective November 1, 2012).

(SI 1999/929)

*19 March 1999.*

ARRANGEMENT OF RULES

CHAPTER 1: GENERAL

Rule
1.1      Citation and commencement
1.2      Interpretation
1.3      Revocation
1.4      Application

CHAPTER 1A: LAY REPRESENTATION

1A.1    Application and interpretation
1A.2    Lay representation for party litigants

CHAPTER 2: SUMMARY APPLICATION RULES

Part I Interpretation

2.1      Interpretation

Part II General Rules

2.2      Application
2.2A    Lay support
2.3      Relief from failure to comply with rules
2.4      The initial writ
2.5      Order for intimation to interested persons by sheriff
2.6      Time-limits
2.7      Warrants, forms and certificate of citation
2.8      *[Omitted by Act of Sederunt (Sheriff Court Caveat Rules) 2006 (SI 2006/198), effective April 28, 2006]*
2.9      *[Omitted by Act of Sederunt (Sheriff Court Caveat Rules) 2006 (SI 2006/198), effective April 28, 2006]*
2.10    Postal service or intimation
2.11    Service within Scotland by sheriff officer
2.12    Service on persons furth of Scotland
2.13    Service where address of person is not known
2.14    Persons carrying on business under trading or descriptive name
2.15    Endorsation unnecessary
2.16    Re-service
2.17    No objection to regularity of citation, service or intimation
2.18    Service of schedule of arrestment
2.19    Arrestment on dependence before service
2.20    Movement of arrested property
2.21    Transfer to another sheriff court
2.22    Applications for time to pay directions
2.23    Remuneration of assessors
2.24    Deposits for expenses
2.25    When decrees extractable
2.26    Form of extract decree
2.27    Form of warrant for execution
2.28    Date of decree in extract

2.29    Decrees in absence where defender furth of Scotland
2.30    Motion procedure
2.31    Power of sheriff to make orders
2.32    Live links
2.33    Representation
2.33i   Enquiry when fixing hearing
2.34    Expenses
2.34i   Vulnerable witness procedure
2.37    Interventions by the CEHR
2.38    Form of intervention
2.39    Interventions by the SCHR
2.40    Invitations to intervene
2.41    Form of intervention

CHAPTER 3: RULES ON APPLICATIONS UNDER SPECIFIC STATUTES

Part I Administration of Justice (Scotland) Act 1972

3.1.1   Interpretation and application
3.1.2   Applications under section 1(1) of the Act

Part II Betting and Gaming Appeals

[Omitted by the Act of Sederunt (Sheriff Court Rules) (Miscellaneous Amendments) 2008 (SSI 2008/223) para.14(3)(effective July 1, 2008).]

Part III Coal Mining Subsidence Act 1991

3.3.1   Interpretation and application
3.3.2   Applications under section 41 of the Act

Part IV Conveyancing and Feudal Reform (Scotland) Act 1970

3.4.1   Application
3.4.2   Disposal of applications under Part II of the Act

Part V Copyright, Designs and Trade Marks

3.5.1   Interpretation
3.5.2   Orders for delivery up, forfeiture, destruction or other disposal
3.5.3   Service of notice on interested persons
3.5.4   Procedure where leave of court required

Part VI Drug Trafficking Act 1994

3.6.1   Interpretation and application
3.6.2   Determination of applications for continued detention of cash
3.6.3   Determination of application for release of cash
3.6.4   Determination of application for forfeiture of cash
3.6.5   Service
3.6.6   Sist of party

Part VII Licensing (Scotland) Act 1976

3.7.1   Interpretation and application
3.7.2   Service
3.7.3   Statement of reasons of licensing board

Part VIII Mental Health (Scotland) Act 1984

3.8.1   Interpretation and application
3.8.2   Appointment of hearing
3.8.3   Service of application
3.8.4   Duties of responsible medical officer
3.8.5   Appointment of curator ad litem
3.8.6   Appointment of solicitor by court

3.8.7 Intimation to representatives
3.8.8 Service by sheriff officer
3.8.9 Variation of conditions of community care order
3.8.10 Hearing
3.8.11 Appeal against community care order

Part IX Proceeds of Crime (Scotland) Act 1995

3.9.1 Interpretation and application
3.9.2 Service of restraint orders
3.9.3 Recall or variation of restraint orders
3.9.4 Applications for interdict
3.9.5 Applications in relation to arrestment
3.9.6 Appeals to the Court of Session
3.9.7 Applications for appointment of administrators
3.9.8 Incidental applications in an administration
3.9.9 Requirements where order to facilitate realisation of property considered
3.9.10 Documents for Accountant of Court
3.9.11 Procedure for fixing and finding caution
3.9.12 Administrator's title to act
3.9.13 Duties of administrator
3.9.14 State of funds and scheme of division
3.9.15 Objections to scheme of division
3.9.16 Application for discharge of administrator
3.9.17 Appeals against determination of outlays and remuneration

Part X Rating (Disabled Persons) Act 1978

3.10.1 Interpretation and application
3.10.2 Appeals under section 6(5) or 6(5A) of the Act

Part XI Representation of the People Act 1983

3.11.1 Interpretation and application
3.11.2 Initiation of proceedings
3.11.3 Security for expenses by bond of caution
3.11.4 Objections to bond of caution
3.11.5 Security by deposit
3.11.6 Amendment of pleadings
3.11.7 Notice of date and place of trial
3.11.8 Clerk of Court
3.11.9 Shorthand writer's charges
3.11.10 Appeals
3.11.11 List of votes objected to and of objections
3.11.12 Petition against undue return
3.11.13 Prescribed officer
3.11.14 Leave to abandon
3.11.15 Death of petitioner
3.11.16 Notice by respondent that he does not oppose petition
3.11.17 Application to be admitted as respondent
3.11.18 Public notice of trial not proceeding
3.11.19 Notice to party's agent sufficient
3.11.20 Cost of publication
3.11.21 Expenses

Part XII Requests or Applications under the Model Law on International Commercial Arbitration

3.12.1    Interpretation
3.12.2    Application
3.12.3    Recognition and enforcement of awards

Part XIII Sex Discrimination Act 1975

*[Omitted by the Act of Sederunt (Ordinary Cause, Summary Application, Summary Cause and Small Claim Rules) Amendment (Equality Act 2006 etc.) 2006 (SSI 2006/509) (effective November 3, 2006).]*

Part XIV Access to Health Records Act 1990

3.14.1    Interpretation and application
3.14.2    Accompanying documents
3.14.3    Time of making application

Part XV Race Relations Act 1976

*[Omitted by the Act of Sederunt (Ordinary Cause, Summary Application, Summary Cause and Small Claim Rules) Amendment (Equality Act 2006 etc.) 2006 (SSI 2006/509) (effective November 3, 2006).]*

Part XVI Adults with Incapacity (Scotland) Act 2000

3.16.1    Interpretation
3.16.2    Appointment of hearing
3.16.3    Place of any hearing
3.16.4    Service of application
3.16.5    Dispensing with service on adult
3.16.6    Hearing
3.16.7    Prescribed forms of application
3.16.8    Subsequent applications
3.16.9    Remit of applications by the Public Guardian etc.
3.16.10   Caution
3.16.11   Appointment of interim guardian
3.16.12   Registration of intervention order or guardianship order relating to heritable property
3.16.13   Non-compliance with decisions of guardians with welfare powers

Part XVII Anti-Terrorism, Crime and Security Act 2001

3.17.1    Interpretation
3.17.2    Applications for extended detention of cash
3.17.3    Applications for release of detained cash
3.17.4    Applications for forfeiture of detained cash
3.17.5    Applications for compensation

Part XVIII Local Government (Scotland) Act 1973

3.18.1    Application
3.18.2    Appeals
3.18.3    Warrant and form of citation

Part IX Proceeds of Crime Act 2002

3.19.1    Interpretation and application
3.19.2    Applications for extended detention of cash
3.19.3    Applications for release of detained cash
3.19.4    Applications for forfeiture of detained cash
3.19.5    Applications for compensation
3.19.6    Service of restraint orders
3.19.7    Recall or variation of restraint orders
3.19.8    Appeals to the Court of Session
3.19.9    Applications in relation to arrestment

3.19.10   Applications for appointment of administrators
3.19.11   Incidental applications in relation to an administration
3.19.12   Documents for Accountant of Court
3.19.13   Procedure for fixing and finding caution
3.19.14   Time for finding caution
3.19.15   Procedure on finding caution
3.19.16   Issue of certified copy interlocutor
3.19.17   Administrator's title to act
3.19.18   Accounts
3.19.19   Application for discharge of administrator
3.19.20   Appeals against determination of outlays and remuneration
3.19.21   Production orders
3.19.22   Search warrants
3.19.23   Customer information orders
3.19.24   Account monitoring orders

Part XX International Criminal Court (Scotland) Act 2001

3.20.1    Interpretation and application
3.20.2    Production or access orders
3.20.3    Search warrants

Part XXI Immigration and Asylum Act 1999

3.21.1    Interpretation
3.21.2    Appeals

Part XXII Crime and Disorder Act 1998

3.22.1    Interpretation
3.22.2    Application for an interim ASBO
3.22.3    Intimation of an ASBO

Part XXIII Ethical Standards in Public Life etc. (Scotland) Act 2000

3.23.1    Application
3.23.2    Appeals
3.23.3    Warrant and form of citation

Part XXIV International Protection of Adults

3.24.1    Interpretation
3.24.2    Application
3.24.3    Intimation of application
3.24.4    Notice to the Public Guardian
3.24.5    Register of recognized foreign measures

Part XXV Sexual Offences Act 2003

3.25.1    Interpretation
3.25.2    Time limit for service of a notice under section 99(3)
3.25.3    Time limit for service of a notice under section 106(11
3.25.4    Time limit for service of a notice under section 116(6)
3.25.5    Remit of original process under section 108(1)
3.25.6    Remit of original process under section 118(1)

Part XXVI Protection of Children (Scotland) Act 2003

3.26.1    Interpretation
3.26.2    Application
3.26.3    Provisional inclusion in the list
3.26.4    Application for removal from the list
3.26.5    Appeal: inclusion in lists under section 5 or 6 of the Act

3.26.6    Appeals: to the sheriff principal or to the Inner House of the Court of Session

### Part XXVII Antisocial Behaviour etc. (Scotland) Act 2004

3.27.1    Interpretation
3.27.2    Applications for variation or revocation of ASBOs to be made by minute n the original process
3.27.3    Application for an interim ASBO
3.27.4    *[Omitted by the Act of Sederunt (Ordinary Cause and Summary Application Rules) Amendment (Miscellaneous) 2006 (SSI 2006/410) (effective August 18, 2006).]*
3.27.5    Parenting orders
3.27.6    Closure notice
3.27.7    Application for closure orders
3.27.8    Application for extension of closure orders
3.27.9    Application for revocation of closure order
3.27.10    Application for access to premises
3.27.11    Applications by summary application 3.27.12
3.27.13    Revocation and suspension of order as to rental income
3.27.14    Revocation of management control order
3.27.15    Review of parenting order
3.27.16    Procedural requirements relating to parenting orders
3.27.17
3.27.18    Enforcement of local authorities' duties under section 71 of the Children (Scotland) Act 1995

### Part XXVIII Land Reform (Scotland) Act 2003

3.28.1    Interpretation
3.28.2    Public notice of appeal against section 14(2) remedial notice
3.28.3    Restriction on number of persons being party to section 14(4) application
3.28.4    Public notice and restriction on number of parties to section 15 application
3.28.5    Public notice and restriction on number of parties to section 28 application

### Part XXIX Risk of Sexual Harm Orders

3.29.1    Interpretation
3.29.2    Variation, renewal or discharge of RSHOs
3.29.3    Interim RSHOs
3.29.4    Service of RSHOs

### Part XXX Mental Health (Care and Treatment) (Scotland) Act 2003

3.30.1    Interpretation
3.30.2    Applications for removal orders
3.30.3    Applications for recall or variation of removal orders
3.30.4    Remit to Court of Session

### Part XXXI Football Banning Orders

3.31.1    Interpretation
3.31.2    Applications for variation or termination of a football banning order

### Part XXXII Animal Health and Welfare

3.32.1    Interpretation
3.32.2    Interim orders
3.32.3    Interim orders pending appeal

### Part XXXIII The Equality Act 2010

3.33.1    Interpretation and application

3.33.2    Relevant commission
3.33.3    Assessor
3.33.4    Taxation of commission expenses
3.33.5    National security
3.33.6    Transfer to Employment Tribunal
3.33.7    Transfer from Employment Tribunal
          Part XXXIV Licensing (Scotland) Act 2005
3.34      Appeals
          Part XXXV Adult Support and Protection (Scotland) Act 2007
3.35.1    Interpretation
3.35.2    Variation or recall of removal order
3.35.3    Applications—banning orders and temporary banning orders
3.35.4    Attachment of power of arrest
3.35.5    Notification to adult at risk
3.35.6    Certificate of delivery of documents
3.35.7    Warrants for entry
3.35.8    Form of appeal to the sheriff principal
3.35.9    Privacy of any hearing
          Part XXXVI UK Borders Act 2007
3.36.1    Interpretation
3.36.2    Appeals
          Part XXXVII Employment Tribunals Act 1996
3.37.1    Conciliation: recovery of sums payable under compromises
          Part XXXVIII Counter-Terrorism Act 2008
3.38      Variation, renewal or discharge of foreign travel restriction order
          Part XXXIX Public Health etc. (Scotland) Act 2008
3.39.1    Interpretation
3.39.2    Application for a public health investigation warrant
3.39.3    Application for an order for medical examination
3.39.4    Application for a quarantine order
3.39.5    Application for a short term detention order
3.39.6    Application for an exceptional detention order
3.39.7    Application for extension of a quarantine order, short term detention order or exceptional detention order
3.39.8    Application for modification of a quarantine order, short term detention order or exceptional detention order
3.39.9    Application for recall of an order granted in the absence of the person to whom it relates
3.39.10   Intimation of applications in relation to a child
3.39.11   Intimation of orders on the person to whom they apply
3.39.12   Appeal to the sheriff against an exclusion order or a restriction order
3.39.13   Application for a warrant to enter premises and take steps under Part 5 of the Act
3.39.14   Application for an order for disposal of a body
3.39.15   Application for appointment of a single arbiter to determine a dispute in relation to compensation
          Part XL Forced Marriage etc. (Protection and Jurisdiction) (Scotland) Act 2011
3.40.1    Interpretation
3.40.2    Applications for leave for a forced marriage protection order
3.40.3    Applications for variation, recall or extension of a forced marriage

protection order

## Part XLI Reporting Restrictions

3.41.1 Interpretation and application of this Part
3.41.2 Interim orders: Notification to interested persons
3.41.3 Interim orders: Representations
3.41.4 Notification of reporting restrictions
3.41.5 Applications for variation or revocation

## Part XLII Regulation of Investigatory Powers Act 2000

3.42.1 Interpretation
3.42.2 Authorisations requiring judicial approval

## Part XLIII Proceeds of Crime Act 2002 (External Investigations) Order 2013

3.43.1 Application of this Part
3.43.2 Applications

## Part XLIV Gender Recognition Act 2004

3.44.1
3.44.2
3.44.3

## Part XLV Mutual Recognition of Protection Measures in Civil Matters

3.45.1 Interpretation
3.45.2 Application of rules 3.45.3 to 3.45.9
3.45.3 Form of application for Article 5 certificate
3.45.4 Issue of Article 5 certificate
3.45.5 Conditions for issue of Article 5 certificate
3.45.6 Notice of issue of Article 5 certificate
3.45.7 Effect of variation of order
3.45.8 Application for rectification or withdrawal of Article 5 certificate
3.45.9 Issue of Article 14 certificate
3.45.10 Form of applications relating to incoming protection measures
3.45.11 Adjustment of incoming protection measures
3.45.12 Attachment of power of arrest to incoming protection measure
3.45.13 Determination that incoming protection measure is a domestic abuse interdict

## PART XLVI Counter-terrorism and Security Act 2015

3.46.1 Interpretation
3.46.2 Applications for extended detention of travel documents
3.46.3 Further applications for extended detention of travel documents

## Schedule 1
Forms
## Schedule 2
Revocations

The Lords of Council and Session, under and by virtue of the powers conferred on them by Schedule 1, paragraphs 24(1), 28D and 28(2), Schedule 2, paragraph 7 and Schedule 3, paragraph 13(3) to the Betting Gaming and Lotteries Act 1963, Schedule 2, paragraphs 33(1), 34(1), 45 and 47, and Schedule 9, paragraph 15 to the Gaming Act 1968, section 32 of the Sheriff Courts (Scotland) Act 1971, sections 66(5A) and 75 of the Sex Discrimination Act 1975, section 39(9) of the Licensing (Scotland) Act 1976, Schedule 3, paragraph 12 to the Lotteries and Amusements Act 1976, sections 136, 139, 146, 147, 152, 153, 182(3) and 185 of the Representation of the People Act 1983, sections 114(3), 204(3) and 231(3) of the Copyright, Designs and Patents Act 1988, section 19(3) of the Trade Marks Act 1994, section 46 of the Drug Trafficking Act 1994, Regulation 5(3) of the Olympics Association Right (Infringement Proceedings) Regulations 1995, and sections 31(5) and 48 of, and Schedule 1, paragraph 11 to, the Proceeds of Crime (Scotland) Act 1995 and of all other powers enabling them in that behalf, having approved draft rules submitted to them by the Sheriff Court Rules Council in accordance with section 34 of the Sheriff Courts (Scotland) Act 1971, do hereby enact and declare:

## CHAPTER 1

## GENERAL

**Citation and commencement**

**1.1**—(1)   This Act of Sederunt may be cited as the Act of Sederunt (Summary Applications, Statutory Applications and Appeals etc. Rules) 1999 and shall come into force on 1st July 1999.

(2)   This Act of Sederunt shall be inserted in the Books of Sederunt.

**Interpretation**

**1.2**—(1)[1]   In this Act of Sederunt, unless the context otherwise requires—

"the 2004 Act" means the Vulnerable Witnesses (Scotland) Act 2004;[2]
"enactment" includes an enactment comprised in, or in an instrument made under, an Act of the Scottish Parliament;
"Ordinary Cause Rules" means the First Schedule to the Sheriff Courts (Scotland) Act 1907;
"sheriff clerk" includes sheriff clerk depute; and
"summary application" has the meaning given by section 3(p) of the Sheriff Courts (Scotland) Act 1907.

(2)   Unless the context otherwise requires, any reference in this Act of Sederunt to a specified Chapter, Part or rule shall be construed as a reference to the Chapter, Part or rule bearing that number in this Act of Sederunt, and a reference to a specified paragraph, sub-paragraph or head shall be construed as a reference to the paragraph, sub-paragraph or head so numbered or lettered in the provision in which that reference occurs.

(3)   Any reference in this Act of Sederunt to a numbered Form shall, unless the context otherwise requires, be construed as a reference to the Form so numbered in Schedule 1 to this Act of Sederunt and includes a form substantially to the same effect with such variation as circumstances may require.

(4)[3]   In this Act of Sederunt, references to a solicitor include a reference to a member of a body which has made a successful application under section 25 of the

---

[1] As amended by the Act of Sederunt (Ordinary Cause, Summary Application, Summary Cause and Small Claim Rules) Amendment (Miscellaneous) 2007 (SSI 2007/6), para.3(2) (effective January 29, 2007).

[2] As inserted by the Act of Sederunt (Ordinary Cause, Summary Application, Summary Cause and Small Claim Rules) Amendment (Vulnerable Witnesses (Scotland) Act 2004) (SSI 2007/463), r.3(2) (effective November 1, 2007).

[3] As inserted by the Act of Sederunt (Sheriff Court Rules Amendment) (Sections 25 to 29 of the Law Reform (Miscellaneous Provisions) (Scotland) Act 1990) 2009 (SSI 2009/164) r.3 (effective May 20, 2009).

Law Reform (Miscellaneous Provisions) (Scotland) Act 1990 but only to the extent
that the member is exercising rights acquired by virtue of section 27 of that Act.

**Revocation**

**1.3** The Acts of Sederunt mentioned in column (1) of Schedule 2 to this Act of
Sederunt are revoked to the extent specified in column (3) of that Schedule.

**Application**

**1.4** Unless otherwise provided in this Act of Sederunt or in any other enactment, any application or appeal to the sheriff shall be by way of summary application and the provisions of Chapter 2 of this Act of Sederunt shall apply accordingly.

CHAPTER 1A[1]

LAY REPRESENTATION

**Application and interpretation**

**1A.1.**—(1) This Chapter is without prejudice to any enactment (including any
other provision in these Rules) under which provision is, or may be, made for a
party to a particular type of case before the sheriff to be represented by a lay
representative.

(2) In this Chapter, a "lay representative" means a person who is not—
    (a) a solicitor;
    (b) an advocate, or
    (c) someone having a right to conduct litigation, or a right of audience, by
        virtue of section 27 of the Law Reform (Miscellaneous Provisions)
        (Scotland) Act 1990.

**Lay representation for party litigants**

**1A.2.**—(1) In any proceedings in respect of which no provision as mentioned in
rule 1A.1(1) is in force, the sheriff may, on the request of a party litigant, permit a
named individual (a "lay representative") to appear, along with the litigant, at a
specified hearing for the purpose of making oral submissions on behalf of the litigant
at that hearing.

(2) An application under paragraph (1)—
    (a) is to be made orally on the date of the first hearing at which the litigant
        wishes a named individual to make oral submissions; and
    (b) is to be accompanied by a document, signed by the named individual, in
        Form A1.

(3) The sheriff may grant an application under paragraph (1) only if the sheriff
is of the opinion that it would assist his or her consideration of the case to grant it.

(4) It is a condition of permission granted by the sheriff that the lay representative does not receive directly or indirectly from the litigant any remuneration or
other reward for his or her assistance.

---

[1] As inserted by the Act of Sederunt (Sheriff Court Rules) (Lay Representation) 2013 (SSI 2013/91) r.3
(effective April 4, 2013).

(5) The sheriff may grant permission under paragraph (1) in respect of one or more specified hearings in the case; but such permission is not effective during any period when the litigant is legally represented.

(6) The sheriff may, of his or her own accord or on the motion of a party to the proceedings, withdraw permission granted under paragraph (1).

(7) Where permission has been granted under paragraph (1), the litigant may—

(a) show the lay representative any document (including a court document); or

(b) impart to the lay representative any information,

which is in his or her possession in connection with the proceedings without being taken to contravene any prohibition or restriction on the disclosure of the document or the information; but the lay representative is then to be taken to be subject to any such prohibition or restriction as if he or she were the litigant.

(8) Any expenses incurred by the litigant in connection with lay representation under this rule are not recoverable expenses in the proceedings.

## CHAPTER 2

## SUMMARY APPLICATION RULES

### Part I

### Interpretation

**Interpretation**

**2.1** In this Chapter, unless the context otherwise requires—

"decree" includes any judgment, deliverance, interlocutor, act, order, finding or authority which may be extracted;

"defender" means any person other than the pursuer who is a party to a summary application; and

"pursuer" means any person making a summary application.

### Part II

### General Rules

**Application**

**2.2** This Part applies to summary applications.

**Lay support**

**2.2A—**[1](1) At any time during proceedings the sheriff may, on the request of a party litigant, permit a named individual to assist the litigant in the conduct of the proceedings by sitting beside or behind (as the litigant chooses) the litigant at hearings in court or in chambers and doing such of the following for the litigant as he or she requires—

(a) providing moral support;

---

[1] As inserted by the Act of Sederunt (Sheriff Court Rules) (Miscellaneous Amendments) (No.2) 2010 (SSI 2010/416) r.3 (effective January 1, 2011).

(b)  helping to manage the court documents and other papers;

(c)  taking notes of the proceedings;

(d)  quietly advising on—

    (i)  points of law and procedure;

    (ii)  issues which the litigant might wish to raise with the sheriff;

    (iii)  questions which the litigant might wish to ask witnesses.

(2)  It is a condition of such permission that the named individual does not receive from the litigant, whether directly or indirectly, any remuneration for his or her assistance.

(3)  The sheriff may refuse a request under paragraph (1) only if—

(a)  the sheriff is of the opinion that the named individual is an unsuitable person to act in that capacity (whether generally or in the proceedings concerned); or

(b)  the sheriff is of the opinion that it would be contrary to the efficient administration of justice to grant it.

(4)  Permission granted under paragraph (1) endures until the proceedings finish or it is withdrawn under paragraph (5); but it is not effective during any period when the litigant is represented.

(5)  The sheriff may, of his or her own accord or on the motion of a party to the proceedings, withdraw permission granted under paragraph (1); but the sheriff must first be of the opinion that it would be contrary to the efficient administration of justice for the permission to continue.

(6)  Where permission has been granted under paragraph (1), the litigant may—

(a)  show the named individual any document (including a court document); or

(b)  impart to the named individual any information,

which is in his or her possession in connection with the proceedings without being taken to contravene any prohibition or restriction on the disclosure of the document or the information; but the named individual is then to be taken to be subject to any such prohibition or restriction as if he or she were the litigant.

(7)  Any expenses incurred by the litigant as a result of the support of an individual under paragraph (1) are not recoverable expenses in the proceedings.

**Relief from failure to comply with rules**

**2.3**—(1)  The sheriff may relieve a party from the consequences of failure to comply with a provision in this Part which is shown to be due to mistake, oversight or other excusable cause, on such conditions as he thinks fit.

(2)  Where the sheriff relieves a party from the consequences of a failure to comply with a provision in this Part of these Rules under paragraph (1), he may make such order as he thinks fit to enable the summary application to proceed as if the failure to comply with the provision had not occurred.

**The initial writ**

**2.4**—(1)  Unless otherwise prescribed by any other enactment, a summary application shall be commenced by initial writ in Form 1.

(2)  The initial writ shall be written, typed or printed on A4 size paper of durable quality and shall not be backed or folded.

(3)  Where the pursuer has reason to believe that an agreement exists prorogating jurisdiction over the subject-matter of the summary application to another court, the initial writ shall contain details of that agreement.

(4)    Where the pursuer has reason to believe that proceedings are pending before another court involving the same cause of action and between the same parties as those named in the instance of the initial writ, the initial writ shall contain details of those proceedings.

(4A)[1]    In an action which relates to a regulated agreement within the meaning given by section 189(1) of the Consumer Credit Act 1974 the initial writ shall include an averment that such an agreement exists and details of the agreement.

(5)    An article of condescendence shall be included in the initial writ averring—

    (a)    the ground of jurisdiction; and

    (b)    the facts upon which the ground of jurisdiction is based.

(6)    Where the residence, registered office or place of business, as the case may be, of the defender is not known and cannot reasonably be ascertained, the pursuer shall set out in the instance of the initial writ that the whereabouts of the defender are not known and aver in the condescendence what steps have been taken to ascertain his present whereabouts.

(7)    The initial writ shall be signed by the pursuer or his solicitor (if any) and the name and address of that solicitor shall be stated on the back of every service copy of that writ.

(8)    The initial writ shall include averments about those persons who appear to the pursuer to have an interest in the application and in respect of whom a warrant for citation is sought.

(9)[2]    Where warrant to arrest on the dependence is sought, the initial writ shall include averments to justify the grant of such a warrant.

## Order for intimation to interested persons by sheriff

**2.5**    The sheriff may make an order for intimation to any person who appears to him to have an interest in the summary application.

## Time limits

**2.6**—(1)[3]    This rule applies to a summary application where the time within which the application being an appeal under statute or an application in the nature of an appeal may be made is not otherwise prescribed.

(2)    An application to which this rule applies shall be lodged with the sheriff clerk within 21 days after the date on which the decision, order, scheme, determination, refusal or other act complained of was intimated to the pursuer.

(3)    On special cause shown, the sheriff may hear an application to which this rule applies notwithstanding that it was not lodged within the period prescribed in paragraph (2).

---

[1]  As inserted by the Act of Sederunt (Sheriff Court Rules) (Miscellaneous Amendments) 2009 (SSI 2009/294) r.3 (effective December 1, 2009) as substituted by the Act of Sederunt (Amendment of the Act of Sederunt (Sheriff Court Rules) (Miscellaneous Amendments) 2009) 2009 (SSI 2009/402) (effective November 30, 2009).

[2]  As inserted by the Act of Sederunt (Ordinary Cause, Summary Application and Small Claim Rules) Amendment (Miscellaneous) 2004 (SSI 2004/197) para.3(2) (effective May 21, 2004).

[3]  As amended by the Act of Sederunt (Ordinary Cause, Summary Application and Small Claim Rules) Amendment (Miscellaneous) 2004 (SSI 2004/197) para.3(3) (effective May 21, 2004).

### Warrants, forms and certificate of citation

**2.7**—[1](1)  Subject to paragraph (2), a warrant for citation or intimation may be signed by the sheriff or sheriff clerk.

(1A)[2]  A warrant for arrestment on the dependence may be signed by the sheriff, if the sheriff considers it appropriate.

(2)  A warrant containing a period of notice shorter than the period of notice to be given to a defender under rule 3.6(1)(a) or (b), as the case may be, of the Ordinary Cause Rules or any other warrant which the sheriff clerk may not sign, shall be signed by the sheriff.

(3)  Where the sheriff clerk refuses to sign a warrant which he may sign, the party presenting the summary application may apply to the sheriff for the warrant.

(4)  Where citation is necessary—

(a)[3, 4]  the warrant of citation shall, subject to paragraphs (5) and (7ZA)(a) and rule 3.18.3(1) (appeals under section 103J of the Local Government (Scotland) Act 1973), be in Form 2; and

(b)[5] [6]  citation shall, subject to paragraphs (7) and (7ZA)(b) and rules 2.13 (service where address of person is not known) and 3.18.3(2) (appeals under section 103J of the Local Government (Scotland) Act 1973), be in Form 3.

(5)  Where a time to pay direction under the Debtors (Scotland) Act 1987 or a time order under the Consumer Credit Act 1974 may be applied for by the defender, the warrant of citation shall be in Form 4.

(6)  Where a warrant of citation in accordance with Form 4 is appropriate, there shall be served on the defender (with the initial writ and warrant) a notice in Form 5.

(7)  Where a time to pay direction under the Debtors (Scotland) Act 1987 or a time order under the Consumer Credit Act 1974 may be applied for by the defender, citation shall be in Form 6 which shall be attached to a copy of the initial writ and warrant of citation.

(7ZA)  In an application for enforcement of security over residential property within the meaning of Part IV of Chapter 3—

(a)  the warrant of citation will be in Form 6ZA;

(b)  citation will be in Form 6ZB which is to be attached to a copy of the initial writ,

Form 11C and warrant of citation.

---

[1] As amended by the Act of Sederunt (Ordinary Cause, Summary Application, Summary Cause and Small Claim Rules) Amendment (Miscellaneous) 2007 (SSI 2007/6), para.3(3) (effective January 29, 2007).

[2] As inserted by the Act of Sederunt (Ordinary Cause, Summary Application and Small Claim Rules) Amendment (Miscellaneous) 2004 (SSI 2004/197) para.3(4) (effective May 21, 2004).

[3] As amended by the Act of Sederunt (Summary Applications, Statutory Applications and Appeals etc. Rules) Amendment (No.2) (Local Government (Scotland) Act 1973) 2002 (SSI 2002/130) para.2(2) (effective March 8, 2002).

[4] As amended by the Act of Sederunt (Sheriff Court Rules)(Miscellaneous Amendments) 2013 (SSI 2013/135) para.2 (effective May 27, 2013).

[5] As amended by the Act of Sederunt (Summary Applications, Statutory Applications and Appeals etc. Rules) Amendment (No.2) (Local Government (Scotland) Act 1973) 2002 (SSI 2002/130) para.2(2) (effective March 8, 2002).

[6] As amended by the Act of Sederunt (Sheriff Court Rules)(Miscellaneous Amendments) 2013 (SSI 2013/135) para.2 (effective May 27, 2013).

(7A)  *[Repealed by the Act of Sederunt (Sheriff Court Rules) (Enforcement of Securities over Heritable Property) 2010 (SSI 2010/324) para.2 (effective September 30, 2010).]*

(8)  Where citation is necessary, the certificate of citation shall be in Form 7 which shall be attached to the initial writ.

(9)  Where citation is by a sheriff officer, one witness shall be sufficient for the execution of citation.

(10)  Where citation is by a sheriff officer, the certificate of citation shall be signed by the sheriff officer and the witness and shall state—

    (a)  the method of citation; and

    (b)  where the method of citation was other than personal or postal citation, the full name and designation of any person to whom the citation was delivered.

(11)  Where citation is executed under paragraph (3) of rule 2.11 (depositing or affixing by sheriff officer), the certificate shall include a statement—

    (a)  of the method of service previously attempted;

    (b)  of the circumstances which prevented such service being executed; and

    (c)  that a copy of the document was sent in accordance with the provisions of paragraph (4) of that rule.

### Orders against which caveats may be lodged

**2.8**  *[Omitted by Act of Sederunt (Sheriff Court Caveat Rules) 2006 (SI 2006/198), effective April 28, 2006]*

### Form, lodging and renewal of caveats

**2.9**  *[Omitted by Act of Sederunt (Sheriff Court Caveat Rules) 2006 (SI 2006/198), effective April 28, 2006]*

### Postal service or intimation

**2.10**—(1)  In any summary application in which service or intimation of any document or citation of any person may be by recorded delivery, such service, intimation or citation shall be by the first class recorded delivery service.

(2)  Notwithstanding the terms of section 4(2) of the Citation Amendment (Scotland) Act 1882 (time from which period of notice reckoned), where service or intimation is by post, any period of notice contained in the warrant of citation shall run from the beginning of the day after the date of posting.

(3)  On the face of the envelope used for postal service or intimation under this rule there shall be written or printed the following notice:—

    "This envelope contains a citation to or intimation from (*specify the court*). If delivery cannot be made at the address shown it is to be returned immediately to:— The Sheriff Clerk (*insert address of sheriff clerk's office*).".

(4)  The certificate of citation or intimation in the case of postal service shall have attached to it any relevant postal receipts.

### Service within Scotland by sheriff officer

**2.11**—(1)  An initial writ, decree, charge, warrant or any other order or writ following upon such initial writ or decree served by a sheriff officer on any person shall be served—

    (a)  personally; or

    (b)  by being left in the hands of a resident at the person's dwelling place or an employee at his place of business.

(2)  Where service is executed under paragraph (1)(b), the certificate of citation or service shall contain the full name and designation of any person in whose hands the initial writ, decree, charge, warrant or other order or writ, as the case may be, was left.

(3)  Where a sheriff officer has been unsuccessful in executing service in accordance with paragraph (1), he may, after making diligent enquiries, serve the document question by—

    (a)  depositing it in that person's dwelling place or place of business; or

    (b)[1]  by leaving it at that person's dwelling place or place of business in such a way that it is likely to come to the attention of that person.

(4)  Subject to rule 2.18 (service of schedule of arrestment), where service is executed under paragraph (3), the sheriff officer shall, as soon as possible after such service, send a letter containing a copy of the document by ordinary first class post to the address at which he thinks it most likely that the person on whom service has been executed may be found.

(5)[2]  Where the firm which employs the sheriff officer has in its possession—

    (a)  the document or a copy of it certified as correct by the pursuer's solicitor, the sheriff officer may serve the writ upon the defender without having the document or certified copy in his possession, in which case he shall if required to do so by the person on whom service is executed and within a reasonable time of being so required, show the document or certified copy to the person; or

    (b)  a certified copy of the interlocutor pronounced allowing service of the document, the sheriff officer may serve the document without having in his possession the certified copy interlocutor if he has in his possession a facsimile copy of the certified copy interlocutor (which he shall show, if required, to the person on whom service is executed).

(6)[3]  Where service is executed under paragraphs (1)(b) or (3), the document and the citation or notice of intimation, as the case may be, must be placed in an envelope bearing the notice "This envelope contains a citation to or intimation from (*insert name of sheriff court*) " and sealed by the sheriff officer.

### Service on persons furth of Scotland

**2.12**—[4, 5](1)  Subject to the following provisions of this rule, an initial writ, decree, charge, warrant or any other order or writ following upon such initial writ or decree served on a person furth of Scotland shall be served—

---

[1] As substituted by the Act of Sederunt (Sheriff Court Rules) (Miscellaneous Amendments) 2011 (SSI 2011/193) r.3 (effective April 4, 2011).

[2] As inserted by the Act of Sederunt (Ordinary Cause, Summary Application, Summary Cause and Small Claim Rules) Amendment (Miscellaneous) 2003 (SSI 2003/26), para.3(3) (effective January 24, 2003).

[3] As inserted by the Act of Sederunt (Sheriff Court Rules) (Miscellaneous Amendments) 2011 (SSI 2011/193) r.3 (effective April 4, 2011).

[4] As amended by the Act of Sederunt (Ordinary Cause, Summary Application, Summary Cause and Small Claim Rules) Amendment (Miscellaneous) 2003 (SSI 2003/26), para.3(4) (effective January 24, 2003).

[5] As amended and inserted by the Act of Sederunt (Ordinary Cause, Summary Application and Small Claim Rules) Amendment (Miscellaneous) 2004 (SSI 2004/197) (effective May 21, 2004), para.3(5)

(a) at a known residence or place of business in England, Wales, Northern Ireland, the Isle of Man, the Channel Islands or any country with which the United Kingdom does not have a convention providing for service of writs in that country—

    (i) in accordance with the rules for personal service under the domestic law of the place in which service is to be executed; or

    (ii) by posting in Scotland a copy of the document in question in a registered letter addressed to the person at his residence or place of business;

(b) in a country which is a party to the Hague Convention on the Service Abroad of Judicial and Extra-Judicial Documents in Civil or Commercial Matters dated 15th November 1965 or the Convention in Schedule 1 or 3C to the Civil Jurisdiction and Judgments Act 1982—

    (i) by a method prescribed by the internal law of the country where service is to be executed for the service of documents in domestic actions upon persons who are within its territory;

    (ii)[1] by or through the central, or other appropriate, authority in the country where service is to be executed at the request of the Scottish Ministers;

    (iii) by or through a British Consular Office in the country where service is to be executed at the request of the Secretary of State for Foreign and Commonwealth Affairs;

    (iv) where the law of the country in which the person resides permits, by posting in Scotland a copy of the document in a registered letter addressed to the person at his residence; or

    (v) where the law of the country in which service is to be executed permits, service by an *huissier*, other judicial officer or competent official of the country where service is to be executed; or

(c) in a country with which the United Kingdom has a convention on the service of writs in that country other than the conventions mentioned in sub-paragraph (b), by one of the methods approved in the relevant convention.

(1A)[2,3] In a country to which the EC Service Regulation applies, service—

(a) may be effected by the methods prescribed in paragraph (1)(b)(ii) or (iii) only in exceptional circumstances; and

(b) is effected only if the receiving agency has informed the person that acceptance of service may be refused on the ground that the document has not been translated in accordance with paragraph (6).

---

and substituted by the Act of Sederunt (Sheriff Court Ordinary Cause, Summary Application, Summary Cause and Small Claims Rules) Amendment (Council Regulation (EC) No. 1348 of 2000 Extension to Denmark) 2007 (SSI 2007/440) r.3(2) (effective October 9, 2007).

[1] As substituted by the Act of Sederunt (Sheriff Court Rules) (Miscellaneous Amendments) 2011 (SSI 2011/193) r.6 (effective April 4, 2011).

[2] As amended and inserted by the Act of Sederunt (Ordinary Cause, Summary Application and Small Claim Rules) Amendment (Miscellaneous) 2004 (SSI 2004/197) (effective May 21, 2004), para.3(5) and substituted by the Act of Sederunt (Sheriff Court Ordinary Cause, Summary Application, Summary Cause and Small Claims Rules) Amendment (Council Regulation (EC) No. 1348 of 2000 Extension to Denmark) 2007 (SSI 2007/440) r.3(2) (effective October 9, 2007).

[3] As amended by the Act of Sederunt (Sheriff Court Rules) (Miscellaneous Amendments) (No.2) 2008 (SSI 2008/365) r.8(a) (effective November 13, 2008).

(2)   Any document which requires to be posted in Scotland for the purposes of this rule shall be posted by a solicitor or a sheriff officer, and on the face of the envelope there shall be written or printed the notice set out in rule 2.10(3).

(3)   In the case of service by a method referred to in paragraph (1)(b)(ii) and (iii), the pursuer shall—

    (a)[1]   send a copy of the writ and warrant of service with citation attached, or other document, as the case may be, with a request for service by the method indicated in the request to the Scottish Ministers or, as the case may be, the Secretary of State for Foreign and Commonwealth Affairs; and

    (b)   lodge in process a certificate signed by the authority which executed service stating that it has been, and the manner in which it was, served.

(4)   In the case of service by a method referred to in paragraph (1)(b)(v), the pursuer or the sheriff officer shall—

    (a)   send a copy of the writ and warrant for service with citation attached, or other document, as the case may be, with a request for service by the method indicated in the request to the official in the country in which service is to be executed; and

    (b)   lodge in process a certificate of the official who executed service stating that it has been, and the manner in which it was, served.

(5)   Where service is executed, in accordance with paragraph (1)(a)(i) or (1)(b)(i) other than on another party in the United Kingdom, the Isle of Man or the Channel Islands, the party executing service shall lodge a certificate by a person who is conversant with the law of the country concerned and who practises or has practised law in that country or is a duly accredited representative of the Government of that country, stating that the method of service employed is in accordance with the law of the place where service was executed.

(6)   Every writ, document, citation or notice on the face of the envelope mentioned in rule 2.10(3) shall be accompanied by a translation in—

    (a)[2]   an official language of the country in which service is to be executed; or

    (b)   in a country to which the EC Service Regulation applies, a language of the member state of transmission that is understood by the person on whom service is being executed.

(7)   A translation referred to in paragraph (6) shall be certified as correct by the person making it and the certificate shall—

    (a)   include his full name, address and qualifications; and

    (b)   be lodged with the execution of citation or service.

(8)[3]   In this rule "the EC Service Regulation" means Regulation (EC) No. 1393/2007 of the European Parliament and of the Council of 13th November 2007 on the service in the Member States of judicial and extrajudicial documents in civil or commercial matters (service of documents), and repealing Council Regulation (EC) No. 1348/2000, as amended from time to time.

---

[1] As amended by the Act of Sederunt (Sheriff Court Rules) (Miscellaneous Amendments) 2011 (SSI 2011/193) r.7 (effective April 4, 2011).

[2] As amended and inserted by the Act of Sederunt (Ordinary Cause, Summary Application and Small Claim Rules) Amendment (Miscellaneous) 2004 (SSI 2004/197) (effective May 21, 2004), para.3(5) and substituted by the Act of Sederunt (Sheriff Court Ordinary Cause, Summary Application, Summary Cause and Small Claims Rules) Amendment (Council Regulation (EC) No. 1348 of 2000 Extension to Denmark) 2007 (SSI 2007/440) r.3(2) (effective October 9, 2007).

[3] As substituted by the Act of Sederunt (Sheriff Court Rules) (Miscellaneous Amendments) (No.2) 2008 (SSI 2008/365) r.8(b) (effective November 13, 2008).

### Service where address of person is not known

**2.13**—(1)   Where the address of a person to be cited or served with a document is not known and cannot reasonably be ascertained, the sheriff shall grant warrant for citation or service upon that person by—

(a)   the publication of an advertisement in Form 9 in a specified newspaper circulating in the area of the last known address of that person; or

(b)   displaying on the walls of court a copy of the instance and crave of the initial writ, the warrant of citation and a notice in Form 10;

and any period of notice contained in the warrant of citation shall run from the date of publication of the advertisement or display on the walls of court, as the case may be.

(2)   Where service requires to be executed under paragraph (1), the pursuer shall lodge a service copy of the initial writ and a copy of any warrant of citation with the sheriff clerk from whom they may be uplifted by the person for whom they are intended.

(3)   Where a person has been cited or served in accordance with paragraph (1) and, after the summary application has commenced, his address becomes known, the sheriff may allow the initial writ to be amended subject to such conditions as to re-service, intimation, expenses or transfer of the summary application as he thinks fit.

(4)   Where advertisement in a newspaper is required for the purpose of citation or service under this rule, a copy of the newspaper containing the advertisement shall be lodged with the sheriff clerk by the pursuer.

(5)   Where display on the walls of court is required under paragraph (1)(b), the pursuer shall supply to the sheriff clerk for that purpose a certified copy of the instance and crave of the initial writ and any warrant of citation.

### Persons carrying on business under trading or descriptive name

**2.14**—(1)   A person carrying on a business under a trading or descriptive name may be designed in the instance of the initial writ by such trading or descriptive name alone, and an extract of a—

(a)   decree pronounced in the sheriff court; or

(b)   decree proceeding upon any deed, decree arbitral, bond, protest of a bill, promissory note or banker's note or upon any other obligation or document on which execution may proceed, recorded in the sheriff court books,

against such person under such trading or descriptive name, shall be a valid warrant for diligence against such person.

(2)   An initial writ, decree, charge, warrant or any other order or writ following upon such initial writ or decree in a summary application in which a person carrying on business under a trading or descriptive name is designed in the instance of the initial writ by that name shall be served—

(a)   at any place of business or office at which such business is carried on within the sheriffdom of the sheriff court in which the cause is brought; or

(b)   where there is no place of business within that sheriffdom, at any place where such business is carried on (including the place of business or office of the clerk or secretary of any company, corporation or association or firm).

**Endorsation unnecessary**

**2.15**   An initial writ, decree, charge, warrant or any other order or writ following upon such initial writ or decree may be served, enforced or otherwise lawfully executed anywhere in Scotland without endorsation by a sheriff clerk and, if executed by a sheriff officer, may be so executed by a sheriff officer of the court which granted it or by a sheriff officer of the sheriff court district in which it is to be executed.

Re-service

**2.16**   Where it appears to the sheriff that there has been any failure or irregularity in citation or service on a person, he may order the pursuer to re-serve the initial writ on such conditions as the sheriff thinks fit.

**No objection to regularity of citation, service or intimation**

**2.17**—(1)   A person who appears in a summary application shall not be entitled to state any objection to the regularity of the execution of citation, service or intimation on him, and his appearance shall remedy any defect in such citation, service or intimation.

(2)   Nothing in paragraph (1) shall preclude a party from pleading that the court has no jurisdiction.

**Service of schedule of arrestment**

**2.18**   If a schedule of arrestment has not been personally served on an arrestee, the arrestment shall have effect only if a copy of the schedule is also sent by registered post or the first class recorded delivery service to—

    (a)   the last known place of residence of the arrestee; or

    (b)   if such a place of residence is not known, or if the arrestee is a firm or corporation, to the arrestee's principal place of business if known, or, if not known, to any known place of business of the arrestee,

and the sheriff officer shall, on the certificate of execution, certify that this has been done and specify the address to which the copy of the schedule was sent.

**Form of schedule of arrestment on the dependence**

**2.18A.**—[1](1)   An arrestment on the dependence shall be served by serving the schedule of arrestment on the arrestee in Form 10A.

(2)   A certificate of execution shall be lodged with the sheriff clerk in Form 10B.

**Arrestment on dependence before service**

**2.19**—(1)   An arrestment on the dependence of a summary application used before service shall cease to have effect if the initial writ is not served within 20 days from the date of arrestment and either—

    (a)   in the case where the pursuer is entitled to minute for decree in absence on the expiry of a period of notice contained in the warrant of citation, decree in absence has not been pronounced within 20 days after the expiry of the period of notice; or

---

[1] As inserted by the Act of Sederunt (Sheriff Court Rules Amendment) (Diligence) 2009 (SSI 2009/107) r.4(effective April 22, 2009).

(b)   in the case where the pursuer is not entitled to minute for decree in absence prior to the first hearing of the summary application, there is no appearance by the pursuer at the first hearing and the summary application drops from the roll.

(2)   After such an arrestment has been executed, the party who executed it shall forthwith report the execution to the sheriff clerk.

### Movement of arrested property

**2.20**—(1)   Any person having an interest may apply by motion for a warrant authorising the movement of a vessel or cargo which is the subject of an arrestment to found jurisdiction or on the dependence of a summary application.

(2)   Where the court grants a warrant sought under paragraph (1), it may make such further order as it thinks fit to give effect to that warrant.

### Transfer to another sheriff court

**2.21**—(1)   The sheriff may, on cause shown, remit a summary application to another sheriff court.

(2)   Subject to paragraph (4), where a summary application in which there are two or more defenders has been brought in the sheriff court of the residence or place of business of one of them, the sheriff may transfer the summary application to any other sheriff court which has jurisdiction over any of the defenders.

(3)   Subject to paragraph (4), where a plea of no jurisdiction is sustained, the sheriff may transfer the summary application to the sheriff court before which it appears to him the summary application ought to have been brought.

(4)   The sheriff shall not transfer a summary application to another sheriff court under paragraph (2) or (3) except—

(a)   on the motion of a party; and

(b)   where he considers it expedient to do so having regard to the convenience of the parties and their witnesses.

(5)   On making an or er under paragraph (1), (2) or (3), the sheriff—

(a)   shall state his reasons for doing so in the interlocutor; and

(b)   may make the order on such conditions as to expenses or otherwise as he thinks fit.

(6)   The court to which a summary application is transferred under paragraph (1), (2) or (3) shall accept the summary application.

(7)   A transferred summary application shall proceed in all respects as if it had been originally brought in the court to which it is transferred.

(8)   *[Repealed by the Act of Sederunt (Rules of the Court of Session, Sheriff Appeal Court Rules and Sheriff Court Rules Amendment) (Sheriff Appeal Court) 2015 (SSI 2015/419) r.9(2) (effective 1 January 2016; as to savings see SSI 2015/419 rule 20(5)(a)).]*

### Applications for time to pay directions or time orders

**2.22**—[1](1)   This rule applies to a summary application in which—

---

[1] As amended by the Act of Sederunt (Ordinary Cause, Summary Application, Summary Cause and Small Claim Rules) Amendment (Miscellaneous) 2007 (SSI 2007/6), para.3(4) (effective January 29, 2007).

    (a)   a time to pay direction may be applied for under the Debtors (Scotland) Act 1987; or

    (b)   a time order may be applied for under the Consumer Credit Act 1987.

  (2)   A defender may apply for a time to pay direction or time order and, where appropriate, for recall or restriction of an arrestment—

    (a)   by appearing and making the appropriate motion at a diet fixed for hearing of the summary application;

    (b)[1]  except where the warrant of citation contains a shorter period of notice than the period of notice to be given to a defender under rule 3.6(1)(a) or (b), as the case may be, of the Ordinary Cause Rules, by completing and returning the appropriate portion of Form 5 to the sheriff clerk at least 14 days before the first diet fixed for hearing of the summary application or the expiry of the period of notice or otherwise, as the case may be in the warrant of citation; or

    (c)   by application to the court at any stage before final decree.

  (3)[2]   On lodging an application under paragraph (2)(b), the defender shall send a copy of it to the pursuer by first class ordinary post.

  (4)[3]   Where the pursuer objects to the application of the defender lodged under paragraph (2)(b) he shall—

    (a)   complete and lodge with the sheriff clerk Form 5A prior to the date fixed for the hearing of the summary application; and

    (b)   send a copy of that form to the defender.

  (5)[4]   The sheriff clerk shall then fix a hearing in relation to the application under paragraph (2)(b) and intimate the hearing to the pursuer and the defender.

  (6)[5]   The sheriff may determine an application under paragraph (2)(c) without the defender having to appear.

## Applications under the Mortgage Rights (Scotland) Act 2001

**2.22A**   *[Repealed by the Act of Sederunt (Sheriff Court Rules) (Enforcement of Securities over Heritable Property) 2010 (SSI 2010/324) para.2 (effective September 30, 2010).]*

## Remuneration of assessors

**2.23**   Where an assessor is appointed by the sheriff to assist him in determining the summary application, the remuneration to be paid to such assessor shall be part of the expenses of the application.

---

[1] As amended by the Act of Sederunt (Sheriff Court Rules) (Miscellaneous Amendments) 2009 (SSI 2009/294) r.3 (effective December 1, 2009).

[2] Para.(3) substituted for paras (3)–(6) by the Act of Sederunt (Sheriff Court Rules) (Miscellaneous Amendments) 2009 (SSI 2009/294) r.3 (effective December 1, 2009).

[3] Para.(3) substituted for paras (3)–(6) by the Act of Sederunt (Sheriff Court Rules) (Miscellaneous Amendments) 2009 (SSI 2009/294) r.3 (effective December 1, 2009).

[4] Para.(3) substituted for paras (3)–(6) by the Act of Sederunt (Sheriff Court Rules) (Miscellaneous Amendments) 2009 (SSI 2009/294) r.3 (effective December 1, 2009).

[5] Para.(3) substituted for paras (3)–(6) by the Act of Sederunt (Sheriff Court Rules) (Miscellaneous Amendments) 2009 (SSI 2009/294) r.3 (effective December 1, 2009).

**Deposits for expenses**

**2.24**  Where, under any enactment, the sheriff requires the pursuer to deposit a sum of money to cover the expenses of an appeal under the enactment, such sum shall, subject to the provisions of that enactment, not exceed an amount which is twenty-five times the amount of the fee payable at that time in respect of lodging the initial writ.

**When decrees extractable**

**2.25**—(1)  Subject to the following paragraphs—
   (a)  subject to sub-paragraph (c), a decree in absence may be extracted after the expiry of 14 days from the date of decree;
   (b)  subject to sub-paragraph (c), any decree pronounced in a defended summary application may be extracted at any time after whichever is the later of the following—
      (i)   the expiry of the period within which an application for leave to appeal may be made and no such application has been made;
      (ii)  the date on which leave to appeal has been refused and there is no right of appeal from such refusal;
      (iii)[1]  the expiry of the period within which an appeal may be made and no appeal has been made; or
      (iv)  the date on which an appeal has been finally disposed of; and
   (c)  where the sheriff has, in pronouncing decree, reserved any question of expenses, extract of that decree may be issued only after the expiry of 14 days from the date of the interlocutor disposing of the question of expenses unless the sheriff otherwise directs.

(2)  The sheriff may, on cause shown, grant a motion to allow extract to be applied for and issued earlier than a date referred to in paragraph (1).

(3)  In relation to a decree referred to in paragraph (1)(b) or (c), paragraph (2) shall not apply unless—
   (a)  the motion under that paragraph is made in the presence of the parties; or
   (b)  the sheriff is satisfied of proper intimation of the motion has been made in writing to every party not present at the hearing of the motion.

(4)  Nothing in this rule shall affect the power of the sheriff to supersede extract.

**Form of extract decree**

**2.26**  The extract of a decree shall be in Form 11.

**Form of warrant for execution**

**2.27**  An extract of a decree on which execution may proceed shall include a warrant for execution in the following terms:— "This extract is warrant for all lawful execution hereon.".

---

[1] As amended by the Act of Sederunt (Rules of the Court of Session, Sheriff Appeal Court Rules and Sheriff Court Rules Amendment) (Sheriff Appeal Court) 2015 (SSI 2015/419) r.9(3) (effective 1 January 2016; as to savings see SSI 2015/419 rule 20(5)(a)).

### Date of decree in extract

**2.28**—[1](1)   Where the Sheriff Appeal Court has adhered to the decision of the sheriff following an appeal, the date to be inserted in the extract decree as the date of decree shall be the date of the decision of the Sheriff Appeal Court.

(2)   Where a decree has more than one date it shall not be necessary to specify in an extract what was done on each date.

### Decrees in absence where defender furth of Scotland

**2.29**—(1)   Where a defender is domiciled in another part of the United Kingdom or in another Contracting State, the sheriff shall not grant decree in absence until it has been shown that the defender has been able to receive the initial writ in sufficient time to arrange for his defence or that all necessary steps have been taken to that end, and for the purposes of this paragraph—

    (a)   the question whether a person is domiciled in another part of the United Kingdom shall be determined in accordance with sections 41 and 42 of the Civil Jurisdiction and Judgments Act 1982;

    (b)   the question whether a person is domiciled in another Contracting State shall be determined in accordance with Article 52 of the Convention in Schedule 1 or 3C to that Act, as the case may be; and

    (c)   the term "Contracting State" has the meaning assigned in section 1 of that Act.

(2)   Where an initial writ has keen served in a country to which the Hague Convention on the Service Abroad of Judicial and Extra-Judicial Documents in Civil or Commercial Matters dated 15th November 1965 applies, decree shall not be granted until it is established to the satisfaction of the sheriff that the requirements of Article 15 of the Convention have been complied with.

### Motion procedure

**2.30**   Except where the sheriff otherwise directs, any motion relating to a summary application shall be made in accordance with, and regulated by, Chapter 15 of the Ordinary Cause Rules.

### Power of sheriff to make orders

**2.31**   The sheriff may make such order as he thinks fit for the progress of a summary application in so far as it is not inconsistent with section 50 of the Sheriff Courts (Scotland) Act 1907.

### Live links

**2.32**—[2](1)   On cause shown, a party may apply by motion for authority for the whole or part of—

    (a)   the evidence of a witness or the party to be given; or

    (b)   a submission to be made,

---

[1] As amended by the Act of Sederunt (Rules of the Court of Session, Sheriff Appeal Court Rules and Sheriff Court Rules Amendment) (Sheriff Appeal Court) 2015 (SSI 2015/419) r.9(4) (effective 1 January 2016; as to savings see SSI 2015/419 rule 20(5)(a)).

[2] As inserted by the Act of Sederunt (Ordinary Cause, Summary Application, Summary Cause and Small Claim Rules) Amendment (Miscellaneous) 2007 (SSI 2007/6), para.3(5) (effective January 29, 2007).

through a live link.

(2)   In paragraph (1)—

"witness" means a person who has been or may be cited to appear before the
court as a witness, except a vulnerable witness within the meaning of section
11(1) of the 2004 Act;[1]

"submission" means any oral submission which would otherwise be made to
the court by the party or his representative in person including an oral
submission in support of a motion; and

"live link" means a live television link or such other arrangement as may be
specified in the motion by which the witness, party or representative, as the
case may be, is able to be seen and heard in the proceedings or heard in the
proceedings and is able to see and hear or hear the proceedings while at a
place which is outside the courtroom.

### Enquiry when fixing hearing

**2.33.**[2]   Where the sheriff fixes a hearing he shall make enquiry whether there is
or is likely to be a vulnerable witness within the meaning of section 11(1) of the
2004 Act who is to give evidence at any proof or hearing, consider any child witness
notice or vulnerable witness application that has been lodged where no order has
been made and consider whether any order under section 12(1) of the 2004 Act
requires to be made.

### Vulnerable witness procedure

**2.34.**[3]   Except where the sheriff otherwise directs, where a vulnerable witness is
to give evidence in a hearing of a summary application any child witness notice or
vulnerable application relating to the vulnerable witness shall be made in accordance with and regulated by Chapter 45 of the Ordinary Cause Rules.

### Representation

**2.35.**—[4](1)   A party may be represented by any person authorised under any
enactment to conduct proceedings in the sheriff court in accordance with the terms
of that enactment.

(2)   The person referred to in paragraph (1) may do everything for the preparation and conduct of an action as may have been done by an individual conducting
his own action.

---

[1] As amended by the Act of Sederunt (Ordinary Cause, Summary Application, Summary Cause and
Small Claim Rules) Amendment (Vulnerable Witnesses (Scotland) Act 2004) 2007 (SSI 2007/463),
r.3(3) (effective November 1, 2007).

[2] As inserted by the Act of Sederunt (Ordinary Cause, Summary Application, Summary Cause and
Small Claim Rules) Amendment (Vulnerable Witnesses (Scotland) Act 2004) 2007 (SSI 2007/463)
r.3(4) (effective November 1, 2007).

[3] As inserted by the Act of Sederunt (Ordinary Cause, Summary Application, Summary Cause and
Small Claim Rules) Amendment (Vulnerable Witnesses (Scotland) Act 2004) 2007 (SSI 2007/463),
r.3(4) (effective November 1, 2007).

[4] As inserted by the Act of Sederunt (Ordinary Cause, Summary Application, Summary Cause and
Small Claim Rules) Amendment (Miscellaneous) 2007 (SSI 2007/6), para.3(5) (effective January 29,
2007).

**Expenses**

**2.36.**—[1](1)  A party who—

    (a)  is or has been represented by a person authorised under any enactment to conduct proceedings in the sheriff court; and

    (b)  would have been found entitled to expenses if he had been represented by a solicitor or an advocate,

May be awarded expenses or outlays to which a party litigant may be found entitled under the Litigants in Person (Costs and Expenses) Act 1975 or any enactment under that Act.

**Interventions by the CEHR**

**2.37.**—[2](1)  In this rule and in rule 2.38, "the CEHR" means the Commission for Equality and Human Rights.

(2)  The CEHR may apply to the sheriff for leave to intervene in any summary application in accordance with this Rule.

(3)  An application for leave to intervene shall be by way of minute of intervention in Form 11AA and the CEHR shall—

    (a)  send a copy of it to all the parties; and

    (b)  lodge it in process, certifying that sub-paragraph (a) has been complied with.

(4)  A minute of intervention shall set out briefly—

    (a)  the CEHR's reasons for believing that the proceedings are relevant to a matter in connection with which the CEHR has a function;

    (b)  the issue in the proceedings which the CEHR wishes to address; and

    (c)  the propositions to be advanced by the CEHR and the CEHR's reasons for believing that they are relevant to the proceedings and that they will assist the sheriff.

(5)  The sheriff may—

    (a)  refuse leave without a hearing;

    (b)  grant leave without a hearing unless a hearing is requested under paragraph (6);

    (c)  refuse or grant leave after such a hearing.

(6)  A hearing, at which the applicant and the parties may address the court on the matters referred to in paragraph (8)(c) may be held if, within 14 days of the minute of intervention being lodged, any of the parties lodges a request for a hearing.

(7)  Any diet in pursuance of paragraph (6) shall be fixed by the sheriff clerk who shall give written intimation of the diet to the CEHR and all the parties.

(8)  The sheriff may grant leave only if satisfied that—

    (a)  the proceedings are relevant to a matter in connection with which the CEHR has a function;

    (b)  the propositions to be advanced by the CEHR are relevant to the proceedings and are likely to assist him; and

    (c)  the intervention will not unduly delay or otherwise prejudice the rights of the parties, including their potential liability for expenses.

---

[1] As renumbered by the Act of Sederunt (Sheriff Court Rules) (Miscellaneous Amendments) 2008 (SSI 2008/223) r.14(2) (effective July 1, 2008).

[2] As inserted by the Act of Sederunt (Sheriff Court Rules) (Miscellaneous Amendments) 2008 (SSI 2008/223) r.5(2) (effective July 1, 2008).

(9)   In granting leave the sheriff may impose such terms and conditions as he considers desirable in the interests of justice, including making provision in respect of any additional expenses incurred by the parties as a result of the intervention.

(10)   The sheriff clerk shall give written intimation of a grant or refusal of leave to the CEHR and all the parties.

(11)   This rule is without prejudice to any other entitlement of the CEHR by virtue of having title and interest in relation to the subject matter of any proceedings by virtue of section 30(2) of the Equality Act 2006 or any other enactment to seek to be sisted as a party in those proceedings.

(12)   Nothing in this rule shall affect the power of the sheriff to make such other direction as he considers appropriate in the interests of justice.

(13)   Any decision of the sheriff in proceedings under this rule and rule 2.38 shall be final and not subject to appeal.

### Form of intervention

**2.38.**—[1](1)   An intervention by the CEHR shall be by way of a written submission which (including any appendices) shall not exceed 5000 words.

(2)   The CEHR shall lodge the submission and send a copy of it to all the parties by such time as the sheriff may direct.

(3)   The sheriff may in exceptional circumstances—

    (a)   allow a longer written submission to be made;

    (b)   direct that an oral submission is to be made.

(4)   Any diet in pursuance of paragraph (3)(b) shall be fixed by the sheriff clerk who shall give written intimation of the diet to the CEHR and all the parties.

### Interventions by the SCHR

**2.39.**—[2](1)   In this rule and in rules 2.40 and 2.41—

    "the Act of 2006" means the Scottish Commission for Human Rights Act 2006;
    "the SCHR" means the Scottish Commission for Human Rights.

(2)   An application for leave to intervene shall be by way of minute of intervention in Form 11AB and the SCHR shall—

    (a)   send a copy of it to all the parties; and

    (b)   lodge it in process, certifying that subparagraph (a) has been complied with.

(3)   In granting leave the sheriff may impose such terms and conditions as he considers desirable in the interests of justice, including making provision in respect of any additional expenses incurred by the parties as a result of the intervention.

(4)   The sheriff clerk shall give written intimation of a grant or refusal of leave to the SCHR and all the parties.

(5)   Any decision of the sheriff in proceedings under this rule and rules 2.40 and 2.41 shall be final and not subject to appeal.

---

[1] As inserted by the Act of Sederunt (Sheriff Court Rules) (Miscellaneous Amendments) 2008 (SSI 2008/223) r.5(2) (effective July 1, 2008).

[2] As inserted by the Act of Sederunt (Sheriff Court Rules) (Miscellaneous Amendments) 2008 (SSI 2008/223) r.5(2) (effective July 1, 2008).

**Invitations to intervene**

**2.40.**—[1](1)  An invitation to intervene under section 14(2)(b) of the Act of 2006 shall be in Form 11AC and the sheriff clerk shall send a copy of it to the SCHR and all the parties.

(2)  An invitation under paragraph (1) shall be accompanied by—

    (a)  a copy of the pleadings in the proceedings; and

    (b)  such other documents relating to those proceedings as the sheriff thinks relevant.

(3)  In issuing an invitation under section 14(2)(b) of the Act of 2006, the sheriff may impose such terms and conditions as he considers desirable in the interests of justice, including making provision in respect of any additional expenses incurred by the parties as a result of the intervention.

**Form of intervention**

**2.41.**—[2](1)  An intervention by the SCHR shall be by way of a written submission which (including any appendices) shall not exceed 5000 words.

(2)  The SCHR shall lodge the submission and send a copy of it to all the parties by such time as the sheriff may direct.

(3)  The sheriff may in exceptional circumstances—

    (a)  allow a longer written submission to be made;

    (b)  direct that an oral submission is to be made.

(4)  Any diet in pursuance of paragraph (3)(b) shall be fixed by the sheriff clerk who shall give written intimation of the diet to the SCHR and all the parties.

**Lodging audio or audio-visual recordings of children**

**2.42.**—[3](1)  In this rule "child" is a person under the age of 16 on the date of commencement of the proceedings and "children" shall be construed accordingly.

(2)  Except where the sheriff otherwise directs, where a party seeks to lodge an audio or audio-visual recording of a child as a production in a summary application, this shall be done in accordance with and regulated by Chapter 50 of the Ordinary Cause Rules.

(3)[4]  A party who has lodged a recording of a child shall—

    (a)  within 14 days after the final determination of the application, where no subsequent appeal has been made, or

    (b)  within 14 days after the disposal of any appeal made on the final determination of the application,

uplift the recording from process.

(4)  Where a recording has not been uplifted as required by paragraph (3), the sheriff clerk shall intimate to—

    (a)  the solicitor who lodged the recording, or

---

[1] As inserted by the Act of Sederunt (Sheriff Court Rules) (Miscellaneous Amendments) 2008 (SSI 2008/223) r.5(2) (effective July 1, 2008).

[2] As inserted by the Act of Sederunt (Sheriff Court Rules) (Miscellaneous Amendments) 2008 (SSI 2008/223) r.5(2) (effective July 1, 2008).

[3] As inserted by the Act of Sederunt (Sheriff Court Rules) (Miscellaneous Amendments) (No.3) 2012 (SSI 2012/271) para.3 (effective November 1, 2012).

[4] As amended by the Act of Sederunt (Rules of the Court of Session, Sheriff Appeal Court Rules and Sheriff Court Rules Amendment) (Sheriff Appeal Court) 2015 (SSI 2015/419) r.9(5) (effective 1 January 2016; as to savings see SSI 2015/419 rule 20(5)(a)).

(b)   where no solicitor is acting, the party or such other party as seems appropriate,

that if he or she fails to uplift the recording within 28 days after the date of such intimation, it will be disposed of in such a manner as the sheriff directs.

## Chapter 3

## Rules on Applications under Specific Statutes

### Part I

### Administration of Justice (Scotland) Act 1972

### Interpretation and application

**3.1.1**—[1](1)   In this Part,

(a)   "the Act" means the Administration of Justice (Scotland) Act 1972; and

(b)   "listed items" means a list of the documents and other property which the applicant in terms of rule 3.1.2 wishes to be made the subject of the order.

(2)   This Part applies to applications under section 1(1) of the Act.

### Applications under section 1(1) of the Act

**3.1.2**—(1)   An application for an order under section 1(1) of the Act (orders for inspection of documents and other property, etc.) shall be made by summary application where the proceedings in respect of which the application is made have not been commenced.

(2)[2]   The summary application shall contain—

(a)   the listed items;

(b)   the address of the premises within which the applicant believes the listed items are to be found; and

(c)   the facts which give rise to the applicant's belief that, were the order not to be granted, the listed items, or any of them, would cease to be available for the purposes of section 1 of the Act.

### Accompanying documents

**3.1.3**[3]   The applicant shall lodge with the summary application—

(a)   an affidavit supporting the averments in the summary application; and

(b)   an undertaking by the applicant that he—

     (i)   will comply with any order of the sheriff as to payment of compensation if it is subsequently discovered that the order, or

---

[1] As amended by the Act of Sederunt (Summary Applications, Statutory Applications and Appeals etc. Rules) Amendment (No.2) (Administration of Justice (Scotland) Act 1972) 2000 (SSI 2000/387) (effective November 20, 2000).

[2] As inserted by the Act of Sederunt (Summary Applications, Statutory Applications and Appeals etc. Rules) Amendment (No.2) (Administration of Justice (Scotland) Act 1972) 2000 (SSI 2000/387) r.2(4) (effective November 20, 2000).

[3] As inserted by the Act of Sederunt (Summary Applications, Statutory Applications and Appeals etc. Rules) Amendment (No.2) (Administration of Justice (Scotland) Act 1972) 2000 (SSI 2000/387) r.2(4) (effective November 20, 2000).

the implementation of the order, has caused loss to the respondent or, where the haver is not the respondent, to the haver;

(ii) will bring within a reasonable time of the execution of the order any proceedings which he decides to bring; and

(iii) will not, without leave of the sheriff, use any information, documents or other property obtained as a result of the order, except for the purpose of any proceedings which he decides to bring and to which the order relates.

## Modification of undertakings

**3.1.4**[1]   The sheriff may, on cause shown, modify, by addition, deletion or substitution, the undertaking mentioned in rule 3.1.3.

## Intimation and service of application

**3.1.5—**[2](1)   Before granting the summary application, the sheriff may order such intimation or service of the summary application to be given or executed, as the case may be, as he thinks fit.

(2)   Any person receiving intimation or service of the summary application by virtue of an order under paragraph (1) may appear and oppose the summary application.

## Form of order

**3.1.6**[3]   An order made under this Part shall—

(a)   be in Form 11A; and

(b)   include in addition a warrant of citation in Form 2.

## Caution and other security

**3.1.7**[4]   On granting, in whole or in part, the summary application the sheriff may order the applicant to find such caution or other security as he thinks fit.

## Execution of an order

**3.1.8**[5]   The order made in terms of rule 3.1.6 shall be served by the Commissioner in person and it shall be accompanied by a copy of the affidavit referred to in rule 3.1.3(a).

---

[1] As inserted by the Act of Sederunt (Summary Applications, Statutory Applications and Appeals etc. Rules) Amendment (No.2) (Administration of Justice (Scotland) Act 1972) 2000 (SSI 2000/387) r.2(4) (effective November 20, 2000).

[2] As inserted by the Act of Sederunt (Summary Applications, Statutory Applications and Appeals etc. Rules) Amendment (No.2) (Administration of Justice (Scotland) Act 1972) 2000 (SSI 2000/387) r.2(4) (effective November 20, 2000).

[3] As inserted by the Act of Sederunt (Summary Applications, Statutory Applications and Appeals etc. Rules) Amendment (No.2) (Administration of Justice (Scotland) Act 1972) 2000 (SSI 2000/387) r.2(4) (effective November 20, 2000).

[4] As inserted by the Act of Sederunt (Summary Applications, Statutory Applications and Appeals etc. Rules) Amendment (No.2) (Administration of Justice (Scotland) Act 1972) 2000 (SSI 2000/387) r.2(4) (effective November 20, 2000).

[5] As inserted by the Act of Sederunt (Summary Applications, Statutory Applications and Appeals etc. Rules) Amendment (No.2) (Administration of Justice (Scotland) Act 1972) 2000 (SSI 2000/387) r.2(4) (effective November 20, 2000).

## Duties of a Commissioner

**3.1.9**[1]  The Commissioner appointed by the sheriff shall, on executing the order—

- (a)  give to the haver a copy of the notice in Form 11B;
- (b)  explain to the haver—
  - (i)  the meaning and effect of the order; and
  - (ii)  that he may be entitled to claim that some or all of the listed items are confidential or privileged;
- (c)[2]  inform the haver of his right to seek legal advice and to ask the sheriff to vary or recall the order;
- (d)  enter the premises and take all reasonable steps to fulfil the terms of the order;
- (e)  where the order has authorised the recovery of any of the listed items, prepare an inventory of all the listed items to be recovered before recovering them; and
- (f)  send any recovered listed items to the sheriff clerk to await the further order of the sheriff.

## Confidentiality

**3.1.10**—[3](1)  Where confidentiality is claimed for any listed item, that listed item shall, where practicable, be enclosed in a sealed envelope.

(2)  A motion to have such a sealed envelope opened may be made by the party who obtained the order and he shall intimate the terms of the motion, by registered post or first class recorded delivery, to the person claiming confidentiality.

(3)  A person claiming confidentiality may oppose a motion made under paragraph (2).

## Restrictions on service

**3.1.11**—[4](1)  Except on cause shown, the order may be served on Monday to Friday only, between the hours of 9am and 5pm only.

(2)  The order shall not be served at the same time as a search warrant granted in the course of a criminal investigation.

(3)  The Commissioner may be accompanied only by—

- (a)  any person whom he considers necessary to assist him to execute the order;
- (b)  such representatives of the applicant as are named in the order, and if it is likely that the premises will be occupied by an unaccompanied female and the Commissioner is not female, one of the people accompanying the Commissioner shall be female.

---

[1]  As inserted by the Act of Sederunt (Summary Applications, Statutory Applications and Appeals etc. Rules) Amendment (No.2) (Administration of Justice (Scotland) Act 1972) 2000 (SSI 2000/387) r.2(4) (effective November 20, 2000).

[2]  As amended by the Act of Sederunt (Sheriff Court Rules) (Miscellaneous Amendments) (No.3) 2011 (SSI 2011/386) para.6 (effective November 28, 2011).

[3]  As inserted by the Act of Sederunt (Summary Applications, Statutory Applications and Appeals etc. Rules) Amendment (No.2) (Administration of Justice (Scotland) Act 1972) 2000 (SSI 2000/387) r.2(4) (effective November 20, 2000).

[4]  As inserted by the Act of Sederunt (Summary Applications, Statutory Applications and Appeals etc. Rules) Amendment (No.2) (Administration of Justice (Scotland) Act 1972) 2000 (SSI 2000/387) r.2(4) (effective November 20, 2000).

(4)   If it appears to the Commissioner when he comes to serve the order that the premises are occupied by an unaccompanied female and the Commissioner is neither female nor accompanied by a female, the Commissioner shall not enter the premises.

### Right of haver to consult

**3.1.12**—[1](1)   The haver may seek legal or other professional advice of his or her choice.

(2)   Where the purpose of seeking this advice is to help the haver to decide whether to ask the sheriff to vary or recall the order, the haver may ask the Commissioner to delay starting the search for up to 2 hours or such other longer period as the Commissioner may permit.

(3)   Where the haver is seeking advice under this rule, he or she must—

    (a)   inform the Commissioner and the applicant's agent of that fact;

    (b)   not disturb or remove any listed items;

    (c)   permit the Commissioner to enter the premises, but not to start the search.

## Part II

### Betting and Gaming Appeals

*[Revoked by the Act of Sederunt (Sheriff Court Rules) (Miscellaneous Amendments) 2008 (SSI 2008/223) para.14(3)(effective July 1, 2008).]*

## Part III

### Coal Mining Subsidence Act 1991

### Interpretation and application

**3.3.1**—(1)   In this Part—

"the Act" means the Coal Mining Subsidence Act 1991;

"agreement or consent" means the agreement or consent referred to in section 41 of the Act);

"person" means a person referred to in section 41 of the Act;

"any person with responsibility for subsidence affecting any land" has the meaning given in section 43 of the Coal Industry Act 1994.

(2)   This Part applies to proceedings under section 41 of the Act.

### Applications under section 41 of the Act

**3.3.2**—(1)   An application under section 41 of the Act (disputes about withholding of agreement or consent) shall specify—

    (a)   the person with whom any person with responsibility for subsidence affecting any land has reached agreement and from whom any person with responsibility for subsidence affecting any land obtained consent; and

---

[1] As inserted by the Act of Sederunt (Summary Applications, Statutory Applications and Appeals etc. Rules) Amendment (No. 2) (Administration of Justice (Scotland) Act 1972) 2000 (SSI 2000/387) (effective November 20, 2000) and substituted by the Act of Sederunt (Sheriff Court Rules) (Miscellaneous Amendments) (No.3) 2011 (SSI 2011/386) para.6 (effective November 28, 2011).

(b) the steps which have been taken to obtain the agreement or consent of the person who is withholding such agreement or consent.

(2) An application under section 41 of the Act made in relation to the exercise of a power under section 5(3) or (5) of the Act, shall, when lodged with the sheriff clerk, be accompanied by the notice of proposed remedial action under section 4(2) of the Act.

Part IV[1]

**Enforcement of Securities over Heritable Property**

*Section 1*

**Interpretation**

**3.4.1.** In this Part—

"the 1894 Act" means the Heritable Securities (Scotland) Act 1894;

"the 1970 Act" means the Conveyancing and Feudal Reform (Scotland) Act 1970;

"application for enforcement of security over residential property" means any of the following—

(a) an application under section 24(1B) of the 1970 Act alone ("a 1970 Act only application");

(b) an application under section 5(1) of the 1894 Act, in a case falling within section 5(2) of that Act, alone ("an 1894 Act only application");

(c) an application under paragraphs (a) and (b) together ("a combined 1970 Act and 1894 Act application");

"entitled resident" means—

(a) in a 1970 Act only application, a person falling within the definition of that expression provided by section 24C of the 1970 Act;

(b) in an 1894 Act only application, a person falling within the definition of that expression provided by section 5D of the 1894 Act;

(c) in a combined 1970 Act and 1894 Act application, a person falling within either of those definitions;

"entitled resident application" means any of the following—

(a) an application under section 24B of the 1970 Act alone;

(b) an application under section 5C of the 1894 Act alone;

(c) an application under paragraphs (a) and (b) together.

"pre-action requirements" means—

(a) in a 1970 Act only application, the requirements specified in sections 24A(2) to (6) of the 1970 Act, together with any provision made under section 24A(8) of that Act;

(b) in an 1894 Act only application, the requirements specified in sections 5B(2) to (6) of the 1894 Act, together with any provision made under section 5B(8) of that Act;

(c) in a combined 1970 Act and 1894 Act application, both of those sets of requirements;

---

[1] As substituted by the Act of Sederunt (Sheriff Court Rules) (Enforcement of Securities over Heritable Property) 2010 (SSI 2010/324) para.2 (effective September 30, 2010).

"a recall of decree application" means any of the following—

    (a)   an application under section 24D of the 1970 Act alone;

    (b)   an application under section 5E of the 1894 Act alone;

    (c)   an application under paragraphs (a) and (b) together.

*Section 2*

## Disposal of applications under Part II of the 1970 Act for non-residential purposes

**3.4.2.**—(1)   This rule applies to an application or counter-application made by virtue of paragraph (3)(2)(b) of the Act of Sederunt (Sheriff Court Rules) (Enforcement of Securities over Heritable Property) 2010.

(2)   An interlocutor of the sheriff disposing of an application or counter-application is final and not subject to appeal except as to a question of title or as to any other remedy granted.

*Section 3*

## Initial writ

**3.4.3.**—(1)   An application for enforcement of security over residential property must include averments that the pre-action requirements have been complied with.

(2)   The pursuer must lodge Form 11C with the initial writ.

(3)   The initial writ must specify the name and particulars of all persons known by the pursuer to be entitled residents; and crave warrant for intimation to such persons.

*Section 4*

## Appointment of Hearing

**3.4.4.**   On an application being submitted under rule 3.4.3, the sheriff must—

    (a)   fix a hearing;

    (b)   appoint service and intimation of the initial writ and Form 11C.

*Section 5*

## Answers

**3.4.5.**—(1)   Where a defender opposes an application, the sheriff may order answers to be lodged within such period that the sheriff specifies.

(2)   The answers must—

    (a)   specify the name and particulars of all persons known by the defender to be entitled residents who have not already been named in the initial writ; and crave warrant for intimation to such persons; or

(b) state that to the best of the defender's knowledge there are no other entitled residents.

## Section 6

**Intimation to known entitled residents**

**3.4.6.** The sheriff must order that a copy of the initial writ together with a notice in Form 11D and Form 11E be intimated to all entitled residents referred to in rules 3.4.3(3) and 3.4.5(2)(a).

## Section 7

**Application to court by entitled residents**

**3.4.7.**—(1) This rule applies to an entitled resident application.

(2) Such application is to be made by lodging a minute in Form 11E in the principal application to which the application relates.

(3) On a Form 11E being lodged, the sheriff must—

(a) fix a hearing of the entitled resident application;

(b) order parties to lodge answers (where the sheriff considers it appropriate to do so) within such period that the sheriff specifies;

(c) order the applicant to serve upon every party and intimate to every entitled resident—

(i) a copy of the entitled resident application;

(ii) a note of the date, time and place of the hearing.

## Section 8

**Recall of decree**

**3.4.8.**—(1) This rule applies to a recall of decree application.

(2) Such application is to be made by lodging a minute in Form 11F.

(3) On a Form 11F being lodged, the sheriff clerk must fix a hearing of the recall of decree application.

(4) Where a hearing has been fixed under paragraph (3) the person seeking recall must, not less than seven days before the date fixed for the hearing, serve upon every party and intimate to every entitled resident—

(a) a copy of the recall of decree application;

(b) a note of the date, time and place of the hearing.

(4A)[1] Where service or intimation under this rule is to be made to a party represented in the cause by a solicitor, a notice sent to such party's solicitor shall be held to be notice to the party.

(5) At a hearing fixed under paragraph (3), the sheriff must recall the decree so far as not implemented and the hearing will then proceed as a hearing held under rule 3.4.4(a).

(6) A minute for recall of a decree, when lodged and served or intimated in terms of this rule, will have the effect of preventing any further action being taken to enforce the decree.

---

[1] As inserted by the Act of Sederunt (Sheriff Court Rules)(Miscellaneous Amendments) 2013 (SSI 2013/135) para.2 (effective May 27, 2013).

(7)   If it appears to the sheriff that there has been any failure or irregularity in service or intimation of the minute for recall of a decree, the sheriff may order re-service or re-intimation of the minute (as the case may be) on such conditions as he or she thinks fit.

(8)   Where the person seeking recall does not appear or is not represented at the hearing for recall, the sheriff will pronounce an interlocutor ordaining that person to appear or be represented at a peremptory diet fixed by the sheriff to state whether or not that person intends to proceed with the person's defence or application, under certification that if that person fails to do so the sheriff may grant decree or make such other order or finding as the sheriff thinks fit.

(9)   The diet fixed in the interlocutor under paragraph (8) must not be less than 14 days after the date of the interlocutor unless the sheriff otherwise orders.

(10)   The sheriff must appoint a party to intimate to the person seeking recall a copy of the interlocutor and a notice in Form 11G.

(11)   Where a person on whom a notice and interlocutor has been intimated under paragraph (10) fails to appear or be represented at a diet fixed under paragraph (8) and to state his or her intention as required by that paragraph, the sheriff may grant decree of new or make such other order or finding as the sheriff thinks fit.

Part V

## Copyright, Designs and Trade Marks

**Interpretation**

**3.5.1**   In this Part

"the 1988 Act" means the Copyright, Designs and Patents Act 1988;
"the 1994 Act" means the Trade Marks Act 1994; and
"the 1995 Regulations" means the Olympics Association Right (Infringement Proceedings) Regulations 1995.

## Orders for delivery up, forfeiture, destruction or other disposal

**3.5.2**   An application to the sheriff made under sections 99, 114, 195, 204, 230, 231 or 298 of the 1988 Act, under sections 16 or 19 of the 1994 Act or under Regulation 3 or 5 of the 1995 Regulations, shall be made—
  (a)   by motion or incidental application, as the case may be, where proceedings have been commenced; or
  (b)   by summary application where no proceedings have been commenced.

## Service of notice on interested persons

**3.5.3**   Where an application has been made under section 114, 204, 231 or 298 of the 1988 Act, section 19 of the 1994 Act or Regulation 5 of the 1995 Regulations—
  (a)   the application shall—
    (i)   specify the name and address of any person known or believed by the applicant to have an interest in the subject matter of the application; or
    (ii)   state that to the best of the applicant's knowledge and belief no other person has such an interest; and

(b) the sheriff shall order that there be intimated to any person who has such an interest, a copy of the pleadings and any motion, incidental application or summary application, as the case maybe.

## Procedure where leave of court required

**3.5.4**—(1) Where leave of the court is required under the 1988 Act before the action may proceed, the pursuer shall lodge along with the initial writ or summons a motion or incidental application, as the case may be, stating the grounds upon which leave is sought.

(2) The sheriff may hear the pursuer on the motion or incidental application and may grant or refuse it or make such other order in relation to it as he considers appropriate prior to determination.

(3) Where such motion or incidental application is granted, a copy of the sheriff's interlocutor shall be served upon the defender along with the warrant of citation.

Part VI

### Drug Trafficking Act 1994

*[Revoked by the Act of Sederunt (Summary Applications, Statutory Applications and Appeals etc. Rules) Amendment (No.5) (Proceeds of Crime Act 2002) 2002 (SSI 2002/563), para.2(3) (effective December 30, 2002), subject to savings outlined in para.2(3).]*

Part VII

### Licensing (Scotland) Act 1976

## Interpretation and application

**3.7.1**—(1) In this Part, "the Act" means the Licensing (Scotland) Act 1976.

(2) This Part applies to appeals under section 39 of the Act.

## Service

**3.7.2** The appellant shall serve a copy of the initial writ on—

(a) the clerk to the licensing board and the chief constable;

(b) if he was the applicant at the hearing before the licensing board, upon all parties who appeared at the hearing; and

(c) if he was an objector at the hearing, upon the applicant.

## Statement of reasons of licensing board

**3.7.3**—(1) Where the appellant has received from the licensing board a statement of reasons for its decision, he shall lodge a copy thereof with the sheriff clerk along with the initial writ.

(2)   The sheriff may, at any time prior to pronouncing a final interlocutor, require the licensing board to state the ground of refusal of an application and to give their reasons for finding such ground to be established.

## Part VIII

## Mental Health (Scotland) Act 1984

### Interpretation and application

**3.8.1**—(1)   In this Part, "the Act" means the Mental Health (Scotland) Act 1984.
(2)   This Part applies to—
- (a)   applications for admission submitted to a sheriff under section 21 of the Act;
- (b)   guardianship applications submitted to a sheriff under section 40 of the Act; and
- (c)   community care applications submitted under section 35A of the Act.

### Appointment of hearing

**3.8.2**—(1)   On an application being submitted, the sheriff shall appoint a hearing subject, in the case of an application for admission, to section 21(3A) of the Act.
(2)   The sheriff may, where he considers it appropriate in all the circumstances, appoint that the hearing of an application shall take place in a hospital or other place.

### Service of application

**3.8.3**—(1)   The sheriff clerk shall serve or cause to be served on the patient a copy of the application, with the exception of any medical recommendation, together with a notice in Form 12.
(2)   Where the patient is not a resident patient in a hospital, the notice and copy application shall be served on him personally by sheriff officer.
(3)   Where the patient is a resident patient in a hospital, the notice and copy application shall be served together with a notice in Form 13 on his responsible medical officer—
- (a)   by first class recorded delivery service; or
- (b)   personally by sheriff officer.

(4)   Where the patient is already the subject of a guardianship order, the notice and copy application (including any medical recommendations) shall, in addition to any other service required by this rule, be served on the guardian—
- (a)   by first class recorded delivery service; or
- (b)   personally a sheriff officer.

### Duties of responsible medical officer

**3.8.4**—(1)   On receipt of a notice in Form 13 the responsible medical officer shall, subject to rule 3.8.5(1)—
- (a)   deliver the notice in Form 12 to the patient; and
- (b)   as soon as practicable thereafter, complete and return to the court a certificate of such delivery in Form 14.

(2)[1]   Where, in the opinion of the responsible medical officer, it would be prejudicial to the patient's health or treatment if the patient were to be present during the proceedings—

    (a)   in an application to which rule 3.8.3(3) applies, the responsible medical officer shall set forth his reasons for his opinion in the certificate in Form 14; and

    (b)   in any other case, the responsible medical officer or the special medical officer, as the case may be, shall set forth his reasons for his opinion in writing and send them to the sheriff clerk.

### Appointment of curator ad litem

**3.8.5**—(1)   Where two medical certificates are produced stating that it would be prejudicial to the health or treatment of the patient if personal service were effected in terms of rule 3.8.3(2) or 3.8.4(1) the sheriff—

    (a)   may dispense with such service; and

    (b)   if he does so, shall appoint a curator ad litem to receive the application and represent the interest of that patient.

(2)   The sheriff may appoint a curator ad litem to represent the interests of the patient where he is satisfied that—

    (a)   the patient should be excluded from the whole or any part of the proceedings under section 113(2) of the Act; or

    (b)   in any other case, it is in all the circumstances appropriate to do so.

(3)   The sheriff clerk shall serve the application on the curator ad litem by handing, or sending by first class recorded delivery service, to him a copy of the application and of the order appointing him as the curator.

### Appointment of solicitor by court

**3.8.6**   Where the patient has indicated that he wishes to be represented at the hearing but has not nominated a representative, the sheriff may appoint a solicitor to take instructions from the patient.

### Intimation to representatives

**3.8.7**   Where in any proceedings under the Act, the sheriff clerk is aware that the patient is represented by any person and that representative would not otherwise receive intimation of any diet, a copy of the notice served on the patient shall be intimated to the representative by the sheriff clerk by first class recorded delivery service.

### Service by sheriff officer

**3.8.8**—(1)   Where a copy of an application and any notice has been served personally by sheriff officer, he shall prepare and return to the court an execution of such service setting forth in detail the manner and circumstances of such service.

(2)   Where a sheriff officer has been unable to effect personal service under this Part, he shall report to the court the reason why service was not effected.

---

[1] As amended by SSI 2003/26, para.3(5) (clerical error).

**Variation of conditions of community care order**

**3.8.9**—(1)   Where, after consulting the persons referred to in subsections (1) and (2) of section 35D of the Act (variation of conditions of community care order), an application is made by the special medical officer for the variation of a community care order under that section, the special medical officer shall—

    (a)   complete Form 22 in Schedule 2 to the Mental Health (Prescribed Forms) (Scotland) Regulations 1996; and

    (b)   lodge that form with the sheriff clerk, together with a certified copy of the community care order to which the application for variation relates.

**Hearing**

**3.8.10**—(1)   Any hearing to determine an application under rule 3.8.9 shall take place within 28 days after receipt by the sheriff clerk of Form 22 and the community care order referred to in that rule.

(2)   Intimation of the date of the hearing referred to in paragraph (1) shall be given by the Stationery sheriff clerk by first class recorded delivery service to such persons as the sheriff may direct; and any intimation of such date to the patient shall be made personally by sheriff officer.

**Appeal against community care order**

**3.8.11**   An application by way of appeal for the revocation of a community care order under section 35F of the Act shall be in Form 15.

Part IX

**Proceeds of Crime (Scotland) Act 1995**

**Interpretation and application**

**3.9.1**—(1)   In this Part—

    "the Act" means the Proceeds of Crime (Scotland) Act 1995; and
    "administrator" means the person appointed under paragraph 1(1) of Schedule 1 to Act.

(2)   This Part applies to proceedings under sections 28, 29, 30, 31 and 33 of, and paragraphs 1, 2, 4, 6 and 12 of Schedule 1 to, the Act.

**Service of restraint orders**

**3.9.2**   Where the sheriff pronounces an interlocutor making a restraint order under section 28(1) of the Act (application for restraint order), the prosecutor shall serve a copy of that interlocutor on every person named in the interlocutor as restrained by the order.

**Recall or variation of restraint orders**

**3.9.3.**—(1)   An application to the sheriff under any of the following provisions of the Act shall be made by note in the process containing the interlocutor malting the restraint order to which the application relates—

    (a)   section 29(4) or (5) (recall of restraint orders in relation to realisable property);

    (b)   section 30(3) or (4) (recall of restraint orders in relation to forfeitable property);

    (c)   section 31(1) (variation or recall of restraint order).

  (2)   In respect of an application by note under paragraph (1)(c) by a person having an interest for an order for variation or recall under section 31(1)(b) of the Act—

    (a)   *[Revoked by the Act of Sederunt (Ordinary Cause, Summary Application, Summary Cause and Small Claim Rules) Amendment (Miscellaneous) 2005 (SSI 2005/648) r.3(2) (effective January 2, 2006).]*

    (b)   the period of notice for lodging answers to the note shall be 14 days or such other period as the sheriff thinks fit.

## Applications for interdict

**3.9.4**—(1)  An application to the sheriff under section 28(8) of the Act (interdict) may be made—

    (a)   in the application made under section 28(1) of the Act; or

    (b)   if made after a restraint order has been made, by note in the process of the application for that order.

  (2)   An application under section 28(8) of the Act by note under paragraph (1)(b) shall not be intimated, served or advertised before that application is granted.

## Applications in relation to arrestment

**3.9.5**—(1)  An application to the sheriff under section 33(1) of the Act (arrestment of property affected by restraint order by the prosecutor for warrant for arrestment may be made—

    (a)   in the application made under section 28(1) of the Act; or

    (b)   if made after a restraint order has been applied for, by note in the process of the application for that order.

  (2)   An application to the sheriff under section 33(2) of the Act, to loose, restrict or recall an arrestment shall be made by note in the process of the application for the restraint order.

  (3)   An application to the sheriff under section 33(4) of the Act (recall or restriction of arrestment) shall be made by note in the process containing the interlocutor making the restraint order to which the application relates.

## Appeals to the Court of Session

**3.9.6**—(1)  This rule applies to appeals against an interlocutor of the sheriff refusing, varying or recalling or refusing to vary or recall a restraint order.

  (2)   An appeal to which this rule applies shall be marked within 14 days after the date of the interlocutor concerned.

  (3)   An appeal to which this rule applies shall be marked by writing a note of appeal on the interlocutor sheet, or other written record containing the interlocutor appealed against, or on a separate sheet lodged with the sheriff clerk, in the following terms:— "The applicant appeals to the Court of Session.".

  (4)   A note of appeal to which this rule applies shall—

    (a)   be signed by the appellant;

    (b)   bear the date on which it is signed; and

    (c)   where the appellant is represented, specify the name and address of the solicitor or other agent who will be acting for him in the appeal.

  (5)   The sheriff clerk shall transmit the process within 4 days after the appeal is marked to the Deputy Principal Clerk of Session.

(6) Within the period specified in paragraph (5), the sheriff clerk shall—

    (a) send written notice of the appeal to every other party; and

    (b) certify on the interlocutor sheet that he has done so.

(7) Failure of the sheriff clerk to comply with paragraph (6) shall not invalidate the appeal.

### Applications for appointment of administrators

**3.9.7**—(1) An application to the sheriff under paragraph 1 of Schedule 1 to the Act (appointment of administrators) shall be made—

    (a) where made after a restraint order has been made, by note in the process of the application for that order; or

    (b) in any other case, by summary application.

(2) The notification to be made by the sheriff clerk under paragraph 1(3)(a) of Schedule 1 to the Act shall be made by intimation of a copy of the interlocutor to the person required to give possession of property to an administrator.

### Incidental applications in an administration

**3.9.8**—(1) An application to the sheriff under any of the following provisions of Schedule to the Act shall be made by note in the process of the application for appointment of the administrator—

    (a) paragraph 1(1) with respect to an application after appointment of an administrator to require a person to give property to him;

    (b) paragraph 1(4) (making or altering a requirement or removal of administrator);

    (c) paragraph 1(5) (appointment of new administrator on death, resignation or removal of administrator);

    (d) paragraph 2(1)(n) (directions as to functions of administrator);

    (e) paragraph 4 (directions for application of proceeds).

(2) An application to the sheriff under any of the following provisions of Schedule 1 to the Act shall be made in the application for appointment of an administrator under paragraph 1(1) of that Schedule or, if made after the application has been made, by note in the process—

    (a) paragraph 2(1)(o) (special powers of administrator);

    (b) paragraph 2(3) (vesting of property in administrator);

    (c) paragraph 12 (order to facilitate the realisation of property).

### Requirements where order to facilitate realisation of property considered

**3.9.9** Where the sheriff considers making an order under paragraph 12 of Schedule 1 to the Act (order to facilitate the realisation of property)—

    (a) the sheriff shall fix a date for a hearing in the first instance; and

    (b) the applicant or noter, as the case may be, shall serve a notice in Form 16 on any person who has an interest in the property.

### Documents for Accountant of Court

**3.9.10**—(1) A person who has lodged any document in the process of an application for the appointment of an administrator shall forthwith send a copy of that document to the Accountant of Court.

(2)   The sheriff clerk shall transmit to the Accountant of Court any part of the process as the Accountant of Court may request in relation to an administration which is in dependence before the sheriff unless such part of the process is, at the time of request, required by the sheriff.

## Procedure for fixing and finding caution

**3.9.11**   Rules 9 to 12 of the Act of Sederunt (Judicial Factors Rules) 1992 (fixing and finding caution in judicial factories) shall, with the necessary modifications, apply to the fixing and finding of caution by an administrator under this Part as they apply to the fixing and finding of caution by a judicial factor.

## Administrator's title to act

**3.9.12**   An administrator appointed under this Part shall not be entitled to act until he has obtained a copy of the interlocutor appointing him.

## Duties of administrator

**3.9.13**—(1)   The administrator shall, as soon as possible, but within three months after the date of his appointment, lodge with the Accountant of Court—
   (a)   an inventory of the property in respect of which he has been appointed;
   (b)   all vouchers, securities, and other documents which are in his possession; and
   (c)   a statement of that property which he has in his possession or intends to realise.

(2)   An administrator shall maintain accounts of his intromissions with the property in his charge and shall, subject to paragraph (3)—
   (a)   within six months after the date of his appointment; and
   (b)   at six monthly intervals after the first account during the subsistence of his appointment,
lodge with the Accountant of Court an account of his intromissions in such form, with such supporting vouchers and other documents, as the Accountant of Court may require.

(3)   The Accountant of Court may waive the lodging of an account where the administrator certifies that there have been no intromissions during a particular accounting period.

## State of funds and scheme of division

**3.9.14**—(1)   The administrator shall—
   (a)   where there are funds available for division, prepare a state of funds after application of sums in accordance with paragraph 4(2) of Schedule 1 to the Act, and a scheme of division amongst those who held property which has been realised under the Act and lodge them and all relevant documents with the Accountant of Court; or
   (b)   where there are no funds available for division, prepare a state of funds only and lodge it with the Accountant of Court, and give to the Accountant of Court such explanations as he shall require.

(2)   The Accountant of Court shall—
   (a)   make a written report on the state of funds and any scheme of division including such observations as he considers appropriate for consideration by the sheriff; and

    (b)   return the state of funds and any scheme of division to the administrator with his report.

(3)   The administrator shall, on receiving the report of the Accountant of Court—

    (a)   lodge in process the report, the state of funds and any scheme of division;

    (b)   intimate a copy of it to the prosecutor; and

    (c)   intimate to each person who held property which has been realised under the Act a notice stating—

        (i)   that the state of funds and scheme of division or the state of funds only, as the case may be, and the report of the Accountant of Court, have been lodged in process; and

        (ii)   the amount for which that person has been ranked, and whether he is to be paid in full, or by a dividend, and the amount of it, or that no funds are available for payment.

## Objections to scheme of division

**3.9.15**—(1)   A person wishing to be heard by the sheriff in relation to the distribution of property under paragraph 4(3) of Schedule 1 to the Act shall lodge a note of objection in the process to which the scheme of division relates within 21 days of the date of the notice intimated under rule 3.9.14(3)(c).

(2)   After the period for lodging a note of objection has expired and no note of objection has been lodged, the administrator may apply by motion for approval of the scheme of division and state of funds, or the state of funds only, as the case may be.

(3)   After the period for lodging a note of objection has expired and a note of objection has been lodged, the sheriff shall dispose of such objection after hearing any objector and the administrator and making such inquiry as he thinks fit.

(4)   If any objection is sustained to any extent, the necessary alterations shall be made to the state of funds and any scheme of division and shall be approved by the sheriff.

## Application for discharge of administrator

**3.9.16**—(1)   Where the scheme of division is approved by the sheriff and the administrator delivered or conveyed to the persons entitled the sums or receipts allocated to them in the scheme, the administrator may apply for his discharge.

(2)   An application to the sheriff for discharge of the administrator shall be made by note in the process of the application under paragraph 1(1) of Schedule 1 to the Act.

**Appeals against determination of outlays and remuneration**

**3.9.17** An appeal to the sheriff under paragraph 6(2) of Schedule 1 to the Act (appeal against a determination by the Accountant of Court) shall be made by note in the process of the application in which the administrator was appointed.

Part X

## Rating (Disabled Persons) Act 1978

**Interpretation and application**

**3.10.1**—(1)   In this Part, "the Act" means the Rating (Disabled Persons) Act 1978.

(2)   This Part applies to appeals under section 6(5) or 6(5A) of the Act.

**Appeals under section 6(5) or 6(5A) of the Act**

**3.10.2**   Any appeal under this Part shall be lodged within 42 days of the date on which the application to the rating authority is refused by the authority.

Part XI

## Representation of the People Act 1983

**Interpretation and application**

**3.11.1**—[1](1)   In this Part—

"sheriff clerk" means, except in rules 3.11.2, 3.11.22 and 3.11.23 the sheriff clerk of the sheriff court district where the trial of the election petition is to take place;

"the Act" means the Representation of the People Act 1983.

(2)   In this Part—

(a)   rules 3.11.2 to 3.11.21 apply to election petitions under the Act; and

(b)   rules 3.11.22 to 3.11.24 apply to registration appeals under section 56 of the Act where the appellant is a person—

(i)   whose entry in the register is an anonymous entry; or

(ii)   who has applied for such an entry.

**Initiation of proceedings**

**3.11.2**—(1)   The election petition shall be lodged with the sheriff clerk of a sheriff court district within which the election questioned has taken place.

(2)   The sheriff clerk shall without delay transmit it to the sheriff principal who shall forthwith appoint—

(a)   the time and place for trial of the petition;

(b)   the amount of the security to be given by the petitioner; and

(c)   if he thinks fit, answers to be lodged within a specified time after service.

---

[1] As substituted by the Act of Sederunt (Summary Applications, Statutory Applications and Appeals etc. Rules) Amendment (Registration Appeals) 2008 (SSI 2008/41), r.2(2) (effective March 17, 2008).

(3)   Service in terms of section 136(3) of the Act (security for costs) shall be effected—

    (a)   personally within—

        (i)   5 days; or

        (ii)   such other period as the sheriff principal may appoint, of the giving of security; or

    (b)   by first class recorded delivery post within—

        (i)   5 days; or

        (ii)   such other period as the sheriff principal may appoint, of the giving of security.

### Security for expenses by bond of caution

**3.11.3**—(1)   If the security proposed is in whole or in part by bond of caution, it shall be given by lodging with the sheriff clerk a bond for the amount specified by the sheriff principal.

(2)   Such bond shall—

    (a)   recite the nature of the petition; and

    (b)   bind and oblige the cautioner and the petitioner jointly and severally, and their respective heirs, executors and successors whomsoever, that the petitioner shall make payment of all costs, charges and expenses that may be payable by him to any person by virtue of any order or decree pronounced in the petition.

(3)   The sufficiency of the cautioner must be attested to the satisfaction of the sheriff clerk, as in the case of judicial bonds of caution.

### Objections to bond of caution

**3.11.4**—(1)   Objections to a bond of caution shall be lodged with the sheriff clerk within 14 days of service in terms of section 136(3) of the Act.

(2)   Objections shall be heard and disposed of by the sheriff clerk.

(3)   If any objection is allowed, it may be removed by a deposit of such sum of money as the sheriff clerk shall determine, made in the manner provided in rule 3.11.5 and within 5 days after the date of the sheriff clerk's determination.

### Security by deposit

**3.11.5**—(1)   Security tendered in whole or in part by deposit of money shall be made in such bank the sheriff clerk may select.

(2)   The deposit receipt shall be—

    (a)   taken in joint name of the petitioner and the sheriff clerk;

    (b)   handed to the sheriff clerk; and

    (c)   held by the sheriff clerk subject to the orders of the court in the petition.

### Amendment of pleadings

**3.11.6**—(1)   Subject to paragraph (2), the sheriff principal shall have power at any stage to allow petition and any answers to be amended upon such condition as to expenses or otherwise as he shall think fit.

(2)   No amendment altering the ground upon which the election was questioned in the petition as presented shall be competent, except to the extent sanctioned by section 129(6) of the Act (time for presentation or amendment of petition questioning local election).

**Notice of date and place of trial**

**3.11.7**—(1)   The sheriff clerk shall, as soon as he receives intimation of the time and place fixed for trial—

    (a)   display a notice thereof on the walls of his principal office; and

    (b)   send by first class post one copy of such notice to—

        (i)   the petitioner;

        (ii)   the respondent;

        (iii)   the Lord Advocate; and

        (iv)   the returning officer.

(2)   The returning officer on receipt of notice from the sheriff clerk shall forthwith publish the time and place fixed for trial in the area for which the election questioned was held.

(3)   Subject to paragraph (4), display of a notice in accordance with paragraph (1)(a) shall be deemed to be notice in the prescribed manner within the meaning of section 139(1) of the Act (trial of petition) and such notice shall not be vitiated by any miscarriage of or relating to all or any copies sent by post.

(4)   At any time before the trial it shall be competent for any party interested to bring any miscarriage of notice sent by post before the sheriff principal, who shall deal therewith as he may consider fit.

**Clerk of court**

**3.11.8**   The sheriff clerk shall attend and act as clerk of court at the trial of the petition.

**Shorthand writer's charges**

**3.11.9**   The shorthand writer's charges, as approved by the sheriff principal, shall be paid in the first instance by the petitioner.

**Appeals**

**3.11.10**   The application to state a special case referred to in section 146(1) of the (special case for determination of the Court of Session) shall be made by minute in the petition proceedings.

**List of votes objected to and of objections**

**3.11.11**—(1)   When a petitioner claims the seat for an unsuccessful candidate, alleging that such candidate had a majority of lawful votes, he and the respondent shall, 5 days before the day fixed for the trial, respectively deliver to the sheriff clerk, and send by first class post to the other party and the Lord Advocate, a list of the votes intended to be objected to, and of the objections to each such vote.

(2)   The sheriff clerk shall allow inspection of such list to all parties concerned.

(3)   No evidence shall be allowed to be given against any vote or in support of any objection not specified in such list, except by leave of the sheriff principal granted upon such terms as to the amendment of the list, postponement of the trial, and payment of expenses as to him may seem fit.

**Petition against undue return**

**3.11.12**—(1)   When on the trial of a petition complaining of an undue return and claiming the office for some person, the respondent intends to give evidence to prove that that person was not duly elected, such respondent shall, 5 days before the day appointed for the trial, deliver to the sheriff clerk, and send by first class post to the petitioner and the Lord Advocate, a list of the objections to the election upon which he intends to rely.

(2) No evidence shall be allowed to be given by a respondent in support of any objection to the election not specified in such list except by leave of the sheriff principal granted upon such terms as to the amendment of the list, postponement of the trial, and payment of expenses as to him may seem fit.

**Prescribed officer**

**3.11.13** The sheriff clerk shall be the prescribed officer for the purposes of sections 143(1) (expense of witnesses) and 155(2) (neglect or refusal to pay costs) of the Act.

**Leave to abandon**

**3.11.14**—(1) Application for leave to withdraw a petition in terms of section 147(1) of the Act (withdrawal of petition), shall be made by minute in Form 17 and shall be preceded by written notice of the intention to make it, sent by first class post to—

    (a) the respondent;

    (b) the Lord Advocate; and

    (c) the returning officer.

(2) The returning officer shall forthwith publish the fact of his having received such notice in the area for which the election questioned was held.

(3) The sheriff principal, upon the application being laid before him, shall by interlocutor, fix the time, not being earlier than 8 days after the date of the interlocutor, and place for hearing it.

(4) The petitioner shall, at least 6 days before the day fixed for the hearing, publish in a newspaper circulating in the district named in the interlocutor a notice in Form 18.

**Death of petitioner**

**3.11.15**—(1) In the event of the death of the sole petitioner, or of the last survivor of several petitioners, the sheriff clerk shall forthwith, upon the fact being brought to his knowledge, insert in a newspaper circulating in the district a notice in Form 19.

(2) The time within which any person who might have been a petitioner in respect of the election may apply to the court by minute in the petition proceedings to be substituted as a petitioner shall be 21 days from the date of publication of such notice.

**Notice by respondent that he does not oppose petition**

**3.11.16**—(1) Notice that a respondent does not intend to oppose a petition shall be given by leaving a written notice to that effect at the office of the sheriff clerk at least 6 days (exclusive of the day of leaving such notice) before the day fixed for the trial.

(2)   On such notice being left with the sheriff clerk, or on its being brought to his knowledge that a respondent other than a returning officer has died, resigned, or otherwise ceased to hold the office to which the petition relates, the sheriff clerk shall forthwith—

(a)   advertise the fact once in a newspaper circulating in the district; and
(b)   send intimation thereof by first class post to—
    (i)   the petitioner;
    (ii)   the Lord Advocate; and
    (iii)   the returning officer, who shall publish the fact in the district.

(3)   The advertisement to be made by the sheriff clerk shall state the last day on which, under this Part, application to be admitted as a respondent to oppose the petition can be made.

## Application to be admitted as respondent

**3.11.17**   Application to be admitted as a respondent to oppose a petition on the occurrence of any of the events mentioned in section 153(1) of the Act (withdrawal and substitution of respondents before trial) must be made by minute in the petition proceedings within 10 days after the date of publication of the advertisement mentioned in rule 3.11.16, unless the sheriff principal on cause shown sees fit to extend the time.

## Public notice of trial not proceeding

**3.11.18**—(1)   This rule applies where after the notice of trial has been published the sheriff clerk receives notice

(a)   the petitioner's intention to apply for leave to withdraw;
(b)   the respondent's intention not to oppose;
(c)   the abatement of the petition by death; or
(d)   the occurrence of any of the events mentioned in section 153(1) of the Act.

(2)   Where this rule applies the sheriff clerk shall forthwith give notice by advertisement inserted once in a newspaper circulating in the district, that the trial will not proceed on the day fixed.

## Notice to a party's agent sufficient

**3.11.19**   Where a party to proceedings under this Part is represented by a solicitor any reference to such party shall, where appropriate, be construed as a reference to the solicitor representing that party and a notice sent to his solicitor shall be held to be notice to the party.

## Cost of publication

**3.11.20**   Where under this Part the returning officer or the sheriff clerk requires to have published a notice or advertisement, the cost shall be paid in the first instance by the petitioner or in the case of a notice under rule 3.11.15 from the estate of the sole or last surviving petitioner and shall form part of the general expenses of the petition.

**Expenses**

**3.11.21**   The expenses of petitions and other proceedings under the Act shall be taxed by the auditor of the sheriff court.

**Application for serial number**

**3.11.22**—[1](1)   Where a person desiring to appeal wishes to prevent his identity being disclosed he may, before lodging the appeal, apply to the sheriff clerk for a serial number to be assigned to him for all purposes connected with the appeal.

(2)   On receipt of an application for a serial number, the sheriff clerk shall assign such a number to the applicant and shall enter a note of it opposite the name of the applicant in the register of such serial numbers.

(3)   The contents of the register of serial numbers and the names of the persons to whom each number relates shall be treated as confidential by the sheriff clerk and shall not be disclosed to any person other than—

(a)   the sheriff;

(b)   the registration officer whose decision or determination is the subject of the appeal.

(4)   In this rule and in rule 3.11.23 "sheriff clerk" means the sheriff clerk of the sheriff court district in which the appeal is or is to be raised.

**Confidentiality**

**3.11.23**[2]   Unless the sheriff otherwise directs, all documents lodged in process of an appeal to which this rule applies are to be available only to the sheriff and the parties; and such documents are to be treated as confidential by all persons involved in, or party to, the proceedings and by the sheriff clerk.

**Hearing**

**3.11.24**[3]   The hearing of an appeal to which this rule applies is to be in private.

Part XII

**Requests or Applications under the Model Law on International Commercial Arbitration**

**Interpretation**

**3.12.1**   In this Part, "the Model Law" means the United Nations Commission on International Trade Law Model Law on International Commercial Arbitration as set out in Schedule 7 to the Law Reform (Miscellaneous Provisions) (Scotland) Act 1990.

---

[1] As inserted by the Act of Sederunt (Summary Applications, Statutory Applications and Appeals etc. Rules) Amendment (Registration Appeals) (SSI 2008/41), r.2(3) (effective March 17, 2008).
[2] As inserted by the Act of Sederunt (Summary Applications, Statutory Applications and Appeals etc. Rules) Amendment (Registration Appeals) (SSI 2008/41), r.2(3) (effective March 17, 2008).
[3] As inserted by the Act of Sederunt (Summary Applications, Statutory Applications and Appeals etc. Rules) Amendment (Registration Appeals) (SSI 2008/41), r.2(3) (effective March 17, 2008).

## Application

**3.12.2**—(1)   Subject to sub-paragraph (2), any request or application which may be made to the sheriff under the Model Law shall be made by summary application.

(2)   Where proceedings involving the same arbitration and the same parties are already pending before the sheriff under this Part, a further application or request may be made by note in the same process.

(3)   The sheriff shall order service of such summary application or note to be made on such persons as he considers appropriate.

## Recognition and enforcement of awards

**3.12.3**—(1)   There shall be lodged along with an application under Article 35 of the Model Law—

   (a)   the original arbitration agreement or certified copy thereof;

   (b)   the duly authenticated original award or certified copy thereof and

   (c)   where appropriate, a duly certified translation in English of the agreement and award.

(2)   An application under this paragraph shall specify whether to the knowledge of the applicant—

   (a)   the arbitral award has been recognised, or is being enforced, in any other jurisdiction; and

   (b)   an application for setting aside or suspension of the arbitral award has been made to a court of the country in which or under whose law the award was made.

(3)   Where the sheriff is satisfied that an arbitral award should be recognised and enforced, he shall so order and shall instruct the sheriff clerk to register the award in the Books of the Sheriff Court for execution.

## Part XIII

### Sex Discrimination Act 1975

*[Omitted by the Act of Sederunt (Ordinary Cause, Summary Application, Summary Cause and Small Claim Rules) Amendment (Equality Act 2006 etc.) 2006 (SSI 2006/ 509) (effective November 3, 2006).]*

## Part XIV[1]

### Access to Health Records Act 1990

## Interpretation and application

**3.14.1**—(1)   In this Part—

"the Act" means the Access to Health Records Act 1990; and
"the Reg" means the Access to Health Records (Steps to Secure Compliance and Complaints Procedures) (Scotland) Regulations 1991.

(2)   This Part applies to applications under section 8(1) of the Act (applications to the court for order to comply with requirement of the Act).

---

[1] As inserted by the Act of Sederunt (Summary Applications, Statutory Applications and Appeals etc. Rules) Amendment 2000 (SSI 2000/148), para.2(2) (effective July 3, 2000).

**Accompanying documents**

**3.14.2**    An application shall specify those steps prescribed in the Regulations which have been taken by the person concerned to secure compliance with any requirement of the Act, and when lodged in process shall be accompanied by—

    (a)   a copy of the application under section 3 of the Act (applications for access to a health record);

    (b)   a copy of the complaint under regulation 3 or 4 of the Regulations (complaint about non-compliance with the Act); and

    (c)   if applicable, a copy of the report under regulation 6 of the Regulations (report in response to complaint).

**Time of making application**

**3.14.3**    The application shall be made where the applicant—

    (a)   has received a report in accordance with regulation 6 of the Regulations, within one year of the date of the report;

    (b)   has not received such a report, within 18 months of the date of the complaint.

Part XV

**Race Relations Act 1976**

*[Omitted by the Act of Sederunt (Ordinary Cause, Summary Application, Summary Cause and Small Claim Rules) Amendment (Equality Act 2006 etc.) 2006 (SSI 2006/ 509) (effective November 3, 2006).]*

Part XVI[1]

**Adults with Incapacity (Scotland) Act 2000**

**Interpretation**

**3.16.1**[2]    In this Part—

    "the 2000 Act" means the Adults with Incapacity (Scotland) Act 2000;

    [3]"the 2003 Act" means the Mental Health (Care and Treatment) (Scotland) Act 2003;

    "adult" means a person who is the subject of an application under the 2000 Act and—

        (a)   has attained the age of 16 years; or

        (b)[4]   in relation to an application for a guardianship order, will attain the age of 16 years within 3 months of the date of the application;

---

[1] As inserted by the Act of Sederunt (Summary Applications, Statutory Applications and Appeals etc. Rules) Amendment (Adults with Incapacity) 2001 (SSI 2001/142) r.3(2).

[2] As amended by the the Mental Health (Care and Treatment) (Scotland) Act 2003 (Modification of Subordinate Legislation) Order 2005 (SSI 2005/445) (effective October 5, 2005).

[3] Inserted by the Mental Health (Care and Treatment) (Scotland) Act 2003 (Modification of Subordinate Legislation) Order 2005 (SSI 2005/445) (effective October 5, 2005).

[4] As substituted by the Act of Sederunt (Summary Applications, Statutory Applications and Appeals etc. Rules) Amendment (Adult Support and Protection (Scotland) Act 2007) 2008 (SSI 2008/111) r.3(1) (effective April 1, 2008).

"authorised establishment" has the meaning ascribed to it in section 35(2) of
the 2000 Act;

"continuing attorney" means a person on whom there has been conferred a
power of attorney granted under section 15(1) of the 2000 Act;

[1] [2]"guardianship order" means an order made under—

(a)   section 57(2)(c) or section 58(1A) of the Criminal Procedure
(Scotland) Act 1995; or

(b)   section 58(4) of the 2000 Act;

"incapable" has the meaning ascribed to it at section 1(6) of the 2000 Act, and
"incapacity" shall be construed accordingly;

[3]"intervention order" means an order made under section 53(1) of the 2000
Act;

"local authority" has the meaning ascribed to it by section 87(1) of the 2000
Act;[4]

"managers" has the meaning ascribed to it in paragraph 1 of Schedule 1 to the
2000 Act;

"Mental Welfare Commission" has the meaning ascribed to it by section 87(1)
of the 2000 Act;[5]

"named person" has the meaning ascribed to it by section 329 of the Mental
Health (Care and Treatment) (Scotland) Act 2003;[6]

"nearest relative" means, subject to section 87(2) of the 2000 Act, the person
who would be, or would be exercising the functions of, the adult's nearest
relative under sections 53 to 57 of the 1984 Act if the adult were a patient
within the meaning of that Act and notwithstanding that the person neither is
or was caring for the adult for the purposes of section 53(3) of that Act;

"power of attorney" includes a factory and commission;

"primary carer" means the person or organisation primarily engaged in caring
for an adult;

"Public Guardian" shall be construed in accordance with section 6 of the 2000
Act; and

"welfare attorney" means a person on whom there has been conferred a power
of attorney granted under section 16(1) of the 2000 Act.

## Appointment of hearing

**3.16.2**   On an application or other proceedings being submitted under or in
pursuance of the 2000 Act the sheriff shall—

(a)   fix a hearing;

(b)   order answers to be lodged (where he considers it appropriate to do so)
within a period that he shall specify; and

---

[1] As amended by the Act of Sederunt (Summary Applications, Statutory Applications and Appeals etc.
Rules) Amendment (No.3) (Adults with Incapacity) 2002 (SSI 2002/146) r.2(2).

[2] As amended by the Act of Sederunt (Summary Applications, Statutory Applications and Appeals etc.
Rules Amendment) (Miscellaneous) 2013 (SSI 2013/293) r.2 (effective November 11, 2013).

[3] As amended by the Act of Sederunt (Summary Applications, Statutory Applications and Appeals etc.
Rules) Amendment (No.3) (Adults with Incapacity) 2002 (SSI 2002/146) r.2(2).

[4] As amended by the Act of Sederunt (Summary Applications, Statutory Applications and Appeals etc.
Rules) Amendment (No.3) (Adults with Incapacity) 2002 (SSI 2002/146) r.2(2).

[5] As amended by the Act of Sederunt (Summary Applications, Statutory Applications and Appeals etc.
Rules) Amendment (No.3) (Adults with Incapacity) 2002 (SSI 2002/146) r.2(2).

[6] As inserted by the Act of Sederunt (Summary Applications, Statutory Applications and Appeals etc.
Rules) Amendment (Adult Support and Protection (Scotland) Act 2007) 2008 (SSI 2008/111) r.2(1)
(effective April 1, 2008).

(c)   appoint service and intimation of the application or other proceedings.

## Place, and privacy, of any hearing

**3.16.3**[1]   The sheriff may, where he considers it appropriate in all the circumstances, appoint that the hearing of an application or other proceedings shall take place—

(a)   in a hospital, or any other place than the court building;

(b)   in private.

## Service of application and renewal proceedings[2]

**3.16.4**—(1)[3] [4]   Service of the application or other proceedings and subsequent proceedings, including proceedings for renewal of guardianship orders, shall be made in Form 20 on—

(a)   the adult;

(b)   the nearest relative of the adult;

(c)   the primary carer of the adult (if any);

(d)   the named person of the adult (if any);

(e)   any guardian, continuing attorney or welfare attorney of the adult who has any power relating to the application or proceedings;

(f)   the Public Guardian;

(g)   where appropriate, the Mental Welfare Commission;

(h)   where appropriate, the local authority;

(i)   where a guardianship order has been made under section 57(2)(c) or section 58(1A) of the Criminal Procedure (Scotland) Act 1995, to the Lord Advocate and, where the order was made by—

    (i)   the High Court of Justiciary, to the Clerk of Justiciary; and

    (ii)   a sheriff, to the sheriff clerk of the Sheriff Court in which the order was made;

(j)   any other person directed by the sheriff.

(2)   Where the applicant is an individual person without legal representation service shall be effected by the sheriff clerk.

(3)   Where the adult is in an authorised establishment the person effecting service shall not serve Form 20 on the adult under paragraph (1)(a) but shall instead serve Forms 20 and 21, together with Form 22, on the managers of that authorised establishment by—

(a)   first class recorded delivery post; or

(b)   personal service by a sheriff officer.

(4)[5]   On receipt of Forms 20 and 21 in terms of paragraph (3) the managers of the authorised establishment shall, subject to rule 3.16.5—

(a)   immediately deliver the notice in Form 20 to the adult; and

---

[1] As substituted by the Act of Sederunt (Ordinary Cause, Summary Application and Small Claim Rules) Amendment (Miscellaneous) 2004 (SSI 2004/197) para.3(7) (effective May 21, 2004).

[2] As amended by the Act of Sederunt (Sheriff Court Rules)(Miscellaneous Amendments) (No.3) 2013 (SSI 2013/171) para.2 (effective June 25, 2013).

[3] As substituted by the Act of Sederunt (Sheriff Court Rules) (Miscellaneous Amendments) (No.3) 2013 (SSI 2013/171) r.2(2) (effective June 25, 2013).

[4] As amended by the Act of Sederunt (Summary Applications, Statutory Applications and Appeals etc. Rules Amendment) (Miscellaneous) 2013 (SSI 2013/293) r.2 (effective November 11, 2013).

[5] As amended by the Act of Sederunt (Summary Applications, Statutory Applications and Appeals etc. Rules Amendment) (Miscellaneous) 2013 (SSI 2013/293) r.2 (effective November 11, 2013).

(b) as soon as practicable thereafter complete, and in any event before the date of the hearing specified in Form 20, and return to the sheriff clerk a certificate of such delivery in Form 22.

(5) Where the application or other proceeding follows on a remit under rule 3.16.9 the order for service of the application shall include an order for service on the Public Guardian or other party concerned.

(6)[1] Where the application is for an intervention order or a guardianship order, copies of the reports lodged in accordance with section 57(3) of the 2000 Act (reports to be lodged in court along with application) shall be served along with Form 20 or Forms 20, 21 and 22 as the case may be.

### Dispensing with service on adult

**3.16.5**—(1) Where, in relation to any application or proceeding under or in pursuance of the 2000 Act, two medical certificates are produced stating that intimation of the application or other proceeding, or notification of any interlocutor relating to such application or other proceeding, would be likely to pose a serious risk to the health of the adult the sheriff may dispense with such intimation or notification.

(2) Any medical certificates produced under paragraph (1) shall be prepared by medical practitioners independent of each other.

(3)[2] In any case where the incapacity of the adult is by reason of mental disorder, one of the two medical practitioners must be a medical practitioner approved for the purposes of section 22(4) of the 2003 Act as having special experience in the diagnosis or treatment of mental disorder.

### Hearing

**3.16.6**—(1)[3] A hearing to determine any application or other proceeding shall take place within 28 days of the interlocutor fixing the hearing under rule 3.16.2 unless any person upon whom the application is to be served is outside Europe.

(2) At the hearing referred to in paragraph (1) the sheriff may determine the application or other proceeding or may order such further procedure as he thinks fit.

### Prescribed forms of application

**3.16.7**—(1) An application submitted to the sheriff under or in pursuance of the 2000 Act, other than an appeal or remitted matter, shall be in Form 23.

(2) An appeal to the sheriff under or in pursuance of the 2000 Act shall be in Form 24.

### Subsequent applications

**3.16.8**—(1)[4] Unless otherwise prescribed in the Part or under the 2000 Act, any application or proceedings subsequent to an initial application or proceeding

---

[1] As amended by the Act of Sederunt (Summary Applications, Statutory Applications and Appeals etc. Rules) Amendment (No.3) (Adults with Incapacity) 2002 (SSI 2002/146) r.2(2).

[2] As amended by the the the Mental Health (Care and Treatment) (Scotland) Act 2003 (Modification of Subordinate Legislation) Order (SSI 2005/445) (effective October 5, 2005).

[3] As amended by the Act of Sederunt (Summary Applications, Statutory Applications and Appeals etc. Rules) Amendment (No.3) (Adults with Incapacity) 2002 (SSI 2002/146), r.2(2) (effective April 1, 2002).

[4] As amended the Act of Sederunt (Summary Applications, Statutory Applications and Appeals etc. Rules) Amendment (No.3) (Adults with Incapacity) 2002 (SSI 2002/146) r.2(2) and the Act of

considered by the sheriff including an application to renew an existing order, shall take the form of a minute lodged in the process.

(1ZA)[1]   Where a guardianship order has been made under section 57(2)(c) or section 58(1A) of the Criminal Procedure (Scotland) Act 1995, an application to renew it shall be made—

(a)   on the first such application, in Form 23;

(b)   on any subsequent application, in the form of a minute lodged in the process.

(1A)[23]   Except where the sheriff otherwise directs, any minute lodged under this rule shall be lodged in accordance with, and regulated by, Chapter 14 of the Ordinary Cause Rules.

(2)   Where any subsequent application or proceedings under paragraph (1) above are made to a court in another sheriffdom the sheriff clerk shall transmit the court process to the court dealing with the current application or proceeding.

(3)   Transmission of the process in terms of paragraph (2) shall be made within 4 days of it being requested by the sheriff clerk of the court in which the current application or proceedings have been raised.

(4)[4]   Where the application is for renewal of a guardianship order, a copy of any report lodged under section 60 of the 2000 Act shall be served along with the minute.

(5)   *[Repealed by the Act of Sederunt (Sheriff Court Rules)(Miscellaneous Amendments) (No.3) 2013 (SSI 2013/171) para.2 (effective June 25, 2013).]*

### Remit of applications by the Public Guardian etc.

**3.16.9**   Where an application is remitted to the sheriff by the Public Guardian or by any other party authorised to do so under the 2000 Act the party remitting the application shall, within 4 days of the decision to remit, transmit the papers relating to the application to the sheriff clerk of the court where the application is to be considered.

### Caution and other security[5]

**3.16.10**—[6](1)   Where the sheriff requires a person authorised under an intervention order or any variation of an intervention order, or appointed as a guardian, to

---

Sederunt (Summary Applications, Statutory Applications and Appeals etc. Rules) Amendment (Adult Support and Protection (Scotland) Act 2007) 2008 (SSI 2008/111) r.3(2)(a) (effective April 1, 2008).

[1] As amended by the Act of Sederunt (Summary Applications, Statutory Applications and Appeals etc. Rules Amendment) (Miscellaneous) 2013 (SSI 2013/293) r.2 (effective November 11, 2013).

[2] As amended the Act of Sederunt (Summary Applications, Statutory Applications and Appeals etc. Rules) Amendment (No.3) (Adults with Incapacity) 2002 (SSI 2002/146) r.2(2) and the Act of Sederunt (Summary Applications, Statutory Applications and Appeals etc. Rules) Amendment (Adult Support and Protection (Scotland) Act 2007) 2008 (SSI 2008/111) r.3(2)(a) (effective April 1, 2008).

[3] As amended by the Act of Sederunt (Summary Applications, Statutory Applications and Appeals etc. Rules Amendment) (Miscellaneous) 2013 (SSI 2013/293) r.2 (effective November 11, 2013).

[4] As amended the Act of Sederunt (Summary Applications, Statutory Applications and Appeals etc. Rules) Amendment (No.3) (Adults with Incapacity) 2002 (SSI 2002/146) r.2(2) and the Act of Sederunt (Summary Applications, Statutory Applications and Appeals etc. Rules) Amendment (Adult Support and Protection (Scotland) Act 2007) 2008 (SSI 2008/111) r.3(2)(a) (effective April 1, 2008).

[5] As amended by the Act of Sederunt (Summary Applications, Statutory Applications and Appeals etc. Rules) Amendment (Adult Support and Protection (Scotland) Act 2007) 2008 (SSI 2008/111) r.4 (effective April 1, 2008).

[6] As inserted by the Act of Sederunt (Summary Applications, Statutory Applications and Appeals etc. Rules) Amendment (No.3) (Adults with Incapacity) 2002 (SSI 2002/146), r.2(2).

find caution he shall specify the amount and period within which caution is to be found in the interlocutor authorising or appointing the person or varying the order (as the case may be).

(1A)[1]   The amount of caution specified by the sheriff in paragraph (1) may be calculated and expressed as a percentage of the value of the adult's estate.

(2)   The sheriff may, on application made by motion before the expiry of the period for finding caution and on cause shown, allow further time for finding caution in accordance with paragraph (1).

(3)   Caution shall be lodged with the Public Guardian.

(4)   Where caution has been lodged to the satisfaction of the Public Guardian he shall notify the sheriff clerk.

(5)   The sheriff may at any time while a requirement to find caution is in force—

(a)   increase the amount of, or require the person to find new, caution; or

(b)   authorise the amount of caution to be decreased.

(6)[2]   Where the sheriff requires the person referred to in paragraph (1) to give security other than caution, the rules of Chapter 27 of the Ordinary Cause Rules shall apply with the necessary modifications.

### Appointment of interim guardian

**3.16.11**[3]   An application under section 57(5) of the 2000 Act (appointment of interim guardian) may be made in the crave of the application for a guardianship order to which it relates or, if made after the submission of the application for a guardianship order, by motion in the process of that application.

### Registration of intervention order or guardianship order relating to heritable property

**3.16.12**[4]   Where an application for an intervention order or a guardianship order seeks to vest in the person authorised under the order, or the guardian, as the case may be, any right to deal with, convey or manage any interest in heritable property which is recorded or capable of being recorded in the General Register of Sasines or is registered or capable of being registered in the Land Register of Scotland, the applicant must specify the necessary details of the property in the application to enable it to be identified in the Register of Sasines or the Land Register of Scotland, as the case may be.

---

[1] As inserted by the Act of Sederunt (Summary Applications, Statutory Applications and Appeals etc. Rules) Amendment (Adult Support and Protection (Scotland) Act 2007) 2008 (SSI 2008/111) r.4 (effective April 1, 2008).

[2] As inserted by the Act of Sederunt (Summary Applications, Statutory Applications and Appeals etc. Rules) Amendment (Adult Support and Protection (Scotland) Act 2007) 2008 (SSI 2008/111) r.4 (effective April 1, 2008).

[3] As inserted by the Act of Sederunt (Summary Applications, Statutory Applications and Appeals etc. Rules) Amendment (No.3) (Adults with Incapacity) 2000 (SSI 2002/146), r.2(2) (effective April 1, 2002).

[4] As inserted by the Act of Sederunt (Summary Applications, Statutory Applications and Appeals etc. Rules) Amendment (No.3) (Adults with Incapacity) 2002 (SSI 2002/146), r.2(2) (effective April 1, 2002).

## Non-compliance with decisions of guardians with welfare powers

**3.16.13**—[1](1)   Where the court is required under section 70(3) of the 2000 Act to intimate an application for an order or warrant in relation to noncompliance with the decision of a guardian with welfare powers, the sheriff clerk shall effect intimation in Form 20 in accordance with paragraphs (2) and (3).

(2)   Intimation shall be effected—

    (a)   where the person is within Scotland, by first class recorded delivery post, or, in the event that intimation by first class recorded delivery post is unsuccessful, by personal service by a sheriff officer; or

    (b)   where the person is furth of Scotland, in accordance with rule 2.12 (service on persons furth of Scotland).

(3)   Such intimation shall include notice of the period within which any objection to the application shall be lodged.

Part XVII[2]

### Anti-Terrorism, Crime and Security Act 2001

## Interpretation

**3.17.1**   In this Part, any reference to a specified paragraph shall be construed as a reference to the paragraph bearing that number in Schedule 1 to the Anti-terrorism, Crime and Security Act 2001.

## Applications for extended detention of cash

**3.17.2**—(1)   An application to the sheriff for an order under paragraph 3(2) (extended detention of seized cash) shall be made by summary application.

(2)   An application for any further order for the detention of cash under paragraph 3(2) shall be made by minute in the original process and shall be proceeded with in accordance with sub-paragraph (3) below.

(3)   On the lodging of an application for any further order the sheriff shall—

    (a)   fix a date for determination of the application; and

    (b)   order service of the application together with notice of such date for determination on any persons whom he considers may be affected.

## Applications for release of detained cash

**3.17.3**—(1)   An application to the sheriff under paragraph 5(2) (application for release of detained cash) or under paragraph 9(1) (application by person who claims that cash belongs to him) shall, where the court has made an order under paragraph 3(2), be made by minute in the original process of the application for that order, and in any other case shall be made by summary application.

(2)   On the lodging of such an application the sheriff shall—

    (a)   fix a date for a hearing; and

    (b)   order service of the application together with notice of such hearing on

---

[1] As inserted by the Act of Sederunt (Summary Applications, Statutory Applications and Appeals etc. Rules) Amendment (No.3) (Adults with Incapacity) 2002 (SSI 2002/146), r.2(2) (effective April 1, 2002).

[2] As inserted by the Act of Sederunt (Summary Applications, Statutory Applications and Appeals etc. Rules) Amendment (Detention and Forfeiture of Terrorist Cash) 2002 (SSI 2002/ 129), para.2(2) (effective March 8, 2002).

the procurator fiscal and any other person whom he considers may be affected by the granting of such an application.

### Applications for forfeiture of detained cash

**3.17.4**—(1)   An application to the sheriff under paragraph 6(1) (application for forfeiture of detained cash) shall, where the court has made an order under paragraph 3(2), be made by minute in the original process of the application for that order, and in any other case shall be made by summary application.

(2)   On the lodging of such an application the sheriff shall—

    (a)   fix a date for a hearing; and

    (b)   order service of the application together with notice of such hearing on any person whom he considers may be affected by the granting of such an application.

### Applications for compensation

**3.17.5**—(1)   An application to the sheriff under paragraph 10(1) (application for compensation) shall, where the court has made an order under paragraph 3(2), be made by minute in the original process of the application for that order, and in any other case shall be made by summary application.

(2)   On the lodging of such an application the sheriff shall—

    (a)   fix a date for a hearing; and

    (b)   order service of the application together with notice of such hearing on any person whom he considers may be affected by the granting of such an application.

Part XVIII[1]

**Local Government (Scotland) Act 1973**

### Application

**3.18.1**—   This Part applies to appeals to the sheriff principal under section 103J of the Local Government (Scotland) Act 1973 (appeals from the Accounts Commission for Scotland).

### Appeals

**3.18.2**—(1)   An appeal under this Part shall be made by summary application.

(2)   A summary application made under paragraph (1) shall include grounds of appeal stating—

    (a)   the finding or sanction or suspension being appealed;

    (b)   reasons why the appeal should be allowed; and

    (c)   the date of sending of the finding or imposition of the sanction or suspension concerned,

and shall be accompanied by a copy of such finding, sanction or suspension.

---

[1] As inserted by the Act of Sederunt (Summary Applications, Statutory Applications and Appeals etc. Rules) Amendment (No.2) (Local Government (Scotland) Act 1973) 2002 (SSI 2002/130), r.2(3) (effective March 8, 2002).

## Warrant and form of citation

**3.18.3**—(1) A warrant for citation in an appeal under this Part shall be in Form 2A and shall state—

    (a) the date by which answers should be lodged; and

    (b) the date and time when the appeal will call.

  (2) Citation in respect of a warrant granted under paragraph (1) shall be in Form 3A.

  (3) Where a party on whom service has been made lodges answers under paragraph (1)(a) that party shall, at the same time, send a copy to the applicant.

  (4) In Schedule 1 (forms)—

    (a) after Form 2 insert Form 2A; and

    (b) after Form 3 insert Form 3A,

as set out in the Schedule to this Act of Sederunt.

---

Part XIX[1]

### Proceeds of Crime Act 2002

*General*

## Interpretation and application

**3.19.1.**—[2](1) In this Part—

"the Act" means the Proceeds of Crime Act 2002;

references to an administrator are to an administrator appointed under section 125(1) or 128(3);

a reference to a specified section is a reference to the section bearing that number in the Act; and any reference to a specified paragraph in a specified Schedule is a reference to the paragraph bearing that number in the Schedule of that number in the Act.

  (2) This Part applies to applications to the sheriff under Parts 3, 5 and 8 of the Act; but it only applies to applications under Part 8 in relation to property that is the subject of a civil recovery investigation.

*Recovery of cash in summary proceedings*

## Applications for extended detention of cash

**3.19.2.**—(1) An application to the sheriff for an order under sections 295(2) and (7) (extended detention of seized cash) shall be made by summary application.

  (2) An application for any further order for the detention of cash under section 295(2) shall be made by minute in the process of the original application for extended detention of seized cash and shall be proceeded with in accordance with sub-paragraph (3) below.

  (3) On the lodging of an application for any further order the sheriff shall—

    (a) fix a date for determination of the application; and

---

[1] As inserted by the Act of Sederunt (Summary Applications, Statutory Applications and Appeals etc. Rules) Amendment (No.5) (Proceeds of Crime Act 2002) 2002 (SSI 2002/563), r.2(2) (effective December 30, 2002).

[2] As substituted by the Act of Sederunt (Summary Applications, Statutory Applications and Appeals etc. Rules) Amendment (No.6) (Proceeds of Crime Act 2002) 2003 (SSI 2003/98), r.2(2)(a) (effective February 24, 2003 for provisions specified in SSI 2003/98 para.1(1)(b)(ii); March 24, 2003 otherwise).

(b)  order service of the application together with notice of such date for determination on any persons whom he considers may be affected.

## Applications for release of detained cash

**3.19.3.**—(1)  An application to the sheriff under section 297(3) (application for release of detained cash) or under section 301(1) (application by person who claims that cash belongs to him) shall, where the court has made an order under section 295(2), be made by minute in the process of the application for that order, and in any other case shall be made by summary application in the course of the proceedings or at any other time.

(2)  On the lodging of such an application the sheriff shall—

    (a)  fix a date for a hearing; and

    (b)  order service of the application together with notice of such hearing on the procurator fiscal and any other person whom he considers may be affected by the granting of such an application.

## Applications for forfeiture of detained cash

**3.19.4.**—(1)  An application to the sheriff under section 298(1)(b) (application by the Scottish Ministers for forfeiture of detained cash) shall, where the court has made an order under section 295(2), be made by minute in the process of the application for that order, and in any other case shall be made by summary application.

(2)  On the lodging of such an application the sheriff shall—

    (a)  fix a date for a hearing; and

    (b)  order service of the application together with notice of such hearing on any person whom he considers may be affected by the granting of such an application.

## Applications for compensation

**3.19.5.**—(1)  An application to the sheriff under section 302(1) (application for compensation) shall, where the court has made an order under section 295(2), be made by minute in the process of the application for that order, and in any other case shall be made by summary application.

(2)  On the lodging of such an application the sheriff shall—

    (a)  fix a date for a hearing; and

    (b)  order service of the application together with notice of such hearing on any person whom he considers may be affected by the granting of such an application.

*Restraint and administration orders[1]*

## Service of restraint orders

**3.19.6.**  The intimation to be made by the prosecutor under section 121(3) shall be made by serving a copy of the interlocutor granting a restraint order on every person named in the interlocutor as restrained by the order.

---

[1] Inserted by the Act of Sederunt (Summary Applications, Statutory Applications and Appeals etc. Rules) Amendment (No.6) (Proceeds of Crime Act 2002) 2003 (SSI 2003/98), r.2(2)(b) (effective February 24, 2003 for provisions specified in SSI 2003/98 para.1(1)(b)(ii); March 24, 2003 otherwise).

**Recall or variation of restraint orders**

**3.19.7.**    An application to the sheriff under section 121(5) (variation or recall of restraint order) shall be made by minute in the process of the application for the restraint order.

**Appeals to the Court of Session**

**3.19.8.**—(1)    An appeal against an interlocutor of the sheriff refusing, varying or recalling or refusing to vary or recall a restraint order shall be marked within 14 days after the date of the interlocutor concerned.

(2)    Such an appeal shall be marked by writing a note of appeal on the interlocutor sheet, or other written record containing the interlocutor appealed against, or on a separate sheet lodged with the sheriff clerk, in the following terms—

"The applicant appeals to the Court of Session.".

(3)    The note of appeal shall—
   (a)    be signed by the appellant;
   (b)    bear the date on which it is signed; and
   (c)    where the appellant is represented, specify the name and address of the solicitor or other agent who will be acting for him in the appeal.

(4)    The sheriff clerk will transmit the process within 4 days after the appeal is marked to the Deputy Principal Clerk of Session.

(5)    Within the period specified in paragraph (4), the sheriff clerk shall—
   (a)    send written notice of the appeal to every other party; and
   (b)    certify on the interlocutor sheet that he has done so.

(6)    Failure of the sheriff clerk to comply with paragraph (5) shall not invalidate the appeal.

**Applications in relation to arrestment**

**3.19.9.**—(1)    An application to the sheriff under section 124(1) (arrestment of property affected by restraint order) by the prosecutor for warrant for arrestment may be made—
   (a)    in the application made under section 121(2) (application for restraint order); or
   (b)    if made after a restraint order has been applied for, by minute in the process of the application for that order.

(2)    An application to the sheriff under section 124(3) (recalling, loosing or restricting arrestment) or under section 124(6) (recall or restriction of arrestment) shall be made by minute in the process of the application for the restraint order.

**Applications for appointment of administrators**

**3.19.10.**—(1)    An application to the sheriff under section 125(1) (appointment of management administrator) shall be made by minute in the process of the application for the restraint order.

(2)    An application to the sheriff under section 128(2) (appointment of enforcement administrator) shall be made—
   (a)    where made after a restraint order has been made, by minute in the process of the application for that order; or
   (b)    in any other case, by summary application.

(3)   The notification to be made by the sheriff clerk under section 125(3) or 128(8) (as the case may be) shall be made by intimation of a copy of the interlocutor to the accused and the persons subject to the order.

### Incidental applications in relation to an administration

**3.19.11.**   An application to the sheriff subsequent to the appointment of an administrator relating to any matter incidental to that appointment shall be made by minute in the process of the application in which the administrator was appointed.

### Documents for Accountant of Court

**3.19.12.**—(1)   A person who has lodged any document in the process of an application for the appointment of an administrator shall forthwith send a copy of that document to the Accountant of Court.

(2)   The sheriff clerk shall transmit to the Accountant of Court any part of the process as the Accountant of Court may request in relation to an administration which is in dependence before the sheriff unless such part of the process is, at the time of request, required by the sheriff.

### Procedure for fixing and finding caution

**3.19.13.**—(1)   The Accountant of Court shall forthwith, on receiving intimation of an application for the appointment of an administrator, fix the caution to be found in the event of appointment being made and shall notify the amount to the sheriff clerk and the applicant.

(2)   During the subsistence of the appointment of the administrator, the Accountant of Court may, at any time—

(a)   require the administrator to increase the amount of or find new or additional caution; or

(b)   authorise the administrator to decrease the amount of existing caution.

### Time for finding caution

**3.19.14.**—(1)   Where the time within which caution is to be found is not stipulated in the interlocutor appointing the administrator, the time allowed for finding caution shall be, subject to paragraph (2) of this rule, limited to one calendar month from the date of the interlocutor.

(2)   The sheriff may, on application made before the expiry of the period for finding caution, and, on cause shown, allow further time for finding caution.

### Procedure on finding caution

**3.19.15.**—(1)   Caution shall be lodged with the Accountant of Court.

(2)   Where caution has been found to the satisfaction of the Accountant of Court, he shall notify the sheriff clerk.

### Issue of certified copy interlocutor

**3.19.16.**—(1)   A certified copy interlocutor of appointment of an administrator shall not be issued by the sheriff clerk until he receives notification from the Accountant of Court in accordance with rule 3.19.15(2).

**Administrator's title to act**

**3.19.17.**    An administrator shall not be entitled to act until he has obtained a certified copy of the interlocutor appointing him.

**Accounts**

**3.19.18.**—(1)   An administrator shall maintain accounts of his intromissions with the property in his charge and shall, subject to paragraph (2)—

(a)   within six months after the date of his appointment; and
(b)   at six monthly intervals after the first account during the subsistence of his appointment,

lodge with the Accountant of Court an account of his intromissions in such form, with such supporting vouchers and other documents, as the Accountant of Court may require.

(2)   The Accountant of Court may waive the lodging of an account where the administrator certifies that there have been no intromissions during a particular accounting period.

**Application for discharge of administrator**

**3.19.19.**    An application to the sheriff for discharge of an administrator shall be made by minute in the process of the application in which the administrator was appointed.

**Appeals against determination of outlays and remuneration**

**3.19.20.**    An appeal to the sheriff under paragraph 9(1) of Schedule 3 (appeal against a determination by the Accountant of Court) shall be made by minute in the process of the application in which the administrator was appointed.

*Detention and realisation of seized property[1]*

**Discharge or variation of detention order**

**3.19.20A**    An application to the sheriff under section 127N(2) (discharge, variation and lapse of detention order) shall be made by minute in the process of the application for an order extending the period for which property may be detained under section 127J.

**Appeals to the Court of Session**

**3.19.20B.**—(1)   This section shall apply to appeals against an interlocutor of the sheriff under the following sections—

(a)   section 127O(1) or (2);
(b)   section 131C(1), (2) or (4).

(2)   An appeal shall be marked by writing a note of appeal on the interlocutor sheet, or other written record containing the interlocutor appealed against, or on a

---

[1] As inserted by the Act of Sederunt (Summary Applications, Statutory Applications and Appeals etc. Rules Amendment) (Policing and Crime Act 2009) 2013 (SSI 2013/241) r.2(2) (effective October 1, 2013).

separate sheet lodged with the sheriff clerk, in the following terms—
The applicant [ or affected person] appeals to the Court of Session.

(3)  The note of appeal shall—

(a)  be signed by the appellant;

(b)  bear the date on which it is signed; and

(c)  where the appellant is represented, specify the name and address of the solicitor or other agent who will be acting for him or her in the appeal.

(4)  The sheriff clerk shall transmit the process within 4 days after the appeal is marked to the Deputy Principal Clerk of Session.

(5)  Within the period specified in paragraph (4), the sheriff clerk shall—

(a)  send written notice of the appeal to every other party; and

(b)  certify on the interlocutor sheet that he or she has done so.

(6)  Failure of the sheriff clerk to comply with paragraph (5) shall not invalidate the appeal.

*Civil recovery investigations[1]*

### Production orders

**3.19.21.**—(1)  An application to the sheriff under section 382(2) (order to grant entry to premises) may be made—

(a)  in the application for the production order; or

(b)  if made after the production order has been made, by minute in the process of the application for that order.

(2)  A report to the sheriff under section 385(4) (report of failure to bring production order made in relation to an authorised government department to the attention of the officer concerned) shall take the form of a letter to the sheriff clerk.

(3)  An application to the sheriff under section 386(4) (discharge or variation of a production order or an order to grant entry) shall be made by minute in the process of the application for the production order.

### Search warrants

**3.19.22.**  An application to the sheriff under section 387(1) (search warrant) shall be in the form of a summary application.

### Customer information orders

**3.19.23.**  An application under section 403(4) (discharge or variation of a customer information order) shall be made by minute in the process of the application for the customer information order.

### Account monitoring orders

**3.19.24.**  An application under section 408(4) (discharge or variation of an account monitoring order) shall be made by minute in the process of the application for the account monitoring order.

---

[1] As inserted by the Act of Sederunt (Summary Applications, Statutory Applications and Appeals etc. Rules) Amendment (No.6) (Proceeds of Crime Act 2002) 2003 (SSI 2003/98), r.2(2)(b) (effective February 24, 2003 for provisions specified in SSI 2003/98 para.1(1)(b)(ii); March 24, 2003 otherwise).

Part XX[1]

## International Criminal Court (Scotland) Act 2001

### *General*

### Interpretation and application

**3.20.1.**—(1)   In this Part—

"the Act" means the International Criminal Court (Scotland) Act 2001;
"ICC crime" has the same meaning as in section 28(1) of the Act; and a reference to a specified section is a reference to the section bearing that number in the Act, and any reference to a specified paragraph in a specified schedule is a reference to the paragraph bearing that number in the schedule of that number to the Act.

(2)   This Part applies to applications to the sheriff under Parts 1 and 2 of schedule 5 to the Act.

### *Investigations of proceeds of ICC crime*

### Production or access orders

**3.20.2.**—(1)   An order under Part 1 of schedule 5 to the Act may be made by the sheriff on a summary application by a person authorised for the purpose under section 19 of the Act.

(2)   Any such application may be made on an ex parte application to a sheriff in chambers.

(3)   Any such application must set out reasonable grounds for suspecting—
  (a)   that a specified person has benefited from an ICC crime; and
  (b)   that the material to which the application relates is likely to be of substantial value (whether by itself or together with other material) to the investigation for the purposes of which the application is made.

(4)   Any application for variation or discharge of an order under Part 1 of schedule 5 to the Act shall be made by minute.

### Search warrants

**3.20.3.**—(1)   On a summary application by a person authorised under section 19 of the Act to the sheriff sitting as a court of civil jurisdiction, the sheriff may issue a warrant under Part 2 of the Act.

(2)   Any such application must set out grounds sufficient to satisfy the sheriff—
  (a)   that a production or access order made in relation to material on the premises has not been complied with;
  (b)   that—
    (i)   there are reasonable grounds for suspecting that a specified person has benefited from an ICC crime;
    (ii)   there are grounds for making a production and access order in relation to material on the premises; and
    (iii)   it would not be appropriate to make a production and access

---

[1] As inserted by the Act of Sederunt (Summary Applications, Statutory Applications and Appeals etc. Rules) Amendment (International Criminal Court) 2003 (SSI 2003/27), r.2(2) (effective January 24, 2003).

order in relation to the material for any of the reasons specified in paragraph 10(4) of schedule 5 to the Act; or

(c) that—

    (i) there are reasonable grounds for suspecting that a specified person has benefited from an ICC crime;

    (ii) there are reasonable grounds for suspecting that there is material on the premises which cannot be particularised at the time of the application, but which—

        (aa) relates to the specified person, or to the question of whether that person has benefited from an ICC crime, or to any question as to the extent or whereabouts of the proceeds of an ICC crime; and

        (bb) is likely to be of substantial value (whether by itself or together with other material) to the investigation for the purposes of which the application is made; and

    (iii) any of the circumstances specified in paragraph 10(6) of schedule 5 to the Act applies.

### Part XXI[1]

## Immigration And Asylum Act 1999

### Interpretation

**3.21.1.** In this Part—

"the Act" means the Immigration and Asylum Act 1999; and

"an appeal" means an appeal to the sheriff under section 35A(1) or section 40B(1) of the Act.

### Appeals

**3.21.2.**—(1) A person making an appeal against a decision by the Secretary of State to impose a penalty under section 32 or a charge under section 40 of the Act must, subject to paragraph (2), bring an appeal within 21 days after receiving the penalty notice or charge notice.

(2) Where the appellant has given notice of objection to the Secretary of State under section 35(4) or section 40A(3) of the Act within the time prescribed for doing so, he must bring an appeal within 21 days after receiving notice of the Secretary of State's decision under section 35(7) or section 40A(6) respectively of the Act in response to the notice of objection.

### Part XXII[2]

## Crime and Disorder Act 1998

*[Revoked by the Act of Sederunt (Summary Applications, Statutory Applications and Appeals etc. Rules) Amendment (Antisocial Behaviour etc. (Scotland) Act 2004)*

---

[1] As inserted by the Act of Sederunt (Summary Applications, Statutory Applications and Appeals etc. Rules) Amendment (Immigration and Asylum) 2003 (SSI 2003/261), r.2(2) (effective May 24, 2003).

[2] As inserted by the Act of Sederunt (Summary Applications, Statutory Applications and Appeals etc. Rules) Amendment (Standards Commission for Scotland) 2003 (SSI 2003/346), r.2(2) (effective July 4, 2003).

*2004 (SSI 2004/455) r.2(2) (effective October 28, 2004: repeal has effect subject to transitional provisions specified in SSI 2004/455 r.2(3)).]*

## Part XXIII[1]

### Ethical Standards in Public Life etc. (Scotland) Act 2000

#### Application

**3.23.1.** This Part applies to appeals to the sheriff principal under sections 22 (appeals from commission) or 26 (appeals by water industry commissioner) of the Ethical Standards in Public Life etc. (Scotland) Act 2000.

#### Appeals

**3.23.2.**—(1) An appeal under this Part shall be made by summary application.

(2) A summary application made under paragraph (1) shall include grounds of appeal stating—

    (a) which of the findings of, or sanction or suspension imposed by, the Standards Commission for Scotland is being appealed;

    (b) reasons why the appeal should be allowed; and

    (c) the date of the sending of that finding, or imposition of that sanction or suspension,

and shall be accompanied by a copy of that finding, sanction or suspension.

#### Warrant and form of citation

**3.23.3.**—(1) A warrant for citation in an appeal under this Part shall be in Form 2A, or a form as near thereto as circumstances permit, and shall state—

    (a) the date by which answers should be lodged; and

    (b) the date and time when the appeal will call.

(2) Citation in respect of a warrant granted under paragraph (1) shall be in Form 3A, or a form as near thereto as circumstances permit.

(3) Where a party on whom service has been made lodges answers under paragraph (1)(a) that party shall, at the same time, send a copy to the appellant.

## Part XXIV[2]

### International Protection of Adults

#### Interpretation

**3.24.1.** In this Part—

    "the Act" means the Adults with Incapacity (Scotland) Act 2000;

    "the Convention" means the Hague Convention of 13th January 2000 on the International Protection of Adults;

---

[1] As inserted by the Act of Sederunt (Summary Applications, Statutory Applications and Appeals etc. Rules) Amendment (Standards Commission for Scotland) 2003 (SSI 2003/346), r.2(2) (effective July 4, 2003).

[2] As inserted by the Act of Sederunt (Summary Applications, Statutory Applications and Appeals etc. Rules) Amendment (International Protection of Adults) 2003 (SSI 2003/556), r.2(2) (effective November 14, 2003).

"international measure" means any measure taken under the law of a country other than Scotland for the personal welfare, or the protection of property, of an adult with incapacity, where—

    (a)  jurisdiction in the other country was based on the adult's habitual residence there; or

    (b)  the other country and the United Kingdom were when that measure was taken parties to the Convention, and jurisdiction in that other country was based on a ground of jurisdiction in the Convention; and

"Public Guardian" shall be construed in accordance with section 6 (the public guardian and his functions) of the Act.

## Application

**3.24.2**—(1)  An application to register an international measure under paragraph 8(1) of schedule 3 to the Act shall be by summary application made under this Part.

(2)  The original document making the international measure, or a copy of that document duly certified as such by an officer of the issuing or a requesting body, shall be lodged with an application under paragraph (1), together with (as necessary) an English translation of that document and that certificate.

(3)  Any translation under paragraph (2) must be certified as a correct translation by the person making it, and the certificate must contain the full name, address and qualifications of the translator.

## Intimation of application

**3.24.3.**—(1)  The sheriff shall order intimation of an application to register an international measure—

    (a)  except where the sheriff is satisfied that the person to whom the international measure relates had an opportunity to be heard in the country where that measure was taken, to that person;

    (b)  which if registered would have the effect of placing the adult to whom the international measure relates in an establishment in Scotland, to the—

        (i)  Scottish Central Authority; and

        (ii)  Mental Welfare Commission;

    (c)  to the Public Guardian; and

    (d)  to any other person whom the sheriff considers appropriate.

(2)  In this rule—

    (a)  "Scottish Central Authority" means an authority—

        (i)  designated under Article 28 of the Convention for the purposes of acting as such; or

        (ii)  appointed by the Scottish Ministers for the purposes of carrying out the functions to be carried out under schedule 3 of the Act by the Scottish Central Authority, where no authority is designated for the purposes of sub paragraph (i); and

    (b)[1]  "Mental Welfare Commission" means the Mental Welfare Commission for Scotland continued in being by section 4 of the Mental Health (Care and Treatment) (Scotland) Act 2003.

---

[1] As amended by the Mental Health (Care and Treatment) (Scotland) Act 2003 (Modification of Subordinate Legislation) Order 2005 (SSI 2005/445) Sch.1 para.29(1)(b) (effective October 5, 2005).

### Notice to the Public Guardian

**3.24.4.** The sheriff clerk shall within 7 days after the date of an order registering an international measure, provide the Public Guardian with—

(a) a copy of that order; and

(b) a copy of the international measure, and of any translation.

### Register of recognised foreign measures

**3.24.5.**—(1) There shall be a register of international measures ("the register") registered by order under this Part.

(2) The register shall include—

(a) the nature of the international measure;

(b) the date of the international measure;

(c) the date of the order under this Part granting recognition of the international measure;

(d) the name and address of—

    (i) the person who applied for recognition of the international measure under this Part;

    (ii) the person in respect of whom the international measure was taken; and

    (iii) if applicable, the person on whom any power is conferred by the international measure; and

(e) a copy of the international measure, and of any translation.

(3) The Public Guardian shall maintain the register, and make it available during normal office hours for inspection by members of the public.

(4) The Public Guardian shall if requested by any person certify that an international measure registered under this Part has been entered in the register.

Part XXV[1]

Sexual Offences Act 2003

### Interpretation

**3.25.1.** In this Part—

"the Act" means the Sexual Offences Act 2003;

"main application" has the same meaning as in section 109(1) of the Act,[2] and words and expressions used in this Part and in the Act shall have the meanings given in the Act.

---

[1] As inserted by the Act of Sederunt (Summary Applications, Statutory Applications and Appeals etc. Rules) Amendment (Sexual Offences Act 2003) 2004 (SSI 2004/222) r.2(2) (effective May 21, 2004).

[2] As inserted by the Act of Sederunt (Summary Applications, Statutory Applications and Appeals etc. Rules) Amendment (Protection of Children and Prevention of Sexual Offences (Scotland) Act 2005) 2005 (SSI 2005/473) r.2(2)(a) (effective October 7, 2005).

**Time limit for service of a notice under section 99(3)**

**3.25.2.** If the person in respect of whom a notification order is sought wishes to serve on the applicant a notice under section 99(3) of the Act, that person must do so no later than 3 working days before the hearing date for the application for the relevant notification order.

**Time limit for service of a notice under section 106(11)**

**3.25.3.** If the person in respect of whom a sexual offences prevention order is sought wishes to serve on the applicant a notice under section 106(11) of the Act, that person must do so no later than 3 working days before the hearing date for the application for the relevant sexual offences prevention order.

**Time limit for service of a notice under section 116(6)**

**3.25.4.** If the person in respect of whom a foreign travel order is sought wishes to serve on the applicant a notice under section 116(6) of the Act, that person must do so no later than 3 working days before the hearing date for the application for the relevant foreign travel order.

**Variation, renewal or discharge of SOPOs**

**3.25.5.**—[1](1) Where an application under section 108(1) of the Act for an order varying, renewing or discharging a sexual offences prevention order is made in a sheriff court other than the sheriff court in which the process relating to the sexual offences prevention order is held—

(a) the initial writ containing the application shall contain averments as to the sheriff court in which the process relating to the sexual offences prevention order is held;

(b) the sheriff clerk with whom the application is lodged shall notify the sheriff clerk of the sheriff court in which the process relating to the sexual offences prevention order is held; and

(c) the sheriff clerk of the sheriff court in which the process relating to the sexual offences prevention order is held shall, not later than 4 days after receipt of such notification, transfer the process relating to the sexual offences prevention order to the sheriff clerk of the sheriff court in which the application is made.

(2) For the purposes of paragraph (1), the sheriff court in which the process relating to the order is held is the sheriff court in which the sexual offences prevention order was granted or, where the process has been transferred under that paragraph, the last sheriff court to which the process has been transferred.

(3) A failure of the sheriff clerk to comply with paragraph (1) shall not invalidate the application.

---

[1] As substituted by the Act of Sederunt (Summary Applications, Statutory Applications and Appeals etc. Rules) Amendment (Protection of Children and Prevention of Sexual Offences (Scotland) Act 2005) 2005 (SSI 2005/473) r.2(2)(b) (effective October 7, 2005).

**Variation, renewal or discharge of FTOs**

**3.25.6.**—[1](1)   Subject to paragraph (2), an application under section 118 of the Act for an order varying, renewing or discharging a foreign travel order shall be made by minute in the process relating to the foreign travel order.

(2)   Where an application under section 118(1) of the Act for an order varying, renewing or discharging a foreign travel order is made in a sheriff court other than the sheriff court in which the process relating to the foreign travel order is held—

    (a)   the application shall be made by summary application;

    (b)   the initial writ containing the application shall contain averments as to the sheriff court in which the process relating to the foreign travel order is held;

    (c)   the sheriff clerk with whom the application is lodged shall notify the sheriff clerk of the sheriff court in which the process relating to the foreign travel order is held; and

    (d)   the sheriff clerk of the sheriff court in which the process relating to the foreign travel order is held shall, not later than 4 days after receipt of such notification, transfer the process relating to the foreign travel order to the sheriff clerk of the sheriff court in which the application is made.

(3)   For the purposes of paragraph (2), the sheriff court in which the process relating to the foreign travel order is held is the sheriff court in which the foreign travel order was granted or, where the process has been transferred under that paragraph, the last sheriff court to which the process has been transferred.

(4)   A minute under paragraph (1) shall be made in accordance with and regulated by Chapter 14 of the Ordinary Cause Rules.

(5)   A failure of the sheriff clerk to comply with paragraph (2) shall not invalidate the application.

**Interim SOPOs**

**3.25.7.**—[2](1)   Subject to paragraph (2), an application under section 109(2) of the Act for an interim sexual offences prevention order shall—

    (a)   be made by crave in the initial writ containing the main application; and

    (b)   once craved, be moved by motion to that effect.

(2)   Where an application under section 109(2) of the Act for an interim sexual offences prevention order is made in a sheriff court other than the sheriff court in which the main application was lodged, the application for an interim sexual offences prevention order shall be made by summary application.

(3)   The initial writ in a summary application under paragraph (2) shall contain averments as to the sheriff court in which the main application was lodged.

(4)   On receipt of a summary application under paragraph (2), the sheriff clerk shall notify the sheriff clerk of the sheriff court in which the main application was lodged.

---

[1] As substituted by the Act of Sederunt (Summary Applications, Statutory Applications and Appeals etc. Rules) Amendment (Protection of Children and Prevention of Sexual Offences (Scotland) Act 2005) 2005 (SSI 2005/473) r.2(2)(b) (effective October 7, 2005).

[2] As inserted by the Act of Sederunt (Summary Applications, Statutory Applications and Appeals etc. Rules) Amendment (Protection of Children and Prevention of Sexual Offences (Scotland) Act 2005) 2005 (SSI 2005/473) r.2(2)(b) (effective October 7, 2005).

(5)   There shall be produced with a summary application under paragraph (2) copies of the following documents, certified as correct by the applicant's solicitor or the sheriff clerk—

    (a)   the initial writ containing the main application;

    (b)   any answers to the main application; and

    (c)   any interlocutors pronounced in the main application.

(6)   The sheriff clerk shall send a certified copy of any interlocutor disposing of a summary application under paragraph (2) to the sheriff clerk of the sheriff court in which the main application was lodged.

(7)   A failure of the sheriff clerk to comply with paragraph (4) or (6) shall not invalidate the main application or the summary application under paragraph (2).

(8)   Paragraphs (3) to (7) shall apply to an application for the variation, renewal or discharge of an interim sexual offences prevention order subject to the following modifications—

    (a)   for references to a summary application under paragraph (2) there shall be substituted references to a summary application for the variation, renewal or discharge of an interim sexual offences prevention order;

    (b)   references to the main application shall include references to any application for an interim sexual offences prevention order and any previous application for the variation, renewal or discharge of such an order; and

    (c)   references to any interlocutors pronounced in the main application shall include any interlocutors pronounced in an application for an interim sexual offences prevention order or previous application for the variation, renewal or discharge of an interim sexual offences prevention order.".

## Part XXVI

## Protection of Children (Scotland) Act 2003

**3.26.1.—3.26.6**   *[Revoked by the Act of Sederunt (Rules of the Court of Session, Sheriff Appeal Court Rules and Sheriff Court Rules Amendment) (Sheriff Appeal Court) 2015 (SSI 2015/419) r.9(6) (effective 1 January 2016).]*

## Part XXVII[1]

## Antisocial Behaviour etc. (Scotland) Act 2004

### Interpretation

**3.27.1.**—(1)   In this Part—

    "the Act" means the Antisocial Behaviour etc. (Scotland) Act 2004;

    "ASBO" means an antisocial behaviour order under section 4(1) of the Act;

    "interim ASBO" means an interim ASBO under section 7(2) of the Act;

---

[1] As inserted by the Act of Sederunt (Summary Applications, Statutory Applications and Appeals etc. Rules) Amendment (Antisocial Behaviour etc. (Scotland) Act 2004) 2004 (SSI 2004/455) r.2(4) (effective January 31, 2005 in relation to the provisions specified in SSI 2004/455 r.1(2)(a); April 4, 2005 in relation to the provisions specified in SSI 2004/455 r.1(2)(b); November 15, 2005 in relation to the provisions specified in SSI 2004/455 r.1(2)(c); October 28, 2004 otherwise).

"parenting order" means a parenting order under section 13 or 102 of the Act; and

"the Principal Reporter" means the Principal Reporter appointed under section 127 of the Local Government etc. (Scotland) Act 1994.

(2)   Any reference to a section shall, unless the context otherwise requires, be a reference to a section of the Act.

## Applications for variation or revocation of ASBO s to be made by minute in the original process

**3.27.2.**—(1)   An application under section 5 (variation and revocation of antisocial behaviour orders) shall be made by minute in the original process of the application for the ASBO in relation to which the variation or revocation is sought.

(2)   Where the person subject to the ASBO is a child, a written statement containing the views of the Principal Reporter on the application referred to in rule 3.27.2(1) shall, where practicable, be lodged with that application.

## Application for an interim ASBO

**3.27.3.**—(1)   An application for an interim ASBO shall be made by crave in the initial writ in which an ASBO is sought.

(2)   An application for an interim ASBO once craved shall be moved by motion to that effect.

(3)   The sheriff shall not consider an application for an interim ASBO until after the initial writ has been intimated to the person in respect of whom that application is made and, where that person is a child, a written statement containing the views of the Principal Reporter on that application has been lodged.

## Notification of making etc. of ASBOs and interim ASBOs

**3.27.4.**   *[Repealed by the Act of Sederunt (Ordinary Cause and Summary Application Rules) Amendment (Miscellaneous) 2006 (SSI 2006/410) r.3(2) (effective August 18, 2006).]*

## Parenting orders

**3.27.5.**—(1)   Where a sheriff is considering making a parenting order under section 13 (sheriffs power to make parenting order), the sheriff shall order the applicant for the ASBO to—

    (a)   intimate to any parent in respect of whom the parenting order is being considered—

        (i)   that the court is considering making a parenting order in respect of that parent;

        (ii)   that if that parent wishes to oppose the making of such a parenting order, he or she may attend or be represented at the hearing at which the sheriff considers the making of the parenting order;

        (iii)   the place, date and time of the hearing set out in sub-paragraph (a)(ii) above; and

        (iv)   that if that parent fails to appear and is not represented at the hearing, a parenting order may be made in respect of the parent; and

    (b)   serve on any parent in respect of whom the parenting order is being considered a copy of the initial writ in which the ASBO is sought.

(2)   Any parent in respect of whom a parenting order under section 13 is being considered may be sisted as a party to the action on their own motion, on the motion of either party or by the sheriff of his own motion.

## Closure notice

**3.27.6.**—(1)   A closure notice served under section 27 (service etc.) shall be in the form of Form 25 and shall (in addition to the requirements set out in section 27(5))—

(a)   state that it has been authorised by a senior police officer;

(b)   specify the date, time and place of the hearing of the application for a closure order under section 28; and

(c)   state that any person living on or having control of, responsibility for or an interest in the premises to which the closure notice relates who wishes to oppose the application should attend or be represented.

(2)   Certification of service of a copy of the closure notice to all persons identified in accordance with section 27(2)(b) shall be in the form of Form 26.

## Application for closure orders

**3.27.7.**   An application to the sheriff for a closure order under section 28 shall be in the form of Form 27.

## Application for extension of closure orders

**3.27.8.**   An application to the sheriff for an extension of a closure order under section 32 shall be by minute in the form of Form 28 lodged in the original process of the application for the closure order in relation to which the extension is sought and shall be lodged not less than 21 days before the closure order to which it relates is due to expire.

## Application for revocation of closure order

**3.27.9.**   An application to the sheriff for revocation of a closure order under section 33 shall be by minute in the form of Form 29 lodged in the original process of the application for the closure order in relation to which the revocation is sought.

## Application for access to premises

**3.27.10.**   An application to the sheriff for an order for access to premises under section 34 shall be by minute in the form of Form 30 lodged in the original process of the application for the closure order in relation to which the access order is sought.

## Applications by summary application

**3.27.11.**   An application under section 35 (Reimbursement of expenditure), 63 (Appeal against graffiti removal notice) or 64 (Appeal against notice under section 61(4)) shall be by summary application.

**3.27.12.**   An application under section 71 (Failure to comply with notice: order as to rental income), 74 (Failure to comply with notice: management control order) or 97 (Appeals against notice under section 94) shall be by summary application.

**Revocation and suspension of order as to rental income**

**3.27.13.**   An application under section 73(2) for the revocation or suspension of
an order relating to rental income shall be by minute lodged in the original process
of the application for the order relating to rental income in relation to which the
order for revocation or suspension is sought.

**Revocation of management control order**

**3.27.14.**   An application under section 76(1) for the revocation of a management
control order shall be by minute lodged in the original process of the application for
the management control order in relation to which the order for revocation is sought.

**Review of parenting order**

**3.27.15.**—(1)   An application under section 105(1) for revocation or variation of
a parenting order shall be by minute lodged in the original process of the application
for the parenting order in relation to which the order for revocation or variation is
sought.

(2)   Where the court that made a parenting order makes an order under section
105(5) that court shall within 4 days transmit the original process relating to the
parenting order to the court specified in that order.

**Procedural requirements relating to parenting orders**

**3.27.16.**   Where the sheriff is considering making a parenting order, or a revocation or variation of a parenting order, and it is practicable, having regard to the age
and maturity of the child to—

   (a)   give the child an opportunity to indicate whether the child wishes to
         express views; and
   (b)   if the child so wishes, give the child an opportunity to express those
         views,

the sheriff shall order intimation in the form of Form 31 to the child in respect of
whom the order was or is proposed to be made.

**3.27.17.**   Where the sheriff is considering making a parenting order or revoking
or varying a parenting order and does not already have sufficient information about
the child, the sheriff shall order intimation in the form of Form 32 to the local authority for the area in which the child resides.

**Enforcement of local authorities' duties under section 71 of the Children
(Scotland) Act 1995**

**3.27.18.**   An application under section 71A(2) of the Children (Scotland) Act
1995 by the Principal Reporter shall be by summary application to the sheriff
principal of the Sheriffdom in which the principal office of the local authority is
situated.

Part XXVIII[1]

---

[1] As inserted by the Act of Sederunt (Summary Applications, Statutory Applications and Appeals, etc.
Rules) Amendment (Land Reform) (Scotland) Act 2005 (SSI 2005/61), r.2(2)(effective February 9,
2005).

## Interpretation

**3.28.1.** In this Part—

"the Act" means the Land Reform (Scotland) Act 2003.

## Public notice of appeal against section 14(2) remedial notice

**3.28.2.** Where an owner of land appeals by summary application undersection 14(4) of the Act against a notice served on him under section 14(2) of the Act, the owner must at the same time as, or as closely in time as practicable to, the lodging of the application, advertise by publication of an advertisement in a newspaper circulating in the area of the land details of the application including details of the notice appealed against.

## Restriction on number of persons being party to section 14(4) application

**3.28.3.** Persons interested in the exercise of access rights over the land to which a summary application under section 14(2) of the Act relates, and persons or bodies representative of such persons, may be parties to the summary application proceedings, but the court may order that any one or more of the persons or bodies who have the same interests and no others, may take an active part in the proceedings.

## Public notice and restriction on number of parties to section 15 application

**3.28.4.** The provisions in rules 3.28.2 and 3.28.3 above apply with necessary modifications to a summary application appealing against a notice served under section 15(2) of the Act.

## Public notice and restriction on number of parties to section 28 application

**3.28.5.**—(1) The provisions in rules 3.28.2 and 3.28.3 above apply with necessary modifications to a summary application for a declaration under section 28(1) or (2) of the Act.

(2) A summary application under section 28(1) or (2) of the Act may be made at any time.

### Part XXIX[1]

### Risk of Sexual Harm Orders

## Interpretation

**3.29.1.** In this Part

"the Act" means the Protection of Children and Prevention of Sexual Offences (Scotland) Act 2005[5];

"main application" has the same meaning as in section 5 of the Act,

---

[1] As inserted by Act of Sederunt (Summary Applications, Statutory Applications and Appeals etc. Rules) Amendment (Protection of Children and Prevention of Sexual Offences (Scotland) Act 2005) 2005 (SSI 2005/473) r.2(3) (effective October 7, 2005).

and words and expressions used in this Part and in the Act shall have the meanings given in the Act.

### Variation, renewal or discharge of RSHOs

**3.29.2.**—(1)  Subject to paragraph (2), an application under section 4(1) of the Act for an order varying, renewing or discharging a risk of sexual harm order shall be made by minute in the process relating to the risk of sexual harm order.

(2)  Where an application under section 4(1) of the Act for an order varying, renewing or discharging a risk of sexual harm order is made in a sheriff court other than the sheriff court in which the process relating to the risk of sexual harm order is held—

    (a)  the application shall be made by summary application;

    (b)  the initial writ containing the application shall contain averments as to the sheriff court in which the process relating to the risk of sexual harm order is held;

    (c)  the sheriff clerk with whom the application is lodged shall notify the sheriff clerk of the sheriff court in which the process relating to the risk of sexual harm order is held; and

    (d)  the sheriff clerk of the sheriff court in which the process relating to the risk of sexual harm order is held shall, not later than 4 days after receipt of such notification, transfer the process relating to the risk of sexual harm order to the sheriff clerk of the sheriff court in which the application is made.

(3)  For the purposes of paragraph (2), the sheriff court in which the process relating to the risk of sexual harm order is held is the sheriff court in which the risk of sexual harm order was granted or, where the process has been transferred under that paragraph, the last sheriff court to which the process has been transferred.

(4)  A minute under paragraph (1) shall be made in accordance with and regulated by Chapter 14 of the Ordinary Cause Rules.

(5)  A failure of the sheriff clerk to comply with paragraph (2) shall not invalidate the application.

### Interim RSHOs

**3.29.3.**—(1)  Subject to paragraph (2), an application under section 5(2) of the Act for an interim risk of sexual harm order shall—

    (a)  be made by crave in the initial writ containing the main application; and

    (b)  once craved, be moved by motion to that effect.

(2)  Where an application under section 5(2) of the Act for an interim risk of sexual harm order is made in a sheriff court other than the sheriff court in which the main application was lodged, the application for an interim risk of sexual harm order shall be made by summary application.

(3)  The initial writ in a summary application under paragraph (2) shall contain averments as to the sheriff court in which the main application was lodged.

(4)  On receipt of a summary application under paragraph (2), the sheriff clerk shall notify the sheriff clerk of the sheriff court in which the main application was lodged.

(5)  There shall be produced with a summary application under paragraph (2) copies of the following documents, certified as correct by the applicant's solicitor or the sheriff clerk:—

(a) the initial writ containing the main application;

(b) any answers to the main application; and

(c) any interlocutors pronounced in the main application.

(6) The sheriff clerk shall send a certified copy of any interlocutor disposing of a summary application under paragraph (2) to the sheriff clerk of the sheriff court in which the main application was lodged.

(7) Rule 3.29.2 (variation, renewal or discharge of RSHOs) shall apply to an application for an order under section 5(6) of the Act for variation, renewal or discharge of an interim risk of sexual harm order subject to the following modifications:—

(a) for references to section 4(1) of the Act there shall be substituted references to section 5(6) of the Act; and

(b) for references to a risk of sexual harm order there shall be substituted references to an interim risk of sexual harm order.

(8) A failure of the sheriff clerk to comply with paragraph (4) or (6) shall not invalidate the main application or the summary application under paragraph (2).

## Service of RSHOs

**3.29.4.**—(1) This rule applies to—

(a) a risk of sexual harm order;

(b) an interim risk of sexual harm order; and

(c) an order varying or renewing an order mentioned in sub-paragraph (a) or (b).

(2)[1] The sheriff clerk shall serve a copy of the order on the person against whom it has effect.

(3)[2] For the purposes of paragraph (2), the copy of the order is served—

(a) where the person against whom the order has effect is present in court when the order is made—

(i) by giving it to the person and obtaining a receipt therefor;

(ii) by sending it to the person by recorded delivery or registered post; or

(iii) by causing it to be served by sheriff officer; or

(b) where the person against whom the order has effect is not present in court when the order is made—

(i) by sending it to the person by recorded delivery or registered post; or

(ii) by causing it to be served by sheriff officer.

(4) A failure by the sheriff clerk to comply with this rule shall not invalidate the order.

### Part XXX[3]

---

[1] As substituted by the Act of Sederunt (Ordinary Cause and Summary Application Rules) Amendment (Miscellaneous) 2006 (SSI 2006/410) r.3(3) (effective August 18, 2006).

[2] As substituted by the Act of Sederunt (Ordinary Cause and Summary Application Rules) Amendment (Miscellaneous) 2006 (SSI 2006/410) r.3(3) (effective August 18, 2006).

[3] As inserted by Act of Sederunt (Summary Applications, Statutory Applications and Appeals etc. Rules) Amendment (Mental Health (Care and Treatment) (Scotland) Act 2003) 2005 (SSI 2005/504) r.2(2) (effective October 6, 2005).

## Mental Health (Care and Treatment) (Scotland) Act 2003

### Interpretation

**3.30.1.** In this Part "the Act" means the Mental Health (Care and Treatment) (Scotland) Act 2003.

### Applications for removal orders

**3.30.2.**—(1) An application under section 293 of the Act (removal order to place of safety) shall be lodged with the sheriff clerk who shall fix a date for hearing the application.

(2) An order fixing a hearing shall be intimated in such manner and within such timescales as may be prescribed by the sheriff.

### Applications for recall or variation of removal orders

**3.30.3.**—(1) An application under section 295 of the Act (recall or variation of removal order) shall be lodged with the sheriff clerk who shall fix a date for hearing the application.

(2) An order fixing a hearing shall be intimated by the sheriff clerk in such manner and within such timescales as may be prescribed by the sheriff.

### Remit to Court of Session

**3.30.4.**—(1) Where the sheriff principal to whom an appeal is made remits the appeal to the Court of Session under section 320 of the Act (appeals), the sheriff clerk shall, within four days after the sheriff principal has pronounced the interlocutor remitting the appeal to the Court of Session, transmit the process to the Deputy Principal Clerk of Session.

(2) On transmitting the process under paragraph (1), the sheriff clerk shall—

    (a) send written notice of the remit and transmission of the process to each party; and

    (b) certify on the interlocutor sheet that he has done so.

Part XXXI[1]

**Football Banning Orders**

### Interpretation

**3.31.1.** In this Part—

"the Act" means the Police, Public Order and Criminal Justice (Scotland) Act 2006;

"football banning order" means an order made under section 52(4) of the Act.

### Applications for variation or termination of a football banning order

**3.31.2.**—(1) An application under—

    (a) section 57(1) of the Act for variation of a football banning order; or

---

[1] As inserted by the Act of Sederunt (Summary Applications, Statutory Applications and Appeals etc. (Rules) Amendment (Miscellaneous) 2006 (SSI 2006/437) r.2(2) (effective September 1, 2006).

(b) section 58(1) of the Act for termination of a football banning order,

shall be made by minute in the process relating to the football banning order.

(2) A minute under paragraph (1) shall be made in accordance with and regulated by Chapter 14 of the Ordinary Cause Rules.

## Part XXXII[1]

### Animal Health and Welfare

**Interpretation**

**3.32.1.** In this Part—

"the 1981 Act" means the Animal Health Act 1981; and

"the 2006 Act" means the Animal Health and Welfare (Scotland) Act 2006.

**Interim orders**

**3.32.2.**—(1) An application for an interim order under—

(a) section 28G(10) of the 1981 Act; or

(b) section 41(9) of the 2006 Act, or

(c)[2] section 48(9) of the Animal Welfare Act 2006,

shall be made by crave in the initial writ in which a seizure order is sought.

(2) An application for an interim order once craved shall be moved by motion to that effect.

**Interim orders pending appeal**

**3.32.3.** An application for an interim order under—

(a) section 28H(2) of the 1981 Act; or

(b) section 43(5) of the 2006 Act, or

(c)[3] section 49(5) of the Animal Welfare Act 2006,

where a seizure order is suspended or inexecutable shall be made by motion.

## Part XXXIII[4]

---

[1] As inserted by the Act of Sederunt (Summary Applications, Statutory Applications and Appeals etc. Rules) Amendment (Miscellaneous) 2006 (SSI 2006/437) r.2(2) (effective September 1, 2006).

[2] As inserted by the Act of Sederunt (Summary Applications, Statutory Applications and Appeals etc. Rules) Amendment (Animal Welfare Act 2006) 2007 (SSI 2007/233) r.2(2) (effective March 26, 2007).

[3] As inserted by the Act of Sederunt (Summary Applications, Statutory Applications and Appeals etc. Rules) Amendment (Animal Welfare Act 2006) 2007 (SSI 2007/233) r.2(3) (effective March 26, 2007).

[4] As inserted by the Act of Sederunt (Ordinary Cause, Summary Application, Summary Cause and Small Claim Rules) Amendment (Equality Act 2006 etc.) 2006 (SSI 2006/509), (effective November 3, 2006). Chapter title amended by the Act of Sederunt (Sheriff Court Rules) (Equality Act 2010) 2010 (SSI 2010/340) para.3 (effective October 1, 2010).

## The Equality Act 2010

### Interpretation and application

**3.33.1.**—[1](1)   In this Part—

"the Commission" means the Commission for Equality and Human Rights; and "the 2010 Act" means the Equality Act 2010.

(2)   This Part applies to claims made by virtue of section 114(1) of the 2010 Act not including a claim for damages.

### Intimation to Commission

**3.33.2.**[2]   The applicant shall, except where the applicant is the Commission, send a copy of the initial writ to the Commission by registered or recorded delivery post.

### Assessor

**3.33.3.**—(1)   The sheriff may, of his own motion or on the motion of any party, appoint an assessor.

(2)   The assessor shall be a person who the sheriff considers has special qualifications to be of assistance in determining the cause.

### Taxation of Commission expenses

**3.33.4.**   *[Omitted by the Act of Sederunt (Sheriff Court Rules) (Miscellaneous Amendments) 2008 (SSI 2008/223) r.5(3)(c) (effective July 1, 2008).]*

### National security

**3.33.5.**—[3](1)   Where, on a motion under paragraph (3) or of the sheriffs own motion, the sheriff considers it expedient in the interests of national security, the sheriff may—

  (a)   exclude from all or part of the proceedings—
   (i)   the pursuer;
   (ii)   the pursuer's representatives;
   (iii)   any assessors;
  (b)   permit a pursuer or representative who has been excluded to make a statement to the court before the commencement of the proceedings or the part of the proceedings, from which he or she is excluded;
  (c)   take steps to keep secret all or part of the reasons for his or her decision in the proceedings.

(2)   The sheriff clerk shall, on the making of an order under paragraph (1) excluding the pursuer or the pursuer's representatives, notify the Advocate General for Scotland of that order.

(3)   A party may apply by motion for an order under paragraph (1).

---

[1] As substituted by the Act of Sederunt (Sheriff Court Rules) (Equality Act 2010) 2010 (SSI 2010/340) para.3 (effective October 1, 2010).

[2] As inserted by the Act of Sederunt (Sheriff Court Rules) (Miscellaneous Amendments) 2008 (SSI 2008/223) r.5(3)(b) (effective July 1, 2008).

[3] As substituted by the Act of Sederunt (Sheriff Court Rules) (Equality Act 2010) 2010 (SSI 2010/340) para.3 (effective October 1, 2010).

(4)　The steps referred to in paragraph (1)(c) may include the following—

- (a)　directions to the sheriff clerk; and
- (b)　orders requiring any person appointed to represent the interests of the pursuer in proceedings from which the pursuer or the pursuer's representatives are excluded not to communicate (directly or indirectly) with any persons (including the excluded pursuer)—
  - (i)　on any matter discussed or referred to;
  - (ii)　with regard to any material disclosed,

during or with reference to any part of the proceedings from which the pursuer or the pursuer's representatives are excluded.

(5)　Where the sheriff has made an order under paragraph (4)(b), the person appointed to represent the interests of the pursuer may apply by motion for authority to seek instructions from or otherwise communicate with an excluded person.

## Transfer to Employment Tribunal

**3.33.6.**—[1](1)　On transferring proceedings to an employment tribunal under section 140(2) of the 2010 Act, the sheriff—

- (a)　shall state his or her reasons for doing so in the interlocutor; and
- (b)　may make the order on such conditions as to expenses or otherwise as he or she thinks fit.

(2)　The sheriff clerk must, within 7 days from the date of such order—

- (a)　transmit the relevant process to the Secretary of the Employment Tribunals (Scotland);
- (b)　notify each party to the proceedings in writing of the transmission under subparagraph (a); and
- (c)　certify, by making an appropriate entry on the interlocutor sheet, that he or she has made all notifications required under subparagraph (b).

(3)　Transmission of the process under paragraph (2)(a) will be valid notwithstanding any failure by the sheriff clerk to comply with paragraph (2)(b) and (c).

## Transfer from Employment Tribunal

**3.33.7.**—[2](1)　On receipt of the documentation in proceedings which have been remitted from an employment tribunal under section 140(3) of the 2010 Act, the sheriff clerk must—

- (a)　record the date of receipt on the first page of the documentation;
- (b)　fix a hearing to determine further procedure not less than 14 days after the date of receipt of the process; and
- (c)　forthwith send written notice of the date of the hearing fixed under subparagraph (b) to each party.

(2)　At the hearing fixed under paragraph (1)(b) the sheriff may make such order as he or she thinks fit to secure so far as practicable that the cause thereafter proceeds in accordance with these Rules.

### Part XXXIV[3]

---

[1] As inserted by the Act of Sederunt (Sheriff Court Rules) (Equality Act 2010) 2010 (SSI 2010/340) para.3 (effective October 1, 2010).
[2] As inserted by the Act of Sederunt (Sheriff Court Rules) (Equality Act 2010) 2010 (SSI 2010/340) para.3 (effective October 1, 2010).
[3] As inserted by the Act of Sederunt (Summary Applications, Statutory Applications and Appeals etc. Rules) Amendment (Licensing (Scotland) Act 2005) 2008 (SSI 2008/9) r.2(2) (effective February 1,

## Licensing (Scotland) Act 2005

### Appeals

**3.34.**—(1)  An appeal under section 131 of the Licensing (Scotland) Act 2005 is to be made by summary application.

(2)  An application under paragraph (1) must be lodged with the sheriff clerk of the sheriff court district in which the principal office of the Licensing Board is situated not later than 21 days after the relevant date.

(3)  In paragraph (2) "relevant date" means—

(a)  the date of the decision of the Licensing Board; or

(b)  where a statement of reasons has been required under section 51(2) of the 2005 Act, the date of issue of the statement of reasons.

## Part XXXV[1]

## Adult Support and Protection (Scotland) Act 2007

### Interpretation

**3.35.1.**  In this Part—

"the Act" means the Adult Support and Protection (Scotland) Act 2007;
"the adult at risk" has the same meaning as in section 3 of the Act.

### Variation or recall of removal order

**3.35.2.**—(1)  An application under section 17 of the Act (variation or recall of removal order) for variation or recall of a removal order shall be made by minute in the process relating to the removal order.

(2)  A minute under paragraph (1) shall be made in accordance with and regulated by Chapter 14 of the Ordinary Cause Rules.

### Applications—banning orders and temporary banning orders

**3.35.3.**—(1)  Where in an application under subsection (1) of section 19 of the Act (banning orders) an order is sought under subsection (2)(a) or (b) of that section there shall, where appropriate and unless the sheriff otherwise directs, be lodged a plan which clearly identifies the area specified in the application.

(2)  An application under section 21 of the Act (temporary banning orders) shall—

(a)  be made by crave in the application for the banning order concerned; and

(b)  once craved, be moved by motion to that effect.

(3)  Where a temporary banning order is granted, the related application for a banning order shall be determined within 6 months of the date of the lodging of that application.

---

2008) and substituted by the Act of Sederunt (Sheriff Court Rules) (Miscellaneous Amendments) (No.2) 2010 (SSI 2010/416) r.9 (effective December 13, 2010).

[1] As inserted by the Act of Sederunt (Summary Applications, Statutory Applications and Appeals etc. Rules) Amendment (Adult Support and Protection (Scotland) Act 2007) (No.2) 2008 (SSI 2008/335) r.2(2) (effective October 29, 2008).

(4)   An application under section 24(1)(a) of the Act (variation or recall of banning order) shall be made by minute in the process relating to the banning order.

(5)   An application under section 24(1)(b) of the Act (variation or recall of temporary banning order) shall be moved by motion to that effect in the process relating to the application for the banning order concerned.

(6)   A minute under paragraph (4) shall be made in accordance with and regulated by Chapter 14 of the Ordinary Cause Rules.

**Attachment of power of arrest**

**3.35.4.**—(1)   The following documents shall be served under section 25(2) of the Act (powers of arrest) along with a power of arrest—

    (a)   a copy of the application for the order;

    (b)   a copy of the interlocutor granting the order and the power of arrest; and

    (c)   where the application to attach the power of arrest was made after the order was granted, a copy of the certificate of service of the order.

(2)   The following documents shall be delivered to the chief constable in accordance with section 27(1) of the Act (notification to police)—

    (a)   a copy of the application for the order;

    (b)   a copy of the interlocutor granting the order;

    (c)   a copy of the certificate of service of the order; and

    (d)   where the application to attach the power of arrest was made after the order was granted—

        (i)   where applicable, a copy of the application for the power of arrest;

        (ii)   a copy of the interlocutor granting it; and

        (iii)   a copy of the certificate of service of the power of arrest and the documents that required to be served along with it in accordance with section 25(2).

(3)   *[Revoked by the Act of Sederunt (Summary Applications, Statutory Applications and Appeals etc. Rules) Amendment (Adult Support and Protection (Scotland) Act 2007) (No.3) 2008 (SSI 2008/375) r.2(2) (effective November 20, 2008).]*

**Notification to adult at risk etc.**

**3.35.5.**[1]   Where section 26(1)(b) of the Act (notification to the adult at risk etc. on the variation or recall of a banning order or temporary banning order) applies, the person prescribed for the purposes of section 26(2) is the sheriff clerk.

**Certificate of delivery of documents**

**3.35.6.**[2]   Where a person is in any circumstances required to comply with section 26(2), 27(1) or 27(2) of the Act he shall, after such compliance, lodge in process a certificate of delivery in Form 34.

---

[1] As substituted by the Act of Sederunt (Summary Applications, Statutory Applications and Appeals etc. Rules) Amendment (Adult Support and Protection (Scotland) Act 2007) (No.3) 2008 (SSI 2008/375) r.2(3) (effective November 20, 2008).

[2] As substituted by the Act of Sederunt (Summary Applications, Statutory Applications and Appeals etc. Rules) Amendment (Adult Support and Protection (Scotland) Act 2007) (No.3) 2008 (SSI 2008/375) r.2(4) (effective November 20, 2008).

### Warrants for entry

**3.35.7.**—(1)  An application for a warrant for entry under section 38(2) of the Act (criteria for granting warrants of entry under section 7) shall be in Form 35.

(2)  The application may be granted without a hearing.

### Applications for leave to appeal to the Sheriff Appeal Court

**3.35.8.**—(1)  *[Omitted by the Act of Sederunt (Rules of the Court of Session, Sheriff Appeal Court Rules and Sheriff Court Rules Amendment) (Sheriff Appeal Court) 2015 (SSI 2015/419) r.9(7) (effective 1 January 2016; as to savings see SSI 2015/419 rule 20(5)(a)).]*

(2)  An application for leave to appeal against an interlocutor of the sheriff granting, or refusing to grant, a temporary banning order under section 51(2) of the Act shall be made within 7 days after the date of the interlocutor concerned.

(3)  *[Omitted by the Act of Sederunt (Rules of the Court of Session, Sheriff Appeal Court Rules and Sheriff Court Rules Amendment) (Sheriff Appeal Court) 2015 (SSI 2015/419) r.9(7) (effective 1 January 2016; as to savings see SSI 2015/419 rule 20(5)(a)).]*

### Privacy of any hearing

**3.35.9.**  The sheriff may, where he considers it appropriate in all the circumstances, appoint that the hearing of an application or other proceedings under this Part shall take place in private.

## Part XXXVI[1]

## UK Borders Act 2007

### Interpretation

**3.36.1.**  In this Part—

"the Act" means the UK Borders Act 2007; and

"an appeal" means an appeal to the sheriff under section 11(1) of the Act.

### Appeals

**3.36.2.**—(1)  Subject to paragraph (2), an appeal must be lodged with the sheriff clerk not later than 21 days after the date the penalty notice was received by the appellant.

(2)  Where the appellant has given notice of objection under section 10(1) of the Act, an appeal must be lodged with the sheriff clerk not later than 21 days after the date that notice of the Secretary of State's decision under section 10(4) of the Act was received by the appellant.

## Part XXXVII[2]

---

[1] As inserted by the Act of Sederunt (Sheriff Court Rules) (Miscellaneous Amendments) (No.2) 2008 (SSI 2008/365) r.6 (effective November 25, 2006).

[2] As inserted by the Act of Sederunt (Summary Applications, Statutory Applications and Appeals etc. Rules) Amendment (Employment Tribunals Act 1996) 2009 (SSI 2009/109) r.2 (effective April 1, 2009).

### Conciliation: recovery of sums payable under compromises

**3.37.1.**—(1)  An application to the sheriff for a declaration under section 19A(4) of the Employment Tribunals Act 1996 shall be made not later than 42 days from the date of issue of the certificate stating that a compromise has been reached.

(2)  An application to the sheriff for a declaration under section 19A(4) of that Act is pending for the purposes of subsection (7) of that section from the date on which it is lodged with the sheriff clerk until the date upon which final judgment on the application has been extracted.

Part XXXVIII[1]

## Counter-Terrorism Act 2008

### Variation, renewal or discharge of foreign travel restriction order

**3.38.**—(1)  Where an application under paragraph 9 of Schedule 5 to the Counter-Terrorism Act 2008 for an order varying, renewing or discharging a foreign travel restriction order is made in a sheriff court other than the sheriff court in which the process relating to the foreign travel restriction order is held—

    (a)  the initial writ containing the application shall contain averments as to the sheriff court in which the process relating to the foreign travel restriction order is held;

    (b)  the sheriff clerk with whom the application is lodged shall notify the sheriff clerk of the sheriff court in which the process relating to the foreign travel restriction order is held; and

    (c)  the sheriff clerk of the sheriff court in which the process relating to the foreign travel restriction order is held shall, not later than 4 days after receipt of such notification, transfer the process relating to the foreign travel restriction order to the sheriff clerk of the sheriff court in which the application is made.

(2)  For the purposes of paragraph (1), the sheriff court in which the process relating to the order is held is the sheriff court in which the foreign travel restriction order was granted or, where the process has been transferred under that paragraph, the last sheriff court to which the process has been transferred.

(3)  A failure of the sheriff clerk to comply with paragraph (1) shall not invalidate the application.

Part XXXIX[2]

---

[1] As inserted by the Act of Sederunt (Sheriff Court Rules) (Miscellaneous Amendments) 2009 (SSI 2009/294) r.18 (effective October 1, 2009).

[2] As inserted by the Act of Sederunt (Summary Applications, Statutory Applications and Appeals etc. Rules) Amendment (Public Health etc. (Scotland) Act 2008) 2009 (SSI 2009/320) r.2 (effective October 1, 2009).

## Public Health etc. (Scotland) Act 2008

### Interpretation

**3.39.1.**   In this Part—

"the Act" means the Public Health etc. (Scotland) Act 2008;

"an investigator" means a person appointed under section 21 of the Act;

"health board competent person" has the same meaning as in section 124 of the Act, and words and expressions used in this Part and in the Act shall have the same meaning given in the Act.

### Application for a public health investigation warrant

**3.39.2.**—(1)   An application made by an investigator for a warrant under section 27(2) of the Act (public health investigation warrants) shall be in Form 36.

(2)   Where such a warrant is granted by the sheriff it shall be in Form 37.

### Application for an order for medical examination

**3.39.3.**—(1)   An application made by a health board for an order under section 34(1) of the Act (order for medical examination) shall be in Form 38.

(2)   On receipt of an application mentioned in paragraph (1), the sheriff may order intimation of the application to such persons, within such a timescale and by such method as he sees fit.

(3)   Where an order for a medical examination is granted by the sheriff it shall be in Form 39.

(4)   Subject to the requirements of section 34(6)(b)(i) and (ii) of the Act, where an order for a medical examination is granted, the sheriff may direct that the order be notified to such persons, within such a timescale and by such method as he sees fit.

(5)   For the avoidance of doubt, the method of intimation or notification referred to in paragraphs (2) and (4) may include intimation or notification by telephone, email or facsimile transmission.

### Application for a quarantine order

**3.39.4.**—(1)   An application made by a health board for a quarantine order under section 40(1) of the Act (quarantine orders) shall be in Form 40.

(2)   On receipt of an application mentioned in paragraph (1), the sheriff may order intimation of the application to such persons, within such a timescale and by such method as he sees fit.

(3)   Where a quarantine order is granted by the sheriff it shall be in Form 41.

(4)   Subject to the requirements of section 40(6)(b)(i) and (ii) of the Act, where a quarantine order is granted, the sheriff may direct that the order be notified to such persons, within such a timescale and by such method as he sees fit.

(5)   For the avoidance of doubt, the method of intimation or notification referred to in paragraphs (2) and (4) may include intimation or notification by telephone, email or facsimile transmission.

### Application for a short term detention order

**3.39.5.**—(1)   An application made by a health board for a short term detention order under section 42(1) of the Act (order for removal to and detention in hospital) shall be in Form 42.

(2)   An application made by a health board for a short term detention order under section 43(1) of the Act (order for detention in hospital) shall be in Form 44.

(3)   On receipt of an application mentioned in paragraph (1) or (2), the sheriff may order intimation of the application to such persons, within such a timescale and by such method as he sees fit.

(4)   Where a short term detention order is granted by the sheriff under section 42(1) of the Act it shall be in Form 43.

(5)   Where a short term detention order is granted by the sheriff under section 43(1) of the Act it shall be in Form 45.

(6)   Subject to the requirements of sections 42(4)(b)(i) and (ii) and 43(4)(b)(i) and (ii) of the Act, where a short term detention order is granted under section 42(1) or 43(1) of the Act, the sheriff may direct that the order be notified to such persons, within such a timescale and by such method as he sees fit.

(7)   For the avoidance of doubt, the method of intimation or notification referred to in paragraphs (3) and (6) may include intimation or notification by telephone, email or facsimile transmission.

### Application for an exceptional detention order

**3.39.6.**—(1)   An application made by a health board for an exceptional detention order under section 45(1) of the Act (exceptional detention order) shall be in Form 46.

(2)   On receipt of an application mentioned in paragraph (1), the sheriff may order intimation of the application to such persons, within such a timescale and by such method as he sees fit.

(3)   Where an exceptional detention order is granted by the sheriff it shall be in Form 47.

(4)   Subject to the requirements of section 45(4)(b)(i) and (ii) of the Act, where an exceptional detention order is granted, the sheriff may direct that the order be notified to such persons, within such a timescale and by such method as he sees fit.

(5)   For the avoidance of doubt, the method of intimation or notification referred to in paragraphs (2) and (4) may include intimation or notification by telephone, email or facsimile transmission.

### Application for extension of a quarantine order, short term detention order or exceptional detention order

**3.39.7.**—(1)   An application made by a health board for an extension to a quarantine order, a short term detention order or an exceptional detention order under section 49(5) of the Act (extension of quarantine and hospital detention orders) shall be in Form 48.

(2)   On receipt of an application mentioned in paragraph (1), the sheriff may order intimation of the application to such persons, within such a timescale and by such method as he sees fit.

(3)   Where an order extending a quarantine order, a short term detention order or an exceptional detention order is granted by the sheriff it shall be in Form 49.

(4)   Subject to the requirements of section 49(10)(b)(i) and (ii) of the Act, where an order mentioned in paragraph (3) is granted, the sheriff may direct that the order be notified to such persons, within such a timescale and by such method as he sees fit.

(5)   For the avoidance of doubt, the method of intimation or notification referred to in paragraphs (2) and (4) may include intimation or notification by telephone, email or facsimile transmission.

### Application for modification of a quarantine order, short term detention order or exceptional detention order

**3.39.8.**—(1)   An application made by a health board for an order modifying a quarantine order, a short term detention order or an exceptional detention order under section 51(1) of the Act (variation of quarantine and hospital detention orders) shall be in Form 50.

(2)   On receipt of an application mentioned in paragraph (1), the sheriff may order intimation of the application to such persons, within such a timescale and by such method as he sees fit.

(3)   Where an order modifying a quarantine order, a short term detention order or an exceptional detention order is granted by the sheriff it shall be in Form 51.

(4)   Subject to the requirements of section 51(5)(b)(i) and (ii) of the Act, where an order mentioned in paragraph (3) is granted, the sheriff may direct that the order be notified to such persons, within such a timescale and by such method as he sees fit.

(5)   For the avoidance of doubt, the method of intimation or notification referred to in paragraphs (2) and (4) may include intimation or notification by telephone, email or facsimile transmission.

### Application for recall of an order granted in the absence of the person to whom it relates

**3.39.9.**—(1)   An application for recall of a quarantine order, a short term detention order or an exceptional detention order under section 59 of the Act (recall of orders granted in absence of persons to whom application relates) shall be in Form 52.

(2)   Subject to section 59(6) of the Act, on receipt of an application mentioned in paragraph (1), the sheriff may order intimation of the application to such persons, within such a timescale and by such method as he sees fit.

(3)   Where an order recalling a quarantine order, a short term detention order or an exceptional detention order is granted by the sheriff it shall be in Form 53.

(4)   Where an order mentioned in paragraph (3) is granted, the sheriff may direct that the order be notified to such persons, within such a timescale and by such method as he sees fit.

(5)   For the avoidance of doubt, the method of intimation or notification referred to in paragraphs (2) and (4) may include intimation or notification by telephone, email or facsimile transmission.

### Intimation of applications in relation to a child

**3.39.10.**—(1)   This rule applies where an application is made under this Part and the person who it is proposed will be subject to the order is under 16.

(2)   On receipt of an application mentioned in paragraph (1), the sheriff may, in particular, order intimation of the application to a person who has day-to-day care or control of the person mentioned in paragraph (1).

### Intimation of orders on the person to whom they apply

**3.39.11.**   Where a sheriff, in the absence of the person to whom it applies, grants—

    (a)   a quarantine order under section 40(1) of the Act;

    (b)   a short term detention order under section 42(1) of the Act;

    (c)   an exceptional detention order under section 45 of the Act,

and the order is intimated to the person to whom it applies, a copy of Form 52 shall be delivered to that person along with the order.

### Appeal to the sheriff against an exclusion order or a restriction order

**3.39.12.**—(1)   An appeal to the sheriff under section 61 of the Act (appeal against exclusion orders and restriction orders) in respect of an exclusion order or a restriction order shall be marked by lodging a note of appeal in Form 54.

(2)   On the lodging of a note of appeal, the sheriff clerk shall send a copy of the note of appeal to—

    (a)   the health board competent person who made the exclusion order or restriction order; and

    (b)   the person in relation to whom the order applies, where that person is not the appellant.

(3)   The sheriff shall make such order as he thinks fit in order to dispose of the appeal.

### Application for a warrant to enter premises and take steps under Part 5 of the Act

**3.39.13.**—(1)   An application made by a local authority for a warrant under section 78(2) of the Act (warrant to enter and take steps) shall be in Form 55.

(2)   Where such a warrant is granted by the sheriff it shall be in Form 56.

### Application for an order for disposal of a body

**3.39.14.**—(1)   An application made by a local authority for an order for the disposal of a body under section 93 of the Act (power of sheriff to order removal to mortuary and disposal) shall be in Form 57.

(2)   Where such an order is granted by the sheriff it shall be in Form 58.

### Application for appointment of a single arbiter to determine a dispute in relation to compensation

**3.39.15.**   An application under sections 30(6), 56(5), 57(3), 58(4) or 82(3) of the Act for the appointment of a single arbiter to determine a dispute in relation to compensation may be made by written application in the form of a letter addressed to the sheriff clerk.

Part XL[1]

## Forced Marriage etc. (Protection and Jurisdiction) (Scotland) Act 2011

### Interpretation

**3.40.1.** In this Part (except where the context otherwise requires) references to terms defined in Part 1 of the Forced Marriage etc. (Protection and Jurisdiction) (Scotland) Act 2011 have the same meaning here as given there.

### Applications for leave for a forced marriage protection order

**3.40.2.**—(1) This rule applies where leave of the court is required to make an application for a forced marriage protection order.

(2) Leave shall be sought at the time of presenting the initial writ by letter addressed to the sheriff clerk.

(3) The letter shall include a statement of—

(a) the grounds on which leave is sought;

(b) whether or not the applicant has applied for legal aid.

(4) Where the applicant has applied for legal aid he or she must also present along with the initial writ written confirmation from the Scottish Legal Aid Board that it has determined, under regulation 7(2)(b) of the Civil Legal Aid (Scotland) Regulations 2002, that notification of the application should be dispensed with or postponed.

(5) An application under paragraph (2) shall not be served or intimated unless the sheriff otherwise directs.

(6) The sheriff may hear the pursuer on the application and may grant or refuse it or make such other order in relation to it as the sheriff considers appropriate.

(7) Where leave is granted, a copy of the interlocutor allowing leave must be served upon the defender along with the warrant of citation.

### Applications for variation, recall or extension of a forced marriage protection order

**3.40.3.**—(1) An application for variation, recall or extension of a forced marriage protection order must be made by minute in the process relating to the forced marriage protection order.

(2) Except where the sheriff otherwise directs, any such minute must be lodged in accordance with, and regulated by, Chapter 14 of the Ordinary Cause Rules.

(3) Paragraph (4) applies where leave of the court is required under section 7(1)(d) or 8(3)(d) of the 2011 Act before an application for variation, or recall or extension of a forced marriage protection order may be made.

(4) Leave shall be sought at the time of presenting the minute by letter addressed to the sheriff clerk.

(5) The letter shall include a statement of—

(a) the grounds on which leave is sought;

(b) whether or not the applicant has applied for legal aid.

(6) Where the applicant has applied for legal aid he or she must also present along with the minute confirmation from the Scottish Legal Aid Board that it has

---

[1] As inserted by the Act of Sederunt (Sheriff Court Rules) (Miscellaneous Amendments) (No.3) 2011 (SSI 2011/386) para.7 (effective November 28, 2011).

determined, under regulation 7(2)(b) of the Civil Legal Aid (Scotland) Regulations 2002, that notification of the application should be dispensed with or postponed.

(7) An application under paragraph (4) shall not be served or intimated unless the sheriff otherwise directs.

(8) The sheriff may hear the applicant on the application and may grant or refuse it or make such other order in relation to it as the sheriff considers appropriate.

(9) Where leave is granted, a copy of the interlocutor allowing leave must be intimated along with the minute.

## PART XLI[1, 2 3]

### REPORTING RESTRICTIONS

**Interpretation and application of this Part**

**3.41.1.**(1)
This Part applies to orders which restrict the reporting of proceedings.

(2) In this Part, "interested person" means a person—

(a)who has asked to see any order made by the sheriff which restricts the reporting of proceedings, including an interim order; and

(b)whose name is included on a list kept by the Lord President for the purposes of this Part.

**Interim orders: notification to interested persons**

**3.41.2.**—(1) Where the sheriff is considering making an order, the sheriff may make an interim order.

(2) Where the sheriff makes an interim order, the sheriff clerk shall immediately send a copy of the interim order to any interested person.

(3) The sheriff shall specify in the interim order why the sheriff is considering making an order.

**Interim orders: representations**

**3.41.3.**—(1) Paragraph (2) applies where the sheriff has made an interim order.

(2) An interested person who would be directly affected by the making of an order shall have an opportunity to make representations to the sheriff before an order is made.

(3) Representations shall—

(a)be made by letter addressed to the sheriff clerk;

(b)where an urgent hearing is sought, include reasons explaining why an urgent hearing is necessary;

(c)be lodged no later than 2 days after the interim order is sent to interested persons in accordance with rule 3.41.2(2).

---

[1] As inserted by the Act of Sederunt (Sheriff Court Rules) (Miscellaneous Amendments) (No.3) 2011 (SSI 2011/386) para.8 (effective November 28, 2011).

[2] As amended by the Act of Sederunt (Sheriff Court Rules) (Miscellaneous Amendments) 2012 (SSI 2012/188) para.12 (effective August 1, 2012).

[3] As substituted by the Act of Sederunt (Rules of the Court of Session and Sheriff Court Rules Amendment No.3) (Reporting Restrictions) 2015 (SSI 2015/85) para.4 (effective April 1, 2015).

(4)   Where the period for lodging representations expires on a Saturday, Sunday, or public or court holiday, it shall be deemed to expire on the next day on which the sheriff clerk's office is open for civil court business.

(5)   On representations being made—
(a)the sheriff shall appoint a date and time for a hearing—
    (i)   on the first suitable court day thereafter; or
    (ii)  where the sheriff is satisfied that an urgent hearing is necessary, at such earlier date and time as the sheriff may determine;
(b)the sheriff clerk shall—
    (i)   notify the date and time of the hearing to the parties to the proceedings and the person who has made representations; and
    (ii)  send a copy of the representations to the parties to the proceedings.

(6)   Where no interested person makes representations in accordance with rule 3.41.3(2), the sheriff clerk shall put the interim order before the sheriff in chambers in order that the sheriff may resume consideration as to whether to make an order.

(7)   Where the sheriff, having resumed consideration under rule 3.41.3(6), makes no order, the sheriff shall recall the interim order.

(8)   Where the court recalls an interim order, the clerk of court shall immediately notify any interested person.

### Notification of reporting restrictions

Where the sheriff makes an order, the sheriff clerk shall immediately—
(a)send a copy of the order to any interested person;
(b)arrange for the publication of the making of the order on the Scottish Court Service website.

### Applications for variation or revocation

**3.41.5.**—(1)   A person aggrieved by an order may apply to the sheriff for its variation or revocation.

(2)   An application shall be made by letter addressed to the sheriff clerk.

(3)   On an application being made—
(a)the sheriff shall appoint the application for a hearing;
(b)the sheriff clerk shall—
    (i)   notify the date and time of the hearing to the parties to the proceedings and the applicant;
    (ii)  send a copy of the application to the parties to the proceedings.

(4)   The hearing shall, so far as reasonably practicable, be before the sheriff who made the order.

Part XLII[1]

Regulation of Investigatory Powers Act 2000

### Interpretation

**3.42.1.**   In this Part—

---

[1] As inserted by the Act of Sederunt (Sheriff Court Rules) (Miscellaneous Amendments) (No.3) 2012 (SSI 2012/271) para.10 (effective November 1, 2012).

"the 2000 Act" means the Regulation of Investigatory Powers Act 2000; and words and expressions used in this Part and in the 2000 Act shall have the same meaning given in the 2000 Act.

### Authorisations requiring judicial approval

**3.42.2.**—(1)   An application under section 23B(1) of the 2000 Act (procedure for judicial approval) for an order under section 23A(2) (authorisations requiring judicial approval)—

(a)approving the grant or renewal of an authorisation; or

(b)the giving or renewal of a notice,

shall be in Form 59, which must be signed by a solicitor on behalf of the local authority.

(2)   The application (and any order made in relation to it) must not be intimated to—

(a)the person to whom the authorisation or notice which is the subject of the application or order relates; or

(b)such person's representatives.

(3)   The application must be heard and determined by the sheriff in private.

(4)   Where an application is granted by the sheriff the order shall be in Form 60.

PART XLIII[1]

PROCEEDS OF CRIMES ACT 2002 (EXTERNAL INVESTIGATIONS) ORDER 2013

### Application of this Part

**3.43.1.**   This Part applies to applications to the sheriff under Part 2 of the Proceeds of Crime Act 2002 (External Investigations) Order 2013.

### Applications

**3.43.2.**—(1)   An application under the following provisions shall be made by summary application—

(a)article 40(1) (production orders);

(b)article 47(1) (search warrants);

(c)article 56(1) (customer information orders);

(d)article 63(1) (account monitoring orders).

(2)   An application under the following provisions shall be made by minute in the process of the original application—

(a)article 46(2) (discharge or variation of a production order or an order to grant entry);

(b)article 62(2) (discharge or variation of a customer information order);

(c)article 67(2) (discharge or variation of an account monitoring order).

(3)   An application under article 42(2) (order to grant entry) shall be made—

(a)in the application for the production order; or

(b)where the application is made after a production order is made, by minute in the process of the application for the production order.

---

[1] As inserted by the Act of Sederunt (Summary Applications, Statutory Applications and Appeals etc. Rules Amendment) (Miscellaneous) 2013 (SSI 2013/293) r.3 (effective November 11, 2013).

Part XLIV[1]

Gender Recognition Act 2004

**3.44.1.** In this Part,—

"the 2004 Act" means the Gender Recognition Act 2004;

"full gender recognition certificate" and "interim gender recognition certificate" have the meanings assigned by section 25 of the 2004 Act;

"Gender Recognition Panels" is to be construed in accordance with Schedule 1 to the 2004 Act.

**3.44.2.**—(1) This rule applies where a party to a protected Scottish marriage who has been issued with an interim gender recognition certificate makes an application to the sheriff under section 4E of the 2004 Act for the issue of a full gender recognition certificate.

(2) The sheriff shall make an order for intimation of the application on the applicant's spouse, but no such order may be made unless there has been produced with the initial writ—

(a) an extract of the relevant entry in the register of marriages; and

(b) the interim gender recognition certificate or, failing that, a certified copy of the interim gender recognition certificate.

(3) For the purpose of this rule, a certified copy of an interim gender recognition certificate shall be a copy of that certificate sealed with the seal of the Gender Recognition Panels and certified to be a true copy by an officer authorised by the President of the Gender Recognition Panels.

(4) On the granting of the application the sheriff clerk shall give the applicant's spouse a certified copy of the full gender recognition certificate.

**3.44.3.** When a full gender recognition certificate has been issued on an application under section 4E of the 2004 Act, an application for a corrected gender recognition certificate under section 6 of the 2004 Act (Errors in certificates) shall be made by minute in the process in the application pursuant to which the full gender recognition certificate was issued.

Part XLV[2]

Mutual Recognition of Protection Measures in Civil Matters

**Interpretation**

**3.45.1.** In this Part—

"Article 5 certificate" means a certificate issued under Article 5 of the Regulation;

"Article 14 certificate" means a certificate issued under Article 14 of the Regulation;

---

[1] As inserted by the Act of Sederunt (Rules of the Court of Session and Sheriff Court Rules Amendment No. 2) (Marriage and Civil Partnership (Scotland) Act 2014) 2014 (SSI 2014/302) para.7 (effective December 16, 2014).

[2] As inserted by the Act of Sederunt Act of Sederunt (Rules of the Court of Session and Sheriff Court Rules Amendment No. 3) (Mutual Recognition of Protection Measures) 2014 (SSI 2014/371) para.4 (effective January 11, 2015).

"incoming protection measure" means a protection measure that has been ordered in a Member State other than the United Kingdom or Denmark;

"interim risk of sexual harm order" has the meaning given by section 5(2) of the Protection of Children and Prevention of Sexual Offences (Scotland) Act 2005;

"interim sexual offences prevention order" has the meaning given by section 109(2) of the Sexual Offences Act 2003;

"Member State" means a Member State of the European Union;

"person causing the risk" has the meaning given by Article 3(3) of the Regulation;

"protected person" has the meaning given by Article 3(2) of the Regulation;

"protection measure" has the meaning given by Article 3(1) of the Regulation;

"registered post service" has the meaning given by section 125(1) of the Postal Services Act 2000;

"risk of sexual harm order" has the meaning given by section 2(1) of the Protection of Children and Prevention of Sexual Offences (Scotland) Act 2005;

"sexual offences prevention order" has the meaning given by section 106(1) of the Sexual Offences Act 2003;

"the Regulation" means Regulation (EU) No. 606/2013 of the European Parliament and of the Council of 12 June 2013 on mutual recognition of protection measures in civil matters.

### Application of rules 3.45.3 to 3.45.9

**3.45.2.** Rules 3.45.3 to 3.45.9 apply for the purpose of—
- (a) the issuing of an Article 5 certificate where the protection measure in respect of which the certificate is sought is—
  - (i) a sexual offences prevention order or an interim sexual offences prevention order; or
  - (ii) a risk of sexual harm order or an interim risk of sexual harm order;
- (b) the rectification or withdrawal of such a certificate; and
- (c) the issuing of an Article 14 certificate subsequent to the issue of such a certificate.

### Form of application for Article 5 certificate

**3.45.3.** An application for the issue of an Article 5 certificate shall be made by lodging Form 61 in process.

### Issue of Article 5 certificate

**3.45.4.** The sheriff shall issue an Article 5 certificate where—
- (a) the order in respect of which the certificate is sought is a protection measure;
- (b) the person applying for the certificate is a protected person in respect of the protection measure;
- (c) the first condition specified in rule 3.45.5 is satisfied; and
- (d) the second condition specified in rule 3.45.5 is satisfied, if the protection measure is an interim order.

### Conditions for issue of Article 5 certificate

**3.45.5.**—(1) The first condition is that—

(a) at the hearing when the order was granted, the person causing the risk was—

    (i)   personally present in court; or

    (ii)  represented by a solicitor or an advocate; or

(b) the order has been—

    (i)   given or sent to the person causing the risk in accordance with section 112(3) of the Sexual Offences Act 2003; or

    (ii)  served on the person causing the risk in accordance with rule 3.29.4.

(2)   The second condition is that either paragraph (3) or (4) applies.

(3)   This paragraph applies where—

(a) the writ containing the crave for the order was intimated on the person causing the risk before the interim order was granted;

(b) the interim order was granted pursuant to an application intimated on the person causing the risk; and

(c) the person causing the risk had a sufficient opportunity to oppose the application, whether or not he or she did so.

(4)   This paragraph applies where the sheriff is satisfied that the person causing the risk has had a sufficient opportunity to apply to have the interim order discharged.

(5)   Where the sheriff requires to be satisfied that any writ, motion or interlocutor has been intimated for the purposes of this rule, it is for the person on whose behalf intimation has been given to lodge in process a certificate of intimation if such a certificate is not already in process.

**Notice of issue of Article 5 certificate**

**3.45.6.**—(1)   Where the sheriff issues an Article 5 certificate, the sheriff clerk shall—

(a) give the protected person—

    (i)   the certificate; and

    (ii)  a certified copy of the interlocutor granting the protection measure; and

(b) give the person causing the risk notice of the issue of the certificate in accordance with paragraphs (2) to (4).

(2)   Where the address of the person causing the risk is known, notice shall be given by sending that person—

(a) a notice in Form 62;

(b) a copy of the certificate; and

(c) a copy of the interlocutor granting the protection measure.

(3)   Where the address of the person causing the risk is outwith the United Kingdom, the sheriff clerk shall send the documents mentioned in paragraph (2) by a registered post service.

(4)   Where the address of the person causing the risk is not known, notice shall be given by displaying on the walls of court a notice in Form 63.

(5)   In this rule, "Article 5 certificate" includes a rectified Article 5 certificate issued under Article 9(1)(a) of the Regulation.

**Effect of variation of order**

**3.45.7.**   Where the order in respect of which an Article 5 certificate is sought has been varied prior to the issue of a certificate—

(a)   the reference to the order in rule 3.45.4(a) is to the order as so varied; and

(b)   the references to the interlocutor granting the protection measure in rule 3.45.6 include a reference to any interlocutor varying the order.

### Application for rectification or withdrawal of Article 5 certificate

**3.45.8.**—(1)   An application to the sheriff under Article 9 of the Regulation for rectification or withdrawal of an Article 5 certificate shall be made by lodging Form 64 in process.

(2)   The sheriff may determine an application without a hearing unless the sheriff considers that a hearing is required.

### Issue of Article 14 certificate

**3.45.9.**—(1)   An application for the issue of an Article 14 certificate shall be made by letter addressed to the sheriff clerk.

(2)   Where the sheriff issues an Article 14 certificate, the sheriff clerk shall send the certificate to the party on whose application the certificate was issued.

### Form of applications relating to incoming protection measures

**3.45.10.**—(1)   The following applications shall be made by summary application—

(a)an application for the adjustment of the factual elements of an incoming protection measure under Article 11 of the Regulation;

(b)an application to refuse the recognition and, where applicable, the enforcement of an incoming protection measure under Article 13 of the Regulation;

(c)a submission under Article 14(2) of the Regulation to suspend or withdraw the effects of the recognition and, where applicable, the enforcement of an incoming protection measure;

(d)an application under section 1(1) of the Protection from Abuse (Scotland) Act 2001 for a power of arrest to be attached to an incoming protection measure;

(e)an application under section 3(1) of the Domestic Abuse (Scotland) Act 2011 for a determination that an incoming protection measure is a domestic abuse interdict.

(2)   Where a process exists in relation to an incoming protection measure, an application mentioned in paragraph (1) shall be made by minute in that process.

### Adjustment of incoming protection measure

**3.45.11.**[1](1)   This rule applies for the purpose of an application under Article 11 of the Regulation to adjust the factual elements of an incoming protection measure.

(2)   Unless the sheriff considers that a hearing is required, the sheriff may—

(a)dispense with intimation of the application; and

(b)determine the application without a hearing.

(3)   Where necessary, the sheriff may grant decree in accordance with Scots law.

---

[1] As amended by the Act of Sederunt (Rules of the Court of Session, Sheriff Appeal Court Rules and Sheriff Court Rules Amendment) (Sheriff Appeal Court) 2015 (SSI 2015/419) r.9(8) (effective 1 January 2016; as to savings see SSI 2015/419 rule 20(5)(a)).

(4)   The sheriff clerk shall give the person causing the risk notice of the adjustment of the protection measure in accordance with paragraphs (5) to (7).

(5)   Where the address of the person causing the risk is known, notice shall be given by sending that person—

(a)a notice in Form 65;

(b)a copy of the interlocutor adjusting the factual elements of the protection measure.

(6)   Where the address of the person causing the risk is outwith the United Kingdom, the sheriff clerk shall send the documents mentioned in paragraph (5) by a registered post service.

(7)   Where the address of the person causing the risk is not known, notice shall be given by displaying on the walls of court a notice in Form 66.

(8)   An appeal against an interlocutor adjusting the factual elements of an incoming protection measure shall be made within 14 days after the date of the interlocutor concerned.

(9)   Where—

(a)the sheriff has dispensed with intimation of the application on the person causing the risk; and

(b)the person causing the risk has not appeared in the application,

the time within which the person causing the risk may make an appeal shall be reckoned from the date on which notice is given in accordance with paragraph (4).

### Attachment of power of arrest to incoming protection measure

**3.45.12.**—(1)   In this rule, "the Act of 2001" means the Protection from Abuse (Scotland) Act 2001.

(2)   Where the sheriff attaches a power of arrest to a protection measure under section 1(2) of the Act of 2001, the following documents shall be served along with the power of arrest in accordance with section 2(1)—

(a)a copy of the protection measure;

(b)a copy of the Article 5 certificate issued by the issuing authority of the Member State of origin; and

(c)a copy of any interlocutor adjusting the factual elements of the protection measure.

(3)   After the power of arrest has been served, the following documents shall be delivered by the protected person to the chief constable of the Police Service of Scotland in accordance with section 3(1)—

(a)a copy of the protection measure;

(b)a copy of the Article 5 certificate issued by the issuing authority of the Member State of origin;

(c)a copy of any interlocutor adjusting the factual elements of the protection measure;

(d)a copy of the application for the attachment of the power of arrest;

(e)a copy of the interlocutor attaching the power of arrest;

(f)a copy of the certificate of service of the power of arrest and the documents that required to be served along with it in accordance with section 2(1) of the Act of 2001; and

(g)where a determination has previously been made in respect of the protection measure under section 3(1) of the Domestic Abuse (Scotland) Act 2011, a copy of the interlocutor making the determination.

(4)   An application under the following provisions of the Act of 2001 shall be made by minute in the process of the application in which the power of arrest was attached—

(a)section 2(3) (extension of power of arrest);

(b)section 2(7) (recall of power of arrest).

(5)   Where the sheriff extends the duration of, or recalls, a power of arrest, the person who obtained the extension, or the recall as the case may be, shall deliver a copy of the interlocutor granting the extension or the recall in accordance with section 3(1) of the Act of 2001.

(6)   Where the sheriff pronounces an interlocutor granting an application mentioned in rule 3.45.10(1)(a) to (c) in respect of an incoming protection measure to which a power of arrest is attached, the applicant shall deliver a copy of that interlocutor to the chief constable of the Police Service of Scotland in accordance with section 3(1) of the Act of 2001.

(7)   Where a person is required to comply with section 3(1) of the Act of 2001, that person shall, after complying with that section, lodge in process a certificate of delivery in Form 67.

### Determination that incoming protection measure is a domestic abuse interdict

**3.45.13.**—(1)   This rule applies where the sheriff makes a determination that an incoming protection measure is a domestic abuse interdict.

(2)   A protected person who serves under 3(4) of the Domestic Abuse (Scotland) Act 2011 a copy of an interlocutor containing a determination under section 3(1) shall lodge in process a certificate of service.

(3)   Paragraph (4) applies where, in respect of the same protection measure—

(a)a power of arrest under section 1 of the Protection from Abuse (Scotland) Act 2001 is in effect; and

(b)a determination is made.

(4)   Where such a determination is made, the person who obtained the determination shall send to the chief constable of the Police Service of Scotland a copy of the interlocutor making the determination and the certificate of service.

(5)   Where a person is required by virtue of this rule to send documents to the chief constable of the Police Service of Scotland, that person must, after such compliance, lodge in process a certificate of sending in Form 68.

### PART XLVI[1]

### COUNTER-TERRORISM AND SECURITY ACT 2015

### Interpretation

**3.46.1.**   In this Part—

"Schedule 1" means Schedule 1 to the Counter-Terrorism and Security Act 2015.

---

[1] As inserted by the Act of Sederunt (Rules of the Court of Session 1994 and Sheriff Court Rules Amendment) (No.3) (Miscellaneous) 2015 (SSI 2015/283) r.7(2) (effective 7 August 2015).

## Applications for extended detention of travel documents

**3.46.2.**(1) An application to the sheriff for an order under paragraph 8(1) of Schedule 1 (extension of 14-day period by judicial authority) is to be in Form 69.

(1A)   Where an applicant seeks an order under paragraph 10(1) of Schedule 1 (order that specified information be withheld), the application for that order is to be included in Form 69.

(2)   On receipt of an application, the sheriff is to fix a date for the determination of the application.

(3)   The applicant must intimate the application to the person to whom it relates—

    (a)in Form 70, which is to be accompanied by a copy of the application; and

    (b)within the timescale and by the method specified by the sheriff.

(4)   Where—

    (a)at any time before intimation of an application, the sheriff grants an order under paragraph 10 of Schedule 1 (order that specified information be withheld); and

    (b)the information to which the order relates includes information contained in the application,

the sheriff may order intimation of the application under deletion of that information.

## Further applications for extended detention of travel documents

**3.46.3.**   A further application under paragraph 8(1) of Schedule 1, by virtue of paragraph 12(1), is to be made by minute in the process relating to the extension of the 14-day period.

SCHEDULE 1

FORMS

**Rule 1.2(3)**

FORM A1[1]

Rule 1A.2(2)(b)

Statement by prospective lay representative for Pursuer/Defender*

Case Ref. No.:

in the cause

SHERIFFDOM OF (*insert name of sheriffdom*)

AT (*insert place of sheriff court*)

[A.B.], (*insert designation and address*), Pursuer

against

[C.D.], (*insert designation and address*), Defender

Court ref. no:

| |
|---|
| Name and address of prospective lay representative who requests to make oral submissions on behalf of party litigant: |
| Identify hearing(s) in respect of which permission for lay representation is sought: |
| The prospective lay representative declares that: |

[1] As inserted by the Act of Sederunt (Sheriff Court Rules) (Lay Representation) 2013 (SSI 2013/91) r.3 (effective April 4, 2013).

| (a) | I have no financial interest in the outcome of the case *or* I have the following financial interest in it:* |
|-----|---|
| (b) | I am not receiving remuneration or other reward directly or indirectly from the litigant for my assistance and will not receive directly or indirectly such remuneration or other reward from the litigant. |
| (c) | I accept that documents and information are provided to me by the litigant on a confidential basis and I undertake to keep them confidential. |
| (d) | I have no previous convictions *or* I have the following convictions: (list convictions)* |
| (e) | I have not been declared a vexatious litigant under the Vexatious Actions (Scotland) Act 1898 *or* I was declared a vexatious litigant under the Vexatious Actions (Scotland) Act 1898 on [insert date].* |

(*Signed*)

[Name of prospective lay representative]

[Date]

(*Insert Place/Date*)

The Sheriff grants/refuses* the application.

[*Signed*]

Sheriff Clerk

[Date]

(**delete as appropriate*)

FORM 1

Rule 2.4(1)

Form of initial writ

SUMMARY APPLICATION UNDER (*title & section of statute or statutory instrument*)

INITIAL WRIT

SHERIFFDOM OF (*insert name of sheriffdom*)

AT (*insert place of sheriff court*)

[A.B.] (*design and state any special capacity in which the pursuer is suing*) Pursuer

against

[C.D.] (*design and state any special capacity in which the defender is being sued*) Defender

The Pursuer craves the court (*here state the specific decree, warrant or order sought*)

CONDESCENDENCE

(*State in numbered paragraphs the facts which form the ground of action*)

PLEAS-IN-LAW

(*State in numbered sentences*)

Signed

[A.B.], Pursuer

or [X.Y.], solicitor for the Pursuer

(*state designation and business address*)

FORM 2

Rule 2.7(4)(a)

[Form of warrant of citation]

(*Insert place and date*). Grants warrant to cite the defender (*insert name and address*) by serving upon him [*or* her] a copy of the writ and warrant [on a period of notice of (*insert period of notice*) days], [and ordains him [*or* her] to answer within the Sheriff Court House (*insert place of sheriff court*) [in Room No. ..........., or in Chambers, *or otherwise, as the case may be*], on the .......... day of .......... at .......... o'clock .......... noon] [*or otherwise, as the case may be*] [and grants warrant to arrest on the dependence].

Signed
Sheriff [*or* sheriff clerk]

Rule 3.18.3(1)                          FORM 2A[1]
Form of warrant of citation

(*Insert place and date*). Grants warrant to cite (*insert name and address of parties specified by sheriff principal*) by serving upon them a copy of the writ and warrant on a period of notice of 21 days and ordains them if they wish to oppose the application—

(a) to lodge answers within the period of notice; and

(b) to be represented within the Sheriff Court House (*insert place and address of sheriff court*) [in Room No............, *or otherwise, as the case may be*], on the..........day of at..........o'clock.......... noon [*or otherwise, as the case may be*].

Signed
Sheriff [*or* sheriff clerk]

Rule 2.7(4)(b)                          FORM 3

Form of citation for summary application
CITATION FOR SUMMARY APPLICATION
SHERIFFDOM OF (*insert name of sheriffdom*)
AT (*insert place of sheriff court*)
[A.B.], (*insert designation and address*) Pursuer
against
[C.D.], (*insert designation and address*) Defender
Court ref. no.

(*Insert place and date*). You [.CD.] are hereby served with this copy writ and warrant, and are required to answer it.

**IF YOU ARE UNCERTAIN AS TO WHAT ACTION TO TAKE** you should consult a solicitor. You may be eligible for legal aid depending on your income, and you can get information about legal aid from a solicitor. You may also obtain advice from any Citizens' Advice Bureau or other advice agency.

**PLEASE NOTE THAT IF YOU DO NOTHING IN ANSWER TO THIS DOCUMENT** the court may regard you as admitting the claim made against you and the pursuer may obtain decree against you in your absence.

Signed
[PQ.], Sheriff Officer,
or [X.Y] (*add designation and
business address*)
Solicitor for the Pursuer

---

[1] Inserted by the Act of Sederunt (Summary Applications, Statutory Applications and Appeals etc. Rules) Amendment (No.2) (Local Government (Scotland) Act 1973) 2002 (S.S.I. 2002 No. 130), para.2(4) and Sched.

Rule 3.18.3(2)                   FORM 3A[1]

Form of citation for summary application
CITATION FOR SUMMARY APPLICATION
SHERIFFDOM OF (*insert name of sheriffdom*)
AT (*insert place of sheriff court*)
[A.B.], (*insert designation and address*), Applicant
against
[C.D.], (*insert designation and address*), Respondent
Court ref. no.

(*Insert place and date*). You [C.D.] are hereby served with this copy writ and warrant, and are required to answer it.

If you wish to oppose the application, you—

(a) must lodge answers with the sheriff clerk at (*insert place and address of sheriff court*) sheriff court, (*insert address*) not later than (*insert date*), and at the same time, send a copy of the answers to the Applicant; and

(b) should be represented within the Sheriff Court House (*insert place and address of sheriff court*) [in Room No..........., or otherwise, as the case may be] on the day of at..........o'clock.......... noon [*or otherwise as the case maybe*].

**PLEASE NOTE THAT IF YOU DO NOTHING IN ANSWER TO THIS DOCUMENT** the court may regard you as admitting the appeal and the Applicant may obtain decree against you in your absence.

Signed
[P.Q.], Sheriff Officer, or [X.Y.]
(*add designation and business address*)
Solicitor for the Applicant

Rule 2.7(5)                      FORM 4[2]

Form of warrant of citation where time to pay direction or time order may be applied for

(*Insert place and date*). *Grants warrant to cite the defender (insert name and address*) by serving a copy of the writ and warrant, together with Form 5, [on a period of notice of (*insert period of notice*) days] and ordains him [*or* her] if he [*or* she]—

(a) intends to defend the action or make any claim [to answer within the Sheriff Court House (*insert place and address of sheriff court*) [in Room No..........., or in Chambers, *or otherwise, as the case may be*], on the..........day of..........at..........o'clock..........noon] [*or otherwise, as the case may be*] or

(b) admits the claim and intends to apply for a time to pay direction or time order (and where appropriate apply for recall or restriction of an arrestment) [either to appear at that diet and make such application or] to lodge the appropriate part of Form 5 duly completed with the sheriff clerk at (*insert place of sheriff court*) at least fourteen days before [the diet or the expiry of the period of notice *or otherwise*, as the case may be] [and grants warrant to arrest on the dependence].

Signed
Sheriff [*or* sheriff clerk]

---

[1] Inserted by the Act of Sederunt (Summary Applications, Statutory Applications and Appeals etc. Rules) Amendment (No.2) (Local Government (Scotland) Act 1973) 2002 (S.S.I. 2002 No. 130), para.2(4) and Sched.

[2] As amended by SSI 2007/6 (effective January 29, 2007) and SSI 2009/294 (effective December 1, 2009).

Rule 2.7(6) and 2.22(2)(b)  FORM 5[1] [2]

Form of notice to be served on defender where time to pay direction or time order may be applied for

Rule 2.7(6) and 2.22(2)(b)  ACTION RAISED BY

PURSUER  DEFENDER

AT...............SHERIFF COURT
(Including address)
COURT REF. NO.

**THIS SECTION MUST BE COMPLETED BY THE PURSUER BEFORE SERVICE**

(1) Time to pay directions

The Debtors (Scotland) Act 1987 gives you the right to apply to the court for a "time to pay direction" which is an order permitting you to pay any sum of money you are ordered to pay to the pursuer (which may include interest and court expenses) either by way of instalments or deferred lump sum. A deferred lump sum means that you must pay all the amount at one time within a period specified by the court.

When making a time to pay direction the court may recall or restrict an arrestment made on your property by the pursuer in connection with the action or debt (for example, your bank account may have been frozen).

(2) Time Orders

The Consumer Credit Act 1974 allows you to apply to the court for a "time order" during a court action, to ask the court to give you more time to pay a loan agreement. **A time order is similar to a time to pay direction, but can only be applied for where the court action is about a credit agreement regulated by the Consumer Credit Act**. The court has power to grant a time order in respect of a regulated agreement to reschedule payment of the sum owed. This means that a time order can change:

- the amount you have to pay each month
- how long the loan will last
- in some cases, the interest rate payable

A time order can also stop the creditor taking away any item bought by you on hire purchase or conditional sale under the regulated agreement, so long as you continue to pay the instalments agreed.

**HOW TO APPLY FOR A TIME TO PAY DIRECTION OR TIME ORDER WHERE YOU ADMIT THE CLAIM AND YOU DO NOT WANT TO DEFEND THE ACTION**

1.  The appropriate application forms are attached to this notice. After completing the appropriate form it should be returned to the Sheriff Court at least fourteen days before the date of the first hearing or expiry of the period of notice or otherwise, as the case may be, in the warrant of citation. The address of the court is shown on page 1 of the application. No court fee is payable when lodging the application.
2.  Before completing the application please read carefully the notes on how to

---

[1] As amended by SSI 2007/6 (effective January 29, 2007) and subtituted by Act of Sederunt (Sheriff Court Rules)(Miscellaneous Amendments) 2009 (SSI 2009/294) r.2 (effective December 1, 2009).

[2] As amended by the Act of Sederunt (Sheriff Court Rules)(Miscellaneous Amendments) 2011 (SSI 2011/193) r.10 (effective April 3, 2011).

complete the application. In the event of difficulty you may contact the court's civil department at the address above or any sheriff clerk's office, solicitor, Citizens Advice Bureau or other advice agency. Written guidance can also be obtained from the Scottish Court Service website (www.scotcourts.gov.uk).

## WHAT WILL HAPPEN NEXT

If the pursuer objects to your application, a hearing will be fixed and the court will advise you in writing of the date and time.

If the pursuer does not object to your application, a copy of the court order for payment (called an extract decree) will be served on you by the pursuer's solicitor advising when instalment payments should commence or deferred payment be made.

Court ref. no.

## APPLICATION FOR A TIME TO PAY DIRECTION UNDER THE DEBTORS (SCOTLAND) ACT 1987

**\*PART A**                        BY

**\*(This section must be completed by pursuer before service)**

DEFENDER
**In an action raised by**
PURSUER

## HOW TO COMPLETE THE APPLICATION
### PLEASE WRITE IN INK USING BLOCK CAPITALS

**PART A** of the application will have been completed in advance by the pursuer and gives details of the pursuer and you as the defender.

**PART B** If you wish to apply to pay by instalments enter the amount and tick the appropriate box at B3(1). If you wish to apply to pay the full sum due in one deferred payment enter the period of deferment you propose at B3(2).

**PART C** Give full details of your financial position in the space provided.

**PART D** If you wish the court, when making the time to pay direction to recall or restrict an arrestment made in connection with the action, enter the appropriate details about what has been arrested and the place and date of the arrestment at D5, and attach the schedule of arrestment or copy.

Sign the application where indicated. Retain the copy initial writ and the form of notice which accompanied this application form as you may need them at a later stage. The application should be returned to the Sheriff Court at least fourteen days before the date of the first hearing or expiry of the period of notice or otherwise, as the case may be, in the warrant of citation. The address of the court is shown on page 1 of the application.

**PART B**                        1. The applicant is a defender in the action brought by the above named pursuer.

2. The defender admits the claim and applies to the court for a time to pay direction.

3. The defender applies

(1) To pay by instalments of £

(Tick one box only)

EACH WEEK        FORTNIGHT        MONTH
OR

(2) To pay the sum ordered in one payment within WEEKS/MONTHS

Please state in this box why you say a time to pay direction should be made. In doing so, please consider the Note below.

**NOTE**

**Under the 1987 Act, the court is required to make a time to pay direction if satisfied that it is reasonable in the circumstances to do so, and having regard in particular to the following matters—**

**The nature of and reasons for the debt in relation to which decree is granted or the order is sought Any action taken by the creditor to assist the debtor in paying the debt**

**The debtor's financial position The reasonableness of any proposal by the debtor to pay that debt**

**The reasonableness of any refusal or objection by the creditor to any proposal or offer by the debtor to pay the debt.**

**PART C**

### 4. Defender's financial position

I am employed /self employed / unemployed

| **My net income is:** weekly, fortnightly or monthly | **My outgoings are:** weekly, fortnightly or monthly |
|---|---|
| Wages £ | Mortgage/rent £ |
| State benefits £ | Council tax £ |
| Tax credits £ | Gas/electricity £ etc |
| Other £ | Food £ |
| | Credit and loans £ |
| | Phone £ |
| | Other £ |
| Total £ | Total £ |

People who rely on your income (e.g. spouse/civil partner/ partner/ children) —how many

Here list all assets (if any) e.g. value of house; amounts in bank or building society accounts; shares or other investments:

Here list any outstanding debts:

**PART D**

5. The defender seeks to recall or restrict an arrestment of which the details are as follows (*please state, and attach the schedule of arrestment or copy*).

6. This application is made under sections 1(1) and 2(3) of the Debtors (Scotland) Act 1987.

Therefore the defender asks the court

*to make a time to pay direction

*to recall the above arrestment

*to restrict the above arrestment (*in which case state restriction wanted*)

Date (*insert date*)

Signed

Defender

**Court ref. no.**

# APPLICATION FOR A TIME ORDER UNDER THE CONSUMER CREDIT ACT 1974

**\*PART A**

**\*(This section must be completed by pursuer before service)**

By

DEFENDER

**In an action raised by**

PURSUER

## HOW TO COMPLETE THE APPLICATION
PLEASE WRITE IN INK USING BLOCK CAPITALS

**PART A** of the application will have been completed in advance by the pursuer and gives details of the pursuer and you as the defender.

**PART B** If you wish to apply to pay by instalments enter the amount and tick the appropriate box at B3. If you wish the court to make any additional orders, please give details at B4. Please give details of the regulated agreement at B5.

**PART C** Give full details of your financial position in the space provided.

Sign the application where indicated. Retain the copy initial writ and the form of notice which accompanied this application form as you may need them at a later stage. The application should be returned to the Sheriff Court at least fourteen days before the date of the first hearing or expiry of the period of notice or otherwise, as the case may be, in the warrant of citation. The address of the court is shown on page 1 of the application.

**PART B**

1. The Applicant is a defender in the action brought by the above named pursuer.

**I/WE WISH TO APPLY FOR A TIME ORDER under the Consumer Credit Act 1974**

2. **Details of order(s) sought**

The defender wishes to apply for a time order under section 129 of the Consumer Credit Act 1974

The defender wishes to apply for an order in terms of section..........of the Consumer Credit Act 1974

### 3. **Proposals for payment**

I admit the claim and apply to pay the arrears and future instalments as follows:

By instalments of £..........per *week/fortnight/month

No time to pay direction or time to pay order has been made in relation to this debt.

### 4. **Additional orders sought**

The following additional order(s) is (are) sought: (*specify*)

The order(s) sought in addition to the time order is (are) sought for the following reasons:

### 5. **Details of regulated agreement**

(*Please attach a copy of the agreement if you have retained it and insert details of the agreement where known*)

(a) Date of agreement

(b) Reference number of agreement

(c) Names and addresses of other parties to agreement

(d) Name and address of person (if any) who acted as surety (guarantor) to the agreement

(e) Place where agreement signed (e.g. the shop where agreement signed, including name and address)

(f) Details of payment arrangements

    i. The agreement is to pay instalments of £..........per week/month

    ii. The unpaid balance is £..........I do not know the amount of arrears

    iii. I am £..........in arrears / I do not know the amount of arrears

**PART C**        **Defender's financial position**

I am employed /self employed / unemployed

| My net income is: | weekly, fortnightly or monthly | My outgoings are: | weekly, fortnightly or monthly |
|---|---|---|---|
| Wages | £ | Mortgage/rent | £ |
| State benefits | £ | Council tax | £ |
| Tax credits | £ | Gas/electricity etc | £ |
| Other | £ | Food | £ |
| | | Credit and loans | £ |
| | | Phone | £ |
| | | Other | £ |
| Total | £ | Total | £ |

People who rely on your income (e.g. spouse/civil partner/partner/children)—how many

Here list all assets (if any) e.g. value of house; amounts in bank or building society accounts; shares or other investments:

Here list any outstanding debts:

Therefore the defender asks the court to make a time order

Date                                    Signed
                                        Defender

Rule 2.22(4)                    FORM 5A[1]

**Form of pursuer's response objecting to application for time to pay direction or time order**

Court ref no:..........

SHERIFFDOM OF (*insert name of sheriffdom*)

AT (*insert place of sheriff court*)

PURSUER'S RESPONSE OBJECTING TO APPLICATION FOR TIME TO PAY DIRECTION OR TIME ORDER

in the cause

[A.B.], (*insert designation and address*), Pursuer

against

[C.D.], (*insert designation and address*), Defender

1. The pursuer received a copy application for a time to pay direction or time order lodged by the defender on (*date*).
2. The pursuer does not accept the offer.
3. The debt is (*please specify the nature of the debt*).
4. The debt was incurred on (*specify date*) and the pursuer has contacted the defender in relation to the debt on (*specify date(s)*).
*5. The contractual payments were (*specify amount*).
*6. (*Specify any action taken by the pursuer to assist the defender to pay the debt*).
*7. The defender has made payment(s) towards the debt of (*specify amount(s)*) on (*specify date(s)*).
*8. The debtor has made offers to pay (*specify amount(s)*) on (*specify date(s)*) which offer(s) was [were] accepted [*or* rejected] and (*specify amount*) was paid on (*specify date(s)*).
9. (*Here set out any information you consider relevant to the court's determination of the application*).

*delete as appropriate

(*Signed*)

Pursuer *or* Solicitor for pursuer

(*Date*)

---

[1] As inserted by the Act of Sederunt (Sheriff Court Rules) (Miscellaneous Amendments) 2009 (SSI 2009/294) r.2 (effective December 1, 2009).

Rule 2.7(7)                                    FORM 6[1]

Form of citation where time to pay direction or time order may be applied for in summary application

SHERIFFDOM OF (*insert name of sheriffdom*)

AT (*insert place of sheriff court*)

[A.B.], (*insert designation and address*) Pursuer

against

[C.D.], (*insert designation and address*) Defender

Court ref. no.

(*Insert place and date*). You [CD.], are hereby served with this copy writ and warrant, together with Form 5 (application for time to pay direction in summary application).

**Form 5** is served on you because it is considered that you may be entitled to apply for a time to pay direction or time order [and for the recall or restriction of an arrestment used on the dependence of the action or in security of the debt referred to in the copy writ]. See Form 5 for further details.

**IF YOU ADMIT THE CLAIM AND WISH TO APPLY FOR A TIME TO PAY DIRECTION OR TIME ORDER,** you must complete Form 5 and return it to the sheriff clerk at the above address at least 7 days before the hearing or the expiry of the period of notice or otherwise, as the case may be, in the warrant of citation.

**IF YOU ADMIT THE CLAIM AND WISH TO AVOID A COURT ORDER BEING MADE AGAINST YOU,** the whole sum claimed including interest and any expenses due should be paid to the pursuer or his solicitor by the court date.

**IF YOU ARE UNCERTAIN AS TO WHAT ACTION TO TAKE** you should consult a solicitor. You may be eligible for legal aid depending on your income, and you can get information about legal aid from a solicitor. You may also obtain advice from any Citizens' Advice Bureau, or other advice agency.

**PLEASE NOTE THAT IF YOU DO NOTHING IN ANSWER TO THIS DOCUMENT** the court may regard you as admitting the claim made against you and the pursuer may obtain decree against you in your absence.

Signed

[P.Q.], Sheriff Officer,

or [X.Y.] (*add designation and business address*)

Solicitor for the Pursuer

FORM 6ZA[2]

Rule 2.7(7ZA)(a)

Form of warrant of citation in an application to which rule 2.7(7ZA)(a) applies

(*Insert place and date*). Grants warrant to cite the defender (*insert name and address*) by serving a copy of the writ and warrant together with Form 6ZB and Form 11C [*on a period of notice of (*insert period of notice*) days] and ordains him [*or* her] if he [*or* she] intends to oppose the application—

To be present or represented at the diet on (*insert date and time*) within (*insert name and address of sheriff court*) [*or otherwise as the case may be*].

Signed

---

[1] As amended by the Act of Sederunt (Ordinary Cause, Summary Application, Summary Cause and Small Claim Rules) Amendment (Miscellaneous) 2007 (SSI 2007/6), para.3(6) (effective January 29, 2007).

[2] As inserted by the Act of Sederunt (Sheriff Court Rules) (Miscellaneous Amendments) 2013 (SSI 2013/135) para.2 (effective May 27, 2013).

Sheriff [*or* sheriff clerk]

(*\*delete as appropriate*)

## FORM 6ZB[1]

Rule 2.7(7ZA)(b)

Form of citation in an application to which rule 2.7(7ZA)(b) applies

SHERIFFDOM OF (*insert name of sheriffdom*)

AT (*insert place of sheriff court*)

[A.B.], (*insert designation and address*), Pursuer

Against

[C.D.], (*insert designation and address*), Defender

Court ref. no:

To: (*insert name and address of defender*)

Attached to this notice is a copy of an application by (*insert name of pursuer*) under [*insert reference to provision or provisions under which application is made*]. **IF THE APPLICATION IS GRANTED, THE PROPERTY AT (*INSERT ADDRESS OF SECURITY SUBJECTS*) MAY BE REPOSSESSED AND YOU WOULD NO LONGER HAVE THE RIGHT TO RESIDE THERE.**

**The hearing will be held at (*insert name and address of sheriff court*) on (*insert date*) at (*insert time*).**

**IF YOU WISH TO OPPOSE THE APPLICATION** you should be present or represented at the hearing.

**IF YOU ARE UNCERTAIN AS TO WHAT ACTION TO TAKE** you should consult a solicitor. You may be eligible for legal aid depending on your income, and you can get information about legal aid from a solicitor. You may also obtain advice from an approved lay representative, or any Citizens' Advice Bureau or other advice agency.

**PLEASE NOTE THAT IF YOU DO NOTHING IN ANSWER TO THIS DOCUMENT** the court may consider the application in the absence of you or your representative.

Signed

[P.Q.], Sheriff Officer,

or [X.Y.], (*add designation and business address*)

Solicitor for the Pursuer

## FORM 6A

*[Repealed by the Act of Sederunt (Sheriff Court Rules) (Enforcement of Securities over Heritable Property) 2010 (SSI 2010/324) para.2 (effective September 30, 2010).]*

## FORM 6B

*[Repealed by the Act of Sederunt (Sheriff Court Rules) (Enforcement of Securities over Heritable Property) 2010 (SSI2010/324) para.2 (effective September 30, 2010).]*

Rule 2.7(8)         FORM 7[2, 3, 4 5]

Form of certificate of citation

---

[1] As inserted by the Act of Sederunt (Sheriff Court Rules) (Miscellaneous Amendments) 2013 (SSI 2013/135) para.2 (effective May 27, 2013).

[2] Inserted by the Act of Sederunt (Amendment of Ordinary Cause Rules and Summary Applications, Statutory Applications and Appeals etc. Rules) Applications under the Mortgage Rights (Scotland) Act 2001) 2002 (SSI 2002/7), para.3(4) and Sch.2.

## CERTIFICATE OF CITATION

(Insert place and date) I, hereby certify that upon the day of I duly cited [CD.], Defender, to answer the foregoing writ. I did this by (*state method of service; [if by officer and not by post, add*: in the presence of [L.M.], (*insert designation*), witness hereto with me subscribing;] *and where service executed by post state whether by registered post or the first class recorded delivery service*).

(*In actions in which a time to pay direction or time order may be applied for, state whether Form 4 and Form 5 were sent in accordance with rule 2.7(5)* and (6).)

(*In applications for enforcement of security over residential property within the meaning of Part IV of Chapter 3 , state whether Forms 6ZA, 6ZB and 11C were provided in accordance with rule 2.7(7ZA)*).

Signed

[P.Q.], Sheriff Officer

[L.M.], witness

or [X.Y.] (*add designation and business address*)

Solicitor for the Pursuer

| | |
|---|---|
| Rule 2.9(1) | FORM 8 |

### Form of caveat

*[Repealed by the Act of Sederunt (Sheriff Court Caveat Rules) 2006 (SI 2006/198), effective April 28, 2006.]*

| | |
|---|---|
| Rule 2.13(1)(a) | FORM 9 |

### Form of advertisement
### NOTICE TO [C.D.]
#### Court ref. no.

An action has been raised in Sheriff Court by [A.B.], Pursuer calling as a Defender [CD.], whose last known address was (*insert last known address of defender*).

If [CD.] wishes to defend the action he [*or* she] should immediately contact the sheriff clerk (*insert address*) from whom the service copy initial writ may be obtained. If he [*or* she] fails to do so decree may pass against him [*or* her] [when the case calls in court on (*date*) or on the expiry of the period of notice *or otherwise, as the case may be in the warrant of citation*].

Signed

[X.Y.], (*add designation and business address*)

Solicitor for the Pursuer

or [P.Q.] (*add business address*)

| | |
|---|---|
| Rule 2.13(1)(b) | FORM 10 |

### Form of notice for walls of court
### NOTICE TO [CD.]
#### Court ref. no.

---

[3] As amended by the Act of Sederunt (Ordinary Cause, Summary Application, Summary Cause and Small Claim Rules) Amendment (Miscellaneous) 2007 (SSI 2007/6), para.3(6) (effective January 29, 2007).

[4] As amended by the Act of Sederunt (Sheriff Court Rules) (Enforcement of Securities over Heritable Property) 2010 (SSI 2010/324) para.2 (effective September 30, 2010).

[5] As amended by the Act of Sederunt (Sheriff Court Rules) (Miscellaneous Amendments) 2013 (SSI 2013/135) para.2 (effective May 27, 2013).

An action has been raised in..........Sheriff Court by [A.B.], Pursuer calling as a Defender [CD.], whose last known address was (*insert last known address of defender*).

If [C.D.] wishes to defend the action he [*or* she] should immediately contact the sheriff clerk at (*insert address*) from whom the service copy initial writ may be obtained. If he [*or* she] fails to do so decree may pass against him [*or* her] [when the case calls in court on (*date*) or on the expiry of the period of notice *or otherwise, as the case may he in the warrant of citation*].

Date (*insert date*)

Signed

Sheriff clerk (*depute*)

Telephone no. (*insert telephone number of sheriff clerk's office*)

Rule 2.18A                                    FORM 10A[1]

Form of schedule of arrestment on the dependence

SCHEDULE OF ARRESTMENT ON THE DEPENDENCE

Date: (*date of execution*)

Time: (*time arrestment executed*)

To: (*name and address of arrested*)

IN HER MAJESTY'S NAME AND AUTHORITY AND IN NAME AND AUTHORITY OF THE SHERIFF.1, (*name*). Sheriff Officer, by virtue of:

- an initial writ containing warrant which has been granted for arrestment on the dependence of the action at the instance of (*name and address of pursuer*) against (*name and address of defender*) and dated (*date*);
- a counterclaim containing a warrant which has been granted for arrestment on the dependence of the claim by (*name and address of creditor*) againts (*name and address of debtor*) and dated (*date of warrant*);
- an order of the Sheriff at (*place*) dated (*dated of order*) granting warrant [for arrestment on the dependence of the action mised at the instance of (*name and address of pursuer*) against (*name and address of defender*).] [or for arrestment on the dependence of the claim in the counterclaim [or third party notice] by (*name and address of creditor*) against (*name and address of debtor*)].

arrest in your hands (i) the sum of (*amount*), in excess of the Protected Minimum Balance; where applicable (*see Note 1*), more or less, due by you to (*defender's name*)[*or name and address of common debtor i common debtor is not the defender*] or to any other person on his [*or* her] [*or* its] [*or* their] behalf, and (ii) all moveable things in your hands belonging or pertaining to the said (*name of common debtor*), to remain in your hands under arrestment until they are made forthcoming to (*name of pursuer*) [*or name and address of creditor if he is not the pursuer*] or until further order of the court.

This I do in the presence of (*name, occupation and address of witness*).

(*Signed*)

Sheriff Officer

(*Address*)

NOTE

1. This Schedule arrests in your hands (i) funds due by you to (*name of common debtor*) and (ii) goods or other moveables held by you for him. **You**

---

[1] As inserted by the Act of Sederunt (Sheriff Court Rules Amendment) (Diligence) 2009 (SSI 2009/107) (effective April 22, 2009).

**should not pay any funds to him or hand over any goods or other moveables to him without taking legal advice**.

2. This Schedule may be used to arrest a ship or cargo. If it is, you should consult your legal adviser about the effect of it.

3. The Protected Minimum Balance is the sum referred to in section 73F(4) of the Debtors (Scotland) Act 1987. This sum is currently set at [*insert current sum*]. The Protected Minimum Balance applies where the arrestment attaches funds standing to the credit of a debtor in an account held by a bank or other financial institution and the debtor is an individual. The Protected Minimum Balance does not apply where the account is held in the name of a company, a limited liability partnership, a partnership or an unincorporated association or where the account is operated by the debtor as a trading account.

4. Under section 73G of the Debtors (Scotland) Act 1987 you must also, within the period of 3 weeks beginning with the day on which the arrestment is executed, disclose to the creditor the nature and value of the funds and/or moveable property which have been attached. This disclosure must be in the form set out in Schedule 8 to the Diligence (Scotland) Regulations 2009. Failure to comply may lead to a financial penalty under section 73G of the Debtors (Scotland) Act 1987 and may also be dealt with as a contempt of court. You must, at the same time, send a copy of the disclosure to the debtor and to any person known to you who owns (or claims to own) attached property and to any person to whom attached funds are (or are claimed to be due), solely or in common with the debtor.

**IF YOU WISH FURTHER ADVICE CONTACT ANY CITIZENS ADVICE BUREAU/LOCAL ADVICE CENTRE/SHERIFF CLERK OR SOLICITOR**

Rule 2.18A                              FORM 10B[1]

Form of certificate of execution of arrestment on the dependence
CERTIFICATE OF EXECUTION

I, (*name*), Sheriff Officer, certify that I executed an arrestment on the dependence, by virtue of an interlocutor of the Sheriff at (*place*) on (*date*) obtained at the instance of (*name and address of party arresting*) against (*name and address of defender*) on (*name of arrestee*)—

* by delivering the schedule of arrestment to (*name of arrestee or other person*) at (*place*) personally on (*date*).

* by leaving the schedule of arrestment with (*name and occupation of person with whom left*) at (*place*) on (*date*) [and by posting a copy of the schedule to the arrestee by registered post or first class recorded delivery to the address specified on the receipt annexed to this certificate].

* by depositing the schedule of arresment in (*place*) on (*date*). (*Specify that enquiry made and reasonable grounds exist for believing that the person on whom service is to be made resides at the place but is not available*) [and by posting a copy of the schedule to the arrestee by registered post or first class recorded delivery to the address specified on the receipt annexed to this certificate].

* by affixing the schedule of arrestment to the door at (*place*) on (*date*). (*Specify that enquiry made and that reasonable grounds exist for believing that the person on whom service is to be made resides at the place but is not available*) [and by

---

[1] As inserted by the Act of Sederunt (Sheriff Court Rules Amendment) (Diligence) 2009 (SSI 2009/107) (effective April 22, 2009).

posting a copy of schedule to the arrestee by registered post or first class recorded delivery to the address specified on the receipt annexed to this certificate].

* by leaving the schedule of arrestment with (*name and occupation of person with whom left*) at (*place of business*) on (*date*) [and by posting a copy of schedule to the arrestee by registered post or first class recorded delivery to the address specified on the receipt annexed to this certificate].

* by depositing the schedule of arresment at (*place of business*) on (*date*). (*Specify that enquiry made and that reasonable grounds exist for believing that the person on whom service is to be made carries on business at that place.*) [and by posting a copy of the schedule to the arrestee by registered post or first class recorded delivery to the address specified on the receipt annexed to this certificate].

* by affixing the schedule of arrestment to the door at (*place of business*) on (*date*). (*Specify that enquiry made and that reasonable grounds exist for believing that the person on whom service is to be made carries on business at that place.*) [and by posting a copy of schedule to the arrestee by registered post or first class recorded delivery to the address specified on the receipt annexed to this certificate].

* by leaving the schedule of arrestment at (*registered office*) on (*date*), in the hands of (*name of person*) [and by posting a copy of the schedule to the arrestee by registered post or first class recorded delivery to the address specified on the receipt annexed to this certificate].

* by depositing the schedule of arrestment at (*registered office*) on (*date*) [and by posting a copy of the schedule to the arrestee by registered post or first class recorded delivery to the address specified on the receipt annexed to this certificate].

* by affixing the schedule of arrestment to the door at (*registered office*) on (*date*) [and by posting a copy of the schedule to the arrestee by registered post or first class recorded delivery to the address specified on the receipt annexed to this certificate].

I did this in the presence of (*name, occupation and address of witness*).

(*Signed*)
Sheriff Officer
(*Address*)
(*Signed*)
(Witness)

*Delele where not applicable

NOTE
A copy of the Schedule of arrestment on the dependence is to be attached to this certificate.

Rule 2.26                      FORM 11

Form of extract decree
EXTRACT DECREE

Sheriff Court                  Court Ref. No.
Date of decree                 *In absence
Pursuer(s)                     Defender(s)
The Sheriff
and granted decree against the        for payment of expenses of £
This extract is warrant for all lawful execution hereon.
Date (*insert date*)                  Sheriff clerk (*depute*)
*Delete as appropriate

Paragraph 5(4)

Rule 2.37(3)                                          FORM 11AA[1]

Form of minute of intervention by the Commission for Equality and Human Rights

SHERIFFDOM OF (*insert name of sher-*   Court ref. no.
*iffdom*)

AT (insert place of sheriff court)

## APPLICATION FOR LEAVE TO INTERVENE BY THE COMMISSION FOR EQUALITY AND HUMAN RIGHTS
in the cause
[A.B.] (*designation and address*), Pursuer
against
[CD.] (*designation and address*), Defender

[*Here set out briefly*:
(a)   the Commission's reasons for believing that the proceedings are relevant to a matter in connection with which the Commission has a function;
(b)   the issue in the proceedings which the Commission wishes to address; and
(c)   the propositions to be advanced by the Commission and the Commission's reasons for believing that they are relevant to the proceedings and that they will assist the court]

Rule 2.39(2)                                          FORM 11AB[2]

Form of minute of intervention by the Scottish Commission for Human Rights

SHERIFFDOM OF (*insert name of sher-*   Court ref. no.
*iffdom*)

AT (*insert place of sheriff court*)

## APPLICATION FOR LEAVE TO INTERVENE BY THE SCOTTISH COMMISSION FOR HUMAN RIGHTS
in the cause
[A.B.] (*designation and address*), Pursuer
against
[C.D.] (*designation and address*), Defender

[*Here set out briefly*:
(a)   *the issue in the proceedings which the Commission intends to address*;
(b)   *a summary of the submission the Commission intends to make.*]

Rule 2.40(1)                                          FORM 11AC[3]

Invitation to the Scottish Commission for Human Rights to intervene

SHERIFFDOM OF (*insert name of sher-*   Court ref. no.
*iffdom*)

AT (*insert place of sheriff court*)

## INVITATION TO THE SCOTTISH COMMISSION FOR HUMAN RIGHTS TO INTERVENE

---

[1] As inserted by the Act of Sederunt (Sheriff Court Rules) (Miscellaneous Amendments) 2008 (SSI 2008/223) para.5(4) (effective July 1, 2008).
[2] As inserted by the Act of Sederunt (Sheriff Court Rules) (Miscellaneous Amendments) 2008 (SSI 2008/223) para.5(4) (effective July 1, 2008).
[3] As inserted by the Act of Sederunt (Sheriff Court Rules) (Miscellaneous Amendments) 2008 (SSI 2008/223) para.5(4) (effective July 1, 2008).

in the cause

[A.B.] (*designation and address*), Pursuer

against

[C.D.] (*designation and address*), Defender

[*Here set out briefly:*

(a)   *the facts, procedural history and issues in the proceedings;*

(b)   *the issue in the proceedings on which the court seeks a submission*]

Rule 3.1.6                                      FORM 11A[1]

Form of order for recovery of documents etc. under the Administration of Justice (Scotland) Act 1972

SHERIFFDOM OF (*insert name of sheriffdom*)

AT (*insert place of sheriff court*)

in the Summary Application

of

[A.B.] (*designation and address*)

Applicant

against

[C.D.] (*designation and address*)

Respondent

Date: (*date of interlocutor*)

To: (*name and address of party or parties or named third party haver, from whom the documents and other property are sought to be recovered*)

**THE SHERIFF** having heard the applicant and being satisfied that it is appropriate to make an order under section 1 of the Administration of Justice (Scotland) Act 1972:

**ORDERS** the Summary Application to be served upon the person(s) named and designed in the application;

**APPOINTS** (*name and designation of Commissioner*) to be Commissioner of the court;

**GRANTS** commission and diligence;

**ORDERS** the Commissioner to explain to the haver on executing the order—

(1)   the meaning and effect of the order;

(2)   that the haver may be entitled to claim that certain of the documents and other property are confidential or privileged;

(3)   that the haver has a right to seek legal or other professional advice of his or her choice and to apply to vary or recall the order;

and to give the haver a copy of the Notice in Form 11B of Schedule 1 to the Act of Sederunt (Summary Applications, Statutory Applications and Appeals etc. Rules) 1999.

*GRANTS* warrant to and authorises the said Commissioner, whether the haver has allowed entry or not—

(1)   to enter, between the hours of 9am and 5pm on Monday to Friday, (*or, where the sheriff has found cause shown under* rule 3.1.11(1), *otherwise specify the time [and day]*) the premises at (*address of premises*) and any other place in Scotland owned or occupied by the haver at which it appears to the Commissioner that any of the items set out in the statement of facts in the application to the court (the "listed items") may be located;

---

[1] As substituted by the Act of Sederunt (Sheriff Court Rules) (Miscellaneous Amendments) (No.3) 2011 (SSI 2011/386) para.6 (effective November 28, 2011).

(2)   to search for and take all other steps which the Commissioner considers necessary to take possession of or preserve (*specify the listed items*);

(3)   to take possession of and to preserve all or any of the listed items and to consign them with the Sheriff Clerk at (*enter name and address of sheriff court*) to be held by him or her pending the further orders of the sheriff;

and for that purpose,

**ORDERS** the haver or his/her servants or agents to allow the Commissioner, any person whom the Commissioner considers necessary to assist him/her, and the Applicant's representatives to enter the premises named in the order and to allow them—

(1)   to search for the listed items and take such other steps as the Commissioner considers it reasonable to take to execute the order;

(2)   to remain in the premises until such time as the search is complete, including allowing them to continue the search on subsequent days if necessary.

**FURTHER ORDERS** the haver or his/her servants or agents—

(1)   (*if appropriate*) to provide access to information stored on any computer owned or used by him/her by supplying or providing the means to overcome any and all security mechanisms inhibiting access thereto;

(2)   to inform the Commissioner immediately of the whereabouts of the listed items;

(3)   to provide the Commissioner with a list of the names and addresses of everyone to whom he or she has given any of the listed items;

and not to destroy, conceal or tamper with any of the listed items except in accordance with the terms of this order;

**FURTHER AUTHORISES** (*specify the representatives*) to be the sole representatives of the Applicant to accompany the Commissioner for the purpose of identification of the said documents and other property.

*(Signed)*

Sheriff

## SCHEDULE TO THE ORDER
### Undertakings given by the Applicant

The Applicant has given the following undertakings—

1.   That he/she will comply with any order of the sheriff as to payment of compensation if it is subsequently discovered that the order, or the implementation of the order, has caused loss to the respondent or, where the respondent is not the haver, to the haver.

2.   That he/she will bring within a reasonable time of the execution of the order any proceedings which he/she decides to bring.

3.   That he/she will not, without leave of the sheriff, use any information, documents or other property obtained as a result of the order, except for the purpose of any proceedings which he/she decides to bring and to which the order relates.

(*or as modified under* rule 3.1.4)

Rule 3.1.9(a)                       FORM 11B[1]

Notice to accompany order in Form 11A when served by Commissioner
### IMPORTANT
### NOTICE TO PERSON ON WHOM THIS ORDER IS SERVED

---

[1] As substituted by the Act of Sederunt (Sheriff Court Rules) (Miscellaneous Amendments) (No.3) 2011 (SSI 2011/386) para.6 (effective November 28, 2011).

1.  This order orders you to allow the person appointed and named in the order as Commissioner to enter your premises to search for, examine and remove or copy the items mentioned in the order.

2.  It also allows entry to the premises to any person appointed and named in the order as a representative of the person who has been granted the order and to any person accompanying the Commissioner to assist him/her.

3.  No-one else is given authority to enter the premises.

4.  You should read the order immediately.

5.  You have the right to seek legal or other professional advice of your choice and you are advised to do so as soon as possible.

6.  Consultation under paragraph 5 will not prevent the Commissioner from entering your premises for the purposes mentioned in paragraph 1 but if the purpose of your seeking advice is to help you to decide if you should ask the sheriff to vary or recall the order you are entitled to ask the Commissioner to delay searching the premises for up to 2 hours or such other longer period as the Commissioner may permit.

7.  The Commissioner is obliged to explain the meaning and effect of the order to you.

8.  The Commissioner is also obliged to explain to you that you are entitled to claim that the items, or some of them, are protected as confidential or privileged.

9.  You are entitled to ask the sheriff to vary or recall the order provided that—

    (a)  you take steps to do so at once; and

    (b)  you allow the Commissioner, any person appointed as a representative of the person who has been granted the order and any person accompanying the Commissioner to assist him/her, to enter the premises meantime.

10. The Commissioner and the persons mentioned as representatives or assistants have a right to enter the premises even if you refuse to allow them to do so, unless—

    (a)  you are female and alone in the premises and there is no female with the Commissioner (where the Commissioner is not herself female), in which case they have no right to enter the premises;

    (b)  the Commissioner serves the order before 9am or after 5pm on a weekday or at any time on a Saturday or Sunday (except where the sheriff has specifically allowed this, which will be stated in the order);

    in which cases you should refuse to allow entry.

11. You are entitled to insist that there is no-one (*or* no-one other than X) present who could gain commercially from anything which might be read or seen on your premises.

12. You are required to hand over to the Commissioner any of the items mentioned in the order which are in your possession.

13. You may be found liable for contempt of court if you refuse to comply with the order.

Rule 3.4.3(2)                          FORM 11C[1, 2]

Form of certificate of completion of pre-action requirements

---

[1] As inserted by the Act of Sederunt (Sheriff Court Rules) (Enforcement of Securities over Heritable Property) 2010 (SSI 2010/324) (effective September 30, 2010).

[2] As amended by the Act of Sederunt (Sheriff Court Rules) (Miscellaneous Amendments) 2013 (SSI 2013/135) para.2 (effective May 27, 2013).

Certificate of completion of pre-action requirements in an application under [insert reference to provision or provisions under which application is made] of the property at (*insert address of security subjects*).

in the cause

SHERIFFDOM OF (*insert name of sheriffdom*)

AT (*insert place of sheriff court*)

[A.B.], (*insert designation and address*), Pursuer

against

[C.D.], (*insert designation and address*), Defender

Court ref. no:

(Insert name of pursuer), pursuer and creditor in the security with (*insert name of defender*), the defender, in respect of the premises at (*insert address of security subjects*) aver(s) that the pre-action requirements, have been complied with (*tick boxes to confirm*)—

1.  As soon as reasonably practicable upon the defender entering into default, the pursuer provided the defender with clear information about—[1]

    (a)  the terms of the security;

    (b)  the amount due to the pursuer under the security, including any arrears and any charges in respect of late payment, broken down so as to show—

    (i)  the total amount of the arrears;

    (ii)  the total outstanding amount due including any charges already incurred;

    (c)  the nature and the level of any charges that may be incurred by virtue of the contract to which the security relates if the default is not remedied; and

    (d)  any other obligation under the security in respect of which the defender is in default.

    Please provide details of (a) the date on which the information mentioned in 1(a) was provided; and (b) how the requirements of 1(b), (c) and (d) were complied with including a copy of the information provided under those paragraphs:

---

[1] As amended by the Act of Sederunt (Sheriff Court Rules) (Miscellaneous Amendments) 2013 (SSI 2013/135) para.2 (effective May 27, 2013).

2.    The pursuer has made reasonable efforts to agree with the defender
      proposals in respect of future payments to the pursuer under the
      security and the fulfilment of any other obligation under the security
      in respect of which the defender is in default, including—[1]

    (a)   making reasonable attempts to contact the defender to discuss the default;

    (b)   providing the defender with details of any proposals made by the pursuer,
      set out in such a way as to allow the defender to consider the proposal;

    (c)   allowing the defender reasonable time to consider any proposals made by
      the pursuer;

    (d)   notifying the defender within a reasonable time of any decision taken by
      the pursuer to accept or reject a proposal made by the defender and, where
      the pursuer rejects such proposal, the pursuer has provided reasons for
      rejecting the proposal in writing within 10 working days of notifying the
      defender it is rejecting the proposal;

    (e)   considering the affordability of any proposal for the defender taking into
      account, where known to the pursuer, the defender's personal and financial
      circumstances.

Provide details:

*3.   Where the defender has failed to comply with a condition of an
      agreement reached with the pursuer in respect of any proposal and
      the defender has not previously failed to comply with a condition of
      the agreement—

    (a)   the pursuer has given the defender notice in writing of its decision to make
      an application under [*insert reference to provision or provisions under
      which application is made*] and the ground of the proposed application
      before making the application;

    (b)   the pursuer has not made an application before the expiry of 15 working
      days**, beginning with the date on which the defender is deemed to have
      received the notice referred to at paragraph (a);

    (c)   the default by the defender in respect of which the application is intended
      to be made has not been remedied during that notice period.

Provide details of the defender's failure to comply with a condition
of the agreement:

*Indicate here if not applicable

**In this paragraph, "working day" means a day that is not a
Saturday or Sunday, or any day that is a bank holiday under the
Banking and Financial Dealings Act 1971 in any part of the United
Kingdom.

4.    The defender has not taken steps that are likely to result in—

    (a)   the payment to the pursuer within a reasonable time of any arrears, or the
      whole amount, due to the pursuer under the security; and

    (b)   fulfilment by the defender within a reasonable time of any other obligation
      under the security in respect of which the defender is in default.

---

[1] As amended by the Act of Sederunt (Sheriff Court Rules) (Miscellaneous Amendments) 2013 (SSI
2013/135) para.2 (effective May 27, 2013).

Indicate what (if any) steps have been taken by the defender and why those steps are not considered to be effective:

5.  The pursuer has provided the defender with information about sources of advice and assistance in relation to management of debt, including—

    (a)  where the security is regulated, any relevant information sheet published by the appropriate regulatory body;

    (b)  a local citizens advice bureau or other advice organisation; and

    (c)  the housing department of the local authority in whose area the property which is subject to the security is situated.

6.  The pursuer has encouraged the defender to contact the local authority in whose area the security subjects are situated.

7.  The pursuer has had regard to any guidance issued by the Scottish Ministers.

(Signed)

[X. Y,], (*add designation and business address*)

Pursuer's solicitor

Rule 3.4.6                                    FORM 11D[1]

Form of notice to entitled residents in an application for enforcement of security over residential property

Notice to an entitled resident in an application for repossession of the property at (*insert address of security subjects*).

**SHERIFFDOM OF** (*insert name of sheriffdom*)

**AT** (*insert place of sheriff court*)

[A.B.], (*insert designation and address*), Pursuer

against

[C.D.], (*insert designation and address*), Defender

Court ref. no:

To: (*insert name and address of entitled resident*)

Attached to this notice is a copy of an application by (*insert name of pursuer*) under [insert reference to provision or provisions under which application is made]. **IF THE APPLICATION IS GRANTED, THE PROPERTY AT (*INSERT ADDRESS OF SECURITY SUBJECTS*) MAY BE REPOSSESSED AND YOU WOULD NO LONGER HAVE THE RIGHT TO RESIDE THERE**. A Form 11E application form is also attached.

This Notice—

(a)  gives you warning that an application has been made to the sheriff court for an order which may affect your interest as an entitled resident under [*insert reference to relevant provision or provisions*] in the property at (*insert address of security subjects*); and

(b)  informs you that an entitled resident may apply to the court to continue the

---

[1] As inserted by the Act of Sederunt (Sheriff Court Rules) (Enforcement of Securities over Heritable Property) 2010 (SSI 2010/324) (effective September 30, 2010).

proceedings or make any other order [*insert reference to relevant provision or provisions*] of that Act.

**IF YOU WISH TO MAKE AN APPLICATION FOR AN ORDER UNDER [INSERT REFERENCE TO RELEVANT PROVISION OR PROVISIONS]** you should complete and lodge Form 11E with the sheriff clerk at (*insert name and address of sheriff court*).

**IF YOU ARE UNCERTAIN AS TO WHAT ACTION TO TAKE** you should consult a solicitor. You may be eligible for legal aid depending on your income, and you can get information about legal aid from a solicitor. You may also obtain advice from an approved lay representative, or any Citizens Advice Bureau or other advice agency.

**PLEASE NOTE THAT IF YOU DO NOTHING IN ANSWER TO THIS DOCUMENT** the court will consider the application in the absence of you or your representative.

(Signed)

[P.Q.], Sheriff Officer, or

[X.Y.] (*add designation and business address*) Solicitor

Rules 3.4.6 and 3.4.7        FORM 11E[1] [2]

Form of application to court by entitled resident

Application to court by an entitled resident in proceedings for repossession of the property at (*insert address of security subjects*).

Sheriff Court:..........

Date:

Court ref. no.

1.     This application is made [by/on behalf of] (*delete as appropriate*) (*insert name and address of entitled resident*).

2.     The applicant is an entitled resident within the meaning of section 24C(1) of the Conveyancing and Feudal Reform (Scotland) Act 1970 and/or, as the case may be, section 5D of the Heritable Securities (Scotland) Act 1894 because his or her sole or main residence is the security subjects (in whole or in part) at (*insert address of security subjects) and (*tick one box as appropriate*)—

      (a)    *he or she is the proprietor of the security subjects (where the proprietor is not the debtor in the security);* ☐

      (b)    *her or she is the non-entitled spouse of the debtor or the proprietor of security subjects which are (in whole or in part) a matrimonial home;* ☐

      (c)    *he or she is the non-entitled civil partner of the debtor or the proprietor of security subjects which are (in whole or in part) a family home;* ☐

      (d)    *he or she is a person living together with the debtor or the proprietor as if* ☐

---

[1] As inserted by the Act of Sederunt (Sheriff Court Rules) (Enforcement of Securities over Heritable Property) 2010 (SSI 2010/324) (effective September 30, 2010).
[2] As amended by the Act of Sederunt (Rules of the Court of Session and Sheriff Court Rules Amendment No. 2) (Marriage and Civil Partnership (Scotland) Act 2014) 2014 (SSI 2014/302) r.7 (effective December 16, 2014).

*they were married to each other;*

    (e)  *he or she lived together with the debtor or the proprietor in a relationship* ☐
        *described in (d) and—*

        (i)  *the security subjects (in whole or in part) are not the sole or main residence of the debtor or the proprietor;*

        (ii)  *he or she lived together with the debtor or the proprietor throughout the period of 6 months ending with the date on which the security subjects ceased to be the sole or main residence of the debtor or the proprietor; and*

        (iii)  *the security subjects (in whole or in part) are the sole or main residence of a child aged under 16 who is a child of both parties in that relationship.*

3.    The applicant believes that the court should consider this application because *(insert relevant details)*—

4.    The applicant asks the court to make an order under section 24B(1) of the Conveyancing and Feudal Reform (Scotland) Act 1970 and/or section 5C(1) of the Heritable Securities (Scotland) Act 1894 for *(insert details of what you wish the court to do and why—)*

*WHAT HAPPENS NEXT:* When you lodge this form at the sheriff clerk's office, the sheriff will fix a hearing for all those with an interest to appear and be heard. You are required to serve upon every party and intimate to every entitled resident a copy of this form, together with details of the date, time and place of the hearing.

*IF YOU ARE UNCERTAIN AS TO WHAT ACTION TO TAKE* you should consult a solicitor. You may be eligible for legal aid depending on your income, and you can get information about legal aid from a solicitor. You may also obtain advice from an approved lay representative or any Citizens Advice Bureau or other advice agency,

Date *(insert date)*

    (Signed)
    [P.Q.], (Applicant),
    or [X.Y.], *(add designation and address of Applicant's representative)*

**DIET ASSIGNED**

At *(insert place)* on *(insert date)*, the court assigns the *(insert date of hearing)* at *(insert time)* at *(insert name of sheriff court)* as a diet for hearing parties on the Form 11E application.

Date *(insert date)*

    *(Signed)*
    Sheriff Clerk

**EXECUTION OF CITATION**

At *(insert place)* on *(insert date)*, I hereby certify that upon the *(insert date)*, I duly served upon every party and intimated to every entitled resident a copy of this Form HE application, together with details of the hearing. This I did by *(insert method of service/intimation)*.

Date *(insert date)*

    *(Signed)*
    [P.Q.], Sheriff Officer, or
    [X.Y.] *(add designation and business address)* Applicant's Solicitor

Rule 3.4.8(2)  FORM 11F[1] [2]

Form of minute for recall of decree

Minute for recall of decree in an application for repossession of the property at (*insert address of security subjects*).

Sheriff Court:..........
Date:
Court ref. no.
A.B. (*pursuer*) against C.D. (*defender(s)*)
(*insert name*), being (*tick one box as appropriate*)—

The Pursuer*; ☐

The Defender*; or ☐

An entitled resident within the meaning of section 24C(1) of the Conveyancing and Feudal Reform (Scotland) Act 1970 and/or, as the case may be, section 5D of the Heritable Securities (Scotland) Act 1894 because my sole or main residence is the security subjects (in whole or in part) at (*insert address of security subjects*) and—*

(a) *I am the proprietor of the security subjects (where the proprietor is not the debtor in the security);* ☐

(b) *I am the non-entitled spouse of the debtor or the proprietor of security subjects which are (in whole or in part) a matrimonial home;* ☐

(c) *I am the non-entitled civil partner of the debtor or the proprietor of security subjects which are (in whole or in part) a family home;* ☐

(d) *I am a person living with the debtor or the proprietor as if we were married to each other;* ☐

(e) *I am a person who lived together with the debtor or the proprietor in a relationship described in (d) and—* ☐

    (i) *the security subjects (in whole or in part) are not the sole or main residence of the debtor or the proprietor;*

    (ii) *I lived together with the debtor or the proprietor throughout the period of 6 months ending with the date on which the security subjects ceased to be the sole or main residence of the debtor or the proprietor; and*

    (iii) *the security subjects (in whole or in part) are the sole or main residence of a child aged under 16 who is a child of both parties in that relationship.*

moves the court to recall the decree pronounced on (*insert date*) in this case.

**WHAT HAPPENS NEXT:** When you lodge this form at the sheriff clerk's office, the sheriff clerk will fix a hearing for all those with an interest to appear and be heard. You are required to serve upon every party and intimate to every entitled resident a copy of this form, together with details of the date, time and place of the hearing.

---

[1] As inserted by the Act of Sederunt (Sheriff Court Rules) (Enforcement of Securities over Heritable Property) 2010 (SSI 2010/324) (effective September 30, 2010).

[2] As amended by the Act of Sederunt (Rules of the Court of Session and Sheriff Court Rules Amendment No. 2) (Marriage and Civil Partnership (Scotland) Act 2014) 2014 (SSI 2014/302) r.7 (effective December 16, 2014).

If you wish to proceed with this application for recall of decree **YOU MUST ATTEND OR BE REPRESENTED AT THAT HEARING**.

**YOU ARE STRONGLY ADVISED TO SEEK IMMEDIATE LEGAL ADVICE FROM A SOLICITOR**. You may be eligible for legal aid depending on your income, and you can get information about legal aid from a solicitor. You may also obtain advice from an approved lay representative or any Citizens Advice Bureau or other advice agency.

Date (*insert date*)

(*Signed*)

[P.Q.], (Applicant),

or [X.Y.], (*add designation and address of Applicant's representative*)

## DIET ASSIGNED

At (*insert place*) on (*insert date*), the court assigns the (*insert date of hearing*) at (*insert time*) at (*insert name of sheriff court*) as a diet for hearing parties on the Form 11F application.

Date (*insert date*)

(*Signed*)

Sheriff Clerk

## EXECUTION OF CITATION

At (*insert place*) on (*insert date*), I hereby certify that upon the (*insert date*), I duly served upon every party and intimated to every entitled resident a copy of this Form 11F application, together with details of the hearing. This I did by (*insert method of service/intimation*).

Date (*insert date*)

(*Signed*)

[P.Q.], Sheriff Officer, or

[X.Y.] (*add designation and business address*) Applicant's Solicitor

Rule 3.4.8(10)                    FORM 11G[1]

Form of intimation where peremptory diet fixed in a recall of decree application

Intimation of peremptory diet fixed in an application for repossession of the property at (*insert address of security subjects*).

**SHERIFFDOM OF** (*insert name of sheriffdom*)

**AT** (*insert place of sheriff court*)

[A.B.], (*insert designation and address*), Pursuer

against

(C.D.], (*insert designation and address*), Defender

Court ref. no:

The court noted that you did not appear at the Hearing to consider your application for recall of decree on (*insert date*). In your absence the decree for repossession of the property at (*insert address of security subjects*) has been recalled. As a result of your non-appearance the sheriff has ordered that you appear or be represented on

---

[1] As inserted by the Act of Sederunt (Sheriff Court Rules) (Enforcement of Securities over Heritable Property) 2010 (SSI 2010/324) (effective September 30, 2010).

(*insert date*) at (*insert time*) within (*insert name and address of sheriff court*) in order to ascertain whether you intend to proceed with your defence or your application.

A copy of the order is attached.

When you appear you will be asked by the sheriff to state whether you intend to proceed with your defence or your application.

**IF YOU ARE UNCERTAIN AS TO WHAT ACTION TO TAKE** you should consult a solicitor. You may be eligible for legal aid depending on your income, and you can get information about legal aid from a solicitor. You may also obtain advice from an approved lay representative or any Citizens Advice Bureau or other advice agency.

**PLEASE NOTE THAT IF YOU DO NOT APPEAR OR ARE NOT REPRESENTED AT THAT HEARING** the sheriff may regard you as no longer wishing to proceed with your defence or your application arid the sheriff may award decree of new against you in your absence and you will not be allowed to make a further application for recall.

Date (*insert date*)            (*Signed*)

                                  (*add designation and address*)

Rule 3.8.3(1)                  FORM 12

FORM OF NOTICE TO BE SERVED ON PERSON WHO IS SUBJECT OF HOSPITAL ORDER, GUARDIANSHIP ORDER OR COMMUNITY CARE ORDER PROCEEDINGS.

To [*name and address of patient*]

Attached to this notice is a copy of—

*an application to the managers of [*name of hospital*] for your admission to that hospital in accordance with section 21 of the Mental Health (Scotland) Act 1984.

*an application to the sheriff at [*name of Sheriff Court*] for a Community Care Order in accordance with section 35A of the Mental Health (Scotland) Act 1984.

*an application to the [*name of local authority*] for your reception into guardianship in accordance with Section 40 of the Mental Health (Scotland) Act 1984.

**The hearing will be held at** [*place*] .......... **on** [*date*] .......... **at** [*time*].

You may appear personally at the hearing of this application unless the court decides otherwise on medical recommendations.

In any event, if you are unable or do not wish to appear personally you may request any person to appear on your behalf.

If you do not appear personally or by representative, the sheriff will consider the application in the absence of you or your representative.

                                       [*Signed*]

                                  Sheriff Clerk

[*Place and date*]

*delete as appropriate

Rule 3.8.3(3)                    |FORM 13

FORM OF NOTICE TO RESPONSIBLE MEDICAL OFFICER

To [*name and address of responsible medical officer*]

In accordance with the Mental Health (Scotland) Act 1984, a copy of the application and notice of hearing is sent with this notice.

1.   You are requested to deliver it personally to [*name of patient*] and to explain the contents of it to him.

2.  You are also required to arrange if the patient so wishes, for the attendance of [*name of patient*] at the hearing at [*place of hearing*] on [*date*] so that he may appear and be heard in person.
3.  You are further requested to complete and return to me in the enclosed envelope the certificate appended hereto before the date of the hearing.
4.  If in your opinion it would be prejudicial to the patient's health or treatment for him to appear and be heard personally you may so recommend in writing, with reasons on the certificate.

[*Signed*]
Sheriff Clerk

[*Place and date*]

**Rule 3.8.4(1)(b) and 3.8.4(2)(a)**                     FORM 14

## FORM OF CERTIFICATE OF DELIVERY BY RESPONSIBLE MEDICAL OFFICER

I, [*name and designation*], certify that—

1.  I have on the..........day of..........personally delivered to [*name of patient*] a copy of the application and the intimation of the hearing; and have explained the contents or purport to him [*or* her].
2.  The patient does [not] wish to attend the hearing.
3.  The patient does [not] wish to be represented at the hearing [and has nominated [*name and address of representative*] to represent him].
4.  I shall arrange for the attendance of the patient at the hearing [*or* in my view it would be prejudicial to the patient's health or treatment for him [*or* her] to appear and be heard in person for the following reasons [*give reasons*]].

[*Signature and designation*]

[*Address and date*]

Rule 3.8.11                     FORM 15

## FORM OF APPEAL FOR REVOCATION OF A COMMUNITY CARE ORDER UNDER SECTION 35F OF THE MENTAL HEALTH (SCOTLAND) ACT 1984

SHERIFFDOM OF (*insert name of sheriffdom*)
AT (*insert name of Sheriff Court*)

I, [*insert name and address of applicant*],
appeal to the sheriff for revocation of a community care order made on [*insert date of order* on the following grounds:—

[*State grounds on which appeal is to proceed*]

The community care order was renewed under section 35C(5) of the Mental Health (Scotland) Act 1984 on [*insert date of renewal*] and is still in force.

The special medical officer specified in the community care order is [*insert name and address of special medical officer*].

[*Signed*]..........
Applicant..........
[*or*          Solicitor          for Applicant*]..........
[*Insert          designation          and address*]..........

**Rule 3.9.9(b)**                     FORM 16

FORM OF NOTICE TO PERSON WITH INTEREST IN PROPERTY SUBJECT
TO AN APPLICATION FOR AN ORDER UNDER PARAGRAPH 12 OF
SCHEDULE 1 TO THE PROCEEDS OF CRIME (SCOTLAND) ACT 1995
IN THE SHERIFF COURT
in the
PETITION [*or* NOTE]
of
[A.B.] (*name and address*)
for an order under paragraph 12 of Schedule 1 to the Proceeds of Crime (Scotland)
Act 1995
in respect of the estates of [CD.] (*name and address*)
*Court Ref No.*

Date: (*date of posting or other method of service*)
To: (name and address of person on whom notice is to be served)
This Notice—

(a) gives you warning that an application has been made to the sheriff court for an order which may affect your interest in property; and

(b) informs you that you have an opportunity to appear and make representations to the court before the application is determined.

TAKE NOTICE

1. That on (*date*) in the sheriff court at (*place*) a confiscation order was made under section 1 of the Proceeds of Crime (Scotland) Act 1995 in respect of [CD.] (name and address).

2. That on (*date*) the administrator appointed under paragraph 1(1)(a) of Schedule 1 to the Proceeds of Crime (Scotland) Act 1995 on (*date*) was empowered to realise property belonging to [CD.].

or

2. That on (*date*) the administrator was appointed under paragraph 1 (1)(b) of Schedule 1 to the Proceeds of Crime (Scotland) Act 1995 on (*date*) to realise property belonging to [CD.].

3. That application has been made by petition [or note] for an order under paragraph 12 of Schedule 1 to the Proceeds of Crime (Scotland) Act 1995 (*here set out briefly the nature of the order sought*). A copy of the petition [*or* note] is attached.

4. That you have the right to appear before the court in person or by counsel or other person having a right of audience and make such representations as you may have in respect of the order applied for. The court has fixed (*insert day and date fixed for hearing the application*), at (*insert time and place fixed for hearing*) as the time when you should appear to do this.

5. That if you do not appear or are not represented on the above date, the order applied for may be made in your absence.

IF YOU ARE UNCERTAIN ABOUT THE EFFECT OF THIS NOTICE, you should consult a Solicitor, Citizen's Advice Bureau or other local advice agency or adviser immediately.

(*Signed*) ..........

Sheriff Officer ..........

[*or* Solicitor [*or* Agent] for petitioner [*or* noter]] ..........

(*Address*)..........

**Rule 3.11.14(1)**          FORM 17

### Representation of the People Act 1983

In the petition questioning the election for the ......... of ........., in which .......... is petitioner and ......... is respondent.

The petitioner desires to withdraw his petition on the following grounds [*state grounds*], and craves that a diet may be appointed for hearing his application. He has, in compliance, with rule 3.11.14 of the Act of Sederunt (Summary Applications, Statutory Applications and Appeals etc. Rules) 1999, given the written notice of his intention to present this application to the respondent, to the Lord Advocate, and to the returning officer.

[*To be signed by the petitioner or his solicitor.*]

**Rule 3.11.14(4)**                    FORM 18

### Representation of the People Act 1983

In the petition questioning the election for the .......... of .........., in which .......... is the petitioner and .......... is respondent.

Notice is hereby given that the above petitioner has applied for leave to withdraw his petition, and that the sheriff principal has, by interlocutor dated the .......... day of .........., assigned the .......... day of .......... at .......... o'clock .......... noon within the .......... as a diet for hearing the application.

Notice is further given that under the Act any person who might have been a petitioner in respect of the said election may at the above diet apply to the sheriff principal to be substituted as a petitioner.

[*To be signed by the petitioner or his solicitor.*]

**Rule 3.11.15(1)**                    FORM 19

### Representation of the People Act 1983

In the petition questioning the election for the .......... of .........., in which .......... was the petitioner [*or* last surviving petitioner] and .......... is the respondent.

Notice is hereby given that the above petition stands abated by the death of the petitioner [*or* last surviving petitioner], and that any person who might have been a petitioner in respect of the said election and who desires to be substituted as a petitioner must, within 21 days from this date, lodge with the undersigned sheriff clerk of [*name sheriff court district*], a minute craving to be so substituted.

Date (*insert date*)

[*To be signed by the sheriff clerk*]

**Rule 3.16.4(1)**                    FORM 20[1]

### FORM OF NOTICE OF AN APPLICATION UNDER THE ADULTS WITH INCAPACITY (SCOTLAND) ACT 2000

To (*insert name and address*)

Attached to this notice is a copy of an application for (*insert type of application*) under the Adults with Incapacity (Scotland) Act 2000.

**The hearing will be held at (insert place) on (insert date) at (insert time)**

You may appear personally at the hearing of this application.

In any event, if you are unable or do not wish to appear personally you may appoint a legal representative to appear on your behalf.

---

[1] As inserted by the Act of Sederunt (Summary Applications, Statutory Applications and Appeals etc. Rules) Amendment (Adults with Incapacity) 2001 (SSI 2001/142), (effective April 2, 2001).

If you are uncertain as to what action to take you should consult a solicitor. You may be eligible for legal aid, and you can obtain information about legal aid from any solicitor. You may also obtain information from any Citizens Advice Bureau or other advice agency.

If you do not appear personally or by legal representative, the sheriff may consider the application in the absence of you or your legal representative.

*(insert place and date)*..........　　　　　　　*(signed)*..........
　　　　　　　　　　　　　　　　　　　Sheriff Clerk ..........
　　　　　　　　　　　　　　　　　　　or
　　　　　　　　　　　　　　　　　　　[P.Q.] Sheriff Officer ..........
　　　　　　　　　　　　　　　　　　　or
　　　　　　　　　　　　　　　　　　　[X.Y.],Solicitor ..........

**Rule 3.16.4(3)**　　　　　　　FORM 21[1][2]

### FORM OF NOTICE TO MANAGERS

To *(insert name and address of manager)*

A copy of an application made under the Adults with Incapacity (Scotland) Act 2000 and notice of hearing is sent with this notice.

1. You are requested immediately on receipt to deliver it personally to (name of adult) and to explain the contents of it to him or her.

2. You are further requested to complete and return to the sheriff clerk in the enclosed envelope the certificate (Form 22) appended hereto before the date of the hearing.

*(insert place and date)*..........　　　　　　　*(signed)*..........
　　　　　　　　　　　　　　　　　　　Sheriff Clerk ..........
　　　　　　　　　　　　　　　　　　　or
　　　　　　　　　　　　　　　　　　　[P.Q.] Sheriff Officer ..........
　　　　　　　　　　　　　　　　　　　or
　　　　　　　　　　　　　　　　　　　[X.Y.],Solicitor ..........

**Rule 3.16.4(4)**　　　　　　　FORM 22[3]

### FORM OF CERTIFICATE OF DELIVERY BY MANAGER

I, *(insert name and designation)*, certify that—

I have on *(insert date)* personally delivered to (name of adult) a copy of the application and the intimation of the hearing and have explained the contents to him/her.

Date *(insert date)*..........　　　　　　　*(signed)*..........
　　　　　　　　　　　　　　　　　　　Manager ..........
　　　　　　　　　　　　　　　　　　　*(add designation and address)*..........

---

[1] As inserted by the Act of Sederunt (Summary Applications, Statutory Applications and Appeals etc. Rules) Amendment (Adults with Incapacity) 2001 (SSI 2001/142), (effective April 2, 2001).

[2] As inserted by the Act of Sederunt (Summary Applications, Statutory Applications and Appeals etc. Rules Amendment) (Miscellaneous) 2013 (SSI 2013/293) r.2, (effective November 11, 2013).

[3] As inserted by the Act of Sederunt (Summary Applications, Statutory Applications and Appeals etc. Rules) Amendment (Adults with Incapacity) 2001 (SSI 2001/142), (effective April 2, 2001).

**Rule 3.16.7(1)**                                             FORM 23[1]

## SUMMARY APPLICATION UNDER THE ADULTS WITH INCAPACITY (SCOTLAND) ACT 2000

SHERIFFDOM OF *(insert name of sheriffdom)*

AT *(insert place of Sheriff Court)*

[A.B.] *(design and state capacity in which the application is made)*, Pursuer

The applicant craves the court *(state here the specific order(s) sought by reference to the provisions in the Adults with Incapacity (Scotland) Act 2000 .)*

**STATEMENTS OF FACT**

*(State in numbered paragraphs the facts on which the application is made, including:*

1. *The designation of the adult concerned (if other than the applicant).*

(a) *the adult's nearest relative;*

(b) *the adult's primary carer;*

(ba) *the adult's named person;*

(c) *any guardian, continuing attorney or welfare attorney of the adult; and*

(d) *any other person who may have an interest in the application.*

3. *The adult's place of habitual residence and/or the location of the property which is the subject of the application.)*

*(insert place and date)* .........                    *(signed)* .........

[A.B.], Pursuer or

[X.Y.], *(state designation and business address)*..........

Solicitor for the Pursuer .........

**Rule 3.16.7(2)**                                             FORM 24[2]

## APPEAL TO THE SHERIFF UNDER THE ADULTS WITH INCAPACITY (SCOTLAND) ACT 2000

SHERIFFDOM OF *(insert name of sheriffdom)*

AT *(insert place of Sheriff Court)*

[A.B.] *(design and state capacity in which the appeal is being made)*, Pursuer

This appeal is made in respect of *(state here the decision concerned, the date on which it was intimated to the pursuer, and refer to the relevant provisions in the Adults with Incapacity (Scotland) Act 2000 ).*

*(State here, in numbered paragraphs:*

1. *The designation of the adult concerned (if other than the applicant).*

2. *The designation of:*

(a) *the adult's nearest relative;*

(b) *the adult's primary carer;*

(ba) *the adult's named person;*

---

[1] As inserted by the Act of Sederunt (Summary Applications, Statutory Applications and Appeals etc. Rules) Amendment (Adults with Incapacity) 2001 (SSI 2001/142), (effective April 2, 2001) and amended by the Act of Sederunt (Summary Applications, Statutory Applications and Appeals etc. Rules) Amendment (Adult Support and Protection (Scotland) Act 2007) (SSI 2008/111) r.2(3) (effective April 1, 2008).

[2] As inserted by the Act of Sederunt (Summary Applications, Statutory Applications and Appeals etc. Rules) Amendment (Adults with Incapacity) 2001 (SSI 2001/142), r.3(3), (effective April 2, 2001) and amended by the Act of Sederunt (Summary Applications, Statutory Applications and Appeals etc. Rules) Amendment (Adult Support and Protection (Scotland) Act 2007) (SSI 2008/111) r.2(3) (effective April 1, 2008).

(c) *any guardian, continuing attorney or welfare attorney of the adult; and*

(d) *any other person who may have an interest in the application.*

3. *The adult's place of habitual residence and/or the location of the property which is the subject of the application.)*

The pursuer appeals against the decision on the following grounds (*state here in separate paragraphs the grounds on which the appeal is made*).

The pursuer craves the court (*state here orders sought in respect of appeal*).

(*insert place and date*) ..........

(*signed*)..........

[A.B.], Pursuer or

[X.Y.], *(state designation and business address)*..........

Solicitor for the Pursuer ..........

**Rule 3.27.6(1)**                    FORM 25[1]

ANTISOCIAL BEHAVIOUR ETC. (SCOTLAND) ACT 2004
CLOSURE NOTICE

Section 27

1. The service of this closure notice is authorised by a senior police officer under section 26(1) of the Antisocial Behaviour etc. (Scotland) Act 2004 ("the Act").

2. The premises to which this closure notice relates are: *(specify premises)*.

3. Access to those premises by any person other than—

(a) a person who habitually resides in the premises; or

(b) the owner of the premises,

is prohibited.

4. Failure to comply with this notice is an offence which may result in a fine of up to £2,500 or imprisonment for a term of up to 3 months (or both). The penalties may be higher for repeated failure to comply with this (or any other) closure notice.

5. An application for the closure of these premises will be made under section 28 of the Act and will be considered at *(insert place including Room No. if appropriate)* on the .......... day of .......... at .......... am/pm.

6. On such an application as set out in paragraph 5 being made, the sheriff may make a closure order under section 29 of the Act in respect of these premises.

7. The effect of the Closure Order in respect of these premises would be to close the premises to all persons (other than any person expressly authorised access by the sheriff in terms of section 29(3) of the Act) for such period not exceeding 3 months as is specified in the order. Measures may be taken to ensure that the premises are securely closed against entry by any person.

8. If you live on or have control of, responsibility for or an interest in the premises to which this closure notice relates and wish to oppose the application for a closure order, you should attend or be represented at the hearing mentioned in paragraph 5 of this notice.

9. If you would like further information or advice about housing or legal matters you can contact—

*(specify at least two persons or organisations (including name and means of contacting) based in the locality of the premises who or which will be able to provide advice about housing and legal matters)*. You also have a legal right to advice from your local authority should you be threatened with possible homelessness.

---

[1] Inserted by SSI 2004/455, para 5 and Sch. (effective October 28, 2004).

**Rule 3.27.6(2)**                                    FORM 26[1]

## ANTISOCIAL BEHAVIOUR ETC. (SCOTLAND) ACT 2004
### CERTIFICATION OF SERVICE

Section 27

I *(insert designation, including address and rank, of police officer)* certify that a
copy of the closure notice which was authorised by *(insert designation of senior
police officer)* on *(insert date on which closure notice was authorised)* in respect of
*(insert details of the premises to which closure notice relates)* was served on: *(insert
name and address of each person to whom a copy of the notice was given, including
date)*

...................

...................

...................

...................

...................

by *(insert designation, including address and rank, of police officer who served
the copy or copies of the closure notice and, if more than one, indicate which police
officer served a copy of the notice on which of the persons listed above).*

...................

Signed
*(insert designation, including rank, of police officer)*

**Rule 3.27.7**                                    FORM 27[2]

## ANTISOCIAL BEHAVIOUR ETC. (SCOTLAND) ACT 2004

Section 28

Sheriff Court.................... 20..........

(Court Ref No.)

**PART A**

APPLICATION FOR CLOSURE ORDER IN RESPECT OF PREMISES AT:

...................

...................

...................

("the Premises")

**PART B**

1. This application is made [by/on behalf of] *(delete as appropriate) (insert name
and rank of senior police officer)* of *(insert details of police force).*

2. Service of a closure notice on the Premises was authorised by *(insert details of
senior police officer)* on the .......... day of ........... A copy of [the authorisation/
written confirmation of such authorisation] *(delete as appropriate)* is attached.

3. A copy of the closure notice was, on the .......... day of ..........,—

(a) fixed to:

*(insert details of all locations in, or used as part of the Premises, to which a copy
of the notice was fixed)*

...................

...................

...................

...................

---

[1] Inserted by SSI 2004/455, para 5 and Sch. (effective October 28, 2004).

[2] Inserted by SSI 2004/455, para 5 and Sch. (effective October 28, 2004) and amended by SSI 2010/
416 (effective December 13, 2010).

......................

......................

(b) given to:
*(insert name and address of each person to whom a copy of the notice was given)*

......................

......................

......................

......................

......................

......................

4. Certification in the prescribed form of service of the closure notice to the persons described at paragraph 3(b) above is attached.

5. This application is made on the following grounds:
*(insert reasons for making application)*

......................

......................

......................

......................

......................

......................

6. The following evidence is [attached/supplied] *(delete as appropriate)* in respect of this application *(insert short details of supporting evidence)*.

**PART C**

7. The applicant asks the court to—

(a) assign the hearing for the .......... day of .......... at .......... am/pm; and

(b) make a closure order in respect of the Premises.

..........Signed

Senior Police Officer for [Police Force] (Applicant)

or [X.Y.] Solicitor for Senior Police Officer

*(add designation and business address)*

FORM OF INTERLOCUTOR

Sheriff Court .......... .......... 20..........

(Court Ref No.)

The sheriff having considered this application assigns .......... at .......... within .......... as a hearing, this date having been previously intimated to known interested persons and published in the closure notice.

..........Signed

Sheriff

FORM OF INTERLOCUTOR

Sheriff Court .................... 20..........

(Court Ref No.)

The sheriff having heard *(insert details of parties who attended the hearing)* and having considered the application [, being satisfied that the conditions mentioned in [section 30(2)] [section 30(2A)] of the Antisocial Behaviour etc. (Scotland) Act 2004 are met] *(delete as appropriate)* and having regard to the matters mentioned in section 30(3) of the Antisocial Behaviour etc. (Scotland) Act 2004 ("the Act"),

*1. makes an order under section 29(1) of the Act that the premises at *(insert details of premises)* are closed to all persons for a period of *(insert period)*.

*2. directs intimation of this interlocutor to *(insert details of all known interested persons)* and by posting a copy thereof at prominent places on the premises at *(indicate where copies have been posted)*.

*3. refuses to make a closure order in respect of the premises at *(insert details of premises)*.

*4. postpones the determination of the application until *(insert date)* at *(insert time)* within *(insert location)*.

*delete as appropriate

..........Signed

Sheriff

**Rule 3.27.8**                              FORM 28[1]

## ANTISOCIAL BEHAVIOUR ETC. (SCOTLAND) ACT 2004

### Minute

Section 32

Application for extension of closure order

Sheriff Court ..........: ............... 20..........

(Court Ref No.)

**PART A**

PREMISES IN RESPECT OF WHICH CLOSURE ORDER HAS BEEN MADE:

.....................

.....................

.....................

("the Premises")

**PART B**

1. This application is made [by/on behalf of] *(delete as appropriate) (insert name and rank of senior police officer)* of *(insert details of police force)*.

2. A copy of the closure order made in respect of the Premises is attached. The closure order has effect until *(enter date)*.

3. The applicant believes that it is necessary to extend the period for which the closure order has effect for the purpose of preventing [relevant harm] [the commission of an exploitation offence] *(delete as appropriate)*, on the following grounds: *(specify reasons for extension)*.

4. *(Insert details of local authority)* has been consulted about the applicant's intention to make this application.

*PART C*

5. The applicant asks the court to—

(c) fix a hearing;

(d) order the applicant to intimate this application and the date of the hearing to such persons as the sheriff considers appropriate; and

(e) extend the closure order in respect of the Premises for a period of .......... [months/days] *(delete as appropriate)* or for such period not exceeding 6 months as the court may consider appropriate.

..........Signed

Senior Police Officer for [Police Force] (Applicant)

or [X.Y.] Solicitor for Senior Police Officer

*(add designation and business address)*

FORM OF INTERLOCUTOR

Sheriff Court.................... 2..........

(Court Ref No.)

---

[1] Inserted by SSI 2004/455, para 5 and Sch. (effective October 28, 2004) and amended by SSI 2010/416 (effective December 13, 2010).

The sheriff having considered this minute orders the applicant to intimate this application and interlocutor to ........., assigns .......... at .......... within .......... as a hearing and directs any person wishing to oppose the granting of the application to appear or be represented at the hearing to show cause why the application should not be granted.

..........Signed

Sheriff

FORM OF INTERLOCUTOR

Sheriff Court ....................20..........

(Court Ref No.)

The sheriff having heard *(insert details of parties who attended the hearing)* [and] having considered this minute [and being satisfied that the condition mentioned in [section 32(1)] [section 32(1 A)] of the Antisocial Behaviour etc. (Scotland) Act 2004 is met] *(delete as appropriate)*,

*1. makes an order extending the closure order made under section 29(1) of the Antisocial Behaviour etc. (Scotland) Act 2004 in respect of the premises at *(insert details of premises)* for a period of *(insert period)*.

*2. directs intimation of this interlocutor to *(insert details of persons to whom sheriff considers it to he appropriate to intimate)* and by posting a copy thereof at prominent places on the premises at *(indicate where copies have been posted)*.

*3. refuses to make an order extending the closure order in respect of the premises at *(insert details of premises)*.

*4. postpones the determination of the application until *(insert date)* at *(insert time)* within *(insert location)*.

*delete as appropriate

..........Signed

Sheriff

**Rule 3.27.9**                    FORM 29[1]

ANTISOCIAL BEHAVIOUR ETC. (SCOTLAND) ACT 2004

Minute

Section 33

Application for revocation of closure order

Sheriff Court .................... 20..........

(Court Ref No.)

**PART A**

PREMISES IN RESPECT OF WHICH CLOSURE ORDER HAS BEEN MADE:

....................

....................

....................

("the Premises")

The applicant is *(insert name and address of applicant)* who is:

*1. a senior police officer of the police force for the area within which the Premises (or part thereof) are situated.

*2. the local authority for the area within which the Premises or part thereof are situated.

---

[1] Inserted by SSI 2004/455, para 5 and Sch. (effective October 28, 2004) and amended by SSI 2010/416 (effective December 13, 2010).

*3. a person on whom a copy of the closure notice relating to the Premises in respect of which the closure order has effect was served under section 27(2)(b) or (3) of the Antisocial Behaviour etc. (Scotland) Act 2004.

*4. a person who has an interest in these premises but on whom the closure notice was not served.

*delete as appropriate.

**PART B**

1.  A copy of the closure order made in respect of the Premises is attached.
2.  The applicant believes that a closure order in respect of the Premises is no longer necessary to prevent [the occurrence of relevant harm][the commission of an exploitation offence] (*delete as appropriate*) for the following reasons (*specify grounds for application for revocation*).

**PART C**

3.  The applicant asks the court to:

    (a)  fix a hearing;
    (b)  order the applicant to intimate this application and the date of the hearing to such persons as the sheriff considers appropriate and, where the applicant is not a senior police officer, to such senior police officer as the sheriff considers appropriate; and
    (c)  order the revocation of the closure order.

..........Signed

Applicant (*include full designation*)

or [X.Y.] Solicitor for Applicant (*include full designation and business address*)

FORM OF INTERLOCUTOR

Sheriff Court.......... ...........20..............

(Court Ref No.)

The sheriff having considered this minute orders the applicant to intimate this application and interlocutor to.........., assigns...........within...........as a hearing and directs any person wishing to oppose the granting of the application to appear or be represented at the hearing to show cause why the application should not be granted.

..........Signed

Sheriff

FORM OF INTERLOCUTOR

Sheriff Court...............20...........

(Court Ref No.)

The sheriff having heard (*insert details of parties who attended the hearing*) [and] having considered this minute [and being satisfied that a closure order is no longer necessary to prevent [the occurrence of relevant harm][the commission of an exploitation offence] (*delete as appropriate*),

*1.  makes an order revoking the closure order made under section 29(1) of the Antisocial Behaviour etc. (Scotland) Act 2004 in respect of the premises at (insert details of the premises).

*2.  directs intimation of this interlocutor to (insert details of persons to whom sheriff considers it to be appropriate to intimate).

*3.  refuses to make an order revoking the closure order in respect of the premises at (insert details of the premises).

*4.  postpones the determination of the application until (*insert date*) at (*insert time*) within (*insert location*).

*delete as appropriate

..........Signed

Sheriff

**Rule 3.27.10**                               FORM 30[1]

### ANTISOCIAL BEHAVIOUR ETC. (SCOTLAND) ACT 2004
Minute

Section 34

Application for access to premises in respect of which a closure order is in force

Sheriff Court.......... ...........20...........

(Court Ref No.)

### PART A

PREMISES IN RESPECT OF WHICH CLOSURE ORDER HAS BEEN MADE:

....................

....................

....................

("the Premises")

PREMISES IN RESPECT OF WHICH APPLICATION FOR ACCESS IS BEING MADE:

....................

....................

....................

### PART B

1.  A copy of the closure order made in respect of the Premises is attached. The closure order has effect until (*insert date*).

2.  The applicant (*insert details of applicant*) [owns/occupies] (*delete as appropriate*) the following [part of] (delete as appropriate) building or structure in which the Premises are situated and in respect of which the closure order does not have effect.

### PART C

3. The applicant asks the court to:

(a)  fix a hearing;

(b)  order the applicant to intimate this application and the date of the hearing to such persons as the sheriff considers appropriate and, where the applicant is not a senior police officer, to such senior police officer as the sheriff considers appropriate; and

(c)  make an order allowing access (detail access provisions requested).

..........Signed

Applicant (*include full designation*)

or [X.Y.] Solicitor for Applicant (*include full designation and business address*)

FORM OF INTERLOCUTOR

Sheriff Court...............20...........

(Court Ref No.)

The sheriff having considered this minute orders the applicant to intimate this application and interlocutor to.........., assigns..........at..........within.......... as a hearing and directs any person wishing to oppose the granting of the application to appear or be represented at the hearing to show cause why the application should not be granted.

..........Signed

Sheriff

FORM OF INTERLOCUTOR

Sheriff Court...............20..........

(Court Ref No.)

---

[1] Inserted by SSI 2004/455, para 5 and Sch. (effective October 28, 2004).

The sheriff having heard (*insert details of parties who attended the hearing*) and having considered this minute,

*1. makes an order an order allowing (*insert name and address*)

....................

....................

....................

access to the following part or parts of the premises at (*insert details of premises*) in relation to which a closure order has been made under section 29(1) of the Antisocial Behaviour etc. (Scotland) Act 2004: (*insert details of parts of premises to which access order is to apply*)

*2. directs intimation of this interlocutor to (*insert details of all known interested persons to whom the sheriff considers it to be appropriate to intimate*).

*3. refuses to make an access order in respect of the premises at (*insert details of premises*).

*4. postpones the determination of the application until (insert date) at (insert time) within (*insert location*).

*delete as appropriate

.......... Signed

Sheriff

**Rule 3.27.16**                                FORM 31

ANTISOCIAL BEHAVIOUR ETC. (SCOTLAND) ACT 2004 Section 13, 102 or 105

Intimation that court may make or revoke or vary a parenting order

Sheriff Court .......... .......... 20 ..........

(Court Ref No.)

**PART A**

**This part must be completed by the applicant's solicitor in language a child is capable of understanding**

To **(1)**

The Sheriff (the person who has to decide about the parenting order) has been asked by **(2)** to decide:—

(a)   **(3)** and **(4)**;

(b)   **(5)**;

(c)   **(6)**.

If you want to tell the Sheriff what you think about the things **(2)** has asked the Sheriff to decide about your future you should complete Part B of this form and send it to the Sheriff Clerk at **(7)** by **(8)**. An envelope which does not need a postage stamp is enclosed for you to use to return the form.

**IF YOU DO NOT UNDERSTAND THIS FORM OR IF YOU WANT HELP TO COMPLETE IT you may get free help from a SOLICITOR or contact the SCOTTISH CHILD LAW CENTRE ON the FREE ADVICE TELEPHONE LINE ON 0800 317 500.**

If you return the form it will be given to the Sheriff. The Sheriff may wish to speak with you and may ask you to come and see him or her.

NOTES FOR COMPLETION

| | |
|---|---|
| (1) Insert name and address of child. | (2) Insert description of party making the application to the court. |
| (3) Insert appropriate wording for parenting order sought. | (4) Insert appropriate wording, if relevant, for Antisocial Behaviour Order. |

| (5) Insert appropriate wording for contact. | (6) Insert appropriate wording for any other order sought or determinations to be made by sheriff. |
|---|---|
| (7) Insert address of sheriff clerk. | (8) Insert the date occurring 21 days after the date on which intimation is given. |
| (9) Insert court reference number. | (10) Insert name and address of parties to the action. |

## PART B
**IF YOU WISH THE SHERIFF TO KNOW YOUR VIEWS ABOUT THE PARENTING ORDER YOU SHOULD COMPLETE THIS PART OF THE FORM**

To the Sheriff Clerk, (7)

Court Ref. No. (9)

(10)..........

**QUESTION (1): DO YOU WISH THE SHERIFF TO KNOW WHAT YOUR VIEWS ARE ABOUT THE PARENTING ORDER?**

(PLEASE TICK BOX)

| YES | |
|---|---|
| NO | |

If you have ticked YES please also answer Question (2) or (3)

**QUESTION (2): WOULD YOU LIKE A FRIEND, RELATIVE OR OTHER PERSON TO TELL THE SHERIFF YOUR VIEWS ABOUT THE PARENTING ORDER?**

(PLEASE TICK BOX)

| YES | |
|---|---|
| NO | |

If you have ticked YES please write the name and address of the person you wish to tell the Sheriff your views in Box (A) below. You should also tell that person what your views are about the parenting order.

| BOX A: | (NAME) | | | |
|---|---|---|---|---|
| | .................. | | | |
| | (ADDRESS) | | | |
| | .................. | | | |
| | .................. | | | |
| | .................. | | | |
| | Is this person— | A friend? | | A relative? |
| | | A teacher? | | Other? |

OR

**QUESTION (3): WOULD YOU LIKE TO WRITE TO THE SHERIFF AND TELL HIM WHAT YOUR VIEWS ARE ABOUT THE PARENTING ORDER?**

(PLEASE TICK BOX)

| YES | |
|---|---|
| NO | |

If you decide that you wish to write to the Sheriff you can write what your views are about the parenting order in Box (B) below or on a separate piece of paper. If you decide to write your views on a separate piece of paper you should send it along with this form to the Sheriff Clerk in the envelope provided.

| BOX B: | WHAT I HAVE TO SAY ABOUT THE PARENTING ORDER:— |
|--------|------------------------------------------------|
|        |                                                |

NAME: ..........
ADDRESS: ..........
DATE: ..........

**Rule 3.27.17**                    FORM 32[1]

ANTISOCIAL BEHAVIOUR ETC. (SCOTLAND) ACT 2004

Section 13, 102 or 105
Form of notice to local authority requesting a report in respect of a child
Sheriff Court.......... .......... 20..........
(Court Ref No.)
To (*insert name and address*)

**1. YOU ARE GIVEN NOTICE** that in an action in the Sheriff Court at (*insert address*) an application for [the variation/revocation of] (*delete as appropriate*) a parenting order is being considered in respect of a parent of the child (*insert name of child*). A copy of the application is enclosed.

2. You are required to submit to the court a report on all the circumstances of the child, including but not limited to:—

(a)   the current or proposed arrangements for the case and upbringing of the child;

(b)   information about the family circumstances of the parent; and

(c)   the likely effect of a parenting order on the family circumstances of the parent and the child.

3. This report should be sent to the Sheriff Court at .......... on or before .......... (*insert date*).

Date (*insert date*)
..........Signed:
Applicant (*include full designation*)
or [X.Y.] Solicitor for Applicant (*include full designation and business address*)
or Sheriff Clerk

**Rule 3.34.2**                    FORM 33

NOTE OF APPEAL UNDER LICENSING (SCOTLAND) ACT 2005
*[Repealed by the Act of Sederunt (Sheriff Court Rules) (Miscellaneous Amendments) (No.2) 2010 (SSI 2010/416) r.8 (effective December 13, 2010).]*

**Rule 3.35.6**                    FORM 34[2]

---

[1] Inserted by SSI 2004/455, para 5 and Sch. (effective October 28, 2004).
[2] As inserted by the Act of Sederunt (Summary Applications, Statutory Applications and Appeals etc. Rules) Amendment (Adult Support and Protection (Scotland) Act 2007) (No.2) 2008 (SSI 2008/335) r.2(3) (effective October 29, 2008) and substituted by the Act of Sederunt (Summary Applications, Statutory Applications and Appeals etc. Rules) Amendment (Adult Support and Protection (Scotland) Act 2007) (No.3) 2008 (SSI 2008/375) para.2(5) (effective November 20, 2008).

Form of certificate of delivery of document under section 26(2), 27(1) or 27(2) of the Adult Support and Protection (Scotland) Act 2007

Court ref no:

(Insert place and date) I, (insert name and designation), hereby certify that on (date) I duly delivered to (insert name and address) (insert details of the document delivered). This I did by (state method of delivery).

*Signed*

*(add designation and address or business address)*

FORM 35[1]

FORM OF APPLICATION FOR WARRANT FOR ENTRY UNDER SECTION 38(2) OF THE ADULT SUPPORT AND PROTECTION (SCOTLAND) ACT 2007

SHERIFFDOM OF *(insert name of sheriffdom)*

AT *(insert place of sheriff court)*

[A.B.] *(design and state capacity in which the application is made)*, Applicant

The applicant craves the court to grant a warrant for entry in terms of sections 37 and 38(2) of the Adult Support and Protection (Scotland) Act 2007 to *(state address of specified place to which entry is sought).*

**Rule 3.39.2(1)**                                           FORM 36[2]

FORM OF APPLICATION FOR WARRANT UNDER SECTION 27 OF THE PUBLIC HEALTH ETC. (SCOTLAND) ACT 2008

SHERIFFDOM OF *(insert name of sheriffdom)*

AT *(insert place of sheriff court)*

[A.B.] (design and state address), Applicant

**Order sought from the court**

The applicant applies to the court to grant warrant to him:

1.  to enter the premises at *(insert address of premises to which entry is sought).*
2.  to take with him any other person he may authorise and, if he has reasonable cause to expect any serious obstruction in obtaining access, a constable.
3.  to take with him any equipment or materials required for any purpose for which the power of entry is being exercised.
4.  to direct that those premises (or any part of them) are, or any thing in or on them is, to be left undisturbed (whether generally or in particular respects) for so long as he considers appropriate.
5.  to exercise any of the powers conferred by sections 23, 24 and 25 of the Public Health etc. (Scotland) Act 2008 ("the Act").

**Statement**

*Delete as appropriate

1.  This application is made pursuant to section 27 of the Act.
2.  The applicant is an investigator duly appointed in terms of section 21(2) of the Act to carry out a public health investigation.
3.  The said premises are*/are not* a dwellinghouse.
4.  The said premises are within the jurisdiction of this court.
5.  The applicant considers it necessary for the purpose of, or in connection

---

[1] As inserted by the Act of Sederunt (Summary Applications, Statutory Applications and Appeals etc. Rules) Amendment (Adult Support and Protection (Scotland) Act 2007) (No.2) 2008 (SSI 2008/335) r.2(3) (effective October 29, 2008).

[2] As inserted by the Act of Sederunt (Summary Applications, Statutory Applications and Appeals etc. Rules) Amendment (Public Health etc. (Scotland) Act 2008) 2009 (SSI 2009/320) r.2 (effective October 1, 2009).

with, a public health investigation to exercise the powers of entry available to him under section 22 of the Act, the other investigatory powers mentioned in section 23 of the Act, the power to ask questions mentioned in section 24 of the Act and any supplementary power mentioned in section 25 of the Act (*insert here a brief statement of reasons*).

*6.  [*If the said premises are a dwellinghouse*] The applicant has in terms of section 26(2) of the Act given 48 hours notice of the proposed entry to a person who appears to be the occupier of the dwellinghouse and the period of notice has expired.

*7.  The applicant is an investigator entitled to enter premises under section 22 of the Act and *the applicant has been refused entry to the said premises, or *the applicant reasonably anticipates that entry will be refused

OR

*7. The said premises are premises which the applicant is entitled to enter and they are unoccupied.

**OR**

*7. The said premises are premises which the applicant is entitled to enter and the occupier thereof is temporarily absent and there is urgency because (*here state briefly why there is urgency*).

**OR**

*7. The applicant is an investigator entitled to exercise a power under section 23 or 24 of the Act and

\*    has been prevented from exercising that power, or

\*    reasonably anticipates being prevented from exercising that power.

**OR**

*7 An application for admission to the said premises would defeat the object of the public health investigation.

8. In the circumstances narrated the applicant is entitled to the warrant sought and it should be granted accordingly.

> (*signed*)
> [A.B.] Applicant
> *or* [X.Y.] (*add designation and business address*)
> Solicitor for applicant
> (*insert date*)

**Rule 3.39.2(2)**                      FORM 37[1]

FORM OF WARRANT FOR A PUBLIC HEALTH INVESTIGATION

Sheriff Court...............20...............

(Court Ref. No.)

* *Delete as appropriate*

The sheriff, having considered an application made under section 27 of the Public Health etc. (Scotland) Act 2008 ("the Act") *[and productions lodged therewith] *[and (*where the premises referred to below are a dwellinghouse*) being satisfied that due notice has been given under section 26(2) of the Act and has expired],

Grants warrant to the applicant (*insert name*) as sought and authorises him:

---

[1] As inserted by the Act of Sederunt (Summary Applications, Statutory Applications and Appeals etc. Rules) Amendment (Public Health etc. (Scotland) Act 2008) 2009 (SSI 2009/320) r.2 (effective October 1, 2009).

(a)   to enter the premises at (*insert address*),

(b)   on entering the premises referred to at paragraph (a), to take—

    (i)   any other person authorised by him and, if he has reasonable cause to expect any serious obstruction in obtaining access, a constable; and

    (ii)   any equipment or materials required for any purpose for which the power of entry is being exercised,

(c)   to direct that—

    (i)   those premises (or any part of them) are; or

    (ii)   any thing in or on those premises is, to be left undisturbed (whether generally or in particular respects) for so long as he considers appropriate.

(d)   to exercise any power mentioned in sections 23 to 25 of the Act.

(*signed*)

Sheriff

## Rule 3.39.3(1)           FORM 38[1]

### FORM OF APPLICATION FOR MEDICAL EXAMINATION OF A PERSON UNDER SECTION 34 OF THE PUBLIC HEALTH ETC. (SCOTLAND) ACT 2008

SHERIFFDOM OF (*insert name of sheriffdom*)

AT (*insert place of sheriff court*)

[A.B.] (*design health board*), Applicant

**Order sought from the court**

\* *Delete as appropriate*

The applicant applies to the court to grant an order under section 34(1) of the Public Health etc. (Scotland) Act 2008 ("the Act") authorising the medical examination of (*insert name, address and date of birth of person to be medically examined*) ("the person").

\*And (*if necessary, request any specialities in connection with the examination, about which the court's additional authority is sought pursuant to* section 34(3) of the Act).

**Statement**

\**Delete as appropriate*

1.   This application is made pursuant to sections 33 and 34 of the Act.
2.   The person is present within the applicant's area. The applicant is a health board operating within the jurisdiction of this court. This court accordingly has jurisdiction.
3.   The person is aged 16 years or over.

**OR**

The person is under 16. The parent or other person who has day-to-day care or control of the person is (*insert name, address and relationship to the person*).

    4.

      (a)   The applicant \*knows/\*suspects that the person—

          \*(i)   has an infectious disease, namely [*insert name of disease*];

          \*(ii)   has been exposed to an organism which causes an infectious disease [*insert name of disease*];

          \*(iii)   is contaminated; or

          \*(iv)   has been exposed to a contaminant,

(*insert here a brief statement indicating the basis upon which these matters are known or suspected by the applicant*)

---

[1] As inserted by the Act of Sederunt (Summary Applications, Statutory Applications and Appeals etc. Rules) Amendment (Public Health etc. (Scotland) Act 2008) 2009 (SSI 2009/320) r.2 (effective October 1, 2009).

**AND**

(b)   It appears to the applicant that as a result—

    (i)   there is or may be a significant risk to public health; and

    (ii)   it is necessary, to avoid or minimise that risk, for the person to be medically examined.

(*Insert here a brief statement indicating the reason why the applicant considers that there is or may be a significant risk to public health and that it is necessary, to avoid or minimise that risk, for the person to be medically examined*).

5. The applicant proposes that the examination be carried out by (*insert proposed class or classes of health care professional*).

6. The applicant proposes that the examination be (*insert nature of the proposed examination*).

\*7. The applicant has explained to the person—

(a)   that there is a significant risk to public health;

(b)   the nature of that risk; and

(c)   why the applicant considers it necessary for the proposed action to be taken in relation to that person.

**OR**

\*7. The applicant states that the person is incapable of understanding any explanation of the matters referred to at section 31(3) of the Act (*state reason*) and has explained to (*insert name and address of a person mentioned in* section 31(5)(a) or (b) of the Act *and their relationship to the person*)—

(a)   that there is a significant risk to public health;

(b)   the nature of that risk; and

(c)   why the applicant considers it necessary for the proposed action to be taken in relation to that person.

**OR**

\*7. The applicant states that no explanation has been given in relation to this application under section 31(3) or (5) of the Act because (*state why it was not reasonably practicable to do so*).

\*8. The applicant states that \*a response was made/\*representations were made on behalf of the person in the following terms (*insert response or representations made*).

9. The applicant attaches to this application a certificate signed by a health board competent person which indicates that the competent person is satisfied as to the matters mentioned in statement 4 [\*and (*in a case where medical examination of a group is sought*) that it is necessary, to avoid or minimise an actual or anticipated significant risk to public health, for all the persons in the group to be medically examined].

10. In the circumstances narrated the applicant is entitled to the order sought and it should be granted accordingly.

                        (*signed*)

                        [X.Y.] (*add designation and business address*)

                        Solicitor for applicant

                        (*insert date*)

FORM 39[1]

---

[1] As inserted by the Act of Sederunt (Summary Applications, Statutory Applications and Appeals etc. Rules) Amendment (Public Health etc. (Scotland) Act 2008) 2009 (SSI 2009/320) r.2 (effective October 1, 2009).

**Rule 3.39.3(3)**

### FORM OF ORDER FOR A MEDICAL EXAMINATION

Sheriff Court................

............... 20.......... at [*insert time*]

(Court Ref. No.)

The sheriff, having considered an application made under section 33(2) of the Public Health etc. (Scotland) Act 2008 ("the Act") *[and productions lodged therewith], and being satisfied as necessary as to the matters mentioned in section 34(2) of the Act,

1. Makes an order in terms of section 34(1) of the Act authorising the medical examination of (insert details of the person as given in the application) and authorises (insert the class or classes of health care professional by whom the medical examination is to be carried out) to carry out the examination,

*And (*add any additional matters to be dealt with in the order in terms of* section 34(3) of the Act).

2. Directs notification of this order (*insert details of method and timing of notice*) to (*the person to whom the order applies*)

*and (*the name and designation of any person to whom an explanation was given under* section 31(5) of the Act)

*and (*insert the name and designation of any other person whom the sheriff considers appropriate*).

* Delete *as appropriate*

(signed)

Sheriff

### FORM 40[1]

**Rule 3.39.4(1)**

### FORM OF APPLICATION FOR QUARANTINE ORDER UNDER SECTION 40 OF THE PUBLIC HEALTH ETC. (SCOTLAND) ACT 2008
### SHERIFFDOM OF (*insert name of sheriffdom*)
### AT (*insert place of sheriff court*)
[A.B.] (*design health board*), Applicant

**Order sought from the court**

* Delete *as appropriate*

The applicant applies to the court for a quarantine order under section 40(1) of the Public Health etc. (Scotland) Act 2008 ("the Act") authorising the quarantining of (*insert name, address and date of birth of person to be quarantined*) (*"the person"*) for a period of (*insert period*).

*and the person's removal to (*insert place of quarantine*) [by (*insert, if sought, the name and designation of a person mentioned in* section 4()(4)(d) of the Act)].

*authorising the taking in relation to the person of the following steps, namely *disinfection/

*disinfestation/*decontamination (*specify which steps are sought*)

*and imposing the following conditions in relation to the quarantine (insert conditions sought).

**Statement**

*Delete *as appropriate*

1. This application is made pursuant to sections 39 and 40 of the Act.

---

[1] As inserted by the Act of Sederunt (Summary Applications, Statutory Applications and Appeals etc. Rules) Amendment (Public Health etc. (Scotland) Act 2008) 2009 (SSI 2009/320) r.2 (effective October 1, 2009).

2. The person is present within the applicant's area. The applicant is a health board operating within the jurisdiction of this court. This court accordingly has jurisdiction.

3. The person is aged 16 years or over.

**OR**

The person is under 16. The parent or other person who has day-to-day care or control of the person is (*insert name, address and relationship to the person*).

4. (a) The applicant *knows/*has reasonable grounds to suspect that the person—

*(i)   has an infectious disease, namely [*insert name of disease*];

*(ii)   has been exposed to an organism which causes an infectious disease [*insert name of disease*];

*(iii)   is contaminated; or

*(iv)   has been exposed to a contaminant,

(*insert here a brief statement indicating the basis upon which these matters are known or suspected by the applicant*)

**AND**

(b) that as a result—

(i)   there is or may be a significant risk to public health; and

(ii)   it is necessary, to avoid or minimise that risk, for the person to be quarantined.

(*Insert here a brief statement indicating the reason why the applicant considers that there is or may be a significant risk to public health and that it is necessary, to avoid or minimise that risk, for the person to be quarantined*).

5. The applicant proposes that the person be quarantined at (*insert place and address*) *[and that he should be removed there by (*insert name and designation of person under* section 40(4) (d) of the Act)]. (*Indicate briefly why this is proposed*).

6. The applicant proposes that the person be quarantined for (*insert period of time*).

7. The applicant considers it necessary to *disinfect/*disinfest/*decontaminate the person (*insert details and reasons*).

*8. The applicant considers the conditions sought to be included in the order to be necessary because (*insert reasons*).

*9. The applicant has explained to the person—

(a)   that there is a significant risk to public health;

(b)   the nature of that risk; and

(c)   why the applicant considers it necessary for the proposed action to be taken in relation to that person.

**OR**

*9. The applicant states that the person is incapable of understanding any explanation of the matters referred to at section 31(3) of the Act (*state reason*) and has explained to (*insert name and address of a person mentioned in* section 31(5) (a) or (b) of the Act *and their relationship to the person*)—

(a)   that there is a significant risk to public health;

(b)   the nature of that risk; and

(c)   why the applicant considers it necessary for the proposed action to be taken in relation to that person.

**OR**

*9 The applicant states that no explanation has been given in relation to this application under section 31(3) or (5) of the Act because (*state why it was not reasonably practicable to do so*).

*10. The applicant states that *a response was made/*representations were made on behalf of the person in the following terms (*insert response or representations made*).

11. The applicant attaches to this application a certificate signed by a health board competent person which indicates that the competent person is satisfied as to the matters mentioned in statement 4.

12. In the circumstances narrated the applicant is entitled to the order sought and it should be granted accordingly.

(*signed*)

[X.Y.] (*add designation and business address*)

Solicitor for applicant

(*insert date*)

## FORM 41[1]

**Rule 3.39.4(3)**

### FORM OF QUARANTINE ORDER

Sheriff Court...............

............... 20..........at (*insert time*)

(Court Ref. No.)

The sheriff, having considered an application made under section 39(2) of the Public Health etc. (Scotland) Act 2008 ("the Act") *[and productions lodged therewith], and being satisfied as necessary as to the matters mentioned in section 40(2) of the Act,

1. Makes an order in terms of section 40(1) of the Act authorising the quarantining of (*insert details of the person as given in the application*) in (*insert the place in which the person is to be quarantined*) for a period of (insert the period for which the person is to be quarantined) and

Authorising the removal of (*insert name of the person*) to (*insert address at which the person is to be quarantined*)

Further (*insert any authorisation for disinfection/disinfestation/decontamination*),

(*Insert any conditions imposed by the order including the name and designation of any person authorised under* section 40(4) (d) of the Act *to effect a removal*), and

2. Directs notification of this order (*insert details of method and timing of notice*) to (the person to whom the order applies)

*and (*the name and designation of any person to whom an explanation was given under* section 31(5) of the Act)

*and (*insert the name and designation of any other person whom the sheriff considers appropriate*).

*Delete as appropriate

(*signed*)

Sheriff

## FORM 42[2]

**Rule 3.39.5(1)**

---

[1] As inserted by the Act of Sederunt (Summary Applications, Statutory Applications and Appeals etc. Rules) Amendment (Public Health etc. (Scotland) Act 2008) 2009 (SSI 2009/320) r.2 (effective October 1, 2009).

[2] As inserted by the Act of Sederunt (Summary Applications, Statutory Applications and Appeals etc. Rules) Amendment (Public Health etc. (Scotland) Act 2008) 2009 (SSI 2009/320) r.2 (effective October 1, 2009).

## FORM OF APPLICATION TO HAVE A PERSON REMOVED TO AND DETAINED IN HOSPITAL UNDER SECTION 42 OF THE PUBLIC HEALTH ETC. (SCOTLAND) ACT 2008

SHERIFFDOM OF (*insert name of sheriffdom*)

AT (*insert place of sheriff court*)

[A.B.] (*design health board*), Applicant

### Order sought from the court

*\*Delete as appropriate*

The applicant applies to the court for a short term detention order under section 42(1) of the Public Health etc. (Scotland) Act 2008 ("the Act") in respect of (*insert name, address and date of birth of person to be subject to the order*) ("the person").

1. authorising the person's removal to hospital *[by (*insert name and designation of a person mentioned in* section 42(1)(a) of the Act)] and the person's detention in hospital for the period of (*insert period*), and

2. authorising the taking in relation to the person of the following steps, namely *disinfection/ *disinfestation/*decontamination (*specify which steps are sought*).

### Statement

*\*Delete as appropriate*

1. This application is made pursuant to sections 41 and 42 of the Act.

2. The person is present within the applicant's area. The applicant is a health board operating within the jurisdiction of this court. This court accordingly has jurisdiction.

3. The person is aged 16 years or over.

### OR

The person is under 16. The parent or other person who has day-to-day care or control of the person is (*insert name, address and relationship to the person*).

4. (a) The applicant knows that the person—

*(i)   has an infectious disease, namely [*insert name of disease*]; or

*(ii)  is contaminated,

(*insert here a brief statement indicating the basis upon which these matters are known to the applicant*)

### AND

(b) it appears to the applicant that as a result—

(i)   there is a significant risk to public health; and

(ii)  it is necessary, to avoid or minimise that risk, for the person to be detained in hospital

(*Insert here a brief statement indicating the reason why the applicant considers that there is a significant risk to public health and that it is necessary, to avoid or minimise that risk, for the person to be detained in hospital*).

5. The applicant proposes that the person be detained at (*insert name and address of hospital*) *[and that he should be removed there by (*insert name and designation of person under* section 42(1)(a) of the Act *and indicate briefly why this is proposed*)].

6. The applicant proposes that the person be detained for (*insert period of time*).

7. The applicant considers it necessary to *disinfect,/*disinfest/*decontaminate the person (*insert details and reasons*).

*8. The applicant has explained to the person—

(a)   that there is a significant risk to public health;

(b)   the nature of that risk; and

(c)   why the applicant considers it necessary for the proposed action to be taken in relation to that person.

### OR

*8. The applicant states that the person is incapable of understanding any explanation of the matters referred to at section 31(3) of the Act (*state reason*) and has explained to (*insert name and address of a person mentioned in* section 31(5)(a) or (b) of the Act *and their relationship to the person*)—

(a)    that there is a significant risk to public health;

(b)    the nature of that risk; and

(c)    why the applicant considers it necessary for the proposed action to be taken in relation to that person.

*OR*

*8. The applicant states that no explanation has been given in relation to this application under section 31(3) or (5) of the Act because (*state why it was not reasonably practicable to do so*).

*9. The applicant states that *a response was made/*representations were made on behalf of the person in the following terms (*insert response or representations made*).

10. The applicant attaches to this application a certificate signed by a health board competent person which indicates that the competent person is satisfied as to the matters mentioned in statement 4.

11. In the circumstances narrated the applicant is entitled to the order sought and it should be granted accordingly.

(*signed*)

*Solicitor for applicant*

*[X. Y.] (add designation and business address)*

(*insert date*)

FORM 43[1]

**Rule 3.39.5(4)**

FORM OF SHORT TERM DETENTION ORDER—REMOVAL TO AND
DETENTION IN HOSPITAL

Sheriff Court...............

............... 20............... at (*insert time*)

(Court Ref. No.)

The sheriff, having considered an application made under section 41(2) of the Public Health etc. (Scotland) Act 2008 ("the Act") *[and productions lodged therewith], and being satisfied as necessary as to the matters mentioned in section 42(2) of the Act,

1. Makes an order in terms of section 42(1) of the Act authorising the short term detention in hospital of (*insert details of the person as given in the application*),

Authorising the removal of that person by (*specify person authorised to carry out removal in terms of* section 42(1)(a) of the Act) to (*specify hospital at which the person is to he detained, including the address*), there to be detained for (*insert period of detention*)

Further (*insert any authorisation for disinfection/disinfestation/decontamination*), and

2. Directs notification of this order (*insert details of method and timing of notice*) to (*the person to whom the order applies*)

*and (*the name and designation of any person to whom an explanation was given under* section 31(5) of the Act)

---

[1] As inserted by the Act of Sederunt (Summary Applications, Statutory Applications and Appeals etc. Rules) Amendment (Public Health etc. (Scotland) Act 2008) 2009 (SSI 2009/320) r.2 (effective October 1, 2009).

*and (*insert the name and designation of any other person whom the sheriff considers appropriate*).

* *Delete as appropriate*
(signed)
Sheriff

FORM 44[1]

**Rule 3.39.5(2)**

FORM OF APPLICATION FOR A SHORT TERM DETENTION ORDER UNDER SECTION 43 OF THE PUBLIC HEALTH ETC. (SCOTLAND) ACT 2008

SHERIFFDOM OF (*insert name of sheriffdom*)

AT (*insert place of sheriff court*)

[A.B.] (*design health hoard*), Applicant

**Order sought from the court**

* *Delete as appropriate*

The applicant applies to the court for a short term detention order under section 43(1) of the Public Health etc. (Scotland) Act 2008 ("the Act") in respect of (*insert name, address and date of birth of person to be subject to the order*) ("the person").

1. authorising the person's detention in hospital for a period of (*insert period*), and

2. authorising the taking in relation to the person of the following steps, namely *disinfection/ *disinfestation/*decontamination (*specify which steps are sought*).

**Statement**

* *Delete as appropriate*

1. This application is made pursuant to sections 41 and 43 of the Act.

2. The person is present within the applicant's area. The applicant is a health board operating within the jurisdiction of this court. This court accordingly has jurisdiction.

3. The person is aged 16 years or over.

**OR**

The person is under 16. The parent or other person who has day-to-day care or control of the person is (*insert name, address and relationship to the person*).

4. (a) The applicant knows that the person—

*(i)   has an infectious disease, namely [*insert name of disease*]; or

*(ii)  is contaminated,

(*insert here a brief statement indicating the basis upon which these matters are known to the applicant*)

**AND**

(b) it appears to the applicant that as a result—

(i)   there is a significant risk to public health; and

(ii)  it is necessary, to avoid or minimise that risk, for the person to be detained in hospital.

(*Insert here a brief statement indicating the reason why the applicant considers that there is a significant risk to public health and that it is necessary, to avoid or minimise that risk, for the person to be detained in hospital*).

5. The person is currently in (*insert name and address of hospital*). The applicant proposes that the person be detained at (*insert name and address of hospital*).

6. The applicant proposes that the person be detained for (*insert period of time*).

---

[1] As inserted by the Act of Sederunt (Summary Applications, Statutory Applications and Appeals etc. Rules) Amendment (Public Health etc. (Scotland) Act 2008) 2009 (SSI 2009/320) r.2 (effective October 1, 2009).

7. The applicant considers it necessary to *disinfect/*disinfest/*decontaminate the person (*insert details and reasons*).

*8. The applicant has explained to the person—

(a)    that there is a significant risk to public health;

(b)    the nature of that risk; and

(c)    why the applicant considers it necessary for the proposed action to be taken in relation to that person.

**OR**

*8. The applicant states that the person is incapable of understanding any explanation of the matters referred to at section 31(3) of the Act (*state reason*) and has explained to (*insert name and address of a person mentioned in* section 31(5)(a) or (b) of the Act *and their relationship to the person*)—

(a)    that there is a significant risk to public health; Release 104: September 2009

(b)    the nature of that risk; and

(c)    why the applicant considers it necessary for the proposed action to be taken in relation to that person.

**OR**

*8. The applicant states that no explanation has been given in relation to this application under section 31(3) or (5) of the Act because {*state why it was not reasonably practicable to do so*).

*9. The applicant states that *a response was made/*representations were made on behalf of the person in the following terms (*insert response or representations made*).

10. The applicant attaches to this application a certificate signed by a health board competent person which indicates that the competent person is satisfied as to the matters mentioned in statement 4.

11. In the circumstances narrated the applicant is entitled to the order sought and it should be granted accordingly.

(*signed*)

[X.Y.] (*add designation and business address*)

Solicitor for applicant

(*insert date*)

FORM 45[1]

**Rule 3.39.5(5)**

FORM OF SHORT TERM DETENTION ORDER—DETENTION IN HOSPITAL

Sheriff Court................

............... 20.......... at (*insert time*)

(Court Ref. No.)

The sheriff, having considered an application made under section 41(2) of the Public Health etc. (Scotland) Act 2008 ("the Act") *[and productions lodged therewith], and being satisfied as necessary as to the matters mentioned in section 43(2) of the Act,

1. Makes an order in terms of section 43(1) of the Act authorising the short term detention in hospital of (*insert details of the person as given in the application*) at (*insert name and address of hospital*) for (*insert period of detention*)

Further (*insert any authorisation for disinfection/disinfestationi/ decontamination*), and

---

[1] As inserted by the Act of Sederunt (Summary Applications, Statutory Applications and Appeals etc. Rules) Amendment (Public Health etc. (Scotland) Act 2008) 2009 (SSI 2009/320) r.2 (effective October 1, 2009).

2. Directs notification of this order (*insert details of method and timing of notice*) to (*the person to whom the order applies*)

*and (*the name and designation of any person to whom an explanation was given under* section 31(5) of the Act)

*and (*insert the name and designation of any other person whom the sheriff considers appropriate*).

*Delete as appropriate*

(*signed*)

Sheriff

FORM 46[1]

**Rule 3.39.6(1)**

FORM OF APPLICATION FOR EXCEPTIONAL DETENTION ORDER UNDER SECTION 45 OF THE PUBLIC HEALTH ETC. (SCOTLAND) ACT 2008

SHERIFFDOM OF (*insert name of sheriffdom*)

AT (*insert place of sheriff court*)

[A.B.] (*design health board*), Applicant

**Order sought from the court**

*Delete as appropriate*

The applicant applies to the court for an exceptional detention order under section 45(1) of the Public Health etc. (Scotland) Act 2008 ("the Act") in respect of (*insert name, address and date of birth of person to be subject to the order*) ("the person").

1. authorising the person's continued detention in hospital for a period of (*insert period*), and

2. authorising the taking in relation to the person of the following steps, namely ""disinfection/ *disinfestation/*decontamination (*specify which steps are sought*).

**Statement**

* *Delete as appropriate*

1. This application is made pursuant to sections 44 and 45 of the Act.

2. The person is presently detained in a hospital within the applicant's area by virtue of a short term detention order. The applicant is a health board operating within the jurisdiction of this court and applied for the short term detention order. This court accordingly has jurisdiction.

3. The person is aged 16 years or over.

**OR**

*The person is under 16. The parent or other person who has day-to-day care or control of the person is (*insert name, address and relationship to the person*).

4. The applicant is satisfied—

(a) that the person—

*(i)   has an infectious disease, namely [*insert name of disease*]; or

*(ii)  is contaminated,

**AND**

(b) that as a result there is a significant risk to public health,

(*insert here a brief statement indicating the basis upon which the applicant is satisfied of these matters*)

**AND**

---

[1] As inserted by the Act of Sederunt (Summary Applications, Statutory Applications and Appeals etc. Rules) Amendment (Public Health etc. (Scotland) Act 2008) 2009 (SSI 2009/320) r.2 (effective October 1, 2009).

(c) that it continues to be necessary, to avoid or minimise that risk, for the person to be detained in hospital (*insert here a brief statement indicating the reason why the applicant considers it necessary for the person to be detained in hospital*),

**AND**

(d) that it is necessary, to avoid or minimise that risk, for the person to be detained for a period exceeding the maximum period for which the person could be detained by virtue of the short term detention order were that order to be extended under section 49(5)(a) of the Act(*insert here a brief statement indicating the reason why the applicant considers it necessary for the person to be detained beyond that maximum period*).

5. The person is currently detained in (*insert name and address of hospital*) by virtue of a short term detention order granted on (*insert date*). The said order is extant until [*insert date*]. The applicant proposes that the person be detained at (*insert name and address of hospital*).

6. The applicant applies to the court to order that the person continue to be detained in (*insert name and address of hospital*) for (*insert period of time*) from (*insert date from which the order is to commence*).

7. The applicant considers it necessary to *disinfect/*disinfest/*decontaminate the person (*insert details and reasons*).

*8. The applicant has explained to the person—

(a)   that there is a significant risk to public health;

(b)   the nature of that risk; and

(c)   why the applicant considers it necessary for the proposed action to be taken in relation to that person.

**OR**

*8. The applicant states that the person is incapable of understanding any explanation of the matters referred to at section 31(3) of the Act (*state reason*) and has explained to (*insert name and address of a person mentioned in* section 31(5) (a) or (b) of the Act *and their relationship to the person*)—

(a)   that there is a significant risk to public health;

(b)   the nature of that risk; and

(c)   why the applicant considers it necessary for the proposed action to be taken in relation to that person.

**OR**

*8. The applicant states that no explanation has been given in relation to this application under section 31(3) or (5) of the Act because (*state why it was not reasonably practicable to do so*).

*9. The applicant states that *a response was made/*representations were made on behalf of the person in the following terms (*insert response or representations made*).

10. The applicant attaches to this application a certificate signed by a health board competent person which indicates that the competent person is satisfied as to the matters mentioned in statement 4.

11. In the circumstances narrated the applicant is entitled to the order sought and it should be granted accordingly.

(*signed*)

[X.Y.] (*add designation and business address*)

Solicitor for applicant

(*insert date*)

## FORM 47[1]

### Rule 3.39.6(3)

### FORM OF EXCEPTIONAL DETENTION ORDER

Sheriff Court..........

..........20..........at (insert time)

(Court Ref. No.)

The sheriff, having considered an application made under section 44(3) of the Public Health etc. (Scotland) Act 2008 ("the Act") *[and productions lodged therewith], and being satisfied as to the matters mentioned in section 45(2) of the Act,

1. Makes an exceptional detention order in terms of section 45(1) of the Act authorising the continued detention of (*insert details of the person as given in the application*) at (*insert name and address of hospital*) for (*insert period of detention*).

Further (*insert any authorisation for disinfection!disinfestation/decontamination*), and

2. Directs notification of this order (*insert details of method and timing of notice*) to (*the person to whom the order applies*)

*and (*the name and designation of any person to whom an explanation was given under* section 31(5) of the Act)

*and (*insert the name and designation of any other person whom the sheriff considers appropriate*).

* *Delete as appropriate*

(*signed*)

Sheriff

## FORM 48[2]

### Rule 3.39.7(1)

### FORM OF APPLICATION FOR EXTENSION OF A QUARANTINE ORDER, SHORT TERM DETENTION ORDER OR EXCEPTIONAL DETENTION ORDER UNDER SECTION 49 OF THE PUBLIC HEALTH ETC. (SCOTLAND) ACT 2008

### SHERIFFDOM OF (*insert name of sheriffdom*)

### AT (*insert place of sheriff court*)

### [A.B.] (*design health hoard*), Applicant

**Order sought from the court**

*\*Delete as appropriate*

The applicant applies to the court to extend for a period of (insert period):

*the quarantine order granted on (*insert date*) in respect of (*insert name, address and date of birth of the person in respect of whom the order was granted*) ("the person") **OR**

*the short term detention order granted on (insert date) in respect of (*insert name, address and date of birth of the person*) ("the person") **OR**

*the exceptional detention order granted on (*insert date*) in respect of (*insert name, address and date of birth of the person*) ("the person").

**Statement**

*\*Delete as appropriate*

---

[1] As inserted by the Act of Sederunt (Summary Applications, Statutory Applications and Appeals etc. Rules) Amendment (Public Health etc. (Scotland) Act 2008) 2009 (SSI 2009/320) r.2 (effective October 1, 2009).

[2] As inserted by the Act of Sederunt (Summary Applications, Statutory Applications and Appeals etc. Rules) Amendment (Public Health etc. (Scotland) Act 2008) 2009 (SSI 2009/320) r.2 (effective October 1, 2009).

1. This application is made pursuant to section 49 of the Public Health etc. (Scotland) Act 2008.

2. The person is presently *quarantined/*detained in hospital within the applicant's area by virtue of *a quarantine order/*a short term detention order/*an exceptional detention order granted on (*insert date*) which expires on (*insert date*). This court accordingly has jurisdiction.

3. The person is aged 16 years or over.

**OR**

The person is under 16. The parent or other person who has day-to-day care or control of the person is (*insert name, address and relationship to the person*).

4. The applicant attaches to this application a certificate signed by a health board competent person which indicates that the competent person is satisfied as to the following matters:

*[*in relation to a proposed extension of a quarantine order*] That it is known, or there are reasonable grounds to suspect, that the person—

*(i)    has an infectious disease;

*(ii)   has been exposed to an organism which causes an infectious disease;

*(iii)  is contaminated; or

*(iv)   has been exposed to a contaminant,

**AND** that as a result there is or may be significant risk to public health,

**AND** that it is necessary, to avoid or minimise that risk, for the person to continue to be quarantined.

**OR**

*[in relation to a proposed extension of a short term detention order or an exceptional detention order] That the person—

*(i)    has an infectious disease; or

*(ii)   is contaminated,

**AND** that as a result there is significant risk to public health,

**AND** that it is necessary, to avoid or minimise that risk, for the person to continue to be detained in hospital.

5. The court is asked to extend the order for a period of (*insert period*) from (*insert date from which the order is to commence*).

*6. An extension of the quarantine order, as sought, will not result in the person being quarantined for a continuous period exceeding 12 weeks.

**OR**

*6 An extension of the short term detention order, as sought, will not result in the person being detained in hospital for a continuous period exceeding 12 weeks.

**OR**

*6 An extension of the exceptional detention order, as sought, will not result in the person being detained in hospital for a continuous period exceeding 12 months.

7. In the circumstances narrated the applicant is entitled to the order sought and it should be granted accordingly.

(*signed*)

[X.Y.] (*add designation and business address*)
Solicitor for applicant
(*insert date*)

FORM 49[1]

**Rule 3.39.7(3)**

---

[1] As inserted by the Act of Sederunt (Summary Applications, Statutory Applications and Appeals etc. Rules) Amendment (Public Health etc. (Scotland) Act 2008) 2009 (SSI 2009/320) r.2 (effective October 1, 2009).

## FORM OF ORDER EXTENDING A QUARANTINE ORDER, SHORT TERM DETENTION ORDER OR EXCEPTIONAL DETENTION ORDER

Sheriff Court.........

.........20.........at (*insert time*)

(Court Ref. No.)

The sheriff, having considered an application made under section 49(2) of the Public Health etc. (Scotland) Act 2008 ("the Act") and productions lodged therewith, and being satisfied as to the matters mentioned in section 49(6) of the Act,

1. Makes an order in terms of section 49(5) of the Act extending *the quarantine order/*the short term detention order/*the exceptional detention order which was granted in respect of (*insert details of the person as given in the application*) on (*insert date*) for a period of (*insert period*) and

2. Directs notification of this order (*insert details of method and timing of notice*) to (*the person to whom the order applies*)

*and (*the name and designation of any person to whom an explanation was given under* section 31(5) of the Act)

*and (*insert the name and designation of any other person whom the sheriff considers appropriate*).

* *Delete as appropriate*

(*signed*)

Sheriff

## FORM 50[1]

**Rule 3.39.8(1)**

## FORM OF APPLICATION FOR MODIFICATION OF A QUARANTINE ORDER, SHORT TERM DETENTION ORDER OR EXCEPTIONAL DETENTION ORDER UNDER SECTION 51 OF THE PUBLIC HEALTH ETC. (SCOTLAND) ACT 2008

**SHERIFFDOM OF** (*insert name of sheriffdom*)

**AT** (*insert place of sheriff court*)

**[A.B.]** (*design health hoard*), Applicant

**Order sought from the court**

**Delete as appropriate*

The applicant applies to the court to modify:

*the quarantine order granted on (insert date) in respect of (insert name, address and date of birth of the person in respect of whom the order was granted) ("the person") **OR**

*the short term detention order granted on (insert date) in respect of (insert name, address and date of birth of the person) ("the person") **OR**

*the exceptional detention order granted on (*insert date*) in respect of (*insert name, address and date of birth of the person*) ("the person")

by (*specify details of the modification sought*).

**Statement**

**Delete as appropriate*

1. This application is made pursuant to sections 50 and 51 of the Public Health etc. (Scotland) Act 2008.

---

[1] As inserted by the Act of Sederunt (Summary Applications, Statutory Applications and Appeals etc. Rules) Amendment (Public Health etc. (Scotland) Act 2008) 2009 (SSI 2009/320) r.2 (effective October 1, 2009).

2. The person is presently *quarantined/*detained in hospital within the applicant's area by virtue of *a quarantine order/*a short term detention order/*an exceptional detention order granted on (*insert date*) which expires on (*insert date*). This court accordingly has jurisdiction.

3. The person is aged 16 years or over.

**OR**

The person is under 16. The parent or other person who has day-to-day care or control of the person is (*insert name, address and relationship to the person*).

4. The applicant attaches to this application a certificate signed by a health board competent person which indicates that the competent person is satisfied as to the following matters:

*[*in relation to a proposed modification of a quarantine order*] That it is known, or there are reasonable grounds to suspect, that the person—

*(i)    has an infectious disease;

*(ii)    has been exposed to an organism which causes an infectious disease;

*(iii)    is contaminated; or

*(iv)    has been exposed to a contaminant,

**AND** that as a result there is or may be significant risk to public health,

**AND** that it is necessary, to avoid or minimise that risk, for the person to continue to be quarantined.

**OR**

*[*in relation to a proposed modification of a short term detention order or an exceptional detention order*] That the person—

*(i)    has an infectious disease; or

*(ii)    is contaminated,

**AND** that as a result there is significant risk to public health

**AND** that it is necessary, to avoid or minimise that risk, for the person to continue to be detained in hospital.

5. The modification is sought for the following reasons (*here insert a brief statement of reasons*).

6. In the circumstances narrated the applicant is entitled to the order sought and it should be granted accordingly.

(*signed*)

[X.Y.] (*add designation and business address*)

Solicitor for applicant

(*insert date*)

## FORM 51[1]

**Rule 3.39.8(3)**

FORM OF MODIFICATION OF A QUARANTINE ORDER, SHORT TERM DETENTION ORDER OR EXCEPTIONAL DETENTION ORDER

Sheriff Court..........

..........20..........at [insert time]

(Court Ref. No.)

The sheriff, having considered an application made under section 50(2) of the Public Health etc. (Scotland) Act 2008 ("the Act") *[and productions lodged therewith], and being satisfied as to the matters mentioned in section 51(2) of the Act,

---

[1] As inserted by the Act of Sederunt (Summary Applications, Statutory Applications and Appeals etc. Rules) Amendment (Public Health etc. (Scotland) Act 2008) 2009 (SSI 2009/320) r.2 (effective October 1, 2009).

1. Makes an order in terms of section 51(1) of the Act modifying *the quarantine order/*the short term detention order/*the exceptional detention order which was granted in respect of (*insert details of the person as given in the application*) on (*insert date*), by

(*insert details of modification and, if applicable, name and designation of person considered appropriate under* section 51(4)(a)(iv) of the Act).

2. Directs notification of this order (*insert details of method and timing of notice*) to (*the person to whom the order applies*)

*and (*the name and designation of any person to whom an explanation was given under* section 31(5) of the Act)

*and (*insert the name and designation of any other person whom the sheriff considers appropriate*).

*Delete as appropriate*
(*signed*)
Sheriff

FORM 52 [1]

Rule 3.39.9(1)

```
Official use only
Court ref:
Date and time of receipt:
```

FORM OF APPLICATION FOR RECALL OF AN ORDER GRANTED IN THE ABSENCE OF THE PERSON TO WHOM IT APPLIES UNDER SECTION 59 OF THE PUBLIC HEALTH ETC. (SCOTLAND) ACT 2008

**NOTES**

This form should be used if you wish to apply to the sheriff for an order recalling a quarantine order OR a short term detention order OR an exceptional detention order which was made in the absence of the person to whom the order applies.

If you are the person to whom the order applies, you or your solicitor should complete and sign **PART A** and deliver it to the sheriff clerk of the sheriff court at which you wish to make your application.

If you are not the person to whom the order applies but instead are a person who has an interest in the welfare of the person to whom the order applies, you or your solicitor should complete and sign **PART B** and deliver it to the sheriff clerk of the sheriff court at which you wish to make your application.

Your application MUST be received by the sheriff clerk before the expiry of the period of 72 hours beginning with the time at which the order which you wish to be recalled was notified to you (or, as the case may be, the person to whom the order applies).

You should note that, despite the making of your application, the order which you wish recalled will REMAIN IN FORCE unless and until it is revoked by the sheriff.

Before determining your application the sheriff must give you and various other parties (who are specified in section 59(7) of the Act) the opportunity of making representations (whether orally or in writing) and of leading, or producing, evidence.

---

[1] As inserted by the Act of Sederunt (Summary Applications, Statutory Applications and Appeals etc. Rules) Amendment (Public Health etc. (Scotland) Act 2008) 2009 (SSI 2009/320) r.2 (effective October 1, 2009).

IF YOU ARE UNCERTAIN WHAT ACTION TO TAKE you should consult a solicitor. You may be entitled to legal aid depending on your financial circumstances, and you can get information about legal aid from a solicitor. You may also obtain advice from any Citizens Advice Bureau or other advice agency.

**PART A**

Sheriff Court (*Insert name of court*)  |  1.

Details of applicant (*Insert full name, address and telephone number and, if available, e-mail address and fax number*)  |  2.

Type of order you wish the sheriff to recall
(*Tick as appropriate*)

3. Quarantine Order ☐
Short Term Detention Order ☐
Exceptional Detention Order ☐

Date of order (*Insert date of order you wish the sheriff to recall*)  |  4.

Sheriff Court at which the order was made, if it was not the court specified in box 1 (*Insert name of court*)  |  5.

If available, a copy of the order which you wish the sheriff to recall should be attached to this application.

Date and time at which the order was notified to you (*Insert date and exact time of day*)  |  6.

I ask the sheriff to recall the order specified in boxes 3 and 4 on the following grounds:

(*State why you wish the order to be recalled. If necessary, continue on a separate sheet of paper*):

Signed:

Date:

(A solicitor should add his or her name and contact details)

**PART B**

Sheriff Court (*Insert name of court*)    1.

Details of applicant (*Insert full name, address and telephone number and, if available, email address and fax number*)    2.

| 3. | Quarantine Order | ☐ |
|---|---|---|
| | Short Term Detention Order | ☐ |
| | | ☐ |
| | Exceptional Detention Order | |

Type of order you wish the sheriff to recall
(*Tick as appropriate*)

Date of order (*Insert date of order you wish the sheriff to recall*)    4.

Sheriff Court at which the order was made, if it was not the court specified in box 1 (*Insert name of court*)    5.

Details of person to whom the order applies (*Insert name, address and telephone number and, if available, e-mail address and fax number*)    6.

If available, a copy of the order which you wish the sheriff to recall should be attached to this application.

Date and time at which the order was notified to the person named in box 6 (*Insert date and exact time of day*)    7.

I have an interest in the welfare of the person named in box 6 for the following reasons:

> *(State why you have an interest in the welfare of this person. If necessary, continue on a separate sheet of paper)*:

I ask the sheriff to recall the order specified in boxes 3 and 4 on the following grounds:

> *(State why you wish the order to he recalled. If necessary, continue on a separate sheet of paper)*:

Signed:
Date:
  (A solicitor should add his or her name and contact details)

**Rule 3.39.9(3)**                    FORM 53[1]

FORM OF ORDER RECALLING A QUARANTINE ORDER, SHORT TERM DETENTION ORDER OR EXCEPTIONAL DETENTION ORDER

Sheriff Court...............
...............20..........
(Court Ref. No.)

The sheriff, having considered an application made under section 59(2) of the Public Health etc. (Scotland) Act 2008 for recall of *the quarantine order/*the short term detention order/*the exceptional detention order which was granted in respect of *(insert details of the person as given in the application)* on *(insert date)*,

Refuses the application and Confirms the said order

OR

*Grants the application and Revokes the said order,

And Directs notification of this order *(insert details of method and timing of notice)* to *(enter details of any other person whom the sheriff considers appropriate)*.

  *Delete as appropriate
  (signed)
  Sheriff

---

[1] As inserted by the Act of Sederunt (Summary Applications, Statutory Applications and Appeals etc. Rules) Amendment (Public Health etc. (Scotland) Act 2008) 2009 (SSI 2009/320) r.2 (effective October 1, 2009).

**Rule 3.39.12(1)**                                    FORM 54[1]

| |
|---|
| Official use only |
| Court ref: |
| Date and time of receipt: |

FORM OF NOTE OF APPEAL UNDER SECTION 61 OF THE PUBLIC HEALTH ETC. (SCOTLAND) ACT 2008

*NOTES*

This form should be used if you wish to appeal to the sheriff under section 61 of the Public Health etc. (Scotland) Act 2008 in relation to an exclusion order OR a restriction order. A copy of the section is set out below.

If you are the person to whom the order applies, you or your solicitor should complete and sign PART A and deliver it to the sheriff clerk of the sheriff court at which you wish to appeal.

If you are not the person to whom the order applies but instead are a person who has an interest in the welfare of the person to whom the order applies, you or your solicitor should complete and sign PART B and deliver it to the sheriff clerk of the sheriff court at which you wish to appeal.

The form MUST be received by the sheriff clerk before the expiry of 14 days beginning with the day on which the order, modification or, as the case may be, decision against which you wish to appeal was made.

IF YOU ARE UNCERTAIN WHAT ACTION TO TAKE you should consult a solicitor. You may be entitled to legal aid depending on your financial circumstances, and you can get information about legal aid from a solicitor. You may also obtain advice from any Citizens Advice Bureau or other advice agency.

**61 Appeal against exclusion orders and restriction orders**

(1) This section applies where a person is subject to—
    (a) an exclusion order; or
    (b) a restriction order.

(2) A person mentioned in subsection (3) may appeal to the sheriff against—
    (a) the making of the order;
    (b) any conditions imposed by the order;
    (c) any modification of the order under section 48(2); or
    (d) a decision of a health board competent person under section 52(4) or 53(3) not to revoke the order.

(3) The person referred to in subsection (2) is—
    (a) the person in relation to whom the order applies; or
    (b) any person who has an interest in the welfare of such a person.

(4) An appeal under this section must be made before the expiry of the period of 14 days beginning with the day on which the order, modification or, as the case may be, decision appealed against is made.

(5) On an appeal under this section, the sheriff may—
    (a) confirm the order appealed against;
    (b) modify the order;
    (c) revoke the order;
    (d) confirm the decision appealed against;
    (e) quash that decision;
    (f) make such other order as the sheriff considers appropriate.

---

[1] As inserted by the Act of Sederunt (Summary Applications, Statutory Applications and Appeals etc. Rules) Amendment (Public Health etc. (Scotland) Act 2008) 2009 (SSI 2009/320) r.2 (effective October 1, 2009).

(6)   In subsection (5)(b), "modify" is to be construed in accordance with section 48.

*PART A*

Sheriff Court (*Insert name of court*)    1. [                    ]

Details of appellant (*Insert full name, address and telephone number and, if available, email address and fax number*)    2. [                    ]

Type of order (*Tick as appropriate to indicate what type of order the appeal is about*)    3. Exclusion Order ☐ Restriction Order ☐

Date of order (*Insert date of order indicated in box 3*)    4. [                    ]

Name and address of person who made the order (*Insert name and address. You should find this on the order*)    5. [                    ]

If available, a copy of the order specified in boxes 3 and 4 should be attached to this application.

I appeal to the sheriff on the following grounds:

*(State here with reasons*
*(i) what it is about the order that you wish to appeal. You should specify at least one of the options given in* section 61(2).
*(ii) what it is that you want the sheriff to do. You should specify one of the options given in* section 61(5). *If you choose the option given in* section 61(5)(f) *you should specify what order you wish the sheriff to make.*
*If necessary, continue on a separate sheet of paper)*

Signed:
  Date:
  (A solicitor should add his or her name and contact details)

**PART B**

Sheriff Court (*Insert name of court*)

> 1.

Details of appellant (*Insert full name, address and telephone number and, if available, email address and fax number*)

> 2.

Type of order (*Tick as appropriate to indicate what type of order the appeal is about*)

> 3. Exclusion Order
> Restriction  Order
> ☐

Date of order (*Insert date of order indicated in box 3*)

> 4.

Name and address of person who made the order (*Insert name and address. You should find this on the order*)

> 5.

Details of person to whom the order applies (*Insert full name, address and telephone number and, if available, email address and fax number*)

> 6.

If available, a copy of the order specified in boxes 3 and 4 should be attached to this application.

I have an interest in the welfare of the person named in box 6 for the following reasons:

> (*State why you have an interest in the welfare of this person. If necessary, continue on a separate sheet of paper*):

I appeal to the sheriff on the following grounds:

> (*State here with reasons
> (i) what it is about the order that you wish to appeal. You should specify at least one of the options given in* section 61(2).
> (ii) *what it is that you want the sheriff to do. You should specify one of the options given in* section 61(5). *If you choose the option given in* section 61(5)(f) *you should specify what order you wish the sheriff to make.*

*If necessary, continue on a separate sheet of paper)*

Signed:
  Date:
  (A solicitor should add his or her name and contact details)

*Rule 3.39.13(1)*                    FORM 55[1]

FORM OF APPLICATION FOR WARRANT TO ENTER PREMISES AND
TAKE STEPS UNDER SECTION 78 OF THE PUBLIC HEALTH ETC.
(SCOTLAND) ACT 2008

SHERIFFDOM OF (*insert name of sheriffdom*)

AT (*insert place of sheriff court*)

[A.B.] (design and state address), Applicant

*Order sought from the court*

The applicant applies to the court to grant warrant to (*insert name*), an officer of
the local authority

1. to enter the premises at (*insert address of premises to which entry is sought*).
2. to take with him any other person he may authorise and, if he has reasonable
   cause to expect any serious obstruction in obtaining access, a constable.
3. to direct that those premises (or any part of them) are, or any thing in or on
   them is to be left undisturbed (whether generally or in particular respects)
   for so long as the officer considers appropriate.
4. to take any step mentioned in section 73(2) of the Public Health etc.
   (Scotland) Act 2008 ("the Act") or to remove any thing from the premises
   for the purpose of taking any such step at any other place.

*Statement*

  *\*Delete as appropriate*

1. This application is made pursuant to section 78 of the Act.
2. The applicant is a local authority and the said officer is an authorised officer
   within the meaning give in section 73(8) of the Act.
3. The said premises *are/\*are not a dwellinghouse within the meaning given
   in section 26 of the Act.
4. The said premises are within the jurisdiction of this court.
5. The applicant considers it necessary that the authorised officer should
   exercise the powers of entry and take the other steps mentioned in section
   73(2) of the Act (*insert here a brief statement of reasons*).

  *6. The authorised officer Release 104: September 2009

*has been refused entry to the said premises, or

  *reasonably anticipates that entry will be refused.

  *OR*

  *6 The said premises are premises which the authorised officer is entitled to
     enter and they are unoccupied.

*OR*

  *6 The said premises are premises which the authorised officer is entitled to
     enter and the occupier thereof is temporarily absent and there is urgency
     because (here state briefly why there is urgency).

*OR*

---

[1] As inserted by the Act of Sederunt (Summary Applications, Statutory Applications and Appeals etc.
Rules) Amendment (Public Health etc. (Scotland) Act 2008) 2009 (SSI 2009/320) r.2 (effective
October 1, 2009).

*6    The authorised officer

*has been prevented from taking any steps which he is entitled to take under Part 5 of the Act, or

*reasonably anticipates being prevented from taking any steps that he is entitled to take under Part 5 of the Act.

*7    [*If the said premises are a dwellinghouse*] The authorised officer has in terms of section 77(2) of the Act given 48 hours notice of the proposed entry to a person who appears to be the occupier of the dwellinghouse and the period of notice has expired.

8.    In the circumstances narrated the applicant is entitled to the warrant sought and it should be granted accordingly.

*(signed)*

[X.Y.[(*add designation and business address*)

Solicitor for applicant

*(insert date)*

---

*Rule 3.39.13(2)*                        FORM 56[1]

## FORM OF WARRANT TO ENTER PREMISES AND TAKE STEPS UNDER PART 5 OF THE PUBLIC HEALTH ETC. (SCOTLAND) ACT 2008

Sheriff Court...............

...............20 ..........

(Court Ref. No.)

*Delete as appropriate*

The sheriff, having considered an application made under section 78 of the Public Health etc. (Scotland) Act 2008 ("the Act") *[and any productions lodged therewith], [*and (where the premises referred to below are a dwellinghouse) being satisfied that due notice has been given under section 77(2) of the Act and has expired],

Grants warrant authorising the authorised person, (insert name):

(a)    to enter the premises at (insert address)

(b)    on entering the premises referred to at paragraph (a), to take any other person authorised by him and, if he has reasonable cause to expect any serious obstruction in obtaining access, a constable; and

(c)    to direct that:

(i)    those premises (or any part of them) are; or

(ii)    any thing in or on those premises is,

to be left undisturbed (whether generally or in particular respects) for so long as he considers appropriate;

(d)    to take any steps mentioned in section 73(2) of the Act; and

(e)    to remove any thing from the premises for the purpose of taking any such step at any other place.

(signed)

Sheriff

*Rule 3.39.14(1)*                        FORM 57[2]

---

[1] As inserted by the Act of Sederunt (Summary Applications, Statutory Applications and Appeals etc. Rules) Amendment (Public Health etc. (Scotland) Act 2008) 2009 (SSI 2009/320) r.2 (effective October 1, 2009).

[2] As inserted by the Act of Sederunt (Summary Applications, Statutory Applications and Appeals etc. Rules) Amendment (Public Health etc. (Scotland) Act 2008) 2009 (SSI 2009/320) r.2 (effective October 1, 2009).

# FORM OF APPLICATION FOR AN ORDER FOR DISPOSAL OF A BODY UNDER SECTION 93 OF THE PUBLIC HEALTH ETC. (SCOTLAND) ACT 2008

SHERIFFDOM OF (*insert name of sheriffdom*)

AT (*insert place of sheriff court*)

[A.B.] (*design local authority*), Applicant

*Order sought from the court*

\* *Delete as appropriate*

\*The applicant applies to the court to make an order authorising the applicant to remove the body of (*insert name and date of birth of deceased person and address of premises in which the body is being retained*) to a mortuary or other similar premises and to dispose of that body before the expiry of (*insert period sought*).

*OR*

The applicant applies to the court to make an order authorising the applicant to dispose of the body of (*insert name and date of birth of deceased person and address of premises in which the body is being retained*) as soon as reasonably practicable.

Statement

\* *Delete as appropriate*

1. This application is made pursuant to section 93 of the Public Health etc. (Scotland) Act 2008.
2. The applicant's area falls within the jurisdiction of the court. The court accordingly has jurisdiction.
3. The body of the said (*insert details of deceased person*) is being retained in (*insert name and address of premises*).
4. The applicant is a local authority in whose area the said premises are situated.
5. The applicant considers that the appropriate arrangements have not been made for the disposal of the said body.
6. The applicant is satisfied that as a result there is a significant risk to public health and it is necessary, to avoid or minimise that risk, for the body to be appropriately disposed of.
\*7 The applicant considers that the risk to public health is such that it is necessary for the body to be disposed of immediately because (*insert here brief reasons why immediate disposal of the body is sought*).
8. The applicant attaches to this application a certificate signed by a local authority competent person which indicates that the competent person is satisfied as to the matters mentioned in statements 3, 4, 5 and 6.
9. In the circumstances narrated the applicant is entitled to the order sought and it should be granted accordingly.

> (*signed*)
>
> [X.Y.] (*add designation and business address*)
>
> Solicitor for applicant
>
> (*insert date*)

*Rule 3.39.14(2)* FORM 58[1]

---

[1] As inserted by the Act of Sederunt (Summary Applications, Statutory Applications and Appeals etc. Rules) Amendment (Public Health etc. (Scotland) Act 2008) 2009 (SSI 2009/320) r.2 (effective October 1, 2009).

## FORM OF ORDER FOR DISPOSAL OF A BODY

Sheriff Court...............

...............20..........

(Court Ref. No.)

*Delete as appropriate*

The sheriff, having considered an application made under section 93 of the Public Health etc. (Scotland) Act 2008 and any productions lodged,

*Being satisfied that there is a significant risk to public health, makes an order authorising the applicant to remove the body of (*insert details of deceased person*) to a mortuary or other similar premises and to dispose of that body before the expiry of (*insert period sought*).

OR

* Being satisfied that the risk to public health is such that it is necessary for the body of (*insert details of deceased person*) to be disposed of immediately, makes an order authorising the applicant to dispose of the body as soon as reasonably practicable.

(*signed*)

Sheriff

## FORM 59

Rule 3.42.2(1)

## FORM OF APPLICATION FOR JUDICIAL APPROVAL UNDER SECTION 23B(1) OF THE REGULATION OF INVESTIGATORY POWERS ACT 2000

Court ref. no.

SHERIFFDOM OF *(insert name of sheriffdom)*

AT *(insert place of sheriff court)*

*[A.B.], (insert designation and address of local authority)*, Applicant

**Order sought from the court**

*Delete as appropriate*

The Applicant applies to the court under section 23B(1) of the Regulation of Investigatory Powers Act 2000 ("the Act") to grant an order under section 23A(2) of the Act approving [*[the grant or renewal of an authorisation] *or* [the giving or renewal of a notice]] to obtain communications data [*about (*insert name and address of person (if known) or other identifying details*] [*from (*insert name and address of postal or telecommunications operator from whom the communications data is to be obtained*)].

**Statement**

*Delete as appropriate*

**1.** This application is made pursuant to section 23B(1) of the Act.

**2.** The Applicant is a local authority the area of which is situated within the jurisdiction of this court. This court accordingly has jurisdiction.

**3.**[1] [*Insert name and office, rank or position of relevant person*], a relevant person within the meaning of section 23A(6) of the Act, has—

*(a)    granted or renewed an authorisation under section 22(3), (3B) or (3F) of the Act;

*(b)    given or renewed a notice under section 22(4) of the Act

(*insert here a brief statement indicating when the authorisation or notice was given, granted or renewed and the terms of such authorisation or notice*)

---

[1] As amended by the Act of Sederunt (Sheriff Court Rules)(Miscellaneous Amendments) 2013 (SSI 2013/135) para.6 (effective May 27, 2013).

**4.** At the time the relevant person [*[*granted or renewed] the authorisation under section [*22(3), (3B) or (3F)]] *or* [*[*gave or renewed] a notice under section 22(4)] of the Act there were reasonable grounds for believing that it was necessary to obtain communications data—

*(a)  in the interests of national security;

*(b)  for the purpose of preventing or detecting crime or of preventing disorder;

*(c)  in the interests of the economic well-being of the United Kingdom;

*(d)  in the interests of public safety;

*(e)  for the purpose of protecting public health;

*(f)  for the purpose of assessing or collecting any tax, duty, levy or other imposition, contribution or charge payable to a government department;

*(g)  for the purpose, in an emergency, of preventing death or injury or any damage to a person's physical or mental health, or of mitigating any injury or damage to a person's physical or mental health; or

*(h)  for any purpose (not falling within paragraphs (a) to (g)) which is specified for the purposes of section 22(2)(h) by an order made by the Secretary of State (*specify relevant details*).

(*insert here a brief statement indicating the basis upon which such grounds were believed to exist*)

**5.** At the time the relevant person [*[*granted or renewed] the authorisation under section [*22(3), (3B) or (3F)]] or [*[*gave or renewed] a notice under section 22(4)] of the Act there were reasonable grounds for believing that obtaining the data in question by the conduct authorised or required by the authorisation or notice was proportionate to what was sought to be achieved by so obtaining the data.

(*insert here a brief statement indicating the basis upon which so obtaining the data was believed to be proportionate*)

**6.** At the time that the authorisation or notice was given, granted or renewed the relevant conditions set out in section 23A(5)(a) or (c) of the Act were satisfied.

(*insert here a brief statement indicating the basis upon which the relevant conditions were satisfied*)

**7.** There remain reasonable grounds for believing that the matters referred to in paragraphs 4, 5 and 6 are satisfied in relation to the authorisation or notice.

(*insert here a brief statement indicating the basis for this averment*)

**8.** In the circumstances narrated the Applicant is entitled to the order sought and it should be granted accordingly.

> (*signed*)
>
> [X.Y.] (*add designation and business address*)
>
> Solicitor for Applicant
>
> (*insert date*)

## FORM 60[1]

Rule 3.42.2(4)

FORM OF ORDER UNDER SECTION 23A(2) OF THE REGULATION OF INVESTIGATORY POWERS ACT 2000

Sheriff Court ..........

.......... 20 ..........

(Court Ref. No.)

---

[1] As amended by the Act of Sederunt (Sheriff Court Rules) (Miscellaneous Amendments) 2013 (SSI 2013/135) para.6 (effective May 27, 2013).

*Delete as appropriate

The sheriff, having considered an application made under section 23B(1) of the Regulation of Investigatory Powers Act 2000 ("the Act") for an order under section 23A(2) of the Act,

*Being satisfied as necessary as to the matters mentioned in section [*23A(3) or 23A(4)] of the Act:

**1.** Makes an order in terms of section 23A(2) of the Act [*approving the grant or renewal of the authorisation OR the giving or renewal of the notice].

[*2. Directs notification of this order by (insert details of method and timing of notice) to (insert name and address of postal or telecommunications operator from whom the communications data is to be obtained).]

OR

*Refuses to approve the [*grant or renewal of the authorisation concerned OR the giving or renewal of the notice concerned] [*and makes an order under section 23B(3) of the Act quashing the authorisation OR notice.]

*Delete as appropriate

(*signed*)

Sheriff

FORM 61[1]

Rule 3.45.3

APPLICATION FOR A CERTIFICATE UNDER ARTICLE 5 OF REGULATION (EU) NO. 606/2013 OF THE EUROPEAN PARLIAMENT AND OF THE COUNCIL OF 12TH JUNE 2013 ON MUTUAL RECOGNITION OF PROTECTION MEASURES IN CIVIL MATTERS

Sheriff Court ...............

Court Ref. No. ..............

1. The applicant is (*design*).
2. The applicant's date of birth is (*insert date of birth*).
3. The applicant's place of birth (*insert place of birth*).
4. The address of the applicant to be used for notification purposes is (*insert address – the address given, which may be disclosed to the person against whom the protection measure was granted, must be an address to which any notification to the applicant can be sent*).
5. The application relates to a sexual offences prevention order (*or an interim sexual offences prevention order, or a risk of sexual harm order, or an interim risk of sexual harm order*) granted on (*insert date of order*) in respect of (*insert name of person against whom protection measure was granted*).
6. The date of birth of the person against whom the order was granted is (*insert date of birth or "not known"*).
7. The place of birth of the person against whom the order was granted is (*insert place of birth or "not known"*).
8. The address of the person against whom the order was granted is (*insert address or "not known"*).
9. The applicant asks the court to issue a certificate pursuant to Article 5(1) of Regulation (EU) No. 606/2013 of the European Parliament and of the Civil Council of 12th June 2013 on mutual recognition of protection measures in civil matters in relation to the order referred to in paragraph 5.

Date (*insert date*)

---

[1] As inserted by the Act of Sederunt Act of Sederunt (Rules of the Court of Session and Sheriff Court Rules Amendment No. 3) (Mutual Recognition of Protection Measures) 2014 (SSI 2014/371) para.4 (effective January 11, 2015).

*(Signed)*
[A.B. *or* C.D.]
[*or* Solicitor for Applicant]
*(add designation and business address)*

FORM 62[1]

Rule 3.45.6(2)(a)

NOTICE OF ISSUE OF CERTIFICATE UNDER ARTICLE 5 OF REGULATION (EU) NO. 606/2013 OF THE EUROPEAN PARLIAMENT AND OF THE COUNCIL OF 12TH JUNE 2013 ON MUTUAL RECOGNITION OF PROTECTION MEASURES IN CIVIL MATTERS

Sheriff Court ...............
Court Ref No ...............
Date: *(insert date of posting or other method of intimation)*
To: *(insert name and address of person causing the risk)*

A certificate has been issued to *(insert name of party to whom certificate was issued)* in accordance with Article 5(1) of Regulation (EU) No. 606/2013 of the European Parliament and of the Council of 12th June 2013 on mutual recognition of protection measures in civil matters. The certificate relates to an order granted by the sheriff on *(insert date of interlocutor containing protection measure)*. A copy of the certificate and a copy of the order accompany this notice.

As a result of the issue of the certificate, *(insert name of person to whom certificate was issued)* can invoke the order in other Member States of the European Union.

If you consider that the certificate was wrongly issued, or that the certificate does not accurately reflect the terms of the order, you can apply to have the certificate withdrawn, or for the issue of a rectified certificate, by lodging an application in Form 64 with the sheriff clerk at the address below.

*(Signed)*
Sheriff Clerk
*(insert address and telephone number)*

FORM 63[2]

Rule 3.45.6(4)

NOTICE FOR WALLS OF COURT OF ISSUE OF CERTIFICATE UNDER ARTICLE 5 OF REGULATION (EU) NO. 606/2013 OF THE EUROPEAN PARLIAMENT AND OF THE COUNCIL OF 12TH JUNE 2013 ON MUTUAL RECOGNITION OF PROTECTION MEASURES IN CIVIL MATTERS

Sheriff Court ...............
Court Ref. No. ...............
Date: *(insert date)*
To: *(insert name and address of person causing the risk)*
TAKE NOTICE

A certificate has been issued to *(insert name of party to whom certificate was issued)* in accordance with Article 5(1) of Regulation (EU) No. 606/2013 of the European Parliament and of the Council of 12th June 2013 on mutual recognition of

---

[1] As inserted by the Act of Sederunt Act of Sederunt (Rules of the Court of Session and Sheriff Court Rules Amendment No. 3) (Mutual Recognition of Protection Measures) 2014 (SSI 2014/371) para.4 (effective January 11, 2015).

[2] As inserted by the Act of Sederunt Act of Sederunt (Rules of the Court of Session and Sheriff Court Rules Amendment No. 3) (Mutual Recognition of Protection Measures) 2014 (SSI 2014/371) para.4 (effective January 11, 2015).

protection measures in civil matters. The certificate relates to an order granted by the sheriff on (*insert date of interlocutor containing protection measure*) against (*insert name of person causing the risk*), whose last known address was (*insert last known address of person causing the risk*).

As a result of the issue of the certificate, (*insert name of person to whom certificate was issued*) can invoke the order in other Member States of the European Union.

If (*insert name of person causing the risk*) wishes to obtain a copy of the certificate and the order, that person should immediately contact the sheriff clerk at the address below.

If (*insert name of person causing the risk*) considers that the certificate was wrongly issued, or that the certificate does not accurately reflect the terms of the order, that person can apply to have the certificate withdrawn, or for the issue of a rectified certificate, by lodging an application in Form 64 with the sheriff clerk at the address below.

(*Signed*)

Sheriff Clerk

(*insert address and telephone number*)

FORM 64[1]

Rule 3.45.8(1)

APPLICATION FOR RECTIFICATION OR WITHDRAWAL OF A CERTIFICATE ISSUED UNDER ARTICLE 5 OF REGULATION (EU) NO. 606/2013 OF THE EUROPEAN PARLIAMENT AND OF THE COUNCIL OF 12TH JUNE 2013 ON MUTUAL RECOGNITION OF PROTECTION MEASURES IN CIVIL MATTERS

Sheriff Court ...............

Court Ref No. ...............

1. The applicant is (*design*).
2. On the application of (*insert name of person on whose application the certificate was issued*), the sheriff has issued a certificate in accordance with Article 5(1) of Regulation (EU) No. 606/2013 of the European Parliament and of the Council of 12th June 2013 on mutual recognition of protection measures in civil matters.
3. The certificate relates to a sexual offences prevention order [*or* an interim sexual offences protection order, *or* a risk of sexual harm order, *or* an interim risk of sexual harm order] granted by the sheriff on (*insert date of order*).
4. The applicant considers that the certificate does not accurately reflect the terms of the order because: (*here specify nature of discrepancy*).

[*or* 4. The applicant considers that the certificate was wrongly issued because: (*here specify the reason the certificate was wrongly issued*).]

5. The applicant asks the court to issue a rectified certificate [*or* to withdraw the certificate].

Date (*insert date*)

(*Signed*)

Applicant

---

[1] As inserted by the Act of Sederunt Act of Sederunt (Rules of the Court of Session and Sheriff Court Rules Amendment No. 3) (Mutual Recognition of Protection Measures) 2014 (SSI 2014/371) para.4 (effective January 11, 2015).

*[or* Solicitor for Applicant]

(*add designation and business address*)

FORM 65[1]

Rule 3.45.11(5)(a)

NOTICE OF ADJUSTMENT OF A PROTECTION MEASURE UNDER ARTICLE 11 OF REGULATION (EU) NO. 606/2013 OF THE EUROPEAN PARLIAMENT AND OF THE COUNCIL OF 12TH JUNE 2013 ON MUTUAL RECOGNITION OF PROTECTION MEASURES IN CIVIL MATTERS

Sheriff Court ...............

Court Ref No. ...............

Date: (*insert date of posting or other method of intimation*)

To: (*insert name and address of person causing the risk*)

This notice relates to a protection measure ordered by (*insert name of issuing authority in Member State of origin*) in respect of which (*insert name of protected person*) is the protected person and you are the person causing the risk.

You are hereby given notice that, in exercise of the power conferred by Article 11(1) of Regulation (EU) No. 606/2013 of the European Parliament and of the Council of 12th June 2013 on mutual recognition of protection measures in civil matters, the sheriff has adjusted the factual elements of the protection measure. A copy of the order adjusting the protection measure accompanies this notice.

As a result of the adjustment, the protection measure falls to be recognised and enforced in the United Kingdom subject to the adjustment.

If you consider that the order adjusting the protection measure was wrongly granted, you have the right to appeal. If you are considering appealing, you are advised to consult a solicitor who will be able to give advice.

(*Signed*)

Sheriff Clerk

(*insert address and telephone number*)

FORM 66[2]

Rule 3.45.11(7)

NOTICE FOR WALLS OF COURT OF ADJUSTMENT UNDER ARTICLE 11 OF REGULATION (EU) NO. 606/2013 OF THE EUROPEAN PARLIAMENT AND OF THE COUNCIL OF 12TH JUNE 2013 ON MUTUAL RECOGNITION OF PROTECTION MEASURES

Sheriff Court ...............

Court Ref. No. ...............

Date: (*insert date*)

To: (*insert name of person causing the risk*)

This notice relates to a protection measure ordered by (*insert name of issuing authority in Member State of origin*) in respect of which (*insert name of protected person*) is the protected person and (*insert name of person causing the risk*) is the person causing the risk. That person's last known address is (*insert last known address of person causing the risk*).

---

[1] As inserted by the Act of Sederunt Act of Sederunt (Rules of the Court of Session and Sheriff Court Rules Amendment No. 3) (Mutual Recognition of Protection Measures) 2014 (SSI 2014/371) para.4 (effective January 11, 2015).

[2] As inserted by the Act of Sederunt Act of Sederunt (Rules of the Court of Session and Sheriff Court Rules Amendment No. 3) (Mutual Recognition of Protection Measures) 2014 (SSI 2014/371) para.4 (effective January 11, 2015).

(*Insert name of person causing the risk*) is hereby given notice that, in exercise of the power conferred by Article 11 of Regulation (EU) No. 606/2013 of the European Parliament and of the Council of 12th June 2013 on mutual recognition of protection measures in civil matters, the sheriff has adjusted the factual elements of the protection measure.

As a result of the adjustment, the protection measure falls to be recognised and enforced in the United Kingdom subject to the adjustment.

If (*insert name of person causing the risk*) wishes to obtain a copy of the order adjusting the protection measure, that person should immediately contact the sheriff clerk at the address below.

If (*insert name of person causing the risk*) considers that the order adjusting the protection measure was wrongly granted, that person has the right to appeal. If that person is considering appealing, that person is advised to consult a solicitor who will be able to give advice.

(*Signed*)

Sheriff Clerk

(*insert address and telephone number*)

## FORM 67[1]

Rule 3.45.12(7)

### FORM OF CERTIFICATE OF DELIVERY OF DOCUMENTS TO CHIEF CONSTABLE

(*insert place and date*) I, hereby certify that upon the day of I duly delivered to the chief constable of the Police Service of Scotland (*insert details of documents delivered*). This I did by (*state method of delivery*).

(Signed)

(*insert name and designation of person delivering documents*)

## FORM 68[2]

Rule 3.45.13(5)

### FORM OF CERTIFICATE OF SENDING OF DOCUMENTS TO CHIEF CONSTABLE

(*insert place and date*) I, hereby certify that upon the day of I duly sent to the chief constable of the Police Service of Scotland (*insert details of documents sent*). This I did by (*state method of delivery*).

(Signed)

(*insert name and designation of person delivering documents*)

## FORM 69[3]

---

[1] As inserted by the Act of Sederunt Act of Sederunt (Rules of the Court of Session and Sheriff Court Rules Amendment No. 3) (Mutual Recognition of Protection Measures) 2014 (SSI 2014/371) para.4 (effective January 11, 2015).

[2] As inserted by the Act of Sederunt Act of Sederunt (Rules of the Court of Session and Sheriff Court Rules Amendment No. 3) (Mutual Recognition of Protection Measures) 2014 (SSI 2014/371) para.4 (effective January 11, 2015).

[3] As inserted by the Act of Sederunt (Rules of the Court of Session 1994 and Sheriff Court Rules Amendment) (No.3) (Miscellaneous) 2015 (SSI 2015/283) Sch.1 para.1 (effective 7 August 2015) and amended by the Act of Sederunt (Rules of the Court of Session 1994 and Sheriff Court Rules Amendment) (Miscellaneous) 2016 (SSI 2016/102) para.4 (effective 21 March 2016).

**Form of application for extension of the 14-day period under** paragraph 8(1) of Schedule 1 to the Counter-Terrorism and Security Act 2015

Rule 3.46.2(1)

SHERIFFDOM OF (*insert name of sheriffdom*)

AT (*insert place of sheriff court*)

[A.B.], (*insert designation, rank and address of applicant*)

APPLICANT

### Order(s) sought from the court

1. The applicant applies to the sheriff under paragraph 8(1) of Schedule 1 to the Counter- Terrorism and Security Act 2015 to extend the period of retention of a travel document relating to (*insert name and address of person to whom the application relates*) ("the person") for a period of (*insert number of days*) from (*insert date of expiry of 14-day period*).

### Withholding of specified information

2. The applicant applies to the sheriff for an order under paragraph 10(1) of Schedule 1 of the Act withholding the information specified in subparagraph (a) for the reasons set out in subparagraph (b).

   (a) The specified information is (*insert details of the information to be withheld*)

   (b) The reasons for withholding that information are (*insert reasons, by reference to paragraph 10(2) of Schedule 1 to the Act*).

### Statement

1. This application is made under paragraph 8(1) of Schedule 1 to the Counter-Terrorism and Security Act 2015 ("the Act").

2. The applicant is a senior police officer (within the meaning of paragraph 1(5) of Schedule 1 to the Act.

3. The travel document to which the application relates is (*insert details of travel document*).

4. The travel document was taken from the person at (*insert place*) on (*insert date*).

5. Authorisation for the retention of the document under paragraph 4 of Schedule 1 to the Act was given by (*insert name and rank of senior police officer who authorised retention*) on (*insert date*).

6. The travel document has since been retained while (*insert reason for retention of travel document by reference to paragraph 5(1) of Schedule 1 to the Act*).

7. (*Insert brief statement of steps taken by reference to paragraph 5(1) of Schedule 1 to the Act*).

(*signed*)

Applicant

[*or* Solicitor for applicant

(*add designation and business address*)]

FORM 70[1]

**Form of intimation of application for extension of the 14-day period under** paragraph 8(1) of Schedule 1 to the Counter-Terrorism and Security Act 2015 Rule 3.46.2(3)

SHERIFFDOM OF (*insert name of sheriffdom*)

AT (*insert place of sheriff court*)

[A.B.], (*insert designation, rank and address of applicant*

APPLICANT

(*Place and date*)

You (*insert designation and address*) are hereby given intimation of the attached application which was lodged with the sheriff clerk at (*insert place*) on (*insert date*).

The hearing of this application will take place at (*insert place and address of sheriff court*), on the ................ day of ................ at ............ o'clock.

If you wish to oppose the application, you must —
(a) provide written representations to the court and the applicant by (*insert date*); or
(b) attend the hearing in person or be legally represented at it if you wish to make oral representations.

**IF YOU ARE UNCERTAIN AS TO WHAT ACTION TO TAKE** you should consult a solicitor. You may be eligible for legal aid depending on your income, and you can get information about legal aid from a solicitor. It might also be possible to obtain advice from any Citizens' Advice Bureau or other advice agency.

(*signed*)

Applicant

[*or* Solicitor for applicant

(*add designation and business address*)]

---

[1] As inserted by the Act of Sederunt (Rules of the Court of Session 1994 and Sheriff Court Rules Amendment) (No.3) (Miscellaneous) 2015 (SSI 2015/283) Sch.1 para.1 (effective 7 August 2015) and amended by the Act of Sederunt (Rules of the Court of Session 1994 and Sheriff Court Rules Amendment) (Miscellaneous) 2016 (SSI 2016/102) para.4 (effective 21 March 2016).

## SCHEDULE 2

### REVOCATIONS

**Rule 1.3**

| (1)<br>Act of Sederunt | (2)<br>Reference | (3)<br>Extent of Revocation |
|---|---|---|
| Codifying Act of Sederunt 1913 | SR & O 1913/638 | Book L, Chapter X (proceedings under the Representation of the People Act 1983) |
| Codifying Act of Sederunt 1913 | SR & O 1913/638 | Book L, Chapter XI (appeals to the Court under the Pilotage Act 1913) |
| Act of Sederunt Regulating Appeals under the Pharmacy and Poisons Act 1933 | SR & O 1935/1313 | The whole Act of Sederunt |
| Act of Sederunt (Betting, Gaming and Lotteries Act Appeals) 1965) | 1965/1168 | The whole Act of Sederunt |
| Act of Sederunt (Housing Appeals) 1966 | 1966/845 | The whole Act of Sederunt |
| Act of Sederunt (Sheriff Court Procedure under Part IV of the Housing (Scotland) Act 1969) 1970 | 1970/1508 | The whole Act of Sederunt |
| Act of Sederunt (Proceedings under Sex Discrimination Act 1975) 1976 | 1976/374 | The whole Act of Sederunt |
| Act of Sederunt (Proceedings under Sex Discrimination Act 1975) No 2 1976 | 1976/1851 | The whole Act of Sederunt |
| Act of Sederunt (Proceedings under Sex Discrimination Act 1975) 1977 | 1977/973 | The whole Act of Sederunt |
| Act of Sederunt (Appeals under the Licensing (Scotland) Act 1976) 1977 | 1977/1622 | The whole Act of Sederunt |
| Act of Sederunt (Betting and Gaming Appeals) 1978 | 1978/229 | The whole Act of Sederunt |
| Act of Sederunt (Appeals under the Rating (Disabled Persons) Act 1978) 1979 | 1979/446 | The whole Act of Sederunt |
| Act of Sederunt (Copyright, Deisgns and Patents) 1990 | 1990/380 | The whole Act of Sederunt |
| Act of Sederunt (Proceedings in the Sheriff Court under the Model Law on International Commercial Arbitration) 1991 | 1991/2214 | The whole Act of Sederunt |
| Act of Sederunt (Coal Mining Subsidence Act 1991) 1992 | 1992/798 | The whole Act of Sederunt |

| (1) Act of Sederunt | (2) Reference | (3) Extent of Revocation |
|---|---|---|
| Act of Sederunt (Applications under Part III of the Criminal Justice (International Co-operation) Act 1990) 1992 | 1992/1077 | The whole Act of Sederunt |
| Act of Sederunt (Sheriff Court Summary Application Rules) 1993 | 1993/3240 | The whole Act of Sederunt |
| Act of Sederunt (Mental Health Rules) 1996 | 1996/2149 | The whole Act of Sederunt |
| Act of Sederunt (Proceeds of Crime Rules) 1996 | 1996/2446 | The whole Act of Sederunt |

# ACT OF SEDERUNT (PROCEEDINGS FOR DETERMINATION OF DEVOLUTION ISSUES RULES) 1999

## (SI 1999/1347)

The Lords of Council and Session, under and by virtue of the powers conferred on them by section 32 of the Sheriff Courts (Scotland) Act 1971, paragraph 37 of Schedule 6 to the Scotland Act 1998, paragraph 38 of Schedule 10 to the Northern Ireland Act 1998 and paragraph 36 of Schedule 8 to the Government of Wales Act 1998 and of all other powers enabling them in that behalf, having approved, draft rules submitted to them by the Sheriff Court Rules Council in accordance with section 34 of the Sheriff Courts (Scotland) Act 1971, do hereby enact and declare:

## Citation

**1.**—(1) This Act of Sederunt may be cited as the Act of Sederunt (Proceedings for Determination of Devolution Issues Rules) 1999 and shall come into force on 6th May 1999.

(2) This Act of Sederunt shall be inserted in the Books of Sederunt.

## Interpretation

**2.**—[1](1) In this Act of Sederunt—

"Advocate General" means the Advocate General for Scotland;
"devolution issue" means a devolution issue within the meaning of—
- (a) Schedule 6 to the Scotland Act 1998;
- (b) Schedule 10 to the Northern Ireland Act 1998; or
- (c) Schedule 9 to the Government of Wales Act 2006;

"initiating document" means the initial writ, summons, petition or other document by which the proceedings are initiated;
"relevant authority" means the Advocate General and—
- (a) in the case of a devolution issue within the meaning of Schedule 6, the Lord Advocate;
- (b) in the case of a devolution issue within the meaning of Schedule 10, the Attorney General for Northern Ireland, the First Minister and the deputy First Minister;
- (c) in the case of a devolution issue within the meaning of Schedule 9, the Counsel General to the Welsh Assembly Government.

(2) Any reference in this Act of Sederunt to a numbered Form shall be construed as a reference to the Form so numbered in Schedule 1 to this Act of Sederunt, and any reference to a rule shall be a reference to the rule so numbered in this Act of Sederunt.

## Proceedings for determination of a devolution issue

**3.** Where the initiating document contains an averment or crave which raises a devolution issue, the initiating document shall include a crave for warrant to intimate it to the relevant authority, unless he is a party to the action.

---

[1] As amended by the Act of Sederunt (Proceedings for Determination of Devolution Issues Rules) Amendment 2007 (SSI 2007/362) r.2(2) (effective August 15, 2007) and by the Act of Sederunt (Devolution Issues) (Appeals and References to the Supreme Court) 2009 (SSI 2009/323) (effective October 1, 2009).

## Time for raising devolution issue

**4.** It shall not be competent for a party to any proceedings to raise a devolution issue after proof is commenced, unless the sheriff, on cause shown, otherwise determines.

## Specification of devolution issue

**5.**—(1) Any party raising a devolution issue shall specify—
  (a) where he initiates the action, in the initiating document;
  (b) in the written defences or answers; or
  (c) in any other case, in Form 1,

the facts and circumstances and contentions of law on the basis of which it is alleged that the devolution issue arises in sufficient detail to enable the sheriff to determine whether such an issue arises in the proceedings.

(2) Where a pay wishes to raise a devolution issue after lodging any writ mentioned in paragraph (1) above he shall do so—
  (a) by way of adjustment or minute of amendment; or
  (b) in proceedings in which there is no procedure for adjustment or amendment, in Form 1,

so as to provide specification of the matters mentioned in that paragraph.

## Intimation of devolution issue

**6.**—(1) Intimation of a devolution issue shall be given to the relevant authority (unless he is a party to the proceedings) in accordance with this rule.

(2) Where the devolution issue is raised in the initiating document, the sheriff shall order intimation of the devolution issue as craved in the warrant for service.

(3) In any case other than that described in paragraph (2) above, the party raising the devolution issue shall lodge a motion or incidental application, as the case may be, craving a warrant for intimation of the devolution issue on the relevant authority, and on considering the motion or incidental application, where it appears to the sheriff that a devolution issue arises, he shall order such intimation of the devolution issue.

(4) Where intimation is ordered in accordance with paragraphs (2) or (3) above, such intimation shall be in Form 2 and be made in such manner as the sheriff considers appropriate in the circumstances.

(5) The intimation of a devolution issue shall specify 14 days, or such other period as the sheriff thinks fit, as the period within which the relevant authority may enter appearance as a party in the proceedings.

(6)[1] Where, after determination at first instance of any proceedings in which a devolution issue has been raised under this Act of Sederunt, a party to those proceedings marks an appeal under rule 31.3 or 31.4 of the Ordinary Cause Rules 1993 in Schedule 1 to the Sheriff Courts (Scotland) Act 1907, that party shall, unless the relevant authority is already a party to the proceedings, intimate the note of appeal to the relevant authority together with a notice in Form 2A.

---

[1] As inserted by the Act of Sederunt (Proceedings for Determination of Devolution Issues Rules) Amendment 2007 (SSI 2007/362) r.2(3) (effective August 15, 2007).

**Response to intimation of devolution issue**

7.—(1)   This rule applies where the relevant authority receives intimation of a devolution issue.

(2)   Where the relevant authority intends to enter an appearance as a party in the proceedings, he shall lodge a minute stating that he intends to do so.

(3)   Upon receipt of the minute lodged in accordance with paragraph (2) above, the sheriff shall sist the relevant authority as a party to the action.

(4)   Upon the relevant authority being sisted as a party in accordance with paragraph (3) above, the sheriff shall order the relevant authority to lodge a note of his written submissions in respect of the devolution issue specifying those matters mentioned in rule 5(1) within 7 days, or such other period as the sheriff thinks fit.

(5)   A copy of the minute lodged in accordance with paragraph (2) above and a copy of any note lodged in accordance with paragraph (4) above shall, at the same time as lodging the minute or any note, be intimated by the party lodging such to all other parties in the proceedings.

(6)   At any time after the note mentioned in paragraph (4) above has been lodged, the sheriff may regulate such further procedure in the proceedings as he thinks fit.

(7)[1]   Where a relevant authority does not take part as a party in the proceedings at first instance the court may allow him to take part as a party in any subsequent appeal to the sheriff principal.

**Intimation under section 102 of the Scotland Act 1998, section 81 of the Northern Ireland Act 1998 or section 153 of the Government of Wales Act 2006**

8.—[2](1)   This rule applies to orders made under—

(a)   section 102 of the Scotland Act 1998 (powers of courts or tribunals to vary retrospective decisions);

(b)   section 81 of the Northern Ireland Act 1998 (powers of courts or tribunals to vary retrospective decisions); or

(c)   section 153 of the Government of Wales Act 2006 (power to vary retrospective decisions).

(2)   Where the sheriff is considering whether to make an order under any of the provisions mentioned in paragraph (1) above, he shall order intimation of that fact to be given to every person to whom intimation is required to be given by that provision.

(3)   The intimation mentioned in paragraph (2) above shall—

(a)   be made forthwith by the sheriff clerk in Form 3 by first class recorded delivery post; and

(b)   specify 14 days, or such other period as the sheriff thinks fit, as the period within which a person may enter an appearance as a party in the proceedings so far as they relate to the making of the order.

**Response to intimation of order under rule 8**

9.—(1)   This rule applies where a person receives intimation in accordance with rule 8.

---

[1] As inserted by the Act of Sederunt (Proceedings for Determination of Devolution Issues Rules) Amendment 2007 (SSI 2007/362) r.2(4) (effective August 15, 2007).

[2] As amended by the Act of Sederunt (Proceedings for Determination of Devolution Issues Rules) Amendment 2007 (SSI 2007/362) r.2(5)–(6) (effective August 15, 2007).

(2)   Where a person intends to enter an appearance as a party in the proceedings, he shall lodge a minute stating that he intends to do so.

(3)   Upon receipt of the minute lodged in accordance with paragraph (2) above, the sheriff shall sist the person as a party to the action.

(4)   Upon a person being sisted as a party in accordance with paragraph (3) above, the sheriff shall order the person to lodge a note of his written submissions in respect of the making of the order within 7 days, or such other period as the sheriff thinks fit.

(5)   A copy of the minute lodged in accordance with paragraph (2) above and a copy of any note lodged in accordance with paragraph (4) above shall, at the same time as lodging the minute or any note, be intimated by the party lodging such to all other parties in the proceedings.

(6)   At any time after the note mentioned in paragraph (4) above has been lodged, the sheriff may regulate such further procedure in the proceedings as he thinks fit.

## Reference of devolution issue to Inner House of the Court of Session or Supreme Court

**10.**—[1](1)   This rule applies where—

(a)   any reference of a devolution issue is made to the Inner House of the Court of Session; or

(b)   the sheriff is required by the relevant authority to refer a devolution issue to the Supreme Court.

(2)   Where a reference is made in accordance with paragraph (1) above, the sheriff shall pronounce an interlocutor giving directions about the manner and time in which the reference is to be drafted and adjusted.

(3)   When the reference has been drafted and adjusted in accordance with paragraph (2) above, the sheriff shall sign the reference.

(4)   The reference shall include such matters as are prescribed in Schedule 2 to this Act of Sederunt, and shall have annexed to it the interlocutor making the reference and any other order of the court in the cause.

(5)   The sheriff clerk shall send a copy of the reference by first class recorded delivery post to—

(a)   the parties to the proceedings; and

(b)   the relevant authority (if he is not already a party) who may have a potential interest in the proceedings,

and shall certify on the back of the principal reference that a copy has been sent and to whom.

## Sist of cause on reference to Inner House of the Court of Session or Supreme Court

**11.**[2]   On a reference being made in accordance with rule 10, the cause shall, unless the sheriff when making the reference otherwise orders, be sisted until the devolution issue has been determined.

---

[1] As amended by the Act of Sederunt (Devolution Issues) (Appeals and References to the Supreme Court) 2009 (SSI 2009/323) (effective October 1, 2009).

[2] As amended by the Act of Sederunt (Devolution Issues) (Appeals and References to the Supreme Court) 2009 (SSI 2009/323) (effective October 1, 2009).

## Interim Orders

**12.**—[1](1)   Notwithstanding the reference of a devolution issue to the Inner House of the Court of Session or to the Supreme Court in accordance with rule 10, the sheriff shall have power to make any interim order which a due regard to the interests of the parties may require.

(2)   The sheriff may recall a sist made under rule 11 for the purpose of making the interim order mentioned in paragraph (1) above.

## Transmission of reference

**13.**—(1)   The sheriff clerk shall forthwith transmit the principal copy of the reference—

    (a)   to the Deputy Principal Clerk of the Court of Session; or

    (b)[2]   together with seven copies, to the Registrar of the Supreme Court, as the case may be.

(2)   Unless the sheriff otherwise directs, the principal copy of the reference shall not be transmitted in accordance with paragraph (1) above, where an appeal against the making of the reference is pending.

(3)   For the purpose of paragraph (2) above, an appeal shall be treated as pending—

    (a)   until the expiry of the time for making that appeal; or

    (b)   where an appeal has been made, until that appeal has been determined.

## Procedure following determination on reference or appeal

**14.**—[3](1)   This rule applies where either the Inner House of the Court of Session or the Supreme Court have determined—

    (a)   a devolution issue referred to them in accordance with rule 10; or

    (b)   an appeal ma to them.

(2)   Upon receipt of the determination of the Inner House of the Court of Session or the Supreme Court, as the case may be, the sheriff clerk shall forthwith place before the sheriff a copy of the determination and the court process.

(3)   The sheriff may *ex proprio motu* or shall upon the lodging of a motion or incidental application by any of the parties to the proceedings, pronounce an interlocutor ordering such further procedure as may be required.

(4)   Where the sheriff *ex proprio motu* pronounces an interlocutor in accordance with paragraph (3) above, the sheriff clerk shall forthwith intimate a copy of the interlocutor to all parties in the proceedings.

SCHEDULE 1

**Rule 2(2)**

Rules 5(1)(c) and 5(2)(b)

FORM 1[4]

---

[1] As amended by the Act of Sederunt (Devolution Issues) (Appeals and References to the Supreme Court) 2009 (SSI 2009/323) (effective October 1, 2009).
[2] As amended by the Act of Sederunt (Devolution Issues) (Appeals and References to the Supreme Court) 2009 (SSI 2009/323) (effective October 1, 2009).
[3] As amended by the Act of Sederunt (Devolution Issues) (Appeals and References to the Supreme Court) 2009 (SSI 2009/323) (effective October 1, 2009).
[4] As amended by the Act of Sederunt (Proceedings for Determination of Devolution Issues Rules) Amendment 2007 (SSI 2007/362) r.2(7)(a) (effective August 15, 2007).

## FORM OF SPECIFICATION OF DEVOLUTION ISSUE

SHERIFFDOM OF (*insert name of sheriffdom*)

AT (*insert place of sheriff court*)..........Court Ref No...........

In the action of

[A.B.] (*designation and address*)

Pursuer

against

[C.D.] (*designation and address*)

Defender

1. The *Pursuer/Defender (*if other please specify*) wishes to raise a devolution issue in the above action.

[*The Pursuer or Defender or other party, as the case may be, should then insert the following information*—

- *the facts and circumstances and contentions of law on the basis of which it is alleged that the devolution issue arises in sufficient detail to enable the sheriff to determine whether such an issue arises in the proceedings;*
- *details of the relevant law including the relevant provisions of the* Scotland Act 1998, the Government of Wales Act 2006 *or the* Northern Ireland Act 1998, *as the case may be; and*
- *the reason why the resolution of the devolution issue is considered necessary for the purpose of disposing of the proceedings*].

Date (*insert date*)

(*Signed*)

Solicitor for the *Pursuer/Defender (*if other please specify*)

*Delete as appropriate

Rule 6(4)

## FORM 2

## FORM OF INTIMATION TO RELEVANT AUTHORITY OF A DEVOLUTION ISSUE RAISED IN CIVIL PROCEEDINGS IN THE SHERIFF COURT

To (*insert name and address*)..........Court Ref No..........

**1.** You are given notice that in the Sheriff Court at (*insert address*),

*an action has been raised which includes a crave in respect of a devolution issue;

*a devolution issue has been raised in an action;

A copy of the * initial writ/pleadings in the case (*as adjusted*) is enclosed. A copy of the interlocutor appointing intimation is also enclosed.

**2.** If you wish to enter appearance as a party to the proceedings, you must lodge with the Sheriff Clerk (*insert name and address*) a notice in writing stating that you intend to appear as a party in the proceedings. The notice must be lodged within 14 days of (*insert date on which intimation was given*).

Date (*insert date*)..........

(*Signed*)..........

Solicitor for *Pursuer/Defender..........

*Delete as appropriate.

Rule 6(6)

## FORM 2A[1]

## FORM OF INTIMATION TO RELEVANT AUTHORITY OF APPEAL IN PROCEEDINGS IN WHICH A DEVOLUTION ISSUE HAS BEEN RAISED

To: (*name and address of relevant authority*).......... Court Ref No:..........

---

[1] As inserted by the Act of Sederunt (Proceedings for Determination of Devolution Issues Rules) Amendment 2007 (SSI 2007/362) r.2(7)(b) (effective August 15, 2007).

You are given notice that an appeal has been marked in proceedings in which a devolution issue has been raised. A copy of the note of appeal is enclosed.

Date (*insert date*).......... (*Signed*)..........

Solicitor for the Appellant
(*add designation and business address*)

FORM 3[1]

FORM OF INTIMATION UNDER *SECTION 102 OF THE SCOTLAND ACT 1998/SECTION 81 OF THE NORTHERN IRELAND ACT 1998/SECTION 153 OF THE GOVERNMENT OF WALES ACT 2006

To (*insert name and address*).......... Court Ref No:..........

**1.** You are given notice that in an action raised in the Sheriff Court at (*insert address*), the sheriff has decided

*that an Act/provision of an Act of the Scottish Parliament is not within the legislative competence of the Parliament;

*a member of the Scottish Executive does not have the power to make, confirm or approve a provision of subordinate legislation he has purported to make, confirm or approve;

A copy of the *initial writ/pleadings in the case (*as adjusted*) is enclosed. A copy of the interlocutor appointing intimation is also enclosed.

2. The sheriff is considering whether to make an order under *section 102 of the Scotland Act 1998/section 81 of the Northern Ireland Act 1998/section 153 of the Government of Wales Act 2006 either removing or limiting the retrospective effect of the decision, or suspending the effect of the decision to allow the defect to be corrected.

**3.** If you wish to enter appearance as a party to the proceedings so far as they relate to the making of the order, you must lodge with the sheriff clerk (insert name and address) a notice in writing stating that you intend to appear as a party in the proceedings. The notice must be lodged within 14 days of (*insert date on which intimation was given*).

Date (*insert date*).......... (*Signed*)

Sheriff Clerk

*Delete as appropriate

SCHEDULE 2[2]

Details to be Included Where Reference Made to *the Inner House of the Court of Session/Supreme Court

**Rule 10(4)**

1. The question(s) referred.
2. The addresses of the parties.
3. A concise statement of the background to the matter, including—
    (i) the facts of the case, including any relevant findings of fact by the referring court; and
    (ii) the main issues in the case and contentions of the parties with regard to them.

---

[1] As amended by the Act of Sederunt (Proceedings for Determination of Devolution Issues Rules) Amendment 2007 (SSI 2007/362) r.2(7)(c) (effective August 15, 2007).

[2] As amended by the Act of Sederunt (Proceedings for Determination of Devolution Issues Rules) Amendment 2007 (SSI 2007/362) r.2(8) (effective August 15, 2007) and by the Act of Sederunt (Devolution Issues) (Appeals and References to the Supreme Court) 2009 (SSI 2009/323) (effective October 1, 2009).

**4.** The relevant law including the relevant provisions of the *Scotland Act 1998/ Government of Wales Act 2006/Northern Ireland Act 1998.

**5.** The reasons why an answer to the question(s) *is/are considered necessary for the purpose of disposing of the proceedings.

*Note*: A copy of the interlocutor making the reference and a copy of any judgment in the proceedings must be annexed to the reference.

*Delete as appropriate.

## ACT OF SEDERUNT (SUMMARY CAUSE RULES) 2002

### (SSI 2002/132)

The Lords of Council and Session, under and by virtue of the powers conferred by section 32 of the Sheriff Courts (Scotland) Act 1971 (a) and of all other powers enabling them in that behalf, having approved draft rules submitted to them by the Sheriff Court Rules Council in accordance with section 34 of the said Act of 1971, do hereby enact and declare:

### Citation and commencement

**1.**—(1)  This Act of Sederunt may be cited as the Act of Sederunt (Summary Cause Rules) 2002 and shall come into force on 10th June 2002.

(2)  This Act of Sederunt shall be inserted in the Books of Sederunt.

### Summary Cause Rules

**2.**  The provisions of Schedule 1 to this Act of Sederunt shall have effect for the purpose of providing rules for a summary cause other than a small claim.

### Transitional provision

**3.**  Nothing in Schedule 1 to this Act of Sederunt shall apply to a summary cause commenced before 10th June 2002 and any such action shall proceed according to the law and practice in force immediately before that date.

### Revocation

**4.**  The Acts of Sederunt mentioned in column (1) of Schedule 2 to this Act of Sederunt are revoked to the extent specified in column (3) of that Schedule except—

(a)  in relation to any summary cause commenced before 10th June 2002; and

(b)  for the purposes of the Act of Sederunt (Small Claim Rules) 1988.

### SCHEDULE 1

### SUMMARY CAUSE RULES 2002

**Paragraph 2**

### Arrangement of Rules

#### Chapter 1
*Citation, interpretation and application*

1.1.      Citation, interpretation and application

#### Chapter 2
*Representation*

2.1.      Representation
2.2.      Lay support

#### Chapter 2A

*Lay Representation*

| | |
|---|---|
| 2A.1 | Application and interpretation |
| 2A.2 | Lay representation for party litigants |

Chapter 3

*Relief from failure to comply with rules*

| | |
|---|---|
| 3.1. | Dispensing power of sheriff |

Chapter 4

*Commencement of action*

| | |
|---|---|
| 4.1. | Form of summons |
| 4.2. | Statement of claim |
| 4.2A. | Actions relating to regulated agreements |
| 4.3. | Defender's copy summons |
| 4.4. | Authentication and effect of summons |
| 4.5. | Period of notice |
| 4.6. | Intimation |

Chapter 5

*Register of Summary Causes, service and return of the summons*

| | |
|---|---|
| 5.1. | Register of Summary Causes |
| 5.2. | Persons carrying on business under trading or descriptive name |
| 5.3. | Form of service and certificate thereof |
| 5.4. | Service within Scotland by sheriff officer |
| 5.5. | Service on persons whose address is unknown |
| 5.6. | Service by post |
| 5.7. | Service on persons outwith Scotland |
| 5.8. | Endorsation by sheriff clerk of defender's residence not necessary |
| 5.9. | Contents of envelope containing defender's copy summons |
| 5.10. | Re-service |
| 5.11. | Defender appearing barred from objecting to service |
| 5.12. | Return of summons |

Chapter 6

*Arrestment*

| | |
|---|---|
| 6.1. | Service of schedule of arrestment |
| 6.2. | Arrestment before service |
| 6.3. | Recall and restriction of arrestment |

Chapter 7

*Undefended action*

| | |
|---|---|
| 7.1. | Undefended action |
| 7.2. | Application for time to pay direction or time order |
| 7.3. | Decree in actions to which the Hague Convention or the Civil Jurisdiction and Judgments Act 1982 apply |

Chapter 8

*Defended action*

| | |
|---|---|
| 8.1. | Response to summons |
| 8.2. | Procedure in defended action |
| 8.3. | Purpose of hearing |

| 8.4. | Remit to person of skill |
| 8.5. | Inspection and recovery of documents |
| 8.6. | Exchange of lists of witnesses |
| 8.7. | Exchange of reports of skilled witnesses |
| 8.8. | Evidence generally |
| 8.9. | Hearing parts of action separately |
| 8.10. | Returning borrowed parts of process before proof |
| 8.11. | Conduct of proof |
| 8.12. | Administration of oath or affirmation to witness |
| 8.13. | Noting of evidence etc. |
| 8.14. | Parties to be heard at close of proof |
| 8.15. | Objections to admissibility of evidence |
| 8.16. | Incidental appeal against rulings on confidentiality of evidence and production of documents |
| 8.17. | Application for time to pay direction or time order in defended action |
| 8.18. | Pronouncement of decision |

Chapter 9

*Incidental applications and sists*

| 9.1. | General |
| 9.2. | Application to sist action |

Chapter 10

*Counterclaim*

| 10.1. | Counterclaim |

Chapter 11

*Third party procedure*

| 11.1 | Application for third party notice |
| 11.2. | Procedure |
| 11.3. | Warrants for diligence on third party notice |

Chapter 12

*Summary decree*

| 12.1. | Application of chapter |
| 12.2 | Application for summary decree |
| 12.3. | Summary decree in a counterclaim etc. |

Chapter 13

*Alteration of summons etc.*

| 13.1. | Alteration of summons etc. |

Chapter 14

*Additional defender*

| 14.1. | Additional defender |

Chapter 14A

*Interventions by the Commission for Equality and Human Rights*

| 14A.1 | Interpretation |
| 14A.2 | Interventions by the CEHR |
| 14A.3 | Applications to intervene |
| 14A.4 | Form of intervention |

## Chapter 14B
### Interventions by the Scottish Commission for Human Rights

14B.1    Interpretation
14B.2    Applications to intervene
14B.3    Invitations to intervene
14B.4    Form of intervention

## Chapter 15
### Application for sist of party and transference

15.1.    Application for sist of party and transference

## Chapter 16
### Transfer and remit of actions

16.1     Transfer to another court
16.2.    Remit between procedures
16.3.    Remit from Court of Session

## Chapter 17
### Productions and documents

17.1.    Lodging of productions
17.2.    Copy productions
17.3.    Borrowing of productions
17.4.    Penalty for failure to return productions
17.5.    Documents lost or destroyed
17.6.    Documents and productions to be retained in custody of sheriff clerk

## Chapter 18
### Recovery of evidence and attendance of witnesses

18.1.    Diligence for recovery of documents
18.2.    Optional procedure before executing commission and diligence
18.2A.   Optional procedure before executing commission and diligence—personal injuries actions
18.3.    Applications for orders under section 1 of the Administration of Justice (Scotland) Act 1972
18.4.    Confidentiality
18.5.    Preservation and obtaining of evidence
18.6.    Warrants for production of original documents from public records
18.7.    Letter of request
18.7A    Taking of evidence in the European Community.
18.8.    Citation of witnesses
18.9.    Citation of witnesses by party litigants
18.10.   Witnesses failing to attend

## Chapter 18A
### Vulnerable Witnesses (Scotland) Act 2004

18A.1.   Interpretation
18A.2.   Child witness notice
18A.3.   Vulnerable witness application
18A.4.   Intimation

18A.5.   Procedure on lodging child witness notice or vulnerable witness application

18A.6.   Review of arrangements for vulnerable witnesses

18A.7.   Intimation of review application

18A.8.   Procedure on lodging a review application

18A.9.   Determination of special measures

18A.10.  Intimation of an order under section 12(1) or (6) or 13(2)

18A.11.  Taking of evidence by commissioner

18A.12.  Commission on interrogatories

18A.13.  Commission without interrogatories

18A.14.  Lodging of video record and documents

18A.15.  Custody of video record and documents

18A.16.  Application for leave for party to be present at the commission

## Chapter 19
### Challenge of documents

19.1.   Challenge of documents

## Chapter 20
### European Court

20.1.   Interpretation of rules 20.2 to 20.5

20.2.   Application for reference

20.3.   Preparation of case for reference

20.4.   Sist of action

20.5.   Transmission of reference

## Chapter 21
### Abandonment

21.1.   Abandonment of action

## Chapter 22
### Decree by default

22.1.   Decree by default

## Chapter 23
### Decrees, extracts, execution and variation

23.1.   Decree

23.2.   Final decree

23.3.   Expenses

23.4.   Correction of interlocutor or note

23.5.   Taxes on funds under control of the court

23.6.   Extract of decree

23.7.   Charge

23.8.   Service of charge where address of defender is unknown

23.9.   Diligence on decree in actions for delivery

23.10.  Applications in same action for variation, etc. of decree

## Chapter 24
### Recall of decree

24.1.   Recall of decree

## Chapter 25

*Appeals*

25.1.    Appeals

25.2.    Effect of and abandonment of appeal

25.3.    Hearing of appeal

25.4.    Appeal in relation to a time to pay direction

25.5.    Sheriff to regulate interim possession

25.6.    Provisions for appeal in actions for recovery of heritable property to which rule 30.2 applies

25.7.    Appeal to the Court of Session

Chapter 26

*Management of damages payable to persons under legal disability*

26.1.    Orders for payment and management of money

26.2.    Methods of management

26.3.    Subsequent orders

26.4.    Management of money paid to sheriff clerk

26.5.    Management of money payable to children

Chapter 27

*Action of multiplepoinding*

27.1.    Application of chapter

27.2.    Application of other rules

27.3.    Pursuer in multiplepoinding

27.4.    Parties

27.5.    Statement of fund or subject in medio

27.6.    Response to summons

27.7.    Procedure where response lodged

27.8.    Objections to fund or subject in medio

27.9.    Claims hearing

27.10.   Procedure at claims hearing

27.11.   Advertisement

27.12.   Consignation and discharge of holder

Chapter 28

*Action of furthcoming*

28.1.    Expenses included in claim

Chapter 29

*Action of count, reckoning and payment*

29.1.    Response to summons

29.2.    Accounting hearing

Chapter 30

*Recovery of possession of heritable property*

30.1.    Action raised under section 38 of the 1907 Act

30.2.    Action against persons in possession of heritable property without right or title

30.3.    Effect of decree

30.4.    Preservation of defender's goods and effects

30.5.    Action of removing where fixed term of removal

30.6.    Form of notices and letter

30.7.    Giving notice of removal

30.8.    Evidence of notice to remove

30.9

## Chapter 31
### Action of sequestration for rent

31.1.    General

31.2.    Appraisal inventory and execution of citation

31.3.    Procedure

31.4.    Sale to be reported within 14 days

31.5.    Recall of sequestration

31.6.    Warrant to eject and re-let where premises displenished

31.7.    Warrant to sequestrate etc.

## Chapter 32
### Action for aliment

32.1.    Recall or variation of decree for aliment

32.2.    Warrant and forms for intimation

## Chapter 33
### Child Support Act 1991

33.1.    Interpretation of rules 33.2 to 33.4

33.2.    Statement of claim

33.3.    Effect of maintenance calculations

33.4.    Effect of maintenance calculations on extracts of decrees relating to aliment

## Chapter 34
### Application and interpretation

34.1.    Application and interpretation of this Chapter

34.2.    Form of summons

34.3.    Defender's copy summons

34.4.    Response to summons

34.5.    Inspection and recovery of documents

### Personal injuries action: application of other rules

34.6.    Application of other rules

### Personal injuries procedure

34.7.    Allocation of diets and timetables

34.8.    Applications for sist or for variation of timetable

34.9.    Statements of valuation of claim

34.10.   Pre-proof conferences

34.11.   Incidental hearings

34.12.   Intimation to connected persons in certain actions of damages

34.13.   Provisional damages for personal injuries

34.14.   Mesothelioma actions: special provisions

## Chapter 35
### Electronic transmission of documents

35.1.    Extent of provision

35.2.    Time of lodgement

## Chapter 36
### *The* Equality Act 2010

36.1    Interpretation and application
36.2    Intimation to Commission
36.3    Assessor
36.4    [Omitted]
36.5    National Security
36.6    Transfer to Employment Tribunal
36.7    Transfer from Employment Tribunal

## Chapter 37
### *Live links*

37.1

## Appendix 1
### Forms

1       Summary cause summons
1a      Summary cause summons—defender's copy—claim for or including payment of money (where time to pay direction or time order may be applied for)
1b      Summary cause summons—defender's copy—claim for or including payment of money (where time to pay direction or time order may not applied for)
1c      Summary cause summons—defender's copy—non-monetary claim
1d      Summary cause summons—defender's copy—multiplepoinding
1e      Summary Cause Summons—Personal Injuries Action
1f      Summary Cause Summons—Personal Injuries Action
2       Claim in a summons for payment of money
3       Claim in a summons for recovery of possession of heritable property
3a      Notice of removal under sections 34, 35 or 36 of the Sheriff Courts (Scotland) Act 1907
3b      Notice of removal under section 37 of the Sheriff Courts (Scotland) Act 1907
3c      Letter of removal
4       Claim in a summons of sequestration for rent
4a      Notice informing defender of right to apply for certain orders under the Debtors (Scotland) Act 1987
4b      Certificate of sequestration
5       Claim in a summons of multiplepoinding
5a      Statement by holder of fund or subject when not the pursuer
5b      Claim on the fund or subject in an action of multiplepoinding
6       Claim in a summons of forthcoming
7       Claim in a summons for delivery
8       Claim in a summons for implement of an obligation
9       Claim in a summons for count, reckoning and payment
10      Form of statement of claim in a personal injuries action
10a     Form of response (action for damages: personal injuries)

| | |
|---|---|
| 10b | Form of order of court for recovery of documents in personal injuries action |
| 10c | Form of docquet for deemed grant of recovery of documents in a personal injuries action |
| 10d | Form of timetable |
| 10e | Form of statement of valuation of claim |
| 10f | Minute of pre-proof conference |
| 10g | Form of intimation to connected persons |
| 10h | Form of claim for provisional damages |
| 10i | Form of application for further damages |
| 10j | Form of notice of application for further damages |
| 11 | Service |
| 12 | Certificate of execution of service |
| 13 | Service on person whose address is unknown—form of advertisement |
| 14 | Service on person whose address is unknown—form of notice to be displayed on the walls of court |
| 15 | Service by post—form of notice |
| 15a | Statement to accompany application for interim diligence |
| 16 | Recall or restriction of arrestment—certificate authorising the release of arrested funds or property |
| 17 | Minute—no form of response lodged by defender |
| 18 | Minute—pursuer not objecting to application for a time to pay direction or time order |
| 19 | Minute—pursuer opposing an application for a time to pay direction or time order |
| 20 | Form of oath for witnesses |
| 21 | Form of affirmation for witnesses |
| 22 | Third party notice |
| 23 | Response to third party notice |
| 24 | Order by the court and certificate in optional procedure for recovery of documents |
| 25 | Minute in an application for letter of request |
| 25a | Letter of request |
| 26 | Witness citation |
| 26a | Certificate of witness citation |
| 27 | Reference to the European Court |
| 28 | Extract decree—basic |
| 28a | Extract decree—payment |
| 28b | Extract decree—recovery of possession of heritable property |
| 28ba | Form of extract decree—recovery of possession of heritable property in accordance with section 16(5A) of the Housing (Scotland) Act 2001 (non-payment of rent) |
| 28bb | Form of extract decree—recovery of possession of heritable property in other cases (non-payment of rent) |
| 28c | Extract decree and warrant to sell in sequestration for rent and sale |

| 28d | Extract decree—warrant for ejection and to re-let in sequestration for rent and sale |
| 28e | Extract decree—furthcoming |
| 28f | Extract decree—delivery |
| 28g | Extract decree—delivery—payment failing delivery |
| 28h | Extract decree—aliment |
| 28i | Extract decree—*adfactum praestandum* |
| 28j | Extract decree—absolvitor |
| 28k | Extract decree—dismissal |
| 29 | Certificate by sheriff clerk—service of charge where address of defender is unknown |
| 30 | Minute for recall of decree |
| 30a | Minute for recall of decree—service copy |
| 31 | Note of appeal to the sheriff principal |
| 32 | Application for leave to appeal against time to pay direction |
| 33 | Appeal against time to pay direction |
| 34 | Application for certificate of suitability for appeal to the Court of Session |
| 35 | Form of receipt for money paid to sheriff clerk |
| 36 | Action for aliment—notice of intimation to children and next of kin where address of defender is unknown |
| 37 | Action for aliment—notice of intimation to children, next of kin and guardian where defender suffers from mental disorder |

Appendix 1A

**Schedule of timetable under personal injuries procedure**

Appendix 2

**Glossary**

## CHAPTER 1

### CITATION, INTERPRETATION AND APPLICATION

**Citation, interpretation and application**

**1.1**—[1](1)   These Rules may be cited as the Summary Cause Rules 2002.

(2)   In these Rules—

"the 1907 Act" means the Sheriff Courts (Scotland) Act 1907;

"the 1971 Act" means the Sheriff Courts (Scotland) Act 1971;

"the 1975 Act" means the Litigants in Person (Costs and Expenses) Act 1975;

"the 2004 Act" means the Vulnerable Witnesses (Scotland) Act 2004;[2]

"authorised lay representative" means a person to whom section 32(1) of the Solicitors (Scotland) Act 1980 (offence to prepare writs) does not apply by virtue of section 32(2)(a) of that Act;

---

[1] As amended by the Act of Sederunt (Ordinary Cause, Summary Application, Summary Cause and Small Claim Rules) Amendment (Miscellaneous) 2007 (SSI 2007/6) r.4(2) (effective January 29, 2007).

[2] As inserted by the Act of Sederunt (Ordinary Cause, Summary Application, Summary Cause and Small Claim Rules) Amendment (Vulnerable Witnesses (Scotland) Act 2004) 2007 (SSI 2007/463) r.4(2) (effective November 1, 2007).

"enactment" includes an enactment comprised in, or in an instrument made under, an Act of the Scottish Parliament;

"small claim" has the meaning assigned to it by section 35(2) of the 1971 Act;

"summary cause" has the meaning assigned to it by section 35(1) of the 1971 Act.

(3)  Any reference to a specified Chapter or rule shall be construed as a reference to the Chapter or rule bearing that number in these Rules, and a reference to a specified paragraph, subparagraph or head shall be construed as a reference to the paragraph, sub-paragraph or head so numbered or lettered in the provision in which that reference occurs.

(4)  A form referred to by number means the form so numbered in Appendix 1 to these Rules or a form substantially of the same effect with such variation as circumstances may require.

(4A)[1]  In these Rules, references to a solicitor include a reference to a member of a body which has made a successful application under section 25 of the Law Reform (Miscellaneous Provisions) (Scotland) Act 1990 but only to the extent that the member is exercising rights acquired by virtue of section 27 of that Act.

(5)  The glossary in Appendix 2 to these Rules is a guide to the meaning of certain legal expressions used in these Rules, but is not to be taken as giving those expressions any meaning which they do not have in law generally.

(6)  These Rules shall apply to a summary cause other than a small claim.

## Chapter 2

### Representation

**Representation**

**2.1.**—[2](1)  A party may be represented by—

(a)  an advocate;

(b)  a solicitor;

(c)  a person authorised under any enactment to conduct proceedings in the sheriff court, in accordance with the terms of that enactment; and

(d)  subject to paragraphs (2) and (4), an authorised lay representative.

(2)  An authorised lay representative shall not appear in court on behalf of a party except at the hearing held in terms of rule 8.2(1) and, unless the sheriff otherwise directs, any subsequent or other calling where the action is not defended on the merits or on the amount of the sum due.

(3)  Subject to the provisions of this rule, the persons referred to in paragraph (1)(c) and (d) above may, in representing a party, do everything for the preparation and conduct of an action as may be done by an individual conducting his own action.

(4)  If the sheriff finds that the authorised lay representative is—

(a)  not a suitable person to represent the party; or

(b)  not in fact authorised to do so,

that person must cease to represent the party.

---

[1] As inserted by the Act of Sederunt (Sheriff Court Rules Amendment) (Sections 25 to 29 of the Law Reform (Miscellaneous Provisions) (Scotland) Act 1990) 2009 (SSI 2009/164) r.4(2) (effective May 20, 2009).

[2] As amended by the Act of Sederunt (Ordinary Cause, Summary Application, Summary Cause and Small Claim Rules) Amendment (Miscellaneous) 2007 (SSI 2007/6) r.4(3) (effective January 29, 2007).

(5)[1]  A party may be represented by a person other than an advocate or solicitor at any stage of any proceedings under the Debtors (Scotland) Act 1987, if the sheriff is satisfied that that person is a suitable person to represent the party at that stage and is authorised to do so.

**Lay support**

**2.2.**—[2](1)  At any time during proceedings the sheriff may, on the request of a party litigant, permit a named individual to assist the litigant in the conduct of the proceedings by sitting beside or behind (as the litigant chooses) the litigant at hearings in court or in chambers and doing such of the following for the litigant as he or she requires—

    (a)   providing moral support;

    (b)   helping to manage the court documents and other papers;

    (c)   taking notes of the proceedings;

    (d)   quietly advising on—

        (i)   points of law and procedure;

        (ii)   issues which the litigant might wish to raise with the sheriff;

        (iii)   questions which the litigant might wish to ask witnesses.

(2)  It is a condition of such permission that the named individual does not receive from the litigant, whether directly or indirectly, any remuneration for his or her assistance.

(3)  The sheriff may refuse a request under paragraph (1) only if—

    (a)   the sheriff is of the opinion that the named individual is an unsuitable person to act in that capacity (whether generally or in the proceedings concerned); or

    (b)   the sheriff is of the opinion that it would be contrary to the efficient administration of justice to grant it.

(4)  Permission granted under paragraph (1) endures until the proceedings finish or it is withdrawn under paragraph (5); but it is not effective during any period when the litigant is represented.

(5)  The sheriff may, of his or her own accord or on the incidental application of a party to the proceedings, withdraw permission granted under paragraph (1); but the sheriff must first be of the opinion that it would be contrary to the efficient administration of justice for the permission to continue.

(6)  Where permission has been granted under paragraph (1), the litigant may—

    (a)   show the named individual any document (including a court document); or

    (b)   impart to the named individual any information,

which is in his or her possession in connection with the proceedings without being taken to contravene any prohibition or restriction on the disclosure of the document or the information; but the named individual is then to be taken to be subject to any such prohibition or restriction as if he or she were the litigant.

---

[1] As amended by the Act of Sederunt (Rules of the Court of Session, Sheriff Appeal Court Rules and Sheriff Court Rules Amendment) (Sheriff Appeal Court) 2015 (SSI 2015/419) r.11 (effective 1 January 2016; as to savings see SSI 2015/419 rule 20(6)(a)).

[2] As inserted by the Act of Sederunt (Sheriff Court Rules) (Miscellaneous Amendments) (No.2) 2010 (SSI 2010/416) r.4 (effective January 1, 2011).

(7) Any expenses incurred by the litigant as a result of the support of an individual under paragraph (1) are not recoverable expenses in the proceedings.

## Chapter 2A[1]

## Lay Representation

### Application and interpretation

**2A.1.**—(1) This Chapter is without prejudice to any enactment (including any other provision in these Rules) under which provision is, or may be, made for a party to a particular type of case before the sheriff to be represented by a lay representative.

(2) In this Chapter, a "lay representative" means a person who is not—

(a) a solicitor;

(b) an advocate, or

(c) someone having a right to conduct litigation, or a right of audience, by virtue of section 27 of the Law Reform (Miscellaneous Provisions) (Scotland) Act 1990.

### Lay representation for party litigants

**2A.2.**—(1) In any proceedings in respect of which no provision as mentioned in rule 2A.1(1) is in force, the sheriff may, on the request of a party litigant, permit a named individual (a "lay representative") to appear, along with the litigant, at a specified hearing for the purpose of making oral submissions on behalf of the litigant at that hearing.

(2) An application under paragraph (1)—

(a) is to be made orally on the date of the first hearing at which the litigant wishes a named individual to make oral submissions; and

(b) is to be accompanied by a document, signed by the named individual, in Form A1.

(3) The sheriff may grant an application under paragraph (1) only if the sheriff is of the opinion that it would assist his or her consideration of the case to grant it.

(4) It is a condition of permission granted by the sheriff that the lay representative does not receive directly or indirectly from the litigant any remuneration or other reward for his or her assistance.

(5) The sheriff may grant permission under paragraph (1) in respect of one or more specified hearings in the case; but such permission is not effective during any period when the litigant is legally represented.

(6) The sheriff may, of his or her own accord or on the motion of a party to the proceedings, withdraw permission granted under paragraph (1).

(7) Where permission has been granted under paragraph (1), the litigant may—

(a) show the lay representative any document (including a court document); or

(b) impart to the lay representative any information,

which is in his or her possession in connection with the proceedings without being taken to contravene any prohibition or restriction on the disclosure of the document or the information; but the lay representative is then to be taken to be subject to any such prohibition or restriction as if he or she were the litigant.

---

[1] As inserted by the Act of Sederunt (Sheriff Court Rules) (Lay Representation) 2013 (SSI 2013/91) r.4 (effective April 4, 2013).

(8)   Any expenses incurred by the litigant in connection with lay representation under this rule are not recoverable expenses in the proceedings.

## Chapter 3

### Relief from failure to comply with rules

**Dispensing power of sheriff**

**3.1.**—(1)   The sheriff may relieve any party from the consequences of any failure to comply with the provisions of these Rules which is shown to be due to mistake, oversight or other excusable cause, on such conditions as he thinks fit.

(2)   Where the sheriff relieves a party from the consequences of the failure to comply with a provision in these Rules under paragraph (1), he may make such order as he thinks fit to enable the action to proceed as if the failure to comply with the provision had not occurred.

## Chapter 4

### Commencement of action

**Form of summons**

**4.1.**—(1)   A summary cause action shall be commenced by summons, which shall be in Form 1.

(2)   The form of claim in a summons may be in one of Forms 2, 3, 4, 5, 6, 7, 8 or 9.

**Statement of claim**

**4.2.**   The pursuer must insert a statement of his claim in the summons to give the defender fair notice of the claim; and the statement must include—

    (a)   details of the basis of the claim including relevant dates; and

    (b)   if the claim arises from the supply of goods or services, a description of the goods or services and the date or dates on or between which they were supplied and, where relevant, ordered.

**Actions relating to regulated agreements**

**4.2A.**[1]   In an action which relates to a regulated agreement within the meaning given by section 189(1) of the Consumer Credit Act 1974 the statement of claim shall include an averment that such an agreement exists and details of the agreement.

**Defender's copy summons**

**4.3.**   A copy summons shall be served on the defender—

    (a)   where the action is for, or includes a claim for, payment of money—

        (i)   in Form 1a where an application for a time to pay direction under the Debtors (Scotland) Act 1987 or time order under the Consumer Credit Act 1974 may be applied for; or

        (ii)   in Form 1b in every other case;

    (b)   where the action is not for, and does not include a claim for, payment of money, in Form 1c; or

    (c)   in an action of multiplepoinding, in Form 1d.

---

[1] As inserted by the Act of Sederunt (Sheriff Court Rules) (Miscellaneous Amendments) 2009 (SSI 2009/294) r.4 (effective December 1, 2009) as substituted by the Act of Sederunt (Amendment of the Act of Sederunt (Sheriff Court Rules) (Miscellaneous Amendments) 2009) 2009 (SSI 2009/402) (effective November 30, 2009).

## Authentication and effect of summons

**4.4.**—(1) A summons shall be authenticated by the sheriff clerk in some appropriate manner except where—

(a) he refuses to do so for any reason;

(b) the defender's address is unknown; or

(c) a party seeks to alter the normal period of notice specified in rule 4.5(2); or

(d)[1] a warrant for arrestment on the dependence, or to found jurisdiction, is sought.

(2) If any of paragraphs (1)(a) to (d) applies, the summons shall be authenticated by the sheriff, if he thinks it appropriate.

(3) The authenticated summons shall be warrant for—

(a) service on the defender; and

(b) where the appropriate warrant has been sought in the summons—

(i) arrestment on the dependence; or

(ii) arrestment to found jurisdiction,

as the case may be.

(4)[2, 3] Where a warrant for arrestment to found jurisdiction, is sought, averments to justify that warrant must be included in the statement of claim.

## Period of notice

**4.5.**—(1) An action shall proceed after the appropriate period of notice of the summons has been given to the defender prior to the return day.

(2) The appropriate period of notice shall be—

(a) 21 days where the defender is resident or has a place of business within Europe; or

(b) 42 days where the defender is resident or has a place of business outwith Europe.

(3) The sheriff may, on cause shown, shorten or extend the period of notice on such conditions as to the form of service as he may direct, but in any case where the period of notice is reduced at least two days' notice must be given.

(4) If a period of notice expires on a Saturday, Sunday, public or court holiday, the period of notice shall be deemed to expire on the next day on which the sheriff clerk's office is open for civil court business.

(5) Notwithstanding the terms of section 4(2) of the Citation Amendment (Scotland) Act 1882, where service is by post the period of notice shall run from the beginning of the day next following the date of posting.

(6) The sheriff clerk shall insert in the summons—

(a) the return day, which is the last day on which the defender may return a form of response to the sheriff clerk; and

(b) the calling date, which is the date set for the action to call in court.

(7)[4] The calling date shall be 14 days after the return day.

---

[1] As inserted by the Act of Sederunt (Ordinary Cause, Summary Application and Small Claim Rules) Amendment (Miscellaneous) (SSI 2004/197) r.4(2) (effective May 21, 2004).

[2] As inserted by the Act of Sederunt (Ordinary Cause, Summary Application and Small Claim Rules) Amendment (Miscellaneous) (SSI 2004/197) r.4(2) (effective May 21, 2004).

[3] As substituted by the Act of Sederunt (Sheriff Court Rules) (Miscellaneous Amendments) 2009 (SSI 2009/294) r.7 (effective October 1, 2009).

[4] As amended by the Act of Sederunt (Sheriff Court Rules) (Miscellaneous Amendments) 2009 (SSI 2009/294) r.7 (effective December 1, 2009).

**Intimation**

**4.6.** Any provision in these Rules requiring papers to be sent to or any intimation to be made to any party, applicant or claimant shall be construed as if the reference to the party, applicant or claimant included a reference to the solicitor representing that party, applicant or claimant.

Chapter 5

Register of Summary Causes, service and return of the summons

**Register of Summary Causes**

**5.1.**—(1) The sheriff clerk shall keep a register of summary cause actions and incidental applications made in such actions, which shall be known as the Register of Summary Causes.

(2) There shall be entered in the Register of Summary Causes a note of all actions, together with a note of all minutes under rule 24.1(1) (recall of decree) and the entry for each action or minute must contain the following particulars where appropriate:—

- (a) the names, designations and addresses of the parties;
- (b) whether the parties were present or absent at any hearing, including an inspection, and the names of their representatives;
- (c) the nature of the action;
- (d) the amount of any claim;
- (e) the date of issue of the summons;
- (f) the method of service;
- (g) the return day;
- (h) the calling date;
- (i) whether a form of response was lodged and details of it;
- (j) the period of notice if shortened or extended in accordance with rule 4.5(3);
- (k) details of any minute by the pursuer regarding an application for a time to pay direction or time order, or minute by the pursuer requesting decree or other order;
- (l) details of any interlocutors issued;
- (m) details of the final decree and the date of it; and
- (n) details of any variation or recall of a decree.

(3) There shall be entered in the Register of Summary Causes in the entry for the action to which they relate details of incidental applications including, where appropriate—

- (a) whether parties are present or absent at the hearing of the application, and the names of their representatives;
- (b) the nature of the application; and
- (c) the interlocutor issued or order made.

(4) The Register of Summary Causes must be—

- (a) authenticated in some appropriate manner by the sheriff in respect of each day any order is made or application determined in an action; and
- (b) open for inspection during normal business hours to all concerned without fee.

(5) The Register of Summary Causes may be kept in electronic or documentary form.

### Persons carrying on business under trading or descriptive name

**5.2.**—(1)  A person carrying on a business under a trading or descriptive name may sue or be sued in such trading or descriptive name alone.

(2)  An extract of—

(a)  a decree pronounced in an action; or

(b)  a decree proceeding upon any deed, decree arbitral, bond, protest of a bill, promissory note or banker's note or upon any other obligation or document on which execution may proceed, recorded in the sheriff court books, against such person under such trading or descriptive name shall be a valid warrant for diligence against such person.

(3)  A summons, decree, charge or other document following upon such summons or decree in an action in which a person carrying on business under a trading or descriptive name sues or is sued in that name may be served—

(a)  at any place of business or office at which such business is carried on within the sheriffdom of the sheriff court in which the action is brought; or

(b)  if there is no place of business within that sheriffdom, at any place where such business is carried on (including the place of business or office of the clerk or secretary of any company, corporation or association or firm).

### Form of service and certificate thereof

**5.3.**—(1)  Subject to rule 5.5 (service where address of defender is unknown), a form of service in Form 11 must be enclosed with the defender's copy summons.

(2)  After service has been effected a certificate of execution of service in Form 12 must be prepared and signed by the person effecting service.

(3)  When service is by a sheriff officer, the certificate of execution of service must—

(a)  be signed by him; and

(b)  specify whether the service was personal or, if otherwise, the mode of service and the name of any person to whom the defender's copy summons was delivered.

(4)  If service is effected in accordance with rule 5.4(2), the certificate must also contain a statement of—

(a)  the mode of service previously attempted; and

(b)  the circumstances which prevented such service from being effected.

### Service within Scotland by sheriff officer

**5.4.**—(1)  A sheriff officer may validly serve any summons, decree, charge or other document following upon such summons or decree issued in an action by—

(a)  personal service; or

(b)  leaving it in the hands of—

(i)  a resident at the person's dwelling place; or

(ii)  an employee at the person's place of business.

(2)  If a sheriff officer has been unsuccessful in effecting service in accordance with paragraph (1), he may, after making diligent inquiries, serve the document—

(a)  by depositing it in the person's dwelling place or place of business by means of a letter box or by other lawful means; or (b)[1]  by leaving it at that person's dwelling place or place of business in such a way that it is likely to come to the attention of that person.

(3)  Subject to the requirements of rule 6.1 (service of schedule of arrestment), if service is effected in accordance with paragraph (2), the sheriff officer must thereafter send by ordinary post to the address at which he thinks it most likely that the person may be found a letter containing a copy of the document.

(4)  In proceedings in or following on an action, it shall be necessary for any sheriff officer to be accompanied by a witness except where service, citation or intimation is to be made by post.

(5)  Where the firm which employs the sheriff officer has in its possession—

(a)  the document or a copy of it certified as correct by the pursuer's solicitor, the sheriff officer may serve the document upon the defender without having the document or certified copy in his possession (in which case he shall if required to do so by the person on whom service is executed and within a reasonable time of being so required, show the document or certified copy to the person); or

(b)  a certified copy of the interlocutor pronounced allowing service of the document, the sheriff officer may serve the document without having in his possession the certified copy interlocutor if he has in his possession a facsimile copy of the certified copy interlocutor (which he shall show, if required, to the person on whom service is executed).

(6)[2]  Where service is executed under paragraphs (1)(b) or (2), the document and the citation or notice of intimation, as the case may be, must be placed in an envelope bearing the notice "This envelope contains a citation to or intimation from (*insert name of sheriff court*)" and sealed by the sheriff officer.

**Service on persons whose address is unknown**

**5.5.**—(A1)[3]  Subject to rule 6.A7, this rule applies to service where the address of a person is not known.

(1)  If the defender's address is unknown to the pursuer and cannot reasonably be ascertained by him, the sheriff may grant warrant to serve the summons—

(a)  by the publication of an advertisement in Form 13 in a newspaper circulating in the area of the defender's last known address; or

(b)  by displaying on the walls of court a notice in Form 14.

(2)  Where a summons is served in accordance with paragraph (1), the period of notice, which must be fixed by the sheriff, shall run from the date of publication of the advertisement or display on the walls of court, as the case may be.

(3)  If service is to be effected under paragraph (1), the pursuer must lodge a service copy of the summons with the sheriff clerk.

(4)  The defender may uplift from the sheriff clerk the service copy of the summons lodged in accordance with paragraph (3).

(5)  If display on the walls of court is required under paragraph (1)(b), the pursuer must supply to the sheriff clerk for that purpose a completed copy of Form 14.

---

[1] As substituted by the Act of Sederunt (Sheriff Court Rules) (Miscellaneous Amendments) 2011 (SSI 2011/193) r.4 (effective April 4, 2011).

[2] As inserted by the Act of Sederunt (Sheriff Court Rules) (Miscellaneous Amendments) 2011 (SSI 2011/193) r.4 (effective April 4, 2011).

[3] As inserted by the Act of Sederunt (Sheriff Court Rules) (Miscellaneous Amendments) 2009 (SSI 2009/294) r.11 (effective October 1, 2009).

(6) In every case where advertisement in a newspaper is required for the purpose of service, a copy of the newspaper containing said advertisement must be lodged with the sheriff clerk.

(7) If service has been made under this rule and thereafter the defender's address becomes known, the sheriff may allow the summons to be amended and, if appropriate, grant warrant for reservice subject to such conditions as he thinks fit.

## Service by post

**5.6.**—(A1) [Repealed by the Act of Sederunt (Sheriff Court Rules) (Miscellaneous Amendments) 2009 (SSI 2009/294) r.11 (effective October 1, 2009).]

(1) If it is competent to serve or intimate any document or to cite any person by recorded delivery, such service, intimation or citation, must be made by the first class recorded delivery service.

(2) On the face of the envelope used for postal service under this rule, there must be written or printed a notice in Form 15.

(3) The certificate of execution of postal service must have annexed to it any relevant postal receipt.

## Service on persons outwith Scotland

**5.7.**—(1) If any summons, decree, charge or other document following upon such summons or decree, or any charge or warrant, requires to be served outwith Scotland on any person, it must be served in accordance with this rule.

(2) If the person has a known home or place of business in—
  (a) England and Wales, Northern Ireland, the Isle of Man or the Channel Islands; or
  (b) any country with which the United Kingdom does not have a convention providing for service of writs in that country,
the document must be served either—
      (i) by posting in Scotland a copy of the document in question in a registered letter addressed to the person at his residence or place of business; or
      (ii) in accordance with the rules for personal service under the domestic law of the place in which the document is to be served.

(3) Subject to paragraph (4), if the document requires to be served in a country which is a party to the Hague Convention on the Service Abroad of Judicial and Extra-Judicial Documents in Civil or Commercial Matters dated 15th November 1965 or the European Convention on Jurisdiction and Enforcement of Judgments in Civil and Commercial Matters as set out in Schedule 1 or 3C to the Civil Jurisdiction and Judgments Act 1982, it must be served—
  (a) by a method prescribed by the internal law of the country where service is to be effected for the service of documents in domestic actions upon persons who are within its territory;
  (b) by or through a British consular authority at the request of the Secretary of State for Foreign and Commonwealth Affairs;
  (c)[1] by or through a central authority in the country where service is to be effected at the request of the Scottish Ministers;

---

[1] As substituted by the Act of Sederunt (Sheriff Court Rules) (Miscellaneous Amendments) 2011 (SSI 2011/193) r.6 (effective April 4, 2011).

(d) where the law of the country in which the person resides permits, by posting in Scotland a copy of the document in a registered letter addressed to the person at his residence; or

(e) where the law of the country in which service is to be effected permits, service by an *huissier*, other judicial officer or competent official of the country where service is to be made.

(4)[1] If the document requires to be served in a country to which the EC Service Regulation applies, service—

(a) may be effected by the methods prescribed in paragraph (3)(b) or (c) only in exceptional circumstances; and

(b) is effected only if the receiving agency has informed the person that acceptance of service may be refused on the ground that the document has not been translated in accordance with paragraph (12).

(5) If the document requires to be served in a country with which the United Kingdom has a convention on the service of writs in that country other than the conventions specified in paragraph (3) or the regulation specified in paragraph (4), it must be served by one of the methods approved in the relevant convention.

(6) Subject to paragraph (9), a document which requires to be posted in Scotland for the purposes of this rule must be posted by a solicitor or a sheriff officer, and the form of service and certificate of execution of service must be in Forms 11 and 12 respectively.

(7) On the face of the envelope used for postal service under this rule there must be written or printed a notice in Form 15.

(8) Where service is effected by a method specified in paragraph (3)(b) or (c), the pursuer must—

(a)[2] send a copy of the summons and warrant for service with form of service attached, or other document, with a request for service to be effected by the method indicated in the request to the Scottish Ministers or, as the case may be, the Secretary of State for Foreign and Commonwealth Affairs; and

(b) lodge in process a certificate of execution of service signed by the authority which has effected service.

(9) If service is effected by the method specified in paragraph (3)(e), the pursuer must—

(a) send to the official in the country in which service is to be effected a copy of the summons and warrant for service, with citation attached, or other document, with a request for service to be effected by delivery to the defender or his residence; and

(b) lodge in process a certificate of execution of service by the official who has effected service.

(10) Where service is executed in accordance with paragraph (2)(b)(ii) or (3)(a) other than on another party in—

(a) the United Kingdom;

(b) the Isle of Man; or

---

[1] As substituted by Act of Sederunt (Ordinary Cause, Summary Application, Summary Cause and Small Claim Rules) Amendment (Miscellaneous) 2004 (SSI 2004/197) r.4(3)(a) (effective May 21, 2004) and amended by the Act of Sederunt (Sheriff Court Rules) (Miscellaneous Amendments) (No.2) 2008 (SSI 2008/365) r.9(a) (effective November 13, 2008).
[2] As amended by the Act of Sederunt (Sheriff Court Rules) (Miscellaneous Amendments) 2011 (SSI 2011/193) r.7 (effective April 4, 2011).

(c) the Channel Islands, the party executing service must lodge a certificate stating that the form of service employed is in accordance with the law of the place where the service was executed.

(11) A certificate lodged in accordance with paragraph (10) shall be given by a person who is conversant with the law of the country concerned and who—

(a) practises or has practised law in that country; or

(b) is a duly accredited representative of the government of that country.

(12)[1] Every summons or document and every citation and notice on the face of the envelope referred to in paragraph (7) must be accompanied by a translation in an official language of the country in which service is to be executed, unless English is—

(a) an official language of the country in which service is to be executed; or

(b) in a country to which the EC Service Regulation applies, a language of the member state of transmission that is understood by the person on whom service is being executed.

(13) A translation referred to in paragraph (12) must be certified as a correct translation by the person making it and the certificate must contain the full name, address and qualifications of the translator and be lodged along with the execution of such service.

(14)[2] In this rule "the EC Service Regulation" means Regulation (EC) No. 1393/2007 of the European Parliament and of the Council of 13th November 2007 on the service in the Member States of judicial and extrajudicial documents in civil or commercial matters (service of documents), and repealing Council Regulation (EC) No. 1348/2000, as amended from time to time.

### Endorsation by sheriff clerk of defender's residence not necessary

**5.8.** Any summons, decree, charge or other document following upon a summons or decree may be served, enforced or otherwise lawfully executed in Scotland without endorsation by a sheriff clerk and, if executed by a sheriff officer, may be so executed by a sheriff officer of the court which granted the summons, or by a sheriff officer of the sheriff court district in which it is to be executed.

### Contents of envelope containing defender's copy summons

**5.9.** Nothing must be included in the envelope containing a defender's copy summons except—

(a) the copy summons;

(b) a response or other notice in accordance with these Rules; and

(c) any other document approved by the sheriff principal.

### Re-service

**5.10.**—(1) If it appears to the sheriff that there has been any failure or irregularity in service upon a defender, the sheriff may order the pursuer to re-serve the summons on such conditions as he thinks fit.

(2) If re-service has been ordered in accordance with paragraph (1) or rule 5.5(7) the action shall proceed thereafter as if it were a new action.

---

[1] As substituted for existing text by the Act of Sederunt (Ordinary Cause, Summary Application, Summary Cause and Small Claim Rules) Amendment (Miscellaneous) 2004 (SSI 2004/197) r.4(3)(b) (effective May 21, 2004) and by the Act of Sederunt (Sheriff Court Rules) (Miscellaneous Amendments) (No.2) 2008 (SSI 2008/365) r.9(a) (effective November 13, 2008).

[2] As substituted by the Act of Sederunt (Sheriff Court Rules) (Miscellaneous Amendments) (No.2) 2008 (SSI 2008/365) r.9(b) (effective November 13, 2008).

### Defender appearing barred from objecting to service

**5.11.**—(1)   A person who appears in an action shall not be entitled to state any objection to the regularity of the execution of service or intimation on him and his appearance shall remedy any defect in such service or intimation.

(2)   Nothing in paragraph (1) shall preclude a party pleading that the court has no jurisdiction.

### Return of summons

**5.12.**—(1)   If any appearance in court is required on the calling date in respect of any party—

   (a)   the summons; and

   (b)   the relevant certificate of execution of service, shall be returned to the sheriff clerk not later than two days before the calling date.

(2)   If no appearance by any party is required on the calling date, only the certificate of execution of service need be returned to the sheriff clerk, not later than two days before the calling date.

(3)   If the pursuer fails to proceed in accordance with paragraph (1) or (2) as appropriate, the sheriff may dismiss the action.

Chapter 6[1]

Interim Diligence

### Interpretation

**6.A1.**   In this Chapter—

   "the 1987 Act" means the Debtors (Scotland) Act 1987; and

   "the 2002 Act" means the Debt Arrangement and Attachment (Scotland) Act 2002.

### Application for interim diligence

**6.A2.**—(1)   The following shall be made by incidental application—

   (a)   an application under section 15D(1) of the 1987 Act for warrant for diligence by arrestment or inhibition on the dependence of an action or warrant for arrestment on the dependence of an admiralty action;

   (b)   an application under section 9C of the 2002 Act for warrant for interim attachment.

(2)   Such an application must be accompanied by a statement in Form 15a.

(3)   A certified copy of an interlocutor granting an application under paragraph (1) shall be sufficient authority for execution of the diligence concerned.

### Effect of authority for inhibition on the dependence

**6.A3.**—(1)   Where a person has been granted authority for inhibition on the dependence of an action, a certified copy of the interlocutor granting the application may be registered with a certificate of execution in the Register of Inhibitions and Adjudications.

[2](2)   A notice of a certified copy of an interlocutor granting authority for inhibition under rule 6.A2 may be registered in the Register of Inhibitions and Adjudica-

---

[1] Chapter renamed and rr.6.A1–6.A7 inserted by the Act of Sederunt (Sheriff Court Rules Amendment) (Diligence) 2008 (SSI 2008/121) r.6 (effective April 1, 2008).

[2] As substituted by the Act of Sederunt (Sheriff Court Rules Amendment) (Diligence) 2009 (SSI 2009/107) r.5 (effective April 22, 2009).

tions; and such registration is to have the same effect as registration of a notice of inhibition under section 155(2) of the Titles to Land Consolidation (Scotland) Act 1868.

### Recall etc of arrestment or inhibition

**6.A4.**—(1)  An application by any person having an interest—

(a)  to loose, restrict, vary or recall an arrestment or an interim attachment; or

(b)  to recall, in whole or in part, or vary, an inhibition,

shall be made by incidental application.

(1A)[1]  An incidental application under paragraph (1) shall—

(a)  specify the name and address of each of the parties;

(b)  where it relates to an inhibition, contain a description of the inhibition including the date of registration in the Register of Inhibitions and Adjudications.

(2)  Paragraph (1) does not apply to an application made orally at a hearing under section 15K that has been fixed under section 15E(4) of the Act of 1987.

### Incidental applications in relation to interim diligence, etc.

**6.A5.**  An application under Part 1A of the 1987 Act or Part 1A of the 2002 Act other than mentioned above shall be made by incidental application.

### Form of schedule of inhibition on the dependence

**6.A6.**  *[Revoked by the Act of Sederunt (Sheriff Court Rules Amendment) (Diligence) 2009 (SSI 2009/107) r.5 (effective April 22, 2009).]*

### Service of inhibition on the dependence where address of defender not known

**6.A7.**—(1)  Where the address of a defender is not known to the pursuer, an inhibition shall be deemed to have been served on the defender if the schedule of inhibition is left with or deposited at the office of the sheriff clerk of the sheriff court district where the defender's last known address is located.

(2)  Where service of an inhibition on the dependence is executed under paragraph (1), a copy of the schedule of inhibition shall be sent by the sheriff officer by first class post to the defender's last known address.

### Form of schedule of arrestment on the dependence

**6.A8.**—(1)[2]  An arrestment on the dependence shall be served by serving the schedule of arrestment on the arrestee in Form 15b.

(2)  A certificate of execution shall be lodged with the sheriff clerk in Form 15c.

### Service of schedule of arrestment

**6.1.**  If a schedule of arrestment has not been personally served on an arrestee, the arrestment shall have effect only if a copy of the schedule is also sent by registered post or the first class recorded delivery service to—

(a)  the last known place of residence of the arrestee; or

(b)  if such place of residence is not known, or if the arrestee is a firm or corporation, to the arrestee's principal place of business if known, or, if not known, to any known place of business of the arrestee,

---

[1]  As inserted by the Act of Sederunt (Rules of the Court of Session and Sheriff Court Rules Amendment No.2) (Miscellaneous) 2014 (SSI 2014/192) r.4 (December 8, 2014).

[2]  As inserted by the Act of Sederunt (Sheriff Court Rules Amendment) (Diligence) 2009 (SSI 2009/107) r.5 (effective April 22, 2009).

and the sheriff officer must, on the certificate of execution, certify that this has been done and specify the address to which the copy of the schedule was sent.

### Arrestment before service

**6.2.**—(1)[1] An arrestment to found jurisdiction used prior to service shall cease to have effect, unless the summons is served within 21 days from the date of execution of the arrestment.

(2) When such an arrestment as is referred to in paragraph (1) has been executed, the party using it must forthwith report the execution to the sheriff clerk.

### Recall and restriction of arrestment

**6.3**—(1) The sheriff may order that an arrestment on the dependence of an action or counterclaim shall cease to have effect if the party whose funds or property are arrested—

    (a) pays into court; or

    (b) finds caution to the satisfaction of the sheriff clerk in respect of, the sum claimed together with the sum of £50 in respect of expenses.

(2) Without prejudice to paragraph (1), a party whose funds or property are arrested may at any time apply to the sheriff to exercise his powers to recall or restrict an arrestment on the dependence of an action or counterclaim, with or without consignation or caution.

(3) An application made under paragraph (2) must be intimated by the applicant to the party who instructed the arrestment.

(4) On payment into court in accordance with paragraph (1), or if the sheriff recalls or restricts an arrestment on the dependence of an action in accordance with paragraph (2) and any condition imposed by the sheriff has been complied with, the sheriff clerk must—

    (a) issue to the party whose funds or property are arrested a certificate in Form 16 authorising the release of any sum or property arrested to the extent ordered by the sheriff; and

    (b) send a copy of the certificate to—

        (i) the party who instructed the arrestment; and

        (ii) the party who has possession of the funds or property that are arrested.

Chapter 7

Undefended action

### Undefended action

**7.1.**—(1) Subject to paragraphs (4), (5) and (6), where the defender has not lodged a form of response on or before the return day—

    (a) the action shall not require to call in court on the calling date; and

    (b) the pursuer must lodge a minute in Form 17 before the sheriff clerk's office closes for business on the second day before the calling date.

(2) If the pursuer does not lodge a minute in terms of paragraph (1), the sheriff must dismiss the action.

(3) If the sheriff is not prepared to grant the order requested in Form 17, the sheriff clerk must—

---

[1] As amended by the Act of Sederunt (Sheriff Court Rules Amendment) (Diligence) 2008 (SSI 2008/121) r.6(5) (effective April 1, 2008).

(a)   fix a date, time and place for the pursuer to be heard; and

(b)   inform the pursuer of—

    (i)   that date, time and place; and

    (ii)   the reasons for the sheriff wishing to hear him.

(4)   Where no form of response has been lodged in an action—

(a)   for recovery of possession of heritable property; or

(b)   of sequestration for rent, the action shall call in court on the calling date and the sheriff shall determine the action as he thinks fit.

(5)   Where no form of response has been lodged in an action of multiplepoinding the action shall proceed in accordance with rule 27.9(1)(a).

(6)   Where no form of response has been lodged in an action of count, reckoning and payment the action shall proceed in accordance with rule 29.2.

(7)   If the defender does not lodge a form of response in time or if the sheriff is satisfied that he does not intend to defend the action on the merits or on the amount of the sum due, the sheriff may grant decree with expenses against him.

### Application for time to pay direction or time order

7.2.—(1)   If the defender admits the claim, he may, where competent—

(a)   make an application for a time to pay direction (including, where appropriate, an application for recall or restriction of an arrestment) or a time order by completing the appropriate part of the form of response contained in the defender's copy summons and lodging it with the sheriff clerk on or before the return day; or

(b)   lodge a form of response indicating that he admits the claim and intends to apply orally for a time to pay direction (including, where appropriate, an application for recall or restriction of an arrestment) or time order.

(1A)[1]   The sheriff clerk must on receipt forthwith intimate to the pursuer a copy of any response lodged under paragraph (1).

(2)[2]   Where the defender has lodged an application in terms of paragraph (1)(a), the pursuer may intimate that he does not object to the application by lodging a minute in Form 18 before the time the sheriff clerk's office closes for business on the day occurring 9 days before the calling date stating that he does not object to the defender's application and seeking decree.

(3)   If the pursuer intimates in accordance with paragraph (2) that he does not object to the application—

(a)   the sheriff may grant decree on the calling date;

(b)   the parties need not attend; and

(c)   the action will not call in court.

(4)[3]   If the pursuer wishes to oppose the application for a time to pay direction or time order made in accordance with paragraph (1)(a) he must before the time the sheriff clerk's office closes for business on the day occurring 9 days before the calling date—

(a)   lodge a minute in Form 19; and

(b)   send a copy of that minute to the defender.

---

[1] As inserted by the Act of Sederunt (Sheriff Court Rules) (Miscellaneous Amendments) 2009 (SSI 2009/294) r.4 (effective December 1, 2009).

[2] As substituted by the Act of Sederunt (Sheriff Court Rules) (Miscellaneous Amendments) 2009 (SSI 2009/294) r.4 (effective December 1, 2009).

[3] As substituted by the Act of Sederunt (Sheriff Court Rules) (Miscellaneous Amendments) 2009 (SSI 2009/294) r.4 (effective December 1, 2009).

(5) Where the pursuer objects to an application in terms of paragraph (1)(a) or the defender has lodged a form of response in accordance with paragraph (1)(b), the action shall call on the calling date when the parties may appear and the sheriff must decide the application and grant decree accordingly.

(6) The sheriff shall decide an application in accordance with paragraph (5) whether or not any of the parties appear.

(7) Where the defender has lodged an application in terms of paragraph (1)(a) and the pursuer fails to proceed in accordance with either of paragraphs (2) or (4) the sheriff may dismiss the claim.

### Decree in actions to which the Hague Convention or Civil Jurisdiction and Judgements Act 1982 apply

**7.3.**—(1) If the summons has been served in a country to which the Hague Convention on the Service Abroad of Judicial and Extra-Judicial Documents in Civil or Commercial Matters dated 15th November 1965 applies, decree must not be granted until it is established to the satisfaction of the sheriff that the requirements of Article 15 of that Convention have been complied with.

(2) Where a defender is domiciled in another part of the United Kingdom or in another Contracting State, the sheriff shall not grant decree until it has been shown that the defender has been able to receive the summons in sufficient time to arrange his defence or that all necessary steps have been taken to that end.

(3) For the purposes of paragraph (2)—

   (a) the question whether a person is domiciled in another part of the United Kingdom shall be determined in accordance with sections 41 and 42 of the Civil Jurisdiction and Judgments Act 1982;

   (b) the question whether a person is domiciled in another Contracting State shall be determined in accordance with Article 52 of the Convention in Schedule 1 or 3C to that Act; and

   (c) the term "Contracting State" has the meaning assigned in section 1 of that Act.

## Chapter 8

## Defended action

### Response to summons

**8.1.**—(1) If the defender intends—

   (a) to challenge the jurisdiction of the court or the competency of the action;

   (b) to defend the action (whether as regards the amount claimed or otherwise); or

   (c) state a counterclaim,

he must complete and lodge with the sheriff clerk on or before the return day the form of response contained in the defender's copy summons including a statement of his response which gives fair notice to the pursuer.

(2) The sheriff clerk must upon receipt intimate to the pursuer a copy of any response lodged under paragraph (1).

### Procedure in defended action

**8.2.**—(1) Where the defender has lodged a form of response in accordance with rule 8.1(1) the action will call in court for a hearing.

(2) The hearing shall be held on the calling date.

(3) The sheriff may continue the hearing to such other date as he considers appropriate.

(4)   The defender must either be present or be represented at the hearing.

(5)   Where the defender—

   (a)   does not appear or is not represented; and

   (b)   the pursuer is present or is represented,

decree may be granted against the defender in terms of the summons.

(6)   Where at the hearing—

   (a)   the pursuer does not appear or is not represented; and

   (b)   the defender is present or represented, the sheriff shall dismiss the action and may grant decree in terms of any counterclaim.

(7)   If all parties fail to appear at the hearing, the sheriff shall, unless sufficient reason appears to the contrary, dismiss the action and any counterclaim.

### Purpose of hearing

**8.3.**—(1)   If, at the hearing, the sheriff is satisfied that the action is incompetent or that there is a patent defect of jurisdiction, he must grant decree of dismissal in favour of the defender or, if appropriate, transfer the action in terms of rule 16.1(2).

(2)   At the hearing, the sheriff shall—

   (a)   ascertain the factual basis of the action and any defence, and the legal basis on which the action and defence are proceeding; and

   (b)   seek to negotiate and secure settlement of the action between the parties.

(3)   If the sheriff cannot secure settlement of the action between the parties, he shall—

   (a)   identify and note on the summons the issues of fact and law which are in dispute;

   (b)   note on the summons any facts which are agreed;

   (c)   where it appears that the claim as stated or any defence stated in response to it is not soundly based in law in whole or in part, hear parties forthwith on that matter and may grant decree in favour of any party; and

   (d)   if satisfied that the claim and any defence have or may have a sound basis in law and that the dispute between the parties depends upon resolution of disputed issues of fact, fix a diet of proof or, alternatively, if satisfied that the claim and any defence have a sound basis in law and that the facts of the case are sufficiently agreed, hear parties forthwith on the merits of the action and may grant decree in whole or in part in favour of any party.

   (e)[1]   enquire whether there is or is likely to be a vulnerable witness within the meaning of section 11(1) of the 2004 Act who is to give evidence at any proof or hearing, consider any child witness notice or vulnerable witness application that has been lodged where no order has been made and consider whether any order under section 12(1) of the 2004 Act requires to be made.

(4)   Where the sheriff fixes a proof, the sheriff clerk shall make up a folder for the case papers.

### Remit to person of skill

**8.4.**—(1)   The sheriff may, on an incidental application by any party or on a joint application, remit to any person of skill, or other person, to report on any matter of fact.

---

[1] As inserted by the Act of Sederunt (Ordinary Cause, Summary Application, Summary Cause and Small Claim Rules) Amendment (Vulnerable Witnesses (Scotland) Act 2004) 2007 (SSI 2007/463) r.4(3) (effective November 1, 2007).

(2)   If a remit under paragraph (1) is made by joint application or of consent of all parties, the report of such person shall be final and conclusive with respect to the matter of fact which is the subject of the remit.

(3)   If a remit under paragraph (1) is made—

    (a)   on the application of one of the parties, the expenses of its execution must, in the first instance, be met by that party; or

    (b)   on a joint application or of consent of all parties, the expenses must, in the first instance, be met by the parties equally, unless the sheriff otherwise orders.

### Inspection and recovery of documents

**8.5.**—(1)   Each party shall, within 28 days after the date of the fixing of a proof, intimate to every other party, and lodge with the sheriff clerk, a list of documents, which are or have been in his possession or control which he intends to use or put in evidence at the proof, including the whereabouts of those documents.

(2)   A party who has received a list of documents from another party under paragraph (1) may inspect those documents which are in the possession or control of the party intimating the list at a time and place fixed by that party which is reasonable to both parties.

(3)   Nothing in this rule shall affect—

    (a)   the law relating, or the right of a party to object, to the inspection of a document on the ground of privilege or confidentiality; or

    (b)   the right of a party to apply under rule 18.1 for a commission and diligence for recovery of documents or under rule 18.3 for an order under section 1 of the Administration of Justice (Scotland) Act 1972.

### Exchange of lists of witnesses

**8.6.**—(1)   Within 28 days after the date of the fixing of a proof, each party shall intimate to every other party, and lodge with the sheriff clerk, a list of witnesses, including any skilled witnesses, whom he intends to call to give evidence.

(2)   A party who seeks to call as a witness a person not on his list intimated and lodged under paragraph (1) shall, if any other party objects to such a witness being called, seek leave of the sheriff to call that person as a witness; and such leave may be granted on such conditions, if any, as the sheriff thinks fit.

(3)[1]   The list of witnesses intimated under paragraph (1) shall include the name, occupation (where known) and address of each intended witness and indicate whether the witness is considered to be a vulnerable witness within the meaning of section 11(1) of the 2004 Act and whether any child witness notice or vulnerable witness application has been lodged in respect of that witness.

### Exchange of reports of skilled witnesses

**8.7.**—(1)   Not less than 28 days before the diet of proof, a party shall—

    (a)   disclose to every other party in the form of a written report the substance of the evidence of any skilled person whom he intends to call as a witness; and

    (b)   lodge a copy of that report in process.

---

[1] As amended by the Act of Sederunt (Ordinary Cause, Summary Application, Summary Cause and Small Claim Rules) Amendment (Vulnerable Witnesses (Scotland) Act 2004) 2007 (SSI 2007/463) r.4(4) (effective November 1, 2007).

(2)   Except on special cause shown, a party may only call as a skilled witness any person the substance of whose evidence has been disclosed in accordance with paragraph (1).

### Evidence generally

**8.8.**   Where possible, the parties shall agree photographs, sketch plans, and any statement or document not in dispute.

### Notices to admit and notices of non-admission

**8.8A.**—[1](1)   At any time after a form of response has been lodged, a party may intimate to any other party a notice or notices calling on him or her to admit for the purposes of that cause only—

  (a)   such facts relating to an issue averred in the statement of claim or form of response as may be specified in the notice;

  (b)   that a particular document lodged with the sheriff clerk and specified in the notice is—

      (i)   an original and properly authenticated document; or

      (ii)   a true copy of an original and properly authenticated document.

(2)   Where a party on whom a notice is intimated under paragraph (1)—

  (a)   does not admit a fact specified in the notice, or

  (b)   does not admit, or seeks to challenge, the authenticity of a document specified in the notice,

he or she must, within 21 days after the date of intimation of the notice under paragraph (1), intimate a notice of non-admission to the party intimating the notice to him or her under paragraph (1) stating that he or she does not admit the fact or document specified.

(3)   A party who fails to intimate a notice of non-admission under paragraph (2) will be deemed to have admitted the fact or document specified in the notice intimated to him or her under paragraph (1); and such fact or document may be used in evidence at a proof if otherwise admissible in evidence, unless the sheriff, on special cause shown, otherwise directs.

(4)   The party serving a notice under paragraph (1) or (2) must lodge a copy of it with the sheriff clerk.

(5)   A deemed admission under paragraph (3) must not be used—

  (a)   against the party by whom it was deemed to be made other than in the cause for the purpose for which it was deemed to be made; or

  (b)   in favour of any person other than the party by whom the notice was given under paragraph (1).

(6)   The sheriff may, at any time, allow a party to amend or withdraw an admission made by him or her on such conditions, if any, as the sheriff thinks fit.

(7)   A party may, at any time, withdraw in whole or in part a notice of non-admission by intimating a notice of withdrawal.

### Hearing parts of action separately

**8.9.**—(1)   In any action which includes a claim for payment of money, the sheriff may—

  (a)   of his own accord; or

  (b)   on the incidental application of any party,

---

[1] As inserted by the Act of Sederunt (Sheriff Court Rules) (Miscellaneous Amendments) 2010 (SSI 2010/279) r.6 (effective July 29, 2010).

order that proof on liability or any specified issue be heard separately from proof on any other issue and determine the order in which the proofs shall be heard.

(2) The sheriff shall pronounce such interlocutor as he thinks fit at the conclusion of the first proof of any action ordered to be heard in separate parts under paragraph (1).

### Returning borrowed parts of process before proof

**8.10.** All parts of process which have been borrowed must be returned to process not later than noon on the day preceding the proof.

### Conduct of proof

**8.11** The pursuer must lead in the proof unless the sheriff, on the incidental application of any of the parties which has been intimated to the other parties not less than seven days before the diet of proof, directs otherwise.

### Administration of oath or affirmation to witness

**8.12.** The sheriff must administer the oath to a witness in Form 20 or, where the witness elects to affirm, the affirmation in Form 21.

### Noting of evidence, etc.

**8.13.**—(1) The sheriff who presides at the proof may make a note of any facts agreed by the parties since the hearing held in terms of rule 8.2(1).

(2) The parties may, and must if required by the sheriff, lodge a joint minute of admissions of the facts upon which they have reached agreement.

(3) The sheriff must—

    (a) make for his own use notes of the evidence led at the proof, including any evidence the admissibility of which is objected to, and of the nature of any such objection; and

    (b) retain these notes until after any appeal has been disposed of.

### Parties to be heard at close of proof

**8.14.**—(1) After all the evidence has been led relevant to the particular proof, the sheriff must hear parties on the evidence.

(2) At the conclusion of that hearing, the sheriff may—

    (a) pronounce his decision; or

    (b) reserve judgment.

### Objections to admissibility of evidence

**8.15.** If in the course of a proof an objection is made to the admissibility of any evidence and that line of evidence is not abandoned by the party pursuing it, the sheriff must except where—

    (a) he is of the opinion that the evidence is clearly irrelevant or scandalous; or

    (b) *[Revoked by the Act of Sederunt (Rules of the Court of Session, Sheriff Appeal Court Rules and Sheriff Court Rules Amendment) (Sheriff Appeal Court) 2015 (SSI 2015/419) r.11 (effective1 January 2016; as to savings see SSI 2015/419 rule 20(6)(a)).]*

### Incidental appeal against rulings on confidentiality of evidence and production of documents

**8.16.** *[Revoked by the Act of Sederunt (Rules of the Court of Session, Sheriff Appeal Court Rules and Sheriff Court Rules Amendment) (Sheriff Appeal Court) 2015 (SSI 2015/419) r.11 (effective1 January 2016; as to savings see SSI 2015/419 rule 20(6)(a)).]*

### Application for time to pay direction or a time order in defended action

**8.17.** A defender in an action which proceeds as defended may, where it is competent to do so, make a incidental application or apply orally at any hearing, at any time before decree is granted, for a time to pay direction (including where appropriate, an order recalling or restricting an arrestment on the dependence) or time order.

### Pronouncement of decision

**8.18.**—(1) If the sheriff pronounces his decision at the end of the hearing held in terms of rule 8.2(1) or any proof, he must state briefly the grounds of his decision, including the reasons for his decision on any question of law or of admissibility of evidence.

(2) If the sheriff pronounces his decision after reserving judgement, he must give to the sheriff clerk within 28 days—

    (a)  a statement of his decision; and

    (b)  a brief note of the matters mentioned in paragraph (1).

(3) The sheriff clerk must send copies of the documents mentioned in paragraphs (2)(a) and (b) to each of the parties.

Chapter 9

Incidental applications and sists

### General

**9.1.**—(1) Except where otherwise provided, any incidental application in an action may be made—

    (a)  orally with the leave of the sheriff during any hearing of the action; or

    (b)  by lodging the application in written form with the sheriff clerk.

(2) An application lodged in accordance with paragraph (1)(b) may only be heard after not less than two days' notice has been given to the other party.

(3) Where the party receiving notice of an incidental application lodged in accordance with paragraph (1)(b) intimates to the sheriff clerk and the party making the application that the application is not opposed, the application shall not require to call in court unless the sheriff so directs.

(4) Any intimation made under paragraph (3) shall be made not later than noon on the day before the application is due to be heard.

### Application to sist action

**9.2.**—(1) Where an incidental application to sist an action is made, the reason for the sist—

    (a)  shall be stated by the party seeking the sist; and

    (b)  shall be recorded in the Register of Summary Causes and on the summons.

(2) Where an action has been sisted, the sheriff may, after giving parties an opportunity to be heard, recall the sist.

Chapter 10

Counterclaim

### Counterclaim

**10.1.**—(1) If a pursuer intends to oppose a counterclaim, he must lodge answers within seven days of the lodging of the form of response.

(2) The pursuer must at the same time as lodging answers intimate a copy of any answers to every other party.

(3)[1]  The defender may apply for warrant for interim diligence in respect of a counterclaim.

(4)–(5)  *[Repealed by the Act of Sederunt (Sheriff Court Rules) (Miscellaneous Amendments) 2009 (SSI 2009/294) r. 11 (effective October 1, 2009).]*

## Chapter 11

## Third party procedure

### Application for third party notice

**11.1.**—(1)  Where in an action a defender claims that—

- (a)  he has in respect of the subject matter of the action a right of contribution, relief or indemnity against any person who is not a party to the action; or
- (b)  a person whom the pursuer is not bound to call as a defender should be made a party to the action along with the defender in respect that such person is—
    - (i)  solely liable, or jointly or jointly and severally liable with the defender to the pursuer in respect of the subject matter of the action; or
    - (ii)  liable to the defender in respect of the claim arising from or in connection with the liability, if any, of the defender to the pursuer,

    he may apply by incidental application for an order for service of a third party notice upon that other person.

(2)  An application for service of a third party notice shall be made at the time when the defender lodges a form of response, unless the sheriff on cause shown shall permit a later application.

(3)  Where—

- (a)  a pursuer against whom a counterclaim is made; or
- (b)  a third party convened in the action,

seeks, in relation to the claim against him, to make against a person who is not a party, a claim mentioned in paragraph (1) as a claim which could be made by a defender against a third party, he shall apply by incidental application for an order for service of a third party notice; and rules 11.2 and 11.3 shall, with the necessary modifications, apply to such a claim as they apply in relation to a counterclaim by a defender.

### Procedure

**11.2.**—(1)  If an application in terms of rule 11.1 is granted, the sheriff shall—

- (a)  fix a date on which he will regulate further procedure; and
- (b)  grant warrant to serve on the third party—
    - (i)  a copy of the summons;
    - (ii)  a copy of the grounds upon which it is claimed that the third party is liable; and
    - (iii)  a notice in Form 22 and a copy of Form 23.

(2)  A copy of the third party notice, and any certificate of execution of service, shall be lodged by the defender before the hearing fixed under paragraph (1)(a).

(3)  A third party seeking to answer the claim against him shall complete and lodge the form of response no later than seven days before the hearing fixed under paragraph (1)(a).

---

[1] As amended by the Act of Sederunt (Sheriff Court Rules) (Miscellaneous Amendments) 2009 (SSI 2009/294) r.11 (effective October 1, 2009).

(4)   The sheriff clerk must upon receipt intimate to the other parties a copy of any response lodged under paragraph (3).

### Warrants for diligence on third party notice

**11.3.**—(1)[1]   A defender who applies for an order for service of a third party notice may apply for—

(a)   a warrant for arrestment to found jurisdiction;

(b)   a warrant for interim diligence,

which would have been permitted had the warrant been sought in an initial writ in a separate action.

(1A)[2]   On an application under paragraph (1)(a) being made—

(a)   the sheriff may grant the application if he thinks it appropriate; and

(b)   the sheriff shall not grant the application unless averments to justify the warrant sought have been made.

(2)   A certified copy of the interlocutor granting warrant for diligence shall be sufficient authority for execution of the diligence.

## Chapter 12

### Summary decree

### Application of chapter

**12.1.**   This chapter applies to any action other than an action of multiplepoinding.

### Application for summary decree

**12.2.**—(1)   A pursuer may at any time after a defender has lodged a form of response apply by incidental application for summary decree against any defender on the ground that there is no defence to the action or any part of it.

(2)   In applying for summary decree the pursuer may ask the sheriff to dispose of the whole or part of the subject matter of the action.

(3)   The pursuer shall intimate an application under paragraph (1) by registered or recorded delivery post to every other party not less than seven days before the date fixed for the hearing of the application.

(4)   On an application under paragraph (1), the sheriff may ordain any party, or a partner, director, officer or office-bearer of any party—

(a)   to produce any relevant document or article; or

(b)   to lodge an affidavit in support of any assertion of fact made in the action or at the hearing of the incidental application.

(5)   Notwithstanding the refusal of an application for summary decree, a subsequent application may be made on a change of circumstances.

---

[1] As substituted by the Act of Sederunt (Sheriff Court Rules) (Miscellaneous Amendments) 2009 (SSI 2009/294) r.11 (effective October 1, 2009).

[2] As inserted by the Act of Sederunt (Ordinary Cause, Summary Application, Summary Cause and Small Claim Rules) Amendment (Miscellaneous) 2004 (SSI 2004/197) r.4(5) (effective May 21, 2004) and amended by the Act of Sederunt (Sheriff Court Rules) (Miscellaneous Amendments) 2009 (SSI 2009/294) r.11 (effective October 1, 2009).

**Summary decree in a counterclaim etc.**

**12.3.** Rule 12.2 shall apply with the necessary modifications to an application by any other party for summary decree.

Chapter 13

Alteration of summons etc.

**Alteration of summons etc.**

**13.1.**—(1) The sheriff may, on the incidental application of a party, allow amendment of the summons, form of response, counterclaim or answers to a counterclaim and adjust the note of disputed issues at any time before final judgment is pronounced on the merits.

(2) In an undefended action, the sheriff may order the amended summons to be re-served on the defender on such period of notice as he thinks fit.

(3) Paragraph (1) includes amendment for the following purposes:-

   (a)   increasing or reducing the sum claimed;

   (b)   seeking a different remedy from that originally sought;

   (c)   correcting or supplementing the designation of a party;

   (d)   enabling a party to sue or be sued in a representative capacity; and

   (e)   sisting a party in substitution for, or in addition to, the original party.

(4) Where an amendment sists an additional or substitute defender to the action the sheriff shall order such service and regulate further procedure as he thinks fit.

Chapter 14

Additional defender

**Additional defender**

**14.1**—(1) Any person who has not been called as a defender may apply by incidental application to the sheriff for leave to enter an action as a defender, and to state a defence.

(2) An application under this rule must specify—

   (a)   the applicant's title and interest to enter the action; and

   (b)   the grounds of the defence which he proposes to state.

(3) On the lodging of an application under this rule—

   (a)   the sheriff must appoint a date for hearing the application; and

   (b)   the applicant must forthwith serve a copy of the application and of the order for a hearing on the parties to the action.

(4) After hearing the applicant and any party to the action the sheriff may, if he is satisfied that the applicant has shown title and interest to enter the action, grant the application.

(5) Where an application is granted under paragraph (4)—

   (a)   the applicant shall be treated as a defender; and

   (b)   the sheriff must forthwith consider whether any decision already taken in the action on the issues in dispute between the parties requires to be reconsidered in light of the terms of the application.

(6)[1] Paragraph (5)(b) does not apply to a personal injuries action raised under Chapter 34.

---

[1] As inserted by the Act of Sederunt (Summary Cause Rules Amendment) (Personal Injuries Actions) 2012 (SSI 2012/144) para.2 (effective September 1, 2012).

(7)[1]  Where an application is granted under paragraph (4) in a personal injuries action raised under Chapter 34, the sheriff may make such further order as the sheriff thinks fit.

Chapter 14A[2]

Interventions by the Commission for Equality and Human Rights

**Interpretation**

**14A.1.**  In this Chapter "the CEHR" means the Commission for Equality and Human Rights.

**Interventions by the CEHR**

**14A.2.**—(1)  The CEHR may apply to the sheriff for leave to intervene in any summary cause action in accordance with this Chapter.

(2)  This Chapter is without prejudice to any other entitlement of the CEHR by virtue of having title and interest in relation to the subject matter of any proceedings by virtue of section 30(2) of the Equality Act 2006 or any other enactment to seek to be sisted as a party in those proceedings.

(3)  Nothing in this Chapter shall affect the power of the sheriff to make such other direction as he considers appropriate in the interests of justice.

(4)  Any decision of the sheriff in proceedings under this Chapter shall be final and not subject to appeal.

**Applications to intervene**

**14A.3.**—(1)  An application for leave to intervene shall be by way of minute of intervention in Form 23A and the CEHR shall-

(a)  send a copy of it to all the parties; and

(b)  lodge it in process, certifying that subparagraph (a) has been complied with.

(2)  A minute of intervention shall set out briefly—

(a)  the CEHR's reasons for believing that the proceedings are relevant to a matter in connection with which the CEHR has a function;

(b)  the issue in the proceedings which the CEHR wishes to address; and

(c)  the propositions to be advanced by the CEHR and the CEHR's reasons for believing that they are relevant to the proceedings and that they will assist the sheriff.

(3)  The sheriff may—

(a)  refuse leave without a hearing;

(b)  grant leave without a hearing unless a hearing is requested under paragraph (4);

(c)  refuse or grant leave after such a hearing.

(4)  A hearing, at which the applicant and the parties may address the court on the matters referred to in paragraph (6)(c) may be held if, within 14 days of the minute of intervention being lodged, any of the parties lodges a request for a hearing.

(5)  Any diet in pursuance of paragraph (4) shall be fixed by the sheriff clerk who shall give written intimation of the diet to the CEHR and all the parties.

---

[1] As inserted by the Act of Sederunt (Summary Cause Rules Amendment) (Personal Injuries Actions) 2012 (SSI 2012/144) para.2 (effective September 1, 2012).

[2] As inserted by the Act of Sederunt (Sheriff Court Rules) (Miscellaneous Amendments) 2008 (SSI 2008/223) r.6(2) (effective July 1, 2008). Originally named Chapter 13B Interventions by the Scottish Commission for Human Rights in a possible drafting error.

(6)  The sheriff may grant leave only if satisfied that—

    (a)  the proceedings are relevant to a matter in connection with which the CEHR has a function;

    (b)  the propositions to be advanced by the CEHR are relevant to the proceedings and are likely to assist him; and

    (c)  the intervention will not unduly delay or otherwise prejudice the rights of the parties, including their potential liability for expenses.

(7)  In granting leave the sheriff may impose such terms and conditions as he considers desirable in the interests of justice, including making provision in respect of any additional expenses incurred by the parties as a result of the intervention.

(8)  The sheriff clerk shall give written intimation of a grant or refusal of leave to the CEHR and all the parties.

**Form of intervention**

**14A.4.**—(1)  An intervention shall be by way of a written submission which (including any appendices) shall not exceed 5000 words.

(2)  The CEHR shall lodge the submission and send a copy of it to all the parties by such time as the sheriff may direct.

(3)  The sheriff may in exceptional circumstances-

    (a)  allow a longer written submission to be made;

    (b)  direct that an oral submission is to be made.

(4)  Any diet in pursuance of paragraph (3)(b) shall be fixed by the sheriff clerk who shall give written intimation of the diet to the CEHR and all the parties.

Chapter 14B[1]

Interventions by the Scottish Commission for Human Rights

**Interpretation**

**14B.1.**  In this Chapter—

"the Act of 2006" means the Scottish Commission for Human Rights Act 2006; and

"the SCHR" means the Scottish Commission for Human Rights.

**Applications to intervene**

**14B.2.**—(1)  An application for leave to intervene shall be by way of minute of intervention in Form 23B and the SCHR shall—

    (a)  send a copy of it to all the parties; and

    (b)  lodge it in process, certifying that subparagraph (a) has been complied with.

(2)  In granting leave the sheriff may impose such terms and conditions as he considers desirable in the interests of justice, including making provision in respect of any additional expenses incurred by the parties as a result of the intervention.

(3)  The sheriff clerk shall give written intimation of a grant or refusal of leave to the SCHR and all the parties.

(4)  Any decision of the sheriff in proceedings under this Chapter shall be final and not subject to appeal.

---

[1] As inserted by the Act of Sederunt (Sheriff Court Rules) (Miscellaneous Amendments) 2008 (SSI 2008/223) r.6(2) (effective July 1, 2008).

**Invitations to intervene**

**14B.3.**—(1)  An invitation to intervene under section 14(2)(b) of the Act of 2006 shall be in Form 23C and the sheriff clerk shall send a copy of it to the SCHR and all the parties.

(2)  An invitation under paragraph (1) shall be accompanied by—

(a)  a copy of the pleadings in the proceedings; and

(b)  such other documents relating to those proceedings as the sheriff thinks relevant.

(3)  In issuing an invitation under section 14(2)(b) of the Act of 2006, the sheriff may impose such terms and conditions as he considers desirable in the interests of justice, including making provision in respect of any additional expenses incurred by the parties as a result of the intervention.

**Form of intervention**

**14B.4.**—(1)  An intervention shall be by way of a written submission which (including any appendices) shall not exceed 5000 words.

(2)  The SCHR shall lodge the submission and send a copy of it to all the parties by such time as the sheriff may direct.

(3)  The sheriff may in exceptional circumstances—

(a)  allow a longer written submission to be made;

(b)  direct that an oral submission is to be made.

(4)  Any diet in pursuance of paragraph (3)(b) shall be fixed by the sheriff clerk who shall give written intimation of the diet to the SCHR and all the parties.

Chapter 15

Application for sist of party and transference

**Application for sist of party and transference**

**15.1.**—(1)  If a party dies or becomes legally incapacitated while an action is depending, any person claiming to represent that party or his estate may apply by incidental application to be sisted as a party to the action.

(2)  If a party dies or becomes legally incapacitated while an action is depending and the provisions of paragraph (1) are not invoked, any other party may apply by incidental application to have the action transferred in favour of or against, as the case may be, any person who represents that party or his estate.

Chapter 16

Transfer and remit of actions

**Transfer to another court**

**16.1.**—(1)  The sheriff may transfer an action to any other sheriff court, whether in the same sheriffdom or not, if the sheriff considers it expedient to do so.

(2)  If the sheriff is satisfied that the court has no jurisdiction, he may transfer the action to any sheriff court in which it appears to the sheriff that it ought to have been brought.

(3)  An action so transferred shall proceed in all respects as if it had been brought originally in the court to which it is transferred.

## Remit from summary cause to ordinary cause

**16.2.**[1](1)   If the sheriff makes a direction that an action is to be treated as an ordinary cause, the sheriff must, at the time of making that direction—

    (a)   direct the pursuer to lodge an initial writ and intimate it to every other party, within 14 days of the date of this direction;

    (b)   direct the defender to lodge defences within 28 days of the date of the direction; and

    (c)   fix a date and time for an Options Hearing and that date is to be the first suitable court day occurring not sooner than ten weeks, or such lesser period as the sheriff considers appropriate, after the last date for lodging the initial writ.

(2)   Where a direction is made under paragraph (1) in relation to a personal injuries action within the meaning of Chapter 34 (action of damages for, or arising from, personal injuries)—

    (a)   the action is to proceed as a personal injuries action within the meaning of Part A1 of Chapter 36 of the Ordinary Cause Rules 1993 in Schedule 1 to the 1907 Act and in particular—

        (i)   the initial writ is to be lodged in the form specified by rule 36.B1 (form of initial writ);

        (ii)   the defences are to be lodged in accordance with rule 9.6 (defences) as modified by rule 36.E1(5) (no note of pleas-in-law);

    (b)   paragraph (1)(c) does not apply.

## Remit from summary cause to all-Scotland sheriff court

**16.2A.**[2](1)   This rule applies where a party applies for an action to be treated as an ordinary cause and transferred to the all-Scotland sheriff court.

(2)   Where the sheriff—

    (a)   directs that the action is to be treated as an ordinary cause; and

    (b)   certifies that the importance or difficulty of the proceedings makes it appropriate to transfer the action to the all-Scotland sheriff court,

the sheriff must make an order transferring the action to that court.

(3)   In this rule—

    (a)   "all-Scotland sheriff court" means the sheriff court specified in the All-Scotland Sheriff Court (Sheriff Personal Injury Court) Order 2015(a) so far as the court is constituted by a sheriff sitting in the exercise of the sheriff's all-Scotland jurisdiction for the purpose of dealing with civil proceedings of a type specified in that Order;

    (b)   the reference to a sheriff's all-Scotland jurisdiction is to be construed in accordance with section 42(3) of the Courts Reform (Scotland) Act 2014.

---

[1] As substituted by the Act of Sederunt (Rules of the Court of Session 1994 and Sheriff Court Rules Amendment) (No. 2) (Personal Injury and Remits) 2015 (SSI 2015/227) r.9 (effective September 22, 2015).

[2] As inserted by the Act of Sederunt (Rules of the Court of Session 1994 and Sheriff Court Rules Amendment) (No. 2) (Personal Injury and Remits) 2015 (SSI 2015/227) r.9 (effective September 22, 2015).

## Remit from ordinary cause or small claim to summary cause

**16.2B.**[1]  If the sheriff directs that an ordinary cause or small claim is to be treated as an action under these Rules—

   (a)  in the case of an ordinary cause, the initial writ is to be deemed to be a summary cause summons;

   (b)  the sheriff must specify the next step of procedure to be followed in the action.

## Remit from Court of Session

**16.3.**[2]  On receipt of the process in an action which has been remitted from the Court of Session under section 93 of the Courts Reform (Scotland) Act 2014 (remit of cases from the Court of Session), the sheriff clerk must—

   (a)  record the date of receipt in the Register of Summary Causes;

   (b)  fix a hearing to determine further procedure on the first court day occurring not earlier than 14 days after the date of receipt of the process; and

   (c)  forthwith send written notice of the date of the hearing fixed under paragraph (b) to each party.

Chapter 17

Productions and documents

## Lodging of productions

**17.1.**—(1)  A party who intends to rely at a proof upon any documents or articles in his possession, which are reasonably capable of being lodged with the court, must—

   (a)  lodge them with the sheriff clerk together with a list detailing the items no later than 14 days before the proof; and

   (b)  at the same time send a copy of the list to the other party.

(2)  The documents referred to in paragraph (1) include any affidavit or other written statement admissible under section 2 (1) of the Civil Evidence (Scotland) Act 1988.

(3)  A party lodging a document under this rule must send a copy of it to every other party, unless it is not practicable to do so.

(4)  Subject to paragraph (5), only documents or articles produced—

   (a)  in accordance with paragraph (1) (and, if it was a document to which rule 8.5 (1) applies, was on the list lodged in accordance with that rule);

   (b)  at a hearing under rule 8.2; or

   (c)  under rule 18.2 (2) or (3), may be used or put in evidence.

(5)  Documents other than those mentioned in paragraph (4) may be used or put in evidence only with the—

   (a)  consent of the parties; or

   (b)  permission of the sheriff on cause shown, and on such terms as to expenses or otherwise as to him seem proper.

---

[1] As inserted by the Act of Sederunt (Rules of the Court of Session 1994 and Sheriff Court Rules Amendment) (No. 2) (Personal Injury and Remits) 2015 (SSI 2015/227) r.9 (effective September 22, 2015).

[2] As amended by the Act of Sederunt (Rules of the Court of Session 1994 and Sheriff Court Rules Amendment) (No. 2) (Personal Injury and Remits) 2015 (SSI 2015/227) r.9 (effective September 22, 2015).

## Copy productions

**17.2.**—(1) A copy of every production, marked with the appropriate number of process of the principal production, must be lodged for the use of the sheriff at a proof not later than 48 hours before the diet of proof.

(2) Each copy production consisting of more than one sheet must be securely fastened together by the party lodging it.

## Borrowing of productions

**17.3.**—(1) Any productions borrowed must be returned not later than noon on the day preceding the date of the proof.

(2) A receipt for any production borrowed must be entered in the list of productions and that list must be retained by the sheriff clerk.

(3) Subject to paragraph (4), productions may be borrowed only by—
  (a)  a solicitor; or
  (b)  his authorised clerk for whom he shall be responsible.

(4) A party litigant or an authorised lay representative may borrow a production only with permission of the sheriff and subject to such conditions as the sheriff may impose.

(5) Productions may be inspected within the office of the sheriff clerk during normal business hours, and copies may be obtained by a party litigant, where practicable, from the sheriff clerk.

## Penalty for failure to return productions

**17.4.**—(1) If a solicitor has borrowed a production and fails to return it for any diet at which it is required, the sheriff may impose upon such solicitor a fine not exceeding £50.

(2) A fine imposed under paragraph (1) shall—
  (a)  be payable to the sheriff clerk; and
  (b)  be recoverable by civil diligence.

(3) An order imposing a fine under this rule shall not be subject to review except that the sheriff who granted it may, on cause shown, recall it.

## Documents lost or destroyed

**17.5.**—(1)  This rule applies to any—
  (a)  summons;
  (b)  form of response;
  (c)  answers to a counterclaim;
  (d)  third party notice or answers to a third party notice;
  (d)  Register of Summary Causes; or
  (e)  other document lodged with the sheriff clerk in connection with an action.

(2)  Where any document mentioned in paragraph (1) is—
  (a)  lost; or
  (b)  destroyed,
a copy of it, authenticated in such manner as the sheriff may require, may be substituted and shall, for the purposes of the action including the use of diligence, be equivalent to the original.

## Documents and productions to be retained in custody of sheriff clerk

**17.6.**—(1)  This rule applies to all documents or other productions which have at any time been lodged or referred to during a hearing or proof.

(2) The sheriff clerk must retain in his custody any document or other production mentioned in paragraph (1) until—

    (a) after the expiry of the period during which an appeal is competent; and

    (b) any appeal lodged has been disposed of.

(3) Each party who has lodged productions in an action shall—

    (a) after the final determination of the claim, where no appeal has been lodged, within 14 days after the appeal period has expired; or

    (b) within 14 days after the disposal of any appeal lodged on the final determination of the action, uplift the productions from the sheriff clerk.

(4) Where any production has not been uplifted as required by paragraph (3), the sheriff clerk shall intimate to—

    (a) the solicitor who lodged the production; or

    (b) where no solicitor is acting, the party himself or such other party as seems appropriate, that if he fails to uplift the production within 28 days after the date of such intimation, it will be disposed of in such manner as the sheriff directs.

Chapter 18

Recovery of evidence and attendance of witnesses

### Diligence for recovery of documents

**18.1.**—(1) At any time after a summons has been served, a party may make an incidental application in writing to the sheriff to grant commission and diligence to recover documents.

(2) A party who makes an application in accordance with paragraph (1) must list in the application the documents which he wishes to recover.

(3) A copy of the incidental application made under paragraph (1) must be intimated by the applicant to—

    (a) every other party; and

    (b) where necessary, the Advocate General for Scotland or the Lord Advocate (and if there is any doubt, both).

(4) The Advocate General for Scotland and the Lord Advocate may appear at the hearing of any incidental application under paragraph (1).

(5) The sheriff may grant commission and diligence to recover those documents in the list mentioned in paragraph (2) which he considers relevant to the action.

### Optional procedure before executing commission and diligence

**18.2.**—(1) Any party who has obtained a commission and diligence for the recovery of documents may, at any time before executing it, serve by first class recorded delivery post on the person from whom the documents are sought to be recovered (or on his known solicitor or solicitors) an order with certificate attached in Form 24.

(2) Documents recovered in response to an order under paragraph (1) must be sent to, and retained by, the sheriff clerk who shall, on receiving them, advise the parties that the documents are in his possession and may be examined within his office during normal business hours.

(3) If the party who served the order is not satisfied that full production has been made under the specification, or that adequate reasons for non-production have been given, he may execute the commission and diligence in normal form, notwithstanding his adoption in the first instance of the foregoing procedure by order.

(4) At the commission, the commissioner shall—

   (a)   administer the appropriate oath or affirmation to any clerk and any shorthand writer appointed for the commission; and

   (b)   administer to the haver the oath in Form 20, or where the haver elects to affirm, the affirmation in Form 21.

(5)  Documents recovered under this rule may be tendered as evidence at any hearing or proof without further formality, and rules 18.4(2), (3) and (4) shall apply to such documents.

### Optional procedure before executing commission and diligence – personal injuries actions

**18.2A.**—[1](1)  This rule applies to actions to which Chapter 34 applies (action of damages for, or arising from, personal injuries) but only where each party is legally represented.

(2)  Any party who has obtained a commission and diligence for the recovery of documents may, at any time before executing it, serve by first class recorded delivery post on the solicitor or solicitors of the person from whom the documents are sought to be recovered an order with certificate attached in Form 10B.

(3)  Documents recovered in response to an order under paragraph (2) must be sent to, and retained by, the party who obtained the order who must, on receiving them, advise the parties that the documents are in his possession and may be examined within his office during normal business hours.

(4)  If the party who served the order is not satisfied that full production has been made under the specification, or that adequate reasons for non-production have been given, he may execute the commission and diligence in normal form, notwithstanding his adoption in the first instance of the foregoing procedure by order.

(5)  At the commission, the commissioner must—

   (a)   administer the appropriate oath or affirmation to any clerk and any shorthand writer appointed for the commission; and

   (b)   administer to the haver the oath in Form 20, or where the haver elects to affirm, the affirmation in Form 21.

(6)  Documents recovered under this rule may be tendered as evidence at any hearing or proof without further formality, and rules 18.4(2), (3) and (4) shall apply to such documents.

### Applications for orders under section 1 of the Administration of Justice (Scotland) Act 1972

**18.3**—(1)  An application by a party for an order under section 1 of the Administration of Justice (Scotland) Act 1972, must be made by incidental application in writing.

(2)  At the time of lodging an incidental application under paragraph (1), a specification of—

   (a)   the document or other property sought to be inspected, photographed, preserved, taken into custody, detained, produced, recovered, sampled or experimented with or upon, as the case may be; or

   (b)   the matter in respect of which information is sought as to the identity of a person who might be a witness or a defender, must be lodged in process.

(3)  A copy of the specification lodged under paragraph (2) and the incidental application made under paragraph (1) must be intimated by the applicant to—

---

[1] As inserted by the Act of Sederunt (Rules of the Court of Session, Ordinary Cause Rules and Summary Cause Rules Amendment) (Miscellaneous) 2014 (SSI 2014/152) r.4 (effective July 7, 2014).

    (a)   every other party;

    (b)   any third party haver; and

    (c)   where necessary, the Advocate General for Scotland or the Lord Advocate (and if there is any doubt, both).

(4)  If the sheriff grants an incidental application under paragraph (1) in whole or in part, he may order the applicant to find such caution or give such other security as he thinks fit.

(5)  The Advocate General for Scotland and the Lord Advocate may appear at the hearing of any incidental application under paragraph (1).

## Confidentiality

**18.4**—(1)[1]  Confidentiality may be claimed for any evidence sought to be recovered under rule 18.2, rule 18.2A or 18.3.

(2)  Where confidentiality is claimed under paragraph (1), the documents or property in respect of which confidentiality is claimed shall be enclosed in a separate, sealed packet.

(3)  A sealed packet referred to in paragraph (2) shall not be opened except by authority of the sheriff obtained on the incidental application of the party who sought the commission and diligence or order.

(4)  The incidental application made under paragraph (3) must be intimated by the applicant to the party or parties from whose possession the documents specified in the commission and diligence or order were obtained.

(5)  Any party received intimation under paragraph (4) may appear at the hearing of the application.

## Preservation and obtaining of evidence

**18.5**—(1)  Evidence in danger of being lost may be taken to be retained until required and, if satisfied that it is desirable so to do, the sheriff may, upon the application of any party at any time, either take it himself or grant authority to a commissioner to take it.

(2)  The interlocutor granting such a commission shall be sufficient authority for citing the witness to appear before the commission.

(3)  The evidence of any witness who—

    (a)   is resident beyond the sheriffdom;

    (b)   although resident within the sheriffdom, resides at some place remote from the court in which the proof is to be held; or

    (c)   is by reason of illness, age, infirmity or other sufficient cause unable to attend the proof, may be taken in the same manner as is provided in paragraph (1).

(4)  On special cause shown, evidence may be taken from any witness or haver on a ground other than one mentioned in paragraph (1) or (3).

(5)  Evidence taken under paragraph (1), (3) or (4) may be taken down by—

    (a)   the sheriff;

    (b)   the commissioner; or

    (c)   a clerk or shorthand writer nominated by the sheriff or commissioner, and such evidence may be recorded in narrative form or by question and

---

[1] As amended by the Act of Sederunt (Rules of the Court of Session, Ordinary Cause Rules and Summary Cause Rules Amendment) (Miscellaneous) 2014 (SSI 2014/152) r.4 (effective July 7, 2014).

answer as the sheriff or commissioner shall direct and the extended notes of such evidence certified by such clerk or shorthand writer shall be the notes of such oral evidence.

(6) At the commission, the commissioner shall or where the sheriff takes evidence himself, the sheriff shall—

(a) administer the appropriate oath or affirmation to any clerk and any shorthand writer appointed for the commission; and

(b) administer to the witness the oath in Form 20, or where the witness elects to affirm, the affirmation in Form 21.

### Warrants for production of original documents from public records

**18.6**—(1)  If a party seeks to obtain from the keeper of any public record production of the original of any register or deed in his custody for the purposes of an action, he must apply to the sheriff by incidental application.

(2)  Intimation of an incidental application under paragraph (1) must be given to the keeper of the public record concerned at least seven days before the incidental application is lodged.

(3)  In relation to a public record kept by the Keeper of the Registers of Scotland or the Keeper of the Records of Scotland—

(a) where it appears to the sheriff that it is necessary for the ends of justice that an incidental application under this rule should be granted, he must pronounce an interlocutor containing a certificate to that effect; and

(b) the party applying for production may apply by letter (enclosing a copy of the interlocutor duly certified by the sheriff clerk), addressed to the Deputy Principal Clerk of Session, for an order from the Court of Session authorising the Keeper of the Registers or the Keeper of the Records, as the case may be, to exhibit the original of any register or deed to the sheriff.

(4)  The Deputy Principal Clerk of Session must submit the application sent to him under paragraph (3) to the Lord Ordinary in chambers who, if satisfied, shall grant a warrant for production or exhibition of the original register or deed sought.

(5)  A certified copy of the warrant granted under paragraph (4) must be served on the keeper of the public record concerned.

(6)  The expense of the production or exhibition of such an original register or deed must be met, in the first instance, by the party who applied by incidental application under paragraph (1).

### Letter of request

**18.7**—(1)[1]  Subject to paragraph (7), this rule applies to an application for a letter of request to a court or tribunal outside Scotland to obtain evidence of the kind specified in paragraph (2), being evidence obtainable within the jurisdiction of that court or tribunal, for the purpose of an action depending before the sheriff.

(2)  An application to which paragraph (1) applies may be made in relation to a request—

(a) for the examination of a witness;

(b) for the inspection, photographing, preservation, custody, detention, production or recovery of, or the taking of samples of, or the carrying out of any experiment on or with, a document or other property, as the case may be;

---

[1] As amended by the Act of Sederunt (Taking of Evidence in the European Community) 2003 (SSI 2003/601) r.5(2) (effective January 1, 2004).

    (c)    for the medical examination of any person;

    (d)    for the taking and testing of samples of blood from any person; or

    (e)    for any other order for obtaining evidence, for which an order could be obtained from the sheriff.

(3)  Such an application must be made by minute in Form 25 together with a proposed letter of request in Form 25a.

(4)  It shall be a condition of granting a letter of request that any solicitor for the applicant, or a party litigant, as the case may be, is to be personally liable, in the first instance, for the whole expenses which may become due and payable in respect of the letter of request to the court or tribunal obtaining the evidence and to any witness who may be examined for the purpose; and he must consign into court such sum in respect of such expenses as the sheriff thinks fit.

(5)  Unless the court or tribunal to which a letter of request is addressed is a court or tribunal in a country or territory—

    (a)    where English is an official language; or

    (b)    in relation to which the sheriff clerk certifies that no translation is required, then the applicant must, before the issue of the letter of request, lodge in process a translation of that letter and any interrogatories and cross-interrogatories into the official language of that court or tribunal.

(6)[1]  The letter of request when issued, any interrogatories and cross-interrogatories and the translations (if any) must be forwarded by the sheriff clerk to the Scottish Ministers or to such person and in such manner as the sheriff may direct.

(7)[2]  This rule does not apply to any request for the taking of evidence under Council Regulation (EC) No. 1206/2001 of 28th May 2001 on cooperation between the courts of the Member States in the taking of evidence in civil or commercial matters.

### Taking of evidence in the European Community

**18.7A.**—[3](1)  This rule applies to any request—

    (a)    for the competent court of another Member State to take evidence under Article 1.1(a) of the Council Regulation; or

    (b)    that the court shall take evidence directly in another Member State under Article 1.1(b) of the Council Regulation.

(2)  An application for a request under paragraph (1) shall be made by minute in Form 25B, together with the proposed request in form A or I (as the case may be) in the Annex to the Council Regulation.

(3)  In this rule, "the Council Regulation" means Council Regulation (EC) No. 1206/2001 of 28th May 2001 on cooperation between the courts of the Member States in the taking of evidence in civil or commercial matters.

### Citation of witnesses

**18.8.**—(1)  The citation of a witness or haver must be in Form 26 and the certificate of it must be in Form 26a.

---

[1] As substituted by the Act of Sederunt (Sheriff Court Rules) (Miscellaneous Amendments) 2011 (SSI 2011/193) r.8 (effective April 4, 2011).

[2] As inserted by the Act of Sederunt (Taking of Evidence in the European Community) 2003 (SSI 2003/601) r.5(2) (effective January 1, 2004).

[3] As inserted by the Act of Sederunt (Taking of Evidence in the European Community) 2003 (SSI 2003/601) r.5(3) (effective January 1, 2004).

(2) A party shall be responsible for securing the attendance of his witnesses or havers at a hearing and shall be personally liable for their expenses.

(3) The summons or the copy served on the defender shall be sufficient warrant for the citation of witnesses and havers.

(4) The period of notice given to witnesses or havers cited in terms of paragraph (3) must be not less than seven days.

(5) A witness or haver shall be cited—

    (a) by registered post or the first class recorded delivery service by the solicitor for the party on whose behalf he is cited; or

    (b) by a sheriff officer—

        (i) personally;

        (ii) by a citation being left with a resident at the person's dwelling place or an employee at his place of business;

        (iii) by depositing it in that person's dwelling place or place of business;

        (iv) by affixing it to the door of that person's dwelling place or place of business; or

        (v) by registered post or the first class recorded delivery service.

(6) Where service is effected under paragraph (5) (b) (iii) or (iv), the sheriff officer shall, as soon as possible after such service, send by ordinary post to the address at which he thinks it most likely that the person may be found, a letter containing a copy of the citation.

### Citation of witnesses by party litigants

**18.9.**—(1) Where a party to an action is a party litigant he shall—

    (a) not later than 28 days before the diet of proof apply to the sheriff by incidental application to fix caution for expenses in such sum as the sheriff considers reasonable having regard to the number of witnesses he proposes to cite and the period for which they may be required to attend court; and

    (b) before instructing a solicitor or a sheriff officer to cite a witness, find caution in the sum fixed in accordance with paragraph (1).

(2) A party litigant who does not intend to cite all the witnesses referred to in his application under paragraph 1(a), may apply by incidental application for variation of the amount of caution.

### Witnesses failing to attend

**18.10.**—(1) A hearing must not be adjourned solely on account of the failure of a witness to appear unless the sheriff, on cause shown, so directs.

(2) A witness or haver who fails without reasonable excuse to answer a citation after having been properly cited and offered his travelling expenses if he has asked for them may be ordered by the sheriff to pay a penalty not exceeding £250.

(3) The sheriff may grant decree for payment of a penalty imposed under paragraph (2) above in favour of the party on whose behalf the witness or haver was cited.

(4) The sheriff may grant warrant for the apprehension of the witness or haver and for bringing him to court.

(5)   A warrant mentioned in paragraph (4) shall be effective in any sheriffdom without endorsation and the expenses of it may be awarded against the witness or haver.

Chapter 18A[1]

Vulnerable Witnesses (Scotland) Act 2004

## Interpretation

**18A.1.**   In this Chapter—

"child witness notice" has the meaning given in section 12(2) of the 2004 Act;

"review application" means an application for review of arrangements for vulnerable witnesses pursuant to section 13 of the 2004 Act;

"vulnerable witness application" has the meaning given in section 12(6) of the 2004 Act.

## Child Witness Notice

**18A.2.**   A child witness notice lodged in accordance with section 12(2) of the 2004 Act shall be in Form 26B.

## Vulnerable Witness Application

**18A.3.**   A vulnerable witness application lodged in accordance with section 12(6) of the 2004 Act shall be in Form 26C.

## Intimation

**18A.4.**—(1)   The party lodging a child witness notice or vulnerable witness application shall intimate a copy of the child witness notice or vulnerable witness application to all the other parties to the proceedings and complete a certificate of intimation.

(2)   A certificate of intimation referred to in paragraph (1) shall be in Form 26D and shall be lodged with the child witness notice or vulnerable witness application.

## Procedure on lodging child witness notice or vulnerable witness application

**18A.5.**—(1)   On receipt of a child witness notice or vulnerable witness application, the sheriff may—

(a)   make an order under section 12(1) or (6) of the 2004 Act without holding a hearing;

(b)   require further information from any of the parties before making any further order;

(c)   fix a date for a hearing of the child witness notice or vulnerable witness application.

(2)   The sheriff may, subject to any statutory time limits, make an order altering the date of the proof or other hearing at which the child or vulnerable witness is to give evidence and make such provision for intimation of such alteration to all parties concerned as he deems appropriate.

(3)   An order fixing a hearing for a child witness notice or vulnerable witness application shall be intimated by the sheriff clerk—

(a)   on the day the order is made; and

(b)   in such manner as may be prescribed by the sheriff,

---

[1] As inserted by the Act of Sederunt (Ordinary Cause, Summary Application, Summary Cause and Small Claim Rules) Amendment (Vulnerable Witnesses (Scotland) Act 2004) 2007 (SSI 2007/463) r.4(5) (effective November 1, 2007).

to all parties to the proceedings and such other persons as are named in the order where such parties or persons are not present at the time the order is made.

**Review of arrangements for vulnerable witnesses**

**18A.6.**—(1)   A review application shall be in Form 26E.

(2)   Where the review application is made orally, the sheriff may dispense with the requirements of paragraph (1).

**Intimation of review application**

**18A.7.**—(1)   Where a review application is lodged, the applicant shall intimate a copy of the review application to all other parties to the proceedings and complete a certificate of intimation.

(2)   A certificate of intimation referred to in paragraph (1) shall be in Form 26F and shall be lodged together with the review application.

**Procedure on lodging a review application**

**18A.8.**—(1)   On receipt of a review application, the sheriff may—

(a)   if he is satisfied that he may properly do so, make an order under section 13(2) of the 2004 Act without holding a hearing or, if he is not so satisfied, make such an order after giving the parties an opportunity to be heard;

(b)   require of any of the parties further information before making any further order;

(c)   fix a date for a hearing of the review application.

(2)   The sheriff may, subject to any statutory time limits, make an order altering the date of the proof or other hearing at which the child or vulnerable witness is to give evidence and such provision for intimation of such alteration to all parties concerned as he deems appropriate.

(3)   An order fixing a hearing for a review application shall be intimated by the sheriff clerk—

(a)   on the day the order is made; and

(b)   in such manner as may be prescribed by the sheriff,

to all parties to the proceedings and such other persons as are named in the order where such parties or persons are not present at the time the order is made.

**Determination of special measures**

**18A.9.**   When making an order under section 12(1) or (6) or 13(2) of the 2004 Act the sheriff may, in light thereof, make such further orders as he deems appropriate in all the circumstances.

**Intimation of an order under section 12(1) or (6) or 13(2)**

**18A.10.**   An order under section 12(1) or (6) or 13(2) of the 2004 Act shall be intimated by the sheriff clerk—

(a)   on the day the order is made; and

(b)   in such manner as may be prescribed by the sheriff,

to all parties to the proceedings and such other persons as are named in the order where such parties or persons are not present at the time the order is made.

**Taking of evidence by commissioner**

**18A.11.**—(1)   An interlocutor authorising the special measure of taking evidence by a commissioner shall be sufficient authority for the citing the witness to appear before the commissioner.

(2)   At the commission the commissioner shall—

(a) administer the oath de fideli administratione to any clerk appointed for the commission; and

(b) administer to the witness the oath in Form 20, or where the witness elects to affirm, the affirmation in Form 21.

(3) The commission shall proceed without interrogatories unless, on cause shown, the sheriff otherwise directs.

### Commission on interrogatories

**18A.12.**—(1) Where interrogatories have not been dispensed with, the party citing or intending to cite the vulnerable witness shall lodge draft interrogatories in process.

(2) Any other party may lodge cross-interrogatories.

(3) The interrogatories and cross-interrogatories, when adjusted, shall be extended and returned to the sheriff clerk for approval and the settlement of any dispute as to their contents by the sheriff.

(4) The party who cited the vulnerable witness shall—

(a) provide the commissioner with a copy of the pleadings (including any adjustments and amendments), the approved interrogatories and any cross-interrogatories and a certified copy of the interlocutor of his appointment;

(b) instruct the clerk; and

(c) be responsible in the first instance for the fee of the commissioner and his clerk.

(5) The commissioner shall, in consultation with the parties, fix a diet for the execution of the commission to examine the witness.

### Commission without interrogatories

**18A.13.** Where interrogatories have been dispensed with, the party citing or intending to cite the vulnerable witness shall—

(a) provide the commissioner with a copy of the pleadings (including any adjustments and amendments) and a certified copy of the interlocutor of his appointment;

(b) fix a diet for the execution of the commission in consultation with the commissioner and every other party;

(c) instruct the clerk; and

(d) be responsible in the first instance for the fees of the commissioner and his clerk.

### Lodging of video record and documents

**18A.14.**—(1) Where evidence is taken on commission pursuant to an order made under section 12(1) or (6) or 13(2) of the 2004 Act the commissioner shall lodge the video record of the commission and relevant documents with the sheriff clerk.

(2) On the video record and any documents being lodged the sheriff clerk shall—

(a) note—

(i) the documents lodged;

(ii) by whom they were lodged; and

(iii) the date on which they were lodged, and

(b) intimate what he has noted to all parties concerned.

### Custody of video record and documents

**18A.15.**—(1) The video record and documents referred to in rule 18A.14 shall, subject to paragraph (2), be kept in the custody of the sheriff clerk.

(2) Where the video record of the evidence of a witness is in the custody of the sheriff clerk under this rule and where intimation has been given to that effect under rule 18A.14(2), the name and address of that witness and the record of his evidence shall be treated as being in the knowledge of the parties; and no party shall be required, notwithstanding any enactment to the contrary—

(a) to include the name of that witness in any list of witnesses; or

(b) to include the record of his evidence in any list of productions.

**Application for leave for party to be present at the commission**

**18A.16.** An application for leave for a party to be present in the room where the commission proceedings are taking place shall be by incidental application..

(2) In rule 37.1(2) (live links) at the end of the definition of "witness" there shall be inserted the following—

", except a vulnerable witness within the meaning of section 11(1) of the 2004 Act.".

(3) In Appendix 1—

(a) for Form 26 there shall be substituted the form in Part 1 of Schedule 2 to this Act of Sederunt; and

(b) after Form 26A there shall be inserted the forms set out in Part 2 of Schedule 2 to this Act of Sederunt.

Chapter 19

Challenge of documents

**Challenge of documents**

**19.1.**—(1) If a party relies on a deed or other document to support his case, any other party may object to the deed or document without having to bring an action of reduction.

(2) If an objection is made, the sheriff may order the objector, if an action of reduction would otherwise have been competent, to find caution or to consign with the sheriff clerk a sum of money as security.

Chapter 20

European Court

**Interpretation of rules 20.2 to 20.5**

**20.1.**—(1) In rules 20.2 to 20.5—

"the European Court" means the Court of Justice of the European Communities;

"reference" means a reference to the European Court for—

(a) a preliminary ruling under Article 234 of the E.E.C. Treaty, Article 150 of the Euratom Treaty or Article 41 of the E.C.S.C. Treaty; or

(b) a ruling on the interpretation of the Conventions, as defined in section 1(1) of the Civil Jurisdiction and Judgments Act 1982, under Article 3 of Schedule 2 to that Act.

(2) The expressions "E.E.C. Treaty", "Euratom Treaty" and "E.C.S.C. Treaty" have the meanings assigned respectively in Schedule 1 to the European Communities Act 1972.

**Application for reference**

**20.2.**—(1) The sheriff may, on the application of a party or of his own accord make a reference.

(2) A reference must be made in the form of a request for a preliminary ruling of the European Court in Form 27.

**Preparation of case for reference**

**20.3.**—(1) If the sheriff decides that a reference shall be made, he must within four weeks draft a reference.

(2) On the reference being drafted, the sheriff clerk must send a copy to each party.

(3) Within four weeks after the date on which copies of the draft have been sent to parties, each party may—

(a) lodge with the sheriff clerk; and

(b) send to every other party, a note of any adjustments he seeks to have made in the draft reference.

(4) Within 14 days after the date on which any such note of adjustments may be lodged, the sheriff, after considering any such adjustments, must make and sign the reference.

(5) The sheriff clerk must forthwith intimate the making of the reference to each party.

**Sist of action**

**20.4.**—(1) Subject to paragraph (2), on a reference being made, the action must, unless the sheriff when making the reference otherwise orders, be sisted until the European Court has given a preliminary ruling on the question referred to it.

(2) The sheriff may recall a sist made under paragraph (1) for the purpose of making an interim order which a due regard to the interests of the parties may require.

**Transmission of reference**

**20.5.** A copy of the reference, certified by the sheriff clerk, must be transmitted by the sheriff clerk to the Registrar of the European Court.

Chapter 21

Abandonment

**Abandonment of action**

**21.1.**—(1) A pursuer may before an order granting absolvitor or dismissing the action has been pronounced, offer to abandon the action.

(2) Where the pursuer offers to abandon the action in accordance with paragraph (1), the sheriff clerk shall, subject to the approval of the sheriff, fix the amount of the defender's expenses to be paid by the pursuer in accordance with rule 23.3 and the action must be continued to the first appropriate court occurring not sooner than 14 days after the amount has been fixed.

(3) If before the continued diet the pursuer makes payment to the defender of the amount fixed under paragraph (2), the sheriff must dismiss the action unless the pursuer consents to absolvitor.

(4)   If before the continued diet the pursuer fails to pay the amount fixed under paragraph (2), the defender shall be entitled to decree of absolvitor with expenses.

## Chapter 22

## Decree by default

**Decree by default**

**22.1.**—(1)   If, after a proof has been fixed under rule 8.3(3)(d), a party fails to appear at a hearing where required to do so, the sheriff may grant decree by default.

(2)   If all parties fail to appear at a hearing or proof where required to do so, the sheriff must, unless sufficient reason appears to the contrary, dismiss the action and any counterclaim.

(3)   If, after a proof has been fixed under rule 8.3(3)(d), a party fails to implement an order of the court, the sheriff may, after giving him an opportunity to be heard, grant decree by default.

(4)   The sheriff shall not grant decree by default solely on the ground that a party has failed to appear at the hearing of an incidental application.

## Chapter 22A[1]

## Dismissal of Action due to Delay

**Dismissal of action due to delay**

**22A.1.**—(1)   Any party to an action may, while that action is depending before the court, apply by written incidental application to the court to dismiss the action due to inordinate and inexcusable delay by another party or another party's agent in progressing the action, resulting in unfairness.

(2)[2]   An application under paragraph (1) shall include a statement of the grounds on which it is proposed that the application should be allowed.

(3)   In determining an application made under this rule, the court may dismiss the action if it appears to the court that—

(a)   there has been an inordinate and inexcusable delay on the part of any party or any party's agent in progressing the action; and

(b)   such delay results in unfairness specific to the factual circumstances, including the procedural circumstances, of that action.

(4)   In determining whether or not to dismiss an action under paragraph (3), the court shall take account of the procedural consequences, both for the parties and for the work of the court, of allowing the action to proceed.

(5)   Rule 9.1 shall, with the necessary modifications, apply to an application under paragraph (1).

## Chapter 23

## Decrees, extracts, execution and variation

**Decree**

**23.1.**   The sheriff must not grant decree against—

(a)   a defender or a third party in respect of a claim; or

---

[1] As inserted by the Act of Sederunt (Sheriff Court Rules) (Miscellaneous Amendments) 2009 (SSI 2009/294) r.15 (effective October 1, 2009).

[2] As amended by the Act of Sederunt (Sheriff Court Rules) (Miscellaneous Amendments) 2010 (SSI 2010/279) r.7 (effective July 29, 2010).

(b)  a pursuer in respect of a counterclaim, under any provision of these Rules unless satisfied that a ground of jurisdiction exists.

**Final decree**

**23.2.**[1] [2]  The final decree of the sheriff shall be granted, where expenses are awarded, only after expenses have been dealt with in accordance with rules 23.3, 23.3A and 23.3B.

**Expenses**

**23.3.**—[3, 4, 5](1)[6]  Subject to rule 23.3A and paragraphs (2) to (4), the sheriff clerk must, with the approval of the sheriff, assess the amount of expenses including the fees and outlays of witnesses awarded in any cause, in accordance with the applicable statutory table of fees.

(2)  A party litigant, who is not represented by a solicitor or advocate and who would have been entitled to expenses if he had been so represented, may be awarded any outlays or expenses to which he might be found entitled by virtue of the 1975 Act or any enactment under that Act.

(3)  A party who is or has been represented by an authorised lay representative or a person authorised under any enactment to conduct proceedings in the sheriff court and who would have been found entitled to expenses if he had been represented by a solicitor or an advocate may be awarded any outlays or expenses to which a party litigant might be found entitled in accordance with paragraph (2).

(4)  A party who is not an individual, and—

    (i)  is or has been represented by an authorised lay representative or a person authorised under any enactment to conduct proceedings in the sheriff court;

    (ii)  if unrepresented, could not represent itself; and

    (iii)  would have been found entitled to expenses if it had been represented by a solicitor or an advocate,

may be awarded any outlays to which a party litigant might be found entitled under the 1975 Act or any enactment made under that Act.

(5)  Except where an account of expenses is allowed to be taxed under rule 23.3A, in every case including an appeal where expenses are awarded, the sheriff clerk shall hear the parties or their solicitors on the claims for expenses including fees, if any, and outlays.

---

[1] As substituted by the Act of Sederunt (Summary Cause Rules) (Amendment) 2002 (SSI 2002/516) r.2(2) (effective January 1, 2003).

[2] As amended by the Act of Sederunt (Rules of the Court of Session, Sheriff Appeal Court Rules and Sheriff Court Rules Amendment) (Sheriff Appeal Court) 2015 (SSI 2015/419) r.11 (effective 1 January 2016; as to savings see SSI 2015/419 rule 20(6)(a)).

[3] As amended by the Act of Sederunt (Summary Cause Rules) (Amendment) 2002 (SSI 2002/516) r.2(3) (effective January 1, 2003).

[4] As amended by the Act of Sederunt (Ordinary Cause, Summary Application, Summary Cause and Small Claim Rules) Amendment (Miscellaneous) 2007 (SSI 2007/6) r.4(4) (effective January 29, 2007).

[5] As amended by the Act of Sederunt (Rules of the Court of Session, Sheriff Appeal Court Rules and Sheriff Court Rules Amendment) (Sheriff Appeal Court) 2015 (SSI 2015/419) r.11 (effective 1 January 2016; as to savings see SSI 2015/419 rule 20(6)(a)).

[6] As amended by the Act of Sederunt (Sheriff Court Rules Amendment) (Sections 25 to 29 of the Law Reform (Miscellaneous Provisions) (Scotland) Act 1990) 2009 (SSI 2009/164) r.4(3) (effective May 20, 2009).

(6)  Except where the sheriff has reserved judgment or where he orders otherwise, the hearing on the claim for expenses must take place immediately upon the decision being pronounced.

(7)  When that hearing is not held immediately, the sheriff clerk must—

(a)  fix the date, time and place when he shall hear the parties or their solicitors; and

(b)  give all parties at least 14 days' notice in writing of the hearing so fixed.

(8)  The party awarded expenses must—

(a)  lodge his account of expenses in court at least seven days prior to the date of any hearing fixed under paragraph (7); and

(b)  at the same time forward a copy of that account to every other party.

(9)  The sheriff clerk must—

(a)  fix the amount of the expenses; and

(b)  report his decision to the sheriff in open court for his approval at a diet which the sheriff clerk has intimated to the parties.

(10)  The sheriff, after hearing parties or their solicitors if objections are stated, must pronounce final decree including decree for payment of expenses as approved by him.

(11)  *[Revoked by the Act of Sederunt (Rules of the Court of Session, Sheriff Appeal Court Rules and Sheriff Court Rules Amendment) (Sheriff Appeal Court) 2015 (SSI 2015/419) r.11 (effective1 January 2016; as to savings see SSI 2015/419 rule 20(6)(a)).]*

(12)  Failure by—

(a)  any party to comply with any of the foregoing provisions of this rule; or

(b)  the successful party or parties to appear at the hearing on expenses, must be reported by the sheriff clerk to the sheriff at a diet which the sheriff clerk has intimated to the parties.

(13)  In either of the circumstances mentioned in paragraphs (12)(a) or (b), the sheriff must, unless sufficient cause be shown, pronounce decree on the merits of the action and find no expenses due to or by any party.

(14)  A decree pronounced under paragraph (13) shall be held to be the final decree for the purposes of these Rules.

(15)  The sheriff may, if he thinks fit, on the application of the solicitor of any party to whom expenses may be awarded, made at or before the time of the final decree being pronounced, grant decree in favour of that solicitor for the expenses of the action.

**Taxation**

**23.3A.**—(1)[1]  Either—

(a)  the sheriff, on his own motion or on the motion of any party; or

(b)  the sheriff clerk on cause shown,

may allow an account of expenses to be taxed by the auditor of court instead of being assessed by the sheriff clerk under rule 23.3.

(2)  Where an account of expenses is lodged for taxation, the account and process shall be transmitted by the sheriff clerk to the auditor of court.

(3)  The auditor of court shall—

---

[1] As inserted by the Act of Sederunt (Summary Cause Rules) (Amendment) 2002 (SSI 2002/516) r.2(4) (effective January 1, 2003).

    (a)   assign a diet of taxation not earlier than 7 days from the date he receives the account from the sheriff clerk; and

    (b)   intimate that diet forthwith from to the party who lodged the account.

  (4)  The party who lodged the account of expenses shall, on receiving intimation from the auditor of court under paragraph (3)—

    (a)   send a copy of the account; and

    (b)   intimate the date, time and place of the diet of taxation, to every other party.

  (5)  After the account has been taxed, the auditor of court shall transmit the process with the account and his report to the sheriff clerk.

  (6)  Where the auditor of court has reserved consideration of the account at the date of the taxation, he shall intimate his decision to the parties who attended the taxation.

  (7)  Where no objections are lodged under rule 23.3B (objections to auditor's report), the sheriff may grant decree for the expenses as taxed.

**23.3B.—**  Objections to auditor's report

  (1)[1]  A party may lodge a note of objections to an account as taxed only where he attended the diet of taxation.

  (2)  Such a note shall be lodged within 7 days after—

    (a)   the diet of taxation; or

    (b)   where the auditor of court reserved consideration of the account under paragraph (6) of rule 23.3A, the date on which the auditor of court intimates his decision under that paragraph.

  (3)  The sheriff shall dispose of the objection in a summary manner, with or without answers.

### Correction of interlocutor or note

**23.4.**  At any time before extract, the sheriff may correct any clerical or incidental error in an interlocutor or note attached to it.

### Taxes on funds under control of the court

**23.5.—(1)**  Subject to paragraph (2), in an action in which money has been consigned into court under the Sheriff Court Consignations (Scotland) Act 1893, no decree, warrant or order for payment to any person shall be granted until there has been lodged with the sheriff clerk a certificate by an authorised officer of the Inland Revenue stating that all taxes or duties payable to the Commissioners of Inland Revenue have been paid or satisfied.

  (2)  In an action of multiplepoinding, it shall not be necessary for the grant of a decree, warrant or order for payment under paragraph (1) that all of the taxes or duties payable on the estate of a deceased claimant have been paid or satisfied.

### Extract of decree

**23.6.—(1)**  Extract of a decree signed by the sheriff clerk may be issued only after the lapse of 14 days from the granting of the decree unless the sheriff on application orders earlier extract.

  (2)  In an action (other than an action to which rule 30.2 applies) where an appeal has been lodged, the extract may not be issued until the appeal has been disposed of.

  (3)  The extract decree—

---

[1] As inserted by the Act of Sederunt (Summary Cause Rules) (Amendment) 2002 (SSI 2002/516) r.2(4) (effective January 1, 2003).

   (a)   may be written on the summons or on a separate paper;

   (b)   may be in one of Forms 28 to 28k; and

   (c)   shall be warrant for all lawful execution.

## Charge

**23.7.**—(1)  The period for payment specified in any charge following on a decree for payment granted in an action shall be—

   (a)   14 days if the person on whom it is served is within the United Kingdom; and

   (b)   28 days if he is outside the United Kingdom or his whereabouts are unknown.

(2)  The period in respect of any other form of charge on a decree in an action shall be 14 days.

## Service of charge where address of defender is unknown

**23.8.**—(1)  If the address of a defender is not known to the pursuer, a charge shall be deemed to have been served on the defender if it is—

   (a)   served on the sheriff clerk of the sheriff court district where the defender's last known address is located; and

   (b)   displayed by the sheriff clerk on the walls of court for the period of the charge.

(2)  On receipt of such a charge, the sheriff clerk must display it on the walls of court and it must remain displayed for the period of the charge.

(3)  The period specified in the charge shall run from the first date on which it was displayed on the walls of court.

(4)  On the expiry of the period of charge, the sheriff clerk must endorse a certificate in Form 29 on the charge certifying that it has been displayed in accordance with this rule and must then return it to the sheriff officer by whom service was executed.

## Diligence on decree in actions for delivery

**23.9.**—(1)  In an action for delivery, the court may, when granting decree, grant warrant to search for and take possession of goods and to open shut and lockfast places.

(2)  A warrant granted under paragraph (1) shall only apply to premises occupied by the defender.

## Applications in same action for variation, etc. of decree

**23.10.**—(1)  If by virtue of any enactment the sheriff, without a new action being initiated, may order that—

   (a)   a decree granted be varied, discharged or rescinded; or

   (b)   the execution of that decree in so far as it has not already been executed be sisted or suspended,

the party requesting the sheriff to make such an order must do so by lodging a minute to that effect, setting out briefly the reasons for the application.

(2)  On the lodging of such a minute by the pursuer, the sheriff clerk must grant warrant for service upon the defender (provided that the pursuer has returned the extract decree).

(3)  On the lodging of such a minute by the defender, the sheriff clerk must grant warrant for service upon the pursuer ordaining him to return the extract decree and may, where appropriate, grant interim sist of execution of the decree.

(4)   Subject to paragraph (5), the minute shall not be heard in court unless seven days' notice of the minute and warrant has been given to the other parties by the party lodging the minute.

(5)   The sheriff may, on cause shown, alter the period of seven days referred to in paragraph (4) but may not reduce it to less than two days.

(6)   This rule shall not apply to any proceedings under the Debtors (Scotland) Act 1987 or to proceedings which may be subject to the provisions of that Act.

Chapter 24

Recall of decree

**Recall of decree**

**24.1.**—[1](1)   A party may apply for recall of a decree granted under any of the following provisions—

    (a)   rule 7.1; or

    (b)   paragraph (5), (6) or (7) of rule 8.2.

(2)   The application is to be by minute in Form 30, which must be lodged with the sheriff clerk.

(3)   The application must include where appropriate (and if not already lodged with the sheriff clerk), the proposed defence or the proposed answer to the counterclaim.

(4)   A party may apply for recall of a decree in the same action on one occasion only.

(5)   A minute for recall of a decree of dismissal must be lodged within 14 days of the date of decree.

(6)   Subject to paragraphs (7) to (9), a minute for recall of any other kind of decree may be lodged at any time before the decree is fully implemented.

(7)   Subject to paragraphs (8) and (9), where a charge or arrestment has been executed following the decree, the minute must be lodged within 14 days of that execution (or the first such execution where there has been more than one).

(8)   Subject to paragraph (9), in the case of a party seeking recall who was served with the action under rule 5.7, the minute must be lodged—

    (a)   within a reasonable time of such party having knowledge of the decree against him or her; but

    (b)   in any event, within one year of the date of decree.

(9)   Where the decree includes a decree for removing from heritable property to which section 216(1) of the Bankruptcy and Diligence etc. (Scotland) Act 2007 applies, the minute may be lodged at any time before the defender has been removed from the subjects or premises.

(10)   On the lodging of a minute for recall of a decree, the sheriff clerk must fix a date, time and place for a hearing of the minute.

(11)   Where a hearing has been fixed under paragraph (10), the party seeking recall must, not less than 7 days before the date fixed for the hearing, serve upon the other party—

    (a)   a copy of the minute in Form 30a; and

    (b)   a note of the date, time and place of the hearing.

---

[1] As substituted by the Act of Sederunt (Sheriff Court Rules) (Miscellaneous Amendments) 2011 (SSI 2011/193) r.16 (effective April 4, 2011).

(12)  At a hearing fixed under paragraph (10), the sheriff must recall the decree so far as not implemented and the hearing must then proceed as a hearing held under rules 8.2(3) to (7) and 8.3.

(13)  A minute for recall of a decree, when lodged and served in terms of this rule, will have the effect of preventing any further action being taken by the other party to enforce the decree.

(14)  On receipt of the copy minute for recall of a decree, any party in possession of an extract decree must return it forthwith to the sheriff clerk.

(15)  If it appears to the sheriff that there has been any failure or irregularity in service of the minute for recall of a decree, the sheriff may order re-service of the minute on such conditions as the sheriff thinks fit.

Chapter 25

Appeals

**Appeals: application for stated case**

**25.1.**[1](1)  An appeal to the Sheriff Appeal Court, other than an appeal to which rule 25.4 applies, must be in Form 31 lodged with the sheriff clerk not later than 14 days after the date of final decree—

    (a)   requesting a stated case; and

    (b)   specifying the point of law upon which the appeal is to proceed.

(2)   The appellant must, at the same time as lodging Form 31, intimate a copy of it to every other party.

(3)   The sheriff must, within 28 days of the lodging of Form 31, issue a draft stated case containing—

    (a)   findings in fact and law or, where appropriate, a narrative of the proceedings before him;

    (b)   appropriate questions of law; and

    (c)   a note stating the reasons for his decisions in law,

and the sheriff clerk must send a copy of the draft stated case to the parties.

(4)   In an appeal where questions of admissibility or sufficiency of evidence have arisen, the draft stated case must contain a description of the evidence led at the proof to which these questions relate.

(5)   Within 14 days of the issue of the draft stated case—

    (a)   a party may lodge with the sheriff clerk a note of any adjustments which he seeks to make;

    (b)   a respondent may state any point of law which he wishes to raise in the appeal; and

    (c)   the note of adjustment and, where appropriate, point of law must be intimated to every other party.

(6)   The sheriff may, on the motion of a party or of his own accord, and must where he proposes to reject any proposed adjustment, allow a hearing on adjustments and may provide for such further procedure under this rule prior to the hearing of the appeal as he thinks fit.

(7)   The sheriff must, within 14 days after—

    (a)   the latest date on which a note of adjustments has been or may be lodged; or

---

[1] As amended by the Act of Sederunt (Rules of the Court of Session, Sheriff Appeal Court Rules and Sheriff Court Rules Amendment) (Sheriff Appeal Court) 2015 (SSI 2015/419) r.11 (effective 1 January 2016; as to savings see SSI 2015/419 rule 20(6)(a)).

(b) where there has been a hearing on adjustments, that hearing, and after considering such note and any representations made to him at the hearing, state and sign the case.

(8) If the sheriff is temporarily absent from duty for any reason, the sheriff principal may extend any period specified in paragraphs (3) or (7) for such period or periods as he considers reasonable.

(9) The stated case signed by the sheriff must include questions of law, framed by him, arising from the points of law stated by the parties and such other questions of law as he may consider appropriate.

(10) After the sheriff has signed the stated case, the appeal is to proceed in accordance with Chapter 29 of the Act of Sederunt (Sheriff Appeal Court Rules) 2015.

**Effect of and abandonment of appeal**

**25.2.** *[Revoked by the Act of Sederunt (Rules of the Court of Session, Sheriff Appeal Court Rules and Sheriff Court Rules Amendment) (Sheriff Appeal Court) 2015 (SSI 2015/419) r.11 (effective1 January 2016; as to savings see SSI 2015/419 rule 20(6)(a)).]*

**Hearing of appeal**

**25.3.** *[Revoked by the Act of Sederunt (Rules of the Court of Session, Sheriff Appeal Court Rules and Sheriff Court Rules Amendment) (Sheriff Appeal Court) 2015 (SSI 2015/419) r.11 (effective1 January 2016; as to savings see SSI 2015/419 rule 20(6)(a)).]*

**Appeal in relation to a time to pay direction**

**25.4.**[1](1) This rule applies to appeals to the Sheriff Appeal Court or to the Court of Session which relate solely to any application in connection with a time to pay direction.

(2) Rule 25.1 shall not apply to appeals under this rule.

(3) An application for leave to appeal against a decision in an application for a time to pay direction or any order connected therewith must—

(a) be made in Form 32 within seven days of that decision, to the sheriff who made the decision; and

(b) must specify the question of law upon which the appeal is to proceed.

(4) If leave to appeal is granted, the appeal must be lodged in Form 33 and intimated by the appellant to every other party within 14 days of the order granting leave and the sheriff must state in writing his reasons for his original decision.

(5) *[Revoked by the Act of Sederunt (Rules of the Court of Session, Sheriff Appeal Court Rules and Sheriff Court Rules Amendment) (Sheriff Appeal Court) 2015 (SSI 2015/419) r.11 (effective1 January 2016; as to savings see SSI 2015/419 rule 20(6)(a)).]*

**Sheriff to regulate interim possession**

**25.5**—(1) Notwithstanding an appeal, the sheriff shall have power—

(a) to regulate all matters relating to interim possession;

(b) to make any order for the preservation of any property to which the action relates or for its sale, if perishable;

---

[1] As amended by the Act of Sederunt (Rules of the Court of Session, Sheriff Appeal Court Rules and Sheriff Court Rules Amendment) (Sheriff Appeal Court) 2015 (SSI 2015/419) r.11 (effective 1 January 2016; as to savings see SSI 2015/419 rule 20(6)(a)).

(c)  to make any order for the preservation of evidence; or

(d)  to make in his discretion any interim order which a due regard for the interests of the parties may require.

(2)  An order under paragraph (1) shall not be subject to review except by the appellate court at the hearing of the appeal.

### Provisions for appeal in actions for recovery of heritable property to which rule 30.2 applies

**25.6.**  In an action to which rule 30.2 applies—

(a)  it shall not be competent to shorten or dispense with the period for appeal specified in rule 25.1;

(b)  it shall be competent to appeal within that period for appeal irrespective of the early issue of an extract decree; and

(c)[1]  the lodging of a Form 31 shall not operate so as to suspend diligence unless the sheriff directs otherwise.

### Appeal to the Court of Session

**25.7.**  *[Revoked by the Act of Sederunt (Rules of the Court of Session, Sheriff Appeal Court Rules and Sheriff Court Rules Amendment) (Sheriff Appeal Court) 2015 (SSI 2015/419) r.11 (effective1 January 2016; as to savings see SSI 2015/419 rule 20(6)(a)).]*

Chapter 26

Management of damages payable to persons under legal disability

### Orders for payment and management of money

**26.1.**—(1)  In an action of damages in which a sum of money becomes payable, by virtue of a decree or an extra-judicial settlement, to or for the benefit of a person under legal disability (other than a person under the age of 18 years), the sheriff shall make such order regarding the payment and management of that sum for the benefit of that person as he thinks fit.

(2)  Any order required under paragraph (1) shall be made on the granting of decree for payment or of absolvitor.

### Methods of management

**26.2.**  In making an order under rule 26.1(1), the sheriff may—

(a)  order the money to be paid to—

(i)  the Accountant of Court; or

(ii)  the guardian of the person under legal disability, as trustee, to be applied, invested or otherwise dealt with and administered under the directions of the sheriff for the benefit of the person under legal disability;

(b)  order the money to be paid to the sheriff clerk of the sheriff court district in which the person under legal disability resides, to be applied, invested or otherwise dealt with and administered, under the directions of the sheriff of that district, for the benefit of the person under legal disability; or

(c)  order the money to be paid directly to the person under legal disability.

---

[1] As amended by the Act of Sederunt (Rules of the Court of Session, Sheriff Appeal Court Rules and Sheriff Court Rules Amendment) (Sheriff Appeal Court) 2015 (SSI 2015/419) r.11 (effective 1 January 2016; as to savings see SSI 2015/419 rule 20(6)(a)).

## Subsequent orders

**26.3.**—(1) If the sheriff has made an order under rule 26.1(1), any person having an interest may apply for an order under rule 26.2, or any other order for the payment or management of the money, by incidental application.

(2) An application for directions under rule 26.2(a) or (b) may be made by any person having an interest by incidental application.

## Management of money paid to sheriff clerk

**26.4.**—(1) A receipt in Form 35 by the sheriff clerk shall be a sufficient discharge in respect of the amount paid to him under rules 26.1 to 26.3.

(2) The sheriff clerk shall, at the request of any competent court, accept custody of any sum of money in an action of damages ordered to be paid to, applied, invested or otherwise dealt with by him, for the benefit of a person under legal disability.

(3) Any money paid to the sheriff clerk under rules 26.1 to 26.3 must be paid out, applied, invested or otherwise dealt with by the sheriff clerk only after such intimation, service and enquiry as the sheriff may order.

(4) Any sum of money invested by the sheriff clerk under rules 26.1 to 26.3 must be invested in a manner in which trustees are authorised to invest by virtue of the Trustee Investments Act 1961.

## Management of money payable to children

**26.5.** If the sheriff has made an order under section 13 of the Children (Scotland) Act 1995, an application by a person for an order by virtue of section 11(1)(d) of that Act must be made in writing.

Chapter 27

Action of multiplepoinding

## Application of Chapter

**27.1.** This Chapter applies to an action of multiplepoinding.

## Application of other rules

**27.2.**—(1) Rule 8.1 shall not apply to an action of multiplepoinding.

(2) Rules 8.2 to 8.17 shall only apply to an action of multiplepoinding in accordance with rule 27.7.

## Pursuer in multiplepoinding

**27.3.** An action of multiplepoinding may be raised by any party holding or having an interest in or claim on the fund or subject *in medio*.

## Parties

**27.4.** The pursuer must call as defenders—

    (a)   all persons so far as known to him as having an interest in the fund or subject *in medio*; and

    (b)   where he is not the holder of the fund or subject, the holder of that fund or subject.

## Statement of fund or subject in medio

**27.5.**—(1) Where the pursuer is the holder of the fund or subject *in medio* he shall include a statement of the fund or subject in his statement of claim.

(2) Where the pursuer is not the holder of the fund or subject *in medio*, the holder shall, before the return day—

    (a)   lodge with the sheriff clerk a statement in Form 5a providing—

> (i) a statement of the fund or subject;
>
> (ii) a statement of any claim or lien which he may profess to have on the fund or subject; and
>
> (iii)[1] a list of all persons known to him as having an interest in the fund or subject; and

(b) intimate the statement in Form 5a to the pursuer, the defenders and all persons listed in the statement as having an interest in the fund or subject.

### Response to summons

**27.6.**—(1) If a defender intends to—

(a) challenge the jurisdiction of the court or the competency of the action;

(b) object to the extent of the fund or subject *in medio*; or

(c) make a claim on the fund, he must complete and lodge with the sheriff clerk on or before the return day the form of response contained in the defender's copy summons as appropriate, including a statement of his response which gives fair notice to the pursuer.

(2) The sheriff clerk must upon receipt intimate to the pursuer a copy of any response lodged under paragraph (1).

### Procedure where response lodged

**27.7.** Where in a form of response a defender states a defence in accordance with rule 27.6(1)(a)—

(a) the provisions of rules 8.2 to 8.17 shall, with the necessary modifications, apply to the resolution of the issues raised under that sub-paragraph; and

(b) rules 27.8 to 27.10 shall apply only once those issues have been so dealt with.

### Objections to fund or subject in medio

**27.8.**—(1) If objections to the fund or subject *in medio* have been lodged, the sheriff must, after disposal of any defence—

(a) fix a hearing; and

(b) state the order in which the claimants shall be heard at the hearing.

(2) If no objections to the fund or subject in medio have been lodged, or if objections have been lodged and disposed of, the sheriff may approve the fund or subject and if appropriate find the holder liable only in one single payment.

### Claims hearing

**27.9.**—(1) This rule applies where—

(a) no defence or objection to the extent of the fund or subject in medio has been stated;

(b) any defence stated has been repelled; or

(c) any such objection stated has been dealt with.

(2) The sheriff must—

(a) order claims in Form 5b to be lodged within 14 days; and

(b) must fix a claims hearing at which all parties may appear or be represented.

(3) The sheriff clerk must intimate to the parties, the order for claims and the date and time of any claims hearing fixed in terms of paragraph (2).

---

[1] As substituted by SSI 2003/26, r.4(3) (clerical error).

**Procedure at claims hearing**

**27.10.**—(1)  If there is no competition between the claimants who appear at the claims hearing, the sheriff may order the holder of the fund or subject *in medio*, or the sheriff clerk if it is consigned with him in terms of rule 27.12, to make it over to the claimants in terms of their claims or otherwise and subject to such provisions as to expenses as he directs.

(2)  If the sheriff is unable at the claims hearing to resolve competing claims, he shall pronounce an order—

(a)  fixing a date, time and place for a further hearing; and

(b)  regulating the nature and scope of the hearing and the procedure to be followed.

(3)  The sheriff may require that evidence be led at the further claims hearing fixed under paragraph (2).

(4)  The sheriff clerk must intimate to all claimants the date, time and place of any hearing fixed under paragraph (2).

(5)  At the conclusion of the claims hearing or the further claims hearing fixed under paragraph (2), the sheriff may either pronounce his decision or reserve judgement in which case he must give his decision in writing within 28 days and the sheriff clerk must forthwith intimate it to the parties.

(6)  In giving his decision under paragraph (5) the sheriff—

(a)  must dispose of the action;

(b)  may order the holder of the fund or subject *in medio*, or the sheriff clerk if it is consigned with him in terms of rule 27.12, to make it over to such claimants and in such quantity or amount as he may determine; and

(c)  must deal with all questions of expenses.

**Advertisement**

**27.11.**  If it appears to the sheriff at any stage in the multiplepoinding that there may be other potential claimants who are not parties to the action, he may order such advertisement or intimation of the order for claims as he thinks proper.

**Consignation and discharge of holder**

**27.12.**—(1)  At any stage in an action of multiplepoinding the sheriff may order that—

(a)  the fund or subject *in medio* be consigned in the hands of the sheriff clerk; or

(b)  any subject *in medio* be sold and the proceeds of sale consigned in the hands of the sheriff clerk.

(2)  After such consignation the holder of the fund or subject may apply for his exoneration and discharge.

(3)  The sheriff may allow the holder of the fund or subject, on his exoneration and discharge, his expenses out of the fund as a first charge on the fund.

Chapter 28

Action of furthcoming

**Expenses included in claim**

**28.1.**  The expenses of bringing an action for furthcoming, including the expenses of the arrestment, shall be deemed to be part of the arrestor's claim which may be paid out of the arrested fund or subject.

Chapter 29

Action of count, reckoning and payment

**Response to summons**

**29.1.**  If a defender wishes to admit liability to account in an action for count, reckoning and payment, this must be stated on the form of response.

**Accounting hearing**

**29.2.**—(1)  This rule applies where in an action of count, reckoning and payment—

(a)  no form of response has been lodged;

(b)  the defender has indicated on the form of response that he admits liability to account;

or

(c)  any defence stated has been repelled.

(2)  Where paragraph 1(a) or (b) applies, the pursuer must lodge with the sheriff clerk a minute in Form 17 before close of business on the second day before the calling date.

(3)  If the pursuer does not lodge a minute in accordance with paragraph (2), the sheriff must dismiss the action.

(4)  Where the pursuer has lodged a minute in accordance with paragraph (2), or any defence stated has been repelled, the sheriff shall pronounce an order—

(a)  for the lodging of accounts within 14 days and objections within such further period as the sheriff may direct;

(b)  fixing a date, time and place for an accounting hearing; and

(c)  regulating the nature and scope of the accounting hearing and the procedure to be followed.

(5)  The sheriff may require that evidence be led at an accounting hearing fixed under paragraph (4) to prove the accounts and in support of any objection taken.

(6)  The sheriff clerk must intimate to all claimants the date, time and place of any hearing fixed under paragraph (4).

Chapter 30

Recovery of possession of heritable property

**Action raised under section 38 of the 1907 Act**

**30.1.**  An action for the recovery of possession of heritable property made in terms of section 38 of the 1907 Act may be raised by—

(a)  a proprietor;

(b)  his factor; or

(c)  any other person authorised by law to pursue a process of removing.

## Action against persons in possession of heritable property without right or title

**30.2.**—(1) Subject to paragraph (2), this rule applies only to an action for recovery of possession of heritable property against a person or persons in possession of heritable property without right or title to possess the property.

(2) This rule shall not apply with respect to a person who has or had a title or other right to occupy the heritable property and who has been in continuous occupation since that title or right is alleged to have come to an end.

(3) Where the name of a person in occupation of a heritable property is not known and cannot reasonably be ascertained, the pursuer shall call that person as a defender by naming him as an "occupier".

(4) Where the name of a person in occupation of the heritable property is not known and cannot reasonably be ascertained, the summons shall be served (whether or not it is also served on a named person), unless the sheriff otherwise directs, by an officer of the court—

(a) affixing a copy of the summons and a citation in Form 11 addressed to "the occupiers" to the main door or other conspicuous part of the premises, and if practicable, depositing a copy of each of those documents in the premises; or

(b) in the case of land only, inserting stakes in the ground at conspicuous parts of the occupied land to each of which is attached a sealed transparent envelope containing a copy of the summons and a citation in Form 11 addressed to "the occupiers".

(5) In an action to which this rule applies, the sheriff may in his discretion, and subject to rule 25.6, shorten or dispense with any period of time provided anywhere in these rules.

(6) An application by a party under this rule to shorten or dispense with any period may be made orally and the provisions in rule 9.1 shall not apply, but the sheriff clerk must enter details of any such application in the Register of Summary Causes.

## Effect of decree

**30.3.** When decree for the recovery of possession is granted, it shall have the same force and effect as—

(a) a decree of removing;

(b) a decree of ejection;

(c) a summary warrant of ejection;

(d) a warrant for summary ejection in common form; or

(e) a decree pronounced in a summary application for removing, in terms of sections 36, 37 and 38 respectively of the 1907 Act.

## Preservation of defender's goods and effects

**30.4.**[1] When decree is pronounced, the sheriff may give such directions as he deems proper for the preservation of the defender's goods and effects.

## Action of removing where fixed term of removal

**30.5.**—(1) Subject to section 21 of the Agricultural Holdings (Scotland) Act 1991—

---

[1] As amended by the Act of Sederunt (Ordinary Cause, Summary Application, Summary Cause and Small Claim Rules) Amendment (Miscellaneous) 2007 (SSI 2007/6) r.4(6) (effective January 29, 2007).

    (a)   if the tenant has bound himself to remove by writing, dated and signed—

        (i)   within 12 months after the term of removal; or

        (ii)  where there is more than one ish, after the ish first in date to remove, an action of removing may be raised at any time; and

    (b)   if the tenant has not bound himself, an action of removing may be raised at any time, but—

        (i)   in the case of a lease of lands exceeding two acres in extent for three years and upwards, an interval of not less than one year nor more than two years must elapse between the date of notice of removal and the term of removal first in date;

        (ii)  in the case of a lease of lands exceeding two acres in extent, whether written or oral, held from year to year or under tacit relocation, or for any other period less than three years, an interval of not less than six months must elapse between the date of notice of removal and the term of removal first in date; and

       (iii)  in the case of a house let with or without land attached not exceeding two acres in extent, as also of land not exceeding two acres in extent without houses, as also of mills, fishings, shootings, and all other heritable subjects excepting land exceeding two acres in extent and let for a year or more, 40 days at least must elapse between the date of notice of removal and the term of removal first in date.

(2)  In any defended action of removing, the sheriff may order the defender to find caution for violent profits.

## Form of notices and letter

**30.6.**—(1)  A notice under section 34, 35 or 36 of the 1907 Act must be in Form 3a.

(2)  A notice under section 37 of the 1907 Act must be in Form 3b.

(3)  A letter of removal must be in Form 3c.

## Giving notice of removal

**30.7.**—(1)  A notice under section 34, 35, 36, 37 or 38 of the 1907 Act may be given by—

    (a)   a sheriff officer;

    (b)   the person entitled to give such notice; or

    (c)   the solicitor or factor of such person,

posting the notice by registered post or the first class recorded delivery service at any post office within the United Kingdom in time for it to be delivered at the address on the notice before the last date on which by law such notice must be given, addressed to the person entitled to receive such notice, and bearing the address of that person at the time, if known, or, if not known, to the last known address of that person.

(2)  A sheriff officer may also give notice under any section of the 1907 Act mentioned in paragraph (1) in any manner in which he may serve an initial writ; and, accordingly, rule 5.4 shall, with the necessary modifications, apply to the giving of notice under this paragraph as it applies to service of a summons.

## Evidence of notice to remove

**30.8.**—(1)  It shall be sufficient evidence that notice has been given if—

    (a)   a certificate of the sending of notice under rule 30.7 dated and endorsed on the lease or an extract of it, or on the letter of removal, is signed by the sheriff officer or the person sending the notice, his solicitor or factor; or

(b) an acknowledgement of the notice is endorsed on the lease or an extract of it, or on the letter of removal, by the party in possession or his agent.

(2) If there is no lease, a certificate of the sending of such notice must be endorsed on a copy of the notice or letter of removal.

**30.9**[1] Where, in response to a summons for the recovery of heritable property which includes a claim for payment of money, a defender makes a written application about payment, he shall not thereby be taken to be admitting the claim for recovery of possession of the heritable property.

### Chapter 31

### Action of sequestration for rent

*[Repealed by the Act of Sederunt (Sheriff Court Rules Amendment) (Diligence) 2008 (SSI 2008/121) r.2(1)(b) (effective April 1, 2008).]*

### Chapter 32

### Action for aliment

#### Recall or variation of decree for aliment

**32.1.**—(1) Applications for the recall or variation of any decree for payment of aliment pronounced in the small debt court under the Small Debt Acts or in a summary cause under the 1971 Act must be made by summons.

(2) The sheriff may make such interim orders in relation to such applications or in relation to actions brought under section 3 of the Sheriff Courts (Civil Jurisdiction and Procedure) (Scotland) Act 1963 as he thinks fit.

(3) In paragraph (1) "the Small Debt Acts" means and includes the Small Debt (Scotland) Acts 1837 to 1889 and Acts explaining or amending the same.

#### Warrant and forms for intimation

**32.2.** In the summons in an action brought under section 3 of the Sheriff Courts (Civil Jurisdiction and Procedure) (Scotland) Act 1963, the pursuer must include an application for a warrant for intimation—

(a) in an action where the address of the defender is not known to the pursuer and cannot reasonably be ascertained, to—

(i) every child of the marriage between the parties who has reached the age of 16 years; and

(ii) one of the next-of-kin of the defender who has reached that age, unless the address of such a person is not known to the pursuer and cannot reasonably be ascertained, and a notice of intimation in Form 36 must be attached to the copy of the summons intimated to any such person; or

(b) in an action where the defender is a person who is suffering from a mental disorder, to—

(i) those persons mentioned in paragraphs (a)(i) and (ii), unless the address of such person is not known to the pursuer and cannot reasonably be ascertained; and

---

[1] As inserted by the Act of Sederunt (Sheriff Court Rules) (Miscellaneous Amendments) 2008 (SSI 2008/223) r.8 (effective July 1, 2008).

    (ii)   the guardian of, the defender, if one has been appointed, and a notice in Form 37 must be attached to the copy of the summons intimated to any such person.

Chapter 33

Child Support Act 1991

### Interpretation of rules 33.2 to 33.4

**33.1.** In rules 33.2 to 33.4 below—

"the 1991 Act" means the Child Support Act 1991;

"child" has the meaning assigned in section 55 of the 1991 Act;

"claim relating to aliment" means a crave for decree of aliment in relation to a child or for recall or variation of such a decree; and

"maintenance calculation" has the meaning assigned in section 54 of the 1991 Act.

### Statement of claim

**33.2.**—(1) Any summons or counterclaim which contains a claim relating to aliment and to which section 8(6), (7), (8) or (10) of the 1991 Act applies must—

  (a)   state, where appropriate—

      (i)   that a maintenance calculation under section 11 of the 1991 Act (maintenance calculations) is in force;

     (ii)   the date of the maintenance calculation;

    (iii)   the amount and frequency of periodical payments of child support maintenance fixed by the maintenance calculation; and

    (iv)   the grounds on which the sheriff retains jurisdiction under section 8(6), (7), (8) or (10) of the 1991 Act; and

  (b)   unless the sheriff on cause shown otherwise directs, be accompanied by any document issued by the Secretary of State to the party intimating the making of the maintenance calculation referred to in sub-paragraph (a).

(2) Any summons or counterclaim which contains a claim relating to aliment and to which section 8(6), (7), (8) or (10) of the 1991 Act does not apply must include a statement—

  (a)   that the habitual residence of the absent parent, person with care or qualifying child, within the meaning of section 3 of the 1991 Act, is outwith the United Kingdom; or

  (b)   that the child is not a child within the meaning of section 55 of the 1991 Act.

(3) A summons or counterclaim which involves parties in respect of whom a decision has been made in any application, review or appeal under the 1991 Act must—

  (a)   include in the statement of claim statements to the effect that such a decision has been made and give details of that decision; and

  (b)   unless the sheriff on cause shown otherwise directs, be accompanied by any document issued by the Secretary of State to the parties intimating that decision.

### Effect of maintenance calculations

**33.3.**—(1) On receiving notification that a maintenance calculation has been made, cancelled or has ceased to have effect so as to affect an order of a kind prescribed for the purposes of section 10 of the 1991 Act, the sheriff clerk must enter in the Register of Summary Causes in respect of that order a note to that effect.

(2)   The note mentioned in paragraph (1) must state that—

(a)   the order ceases or ceased to have effect from the date two days after the making of the maintenance calculation; or

(b)   the maintenance calculation has been cancelled or has ceased to have effect.

### Effect of maintenance calculations on extacts of decrees relating to aliment

**33.4**—(1)   Where a decree relating to aliment is affected by a maintenance calculation, any extract of that decree issued by the sheriff clerk must be endorsed with the following certificate:—

"A maintenance calculation having been made under the Child Support Act 1991 on (*insert date*), this order, in so far as it relates to the making or securing of periodical payments to or for the benefit of (*insert name(s) of child/children*), ceases to have effect from (*insert date two days after the date on which the maintenance calculation was made*).".

(2)   Where a decree relating to aliment has ceased to have effect on the making of a maintenance calculation and that maintenance calculation is later cancelled or ceases to have effect, any extract of that order issued by the sheriff clerk must be endorsed also with the following certificate:—

"The jurisdiction of the child support officer under the Child Support Act 1991 having terminated on (*insert date*), this order, in so far as it relates to (*insert name(s) of child/children*), again shall have effect as of (*insert date of termination of child support officer's jurisdiction*).".

### Chapter 34[1]

### Action of Damages for, or Arising from, Personal Injuries

*Application and interpretation*

### Application and interpretation of this Chapter

**34.1.**—(1)   This Chapter applies to a personal injuries action.

(2)   In this Chapter—

"personal injuries action" means an action of damages for, or arising from, personal injuries or death of a person from personal injuries;

"personal injuries procedure" means the procedure that applies to a personal injuries action as established by rules 34.7 to 34.11;

"1982 Act" means the Administration of Justice Act 1982.

(3)   In the definition of "personal injuries action", "personal injuries" includes any disease or impairment, whether physical or mental.

---

[1] As substituted by the Act of Sederunt (Summary Cause Rules Amendment) (Personal Injuries Actions) 2012 (SSI 2012/144) para.2 (effective September 1, 2012; not applicable to an action raised before September 1, 2012).

*Raising a personal injuries action*

## Form of summons

**34.2.**—(1)  In a personal injuries action the form of claim to be inserted in box 4 of Form 1 (summary cause summons) shall be in Form 2 (form of claim in a summons for payment of money).

(2)  The pursuer must, instead of stating the details of claim in box 7 of Form 1, attach to Form 1 a statement of claim in Form 10 (form of statement of claim in a personal injuries action), which must give the defender fair notice of the claim and include—

(a)  a concise statement of the grounds of the claim in numbered paragraphs relating only to those facts necessary to establish the claim;

(b)  the names of every medical practitioner from whom, and every hospital or other institution in which, the pursuer or, in an action in respect of the death of a person, the deceased, received treatment for the personal injuries.

(3)  A summons may include—

(a)  an application for warrants for intimation so far as permitted under these Rules; and

(b)  a specification of documents containing such of the calls in Form 10b (form of order of court for recovery of documents etc.) as the pursuer considers appropriate.

## Defender's copy summons

**34.3.**—(1)  A copy summons shall be served on the defender—

(a)  in Form 1e where an application for a time to pay direction under the Debtors (Scotland) Act 1987 may be applied for; or

(b)  in Form 1f in every other case,

in each case, including a copy statement of claim in Form 10.

(2)  A form of response in Form 10a shall accompany the defender's copy summons when it is served on the defender.

## Response to summons

**34.4.**—(1)  If a defender intends to—

(a)  challenge the jurisdiction of the court or the competency of the action;

(b)  defend the action (whether as regards the amount claimed or otherwise); or

(c)  state a counterclaim,

the defender must complete and lodge with the sheriff clerk on or before the return day the form of response contained in the defender's copy summons and Form 10a stating, in a manner which gives the pursuer fair notice, the grounds of fact and law on which the defender intends to resist the claim.

(2)  A counterclaim may include—

(a)  an application for warrants for intimation so far as permitted under these Rules; and

(b)  a specification of documents containing such of the calls in Form 10b as the defender considers appropriate.

(3)  The sheriff clerk must, upon receipt, intimate to the pursuer a copy of any response lodged under paragraph (1).

(4) Within 7 days of receipt of intimation under paragraph (3), the pursuer shall return to the sheriff clerk the summons and the relevant certificate of execution of service.

**Inspection and recovery of documents**

**34.5.**—(1) This rule applies where the summons or counterclaim in a personal injuries action contains a specification of documents by virtue of rule 34.2(3)(b) or rule 34.4(2)(b).

(2) On the summons being authenticated or counterclaim received, an order granting commission and diligence for the production and recovery of the documents mentioned in the specification shall be deemed to have been granted and the sheriff clerk shall certify Form 10b to that effect by attaching thereto a docquet in Form 10c (form of docquet etc.).

(3) An order which is deemed to have been granted under paragraph (2) shall be treated for all purposes as an interlocutor granting commission and diligence signed by the sheriff.

(4) The pursuer or defender in the case of a counterclaim may serve an order under paragraph (2) and the provisions of Chapter 18 (recovery of evidence and attendance of witnesses) shall thereafter apply, subject to any necessary modifications, as if the order were an order obtained on an incidental application made under rule 18.1 (diligence for recovery of documents).

(5) Nothing in this rule shall affect the right of a party to apply under rule 18.1 for a commission and diligence for recovery of documents or under rule 18.3 for an order under section 1 of the Administration of Justice (Scotland) Act 1972 in respect of any document or other property whether or not mentioned in the specification annexed to the summons.

*Personal injuries action: application of other rules*

**Application of other rules**

**34.6.**—(1) The following rules do not apply to a personal injuries action—

rule 4.1(2) (form of claim in a summons);

rule 4.2 (statement of claim);

rule 4.3 (defender's copy summons);

rule 8.1 (response to summons);

rule 8.2 (procedure in defended action);

rule 8.3 (purpose of hearing);

rule 8.5 (inspection and recovery of documents);

rule 8.6 (exchange of lists of witnesses);

rule 8.13(1) (noting of evidence, etc.).

(2) In the application of Chapter 11 (third party procedure)—

    (a)   rule 11.1(2) (application for third party notice) shall not apply;

    (b)   in the application of rule 11.2(1) (procedure) a copy of Form 10 and any timetable already issued in terms of rule 34.7(1)(c) shall also be served on the third party; and

    (c)   where a third party lodges a form of response under rule 11.2(3), any timetable already issued under rule 34.7(1)(c) shall apply to the third party.

(3) In respect of adjustments to the parties' respective statements made in accordance with the timetable issued under rule 34.7(1)(c), the requirement under rule 13.1 (alteration of summons etc.) to make an incidental application in respect of such adjustments shall not apply.

(4) In relation to an action proceeding in accordance with personal injuries procedure references elsewhere in these Rules to the statement of claim in the summons shall be construed as references to the statement required under rule 34.2(2) and the numbered paragraphs of that statement.

*Personal injuries procedure*

**Allocation of diets and timetables**

**34.7.**—(1) The sheriff clerk shall, on the lodging of the form of response in pursuance of rule 34.4(1) or, where there is more than one defender, the first lodging of a form of response—

    (a) discharge the hearing assigned to take place on the calling date specified in the summons;

    (b) allocate a diet for proof of the action, which shall be no earlier than 4 months (unless the sheriff on cause shown directs an earlier diet to be fixed) and no later than 9 months from the date of the first lodging of the form of response; and

    (c) issue a timetable stating—

        (i) the date of the diet mentioned in subparagraph (b); and

        (ii) the dates no later than which the procedural steps mentioned in paragraph (2) are to take place.

(2) Those procedural steps are—

    (a) application for a third party notice under rule 11.1;

    (b) the pursuer serving a commission for recovery of documents under rule 34.5;

    (c) the parties adjusting their respective statements;

    (d) the pursuer lodging with the sheriff clerk a statement of valuation of claim;

    (e) the pursuer lodging with the sheriff clerk a certified adjusted statement of claim;

    (f) the defender (and any third party to the action) lodging with the sheriff clerk a certified adjusted response to statement of claim;

    (g) the defender (and any third party to the action) lodging with the sheriff clerk a statement of valuation of claim;

    (h) the parties lodging with the sheriff clerk a list of witnesses together with any productions upon which they wish to rely; and

    (i) the pursuer lodging with the sheriff clerk the minute of the pre-proof conference.

(3) The dates mentioned in paragraph (1)(c)(ii) are to be calculated by reference to periods specified in Appendix 1A, which, with the exception of the period specified in rule 34.10(2), the sheriff principal may vary for his or her sheriffdom or for any court within his or her sheriffdom.

(4) A timetable issued under paragraph (1)(c) shall be in Form 10d and shall be treated for all purposes as an interlocutor signed by the sheriff; and so far as the timetable is inconsistent with any provision in these Rules which relates to a matter to which the timetable relates, the timetable shall prevail.

(5)[1] Where a party fails to comply with any requirement of a timetable other than that referred to in rule 34.10(3), the sheriff clerk may fix a date and time for the parties to be heard by the sheriff.

---

[1] As amended by the Act of Sederunt (Rules of the Court of Session, Ordinary Cause Rules and Summary Cause Rules Amendment) (Miscellaneous) 2014 (SSI 2014/152) r.4 (effective July 7, 2014).

(6) The relevant parties must lodge with the sheriff clerk the following documents by the date specified in the timetable and intimate that fact to the other parties at the same time—

(a) in the case of the pursuer, a certified adjusted statement of claim; and

(b) in the case of the defender (and any third party to the action), a certified adjusted response to statement of claim.

(7) The pursuer shall, on lodging the certified adjusted statement of claim required by paragraph (6)(a), apply by incidental application to the sheriff, craving the court—

(a) to allow parties a preliminary proof on specified matters;

(b) to allow a proof; or

(c) to make some other specified order.

(8) The application lodged under paragraph (7) shall specify the anticipated length of the preliminary proof, or proof, as the case may be.

(9) In the event that any party proposes to crave the court to make any order other than an order allowing a proof under paragraph (7)(b), that party shall, on making or opposing (as the case may be) the pursuer's application, specify the order to be sought and give full notice of the grounds of their application or their grounds of opposition to such application.

(10) *[As repealed by the Act of Sederunt (Rules of the Court of Session, Ordinary Cause Rules and Summary Cause Rules Amendment) (Miscellaneous) 2014 (SSI 2014/152) r.4 (effective July 7, 2014).]*

(11) A party who seeks to rely on the evidence of a person not on his or her list lodged in accordance with paragraph (2)(h) must, if any other party objects to such evidence being admitted, seek leave of the sheriff to admit that evidence whether it is to be given orally or not; and such leave may be granted on such conditions, if any, as the sheriff thinks fit.

(12) The list of witnesses intimated in accordance with paragraph (2)(h) must include the name, occupation (where known) and address of each intended witness and indicate whether the witness is considered to be a vulnerable witness within the meaning of section 11(1) of the 2004 Act and whether any child witness notice or vulnerable witness application has been lodged in respect of that witness.

(13) A production which is not lodged in accordance with paragraph (2)(h) shall not be used or put in evidence at proof unless—

(a) by consent of the parties; or

(b) with the leave of the sheriff on cause shown and on such conditions, if any, as to expenses or otherwise as the sheriff thinks fit.

(14) In a cause which is one of a number of causes arising out of the same cause of action, the sheriff may—

(a) on the application of a party to that cause; and

(b) after hearing parties to all those causes,

appoint that cause or any part of those causes to be the leading cause and to sist the other causes pending the determination of the leading cause.

(15) In this rule, "pursuer" includes additional pursuer or applicant as the case may be.

## Applications for sist or for variation of timetable

**34.8.**—(1) The action may be sisted or the timetable varied by the sheriff on the incidental application of any party to the action.

(2) An application under paragraph (1)—

(a) shall be placed before the sheriff; and

(b)[1]   shall be granted only on cause shown.

(3)   Any sist of an action in terms of this rule shall be for a specific period.

(4)   Where the timetable issued under rule 34.7(1)(c) is varied under this rule, the sheriff clerk shall issue a revised timetable in Form 10d.

(5)   A revised timetable issued under paragraph (4) shall have effect as if it were a timetable issued under rule 34.7(1)(c) and any reference in this Chapter to any action being taken in accordance with the timetable shall be construed as a reference to its being taken in accordance with the timetable as varied under this rule.

### Statements of valuation of claim

**34.9.**—(1)   Each party to the action shall make a statement of valuation of claim in Form 10e.

(2)   A statement of valuation of claim (which shall include a list of supporting documents) shall be lodged with the sheriff clerk.

(3)   Each party shall, on lodging a statement of valuation of claim—

(a)   intimate the list of documents included in the statement of valuation of claim to every other party; and

(b)   lodge each of those documents with the sheriff clerk.

(4)   Nothing in paragraph (3) shall affect—

(a)   the law relating to, or the right of a party to object to, the recovery of a document on the ground of privilege or confidentiality; or

(b)   the right of a party to apply under rule 18.1 for a commission and diligence for recovery of documents or under rule 18.3 for an order under section 1 of the Administration of Justice (Scotland) Act 1972.

(5)   Without prejudice to rule 34.11(2), where a party has failed to lodge a statement of valuation of claim in accordance with a timetable issued under rule 34.7(1)(c), the sheriff may, at any hearing under paragraph (5) of that rule—

(a)   where the party in default is the pursuer, dismiss the action; or

(b)   where the party in default is the defender, grant decree against the defender for an amount not exceeding the pursuer's valuation.

### Pre-proof conferences

**34.10.**—(1)   For the purposes of this rule, a pre-proof conference is a conference of the parties, which shall be held not later than four weeks before the date assigned for the proof—

(a)   to discuss settlement of the action; and

(b)   to agree, so far as is possible, the matters which are not in dispute between them.

(2)   Subject to any variation of the timetable in terms of rule 34.8, a joint minute of a pre-proof conference, made in Form 10f, shall be lodged with the sheriff clerk by the pursuer not later than three weeks before the date assigned for proof.

(3)   Where a joint minute in Form 10f has not been lodged in accordance with paragraph (2) and by the date specified in the timetable the sheriff clerk must fix a date and time for the parties to be heard by the sheriff.

(4)   If a party is not present during the pre-proof conference, the representative of such party shall have access to the party or another person who has authority to commit the party in settlement of the action.

---

[1] As amended by the Act of Sederunt (Rules of the Court of Session, Ordinary Cause Rules and Summary Cause Rules Amendment) (Miscellaneous) 2014 (SSI 2014/152) r.4 (effective July 7, 2014).

**Incidental hearings**

**34.11.**—(1) Where the sheriff clerk fixes a date and time for a hearing under rules 34.7(5) or (10) or rule 34.10(3), the sheriff clerk must—

    (a) fix a date not less than seven days after the date of the notice referred to in subparagraph (b);

    (b) give notice to the parties to the action—

        (i) of the date and time of the hearing; and

        (ii) requiring the party in default to lodge with the sheriff clerk a written explanation as to why the timetable has not been complied with and to intimate a copy to all other parties not less than two clear working days before the date of the hearing.

(2) At the hearing, the sheriff—

    (a) must consider any explanation provided by the party in default;

    (b) may award expenses against that party; and

    (c) may make any other appropriate order, including decree of dismissal.

*Personal injuries action: additional provisions*

**Intimation to connected persons in certain actions of damages**

**34.12.**—(1) This rule applies to an action of damages in which, following the death of any person from personal injuries, damages are claimed—

    (a) in respect of the injuries from which the deceased died; or

    (b) in respect of the death of the deceased.

(2) In this rule "connected person" means a person, not being a party to the action, who has title to sue the defender in respect of the personal injuries from which the deceased died or in respect of his or her death.

(3) The pursuer shall state in the summons, as the case may be—

    (a) that there are no connected persons;

    (b) that there are connected persons, being the persons specified in the application for warrant for intimation; or

    (c) that there are connected persons in respect of whom intimation should be dispensed with on the ground that—

        (i) the names or whereabouts of such persons are not known to, and cannot reasonably be ascertained by, the pursuer; or

        (ii) such persons are unlikely to be awarded more than £200 each.

(4) Where the pursuer makes a statement in accordance with paragraph (3)(b), the summons shall include an application for warrant for intimation to any such persons.

(5) A notice of intimation in Form 10g shall be attached to the copy of the summons, where intimation is given on a warrant under paragraph (4).

(6) Where the pursuer makes a statement in accordance with paragraph (3)(c), the summons shall include an application for an order to dispense with intimation.

(7) In determining an application under paragraph (6), the sheriff shall have regard to—

    (a) the desirability of avoiding a multiplicity of actions; and

    (b) the expense, inconvenience or difficulty likely to be involved in taking steps to ascertain the name or whereabouts of the connected person.

(8) Where the sheriff is not satisfied that intimation to a connected person should be dispensed with, the sheriff may—

    (a)   order intimation to a connected person whose name and whereabouts are known;

    (b)   order the pursuer to take such further steps as the sheriff may specify in the interlocutor to ascertain the name or whereabouts of any connected person; and

    (c)   order advertisement in such manner, place and at such times as the sheriff may specify in the interlocutor.

(9)  Where the name or whereabouts of a person, in respect of whom the sheriff has dispensed with intimation on a ground specified in paragraph (3)(c), subsequently becomes known to the pursuer, the pursuer shall apply to the sheriff by incidental application for a warrant for intimation to such a person; and such intimation shall be made in accordance with paragraph (5).

(10)  A connected person may apply by incidental application to be sisted as an additional pursuer to the action.

(11)  An application under paragraph (10) shall also seek leave of the sheriff to adopt the existing grounds of action and to amend the summons and statement of claim.

(12)  Where an application under paragraph (10) is granted, any timetable already issued under rule 34.7(1)(c)—

    (a)   shall apply to such connected person; and

    (b)   must be intimated to such person by the sheriff clerk.

(13)  Where a connected person to whom intimation is made—

    (a)   does not apply to be sisted as an additional pursuer to the action;

    (b)   subsequently raises a separate action against the same defender in respect of the same personal injuries or death; and

    (c)   would, apart from this rule, be awarded the expenses or part of the expenses of that action,

such person shall not be awarded those expenses except on cause shown.

### Provisional damages for personal injuries

**34.13.**—(1)  In this rule—

"further damages" means the damages referred to in section 12(4)(b) of the 1982 Act; and

"provisional damages" means the damages referred to in section 12(4)(a) of the 1982 Act.

(2)  An application for an order under section 12(2)(a) of the 1982 Act (application for provisional damages) shall be made by including in the summons a claim for provisional damages in Form 10h, and where such application is made, a concise statement as to the matters referred to in paragraphs (a) and (b) of section 12(1) of that Act must be included in the statement of claim.

(3)  An application for further damages by a pursuer in respect of whom an order has been made under section 12(2)(b) of the 1982 Act (application for further damages) shall be made by lodging an incidental application with the sheriff clerk in Form 10i, which shall include—

    (a)   a claim for further damages;

    (b)   a concise statement of the facts supporting that claim;

    (c)   an application for warrant to serve the incidental application on—

        (i)   every other party; and

        (ii)   where such other parties are insured or otherwise indemnified, their insurer or indemnifier, if known to the pursuer; and

(d)    a request for the sheriff to fix a hearing on the application.

(4)    A notice of intimation in Form 10j shall be attached to every copy of the incidental application served on a warrant granted under paragraph (3)(c).

(5)    At the hearing fixed under paragraph (3)(d), the sheriff may determine the application or order such further procedure as the sheriff thinks fit.

**Mesothelioma actions: special provisions**

**34.14.**—[1](1)    This rule applies where liability to a relative of the pursuer may arise under section 5 of the Damages (Scotland) Act 2011 (discharge of liability to pay damages: exception for mesothelioma).

(2)    On settlement of the pursuer's claim, the pursuer may apply by incidental application for all or any of the following—

(a)    a sist for a specified period;

(b)    discharge of any diet;

(c)    where the action is one to which the personal injuries procedure applies, variation of the timetable issued under rule 34.7(1)(c).

(3)    Paragraphs (4) to (7) apply where an application under paragraph (2) has been granted.

(4)    As soon as reasonably practicable after the death of the pursuer, any agent who immediately prior to the death was instructed in a cause by the deceased pursuer shall notify the court of the death.

(5)    The notification under paragraph (4) shall be by letter to the sheriff clerk and shall be accompanied by a certified copy of the death certificate relative to the deceased pursuer.

(6)    A relative of the deceased may apply by incidental application for the recall of the sist and for an order for further procedure.

(7)    On expiration of the period of any sist pronounced on an application under paragraph (2), the sheriff clerk may fix a date and time for the parties to be heard by the sheriff.

### Chapter 35

### Electronic transmission of documents

**Extent of provision**

**35.1.**—(1)    Any document referred to in these rules which requires to be—

(a)    lodged with the sheriff clerk;

(b)    intimated to a party; or

(c)    sent by the sheriff clerk,

may be in electronic or documentary form, and if in electronic form may be lodged, intimated or sent by e-mail or similar means.

(2)    Paragraph (1) does not apply to any certificate of execution of service, citation or arrestment, or to a decree or extract decree of the court.

(3)    Where any document is lodged by e-mail or similar means the sheriff may require any principal document to be lodged.

---

[1] In relation to any action raised in respect of any death occurring before July 7, 2011, rule 34.14 of the Summary Cause Rules shall be construed in accordance with art.4 of the Damages (Scotland) Act 2011 (Commencement, Transitional Provisions and Savings) Order 2011.

## Time of lodgement

**35.2.** The time of lodgement, intimation or sending shall be the time when the document was sent or transmitted.

Chapter 36[1]

The Equality Act 2010

## Interpretation and application

**36.1.**—[2](1)  In this Chapter—

"the Commission" means the Commission for Equality and Human Rights; and "the 2010 Act" means the Equality Act 2010.

(2)  This Chapter applies to claims made by virtue of section 114(1) of the 2010 Act including a claim for damages.

## Intimation to Commission[3]

**36.2.** The pursuer shall send a copy of the summons to the Commission by registered or recorded delivery post.

## Assessor

**36.3.**—(1)  The sheriff may, of his own motion or on the incidental application of any party, appoint an assessor.

(2)  The assessor shall be a person who the sheriff considers has special qualifications to be of assistance in determining the cause.

## Taxation of Commission expenses

**36.4.** *[Repealed by the Act of Sederunt (Sheriff Court Rules) (Miscellaneous Amendments) 2008 (SSI 2008/223) r.6(3)(c) (effective July 1, 2008).]*

## National security

**36.5.**—[4](1)  Where, on an incidental application under paragraph (3) or of the sheriff's own motion, the sheriff considers it expedient in the interests of national security, the sheriff may—

   (a)  exclude from all or part of the proceedings—

    (i)   the pursuer;

    (ii)  the pursuer's representatives;

    (iii) any assessors;

   (b)  permit a pursuer or representative who has been excluded to make a statement to the court before the commencement of the proceedings or the part of the proceedings, from which he or she is excluded;

   (c)  take steps to keep secret all or part of the reasons for his or her decision in the proceedings.

---

[1] As inserted by the Act of Sederunt (Ordinary Cause, Summary Application, Summary Cause and Small Claim Rules) Amendment (Equality Act 2006 etc.) 2006 (SSI 2006/509) r.4(2) (effective November 3, 2006). Chapter title amended by the Act of Sederunt (Sheriff Court Rules) (Equality Act 2010) 2010 (SSI 2010/340) para.4 (effective October 1, 2010).

[2] As substituted by the Act of Sederunt (Sheriff Court Rules) (Equality Act 2010) 2010 (SSI 2010/340) para.4 (effective October 1, 2010).

[3] As substituted by the Act of Sederunt (Sheriff Court Rules) (Miscellaneous Amendments) 2008 (SSI 2008/223) r.6(3)(b) (effective July 1, 2008).

[4] As substituted by the Act of Sederunt (Sheriff Court Rules) (Equality Act 2010) 2010 (SSI 2010/340) para.4 (effective October 1, 2010).

(2)   The sheriff clerk shall, on the making of an order under paragraph (1) excluding the pursuer or the pursuer's representatives, notify the Advocate General for Scotland of that order.

(3)   A party may make an incidental application for an order under paragraph (1).

(4)   The steps referred to in paragraph (1)(c) may include the following—

    (a)   directions to the sheriff clerk; and

    (b)   orders requiring any person appointed to represent the interests of the pursuer in proceedings from which the pursuer or the pursuer's representatives are excluded not to communicate (directly or indirectly) with any persons (including the excluded pursuer)—

        (i)   on any matter discussed or referred to;

        (ii)   with regard to any material disclosed,

during or with reference to any part of the proceedings from which the pursuer or the pursuer's representatives are excluded.

(5)   Where the sheriff has made an order under paragraph (4)(b), the person appointed to represent the interests of the pursuer may make an incidental application for authority to seek instructions from or otherwise communicate with an excluded person.

(6)   The sheriff may, on the application of a party intending to lodge an incidental application in written form, reduce the period of notice of two days specified in rule 9.1(2) or dispense with notice.

(7)   An application under paragraph (6) shall be made in the written incidental application, giving reasons for such reduction or dispensation.

## Transfer to Employment Tribunal

**36.6.**—[1](1)   On transferring proceedings to an employment tribunal under section 140(2) of the 2010 Act, the sheriff —

    (a)   shall state his or her reasons for doing so in the interlocutor; and

    (b)   may make the order on such conditions as to expenses or otherwise as he or she thinks fit.

(2)   The sheriff clerk must, within 7 days from the date of such order—

    (a)   transmit the relevant process to the Secretary of the Employment Tribunals (Scotland);

    (b)   notify each party to the proceedings in writing of the transmission under subparagraph (a); and

    (c)   certify, by making an appropriate entry in the Register of Summary Causes, that he or she has made all notifications required under subparagraph (b).

(3)   Transmission of the process under paragraph (2)(a) will be valid notwithstanding any failure by the sheriff clerk to comply with paragraph (2)(b) and (c).

## Transfer from Employment Tribunal

**36.7.**—[2](1)   On receipt of the documentation in proceedings which have been remitted from an employment tribunal under section 140(3) of the 2010 Act, the sheriff clerk must—

---

[1] As inserted by the Act of Sederunt (Sheriff Court Rules) (Equality Act 2010) 2010 (SSI 2010/340) para.4 (effective October 1, 2010).

[2] As inserted by the Act of Sederunt (Sheriff Court Rules) (Equality Act 2010) 2010 (SSI 2010/340) para.4 (effective October 1, 2010).

   (a)   record the date of receipt on the first page of the documentation;

   (b)   fix a hearing to determine further procedure not less than 14 days after the date of receipt of the process; and

   (c)   forthwith send written notice of the date of the hearing fixed under subparagraph (b) to each party.

(2)  At the hearing fixed under paragraph (1)(b) the sheriff may make such order as he or she thinks fit to secure so far as practicable that the cause thereafter proceeds in accordance with these Rules.

Chapter 37[1]

Live Links

**37.1.**—(1)  On cause shown, a party may apply by incidental application for authority for the whole or part of—

   (a)   the evidence of a witness or the party to be given; or

   (b)   a submission to be made,

through a live link.

(2)  in paragraph (1)—

"witness" means a person who has been or may be cited to appear before the court as a witness except a vulnerable witness within the meaning of section 11(1) of the Act of 2004;[2]

"submission" means any oral submission which would otherwise be made to the court by the party or his representative in person including an oral submission in support of an incidental application; and

"live link" means a live television link or such other arrangement as may be specified in the incidental application by which the witness, party or representative, as the case may be, is able to be seen and heard in the proceedings or heard in the proceedings and is able to see and hear or hear the proceedings while at a place which is outside the court room.

**Appendix 1**

**FORMS**

**Rule 1.1(4)**

Rule 4.1(1)

[3]FORM A1

Rule 2A.2(2)(b)

Statement by prospective lay representative for Pursuer/Defender*

Case Ref. No.:

in the cause

SHERIFFDOM OF (*insert name of sheriffdom*)

AT (*insert place of sheriff court*)

[A.B.], (*insert designation and address*), Pursuer

against

---

[1] As inserted by the Act of Sederunt (Ordinary Cause, Summary Application, Summary Cause and Small Claim Rules) Amendment (Miscellaneous) 2007 (SSI 2007/6) r.4(7) (effective January 29, 2007).

[2] As amended by the Act of Sederunt (Ordinary Cause, Summary Application, Summary Cause and Small Claim Rules) Amendment (Vulnerable Witnesses (Scotland) Act 2004) 2007 (SSI 2007/463) r.4(6) (effective November 1, 2007).

[3] As inserted by the Act of Sederunt (Sheriff Court Rules) (Lay Representation) 2013 (SSI 2013/91) r.4 (effective April 4, 2013).

[C.D.], (*insert designation and address*), Defender
Court ref. no:

| | Name and address of prospective lay representative who requests to make oral submissions on behalf of party litigant: |
|---|---|
| | Identify hearing(s) in respect of which permission for lay representation is sought: |
| | The prospective lay representative declares that: |
| (a) | I have no financial interest in the outcome of the case *or* I have the following financial interest in it:* |
| (b) | I am not receiving remuneration or other reward directly or indirectly from the litigant for my assistance and will not receive directly or indirectly such remuneration or other reward from the litigant. |
| (c) | I accept that documents and information are provided to me by the litigant on a confidential basis and I undertake to keep them confidential. |
| (d) | I have no previous convictions *or* I have the following convictions: (list convictions)* |
| (e) | I have not been declared a vexatious litigant under the Vexatious Actions (Scotland) Act 1898 *or* I was declared a vexatious litigant under the Vexatious Actions (Scotland) Act 1898 on [insert date].* |

*(Signed)*
[Name of prospective lay representative]
[Date]

*(Insert Place/Date)*
The Sheriff grants/refuses* the application.

*[Signed]*
Sheriff Clerk
[Date]

*(\*delete as appropriate)*

[1]FORM 1
*Summons*

FORM 1

**Summary Cause Summons**

Action for/of
(state type, e.g. payment of money)

OFFICIAL USE ONLY
SUMMONS No.

| Sheriff Court (name, address, e-mail and telephone no.) | **1** | |
| Name and address of person raising the action (**pursuer**) | **2** | |
| Name and address of person against whom action raised (**defender, arrestee, etc.**) | **3** | |

---

[1] As amended by the Act of Sederunt (Sheriff Court Rules Amendment) (Diligence) 2008 (SSI 2008/121) r.6(6) (effective April 1, 2008) and by the Act of Sederunt (Summary Cause Rules Amendment) (Personal Injuries Actions) 2012 (SSI 2012/144) para.2 (effective September 1, 2012).

| | | | | |
|---|---|---|---|---|
| Name(s) and address(s) of any interested party (eg. connected person) | **3a** | | | |

| | | |
|---|---|---|
| Claim (form of decree or other order sought) | **4** | |

| | | |
|---|---|---|
| Name, full address, telephone no, and e-mail address of pursuer's solicitor or representative (if any) acting in the case | **5** | |

| | | |
|---|---|---|
| Fee Details (Enter these only if forms sent electronically to court) | **5a** | |

| | |
|---|---|
| **6** | **RETURN DAY**      20 |
| | **CALLING DATE**      20    at    am. |
| *Sheriff Clerk to delete as appropriate | The pursuer is authorised to serve a copy summons in form *1a/1b/1c/1d/1e/1f, on the defender, and give intimation to any interested party, not less than * 21/42 days before the **RETURN DAY** shown in the box above. The summons is warrant for service, and for citation of witnesses to attend court on any future date at which evidence may be led. |
| *Court Authentication* | Sheriff clerk depute (name)     Date:.......... 20 |

**NOTE: The pursuer should complete boxes 1 to 5a above and box 7 on page 2. The sheriff clerk will complete box 6.**

| | |
|---|---|
| 7. | **STATE DETAILS OF CLAIM HERE (all cases) and PARTICULARS OF ARREST-MENT (furthcoming actions only)** |
| | **(To be completed by the pursuer. If space is insufficient, a separate sheet may be attached)** |
| | The details of the claim are:............... |

**FOR OFFICIAL USE ONLY**

Sheriff's notes as to:

1. Issues of fact and law in dispute

> 2. Facts agreed
>
> 3. Reasons for any final disposal at the hearing held on the calling date.

<br>

[1][2] FORM 1a

Rule 4.3(a)

*Defender's copy summons—claim for or including payment of money where time to pay direction or time order may be applied for*

| OFFICIAL USE ONLY |
| :--- |
| SUMMONS No. |

## Summary Cause Summons
### Action for/of
(state type, e.g. payment of money)

**DEFENDER'S COPY: Claim for or including payment of money (where time to pay direction or time order may be applied for)**

| | | |
| :--- | :--- | :--- |
| Sheriff Court (name, address, e-mail and telephone no.) | **1** | |
| Name and address of person raising the action (**pursuer**) | **2** | |
| Name and address of person against whom action raised (**defender, arrestee, etc.**) | **3** | |
| Name(s) and address(s) of any interested party (e.g. connected person) | **3a** | |

---

[1] As amended by the Act of Sederunt (Sheriff Court Rules Amendment) (Diligence) 2008 (SSI 2008/121) r.6(8) (effective April 1, 2008) and substituted by the Act of Sederunt (Sheriff Court Rules) (Miscellaneous Amendments) 2009 (SSI 2009/294) r.4 (effective December 1, 2009).

[2] As amended by the Act of Sederunt (Sheriff Court Rules) (Miscellaneous Amendments) 2011 (SSI 2011/193) r.11 (effective April 4, 2011) and by the Act of Sederunt (Summary Cause Rules Amendment) (Personal Injuries Actions) 2012 (SSI 2012/144) para.2 (effective September 1, 2012).

Claim (form of decree **4**
or other order sought)

Name, full address, **5**
telephone no., and
e-mail address of pur-
suer's solicitor or rep-
resentative (if any) act-
ing in the case

| **6** | **RETURN DAY** | **20** | | |
|---|---|---|---|---|
| | **CALLING DATE** | **20** | **at** | **am.** |

**NOTE: You will find details of claim on page 2.**

**PAGE 1**

| **7.** | STATEMENT OF CLAIM |
|---|---|

**PARTICULARS OF ARRESTMENT (furthcoming actions only)**

**(To be completed by the pursuer. If space is insufficient, a separate sheet may be attached)**

The details of the claim are:

**8.** **SERVICE ON DEFENDER**

**(PLACE)**...............

**(DATE)**..........

**To:**...............

**(Defender)**..........

**You are hereby served with a copy of the above summons**.

**Solicitor/sheriff officer**
*delete as appropriate*

```

```

NOTE: The pursuer should complete boxes 1 to 6 on page 1, the statement of claim in box 7 on page 2 and section A on page 6 before service on the defender. The person serving the Summons will complete box 8, above.

**PAGE 2**

## WHAT MUST I DO ABOUT THIS SUMMONS?

The RETURN DAY (on page 1 of this summons) is the deadline by which you need to reply to the court. You must send the correct forms back (see below for details) by this date if you want the court to hear your case. If you do not do this, in most cases there will not be a hearing about your case and the court will make a decision in your absence.

The CALLING DAY (on page 1 of this summons) is the date for the court hearing.

Note: If your case is about **recovery of possession of heritable property** (eviction) there will be a hearing even if you do not send back the forms, so you should attend court on the calling date. If you make an application for time to pay in such a case and the court accepts your application, it may still make an order for eviction, so you should attend court if you wish to defend the action for eviction.

**You should decide whether you wish to dispute the claim and/or whether you owe any money or not, and how you wish to proceed**. Then, look at the 5 options listed below. Find the one that covers your decision and follow the instructions given there.

If you are not sure what you need to do, contact the sheriff clerk's office before the return day. Written guidance can also be obtained from the Scottish Court Service website (www.scotcourts.gov.uk).

## OPTIONS

1. **ADMIT LIABILITY FOR THE CLAIM and settle it with the pursuer now.**

    If you wish to avoid the possibility of a court order passing against you, you should settle the claim (including any question of expenses) with the pursuer or his representative **in good time before the return day**. Please do not send any payment direct to the court. Any payment should be made to the pursuer or his representative.

2. **ADMIT LIABILITY FOR THE CLAIM and make written application to pay by instalments or by deferred lump sum.**

    **Complete Box 1 of section B on page 6 of this form and return pages 6, 8 and 9 to the court to arrive on or before the return day**. You should then contact the court to find out whether or not the pursuer has accepted your offer. If he has not accepted it, the case will then call in court on the calling date, when the court will decide how the amount claimed is to be paid.

    **NOTE: If you fail to return pages 6, 8 and 9 as directed, or if, having returned them, you fail to attend or are not represented at the calling date if the case is to call, the court may decide the claim in your absence.**

3. **ADMIT LIABILITY FOR THE CLAIM and attend at court to make application to pay by instalments or deferred lump sum.**

    **Complete Box 2 on page 6. Return page 6 to the court so that it arrives on or before the return day**.

**PAGE 3**

You must attend personally, or be represented, at court on the calling date. Your representative may be a Solicitor, or someone else having your authority. It may be helpful if you or your representative bring pages 1 and 2 of this form to the court.

NOTE: If you fail to return page 6 as directed, or if, having returned it, you fail to attend or are not represented at the calling date, the court may decide the claim in your absence.

4. **DISPUTE THE CLAIM and attend at court to do any of the following:**

- Challenge the jurisdiction of the court or the competency of the action
- Defend the action (whether as regards the sum claimed or otherwise)
- State a counterclaim

Complete Box 3 on page 6. Return page 6 to the court so that it arrives **on or before the return day. You must attend personally, or be represented, at court on the calling date**.

Your representative may be a solicitor, or someone else having your authority. It may be helpful if you or your representative bring pages 1 and 2 of this form to the court.

**NOTE: If you fail to return page 6 as directed, or if, having returned it, you fail to attend or are not represented at the calling date, the court may decide the claim in your absence.**

### WRITTEN NOTE OF PROPOSED DEFENCE

You must send to the court by the return day a written note of any proposed defence, or intimate that you intend to dispute the sum claimed or wish to dispute the court's jurisdiction. You must also attend or be represented at court on the calling date.

5. **ADMIT LIABILITY FOR THE CLAIM and make written application for a time order under the Consumer Credit Act 1974.**

Complete Box 4 on page 6 and return pages 6 and 10 to 12 to the court to arrive on or before the return day. You should then contact the court to find out whether or not the pursuer has accepted your offer. Where you have been advised that the pursuer has not accepted your offer then the case will call in court on the calling date. You should appear in court on the calling date as the court will decide how the amount claimed is to be paid.

NOTE: If you fail to return pages 6 and 10 to 12 as directed, or if, having returned them, you fail to attend or are not represented at the calling date if the case is to call, the court may decide the claim in your absence.

### PLEASE NOTE

If you do nothing about this summons, the court will almost certainly, where appropriate, grant decree against you and order you to pay the pursuer the sum claimed, including any interest and expenses found due.

**YOU ARE ADVISED TO KEEP PAGES 1 AND 2, AS THEY MAY BE USEFUL AT A LATER STAGE OF THE CASE.**

**PAGE 4**

Notes:

(1) **Time to pay directions**

The Debtors (Scotland) Act 1987 gives you the right to apply to the court for a "time to pay direction". This is an order which allows you to pay any sum which the court orders you to pay either in instalments or by deferred lump sum. A "deferred lump sum" means that you will be ordered by the court to pay the whole amount at one time within a period which the court will specify.

If the court makes a time to pay direction it may also recall or restrict any arrestment made on your property by the pursuer in connection with the action or debt (for example, your bank account may have been frozen).

No court fee is payable when making an application for a time to pay direction.

If a time to pay direction is made, a copy of the court order (called an extract decree) will be sent to you by the pursuer telling you when payment should start or when it is you have to pay the lump sum.

If a time to pay direction is not made, and an order for immediate payment is made against you, an order to pay (called a charge) may be served on you if you do not pay.

(2)  **Determination of application**

Under the 1987 Act, the court is required to make a time to pay direction if satisfied that it is reasonable in the circumstances to do so, and having regard in particular to the following matters—

- The nature of and reasons for the debt in relation to which decree is granted
- Any action taken by the creditor to assist the debtor in paying the debt
- The debtor's financial position
- The reasonableness of any proposal by the debtor to pay that debt
- The reasonableness of any refusal or objection by the creditor to any proposal or offer by the debtor to pay the debt.

(3)  **Time Orders**

The Consumer Credit Act 1974 allows you to apply to the court for a "time order" during a court action, to ask the court to give you more time to pay a loan agreement. **A time order is similar to a time to pay direction, but can only be applied for where the court action is about a credit agreement regulated by the Consumer Credit Act.** The court has power to grant a time order in respect of a regulated agreement to reschedule payment of the sum owed. This means that a time order can change:

- the amount you have to pay each month
- how long the loan will last
- in some cases, the interest rate payable

A time order can also stop the creditor taking away any item bought by you on hire purchase or conditional sale under the regulated agreement, so long as you continue to pay the instalments agreed.

No court fee is payable when making an application for a time order.

**PAGE 5**

**SECTION A**

This section must be completed before service

| | Summons No |
| --- | --- |
| | Return Day |
| | Calling Date |

SHERIFF COURT (Including address)

PURSUER'S FULL NAME AND ADDRESS

DEFENDER'S FULL NAME AND ADDRESS

**SECTION B**          **DEFENDER'S RESPONSE TO THE SUMMONS**
                    ** Delete those boxes which do <u>not</u> apply

| | |
|---|---|
| **\*\*Box 1** | **ADMIT LIABILITY FOR THE CLAIM and make** <u>written</u> **application to pay by instalments or by** <u>deferred</u> **lump sum**.<br><br>I do not intend to defend the case but admit liability for the claim.<br><br>I wish to make a written application about payment.<br><br>I have completed the application form on pages 8 and 9. |
| **\*\*Box 2** | **ADMIT LIABILITY FOR THE CLAIM and** <u>attend at court</u> **to make application to pay by instalments or deferred lump sum**.<br><br>I admit liability for the claim.<br><br>I intend to appear or be represented at court on the calling date. |
| **\*\*Box 3** | **DISPUTE THE CLAIM (or the amount due) and attend at court**<br><br>\*I intend to challenge the jurisdiction of the court.<br><br>\*I intend to challenge the competency of the action.<br><br>\*I intend to defend the action.<br><br>\*I wish to dispute the amount due only.<br><br>\*I apply for warrant to serve a third party notice (see page 14).<br><br>I intend to appear or be represented in court on the calling date.<br><br>.............<br><br>\*I attach a note of my proposed defence/counterclaim.<br><br>*\*delete as necessary* |
| **\*\*Box 4** | **ADMIT LIABILITY FOR THE CLAIM and apply for a time order under the** Consumer Credit Act 1974.<br><br>I do not intend to defend the case but admit liability for the claim.<br><br>I wish to apply for a time order under the Consumer Credit Act 1974.<br><br>I have completed the application form on pages 10 to 12. |

**PAGE 6**

---

**WRITTEN NOTE OF PROPOSE DEFENCE / COUNTERCLAIM**

State which facts in the statement of claim are admitted:

State briefly any facts regarding the circumstances of the claim on which you intent to rely:

State details of counterclaim, if any:

**PLEASE REMEMBER:** You must send your response to the court to **arrive on or before the return day** if you have completed a response in Section B. If you have admitted the claim, please do not send any payment direct to the court. **Any payments you wish to make should be made to the pursuer or his solicitor**.

Page 7

## APPLICATION IN WRITING FOR A TIME TO PAY DIRECTION UNDER THE DEBTORS (SCOTLAND) ACT 1987

**I WISH TO APPLY FOR A TIME TO PAY DIRECTION**

*I admit the claim* and make application to pay as follows:

(1) By instalments of £ .......... per *week / fortnight / month

**OR**

(2) In one payment within .......... *weeks / months from the date of the court order.

The debt is for (*specify the nature of the debt*) and has arisen (*here set out the reasons the debt has arisen*)

Please also state why you say a time to pay direction should be made. In doing so, please consider the Notes (1) and (2) on page 5.

To help the court please provide details of your financial position in the boxes below.

I am employed / self-employed / unemployed

**\*Please also indicate whether payment/receipts are weekly, fortnightly or monthly**

| My outgoings are: | *Weekly / fortnightly/ monthly | | My net income is | *Weekly / fortnightly/ monthly |
|---|---|---|---|---|
| Rent/mortgage | £ | | Wages/pensions | £ |
| Council tax | £ | | State benefits | £ |
| Gas/electricity etc | £ | | Tax credits | £ |
| Food | £ | | Other | £ |
| Loans and credit agreements | £ | | | |
| Phone | £ | | | |
| Other | £ | | | |
| Total | £ | | Total | £ |

| | |
|---|---|
| People who rely on your income (e.g. spouse/ civil partner/ partner/children)— how many | |

**Page 8**

Please list details of all capital held, e.g. value of house; amount in savings account, shares or other investments:

I am of the opinion that the payment offer is reasonable for the following reason(s):

*Here set out any information you consider relevant to the court's determination of the application. In doing so, please consider Note (2) on page 5.*

**\*APPLICATION FOR RECALL OR RESTRICTION OF AN ARRESTMENT**

I seek the recall or restriction of the arrestment of which the details are as follows:

Date:

   *Delete if inapplicable*

**Page 9**

| | |
|---|---|
| | **APPLICATION FOR A TIME ORDER UNDER THE CONSUMER CREDIT ACT 1974** |
| | By |
| | DEFENDER |
| | **In an action raised by** |
| | PURSUER |
| | PLEASE WRITE IN INK USING BLOCK CAPITALS |
| | If you wish to apply to pay by instalments enter the amount at box 3.<br><br>If you wish the court to make any additional orders, please give details at box 4. Please give details of the regulated agreement at box 5 and details of your financial position in the spaces provided below box 5.<br><br>Sign and date the application where indicated. You should ensure that your application arrives at the court along with the completed page 6 on or before the return day. |
| | 1. The Applicant is a defender in the action brought by the above named pursuer.<br><br>**I/WE WISH TO APPLY FOR A TIME ORDER under the Consumer Credit Act 1974** |
| | 2. **Details of order(s) sought**<br><br>The defender wishes to apply for a time order under section 129 of the Consumer Credit Act 1974<br><br>The defender wishes to apply for an order in terms of section .......... of the Consumer Credit Act 1974 |
| | 3. **Proposals for payment**<br><br>I admit the claim and apply to pay the arrears and future instalments as follows:<br><br>By instalments of £ .......... per *week/fortnight/month<br><br>No time to pay direction or time to pay order has been made in relation to this debt. |
| | 4. **Additional orders sought** |

|  | The following additional order(s) is (are) sought: (*specify*) |
|  | The order(s) sought in addition to the time order is (are) sought for the following reasons: |
|  | **5. Details of regulated agreement**<br><br>*(Please attach a copy of the agreement if you have retained it and insert details of the agreement where known)*<br><br>(a) Date of agreement<br><br>(b) Reference number of agreement |
|  | (c) Names and addresses of other parties to agreement<br><br>(d) Name and address of person (if any) who acted as surety (guarantor) to the agreement<br><br>(e) Place where agreement signed (e.g. the shop where agreement signed, including name and address)<br><br>(f) Details of payment arrangements<br>i. The agreement is to pay instalments of £ .......... per week/month<br>ii. The unpaid balance is £ .......... / I do not know the amount of arrears<br>iii. I am £ .......... in arrears / I do not know the amount of arrears |

**PAGE 11**

| | **Defender's financial position** | | | |
|---|---|---|---|---|
| | I am employed /self employed / unemployed | | | |
| | **My net income is:** | weekly, fort-nightly or monthly | **My outgoings are:** | weekly, fort-nightly or monthly |
| | Wages | £ | Mortgage/rent | £ |
| | State benefits | £ | Council tax | £ |
| | Tax credits | £ | Gas/electricity etc | £ |
| | Other | £ | Food | £ |
| | | | Credit and loans | £ |
| | | | Phone | £ |
| | | | Other | £ |
| | Total | £ | Total | £ |
| | People who rely on your income (e.g. spouse/civil partner/partner/children)— how many | | | |
| | Here list all assets (if any) e.g. value of house; amounts in bank or building society accounts; shares or other investments:................... | | | |
| | Here list any outstanding debts:................... | | | |
| | Therefore the defender asks the court to make a time order | | | |

| Date:............... | Signed:............... |
| | Defender:............... |

## APPLICATION FOR SERVICE OF A THIRD PARTY NOTICE
NOTE:
You can apply to have another party added to the action if:

(A)      **You think that, as regards the matter which the action is about, that other party has a duty to:**

1. Indemnify you; or
2. Make a contribution in respect of the matter; or
3. Relieve you from any responsibility as regards it.

**or**

(B)      **You think that other party is:**

1. Solely liable to the pursuer; or
2. Liable to the pursuer along with you; or
3. Has a liability to you as a result of the pursuer's claim against you.

You may apply for warrant to found jurisdiction if you wish to do so.

FORM OF APPLICATION

**(TO BE RETURNED TO THE COURT ALONG WITH YOUR RESPONSE)**

I request the court to grant warrant for service of a third party notice on the following party:

**Name:** ...............

**Address:** ...............

The reason I wish a third party notice to be served on the party mentioned above is as follows:
**(Give details below of the reasons why you wish the party to be made a defender in the action.)**

*****I** apply for warrant to found jurisdiction

```
*delete as appropriate

Date: ...............
```

¹ FORM 1b

Rule 4.3(a)

*Defender's copy summons - claim for or including payment of money (where time to pay direction or time order may not be applied for)*

**FORM 1b**

**Summary Cause Summons**
**Action for/of**
(state type, e.g. payment of money)

OFFICIAL USE ONLY
SUMMONS No.

**DEFENDER'S COPY: Claim for or including payment of money (where time to pay direction or time order may not be applied for)**

| | | |
|---|---|---|
| Sheriff Court (name, address, e-mail and telephone no.) | **1** | |
| Name and address of person raising the action (**pursuer**) | **2** | |
| Name and address of person against whom action raised (**defender, arrestee, etc.**) | **3** | |
| Name(s) and address(s) of any interested party (e.g. connected person) | **3a** | |
| Claim (Form of decree or other order sought) | **4** | |
| Name, full address, telephone no., and e-mail address of pur- | **5** | |

---

¹ As amended by the Act of Sederunt (Sheriff Court Rules Amendment) (Diligence) 2008 (SSI 2008/121) r.6(8) (effective April 1, 2008) and by the Act of Sederunt (Summary Cause Rules Amendment) (Personal Injuries Actions) 2012 (SSI 2012/144) para.2 (effective September 1, 2012).

suer's solicitor or rep-
resentative (if any)

| 6 | **RETURN DAY** | 20 | | |
|---|---|---|---|---|
| | **CALLING DATE** | 20 | at | am. |

**NOTE: You will find details of claim on page 2.**

**PAGE 1**

| 7. | **STATEMENT OF CLAIM** |
|---|---|

**PARTICULARS OF ARRESTMENT (furthcoming actions only.)**

(To be completed by the pursuer. If space is insufficient, a separate sheet may be attached)

The details of the claim are:

8. **SERVICE ON DEFENDER**

(Place).............       (Date)..........

To:.............       (defender)..........

You are hereby served with a copy of the above summons.

Solicitor / sheriff officer

*delete as appropriate*

**NOTE: The pursuer should complete boxes 1 to 6 on page 1, the statement of claim in box 7 on page 2 and section A on page 5 before service on the defender. The person serving the Summons will complete box 8.**

WHAT MUST I DO ABOUT THIS SUMMONS?

Decide whether you wish to dispute the claim, or admit any liability for the claim and whether you owe any money or not, and how you wish to proceed. Thereafter, look at the 2 options listed below. Find the one which covers your decision and follow the instructions given there. You will find the RETURN DAY and the CALLING DATE on page one of the summons.

Written guidance on summary cause procedure can be obtained from the sheriff clerk at any sheriff clerk's office. Further advice can also be obtained by contacting any of the following:

Citizen's Advice Bureau, Consumer Advice Centre, Trading Standards or Consumer Protection Department or a Solicitor. (Addresses can be found in the guidance booklets)

**Options**

**1. ADMIT LIABILITY FOR THE CLAIM and settle it with the pursuer now.**

If you wish to avoid the possibility of a court order passing against you, you should settle the claim (including any question of expenses) with pursuer or his representative **in good time before the return day**. Please do not send any payment direct to the court. Any payment should be made to the pursuer or his representative.

**2. DISPUTE THE CLAIM and attend at court to do any of the following:**

- Challenge the jurisdiction of the court or the competency of the action
- Defend the action
- Dispute the sum claimed
- State a counterclaim

973

Complete Section B on page 4. Return your response to the court so that it arrives **on or before the return day. You must attend personally, or be represented, at court on the calling date.**

Your representative may be a solicitor, or someone else having your authority. It may be helpful if you or your representative bring pages 1 and 2 of this form to the court.

**NOTE: If you fail to return your response as directed, or if, having returned it, you fail to attend or are not represented at the calling date, the court will almost certainly decide the claim in your absence.**

### Written Note of Proposed Defence

You must send to the court by the return day a written note of any proposed defence, or intimate that you intend to dispute the sum claimed or wish to challenge the court's jurisdiction. You must also attend or be represented at court on the calling date.

### Please Note:

If you do nothing about this summons, the court will almost certainly, where appropriate, grant decree against you and order you to pay the pursuer the sum claimed, including any interest and expenses found due.

**You Are Advised to Keep Pages 1 And 2, as They May Be Useful at a Later Stage of the Case**.

| SECTION A | | | |
|---|---|---|---|
| This section must be completed before service | | Summons No | |
| | | Return Day | |
| | | Calling Date | |
| | SHERIFF COURT (Including address) | | |
| | PURSUER'S FULL NAME AND ADDRESS | DEFENDER'S FULL NAME AND ADDRESS | |

**SECTION B** — **DEFENDER'S RESPONSE TO THE SUMMONS**

**DISPUTE THE CLAIM (or the amount due) and attend at court**

* I intend to challenge the jurisdiction of the court.
* I intend to challenge the competency of the action.
* I intend to defend the claim.
* I wish to dispute the amount due only.
* I apply for warrant to serve a third party notice (see page 6).
* I intend to appear or be represented in court on the calling date.

....................

* I attach a note of my proposed defence/counterclaim (see page 5).
* *delete as necessary*

**WRITTEN NOTE OF PROPOSED DEFENCE / COUNTERCLAIM**

State which facts in the statement of claim are admitted:

State briefly any facts regarding the circumstances of the claim on which you intend to rely:

State details of counterclaim, if any:

**PLEASE REMEMBER:** You must send your response to the court to **arrive on or before the return day** if you have completed a response in Section B. If you have admitted the claim, please do not send any payment direct to the court. **Any payments you wish to make should be made to the pursuer or his solicitor.**

### APPLICATION FOR SERVICE OF A THIRD PARTY NOTICE

**NOTE:**

You can apply to have another party added to the action if:

**(A) You think that, as regards the matter which the action is about, that other party has a duty to:**

1. Indemnify you; or
2. Make a contribution in respect of the matter; or
3. Relieve you from any responsibility as regards it.

**or**

**(B) You think that other party is:**

4. Solely liable to the pursuer; or
5. Liable to the pursuer along with you; or
6. Has a liability to you as a result of the pursuer's claim against you.

You may apply for warrant to found jurisdiction if you wish to do so.

FORM OF APPLICATION

**(TO BE RETURNED TO THE COURT ALONG WITH YOUR RESPONSE)**

**I request the court to grant warrant for service of a third party notice on the following party:**

Name:...............

Address:...............

**The reason I wish a third party notice to be served on the party mentioned above is as follows:** (Give details below of the reasons why you wish the party to be made a defender in the action.)

> \* I apply for warrant to found jurisdiction
>
> \* delete as appropriate

Form 1c[1]

> *Defender's copy summons — non monetary claim*
> Rule 4.3(b)

**FORM 1c**

# Summary Cause Summons
## Action for/of
(state type, e.g. delivery)

OFFICIAL USE ONLY
SUMMONS No.

## DEFENDER'S COPY: Non Monetary Claim

| | | |
|---|---|---|
| Sheriff Court (name, address, e-mail and telephone no.) | **1** | |
| Name and address of person raising the action (**pursuer**) | **2** | |
| Name and address of Person against whom Action raised (**defender**) | **3** | |
| Claim (Form of decree or other order sought) | **4** | |
| Name, full address, telephone no, and e-mail address of pursuer's solicitor or representative (if any) | **5** | |

| | | | | |
|---|---|---|---|---|
| **6** | RETURN DAY | 20 | | |
| | CALLING DATE | 20 | at | am. |

### NOTE: You will find details of claim on page 2.

---

[1] As amended by the Act of Sederunt (Sheriff Court Rules Amendment) (Diligence) 2008 (SSI 2008/121) r.6(8) (effective April 1, 2008).

7. **STATE DETAILS OF CLAIM HERE OR ATTACH A STATEMENT OF CLAIM**
**(to be completed by the pursuer. If space is insufficient, a separate sheet may be attached)**

The details of the claim are:

8. **SERVICE ON DEFENDER**

(Place)...............                                          (Date).........

To:...............                                              (defender)

You are hereby served with a copy of the above summons.

\* Solicitor / sheriff officer
(delete as appropriate)

NOTE: The pursuer should complete boxes 1 to 6 on page 1, the statement of claim in box 7 on page 2 and section A on page 5 before service on the defender. The person serving the Summons will complete box 8.

## WHAT MUST I DO ABOUT THIS SUMMONS?

**Decide whether you wish to dispute the action and how you wish to proceed.** Thereafter, look at the 2 options listed below. Find the one which covers your decision and follow the instructions given there. You will find the RETURN DAY and the CALLING DATE on page one of the summons.

**Written guidance on summary cause procedure can be obtained from the sheriff clerk at any sheriff clerk's office. Further advice can also be obtained by contacting any of the following:**

**Citizen's Advice Bureau, Consumer Advice Centre, Trading Standards or Consumer Protection Department or a Solicitor. (Addresses can be found in the guidance booklets)**

### Options

**1. ADMIT LIABILITY FOR THE CLAIM and settle it with the pursuer now.**

If you wish to avoid the possibility of a court order passing against you, you should settle the claim (including any liability for expenses) with the pursuer or his representative in good time before the return day.

**2. DISPUTE THE CLAIM and attend at court to do any of the following:**
- Challenge the jurisdiction of the court or the competency of the action
- Defend the action
- State a counterclaim

Complete Section B on page 4. Return page 4 to the court so that it arrives **on or before the return day. You must attend personally, or be represented, at court on the calling date.**

Your representative may be a solicitor, or someone else having your authority. It may be helpful if you or your representative bring pages 1 and 2 of this form to the court.

**NOTE: If you fail to return page 4 as directed, or if, having returned it, you fail to attend or are not represented at the calling date, the court will almost certainly decide the claim in your absence**.

### Written Note of Proposed Defence

You must send to the court by the return day a written note of any proposed defence, or intimate that you wish to challenge the jurisdiction of the court. You must also attend or be represented at court on the calling date.

### Please Note

If you do nothing about this summons, the court will almost certainly, where appropriate, grant decree against you, including any interest and expenses found due.

**You Are Advised to Keep Pages 1 And 2, as They May Be Useful at a Later Stage of the Case**.

**SECTION A**
This section must
Be completed
Before service

| Summons No |
| --- |
| Return Day |
| Calling Date |

SHERIFF COURT (Including address)

PURSUER'S FULL NAME AND ADDRESS

DEFENDER'S FULL NAME AND ADDRESS

**SECTION B**  **DEFENDER'S RESPONSE TO THE SUMMONS**

DISPUTE THE CLAIM and attend at court

* I intend to challenge the jurisdiction of the court.

* I intend to challenge the competency of the court.

* I wish to defend the action.

* I apply for warrant to serve a third party notice (see page 6).

I intend to appear or be represented in court on the calling date.

*I attach a note of my proposed defence/counterclaim (see page 5).

* *delete as necessary*

**WRITTEN NOTE OF PROPOSED DEFENCE / COUNTERCLAIM**

State which facts in the statement of claim are admitted:

State briefly any facts regarding the circumstances of the claim on which you intend to rely:

State details of counterclaim, if any:

**PLEASE REMEMBER:** You must send your response to the court to **arrive** on or **before the return day** if you have completed a response in Section B.

### APPLICATION FOR SERVICE OF A THIRD PARTY NOTICE

### NOTE:

You can apply to have another party added to the action if:

**(A) You think that, as regards the matter which the action is about, that other party has a duty to:**

1. Indemnify you; or
2. Make a contribution in respect of the matter; or
3. Relieve you from any responsibility as regards it.

or

(B) You think that other party is:

4. Solely liable to the pursuer; or

5. Liable to the pursuer along with you; or

6. Has a liability to you as a result of the pursuer's claim against you.

You may apply for warrant to found jurisdiction if you wish to do so.

---

**Form of Application**

(TO BE RETURNED TO THE COURT ALONG WITH YOUR RESPONSE)

**I request the court to grant warrant for service of a third party notice on the following party:**

Name:...............

Address:...............

**The reason I wish a third party notice to be served on the party mentioned above is as follows:**
(Give details below of the reasons why you wish the party to be made a defender in the action.)

**\* I apply for warrant to found jurisdiction**

delete as appropriate

```
┌──────────────────────────────────────────────────┐
│                                                    │
│                                                    │
└──────────────────────────────────────────────────┘
```

Form 1d

Defender's copy summons - multiplepoinding

Rule 4.3(c)

**FORM 1d**

## Summary Cause Summons

Action of Multiplepoinding

| OFFICIAL USE ONLY |
| --- |
| SUMMONS No. |

**DEFENDER'S COPY**

| | | |
| --- | --- | --- |
| Sheriff Court (name, address, e-mail and telephone no.) | **1** | |
| Name and address of person raising the action (**pursuer**) | **2** | |
| Name and address of person against whom action raised (**defenders**) | **3** | |
| Claim (Form of decree or other order sought - see Form 5) | **4** | |
| Name, full address, telephone no., and e-mail address of pursuer's solicitor (if any) | **5** | |

| | |
| --- | --- |
| **6** | **RETURN DAY** 20 |
| | **CALLING DATE** 20 at am. |

**NOTE: You will find details of claim on page 2.**

7. **STATE DETAILS OF CLAIM HERE OR ATTACH A STATE-MENT OF CLAIM**

**(to be completed by the pursuer. If space is insufficient, a separate sheet may be attached)**

The details of the claim are:

8. **SERVICE ON DEFENDER**

(Place)............... (Date)..........

To:............... (Defender.)

You are hereby served with the above summons. The pursuer has been authorised by the court to serve it on you.

Solicitor / sheriff officer
(delete as appropriate)

**NOTE: The Pursuer should complete boxes 1 to 6 on page 1, the statement of claim in box 7 on page 2 and section A on page 5 before service on the defender. The person serving the Summons will complete box 8.**

## WHAT MUST I DO ABOUT THIS SUMMONS?

**Decide whether you wish to dispute the action and how you wish to proceed**. Thereafter, look at the 2 options listed below. Find the one which covers your decision and follow the instructions given there. You will find the RETURN DAY and the CALLING DATE on page one of the summons.

**Written guidance on summary cause procedure can be obtained from the sheriff clerk at any sheriff clerk's office. Further advice can also be obtained by contacting any of the following:**

**Citizen's Advice Bureau, Consumer Advice Centre, Trading Standards or Consumer Protection Department or a solicitor. (Addresses can be found in the guidance booklets)**

## OPTIONS

1. ADMIT LIABILITY FOR THE CLAIM and settle it with the pursuer now.

If you wish to avoid the possibility of a court order passing against you, you should attempt to settle the claim (including any liability for expenses) with the pursuer or his Solicitor **in good time before the return day**.

**2. DISPUTE THE CLAIM and attend at court to do any of the following:**

- Challenge the jurisdiction of the court or the competency of the action.
- Object to the extent of the fund or subject detailed in the statement of claim on page 2.
- Make a claim on the fund or subject.

Complete Section B on page 4. Return page 4 to the court so that it arrives **on or before the return day. You must attend personally, or be represented, at court on the calling date**.

Your representative may be a Solicitor, or someone else having your authority. It may be helpful if you or your representative bring pages 1 and 2 of this form to the court.

**NOTE: If you fail to return page 4 as directed, or if, having returned it, you fail to attend or are not represented at the calling date, the court will almost certainly deal with the action in your absence**.

**NOTES:**

1. If you do nothing about this summons, the court will almost certainly deal with the action in your absence.

2. **IF YOU ARE THE HOLDER OF THE FUND,** you must complete the enclosed form 5a and send it to the sheriff clerk before the return day. You must also, before the return day, send a copy of form 5a to the pursuer, the other defenders in the action and to all the persons you have listed in form 5a as having an interest in the fund or subject.

**YOU ARE ADVISED TO KEEP PAGES 1 AND 2, AS THEY MAY BE USEFUL AT A LATER STAGE OF THE CASE**.

| SECTION A This section must be completed Before service | | Summons No |
| --- | --- | --- |
| | | Return Day |
| | | Calling Date |

SHERIFF COURT (Including address)

PURSUER'S FULL NAME AND ADDRESS

DEFENDER'S FULL NAME AND ADDRESS

**SECTION B**   **DEFENDER'S RESPONSE TO THE SUMMONS**

---

**DISPUTE THE CLAIM and attend at court**

**I intend to:**

\* (1) Challenge the jurisdiction of the court or the competency of the action.

\* (2) Object to the extent of the fund or subject detailed in the statement of claim.

\* (3) Make a claim on the fund or subject.

I intend to appear or be represented in court on the calling date.

*\* delete as necessary*

> **Please give below brief details of your reason(s) for disputing the claim in accordance with your response to 1, 2 or 3 above:**

¹ FORM 1e

Form 1e

> OFFICIAL USE ONLY
> SUMMONS No.

Rule 34.3(1)(a)

*Summary Cause Summons—Personal Injuries Action*

**DEFENDER'S COPY: Claim for payment of money in a personal injuries action (where time to pay direction may be applied for)**

| | |
|---|---|
| Sheriff Court **1** (name, address, e-mail and telephone no.) | |
| Name and address **2** of person raising the action (**pursuer**) | |
| Name and address **3** of person against whom action raised (**defender, arrestee, etc.**) | |
| Name(s) and address(es) of any interested party (e.g. connected person) **3a** | |
| Claim (form of **4** decree of other order sought) | |
| Name, full address, telephone **5** | |

---

¹ As inserted by the Act of Sederunt (Summary Cause Rules Amendment) (Personal Injuries Actions) 2012 (SSI 2012/144) para.2 (effective September 1, 2012; not applicable to an action raised before September 1, 2012).

| no., and e-mail address of pursuer's solicitor or representative (if any) acting in the case | |
|---|---|

| 6 | RETURN DAY | 20 | | |
|---|---|---|---|---|
| | CALLING DATE | 20 | at | am. |

**NOTE: You will find details of the claim in the attached Form 10 (statement of claim in a personal injuries action).**

| 7. | STATEMENT OF CLAIM |
|---|---|
| | **(Pursuer to attach copy Form 10 (statement of claim in a personal injuries action))** |
| | The details of the claim are as stated in the attached copy Form 10. |

| 8. | SERVICE ON DEFENDER |
|---|---|
| | (Place)............... (Date).......... |
| | To:............... (Defender).......... |
| | **You are hereby served with a copy of the above summons.** |
| | Solicitor / sheriff officer |
| | *delete as appropriate* |

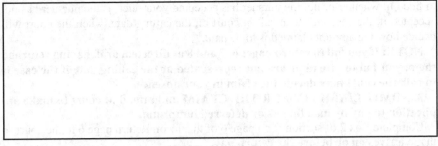

NOTE: The pursuer should complete boxes 1 to 6 on page 1, attach a copy of the Form 10, (statement of claim) and complete section A on page 6 before service on the defender. The pursuer should also enclose a form of response in Form 10a. The person serving the Summons will complete box 8, above.

**PAGE 2**

## WHAT MUST I DO ABOUT THIS SUMMONS?

The RETURN DAY (on page 1 of this summons) is the deadline by which you need to reply to the court. You must send the correct forms back (see below for details) by this date if you want the court to hear your case. If you do not do this, in most cases there will not be a hearing about your case and the court will make a decision in your absence.

The CALLING DAY (on page 1 of this summons) is the date when the court will deal with your case should you not respond to this summons, or the date of the court hearing should you admit the claim and the court is required to consider your application to pay the sum claimed by instalments or by deferred lump sum.

**You should decide whether you wish to dispute the claim and/or whether you owe any money or not, and how you wish to proceed.** Then, look at the 4 options listed below. Find the one that covers your decision and follow the instructions given there.

You may have a policy of insurance that could indemnify you against this claim. This could be motor, home contents, buildings, travel or some other form of liability insurance that may offer cover to meet legal costs to defend this claim or to meet any claim against you that is admitted or proved. If you believe you have any such insurance cover, you should **immediately** contact your insurer and take steps to forward to them details of this claim.

**IF YOU ARE UNCERTAIN WHAT ACTION TO TAKE** you should consult a solicitor. You may also obtain advice from a Citizens Advice Bureau or other advice agency. Alternatively, if you are not sure what you need to do, contact the sheriff clerk's office before the return day. Written guidance is available from the Scottish Court Service website (www.scotcourts.gov.uk).

## OPTIONS

**1. ADMIT LIABILITY FOR THE CLAIM and settle it with the pursuer now.**

If you wish to avoid the possibility of a court order passing against you, you should settle the claim (including any question of expenses) with the pursuer or their representative **in good time before the return day.** Please do not send any payment direct to the court. Any payment should be made to the pursuer or their representative.

**2. ADMIT LIABILITY FOR THE CLAIM and make written application to pay by instalments or by deferred lump sum.**

Complete Box 1 of section B on page 6 of this form and return pages 6, 7 and 8 to the court **to arrive on or before the return day.** You should then contact the court to find out whether or not the pursuer has accepted your offer. If the pursuer has not accepted it, the case will then call in court on the calling date, when the court will decide how the amount claimed is to be paid.

**NOTE: If you fail to return pages 6, 7 and 8 as directed, or if, having returned them, you fail to attend or are not represented at the calling date if the case is to call, the court may decide the claim in your absence.**

**3. ADMIT LIABILITY FOR THE CLAIM and attend at court to make application to pay by instalments or deferred lump sum.**

Complete Box 2 of section B on page 6 of this form. Return page 6 to the court so that it arrives **on or before the return day.**

**PAGE 3**

**You must attend personally, or be represented, at court on the calling date.** Your representative may be a solicitor, or someone else having your authority. It may be helpful if you or your representative bring pages 1 and 2 of this Form and Form 10 to the court.

**NOTE: If you fail to return page 6 as directed, or if, having returned it, you fail to attend or are not represented at the calling date, the court may decide the claim in your absence.**

**4. DISPUTE THE CLAIM for any of the following reasons:**
- Challenge the jurisdiction of the court or the competency of the action;
- Defend the action;
- Dispute the sum claimed; or
- State a counterclaim.

You must complete Box 3 of Section B on page 6 and the attached form of response in Form 10a, stating in a manner which gives the pursuer fair notice, the grounds of fact and law on which you intend to resist the claim, or counterclaim, and return these to the court so that they arrive **on or before the return day.** Thereafter, the case **will not** call in court on the calling date and you do not require to attend or be represented at court on that date. The sheriff clerk will send to you or your representative a timetable confirming the anticipated date for the hearing of evidence and the dates by which various procedural matters must be undertaken. Your representative may be a solicitor or someone else having your authority.

**NOTE: If you fail to return page 6 and the completed Form 10a as directed, the case may call on the calling date, and the court may decide the claim in your absence.**

**PLEASE NOTE**

If you do nothing about this summons, the court will almost certainly, where appropriate, grant decree against you and order you to pay the pursuer the sum claimed, including any interest and expenses found due.

**YOU ARE ADVISED TO KEEP PAGES 1 AND 2 AND FORM 10, AS THEY MAY BE USEFUL AT A LATER STAGE OF THE CASE.**

**PAGE 4**

**Notes:**

**(1) Time to pay directions**

The Debtors (Scotland) Act 1987 gives you the right to apply to the court for a "time to pay direction". This is an order which allows you to pay any sum which the court orders you to pay either in instalments or by deferred lump sum. A "deferred lump sum" means that you will be ordered by the court to pay the whole amount at one time within a period which the court will specify.

If the court makes a time to pay direction it may also recall or restrict any arrestment made on your property by the pursuer in connection with the action or debt (for example, your bank account may have been frozen).

No court fee is payable when making an application for a time to pay direction.

If a time to pay direction is made, a copy of the court order (called an extract decree) will be sent to you by the pursuer telling you when payment should start or when it is you have to pay the lump sum.

If a time to pay direction is not made, and an order for immediate payment is made against you, an order to pay (called a charge) may be served on you if you do not pay.

**(2) Determination of application**

Under the 1987 Act, the court is required to make a time to pay direction if satisfied that it is reasonable in the circumstances to do so, and having regard in particular to the following matters—

- The nature of and reasons for the debt in relation to which decree is granted
- Any action taken by the creditor to assist the debtor in paying the debt
- The debtor's financial position
- The reasonableness of any proposal by the debtor to pay that debt
- The reasonableness of any refusal or objection by the creditor to any proposal or offer by the debtor to pay the debt.

**PAGE 5**

| | |
|---|---|
| **SECTION A** This section must be completed before service | Summons No / Return Day / Calling Date |

SHERIFF COURT (Including address)

PURSUER'S FULL NAME AND ADDRESS

DEFENDER'S FULL NAME AND ADDRESS

**SECTION B**     **DEFENDER'S RESPONSE TO THE SUMMONS**
** Delete those boxes which do not apply

**Box 1**

**ADMIT LIABILITY FOR THE CLAIM and make written application to pay by instalments or by deferred lump sum**.

I do not intend to defend the case but admit liability for the claim.

I wish to make a written application about payment.

|  | I have completed the application form on pages 7 and 8. |
|---|---|
| **Box 2 | **ADMIT LIABILITY FOR THE CLAIM and attend at court to make application to pay by instalments or deferred lump sum.**<br>I admit liability for the claim.<br>I intend to appear or be represented at court on the calling date. |
| **Box 3 | **DISPUTE THE CLAIM (or the amount due)**<br>*I intend to challenge the jurisdiction of the court.<br>*I intend to challenge the competency of the action.<br>*I intend to defend the action/state a counterclaim.<br>*I wish to dispute the amount due only.<br>*I apply for warrant to serve a third party notice (see page 10).<br>*delete as necessary<br>...............<br>I attach completed Form 10a stating my proposed defence/counterclaim. |

**PLEASE REMEMBER:** You must send your response to the court to **arrive on or before the return day** if you have completed a response in Section B. If you have admitted the claim, please do not send any payment direct to the court. **Any payments you wish to make should be made to the pursuer or their solicitor.**

PAGE 6

## APPLICATION IN WRITING FOR A TIME TO PAY DIRECTION UNDER THE DEBTORS (SCOTLAND) ACT 1987

**I WISH TO APPLY FOR A TIME TO PAY DIRECTION**
**I admit the claim** and make application to pay as follows:

(1) By instalments of £ .......... per *week / fortnight / month

**OR**

(2) In one payment within .......... *weeks / months from the date of the court order.

The debt is for (*specify the nature of the debt*) and has arisen (*here set out the reasons the debt has arisen*)

Please also state why you say a time to pay direction should be made. In doing so, please consider the Notes (1) and (2) on page 5.

To help the court please provide details of your financial position in the boxes below.

I am employed / self-employed / unemployed

**\*Please also indicate whether payment/receipts are weekly, fortnightly or monthly**

| My outgoings are: | \*Weekly / fortnightly/ monthly | My net income is | \*Weekly / fortnightly/ monthly |
|---|---|---|---|
| Rent/ mortgage | £ | Wages/ pensions | £ |
| Council tax | £ | State benefits | £ |
| Gas/ electricity etc | £ | Tax credits | £ |
| Food | £ | Other | £ |
| Loans and credit agreements | £ | | |
| Phone | £ | | |
| Other | £ | | |
| Total | £ | Total | £ |

People who rely on your income (e.g. spouse/civil partner/ partner/ children)— how many

**Please list details of all capital held, e.g. value of house; amount in savings account, shares or other investments:**

I am of the opinion that the payment offer is reasonable for the following reason(s):

*Here set out any information you consider relevant to the court's determination of the application. In doing so, please consider Note (2) on page 5.*

---

**\*APPLICATION FOR RECALL OR RESTRICTION OF AN ARREST-MENT**

I seek the recall or restriction of the arrestment of which the details are as follows:

*\*Delete if inapplicable*

---

Date:

**PAGE 8**

APPLICATION FOR SERVICE OF A THIRD PARTY NOTICE
NOTE:
You can apply to have another party added to the action if:

(A)        **You think that, as regards the matter which the action is about, that other party has a duty to:**

       1. Indemnify you; or
       2. Make a contribution in respect of the matter; or
       3. Relieve you from any responsibility as regards it.

                **or**

(B)        **You think that other party is:**
       1. Solely liable to the pursuer; or
       2. Liable to the pursuer along with you; or
       3. Has a liability to you as a result of the pursuer's claim against you.

You may apply for warrant to found jurisdiction if you wish to do so.

**PAGE 9**

---

FORM OF APPLICATION

**(TO BE RETURNED TO THE COURT ALONG WITH YOUR RESPONSE)**

I request the court to grant warrant for service of a third party notice on the following party:

**Name:**...............

**Address:**...............

---

The reason I wish a third party notice to be served on the party mentioned above is as follows:

**(Give details below of the reasons why you wish the party to be made a defender in the action.)**

---

*I apply for warrant to found jurisdiction

*delete as appropriate*

Date:...............

**PAGE 10**

¹ FORM 1f

Form 1f

OFFICIAL USE ONLY
SUMMONS No.

Rule 34.3(1)(b)

*Summary Cause Summons—Personal Injuries Action*

**DEFENDER'S COPY: Claim for payment of money in a personal injuries action (where time to pay direction may be applied for)**

---

¹ As inserted by the Act of Sederunt (Summary Cause Rules Amendment) (Personal Injuries Actions) 2012 (SSI 2012/144) para.2 (effective September 1, 2012; not applicable to an action raised before September 1, 2012).

| | | |
|---|---|---|
| Sheriff Court (name, address, e-mail and telephone no.) | **1** | |
| Name and address of person raising the action (**pursuer**) | **2** | |
| Name and address of person against whom action raised (**defender, arrestee, etc.**) | **3** | |
| Name(s) and address(es) of any interested party (e.g. connected person) | **3a** | |
| Claim (form of decree of other order sought) | **4** | |
| Name, full address, telephone no., and e-mail address of pursuer's solicitor or representative (if any) acting in the case | **5** | |

| | | | | |
|---|---|---|---|---|
| **6** | **RETURN DAY** | | 20 | |
| | **CALLING DATE** | | 20 | at am. |

**NOTE: You will find details of the claim in the attached Form 10 (statement of claim in a personal injuries action).**

**PAGE 1**

| | |
|---|---|
| 7. | **STATEMENT OF CLAIM** |
| | **(Pursuer to attach copy Form 10 (statement of claim in a personal injuries action))** |
| | The details of the claim are as stated in the attached copy Form 10. |

8.          **SERVICE ON DEFENDER**

          (Place)...............                              (Date).........

          To:...............                                  (Defender)..........

          **You are hereby served with a copy of the above summons.**

                                                              Solicitor / sheriff
                                                              officer
                                                              *delete as appropri-
                                                              ate*

NOTE: The pursuer should complete boxes 1 to 6 on page 1, attach a copy of the Form 10, (statement of claim) and complete section A on page 6 before service on the defender. The pursuer should also enclose a form of response in Form 10a. The person serving the Summons will complete box 8, above.

**PAGE 2**

## WHAT MUST I DO ABOUT THIS SUMMONS?

The RETURN DAY (on page 1 of this summons) is the deadline by which you need to reply to the court. You must send the correct forms back (see below for details) by this date if you want the court to hear your case. If you do not do this, in most cases there will not be a hearing about your case and the court will make a decision in your absence.

The CALLING DAY (on page 1 of this summons) is the date when the court will deal with your case should you not respond to this summons.

**You should decide whether you wish to dispute the claim and/or whether you owe any money or not, and how you wish to proceed.** Then, look at the 2 options listed on the next page. Find the one that covers your decision and follow the instructions given there.

You may have a policy of insurance that could indemnify you against this claim. This could be motor, buildings, travel or some other form of liability insurance that may offer cover to meet legal costs to defend this claim or to meet any claim against you that is admitted or proved. If you believe you have any such insurance cover, you should **immediately** contact your insurer and take steps to forward to them details of this claim.

**IF YOU ARE UNCERTAIN WHAT ACTION TO TAKE** you should consult a solicitor. You may also obtain advice from a Citizens Advice Bureau or other advice agency. Alternatively, if you are not sure what you need to do, contact the sheriff clerk's office before the return day. Written guidance is available from the Scottish Court Service website (www.scotcourts.gov.uk).

PAGE 3

## OPTIONS
**1. ADMIT LIABILITY FOR THE CLAIM and settle it with the pursuer now.**

If you wish to avoid the possibility of a court order passing against you, you should settle the claim (including any question of expenses) with the pursuer or their representative **in good time before the return day.** Please do not send any payment direct to the court. Any payment should be made to the pursuer or their representative.

**2. DISPUTE THE CLAIM for any of the following reasons:**
- Challenge the jurisdiction of the court or the competency of the action;
- Defend the action;
- Dispute the sum claimed; or
- State a counterclaim.

You must complete Section B on page 5 and the attached form of response in Form 10a, stating in a manner which gives the pursuer fair notice, the grounds of fact and law on which you intend to resist the claim, or counterclaim, and return these to the court so that they arrive **on or before the return day**. Thereafter, the case **will not** call in court on the calling date and you do not require to attend or be represented at court on that date. The sheriff clerk will send to you or your representative a timetable confirming the anticipated date for the hearing of evidence and the dates by which various procedural matters must be undertaken. Your representative may be a solicitor or someone else having your authority.

**NOTE: If you fail to return page 5 and the completed Form 10a as directed, the case may call on the calling date, and the court may decide the claim in your absence.**

## PLEASE NOTE
If you do nothing about this summons, the court will almost certainly, where appropriate, grant decree against you and order you to pay the pursuer the sum claimed, including any interest and expenses found due.

**YOU ARE ADVISED TO KEEP PAGES 1 AND 2 AND FORM 10, AS THEY MAY BE USEFUL AT A LATER STAGE OF THE CASE.**

Page 4

**SECTION A**

This section must be completed before service

| |
| --- |
| |
| |
| |
| |

| Summons No |
| --- |
| Return Day |
| Calling Date |

SHERIFF COURT
(Including address)

| |
| --- |
| |
| |
| |
| |

| |
| --- |
| |
| |
| |
| |

PURSUER'S FULL NAME AND ADDRESS

DEFENDER'S FULL NAME AND ADDRESS

**SECTION B**    **DEFENDER'S RESPONSE TO THE SUMMONS**
** Delete those boxes which do not apply

| **DISPUTE THE CLAIM (or the amount due)** |
| --- |
| *I intend to challenge the jurisdiction of the court. |
| *I intend to challenge the competency of the action. |
| *I intend to defend the action/state a counterclaim. |
| *I wish to dispute the amount due only. |
| *I apply for warrant to serve a third party notice (see page 6). |
| *delete as necessary |
| ............... |
| I attach completed Form 10a stating my proposed defence/counterclaim. |

**PLEASE REMEMBER:** You must send your response to the court to **arrive on or before the return day** if you have completed a response in Section B. If you have admitted the claim, please do not send any payment direct to the court. **Any payments you wish to make should be made to the pursuer or their solicitor**.

**PAGE 5**

APPLICATION FOR SERVICE OF A THIRD PARTY NOTICE
NOTE:
You can apply to have another party added to the action if:

(A)     **You think that, as regards the matter which the action is about, that other party has a duty to:**

1.                                                          Indemnify you; or

2.                                                          Make a contribution in respect of the matter; or

3.                                                          Relieve you from any responsibility as regards it.

                                                            **or**

(B)     **You think that other party is:**

1.                                                          Solely liable to the pursuer; or

2.                                                          Liable to the pursuer along with you; or

3.                                                          Has a liability to you as a result of the pursuer's claim against you.

You may apply for warrant to found jurisdiction if you wish to do so.

**PAGE 6**

---

FORM OF APPLICATION

### (TO BE RETURNED TO THE COURT ALONG WITH YOUR RESPONSE)

I request the court to grant warrant for service of a third party notice on the following party:

Name:...............

Address:...............

The reason I wish a third party notice to be served on the party mentioned above is as follows:

**(Give details below of the reasons why you wish the party to be made a defender in the action.)**

---

```
*I apply for warrant to found jurisdiction

*delete as appropriate

Date:..............
```

**PAGE 7**

**Rule 4.1(2)**                    FORM 2

Form of claim in a summons for payment of money..........The pursuer claims from the defender(s) the sum of £..........with..........interest on that sum at the rate of..........annually from the date of service, together with the expenses of bringing the action.

**Rule 4.1(2)**                    FORM 3

Form of claim in a summons for recovery of possession of heritable property The pursuer claims that, in the circumstances described in the statement contained on page 2 of this copy summons, he is entitled to recover possession of the property at (*address*), and that you refuse or delay to remove from said property.

The pursuer therefore asks the court to grant a decree against you, removing you, and your family, sub-tenants and dependants (if any) with your goods and possessions from the said property.

The pursuer also claims from you the expenses of bringing the action.

**Rule 30.6(1)**                    FORM 3A

Form of notice of removal under sections 34, 35 or 36 of the Sheriff Courts (Scotland) Act 1907

To: (*name, designation and address of party in possession*)

You are hereby required to remove from (*describe subjects*) at the term of (*or, if different terms, state them and the subjects to which they apply*), in terms of (*describe lease, terms of letter of removal or otherwise*).

(*date*)                                        (*signature, designation and address*)

**Rule 30.6(2)**                    FORM 3B

997

Form of notice of removal under section 37 of the Sheriff Courts (Scotland) Act 1907

NOTICE OF REMOVAL UNDER SECTION 37 OF THE SHERIFF COURTS (SCOTLAND) ACT 1907

To:...............

*(name, designation and address)*

You are hereby required to remove from *(describe subjects)* at the term of *(Whitsunday or Martinmas), (date).*

*(date)*                 signature, designation and address)*

**Rule 30.6(3)**          FORM 3C

Form of letter of removal

To: *(name, designation and address)*...............*(place and date).* I am to remove from (describe subjects by usual name or give a short description sufficient for identification) at the term of *(insert term and date).*

*(date)*              *(signature, designation and address)*

**Rule 4.1(2)**          FORM 4

Form of claim in a summons of sequestration for rent

*[Repealed by the Act of Sederunt (Sheriff Court Rules Amendment) (Diligence) 2008 (SSI 2008/121) r.2(1)(b) (effective April 1, 2008).]*

**Rule 31.2(2)**          FORM 4A

Notice informing defender of right to apply for certain orders under the Debtors (Scotland) Act 1987

*[Repealed by the Act of Sederunt (Sheriff Court Rules Amendment) (Diligence) 2008 (SSI 2008/121) r.2(1)(b) (effective April 1, 2008).]*

**Rule 31.2(2)**          FORM 4B

Certificate of Sequestration

*[Repealed by the Act of Sederunt (Sheriff Court Rules Amendment) (Diligence) 2008 (SSI 2008/121) r.2(1)(b) (effective April 1, 2008).]*

**Rule 4.1(2)**          FORM 5

Form of claim in a summons of multiplepoinding

The pursuer claims that, in the circumstances described in the statement contained on page 2 of this copy summons, the *(state party)* is the holder of a fund *(or subject)* valued at £.......... on which competing claims are being made by the defenders.

The pursuer therefore asks the court to grant a decree finding the holder of the said fund or subject liable to make payment of, or to deliver, same to the party found by the court to be entitled thereto.

The pursuer also asks that the expenses of bringing the action be deducted from the value of the said fund or subject before payment is made.

**Rule 27.5(2)(a)**          FORM 5A

Form of statement by holder of fund or subject when not the pursuer

(1) I, (*name, address*), hereby state that the fund or subject in the summary cause summons raised at the instance of AB (*design*) against CD, *(EF and GH) (design)* is as follows: (*description and details of fund or subject*).

(2) I have the following claim or lien on said fund or subject (give details, including a reference to any document founded upon in support of the claim).

(3) I am aware that the persons listed below have an interest in the said fund/subject:

(*list names and addresses*)

(4) I certify that I have today intimated a copy of this statement to each of the persons contained in the list at (3) above.

(*date*)

**Rule 27.9(2)(a)**                                   FORM 5B

Form of claim on the fund or subject in action of multiplepoinding

I, EF, claim to be preferred on the fund in the multiplepoinding raised in the name of AB against CD, EF etc. for the sum of £.......... by reason of (*state ground of claim, including a reference to any document founded upon in support thereof*) with interest thereon from (*date*).

I also claim any appropriate court expenses which I may incur by appearing in this action.

(*signature*)

**Rule 4.1(2)**                                   FORM 6

Form of claim in a summons of furthcoming

The pursuer claims that, in the circumstances described in the statement contained on page 2 of this copy summons, the said (*name of common debtor*) is due to him the sum of £...........

He further claims that he has lawfully arrested in the hands of the said (*name of arrestee*) the goods or money valued at £.......... and described in the said statement of claim, which ought to be made furthcoming to him.

He therefore asks the court to order that you make furthcoming and deliver to him the said arrested goods or money or so much thereof as will satisfy (*or part satisfy*) the said sum of £.......... owing to him.

The pursuer also claims from you the expenses of bringing this action. If the value of the arrested funds are insufficient to meet the sum owing to the pursuer plus the expenses of the action, the pursuer claims those expenses from the said (*name of common debtor*).

**Rule 4.1(2)**                                   FORM 7

Form of claim in a summons for delivery

The pursuer claims that, in the circumstances described in the statement contained on page 2 of this copy summons, he has right to the possession of the article(s) described therein.

He therefore asks the court to grant a decree ordering you to deliver the said articles to the pursuer.

Alternatively, if you do not deliver said articles, the pursuer asks the court to grant a decree ordering you to pay to him the sum of £.......... with interest on that sum at the rate of.......... % annually from (*date*) until payment.

The pursuer also claims from you the expenses of bringing the action.

**Rule 4.1(2)**                                   FORM 8

Form of claim in a summons for implement of an obligation

The pursuer claims that, in the circumstances described in the statement contained on page 2 of this copy summons, you are obliged to

He therefore asks the court to grant a decree ordering you to implement the said obligation.

Alternatively, if you do not fulfil the obligation, the pursuer asks the court to grant a decree ordering you to pay to him the sum of £.......... with interest on that sum at the rate of.......... % annually from (*date*) until payment.

The pursuer also claims from you the expenses of bringing the action.

**Rule 4.1(2)**                                FORM 9

Form of claim in a summons for count, reckoning and payment

The pursuer claims that, in the circumstances described in the statement contained on page 2 of this copy summons, you have intromitted with (*describe briefly the fund or estate*), in which he has an interest.

He therefore asks the court to grant a decree ordering you to produce a full account of your intromissions therewith, and for payment to him of the sum of £.........., or such other sum as appears to the court to be the true balance due by you, with interest thereon at the rate of.......... % annually from (*date*) until payment.

Alternatively, if you do not produce such an account, the pursuer asks the court to grant a decree ordering you to pay to him the said sum of £.......... with interest thereon at the rate of.......... % annually from (*date*) until payment.

The pursuer also claims from you the expenses of bringing the action.

**Rule 34.2(2)**                                FORM 10 [1]

Form of statement of claim in a personal injuries action

1.  The pursuer is (*state designation, address, occupation, date of birth and National Insurance number (where applicable) of the pursuer*). (*In an action arising out of the death of a relative state designation of the deceased and relation to the pursuer*).
2.  The defender is (*state designation, address and occupation of the defender*).
3.  The court has jurisdiction to hear this claim against the defender because (*state briefly ground of jurisdiction*).
4.  (*State briefly the facts necessary to establish the claim*).
5.  (*State briefly the personal injuries suffered and the heads of claim. Give names and addresses of medical practitioners and hospitals or other institutions in which the person injured received treatment*).
6.  (*State whether claim based on fault at common law or breach of statutory duty; if breach of statutory duty, state provision of enactment*).

**Rules 34.3(2)** and **34.4(1)**                FORM 10A [2]

Form of response (action for damages: personal injuries)

Court ref. no:

SHERIFFDOM OF (*insert name of sheriffdom*)
AT (*insert place of sheriff court*)

---

[1] As inserted by the Act of Sederunt (Summary Cause Rules Amendment) (Personal Injuries Actions) 2012 (SSI 2012/144) para.2 (effective September 1, 2012; not applicable to an action raised before September 1, 2012).

[2] As inserted by the Act of Sederunt (Summary Cause Rules Amendment) (Personal Injuries Actions) 2012 (SSI 2012/144) para.2 (effective September 1, 2012; not applicable to an action raised before September 1, 2012).

*in the cause*
[A.B.], (*insert name and address*), Pursuer
against
[C.D.], (*insert name and address*), Defender
RESPONSE TO STATEMENT OF CLAIM

| Question | Response |
|---|---|
| 1. Is it intended to dispute the description and designation of the pursuer? If so, why? | |
| 2. Is the description and designation of the defender disputed? If so, why? | |
| 3. Is there any dispute that the court has jurisdiction to hear the claim? If so, why? | |
| 4. (a) State which facts in paragraph 4 of the statement of claim are admitted. | |
| (b) State any facts regarding the circumstances of the claim upon which the defender intends to rely. | |
| 5. (a) State whether the nature and extent of the pursuer's injuries is disputed and whether medical reports can be agreed. | |
| (b) If the defender has a medical report upon which he or she intends to rely to contradict the pursuer's report in any way, state the details. | |
| (c) State whether the claims for other losses are disputed in whole or in part. | |
| 6. (a) Does the defender accept that the common law duty or duties in the statement of claim were incumbent upon them in the circumstances? If not, state why. | |
| (b) Does the defender accept that the statutory duty or duties alleged in the statement of claim were incumbent upon them in the circumstances? If not, state why. | |
| (c) State any other provisions or propositions upon which the defender proposes to rely in relation to the question of their liability for the accident including, if appropriate, details of any allegation of contributory negligence. | |
| (d) Does the defender allege that the accident was caused by any other wrongdoer? If so, give details. | |
| (e) Does the defender allege that they are entitled to be indemnified or relieved from any liability they might have to the pursuer? If so, give details. | |

| Question | Response |
|---|---|
| 7. Does the defender intend to pursue a counterclaim against the pursuer? If so, give details. | |
| *(Insert date)* | *(signature, designation and address)* |

**Rules 34.2(3)(b)** and **34.4(2)(b)**          FORM 10B [1,2]

Form of order of court for recovery of documents in personal injuries action

Court ref. no:

SHERIFFDOM OF *(insert name of sheriffdom)*

AT *(insert place of sheriff court)*

SPECIFICATION OF DOCUMENTS

*in the cause*

[A.B.], *(insert name and address, or, as the case may be, the party who obtained the order.)*, Pursuer

against

[C.D.], *(insert name and address)*, Defender

To: *(insert name and address of party or parties from whom the following documents are sought to be recovered)*.

You are hereby required to produce to the sheriff clerk at *(insert address)* within seven days of the service on you of this Order:

*[Insert such of the following calls as are required]*

1. All books, medical records, reports, charts, X-rays, notes and other documents of *(specify the name of each medical practitioner or general practitioner practice named in summons in accordance with rule 34.2(2)(b))*, and relating to the pursuer *[or, as the case may be, the deceased]* from *(insert date)*, in order that excerpts may be taken therefrom at the sight of the Commissioner of all entries showing or tending to show the nature, extent and cause of the pursuer's *[or, as the case may be, the deceased's]* injuries when he or she attended his or her doctor on or after *(specify date)* and the treatment received by him or her since that date.

2. All books, medical records, reports, charts, X-rays, notes and other documents of *(specify, in separate calls, the name of each hospital or other institution named in summons in accordance with* rule 34.2(2)(b))*, and relating to the pursuer *[or, as the case may be, the deceased]* from *(insert date)*, in order that excerpts may be taken therefrom at the sight of the Commissioner of all entries showing or tending to show the nature, extent and cause of the pursuer's *[or, as the case may be, the deceased's]* injuries when he or she was admitted to that institution on or about *(specify date)*, the treatment received by him or her since that date and his or her certificate of discharge, if any.

3. The medical records and capability assessments held by the defender's occupational health department relating to the pursuer *[or, as the case may be, the deceased]*, except insofar as prepared for or in contemplation of litigation, in order that excerpts may be taken therefrom at the sight of the Commissioner of all entries showing or tending to show the nature and extent of any injuries, symptoms and

---

[1] As inserted by the Act of Sederunt (Summary Cause Rules Amendment) (Personal Injuries Actions) 2012 (SSI 2012/144) para.2 (effective September 1, 2012; not applicable to an action raised before September 1, 2012).

[2] As amended by the Act of Sederunt (Rules of the Court of Session, Ordinary Cause Rules and Summary Cause Rules Amendment) (Miscellaneous) 2014 (SSI 2014/152) r.4 (effective July 7, 2014).

conditions from which the pursuer [or, as the case may be, the deceased] was suffering and the nature of any assessment and diagnosis made thereof on or subsequent to (specify date).

4. All wage books, cash books, wage sheets, computer records and other earnings information relating to the pursuer [or, as the case may be, the deceased] (N.I. number (specify number)) held by or on behalf of (specify employer), for the period (specify dates commencing not earlier than 26 weeks prior to the date of the accident or the first date of relevant absence, as the case may be) in order that excerpts may be taken therefrom at the sight of the Commissioner of all entries showing or tending to show—

(a) the pursuer's [or, as the case may be, the deceased's] earnings, both gross and net of income tax and employee National Insurance Contributions, over the said period;

(b) the period or periods of the pursuer's [or, as the case may be, the deceased's] absence from employment over the said period and the reason for absence;

(c) details of any increases in the rate paid over the period (specify dates) and the dates on which any such increases took effect;

(d) the effective date of, the reasons for and the terms (including any terms relative to any pension entitlement) of the termination of the pursuer's [or, as the case may be, the deceased's] employment;

(e) the nature and extent of contributions (if any) to any occupational pension scheme made by the pursuer [or, as the case may be, the deceased] and his or her employer;

(f) the pursuer's present entitlement (if any) to any occupational pension and the manner in which said entitlement is calculated.

5. All accident reports, memoranda or other written communications made to the defender or anyone on his or her behalf by an employee of the defender who was present at or about the time at which the pursuer [or, as the case may be, the deceased] sustained the injuries in respect of which the summons in this cause was issued and relevant to the matters contained in the statement of claim.

6. Any assessment current at the time of the accident referred to in the summons or at the time of the circumstances referred to in the summons giving rise to the cause of action (as the case may be) undertaken by or on behalf of the defender for the purpose of regulation 3 of the Management of Health and Safety at Work Regulations 1992 and subsequently regulation 3 of the Management of Health and Safety at Work Regulations 1999 [or (specify the regulations or other legislative provision under which the risk assessment is required)] in order that excerpts may be taken therefrom at the sight of the Commissioner of all entries relating to the risks posed to workers [or (specify the matters set out in the statement of claim to which the risk assessment relates)].

7. Failing principals, drafts, copies or duplicates of the above or any of them.

Date (insert date of posting or other  (Insert signature, name and business address of the agent for the pursuer)
method of service)

**NOTES:**

1. The documents recovered will be considered by the parties to the action and they may or may not be lodged with the sheriff clerk. A written receipt will be given or sent to you by the sheriff clerk, who may thereafter allow them to be inspected by the parties. The party in whose possession the documents are will be responsible for their safekeeping.

2. Payment may be made, within certain limits, in respect of claims for outlays incurred in relation to the production of documents. Claims should be made in writing to the person who has obtained an order that you produce the documents.

3. If you claim that any of the documents produced by you is **confidential** you must still produce such documents but may place them in a separate sealed packet by themselves, marked "CONFIDENTIAL". Any party who wishes to open the sealed packet must apply to the sheriff by incidental application. A party who makes such an application must intimate the application to you.

4. Subject to paragraph 3 above, you may produce these documents by sending them by registered post or by recorded delivery service, or by hand delivery to the sheriff clerk at (*insert address*).

## CERTIFICATE

I hereby certify with reference to the above order of the sheriff at (*insert name of sheriff court*) in the case (*insert court reference number*) and the enclosed specification of documents, served on me and marked respectively X and Y—

1. That the documents which are produced and which are listed in the enclosed inventory signed by me and marked Z, are all the documents in my possession falling within the specification.

*or*

That I have no documents in my possession falling within the specification.

2. That, to the best of my knowledge and belief, there are in existence other documents falling within the specification, but not in my possession. These documents are as follows—(*describe them by reference to the descriptions of documents in the specification*). They were last seen by me on or about (*date*), at (*place*), in the hands of (*insert name and address of the person*).

*or*

That I know of the existence of no documents in the possession of any person, other than me, which fall within the specification.

(*Insert date*)                                    (*Signed*)

                                                  (*Name and address*)


**Rule 34.5(2)**                              FORM 10C [1]

Form of docquet for deemed grant of recovery of documents in a personal injuries action

Court ref. no:

Court (*insert court*)

Commission and diligence for the production and recovery of the documents called for in this specification of documents is deemed to have been granted.

Date (*insert date*)                          (*Signed*)

                                              Sheriff Clerk (depute)


**Rule 34.7(1)(c) and (4)**                   FORM 10D [2]

---

[1] As inserted by the Act of Sederunt (Summary Cause Rules Amendment) (Personal Injuries Actions) 2012 (SSI 2012/144) para.2 (effective September 1, 2012; not applicable to an action raised before September 1, 2012).

[2] As inserted by the Act of Sederunt (Summary Cause Rules Amendment) (Personal Injuries Actions) 2012 (SSI 2012/144) para.2 (effective September 1, 2012; not applicable to an action raised before September 1, 2012).

Form of timetable

Court ref. no:

TIMETABLE
*in the cause*
[A.B.], (*insert name and address*), Pursuer
against
[C.D.], (*insert name and address*), Defender
This timetable has effect as if it were an interlocutor of the sheriff.

1. The diet allocated for the proof in this action will begin on (*date*). Subject to any variation under rule 34.8, this order requires the parties to undertake the conduct of this action within the periods specified in paragraphs 2 to 10 below.

2. An application under rule 11.1 (third party procedure) shall be made by (*date*).

3. Where the pursuer has obtained a commission and diligence for the recovery of documents by virtue of rule 34.5, the pursuer shall serve the order not later than (*date*).

4. For the purposes of rule 34.7(2)(c), the adjustment period shall end on (*date*).

5. The pursuer shall lodge with the sheriff clerk a statement of valuation of claim under rule 34.9 not later than (*date*).

6. The pursuer shall lodge with the sheriff clerk a certified adjusted statement of claim not later than (*date*).

7. The defender (and any third party to the action) shall lodge with the sheriff clerk a certified adjusted response to statement of claim not later than (*date*).

8. The defender (and any third party to the action) shall lodge with the sheriff clerk a statement of valuation of claim under rule 34.9 not later than (*date*).

9. Not later than (*date*) the parties shall lodge with the sheriff clerk lists of witnesses and productions.

10. Not later than (*date*) the pursuer shall lodge with the sheriff clerk a pre-proof minute under rule 34.10.

(*Insert date*)                    (*Signed*)

Sheriff Clerk (depute)

**Rule 34.9**                    FORM 10E[1]

Form of statement of valuation of claim

Court ref. no:

SHERIFFDOM OF (*insert name of sheriffdom*)
AT (*insert place of sheriff court*)
STATEMENT OF VALUATION OF CLAIM
*in the cause*
[A.B.], (*insert name and address*), Pursuer
against
[C.D.], (*insert name and address*), Defender

| Head of Claim | Components | Valuation |
|---|---|---|
| Solatium | Past | £x |
|  | Future | £x |

[1] As inserted by the Act of Sederunt (Summary Cause Rules Amendment) (Personal Injuries Actions) 2012 (SSI 2012/144) para.2 (effective September 1, 2012; not applicable to an action raised before September 1, 2012).

| Head of Claim | Components | Valuation |
|---|---|---|
| Interest on past solatium | Percentage applied to past solatium (*state percentage rate*) | £x |
| Past wage loss | Date from which wage loss claimed: (*date*) | £x |
| | Date to which wage loss claimed: (*date*) | |
| | Rate of net wage loss (*per week, per month or per annum*) | |
| Interest on past wage loss | Percentage applied to past wage loss: (*state percentage rate*) | £x |
| Future wage loss | Multiplier: (*state multiplier*) | £x |
| | Multiplicand: (*state multiplicand and show how calculated*) | |
| | Discount factor applied (if appropriate): (*state factor*) | |
| | Or specify any other method of calculation | |
| Past services | Date from which services claimed: (*date*) | £x |
| | Date to which services claimed: (*date*) | |
| | Nature of services: (............) | |
| | Person by whom services provided: (............) | |
| | Hours per week services provided: (............) | |
| | Net hourly rate claimed: (..........) | |
| | Total amount claimed: (..........) | |
| | Interest | |
| Future loss of capacity to provide personal services | Multiplier: (*insert multiplier*) | £x |
| | Multiplicand: (*insert multiplicand, showing how calculated*) | |
| Needs and other expenses | One off | £x |
| | Multiplier: (*insert multiplier*) | |
| | Multiplicand: (*insert multiplicand*) | |
| | Interest | |
| Any other heads as appropriate (*specify*) | | £x |
| Total | | £x (*insert total valuation of claim*) |
| List of Supporting Documents:— | | |

(*Insert date*)                              (*Signed*)

                                             (*Name and address*)

**Rule 34.10(2)**                     FORM 10F [1]

Minute of pre-proof conference

                                                  Court ref. no.:

SHERIFFDOM OF (*insert sheriffdom*)

AT (*insert place of sheriff court*)

JOINT MINUTE OF PRE-PROOF CONFERENCE

in the cause

[*A.B.*], Pursuer

against

[*C.D.*], Defender

[E.F.] for the pursuer and

[G.H.] for the defender hereby state to the court:

1. That the pre-proof conference was held in this case [*at (place) or by (telephone conference or video conference or other remote means)*] on [*date*].

2. That the following persons were present—

(*State names and designations of persons attending conference*)

3. That the following persons were available to provide instructions by telephone or video conference—

(*State names and designations or persons available to provide instructions by telephone or video conference*)

4. That the persons participating in the conference discussed settlement of the action.

5. That the following questions were addressed—

**Section 1**

|    |    | Yes | No |
|----|----|-----|----|
| 1. | Is the diet of proof still required? | | |
| 2. | If the answer to question 1 is "yes", does the defender admit liability? (If "no", complete section 2)<br><br>If yes, does the defender plead contributory negligence?<br><br>If yes, is the degree of contributory negligence agreed?<br><br>If yes, state % degree of fault attributed to the pursuer. | | |
| 3. | If the answer to question 1 is "yes", is the quantum of damages agreed? (If "no", complete section 3) | | |

**Section 2**

[*To be inserted only if the proof is still required*]

It is estimated that the hearing will last [*insert number*] [*days/hours*].

---

[1] As inserted by the Act of Sederunt (Summary Cause Rules Amendment) (Personal Injuries Actions) 2012 (SSI 2012/144) para.2 (effective September 1, 2012; not applicable to an action raised before September 1, 2012).

*NB. If the estimate is more than one day then this should be brought to the attention of the sheriff clerk. This may affect prioritisation of the case.*

During the course of the pre-proof conference, the pursuer called on the defender to agree certain facts, questions of law and matters of evidence.

Those calls, and the defender's responses, are as follows—

| Call | Response | |
|---|---|---|
| | *Admitted* | *Denied* |
| 1. | | |
| 2. | | |
| 3. | | |
| 4. | | |

During the course of the pre-proof conference, the defender called on the pursuer to agree certain facts, questions of law and matters of evidence.

Those calls, and the pursuer's responses, are as follows—

| Call | Response | |
|---|---|---|
| | *Admitted* | *Denied* |
| 1. | | |
| 2. | | |
| 3. | | |
| 4. | | |

**Section 3**

Quantum of damages

Please indicate where agreement has been reached on an element of damages

| Head of claim | Components | Not agreed | Agreed at |
|---|---|---|---|
| Solatium | Past Future | | |
| Interest on past solatium | Percentage applied to past solatium (*state percentage*) | | |
| Past wage loss | Date from which wage loss claimed | | |
| | Date to which wage loss claimed | | |
| | Rate of net wage loss (*per week, per month or per annum*) | | |
| Interest on past wage loss | | | |
| Future wage loss | Multiplier | | |
| | Multiplicand (*showing how calculated*) | | |
| Past necessary services | Date from which services claimed | | |
| | Date to which services claimed | | |

| Head of claim | Components | Not agreed | Agreed at |
|---|---|---|---|
| | Hours per week services provided | | |
| | Net hourly rate claimed | | |
| Past personal services | Date from which services claimed | | |
| | Date to which services claimed | | |
| | Hours per week services provided | | |
| | Net hourly rate claimed | | |
| Interest on past services | | | |
| Future necessary services | Multiplier | | |
| | Multiplicand (*showing how calculated*) | | |
| Future personal services | Multiplier | | |
| | Multiplicand (*showing how calculated*) | | |
| Needs and other expenses | One off | | |
| | Multiplier | | |
| | Multiplicand (*showing how calculated*) | | |
| Any other heads as appropriate (specify) | | | |

(*Insert date of signature*)        (*Signed by each party/his or her solicitor*)

**Rule 34.12(5)**                    FORM 10G[1]

Form of intimation to connected persons

Court ref. no:

SHERIFFDOM OF (*insert sheriffdom*)
AT (*insert place of sheriff court*)
in the cause
[*A.B.*], Pursuer
against
[*C.D.*], Defender
To: (*insert name and address as in warrant*)

---

[1] As inserted by the Act of Sederunt (Summary Cause Rules Amendment) (Personal Injuries Actions) 2012 (SSI 2012/144) para.2 (effective September 1, 2012; not applicable to an action raised before September 1, 2012).

You are hereby given notice that an action has been raised in the above sheriff court against (*insert name of defender*), by your (*insert relationship, e.g. father, brother or other relative as the case may be*). A copy of the summons is attached.

It is believed that you may have a title or interest to sue (*name of defender*) in this action, which is based upon (*the injuries from which the late (insert name and designation) died) (or the death of the late (insert name and designation)*). You may therefore be entitled to enter this action as an additional pursuer. This may be done by lodging an incidental application with the sheriff clerk at (*insert address of sheriff court*).

If you wish to appear as a party in the action, or are uncertain about what action to take, you should contact a solicitor. You may, depending on your financial circumstances, be entitled to legal aid, and you can get information about legal aid from a solicitor.

You may also obtain advice from any Citizen's Advice Bureau, other advice agency or any sheriff clerk's office.

(*Insert date of signature*)                    (*Signed*)

                                                (*Solicitor for the pursuer*)


**Rule 34.13(2)**                          FORM 10H[1]

Form of claim for provisional damages

Court ref. no:

SHERIFFDOM OF (*insert sheriffdom*)
AT (*insert place of sheriff court*)
in the cause
[*A.B.*], Pursuer
against
[*C.D.*], Defender

For payment to the pursuer by the defender of the sum of (*amount in words and figures*) as provisional damages under section 12(2)(a) of the Administration of Justice Act 1982.

(*Statements to include that there is a risk that the pursuer will as result of the act or omission which gave rise to the cause of action develop serious disease or serious deterioration of condition in the future; and that the defender was, at the time of the act or omission which gave rise to the cause of action, a public authority, public corporation or insured or otherwise indemnified in respect of the claim*).

(*Insert date of signature*)                    (*Signed*)

                                                (*Solicitor for the pursuer*)


**Rule 34.13(3)**                          FORM 10I[2]

Form of application for further damages

Court ref. no:

SHERIFFDOM OF (*insert sheriffdom*)

---

[1] As inserted by the Act of Sederunt (Summary Cause Rules Amendment) (Personal Injuries Actions) 2012 (SSI 2012/144) para.2 (effective September 1, 2012; not applicable to an action raised before September 1, 2012).
[2] As inserted by the Act of Sederunt (Summary Cause Rules Amendment) (Personal Injuries Actions) 2012 (SSI 2012/144) para.2 (effective September 1, 2012; not applicable to an action raised before September 1, 2012).

AT (*insert place of sheriff court*)
APPLICATION FOR FURTHER DAMAGES
in the cause
[*A.B.*], Pursuer
against
[*C.D.*], Defender

The pursuer claims payment from the defender of the sum (*insert amount* in words and figures) as further damages under section 12(2)(b) of the Administration of Justice Act 1982.

(*Insert concise statement of facts supporting claim for further damages*).

The pursuer requests the sheriff to fix a hearing on this incidental application and applies for warrant to serve the application on—

(*Here state names and addresses of other parties to the action; and, where such other parties are insured or otherwise indemnified, their insurers or indemnifiers, if known to the pursuer*).

(*Insert date of signature*)　　　　　(*Signed*)
　　　　　　　　　　　　　　　　　　(*Solicitor for the pursuer*)

**Rule 34.13(4)**　　　　　　　　　FORM 10J[1]

Form of application for further damages

Court ref. no:

SHERIFFDOM OF (*insert sheriffdom*)
AT (*insert place of sheriff court*)
APPLICATION FOR FURTHER DAMAGES
in the cause
[*A.B.*], Pursuer
against
[*C.D.*], Defender

To:
TAKE NOTICE

(*Pursuer's name and address*), pursuer, raised an action against (*defender's name and address*), defender, in the sheriff court at (*insert name of sheriff court*).

In the action, the sheriff on (*date*) made an award of provisional damages in accordance with section 12(2)(a) of the Administration of Justice Act 1982 in favour of the pursuer against (*you* or *name of party*). [The sheriff specified that the pursuer may apply for an award of further damages under section 12(2)(b) of that Act at any time before (*date*)]. The pursuer has applied by incidental application for an award of further damages against you [or name of party]. A copy of the incidental application is attached.

A hearing on the incidental application has been fixed for (*date and time*) at (*place of sheriff court*). If you wish to be heard on the incidental application, you should attend or be represented at court on that date.

(*Insert date of signature*)　　　　　(*Signed*)
　　　　　　　　　　　　　　　　　　(*Solicitor for the pursuer*)

---

[1] As inserted by the Act of Sederunt (Summary Cause Rules Amendment) (Personal Injuries Actions) 2012 (SSI 2012/144) para.2 (effective September 1, 2012; not applicable to an action raised before September 1, 2012).

**Rule 5.3(1)** FORM 11

Form of service

XY, you are hereby served with a copy of the above (or attached) summons.

*(signature of solicitor or sheriff officer)*

**Rule 5.3(2)** FORM 12

Form of certificate of execution of service

Case name:

Court ref: no:

*(Place and date)*...............

I,..........,hereby certify that on the..........day of.........., 20..........,I duly cited XY to answer the foregoing summons. This I did by (*set forth the mode of service*).

*(Signature of solicitor or sheriff officer)*

**Rule 5.5(1)(a)** FORM 13

Service on person whose address is unknown Form of advertisement

A summary cause action has been raised in the sheriff court at..........by AB, pursuer against CD, defender, whose last known address was..........

If the said CD wishes to defend the action he should immediately contact the sheriff clerk's office at the above court.

Address of court:

Telephone no:

Fax no:

E-mail address:

**Rule 5.5(1)(b)** FORM 14

Service on person whose address is unknown
Form of notice to be displayed on the walls of court

A summary cause action has been raised in this court by AB, pursuer against CD, defender, whose last known address was...............

If the said CD wishes to defend the action he should immediately contact the sheriff clerk's office.

*(Date)* Displayed on the walls of court
of this date.

Sheriff clerk depute

**Rule 5.6(2)** FORM 15

Service by post—form of notice

This letter contains a citation to or intimation from the sheriff court at..........

If delivery cannot be made the letter must be returned immediately to the sheriff clerk at (*insert full address*).

**Rule 6.A2(2)** FORM 15A [1]

Statement to accompany application for interim diligence
DEBTORS (SCOTLAND) ACT 1987 Section 15D [or DEBT ARRANGEMENT
AND ATTACHMENT (SCOTLAND) ACT 2002 Section 9C]

---

[1] As inserted by the Act of Sederunt (Sheriff Court Rules Amendment) (Diligence) 2008 (SSI 2008/ 121) r.6(9) (effective April 1, 2008).

Sheriff Court:...............

In the Cause (Cause Reference No. )

[A.B.] (*designation and address*)

Pursuer

against

[C.D.] (*designation and address*)

Defender

## STATEMENT

1. The applicant is the pursuer [*or* defender] in the action by [A.B] (*design*) against [C.D.] (*design*).

2. [The following persons have an interest [*specify names and addresses*].]

3. The application is [*or* is not] seeking the grant under section 15E(1) of the 1987 Act of warrant for diligence [or section 9D(1) of the 2002 Act of interim attachment] in advance of a hearing on the application.

4. [*Here provide such other information as may be prescribed by regulations made by the Scottish Ministers under* section 15D(2)(d) of the 1987 Act *or* 9C(2)(d,) of the 2002 Act]

(*Signed*)

Solicitor [*or* Agent] for A.B. [*or* C.D.]

(*include full designation*)

**Rule 6.A8**                    FORM 15B [1]

Form of schedule of arrestment on the dependence

SCHEDULE OF ARRESTMENT ON THE DEPENDENCE

**Rule 6.A8**                    FORM 15C [2]

Form of certificate of execution of arrestment on the dependence

CERTIFICATE OF EXECUTION

\* by affixing the schedule of arrestment to the door at (*place*) on (*date*). (*Specify that enquiry made and that reasonable grounds exist for believing that the person on whom service is to be made resides at the place but is not available*) [and by posting a copy of the schedule to the arrestee by registered post or first class recorded delivery to the address specified on the receipt annexed to this certificate].

\* by leaving the schedule of arrestment with (*name and occupation of person with whom left*) at (*place of business*) on (*date*).[and by posting a copy of the schedule to the arrestee by registered post or first class recorded delivery to the address specified on the receipt annexed to this certificate].

\* by depositing the schedule of arrestment at (*place of business*) on (*date*). (*Specify that enquiry made and that reasonable grounds exist for believing that the person on whom service is to be made carries on business at that place.*) [and by posting a copy of the schedule to the arrestee by registered post or first class recorded delivery to the address specified on the receipt annexed to this certificate].

\* by affixing the schedule of arrestment to the door at (*place of business*) on (*date*). (*Specify that enquiry made and that reasonable grounds exist for believing that the person on whom service is to be made carries on business at that place.*)

---

[1] As inserted by the Act of Sederunt (Sheriff Court Rules Amendment) (Diligence) 2008 (SSI 2008/ 121) r.6(9) (effective April 1, 2008) and substituted by the Act of Sederunt (Sheriff Court Rules Amendment) (Diligence) 2009 (SSI 2009/107) (effective April 22, 2009).

[2] As inserted by the Act of Sederunt (Sheriff Court Rules Amendment) (Diligence) 2008 (SSI 2008/ 121) r.6(9) (effective April 1, 2008) and substituted by the Act of Sederunt (Sheriff Court Rules Amendment) (Diligence) 2009 (SSI 2009/107) (effective April 22, 2009).

[and by posting a copy of the schedule to the arrestee by registered post or first class recorded delivery to the address specified on the receipt annexed to this certificate].

\* by leaving the schedule of arrestment at (*registered office*) on (*date*), in the hands of (*name of person*) [and by posting a copy of the schedule to the arrestee by registered post or first class recorded delivery to the address specified on the receipt annexed to this certificate].

\* by depositing the schedule of arrestment at (*registered office*) on (*date*) [and by posting a copy of the schedule to the arrestee by registered post or first class recorded delivery to the address specified on the receipt annexed to this certificate].

\* by affixing the schedule of arrestment to the door at (*registered office*) on (*date*). [and by posting a copy of the schedule to the arrestee by registered post or first class recorded delivery to the address specified on the receipt annexed to this certificate].

I did this in the presence of (*name, occupation and address of witness*).

(*Signed*)
Sheriff Officer
(*Address*)
(*Signed*)
(Witness)

*Delete where not applicable
**NOTE**
**A copy of the Schedule of arrestment on the dependence is to be attached to this certificate.**

**Rule 6.3(4)(a)**                    FORM 16

Recall or restriction of arrestment
Certificate authorising the release of arrested funds or property
Sheriff court, (*place*)...............
Court ref. no.:..........AB (pursuer) against CD (defender)

I, (*name*), hereby certify that the sheriff on (*date*) authorised the release of the funds or property arrested on the *dependence of the action/counterclaim/third party notice to the following extent:
(*details of sheriff's order*)

(*Date*)                         Sheriff clerk depute

*delete as appropriate
Copy to:
Party instructing arrestment
Party possessing arrested funds/property

**Rule 7.1(1)**                    FORM 17

Form of minute—no form of response lodged by defender
Sheriff court, (*place*)...............
Calling date:...............

In respect that the defender(s) has/have failed to lodge a form of response to the summons, the pursuer respectfully craves the court to make the orders specified in the following case(s):

| Court ref. No | Name(s) of defender(s) | Minute(s) |
| --- | --- | --- |

**Rule 7.1(2)**                         FORM 18 [1]

Form of minute—pursuer not objecting to application for a time to pay direction or time order

Sheriff court, (*place*)...............
Court ref. no.:...............
Name(s) of defender(s)...............
Calling date:...............
I do not object to the defender's application for
*a time to pay direction
*recall or restriction of an arrestment
*a time order
The pursuer requests the court to grant decree or other order in terms of the following minute(s)
*delete as appropriate

FORM 19 [2]

Rule 7.2(4)

Form of minute—pursuer opposing an application for a time to pay direction or time order

**Sheriff court (place):**...............
**Court ref no:**...............
Name(s) of defender(s):...............
Calling date:...............
I oppose the defender's application for
*a time to pay direction
*recall or restriction of arrestment
*a time order
* delete as appropriate
1. The debt is (*please specify the nature of the debt*).
2. The debt was incurred on (*specify date*) and the pursuer has contacted the defender in relation to the debt on (*specify date(s)*).
*3. The contractual payments were (*specify amount*).
*4. (*Specify any action taken by the pursuer to assist the defender to pay the debt*).
*5. The defender has made payment(s) towards the debt of (*specify amount(s)*) on (*specify date(s)*).
*6. The debtor has made offers to pay (*specify amount(s)*) on (*specify date(s)*) which offer(s) was [were] accepted] [or rejected] and (*specify amount*) was paid on (*specify date(s)*).
7. (*Here set out any information you consider relevant to the court's determination of the application*).
8. The pursuer requests the court to grant decree.
* delete as appropriate

(*Signed*)
Pursuer [*or* Solicitor for Pursuer]
(*Date*)

---

[1] As amended by the Act of Sederunt (Ordinary Cause, Summary Application, Summary Cause and Small Claim Rules) Amendment (Miscellaneous) 2003 (SSI 2003/26) r.4(4)(b) (effective January 24, 2003).

[2] As substituted by the Act of Sederunt (Sheriff Court Rules) (Miscellaneous Amendments) 2009 (SSI 2009/294) r.4 (effective December 1, 2009)

Rule 8.12

## FORM 20
### Form of oath for witnesses

I swear by Almighty God that I will tell the truth, the whole truth and nothing but the truth.

Rule 8.12

## FORM 21
### Form of affirmation for witnesses

I solemnly, sincerely and truly declare and affirm that I will tell the truth, the whole truth and nothing but the truth.

Rule 11.2(1)(b)(iii)

## FORM 22
### Form of third party notice

Court ref. no.

SHERIFF COURT, (*place*)

### THIRD PARTY NOTICE
in the cause
(AB) (*insert designation and address*), pursuer
against
(CD) (*insert designation and address*), defender

To (EF)

You are given notice by (CD) of an order granted by the sheriff at (*insert place of court*) in which (AB) is the pursuer and (CD) is the defender. A copy of the order is enclosed herewith.

In the action, the pursuer claims from the defender (*insert a brief account of the circumstances of the claim*) as more fully appears in the copy summons enclosed.

The defender claims that,...............(* *delete as appropriate*).

*if he is liable to the pursuer, you are liable to relieve him wholly/partially of his liability, as more fully appears in the copy grounds upon which the defender relies for this, which are also enclosed.

*he is not liable to the pursuer for the claim made against him. He maintains that any liability to the pursuer in respect of this claim rests solely on you, as more fully appears in the copy grounds upon which the defender relies for this, which are also enclosed.

*if he is liable to the pursuer in respect of this claim, he shares that liability with you, as more fully appears in the copy grounds upon which the defender relies for this, which are also enclosed.

*You are liable to him in respect of the claim, as more fully appears in the copy grounds upon which the defender relies for this, which are also enclosed.

If you wish to resist the claim(s) made by the defender as detailed above, you must—

(a) return the form of response enclosed to the sheriff clerk at (*address*) by (*date seven days before the date of hearing*); and

(b) attend or be represented at a hearing on (*date and time*).

(*Date*)...............(*Signature of person serving notice*)

Rule 11.2(1)(b)(iii)

## FORM 23
### Form of response to third party notice
in the cause
(AB) (*insert designation and address*), pursuer
against
(CD) (*insert designation and address*), defender

I wish to answer the claim made against me by (CD), defender. (*here state briefly the grounds of opposition to the defender's claim.*)

(*date*)

Rule 14A.3(1)

### FORM 23A [1]

Form of minute of intervention by the Commission for Equality and Human Rights

SHERIFF COURT, (place)..........Court ref. no...........

## APPLICATION FOR LEAVE TO INTERVENE BY THE COMMISSION FOR EQUALITY AND HUMAN RIGHTS

in the cause

[A.B.] (designation and address), Pursuer

against

[C.D.] (designation and address), Defender

[Here set out briefly:

(a)    the Commission's reasons for believing that the proceedings are relevant to a matter in connection with which the Commission has a function;

(b)    the issue in the proceedings which the Commission wishes to address; and

(c)    the propositions to be advanced by the Commission and the Commission's reasons for believing that they are relevant to the proceedings and that they will assist the court.]

Rule 14B.2(1)

### FORM 23B [2]

Form of minute of intervention by the Scottish Commission for Human Rights

SHERIFF COURT, (place)..........Court ref. no...........

## APPLICATION FOR LEAVE TO INTERVENE BY THE SCOTTISH COM- MISSION FOR HUMAN RIGHTS

in the cause

[A.B.] (designation and address), Pursuer

against

[C.D.] (designation and address), Defender

[Here set out briefly:

(a)    the issue in the proceedings which the Commission intends to address; and

(b)    a summary of the submission the Commission intends to make.]

Rule 14B.3(1)

### FORM 23C [3]

Invitation to the Scottish Commission for Human Rights to intervene

SHERIFF COURT, (place)..........Court ref. no...........

## INVITATION TO THE SCOTTISH COMMISSION FOR HUMAN RIGHTS TO INTERVENE

in the cause

[A.B.] (designation and address), Pursuer

against

[C.D.] (designation and address), Defender

[Here set out briefly:

(a)    the facts, procedural history and issues in the proceedings;

---

[1] As inserted by the Act of Sederunt (Sheriff Court Rules) (Miscellaneous Amendments) 2008 (SSI 2008/223) Sch.3 (effective July 1, 2008).

[2] As inserted by the Act of Sederunt (Sheriff Court Rules) (Miscellaneous Amendments) 2008 (SSI 2008/223) Sch.3 (effective July 1, 2008).

[3] As inserted by the Act of Sederunt (Sheriff Court Rules) (Miscellaneous Amendments) 2008 (SSI 2008/223) Sch.3 (effective July 1, 2008).

(b)   the issue in the proceedings on which the court seeks a submission.]
Rule 18.2(1)

## FORM 24 [1]

Order by the court and certificate in optional procedure for recovery of documents
Sheriff Court, (*place and address*)

In the cause (*court ref. no.*)
in which
AB (*design*) is the pursuer
and
CD (*design*) is the defender

To: (*name and designation of party or haver from whom the documents are sought to be recovered.*)

You are required to produce to the sheriff clerk at (*address*) within..........days of the service upon you of this order:

(1) This order itself (which must be produced intact);

(2) The certificate marked 'B' attached;

(3) All documents within your possession covered by the specification which is enclosed; and

(4) A list of those documents. You can produce the items listed above either:

(a) by delivering them to the sheriff clerk at the address shown above; or

(b) sending them to the sheriff clerk by registered or recorded delivery post.

(*date*)..........(*Signature, name, address and designation of person serving order*)

PLEASE NOTE:

If you claim confidentiality for any of the documents produced by you, you must still produce them. However, they may be placed in a separate envelope by themselves, marked "confidential". The court will, if necessary, decide whether the envelope should be opened or not.

Claims for necessary outlays within certain specified limits may be paid. Claims should be made in writing to the person who has obtained an order that you produce the documents.

## CERTIFICATE

B

Sheriff Court, (*place and address*)

In the cause (*court ref. no.*)
in which
AB (*design*) is the pursuer
and
CD (*design*) is the defender.
Order for recovery of documents dated..........

With reference to the above order and relative specification of documents, I certify:

*delete as appropriate*

*that the documents produced herewith and the list signed by me which accompanies them are all the documents in my possession which fall under the specification.

* I have no documents in my possession falling under the specification.

* I believe that there are other documents falling within the specification which are not in my possession. These documents are (*list the documents as described in*

---

[1] As substituted by Act of Sederunt (Ordinary Cause, Summary Application, Summary Cause and Small Claim Rules) Amendment (Miscellaneous) 2005 (SSI 2005/648) (effective January 2, 2006).

*the specification)* These documents were last seen by me on *(date)* in the possession of *(name and address of person/company, if known).*

\* I know of no documents falling within the specification which are in the possession of any other person.

*(name) (date)*

Rule 18.7(3)

### FORM 25

Form of minute in an application for letter of request

Sheriff Court, *(place and address)*

MINUTE

for *(designation)*

In the cause (court ref. no.)

in which

AB *(design)* is the pursuer

and

CD *(design)* is the defender.

The minuter states to the court that the evidence specified in the proposed letter of request lodged with this minute is required for the purpose of this cause. The minuter respectfully asks the court to issue a letter of request in terms of the proposed letter of request to *(central authority of the country or territory in which the evidence is to be obtained)* in order to obtain the evidence so specified.

*(designation of minuter)*

Rule 18.7(3)

### FORM 25A

Form of letter of request

PART A—items to be included in every letter of request

1. Sender *(Identity and address)*..........
   ...............

2. Central authority of the requested state *(Identity and address)*..........
   ...............

3. Persons to whom the executed request *(Identity and address)*..........
   is to be returned

   ...............

4. The undersigned applicant has the honour to submit the following request:

5. a. Requesting Judicial authority *(Identity and address)*..........
   ...............

   b. To the competent authority *(the requested state)*..........
   ...............

6. Names and addresses of the parties and their representatives
   a. pursuer ...............
   b. defender ...............
   c. other parties ...............

7. Nature and purpose of the proceedings ...............
   and summary of the facts

   ...............

8. Evidence to be obtained or other judi- ...............
cial act to be performed

...............

PART B—items to be completed where applicable

9. Identity and address of any person to be ...............
examined

...............

10. Questions to be put to the person to be *(or, see attached list)*..........
examined, or statement of the subject
matter about which they are to be examined

...............

...............

...............

11. Documents or other property to be in- *(specify whether to be produced,*
spected *copied,*
*valued etc.)*...............

12. Any requirement that the evidence be *(in the event that the evidence can-*
given on oath or affirmation and any *not be taken in the manner re-*
special form to be used *quested, specify whether it is to be*
*taken in such manner as provided*
*by local law for the formal taking*
*of evidence)*

13. Special methods or procedure to be fol- ...............
lowed

...............

14. Request for notification of the time and ...............
place for the execution of the request
and identity and address of any person
to be notified

...............

...............

...............

15. Request for attendance or participation ...............
of judicial personnel of the requesting
authority at the execution of the letter
of request

...............

...............

...............

16. Specification of privilege or duty to ...............
refuse to give evidence under the law of
the state of origin

...............

...............

17. The fees and expenses incurred will be *(identity and address)*..........
borne by

PART C—to be included in every letter of request

18.  Date of request, signature and seal of ...............
     the requesting authority

     ...............

**Rule 18.7A(2)**

FORM 25B [1]

Form of minute in application for taking of evidence in the European Community
Sheriff Court, (*place and address*)

MINUTE

for (*designation*)

In the cause (court ref. no.)

in which

AB (*design*) is the pursuer

and

CD (*design*) is the defender.

The minuter states to the court that the evidence specified in the proposed Form A
[or Form I] lodged with this minute is required for the purpose of this cause. The
minuter respectfully asks the court to issue that Form to (*specify the applicable
court, tribunal, central body or competent authority*) in order to obtain the evidence
specified.

Signed (*designation of minuter*)

**Rule 18.8(1)**

FORM 26 [2]

Form of citation of witness or haver

(*date*)

CITATION

SHERIFFDOM OF (*insert name of sheriffdom*)

AT (*insert place of sheriff court*)

TO [*A.B.*] (design)

(*Name*) who is pursuing/defending a case against (*name*) [*or is a (specify) in the
case of (name) against (name)]* has asked you to be a witness. You must attend the
above sheriff court on (*insert date*) at (*insert time*) for that purpose, [*and bring with
you (specify documents)].*

If you

• would like to know more about being a witness

• are a child under the age of 16

• think you may be a vulnerable witness within the meaning of section 11(1) of
the Vulnerable Witnesses (Scotland) Act 2004 (that is someone the court considers
may be less able to give their evidence due to mental disorder or fear or distress
connected to giving your evidence at the court hearing).

you should contact (*specify the solicitor acting for the party or the party litigant
citing the witness*) for further information.

---

[1] As inserted by the Act of Sederunt (Taking of Evidence in the European Community) 2003 (SI 2003/
601).
[2] As substituted by the Act of Sederunt (Ordinary Cause, Summary Application, Summary Cause and
Small Claim Rules) Amendment (Vulnerable Witnesses (Scotland) Act 2004) 2007 (SSI 2007/463)
(effective November 1, 2007).

If you are a vulnerable witness (including a child under the age of 16) then you should be able to use a special measure (such measures include use of a screen, a live TV link or a supporter, or a commissioner) to help you give evidence.

**Expenses**

You may claim back money which you have had to spend and any earnings you have lost within certain specified limits, because you have to come to court on the above date. These may be paid to you if you claim within specified time limits. Claims should be made to the person who has asked you to attend court. Proof of any loss of earnings should be given to that person.

If you wish your travelling expenses to be paid before you go to court, you should apply for payment to the person who has asked you to attend court.

**Failure to attend**

**It is very important that you attend court and you should note that failure to do so may result in a warrant being granted for your arrest. In addition, if you fail to attend without any good reason, having requested and been paid your travelling expenses, you may be ordered to pay a penalty not exceeding £250.**

If you have any questions about anything in this citation, please contact (*specify the solicitor acting for the party or the party litigant citing the witness*) for further information.

Signed

[P.Q.] Sheriff Officer

or [X.Y.], (*add designation and business address*)

Solicitor for the pursuer *[or defender] [or (specify)]*

Rule 18.8(1)

FORM 26A

Form of certificate of witness citation

I certify that on (*date*) I duly cited AB (*design*) to attend at (*name of court*) on (*date*) at (*time*) as a witness for the (*design party*) in the action at the instance of CD (*design*) against EF (*design*) (and I required him to bring with him ....). This I did by ....

(*Signature of solicitor or sheriff officer*)

**Rule 18A.2**

FORM 26B [1] [2]

Form of child witness notice

VULNERABLE WITNESSES (SCOTLAND) ACT 2004 SECTION 12

*Received the..........day of..........20*

(*Date of receipt of this notice*)

...............(*signed*)

Sheriff Clerk

CHILD WITNESS NOTICE

Sheriff Court...............20

Court Ref. No.

1. The applicant is the pursuer [or defender] in the action by [A.B.] (*design*) against [C.D.] (*design*).

2. The applicant has cited *[or intends to cite]* [E.F.] (*date of birth*) as a witness.

---

[1] As inserted by the Act of Sederunt (Ordinary Cause, Summary Application, Summary Cause and Small Claim Rules) Amendment (Vulnerable Witnesses (Scotland) Act 2004) 2007 (SSI 2007/463) (effective November 1, 2007).

[2] As amended by the Act of Sederunt (Rules of the Court of Session 1994 and Sheriff Court Rules Amendment) (No.3) (Miscellaneous) 2015 (SSI 2015/283) r.5(2) (effective 1 September 2015).

3. [E.F.] is a child witnesses under section 11 of the Vulnerable Witnesses (Scotland) Act 2004 [and was under the age of eighteen on the date of the commencement of proceedings].

4. The applicant considers that the following special measure[s] is [are] the most appropriate for the purpose of taking the evidence of [E.F.] *[or that [E.F.] should give evidence without the benefit of any special measure]*:—

(*delete as appropriate and specify any special measure(s) sought*).

5. [(a) The reason] [s] this [these] special measure[s] is [are] considered the most appropriate is [are] as follows:—

(*here specify the reason(s) for the special measure(s) sought*).

OR

[(b) The reason] [s] it is considered that [E.F.] should give evidence without the benefit of any special measure is [are]:—

(*here explain why it is felt that no special measures are required*).

6. [E.F.] and the parent[s] of *[or person[s] with parental responsibility for]* [E.F.] has [have] expressed the following view[s] on the special measure[s] that is [are] considered most appropriate *[or the appropriateness of [E.F.] giving evidence without the benefit of any special measure]*:—

(*delete as appropriate and set out the views(s) expressed and how they were obtained*)

7. Other information considered relevant to this application is as follows:—

(*here set out any other information relevant to the child witness notice*).

8. The applicant asks the court to —

(a) consider this child witness notice;

(b) make an order authorising the special measure[s] sought;

*or*

(c) make an order authorising the giving of evidence by [E.F.] without the benefit of special measures.

(*delete as appropriate*)

(*Signed*)

[A.B. *or* C.D.]

[or Representative of A.B. *[or C.D.]]* (*include full designation*)

*NOTE: This form should he suitably adapted where* section 16 of the Act of 2004 *applies.*

FORM 26C[1]

Form of vulnerable witness application

Rule 18A.3

VULNERABLE WITNESSES (SCOTLAND) ACT 2004 Section 12

Received the..........day of..........20..........

(*Date of receipt of this notice*)

..........(*signed*)

Sheriff Clerk

VULNERABLE WITNESS APPLICATION

Sheriff Court................ ..........20..........

Court Ref. No.

1. The applicant is the pursuer *[or defender]* in the action by [A.B] (*design*) against [C.D.] (*design*).

2. The applicant has cited *[or intends to cite]* [E.F.] (*date of birth*) as a witness.

---

[1] As inserted by the Act of Sederunt (Ordinary Cause, Summary Application, Summary Cause and Small Claim Rules) Amendment (Vulnerable Witnesses (Scotland) Act 2004) 2007 (SSI 2007/463) (effective November 1, 2007).

3. The applicant considers that [E.F.] is a vulnerable witness under section 11(1)(b) of the Vulnerable Witnesses (Scotland) Act 2004 for the following reasons:—

(*here specify reasons witness is considered to be a vulnerable witness*).

4. The applicant considers that the following special measure[s] is [are] the most appropriate for the purpose of taking the evidence of [E.F.]:—

(*specify any special measure(s) sought*).

5. The reason[s] this [these] special measure[s] is [are] considered the most appropriate is [are] as follows:—

(*here specify the reason(s) for the special measures(s) sought*).

6. [E.F.] has expressed the following view[s] on the special measure[s] that is [are] considered most appropriate:—

(*set out the views expressed and how they were obtained*).

7. Other information considered relevant to this application is as follows:—

(*here set out any other information relevant to the vulnerable witness application*).

8. The applicant asks the court to—

(a)  consider this vulnerable witness application;

(b)  make an order authorising the special measure[s] sought.

(*Signed*)
[A.B. or CD]
*[or Representative of A.B. [or C.D.]] (include full designation)*
*NOTE: This form should be suitably adapted where section 16 of the Act of 2004 applies.*

FORM 26D[1]

Form of certificate of intimation

Rule 18A.4(2)

VULNERABLE WITNESSES (SCOTLAND) ACT 2004 Section 12
CERTIFICATE OF INTIMATION

Sheriff Court.................... 20

Court Ref. No.

I certify that intimation of the child witness notice *[or vulnerable witness application]* relating to (*insert name of witness*) was made to (*insert names of parties or solicitors for parties, as appropriate*) by (*insert method of intimation; where intimation is by facsimile transmission, insert fax number to which intimation sent*) on (*insert dale of intimation*).

Date:..........

(*Signed*)
Solicitor/or Sheriff Officer
(*include full business designation*)

FORM 26E[2]

Form of application for review

Rule 18A.6(1)

VULNERABLE WITNESSES (SCOTLAND) ACT 2004 Section 13

Received the...........day of..........20..........

---

[1] As inserted by the Act of Sederunt (Ordinary Cause, Summary Application, Summary Cause and Small Claim Rules) Amendment (Vulnerable Witnesses (Scotland) Act 2004) 2007 (SSI 2007/463) (effective November 1, 2007).

[2] As inserted by the Act of Sederunt (Ordinary Cause, Summary Application, Summary Cause and Small Claim Rules) Amendment (Vulnerable Witnesses (Scotland) Act 2004) 2007 (SSI 2007/463) (effective November 1, 2007).

(*date of receipt of this notice*)

................(*signed*)

Sheriff Clerk

## APPLICATION FOR REVIEW OF ARRANGEMENTS FOR VULNERABLE WITNESS

Sheriff Court....................20.....

Court Ref. No.

1. The applicant is the pursuer *[or* defender] in the action by [A.B.] (*design*) against [C.D.] (*design*).
2. A proof *[or* hearing] is fixed for (*date*) at (*time*).
3. [E.F.] is a witness who is to give evidence at, or for the purposes of, the proof *[or* hearing]. [E.F.] is a child witness *[or* vulnerable witness] under section 11 of the Vulnerable Witnesses (Scotland) Act 2004.
4. The current arrangements for taking the evidence of [E.F.] are (*here specify current arrangements*).
5. The current arrangements should be reviewed as (*here specify reasons for review*).
6. [E.F.] [and the parent[s] of *[or* person[s] with parental responsibility for] [E.F.]] has [have] expressed the following view[s] on [the special measure[s] that is [are] considered most appropriate] *[or* the appropriateness of [E.F.] giving evidence without the benefit of any special measure]:–

(*delete as appropriate and set out the view(s) expressed and how they were obtained*).

7. The applicant seeks (here specify the order sought).

(*Signed*)

[A.B. or C.D.]

*[or* Representative of A.B. *[or* C.D.]] (*include full designation*)

*NOTE: This form should be suitably adapted where* section 16 of the Act of 2004 *applies.*

### FORM 26F[1]

Form of certificate of intimation

Rule 18A.7(2)

### VULNERABLE WITNESSES (SCOTLAND) ACT 2004 Section 13
### CERTIFICATE OF INTIMATION

Sheriff Court.........................20..........

Court Ref. No.

I certify that intimation of the review application relating to (*insert name of witness*) was made to (*insert names of parties or solicitors for parties, as appropriate*) by (*insert method of intimation; where intimation is by facsimile transmission, insert fax number to which intimation sent*) on (*insert date of intimation*).

Date:..........

(*Signed*)

Solicitor *[or* Sheriff Officer]

(*include full business designation*)

### FORM 27

Form of reference to the European Court

Rule 20.2(2)

### REQUEST

---

[1] As inserted by the Act of Sederunt (Ordinary Cause, Summary Application, Summary Cause and Small Claim Rules) Amendment (Vulnerable Witnesses (Scotland) Act 2004) 2007 (SSI 2007/463) (effective November 1, 2007).

for
PRELIMINARY RULING
of
THE COURT OF JUSTICE OF THE EUROPEAN COMMUNITIES
from
THE SHERIFFDOM OF (*insert name of sheriffdom*) at (*insert place of court*)
In the cause
AB (*insert designation and address*),

Pursuer

Against
CD (*insert designation and address*)

Defender

(*Here set out a clear and succinct statement of the case giving rise to the request for a ruling of the European Court in order to enable the European Court to consider and understand the issues of Community law raised and to enable governments of Member states and other interested parties to submit observations. The statement of the case should include*:

(a)  *particulars of the parties*;
(b)  *the history of the dispute between the parties*;
(c)  *the history of the proceedings*;
(d)  *the relevant facts as agreed by the parties or found by the court or, falling such agreement or finding, the contentions of the parties on such facts*;
(e)  *the nature of the issues of law and fact between the parties*;
(f)  *the Scots law, so far as relevant*;
(g)  *the Treaty provisions or other acts, instruments or rules of Community law concerned*;
(h)  *an explanation of why the reference is being made*).

The preliminary ruling of the Court of Justice of the European Communities is accordingly requested on the following questions:

1,2,etc. (*Here set out the question(s) on which the ruling is sought, identifying the Treaty provisions or other acts, instruments or rules of Community law concerned.*)

Dated..........the..........day of..........20

FORM 28
Form of extract decree–basic
Rule 23.6(3)

Sheriff Court                                                    Court ref. no.
Date of decree                                                  *in absence
Pursuer(s)                                                      Defender(s)
The sheriff

and granted decree against..........the for payment of expenses of £..........against the (name of party).

This extract is warrant for all lawful execution thereon.

Date                                      Sheriff clerk depute

*delete as appropriate*

FORM 28A
Form of extract decree–payment
Rule 23.6(3)

Sheriff Court                                                    Court ref. no.

Date of decree                                    *in absence
Pursuer(s)                                        Defender(s)

The sheriff granted decree against the..........for payment to the..........the undernoted sums:
 (1)  Sum(s) decerned for: £
 (2)  Interest at per cent per year from (*date*) until payment.
 (3)  Expenses of £..........against the (*name of party*).
*A time to pay direction was made under section 1(1) of the Debtors (Scotland) Act 1987.
 *A time order was made under section 129(1) of the Consumer Credit Act 1974.
 *The amount is payable by instalments of £percommencing within
 *days/weeks/months of intimation of this extract decree.
 *The amount is payable by lump sum within*days/weeks/months of intimation of this extract decree.
 This extract is warrant for all lawful execution thereon.

Date                              Sheriff clerk depute

*delete as appropriate*

## FORM 28B [1]
Form of extract decree—recovery of possession of heritable property (no rent arrears)

Rule 23.6(3)

Sheriff Court                                     Court ref. no.
Date of decree                                    *in absence
Pursuer(s)                                        Defender(s)
The sheriff

 (1)  granted warrant for ejecting the defender (and others mentioned in the summons) from the premises at.........., such ejection being not sooner than (*date*) at 12 noon.
 (2)  granted decree against the defender for payment to the pursuer of the sum of £.......... of expenses.
This extract is warrant for all lawful execution thereon.

Date                              Sheriff clerk depute

Rule 23.6(3)

## FORM 28BA [2]
Form of extract decree—recovery of possession of heritable property in accordance with section 16(5A) of the Housing (Scotland) Act 2001 (non-payment of rent)

Sheriff Court                                     Court ref no.
Date of decree                                    * in absence
Pursuer(s)                                        Defender(s)
The sheriff—

---

[1] As amended by the Act of Sederunt (Sheriff Court Rules) (Miscellaneous Amendments) 2012 (SSI 2012/188) para.11 (effective August 1, 2012).
[2] As inserted by the Act of Sederunt (Sheriff Court Rules) (Miscellaneous Amendments) 2012 (SSI 2012/188) para.11 (effective August 1, 2012).

(1)  granted warrant for ejecting the defender (and others mentioned in the summons) from the premises at (*insert address of premises*) on (*insert date*) and specified a period of (*number*) (*days/weeks/months\**) from that date as the period for which the pursuer's right to eject shall have effect.

(2)  granted decree against the defender for payment to the pursuer of the undernoted sums:

(a)  Sum(s) decerned for: £(*insert sum*).

(b)  Interest at (*insert rate of interest*) per cent per year from (*insert date*) until payment.

(c)  Expenses of £(*insert amount*) against the (*insert name of party*).

\*A time to pay direction was made under section 1(1) of the Debtors (Scotland) Act 1987.

\*The amount is payable by instalments of £(*insert sum*) per (*insert period*) commencing within (*insert timescale*) \*days/weeks/months of intimation of this extract decree.

The amount is payable by lump sum within (*insert timescale*) \*days/weeks/months of intimation of this extract decree.

This extract is warrant for all lawful execution thereon.

Date                                    (Sheriff clerk depute)

\**delete as appropriate*

## FORM 28BB[1][2]

Rule 23.6(3)

Form of extract decree—recovery of possession of heritable property in other cases
(non-payment of rent)

| | |
|---|---|
| Sheriff Court | Court ref no. |
| Date of decree | \*in absence |
| Pursuer(s) | Defender(s) |

The sheriff—

(1)  granted warrant for ejecting the defender (and others mentioned in the summons) from the premises at (*insert address of premises*), such ejection being not sooner than (*insert date*) at 12 noon.

(2)  granted decree against the defender for payment to the pursuer of the undernoted sums:

(a)  Sum(s) decerned for: £(*insert sum*).

(b)  Interest at (*insert rate of interest*) per cent per year from (*insert date*) until payment.

(c)  Expenses of £(*insert amount*) against the (*insert name of party*).

\*A time to pay direction was made under section 1(1) of the Debtors (Scotland) Act 1987.

\*The amount is payable by instalments of £(*insert sum*) per (*insert period*) commencing within (*insert timescale*) \*days/weeks/months of intimation of this extract decree.

\* The amount is payable by lump sum within (*insert timescale*) \*days/weeks/months of intimation of this extract decree.

---

[1] As inserted by the Act of Sederunt (Sheriff Court Rules) (Miscellaneous Amendments) 2013 (SSI 2013/135) para.3 (effective May 27, 2013).

[2] As amended by the Act of Sederunt (Sheriff Court Rules) (Miscellaneous Amendments) (No.3) 2013 (SSI 2013/171) para.5 (effective June 25, 2013).

This extract is warrant for all lawful execution thereon.

Date                                    *(Sheriff clerk depute)*

*delete as appropriate*

## FORM 28C

Form of extract decree and warrant to sell in sequestration for rent and sale

Rule 23.6(3)

*[Repealed by the Act of Sederunt (Sheriff Court Rules Amendment) (Diligence) 2008 (SSI 2008/121) r.2(1)(b) (effective April 1, 2008).]*

## FORM 28D

Form of extract—warrant for ejection and to re-let in sequestration for rent and sale

Rule 23.6(3)

*[Repealed by the Act of Sederunt (Sheriff Court Rules Amendment) (Diligence) 2008 (SSI 2008/121) r.2(1)(b) (effective April 1, 2008).]*

## FORM 28E

Form of extract decree—forthcoming

Rule 23.6(3)

Sheriff Court                                    Court ref. no.

Date of decree                                    *in absence

Date of original decree

Pursuer(s)

Defender(s)/Arrestee(s)

Common debtor

The sheriff granted decree
(1)    against the arrestee(s) for payment of £, or such other sum(s) as may be owing by the arrestee(s) to the common debtor(s) by virtue of the original decree mentioned above in favour of the pursuer(s) against the common debtor(s).
(2)    for expenses of £
*payable out of the arrested fund.
    *payable by the common debtor.
    *delete as appropriate*
This extract is warrant for all lawful execution thereon.

Date                                    Sheriff clerk depute

## FORM 28F

Form of extract decree—delivery

Rule 23.6(3)

Sheriff Court                                    Court ref. no.

Date of decree                                    *in absence

Pursuer(s)

Defender(s)

The sheriff granted decree against the defender
(1)    for delivery to the pursuer of (*specify articles*)
(2)    for expenses of £
*Further, the sheriff granted warrant to officers of court to (1) open shut and lockfast places occupied by the defender and (2) search for and take possession of said goods in the possession of the defender.
    *delete as appropriate*
This extract is warrant for all lawful execution thereon.

Date                                        Sheriff clerk depute

### FORM 28G
Form of extract decree—delivery—payment failing delivery
Rule 23.6(3)

Sheriff Court                                        Court ref. no.
Date of decree                                       *in absence
Pursuer(s)
Defender(s)

The sheriff, in respect that the defender has failed to make delivery in accordance with the decree granted in this court on (*date*), granted decree for payment against the defender of the undernoted sums:

(1)  Sum(s) decerned for: £.........., being the alternative crave claimed.
(2)  Interest at..........per cent per year from (*date*) until payment.
(3)  Expenses of £..........against the (*name of party*).

*A time to pay direction was made under section 1(1) of the Debtors (Scotland) Act 1987.

*A time order was made under section 129(1) of the Consumer Credit Act 1974.

*The amount is payable by instalments of £..........per...........commencing within..........*days/weeks/months..........of intimation of this extract decree.

*The amount is payable by lump sum within..........*days/weeks/months of intimation of this extract decree.

*delete as appropriate

This extract is warrant for all lawful execution thereon.

Date                                        Sheriff clerk depute

### FORM 28H
Form of extract decree—aliment
Rule 23.6(3)

Sheriff Court                                        Court ref. no.
Date of decree                                       *in absence
Pursuer(s)
Defender(s)
The sheriff

Granted decree against the defender for payment to the pursuer of aliment at the rate of £.......... per *week/month.

*delete as appropriate

This extract is warrant for all lawful execution thereon.

Date                                        Sheriff clerk depute

### FORM 28I
Form of extract decree—ad factum praestandum
Rule 23.6(3)

Sheriff Court                                        Court ref. no.
Date of decree                                       *in absence
Pursuer(s)
Defender(s)

The sheriff
  (1)   ordained the defender(s)
  (2)   granted decree for payment of expenses of £against the defender(s).
*delete as appropriate
   This extract is warrant for all lawful execution thereon.

Date                                            Sheriff clerk depute

## FORM 28J
### Form of extract decree—absolvitor
   Rule 23.6(3)

Sheriff Court                             Court ref. no.
Date of decree                           *in absence
Pursuer(s)
Defender(s)

The sheriff
  (1)   absolved the defender(s)
  (2)   granted decree for payment of expenses of £.......... against the
*delete as appropriate
   This extract is warrant for all lawful execution thereon.

Date                                            Sheriff clerk depute

## FORM 28K
### Form of extract decree—dismissal
   Rule 23.6(3)

Sheriff Court                             Court ref. no.
Date of decree                           *in absence
Pursuer(s)
Defender(s)

The sheriff
  (1)   dismissed the action against the defender(s)
*(2)   granted decree for payment of expenses of £.......... against the
*(3)   found no expenses due to or by either party
*delete as appropriate
   This extract is warrant for all lawful execution thereon.

Date                                            Sheriff clerk depute

## FORM 29
### Form of certificate by sheriff clerk
#### Service of charge where address of defender is unknown
   Rule 23.8(4)
   I certify that the foregoing charge was displayed on the walls of court on (date)
and that it remained so displayed for a period of (period of charge) from that date.

(date)                                          Sheriff clerk depute

## FORM 30 [1]
### Minute for recall of decree
Rule 24.1(1)

Sheriff Court:                                              (place)
Court ref. no.:

AB (*pursuer*) against CD (*defender(s)*)

The *(*pursuer/defender/third party*) moves the court to recall the decree pronounced on (*date*) in this case * and in which execution of a charge/arrestment was effected on (*date*)

*Proposed defence/answer:

**delete as appropriate*

Rule 24.1(6)(a)

## FORM 30A [2]
### Minute for recall of decree—service copy

Sheriff Court:..........(*place*)

Court ref. no.:..........

AB (*pursuer*) against CD (*defender(s)*)

The *(*pursuer/defender/third party*) moves the court to recall the decree pronounced on (*date*) in this case * and in which execution of a charge/arrestment was effected on (*date*)

*Proposed defence/answer:

**delete as appropriate*

NOTE: You must return the summons to the sheriff clerk at the court mentioned at the top of this form by (*insert date 2 days before the date of the hearing.*)

Rule 25.1(1)

## FORM 31 [3]
### Form of application for stated case

SHERIFF COURT (*place*)

Court ref. no...........AB (pursuer) against CD (defender)

The pursuer/defender appeals the sheriff's interlocutor of (*date*) to the Sheriff Appeal Court and requests the sheriff to state a case.

The point(s) of law upon which the appeal is to proceed is/are: (*give brief statement*)

(*date*)

Rule 25.4(3)(a)

## FORM 32 [4]
### Application for leave to appeal against time to pay direction

SHERIFF COURT (*place*)

Court ref. no........... AB (pursuer) against CD (defender)

---

[1] As amended by the Act of Sederunt (Sheriff Court Rules) (Miscellaneous Amendments) 2011 (SSI 2011/193) r.16 (effective April 4, 2011).

[2] As amended by the Act of Sederunt (Sheriff Court Rules) (Miscellaneous Amendments) 2011 (SSI 2011/193) r.16 (effective April 4, 2011).

[3] As amended by the Act of Sederunt (Rules of the Court of Session, Sheriff Appeal Court Rules and Sheriff Court Rules Amendment) (Sheriff Appeal Court) 2015 (SSI 2015/419) r.11 (effective 1 January 2016; as to savings see SSI 2015/419 rule 20(6)(a)).

[4] As amended by the Act of Sederunt (Rules of the Court of Session, Sheriff Appeal Court Rules and Sheriff Court Rules Amendment) (Sheriff Appeal Court) 2015 (SSI 2015/419) r.11 (effective 1 January 2016; as to savings see SSI 2015/419 rule 20(6)(a)).

The pursuer/defender requests the sheriff to grant leave to appeal the decision made on (*date*) in respect of the defender's application for a time to pay direction to the Sheriff Appeal Court/Court of Session.

The point(s) of law upon which the appeal is to proceed is/are: (*give brief statement*)

(*date*)

Rule 25.4(4)

## FORM 33[1]
### Appeal against time to pay direction

SHERIFF COURT (*place*)

Court ref. no........... AB (pursuer) against CD (defender)

The pursuer/defender appeals the decision made on (*date*) in respect of the defender's application for a time to pay direction to the Sheriff Appeal Court/Court of Session.

(*date*)

Rule 25.7(1)

## FORM 34
### Application for certificate of suitability for appeal to the Court of Session

*[Repealed by the Act of Sederunt (Rules of the Court of Session, Sheriff Appeal Court Rules and Sheriff Court Rules Amendment) (Sheriff Appeal Court) 2015 (SSI 2015/419) r.11 (effective 1 January 2016; as to savings see SSI 2015/419 rule 20(6)(a)).]*

Rule 26.4(1)

## FORM 35
### Form of receipt for money paid to the sheriff clerk

In the sheriff court of (*name of sheriffdom*) at (*place of sheriff court*).

In the cause (*state names of parties or other appropriate description*)

AB (*designation*) has this day paid into court the sum of £........., being a payment made in terms of rule 26(4)(1) of the Summary Cause Rules 2002.

*Custody of this money has been accepted at the request of (*insert name of court making the request*)

**delete as appropriate*

(Date)                                                              Sheriff clerk depute

Rule 32.2(a)

## FORM 36
### Action for aliment
Form of notice of intimation to children and next of kin where address of defender is unknown

Court ref. no.

To: (*insert name and address as in warrant*)

You are hereby given notice that an action for aliment has been raised against (*name*), your (*insert relationship, e.g, father, brother or other relative as the case may be*). A copy of the summons is enclosed.

If you know of his/her present address, you are requested to inform the sheriff clerk at (*insert full address*) in writing immediately.

---

[1] As amended by the Act of Sederunt (Rules of the Court of Session, Sheriff Appeal Court Rules and Sheriff Court Rules Amendment) (Sheriff Appeal Court) 2015 (SSI 2015/419) r.11 (effective 1 January 2016; as to savings see SSI 2015/419 rule 20(6)(a)).

If you wish to appear as a party in the action, or are uncertain about what action to take, you should contact a solicitor. You may, depending on your financial circumstances, be entitled to legal aid, and you can get information about legal aid from a solicitor.

You may also obtain advice from any Citizen's Advice Bureau, other advice agency or any sheriff clerk's office.

Rule 32.2(b)

## FORM 37
### Action for aliment
Form of notice of intimation to children, next of kin and guardian where defender suffers from mental disorder

Court ref. no.

To: (*insert name and address as in warrant*)

You are hereby given notice that an action for aliment has been raised against (*name*), your (*insert relationship, e.g. father or other relative, or ward, as the case may be*). A copy of the summons is enclosed.

If you wish to appear as a party in the action, or are uncertain about what action to take, you should contact a solicitor immediately. You may, depending on your financial circumstances, be entitled to legal aid, and you can get information about legal aid from a solicitor.

You may also obtain advice from any Citizen's Advice Bureau, other advice agency or any sheriff clerk's office.

### Appendix IA[1]

**SCHEDULE OF TIMETABLE UNDER PERSONAL INJURIES PROCEDURE**

| Steps referred to under rule 34.7(1)(c) | Period of time within which action must be carried out* |
|---|---|
| Application for a third party notice under rule 11.1 (rule 34.7(2)(a)) | Not later than 28 days after the form of response has been lodged |
| Pursuer serving a commission for recovery of documents under rule 34.5 (rule 34.7(2)(b)) | Not later than 28 days after the form of response has been lodged |
| Parties adjusting their respective statements (rule 34.7(2)(c)) | Not later than 8 weeks after the form of response has been lodged |
| Pursuer lodging a statement of valuation of claim (rule 34.7(2)(d)) | Not later than 8 weeks after the form of response has been lodged |
| Pursuer lodging a certified adjusted statement of claim (rule 34.7(2)(e)) | Not later than 10 weeks after the form of response has been lodged |
| Defender (and any third party to the action) lodging a certified adjusted response to statement of claim (rule 34.7(2)(f)) | Not later than 10 weeks after the form of response has been lodged |
| Defender (and any third party to the action) lodging a statement of valuation of claim (rule 34.7(2)(g)) | Not later than 12 weeks after the form of response has been lodged |
| Parties lodging a list of witnesses together with any productions on which they wish to rely (rule 34.7(2)(h)) | Not later than 8 weeks before the date assigned for the proof |
| Pursuer lodging the minute of the pre- | Not later than 21 days before the date assigned for the proof |

---

[1] As inserted by the Act of Sederunt (Summary Cause Rules Amendment) (Personal Injuries Actions) 2012 (SSI 2012/144) para.2 (effective September 1, 2012; not applicable to an action raised before September 1, 2012).

| Steps referred to under rule 34.7(1)(c) | Period of time within which action must be carried out* |
|---|---|
| proof conference (rule 34.7(2)(i)) | |

*NOTE: Where there is more than one defender in an action, references in the above table to the form of response having been lodged should be read as references to the first lodging of a form of response.

## Appendix 2

## GLOSSARY

*Absolve*

To find in favour of and exonerate the defender.

*Absolvitor*

An order of the court granted in favour of and exonerating the defender which means that the pursuer is not allowed to bring the same matter to court again.

*Action of count, reckoning and payment*

A legal procedure for requiring someone to account for their dealings with assets under their stewardship. For example, a trustee might be subject to such an action.

*Action of furthcoming*

A final stage of diligence or enforcement. It results in whatever has been subject to arrestment being made over to the person who is suing. For example, where a bank account has been arrested this results in the appropriate amount being transferred to the pursuer.

*Appellant*

A person making an appeal against the sheriff's decision. This might be the pursuer or the defender.

*Arrestee*

A person subject to an arrestment.

*Arrestment on the dependence*

A court order to freeze the goods or bank account of the defender until the court has heard the case.

*Arrestment to found jurisdiction*

A court order to used against a person who has goods or other assets in Scotland to give the court jurisdiction to hear a case. This is achieved by preventing anything being done with the goods or assets until the case has been disposed of.

*Authorised lay representative*

A person other than a lawyer who represents a party to a summary cause.

*Calling date*

The date on which the case will first be heard in court.

*Cause*

Another word for case or claim.

*Caution (pronounced kay-shun)*

A security, usually a sum of money, given to ensure that some obligation will be carried out.

*Certificate of execution of service*

The document recording that an application to, or order or decree of, the court for service of documents has been effected.

*Charge*

An order to obey a decree of a court. A common type is one served on the defender by a sheriff officer on behalf of the pursuer who has won a case demanding payment of a sum of money.

*Claim*

The part of the summons which sets out the legal remedy which the pursuer is seeking.

*Commission and diligence*

Authorisation by the court for someone to take the evidence of a witness who cannot attend court or to obtain the production of documentary evidence. It is combined with a diligence authorising the person appointed to require the attendance of the witness and the disclosure of documents.

*Consignation*

The deposit in court, or with a third party, of money or an article in dispute.

*Continuation*

An order made by the sheriff postponing the completion of a hearing until a later date or dates.

*Contribution, Right of*

The right of one person who is legally liable to pay money to someone to claim a proportionate share from others who are also liable.

*Counterclaim*

A claim made by a defender in response to the pursuer's case and which is not necessarily a defence to that case. It is a separate but related case against the pursuer which is dealt with at the same time as the pursuer's case.

*Damages*

Money compensation payable for a breach of contract or some other legal duty.

*Declarator of irritancy of a lease*

A decision of a court finding that a tenant has failed to observe a term of a lease which may lead to the termination of the lease.

*Decree*

An order of the court containing the decision of the case in favour of one of the parties and granting the remedy sought or disposing of the case.

*Decree of ejection*

A decree ordering someone to leave land or property which they are occupying. For example, it is used to remove tenants in arrears with their rent.

*Decree of removing*

A court order entitling someone to recover possession of heritable property and ordering a person to leave land which he is occupying. For example, it is used to remove tenants in arrears with their rent.

*Defender*

Person against whom a summary cause is started.

*Deliverance*

A decision or order of a court.

*Diet*

Date for a court hearing.

*Diligence*

The collective term for the procedures used to enforce a decree of a court. These include arrestment of wages, goods or a bank account.

*Dismissal*

An order bringing to an end the proceedings in a summary cause. It is usually possible for a new summary cause to be brought if not time barred.

*Domicile*

The place where a person is normally resident or where, in the case of a company, it has its place of business or registered office.

*Execution of service*

See *Certificate of execution of service.*

*Execution of a charge*

The intimation of the requirement to obey a decree or order of a court.

*Execution of an arrestment*

The carrying out of an order of arrestment.

*Expenses*

The costs of a court case.

*Extract decree*

The document containing the order of the court made at the end of the summary cause. For example, it can be used to enforce payment of a sum awarded.

*Fund in medio*

See *Multiplepoinding.*

*Haver*

A person who holds documents which are required as evidence in a case.

*Heritable property*

Land and buildings as opposed to moveable property.

*Huissier*

An official in France and some other European countries who serves court documents.

*Incidental application*

An application that can be made during the course of a summary cause for certain orders. Examples are applications for the recovery of documents or to amend the statement of claim.

*Interlocutor*

The official record of the order or judgment of a court.

*Interrogatories*

Written questions put to someone in the course of a court case and which must be answered on oath.

*Intimation*

Giving notice to another party of some step in a summary cause.

*Jurisdiction*

The authority of a court to hear particular cases.

*Ish*

The date on which a lease terminates.

*Letter of request*

A document issued by the sheriff court requesting a foreign court to take evidence from a specified person within its jurisdiction or to serve Scottish court documents on that person.

*Messenger at arms*

Officers of court who serve documents issued by the Court of Session.

*Minute*

A document produced in the course of a case in which a party makes an application or sets out his position on some matter.

*Minute for recall*

A form lodged with the court by one party asking the court to recall a decree.

*Multiplepoinding* (pronounced "multiple pinding")

A special type of summary cause in which the holder of property, etc. (referred to as the fund *in medio*) requires claimants upon it to appear and settle claims in court. For example, where the police come into possession of a stolen car of which two or more people claim to be owner this procedure could be used.

*Options Hearing*

A preliminary stage in an ordinary cause action.

*Ordinary cause*

Another legal procedure for higher value cases available in the sheriff court.

*Party litigant*

A person who conducts his own case.

*Process*

The court file containing the collection of documents relating to a case.

*Productions*

Documents or articles which are used in evidence.

*Pursuer*

The person who starts a summary cause.

*Recall of an arrestment*

A court order withdrawing an arrestment.

*Restriction of an arrestment*

An order releasing part of the money or property arrested.

*Recall of a decree*

An order revoking a decree which has been granted.

*Recovery of documents*

The process of obtaining documentary evidence which is not in the possession of the person seeking it (e.g. hospital records necessary to establish the extent of injuries received in a road accident).

*Remit between procedures*

A decision of the sheriff to transfer the summary cause to another court procedure e.g. small claim or ordinary cause procedure.

*Respondent*

When a decision of the sheriff is appealed against, the person making the appeal is called the appellant. The other side in the appeal is called the respondent.

*Return day*

The date by which the defender must send a written reply to the court and, where appropriate, the pursuer must return the summons to court.

*Schedule of arrestment*

The list of items which may be arrested.

*Serve / service*

Sending a copy of the summons or other court document to the defender or another party.

*Sheriff clerk*

The court official responsible for the administration of the sheriff court.

*Sheriff officer*

A person who serves court documents and enforces court orders.

*Sist of action*

The temporary suspension of a court case by court order.

*Sist as a party*

To add another person as a litigant in a case.

*Small claim*

Another legal procedure in the sheriff court for claims having a lower value than summary cause.

*Specification of documents*

A list lodged in court of documents for the recovery of which a party seeks a court order.

*Stated case[1]*

An appeal procedure where the sheriff sets out his findings and the reasons for his decision and states the issues on which the decision of the Sheriff Appeal Court is requested.

*Statement of claim*

The part of the summons in which pursuers set out details of their cases against defenders.

*Summons*

The form which must be filled in to begin a summary cause.

*Time to pay direction*

A court order for which a defender who is an individual may apply permitting a sum owed to be paid by instalments or by a single payment at a later date.

*Time order*

A court order which assists debtors who have defaulted on an agreement regulated by the Consumer Credit Act 1974 (c.39) and which may be applied for during a court action.

*Warrant for diligence*

Authority to carry out one of the diligence procedures.

*Writ*

A legally significant writing.

# SCHEDULE 2

## REVOCATIONS

**Paragraph 4**

| (1)<br>**Act of Sederunt** | (2)<br>**Refer-<br>ence** | (3)<br>**Extent of revoca-<br>tion** |
|---|---|---|
| Act of Sederunt (Summary Cause Rules, Sheriff Court) 1976 | S.I. 1976/ 476 | The whole Act of Sederunt |
| Act of Sederunt (Summary Cause Rules, Sheriff Court) (Amendment) 1978 | S.I. 1978/ 112 | The whole Act of Sederunt |
| Act of Sederunt (Summary Cause Rules, Sheriff court) (Amendment no. 2) 1978 | S.I. 1978/ 1805 | The whole Act of Sederunt |
| Act of Sederunt (Summary Cause Rules, Sheriff Court) (Amendment) 1980 | S.I. 1980/ 455 | The whole Act of Sederunt |
| Act of Sederunt (Ordinary Cause Rules, Sheriff Court) 1983 | S.I. 983/ 747 | Paragraph 4 |
| Act of Sederunt (Civil Jurisdiction of the Sheriff Court) 1986 | S.I. 1986/ 1946 | Paragraph 3 |

---

[1] As amended by the Act of Sederunt (Rules of the Court of Session, Sheriff Appeal Court Rules and Sheriff Court Rules Amendment) (Sheriff Appeal Court) 2015 (SSI 2015/419) r.11 (effective 1 January 2016; as to savings see SSI 2015/419 rule 20(6)(a)).

| (1)<br>Act of Sederunt | (2)<br>Refer-<br>ence | (3)<br>Extent of revoca-<br>tion |
|---|---|---|
| Act of Sederunt (Miscellaneous Amendments) 1986 | S.I. 1986/1966 | Paragraph 3 |
| Act of Sederunt (Small Claim Rules) 1988 | S.I. 1988/1976 | Paragraph 3 |
| Act of Sederunt (Amendment of Sheriff Court Ordinary Cause, and Summary Cause, Rules) 1988 | S.I. 1988/1978 | Paragraphs 19 to 35 and Schedule 2 |
| Act of Sederunt (Amendment of Ordinary Cause and Summary Cause Rules) (Written Statements) 1989 | S.I. 1989/436 | Paragraph 3 |
| Act of Sederunt (Amendment of Sheriff Court Ordinary Cause, Summary Cause and Small Claim, Rules) 1990 | S.I. 1990/661 | Paragraph 3 |
| Act of Sederunt (Amendment of Sheriff Court Ordinary Cause, Summary Cause and Small Claim, Rules) (No. 2) 1990 | S.I. 1990/2105 | Paragraph 3 |
| Act of Sederunt (Amendment of Summary Cause and Small Claim Rules) 1991 | S.I. 1991/821 | The whole Act of Sederunt |
| Act of Sederunt (Amendment of Ordinary Cause, Summary Cause and Small Claim Rules) 1992 | S.I. 1992/249 | Paragraph 3 |
| Act of Sederunt (Child Support Act 1991) (Amendment of Ordinary Cause and Summary Cause Rules) 1993 | S.I. 1993/919 | Paragraph 4 |
| Act of Sederunt (Sheriff Court Ordinary Cause Rules) 1993 | S.I. 1993/1956 | Paragraph 3 |

# ACT OF SEDERUNT (SMALL CLAIM RULES) 2002

## (SSI 2002/133)

*10 June 2002.*

The Lords of Council and Session, under and by virtue of the powers conferred by section 32 of the Sheriff Courts (Scotland) Act 1971 and of all other powers enabling them in that behalf, having approved draft rules submitted to them by the Sheriff Court Rules Council in accordance with section 34 of the said Act of 1971, do hereby enact and declare:

### Citation and commencement

**1.**—(1) This Act of Sederunt may be cited as the Act of Sederunt (Small Claim Rules) 2002 and shall come into force on 10th June 2002.

(2) This Act of Sederunt shall be inserted in the Books of Sederunt.

### Small Claim Rules

**2.** The provisions of Schedule 1 to this Act of Sederunt shall have effect for the purpose of providing rules for the form of summary cause process known as a small claim.

### Transitional provision

**3.** Nothing in Schedule 1 to this Act of Sederunt shall apply to a small claim commenced before 10th June 2002 and any such claim shall proceed according to the law and practice in force immediately before that date.

### Revocation

**4.** The Acts of Sederunt mentioned in column (1) of Schedule 2 to this Act of Sederunt are revoked to the extent specified in column (3) of that Schedule except in relation to any small claim commenced before 10th June 2002.

## SCHEDULE 1

### SMALL CLAIM RULES 2002

Arrangement of Rules

*Chapter 1*

*Citation, interpretation and application*

1.1.     Citation, interpretation and application

*Chapter 2*

*Representation*

2.1.     Representation
2.2.     Lay support

*Chapter 2A*

*Lay Representation*

2A.1     Application and interpretation

2A.2        Lay representation for party litigants

*Chapter 3*

*Relief from failure to comply with rules*

3.1.        Dispensing power of sheriff

*Chapter 4*

*Commencement of claim*

4.1.        Form of summons
4.2.        Statement of claim
4.2A.       Actions relating to regulated agreements
4.3.        Defender's copy summons
4.4.        Authentication and effect of summons
4.5.        Period of notice
4.6.        Intimation

*Chapter 5*

*Register of Small Claims*

5.1.        Register of Small Claims

*Chapter 6*

*Service and return of the summons*

6.1.        Persons carrying on business under trading or descriptive name
6.2.        Form of service
6.3.        Service of the summons
6.4.        Service within Scotland by sheriff officer
6.5.        Service on persons outwith Scotland
6.6.        Service where address of defender is unknown
6.7.        Endorsation by sheriff clerk of defender's residence not necessary
6.8.        Contents of envelope containing defender's copy summons
6.9.        Re-service
6.10.       Defender appearing barred from objecting to service
6.11.       Return of summons and execution

*Chapter 7*

*Arrestment*

7.1.        Service of schedule of arrestment
7.2.        Arrestment before service
7.3.        Recall and restriction of arrestment

*Chapter 8*

*Undefended claim*

8.1.        Undefended claim
8.2.        Application for time to pay direction or time order
8.3.        Decree in claims to which the Hague Convention or the Civil Jurisdiction and Judgments Act 1982 apply

*Chapter 9*

*Defended claim*

9.1.        The Hearing
9.2.        Purpose of the Hearing
9.3.        Conduct of hearings

9.4.      Inspection of places and objects
9.5.      Remit to determine matter of fact
9.6.      Noting of evidence
9.7.      Application for a time to pay direction or time order in defended claim
9.8.      Pronouncement of decision

*Chapter 10*
*Incidental applications and sists*

10.1.     General
10.2.     Application to sist claim

*Chapter 11*
*Counterclaim*

11.1.     Counterclaim

*Chapter 12*
*Alteration of summons etc.*

12.1.     Alteration of summons etc.

*Chapter 13*
*Additional defender*

13.1.     Additional defender

*Chapter 13A*
*Interventions by the Commission for Equality and Human Rights*

13A.1     Interpretation
13A.2     Interventions by the CEHR
13A.3     Applications to intervene
13A.4     Form of intervention

*Chapter 13B*
*Interventions by the Scottish Commission for Human Rights*

13B.1     Interpretation
13B.2     Applications to intervene
13B.3     Invitations to intervene
13B.4     Form of intervention

*Chapter 14*
*Applications for sist of party and transference*

14.1.     Applications for sist of party and transference

*Chapter 15*
*Transfer and remit of claims*

15.1.     Transfer to another court
15.2.     Remit between procedures

*Chapter 16*
*Productions and documents*

16.1.     Lodging of productions
16.2.     Borrowing of productions
16.3.     Documents lost or destroyed
16.4.     Documents and productions to be retained in custody of sheriff clerk

*Chapter 17*
*Recovery of documents and attendance of witnesses*

| 17.1. | Diligence for recovery of documents |
| 17.2. | Optional procedure before executing commission and diligence |
| 17.3. | Confidentiality of documents |
| 17.4. | Witnesses |
| 17.5. | Citation of witnesses by party litigants |
| 17.6. | Witnesses failing to attend |

### Chapter 17A
### *Vulnerable Witnesses (Scotland) Act 2004*

| 17A.1. | Interpretation |
| 17A.2. | Child witness notice |
| 17A.3. | Vulnerable witness application |
| 17A.4. | Intimation |
| 17A.5. | Procedure on lodging child witness notice or vulnerable witness application |
| 17A.6. | Review of arrangements for vulnerable witnesses |
| 17A.7. | Intimation of review application |
| 17A.8. | Procedure on lodging a review application |
| 17A.9. | Determination of special measures |
| 17A.10. | Intimation of an order under section 12(1) or (6) or 13(2) |
| 17A.11. | Taking of evidence by commissioner |
| 17A.12. | Commission on interrogatories |
| 17A.13. | Commission without interrogatories |
| 17A.14. | Lodging of video record and documents |
| 17A.15. | Custody of video record and documents |
| 17A.16. | Application for leave for party to be present at the commission |

### Chapter 18
### *European Court*

| 18.1. | Interpretation of rules 18.2 to 18.5 |
| 18.2. | Application for reference |
| 18.3. | Preparation of case for reference |
| 18.4. | Sist of claim |
| 18.5. | Transmission of reference |

### Chapter 19
### *Abandonment*

| 19.1. | Abandonment of claim |

### Chapter 20
### *Decree by default*

| 20.1. | Decree by default |

### Chapter 21
### *Decrees, extracts, execution and variation*

| 21.1. | Decree |
| 21.2. | Decree for alternative claim for payment |
| 21.3. | Taxes on funds under control of the court |
| 21.4. | Correction of interlocutor or note |
| 21.5. | Extract of decree |

21.6.    Expenses

21.7.    Charge

21.8.    Service of charge where address of defender is unknown

21.9.    Diligence on decree in claim for delivery

21.10.   Applications in same claim for variation etc. of decree

### Chapter 22
### Recall of decree

22.1.    Recall of decree

### Chapter 23 Appeals

23.1.    Appeals

23.2.    Effect of and abandonment of appeal

23.3.    Hearing of appeal

23.4.    Appeal in relation to a time to pay direction

23.5.    Sheriff to regulate interim possession

### Chapter 24
### Management of damages payable to persons under legal disability

24.1.    Orders for payment and management of money

24.2.    Methods of management

24.3.    Subsequent orders

24.4.    Management of money paid to sheriff clerk

24.5.    Management of money payable to children

### Chapter 25
### Electronic transmission of documents

25.1.    Extent of provision

25.2.    Time of lodgement

### Chapter 26
### The Equality Act 2010

26.1.    Interpretation and application

26.2.    Intimation to Commission

26.3.    Assessor

26.4.    Taxation of Commission expenses

26.5.    National security

26.6.    Transfer to Employment Tribunal

26.7.    Transfer from Employment Tribunal

### Chapter 27
### Live Links

27.1.

### Appendix 1
### FORMS

1     Small claim summons

1a    Small claim summons—defender's copy—claim for or including payment of money (where time to pay direction or time order may be applied for)

1b    Small claim summons—defender's copy—all other claims

2     Claim in a summons for payment of money

3     Claim in a summons for delivery

4     Claim in a summons for implement of an obligation

5     Form of service

6     Certificate of execution of service

7     Postal service—form of notice

8     Service on person who address is unknown—form of advertisement

9     Service on person whose address is unknown—form of notice to be displayed on the walls of court

10    Recall or restriction of arrestment—certificate authorising the release of arrested funds or property

11    Minute—no form of response lodged by defender

12    Minute—pursuer not objecting to application for a time to pay direction or time order

13    Minute—pursuer opposing an application for a time to pay direction or time order

14    Counterclaim—form of intimation by sheriff clerk where pursuer fails to appear

15    Order by the court and certificate in optional procedure for recovery of documents

16    Witness citation

16a   Certificate of execution of witness citation

17    Reference to the European Court

18    Extract decree—(basic)

18a   Extract decree—payment

18b   Extract—delivery

18c   Extract decree—delivery—payment failing delivery

18d   Extract decree—recovery of possession of moveable property

18e   Extract decree—recovery of possession of moveable property—payment failing recovery

18f   Extract decree—*ad factum praestandum*

18g   Extract decree—*ad factum praestandum*—payment upon failure to implement obligation

18h   Extract decree—absolvitor

18i   Extract decree—dismissal

19    Certificate by sheriff clerk—service of charge were address of defender is unknown

20    Minute for recall of decree

20a   Minute for recall of decree—service copy

21    Note of appeal to the sheriff principal

22    Application for leave to appeal against time to pay direction

23    Appeal against time to pay direction

24    Form of receipt for money paid to sheriff clerk

**Appendix 2**

**GLOSSARY**

# CHAPTER 1

## CITATION, INTERPRETATION AND APPLICATION

## Citation, interpretation and application

**1.1.**—[1](1)   These Rules may be cited as the Small Claim Rules 2002.

(2)   In these rules—

---

[1] As amended by the Act of Sederunt (Ordinary Cause, Summary Application, Summary Cause and Small Claim Rules) Amendment (Miscellaneous) 2007 (SSI 2007/6) r.5(a) (effective January 29, 2007).

"the 1971 Act" means the Sheriff Courts (Scotland) Act 1971;

"the 1975 Act" means the Litigants in Person (Costs and Expenses) Act 1975;

"the 2004 Act" means the Vulnerable Witnesses (Scotland) Act 2004;[1]

"authorised lay representative" means a person to whom section 32(1) of the Solicitors (Scotland) Act 1980 (offence to prepare writs) does not apply by virtue of section 32(2)(a) of that Act;

"enactment" includes an enactment comprised in, or in an instrument made under, an Act of the Scottish Parliament;

"small claim" has the meaning assigned to it by section 35(2) of the 1971 Act;

"summary cause" has the meaning assigned to it by section 35(1) of the 1971 Act.

(3)  Any reference in these Rules to a specified rule shall be construed as a reference to the rule bearing that number in these Rules, and a reference to a specified paragraph, sub-paragraph or head shall be construed as a reference to the paragraph, sub-paragraph or head so numbered or lettered in the provision in which that reference occurs.

(4)  A form referred to by number in these Rules means the form so numbered in Appendix 1 to these rules or a form substantially of the same effect with such variation as circumstances may require.

(4A)[2]  In these Rules, references to a solicitor include a reference to a member of a body which has made a successful application under section 25 of the Law Reform (Miscellaneous Provisions) (Scotland) Act 1990 but only to the extent that the member is exercising rights acquired by virtue of section 27 of that Act.

(5)  The glossary in Appendix 2 to these Rules is a guide to the meaning of certain legal expressions used in these Rules, but is not to be taken as giving those expressions any meaning which they do not have in law generally.

(6)  These Rules shall apply to a small claim.

## CHAPTER 2

### REPRESENTATION

## Representation

**2.1.**—[3](1)  A party may be represented by—

(a)  an advocate;

(b)  a solicitor;

(c)  a person authorised under any enactment to conduct proceedings in the sheriff court, in accordance with the terms of that enactment; and

(d)  subject to paragraph (3), an authorised lay representative.

(2)  The persons referred to in paragraph (1)(c) and (d) above may in representing a party do everything for the preparation and conduct of a small claim as may be done by an individual conducting his own claim.

(3)  If the sheriff finds that the authorised lay representative is—

---

[1] As inserted by the Act of Sederunt (Ordinary Cause, Summary Application, Summary Cause and Small Claim Rules) Amendment (Vulnerable Witnesses (Scotland) Act 2004) 2007 (SSI 2007/463) r.5(2) (effective November 1, 2007).

[2] As inserted by the Act of Sederunt (Sheriff Court Rules Amendment) (Sections 25 to 29 of the Law Reform (Miscellaneous Provisions) (Scotland) Act 1990) 2009 (SSI 2009/164) r.5(2) (effective May 20, 2009).

[3] As amended by the Act of Sederunt (Ordinary Cause, Summary Application, Summary Cause and Small Claim Rules) Amendment (Miscellaneous) 2007 (SSI 2007/6) r.5(b) (effective January 29, 2007).

    (a)   not a suitable person to represent the party; or

    (b)   not in fact authorised to do so,

that person must cease to represent the party.

## Lay support

**2.2**—[1](1)  At any time during proceedings the sheriff may, on the request of a party litigant, permit a named individual to assist the litigant in the conduct of the proceedings by sitting beside or behind (as the litigant chooses) the litigant at hearings in court or in chambers and doing such of the following for the litigant as he or she requires—

    (a)   providing moral support;

    (b)   helping to manage the court documents and other papers;

    (c)   taking notes of the proceedings;

    (d)   quietly advising on—

        (i)   points of law and procedure;

        (ii)   issues which the litigant might wish to raise with the sheriff;

        (iii)   questions which the litigant might wish to ask witnesses.

  (2)  It is a condition of such permission that the named individual does not receive from the litigant, whether directly or indirectly, any remuneration for his or her assistance.

  (3)  The sheriff may refuse a request under paragraph (1) only if—

    (a)   the sheriff is of the opinion that the named individual is an unsuitable person to act in that capacity (whether generally or in the proceedings concerned); or

    (b)   the sheriff is of the opinion that it would be contrary to the efficient administration of justice to grant it.

  (4)  Permission granted under paragraph (1) endures until the proceedings finish or it is withdrawn under paragraph (5); but it is not effective during any period when the litigant is represented.

  (5)  The sheriff may, of his or her own accord or on the incidental application of a party to the proceedings, withdraw permission granted under paragraph (1); but the sheriff must first be of the opinion that it would be contrary to the efficient administration of justice for the permission to continue.

  (6)  Where permission has been granted under paragraph (1), the litigant may—

    (a)   show the named individual any document (including a court document); or

    (b)   impart to the named individual any information,

which is in his or her possession in connection with the proceedings without being taken to contravene any prohibition or restriction on the disclosure of the document or the information; but the named individual is then to be taken to be subject to any such prohibition or restriction as if he or she were the litigant.

  (7)  Any expenses incurred by the litigant as a result of the support of an individual under paragraph (1) are not recoverable expenses in the proceedings.

---

[1] As inserted by the Act of Sederunt (Sheriff Court Rules) (Miscellaneous Amendments) (No.2) 2010 (SSI 2010/416) r.5 (effective January 1, 2011).

## Chapter 2A[1]

### Lay Representation

**Application and interpretation**

**2A.1.**—(1)  This Chapter is without prejudice to any enactment (including any other provision in these Rules) under which provision is, or may be, made for a party to a particular type of case before the sheriff to be represented by a lay representative.

(2)  In this Chapter, a "lay representative" means a person who is not—

(a)  a solicitor;

(b)  an advocate, or

(c)  someone having a right to conduct litigation, or a right of audience, by virtue of section 27 of the Law Reform (Miscellaneous Provisions) (Scotland) Act 1990.

**Lay representation for party litigants**

**2A.2.**—(1)  In any proceedings in respect of which no provision as mentioned in rule 2A.1(1) is in force, the sheriff may, on the request of a party litigant, permit a named individual (a "lay representative") to appear, along with the litigant, at a specified hearing for the purpose of making oral submissions on behalf of the litigant at that hearing.

(2)  An application under paragraph (1)—

(a)  is to be made orally on the date of the first hearing at which the litigant wishes a named individual to make oral submissions; and

(b)  is to be accompanied by a document, signed by the named individual, in Form A1.

(3)  The sheriff may grant an application under paragraph (1) only if the sheriff is of the opinion that it would assist his or her consideration of the case to grant it.

(4)  It is a condition of permission granted by the sheriff that the lay representative does not receive directly or indirectly from the litigant any remuneration or other reward for his or her assistance.

(5)  The sheriff may grant permission under paragraph (1) in respect of one or more specified hearings in the case; but such permission is not effective during any period when the litigant is legally represented.

(6)  The sheriff may, of his or her own accord or on the motion of a party to the proceedings, withdraw permission granted under paragraph (1).

(7)  Where permission has been granted under paragraph (1), the litigant may—

(a)  show the lay representative any document (including a court document); or

(b)  impart to the lay representative any information, which is in his or her possession in connection with the proceedings without being taken to contravene any prohibition or restriction on the disclosure of the document or the information; but the lay representative is then to be taken to be subject to any such prohibition or restriction as if he or she were the litigant.

---

[1] As inserted by the Act of Sederunt (Sheriff Court Rules) (Lay Representation) 2013 (SSI 2013/91) r.5 (effective April 4, 2013).

(8)   Any expenses incurred by the litigant in connection with lay representation under this rule are not recoverable expenses in the proceedings.

## CHAPTER 3

### RELIEF FROM FAILURE TO COMPLY WITH RULES

**Dispensing power of sheriff**

**3.1.**—(1)   The sheriff may relieve any party from the consequences of any failure to comply with the provisions of these Rules which is shown to be due to mistake, oversight or other excusable cause, on such conditions as he thinks fit.

(2)   Where the sheriff relieves a party from the consequences of the failure to comply with a provision in these Rules under paragraph (1), he may make such order as he thinks fit to enable the claim to proceed as if the failure to comply with the provision had not occurred.

## CHAPTER 4

### COMMENCEMENT OF CLAIM

**Form of summons**

**4.1.**—(1)   A small claim shall be commenced by summons, which shall be in Form 1.

(2)   The claim in a small claim summons may be in one of Forms 2 to 4.

**Statement of claim**

**4.2.**   The pursuer must insert a statement of his claim in the summons to give the defender fair notice of the claim; and the statement must include—

(a)   details of the basis of the claim including relevant dates; and

(b)   if the claim arises from the supply of goods or services, a description of the goods or services and the date or dates on or between which they were supplied and, where relevant, ordered.

**Actions relating to regulated agreements**

**4.2A.**[1]   In an action which relates to a regulated agreement within the meaning given by section 189(1) of the Consumer Credit Act 1974 the statement of claim shall include an averment that such an agreement exists and details of the agreement.

**Defender's copy summons**

**4.3.**   A copy summons shall be served on the defender—

(a)   in Form 1 a where—

(i)   the small claim is for, or includes a claim for, payment of money; and

(ii)   an application for a time to pay direction under the Debtors (Scotland) Act 1987 or time order under the Consumer Credit Act 1974 may be applied for;

or

(b)   in Form 1b in every other case.

---

[1] As inserted by the Act of Sederunt (Sheriff Court Rules) (Miscellaneous Amendments) 2009 (SSI 2009/294) r.5 (effective December 1, 2009) as substituted by the Act of Sederunt (Amendment of the Act of Sederunt (Sheriff Court Rules) (Miscellaneous Amendments) 2009) 2009 (SSI 2009/402) (effective November 30, 2009).

## Authentication and effect of summons

**4.4.**—(1) A summons shall be authenticated by the sheriff clerk in some appropriate manner except where—

    (a)  he refuses to do so for any reason;

    (b)  the defender's address is unknown; or

    (c)  a party seeks to alter the normal period of notice specified in rule 4.5(2); or

    (d)[1]  a warrant for arrestment on the dependence, or to found jurisdiction, is sought

(2)[2] If any of paragraphs (1)(a) to (d) applies, the summons shall be authenticated by the sheriff, if he thinks it appropriate.

(3) The authenticated summons shall be warrant for—

    (a)  service on the defender; and

    (b)  where the appropriate warrant has been sought in the summons—

        (i)  arrestment on the dependence; or

        (ii)  arrestment to found jurisdiction, as the case may be.

(4)[3] Where a warrant for arrestment to found jurisdiction, is sought, averments to justify that warrant must be included in the statement of claim.

## Period of notice

**4.5.**—(1) A claim shall proceed after the appropriate period of notice of the summons has been given to the defender prior to the return day.

(2) The appropriate period of notice shall be—

    (a)  21 days where the defender is resident or has a place of business within Europe; or

    (b)  42 days where the defender is resident or has a place of business outwith Europe.

(3) The sheriff may, on cause shown, shorten or extend the period of notice on such conditions as to the form of service as he may direct, but in any case where the period of notice is reduced at least two days' notice must be given.

(4) If a period of notice expires on a Saturday, Sunday, public or court holiday, the period of notice shall be deemed to expire on the next day on which the sheriff clerk's office is open for civil court business.

(5) Notwithstanding the terms of section 4(2) of the Citation Amendment (Scotland) Act 1882, where service is by post the period of notice shall run from the beginning of the day next following the date of posting.

(6) The sheriff clerk shall insert in the summons—

    (a)  the return day, which is the last day on which the defender may return a form of response to the sheriff clerk; and

    (b)  the hearing date, which is the date set for the hearing of the claim.

---

[1] As inserted by the Act of Sederunt (Ordinary Cause, Summary Application and Small Claim Rules) Amendment (Miscellaneous) 2004 (SSI 2004/197) r.5(2) (effective May 21, 2004) and amended by the Act of Sederunt (Sheriff Court Rules) (Miscellaneous Amendments) 2009 (SSI 2009/294) r.12 (effective October 1, 2009).

[2] As substituted by the Act of Sederunt (Ordinary Cause, Summary Application, Summary Cause and Small Claim Rules) Amendment (Miscellaneous) 2004 (SSI 2004/197) r.5(2)(b) (effective May 21, 2004).

[3] As inserted by the Act of Sederunt (Ordinary Cause, Summary Application and Small Claim Rules) Amendment (Miscellaneous) 2004 (SSI 2004/197) r.5(2) (effective May 21, 2004) and amended by the Act of Sederunt (Sheriff Court Rules) (Miscellaneous Amendments) 2009 (SSI 2009/294) r.12 (effective October 1, 2009).

**Intimation**

**4.6.** Any provision in these Rules requiring papers to be sent to or any intimation to be made to any party or applicant shall be construed as if the reference to the party or applicant included a reference to the solicitor representing that party or applicant.

## CHAPTER 5

### REGISTER OF SMALL CLAIMS

**Register of Small Claims**

**5.1.**—(1) The sheriff clerk shall keep a register of claims and incidental applications made in claims, which shall be known as the Register of Small Claims.

(2) There shall be entered in the Register of Small Claims a note of all claims, together with a note of all minutes under rule 22.1(1) (recall of decree) and the entry for each claim or minute must contain the following particulars where appropriate:—

    (a) the names, designations and addresses of the parties;

    (b) whether the parties were present or absent at any hearing, including an inspection, and the names of their representatives;

    (c) the nature of the claim;

    (d) the amount of any claim;

    (e) the date of issue of the summons;

    (f) the method of service;

    (g) the return day;

    (h) the hearing date;

    (i) whether a form of response was lodged and details of it;

    (j) the period of notice if shortened or extended in accordance with rule 4.5(3);

    (k) details of any minute by the pursuer regarding a time to pay direction or time order, or minute by the pursuer requesting decree or other order;

    (l) details of any interlocutors issued;

    (m) details of the final decree and the date of it; and

    (n) details of any variation or recall of a decree by virtue of the Debtors (Scotland) Act 1987.

(3) There shall be entered in the Register of Small Claims, in the entry for the claim to which they relate, details of incidental applications including, where appropriate—

    (a) whether parties are present or absent at the hearing of the application, and the names of their representatives;

    (b) the nature of the application; and

    (c) the interlocutor issued or order made.

(4) The Register of Small Claims must be—

    (a) authenticated in some appropriate manner by the sheriff in respect of each day any order is made or application determined in a claim; and

    (b) open for inspection during normal business hours to all concerned without fee.

(5) The Register of Small Claims may be kept in electronic or documentary form.

## CHAPTER 6

### SERVICE AND RETURN OF THE SUMMONS

**Persons carrying on business under trading or descriptive name**

**6.1.**—(1) A person carrying on a business under a trading or descriptive name may sue or be sued in such trading or descriptive name alone.

(2) An extract of a decree pronounced in a claim against such person under such trading or descriptive name shall be a valid warrant for diligence against that person.

(3) A summons, decree, charge or other document following upon such summons or decree in a claim in which a person carrying on business under a trading or descriptive name sues or is sued in that name may be served—

(a) at any place of business or office at which such business is carried on within the sheriffdom of the sheriff court in which the claim is brought; or

(b) if there is no place of business within that sheriffdom, at any place where such business is carried on (including the place of business or office of the clerk or secretary of any company, corporation or association or firm).

**Form of service**

**6.2.**—(1) Subject to rule 6.6 (service where address of defender is unknown), a form of service in Form 5 must be enclosed with the defender's copy summons.

(2) After service has been effected a certificate of execution of service in Form 6 must be prepared and signed by the person effecting service.

(3) When service is effected by a sheriff officer the certificate of execution of service must specify whether the service was personal or, if otherwise, the mode of service and the name of any person to whom the defender's copy summons was delivered.

(4) If service is effected in accordance with rule 6.4(2) (service within Scotland by sheriff officer where personal service etc. unsuccessful) the certificate must also contain a statement of—

(a) the mode of service previously attempted; and

(b) the circumstances which prevented the service from being effected.

**Service of the summons**

**6.3.**—(1) Subject to rule 6.5 (service on persons outwith Scotland), a copy summons may be served on the defender—

(a) by the pursuer's solicitor, a sheriff officer or the sheriff clerk sending it by first class recorded delivery post; or

(b) in accordance with rule 6.4 (service within Scotland by sheriff officer).

(2) On the face of the envelope used for postal service in terms of this rule, there must be printed or written a notice in Form 7.

(3) The certificate of execution of service in the case of postal service must have annexed to it any relevant postal receipt.

(4) If the pursuer requires the sheriff clerk to effect service on his behalf by virtue of section 36A of the 1971 Act (pursuer not being a partnership, body corporate or acting in a representative capacity) under paragraph (1), he may require the sheriff clerk to supply him with a copy of the summons.

### Service within Scotland by sheriff officer

**6.4.**—(1)  A sheriff officer may validly serve any summons, decree, charge or other document following upon such summons or decree issued in a claim by—

>  (a)   personal service; or

>  (b)   leaving it in the hands of—

>>   (i)[1]   a resident at the person's dwelling place; or

>>   (ii)   an employee at the person's place of business.

(2)  If a sheriff officer has been unsuccessful in effecting service in accordance with paragraph (1), he may, after making diligent inquiries, serve the document—

>  (a)   by depositing it in the person's dwelling place or place of business by means of a letter box or by other lawful means; or

>  (b)[2]   by leaving it at that person's dwelling place or place of business in such a way that it is likely to come to the attention of that person.

(3)   If service is effected in accordance with paragraph (2), the sheriff officer must thereafter send by ordinary post to the address at which he thinks it most likely that the person may be found a letter containing a copy of the document.

(4)   In proceedings in or following on a claim, it shall be necessary for any sheriff officer to be accompanied by a witness except where service, citation or intimation is to be made by post.

(5)   Where the firm which employs the sheriff officer has in its possession—

>  (a)   the document or a copy of it certified as correct by the pursuer's solicitor or the sheriff clerk, the sheriff officer may serve the document upon the defender without having the document or certified copy in his possession (in which case he shall if required to do so by the person on whom service is executed and within a reasonable time of being so required, show the document or certified copy to the person); or

>  (b)   a certified copy of the interlocutor pronounced allowing service of the document, the sheriff officer may serve the document without having in his possession the certified copy interlocutor if he has in his possession a facsimile copy of the certified copy interlocutor (which he shall show, if required, to the person on whom service is executed).

(6)   If the pursuer requires the sheriff clerk to effect service of the summons on his behalf by virtue of section 36A of the 1971 Act, the sheriff clerk may instruct a sheriff officer to effect service in accordance with this rule on payment to the sheriff clerk by the pursuer of the fee prescribed by order of the Scottish Ministers.

(7)[3]   Where service is executed under paragraphs (1)(b) or (2), the document and the citation or notice of intimation, as the case may be, must be placed in an envelope bearing the notice "This envelope contains a citation to or intimation from (*insert name of sheriff court*)" and sealed by the sheriff officer.

### Service on persons outwith Scotland

**6.5.**—(1)  If any summons, decree, charge or other document following upon such summons or decree, or any charge or warrant, requires to be served outwith Scotland on any person, it must be served in accordance with this rule.

---

[1]  As substituted by the Act of Sederunt (Sheriff Court Rules) (Miscellaneous Amendments) 2011 (SSI 2011/193) r.5 (effective April 4, 2011).

[2]  As substituted by the Act of Sederunt (Sheriff Court Rules) (Miscellaneous Amendments) 2011 (SSI 2011/193) r.5 (effective April 4, 2011).

[3]  As inserted by the Act of Sederunt (Sheriff Court Rules) (Miscellaneous Amendments) 2011 (SSI 2011/193) r.5 (effective April 4, 2011).

(2)   If the person has a known home or place of business in—

(a)   England and Wales, Northern Ireland, the Isle of Man or the Channel Islands; or

(b)   any country with which the United Kingdom does not have a convention providing for service of writs in that country,

the document must be served either—

(i)   by posting in Scotland a copy of the document in question in a registered letter addressed to the person at his residence or place of business; or

(ii)   in accordance with the rules for personal service under the domestic law of the place in which the document is to be served.

(3)   Subject to paragraph (4), if the document requires to be served in a country which is a party to the Hague Convention on the Service Abroad of Judicial and Extra-Judicial Documents in Civil or Commercial Matters dated 15th November 1965 or the European Convention on Jurisdiction and Enforcement of Judgments in Civil and Commercial Matters as set out in Schedule 1 or 3C to the Civil Jurisdiction and Judgments Act 1982, it must be served—

(a)   by a method prescribed by the internal law of the country where service is to be effected for the service of documents in domestic actions upon persons who are within its territory;

(b)   by or through a British consular authority at the request of the Secretary of State for Foreign and Commonwealth Affairs;

(c)[1]   by or through a central authority in the country where service is to be effected at the request of the Scottish Ministers;

(d)   where the law of the country in which the person resides permits, by posting in Scotland a copy of the document in a registered letter addressed to the person at his residence; or

(e)   where the law of the country in which service is to be effected permits, service by an *huissier*, other judicial officer or competent official of the country where service is to be made.

(4)[2, 3]   If the document requires to be served in a country to which the EC Service Regulation applies, service—

(a)   may be effected by the methods prescribed in paragraph (3)(b) or (c) only in exceptional circumstances; and

(b)   is effected only if the receiving agency has informed the person that acceptance of service may be refused on the ground that the document has not been translated in accordance with paragraph (12).

(5)   If the document requires to be served in a country with which the United Kingdom has a convention on the service of writs in that country other than the conventions specified in paragraph (3) or the regulation specified in paragraph (4), it must be served by one of the methods approved in the relevant convention.

---

[1] As substituted by the Act of Sederunt (Sheriff Court Rules) (Miscellaneous Amendments) 2011 (SSI 2011/193) r.6 (effective April 4, 2011).

[2] As substituted by the Act of Sederunt (Ordinary Cause, Summary Application, Summary Cause and Small Claim Rules) Amendment (Miscellaneous) 2004 (SSI 2004/197) r.5(3) (effective May 21, 2004).

[3] As substituted by Act of Sederunt (Sheriff Court Rules) (Miscellaneous Amendments) (No.2) 2008 (SSI 2008/365) r.10(a) (effective November 13, 2008).

(6) Subject to paragraph (9), a document which requires to be posted in Scotland for the purposes of this rule must be posted by a solicitor, the sheriff clerk or a sheriff officer, and the form for service and the certificate of execution of service must be in Forms 5 and 6 respectively.

(7) On the face of the envelope used for postal service under this rule there must be written or printed a notice in Form 7.

(8) Where service is effected by a method specified in paragraph (3)(b) or (c), the pursuer must—

(a)[1]    send a copy of the summons and warrant for service with form of service attached, or other document, with a request for service to be effected by the method indicated in the request to the Scottish Ministers or, as the case may be, the Secretary of State for Foreign and Commonwealth Affairs; and

(b)    lodge in process a certificate of execution of service signed by the authority which has effected service.

(9) If service is effected by the method specified in paragraph (3)(e), the pursuer must—

(a)    send to the official in the country in which service is to be effected a copy of the summons and warrant for service, with citation attached, or other document, with a request for service to be effected by delivery to the defender or his residence; and

(b)    lodge in process a certificate of execution of service by the official who has effected service.

(10) Where service is executed in accordance with paragraph (2)(b)(ii) or (3)(a) other than on another party in—

(a)    the United Kingdom;

(b)    the Isle of Man; or

(c)    the Channel Islands,

the party executing service must lodge a certificate stating that the form of service employed is in accordance with the law of the place where the service was executed.

(11) A certificate lodged in accordance with paragraph (10) shall be given by a person who is conversant with the law of the country concerned and who—

(a)    practises or has practised law in that country; or

(b)    is a duly accredited representative of the government of that country.

(12)[2] Every summons or document and every citation and notice on the face of the envelope referred to in paragraph (7) must be accompanied by a translation in—

(a)    an official language of the country in which service is to be executed; or

(b)[3]    in a country to which the EC Service Regulation applies, a language of the member state of transmission that is understood by the person on whom service is being executed.

---

[1] As amended by the Act of Sederunt (Sheriff Court Rules) (Miscellaneous Amendments) 2011 (SSI 2011/193) r.7 (effective April 4, 2011).

[2] As substituted by the Act of Sederunt (Ordinary Cause, Summary Application, Summary Cause and Small Claim Rules) Amendment (Miscellaneous) 2004 (SSI 2004/197) r.5(3) (effective May 21, 2004).

[3] As substituted by Act of Sederunt (Sheriff Court Rules) (Miscellaneous Amendments) (No.2) 2008 (SSI 2008/365) r.10(a) (effective November 13, 2008).

(13) A translation referred to in paragraph (12) must be certified as a correct translation by the person making it and the certificate must contain the full name, address and qualifications of the translator and be lodged along with the execution of such service.

(14) If the pursuer requires the sheriff clerk to effect service on his behalf under this rule by virtue of section 36A of the 1971 Act (pursuer not a partnership, body corporate or acting in a representative capacity)—

(a) the cost must be borne by the pursuer;

(b) no service shall be instructed by the sheriff clerk until such cost has been paid to him by the pursuer; and

(c) the pursuer may require the sheriff clerk to supply him with a copy of the summons.

(15)[1] In this rule "the EC Service Regulation" means Regulation (EC) No. 1393/2007 of the European Parliament and of the Council of 13th November 2007 on the service in the Member States of judicial and extrajudicial documents in civil or commercial matters (service of documents), and repealing Council Regulation (EC) No. 1348/2000, as amended from time to time.

### Service where address of defender is unknown

**6.6.**—(A1)[2] Subject to rule 7.A7 this rule applies to service where the address of a person is not known.

(1) If the defender's address is unknown to the pursuer and cannot reasonably be ascertained by him, the sheriff may grant warrant to serve the summons—

(a) by the publication of an advertisement in Form 8 in a newspaper circulating in the area of the defender's last known address; or

(b) by displaying on the walls of court a copy of a notice in Form 9.

(2) Where a summons is served in accordance with paragraph (1), the period of notice, which must be fixed by the sheriff, shall run from the date of publication of the advertisement or display on the walls of court, as the case may be.

(3) If service is to be effected under paragraph (1), the pursuer must lodge a defender's copy summons with the sheriff clerk.

(4) The defender may uplift from the sheriff clerk the copy summons lodged in accordance with paragraph (3).

(5) If the pursuer requires the sheriff clerk to effect service on his behalf under paragraph (1) by virtue of section 36A of the 1971 Act (pursuer not a partnership, body corporate or acting in a representative capacity)—

(a) the cost of any advertisement required under sub-paragraph (a) of that paragraph must be borne by the pursuer;

(b) no advertisement required under sub-paragraph (a) of that paragraph shall be instructed by the sheriff clerk until such cost has been paid to him by the pursuer; and

---

[1] As inserted by the Act of Sederunt (Ordinary Cause, Summary Application, Summary Cause and Small Claim Rules) Amendment (Miscellaneous) 2004 (SSI 2004/197) r.5(3) (effective May 21, 2004) and substituted by the Act of Sederunt (Sheriff Court Ordinary Cause, Summary Application, Summary Cause and Small Claim Rules) Amendment (Council Regulation (EC) No.1348 of 2000 Extension to Denmark) 2007 (SSI 2007/440) (effective October 9, 2007) and the Act of Sederunt (Sheriff Court Rules) (Miscellaneous Amendments) (No.2) 2008 (SSI 2008/365) r.10(b) (effective November 13, 2008).

[2] As inserted by the Act of Sederunt (Sheriff Court Rules Amendment) (Diligence) 2008 (SSI 2008/121) r.7(2) (effective April 1, 2008).

    (c)   the pursuer may require the sheriff clerk to supply him with a copy of the summons.

(6)  A copy of the newspaper containing the advertisement referred to in paragraph (1)(a) must be lodged with the sheriff clerk unless the sheriff clerk instructed such advertisement.

(7)  If display on the walls of court is required under paragraph (1)(b), the pursuer must supply to the sheriff clerk for that purpose a completed copy of Form 9.

(8)  If service has been made under this rule and thereafter the defender's address becomes known, the sheriff may allow the summons to be amended and, if appropriate, grant warrant for resservice subject to such conditions as he thinks fit.

### Endorsation by sheriff clerk of defender's residence not necessary

**6.7.**  Any summons, decree, charge or other document following upon a summons or decree may be served, enforced or otherwise lawfully executed in Scotland without endorsation by a sheriff clerk and, if executed by a sheriff officer, may be so executed by a sheriff officer of the court which granted the summons, or by a sheriff officer of the sheriff court district in which it is to be executed.

### Contents of envelope containing defender's copy summons

**6.8.**  Nothing must be included in the envelope containing a defender's copy summons except—

    (a)   the copy summons;

    (b)   a response or other notice in accordance with these Rules; and

    (c)   any other document approved by the sheriff principal.

### Re-service

**6.9.**—(1)  If it appears to the sheriff that there has been any failure or irregularity in service upon a defender, the sheriff may order the pursuer to re-serve the summons on such conditions as he thinks lit.

(2)  If re-service has been ordered in accordance with paragraph (1) or rule 6.6(8), the claim shall proceed thereafter as if it were a new claim.

### Defender appearing barred from objecting to service

**6.10.**—(1)  A person who appears in any claim shall not be entitled to state any objection to the regularity of the execution of service or intimation on him and his appearance shall remedy any defect in such service or intimation.

(2)  Nothing in paragraph (1) shall preclude a party pleading that the court has no jurisdiction.

### Return of summons and execution

**6.11.**—(1)  If—

    (a)   someone other than the sheriff clerk has served the summons; and

    (b)   the case requires to call in court for any reason on the hearing date, the pursuer must return the summons and the certificate of execution of service to the sheriff clerk at least two days before the hearing date.

(2)  If the case does not require to call in court on the hearing date, the pursuer must return the certificate of execution of service to the sheriff clerk by the date mentioned in paragraph (1) above.

(3)   If the pursuer fails to return the summons or certificate of execution of service in accordance with paragraph (1) or (2) as appropriate, the sheriff may dismiss the claim.

CHAPTER 7

INTERIM DILIGENCE[1]

## Interpretation

**7.A1.**[2]   In this Chapter—

"the 1987 Act" means the Debtors (Scotland) Act 1987; and
"the 2002 Act" means the Debt Arrangement and Attachment (Scotland) Act 2002.

## Application for interim diligence

**7.A2.**—[3](1)   The following shall be made by incidental application—

(a)   an application under section 15D(1) of the 1987 Act for warrant for diligence by arrestment or inhibition on the dependence of an action or warrant for arrestment on the dependence of an admiralty action;

(b)   an application under section 9C of the 2002 Act for interim attachment.

(2)   Such an application must be accompanied by a statement in Form 9a.

(3)   A certified copy of an interlocutor granting an application under paragraph (1) shall be sufficient authority for execution of the diligence concerned.

## Effect of authority for inhibition on the dependence

**7.A3.**—[4](1)   Where a person has been granted authority for inhibition on the dependence of an action, a certified copy of the interlocutor granting the application may be registered with a certificate of execution in the Register of Inhibitions and Adjudications.

(2)[5]   A notice of a certified copy of an interlocutor granting authority for inhibition under rule 7.A2 may be registered in the Register of Inhibitions and Adjudications; and such registration is to have the same effect as registration of a notice of inhibition under section 155(2) of the Titles to Land Consolidation (Scotland) Act 1868.

## Recall etc of arrestment or inhibition

**7.A4.**—[6](1)   An application by any person having an interest—

(a)   to loose, restrict, vary or recall an arrestment or an interim attachment; or

(b)   to recall, in whole or in part, or vary, an inhibition,

shall be made by incidental application.

---

[1] Chapter renamed by the Act of Sederunt (Sheriff Court Rules Amendment) (Diligence) 2008 (SSI 2008/121) r.7(3) (effective April 1, 2008).

[2] As inserted by the Act of Sederunt (Sheriff Court Rules Amendment) (Diligence) 2008 (SSI 2008/121) r.7(4) (effective April 1, 2008).

[3] As inserted by the Act of Sederunt (Sheriff Court Rules Amendment) (Diligence) 2008 (SSI 2008/121) r.7(4) (effective April 1, 2008).

[4] As inserted by the Act of Sederunt (Sheriff Court Rules Amendment) (Diligence) 2008 (SSI 2008/121) r.7(4) (effective April 1, 2008).

[5] As substituted by the Act of Sederunt (Sheriff Court Rules Amendment) (Diligence) 2009 (SSI 2009/107) r.6 (effective April 22, 2009).

[6] As inserted by the Act of Sederunt (Sheriff Court Rules Amendment) (Diligence) 2008 (SSI 2008/121) r.7(4) (effective April 1, 2008).

(1A)[1]  An incidental application under paragraph (1) shall—

(a)  specify the name and address of each of the parties;

(b)  where it relates to an inhibition, contain a description of the inhibition including the date of registration in the Register of Inhibitions and Adjudications.

(2)  Paragraph (1) does not apply to an application made orally at a hearing under section 15K that has been fixed under section 15E(4) of the Act of 1987.

### Incidental applications in relation to interim diligence, etc

**7.A5.**[2]  An application under Part 1A of the 1987 Act or Part 1A of the 2002 Act other than mentioned above shall be made by incidental application.

### Form of schedule of inhibition on the dependence

**7.A6.**  *[Revoked by the Act of Sederunt (Sheriff Court Rules Amendment) (Diligence) 2009 (SSI 2009/107) r.6 (effective April 22, 2009).]*

### Service of inhibition on the dependence where address of defender not known

**7.A7.**—[3](1)  Where the address of a defender is not known to the pursuer, an inhibition shall be deemed to have been served on the defender if the schedule of inhibition is left with or deposited at the office of the sheriff clerk of the sheriff court district where the defender's last known address is located.

(2)  Where service of an inhibition on the dependence is executed under paragraph (1), a copy of the schedule of inhibition shall be sent by the sheriff officer by first class post to the defender's last known address.

### Form of schedule of arrestment on the dependence

**7.A8.**—[4](1)  An arrestment on the dependence shall be served by serving the schedule of arrestment on the arrestee in Form 9b.

(2)  A certificate of execution shall be lodged with the sheriff clerk in Form 9c.

### Service of schedule of arrestment

**7.1.**  If a schedule of arrestment has not been personally served on an arrestee, the arrestment shall have effect only if a copy of the schedule is also sent by registered post or the first class recorded delivery service to—

(a)  the last known place of residence of the arrestee; or

(b)  if such place of residence is not known, or if the arrestee is a firm or corporation, to the arrestee's principal place of business if known, or, if not known, to any known place of business of the arrestee,

and the sheriff officer must, on the certificate of execution, certify that this has been done and specify the address to which the copy of the schedule was sent.

---

[1] As inserted by the Act of Sederunt (Court of Session and Sheriff Court Rules Amendment No.2) (Miscellaneous) 2014 (SSI 2014/291) r.5 (effective December 8, 2014).

[2] As inserted by the Act of Sederunt (Sheriff Court Rules Amendment) (Diligence) 2008 (SSI 2008/121) r.7(4) (effective April 1, 2008).

[3] As inserted by the Act of Sederunt (Sheriff Court Rules Amendment) (Diligence) 2008 (SSI 2008/121) r.7(4) (effective April 1, 2008).

[4] As inserted by the Act of Sederunt (Sheriff Court Rules Amendment) (Diligence) 2009 (SSI 2009/107) r.6 (effective April 22, 2009).

## Arrestment on dependence before service

**7.2**—[1](1) An arrestment to found jurisdiction used prior to service shall cease to have effect, unless the summons is served within 21 days from the date of execution of the arrestment.

(2) When such an arrestment as is referred to in paragraph (1) has been executed, the party using it must forthwith report the execution to the sheriff clerk.

## Recall and restriction of arrestment

**7.3.**—(1) The sheriff may order that an arrestment on the dependence of a claim or counterclaim shall cease to have effect if the party whose funds or property are arrested—

  (a)  pays into court; or
  (b)  finds caution to the satisfaction of the sheriff clerk in respect of, the sum claimed together with the sum of £50 in respect of expenses.

(2) Without prejudice to paragraph (1), a party whose funds or property are arrested may at any time apply to the sheriff to exercise his powers to recall or restrict an arrestment on the dependence of a claim or counterclaim, with or without consignation or caution.

(3) An application made under paragraph (3) must be intimated by the applicant to the party who instructed the arrestment.

(4) On payment into court or the finding of caution to the satisfaction of the sheriff clerk in accordance with paragraph (1), or if the sheriff recalls or restricts an arrestment on the dependence of a claim in accordance with paragraph (2) and any condition imposed by the sheriff has been complied with, the sheriff clerk must—

  (a)  issue to the party whose funds or property are arrested a certificate in Form 10 authorising the release of any sum or property arrested to the extent ordered by the sheriff; and
  (b)  send a copy of the certificate to—
       (i)   the party who instructed the arrestment; and
       (ii)  the party who has possession of the funds or property that are arrested.

CHAPTER 8

UNDEFENDED CLAIM

## Undefended claim

**8.1.**—(1) Where the defender has not lodged a form of response on or before the return day, the claim shall not require to call in court.

(2) Where paragraph (1) applies, the pursuer must lodge a minute in Form 11 before the sheriff clerk's office closes for business on the second day before the date set for the hearing.

(3) Where the pursuer has lodged a minute in accordance with paragraph (2), the sheriff may grant decree or other competent order sought in terms of that minute.

(4) Where the pursuer has not lodged a minute in accordance with paragraph (2), the sheriff must dismiss the claim.

---

[1] As amended by the Act of Sederunt (Sheriff Court Rules Amendment) (Diligence) (SSI 2008/121) r.7(5) (effective April 1, 2008). This rule as it applied immediately before April 1, 2008 continues to have effect for the purpose of any application for arrestment on the dependence made before that date.

### Application for time to pay direction or time order

**8.2.**—(1)  If the defender admits the claim, he may, where competent—

    (a)  make an application for a time to pay direction (including, where appropriate, an application for recall or restriction of an arrestment) or a time order by completing the appropriate parts of the Form 1a and lodging it with the sheriff clerk on or before the return day; or

    (b)  lodge a form of response indicating that he admits the claim and intends to apply orally for a time to pay direction (including, where appropriate, an application for recall or restriction of an arrestment) or time order.

(1A)[1]  The sheriff clerk must on receipt forthwith intimate to the pursuer a copy of any response lodged under paragraph (1).

(2)[2]  Where the defender has lodged an application in terms of paragraph (1)(a), the pursuer may intimate that he does not object to the application by lodging a minute in Form 12 before the time the sheriff clerk's office closes for business on the day occurring 9 days before the hearing date stating that he does not object to the defender's application and seeking decree.

(3)  If the pursuer intimates in accordance with paragraph (2) that he does not object to the application—

    (a)  the sheriff may grant decree on the hearing date;

    (b)  the parties need not attend; and

    (c)  the action will not call in court.

(4)[3]  If the pursuer wishes to oppose the application for a time to pay direction or time order made in accordance with paragraph (1)(a) he must before the time the sheriff clerk's office closes for business on the day occurring 9 days before the hearing date—

    (a)  lodge a minute in Form 13; and

    (b)  send a copy of that minute to the defender.

(5)  Where the pursuer objects to an application in terms of paragraph (1)(a) or the defender has lodged a form of response in accordance with paragraph (1)(b), the action shall call in court on the hearing date when the parties may appear and the sheriff must decide the application and grant decree accordingly.

(6)  The sheriff shall decide an application in accordance with paragraph (5) whether or not any of the parties appear.

(7)  Where the defender has lodged an application in terms of paragraph (1)(a) and the pursuer fails to proceed in accordance with either of paragraphs (2) or (4) the sheriff may dismiss the claim.

### Decree in claims to which the Hague Convention or the Civil Jurisdiction and Judgments Act 1982 apply

**8.3.**—(1)  If the summons has been served in a country to which the Hague Convention on the Service Abroad of Judicial and Extra-Judicial Documents in Civil or Commercial Matters dated 15th November 1965 applies, decree must not be granted until it is established to the satisfaction of the sheriff that the requirements of Article 15 of that Convention have been complied with.

---

[1]  As inserted by the Act of Sederunt (Sheriff Court Rules) (Miscellaneous Amendments) 2009 (SSI 2009/294) r.5 (effective December 1, 2009).

[2]  As substituted by the Act of Sederunt (Sheriff Court Rules) (Miscellaneous Amendments) 2009 (SSI 2009/294) r.5 (effective December 1, 2009).

[3]  As substituted by the Act of Sederunt (Sheriff Court Rules) (Miscellaneous Amendments) 2009 (SSI 2009/294) r.5 (effective December 1, 2009).

(2) Where a defender is domiciled in another part of the United Kingdom or in another Contracting State, the sheriff shall not grant decree until it has been shown that the defender has been able to receive the summons in sufficient time to arrange his defence or that all necessary steps have been taken to that end.

(3) For the purposes of paragraph (2)—

(a) the question whether a person is domiciled in another part of the United Kingdom shall be determined in accordance with sections 41 and 42 of the Civil Jurisdiction and Judgments Act 1982;

(b) the question whether a person is domiciled in another Contracting State shall be determined in accordance with Article 52 of the Convention in Schedule 1 or 3C to that Act; and

(c) the term "Contracting State" has the meaning assigned in section 1 of that Act.

## CHAPTER 9

### DEFENDED CLAIM

**The Hearing**

**9.1.**—(1) Where a defender intends to—

(a) challenge the jurisdiction of the court;

(b) state a defence (including, where appropriate, a counterclaim); or

(c) dispute the amount of the claim, he must complete the form of response part of Form 1a or 1b as appropriate indicating that intention and lodge it with the sheriff clerk on or before the return day.

(2) Where the defender has lodged a form of response in accordance with paragraph (1) the claim will call in court for a hearing ("the Hearing").

(3)[1] The Hearing shall be held on the hearing date which shall be 14 days after the return day.

(4) If the claim is not resolved at the Hearing, the sheriff may continue the Hearing to such other date as he considers to be appropriate.

(5) The defender must attend or be represented at the Hearing and the sheriff shall note any challenge, defence or dispute, as the case may be, on the summons.

(6) Where at the Hearing the defender—

(a) does not appear or is not represented; and

(b) the pursuer is present or is represented, decree may be granted against the defender in terms of the summons.

(7) Where at the Hearing—

(a) the pursuer does not appear or is not represented; and

(b) the defender is present or represented, the sheriff may grant decree of dismissal.

(8) If all parties fail to appear at the Hearing, the sheriff shall, unless sufficient reason appears to the contrary, dismiss the claim.

**Purpose of the Hearing**

**9.2.**—(1) If, at the Hearing, the sheriff is satisfied that the claim is incompetent or that there is a patent defect of jurisdiction, he must grant decree of dismissal in favour of the defender or, if appropriate, transfer the claim in terms of rule 15.1(2).

(2) At the Hearing, the sheriff shall—

---

[1] As substituted by the Act of Sederunt (Sheriff Court Rules) (Miscellaneous Amendments) 2009 (SSI 2009/294) r.7 (effective December 1, 2009).

(a) ascertain the factual basis of the claim and any defence, and the legal basis on which the claim and defence are proceeding; and

(b) seek to negotiate and secure settlement of the claim between the parties.

(3) If the sheriff cannot secure settlement of the claim between the parties, he shall—

(a) identify and note on the summons the issues of fact and law which are in dispute;

(b) note on the summons any facts which are agreed; and

(c) if possible reach a decision on the whole dispute on the basis of the information before him.

(d)[1] enquire whether there is or is likely to be a vulnerable witness within the meaning of section 11(1) of the 2004 Act who is to give evidence at any proof or hearing, consider any child witness notice or vulnerable witness application that has been lodged where no order has been made and consider whether any order under section 12(1) of the 2004 Act requires to be made.

(4) Where evidence requires to be led for the purposes of reaching a decision on the dispute, the sheriff shall—

(a) direct parties to lead evidence on the disputed issues of fact which he has noted on the summons;

(b) indicate to the parties the matters of fact that require to be proved, and may give guidance on the nature of the evidence to be led; and

(c) fix a hearing on evidence for a later date for that purpose.

## Conduct of hearings

**9.3.**—(1) Any hearing in a claim shall be conducted in accordance with the following paragraphs of this rule.

(2) A hearing shall be conducted as informally as the circumstances of the claim permit.

(3) The procedure to be adopted at a hearing shall be such as the sheriff considers—

(a) to be fair;

(b) best suited to the clarification and determination of the issues before him; and

(c) gives each party sufficient opportunity to present his case.

(4) Before proceeding to hear evidence, the sheriff shall explain to the parties the form of procedure which he intends to adopt.

(5) Having considered the circumstances of the parties and whether (and to what extent) they are represented, the sheriff—

(a) may, in order to assist resolution of the disputed issues of fact, put questions to parties and to witnesses; and

(b) shall (if he considers it necessary for the fair conduct of the hearing) explain any legal terms or expressions which are used.

(6) Evidence will normally be taken on oath or affirmation but the sheriff may dispense with that requirement if it appears reasonable to do so.

---

[1] As inserted by the Act of Sederunt (Ordinary Cause, Summary Application, Summary Cause and Small Claim Rules) Amendment (Vulnerable Witnesses (Scotland) Act 2004) 2007 (SSI 2007/463) r.5(3) (effective November 1, 2007).

## Inspection of places and objects

**9.4.**—(1)  If, at any hearing, a disputed issue noted by the sheriff is the quality or condition of an object, the sheriff may inspect the object in the presence of the parties or their representatives in court or, if it is not practicable to bring the object to court, at the place where the object is located.

(2)  The sheriff may, if he considers it appropriate, inspect any place that is material to the disputed issues in the presence of the parties or their representatives.

## Remit to determine matter of fact

**9.5.**—(1)  The sheriff may, where parties agree, remit to any suitable person to report on any matter of fact.

(2)  Where a remit is made under paragraph (1) above, the report of such person shall be final and conclusive with respect to the matter of fact which is the subject of the remit.

(3)  A remit shall not be made under paragraph (1) of this rule unless parties have previously agreed the basis upon which the fees, if any, of such person shall be met.

## Noting of evidence

**9.6.**  The sheriff must make notes of the evidence at a hearing for his own use and must retain these notes until after any appeal has been disposed of.

## Application for time to pay direction or time order in defended claim

**9.7.**  A defender in a claim which proceeds as defended may, where it is competent to do so, make an incidental application or apply orally at any hearing, at any time before decree is granted, for a time to pay direction (including where appropriate, an order recalling or restricting an arrestment on the dependence) or a time order.

## Pronouncement of decision

**9.8.**—(1)  The sheriff must, where practicable, give his decision and a brief statement of his reasons at the end of the hearing of a claim, or he may reserve judgment.

(2)  If the sheriff reserves judgment, he must, within 28 days of the hearing, give his decision in writing together with a brief note of his reasons, and the sheriff clerk must send a copy to the parties.

(3)  After giving his judgment, the sheriff must—

    (a)  deal with the question of expenses and, where appropriate, make an award of expenses; and

    (b)  grant decree as appropriate

(4)  The decree of the sheriff shall be a final decree.

## CHAPTER 10

### INCIDENTAL APPLICATIONS AND SISTS

## General

**10.1.**—(1)  Except where otherwise provided, any incidental application in a claim may be made—

    (a)  orally with the leave of the sheriff during any hearing of the claim; or

    (b)  by lodging the application in written form with the sheriff clerk.

(2)  An application lodged in accordance with paragraph (1)(b) may only be heard after not less than two days' notice has been given to the other party.

(3)  A party who is not—

(a)   a partnership or a body corporate; or

(b)   acting in a representative capacity, and is not represented by a solicitor,

may require the sheriff clerk to intimate to the other party a copy of an incidental application.

(4)   Where the party receiving notice of an incidental application lodged in accordance with paragraph (1)(b) intimates to the sheriff clerk and the party making the application that it is not opposed, the application shall not require to call in court unless the sheriff so directs.

(5)   Any intimation under paragraph (4) shall be made not later than noon on the day before the application is due to be heard.

### Application to sist claim

**10.2.**—(1)   Where an incidental application to sist a claim is made, the reason for the sist—

(a)   shall be stated by the party seeking the sist; and

(b)   shall be recorded in the Register of Small Claims and on the summons.

(2)   Where a claim has been sisted, the sheriff may, after giving parties an opportunity to be heard, recall the sist.

## CHAPTER 11

### COUNTER CLAIM

### Counterclaim

**11.1.**—(1)   If a defender intends to state a counterclaim he must—

(a)   indicate that on the form of response; and

(b)   state the counterclaim—

(i)   in writing on the form of response; or

(ii)   orally at the Hearing.

(2)   Where a defender states a counterclaim in accordance with paragraph (1)(b)(i) he must at the same time send a copy of the form of response to—

(a)   the pursuer; and

(b)   any other party.

(3)   *[Repealed by the Act of Sederunt (Sheriff Court Rules) (Miscellaneous Amendments) 2009 (SSI 2009/294) r.12 (effective October 1, 2009).]*

(5)   Where a defender has indicated in terms of paragraph (1)(a) that he intends to state a counterclaim orally at the Hearing the sheriff may continue the Hearing to allow an answer to the counterclaim to be stated.

(6)   The defender may state a counterclaim after—

(a)   the Hearing; or

(b)   any continuation of the Hearing,

as the case may be, only with the leave of the sheriff.

(7)   If a counterclaim has been stated orally at any hearing at which the pursuer fails to appear or be represented the sheriff may continue that hearing after noting the counterclaim and the factual basis of it to allow the pursuer to appear.

(8)   Intimation of a continued hearing fixed under paragraph (7) shall be given to the pursuer by the sheriff clerk in Form 14 advising him that if he fails to appear or be represented at the continued hearing decree may be granted in terms of the counterclaim.

## Chapter 12

### Alteration of summons etc.

**Alteration of summons etc.**

**12.1.**—(1)   The sheriff may, on the incidental application of a party allow amendment of the summons, form of response or any counterclaim, and adjust the note of disputed issues at any time before final judgment is pronounced on the merits.

(2)   In an undefended claim, the sheriff may order the amended summons to be re-served on the defender on such period of notice as he thinks fit.

## Chapter 13

### Additional defender

**Additional defender**

**13.1.**—(1)   Any person who has not been called as a defender may apply by incidental application to the sheriff for leave to enter a claim as a defender, and to state a defence.

(2)   An application under this rule must specify—

(a)   the applicant's title and interest to enter the claim; and

(b)   the grounds of the defence which he proposes to state.

(3)   On the lodging of an application under this rule—

(a)   the sheriff must fix a date for hearing the application; and

(b)   the applicant must forthwith serve a copy of the application and of the order for a hearing on the parties to the claim.

(4)   After hearing the applicant and any party to the claim the sheriff may, if he is satisfied that the applicant has shown title and interest to enter the claim, grant the application.

(5)   Where an application is granted under paragraph (4)—

(a)   the applicant shall be treated as a defender; and

(b)   the claim shall proceed against him as if was the Hearing in terms of rule 9.2.

## Chapter 13A[1]

### Interventions by the Commission for Equality and Human Rights

**Interpretation**

**13A.1.**   In this Chapter "the CEHR" means the Commission for Equality and Human Rights.

**Interventions by the CEHR**

**13A.2.**—(1)   The CEHR may apply to the sheriff for leave to intervene in any small claim in accordance with this Chapter.

---

[1] As inserted by the Act of Sederunt (Sheriff Court Rules) (Miscellaneous Amendments) 2008 (SSI 2008/223) r.7(2) (effective July 1, 2008).

(2) This Chapter is without prejudice to any other entitlement of the CEHR by virtue of having title and interest in relation to the subject matter of any proceedings by virtue of section 30(2) of the Equality Act 2006 or any other enactment to seek to be sisted as a party in those proceedings.

(3) Nothing in this Chapter shall affect the power of the sheriff to make such other direction as he considers appropriate in the interests of justice.

(4) Any decision of the sheriff in proceedings under this Chapter shall be final and not subject to appeal.

### Applications to intervene

**13A.3.**—(1) An application for leave to intervene shall be by way of minute of intervention in Form 14A and the CEHR shall—
- (a) send a copy of it to all the parties; and
- (b) lodge it in process, certifying that subparagraph (a) has been complied with.

(2) A minute of intervention shall set out briefly—
- (a) the CEHR's reasons for believing that the proceedings are relevant to a matter in connection with which the CEHR has a function;
- (b) the issue in the proceedings which the CEHR wishes to address; and
- (c) the propositions to be advanced by the CEHR and the CEHR's reasons for believing that they are relevant to the proceedings and that they will assist the sheriff.

(3) The sheriff may—
- (a) refuse leave without a hearing;
- (b) grant leave without a hearing unless a hearing is requested under paragraph (4);
- (c) refuse or grant leave after such a hearing.

(4) A hearing, at which the applicant and the parties may address the court on the matters referred to in paragraph (6)(c) may be held if, within 14 days of the minute of intervention being lodged, any of the parties lodges a request for a hearing.

(5) Any diet in pursuance of paragraph (4) shall be fixed by the sheriff clerk who shall give written intimation of the diet to the CEHR and all the parties.

(6) The sheriff may grant leave only if satisfied that—
- (a) the proceedings are relevant to a matter in connection with which the CEHR has a function;
- (b) the propositions to be advanced by the CEHR are relevant to the proceedings and are likely to assist him; and
- (c) the intervention will not unduly delay or otherwise prejudice the rights of the parties, including their potential liability for expenses.

(7) In granting leave the sheriff may impose such terms and conditions as he considers desirable in the interests of justice, including, subject to section 36B of the Sheriff Courts (Scotland) Act 1971, making provision in respect of any additional expenses incurred by the parties as a result of the intervention.

(8) The sheriff clerk shall give written intimation of a grant or refusal of leave to the CEHR and all the parties.

### Form of intervention

**13A.4.**—(1) An intervention shall be by way of a written submission which (including any appendices) shall not exceed 5000 words.

(2) The CEHR shall lodge the submission and send a copy of it to all the parties by such time as the sheriff may direct.

(3) The sheriff may in exceptional circumstances—

    (a)   allow a longer written submission to be made;

    (b)   direct that an oral submission is to be made.

(4) Any diet in pursuance of paragraph (3)(b) shall be fixed by the sheriff clerk who shall give written intimation of the diet to the CEHR and all the parties.

CHAPTER 13B[1]

INTERVENTIONS BY THE SCOTTISH COMMISSION FOR HUMAN RIGHTS

**Interpretation**

**13B.1.**  In this Chapter—

    "the Act of 2006" means the Scottish Commission for Human Rights Act 2006; and

    "the SCHR" means the Scottish Commission for Human Rights.

**Applications to intervene**

**13B.2.**—(1)  An application for leave to intervene shall be by way of minute of intervention in Form 14B and the SCHR shall—

    (a)   send a copy of it to all the parties; and

    (b)   lodge it in process, certifying that subparagraph (a) has been complied with.

(2) In granting leave the sheriff may impose such terms and conditions as he considers desirable in the interests of justice, including, subject to section 36B of the Sheriff Courts (Scotland) Act 1971, making provision in respect of any additional expenses incurred by the parties as a result of the intervention.

(3) The sheriff clerk shall give written intimation of a grant or refusal of leave to the SCHR and all the parties.

(4) Any decision of the sheriff in proceedings under this Chapter shall be final and not subject to appeal.

**Invitations to intervene**

**13B.3.**—(1)  An invitation to intervene under section 14(2)(b) of the Act of 2006 shall be in Form 14C and the sheriff clerk shall send a copy of it to the SCHR and all the parties.

(2) An invitation under paragraph (1) shall be accompanied by—

    (a)   a copy of the pleadings in the proceedings; and

    (b)   such other documents relating to those proceedings as the sheriff thinks relevant.

(3) In issuing an invitation under section 14(2)(b) of the Act of 2006, the sheriff may impose such terms and conditions as he considers desirable in the interests of justice, including, subject to section 36B of the Sheriff Courts (Scotland) Act 1971, making provision in respect of any additional expenses incurred by the parties as a result of the intervention.

**Form of intervention**

**13B.4.**—(1)  An intervention shall be by way of a written submission which (including any appendices) shall not exceed 5000 words.

---

[1] As inserted by the Act of Sederunt (Sheriff Court Rules) (Miscellaneous Amendments) 2008 (SSI 2008/223) r.7(2) (effective July 1, 2008).

(2) The SCHR shall lodge the submission and send a copy of it to all the parties by such time as the sheriff may direct.

(3) The sheriff may in exceptional circumstances—

    (a) allow a longer written submission to be made;

    (b) direct that an oral submission is to be made.

(4) Any diet in pursuance of paragraph (3)(b) shall be fixed by the sheriff clerk who shall give written intimation of the diet to the SCHR and all the parties.

## CHAPTER 14

### APPLICATIONS FOR SIST OF PARTY AND TRANSFERENCE

**Application for sist of party and transference**

**14.1.**—(1) If a party dies or becomes legally incapacitated while a claim is depending, any person claiming to represent that party or his estate may apply by incidental application to be sisted as a party to the claim.

(2) If a party dies or becomes legally incapacitated while a claim is depending and the provisions of paragraph (1) are not invoked, any other party may apply by incidental application to have the claim transferred in favour of or against, as the case may be, any person who represents that party or his estate.

## CHAPTER 15

### TRANSFER AND REMIT OF CLAIMS

**Transfer to another court**

**15.1.**—(1) The sheriff may transfer a claim to any other sheriff court, whether in the same sheriffdom or not, if the sheriff considers it expedient to do so.

(2) If the sheriff is satisfied that the court has no jurisdiction, he may transfer the claim to any sheriff court in which it appears to the sheriff that it ought to have been brought.

(3) A claim so transferred shall proceed in all respects as if it had been brought originally in the court to which it is transferred.

**Remit between procedures**

**15.2.**—(1) If the sheriff makes a direction that a claim is to be treated as an ordinary cause, he must, at the time of making that direction—

    (a) direct the pursuer to lodge an initial writ, and intimate it to every other party, within 14 days of the date of the direction;

    (b) direct the defender to lodge defences within 28 days of the date of the direction; and

    (c) fix a date and time for an Options Hearing and that date shall be the first suitable court day occurring not sooner than ten weeks, or such lesser period as he considers appropriate, after the last date for lodging the initial writ.

(2) If the sheriff directs that a claim is to be treated as a summary cause he must specify the next step of procedure to be followed.

(3) If the sheriff directs that an ordinary cause or a summary cause is to be treated as a claim under these rules it shall call for the Hearing held in terms of rule 9.1(2).

## CHAPTER 16

### PRODUCTIONS AND DOCUMENTS

**Lodging of productions**

**16.1.**—(1) A party who intends to rely at a hearing at which evidence is to be led, upon any documents or articles in his possession, which are reasonably capable of being lodged with the court, must—

    (a) lodge them with the sheriff clerk together with a list detailing the items no later than 14 days before the hearing; and

    (b) at the same time send a copy of the list to the other party.

(2) The documents referred to in paragraph (1) include any affidavit or other written statement admissible under section 2(1) of the Civil Evidence (Scotland) Act 1988.

(3) Subject to paragraph (4), only documents or articles produced—

    (a) in accordance with paragraph (1);

    (b) at an earlier hearing; or

    (c) under rule 17.2(3) or (4), may be used or put in evidence.

(4) Documents other than those mentioned in paragraph (3) may be used or put in evidence only with the—

    (a) consent of the parties; or

    (b) permission of the sheriff on cause shown, and on such terms as to expenses or otherwise as to him seem proper.

**Borrowing of productions**

**16.2.**—(1) Any productions borrowed must be returned not later than noon on the day preceding the date of any hearing.

(2) A receipt for any production borrowed must be entered in the list of productions and that list must be retained by the sheriff clerk.

(3) Subject to paragraph (4), productions may be borrowed only by—

    (a) a solicitor; or

    (b) his authorised clerk for whom he shall be responsible.

(4) A party litigant or an authorised lay representative may borrow a production only with permission of the sheriff and subject to such conditions as the sheriff may impose.

(5) Productions may be inspected within the office of the sheriff clerk during normal business hours, and copies may be obtained by a party litigant, where practicable, from the sheriff clerk.

**Documents lost or destroyed**

**16.3.**—(1) This rule applies to any—

    (a) summons;

    (b) form of response;

    (c) counterclaim;

    (d) Register of Small Claims; or

    (e) other document lodged with the sheriff clerk in connection with a claim.

(2) Where any document mentioned in paragraph (1) is—

    (a) lost; or

    (b) destroyed,

a copy of it, authenticated in such manner as the sheriff may require, may be substituted and shall, for the purposes of the claim including the use of diligence, be equivalent to the original.

### Documents and productions to be retained in custody of sheriff clerk

**16.4.**—(1) This rule applies to all documents or other productions which have at any time been lodged or referred to during a hearing.

(2) The sheriff clerk must retain in his custody any document or other production mentioned in paragraph (1) until—

    (a) after the expiry of the period during which an appeal is competent; and

    (b) any appeal lodged has been disposed of.

(3) Each party who has lodged productions in a claim shall—

    (a) after the final determination of the claim, where no appeal has been lodged, within 14 days after the appeal period has expired; or

    (b) within 14 days after the disposal of any appeal lodged on the final determination of the claim, uplift the productions from the sheriff clerk.

(4) Where any production has not been uplifted as required by paragraph (3), the sheriff clerk shall intimate to—

    (a) the solicitor who lodged the production; or

    (b) where no solicitor is acting, the party himself or such other party as seems appropriate, that if he fails to uplift the production within 28 days after the date of such intimation, it will be disposed of in such manner as the sheriff directs.

CHAPTER 17

RECOVERY OF DOCUMENTS AND ATTENDANCE OF WITNESSES

### Diligence for recovery of documents

**17.1**—(1) At any time after a summons has been served, a party may make an incidental application in writing to the sheriff to grant commission and diligence to recover documents.

(2) A party who makes an application in accordance with paragraph (1) must list in the application the documents which he wishes to recover.

(3) The sheriff may grant commission and diligence to recover those documents in the list mentioned in paragraph (2) which he considers relevant to the claim.

### Optional procedure before executing commission and diligence

**17.2.**—(1) Any party who has obtained a commission and diligence for the recovery of documents may, at any time before executing it, serve by first class recorded delivery post on the person from whom the documents are sought to be recovered (or on his known solicitor or solicitors) an order with certificate attached in Form 15.

(2) If in a claim the party in whose favour the commission and diligence has been granted is not—

    (a) a partnership or body corporate; or

    (b) acting in a representative capacity, and is not represented by a solicitor, service under paragraph (1) must be effected by the sheriff clerk posting a copy of the order together with a certificate in Form 15 by first class recorded delivery post or, on payment of the fee prescribed by the Scottish Ministers by order, by sheriff officer.

(3) Documents recovered in response to an order under paragraph (1) must be sent to, and retained by, the sheriff clerk who shall, on receiving them, advise the parties that the documents are in his possession and may be examined within his office during normal business hours.

(4) If the party who served the order is not satisfied that—

(a) full production has been made under the specification; or

(b) that adequate reasons for non-production have been given, he may execute the commission and diligence in normal form, notwithstanding his adoption in the first instance of the procedure in paragraph (1) above.

(5) Documents recovered under this rule may be submitted as evidence at any hearing without further formality, and rule 17.3(3) and (4) shall apply to such documents.

## Confidentiality of documents

**17.3.**—(1) In any claim where a party has obtained a commission and diligence to recover documents and the documents have been produced either—

(a) before the execution of the commission and diligence; or

(b) following execution of the commission and diligence, confidentiality may be claimed for any document produced.

(2) Where confidentiality is claimed under paragraph (1), the documents in respect of which confidentiality is claimed shall be enclosed in a separate, sealed packet.

(3) A sealed packet referred to in paragraph (2) shall not be opened except by authority of the sheriff obtained on the application of the party who sought the commission and diligence.

(4) Before the sheriff grants an application made in accordance with paragraph (3), he shall offer to hear the party or parties from whose possession the documents specified in the commission and diligence were obtained.

## Witnesses

**17.4.**—(1) A party shall be responsible for securing the attendance of his witnesses or havers at a hearing and shall be personally liable for their expenses.

(2) The summons or the copy served on the defender shall be sufficient warrant for the citation of witnesses or havers.

(3) The citation of a witness or haver must be in Form 16 and the certificate of execution of citation must be in Form 16a.

(4) The period of notice given to witnesses or havers cited in terms of paragraph (3) must be not less than seven days.

(5) A witness or haver shall be cited—

(a) by registered post or the first class recorded delivery service by the solicitor for the party on whose behalf he is cited;

(b) by a sheriff officer—

(i) personally;

(ii) by a citation being left with a resident at the person's dwelling place or an employee at his place of business;

(iii) by depositing it in that person's dwelling place or place of business;

(iv) by affixing it to the door of that person's dwelling place or place of business; or

(v) by registered post or the first class recorded delivery service.

(6) Where service is effected under paragraph 5(b)(iii) or (iv), the sheriff officer shall, as soon as possible after such service, send by ordinary post to the address at which he thinks it most likely that the person may be found, a letter containing a copy of the citation.

### Citation of witnesses by party litigants

**17.5.**—(1) Where a party to a claim is a party litigant he shall—

(a) not later than 28 days before any hearing on evidence apply to the sheriff to fix caution for expenses in such sum as the sheriff considers reasonable having regard to the number of witnesses he proposes to cite and the period for which they may be required to attend court; and

(b) before instructing a solicitor or a sheriff officer to cite a witness, find the sum fixed in accordance with paragraph (1)(a).

(2) A party litigant who does not intend to cite all the witnesses referred to in his application under paragraph (1)(a) may apply for variation of the amount of caution.

### Witnesses failing to attend

**17.6.**—(1) A hearing must not be adjourned solely on account of the failure of a witness to appear unless the sheriff, on cause shown, so directs.

(2) A witness or haver who fails without reasonable excuse to answer a citation after having been properly cited and offered his travelling expenses if he has asked for them may be ordered by the sheriff to pay a penalty not exceeding £250.

(3) The sheriff may grant decree for payment of a penalty imposed under paragraph (2) above in favour of the party on whose behalf the witness or haver was cited.

(4) The sheriff may grant warrant for the apprehension of the witness or haver and for bringing him to court.

(5) A warrant mentioned in paragraph (4) shall be effective in any sheriffdom without endorsation and the expenses of it may be awarded against the witness or haver.

CHAPTER 17A[1]

VULNERABLE WITNESSES (SCOTLAND) ACT 2004

### Interpretation

**17A.1.** In this Chapter—

"child witness notice" has the meaning given in section 12(2) of the 2004 Act;
"review application" means an application for review of arrangements for vulnerable witnesses pursuant to section 13 of the 2004 Act;
"vulnerable witness application" has the meaning given in section 12(6) of the 2004 Act.

### Child Witness Notice

**17A.2.** A child witness notice lodged in accordance with section 12(2) of the 2004 Act shall be in Form 16B.

---

[1] As inserted by the Act of Sederunt (Ordinary Cause, Summary Application, Summary Cause and Small Claim Rules) Amendment (Vulnerable Witnesses (Scotland) Act 2004) 2007 (SSI 2007/463) r.5(5) (effective November 1, 2007).

## Vulnerable Witness Application

**17A.3.** A vulnerable witness application lodged in accordance with section 12(6) of the 2004 Act shall be in Form 16C.

## Intimation

**17A.4.**—(1) The party lodging a child witness notice or vulnerable witness application shall intimate a copy of the child witness notice or vulnerable witness application to all the other parties to the proceedings and complete a certificate of intimation.

(2) A certificate of intimation referred to in paragraph (1) shall be in Form 16D and shall be lodged with the child witness notice or vulnerable witness application.

## Procedure on lodging child witness notice or vulnerable witness application

**17A.5.**—(1) On receipt of a child witness notice or vulnerable witness application, the sheriff may—

(a) make an order under section 12(1) or (6) of the 2004 Act without holding a hearing;

(b) require further information from any of the parties before making any further order;

(c) fix a date for a hearing of the child witness notice or vulnerable witness application.

(2) The sheriff may, subject to any statutory time limits, make an order altering the date of the proof or other hearing at which the child or vulnerable witness is to give evidence and make such provision for intimation of such alteration to all parties concerned as he deems appropriate.

(3) An order fixing a hearing for a child witness notice or vulnerable witness application shall be intimated by the sheriff clerk—

(a) on the day the order is made; and

(b) in such manner as may be prescribed by the sheriff,

to all parties to the proceedings and such other persons as are named in the order where such parties or persons are not present at the time the order is made.

## Review of arrangements for vulnerable witnesses

**17A.6.**—(1) A review application shall be in Form 16E.

(2) Where the review application is made orally, the sheriff may dispense with the requirements of paragraph (1).

## Intimation of review application

**17A.7.**—(1) Where a review application is lodged, the applicant shall intimate a copy of the review application to all other parties to the proceedings and complete a certificate of intimation.

(2) A certificate of intimation referred to in paragraph (1) shall be in Form 16F and shall be lodged together with the review application.

## Procedure on lodging a review application

**17A.8.**—(1) On receipt of a review application, the sheriff may—

(a) if he is satisfied that he may properly do so, make an order under section 13(2) of the 2004 Act without holding a hearing or, if he is not so satisfied, make such an order after giving the parties an opportunity to be heard;

(b) require of any of the parties further information before making any further order;

(c)   fix a date for a hearing of the review application.

(2)   The sheriff may, subject to any statutory time limits, make an order altering the date of the proof or other hearing at which the child or vulnerable witness is to give evidence and make such provision for intimation of such alteration to all parties concerned as he deems appropriate.

(3)   An order fixing a hearing for a review application shall be intimated by the sheriff clerk—

(a)   on the day the order is made; and

(b)   in such manner as may be prescribed by the sheriff,

to all parties to the proceedings and such other persons as are named in the order where such parties or persons are not present at the time the order is made.

### Determination of special measures

**17A.9.**   When making an order under section 12(1) or (6) or 13(2) of the 2004 Act the sheriff may, in light thereof, make such further orders as he deems appropriate in all the circumstances.

### Intimation of an order under section 12(1) or (6) or 13(2)

**17A.10.**   An order under section 12(1) or (6) or 13(2) of the 2004 Act shall be intimated by the sheriff clerk—

(a)   on the day the order is made; and

(b)   in such manner as may be prescribed by the sheriff,

to all parties to the proceedings and such other persons as are named in the order where such parties or persons are not present at the time the order is made.

### Taking of evidence by commissioner

**17A.11.**—(1)   An interlocutor authorising the special measure of taking evidence by a commissioner shall be sufficient authority for the citing the witness to appear before the commissioner.

(2)   At the commission the commissioner shall—

(a)   administer the oath *de fideli administratione* to any clerk appointed for the commission; and

(b)   administer to the witness the oath, or where the witness elects to affirm, the affirmation.

(3)   The commission shall proceed without interrogatories unless, on cause shown, the sheriff otherwise directs.

### Commission on interrogatories

**17A.12.**—(1)   Where interrogatories have not been dispensed with, the party citing or intending to cite the vulnerable witness shall lodge draft interrogatories in process.

(2)   Any other party may lodge cross-interrogatories.

(3)   The interrogatories and cross-interrogatories, when adjusted, shall be extended and returned to the sheriff clerk for approval and the settlement of any dispute as to their contents by the sheriff.

(4)   The party who cited the vulnerable witness shall—

(a)   provide the commissioner with a copy of the pleadings (including any adjustments and amendments), the approved interrogatories and any cross-interrogatories and a certified copy of the interlocutor of his appointment;

(b)   instruct the clerk; and

(c)   be responsible in the first instance for the fee of the commissioner and his clerk.

(5) The commissioner shall, in consultation with the parties, fix a diet for the execution of the commission to examine the witness.

### Commission without interrogatories

**17A.13.** Where interrogatories have been dispensed with, the party citing or intending to cite the vulnerable witness shall—

(a) provide the commissioner with a copy of the pleadings (including any adjustments and amendments) and a certified copy of the interlocutor of his appointment;

(b) fix a diet for the execution of the commission in consultation with the commissioner and every other party;

(c) instruct the clerk; and

(d) be responsible in the first instance for the fees of the commissioner and his clerk.

### Lodging of video record and documents

**17A.14.**—(1) Where evidence is taken on commission pursuant to an order made under section 12(1) or (6) or 13(2) of the 2004 Act the commissioner shall lodge the video record of the commission and relevant documents with the sheriff clerk.

(2) On the video record and any documents being lodged the sheriff clerk shall—

(a) note—

(i) the documents lodged;

(ii) by whom they were lodged; and

(iii) the date on which they were lodged, and

(b) intimate what he has noted to all parties concerned.

### Custody of video record and documents

**17A.15.**—(1) The video record and documents referred to in rule 17A.14 shall, subject to paragraph (2), be kept in the custody of the sheriff clerk.

(2) Where the video record of the evidence of a witness is in the custody of the sheriff clerk under this rule and where intimation has been given to that effect under rule 17A.14(2), the name and address of that witness and the record of his evidence shall be treated as being in the knowledge of the parties; and no party shall be required, notwithstanding any enactment to the contrary—

(a) to include the name of that witness in any list of witnesses; or

(b) to include the record of his evidence in any list of productions.

### Application for leave for party to be present at the commission

**17A.16.** An application for leave for a party to be present in the room where the commission proceedings are taking place shall be by incidental application..

(4) In Appendix 1—

(a) for Form 16 there shall be set out the form in Part 1 of Schedule 3 to this Act of Sederunt; and

(b)  after Form 16A there shall be inserted the forms set out in Part 2 of Schedule 3 to this Act of Sederunt.

## CHAPTER 18

## EUROPEAN COURT

### Interpretation of rules 18.2 to 18.5

**18.1.**—[1](1)  In rules 18.2 to 18.5—

"the European Court" means the Court of Justice of the European Communities;

"reference" means a reference to the European Court for—

(a)  a preliminary ruling under Article 267 of the Treaty on the Functioning of the European Union, Article 150 of the Euratom Treaty or Article 41 of the E.C.S.C. Treaty; or

(b)  a ruling on the interpretation of the Conventions, as defined in section 1(1) of the Civil Jurisdiction and Judgments Act 1982, under Article 3 of Schedule 2 to that Act.

(2)  The expressions "Euratom Treaty" and "E.C.S.C. Treaty" have the meanings assigned respectively in Schedule 1 to the European Communities Act 1972.

(3)[2]  In paragraph (1), "the Treaty on the Functioning of the European Union" means the treaty referred to in section 1(2)(s) of the European Communities Act 1972.

### Application for reference

**18.2.**—(1)  The sheriff may, on the incidental application of a party, or of his own accord, make a reference.

(2)  A reference must be made in the form of a request for a preliminary ruling of the European Court in Form 17.

### Preparation of case for reference

**18.3.**—(1)  If the sheriff decides that a reference shall be made, he must within four weeks draft a reference.

(2)  On the reference being drafted, the sheriff clerk must send a copy to each party.

(3)  Within four weeks after the date on which copies of the draft have been sent to parties, each party may—

(a)  lodge with the sheriff clerk; and

(b)  send to every other party, a note of any adjustments he seeks to have made in the draft reference.

(4)  Within 14 days after the date on which any such note of adjustments may be lodged, the sheriff, after considering any such adjustments, must make and sign the reference.

(5)  The sheriff clerk must forthwith intimate the making of the reference to each party.

---

[1] As amended by the Act of Sederunt (Sheriff Court Rules) (Miscellaneous Amendments) (No.3) 2012 (SSI 2012/271) para.8 (effective November 1, 2012).

[2] As inserted by the Act of Sederunt (Sheriff Court Rules) (Miscellaneous Amendments) (No.3) 2012 (SSI 2012/271) para.8 (effective November 1, 2012).

**Sist of claim**

**18.4.**—(1) Subject to paragraph (2), on a reference being made, the claim must, unless the sheriff when making the reference otherwise orders, be sisted until the European Court has given a preliminary ruling on the question referred to it.

(2) The sheriff may recall a sist made under paragraph (1) for the purpose of making an interim order which a due regard to the interests of the parties may require.

**Transmission of reference**

**18.5.** A copy of the reference, certified by the sheriff clerk, must be transmitted by the sheriff clerk to the Registrar of the European Court.

CHAPTER 19

ABANDONMENT

**Abandonment of claim**

**19.1.**—(1) At any time prior to decree being granted, the pursuer may offer to abandon the claim.

(2) If the pursuer offers to abandon, the sheriff clerk must assess the expenses payable by the pursuer to the defender on such basis as the sheriff may direct subject to the provisions of section 36B of the 1971 Act and rule 21.6, and the claim must be continued to the first appropriate court occurring not sooner than 14 days thereafter.

(3) If before the continued diet the pursuer makes payment to the defender of the amount fixed under paragraph (2), the sheriff must dismiss the action unless the pursuer consents to absolvitor.

(4) If before the continued diet the pursuer fails to pay the amount fixed under paragraph (2), the defender shall be entitled to decree of absolvitor with expenses.

CHAPTER 20

DECREE BY DEFAULT

**Decree by default**

**20.1.**—(1) If, after the sheriff has fixed a hearing on evidence under rule 9.2(4), any party fails to appear or be represented at a hearing, the sheriff may grant decree by default.

(2) If all parties fail to appear or be represented at a hearing referred to at paragraph (1) the sheriff must, unless sufficient reason appears to the contrary, dismiss the claim and any counterclaim.

(3) If, after a defence has been stated, a party fails to implement an order of the court, the sheriff may, after giving him an opportunity to be heard, grant decree by default.

(4) The sheriff shall not grant decree by default solely on the ground that a party has failed to appear at the hearing of an incidental application.

CHAPTER 21

DECREES, EXTRACTS, EXECUTION AND VARIATION

**Decree**

**21.1.**—(1) The sheriff must not grant decree against—

    (a) a defender in respect of a claim; or

    (b) a pursuer in respect of a counterclaim,

under any provision of these Rules unless satisfied that a ground of jurisdiction exists.

### Decree for alternative claim for payment

**21.2.**—(1)  If the sheriff has granted decree for—

 (a)   delivery;

 (b)   recovery of possession of moveable property; or

 (c)   implement of an obligation,

and the defender fails to comply with that decree, the pursuer may lodge with the sheriff clerk an incidental application for decree in terms of the alternative claim for payment.

(2)  If the pursuer lodges an incidental application in terms of paragraph (1), he must intimate it to the defender at or before the time it is lodged with the sheriff clerk.

(3)  The pursuer must appear at the hearing of an incidental application under paragraph (1).

### Taxes on funds under control of the court

**21.3.**  In a claim in which money has been consigned into court under the Sheriff Court Consignations (Scotland) Act 1893, no decree, warrant or order for payment to any person shall be granted until there has been lodged with the sheriff clerk a certificate by an authorised officer of the Inland Revenue stating that all taxes or duties payable to the Commissioners of Inland Revenue have been paid or satisfied.

### Correction of interlocutor or note

**21.4.**  At any time before extract, the sheriff may correct any clerical or incidental error in an interlocutor or note attached to it.

### Extract of decree

**21.5.**—(1)  Unless the sheriff on application authorises earlier extract, extract of a decree signed by the sheriff clerk may be issued only after the lapse of 14 days from the granting of the decree.

(2)  An application for early extract shall be made by incidental application.

(3)  In a claim where an appeal has been lodged, the extract may not be issued until the appeal has been disposed of.

(4)  The extract decree—

 (a)   may be written on the summons or on a separate paper;

 (b)   may be in one of Forms 18 to 18i; and

 (c)   shall be warrant for all lawful execution.

### Expenses

**21.6.**[1](1)[2]  This rule applies, subject to section 36B of the 1971 Act, to the determination of expenses—

 (a)   in a claim, where the defender has—

  (i)   not stated a defence;

  (ii)   having stated a defence, has not proceeded with it; or

---

[1] As amended by the Act of Sederunt (Rules of the Court of Session, Sheriff Appeal Court Rules and Sheriff Court Rules Amendment) (Sheriff Appeal Court) 2015 (SSI 2015/419) r.12 (effective 1 January 2016; as to savings see SSI 2015/419 r.20(7)(a)).

[2] As substituted by Act of Sederunt (Ordinary Cause, Summary Application, Summary Cause and Small Claim Rules) Amendment (Miscellaneous) 2005 (SSI 2005/648) r.5(2) (effective January 2, 2006).

      (iii)   having stated a defence, has not acted in good faith as to its merits;

(b)   in a claim where there has been unreasonable conduct on the part of a party to that claim in relation to the proceedings or the claim;

(c)   *[Revoked by the Act of Sederunt (Rules of the Court of Session, Sheriff Appeal Court Rules and Sheriff Court Rules Amendment) (Sheriff Appeal Court) 2015 (SSI 2015/419) r.12 (effective 1 January 2016; as to savings see SSI 2015/419 r.20(7)(a)).]*

(2)[1]  Subject to paragraphs (3) to (5), the sheriff clerk must, with the approval of the sheriff, assess the amount of expenses including the fees and outlays of witnesses awarded in any claim, in accordance with the applicable statutory table of fees.

(3)[2]  Paragraph (4) applies to a party who—

(a)   represents himself;

(b)   is represented by an authorised lay representative or a person authorised under any enactment to conduct proceedings in the sheriff court; or

(c)   is not an individual and—

      (i)   is represented by an authorised lay representative or a person authorised under any enactment to conduct proceedings in the sheriff court; and

      (ii)   if unrepresented could not represent itself.

(4)  A party mentioned in paragraph (3) who, if he had been represented by a solicitor or advocate would have been entitled to expenses, may be awarded any outlays or expenses to which he might be found entitled by virtue of the 1975 Act or any enactment under that Act.

(5)  In every case including an appeal where expenses are awarded, the sheriff clerk shall hear the parties or their solicitors on the claims for expenses including fees, if any, and outlays.

(6)  Except where the sheriff has reserved judgment or where he orders otherwise, the hearing on the claim for expenses must take place immediately upon the decision being pronounced.

(7)  When that hearing is not held immediately, the sheriff clerk must—

(a)   fix the date, time and place when he shall hear the parties or their solicitors; and

(b)   give all parties at least 14 days' notice in writing of the hearing so fixed.

(8)  The party awarded expenses must—

(a)   lodge his account of expenses in court at least seven days prior to the date of any hearing fixed under paragraph (7); and

(b)   at the same time forward a copy of that account to every other party.

(9)  The sheriff clerk must—

(a)   fix the amount of the expenses; and

(b)   report his decision to the sheriff in open court for his approval at a diet which the sheriff clerk has intimated to the parties.

(10)  The sheriff, after hearing parties or their solicitors if objections are stated, must pronounce final decree including decree for payment of expenses as approved by him.

---

[1] As amended by the Act of Sederunt (Sheriff Court Rules Amendment) (Sections 25 to 29 of the Law Reform (Miscellaneous Provisions) (Scotland) Act 1990) 2009 (SSI 2009/164) r.5(3) (effective May 20, 2009).

[2] As amended by the Act of Sederunt (Ordinary Cause, Summary Application, Summary Cause and Small Claim Rules) Amendment (Miscellaneous) 2007 (SSI 2007/6) r.5(c) (effective January 29, 2007).

(11) *[Revoked by the Act of Sederunt (Rules of the Court of Session, Sheriff Appeal Court Rules and Sheriff Court Rules Amendment) (Sheriff Appeal Court) 2015 (SSI 2015/419) r.12 (effective 1 January 2016; as to savings see SSI 2015/419 r.20(7)(a)).]*

(12) Failure by—

    (a)   any party to comply with any of the foregoing provisions of this rule; or

    (b)   the successful party or parties to appear at the hearing on expenses, must be reported by the sheriff clerk to the sheriff at a diet which the sheriff clerk has intimated to the parties.

(13) In either of the circumstances mentioned in paragraphs (12)(a) or (b), the sheriff must, unless sufficient cause be shown, pronounce decree on the merits of the claim and find no expenses due to or by any party.

(14) A decree pronounced under paragraph (13) shall be held to be the final decree for the purposes of these Rules.

(15) The sheriff may, if he thinks fit, on the application of the solicitor of any party to whom expenses may be awarded, made at or before the time of the final decree being pronounced, grant decree in favour of that solicitor for the expenses of the claim.

## Charge

**21.7.**—(1) The period for payment specified in any charge following on a decree for payment granted in a claim shall be—

    (a)   14 days if the person on whom it is served is within the United Kingdom; and

    (b)   28 days if he is outside the United Kingdom or his whereabouts are unknown.

(2) The period in respect of any other form of charge on a decree granted in a claim shall be 14 days.

## Service of charge where address of defender is unknown

**21.8.**—(1) If the address of a defender is not known to the pursuer, a charge shall be deemed to have been served on the defender if it is—

    (a)   served on the sheriff clerk of the sheriff court district where the defender's last known address is located; and

    (b)   displayed by the sheriff clerk on the walls of court for the period of the charge.

(2) On receipt of such a charge, the sheriff clerk must display it on the walls of court and it must remain displayed for the period of the charge.

(3) The period specified in the charge shall run from the first date on which it was displayed on the walls of court.

(4) On the expiry of the period of charge, the sheriff clerk must endorse a certificate in Form 19 on the charge certifying that it has been displayed in accordance with this rule and must thereafter return the charge to the sheriff officer by whom service was executed.

## Diligence on decree in claim for delivery

**21.9.**—(1) In a claim for delivery, the court may, when granting decree, grant warrant to search for and take possession of goods and to open shut and lockfast places.

(2) A warrant granted under paragraph (1) shall only apply to premises occupied by the defender.

### Applications in same claim for variation, etc. of decree

**21.10.**—(1)  If by virtue of any enactment the sheriff, without a new action being initiated, may order that—

    (a)   a decree granted be varied, discharged or rescinded; or

    (b)   the execution of that decree in so far as it has not already been executed be sisted or suspended, the party requesting the sheriff to make such an order must do so by lodging a minute to that effect, setting out briefly the reasons for the application.

(2)  On the lodging of such a minute by the pursuer, the sheriff clerk must grant warrant for service upon the defender (provided that the pursuer has returned the extract decree).

(3)  On the lodging of such a minute by the defender, the sheriff clerk must grant warrant for service upon the pursuer ordaining him to return the extract decree and may, where appropriate, grant interim sist of execution of the decree.

(4)  Subject to paragraph (5), the minute shall not be heard in court unless seven days' notice of the minute and warrant has been given to the other parties by the party lodging the minute.

(5)  The sheriff may, on cause shown, alter the period of seven days referred to in paragraph (4) but may not reduce it to less than two days.

(6)  This rule shall not apply to any proceedings under the Debtors (Scotland) Act 1987 or to proceedings which may be subject to the provisions of that Act.

CHAPTER 22

RECALL OF DECREE

### Recall of decree

**22.1.**—[1](1)  A party may apply for recall of a decree granted under any of the following provisions—

    (a)   rule 8.1(3);

    (b)   paragraph (6), (7) or (8) of rule 9.1; or

    (c)   rule 11.1(8).

(2)  The application is to be by minute in Form 20, which must be lodged with the sheriff clerk.

(3)  The application must include where appropriate (and if not already lodged with the sheriff clerk), the proposed defence or the proposed answer to the counterclaim.

(4)  A party may apply for recall of a decree in the same claim on one occasion only.

(5)  A minute for recall of a decree of dismissal must be lodged within 14 days of the date of decree.

(6)  Subject to paragraphs (7) and (8), a minute for recall of any other kind of decree may be lodged at any time before the decree is fully implemented.

(7)  Subject to paragraph (8), where a charge or arrestment has been executed following the decree, the minute must be lodged within 14 days of that execution (or the first such execution where there has been more than one).

(8)  In the case of a party seeking recall who was served with the action under rule 6.5, the minute must be lodged—

---

[1] As substituted by the Act of Sederunt (Sheriff Court Rules) (Miscellaneous Amendments) 2011 (SSI 2011/193) r.17 (effective April 4, 2011).

    (a)   within a reasonable time of such party having knowledge of the decree against him or her; but

    (b)   in any event, within one year of the date of decree.

(9)  On the lodging of a minute for recall of a decree, the sheriff clerk must fix a date, time and place for a hearing of the minute.

(10)  Where a hearing has been fixed under paragraph (9), the party seeking recall must, not less than 7 days before the date fixed for the hearing, serve upon the other party—

    (a)   a copy of the minute in Form 20a; and

    (b)   a note of the date, time and place of the hearing.

(11)  Paragraph (12) applies if the party seeking recall—

    (a)   is not a partnership or body corporate;

    (b)   is not acting in a representative capacity; and

    (c)   is not represented by a solicitor.

(12)  The sheriff clerk must assist such party to complete and lodge the minute for recall and arrange service of the minute for recall—

    (a)   by first class recorded delivery post; or

    (b)   on payment of the fee prescribed by the Scottish Ministers by order, by sheriff officer.

(13)  At a hearing fixed under paragraph (9), the sheriff must recall the decree so far as not implemented and the hearing must then proceed as a hearing held under rules 9.1(4) to (8) and 9.2.

(14)  A minute for recall of a decree, when lodged and served in terms of this rule, will have the effect of preventing any further action being taken by the other party to enforce the decree.

(15)  On receipt of the copy minute for recall of a decree, any party in possession of an extract decree must return it forthwith to the sheriff clerk.

(16)  If it appears to the sheriff that there has been any failure or irregularity in service of the minute for recall of a decree, the sheriff may order re-service of the minute on such conditions as the sheriff thinks fit.

CHAPTER 23

APPEALS

### Appeals: application for stated case

**23.1.**[1](1)  An appeal to the Sheriff Appeal Court, other than an appeal to which rule 23.4 applies, must be in Form 21 and lodged with the sheriff clerk not later than 14 days after the date of final decree—

    (a)   requesting a stated case; and

    (b)   specifying the point of law upon which the appeal is to proceed.

(2)  The appellant must, at the same time as lodging Form 21, intimate a copy of it to every other party.

(3)  The sheriff must, within 28 days of the lodging of Form 21, issue a draft stated case containing—

    (a)   findings in fact and law or, where appropriate, a narrative of the proceedings before him;

---

[1] As amended by the Act of Sederunt (Rules of the Court of Session, Sheriff Appeal Court Rules and Sheriff Court Rules Amendment) (Sheriff Appeal Court) 2015 (SSI 2015/419) r.12 (effective 1 January 2016; as to savings see SSI 2015/419 rule 20(7)(a)).

(b)    appropriate questions of law; and

(c)    a note stating the reasons for his decisions in law, and the sheriff clerk must send a copy of the draft stated case to the parties.

(4)   Within 14 days of the issue of the draft stated case—

(a)    a party may lodge with the sheriff clerk a note of any adjustments which he seeks to make;

(b)    a respondent may state any point of law which he wishes to raise in the appeal; and

(c)    the note of adjustment and, where appropriate, point of law must be intimated to every other party.

(5)   The sheriff may, on the motion of a party or of his own accord, and must where he proposes to reject any proposed adjustment, allow a hearing on adjustments and may provide for such further procedure under this rule prior to the hearing of the appeal as he thinks fit.

(6)   The sheriff must, within 14 days after—

(a)    the latest date on which a note of adjustments has been or may be lodged; or

(b)    where there has been a hearing on adjustments, that hearing, and after considering such note and any representations made to him at the hearing, state and sign the case.

(7)   If the sheriff is temporarily absent from duty for any reason, the sheriff principal may extend any period specified in paragraphs (3) or (6) for such period or periods as he considers reasonable.

(8)   The stated case signed by the sheriff must include questions of law, framed by him, arising from the points of law stated by the parties and such other questions of law as he may consider appropriate.

(9)[1]   After the sheriff has signed the stated case, the appeal is to proceed in accordance with Chapter 29 of the Act of Sederunt (Sheriff Appeal Court Rules) 2015.

(10)   After the sheriff has signed the stated case, the appeal is to proceed in accordance with Chapter 29 of the Act of Sederunt (Sheriff Appeal Court Rules) 2015.

## Effect of and abandonment of appeal

**23.2.**    *[Revoked by the Act of Sederunt (Rules of the Court of Session, Sheriff Appeal Court Rules and Sheriff Court Rules Amendment) (Sheriff Appeal Court) 2015 (SSI 2015/419) r.12 (effective 1 January 2016; as to savings see SSI 2015/419 r.20(7)(a)).]*

## Hearing of appeal

**23.3.**    *[Revoked by the Act of Sederunt (Rules of the Court of Session, Sheriff Appeal Court Rules and Sheriff Court Rules Amendment) (Sheriff Appeal Court) 2015 (SSI 2015/419) r.12 (effective 1 January 2016; as to savings see SSI 2015/419 r.20(7)(a)).]*

## Appeal in relation to a time to pay direction

**23.4.**[2](1)    This rule applies to appeals to the Sheriff Appeal Court or to the Court of Session which relate solely to any application in connection with a time to pay direction.

(2)   Rule 23.1 shall not apply to appeals under this rule.

---

[1] As substituted by the Act of Sederunt (Sheriff Appeal Court Rules 2015 and Sheriff Court Rules Amendment) (Miscellaneous) 2016 (SSI 2016/194) r.5 (effective 7 July 2016).

[2] As amended by the Act of Sederunt (Rules of the Court of Session, Sheriff Appeal Court Rules and Sheriff Court Rules Amendment) (Sheriff Appeal Court) 2015 (SSI 2015/419) r.12 (effective 1 January 2016; as to savings see SSI 2015/419 r.20(7)(a)).

(3) An application for leave to appeal against a decision in an application for a time to pay direction or any order connected therewith must—

    (a) be made in Form 22, within seven days of that decision, to the sheriff who made the decision; and

    (b) must specify the question of law upon which the appeal is to proceed.

(4) If leave to appeal is granted, the appeal must be lodged in Form 23 and intimated by the appellant to every other party within 14 days of the order granting leave and the sheriff must state in writing his reasons for his original decision.

(5) *[Revoked by the Act of Sederunt (Rules of the Court of Session, Sheriff Appeal Court Rules and Sheriff Court Rules Amendment) (Sheriff Appeal Court) 2015 (SSI 2015/419) r.12 (effective 1 January 2016; as to savings see SSI 2015/419 r.20(7)(a)).]*

### Sheriff to regulate interim possession

**23.5.**—(1) Notwithstanding an appeal, the sheriff shall have power—

    (a) to regulate all matters relating to interim possession;

    (b) to make any order for the preservation of any property to which the claim relates or for its sale, if perishable;

    (c) to make any order for the preservation of evidence; or

    (d) to make in his discretion any interim order which a due regard for the interests of the parties may require.

(2) An order under paragraph (1) shall not be subject to review except by the appellate court at the hearing of the appeal.

## Chapter 24

### Management of damages payable to persons under legal disability

### Orders for payment and management of money

**24.1.**—(1) In a claim of damages in which a sum of money becomes payable, by virtue of a decree or an extra-judicial settlement, to or for the benefit of a person under legal disability (other than a person under the age of 18 years), the sheriff shall make such order regarding the payment and management of that sum for the benefit of that person as he thinks fit.

(2) Any order required under paragraph (1) shall be made on the granting of decree for payment or of absolvitor.

### Methods of management

**24.2.** In making an order under rule 24.1 (1), the sheriff may—

    (a) order the money to be paid to—

        (i) the Accountant of Court, or

        (ii) the guardian of the person under legal disability, as trustee, to be applied, invested or otherwise dealt with and administered under the directions of the sheriff for the benefit of the person under legal disability;

    (b) order the money to be paid to the sheriff clerk of the sheriff court district in which the person under legal disability resides, to be applied, invested or otherwise dealt with and administered, under the directions of the sheriff of that district, for the benefit of the person under legal disability; or

    (c) order the money to be paid directly to the person under legal disability.

## Subsequent orders

**24.3.**—(1) If the sheriff has made an order under rule 24.1(1), any person having an interest may apply for an order under rule 24.2, or any other order for the payment or management of the money, by incidental application.

(2) An application for directions under rule 24.2(a) or (b) may be made by any person having an interest by incidental application.

## Management of money paid to sheriff clerk

**24.4.**—(1) A receipt in Form 24 by the sheriff clerk shall be a sufficient discharge in respect of the amount paid to him under rules 24.1 to 24.3.

(2) The sheriff clerk shall, at the request of any competent court, accept custody of any sum of money in an claim of damages ordered to be paid to, applied, invested or otherwise dealt with by him, for the benefit of a person under legal disability.

(3) Any money paid to the sheriff clerk under rules 24.1 to 24.3 must be paid out, applied, invested or otherwise dealt with by the sheriff clerk only after such intimation, service and enquiry as the sheriff may order.

(4) Any sum of money invested by the sheriff clerk under rules 24.1 to 24.3 must be invested in a manner in which trustees are authorised to invest by virtue of the Trustee Investments Act 1961.

## Management of money payable to children

**24.5.** If the sheriff has made an order under section 13 of the Children (Scotland) Act 1995, an application by a person for an order by virtue of section 11(1)(d) of that Act must be made in writing.

CHAPTER 25

ELECTRONIC TRANSMISSION OF DOCUMENTS

## Extent of provision

**25.1.**—(1) Any document referred to in these rules which requires to be—
  (a) lodged with the sheriff clerk;
  (b) intimated to a party; or
  (c) sent by the sheriff clerk, may be in electronic or documentary form, and if in electronic form may be lodged, intimated or sent by e-mail or similar means.

(2) Paragraph (1) does not apply to any certificate of execution of service, citation or arrestment, or to a decree or extract decree of the court.

(3) Where any document is lodged by e-mail or similar means the sheriff may require any principal document to be lodged.

## Time of lodgement

**25.2.** The time of lodgement, intimation or sending shall be the time when the document was sent or transmitted.

## CHAPTER 26[1]

## THE EQUALITY ACT 2010

### Interpretation and application

**26.1.**—[2](1) In this Chapter—

"the Commission" means the Commission for Equality and Human Rights; and "the 2010 Act" means the Equality Act 2010.

(2) This Chapter applies to claims made by virtue of section 114(1) of the 2010 Act including a claim for damages.

### Intimation to Commission

**26.2.**[3] The pursuer shall send a copy of the summons to the Commission by registered or recorded delivery post.

### Assessor

**26.3.**—(1) The sheriff may, of his own motion or on the incidental application of any party, appoint an assessor.

(2) The assessor shall be a person who the sheriff considers has special qualifications to be of assistance in determining the cause.

### Taxation of Commission expenses

**26.4.** *[Omitted by the Act of Sederunt (Sheriff Court Rules) (Miscellaneous Amendments) 2008 (SSI 2008/223) para.7(3)(c) (effective July 1, 2008).]*

### National security

**26.5.**—[4](1) Where, on an incidental application under paragraph (3) or of the sheriffs own motion, the sheriff considers it expedient in the interests of national security, the sheriff may—

    (a) exclude from all or part of the proceedings—
        (i) the pursuer;
        (ii) the pursuer's representatives;
        (iii) any assessors;
    (b) permit a pursuer or representative who has been excluded to make a statement to the court before the commencement of the proceedings or the part of the proceedings, from which he or she is excluded;
    (c) take steps to keep secret all or part of the reasons for his or her decision in the proceedings.

(2) The sheriff clerk shall, on the making of an order under paragraph (1) excluding the pursuer or the pursuer's representatives, notify the Advocate General for Scotland of that order.

(3) A party may make an incidental application for an order under paragraph (1).

---

[1] As inserted by the Act of Sederunt (Ordinary Cause, Summary Application, Summary Cause and Small Claim Rules) Amendment (Equality Act 2006 etc.) 2006 (SSI 2006/509) r.5(2) (effective November 3, 2006). Chapter title amended by the Act of Sederunt (Sheriff Court Rules) (Equality Act 2010) 2010 (SSI 2010/340) para.5 (effective October 1, 2010).

[2] As substituted by the Act of Sederunt (Sheriff Court Rules) (Equality Act 2010) 2010 (SSI 2010/340) para.5 (effective October 1, 2010).

[3] As substituted by the Act of Sederunt (Sheriff Court Rules) (Miscellaneous Amendments) 2008 (SSI 2008/223) r.7(3)(b) (effective July 1, 2008).

[4] As inserted by the Act of Sederunt (Sheriff Court Rules) (Equality Act 2010) 2010 (SSI 2010/340) para.5 (effective October 1, 2010).

(4)  The steps referred to in paragraph (1)(c) may include the following—

(a)  directions to the sheriff clerk; and

(b)  orders requiring any person appointed to represent the interests of the pursuer in proceedings from which the pursuer or the pursuer's representatives are excluded not to communicate (directly or indirectly) with any persons (including the excluded pursuer)—

(i)  on any matter discussed or referred to;

(ii)  with regard to any material disclosed, during or with reference to any part of the proceedings from which the pursuer or the pursuer's representatives are excluded.

(5)  Where the sheriff has made an order under paragraph (4)(b), the person appointed to represent the interests of the pursuer may make an incidental application for authority to seek instructions from or otherwise communicate with an excluded person.

(6)  The sheriff may, on the application of a party intending to lodge an incidental application in written form, reduce the period of notice of two days specified in rule 10.1(2) or dispense with notice.

(7)  An application under paragraph (6) shall be made in the written incidental application, giving reasons for such reduction or dispensation.

### Transfer to Employment Tribunal

**26.6.**—[1](1)  On transferring proceedings to an employment tribunal under section 140(2) of the 2010 Act, the sheriff —

(a)  shall state his or her reasons for doing so in the interlocutor; and

(b)  may make the order on such conditions as to expenses or otherwise as he or she thinks fit.

(2)  The sheriff clerk must, within 7 days from the date of such order—

(a)  transmit the relevant process to the Secretary of the Employment Tribunals (Scotland);

(b)  notify each party to the proceedings in writing of the transmission under subparagraph (a); and

(c)  certify, by making an appropriate entry in the Register of Small Claims, that he or she has made all notifications required under subparagraph (b).

(3)  Transmission of the process under paragraph (2)(a) will be valid notwithstanding any failure by the sheriff clerk to comply with paragraph (2)(b) and (c).

### Transfer from Employment Tribunal

**26.7.**—[2](1)  On receipt of the documentation in proceedings which have been remitted from an employment tribunal under section 140(3) of the 2010 Act, the sheriff clerk must—

(a)  record the date of receipt on the first page of the documentation;

(b)  fix a hearing to determine further procedure not less than 14 days after the date of receipt of the process; and

(c)  forthwith send written notice of the date of the hearing fixed under subparagraph (b) to each party.

---

[1] As inserted by the Act of Sederunt (Sheriff Court Rules) (Equality Act 2010) 2010 (SSI 2010/340) para.5 (effective October 1, 2010).

[2] As inserted by the Act of Sederunt (Sheriff Court Rules) (Equality Act 2010) 2010 (SSI 2010/340) para.5 (effective October 1, 2010).

(2)   At the hearing arranged under paragraph (1)(b), the sheriff may make such order as he or she thinks fit to secure so far as practicable that the cause thereafter proceeds in accordance with these Rules.

## CHAPTER 27[1]

### LIVE LINKS

**27.1.**—(1)   On cause shown, a party may apply by incidental application for authority for the whole or part of—

(a)   the evidence of a witness or the party to be given; or

(b)   a submission to be made,

through a live link.

(2)   in paragraph (1)—

"witness"[2] means a person who has been or may be cited to appear before the court as a witness, except a vulnerable witness within the meaning of section 11(1) of the 2004 Act;

"submission" means any oral submission which would otherwise be made to the court by the party or his representative in person including an oral submission in support of an incidental application; and

"live link" means a live television link or such other arrangement as may be specified in the incidental application by which the witness, party or representative, as the case may be, is able to be seen and heard in the proceedings or heard in the proceedings and is able to see and hear or hear the proceedings while at a place which is outside the courtroom.

**Appendix 1**

**FORMS**

**Rule 1.1(4)**

Form A1[3]

Rule 2A.2(2)(b)

Statement by prospective lay representative for Pursuer/Defender*

Case Ref. No.:

in the cause

SHERIFFDOM OF (*insert name of sheriffdom*)

AT (*insert place of sheriff court*)

[A.B.], (*insert designation and address*), Pursuer

against

[C.D.], (*insert designation and address*), Defender

Court ref. no:

| |
|---|
| Name and address of prospective lay representative who requests to make oral submissions on behalf of party litigant: |
| Identify hearing(s) in respect of which permission for lay representation is sought: |
| The prospective lay representative declares that: |

---

[1] As inserted by the Act of Sederunt (Ordinary Cause, Summary Application, Summary Cause and Small Claim Rules) Amendment (Miscellaneous) (SSI 2007/6) r.5(e) (effective January 29, 2007).

[2] As amended by the Act of Sederunt (Ordinary Cause, Summary Application, Summary Cause and Small Claim Rules) Amendment (Vulnerable Witnesses (Scotland) Act 2004) 2007 (SSI 2007/463) r.5(4) (effective November 1, 2007).

[3] As inserted by the Act of Sederunt (Sheriff Court Rules) (Lay Representation) 2013 (SSI 2013/91) r.5 (effective April 4, 2013).

| (a) | I have no financial interest in the outcome of the case *or* I have the following financial interest in it:* |
|-----|---|
| (b) | I am not receiving remuneration or other reward directly or indirectly from the litigant for my assistance and will not receive directly or indirectly such remuneration or other reward from the litigant. |
| (c) | I accept that documents and information are provided to me by the litigant on a confidential basis and I undertake to keep them confidential. |
| (d) | I have no previous convictions *or* I have the following convictions: (list convictions)* |
| (e) | I have not been declared a vexatious litigant under the Vexatious Actions (Scotland) Act 1898 *or* I was declared a vexatious litigant under the Vexatious Actions (Scotland) Act 1898 on [insert date].* |

*(Signed)*
[Name of prospective lay representative]
[Date]

*(Insert Place/Date)*
The Sheriff grants/refuses* the application.

*[Signed]*
Sheriff Clerk
[Date]

Rule 4(1)(c)
(**delete as appropriate*)

**Form 1**[1]
*Summons*

FORM 1

OFFICIAL USE ONLY
SUMMONS No.

## Small Claim Summons
**Action for/of**
(state type, e.g., payment of money)

| | | |
|---|---|---|
| Sheriff Court (name, address, e-mail and telephone no.) | **1** | |
| Name and address of person making the claim (**pursuer**) | **2** | |
| Name and address of person against whom claim made (**defender**) | **3** | |
| Claim (form of decree or other order sought) | **4** | |
| Name, full address, telephone no, and e-mail address of pursuer's solicitor or authorised lay representative (if any) acting in the claim | **5** | |
| Fee Details (Enter these only if forms sent | **5a** | |

---

[1] As amended by the Act of Sederunt (Sheriff Court Rules Amendment) (Diligence) (SSI 2008/121) r.7(6) (effective April 1, 2008). This form as it applied immediately before April 1, 2008 continues to have effect for the purpose of any application for arrestment on the dependence made before that date.

electronically to court)

|   |   |   |
|---|---|---|
| 6 | **RETURN DAY** | **20** |
|   | **HEARING DATE** | 20 at am. |

*Sheriff Clerk to delete as appropriate*

The pursuer is authorised to serve a copy summons in Form *1a/1b, on the defender(s) not less than *21/42 days before the **RETURN DAY** shown in the box above. The summons is warrant for service, and for citation of witnesses to attend court on any future date at which evidence may be led.

*Court Authentication*

**NOTE: The pursuer should complete boxes 1 to 5a, and the statement of claim on page 2. The sheriff clerk will complete box 6.**

7. **STATE DETAILS OF CLAIM HERE (all cases) and PARTICULARS OF ARREST-MENT (furthcoming actions only)**

   **(To be completed by the pursuer. If space is insufficient, a separate sheet may be attached)**

   The details of the claim are:

   **FOR OFFICIAL USE ONLY**

   Sheriffs notes as to:

   1. Issues of fact and law in dispute
   2. Facts agreed
   3. Reasons for any final disposal at the hearing held on the calling date.

(note 1,2)FORM 1a

*Defender's copy summons—claim for or including claim for payment of money where time to pay direction or time order may be applied for*

|   |
|---|
| OFFICIAL USE ONLY |
| SUMMONS No. |

**Small Claim Summons**
   **Action for/of**
   (state type, e.g. payment of money)
   **DEFENDER'S COPY: Claim for or including payment of money (where time to pay direction or time order may be applied for)**

| | | |
|---|---|---|
| Sheriff Court<br>(name, address, e-mail and telephone no.) | **1** | |
| Name and address of person making the claim (**pursuer**) | **2** | |
| Name and address of person against whom claim made (**defender**) | **3** | |
| Claim (form of decree or other order sought—complete as in section 4 of Form 1) | **4** | |
| Name, full address, telephone no., and e-mail address of pursuer's solicitor or authorised lay representative (if any) acting in the claim | **5** | |

| | |
|---|---|
| **6** | **RETURN DAY** 20 |
| | **HEARING DATE** 20 at am. |

## NOTE: You will find details of claim on page 2.

| | |
|---|---|
| **7.** | **STATE DETAILS OF CLAIM HERE OR ATTACH A STATEMENT OF CLAIM** |
| | (To be completed by the pursuer. If space is insufficient, a separate sheet may be attached) |
| | The details of the claim are: |

| | |
|---|---|
| **8.** | **SERVICE ON DEFENDER** |

(Place)                                           (Date)

To:                                            (Defender)

You are hereby served with a copy of the above summons.

Solicitor / sheriff officer
*delete as appropriate*

## NOTE: The pursuer should complete boxes 1 to 6 on page 1, the statement of claim in box 7 on page 2 and section A on page 7 before service on the defender. The person serving the Summons will complete box 8, above.

## WHAT MUST I DO ABOUT THIS SUMMONS?

The RETURN DAY (on page 1 of this summons) is the deadline by which you need to reply to the court. You must send the correct forms back (see below for details) by this date if you want the court to hear your case. If you do not do this, in most cases there will not be a hearing about your case and the court will make a decision in your absence.

The HEARING DATE (on page 1 of this summons) is the date for the court hearing.

**You should decide whether you wish to dispute the claim, admit liability for the claim and whether you owe any money or not, and how you wish to proceed.** Then, look at the 5 options listed below. Find the one that covers your decision and follow the instructions given there.

If you are not sure what you need to do, contact the sheriff clerk's office before the return day. Written guidance can also be obtained from the Scottish Court Service website (www.scot-courts.gov.uk).

## OPTIONS

**1. ADMIT LIABILITY FOR THE CLAIM and settle it with the pursuer now.**

**If you wish to avoid the possibility of a court order passing against you, you should settle the claim (including any question of expenses) with the pursuer or his representative in good time before the return day.** Please do not send any payment direct to the court. Any payment should be made to the pursuer or his representative.

**2. ADMIT LIABILITY FOR THE CLAIM and make written application to pay by instalments or by deferred lump sum.**

Complete Box 1 of section **B** on page 7 of this form and return pages 7, 9 and 10 to the court **to arrive on or before the return day**. You should then contact the court to find out whether or not the pursuer has accepted your offer. If he has not accepted it, the case will then call in court on the calling date, when the court will decide how the amount claimed is to be paid.

If your claim is for delivery, or implement of an obligation, and you wish to pay the alternative amount claimed, you may also wish to make an application about the method of payment. If so, follow the instructions in the previous paragraph.

**NOTE: If you fail to return pages 7, 9 and 10 as directed, or if, having returned them, you fail to attend or are not represented at the calling date if the case is to call, the court may decide the claim in your absence.**

**3. ADMIT LIABILITY FOR THE CLAIM and attend at court to make application to pay by instalments or deferred lump sum.**

Complete Box 2 on page 7. Return page 7 to the court so that it arrives **on or before the return day.**

**If the claim for delivery, or implement of an obligation, you may wish to pay the alternative amount claimed and attend at court to make an application about the method of payment.**

**You must attend personally, or be represented, at court on the hearing date.** Your representative may be a solicitor, or someone else having your authority. It may be helpful if you or your representative bring pages 1 and 2 of this form to the court.

**NOTE: If you fail to return page 7 as directed, or if, having returned it, you fail to attend or are not represented at the hearing date, the court may decide the claim in your absence.**

**4. DISPUTE THE CLAIM and attend at court to do any of the following:**
- Challenge the jurisdiction of the court
- State a defence
- State a counterclaim
- Dispute the amount of the claim

Complete Box 3 on page 7. Return page 7 to the court so that it arrives **on or before the return day. You must attend personally, or be represented, at court on the hearing date.**

Your representative may be a solicitor, or someone else having your authority. It may be helpful if you or your representative bring pages 1 and 2 of this form to the court.

**NOTE: If you fail to return page 7 as directed, or if, having returned it, you fail to attend or are not represented at the hearing date, the court may decide the claim in your absence.**

**WRITTEN NOTE OF PROPOSED COUNTERCLAIM**

**You must send to the court a written note of any counterclaim. If you do, you should also send a copy to the pursuer. You must also attend or be represented at court on the hearing date.**

**5. ADMIT LIABILITY FOR THE CLAIM and make written application for a time order under the Consumer Credit Act 1974.**

Complete Box 4 on page 8 and return pages 7 and 8 and 11 to 13 to the court to arrive on or before the return day. You should then contact the court to find out whether or not the pursuer has accepted your offer. Where you have been advised that the pursuer has not accepted your offer then the case will call in court on the hearing date. You should appear in court on the hearing date as the court will decide how the amount claimed is to be paid.

**NOTE: If you fail to return pages 8 and 9 and 11 to 13 as directed, or if, having returned them, you fail to attend or are not represented at the hearing date, if the case is to call, the court may decide the claim in your absence.**

**Please Note**

If you do nothing about this summons, the court will almost certainly, where appropriate, grant decree against you and order you to pay the pursuer the sum claimed, including any interest and expenses found due.

If the summons is for delivery, or implement of an obligation, the court may order you to deliver the article or perform the duty in question within a specified period. If you fail to do so, the court may order you to pay to the pursuer the alternative amount claimed, including interest and expenses.

**You Are Advised to Keep Pages 1 And 2, as They May Be Useful at a Later Stage of the Case.**

**Notes**

**(1) Time to pay directions**

The Debtors (Scotland) Act 1987 gives you the right to apply to the court for a "time to pay direction". This is an order which allows you to pay any sum which the court orders you to pay either in instalments or by deferred lump sum. A "deferred lump sum" means that you will be ordered by the court to pay the whole amount at one time within a period which the court will specify.

If the court makes a time to pay direction it may also recall or restrict any arrestment made on your property by the pursuer in connection with the action or debt (for example, your bank account may have been frozen).

No court fee is payable when making an application for a time to pay direction.

If a time to pay direction is made, a copy of the court order (called an extract decree) will be sent to you by the pursuer telling you when payment should start or when it is you have to pay the lump sum.

If a time to pay direction is not made, and an order for immediate payment is made against you, an order to pay (called a charge) may be served on you if you do not pay.

**(2) Determination of application**

Under the 1987 Act, the court is required to make a time to pay direction if satisfied that it is reasonable in the circumstances to do so, and having regard in particular to the following matters—

- The nature of and reasons for the debt in relation to which decree is granted
- Any action taken by the creditor to assist the debtor in paying the debt
- The debtor's financial position
- The reasonableness of any proposal by the debtor to pay that debt
- The reasonableness of any refusal or objection by the creditor to any proposal or offer by the debtor to pay the debt.

### (3) Time Orders

The Consumer Credit Act 1974 allows you to apply to the court for a "time order" during a court action, to ask the court to give you more time to pay a loan agreement. **A time order is similar to a time to pay direction, but can only be applied for where the court action is about a credit agreement regulated by the Consumer Credit Act**. The court has power to grant a time order in respect of a regulated agreement to reschedule payment of the sum owed. This means that a time order can change:

- the amount you have to pay each month
- how long the loan will last
- in some cases, the interest rate payable

A time order can also stop the creditor taking away any item bought by you on hire purchase or conditional sale under the regulated agreement, so long as you continue to pay the instalments agreed.

No court fee is payable when making an application for a time order.

| SECTION A  This section must be  be completed  complete before service | | Summons No |
| --- | --- | --- |
| | | Return Day |
| | | Hearing Date |

SHERIFF COURT (Including address)

| | |
| --- | --- |
| | |

PURSUER'S FULL NAME AND ADDRESS

DEFENDER'S FULL NAME AND ADDRESS

### SECTION B DEFENDER'S RESPONSE TO THE SUMMONS
  ** Delete those boxes which do not apply

**Box 1

**ADMIT LIABILITY FOR THE CLAIM and make written application to pay by instalments or by deferred lump sum.**

I do not intend to defend the case but admit liability for the claim and wish to pay the sum of money claimed.

| | |
|---|---|
| | I wish to make a written application about payment. |
| | I have completed the application form on pages 9 and 10. |
| **Box 2 | **ADMIT LIABILITY FOR THE CLAIM and attend at court.** |
| | I admit liability for the claim. |
| | I wish to make an application to pay the sum claimed by instalments or by deferred lump sum. |
| | I intend to appear or be represented at court. |
| **Box 3 | **DISPUTE THE CLAIM (or the amount due) and attend at court** |
| | *I wish to dispute the amount due only. |
| | *I intend to challenge the jurisdiction of the court. |
| | *I intend to state a defence. |
| | *I intend to state a counterclaim. |
| | *I intend to appear or be represented in court. |
| | .............. |
| | *I attach a note of my proposed counterclaim which has been copied to the pursuer. |
| | *delete as necessary |
| **Box 4 | **ADMIT LIABILITY FOR THE CLAIM and apply for a time order under the Consumer Credit Act 1974**. |
| | I do not intend to defend the case but admit liability for the claim. |
| | I wish to apply for a time order under the Consumer Credit Act 1974. |
| | I have completed the application form on pages 11 to 13. |

**NOTE: Please remember to send your response to the court to arrive on or before the return day if you have completed any of the responses above.**

I WISH TO APPLY FOR A *TIME TO PAY DIRECTION

**I WISH TO APPLY FOR A *TIME TO PAY DIRECTION**

**I admit the claim** and make application to pay as follows:

(1) by instalments of £...............per *week / fortnight / month

**OR**

(2) in one payment within...............*weeks / months from the date of the court order.

The debt is for *(specify the nature of the debt)* and has arisen *(here set out the reasons the debt has arisen)*

Please also state why you say a time to pay direction should be made. In doing so, please consider Notes (1) and (2) on page 5.

To help the court please provide details of your financial position in the boxes below.

I am employed / self-employed / unemployed

***Please also indicate whether payment/receipts are weekly, fortnightly or monthly**

| My outgoings are: | *Weekly fortnightly/ monthly / | | My net income is | *Weekly fortnightly/ monthly / |
|---|---|---|---|---|
| Rent/mortgage | £ | | Wages/pensions | £ |
| Council tax | £ | | State benefits | £ |
| Gas/electricity etc | £ | | Tax credits | £ |
| Food | £ | | Other | £ |
| Loans and credit agreements | £ | | | |
| Phone | £ | | | |
| Other | £ | | | |
| Total | £ | | Total | £ |
| People who rely on your income (e.g. spouse/civil partner/ partner/children)— how many | | | | |

## Please list details of all capital held, e.g. value of house; amount in savings account, shares or other investments:

I am of the opinion that the payment offer is reasonable for the following reason(s):

*Here set out any information you consider relevant to the court's determination of the application. In doing so, please consider Note (2) on page 5.*

### *APPLICATION FOR RECALL OR RESTRICTION OF AN ARRESTMENT

I seek the recall or restriction of the arrestment of which the details are as follows:
Date:

*Delete if inapplicable*

### Application for a Time Order under the Consumer Credit Act 1974

By

Defender

### In an action raised by

Pursuer

Please Write In Ink Using Block Capitals

If you wish to apply to pay by instalments enter the amount at box 3.

If you wish the court to make any additional orders, please give details at box 4. Please give details of the regulated agreement at box 5 and details of your financial position in the space provided below at box 5.

Sign and date the application where indicated.

You should ensure that your application arrives at the court along with completed pages 7 and 8 on or before the return day.

1. The Applicant is a defender in the action brought by the above named pursuer.

### I/we Wish to Apply for a Time Order under the Consumer Credit Act 1974

### 2. Details of order(s) sought

The defender wishes to apply for a time order under section 129 of the Consumer Credit Act 1974.

The defender wishes to apply for an order in terms of section..........of the Consumer Credit Act 1974.

### 3. Proposals for payment

I admit the claim and apply to pay the arrears and future instalments as follows:...............

By instalments of £..........per *week/fortnight/month

No time to pay direction or time to pay order has been made in relation to this debt.

### 4. Additional orders sought

The following additional order(s) is (are) sought: (*specify*)

The order(s) sought in addition to the time order is (are) sought for the following reasons:

### 5. Details of regulated agreement

(*Please attach a copy of the agreement if you have retained it and insert details of the agreement where known*)

(a) Date of agreement

(b) Reference number of agreement

(c) Names and addresses of other parties to agreement

(d) Name and address of person (if any) who acted as surety (guarantor) to the agreement

(e) Place where agreement signed (e.g. the shop where agreement signed, including name and address)

(f) Details of payment arrangements

    i. The agreement is to pay instalments of £..........per week/ month

    ii. The unpaid balance is £........../ I do not know the amount of arrears

    iii. I am £..........in arrears / I do not know the amount of arrears

### Defender's financial position

I am employed /self employed / unemployed

### Defender's financial position

I am employed /self employed / unemployed

| My net income is: | weekly, fortnightly or monthly | My outgoings are: | weekly, fortnightly or monthly |
|---|---|---|---|
| Wages | £ | Mortgage/rent | £ |
| State benefits | £ | Council tax | £ |
| Tax credits | £ | Gas/electricity etc | £ |
| Other | £ | Food | £ |
| | | Credit and loans | £ |
| | | Phone | £ |
| | | Other | £ |
| Total | £ | Total | £ |

People who rely on your income (e.g. spouse/civil partner/partner/children)—how many

Here list all assets (if any) e.g. value of house; amounts in bank or building society accounts; shares or other investments:

Here list any outstanding debts:

Therefore the defender asks the court to make a time order

Date: ............... Signed: ...............

Defender: ...............

1. As amended by SSI 2008/121 and substituted by the Act of Sederunt (Sheriff Court Rules) (Miscellaneous Amendments) 2009 (SSI 2009/294) r.5 (effective December 1, 2009).

2. As amended by the Act of Sederunt (Sheriff Court Rules) (Miscellaneous Amendments) 2011 (SSI 2011/193) r.12 (effective April 4, 2011).

Rule 4.3(b)

### FORM 1b
*Defender's copy summons - all other claims*

**FORM 1b**

# Small Claim Summons
## Action for/of
(state type, e.g., payment of money)

| OFFICIAL USE ONLY |
| SUMMONS No. |

**DEFENDER'S COPY: (Claim other than claim for or including payment of money where time to pay direction or time order may be applied for)**

| Sheriff Court (name, address, e-mail and telephone no.) | 1 | |
|---|---|---|
| Name and address of person making the claim (**pursuer**) | 2 | |
| Name and address of person against whom claim made (**defender**) | 3 | |
| Claim (form of decree or other order sought — *complete as in section 4 of Form 1*) | 4 | |
| Name, full address, telephone no., and e-mail address of pursuer's solicitor or authorised lay representative (if any) | 5 | |

| 6 | RETURN DAY | 20 |
|---|---|---|
| | HEARING DATE | 20 at am. |

**NOTE: You will find details of claim on page 2.**

| 7. | STATE DETAILS OF CLAIM HERE OR ATTACH A STATEMENT OF CLAIM |
|---|---|

**(To be completed by the pursuer. If space is insufficient, a separate sheet may be attached)**

The details of the claim are:

**8. SERVICE ON DEFENDER**

(Place).............. (Date)..............

To:.............. (defender)..........

You are hereby served with a copy of the above summons.

Solicitor / sheriff officer
*delete as appropriate*

The pursuer should complete boxes 1 to 6 on page 1, the statement of claim in box 7 on page 2 and section A on page 4 before service on the defender. The person serving the summons will complete box 8.

### WHAT MUST I DO ABOUT THIS SUMMONS?

**Decide whether you wish to dispute the claim and/or whether you owe any money or not, and how you wish to proceed.** Then, look at the 2 options listed below. Find the one which covers your decision and follow the instructions given there. You will find the RETURN DAY and the HEARING DATE on page one of the summons.

**Written guidance on small claims procedure can be obtained from the sheriff clerk at any Sheriff Clerk's office.**

**Further advice can also be obtained by contacting any of the following:**

**Citizen's Advice Bureau, Consumer Advice Centre, Trading Standards or Consumer Protection Department or a solicitor. (Addresses can be found in the guidance booklets).**

### OPTION

1. **ADMIT LIABILITY FOR THE CLAIM and settle it with the pursuer now.**

If you wish to avoid the possibility of a court order passing against you, you should settle the claim (including any question of expenses) with pursuer or his representative **in good time before the return day**. Please do not send any payment direct to the court. Any payment should be made to the pursuer or his representative.

2. **DISPUTE THE CLAIM and attend at court to do any of the following:**
   - Challenge the jurisdiction of the court
   - State a defence
   - State a counterclaim
   - Dispute the amount of the claim

Complete Section B on page 4. Return page 4 to the court so that it arrives **on or before the return day. You must attend personally, or be represented, at court on the hearing date.**

Your representative may be a solicitor, or someone else having your authority. It may be helpful if you or your representative bring pages 1 and 2 of this form to the court.

**NOTE: If you fail to return page 4 as directed, or if, having returned it, you fail to attend or are not represented at the hearing date, the court will almost certainly decide the claim in your absence.**

**Written Note of Proposed Counterclaim**

You may send to the court a written note of any counterclaim. If you do, you should also send a copy to the pursuer. You must also attend or be represented at court on the hearing date.

### Please Note

If you do nothing about this summons, the court will almost certainly, where appropriate, grant decree against you and order you to pay to the pursuer the sum claimed, including any interest and expenses found due.

If the summons is for delivery, or implement of an obligation, the court may order you to deliver the article or perform the duty in question within a specified period. If you fail to do so, the court may order you to pay to the pursuer the alternative amount claimed, including interest and expenses.

**You Are Advised to Keep Pages 1 And 2, as They May Be Useful at a Later Stage of the Case.**

| SECTION A |  | Summons No |
|---|---|---|
| This section must be completed before service |  | Return Day |
|  |  | Hearing Date |

SHERIFF COURT (Including address)

| PURSUER'S FULL NAME AND ADDRESS | DEFENDER'S FULL NAME AND ADDRESS |
|---|---|

**SECTION B**      **DEFENDER'S RESPONSE TO THE SUMMONS**

DISPUTE THE CLAIM (or the amount due) and attend at court

* I wish to dispute the amount due only.

* I intend to challenge the jurisdiction of the court.

* I intend to state a defence.

* I intend to state a counterclaim.

I intend to appear or be represented in court.

* I attach a note of my proposed counterclaim which has been copied to the pursuer.

* delete as necessary

**PLEASE REMEMBER:** You must send this page to the court **to arrive on or before the return day** if you have completed Section B above.

If you have admitted the claim, please do not send any payment direct to the court. Any payment should be made to the pursuer or his solicitor.

## FORM 2

Form of claim in a summons for payment of money

Rule 4.1(2)

The pursuer claims from the defender(s) the sum of £.......... with interest on that sum at the rate of ..........% annually from the date of service, together with the expenses of bringing the claim.

## FORM 3

Rule 4.1(2)

Form of claim in a summons for delivery

The pursuer claims that, in the circumstances described in the statement contained on page 2 of this copy summons, he has right to the possession of the article(s) described therein.

He therefore asks the court to grant a decree ordering you to deliver the said articles to the pursuer.

*Alternatively*, if you do not deliver said articles, the pursuer asks the court to grant a decree ordering you to pay to him the sum of £.......... with interest on that sum at the rate of ..........% annually from ..........until payment.

The pursuer also claims from you the expenses of bringing the claim.

## FORM 4

Rule 4.1(2)

Form of claim in a summons for implement of an obligation

The pursuer claims that, in the circumstances described in the statement contained on page 2 of the summons, you are obliged to...............

He therefore asks the court to grant a decree ordering you to implement the said obligation.

*Alternatively*, if you do not fulfil the obligation, the pursuer asks the court to grant a decree ordering you to pay to him the sum of £.......... with interest on that sum at the rate of ..........% annually from until payment.

The pursuer also claims from you the expenses of bringing the claim.

## FORM 5

Rule 6.2(1)

Form of service

XY, you are hereby served with a copy of the above (or attached) summons.

*(signature of solicitor or sheriff officer)*

## FORM 6

Form of certificate of execution of service

Rule 6.2(2)

*(place and date)*

I,.......... , hereby certify that on the.......... day of.......... 20, I duly cited XY to answer the foregoing summons. This I did by *(set forth the mode of service)*

*(signature of solicitor or sheriff officer)*

## FORM 7

Postal service—form of notice

Rule 6.3(2)

This letter contains a citation to or intimation from the sheriff court at

If delivery cannot be made the letter must be returned immediately to the sheriff clerk at *(insert full address)*.

## FORM 8

Service on person whose address is unknown—form of advertisement.

Rule 6.6(1)(a)

A small claim has been raised in the sheriff court at.........., by AB., pursuer, against CD, defender, whose last known address was...............

If the said CD wishes to defend the claim he should immediately contact the sheriff clerk's office at the above court, from whom the defender's copy summons may be obtained.

Address of court:...............

Telephone no:...............

Fax no:...............

E mail address:...............

## FORM 9

Service on person whose address is unknown

Rule 6.6(1)(b)

Form of notice to be displayed on the walls of court

A small claim has been raised in this court by AB, pursuer against CD, defender, whose last known address was...............

If the said CD wishes to defend the claim he should immediately contact the sheriff clerk's office, from whom the defender's copy summons may be obtained.

(*date*)Displayed on the walls of court of this date.

Sheriff clerk depute

## FORM 9A[1]

Statement to accompany application for interim diligence

Rule 7.A2(2)

DEBTORS (SCOTLAND) ACT 1987 Section 15D[or DEBT ARRANGEMENT AND ATTACHMENT (SCOTLAND) ACT 2002 Section 9C]

Sheriff Court..........

In the Cause (Cause Reference No. )

[A.B.] (*designation and address*)

Pursuer

against

[C.D.] (*designation and address*)

Defender

Statement

1. The applicant is the pursuer [*or* defender] in the action by [A.B] (*design*) against [C.D.] (*design*).

2. [The following persons have an interest [*specify names and addresses*]]

3. The application is [*or* is not] seeking the grant under section 15E(1) of the 1987 Act of warrant for diligence [or section 9D(1) of the 2002 Act of interim attachment] in advance of a hearing on the application.

4. [Here provide such other information as may be prescribed by regulations made by the Scottish Ministers under section 15D(2)(d) or 9C(2)(d) of the 1987 Act]

(*Signed*)

Solicitor [*or* Agent] for A.B. [or C.D.]

(*include full designation*)

**Rule 7.A8**

## FORM 9B[2]

Form of schedule of arrestment on the dependence

**SCHEDULE OF ARRESTMENT ON THE DEPENDENCE**

Date: (*date of execution*)...............

Time: (*time arrestment executed*)...............

To: (*name and address of arrestee*)...............

IN HER MAJESTY'S NAME AND AUTHORITY AND IN NAME AND AUTHORITY OF THE SHERIFF, I, (*name*), Sheriff Officer, by virtue of:

- a summons containing warrant which has been granted for arrestment on the dependence of the action at the instance of (*name and address of pursuer*) against (*name and address of defender*) and dated (*date*);
- a counterclaim containing a warrant which has been granted for arrestment on the dependence of the claim by (*name and address of creditor*) against (*name and address of debtor*) and dated (*date of warrant*);

---

[1] As inserted by the Act of Sederunt (Sheriff Court Rules Amendment) (Diligence) 2008 (SSI 2008/121) r.7(8) (effective April 1, 2008).

[2] As inserted by the Act of Sederunt (Sheriff Court Rules Amendment) (Diligence) 2008 (SSI 2008/121) r.7(8) (effective April 1, 2008) and substituted by the Act of Sederunt (Sheriff Court Rules Amendment) (Diligence) 2009 (SSI 2009/107) (effective April 22, 2009).

- an order of the Sheriff at (*place*) dated (*date of order*) granting warrant [for arrestment on the dependence of the action raised at the instance of (*name and address of pursuer*) against (*name and address of defender*)] [*or* for arrestment on the dependence of the claim in the counterclaim by (*name and address of creditor*) against (*name and address or debtor*)],

arrest in your hands (i) the sum of (*amount*), in excess of the Protected Minimum Balance, where applicable (*see Note 1*), more or less, due by you to (*defender's name*) [*or name and address of common debtor if common debtor is not the defender*] or to any other person on his [*or* her] [*or* its] [*or* their] behalf; and (ii) all moveable things in your hands belonging or pertaining to the said (*name of common debtor*), to remain in your hands under arrestment until they are made forthcoming to (*name of pursuer*) [*or name and address of creditor if he is not the pursuer*] or until further order of the court.

This I do in the presence of (*name, occupation and address of witness*).

*(Signed)*

Sheriff Officer

*(Address)*

## NOTE

1. This Schedule arrests in your hands (i) funds due by you to (*name of common debtor*) and (ii) goods or other moveables held by you for him. **You should not pay any funds to him or hand over any goods or other moveables to him without taking legal advice.**

2. This Schedule may be used to arrest a ship or cargo. If it is, you should consult your legal adviser about the effect of it.

3. The Protected Minimum Balance is the sum referred to in section 73F(4) of the Debtors (Scotland) Act 1987. This sum is currently set at [*insert current sum*]. The Protected Minimum Balance applies where the arrestment attaches funds standing to the credit of a debtor in an account held by a bank or other financial institution and the debtor is an individual. The Protected Minimum Balance does not apply where the account is held in the name of a company, a limited liability partnership, a partnership or an unincorporated association or where the account is operated by the debtor as a trading account.

4. Under section 73G of the Debtors (Scotland) Act 1987 you must also, within the period of 3 weeks beginning with the day on which the arrestment is executed, disclose to the creditor the nature and value of the funds and/or moveable property which have been attached. This disclosure must be in the form set out in Schedule 8 to the Diligence (Scotland) Regulations 2009. Failure to comply may lead to a financial penalty under section 73G of the Debtors (Scotland) Act 1987 and may also be dealt with as a contempt of court. You must, at the same time, send a copy of the disclosure to the debtor and to any person known to you who owns (or claims to own) attached property and to any person to whom attached funds are (or are claimed to be due), solely or in common with the debtor.

## IF YOU WISH FURTHER ADVICE CONTACT ANY CITIZENS ADVICE BUREAU/ LOCAL ADVICE CENTRE/SHERIFF CLERK OR SOLICITOR

Rule 6.A8

### FORM 9C[1]

Form of certificate of execution of arrestment on the dependence

### CERTIFICATE OF EXECUTION

I, (*name*), Sheriff Officer, certify that I executed an arrestment on the dependence, by virtue of an interlocutor of the Sheriff at (*place*) on (*date*) obtained at the instance of (*name and address of party arresting*) against (*name and address of defender*) on (*name of arrestee*)—

---

[1] As inserted by the Act of Sederunt (Sheriff Court Rules Amendment) (Diligence) 2008 (SSI 2008/121) r.7(8) (effective April 1, 2008) and substituted by the Act of Sederunt (Sheriff Court Rules Amendment) (Diligence) 2009 (SSI 2009/107) (effective April 22, 2009).

* by delivering the schedule of arrestment to (*name of arrestee or other person*) at (*place*) personally on (*date*).

* by leaving the schedule of arrestment with (*name and occupation of person with whom left*) at (*place*) on (*date*) [and by posting a copy of the schedule to the arrestee by registered post or first class recorded delivery to the address specified on the receipt annexed to this certificate].

* by depositing the schedule of arrestment in (*place*) on (*date*). (*Specify that enquiry made and reasonable grounds exist for believing that the person on whom service is to be made resides at the place but is not available*) [and by posting a copy of the schedule to the arrestee by registered post or first class recorded delivery to the address specified on the receipt annexed to this certificate].

* by affixing the schedule of arrestment to the door at (*place*) on (*date*). (*Specify that enquiry made and that reasonable grounds exist for believing that the person on whom service is to be made resides at the place but is not available*) [and by posting a copy of the schedule to the arrestee by registered post or first class recorded delivery to the address specified on the receipt annexed to this certificate].

* by leaving the schedule of arrestment with (*name and occupation of person with whom left*) at (*place of business*) on (*date*) [and by posting a copy of the schedule to the arrestee by registered post or first class recorded delivery to the address specified on the receipt annexed to this certificate].

* by depositing the schedule of arrestment at (*place of business*) on (*date*). (*Specify that enquiry made and that reasonable grounds exist for believing that the person on whom service is to be made carries on business at that place.*) [and by posting a copy of the schedule to the arrestee by registered post or first class recorded delivery to the address specified on the receipt annexed to this certificate].

* by affixing the schedule of arrestment to the door at (*place of business*) on (*date*). (*Specify that enquiry made and that reasonable grounds exist for believing that the person on whom service is to be made carries on business at that place.*) [and by posting a copy of the schedule to the arrestee by registered post or first class recorded delivery to the address specified on the receipt annexed to this certificate].

* by leaving the schedule of arrestment at (*registered office*) on (*date*), in the hands of (*name of person*) [and by posting a copy of the schedule to the arrestee by registered post or first class recorded delivery to the address specified on the receipt annexed to this certificate].

* by depositing the schedule of arrestment at (*registered office*) on (*date*) [and by posting a copy of the schedule to the arrestee by registered post or first class recorded delivery to the address specified on the receipt annexed to this certificate].

* by affixing the schedule of arrestment to the door at (*registered office*) on (*date*) [and by posting a copy of the schedule to the arrestee by registered post or first class recorded delivery to the address specified on the receipt annexed to this certificate].

I did this in the presence of (*name, occupation and address of witness*).

(*Signed*)
Sheriff Officer
(*Address*)
(*Signed*)
(Witness)

*Delete where not applicable
**NOTE**
A copy of the Schedule of arrestment on the dependence is to be attached to this certificate

FORM 10

Rule 7.3(4)(a)

Recall or restriction of arrestment Certificate authorising the release of arrested funds or property

Sheriff court at (*place*)

Court ref. no.:...............

AB (pursuer) against CD (defender)

I, (*name*), hereby certify that the sheriff on (*date*) authorised the release of the funds or property arrested on the *dependence of the action / counterclaim to the following extent:

(*details of sheriff's order*)

(*date*)

Sheriff clerk depute

*delete as appropriate*

Copy to:

Party instructing arrestment

Party possessing arrested funds/property

## FORM 11

Rule 8.1(2)

Form of minute—no form of response lodged by defender

Sheriff court at (*place*)

Hearing date:...............

In respect that the defender(s) has/have failed to lodge a form of response to the summons, the pursuer requests the court to make the orders specified in the following case(s):

Court ref. no.: ......... Name(s) of defender(s) .......... Minute(s) ..........

## FORM 12[1]

Rule 8.2(2)

Form of minute—pursuer not objecting to application for a time to pay direction or time order

Sheriff court at (*place*)

Court ref. no.: ...............

Name(s) of defender(s) ...............

Hearing date: ...............

I do not object to the defender's application for

* a time to pay direction
* recall or restriction of an arrestment
* a time order

The pursuer requests the court to grant decree or other order in terms of the following minute(s)

*delete as appropriate*

## FORM 13[2]

Rule 8.2(4)

Form of minute—pursuer opposing an application for a time to pay direction or time order

**Sheriff court (place): ...............**

**Court ref no: ...............**

Name(s) of defender(s): ...............

---

[1] As amended by the Act of Sederunt (Ordinary Cause, Summary Application, Summary Cause and Small Claim Rules) Amendment (Miscellaneous) 2003 (SSI 2003/26), para.5(2)(b) (effective January 24, 2003).

[2] As substituted by the Act of Sederunt (Sheriff Court Rules) (Miscellaneous Amendments) 2009 (SSI 2009/294) r.5 (effective December 1, 2009).

Hearing date: ...............

I oppose the defender's application for

* a time to pay direction
* recall or restriction of arrestment
* a time order

*delete as appropriate

1. The debt is (please specify the nature of the debt and any reason known to the pursuer for the debt).
2. The debt was incurred on (specify date) and the pursuer has contacted the defender in relation to the debt on (specify date(s)).
*3. The contractual payments were (specify amount).
*4. (Specify any action taken by the pursuer to assist the defender to pay the debt).
*5. The defender has made payment(s) towards the debt of (specify amount(s)) on (specify date(s)).
*6. The debtor has made offers to pay (specify amount(s)) on (specify date(s)) which offer(s) was [were] accepted] [or rejected] and (specify amount) was paid on (specify date(s)).
7. (Here set out any information you consider relevant to the court's determination of the application.)
8. The pursuer requests the court to grant decree.

*delete as appropriate

(Signed)

Pursuer [or Solicitor for Pursuer]

(Date)

## FORM 14

Rule 11.1(8)

Counterclaim—form of intimation by sheriff clerk where pursuer fails to appear

Court ref. no.: ...............

(AB) (insert address), pursuer

against

(CD) (insert address), defender

When the above case called in court on (insert date), the defender appeared (or was represented) and stated a counterclaim to the claim made by you against him.

The court continued the case until (date) at (time).

**Please note that, if you fail to appear or be represented at the continued diet, the court may grant decree against you in terms of the counterclaim.**

(date)

Sheriff clerk depute

Rule 13A.3(1)

Paragraph 7(4)

## FORM 14A[1]

Form of minute of intervention by the Commission for Equality and Human Rights

Sheriff Court at (place) ............... Court ref. no...............

APPLICATION FOR LEAVE TO INTERVENE BY THE COMMISSION FOR EQUALITY AND HUMAN RIGHTS

in the cause

[A.B.] (designation and address), Pursuer

against

[C.D.] (designation and address), Defender

[Here set out briefly:

(a) the Commission's reasons for believing that the proceedings are relevant to a matter in connection with which the Commission has a function;

---

[1] As inserted by the Act of Sederunt (Sheriff Court Rules) (Miscellaneous Amendments) 2008 (SSI 2008/223) para.7(4) (effective July 1, 2008).

(b)   *the issue in the proceedings which the Commission wishes to address; and*

(c)   *the propositions to be advanced by the Commission and the Commission's reasons for believing that they are relevant to the proceedings and that they will assist the court.]*

## FORM 14B[1]

Rule 13B.2(1)

Form of minute of intervention by the Scottish Commission for Human Rights

Sheriff Court at (*place*) ............... Court ref. no.

APPLICATION FOR LEAVE TO INTERVENE BY THE SCOTTISH COMMIS-SION FOR HUMAN RIGHTS

in the cause

[A.B.] (*designation and address*), Pursuer

against

[C.D.] (*designation and address*), Defender

*[Here set out briefly:*

(a)   *the issue in the proceedings which the Commission intends to address;*

(b)   *a summary of the submission which the Commission intends to make.]*

## FORM 14C[2]

Rule 13B.3(1)

Invitation to the Scottish Commission for Human Rights to intervene

SHERIFFDOM OF (*insert name of sheriffdom*) ...............Court ref. no.

AT (*insert place of sheriff court*) ...............

INVITATION TO THE SCOTTISH COMMISSION FOR HUMAN RIGHTS TO INTERVENE

in the cause

[A.B.] (*designation and address*), Pursuer

against

[C.D.] (*designation and address*), Defender

*[Here set out briefly:*

(a)   *the facts, procedural history and issues in the proceedings;*

(b)   *the issue in the proceedings on which the court seeks a submission.]*

## FORM 15[3]

Rule 17.2(1)

**Sheriff court at** (*place*) ...............

In the claim (*court ref. no.*)

in which

AB (*design*) is the pursuer

and

C.D. (*design*) is the defender

To: (*name and designation of party or haver from whom the documents are sought to be recovered*).

You are hereby required to produce to the sheriff clerk at (*address*) within days of the service upon you of this order:

1.   This order itself (which must be produced intact);

2.   The certificate marked "B" attached;

3.   All documents within your possession covered by the specification which is enclosed; and

4.   A list of those documents.

---

[1] As inserted by the Act of Sederunt (Sheriff Court Rules) (Miscellaneous Amendments) 2008 (SSI 2008/223) para.7(4) (effective July 1, 2008).

[2] As inserted by the Act of Sederunt (Sheriff Court Rules) (Miscellaneous Amendments) 2008 (SSI 2008/223) para.7(4) (effective July 1, 2008).

[3] Substituted by Act of Sederunt (Ordinary Cause, Summary Application, Summary Cause and Small Claim Rules) Amendment (Miscellaneous) 2005 (SSI 2005/648) (effective January 2, 2006).

You can produce the items listed above either:

    (a)    by delivering them to the sheriff clerk at the address shown above; or

    (b)    sending them to the sheriff clerk by registered or recorded delivery post.

(*date*)

    (*signature, name, address and designation of person serving order*)

**PLEASE NOTE:**

If you claim confidentiality for any of the documents produced by you, you must still produce them. However, they may be placed in a separate envelope by themselves, marked "confidential". The court will, if necessary, decide whether the envelope should be opened or not.

Where the person ordering you to produce the document is **not** the sheriff clerk, claims for necessary outlays within certain specified limits may be paid. Claims should be made in writing to the person who has obtained an order that you produce the documents.

**CERTIFICATE**

**B**

Sheriff Court at (*place*)

In the claim (*court ref. no.*)

in which

AB (*design*) is the pursuer

and

CD (*design*) is the defender

Order for recovery of documents dated (*insert date*).

With reference to the above order and relative specification of documents, I hereby certify:

* that the documents produced herewith and the list signed by me which accompanies them are all the documents in my possession which fall under the specification.

* I have no documents in my possession falling under the specification.

* I believe that there are other documents falling within the specification which are not in my possession. These documents are (*list the documents as described in the specification.*) These documents were last seen by me on (*date*) in the possession of (*name and address of person/ company, if known*).

* I know of no documents falling within the specification which are in the possession of any other person.

* *delete as appropriate*

(*name*) (*date*)

[1] FORM 16

Rule 17.4(3)

Form of citation of witness or haver

(*date*)

CITATION

SHERIFFDOM OF (*insert name of sheriffdom*)

**At (insert place of sheriff court)**

**To [A.B.] (design)**

---

[1] As substituted by the Act of Sederunt (Ordinary Cause, Summary Application, Summary Cause and Small Claim Rules) Amendment (Vulnerable Witnesses (Scotland) Act 2004) 2007 (SSI 2007/463) (effective November 1, 2007).

(*Name*) who is pursuing/defending a case against (*name*) [*or* is a (*specify*) in the case of (*name*) against (*name*)] has asked you to be a witness. You must attend the above sheriff court on (*insert date*) at (*insert time*) for that purpose, [and bring with you (*specify documents*)].

If you

- would like to know more about being a witness
- are a child under the age of 16
- think you may be a vulnerable witness within the meaning of section 11(1) of the Vulnerable Witnesses (Scotland) Act 2004 (that is someone the court considers may be less able to give their evidence due to mental disorder or fear or distress connected to giving your evidence at the court hearing).

you should contact (*specify the solicitor acting for the party or the party litigant citing the witness*) for further information.

If you are a vulnerable witness (including a child under the age of 16) then you should be able to use a special measure (such measures include use of a screen, a live TV link or a supporter, or a commissioner) to help you give evidence.

**Expenses**

You may claim back money which you have had to spend and any earnings you have lost within certain specified limits, because you have to come to court on the above date. These may be paid to you if you claim within specified time limits. Claims should be made to the person who has asked you to attend court. Proof of any loss of earnings should be given to that person.

If you wish your travelling expenses to be paid before you go to court, you should apply for payment to the person who has asked you to attend court.

**Failure to attend**

**It is very important that you attend court and you should note that failure to do so may result in a warrant being granted for your arrest. In addition, if you fail to attend without any good reason, having requested and been paid your travelling expenses, you may be ordered to pay a penalty not exceeding £250.**

If you have any questions about anything in this citation, please contact (*specify the solicitor acting for the party or the party litigant citing the witness*) for further information.

Signed

[P.Q.] Sheriff Officer
or [X.Y.], (*add designation and business address*)
Solicitor for the pursuer [*or* defender][*or* (*specify*)]

FORM 16A

Rule 17.4(3)

Form of certificate of execution of witness citation

I certify that on (*date*) I duly cited AB (*design*) to attend at (*name of court*) on (*date*) at (*time*) as a witness for the (*design party*) in the action at the instance of CD (*design*) against EF (*design*) (*and I required him to bring with him..........*). This I did by

(*signature of solicitor or sheriff officer*)

FORM 16B[1] [2]

Form of child witness notice

**Rule 11A.2**

---

[1] As inserted by the Act of Sederunt (Ordinary Cause, Summary Application, Summary Cause and Small Claim Rules) Amendment (Vulnerable Witnesses (Scotland) Act 2004) 2007 (SSI 2007/463) (effective November 1, 2007).

[2] As amended by the Act of Sederunt (Rules of the Court of Session 1994 and Sheriff Court Rules Amendment) (No. 3) (Miscellaneous) 2015 (SSI 2015/283) r.6(2) (effective 1 September 2015).

## VULNERABLE WITNESSES (SCOTLAND) ACT 2004 SECTION 12

*Received the day* .......... *of* .......... 20
*(Date of receipt of this notice)*
.............. *(signed)*
Sheriff Clerk

### CHILD WITNESS NOTICE

Sheriff court ...............20..........
...............Court Ref. No.

1. The applicant is the pursuer [*or* defender] in the action by [A.B.] (*design*) against [C.D.] (*design*).

2. The applicant has cited [*or* intends to cite] [E.F.] (*date of birth*) as a witness.

3. [E.F.] is a child witnesses under section 11 of the Vulnerable Witnesses (Scotland) Act 2004 [and was under the age of eighteen on the date of the commencement of proceedings].

4. The applicant considers that the following special measure[s] is [are] the most appropriate for the purpose of taking the evidence of [E.F.][*or* that [E.F.] should give evidence without the benefit of any special measure]:-
*(delete as appropriate and specify any special measure(s) sought).*

5. [(a) The reason[s] this [these] special measure[s] is [are] considered the most appropriate is [are] as follows:-
*(here specify the reason(s) for the special measure(s) sought)*].

OR

[(b) The reason[s] it is considered that [E.F.] should give evidence without the benefit of any special measure is [are]:-
*(here explain why it is felt that no special measures are required)*].

6. [E.F.] and the parent[s] of [*or* person[s] with parental responsibility for] [E.F.] has [have] expressed the following view[s] on the special measure[s] that is [are] considered most appropriate [*or* the appropriateness of [E.F.] giving evidence without the benefit of any special measure]:
*(delete as appropriate and set out the views(s) expressed and how they were obtained)*

7. Other information considered relevant to this application is as follows:—
*(here set out any other information relevant to the child witness notice).*

8. The applicant asks the court to—
(a)   consider this child witness notice;
(b)   make an order authorising the special measure[s] sought; *or*
(c)   make an order authorising the giving of evidence by [E.F.] without the benefit of special measures.

*(delete as appropriate)*
*(Signed)*

[A.B. *or* C.D.]
[*or* Representative of A.B. [*or* C.D.]] (*include full designation*)
*NOTE: This form should be suitably adapted where section 16 of the Act of 2004 applies.*

### FORM 16C[1]
Form of vulnerable witness application

Rule 17A.3

## VULNERABLE WITNESSES (SCOTLAND) ACT 2004 Section 12

---

[1] As inserted by the Act of Sederunt (Ordinary Cause, Summary Application, Summary Cause and Small Claim Rules) Amendment (Vulnerable Witnesses (Scotland) Act 2004) 2007 (SSI 2007/463) (effective November 1, 2007).

Received the..........day of..........20..........
*(Date of receipt of this notice)*
..........*(signed)*
Sheriff Clerk

## VULNERABLE WITNESS APPLICATION

Sheriff Court.................... ..........20..........

Court Ref. No.

1. The applicant is the pursuer [*or* defender] in the action by [A.B] (*design*) against [C.D.] (*design*).

2. The applicant has cited [or intends to cite] [E.F.] (*date of birth*) as a witness.

3. The applicant considers that [E.F.] is a vulnerable witness under section 11(1)(b) of the Vulnerable Witnesses (Scotland) Act 2004 for the following reasons:—

(*here specify reasons witness is considered to be a vulnerable witness*).

4. The applicant considers that the following special measure[s] is [are] the most appropriate for the purpose of taking the evidence of [E.F.].

(*specify any special measure(s) sought*)

5. The reason[s] this [these] special measure[s] is [are] considered the most appropriate is [are] as follows:—

(*here specify the reason(s) for the special measures(s) sought*).

6. [E.F.] has expressed the following view[s] on the special measure[s] that is [are] considered most appropriate:—

(*set out the views expressed and how they were obtained*).

7. Other information considered relevant to this application is as follows:—

(*here set out any other information relevant to the vulnerable witness application*).

8. The applicant asks the court to—

(a)    consider this vulnerable witness application;

(b)    make an order authorising the special measure[s] sought.

(*Signed*)
[A.B. *or* C.D.]
[ *or* Representative of A.B. [ *or* C.D. ]] (*include full designation*)
*NOTE: This form should be suitably adapted where* section 16 of the Act of 2004 *applies.*

## FORM 16D[1]

### FORM OF CERTIFICATE OF INTIMATION

**Rule 17A.4(2)**

### VULNERABLE WITNESSES (SCOTLAND) ACT 2004 Section 12
### CERTIFICATE OF INTIMATION

Sheriff Court.......... ..........20..........

Court Ref. No.

I certify that intimation of the child witness notice [*or* vulnerable witness application] relating to (*insert name of witness*) was made to (*insert names of parties or solicitors for parties, as appropriate) by (insert method of intimation: where intimation is by facsimile transmission, insert fax number to which intimation sent*) on (*insert date of intimation*).

Date:..........

---

[1] As inserted by the Act of Sederunt (Ordinary Cause, Summary Application, Summary Cause and Small Claim Rules) Amendment (Vulnerable Witnesses (Scotland) Act 2004) 2007 (SSI 2007/463) (effective November 1, 2007).

(*Signed*)
Solicitor [*or* Sheriff Officer]
(*include full business designation*)

## FORM 16E[1]

### FORM OF APPLICATION FOR REVIEW

**Rule 17A.6(1)**

VULNERABLE WITNESSES (SCOTLAND) ACT 2004 Section 13
Received the...............day of...............20.........
(*date of receipt of this notice*)
....................(*signed*)
Sheriff Clerk

APPLICATION FOR REVIEW OF ARRANGEMENTS FOR VULNERABLE
WITNESS

Sheriff Court.................... ...........20.........

Court Ref. No.

1. The applicant is the pursuer |*or* defender| in the action by |A.B.| (*design*) against |C.D.| (design).

2. A proof |*or* hearing| is fixed for (*date*) at (*time*).

3. [E.F.] is a witness who is to give evidence at, or for the purposes of, the proof [*or* hearing]. [E.F.] is a child witness [*or* vulnerable witness] under section 11 of the Vulnerable Witnesses (Scotland) Act 2004.

4. The current arrangements for taking the evidence of [E.F.] are (*here specify current arrangements*).

5. The current arrangements should be reviewed as (*here specify reasons for review*).

6. [E.F.] [and the parent[s] of [*or* person[s] with parental responsibility for] [E.F.]] has [have] expressed the following view[s] on [the special measure[s] that is [are] considered most appropriate] [*or* the appropriateness of [E.F] giving evidence without the benefit of any special measure]:—
(*delete as appropriate and set out the view(s) expressed and how they were obtained*).

7. The applicant seeks (here specify the order sought).

(*Signed*)
|A.B. *or* C.D.|
[*or* Representative of A.B. [*or* C.D.]] (*include full designation*)
*NOTE: This form should be suitably adapted where* section 16 of the Act of 2004 applies.

## FORM 16F[2]

### FORM OF CERTIFICATE OF INTIMATION

**Rule 17A.7(2)**

VULNERABLE WITNESSES (SCOTLAND) ACT 2004 Section 13
CERTIFICATE OF INTIMATION

---

[1] As inserted by the Act of Sederunt (Ordinary Cause, Summary Application, Summary Cause and Small Claim Rules) Amendment (Vulnerable Witnesses (Scotland) Act 2004) 2007 (SSI 2007/463) (effective November 1, 2007).

[2] As inserted by the Act of Sederunt (Ordinary Cause, Summary Application, Summary Cause and Small Claim Rules) Amendment (Vulnerable Witnesses (Scotland) Act 2004) 2007 (SSI 2007/463) (effective November 1, 2007).

Sheriff Court.......... ..........20..........

Court Ref. No.

I certify that intimation of the review application relating to (*insert name of witness*) was made to (*insert names of parties or solicitors for parties, as appropriate*) by (*insert method of intimation; where intimation is by facsimile transmission, insert fax number to which intimation sent*) on (*insert date of intimation*).

Date:..........

(*Signed*)

Solicitor [*or* Sheriff Officer]

(*include full business designation*)

## FORM 17

### FORM OF REFERENCE TO THE EUROPEAN COURT

**Rule 18.2(2)**

REQUEST
for
PRELIMINARY RULING
of
THE COURT OF JUSTICE OR THE EUROPEAN COMMUNITIES
from
THE SHERIFFDOM OF (*insert name of sheriffdom*) at (*insert place of court*)
in the cause
AB (*insert designation and address*), pursuer
against
CD (*insert designation and address*), defender

(Here set out a clear and succinct statement of the case giving rise to the request for a ruling of the European Court in order to enable the European Court to consider and understand the issues of Community law raised and to enable governments of Member states and other interested parties to submit observations. The statement of the case should include:

(a) particulars of the parties;

(b) the history of the dispute between the parties;

(c) the history of the proceedings;

(d) the relevant facts as agreed by the parties or found by the court or, failing such agreement or finding, the contentions of the parties on such facts;

(e) the nature of the issues of law and fact between the parties;

(f) the Scots law, so far as relevant;

(g) the Treaty provisions or other acts, instruments or rules of Community law concerned;

(h) an explanation of why the reference is being made).

The preliminary ruling of the Court of Justice of the European Communities is accordingly requested on the following questions:

1,2, etc. (*Here set out the question (s) on which the ruling is sought, identifying the Treaty provisions or other acts, instruments or rules of Community law concerned.*)

Dated the.......... day of..........20

## FORM 18

### FORM OF EXTRACT DECREE (BASIC)

**Rule 21.5(4)(b)**

Sheriff court.................... Court ref. no.:

Date of decree....................*in absence

Pursuer(s).................... Defender(s)

The sheriff
and granted decree against the.................... for payment of expenses of £..........
against the (name of party).

This extract is warrant for all lawful execution thereon.

Date.................... Sheriff clerk depute

*delete as appropriate

## FORM 18A

### FORM OF EXTRACT DECREE FOR PAYMENT

**Rule 21.5(4)(b)**

Sheriff court .................... Court ref. no.

Date of decree .................... *in absence

Pursuer(s) .................... Defender(s)

The sheriff granted decree against the .................... for payment to the ....................
of the undernoted sums:

(1)   Sum(s) decerned for: £

(2)   Interest atper cent per year from (*date*) until payment.

(3)   Expenses of £.......... against the (*name of party*).

*A time to pay direction was made under section 1(1) of the Debtors (Scotland) Act
1987.

*A time order was made under section 129 (1) of the Consumer Credit Act 1974.

*The amount is payable by instalments of £.......... per .......... commencing within
.......... *days/weeks/months of intimation of this extract decree.

*The amount is payable by lump sum within .......... *days/weeks/months of
intimation of this extract decree.

This extract is warrant for all lawful execution thereon.

Date .................... Sheriff clerk depute

**delete as appropriate*

## FORM 18B

### FORM OF EXTRACT DECREE IN AN ACTION OF DELIVERY

**Rule 21.5(4)(b)**

Sheriff court .................... Court ref. no.:

Date of decree .................... *in absence

Pursuer(s)

Defender(s)

The sheriff granted decree against the defender

(1)   for delivery to the pursuer of (*specify articles*)

(2)   for expenses of £..........

* Further, the sheriff granted warrant to officers of court to (1) open shut and lockfast
places occupied by the defender and (2) search for and take possession of said goods
in the possession of the defender.

**delete as appropriate*

This extract is warrant for all lawful execution thereon.

Date .................... Sheriff clerk depute

## FORM 18C

FORM OF EXTRACT DECREE IN AN ACTION OF DELIVERY—PAYMENT FAILING
DELIVERY

**Rule 21.5(4)(b)**

Sheriff court .................... Court ref. no.:

Date of decree .................... *in absence

Pursuer(s)

Defender(s)

The sheriff, in respect that the defender has failed to make delivery in accordance
with the decree granted in this court on (*date*), granted decree for payment against
the defender of the undernoted sums:

(1)  Sum(s) decerned for: £.........., being the alternative amount claimed.

(2)  Interest at .......... per cent per year from (*date*) until payment.

(3)  Expenses of £.......... against the (*name of party*).

*A time to pay direction was made under section 1 (1) of the Debtors (Scotland) Act
1987.

The amount is payable by instalments of £.......... per .......... commencing within
.......... *days/weeks/monthsof intimation of this extract decree.

The amount is payable by lump sum within .......... *days/weeks/months of intimation of this extract decree.

*delete as appropriate*

This extract is warrant for all lawful execution thereon.

Date .................... Sheriff clerk depute

## FORM 18D

FORM OF EXTRACT DECREE RECOVERY OF POSSESSION OF MOVEABLE PROPERTY

**Rule 21.5(4)(b)**

Sheriff court .................... Court ref. no.:

Date of decree .................... *in absence

Pursuer(s) .................... Defender(s)

The sheriff granted decree against the defender:

(1)  Finding the pursuer entitled to recovery of possession of the article(s) (*specify*)

(2)  for expenses of £

* Further, the sheriff granted warrant to officers of court to (1) open shut and lockfast
places occupied by the defender and (2) search for and take possession of said goods
in the possession of the defender.

*delete as appropriate*

This extract is warrant for all lawful execution thereon.

Date .................... Sheriff clerk depute

## FORM 18E

FORM OF EXTRACT DECREE

**Rule 21.5(4)(b)**

Recovery of possession of moveable property—payment failing recovery

Sheriff court .................... Court ref. no.:

Date of decree .................... *in absence

Pursuer(s) .................... Defender(s)

The sheriff, in respect that the defender has failed to recover possession in accordance with the decree granted in this court on (*date*), granted decree for payment against the defender of the undernoted sums:

Sum(s) decerned for: £.......... , being the alternative amount claimed.

Interest at .......... per cent per year from (*date*) until payment.

Expenses of £.......... against the (*name of party*).

*A time to pay direction was made under section 1 (1) of the Debtors (Scotland) Act 1987.

*The amount is payable by instalments of £.......... per .......... commencing within .......... *days/weeks/monthsof intimation of this extract decree.

*The amount is payable by lump sum within .......... *days/weeks/months of intimation of this extract decree.

* *delete as appropriate*

This extract is warrant for all lawful execution thereon.

Date .................... Sheriff clerk depute

## FORM 18F

### FORM OF EXTRACT DECREE AD FACTUM PRAESTANDUM

**Rule 21.5(4)(b)**

Sheriff .................... court Court ref. no.:

Date of decree .................... *in absence

Pursuer(s)

Defender(s)

The sheriff

(1)   ordained the defender(s)

(2)   granted decree for payment of expenses of £.......... against the defender(s).

This extract is warrant for all lawful execution thereon.

Date .................... Sheriff clerk depute

## FORM 18G

### FORM OF EXTRACT DECREE AD FACTUM PRAESTANDUM—PAYMENT UPON FAILURE TO IMPLEMENT OBLIGATION

**Rule 21.5(4)(b)**

Sheriff court .................... Court ref. no.:

Date of decree .................... *in absence

Pursuer(s)

Defender(s)

The sheriff, in respect that the defender has failed to implement the obligation contained in and in accordance with the decree granted in this court on (*date*), granted decree for payment against the defender of the undernoted sums:

(1)   Sum(s) decerned for: £.......... ,being the alternative amount claimed.

(2)   Interest at .......... per cent per year from (*date*) until payment.

(3)   Expenses of £.......... against the (*name of party*).

*A time to pay direction was made under section 1(1) of the Debtors (Scotland) Act 1987.

The amount is payable by instalments of £.......... per .......... commencing within ............... *days/weeks/monthsof intimation of this extract decree.

*The amount is payable by lump sum within .......... *days/weeks/months of intimation of this extract decree.

* *delete as appropriate*

This extract is warrant for all lawful execution thereon.

Date .................... Sheriff clerk depute

## FORM 18H

### FORM OF EXTRACT DECREE OF ABSOLVITOR

**Rule 21.5(4)(b)**

Sheriff court .................... Court ref. no.:

Date of decree .................... *in absence

Pursuer(s)

Defender(s)

The sheriff

(1)   absolved the defender(s).

(2)   granted decree for payment of expenses of £.......... against the

This extract is warrant for all lawful execution thereon.

Date .................... Sheriff clerk depute

## FORM 18I

### FORM OF EXTRACT DECREE OF DISMISSAL

**Rule 21.5(4)(b)**

Sheriff court .................... Court ref. no.:

Date of decree .................... *in absence

Pursuer(s)

Defender(s)

The sheriff

(1)   dismissed the action against the defender(s).

(2)   granted decree for payment of expenses of £.......... against the

This extract is warrant for all lawful execution thereon.

Date .................... Sheriff clerk depute

## FORM 19

### FORM OF CERTIFICATE BY SHERIFF CLERK

**Rule 21.8(4)**

Service of charge where address of defender is unknown

I certify that the foregoing charge was displayed on the walls of court on (*date*) and that it remained so displayed for a period of (*period of charge*) from that date.

(date) .................... Sheriff clerk depute

## FORM 20[1]

### MINUTE FOR RECALL OF DECREE

**Rule 21.1(1)**

Sheriff court: (*place*)

Court ref. no.:

AB (*pursuer*) against CD (*defender(s)*)

The *(*pursuer / defender*) moves the court to recall the decree pronounced on (*date*) in this case * and in which execution of a charge/arrestment was effected on (*date*).

*Proposed defence/answer:

Date

---

[1]  As amended by the Act of Sederunt (Sheriff Court Rules) (Miscellaneous Amendments) 2011 (SSI 2011/193) r.17 (effective April 4, 2011).

*delete as appropriate

## FORM 20A[1]

### Minute for Recall of Decree — Service Copy

**Rule 22.1(6)**

Sheriff court: (*place*)

Court ref. no.:

AB (*pursuer*) against CD (*defender(s)*)

The *(*pursuer / defender*) moves the court to recall the decree pronounced on (*date*) in this case * and in which execution of a charge/arrestment was effected on (*date*).

*Proposed defence/answer:

Date

*delete as appropriate

**NOTE: You must return the summons to the sheriff clerk at the court mentioned at the top of this form by (insert date 2 days before the date of the hearing).**

## FORM 21[2]

### Form of Application for Stated Case

**Rule 23.1(1)**

Sheriff court (*place*)

Court ref. no:

AB (pursuer) against CD (defender(s))

The pursuer/defender appeals the sheriffs interlocutor of (*date*) to the Sheriff Appeal Court and requests the sheriff to state a case.

The point(s) of law upon which the appeal is to proceed is/are: (*give brief statement*).

(*date*)

## FORM 22[3]

### Application for Leave to Appeal against Time to Pay Direction

**Rule 23.4(3)(a)**

Sheriff court (*place*)

Court ref. no.:

AB (pursuer) against CD (defender(s))

The pursuer/defender requests the sheriff to grant leave to appeal the decision made on (*date*) in respect of the defender's application for a time to pay direction to the Sheriff Appeal Court/Court of Session.

The point(s) of law upon which the appeal is to proceed is/are: (give brief statement).

(*date*)

---

[1] As amended by the Act of Sederunt (Sheriff Court Rules) (Miscellaneous Amendments) 2011 (SSI 2011/193) r.17 (effective April 4, 2011).

[2] As amended by the Act of Sederunt (Rules of the Court of Session, Sheriff Appeal Court Rules and Sheriff Court Rules Amendment) (Sheriff Appeal Court) 2015 (SSI 2015/419) r.12 (effective 1 January 2016; as to savings see SSI 2015/419 r.20(7)(a)).

[3] As amended by the Act of Sederunt (Rules of the Court of Session, Sheriff Appeal Court Rules and Sheriff Court Rules Amendment) (Sheriff Appeal Court) 2015 (SSI 2015/419) r.12 (effective 1 January 2016; as to savings see SSI 2015/419 r.20(7)(a)).

Form 23[1]

Appeal against time to pay direction

**Rule 23.4(4)**

Sheriff court (*place*)

Court ref. no.:

AB (pursuer) against CD (defender(s))

The pursuer/defender appeals the decision made on (*date*) in respect of the defender's application for a time to pay direction to the Sheriff Appeal Court/Court of Session.

(*date*)

Form 24

Form of receipt for money paid to sheriff clerk

**Rule 24.4(1)**

In the sheriff court of (*name of sheriffdom*) at (*place of sheriff court*).

In the claim (*state names of parties or other appropriate description*)

AB (*designation*) has this day paid into court the sum of £.........., being a payment made in terms of Chapter 24 of the Small Claim Rules 2002.

\*Custody of this money has been accepted at the request of (*insert name of court making the request*).

\**delete as appropriate*

(Date)

Sheriff clerk depute

**Appendix 2**
**GLOSSARY**

**Rule 1.1(5)**

*Absolve*

To find in favour of and exonerate the defender.

*Absolvitor*

An order of the court granted in favour of and exonerating the defender which means that the pursuer is not allowed to bring the same matter to court again.

*Appellant*

A person making an appeal against the sheriff's decision. This might be the pursuer or the defender.

*Arrestee*

A person subject to an arrestment.

*Arrestment on the dependence*

A court order to freeze the goods or bank account of the defender until the court has heard the case.

*Arrestment to found jurisdiction*

---

[1] As amended by the Act of Sederunt (Rules of the Court of Session, Sheriff Appeal Court Rules and Sheriff Court Rules Amendment) (Sheriff Appeal Court) 2015 (SSI 2015/419) r.12 (effective 1 January 2016; as to savings see SSI 2015/419 r.20(7)(a)).

1121

A court order used against a person who has goods or other assets in Scotland to give the court jurisdiction to hear a claim. This is achieved by preventing anything being done with the goods or assets until the case has been disposed of.

*Authorised lay representative*

A person other than a lawyer who represents a party to a small claim.

*Cause*

Another word for case or claim, used for cases under the summary cause procedure.

*Caution (pronounced kay-shun)*

A security, usually a sum of money, given to ensure that some obligation will be carried out.

*Certificate of execution of service*

The document recording that an application to, or order or decree of, the court for service of documents has been effected.

*Charge*

An order to obey a decree of a court. A common type is one served on the defender by a sheriff officer on behalf of the pursuer who has won a case demanding payment of a sum of money.

*Commission and diligence*

Authorisation by the court for someone to take the evidence of a witness who cannot attend court or to obtain the production of documentary evidence. It is combined with a diligence authorising the person appointed to require the attendance of the witness and the disclosure of documents.

*Consignation*

The deposit in court, or with a third party, of money or an article in dispute.

*Continuation*

An order made by the sheriff postponing the completion of a hearing until a later date or dates.

*Counterclaim*

A claim made by a defender in response to the pursuer's claim and which is not a defence to that claim. It is a separate but related claim against the pursuer which is dealt with at the same time as the pursuer's claim.

*Damages*

Money compensation payable for a breach of contract or some other legal duty.

*Decree*

An order of the court containing the decision of the claim in favour of one of the parties and granting the remedy sought or disposing of the claim.

*Defender*

Person against whom a claim is made.

*Deliverance*

A decision or order of a court.

*Depending*

A case is said to be depending when it is going through a court procedure. Technically, this begins with citation of the defender and ends with any final appeal.

*Diet*

Date for a court hearing.

*Diligence*

The collective term for the procedures used to enforce a decree of a court. These include arrestment of wages, goods or a bank account.

*Dismissal*

An order bringing to an end the proceedings in a claim. It is usually possible for a new claim to be brought if not time barred.

*Domicile*

The place where a person is normally resident or where, in the case of a company, it has its place of business or registered office.

*Execution of service*

See Certificate of execution of service.

*Execution of a charge*

The intimation of the requirement to obey a decree or order of a court.

*Execution of an arrestment*

The carrying out of an order of arrestment.

*Expenses*

The costs of a court case.

*Extra-judicial settlement*

An agreement between the parties to a case to settle it themselves rather than to await a decision by the sheriff.

*Extract decree*

The document containing the order of the court made at the end of the claim. For example, it can be used to enforce payment of a sum awarded.

*Haver*

A person who holds documents which are required as evidence in a case.

*Huissier*

An official in France and some other European countries who serves court documents.

*Incidental application*

An application that can be made during the course of a small claim for certain orders. Examples are applications for the recovery of documents or to amend the statement of claim.

*Interlocutor*

The official record of the order or judgment of a court.

*Intimation*

Giving notice to another party of some step in the small claim.

*Jurisdiction*

The authority of a court to hear particular cases.

*Messenger at arms*

Officers of court who serve documents issued by the Court of Session.

*Minute*

A document produced in the course of a case in which a party makes an application or sets out his position on some matter.

*Minute for recall*

A form lodged with the court by one party asking the court to recall a decree.

*Options Hearing*

A preliminary stage in an ordinary cause action.

*Ordinary cause*

Another legal procedure for higher value claims available in the sheriff court.

*Party litigant*

A person who conducts his own case.

*Productions*

Documents or articles which are used in evidence.

*Pursuer*

The person making a claim.

*Recall of an arrestment*

A court order withdrawing an arrestment.

*Restriction of an arrestment*

An order releasing part of the money or property arrested.

*Recall of a decree*

An order revoking a decree which has been granted.

*Recovery of documents*

The process of obtaining documentary evidence which is not in the possession of the person seeking it (e.g. hospital records necessary to establish the extent of injuries received in a road accident).

*Remit between procedures*

A decision of the sheriff to transfer the claim to another court procedure e.g. summary cause or ordinary cause procedure.

*Respondent*

When a decision of the sheriff is appealed against, the person making the appeal is called the appellant. The other side in the appeal is called the respondent.

*Return day*

The date by which the defender must send a written reply to the court and, where appropriate, the pursuer must return the summons to court.

*Schedule of arrestment*

The list of items which may be arrested.

*Serve/Service*

Sending a copy of the summons or other court document to the defender or another party.

*Sheriff clerk*

The court official responsible for the administration of the sheriff court.

*Sheriff officer*

A person who serves court documents and enforces court orders.

*Sist of action*

The temporary suspension of a court case by court order.

*Sist as a party*

To add another person as a litigant in a case.

*Stated case*[1]

An appeal procedure where the sheriff sets out his findings and the reasons for his decision and states the issues on which the decision of the Sheriff Appeal Court is requested.

*Statement of claim*

The part of the summons in which pursuers set out details of their claims against defenders.

*Summary cause*

Another legal procedure available in the Sheriff Court. It is used for certain types of claim usually having a higher value than small claims though less than those dealt with as ordinary causes.

*Summons*

The form which must be filled in to begin a small claim.

*Time to pay direction*

A court order for which a defender who is an individual may apply permitting a sum owed to be paid by instalments or by a single payment at a later date.

*Time order*

---

[1] As amended by the Act of Sederunt (Rules of the Court of Session, Sheriff Appeal Court Rules and Sheriff Court Rules Amendment) (Sheriff Appeal Court) 2015 (SSI 2015/419) r.12 (effective 1 January 2016; as to savings see SSI 2015/419 r.20(7)(a)).

A court order which assists debtors who have defaulted on an agreement regulated by the Consumer Credit Act 1974 (c.39) and which may be applied for during a court action.

*Warrant for diligence*
Authority to carry out one of the diligence procedures.
*Writ*
A legally significant writing.

## SCHEDULE 2

### REVOCATIONS

**Paragraph 4**

| (1)<br>Act of Sederunt | (2)<br>Reference | (3)<br>Extent of revocation |
|---|---|---|
| Act of Sederunt (Small Claim Rules) 1988 | S.I. 1988/1976 | The whole Act of Sederunt |
| Act of Sederunt (Amendment of Sheriff Court Ordinary Cause, Summary Cause and Small Claim, Rules) 1990 | S.I. 1990/661 | Paragraph 4 |
| Act of Sederunt (Amendment of Sheriff Court Ordinary Cause, Summary Cause and Small Claim, Rules) (No. 2) 1990 | S.I. 1990/2105 | Paragraph 4 |
| Act of Sederunt (Amendment of Summary Cause and Small Claim Rules) 1991 | S.I. 1991/821 | Paragraph 3 |
| Act of Sederunt (Amendment of Ordinary Cause, Summary Cause and Small Claim Rules) 1992 | S.I. 1992/249 | Paragraph 3 |
| Act of Sederunt (Sheriff Court Ordinary Cause Rules) 1993 | S.I. 1993/1956 | Paragraph 4 |

# ACT OF SEDERUNT (SHERIFF COURT CAVEAT RULES) 2006

## (SSI 2006/198)

### *28 April 2006.*

The Lords of Council and Session, under and by virtue of the powers conferred by section 32 of the Sheriff Courts (Scotland) Act 1971 and of all other powers enabling them in that behalf, having approved draft rules submitted to them by the Sheriff Court Rules Council in accordance with section 34 of the Sheriff Courts (Scotland) Act 1971, do hereby enact and declare:

### Citation and commencement

**1.**—(1) This Act of Sederunt may be cited as the Act of Sederunt (Sheriff Court Caveat Rules) 2006 and shall come into force on 28th April 2006.

(2) This Act of Sederunt shall be inserted into the Books of Sederunt.

### Orders against which caveats may be lodged

**2.**—(1) Subject to paragraphs (2) and (3), a person may lodge a caveat against only—

(a) an interim interdict sought against the person in an ordinary cause before the person has lodged a notice of intention to defend;

(b) an interim order sought against the person in an ordinary cause before the expiry of the period within which the person could lodge a notice of intention to defend;

(c) an interim order sought against the person in a summary application before service of the initial writ;

(d) an order for intimation, service and advertisement of a petition to wind up, or appoint an administrator to, a company in which he has an interest;

(e) an order for intimation, service and advertisement of a petition for his sequestration; and

(f) the disposal of a commissary application.

(2) In this rule—

(a) "interim order" does not include an order under section 1 of the Administration of Justice (Scotland) Act 1972 (orders for inspection of documents and other property etc.); and

(b) "commissary application" means an application for—

(i) confirmation;

(ii) appointment of an executor; or

(iii) restriction of caution in respect of an executor.

(3) A person may lodge a caveat against an order mentioned in paragraph (1)(d) only where the person is a company, debenture holder, holder of a floating charge, receiver, shareholder of the company or other person claiming an interest.

### Form, lodging and renewal of caveats

**3.**—(1) A caveat shall be in the form set out in the Schedule to this Act of Sederunt, or a form substantially to the same effect with such variation as circumstances may require, and shall be lodged with the sheriff clerk.

(2) A caveat shall remain in force for a period of one year from the date on which it was lodged and may be renewed on its expiry for a further period of one year and yearly thereafter.

(3) An application for the renewal of a caveat shall be made in writing to the sheriff clerk not less than 7 days before its expiry.

(4) Where a caveat has been lodged and has not expired, no order in respect of which the caveat was lodged may be pronounced unless the sheriff is satisfied that all reasonable steps have been taken to afford the person lodging the caveat an opportunity of being heard; and the sheriff may continue the hearing on such an order until he is satisfied that such steps have been taken.

## Amendments

**4.**—(1) Rule 20 of the Act of Sederunt (Sheriff Court Company Insolvency Rules) 1986 shall be omitted.

(2) Chapter 4 of, and Form G2 in Appendix 1 to, the Ordinary Cause Rules 1993 in Schedule 1 to the Sheriff Courts (Scotland) Act 1907 shall be omitted.

(3) Rules 2.8 and 2.9 of, and Form 8 in Schedule 1 to, the Act of Sederunt (Summary Applications, Statutory Applications, and Appeals etc. Rules) 1999 shall be omitted.

## Transitional and savings provision

**5.**—(1) Subject to paragraph (2), nothing in this Act of Sederunt shall affect a caveat lodged prior to 28th April 2006.

(2) A caveat lodged prior to 28th April 2006 may not be renewed unless the caveat complies with the requirements of this Act of Sederunt.

## SCHEDULE

**Rule 3(1)**

### Form of Caveat

SHERIFFDOM OF (*insert name of sheriffdom*)

AT (*insert place of sheriff court*)

CAVEAT for A.B. (*insert designation and address\**)

Should any application be made for (*here specify, under reference to sub-paragraphs of* rule 2(1), *the application(s) to which this caveat is to apply*) [before the lodging of a notice of intention to defend *[or (specify for each application which of the following alternatives is to apply*: the expiry of the period within which a notice of intention to defend may be lodged; before service of the initial writ or petition)]], it is requested that intimation be made to the caveator before any order is pronounced.

Date (*insert date*)...................Signed

...............[A.B.]...............

or [X.Y.] Solicitor for [A.B.] (*add designation, business address and email address*)

Caveator's telephone and fax number (*insert where caveat is not lodged by solicitors*)

Solicitor (*insert name and address, telephone and fax number and reference*)

Out of hours contacts:

1. (*insert name and telephone number*)
2. (*insert name and telephone number*)

\* State whether the caveat is lodged in an individual capacity, or a specified representative capacity (e.g. as a trustee of a named trust) or both. Where appropriate, state the nature of the caveator's interest (e.g. shareholder, debenture holder).

# ACT OF SEDERUNT (SIMPLE PROCEDURE) 2016

## (SSI 2016/200)

*28 November 2016.*

In accordance with section 4 of the Scottish Civil Justice Council and Criminal Legal Assistance Act 2013, the Court of Session has, taking into consideration the matters in section 75 of the Courts Reform (Scotland) Act 2014, approved draft rules submitted to it by the Scottish Civil Justice Council with such modifications as it thinks appropriate.

The Court of Session therefore makes this Act of Sederunt under the powers conferred by section 14(7) of the Scottish Commission for Human Rights Act 2006, section 104(1) of the Courts Reform (Scotland) Act 2014 and all other powers enabling it to do so.

## Citation and commencement, etc.

**1.**—(1)   This Act of Sederunt may be cited as the Act of Sederunt (Simple Procedure) 2016.

(2)   It comes into force on 28th November 2016.

(3)   A certified copy is to be inserted in the Books of Sederunt.

## The Simple Procedure Rules

**2.**—(1)   Schedule 1 contains rules for simple procedure cases and may be cited as the Simple Procedure Rules.

(2)   A form referred to in the Simple Procedure Rules means—

   (a)   the form with that name in Schedule 2, or

   (b)   an electronic version of the form with that name in Schedule 2, adapted for use by the Scottish Courts and Tribunals Service with the portal on its website.

(3)   Where the Simple Procedure Rules require a form to be used, that form may be varied where the circumstances require it.

## Interpretation of the Simple Procedure Rules

**3.**—(1)   In the Simple Procedure Rules—

   "a case where the expenses of a claim are capped" means a simple procedure case—

   (a)   to which an order made under section 81(1) of the Courts Reform (Scotland) Act 2014 applies; or

   (b)   in which the sheriff has made a direction under section 81(7) of that Act;

   "a decision absolving the responding party" means a decree of absolvitor;

   "a decision ordering the responding party to deliver something to the claimant" means a decree for delivery or for recovery of possession;

   "a decision ordering the responding party to do something for the claimant" means a decree ad factum praestandum;

   "advocate" means a practising member of the Faculty of Advocates;

"any time before the decision of the sheriff has been fully implemented" means, where a charge or arrestment has been executed, any time within 14 days of that execution (or, where there has been more than one, the first such execution);

"a person otherwise entitled to conduct proceedings in the sheriff court" means any person so entitled, including a member of a body which has made a successful application under section 25 of the Law Reform (Miscellaneous Provisions) (Scotland) Act 1990, but only to the extent that the member is exercising rights acquired by virtue of section 27 of that Act;

"a question of EU law" means a question which might lead to a reference to the Court of Justice of the European Union for—

    (a)    a preliminary ruling under Article 267 of the Treaty on the Functioning of the European Union;

    (b)    a ruling on the interpretation of the Conventions mentioned in Article 1 of Schedule 2 to the Civil Jurisdiction and Judgments Act 1982 under Article 3 of that Schedule; or

    (c)    a preliminary ruling on the interpretation of the instruments mentioned in Article 1 of Schedule 3 to the Contracts (Applicable Law) Act 1990 under Article 2 of that Schedule;

"child's property administration order" means an order under section 11(1) of the Children (Scotland) Act 1995;

"Child Witness Notice" means a child witness notice under section 12(2) of the Vulnerable Witnesses (Scotland) Act 2004;

"damages management order" means an order about how a sum of money awarded as damages is to be paid to and managed for a person under a legal disability;

"Equality Act 2010 claim" means a claim which, in Scotland, the sheriff has jurisdiction to determine as a result of section 114(1) of the Equality Act 2010;

"EU member state" means a state which is a member of the European Union, within the meaning of Part II of Schedule 1 to the European Communities Act 1972;

"Hague Convention country" means a country in respect of which the Convention of 15 November 1965 on the Service Abroad of Judicial and Extrajudicial Documents in Civil or Commercial Matters is in force, other than an EU member state;

"independent person" means a commissioner before whom evidence is taken in accordance with section 19 of the Vulnerable Witnesses (Scotland) Act 2004;

"next-day postal service which records delivery" means a postal service which—

    (a)    seeks to deliver documents or other things by post no later than the next working day in all or the majority of cases; and

    (b)    provides for the delivery of documents or other things by post to be recorded;

"order for time to pay" means—

    (a)    a time to pay direction under section 1 of the Debtors (Scotland) Act 1987;

    (b)    a time to pay order under section 5 of of the Debtors (Scotland) Act 1987;

    (c)    a time order under section 129 of the Consumer Credit Act 1974.

"ordinary cause" means an action under the Ordinary Cause Rules 1993;

"pause a case" means sist a case;

"postal service which records delivery" means a postal service which provides for the delivery of documents or other things by post to be recorded;

"provisional order" means a warrant for—

    (a)   arrestment on the dependence or inhibition on the dependence under section 15A(1) of the Debtors (Scotland) Act 1987; or

    (b)   interim attachment under section 9A(1) of the Debt Arrangement and Attachment (Scotland) Act 2002;

"Provisional Orders Reconsideration Application" means an application under—

    (a)   section 15K(2) or 15L(1) of the Debtors (Scotland) Act 1987; or

    (b)   section 9M(2) or 9N(1) of the Debt Arrangement and Attachment (Scotland) Act 2002;

"provisional orders review hearing" means a hearing under—

    (a)   section 15K(4) or 15L(3) of the Debtors (Scotland) Act 1987; or

    (b)   section 9M(4) or 9N(3) of the Debt Arrangement and Attachment (Scotland) Act 2002;

"restart a case" means recall a sist;

"schedule of inhibition" means a schedule of inhibition in the form prescribed by regulation 3(1)(a) of and Schedule 1 to the Diligence (Scotland) Regulations 2009;

"Service Regulation" means Regulation (EC) No. 1393/2007 of the European Parliament and of the Council of 13 November 2007 on the service in the Member States of judicial and extrajudicial documents in civil or commercial matters (service of documents), and repealing Council Regulation (EC) No. 1348/2000, as amended from time to time and as applied by the Agreement made on 19 October 2005 between the European Community and the Kingdom of Denmark on the service of judicial and extrajudicial documents in civil and commercial matters;

"Sheriff Personal Injury Court" means the all-Scotland sheriff court sitting by virtue of the All-Scotland Sheriff Court (Sheriff Personal Injury Court) Order 2015;

"Special Measures Review Application" means an application under section 13 of the Vulnerable Witness (Scotland) Act 2004;

"solicitor" means a qualified solicitor under section 4 of the Solicitors (Scotland) Act 1980;

"standard order" means one of the standard orders in Schedule 3;

"the principles of simple procedure" means the principles in rule 1.2;

"trading name" means the trading or descriptive name of a person, partnership, limited liability partnership or company;

"Vulnerable Witness Application" means a vulnerable witness application under section 12(6) of the Vulnerable Witnesses (Scotland) Act 2004.

(2)   In Part 2 of the Simple Procedure Rules, "other legislation" means any enactment which entitles a person to act as a lay representative in a simple procedure case.

(3)   In Part 11 of the Simple Procedure Rules, "supporter" means a supporter within the meaning of section 22(1) of the Vulnerable Witnesses (Scotland) Act 2004.

(4)   In Part 17 of the Simple Procedure Rules, "initial writ", "intimate", "defences", "options hearing" and "lodging" have the meaning they have in the Ordinary Cause Rules 1993.

## Warrants

**4.**—(1)   In the Simple Procedure Rules—

(a)   a claim being registered—

(i)   is warrant for the service of the Claim Form on the respondent;

(ii)   is warrant for the citation of witnesses;

(b)   a Response Form being registered is warrant for the citation of witnesses;

(c)   a certified copy of a written order granting a provisional order is sufficient authority for execution of the diligence specified in the provisional order;

(d)   in Part 11, a sheriff ordering a witness to be brought to court—

(i)   is warrant for the apprehension of that witness and for having that witness brought to court,

(ii)   that warrant is effective in all sheriffdoms without endorsation, and

(iii)   the expenses of that warrant may be awarded against the witness.

(2)   In a claim for delivery in a simple procedure case, the court may—

(a)   grant warrant to search for and take possession of goods and to open shut and lockfast places, and

(b)   that warrant only applies to premises occupied by the respondent.

## Arrestment to found jurisdiction

**5.**—(1)   This paragraph applies to a simple procedure case where the claimant has used an arrestment to found jurisdiction before the Claim Form is formally served on the respondent.

(2)   The service of the arrestment must be reported to the sheriff clerk as soon as possible.

(3)   The arrestment ceases to have effect unless the Claim Form is formally served on the respondent within 21 days from the date of formal service of the arrestment.

SCHEDULE 1

THE SIMPLE PROCEDURE RULES

**Paragraph 2(1)**

**Part 1  An overview of simple procedure**

1.1  *The simple procedure is a court process designed to provide a speedy, inexpensive and informal court way to resolve disputes.*

1.2  What are the principles of simple procedure?

1.3  Who takes part in a simple procedure case?

1.4  What are the sheriff's responsibilities?

1.5  What are parties' responsibilities?

1.6  What are representatives' responsibilities?

1.7  What are the sheriff clerk's responsibilities?

1.8  What are the sheriff's powers?

**Part 2  Representation and support**

2.1  *This Part is about who may represent a party, and what that representative may and may not do.*

*This Part is also about who may provide support to a party in the courtroom, and what that courtroom supporter may and may not do.*

*Representation*

2.2  Who can be a representative?

2.3  What can a representative do?

2.4  Who is entitled by these Rules to be a lay representative?

*Support*

2.5  Who can be a courtroom supporter?

2.6  What can a courtroom supporter do?

**Part 3  How to make a claim**

3.1  *This Part is about how the claimant makes a claim and what the court will do with that claim.*

3.2  How is a claim made?

3.3  How do you complete a Claim Form?

3.4  What if there is more than one claimant?

3.5  What if there are more than two respondents?

3.6  What if the respondent uses a trading name?

3.7  What do you do with a completed Claim Form?

3.8  How do you ask for provisional orders to be made?

3.9  What will the court do with the Claim Form?

3.10  What happens next?

3.11  What is the last date for service?

3.12  What is the last date for a response?

3.13  How can the timetable be changed?

**Part 4  How to respond to a claim**

4.1 *This Part is about how the respondent responds to a claim and what the court will do with that response.*

4.2 How do you respond to a claim?

4.3 What responses can you make?

4.4 What has to go in the Response Form?

4.5 What will the court do with the Response Form?

**Part 5 How to ask for time to pay**

5.1 *This Part is about how the respondent may ask for time to pay if a claim for payment of a sum of money is admitted, and how the claimant can consent or object to that.*

5.2 What is an order for time to pay?

5.3 How can a respondent ask for time to pay?

5.4 What will the court do with a Time to Pay Application?

5.5 How can the claimant consent to a Time to Pay Application?

5.6 How can the claimant object to a Time to Pay Application?

5.7 What if the claimant does not consent or object to a Time to Pay Application?

**Part 6 Sending and formal service**

6.1 *This Part is about what has to be done when these Rules require something to be sent to someone.*

*This Part is also about what has to be done when these Rules require a document to be formally served on someone.*

6.2 What is the difference between sending and formally serving?

6.3 When must something be sent or formally served?

6.4 Can a party object to how sending or formal service was done?

*Sending*

6.5 How can the court send something to a party?

6.6 How can a party send something to the court?

6.7 How can a party send something to another party?

*Formal service*

6.8 How can you formally serve a document on someone living within Scotland?

6.9 How can you formally serve a document on someone living outside Scotland?

6.10 What if a person uses a trading name?

6.11 How can the Claim Form be formally served on the respondent?

6.12 What if the claimant does not know the respondent's address?

6.13 What if the sheriff considers that formal service of the Claim Form has not been done properly?

**Part 7 What happens to a case**

7.1 *This Part is about what happens after a Response Form has been received and what happens if no Response Form is received.*

*Admitted claims*

7.2 What if parties settle the claim before the last date for a response?

7.3 What if the respondent makes a Time to Pay Application?

7.4 What if no Response Form is received by the court?

*Disputed claims*

7.5 What if the respondent disputes the claim?

7.6 What will be in the first written orders?

7.7 What is a case management discussion?

7.8 What is a hearing?

**Part 8 Orders**

8.1 *This Part is about the orders which the sheriff can give to manage or decide a case.*

8.2 What are orders?

8.3 What are standard orders?

8.4 What are unless orders?

8.5 What if a party does not follow an order?

**Part 9 Applications**

9.1 *This Part is about applications which parties may make to the court to ask for things to be done in a case.*

*Pausing and restarting cases*

9.2 How can a party ask for the progress of a case to be paused?

9.3 What happens if the progress of a case is paused?

9.4 How can a party ask for a paused case to be restarted?

9.5 What can the court do with a paused case?

*Miscellaneous applications*

9.6 How can a person become an additional respondent in a case?

9.7 How can a party ask to amend the Claim Form or the Response Form?

9.8 How can a claimant abandon a claim?

9.9 What can happen if a party dies or becomes legally incapacitated?

9.10 How can a party ask the sheriff to make any other orders?

**Part 10 Documents and other evidence**

10.1 *This Part is about how parties should lodge documents and other evidence with the court before a hearing.*

*This Part is also about how parties can apply for orders to recover documents from other people.*

*Lodging documents and other evidence*

10.2 How can you lodge documents and other evidence with the court?

10.3 What documents and other evidence can a party bring to a hearing?

10.4 How can other parties borrow or inspect documents and other evidence lodged with the court?

10.5 How long will the court keep documents and other evidence for?

*Orders to recover documents*

10.6 How can a party recover documents to lodge them with the court?

10.7 What happens when an order to recover documents is made?

10.8 What happens if the person who has the documents claims they are confidential?

10.9 What happens if a party does not believe that an order to recover documents has been complied with?

10.10 What happens when a special order to recover documents is made?

10.11 What happens if the person who has the documents claims they are confidential?

## Part 11 Witnesses

11.1 *This Part is about the citation of witnesses and their attendance at hearings.*

*This Part is also about measures that the court can take to assist vulnerable witnesses in giving evidence.*

### The citation of witnesses

11.2 How can a party arrange the attendance of witnesses at a hearing?

11.3 What if a witness does not appear at a hearing?

### Vulnerable witnesses

11.4 How will the court treat a child witness?

11.5 How will the court treat other vulnerable witnesses?

11.6 What are special measures?

11.7 How can a party ask the court to review the arrangements for a child witness or a vulnerable witness?

11.8 What happens when evidence is to be given before an independent person?

## Part 12 The hearing

12.1 *This Part is about the hearing at which the dispute between the parties should be resolved.*

12.2 What is the purpose of the hearing?

12.3 How will the dispute between the parties be resolved?

12.4 What will the sheriff do at the hearing?

12.5 What if a party does not come to the hearing?

12.6 How will evidence be given at the hearing?

## Part 13 The decision

13.1 *This Part is about the decisions which the sheriff can make to resolve a dispute.*

*This Part is also about the circumstances in which a party can apply to have a decision recalled.*

13.2 When must the sheriff make the decision?

13.3 How will the sheriff make the decision?

13.4 What sort of decisions can the sheriff make?

### Recalling a decision

13.5 When can a decision of the sheriff be recalled?

13.6 How can a party apply to have a decision of the sheriff recalled?

13.7 What happens when a sheriff decides to recall a decision?

## Part 14 Expenses

14.1 *This Part is about the expenses of a claim which the sheriff can order a party to pay for.*

14.2 What orders about expenses can the sheriff make?

14.3 When will the sheriff make an order about expenses?

14.4 What if the sheriff does not make an order about expenses when deciding the claim?

14.5 What is an expenses hearing?

## Part 15 How to enforce a decision

15.1 *This Part is about the steps which a successful party must take to enforce a decision.*

15.2 When can a party enforce a decision?

15.3 How can a party enforce a decision?

15.4 What if the claimant does not know the respondent's address?

15.5 What if the respondent does not comply with a decision?

**Part 16  How to appeal a decision**

16.1 *This Part is about how a party can appeal a decision and how the sheriff and Sheriff Appeal Court will deal with an appeal.*

16.2 How do you appeal a decision?

16.3 What will the sheriff do with an appeal?

16.4 What will the Sheriff Appeal Court do with an appeal?

**Part 17  Miscellaneous matters**

17.1 This Part is about some miscellaneous matters which can arise during a case.

17.2 How can a case be transferred out of the simple procedure?

17.3 How can the sheriff make a reference to the Court of Justice of the European Union?

17.4 How can the Commission for Equality and Human Rights ("CEHR") or the Scottish Commission for Human Rights ("SCHR") intervene?

17.5 What can the CEHR or the SCHR do in an intervention?

*Management of damages*

17.6 When is a damages management order available?

17.7 When must the sheriff make a damages management order?

17.8 What can the sheriff do in a damages management order?

17.9 How can the damages management order be changed?

17.10 How can further instructions about managing the money be given?

17.11 When can someone apply for a child's property administration order?

17.12 How can someone apply for a child's property administration order?

*The Equality Act 2010*

17.13 What is an Equality Act 2010 claim?

17.14 How can the Commission for Equality and Human Rights ("the CEHR") be notified of an Equality Act 2010 claim?

17.15 How can an Equality Act 2010 claim be transferred to the Employment Tribunal?

17.16 How can an Employment Tribunal case be transferred to simple procedure?

17.17 What if a question of national security arises in an Equality Act 2010 claim?

**Part 18  Formal service in Scotland**

18.1 *This Part is about how to formally serve a document on someone living in Scotland.*

18.2 How can you formally serve a document on someone who lives in Scotland?

18.3 What if service by post does not work?

**Part 19  Formal service outside Scotland**

19.1 *This Part is about how to formally serve a document on someone outside Scotland.*

19.2 How can you formally serve a document on someone who lives outside Scotland?

19.3 How can you formally serve a document on someone who lives in England and Wales, Northern Ireland, the Isle of Man or the Channel Islands?

19.4 How can you formally serve a document on someone who lives in an EU member state (including Denmark) under the Service Regulation?

19.5 How can you formally serve a document on someone who lives in a Hague Convention country (other than an EU member state)?

19.6 How can you formally serve a document on someone who lives in a country with which the United Kingdom has a convention about how to serve court documents?

19.7 How can you formally serve a document on someone who lives in any other country?

**Part 20  Provisional orders**

20.1 *This Part is about provisional orders which protect or secure the claimant's position before the sheriff makes a final decision in a case.*

20.2 When can a claimant ask for provisional orders to be made?

20.3 What happens when the court receives a Provisional Orders Application?

20.4 How can the claimant tell the respondent or an interested party about a hearing?

20.5 How can you ask the court to reconsider provisional orders that it has made?

20.6 How can you ask the court to consider other applications about provisional orders?

20.7 How are provisional orders made effective?

20.8 How is an arrestment on the dependence made effective?

20.9 How is an inhibition on the dependence made effective if the claimant does not know the respondent's address?

**Part 21  Glossary**

21.1 *This Part contains a guide for litigants, lay representatives and courtroom supporters to the meaning of certain legal words and expressions used in these rules.*

# PART 1: AN OVERVIEW OF SIMPLE PROCEDURE

## PART 1

### AN OVERVIEW OF SIMPLE PROCEDURE

**What is simple procedure?**

**1.1**(1) Simple procedure is a court process designed to provide a speedy, inexpensive and informal way to resolve disputes.

**What are the principles of simple procedure?**

**1.2**(1) Cases are to be resolved as quickly as possible, at the least expense to parties and the courts.

(2) The approach of the court to a case is to be as informal as is appropriate, taking into account the nature and complexity of the dispute.

(3) Parties are to be treated even-handedly by the court.

(4) Parties are to be encouraged to settle their disputes by negotiation or alternative dispute resolution, and should be able to do so throughout the progress of a case.

(5) Parties should only have to come to court when it is necessary to do so to progress or resolve their dispute.

**Who takes part in a simple procedure case?**

**1.3**(1) A simple procedure case involves a claim being made in the sheriff court.

(2) The person who makes the claim is the claimant.

(3) The person the claim is made against is the respondent.

(4) The claimant and the respondents are the parties.

(5) The case will be decided by the sheriff, who is in charge of the court.

(6) The sheriff clerk provides administrative support to the sheriff.

(7) A claim which is registered by the sheriff clerk is a simple procedure case.

(8) Parties may represent themselves or have representatives.

(9) Parties may be assisted by courtroom supporters.

**What are the sheriff's responsibilities?**

**1.4**(1) The sheriff must take into account the principles of simple procedure when managing cases and when interpreting these rules.

(2) The sheriff must ensure that parties who are not represented, or parties who do not have legal representation, are not unfairly disadvantaged.

(3) The sheriff must encourage cases to be resolved by negotiation or alternative dispute resolution, where possible.

(4) If a case cannot be resolved by negotiation or alternative dispute resolution, the sheriff must decide the case.

**What are parties' responsibilities?**

**1.5**(1) Parties must respect the principles of simple procedure.

(2) Parties must be honest with each other, with representatives and with the sheriff.

(3) Parties must be respectful and courteous to each other, to representatives, to witnesses and to the sheriff.

(4) Parties must not try to make a witness give misleading evidence.

(5) Parties must consider throughout the progress of a case whether their dispute could be resolved by negotiation or alternative dispute resolution.

(6) Parties must approach any negotiation or alternative dispute resolution with an open and constructive attitude.

(7) Parties must follow the sheriff's orders.

## What are representatives' responsibilities?

**1.6**(1) Representatives must respect the principles of simple procedure.

(2) Representatives must be honest with each other, with parties and with the sheriff.

(3) Representatives must be respectful and courteous to each other, to parties, to witnesses and to the sheriff.

(4) Representatives must act in the best interests of the person being represented, and not allow any personal interest to influence their advice or actions.

(5) Representatives must not knowingly make claims or arguments which have no factual or legal basis.

(6) Representatives must maintain client confidentiality.

(7) Representatives must not try to make a witness give misleading evidence.

(8) Representatives must not act where they have a conflict of interest.

(9) When appearing against a party who is not represented, or who is not legally represented, representatives must not take advantage of that party.

(10) When appearing against a party who is not represented, or who is not legally represented, representatives must help the court to allow that person to argue a case fairly.

(11) Representatives must follow the sheriff's orders.

## What are the sheriff clerk's responsibilities?

**1.7**(1) The sheriff clerk must maintain a register of simple procedure cases.

(2) The sheriff clerk must send the sheriff's written orders to the parties.

## What are the sheriff's powers?

**1.8**(1) The sheriff may give orders to the parties, either in person or by giving written orders.

(2) The sheriff may do anything or give any order considered necessary to encourage negotiation or alternative dispute resolution between the parties.

(3) The sheriff may do anything or give any order considered necessary to decide the case.

(4) The sheriff may relieve a party from the consequences of failing to comply with any of the Simple Procedure Rules. When doing so, the sheriff may impose conditions or make orders about expenses.

(5) The sheriff may give orders which vary a deadline or period of time set out in the Simple Procedure Rules.

(6) The sheriff may make decisions about the form, location and conduct of a discussion in court, case management discussion or hearing. The sheriff must explain to parties why these decisions were made.

(7) The sheriff may combine separate cases, so that any discussion in court, case management discussion or hearing in the cases is held at the same time.

(8) The sheriff may continue any discussion in court, case management discussion or hearing to another day only if it is necessary to do so.

(9) The sheriff may pause and restart the progress of a case.

(10) The sheriff may decide a case without a hearing.

(11)   If a claim, or part of a claim, obviously has no real prospect of success, the sheriff may dismiss the claim or that part of it at any time.

(12)   If a claim, or part of claim, obviously will not succeed because it is incompetent, the sheriff may dismiss the claim or that part of it at any time.

(13)   If a response, or part of a response, obviously will not succeed because it is incompetent, the sheriff may decide a case, or that part of it, at any time.

(14)   The sheriff may make provisional orders or interim orders which protect or secure a claimant's position before a hearing.

(15)   The sheriff may order an authenticated copy of any document to be treated as an original, where the original is lost or destroyed.

(16)   The sheriff may transfer a simple procedure case to another court, whether in the same sheriffdom or not.

(17)   If a claim should have been raised in a different sheriff court the sheriff must transfer the claim to a court in which the claim could have been raised, unless the sheriff is satisfied that there is a good reason not to.

## PART 2: REPRESENTATION AND SUPPORT

PART 2

REPRESENTATION AND SUPPORT

**What is this Part about?**

**2.1**(1)  This Part is about who may represent a party, and what that representative may and may not do.

(2)  This Part is also about who may provide support to a party in the courtroom, and what that courtroom supporter may and may not do.

*Representation*

**Who can be a representative?**

**2.2**(1)  A party may be represented by a legal representative or a lay representative.

(2)  A legal representative is a person who is an advocate, a solicitor or a person otherwise entitled to conduct proceedings in the sheriff court.

(3)  A lay representative is a person who is not a legal representative but is entitled to be a lay representative, either by these Rules or by other legislation.

**What can a representative do?**

**2.3**(1)  A representative may do anything involved in the preparation or conduct of a case that a party can do.

**Who is entitled by these Rules to be a lay representative?**

**2.4**(1)  If a party wants to be represented by a lay representative throughout a case, then that lay representative must complete a Lay Representation Form and send it to the court when the Claim Form or the Response Form is sent to court.

(2)  If a party wants to be represented by a lay representative during a particular discussion or hearing only, then the lay representative must complete a Lay Representation Form and give it to the sheriff clerk in person at court at that discussion or hearing.

(3)  The sheriff may at any time order a person to stop acting as a lay representative if the sheriff considers that person unsuitable.

(4)  For the purposes of considering suitability, the sheriff may take into account any interest that person has in the case and whether that person has been declared a vexatious litigant.

(5)  A person is unsuitable to act as a lay representative if their behaviour does not respect the principles of simple procedure.

(6)  A person may only act as a lay representative if that person agrees not to receive any remuneration from the party, whether directly or indirectly, for acting as a lay representative. This rule does not apply where the party is a company, limited liability partnership or partnership.

*Support*

**Who can be a courtroom supporter?**

**2.5**(1)  A courtroom supporter is a person (for example, a family member, friend or colleague) who may accompany a party in court in order to provide quiet support, encouragement and advice during a hearing.

(2)   A party may ask the sheriff in court for permission for someone to be a courtroom supporter.

(3)   The sheriff may permit a person to act as a courtroom supporter only if that person agrees not to receive any remuneration from the party, whether directly or indirectly, for acting as a courtroom supporter.

(4)   If at any point the sheriff considers that a person is not suitable to act as a courtroom supporter, the sheriff may withdraw permission to act as a courtroom supporter.

(5)   A person is unsuitable to act as a courtroom supporter if their behaviour does not respect the principles of simple procedure.

**What can a courtroom supporter do?**

**2.6**(1)   A courtroom supporter may sit beside or behind the party in court.

(2)   A courtroom supporter may provide moral support to the party.

(3)   A courtroom supporter may help to manage the party's court documents and other papers.

(4)   A courtroom supporter may take notes in court.

(5)   A courtroom supporter may quietly advise the party on points of law and procedure, on issues the party might wish to raise with the sheriff or on questions the party might want to ask any witness.

(6)   A courtroom supporter may be given any document or information connected to the case.

(7)   However, if disclosure of that document or that information is prohibited or restricted in any way, then the courtroom supporter must respect that prohibition or restriction.

PART 3

HOW TO MAKE A CLAIM

**What is this Part about?**

**3.1**(1)   This Part is about how the claimant makes a claim and what the court will do with that claim.

**How is a claim made?**

**3.2**(1)   The process for making a claim is:
(a)   the claimant completes a Claim Form (see rule 3.3),
(b)   the claimant sends the Claim Form to the court (see rule 3.7),
(c)   the sheriff clerk checks and registers the Claim Form (see 3.9),
(d)   the sheriff clerk issues a timetable for the case (see rule 3.10), and
(e)   the Claim Form is formally served on the respondent, either by the sheriff clerk, a solicitor or a sheriff officer (see Part 6).

**How do you complete a Claim Form?**

**3.3**(1)   The claimant must set out the following information in the Claim Form:
(a)   the identity of the claimant, including the claimant's address and whether the claimant is an individual, a company or another type of organisation,
(b)   the identity of the respondent, including the respondent's address (where known) and whether the respondent is an individual, a company or another type of organisation,
(c)   the essential factual background to the dispute,
(d)   what the claimant wants from the respondent if the claim is successful,
(e)   why the claim should succeed,
(f)   what steps the claimant has already taken (if any) to try to resolve the dispute with the respondent.

(2)   The claimant must list in the Claim Form any documents or other evidence that the claimant thinks support the claim.

(3)   The claimant must list in the Claim Form any witnesses (other than the claimant and the respondent) that the claimant thinks support the claim.

**What if there is more than one claimant?**

**3.4**(1)   If there is more than one claimant, the claimant must complete a Further Claimant Form for each further claimant.

(2)   The Further Claimant Form must identify the further claimant, including the further claimant's address and whether the further claimant is an individual, a company or another type of organisation.

**What if there are more than two respondents?**

**3.5**(1)   If there are more than two respondents, the claimant must set out the claim against all respondents in the Claim Form.

(2)   The claimant must also complete a Further Respondent Form for each further respondent.

(3)   The Further Respondent Form must identify the further respondent, including the further respondent's address (where known) and whether the further respondent is an individual, a company or another type of organisation.

**What if the respondent uses a trading name?**

**3.6**(1) If the respondent uses a trading name, a claim may be made against them using that trading name.

**What do you do with a completed Claim Form?**

**3.7**(1) The completed Claim Form must be sent to the sheriff court.

(2) If the Claim Form has been completed on paper then two copies must be sent to the sheriff court.

**How do you ask for provisional orders to be made?**

**3.8**(1) Provisional orders are orders which protect or secure the claimant's position before the sheriff makes a final decision in a case.

(2) There are three types of provisional order:
- (a) an arrestment on the dependence under section 15A(1) of the Debtors (Scotland) Act 1987 (this is an order freezing the respondent's goods or money held by a third party),
- (b) an inhibition on the dependence under section 15A(1) of the Debtors (Scotland) Act 1987 (this is an order preventing the respondent from selling their home or other land, or taking out a secured loan), and
- (c) an interim attachment under section 9A(1) of the Debt Arrangement and Attachment (Scotland) Act 2002 (this is an order preventing the respondent from selling or removing their goods).

(3) Part 20 of these Rules is about how the claimant may apply for provisional orders.

**What will the court do with the Claim Form?**

**3.9**(1) The sheriff clerk will check the Claim Form for problems which mean that it cannot be registered. Such problems might include:
- (a) the Claim Form not being accompanied by the correct fee,
- (b) the Claim Form being sent to the wrong sheriff court,
- (c) the Claim Form asking for something that is not possible in simple procedure, such as making a claim for over £5,000,
- (d) the Claim Form being incomplete.

(2) If there are no such problems, the sheriff clerk must register the claim.

(3) The sheriff clerk must ask for the approval of the sheriff before registering the claim if:
- (a) the respondent's address is unknown,
- (b) the claimant is seeking provisional orders or interim orders, or
- (c) the sheriff clerk thinks that the claim requires the attention of the sheriff for some other reason.

**What happens next?**

**3.10**(1) After registering a claim, the sheriff clerk must send the claimant a Timetable.

(2) The Timetable must set out the timetable for the case, including:
- (a) the last date for service, and
- (b) the last date for a response.

**What is the last date for service?**

**3.11**(1) The last date for service is the date by which the Claim Form must be formally served on the respondent.

(2)   This must normally be 3 weeks before the last date for a response.

(3)   If the respondent does not live in an EU member state, the last date for service must normally be 6 weeks before the last date for a response.

(4)   If the respondent is a business with no place of business in an EU member state, the last date for service must normally be 6 weeks before the last date for a response.

**What is the last date for a response?**

**3.12**(1)   The last date for a response is the date by which the respondent must send a Response Form to the court and to the claimant.

**How can the timetable be changed?**

**3.13**(1)   The sheriff may change the timetable at the request of the sheriff clerk or at the request of one of the parties.

(2)   The claimant may request a change (if, for example, there has been a difficulty serving the Claim Form on the respondent) by sending the court a Change of Timetable Application.

(3)   The respondent may request a change (if, for example, the Claim Form was formally served on them late) by sending the court a Change of Timetable Application.

(4)   If the sheriff changes the timetable, the sheriff clerk must send a new Timetable to the claimant or to the parties.

# PART 4: HOW TO RESPOND TO A CLAIM

PART 4

HOW TO RESPOND TO A CLAIM

## What is this Part about?

**4.1**(1)   This Part is about how the respondent responds to a claim and what the court will do with that response.

## How do you respond to a claim?

**4.2**(1)   The respondent must send a completed Response Form to the court by the last date for a response.

(2)   The respondent must also send a copy of the completed Response Form to the claimant by the last date for a response.

## What responses can you make?

**4.3**(1)   There are three ways in which the respondent may respond to the claim.

(2)   The respondent may:
  (a)   admit the claim and settle it before the last date for a response,
  (b)   admit the claim and ask the court for time to pay (see Part 5), or
  (c)   dispute the claim or part of the claim (such as the amount the respondent should pay the claimant).

(3)   This flow-chart sets out how the respondent may respond to a claim:

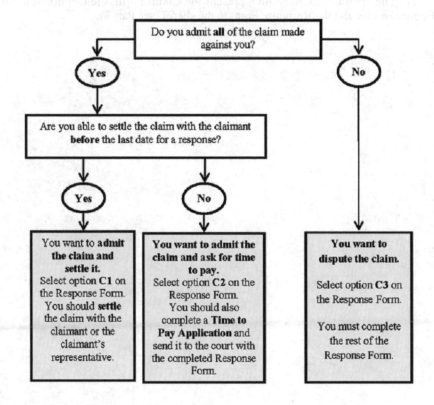

**What has to go in the Response Form?**

**4.4**(1)   The respondent must set out in the Response Form the following information:

    (a)   which facts (if any) set out in the Claim Form that the respondent agrees with,

    (b)   which facts (if any) set out in the Claim Form that the respondent disagrees with and why,

    (c)   why the respondent thinks that the claimant should not get what was asked for in the Claim Form, or why the claimant should only get some of what was asked for in the Claim Form,

    (d)   what steps the respondent has already taken (if any) to try to resolve the dispute with the claimant.

(2)   The respondent must indicate in the Response Form if the respondent thinks that there should be any additional respondents.

(3)   The respondent must list in the Response Form any documents, files, or other evidence that the respondent thinks support the response.

(4)   The respondent must list in the Response Form any witnesses that the respondent thinks support the response.

**What will the court do with the Response Form?**

**4.5**(1)   When the court receives a Response Form, the sheriff clerk must register it.

(2)   The sheriff clerk must then present the Claim Form, the Confirmation of Formal Service and the Response Form to the sheriff (see Part 7).

# PART 5: HOW TO ASK FOR TIME TO PAY

## PART 5

### HOW TO ASK FOR TIME TO PAY

**What is this Part about?**

**5.1**(1)   This Part is about how the respondent may ask for time to pay if a claim for payment of a sum of money is admitted, and how the claimant can consent or object to that.

**What is an order for time to pay?**

**5.2**(1)   An order for time to pay is an order of the sheriff that the respondent must pay the claimant a sum of money in a particular way, such as by instalments or by a delayed payment.

**How can a respondent ask for time to pay?**

**5.3**(1)   The respondent may ask for time to pay in three ways:
  (a)   by completing a Time to Pay Application and sending it to court with the completed Response Form,
  (b)   by completing a Time to Pay Application and giving it to the sheriff clerk at a discussion in court, case management discussion or a hearing, or
  (c)   by completing a Time to Pay Application and sending it to court after the sheriff has made a decision.

**What will the court do with a Time to Pay Application?**

**5.4**(1)   If the respondent sends a Time to Pay Application to the court, the sheriff clerk must send a copy of it to the claimant along with a Time to Pay Notice.

**How can the claimant consent to a Time to Pay Application?**

**5.5**(1)   To consent to a Time to Pay Application, the claimant must indicate consent on the Time to Pay Notice and send it to the court within 2 weeks after the claimant is sent the Time to Pay Notice.

(2)   The sheriff may then grant the Time to Pay Application and decide the case.

**How can the claimant object to a Time to Pay Application?**

**5.6**(1)   To object to a Time to Pay Application, the claimant must indicate objection on the Time to Pay Notice and send it to the court within 2 weeks after the claimant is sent the Time to Pay Notice.

(2)   When the court receives an objection to a Time to Pay Application, the sheriff must give the parties order arranging a time to pay hearing.

(3)   At a time to pay hearing, the sheriff must decide the case and decide whether to grant or refuse the Time to Pay Application.

**What if the claimant does not consent or object to a Time to Pay Application?**

**5.7**(1)   If the claimant has not consented or objected to a Time to Pay Application within 2 weeks after the claimant is sent the Time to Pay Notice, the sheriff must decide the case (if the case has not yet been decided) and grant or refuse the Time to Pay Application.

PART 6

SENDING AND FORMAL SERVICE

## What is this Part about?

**6.1**(1)   This Part is about what has to be done when these Rules require something to be sent to someone.

(2)   This Part is also about what has to be done when these Rules require a document to be formally served on someone.

## What is the difference between sending and formally serving?

**6.2**(1)   When these Rules require something to be "sent", that may be done by anyone and in a number of ways.

(2)   When these Rules require a document to be "formally served" on someone, that may only be done by certain people (sheriff officers, sheriff clerks or solicitors) and may only be done in certain ways.

## When must something be sent or formally served?

**6.3**(1)   If these Rules say that something must be sent or formally served within a period or number of days, it must be sent or formally served in time for it to arrive before the end of that period or the last day.

(2)   If these Rules say that something must be sent or formally served by a particular day, it must be sent or formally served in time for it to arrive before the end of that day.

(3)   If these Rules say that something must be sent to court within a period, number of days or by a particular day and the end of that period or that day is a Saturday, Sunday, public holiday or court holiday, then it must be sent so that it will be received before the end of the next working day.

## Can a party object to how sending or formal service was done?

**6.4**(1)   A party who responds to something (such as sending a Response Form in response to a Claim Form or objecting to an application) may not object to how that thing was sent or formally served.

### *Sending*

## How can the court send something to a party?

**6.5**(1)   The court may send something to a party in one of 4 ways:
   (a)   handing it to that party or to that party's representative in person,
   (b)   posting it to that party or that party's representative,
   (c)   emailing it to that party or that party's representative, using an email address given on the Claim Form or Response Form,
   (d)   making it available to that party using the portal on the Scottish Courts and Tribunals Service website.

## How can a party send something to the court?

**6.6**(1)   A party may send something to the court in one of three ways:
   (a)   handing it in to the court in person,
   (b)   posting it to the court using a postal service which records delivery,
   (c)   submitting it to the court using the portal on the Scottish Courts and Tribunals Service website.

### How can a party send something to another party?

**6.7**(1)   A party may send something to another party in one of three ways:

(a)   posting it to that party or that party's representative using a next-day postal service which records delivery,

(b)   emailing it to that party or that party's representative, using an email address given on the Claim Form or Response Form,

(c)   making it available to that party using the portal on the Scottish Courts and Tribunals Service website.

*Formal service*

### How can you formally serve a document on someone living within Scotland?

**6.8**(1)   Part 18 of these Rules is about formal service on someone living in Scotland.

### How can you formally serve a document on someone living outside Scotland?

**6.9**(1)   Part 19 of these Rules is about formal service on someone living outside Scotland.

### What if a person uses a trading name?

**6.10**(1)   If a person uses a trading name, a document may be formally served on that person at any place of business or office at which that business is carried on within the sheriffdom.

(2)   If that person does not have a place of business or office within the sheriffdom, a document may be formally served on that person at any place where that business is carried on (including the office of the clerk or secretary of a company, association or firm).

### How can the Claim Form be formally served on the respondent?

**6.11**(1)   As well as following the rules for formal service in Part 18 or Part 19, there are some additional requirements when formally serving the Claim Form.

(2)   The sheriff clerk may formally serve the Claim Form if:

(a)   the claimant is not a company, limited liability partnership or partnership, and

(b)   the claimant is not legally represented.

(3)   When formally serving a Claim Form, the envelope must contain only the following:

(a)   a copy of the Claim Form,

(b)   any Further Claimant Forms or Further Respondent Forms,

(c)   a blank Response Form,

(d)   a copy of the Notice of Claim,

(e)   a copy of the Timetable,

(f)   if the respondent can apply for time to pay, a blank Time to Pay Application, and

(g)   any other document approved by the sheriff principal in that sheriffdom.

(4)   If a solicitor or sheriff officer has formally served the Claim Form, then a Confirmation of Formal Service must be sent to the court at least 2 days before the last date for a response.

## What if the claimant does not know the respondent's address?

**6.12**(1)  The claimant must take all reasonable steps to find out the respondent's address.

(2)  If the claimant does not know the respondent's address and cannot find it out, then the claimant does not need to formally serve a copy of the Claim Form on the respondent.

(3)  The claimant must instead complete a Service by Advertisement Application and send it to court with the Claim Form.

(4)  The sheriff may order the details of the claim to be publicised by advertisement on the Scottish Courts and Tribunals Service website.

(5)  The sheriff clerk must make a copy of the Claim Form available for the respondent to collect at the sheriff court.

(6)  If the respondent's address becomes known, the sheriff must order:

   (a)  the Claim Form to be amended,
   (b)  the claimant to formally serve the Claim Form on the respondent,
   (c)  a change to the timetable.

## What if the sheriff considers that formal service of the Claim Form has not been done properly?

**6.13**(1)  If the sheriff considers that formal service of the Claim Form was not done correctly, then the sheriff may change the timetable.

(2)  If the sheriff changes the timetable, the sheriff clerk must send a new Timetable to the claimant or to the parties.

PART 7

WHAT HAPPENS TO A CASE

## What is this Part about?

**7.1**(1)   This Part is about what happens after a Response Form has been received and what happens if no Response Form is received.

*Admitted claims*

## What if parties settle the claim before the last date for a response?

**7.2**(1)   If the Response From indicates that the respondent admits the claim and will settle it before the last date for a response, then the sheriff does not have to send written orders to the parties.

(2)   If the claimant then sends an Application for a Decision to the court within 2 weeks from the last date for a response, the sheriff may do one of three things:

    (a)   dismiss the claim,

    (b)   make a decision awarding the claimant some or all of what was asked for in the Claim Form,

    (c)   if the sheriff considers that a decision cannot be made awarding the claimant some or all of what was asked for in the Claim Form, order the claimant to come to court to discuss the terms of the decision.

(3)   The claimant must, at the same time, send the court evidence that the Claim Form was formally served on the respondent.

(4)   If the claimant does not send an Application for a Decision to the court within 2 weeks from the last date for a response, the sheriff must dismiss the claim.

## What if the respondent makes a Time to Pay Application?

**7.3**(1)   If the respondent admits the claim and asks for time to pay, then the sheriff does not have to send written orders to the parties.

(2)   Part 5 of these Rules is about what happens when a Time to Pay Application is made.

## What if no Response Form is received by the court?

**7.4**(1)   If no Response Form has been received by the court by the last date for a response, then the sheriff does not have to send written orders to the parties.

(2)   If the claimant sends an Application for a Decision to the court within 2 weeks from the last date for a response, then the sheriff may make a decision awarding the claimant some or all of what was asked for in the Claim Form.

(3)   If the sheriff considers that a decision cannot be made awarding the claimant some or all of what was asked for in the Claim Form, then the sheriff may order the claimant to come to court to discuss the terms of the decision.

(4)   If the claimant does not send an Application for a Decision to the court within 2 weeks from the last date for a response, then the sheriff must dismiss the claim.

*Disputed claims*

## What if the respondent disputes the claim?

**7.5**(1)   If the respondent disputes the claim, the sheriff must consider the case in private.

(2)   The sheriff must then send the parties the first written orders within 2 weeks from the date the court received the Response Form.

(3)   If the Response Form indicates that the respondent thinks that there should be additional respondents, then the sheriff does not have to send first written orders to the parties.

(4)   Instead, the sheriff may order that the Claim Form and Response From should be formally served on those persons by the respondent before the sheriff issues the first written orders.

### What will be in the first written orders?

7.6(1)   The first written orders may do any of 5 things:
- (a)   refer parties to alternative dispute resolution,
- (b)   arrange a case management discussion,
- (c)   arrange a hearing,
- (d)   if the sheriff thinks that a decision could be made without a hearing, indicate that the sheriff is considering doing so,
- (e)   use the sheriff's powers to dismiss a claim or decide a case under rule 1.8(11), (12) and (13).

### What is a case management discussion?

7.7(1)   A case management discussion may take place in a courtroom, by videoconference, conference call, or in any other form or location ordered by the sheriff.

(2)   The purpose of a case management discussion is so that the sheriff may:
- (a)   discuss the claim and response with the parties and clarify any concerns the sheriff has,
- (b)   discuss negotiation and alternative dispute resolution with the parties,
- (c)   give the parties, in person, guidance and orders about the witnesses, documents and other evidence which they need to bring to a hearing,
- (d)   give the parties, in person, orders which arrange a hearing.

(3)   The sheriff may refer parties to alternative dispute resolution at a case management discussion.

(4)   The sheriff may do anything at a case management discussion that can be done at a hearing, including making a decision in a case or part of a case.

### What is a hearing?

7.8(1)   The purpose of a hearing is to help the sheriff to resolve the dispute between the parties.

(2)   Part 12 of these Rules is about hearings.

PART 8

ORDERS

## What is this Part about?

**8.1**(1) This Part is about the orders which the sheriff can give to manage or decide a case.

## What are orders?

**8.2**(1) Orders are the way that the sheriff uses the powers of the sheriff to manage or decide a case.

(2) Orders may be given to the parties in writing, using the Order of the Sheriff Form.

(3) Orders may be given to the parties in person at a hearing, case management discussion or discussion in court.

(4) Written orders must be signed or authenticated electronically by either the sheriff or the sheriff clerk.

## What are standard orders?

**8.3**(1) There are standard orders which the sheriff may give in typical situations.

(2) The sheriff may do one of three things:
  (a) give parties a standard order,
  (b) give parties an amended version of a standard order, or
  (c) give parties an order customised to their case.

## What are unless orders?

**8.4**(1) The sheriff may give a party an order which states that unless that party does something or takes a step, then the sheriff will make a decision in the case, including:
  (a) dismissing the claim,
  (b) awarding the claimant some or all of what was asked for in the Claim Form.

(2) If that party does not do the thing or take the step that the party was ordered to, then the decision in the case must be made.

## What if a party does not follow an order?

**8.5**(1) Where a party does not follow an order the sheriff may make a decision in the case, including:
  (a) dismissing the claim or part of the claim,
  (b) awarding the claimant some or all of what was asked for in the Claim Form.

# PART 9: APPLICATIONS

PART 9

APPLICATIONS

**What is this Part about?**

**9.1**(1)   This Part is about applications which parties may make to the court to ask for things to be done in a case.

*Pausing and restarting cases*

**How can a party ask for the progress of a case to be paused?**

**9.2**(1)   A party may apply to have the progress of a case paused by sending the other party an Application to Pause.

(2)   That party must at the same time send the court a copy of the Application to Pause with evidence that it was sent to the other party (for example a postal receipt or a copy of an email).

(3)   The Application to Pause must set out why the progress of a case should be paused.

(4)   If the party who has been sent the Application to Pause objects to having the progress of the case paused, that party must send that Application to Pause to the court within 10 days of it being sent, setting out that objection.

(5)   After considering the Application to Pause, and any objection that may have been sent, the sheriff may do one of three things:

(a)   grant the application, and pause the progress of the case,

(b)   refuse the application, and the progress of the case continues, or

(c)   order both parties to appear at a discussion in court, where the sheriff will consider whether to pause the progress of the case.

**What happens if the progress of a case is paused?**

**9.3**(1)   If the progress of a case is paused, then any discussions or hearings in the case are cancelled and the case will not progress until it is restarted.

**How can a party ask for a paused case to be restarted?**

**9.4**(1)   A party may apply to have a paused case restarted by sending the other party an Application to Restart.

(2)   That party must at the same time send the court a copy of the Application to Restart with evidence that it was sent to the other party (for example a postal receipt or a copy of an email).

(3)   The Application to Restart must set out why the paused case should be restarted.

(4)   If the party who has been sent the Application to Restart objects to having the paused case restarted, that party must send that Application to Restart to the court within 10 days of it being sent, setting out that objection.

(5)   After considering the Application to Restart, and any objection that may have been sent, the sheriff may do one of three things:

(a)   grant the application, and restart the case,

(b)   refuse the application, and the case continues to be paused, or

(c)   order both parties to appear at a discussion in court, where the sheriff will consider whether to restart the case.

## What can the court do with a paused case?

**9.5**(1)   The sheriff clerk must present to the sheriff a case which has been paused for 6 months or more.

(2)   The sheriff may then send the parties written orders that unless a party (or parties) does something or takes a step, then the sheriff will dismiss the claim.

(3)   If that party (or the parties) does not do the thing or take the step ordered, then the claim must be dismissed.

### *Miscellaneous applications*

## How can a person become an additional respondent in a case?

**9.6**(1)   A person who is not a respondent may apply to become a respondent in a case by sending an Additional Respondent Application to the court.

(2)   The Additional Respondent Application must set out why that person has an interest in becoming a respondent.

(3)   The Additional Respondent Application must have attached to it a draft Response Form.

(4)   The sheriff may grant the application without a discussion in court, but must order a discussion in court if considering refusing the application.

(5)   If ordering a discussion in court, the sheriff must also order the person wishing to become a respondent to formally serve a copy of the Additional Respondent Application, the draft Response Form and notice of the discussion on all parties.

(6)   If granting the application, the sheriff must give orders that allow the additional respondent to participate in the case as a respondent.

## How can a party ask to amend the Claim Form or the Response Form?

**9.7**(1)   A claimant may apply to amend a Claim Form by sending the respondent an Application to Amend.

(2)   The claimant must at the same time send the court a copy of the Application to Amend with evidence that it was sent to the respondent (for example a postal receipt or a copy of an email).

(3)   A respondent may apply to amend a Response Form by sending the claimant an Application to Amend.

(4)   The respondent must at the same time send the court a copy of the Application to Amend with evidence that it was sent to the claimant (for example a postal receipt or a copy of an email).

(5)   The Application to Amend must set out why the form should be amended.

(6)   The Application to Amend must set out the proposed amendments.

(7)   If the party who has been sent the Application to Amend objects to the proposed amendments, that party must send that Application to Amend to the court within 10 days of it being sent, setting out that objection.

(8)   After considering the Application to Amend, and any objection that may have been sent, the sheriff may do one of three things:

    (a)   grant the application, and allow the proposed amendments (or some of them),

    (b)   refuse the application, and not allow any amendment, or

    (c)   order both parties to appear at a discussion in court, where the sheriff will consider whether to allow the proposed amendments.

### How can a claimant abandon a claim?

**9.8**(1)   A claimant may abandon a claim any time before the sheriff decides a case by sending an Abandonment Notice to the respondent.

(2)   That claimant must at the same time send the court a copy of the Abandonment Notice with evidence that it was sent to the respondent (for example a postal receipt or a copy of an email).

(3)   When the court receives the Abandonment Notice, the sheriff must give the parties written orders.

(4)   Those orders may dismiss the claim.

(5)   Those orders may do one of three further things:
   (a)   order that no expenses are to be awarded to any party,
   (b)   order that a sum of money is to be paid to a party or to a party's solicitor, as assessed by the sheriff clerk, or
   (c)   arrange an expenses hearing (see Part 15).

### What can happen if a party dies or becomes legally incapacitated?

**9.9**(1)   If a party dies or becomes legally incapacitated before a sheriff decides a case, then a person who asserts a right to represent that party or that party's estate may apply to represent that party, by sending an Application to Represent to the other party.

(2)   That person must at the same time send the court a copy of the Application to Represent with evidence that it was sent to other parties (for example a postal receipt or a copy of an email).

(3)   If the party who has been sent the Application to Represent objects to the proposed representation, that party must send that Application to Represent to the court within 10 days of it being sent, setting out that objection.

(4)   After considering the Application to Represent, and any objection that may have been sent, the sheriff may do one of three things:
   (a)   grant the application, and allow the person to represent that party,
   (b)   refuse the application, and not allow the person to represent that party, or
   (c)   order the parties and the person making the application to appear at a discussion in court, where the sheriff will consider whether to allow the person to represent that party.

### How can a party ask the sheriff to make any other orders?

**9.10**(1)   A party may ask the sheriff to make any other orders by sending an Incidental Orders Application to the other party.

(2)   That party must at the same time send the court a copy of the Incidental Orders Application with evidence that it was send to the other party (for example a postal receipt or a copy of an email).

(3)   If the party who has been sent the Incidental Orders Application objects to the proposed orders, that party must send that Incidental Orders Application to the court within 10 days of it being sent, setting out that objection.

(4)   After considering the Incidental Orders Application, and any objection that may have been sent, the sheriff may do one of three things:
   (a)   grant the application, and send written orders to the parties,
   (b)   refuse the application, and make no orders, or
   (c)   order the parties to appear at a discussion in court, where the sheriff will consider whether to make any orders.

PART 10:

DOCUMENTS AND OTHER EVIDENCE

**What is this Part about?**

**10.1**(1)   This Part is about how parties should lodge documents and other evidence with the court before a hearing.

(2)   This Part is also about how parties can apply for orders to recover documents from other people.

*Lodging documents and other evidence*

**How can you lodge documents and other evidence with the court?**

**10.2**(1)   Parties must send each other and the court a List of Evidence Form at least 2 weeks before the hearing.

(2)   The List of Evidence Form must set out the documents and other evidence that they are lodging with the court.

(3)   All documents and other evidence must be lodged with the court at least 2 weeks before the hearing.

(4)   Documents and other evidence may be lodged with the court by sending them to the sheriff clerk.

(5)   If a party considers that there would be practical difficulties involved in sending evidence to the sheriff clerk, that party must contact the sheriff clerk.

(6)   In that situation, the sheriff clerk may give that party permission to lodge only a brief description of the evidence. The party must bring the evidence to any hearing.

**What documents and other evidence can a party bring to a hearing?**

**10.3**(1)   A party may bring to a hearing documents and other evidence which have not been lodged with the court.

(2)   The sheriff may refuse to consider these.

**How can other parties borrow or inspect documents and other evidence lodged with the court?**

**10.4**(1)   A solicitor, or the authorised assistant of a solicitor, may borrow any documents or other evidence which have been lodged with the court.

(2)   Any documents or other evidence borrowed must be returned to the court before midday (1200 hours) on the last day the court is open before the hearing.

(3)   A party who is not represented by a solicitor may, during normal business hours, inspect documents or other evidence at the sheriff clerk's office.

(4)   Where it is possible to do so, that party may take copies or photographs of documents or other evidence.

**How long will the court keep documents and other evidence for?**

**10.5**(1)   The court must keep the documents and other evidence for at least 4 weeks after the sheriff has made a decision.

(2)   If a party has appealed the sheriff's decision, the court must keep the documents and other evidence until that appeal has been decided.

(3)   Each party must collect the documents and other evidence which that party lodged within 2 weeks of the end of either the 4 week period or the appeal being decided, whichever is later.

(4)  If a party has not collected the documents and other evidence by the end of that 2 weeks, the sheriff clerk must send the party a warning that if the documents and other evidence is not collected within 2 weeks of the warning, then it will be destroyed or disposed of.

(5)  If the documents and other evidence are not collected by the end of that further 2 weeks, the sheriff must order it to be destroyed or disposed of.

*Orders to recover documents*

### How can a party recover documents to lodge them with the court?

**10.6**(1)  Where a party wants to lodge a document which they do not possess, the sheriff may make an order to recover a document from the person who possesses it.

(2)  A party may ask the sheriff to make an order to recover documents by sending a Recovery of Documents Application to the court and the other party.

(3)  A party may object to the proposed recovery of documents by returning that Recovery of Documents Application to the court within 10 days of it being sent, setting out that objection.

(4)  After considering the Recovery of Documents Application, and any objection that may have been sent, the sheriff may do one of 4 things:

   (a)   grant the application, and make an order to recover documents,
   (b)   grant the application in part, and make an order to recover documents,
   (c)   refuse the application,
   (d)   order the parties to appear at a discussion in court, where the sheriff will consider whether to make an order to recover documents.

### What happens when an order to recover documents is made?

**10.7**(1)  A party who has been granted an order to recover documents must formally serve it on the person who is named in the order.

(2)  When the sheriff clerk receives documents in response to an order to recover documents, the sheriff clerk must lodge them and send the parties a notice indicating that the documents have been received and lodged.

### What happens if the person who has the documents claims they are confidential?

**10.8**(1)  A person who has documents mentioned in an order to recover documents must tell the court if that person believes them to be confidential.

(2)  This is done by:

   (a)   sealing the confidential documents in an envelope, marked as confidential,
   (b)   completing the confidential documents part of the order to recover documents, and
   (c)   sending these to the court.

(3)  If the party who obtained the order to recover documents wishes to open the sealed envelope containing the confidential document, the party must send an Application to Open Confidential Document to the court, the other party and the person who sent the document to the court.

(4)  If a person who has been sent the Application to Open Confidential Document objects to the confidential document being seen by the parties, that party must send that Application to Open Confidential Document to the court within 10 days of it being sent, setting out that objection.

(5)  After considering the Application to Open Confidential Document, and any objection that may have been sent, the sheriff may do one of three things:

(a)   grant the application, and allow the sealed envelope containing the confidential document to be opened,

(b)   refuse the application,

(c)   order the parties and the person who sent the document to the court to appear at a discussion in court, where the sheriff will consider whether to allow the sealed envelope containing the confidential document to be opened.

(6)   When granting an application, the sheriff may order parts of the document to be redacted.

### What happens if a party does not believe that an order to recover documents has been complied with?

**10.9**(1)   The party who obtained the order to recover documents can ask the sheriff to make a special order to recover documents by sending a Special Recovery of Documents Application to the court and the other party.

(2)   If the party who has been sent the Special Recovery of Documents Application objects to the proposed recovery of documents, that party must send that Special Recovery of Documents Application to the court within 10 days of it being sent, setting out that objection.

(3)   After considering the Special Recovery of Documents Application, and any objection that may have been sent, the sheriff may do one of three things:

(a)   grant the application, and send a special order to recover documents to the parties,

(b)   refuse the application,

(c)   order the parties to appear at a discussion in court, where the sheriff will consider whether to make a special order to recover documents.

### What happens when a special order to recover documents is made?

**10.10**(1)   A special order to recover documents appoints a person to recover the documents mentioned in the order for the court. This person is called a commissioner.

(2)   The party who obtained the special order to recover documents must send it to the commissioner.

(3)   The commissioner must carry out the recovery of documents mentioned in the order.

(4)   When the sheriff clerk receives documents from the commissioner, the sheriff clerk must lodge them and send the parties a notice explaining that the documents have been received and lodged.

### What happens if the person who has the documents claims they are confidential?

**10.11**(1)   A person who has documents mentioned in a special order to recover documents must tell the court that the person believes them to be confidential

(2)   This is done by telling the commissioner why the document is considered to be confidential and giving the commissioner the confidential document in a sealed envelope.

(3)   If the party who obtained the special order to recover documents wishes to open the sealed envelope containing the confidential document, the party must send an Application to Open Confidential Document to the court, the other party and the person who sent the document to the court.

(4)   If anyone who has been sent the Application to Open Confidential Document objects to the confidential document being seen by the parties, that party must send that Application to Open Confidential Document to the court within 10 days of it being sent, setting out that objection.

(5)   After considering the Application to Open Confidential Document, and any objection that may have been sent, the sheriff may do one of three things:

    (a)   grant the application, and allow the sealed envelope containing the confidential document to be opened,

    (b)   refuse the application,

    (c)   order the parties and the person who sent the document to the court to appear at a discussion in court, where the sheriff will consider whether to allow the sealed envelope containing the confidential document to be opened.

(6)   When granting an application, the sheriff may order parts of the document to be redacted.

## PART 11

### WITNESSES

#### What is this Part about?

**11.1**(1)   This Part is about the citation of witnesses and their attendance at hearings.

(2)   This Part is also about measures that the court can take to assist vulnerable witnesses in giving evidence.

### *The citation of witnesses*

#### How can a party arrange the attendance of witnesses at a hearing?

**11.2**(1)   Parties must send each other and the court a List of Witnesses Form at least 2 weeks before the hearing.

(2)   The List of Witnesses Form must set out the witnesses that they want to appear at a hearing.

(3)   A party only needs to cite a witness to appear at a hearing if the party is unable otherwise to arrange for that witness to appear.

(4)   A witness may be cited to appear at a hearing by formally serving on that witness a Witness Citation Notice.

(5)   The Witness Citation Notice must be formally served on the witness at least 3 weeks before the hearing.

#### What if a witness does not appear at a hearing?

**11.3**(1)   If a witness is cited to appear at a hearing, the witness must appear at that hearing.

(2)   If a witness who has been cited does not appear at a hearing, the sheriff may order the witness to be brought to court.

(3)   The sheriff must not continue a hearing to another day solely because a witness did not appear.

### *Vulnerable witnesses*

#### How will the court treat a child witness?

**11.4**(1)   If a party cites (or intends to arrange the attendance of) a child as a witness, that party must send the court and the other party a Child Witness Notice.

(2)   A Child Witness Notice asks the sheriff to authorise the use of a special measure in taking the child witness's evidence, or to decide that the child witness is to give evidence without the benefit of any special measure.

(3)   Before the sheriff decides how to deal with the Child Witness Notice, the sheriff may order the parties to provide further information.

(4)   The sheriff may decide to make the orders requested in the Child Witness Notice with or without ordering a discussion in court.

(5)   Where the sheriff decides to have a discussion, the sheriff clerk must send the parties notice of when it will be held.

(6)   At the discussion, the sheriff must consider the Child Witness Notice and decide whether to authorise the use of a special measure in taking the child witness's evidence, or that the child witness is to give evidence without the benefit of any special measure.

### How will the court treat other vulnerable witnesses?

**11.5**(1)   If a party cites (or intends to arrange the attendance of) a witness who is not a child, but the party thinks that the witness is a vulnerable witness, that party may send the court and the other party a Vulnerable Witness Application.

(2)   A Vulnerable Witness Application asks the sheriff to decide whether the witness is a vulnerable witness. If the sheriff agrees, the sheriff may authorise the use of a special measure in taking the vulnerable witness's evidence.

(3)   Before the sheriff decides how to deal with the Vulnerable Witness Application, the sheriff may order the parties to provide further information.

(4)   The sheriff may decide to make the orders requested in the Vulnerable Witness Application with or without a discussion in court.

(5)   Where the sheriff decides to have a discussion, the sheriff clerk must send the parties notice of when it will be held.

(6)   At the discussion, the sheriff must consider the Vulnerable Witness Application and decide whether the witness is a vulnerable witness. If the sheriff agrees, the sheriff may authorise the use of a special measure in taking the vulnerable witness's evidence.

### What are special measures?

**11.6**(1)   Special measures are ways of taking the evidence of a child witness or a vulnerable witness.

(2)   The sheriff may authorise the use of any of these special measures:
- (a)   allowing that witness to give evidence before an independent person,
- (b)   allowing that witness to give evidence by live television link,
- (c)   allowing that witness to use a screen while giving evidence,
- (d)   allowing that witness to be supported by someone while giving evidence.

### How can a party ask the court to review the arrangements for a child witness or a vulnerable witness?

**11.7**(1)   The party who sent a Child Witness Notice or Vulnerable Witness Application to the court may ask the sheriff to review the arrangements for the child witness or vulnerable witness to give evidence by sending the court and the other party a Special Measures Review Application.

(2)   A Special Measures Review Application asks the sheriff to vary or revoke the current arrangements for the child witness or vulnerable witness to give evidence.

(3)   When a Special Measures Review Application is received, the sheriff may do one of 4 things:
- (a)   add a new special measure,
- (b)   substitute a new special measure for an existing one,
- (c)   delete a special measure, or
- (d)   revoke the order authorising the use of special measures entirely.

(4)   Before the sheriff decides how to deal with the Special Measures Review Application, the sheriff may order the parties to provide further information.

(5)   The sheriff may decide to make the orders requested in the Special Measures Review Application with or without a discussion in court.

(6)   Where the sheriff decides to have a discussion, the sheriff clerk must send the parties notice of when it will be held.

(7)   At the discussion, the sheriff must consider the Special Measures Review Application and decide whether to vary or revoke the current arrangements for the child witness or vulnerable witness to give evidence.

## What happens when evidence is to be given before an independent person?

**11.8**(1)   Where the sheriff authorises a child witness or a vulnerable witness to give evidence before an independent person, the hearing at which the evidence is taken is to be video recorded.

(2)   A party may be present when a child witness or vulnerable witness gives evidence before an independent person only if the sheriff has given permission for this to happen.

(3)   The independent person must send the video recording and any relevant documents from the hearing to the sheriff clerk.

(4)   The sheriff clerk must send the parties a notice indicating that the video recording has been received.

(5)   If any relevant documents or other evidence are also received, the sheriff clerk must send the parties notice of what they are and when they were received.

PART 12

THE HEARING

## What is this Part about?

**12.1**(1) This Part is about the hearing at which the dispute between the parties should be resolved.

## What is the purpose of the hearing?

**12.2**(1) The purpose of the hearing is to help the sheriff to resolve the dispute between the parties.

## How will the dispute between the parties be resolved?

**12.3**(1) The sheriff may refer parties to alternative dispute resolution at a hearing.

(2) If the sheriff thinks a negotiated settlement is possible, the sheriff must help the parties to negotiate a settlement to the dispute.

(3) If no negotiated settlement is possible, the sheriff must resolve the dispute by deciding it at that hearing.

(4) The sheriff may continue the hearing to another day without resolving the dispute only if it is necessary to do so.

## What will the sheriff do at the hearing?

**12.4**(1) The sheriff must ask the parties about their attitudes to negotiation and alternative dispute resolution.

(2) The sheriff must identify the factual basis and legal basis of the claim and the response to the claim.

(3) The sheriff must identify the factual and legal matters genuinely in dispute between the parties.

(4) The sheriff must take a note of the hearing. This note is for the sheriff's own purposes and must be kept until any appeal is no longer possible or until any appeal has been concluded.

## What if a party does not come to the hearing?

**12.5**(1) If the claimant does not come to the hearing or is not represented at the hearing, the sheriff may dismiss the claim.

(2) If the respondent does not come to the hearing or is not represented at the hearing, the sheriff may make a decision in the case at that hearing.

(3) If neither party comes to the hearing and neither party is represented at the hearing, the sheriff must dismiss the claim.

## How will evidence be given at the hearing?

**12.6**(1) Before evidence is heard, the sheriff must explain to the parties the way the sheriff has decided to consider evidence at the hearing.

(2) The sheriff may impose conditions on how evidence is presented or dealt with, including conditions on how witnesses are questioned or setting time limits on how long witnesses may be questioned.

(3) The sheriff may decide whether the evidence of a witness is to be taken on oath or affirmation or not.

(4) The sheriff may ask questions to the parties or to witnesses.

(5)   The sheriff may inspect any evidence with the parties or their representatives present.

(6)   The sheriff may inspect any place with the parties or their representatives present.

PART 13

THE DECISION

## What is this Part about?

**13.1**(1)   This Part is about the decisions which the sheriff can make to resolve a dispute.

(2)   This Part is also about the circumstances in which a party can apply to have a decision recalled.

## When must the sheriff make the decision?

**13.2**(1)   At the end of the hearing, the sheriff may either make a decision there and then, or may take time to consider before making a decision.

(2)   If the sheriff takes time to consider a decision, the decision must be made within 4 weeks from the date of the hearing.

## How will the sheriff make the decision?

**13.3**(1)   If the sheriff makes a decision there and then, the sheriff must explain the reasons for that decision to the parties in person.

(2)   If the sheriff takes time to consider a decision, the sheriff must prepare a note of the reasons for the decision, and the sheriff clerk must send that note to the parties.

(3)   In every case, the sheriff must set out the decision in the case in a Decision Form.

(4)   The sheriff may correct any errors in a Decision Form before it is sent to a party.

## What sort of decisions can the sheriff make?

**13.4**(1)   The sheriff may make any decision which resolves the dispute between the parties, including a decision which:

    (a)   orders the respondent to pay the claimant a sum of money,

    (b)   orders the respondent to deliver something to the claimant,

    (c)   orders the respondent to do something for the claimant,

    (d)   dismisses the claim (or part of the claim) made by the claimant,

    (e)   absolves the respondent of the claim (or part of the claim) made by the claimant.

(2)   A decision which absolves the respondent in a claim means that the claimant cannot make a claim about the same subject against the respondent again.

*Recalling a decision*

## When can a decision of the sheriff be recalled?

**13.5**(1)   A party may apply to have a decision of the sheriff recalled in 6 situations:

    (a)   where the sheriff dismissed a claim or made a decision under rule 7.2(2), because the claimant did not send the court an Application for a Decision within 2 weeks from the last date for a response,

    (b)   where the sheriff made a decision under rule 7.4(2), because the respondent did not send the court a Response Form by the last date for a response,

    (c)   where the sheriff dismissed a claim under rule 7.4(4), because the claimant did not send the court an Application for a decision within 2 weeks from the last date for a response,

    (d)    where the sheriff dismissed a claim under rule 12.5(1), because the claimant did not attend the hearing,

    (e)    where the sheriff made a decision under rule 12.5(2), because the respondent did not attend the hearing, and

    (f)    where the sheriff dismissed a claim under rule 12.5(3), because neither party attended the hearing.

(2)  If the sheriff dismissed the claim, a party may only apply for recall within 2 weeks of the claim being dismissed.

(3)  If the sheriff made a decision (other than dismissal) in the case, a party may apply for recall at any time before the decision of the sheriff has been fully implemented.

### How can a party apply to have a decision of the sheriff recalled?

**13.6**(1)  A party may apply to have a decision of the sheriff recalled by completing the Application to Recall and sending it to the other party.

(2)  That party must at the same time send the court a copy of the Application to Recall with evidence that it was sent to the other party (for example a postal receipt or a copy of an email).

(3)  If the sheriff made a decision following an Application for a Decision, the respondent must include a completed Response Form with the Application to Recall.

(4)  If the party who has been sent the Application to Recall objects to the recall, that party must send that Application to Recall to the court within 10 days of it being sent, setting out that objection.

(5)  After considering the Application to Recall, and any objection that may have been sent, the sheriff may do one of three things:

    (a)    grant the application, and recall the decision,

    (b)    refuse the application, or

    (c)    order the parties to appear at a discussion in court, where the sheriff will consider whether to recall the decision.

### What happens when a sheriff decides to recall a decision?

**13.7**(1)  If the sheriff recalls a decision then the sheriff must give each party orders setting out the next steps they are to take to allow the dispute to be resolved.

# PART 14: EXPENSES

PART 14

EXPENSES

**What is this Part about?**

**14.1**(1)   This Part is about the expenses of a claim which the sheriff can order a party to pay for.

**What orders about expenses can the sheriff make?**

**14.2**(1)   Once a claim has been resolved, the sheriff must make an order about expenses, such as:

  (a)   that no payments are to be made in respect of the expenses of any party,

  (b)   that a payment is to be made to a party or to a party's solicitor.

  (2)   Expenses incurred by a party to do with a courtroom supporter may not be part of an order about expenses.

**When will the sheriff make an order about expenses?**

**14.3**(1)   In a case where the expenses of a claim are capped, the sheriff must make an order about expenses when deciding the claim.

  (2)   In any other case, the sheriff must, if able to, make an order about expenses when deciding the claim.

  (3)   If not able to make an order about expenses when deciding the claim, the sheriff may make an order about expenses after deciding the claim.

**What if the sheriff does not make an order about expenses when deciding the claim?**

**14.4**(1)   If the sheriff makes an order about expenses after deciding the claim, then the sheriff must not set out the final decision in a case in a Decision Form until the order about expenses is made.

  (2)   If the sheriff does not make an order about expenses when deciding the claim, the sheriff must give the parties written orders.

  (3)   Those orders must arrange an expenses hearing.

  (4)   Those orders may require a party to send an account of expenses to the court and to each other before the expenses hearing.

  (5)   Those orders may then require the sheriff clerk to assess the level of expenses (if any) that should be awarded to a party and to send notice of that assessment to the parties before the expenses hearing.

**What is an expenses hearing?**

**14.5**(1)   The purpose of an expenses hearing is to assess the level of expenses (if any) that should be awarded to a party.

  (2)   At the expenses hearing, the sheriff must make an order about expenses, such as:

  (a)   that no payments are to be made in respect of the expenses of any party,

  (b)   that a payment is to be made to a party or to a party's solicitor.

# PART 15: HOW TO ENFORCE A DECISION

PART 15:

HOW TO ENFORCE A DECISION

## What is this Part about?

**15.1**(1)   This Part is about the steps which a successful party must take to enforce a decision.

## When can a party enforce a decision?

**15.2**(1)   After the Decision Form is sent, a party must wait 4 weeks before enforcing a decision.

(2)   A party must not enforce a decision if that decision is being appealed (see Part 16).

(3)   A party who is sent an Application to Recall must not enforce a decision until the sheriff has decided whether to recall the decision.

(4)   A party must not enforce a decision which has been recalled.

## How can a party enforce a decision?

**15.3**(1)   If a party uses a trading name, a decision which names the party using that trading name may be enforced against the party by that name.

(2)   Before enforcing a decision for payment of a sum of money, the successful party must formally serve a Charge on the other party.

(3)   The purpose of formally serving the Charge is to give the other party one last chance to pay the sum of money ordered by the court.

(4)   The Charge must demand payment:
  (a)   within 2 weeks if the other party is in the United Kingdom,
  (b)   within 4 weeks if the other party is outside the United Kingdom,
  (c)   within 4 weeks if the other party's address is unknown.

(5)   If the demand in the Charge is not complied with, then the successful party may instruct a sheriff officer to enforce the decision.

## What if the claimant does not know the respondent's address?

**15.4**(1)   Where the claimant is successful but does not know the respondent's address, the claimant must take all reasonable steps to find out the respondent's address.

(2)   If the claimant does not know the respondent's address, then instead of formally serving the Charge on the respondent, the claimant must formally serve it on the sheriff clerk in the sheriff court district where the respondent's last known address was.

(3)   The sheriff clerk must then publicise the Charge by advertising its details on the Scottish Courts and Tribunals Service website for 4 weeks.

(5)   After that 4 weeks, the sheriff clerk must certify on the Charge that the advertisement took place and send it to the sheriff officer who formally served it.

(6)   The claimant may then instruct a sheriff officer to enforce the decision.

## What if the respondent does not comply with a decision?

**15.5**(1)   A claimant may make an Alternative Decision Application where the respondent does not comply with a decision which:
  (a)   orders the respondent to deliver something to the claimant, or
  (b)   orders the respondent to do something for the claimant.

(2) An Alternative Decision Application may only be made where the sheriff alternatively ordered the respondent to pay the claimant a sum of money.

(3) The application is made by sending an Alternative Decision Application to the court.

(4) After considering the Alternative Decision Application, and any objection that may have been sent, the sheriff may do one of three things:

    (a) grant the application, and order the respondent to pay the claimant a sum of money,

    (b) refuse the application,

    (c) order the claimant to appear at a discussion in court, where the sheriff will consider whether to make any orders.

PART 16

HOW TO APPEAL A DECISION

## What is this Part about?

**16.1**(1) This Part is about how a party can appeal a decision and how the sheriff and Sheriff Appeal Court will deal with an appeal.

## How do you appeal a decision?

**16.2**(1) A party may appeal a decision within 4 weeks from the Decision Form being sent.

(2) A party may appeal a decision by sending a completed Appeal Form to the sheriff court.

(3) That party must at the same time send a copy of the completed Appeal Form to the other party.

(4) The Appeal Form must set out the legal points which the party making the appeal wants the Sheriff Appeal Court to answer.

(5) A party may not appeal a decision if that party can apply to have that decision recalled (see Part 13).

## What will the sheriff do with an appeal?

**16.3**(1) The sheriff must prepare a draft Appeal Report within 4 weeks of the court receiving an Appeal Form.

(2) The draft Appeal Report must set out the factual and legal basis for the decision which the sheriff came to.

(3) The draft Appeal Report must set out legal questions for the Sheriff Appeal Court to answer.

(4) The sheriff clerk must send the draft Appeal Report to all parties.

(5) All parties may, within 2 weeks of the draft Appeal Report being sent to them, send the sheriff a note of any other legal points they wish the Sheriff Appeal Court to answer and any factual points in the draft Appeal Report they disagree with.

(6) The sheriff may order a discussion in court to consider whether amendments should be made to the Appeal Report.

(7) The sheriff may then amend the Appeal Report.

(8) The sheriff must then sign the Appeal Report.

(9) The sheriff clerk must send a copy of the signed Appeal Report to each party.

(10) The sheriff clerk must transmit the following to the Clerk of the Sheriff Appeal Court:

  (a) the note of the reasons for the sheriff's decision (if one was prepared),

  (b) a copy of the Decision Form,

  (c) all written orders,

  (d) the signed Appeal Report, and

  (e) any note sent to the court by a party.

## What will the Sheriff Appeal Court do with an appeal?

**16.4**(1) The Clerk of the Sheriff Appeal Court must, within 2 weeks of receiving the signed Appeal Report, arrange an appeal hearing and send all parties notice of where and when the appeal hearing is to be held.

(2) Unless the Sheriff Appeal Court orders otherwise, an appeal hearing must be before one Appeal Sheriff.

(3) At the end of the appeal hearing, the Sheriff Appeal Court may either make a decision there and then, or may take time to consider the decision.

(4) If the Sheriff Appeal Court takes time to consider the decision, the decision must be made within 4 weeks from the date of the appeal hearing.

(5) If the Sheriff Appeal Court makes a decision there and then, it must explain the reasons for that decision to the parties in person.

(6) If the Sheriff Appeal Court takes time to consider a decision, the court must prepare a note of the reasons for the decision, and the Clerk of the Sheriff Appeal Court must send that note to the parties.

(7) The Sheriff Appeal Court may alter the decision which the sheriff made by either amending the Decision Form or issuing a new Decision Form.

# PART 17: MISCELLANEOUS MATTERS

PART 17:

MISCELLANEOUS MATTERS

**What is this Part about?**

**17.1**(1)   This Part is about some miscellaneous matters which can arise during a case.

**How can a case be transferred out of the simple procedure?**

**17.2**(1)   Where a sheriff orders that a case should no longer proceed subject to these rules, that order must identify the procedure under which the case is to continue.

(2)   If the sheriff orders that the case should proceed as an ordinary cause, the sheriff must also order three things:

    (a)   that the claimant must lodge an initial writ and intimate it to every other party within 2 weeks from the date of the order,

    (b)   that the respondent must lodge defences within 4 weeks from the date of the order, and

    (c)   that an options hearing is to be held on the first suitable court day occurring not sooner than 10 weeks (or such lesser period as the sheriff considers appropriate) after the last date for lodging the initial writ.

(3)   If the sheriff orders that the case should proceed as an ordinary cause the sheriff may also certify in the order that the importance or difficulty of the proceedings makes it appropriate to transfer the case to the Sheriff Personal Injury Court.

**How can the sheriff make a reference to the Court of Justice of the European Union?**

**17.3**(1)   If a question of EU law arises in a case, the sheriff may refer that question to the Court of Justice of the European Union using the CJEU Reference Form.

(2)   The sheriff may decide to do this when asked to by a party, or without being asked.

(3)   The sheriff must draft the reference within 4 weeks of deciding to do so.

(4)   Once a reference has been drafted, the sheriff clerk must send a copy to the parties.

(5)   Once the draft reference has been sent to the parties, each party has 4 weeks to send suggested amendments of that reference to the sheriff.

(6)   Once that 4 weeks has passed, the sheriff has 2 weeks to consider any suggested amendments.

(7)   At the end of that period of 2 weeks, the sheriff must finalise and sign the reference.

(8)   The sheriff clerk must transmit the reference to the Court of Justice of the European Union and inform parties that the reference has been made.

**How can the Commission for Equality and Human Rights ("CEHR") or the Scottish Commission for Human Rights ("SCHR") intervene?**

**17.4**(1)   The CEHR and the SCHR may apply to the sheriff to intervene in a case by sending to the court and to the parties an Application to Intervene.

(2)   The Application to Intervene must set out the reasons for the proposed intervention, the issues which the intervention would address, and the reasons why the intervention would assist the sheriff.

(3)   The sheriff may grant the application with or without a discussion, but there must be a discussion if a party asks for one.

(4)   The sheriff may grant the Application to Intervene only if satisfied that:

    (a)   the case has a relevant connection to one of the functions of the CEHR or the SCHR,

    (b)   the intervention is likely to assist the sheriff, and

    (c)   the intervention will not unduly delay or otherwise prejudice the interests of the parties, including their liability for expenses.

(5)   The sheriff may impose conditions on the intervention.

(6)   The sheriff may invite the CEHR or SCHR to intervene in a simple procedure case by sending to the CEHR or SCHR and to all parties an Invitation to Intervene.

(7)   An Invitation to Intervene must be accompanied by a copy of the Claim Form and the Response Form, and any other documents relevant to the reasons for the proposed intervention.

(8)   The sheriff may impose conditions on an intervention when making an invitation.

### What can the CEHR or the SCHR do in an intervention?

**17.5**(1)   An intervention is a written submission of 5,000 words or less (including any appendices).

(2)   A copy of the intervention must be sent to all parties.

(3)   In exceptional circumstances, the sheriff may allow a longer written submission or an oral submission.

*Management of damages*

### When is a damages management order available?

**17.6**(1)   Damages management orders are available:

    (a)   where a claimant who is under a legal disability asks for the payment of a sum of money as damages,

    (b)   where another person makes a claim on behalf of a person who is under a legal disability asking for the payment of a sum of money as damages.

(2)   In either case, a damages management order is only available if the person who is under a legal disability is 16 years of age or older.

### When must the sheriff make a damages management order?

**17.7**(1)   The sheriff must make a damages management order if the sheriff orders the respondent to pay the claimant a sum of money as damages.

(2)   The sheriff must also make a damages management order if the claimant accepts an offer from the respondent to pay a sum of money as damages to settle the claim.

### What can the sheriff do in a damages management order?

**17.8**(1)   The sheriff must make an order about how the money is to be paid to and managed for the person under a legal disability.

(2)   The sheriff may order the money to be paid to different people to be managed for the benefit of the person under a legal disability.

(3)   The sheriff may order the money to be paid to:

    (a)   the Accountant of Court,

    (b)   the sheriff clerk, or

    (c)   the guardian of the person who is under a legal disability.

(4)   Alternatively, the sheriff may decide that the person under a legal disability is capable of managing the money and order that the money is paid directly to that person.

(5)   Where the sheriff orders the money to be paid to the sheriff clerk or a guardian, the sheriff may also tell that person how to manage the money for the benefit of the person under a legal disability.

### How can the damages management order be changed?

**17.9**(1)   An interested person can ask the sheriff to change the damages management order by sending an Application to Change a Damages Management Order to the court and every party.

(2)   If a person who has been sent the Application to Change a Damages Management Order objects to the proposed orders, that person must send that Application to Change a Damages Management Order to the court within 10 days of it being sent, setting out that objection.

(3)   After considering the Application to Change a Damages Management Order, and any objection that may have been sent, the sheriff may do one of three things:

(a)   grant the application, and send written orders to the parties and the interested person,

(b)   refuse the application,

(c)   order the parties and the interested person to appear at a discussion in court, where the sheriff will consider whether to make any orders.

### How can further instructions about managing the money be given?

**17.10**(1)   An interested person can also ask the sheriff to tell the sheriff clerk or a guardian how to manage the money by sending an Application for Instructions about a Damages Management Order to the court and every party.

(2)   If a guardian is managing the money, the Application for Instructions about a Damages Management Order must also be sent to the guardian.

(3)   If a person who has been sent the Application for Instructions about a Damages Management Order, objects to the proposed instructions, that person must send that Application for Instructions about a Damages Management Order to the court within 10 days of it being sent, with a note setting out that objection.

(4)   After considering the Application for Instructions about a Damages Management Order, and any objection that may have been sent, the sheriff may do one of three things:

(a)   grant the application, and send further instructions to the parties, the interested person and the sheriff clerk or guardian,

(b)   refuse the application,

(c)   order the parties, the interested person and the guardian (if there is one) to appear at a discussion in court, where the sheriff will consider whether to give further instructions.

### When can someone apply for a child's property administration order?

**17.11**(1)   A person may ask the sheriff to make a child's property administration order in any simple procedure case where the sheriff has made an order under section 13 of the Children (Scotland) Act 1995 (section 13 is about the payment and management of money to (or for the benefit of) a child).

## How can someone apply for a child's property administration order?

**17.12**(1)  A person can ask the sheriff to make a child's property administration order by sending an Application for a Child's Property Administration Order to the court and every party.

(2)  If a person who has been sent the Application for a Child's Property Administration Order objects to the proposed orders, that person must send that Application for a Child's Property Administration Order to the court within 10 days of it being sent, setting out that objection.

(3)  After considering the Application for a Child's Property Administration Order, and any objection that may have been sent, the sheriff may do one of three things:

- (a)  grant the application, and send written orders to the parties and the applicant,
- (b)  refuse the application,
- (c)  order the parties and the applicant to appear at a discussion in court, where the sheriff will consider whether to make any orders.

### *The Equality Act 2010*

## What is an Equality Act 2010 claim?

**17.13**(1)  An Equality Act 2010 claim is a claim made under section 114(1) of the Equality Act 2010 (section 114 is about claims related to the provision of services, the exercise of public functions, the disposal and management of premises, education (other than in relation to disability), and associations).

## How can the Commission for Equality and Human Rights ("the CEHR") be notified of an Equality Act 2010 claim?

**17.14**(1)  The claimant must send a copy of the Claim Form in an Equality Act 2010 claim to the CEHR.

## How can an Equality Act 2010 claim be transferred to the Employment Tribunal?

**17.15**(1)  The sheriff may order an Equality Act 2010 claim to be transferred to the Employment Tribunal.

(2)  The sheriff must state in that order the reasons for making it.

(3)  That order may include an order about expenses.

(4)  When the sheriff makes that order, the sheriff clerk must transmit, within one week of the order, the following things to the Employment Tribunal:

- (a)  the Claim Form,
- (b)  the Response Form,
- (c)  any written orders, and
- (d)  any other document the sheriff orders to be transmitted.

## How can an Employment Tribunal case be transferred to simple procedure?

**17.16**(1)  When proceedings are transferred to simple procedure from the Employment Tribunal under section 140(3) of the Equality Act 2010, the sheriff clerk must register those proceedings as a claim.

(2)  The sheriff must, within 2 weeks of the claim being registered, order a case management discussion.

## What if a question of national security arises in an Equality Act 2010 claim?

**17.17**(1)   Where the sheriff considers it expedient in the interests of national security, the sheriff may order any of the following persons to be excluded from any or all hearings, case management discussions or discussions in court of an Equality Act 2010 claim:

    (a)   the claimant,

    (b)   the claimant's representative,

    (c)   the claimant's courtroom supporter.

(2)   That order may allow an excluded claimant or representative to send a written statement to the court before the case (or part of the case) from which they have been excluded.

(3)   When the sheriff makes an order excluding persons, the sheriff clerk must send a copy of the order to the Advocate General for Scotland.

(4)   Where the sheriff considers it expedient in the interests of national security, the sheriff may take any steps or make any order required to keep secret any or all of the reasons for the sheriff's decision in an Equality Act 2010 claim.

PART 18

FORMAL SERVICE IN SCOTLAND

## What is this Part about?

**18.1**(1)   This Part is about how to formally serve a document on someone living in Scotland.

## How can you formally serve a document on someone who lives in Scotland?

**18.2**(1)   When these Rules require a document to be formally served, the first attempt must be by a next-day postal service which records delivery.

(2)   That may only be done by one of three persons:

(a)   the party's solicitor,

(b)   a sheriff officer instructed by the party,

(c)   the sheriff clerk (where provided for by rule 6.10(2)).

(3)   The envelope which contains the document must have the following label written or printed on it:

---

**THIS ENVELOPE CONTAINS A [NAME OF DOCUMENT] FROM
[NAME OF SHERIFF COURT]
IF DELIVERY CANNOT BE MADE, THE LETTER MUST BE
RETURNED TO THE SHERIFF CLERK AT
[FULL ADDRESS OF SHERIFF COURT]**

---

(4)   After formally serving a document, a Confirmation of Formal Service must be completed and any evidence of delivery attached to it.

(5)   Where a solicitor or sheriff officer has formally served the document, then the Confirmation of Formal Service must be sent to the sheriff court within one week of service taking place.

## What if service by post does not work?

**18.3**(1)   If service by post has not worked, a sheriff officer may formally serve a document in one of three ways:

(a)   delivering it personally,

(b)   leaving it in the hands of a resident at the person's home,

(c)   leaving it in the hands of an employee at the person's place of business.

(2)   If none of those ways has worked, the sheriff officer must make diligent inquiries about the person's whereabouts and current residence, and may then formally serve the document in one of two ways:

(a)   depositing it in the person's home or place of business by means of a letter box or other lawful way of doing so, or

(b)   leaving it at the person's home or place of business in such a way that it is likely to come to the attention of that person.

(3)   If formal service is done in either of those ways, the sheriff officer must also do two more things:

(a)   send a copy of the document to the person by post to the address at which the sheriff officer thinks the person is most likely to be found, and

(b)   write or print on the envelope containing the document the following label:

> **THIS ENVELOPE CONTAINS A [NAME OF DOCUMENT] FROM**
> **[NAME OF SHERIFF COURT]**

Part 1—Service in Scotland

*What is the Procedure?*

18.01) The rules about how to formally serve a document on somebody living in Scotland.

*How can you formally serve a document on someone who lives in Scotland?*

18.02) Where the rules require a document to be served, it may be served in a different way from a next-day-recorded service of a document.

(2) This may only be done by one of three persons—

   (a) the sheriff's officer;

   (b) a person chosen in terms of by-laws; or

   (c) the sheriff clerk, who is provided for by the rules.

(3) The envelope which contains the document must have the following wording on the face of it—

> THIS ENVELOPE CONTAINS A [NAME OF DOCUMENT] FROM
> [NAME OF SHERIFF COURT]
> BEFORE YOU CAN OPEN THE LETTER MUST BE
> RETURNED TO THE SHERIFF CLERK AT
> [THE ADDRESS OF SHERIFF COURT]

1. When formally serving a document, a Certification of Formal Service must be sent, together with a copy of the document delivered, attached to it.

(2) By force of handing or sent in other ways, this Form of serving a document, then the Certification of Formal Service, may be sent to the sheriff court which has sent service in this place.

*What if service by post does not work?*

18.03) (1) If service by post has not worked, a sheriff officer may in this way send a document in one of three ways—

   (a) delivering it personally;

   (b) leaving it in the hands of a resident at the place's home;

   (c) leaving it in the hands of an employee at the person's place of business.

(2) If none of these ways has worked, the sheriff officer must make enquiries about the person's whereabouts and current residence, and may that officially serve the document in one of two ways—

   (a) depositing it in the person's letter-box or place of business, by means of a letter, but leave a notice-to-leave notice, that a

(3) leaving the person's home or place of business in a way that the document was to come to the attention of that person.

18.04) In circumstances where the sheriff officer must also do two more things—

   (a) send a copy of the document to the person by post to the address which the sheriff officer thinks the person is most likely to be found; and

   (b) write on the envelope containing the document the following label:

PART 19

FORMAL SERVICE OUTSIDE SCOTLAND

**What is this Part about?**

**19.1**(1)   This Part is about how to formally serve a document on someone outside Scotland.

**How can you formally serve a document on someone who lives outside Scotland?**

**19.2**(1)   Different rules apply depending on the country that the person lives in.

(2)   If the person lives in England and Wales, Northern Ireland, the Isle of Man or the Channel Islands, see rule 19.3.

(3)   If the person lives in an EU member state (including Denmark), see rule 19.4.

(4)   If the person lives in a Hague Convention country (other than an EU member state), see rule 19.5.

(5)   If the person lives in a country with which the United Kingdom has a convention about how to serve court documents (such as Algeria, Libya and the United Arab Emirates), see rule 19.6.

(6)   If none of the above applies, see rule 19.7.

**How can you formally serve a document on someone who lives in England and Wales, Northern Ireland, the Isle of Man or the Channel Islands?**

**19.3** *Method*

(1)   There are two ways to formally serve a document on someone who lives in England and Wales, Northern Ireland, the Isle of Man or the Channel Islands.

(2)   It may be done by posting the document to the person's home or business address using a postal service which records delivery. This is called postal service.

(3)   It may also be done by using the rules for personal service under the domestic law of the country where the document is to be served. This is called personal service.

*Who can formally serve the document?*

(4)   The sheriff clerk may formally serve a Claim Form on the respondent by postal service only if:

(a)   the claimant is not a company or a partnership, and

(b)   the claimant is not legally represented.

(5)   Otherwise, postal service may only be done by one of two persons:

(a)   the party's solicitor,

(b)   a sheriff officer instructed by the party.

(6)   Personal service may be done by a person who is authorised to do so under the domestic law of the country where the document is to be served.

*Additional requirements*

(7)   Where postal service is used, the envelope containing the document must have the following label printed or written on it:

> **THIS ENVELOPE CONTAINS A [NAME OF DOCUMENT] FROM [NAME OF SHERIFF COURT], SCOTLAND**
> **IF DELIVERY CANNOT BE MADE, THE LETTER MUST BE RETURNED TO THE SHERIFF CLERK AT**

| [FULL ADDRESS OF SHERIFF COURT] |
|---|

(8)   After formally serving a document, a Confirmation of Formal Service must be signed by the person who served it.

(9)   If postal service has been used, any postal receipts must be attached to the Confirmation of Formal Service.

(10)   If a solicitor or a sheriff officer has formally served a document, the Confirmation of Formal Service must be sent to the sheriff court within one week of service taking place.

## How can you formally serve a document on someone who lives in an EU member state (including Denmark) under the Service Regulation?

**19.4**   *Method*

(1)   There are up to 4 ways to formally serve a document on someone who lives in an EU member state (including Denmark) under the Service Regulation, depending on what the law of that member state permits.

(2)   It may be done by posting the document to the person's home or business address using a postal service which records delivery. This is called postal service.

(3)   It may be done by sending the document to a messenger-at-arms and asking them to arrange for it to be served. This is called service by transmitting agency.

(4)   It may be done by sending the document to a person who is entitled to serve court documents in that member state and asking them to arrange for it to be formally served. This is called direct service. This method can only be used if the law of the member state permits it.

(5)   It may be done by sending the document to the Secretary of State for Foreign and Commonwealth Affairs and asking the Secretary of State to arrange for it to be formally served by a British consular authority. This is called consular service. This method can always be used if the document is being served on a British national. Otherwise, it can only be used if the law of the member state permits it.

*Who can formally serve the document?*

(6)   The sheriff clerk may formally serve a Claim Form on the respondent by postal service only if:

(a)   the claimant is not a company or a partnership, and

(b)   the claimant is not legally represented.

(7)   Otherwise, postal service may only be done by one of two persons:

(a)   the party's solicitor,

(b)   a sheriff officer instructed by the party.

(8)   For the other methods of formal service, the party sends the document to the Secretary of State for Foreign and Commonwealth Affairs or a person who is entitled to serve court documents in the country where the Form or Notice is to be formally served. That person will make the necessary arrangements for formal service.

*Additional requirements*

(9)   Where a party chooses service by transmitting agency, the party must give the messenger-at-arms a translation of the document into a language which the recipient understands or an official language of the member state where the document is to be served.

(10)   After translating a document, the translator must sign a Translation Certificate and give it to the party who is formally serving the document.

(11)   Where postal service is used, the envelope containing the document must have the following label printed or written on it:

> **THIS ENVELOPE CONTAINS A [NAME OF DOCUMENT] FROM [NAME OF SHERIFF COURT], SCOTLAND IF DELIVERY CANNOT BE MADE, THE LETTER MUST BE RETURNED TO THE SHERIFF CLERK AT [FULL ADDRESS OF SHERIFF COURT]**

(12)   That label must also be translated into an official language of the country where the document is to be served, unless English is an official language of that country.

(13)   After formally serving a document by postal service, a Confirmation of Formal Service must be signed by the person who formally served it.

(14)   Any postal receipts must be attached to the Confirmation of Formal Service.

(15)   If a solicitor or a sheriff officer has used postal service, the Confirmation of Formal Service must be sent to the sheriff court within one week of formal service taking place.

(16)   If any other method of formal service was used, the party who requested service of the document must send the certificate that the party receives from the person who served the document to the sheriff court within one week of receiving it.

(17)   If the document was translated into another language, the Translation Certificate must be sent to the sheriff court with the Confirmation of Formal Service or the certificate from the person who served the document.

### How can you formally serve a document on someone who lives in a Hague Convention country (other than an EU member state)?

#### 19.5  *Method*

(1)   There are up to 4 ways to formally serve a document on someone who lives in a Hague Convention country, depending on what the law of that country permits.

(2)   It may be done by posting the document to the person's home or business address using a postal service which records delivery. This is called postal service. This method can only be used if the law of the country permits it.

(3)   It may be done by sending the document to the Scottish Ministers and asking them to arrange for it to be formally served. This is called service via central authority. This method can always be used.

(4)   It may be done by sending the document to the Secretary of State for Foreign and Commonwealth Affairs and asking the Secretary of State to arrange for it to be formally served by a British consular authority. This is called consular service. This method can always be used if the document is being formally served on a British national. Otherwise, it can only be used if the law of the country permits it.

(5)   It may be done by sending the document to a person who is entitled to serve court documents in that country and asking them to arrange for it to be formally served. This is called service by competent person. This method can only be used if the law of the country permits it.

#### Who can formally serve the document?

(6)   The sheriff clerk may formally serve a Claim Form on the respondent by postal service only if:

   (a)   the claimant is not a company or a partnership, and
   (b)   the claimant is not legally represented.

(7)   Otherwise, postal service may only be done by one of two persons:

   (a)   the party's solicitor,
   (b)   a sheriff officer instructed by the party.

(8)   For the other methods of formal service, the party sends the Form or Notice to the Scottish Ministers, the Secretary of State for Foreign and Commonwealth Affairs or a person who is entitled to serve court documents in the country where the Form or Notice is to be formally served. That person will make the necessary arrangements for formal service.

*Additional requirements*

(9)   Any document must be accompanied by a translation into an official language of the country where it is to be formally served, unless English is an official language of that country.

(10)   After translating a document, the translator must sign a Translation Certificate and give it to the party who is formally serving the Form or Notice.

(11)   Where postal service is used, the envelope containing the document must have the following label printed or written on it:

> **THIS ENVELOPE CONTAINS A [NAME OF DOCUMENT] FROM [NAME OF SHERIFF COURT], SCOTLAND**
> **IF DELIVERY CANNOT BE MADE, THE LETTER MUST BE RETURNED TO THE SHERIFF CLERK AT [FULL ADDRESS OF SHERIFF COURT]**

(12)   That label must also be translated into an official language of the country where the Form or Notice is to be served, unless English is an official language of that country.

(13)   After formally serving a document by postal service, a Confirmation of Formal Service must be signed by the person who served it.

(14)   Any postal receipts must be attached to the Confirmation of Service.

(15)   If a solicitor or a sheriff officer has used postal service, the Confirmation of Formal Service must be sent to the sheriff court within one week of service taking place.

(16)   If any other method of formal service was used, the party who requested formal service of the document must send the certificate that the party receives from the person who formally served the document to the sheriff court within one week of receiving it.

(17)   If the document was translated into another language, the Translation Certificate must be sent to the sheriff court with the Confirmation of Formal Service or the certificate from the person who served the document.

**How can you formally serve a document on someone who lives in a country with which the United Kingdom has a convention about how to serve court documents?**

**19.6**   *Method*

(1)   The ways of formally serving a document on someone who lives in a country with which the United Kingdom has a convention about how to serve court documents depends on the convention between the United Kingdom and that country.

(2)   Accordingly, a document can be formally served in any way that is allowed in the convention between the United Kingdom and the country where it is to be served.

*Who can formally serve the document?*

(3)   A document can be formally served by a person who is authorised to do so by the convention between the United Kingdom and the country where it is to be served.

*Additional requirements*

(4) Where the convention requires that a document must be accompanied by a translation into an official language of the country where it is to be served, the translator must sign a Translation Certificate and give it to the party who is serving the document.

(5) The party who requested formal service of the document must send the certificate that the party receives from the person who served the document to the sheriff court within one week of receiving it.

(6) If the document was translated into another language, the Translation Certificate must be sent to the sheriff court with the certificate from the person who served the document.

## How can you formally serve a document on someone who lives in any other country?

### 19.7 *Method*

(1) There are two ways to formally serve a document on someone who lives in a country where none of the other rules apply.

(2) It can be done by posting the document to the person's home or business address using a postal service which records delivery. This is called postal service.

(3) It can also be done by using the rules for personal service under the domestic law of the country where the document is to be served. This is called personal service.

*Who can formally serve the document?*

(4) The sheriff clerk may formally serve a Claim Form on the respondent by postal service only if:

    (a) the claimant is not a company or a partnership, and

    (b) the claimant is not legally represented.

(5) Otherwise, postal service many only be done by one of two persons:

    (a) the party's solicitor,

    (b) a sheriff officer instructed by the party.

(6) Personal service may be done by a person who is authorised to do so under the domestic law of the country where the document is to be served.

*Additional requirements*

(7) Any document must be accompanied by a translation into an official language of the country where it is to be formally served, unless English is an official language of that country.

(8) After translating a document, the translator must sign a Translation Certificate and give it to the party who is formally serving the Form or Notice.

(9) Where postal service is used, the envelope containing the document must have the following label printed or written on it:

> **THIS ENVELOPE CONTAINS A [NAME OF DOCUMENT] FROM**
> **[NAME OF SHERIFF COURT], SCOTLAND**
> **IF DELIVERY CANNOT BE MADE, THE LETTER MUST BE**
> **RETURNED TO THE SHERIFF CLERK AT**
> **[FULL ADDRESS OF SHERIFF COURT]**

(10) That label must also be translated into an official language of the country where the document is to be served, unless English is an official language of that country.

(11)  After formally serving a document by postal service, a Confirmation of Formal Service must be signed by the person who served it.

(12)  Any postal receipts must be attached to the Confirmation of Formal Service.

(13)  If a solicitor or a sheriff officer has used postal service, the Confirmation of Formal Service must be sent to the sheriff court within one week of service taking place.

(14)  If any other method of formal service was used, the party who requested formal service of the document must send the certificate that the party receives from the person who formally served the document to the sheriff court within one week of receiving it.

(15)  If any other method of formal service was used, the party who requested formal service of the document must also send a Method of Service Abroad Certificate to the sheriff court with the certificate that the party receives from the person who served the document to the sheriff court within one one week of receiving it.

(16)  If the document was translated into another language, the Translation Certificate must be sent to the sheriff court with the Confirmation of Formal Service Notice or the certificate from the person who formally served the document.

# PART 20: PROVISIONAL ORDERS

Part 20

Provisional orders

### What is this Part about?

**20.1**(1) This Part is about provisional orders which protect or secure the claimant's position before the sheriff makes a final decision in a case.

### When can a claimant ask for provisional orders to be made?

**20.2**(1) The claimant may apply for provisional orders to be made by completing a Provisional Orders Application and sending it to the sheriff court with the Claim Form.

(2) The claimant may also apply for provisional orders at any time before the sheriff makes a final decision in a case by completing a Provisional Orders Application and sending it to the sheriff court.

(3) The claimant must also send the Provisional Orders Application to the respondent and any interested person, unless the claimant has asked the court to make the provisional orders without holding a provisional orders hearing.

### What happens when the court receives a Provisional Orders Application?

**20.3**(1) The next steps depend on whether the claimant has asked the court to make the provisional orders with or without holding a provisional orders hearing.

(2) If the claimant has asked the court to make the provisional orders without holding a provisional orders hearing, the sheriff may do two things:

(a) grant the application and send the claimant written orders containing the provisional orders, or

(b) refuse to grant the application without a hearing and send the claimant notice of when and where the provisional orders hearing is to be held.

(3) Where the sheriff grants the application, the sheriff must also fix a provisional orders review hearing and order the claimant to tell the respondent and any interested person when and where it is to be held.

(4) If the sheriff refuses to grant the application without a hearing, the sheriff must also order the complainant to send the respondent and any interested person notice of when and where the provisional orders hearing is to be held.

### How can the claimant tell the respondent or an interested party about a hearing?

**20.4**(1) The claimant can tell the respondent or an interested party about any hearing under this Part by sending a Provisional Orders Hearing Notice to the respondent or interested party.

### How can you ask the court to reconsider provisional orders that it has made?

**20.5**(1) The respondent can ask the sheriff to reconsider a provisional order by sending a Provisional Orders Reconsideration Application to the court, the claimant and any interested person.

(2) An interested person can ask the sheriff to reconsider a provisional order by sending a Provisional Orders Reconsideration Application to the court, the claimant, the respondent and any other interested person.

(3) When the court receives a Provisional Orders Reconsideration Application, the sheriff must order every person to whom the application was sent to appear at a provisional orders review hearing where the sheriff will consider whether to change the provisional order.

(4) The sheriff may also order notice of the provisional orders review hearing to be given to any other person that the sheriff is satisfied has an interest.

## How can you ask the court to consider other applications about provisional orders?

**20.6**(1) A party may make any other application mentioned in Part 1A of the Debtors (Scotland) Act 1987 or Part 1A of the Debt Arrangement and Attachment (Scotland) Act 2002 by sending an Incidental Orders Application to the court, the other party and any interested person.

(2) An interested person may make any other application mentioned in Part 1A of the Debtors (Scotland) Act 1987 or Part 1A of the Debt Arrangement and Attachment (Scotland) Act 2002 by sending an Incidental Orders Application to the court, the parties and any other interested person.

(3) When the court receives such an Incidental Orders Application, the sheriff must order every person to whom the application was sent to appear at a provisional orders discussion in court, where the sheriff will consider whether to make any orders.

## How are provisional orders made effective?

**20.7**(1) The method for making a provisional order effective depends on the type of provisional order.

(2) An arrestment on the dependence (see rule 3.8(2)(a)) is made effective in accordance with rule 20.6.

(3) An inhibition on the dependence (see rule 3.8(2)(b)) is made effective in accordance with section 148(3)(b) of the Bankruptcy and Diligence (Scotland) Act 2007 and the Diligence (Scotland) Regulations 2009 (but see rule 20.9 if the respondent's address is not known).

(4) An interim attachment (see rule 3.8(2)(c)) is made effective in accordance with Chapter 1A of the Rules for Applications in the Sheriff Court under the Debt Arrangement and Attachment (Scotland) Act 2002.

## How is an arrestment on the dependence made effective?

**20.8**(1) An arrestment on the dependence is made effective by formally serving an Arrestment Notice on the person named in the provisional order who holds the respondent's goods or money.

(2) An arrestment Notice must be formally served by a sheriff officer. The sheriff officer must use one of the methods of formal service mentioned in rule 18.3.

(3) After formally serving an Arrestment Notice, the sheriff officer must complete a Confirmation of Formal Service of Arrestment Notice and send it to the sheriff court within one week of service taking place.

## How is an inhibition on the dependence made effective if the claimant does not know the respondent's address?

**20.9**(1) If the claimant does not know the respondent's address, an inhibition on the dependence is made effective if the sheriff officer does two additional things:

    (a) send the schedule of inhibition to the sheriff clerk of the sheriff court district where the respondent's last known address is located;

(b) send a copy of the schedule of inhibition by post to the respondent's last known address.

# PART 21: GLOSSARY

## What is this Part about?

**21.1**(1) This Part contains a guide for litigants, lay representatives and courtroom supporters to the meaning of certain legal words and expressions used in these rules.

| Word or expression | Meaning |
|---|---|
| *Additional respondent* | A person who is not named as a respondent by the claimant in the Claim Form but who enters the case later. |
| *Admitting a claim* | Where the respondent accepts the claim made by the claimant, including the things which the claimant wants from the respondent. |
| *Appeal* | Asking the Sheriff Appeal Court to reverse or vary the decision of a sheriff on a point of law. |
| *Application* | A way for a party to ask the court to do something by sending it and other parties a written application in a special form. |
| *Arrestment on the dependence* | An order freezing the respondent's funds or good held by a third party (typically money held in a bank account), in advance of the sheriff making a decision in a case. |
| *Case management discussion* | An informal discussion of how a case is progressing, involving the sheriff and the parties. |
| *Cite a witness* | Demand that a witness attend a hearing by an officer of court formally serving a Witness Citation Notice. |
| *Claim* | The things which the claimant wants from the respondent. |
| *Claimant* | The person making a claim. |
| *Courtroom supporter* | A person who may accompany a party in court to provide moral support. |
| *Decision* | The final order which the sheriff makes about the merits of a case, setting out who has been successful. |
| *Discussion* | A discussion of a particular issue (such as an application), involving the sheriff and the parties, which may take place in court. |

| Word or expression | Meaning |
|---|---|
| *Dismissing a claim* | An order by the sheriff ending the case without deciding which party has been successful. |
| *Expenses* | The contribution the court can order one party to make towards how much it costs another party to conduct a case. |
| *Formal service* | The formal process of sending a copy of a court document to a party or other person. |
| *Hearing* | An appearance by both parties in court at which witnesses and evidence can be considered and the sheriff will make a decision. |
| *Last date for a response* | The date by which the Respondent must send a Response Form to the court and to the claimant. |
| *Last date for service* | The date by which the Claim Form must be formally served on the respondent. |
| *Lay representative* | A representative who is not a lawyer. |
| *Legal representative* | A representative who is a lawyer. |
| *Lodge* | To deposit documents and other evidence to the sheriff clerk before a hearing, for their use at that hearing. |
| *Order* | A direction given by the sheriff to the parties telling them what they must do or what will happen next in a case. |
| *Party* | A person involved on one side of a simple procedure case – either a claimant or a respondent. |
| *Pause* | Temporarily suspend the progress of a case. |
| *Portal on the Scottish Courts and Tribunals Service website* | The portal for conducting a simple procedure case at http://www.scotcourts.gov.uk/. |
| *Principles of simple procedure* | The 5 principles listed in rule 1.2. |
| *Provisional order* | An order which protects or secures a claimant's position before a hearing, such as freezing a sum of money in the respondent's bank account. |
| *Recall* | An order cancelling a decision made by the sheriff. |
| *Representative* | A person who assists a party and speaks on their behalf in court, who may be either a legal representative or a lay representative. |

| Word or expression | Meaning |
|---|---|
| *Respondent* | The person a claim is made against. Response The respondent's reasons why the claim should not be successful. |
| *Restart* | Resuming the progress of a paused case. |
| *Send* | Sending something in a way provided for in Part 6 of the rules. |
| *Sheriff* | The judge who will decide a simple procedure case. |
| *Sheriff clerk* | A court official who provides administrative support to the sheriff. |
| *Sheriff officer* | A court officer who may formally serve court documents. |
| *Simple procedure case* | A claim which is registered by the sheriff clerk. |
| *Timetable* | The dates by which the first two steps that the parties must take in a simple procedure case are to be completed – the last date for service and the last date for a response. |
| *Time to pay* | An order giving the respondent time to pay the claimant in instalments or in a deferred lump sum. |
| *Trading name* | A name under which a person, partnership or company carries out its business. |

## SCHEDULE 2 FORMS

SCHEDULE 2

FORMS

**Paragraph 2(2)**

**PART 2**
2A. Lay Representation Form
**PART 3**
3A. Claim Form
3B. Further Claimant Form
3C. Further Respondent Form
3D. Timetable
3E. Change of Timetable Application
**PART 4**
4A. Response Form
**PART 5**
5A. Time to Pay Application
5B. Time to Pay Notice
**PART 6**
6A. Notice of Claim
6B. Service by Advertisement Application
6C. Confirmation of Formal Service
**PART 7**
7A. Application for a Decision
**PART 8**
8A. Order of the Sheriff
**PART 9**
9A. Application to Pause
9B. Application to Restart
9C. Additional Respondent Application
9D. Application to Amend
9E. Abandonment Notice
9F. Application to Represent
9G. Incidental Orders Application
**PART 10**
10A. List of Evidence Form
10B. Recovery of Documents Application
10C. Application to Open Confidential Document
10D. Special Recovery of Documents Application
**PART 11**
11A. List of Witnesses Form
11B. Witness Citation Notice
11C. Child Witness Notice

11D. Vulnerable Witness Application

11E. Special Measures Review Application

**PART 13**

13A. Decision Form

13B. Application to Recall

**PART 15**

15A. Charge to Pay

15B. Alternative Decision Application

**PART 16**

16A. Appeal Form

16B. Appeal Report

**PART 17**

17A. CJEU Reference Form

17B. Application to Intervene

17C. Invitation to Intervene

17D. Application to Change a Damages Management Order

17E. Application for Instructions about a Damages Management Order

17F. Application for a Child's Property Administration Order

**PART 19**

19A. Translation Certificate

19B. Method of Service Abroad Certificate

**PART 20**

20A. Provisional Orders Application

20B. Provisional Orders Hearing Notice

20C. Provisional Orders Reconsideration Application

20D. Arrestment Notice

20E. Confirmation of Formal Service of Arrestment Notice

**FORM 2A**

# The Simple Procedure
# Lay Representation Form

This is the Lay Representation Form. You must complete it if you are acting as a lay representative in a simple procedure case.

Before completing this form, you should read Part 2 of the Simple Procedure Rules, which is about lay representation.

If you are representing a party throughout a simple procedure case, you must complete this form and send it to the court with the Claim Form or the Response Form.

Otherwise, if you are representing a person only during a particular discussion or hearing in a simple procedure case, you must complete this form and give it to the sheriff clerk in person at court.

If you are representing an individual, you must complete Parts A to C. If you are representing a company, limited liability partnership, partnership or unincorporated association, you must also complete Part D.

## A. ABOUT THE CASE

| | |
|---|---|
| Sheriff Court | |
| Claimant | |
| Respondent | |
| Case reference number (if known) | |

## B. ABOUT YOU

### B1. What is your full name?

| | |
|---|---|
| Name | |
| Middle name | |
| Surname | |

### B2. Are you from an advice or advocacy organisation?

ⓘ A lay representative may be a family member or friend, may be someone from an advice or advocacy organisation, or may be someone else.

☐ Yes

☐ No

**B3. If you have answered 'Yes', which organisation are you from?**

Name of organisation

**B4. Are you representing a non-natural person?**

ⓘ A non-natural person is a company, limited liability partnership, partnership or unincorporated association.

ⓘ If you are representing a non-natural person, then as well as completing part C, you must also complete part D.

☐ Yes

☐ No

## C. DECLARATIONS

ⓘ To comply with simple procedure rules, and so that the sheriff can decide if you are a suitable person to act as a lay representative, you must complete this section.

ⓘ Tick the box next to each declaration that applies to you and complete any sections that apply to you.

☐ I am authorised by the person to conduct these proceedings.

☐ I am not receiving and will not receive from the person I represent any remuneration, whether directly or indirectly, for acting as a lay representative.

☐ I accept that documents and information are provided to me by the parties on a confidential basis and I undertake to keep them confidential.

☐ I have not been declared a vexatious litigant under the Vexatious Litigants (Scotland) Act 1898.

☐ I was declared a vexatious litigant on:

[date]

☐ I have no financial interest in the outcome of this case.

☐ I have the following financial interest in the outcome of this case:

[explain]

## D. ADDITIONAL DECLARATIONS: REPRESENTING A NON-NATURAL PERSON

ⓘ If you selected 'Yes' at B4, you must complete this Part, so that the sheriff can decide if you are a suitable person to act as a lay representative.

ⓘ Tick the box next to each declaration that applies to you and complete any sections that apply to you.

☐ **The relevant position I hold with the non-natural person is:**

[director / secretary of the company, a member of the limited liability partnership or partnership, or a member or office holder of the association]

☐ **My responsibilities do not consist wholly or mainly of conducting legal proceedings on behalf of the non-natural person or another person.**

☐ **I do not have a personal interest in the subject matter of the proceedings.**

Signature

Date

FORM 3A

# The Simple Procedure
# Claim Form

The Simple Procedure is a speedy, inexpensive and informal court procedure for settling or determining disputes with a value of **£5,000 or less**.

The Simple Procedure Rules should be read alongside this form. They can be found on the Scottish Courts and Tribunals Service website. Please **read the whole Claim Form** before beginning to complete it. There are guidance notes above each section of the form.

To make a claim using the Simple Procedure, you must **complete this Claim Form** and send it to the sheriff court to register your case. You should either complete the form yourself or, if you have someone assisting or representing you, you should complete the form with them.

## A. ABOUT YOU

ⓘ Set out information about you, so that the court knows who you are and how to contact you.

A1. Are you an individual, a company or an organisation?

☐ An individual (including a sole trader) (please fill out A2)

☐ A company or organisation (please fill out A3)

A2. What is your full name?

| | |
|---|---|
| Name | |
| Middle name | |
| Surname | |
| Trading name or representative capacity (if any) | |

A3. What is the name of the company or organisation?

| | |
|---|---|
| Name | |
| Company type | |
| Company registration number (if limited company or LLP) | |
| Trading name (if any) | |

**A4. What are your contact details?**

| | |
|---|---|
| Address | |
| City | |
| Postcode | |
| Email address | |

**A5. How would you prefer the court and the responding party to contact you?**

☐   By post

☐   Email

## B. ABOUT YOUR REPRESENTATION

ⓘ Set out information about how you will be represented.

**B1. How will you be represented during this case?**

☐   I will represent myself

☐   I will be represented by a solicitor

☐   I will be represented by a non-solicitor (e.g. a family member, friend, or someone from an advice or advocacy organisation)

**B2. Who is your representative?**

ⓘ If a family member or friend, please give their full name. If someone from an advice or advocacy organisation, please also give the name of that organisation.

| | |
|---|---|
| Name | |
| Surname | |
| Organisation / firm name | |

**B3. What is the address of your representative?**

ⓘ If your representative works for a solicitors' firm or an advocacy organisation, please give the address of that firm or organisation.

| | |
|---|---|
| Address | |
| City | |
| Postcode | |
| Email address | |

**B4. Would you like us to contact you through your representative?**

ⓘ If you select 'yes', then the court will send orders and information in this case to your representative.

☐ Yes

☐ No

**B5. How would your representative prefer the court to contact them?**

☐ By post

☐ Online

## C. ABOUT THE RESPONDENT(S)

ⓘ The person who you are making the claim against is called the respondent. In this part, you must fill in information about that person so that the court knows who they are and how to contact them.

ⓘ If there are more than two respondents, you must select 'more than two respondents' at C1 and complete a Further Respondent Form for each further respondent.

**C1. Is there one respondent, two respondents or more than two respondents?**

☐ One respondent

☐ Two respondents

☐ More than two respondents

**C2. Is the first respondent an individual, a company or an organisation?**

☐ An individual (including a sole trader) (please complete C3)

☐ A company or organisation (please complete C4)

**C3. What is the first respondent's full name?**

ⓘ If the respondent is an individual trading under a name, please also give that name.

Name

Middle name

Surname

Trading name (if any)

**C4. What is the first respondent's company name or organisation name?**

ⓘ If the respondent is a company (which might be indicated by 'Limited', 'Ltd' or 'plc' after its name), please give the full name of that company and the company registration number.

ⓘ You can check the name of a company on the Companies House website.

Name

Company type

Company registration number (if limited company or LLP)

| Trading name (if any) | |
|---|---|

## C5. What are the first respondent's contact details?

| Address | |
|---|---|
| City | |
| Postcode | |
| Email address | |

## C6. Is the second respondent an individual, a company or an organisation?

☐   An individual (including a sole trader) (please complete C7)

☐   A company or organisation (please complete C8)

## C7. What is the second respondent's full name?

ⓘ If the respondent is an individual trading under a name, please also give that name.

| Name | |
|---|---|
| Middle name | |
| Surname | |
| Trading name (if any) | |

## C8. What is the second respondent's company name or organisation name?

ⓘ If the respondent is a company (which might be indicated by 'Limited', 'Ltd' or 'plc' after its name), please give the full name of that company and the company registration number.

ⓘ You can check the name of a company on the Companies House website.

| Name | |
|---|---|
| Company type | |
| Company registration number (if limited company or LLP) | |
| Trading name (if any) | |

## C9. What are the second respondent's contact details?

| Address | |
|---|---|
| City | |
| Postcode | |

Email address

### C10. Would you like the court to formally serve this Claim Form on your behalf?

ⓘ The court cannot formally serve this Claim Form on your behalf if you are a company or if you are represented by a solicitor. You will have to arrange formal service yourself.

☐ Yes

☐ No

## D. ABOUT YOUR CLAIM

ⓘ In this part, you must fill in information about the claim you are making against the respondent.

### D1. What is the background to your claim?

ⓘ In this section, you should briefly describe the essential facts about the story behind your claim. You do not need to set out every detail of the story. You should focus on the parts which are important for you to establish your claim.

ⓘ You should include:

– key dates,

– if there was an agreement, what you agreed to do and what the respondent agreed to do,

– when you became aware of the problem or dispute,

– whether any payments have been made so far, and if so what,

– whether any services have been provided so far, and if so what.

ⓘ If this is insufficient space to describe the essential factual background, you may use another sheet of paper, which must be headed 'D1' and must be attached to the Claim Form.

### D2. Where did this take place?

ⓘ You should set out where the events described above took place. If any part happened online, please state this.

ⓘ This is so that the court and the respondent can make sure that this is the right court to hear this claim.

| Address | |
|---|---|
| City | |
| Postcode | |
| Details | |

### D3. Does this claim relate to a consumer credit agreement?

ⓘ You should select 'Yes' if the claim is about an agreement between you and the respondent in which you provided the respondent with credit of any amount.

☐ **Yes (please complete D4)**

☐ **No**

### D4. What are the details of the consumer credit agreement?

ⓘ Set out the following information:

- the date of the agreement and its reference number

- the name and address of any person who acted as guarantor

- the details of the agreed repayment arrangements

- the unpaid balance or amount of arrears.

### D5. If your claim is successful, what do you want from the respondent?

ⓘ You should select the option(s) that best describes the type of order you would like the court to make if your claim is successful. You can ask for more than one type of order to be made in a claim.

ⓘ You can also ask for alternative orders. For example, you could ask for the respondent to be ordered to repair something of yours or, failing that, to give you money to buy a new item.

ⓘ You should set out the detail of what you would like the court to order next to each option that you select.

☐ **I want the respondent to be ordered by the court to pay me a sum of money:**

> I want the court to order the respondent to pay me the sum of £_____.___.
>
> I want the court to order the respondent to pay me interest on that sum at the rate of __%
> annually from the last date for service.

&#9432; You should provide a breakdown to explain the sum of money you are claiming

&#9432; You should also set out the date from which you would like the court to order interest
to run from and the rate of interest you would like the court to order.

☐ **I want the respondent to be ordered by the court to deliver something to me:**

> I want the court to order the respondent to deliver to me the following items:
>    1. [list]
>
> Alternatively, if the respondent does not deliver [that item / those items], I want the court to
> order the respondent to pay me the sum of £_____.___, with interest on that sum at the rate of
> __% annually from the last date for service.

&#9432; Set out the item(s) you want to be delivered to you.

&#9432; You may want to set out an alternative claim for payment of a sum of money in case
the respondent does not deliver the items to you.

☐ **I want the respondent to be ordered by the court to do something for me:**

> I want the court to order the respondent to do the following:
>    1. [list]
>
> Alternatively, if the respondent does not do that, I want the court to order the respondent to
> pay me the sum of £_____.___, with interest on that sum at the rate of __% annually from the
> last date for service.

&#9432; Set out exactly what you want the respondent to be ordered to do.

&#9432; You may want to set out an alternative claim for payment of a sum of money in case
the respondent does not do what the court has ordered.

**D6. If your claim is successful, would you like the court to order the respondent to pay you a
sum of money for the expenses of the claim?**

&#9432; If your claim is successful, the court can order the respondent to pay you a sum of
money to compensate you for the expense of making this claim.

☐ Yes

☐ No

## D7. Why should your claim be successful?

ⓘ ⓘ You should set out briefly the reasons why your claim should be successful, and the court should make the orders which you have asked for, for example:

– "The respondent breached a contract with me by not completing work satisfactorily"

– "The respondent caused damage or financial loss to me by breaking something belonging to me"

– "The respondent have kept something belonging to me without the right to do."

## D8. What steps have you taken, if any, to try to settle the dispute with the respondent?

ⓘ It is an important principle of simple procedure that parties should be encouraged to settle their disputes by negotiation, where possible.

ⓘ You should set out any steps you have taken, if any, to try to settle the dispute with the respondent.

ⓘ The court will use this information to assess whether more negotiation would help you and the respondent settle your dispute.

## E. WITNESSES, DOCUMENTS AND EVIDENCE

**E1. Set out in a numbered list any witnesses you might to bring to a hearing to support your claim, their name and address, and what their relationship to the claim is.**

ⓘ You should list any witnesses you think you might bring to a hearing. You do not need to list yourself or the respondent.

ⓘ You should provide the full name and address of any witnesses.

ⓘ Your claim may require no witnesses other than you and the respondent. You do not need to bring a witness if the evidence which they might give can be shown in some other way, e.g. by photographs.

(i) You should describe the relationship of each witness to the claim. For example, you might indicate that a witness:

- was the person with whom you made an agreement

- was present when damage took place

- inspected some work which you consider to have not been completed satisfactorily.

(i) If the court orders a hearing, Part 11 of the Simple Procedure Rules tells you what you need to do to arrange the attendance of your witnesses.

1. [ Name ]
   [ Address]
   [ Relationship to the claim ]

2. [ Name ]
   [ Address ]
   [ Relationship to the claim ]

3. [ Name ]
   [ Address ]
   [ Relationship to the claim ]

[...]

**E2. Set out in a numbered list any documents you might bring to court to support your claim.**

(i) You should list any documents you think you might bring to a hearing. This includes photographs and other printed material which may be kept in a file.

(i) When preparing these documents for a hearing, it is useful if they are indexed with numbers.

(i) If the court orders a hearing, Part 10 of the Simple Procedure Rules tells you what you need to do to lodge documents.

1.
2.
3.
4.
5.

[...]

**E3. Set out any other pieces of evidence you intend to bring to a hearing to support your claim.**

(i) You should list any other evidence you think you might bring to a hearing.

(i) This includes objects, but not printed material.

(i) For example, if the claim was about damage caused to an item of clothing, you might list the item of clothing. You do not need to bring a piece of evidence if the important point can be shown in some other way, e.g. by photographs.

(i) If the court orders a hearing, Part 10 of the Simple Procedure Rules tells you what you need to do to lodge evidence.

1.

2.

3.

4.

5.

[...]

**PLEASE CHECK THIS FORM BEFORE SENDING IT.**

FORM 3B

# The Simple Procedure
# Further Claimant Form

To make a claim for more than one claimant, you must complete a Further Claimant Form for each extra claimant after the claimant you named in the Claim Form and send it to the sheriff court along with the Claim Form.

## A. ABOUT THE FIRST CLAIMANT

ⓘ Fill in information about the claimant named on the Claim Form, so that the court knows who you are and how to contact you.

A1. Are you an individual, a company or an organisation?

☐ An individual (including a sole trader) (please fill out A2)

☐ A company or organisation (please fill out A3)

A2. What is your full name?

| | |
|---|---|
| Name | |
| Middle name | |
| Surname | |
| Trading name or representative capacity (if any) | |

A3. What is the name of the company or organisation?

| | |
|---|---|
| Name | |
| Company type | |
| Company registration number (if limited company or LLP) | |
| Trading name (if any) | |

A4. What is your address?

| | |
|---|---|
| Address | |
| City | |
| Postcode | |

Email address [                    ]

## C. ABOUT THE FURTHER CLAIMANT

**C1. Is the further claimant an individual, a company or an organisation?**

☐ An individual (including a sole trader) (please complete C2)

☐ A company or organisation (please complete C3)

**C2. What is the further claimant's full name?**

ⓘ If the further claimant is an individual trading under a business name, please also give that name.

Name [                    ]

Middle name [                    ]

Surname [                    ]

Trading name (if any) [                    ]

**C3. What is the further claimant's company name or organisation name?**

ⓘ If the further claimant is a company (which might be indicated by 'Limited', 'Ltd' or 'plc' after its name), please give the full name of that company and the company registration number.

ⓘ You can check the name of a company on the Companies House website.

Name [                    ]

Company type [                    ]

Company registration number (if limited company or LLP) [                    ]

Trading name (if any) [                    ]

**C5. What are the further claimant's contact details?**

Address [                    ]

City [                    ]

Postcode [                    ]

Email address [                    ]

FORM 3C

# The Simple Procedure
# Further Respondent Form

To make a claim against more than two respondents, you must complete a Further Respondent Form for each extra respondent after the two respondents you named in the Claim Form and send it to the sheriff court along with the Claim Form.

## A. ABOUT THE FIRST CLAIMANT

ⓘ Fill in information about the claimant named on the Claim Form, so that the court knows who you are and how to contact you.

A1. Are you an individual, a company or an organisation?

☐ An individual (including a sole trader) (please fill out A2)

☐ A company or organisation (please fill out A3)

A2. What is your full name?

| | |
|---|---|
| Name | |
| Middle name | |
| Surname | |
| Trading name or representative capacity (if any) | |

A3. What is the name of the company or organisation?

| | |
|---|---|
| Name | |
| Company type | |
| Company registration number (if limited company or LLP) | |
| Trading name (if any) | |

A4. What is your address?

| | |
|---|---|
| Address | |
| City | |
| Postcode | |

Email address [                    ]

## C. ABOUT THE FURTHER RESPONDENT

### C1. What is the first respondent's full name or company name?

ⓘ You must fill in information about the first respondent you named in part C of the Claim Form so that the court knows which claim this relates to.

[                    ]

### C2. What is the second respondent's full name or company name?

ⓘ You must fill in information about the second respondent you named in part C of the Claim Form so that the court knows which claim this relates to.

[                    ]

### C3. Is the further respondent an individual, a company or an organisation?

☐ An individual (including a sole trader) (please complete C3)

☐ A company or organisation (please complete C4)

### C4. What is the further respondent's full name?

ⓘ If the further respondent is an individual trading under a business name, please also give that name.

Name [                    ]

Middle name [                    ]

Surname [                    ]

Trading name (if any) [                    ]

### C5. What is the further respondent's company name or organisation name?

ⓘ If the further respondent is a company (which might be indicated by 'Limited', 'Ltd' or 'plc' after its name), please give the full name of that company and the company registration number.

ⓘ You can check the name of a company on the Companies House website.

Name [                    ]

Company type [                    ]

Company registration number (if limited company or LLP) [                    ]

Trading name (if any) [                    ]

**C6. What are the further respondent's contact details?**

| | |
|---|---|
| Address | |
| City | |
| Postcode | |
| Email address | |

FORM 3D
# The Simple Procedure Timetable

Your claim has been registered.

This is the timetable for your case. It sets out the two important dates by which certain things must be done in this simple procedure case

## A. ABOUT THE CASE

| | |
|---|---|
| Sheriff Court | |
| Claimant | |
| Respondent | |
| Case reference number | |

## B. LAST DATE FOR SERVICE

ⓘ The last date for service is the date by which the Claim Form must be formally served on the respondent.

ⓘ Part 6 of the Simple Procedure Rules is about how formal service can be arranged.

Last date for service:

## C. LAST DATE FOR A RESPONSE

ⓘ The last date for a response is the date by which the respondent must send a Response Form to the court and to the claimant.

ⓘ Part 7 of the Simple Procedure Rules is about what happens if the respondent sends the court a Response Form and what can happen if they don't.

Last date for a response:

FORM 3E

# The Simple Procedure
# Change of Timetable
# Application

This is a Change of Timetable Application. You can use this Application to ask to change the timetable in a simple procedure case, including:

- changing the last date for service, or

- changing the last date for a response.

Before completing this form, you should read rule 3.13 of the Simple Procedure Rules, which is about how to apply for a change of timetable.

## A. ABOUT THE CASE

| | |
|---|---|
| Sheriff Court | |
| Claimant | |
| Respondent | |
| Case reference number | |

## B. ABOUT YOU

B1. What is your full name?

| | |
|---|---|
| Name | |
| Middle name | |
| Surname | |
| Trading name or representative capacity (if any) | |

B2. Which party in this case are you?

☐ Claimant

☐ Respondent

## C. THE APPLICATION

C1. Why does the timetable for this case need to be changed?

**C1. Why does the timetable for this case need to be changed?**

ⓘ Set out why the original timetable for this case can no longer be complied with (e.g. because of difficulties with service).

**C2. What new timetable would allow this case to progress?**

ⓘ Set out your suggestion for new dates which would allow this case to progress (e.g. how long do you think it will take you to formally serve something?).

# PART 4

PART 4

FORM 4A

# The Simple Procedure
# Response Form

The Simple Procedure is a speedy, inexpensive and informal court procedure for settling or determining disputes with a value of **£5,000 or less**.

A claim has been raised against you under the Simple Procedure. You have been provided with a copy of the Claim Form which sets out the claim made against you.

The Simple Procedure Rules should be read alongside this form. They can be found on the Scottish Courts and Tribunals Service website. Please **read the whole Response Form** before beginning to complete it. There are guidance notes for each part of the form.

Please note that if you **do nothing**, the court will almost certainly, if appropriate, award the claim to the claimant and order you to make a payment, including interest and expenses.

## A. ABOUT YOU

ⓘ Set out information about you, so that the court knows who you are and how to contact you.

A1. Are you an individual, a company or an organisation?

☐ An individual (including a sole trader) (please fill out A2)

☐ A company or organisation (please fill out A3)

A2. What is your full name?

| | |
|---|---|
| Name | |
| Middle name | |
| Surname | |
| Trading name or representative capacity (if any) | |

A3. What is the name of the company or organisation?

| | |
|---|---|
| Name | |
| Company type | |
| Company registration number (if limited company or LLP) | |

1231

| Trading name (if any) | |
|---|---|

## A4. What are your contact details?

| Address | |
|---|---|
| City | |
| Postcode | |
| Email address | |

## A5. How would you prefer the court and the responding party to contact you?

☐ By post

☐ Email

## B. ABOUT YOUR REPRESENTATION

ⓘ Set out information about how you will be represented.

## B1. How will you be represented during this case?

☐ I will represent myself

☐ I will be represented by a solicitor

☐ I will be represented by a non-solicitor (e.g. a family member, friend, or someone from an advice or advocacy organisation)

## B2. Who is your representative?

ⓘ If a family member or friend, give their full name. If someone from an advice or advocacy organisation, also give the name of that organisation.

| Name | |
|---|---|
| Surname | |
| Organisation / firm name | |

## B3. What are the contact details of your representative?

ⓘ If your representative works for a solicitors' firm or an advice or advocacy organisation, give the address of that firm or organisation.

| Address | |
|---|---|
| City | |
| Postcode | |
| Email address | |

## B4. Would you like us to contact you through your representative?

ⓘ If you select 'yes', then the court will send orders and information in this case to your representative.

☐ Yes

☐ No

**B5. How would your representative prefer the court to contact them?**

☐ By post

☐ Email

## C. YOUR RESPONSE TO THE CLAIM

ⓘ You should decide now how you intend to respond to this claim. There are three options. Please mark the box next to the option you choose and follow those instructions.

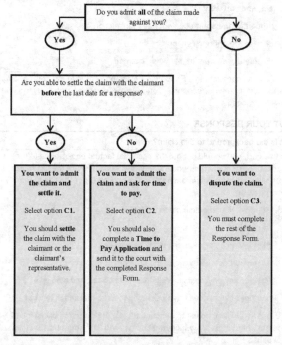

☐ C1. I want to **admit the claim** and settle it before the last date for a response.

ⓘ You should select this option if you accept that the claim against you is correct and you are able to settle it with the claimant now.

ⓘ You do not need to complete Parts D and E.

ⓘ You should send this Response Form to the court and to the claimant. You should settle the claim with the claimant or the claimant's representative by the last date for a response.

☐ **C2. I want to admit the claim and apply for time to pay.**

ⓘ You should select this option if you accept that the claim against you is correct but you want to be given time to may a payment, or time to make payments in instalments.

ⓘ You do not need to complete Parts D and E.

ⓘ You should also complete a Time to Pay Application and send it with this completed Response Form to the court and to the claimant by the last date for a response.

☐ **C3. I want to dispute the claim.**

ⓘ You should select this option if you do not accept that the claim against you is correct, and you want to:

- argue that the court does not have jurisdiction,

- dispute the entire claim, or

- dispute the amount that is being claimed.

ⓘ You should complete this Response Form and send it to the court and to the claimant by the last date for a response. You will be sent written orders by the court telling you how to proceed.

## D. ABOUT YOUR RESPONSE

### D1. What is the background to this claim?

ⓘ In this part, you should set out the essential factual background to the claim. The claimant has set out their understanding in section D1 of the Claim Form. In particular, you should set out anything in section D1 of the Claim Form which you disagree with.

ⓘ For example, you should include:

- key dates

- if there was an agreement, what was agreed

- when you became aware of the problem or dispute

- whether any payments have been made so far, and if so what

- whether any services have been provided so far, and if so what.

ⓘ If this is insufficient space to describe the essential factual background, you may use another sheet of paper, which must be headed 'D1' and must be attached to the Response Form.

[ ]

## D2. Why should the claim not be successful?

ⓘ You should set out briefly the reasons why the claim made against you should not be successful, and the court should not make the orders which the claimant has asked for in section D3 of the Claim Form.

ⓘ For example, reasons might include:

– that you did not breach a contract with the claimant (e.g. work was completed satisfactorily)

– that you did not cause the claimant damage or financial loss

– that you have the right to keep something belonging to the claimant (e.g. because a repair has not been paid for).

ⓘ If this is insufficient space set out these reasons, you may use another sheet of paper, which must be headed 'D2' and must be attached to the Response Form.

[ ]

## D3. Are there any additional respondents you think should be responding to this claim?

ⓘ You should complete this section if you think that:

– you have a right of contribution, relief or indemnity against someone who is already a respondent

    –  someone else should be made a respondent in this claim, as they are solely, jointly, or jointly and severally liable with you for the claim made against you

    –  someone else should be made a respondent in this claim as they are liable to you for the claim made against you.

ⓘ If you complete this section then the court may order you to formally serve the Claim Form and the Response Form on any additional respondents.

☐  **Yes (please complete D4)**

☐  **No**

**D4. Which additional respondents do you think should be responding to this claim?**

ⓘ Set out below the full names and addresses of any additional respondents you think should be responding to the claim made against you.

ⓘ Set out the reasons why each person should be an additional respondent to the claim made against you.

> 1. [ Name ]
>
>    [ Address]
>
>    [ Reasons why this person should be an additional respondent ]
>
> 2. [ Name ]
>
>    [ Address ]
>
>    [ Reasons why this person should be an additional respondent ]
>
> [...]

**D5. What steps have you taken, if any, to try to settle the dispute with the claimant?**

ⓘ It is an important principle of simple procedure that parties should be encouraged to settle their disputes by negotiation, where possible.

ⓘ The court will use this information to assess whether more negotiation would help you and the responding party settle your dispute.

**E. WITNESSES, DOCUMENTS AND EVIDENCE**

**E1. Set out in a numbered list any witnesses you might to bring to a hearing to support your response, their name and address, and what their relationship to the claim or response is.**

ⓘ You should list any witnesses you think you might bring to a hearing. You do not need to list yourself or the claimant.

ⓘ You should provide the full name and address of any witnesses.

(i) Your claim may require no witnesses other than you and the claimant. You do not need to bring a witness if the evidence which they might give can be shown in some other way, e.g. by photographs.

(i) You should describe the relationship of each witness to the claim or response. For example, you might indicate that a witness:

- was the person with whom you made an agreement,
- was present when the alleged damage took place,
- inspected some work which you consider to have been completed satisfactorily.

(i) If the court orders a hearing, Part 11 of the Simple Procedure Rules tells you what you need to do to arrange the attendance of your witnesses.

```
1. [ Name ]
   [ Address]
   [ Relationship to the claim or response ]

2. [ Name ]
   [ Address ]
   [ Relationship to the claim or response ]

3. [ Name ]
   [ Address ]
   [ Relationship to the claim or response ]
[...]
```

**E2. Set out in a numbered list any documents you might bring to court to support your response.**

(i) You should list any documents you think you might bring to a hearing. This includes photographs and other printed material which may be kept in a file.

(i) When preparing these documents for a hearing, it is useful if they are indexed with numbers.

(i) If the court orders a hearing, Part 10 of the Simple Procedure Rules tells you what you need to do to lodge documents before that hearing.

```
1.
2.
3.
4.
5.
[...]
```

**E3. Set out any other pieces of evidence you intend to bring to a hearing to support your response.**

(i) You should list any other evidence you think you might bring to a hearing.

(i) This includes objects, but not printed material. For example, if the claim was about damage caused to an item of clothing, you might list the item of clothing. You do not need to bring a piece of evidence if the important point can be shown in some other way, e.g. by photographs.

(i) If the court orders a hearing, Part 10 of the Simple Procedure Rules tells you what you need to do to lodge other evidence before that hearing.

1.

2.

3.

4.

5.

[…]

## PLEASE CHECK THIS FORM BEFORE SENDING IT.

**FORM 5A**

# The Simple Procedure
# Time to Pay Application

This is a Time to Pay Application. It is used to ask the sheriff to make an order giving the respondent time to pay (where such an order is available).

**You can only apply for time to pay where you admit the claim made against you by the claimant.**

The respondent may ask for time to pay by completing this application and either:

(a)    sending it to court with the completed Response Form, or

(b)    bringing it to court at a discussion in court, case management discussion or a hearing.

Before completing this form, you should read Part 5 of the Simple Procedure Rules, which is about asking for time to pay.

There are two situations in which the court can make a time to pay order: under the Debtors (Scotland) Act 1987 and under the Consumer Credit Act 1974.

**Time to pay under the Debtors (Scotland) Act 1987**

The Debtors (Scotland) Act 1987 gives you the right to apply to the court for time to pay. This is an order which allows you to pay any sum which the court orders you to pay either in instalments or by deferred lump sum. A "deferred lump sum" means that you will be ordered by the court to pay the whole amount at one time within a period which the court will specify.

If the court makes an order, it may also recall or restrict any arrestment made on your property by the pursuer in connection with the action or debt (for example, your bank account may have been frozen).

If an order is made, a copy of the Decision Form will be sent to you by the pursuer telling you when payment should start or when it is you have to pay the lump sum.

If an order is not made, and an order for immediate payment is made against you, a Charge may be served on you if you do not pay.

Under the 1987 Act, the court is required to make an order if satisfied that it is reasonable in the circumstances to do so, and having regard in particular to the following matters:

- The nature of and reasons for the debt in relation to which decree is granted

- Any action taken by the creditor to assist the debtor in paying the debt

- The debtor's financial position

- The reasonableness of any proposal by the debtor to pay that debt

- The reasonableness of any refusal or objection by the creditor to any proposal or offer by the debtor to pay the debt.

**Time to pay under the Consumer Credit Act 1974**

The Consumer Credit Act 1974 allows you to apply to the court for an order asking the court to give you more time to pay a loan agreement. This order can only be applied for where the claim is about a credit agreement regulated by the Consumer Credit Act. The court has power to make an order in respect of a regulated agreement to reschedule payment of the sum owed. This means that an order can change:

- the amount you have to pay each month

- how long the loan will last

- in some cases, the interest rate payable

A time order can also stop the creditor taking away any item bought by you on hire purchase or conditional sale under the regulated agreement, so long as you continue to pay the instalments agreed.

**A. ABOUT YOU**

**A1. What is your full name?**

| Name | |
|---|---|
| Middle name | |
| Surname | |
| Trading name or representative capacity (if any) | |
| Date of application | |

**B. ABOUT YOUR APPLICATION**

ⓘ Set out how you think that you are able to pay the claimant the sum of money which you owe.

**B1. I admit the claim** and would like to apply to pay the sum of money as follows:

☐ By instalments of: £_____ **per** week / fortnight / month

☐ In one lump sum within: [        ] [weeks / months] from today.

## B2. How did you get into this debt?

ⓘ Set out the reasons for you getting into this debt.

[        ]

## B3. Why should the court give you time to pay?

ⓘ Set out the reasons why the court should give you time to pay.

[        ]

## B4. Why is the payment offer you have made reasonable?

ⓘ Set out any information which explains why the offer you have made is a reasonable one (i.e. why you can afford that offer but not a higher one).

[        ]

## B5. Are you apply to have an arrestment recalled or restricted?

ⓘ When making an order the court may recall or restrict an arrestment (i.e. unfreeze your bank account if it has been frozen).

☐ Yes (explain below)

☐ No

ⓘ Set out the details of the arrestment, including the date on which it occurred.

[        ]

## C. ABOUT YOUR FINANCES

ⓘ To help the court decide whether to make an order and what that order should be, please provide some details of your financial situation.

**C1. What is your employment situation?**

☐ Employed

☐ Self-employed

☐ Unemployed

**C2. What are your outgoings?**

ⓘ Set out any regular payments you have to make and whether these are made weekly, fortnightly or monthly.

Rent or mortgage £___ **each** week / fortnight / month

Council tax £___ **each** week / fortnight / month

Utilities (gas, electricity, etc) £___ **each** week / fortnight / month

Food £___ **each** week / fortnight / month

Loans and credit agreements £___ **each** week / fortnight / month

Phone £___ **each** week / fortnight / month

Other £___ **each** week / fortnight / month

Total £___ **each** week / fortnight / month

**C3. What income do you receive?**

ⓘ Set out any regular income you receive and whether you get this weekly, fortnightly or monthly.

Wages or pension £___ **each** week / fortnight / month

Benefits £___ **each** week / fortnight / month

Tax credits £___ **each** week / fortnight / month

Other £___ **each** week / fortnight / month

Total £___ **each** week / fortnight / month

**C4. Does anyone rely on your income?**

ⓘ Set out how many people (if any) rely on your income and who they are (e.g. spouse / civil partner / children).

**C5. Do you have any capital?**

ⓘ Set out any capital which you hold. For example, money in savings accounts, shares, investments or houses owned.

FORM 5B

# The Simple Procedure
# Time to Pay Notice

The respondent has admitted the claim you made against them and applied to the court for time to pay the sum of money which you claimed.

A copy of the Time to Pay Application is attached.

Before completing this form, you should read Part 5 of the Simple Procedure Rules, which is about asking for time to pay.

You must send this Time to Pay Notice back to the court within 14 days of the date above or else the court will dismiss your claim.

## A. ABOUT THE CASE

| | |
|---|---|
| Sheriff Court | |
| Name of claimant | |
| Name of respondent | |
| Case reference number | |
| Date of notice | |

## B. ABOUT YOU

ⓘ This is so that the court knows who you are.

### B1. What is your full name?

| | |
|---|---|
| Name | |
| Middle name | |
| Surname | |
| Trading name or representative capacity (if any) | |

## C. YOUR RESPONSE

ⓘ This will assist the court in deciding whether or not to grant the respondent time to pay.

**B1. How do you respond to the Time to Pay Application?**

ⓘ Set out whether you are content or not for the court to give the respondent time to pay the sum of money in your claim.

☐ I am **content** with the proposal for time to pay.

☐ I am **not content** with the proposal for time to pay.

FORM 6A

# The Simple Procedure
# Notice of Claim

The Simple Procedure is a speedy, inexpensive and informal court procedure for settling or determining disputes with a value of **£5,000 or less**.

You have been **formally served** with a simple procedure claim.

### What is this envelope?

You have received this envelope because a claim is being made against you in court. The claim is being made under the Simple Procedure. The Simple Procedure is a speedy, inexpensive and informal court procedure for settling or determining disputes with a value of £5,000 or less. The Simple Procedure Rules are available on the Scottish Courts and Tribunals Service website.

In the Simple Procedure, the person who is making a claim against you is known as the claimant. You, the person the claim is being made against, are known as the respondent.

This envelope should contain:

- this Notice of Claim,
- a Timetable,
- a completed Claim Form,
- if you are able to apply to the court for time to pay, a Time to Pay Application,
- a blank Response Form.

### What should you do next?

You should read the completed Claim Form carefully, because it sets out the claim being made against you, including the identity of the claimant, what the claimant says happened and what the claimant wants from you if their claim is successful in court.

You should read the Timetable carefully. This sets out what the last date for a response is. This is the date by which, if you want to dispute the claim, you must send a completed Response Form to the court and to the claimant. If you do not do this, the court will almost certainly, if appropriate, award the claim to the claimant and order you to make a payment, including interest and expenses.

### What help is available?

If you are not sure what to do next, you can contact the office of the sheriff clerk at the sheriff court.

If you need help to decide how to respond to the claim, how to complete the Response Form or help by representing you in court at a hearing, you should contact a solicitor, the Citizens Advice Bureau or another advocacy or assistance organisation.

FORM 6B

# The Simple Procedure Service by Advertisement Application

This is a Service by Advertisement Application. You should complete this application if, after taking all reasonable steps to find out the respondent's address, you do not know what the respondent's address is.

If you complete this application and send it to court with the Claim Form, then the court may order the details of the claim to be publicised by advertisement on the Scottish Courts and Tribunals Service website.

Before completing this form, you should read rule 6.11 of the Simple Procedure Rules, which is about service by advertisement.

## A. ABOUT YOU

ⓘ Fill in information about you, so that the court knows who you are and how to contact you.

A1. Are you an individual, a company or an organisation?

☐ An individual (including a sole trader) (please fill out A2)

☐ A company or organisation (please fill out A3)

A2. What is your full name?

| | |
|---|---|
| Name | |
| Middle name | |
| Surname | |
| Trading name or representative capacity (if any) | |

A3. What is the name of the company or organisation?

| | |
|---|---|
| Name | |
| Company type | |
| Company registration number (if limited company or LLP) | |
| Trading name (if any) | |

**A4. What are your contact details?**

Address

City

Postcode

Email address

## B. SERVICE BY ADVERTISEMENT

**C1. What steps have you taken to find out the respondent's address?**

ⓘ The court will only grant this application if you have taken all reasonable steps to find out the respondent's address.

FORM 6C

# The Simple Procedure Confirmation of Formal Service

This is a Confirmation of Formal Service. It is used to inform the court when and how something has been formally served.

It must be completed and sent to the court whenever you are required to formally serve something on someone under the rules.

## A. ABOUT THE CASE

| | |
|---|---|
| Sheriff Court | |
| Claimant | |
| Representative | |
| Case reference number | |

## B. ABOUT YOU

### B1. What is your full name?

| | |
|---|---|
| Name | |
| Middle name | |
| Surname | |
| Firm or organisation | |

### B2. What is your profession?

☐ Sheriff officer

☐ Sheriff clerk

☐ Solicitor

## C. ABOUT FORMAL SERVICE

### C1. Who did you formally serve something on?

ⓘ You must identify the person who you were required to serve something on.

> _____

**C2.How did you formally serve it?**

ⓘ You must describe the method of formal service used.

☐ By a next-day postal service which records delivery

☐ Delivering it personally

☐ Leaving it in the hands of a resident or employee

☐ Depositing it in a home or place of business by letter box or other lawful way

☐ Leaving it at a home or place of business in a way likely to come to the person's attention

☐ Other

ⓘ If you have selected 'Other' or need to give more details about the manner of formal service, please set this out below.

> _____

**C3. When did you formally serve it?**

ⓘ You must identify when service was performed.

> _____

PART 7

**FORM 7A**

# The Simple Procedure
# Application for a Decision

This is an Application for a Decision. You can use this Application in two situations:

- to ask the court to make the orders which you asked for in your Claim Form if the responding party has not returned a Response Form to the court by the last date for a response, or

- to ask the court to dismiss a claim or make a decision awarding you some or all of your claim if the claim has been settled before the last date for a response.

Before completing this form, you should read rules 7.2 to 7.4 of the Simple Procedure Rules, which are about applying for a decision.

## A. ABOUT THE CASE

| | |
|---|---|
| Sheriff Court | |
| Claimant | |
| Representative | |
| Case reference number | |

## B. ABOUT YOU

B1. What is your full name?

| | |
|---|---|
| Name | |
| Middle name | |
| Surname | |
| Trading name or representative capacity (if any) | |

## C. ABOUT THE CASE

ⓘ Set out what has happened that entitles you to make this Application.

☐ No Response Form has been sent to the court by the last date for a response.

☐ The respondent has admitted the claim and wants to settle it by the last date for a response.

## D. ABOUT THE DECISION

ⓘ You must set out which orders you would like the sheriff to make.

☐ I would like the sheriff to dismiss the claim.

☐ I would like the sheriff to make all of the orders I asked for in the Claim Form.

☐ I would like the sheriff to make the following orders I asked for in the Claim Form:

**FORM 8A**

# The Simple Procedure
# Order of the Sheriff

This is an order of the sheriff in a case which you are a party in. You should **read it** and **follow it**.

You should also read Part 8 of the Simple Procedure Rules, which is about orders of the sheriff.

| | |
|---|---|
| **Sheriff Court:** | |
| **Date of order:** | |
| **Claimant:** | |
| **Respondent:** | |
| **Court ref no:** | |

[Text of order]

**Signed by:**

Sheriff of [sheriffdom] at [sheriff court]

FORM 9A

# The Simple Procedure
# Application to Pause

Before completing this form, you should read rule 9.2 of the Simple Procedure Rules, which is about applying to have a case paused.

**If you are applying to have the case paused:**

This is an Application to Pause.

If the court grants this application then any hearings arranged in this case will be cancelled and the case will not progress until it is restarted.

You must send fill in parts A, B and C of this application and send it to the court and to the other party in this case. So if you are the claimant, it must be sent to respondents. If you are a respondent it must be sent to the claimant.

**If you have been sent this application:**

This is an Application to Pause.

If the court grants this application then any hearings arranged in this case will be cancelled and the case will not progress until it is restarted.

You have received this application because someone has applied to have a simple procedure case you are involved in paused.

You must fill in part D of this application ('the reply') and return it to the court within 10 days of it being sent to you. The court will then do one of three things: pause the case, refuse to pause the case, or order a discussion in court.

## A. ABOUT THE CASE

| | |
|---|---|
| Sheriff Court | |
| Claimant | |
| Respondent | |
| Case reference number | |

## B. ABOUT YOU

B1. What is your full name?

| | |
|---|---|
| Name | |
| Middle name | |

| Surname | |
|---|---|

| Trading name or representative capacity (if any) | |
|---|---|

**B2. Which party in this case are you?**

☐ Claimant

☐ Respondent

## C. THE APPLICATION

ⓘ If you are the party replying to this application, do not fill in this part. You should fill in part D.

### C1. Why should this case be paused?

ⓘ The party making the application must set out why the court should pause the case.

### C2. When was this application sent to the court?

ⓘ Set out the date on which the application was sent to the court (i.e. the date on which the email was sent, or the date on which the application was posted).

ⓘ Any reply to this application must be sent to the court within 10 days of this application being sent.

## D. THE REPLY

ⓘ If you are the party making this application, do not fill in this part. You should fill in parts A, B and C.

### D1. What is your full name?

| Name | |
|---|---|

| Middle name | |
|---|---|

| Surname | |
|---|---|

| Trading name or representative capacity (if any) | |
|---|---|

### D2. Should this case be paused?

☐ Yes

☐ No

### D3. If you answered 'no', why should this case not be paused?

ⓘ If the party replying to the application objects to the case being paused, they should
set out why the court should not pause the case.

FORM 9B

# The Simple Procedure
# Application to Restart

Before completing this form, you should read rule 9.4 of the Simple Procedure Rules, which is about applying to have a paused case restarted.

**If you are applying to have the case restarted:**

This is an Application to Restart.

If the court grants this application then the progress of this case will resume and a hearing may be arranged.

You must fill in parts A, B and C of this application and send it to the court and to the other party in this case. So if you are the claimant, it must be sent to the responding party. If you are the responding party it must be sent to the claimant.

**If you have been sent this application:**

This is an Application to Restart.

If the court grants this application then the progress of this case will resume and a hearing may be arranged.

You have received this application because someone has applied to have a simple procedure case you are involved in restarted.

You must fill in part D of this application ('the reply') and return it to the court. The court will then do one of three things: restart the case, refuse to restart the case, or order a discussion in court.

## A. ABOUT THE CASE

| | |
|---|---|
| Sheriff Court | |
| Claimant | |
| Respondent | |
| Case reference number | |

## B. ABOUT YOU

B1. What is your full name?

| | |
|---|---|
| Name | |
| Middle name | |
| Surname | |

B2. Which party in this case are you?

☐ Claimant

☐ Respondent

## C. THE APPLICATION

ⓘ If you are the party replying to this application, do not fill in this part. You should fill in part D.

### C1. Why should this case be restarted?

ⓘ The party making the application must set out why the court should restart the case.

### C2. When was this application sent to the court?

ⓘ Set out the date on which the application was sent to the court (i.e. the date on which the email was sent, or the date on which the application was posted).

ⓘ Any reply to this application must be sent to the court within 10 days of this application being sent.

## D. THE REPLY

ⓘ If you are the party making this application, do not fill in this part. You should fill in parts A, B and C.

### D1. What is your full name?

| | |
|---|---|
| Name | |
| Middle name | |
| Surname | |
| Trading name or representative capacity (if any) | |

### D2. Should this case be restarted?

☐ Yes

☐ No

### D3. If you answered 'no', why should this case not be restarted?

ⓘ If the party replying to the application objects to the case being restarted, they should set out why the court should not restart the case.

**FORM 9C**

# The Simple Procedure
# Additional Respondent
# Application

Before completing this form, you should read rule 9.6 of the Simple Procedure Rules, which is about applying to be an additional respondent.

This is an Additional Respondent Application. If the court grants this application then the person making it will become a respondent in this simple procedure case. The court cannot refuse this application without ordering a discussion in court.

A draft Response Form must be attached to this application.

## A. ABOUT THE CASE

| | |
|---|---|
| Sheriff Court | |
| Claimant | |
| Respondent | |
| Case reference number | |

## B. ABOUT YOU

B1. What is your full name?

| | |
|---|---|
| Name | |
| Middle name | |
| Surname | |

## C. THE APPLICATION

C1. What is your interest in becoming a respondent?

ⓘ You must set out what your interest in this simple procedure case is and why the court should allow you to participate in it as a respondent.

FORM 9D

# The Simple Procedure
# Application to Amend

Before completing this form, you should read rule 9.7 of the Simple Procedure Rules, which is about applying to amend a Claim Form or Response Form.

**If you are applying to have a Form amended:**

This is an Application to Amend.

If the court grants this application then it will make the amendments you have asked for.

You must fill in parts A, B and C of this application and send it to the court and to the other party in this case. So if you are the claimant, it must be sent to the respondent. If you are the respondent it must be sent to the claimant.

**If you have been sent this application:**

This is an Application to Amend.

If the court grants this application then it will make the amendments which have been asked for.

You have received this application because someone has applied to have a Form amended in a simple procedure case you are involved in.

You must fill in part D of this application ('the reply') and return it to the court within 10 days of it being sent to you. The court will then do one of three things: allow the amendment, refuse the amendment, or order a discussion in court.

## A. ABOUT THE CASE

| | |
|---|---|
| Sheriff Court | |
| Claimant | |
| Representative | |
| Case reference number | |

## B. ABOUT YOU

B1. What is your full name?

| | |
|---|---|
| Name | |
| Middle name | |

| Surname | |
|---|---|

| Trading name or representative capacity (if any) | |
|---|---|

**B2. Which party in this case are you?**

☐ Claimant

☐ Respondent

## C. THE APPLICATION

ⓘ If you are the party replying to this application, do not fill in this part. You should fill in part D.

**C1. What amendments should be made?**

ⓘ The party making the application must set out the amendments they want to be made to the Claim Form or Response Form.

ⓘ It might be best to do this as a track-changes version of the original text, attached to this application.

**C2. Why should these amendments be made?**

ⓘ Set out why the court should allow these amendments to be made?

**C3. When was this application sent to the court?**

ⓘ Set out the date on which the application was sent to the court (i.e. the date on which the email was sent, or the date on which the application was posted).

ⓘ Any reply to this application must be sent to the court within 10 days of this application being sent.

## D. THE REPLY

ⓘ If you are the party making this application, do not fill in this part. You should fill in parts A, B and C.

**D1. What is your full name?**

1266

| Name | |
|---|---|
| Middle name | |
| Surname | |
| Trading name or representative capacity (if any) | |

**D2. Should these amendments be allowed?**

☐ Yes

☐ No

**D3. If you answered 'no', why should these amendments not be allowed?**

ⓘ If the party replying to the application objects to these amendments, they should set out why.

FORM 9E

# The Simple Procedure
# Abandonment Notice

Before completing this form, you should read rule 9.8 of the Simple Procedure Rules, which is about applying to abandon a case.

| If you are abandoning your claim: | If you have been sent this notice: |
|---|---|
| This is an Abandonment Notice. | This is an Abandoment Notice. |
| You must fill in this Notice and sent it to the court and the respondent. | You have been sent it because the claimant has abandoned a claim made against you. |
| You will be sent written orders. | You will be sent further written orders. |

## A. ABOUT THE CASE

| | |
|---|---|
| Sheriff Court | |
| Claimant | |
| Respondent | |
| Case reference number | |

## B. ABOUT YOU

B1. What is your full name?

| | |
|---|---|
| Name | |
| Middle name | |
| Surname | |

## C. ABANDONMENT

C1. Which respondent are you abandoning your claim against?

| | |
|---|---|
| Name of respondent | |

ⓘ You must check the box below to confirm that you are abandoning your claim against this respondent and that you are aware that this will normally mean that you are ordered to pay that respondent a sum of expenses.

☐ I am abandoning my claim against this respondent.

FORM 9F

# The Simple Procedure
# Application to Represent

Before completing this form, you should read rule 9.9 of the Simple Procedure Rules, which is about applying to represent a deceased or incapacitated party.

**If you are applying to represent a party:**

This is an Application to Represent.

If the court grants this application then you will be allowed to represent a deceased or legally incapacitated party in this simple procedure case.

You must send fill in parts A, B and C of this application and send it to the court and to the other party in this case. So if you are the claimant, it must be sent to the respondent. If you are the respondent it must be sent to the claimant.

**If you have been sent this application:**

This is an Application to Represent.

If the court grants this application then it will allow someone to represent a deceased or legally incapacitated party in this simple procedure case.

You have received this application because someone has applied to represent a dead or legally incapacitated party in a simple procedure case you are involved in.

You must fill in part D of this application ('the reply') and return it to the court within 10 days of it being sent to you. The court will then do one of three things: allow that person to represent the party, not allow that person to represent that party, or order a discussion in court.

## A. ABOUT THE CASE

| | |
|---|---|
| Sheriff Court | |
| Claimant | |
| Respondent | |
| Case reference number | |

## B. ABOUT YOU

B1. What is your full name?

| | |
|---|---|
| Name | |

| Middle name | |
|---|---|

| Surname | |
|---|---|

| Trading name or representative capacity (if any) | |
|---|---|

## B2. Which party in this case would you like to represent?

| Name | |
|---|---|

| Middle name | |
|---|---|

| Surname | |
|---|---|

| Trading name (if any) | |
|---|---|

## B3. Which party in this case is that person?

☐ Claimant

☐ Respondent

## C. THE APPLICATION

ⓘ If you are the party replying to this application, do not fill in this part. You should fill in part D.

## C1. Why should the court let you represent that person in this case?

ⓘ Set out what has happened to the party in this simple procedure case, and why you represent that person or that person's estate.

ⓘ If you have any documents (e.g. a death certificate) which might help the court make a decision in this application, you should send them to the court with this application.

## C2. When was this application sent to the court?

ⓘ Set out the date on which the application was sent to the court (i.e. the date on which the email was sent, or the date on which the application was posted).

ⓘ Any reply to this application must be sent to the court within 10 days of this application being sent.

## D. THE REPLY

ⓘ If you are the party making this application, do not fill in this part. You should fill in parts A, B and C.

## D1. What is your full name?

| | |
|---:|---|
| Name | |
| Middle name | |
| Surname | |
| Trading name or representative capacity (if any) | |

**D2. Should this person be allowed to represent this party?**

☐   Yes

☐   No

**D3. If you answered 'no', why should this person not be allowed to represent this party?**

ⓘ If the party replying to the application objects, they should set out why the court should not allow this person to represent this party.

FORM 9G
# The Simple Procedure
# Incidental Orders
# Application

Before completing this form, you should read rule 9.10 of the Simple Procedure Rules, which is about applying for the sheriff to make incidental orders.

**If you are applying for the sheriff to make orders:**

This is an Incidental Orders Application.

You can use this Application to ask the sheriff to make any orders that are not specifically provided for by the Simple Procedure Rules.

**If you have been sent this application:**

This is an Incidental Orders Application.

If the court grants this application then it will make the orders which have been asked for below.

You must fill in part D of this application ('the reply') and return it to court within 10 days of it being sent to you. The court will then either grant the application and send written orders to the parties, or make no orders.

## A. ABOUT THE CASE

| | |
|---|---|
| Sheriff Court | |
| Claimant | |
| Respondent | |
| Case reference number | |

## B. ABOUT YOU

B1. What is your full name?

| | |
|---|---|
| Name | |
| Middle name | |
| Surname | |

B2. Which party in this case are you?

☐ Claimant

☐ Respondent

## C. THE APPLICATION

ⓘ If you are the party replying to this application, do not fill in this part. You should fill in part D.

### C1. What orders would you like the court to make?

ⓘ The party making the application must set out the terms of the orders the court is being asked to make.

 

### C2. Why should the court make these orders?

ⓘ The party making the application must set out why the court should make the orders asked for.

 

### When was this application sent to the court?

ⓘ Set out the date on which the application was sent to the court (i.e. the date on which the email was sent, or the date on which the application was posted).

ⓘ Any reply to this application must be sent to the court within 10 days of this application being sent.

 

## D. THE REPLY

ⓘ If you are the party making this application, do not fill in this part. You should fill in parts A, B and C.

### D1. What is your full name?

| | |
|---|---|
| Name | |
| Middle name | |
| Surname | |
| Trading name or representative capacity (if any) | |

### D2. Should the court make these orders?

☐ Yes

☐ No

**D3. If you answered 'no', why should the court not make these orders?**

ⓘ If the party replying to the application objects to proposed orders, they should set out why the court should not make these orders.

FORM 10A

# The Simple Procedure
# List of Evidence Form

Before completing this form, you should read Part 10 of the Simple Procedure Rules, which is about documents and other evidence.

This is the List of Evidence Form. Parties must send a copy to each other and to the court at least 14 days before the hearing.

All documents and other evidence must be lodged with the court by sending them to the sheriff clerk at least 14 days before the hearing. If you think that there will be practical difficulties involved with sending evidence to the court (e.g. because of size, or because something might go off) you must contact the sheriff clerk before sending that evidence to be lodged.

## A. ABOUT THE CASE

| | |
|---|---|
| Sheriff Court | |
| Claimant | |
| Respondent | |
| Case reference number | |

## B. ABOUT YOU

B1. What is your full name?

| | |
|---|---|
| Name | |
| Middle name | |
| Surname | |
| Trading name or representative capacity (if any) | |

B2. Which party in this case are you?

☐   Claimant

☐   Respondent

## C. LIST OF EVIDENCE

ⓘ Set out all evidence or other documents you are lodging with the court.

ⓘ Set out a brief description of each item of evidence and explain its relationship to the case. This means the reason why you think this item of evidence is necessary for the court to make a decision in this case.

ⓘ It is useful to the court if documents and other evidence being lodged can be numbered using the numbers (C1, C2, etc) below. If bigger documents do not already have page numbers, then adding page numbers can help the court read and understand these documents.

ⓘ If you think that you need more than 10 items of evidence, please fill out a further List of Evidence Form and attach it to this one.

**C1. Item of evidence**

| Brief description of document or other evidence | |
|---|---|
| Relationship to the case | |

**C2. Item of evidence**

| Brief description of document or other evidence | |
|---|---|
| Relationship to the case | |

**C3. Item of evidence**

| Brief description of document or other evidence | |
|---|---|
| Relationship to the case | |

**C4. Item of evidence**

| Brief description of document or other evidence | |
|---|---|
| Relationship to the case | |

**C5. Item of evidence**

| Brief description of document or other evidence | |
|---|---|
| Relationship to the case | |

## C6. Item of evidence

Brief description of
document or other evidence

Relationship to the case

## C7. Item of evidence

Brief description of
document or other evidence

Relationship to the case

## C8. Item of evidence

Brief description of
document or other evidence

Relationship to the case

## C9. Item of evidence

Brief description of
document or other evidence

Relationship to the case

## C10. Item of evidence

Brief description of
document or other evidence

Relationship to the case

FORM 10B

# The Simple Procedure Recovery of Documents Application

**If you are applying for the sheriff to make orders:**

**If you have been sent this Application:**

This is a Recovery of Documents Application.

If you do not possess a document that you want to lodge with the court, you can use this Application to ask the court for an order to recover documents.

That order tells the person who has the document to send it to the court.

This is a Recovery of Documents Application.

If the court grants this application then it will make the orders which have been asked for below.

You must fill in part D of this application ('the reply') and return it to court within 10 days of it being sent to you.

The court will then either grant the application and send an order to recover documents to the parties, refuse the application and make no orders, or order you to appear at a discussion in court where the sheriff will consider whether to make an order.

## A. ABOUT THE CASE

| | |
|---|---|
| Sheriff Court | |
| Claimant | |
| Respondent | |
| Case reference number | |

## B. ABOUT YOU

B1. What is your full name?

| | |
|---|---|
| Name | |

| Middle name | |
|---|---|

| Surname | |
|---|---|

## B2. Which party in this case are you?

☐ Claimant

☐ Respondent

## C. THE APPLICATION

ⓘ If you are the party replying to this application, do not fill in this part. You should fill in part D.

## C1. What documents would you like to recover?

ⓘ The party making the application must identify every document that the party wants to recover. Use a new line for each document.

## C2. Who has these documents?

ⓘ The party making the application must set out who possesses each of the documents.

## C3. Why should the court make an order to recover these documents?

ⓘ The party making the application must set out why the court should make an order for recovery of these documents.

## C4. When was this application sent to the court?

ⓘ Set out the date on which the application was sent to the court (i.e. the date on which the email was sent, or the date on which the application was posted).

ⓘ Any reply to this application must be sent to the court within 10 days of this application being sent.

## D. THE REPLY

ⓘ If you are the party making this application, do not fill in this part. You should fill in parts A, B and C.

### D1. What is your full name?

Name

Middle name

Surname

Trading name or representative capacity (if any)

### D2. Should the court make an order to recover these documents?

☐ Yes

☐ No

### D3. If you answered 'no', why should the court not make an order to recover these documents?

ⓘ If the party replying to the application objects to the proposed order, they should set out why the court should not make an order to recover these documents.

**FORM 10C**

# The Simple Procedure
# Application to Open
# Confidential Document

**If you are applying for the sheriff to make orders:**

This is an Application to Open Confidential Document.

It is used where someone has claimed that documents are confidential in response to an order to recover documents or a special order to recover documents. That person has given the documents to the court in a sealed envelope.

You can use this Application to ask the court to open the sealed envelope so that the documents can be used in your simple procedure case.

**If you have been sent this Application:**

This is an Application to Open Confidential Document.

If the court grants this application then it will make the orders which have been asked for below.

You must fill in part D of this application ('the reply') and return it to court within 10 days of it being sent to you.

The court will then either grant the application and allow the sealed envelope containing the confidential document to be opened, refuse the application and make no orders, or order you to appear at a discussion in court where the sheriff will consider whether to make an order.

## A. ABOUT THE CASE

| | |
|---|---|
| Sheriff Court | |
| Claimant | |
| Respondent | |
| Case reference number | |

## B. ABOUT YOU

**B1. What is your full name?**

| | |
|---|---|
| Name | |
| Middle name | |

| Surname | |
|---------|---|

**B2. What is your role in this case?**

☐ Claimant

☐ Respondent

## C. THE APPLICATION

ⓘ If you are replying to this application, do not fill in this part. You should fill in part D.

**C1. Which sealed envelope would you like to open?**

ⓘ The party making the application must identify which sealed envelope they wish to have opened.

[Include the date on which the envelope was sent the court and who sent it]

**C3. Why should the court make an order allowing this sealed envelope to be opened?**

ⓘ The party making the application must set out why the court should make an order allowing the sealed envelope to be opened.

[Give reasons why the envelope should be opened]

**C4. When was this application sent to the court?**

ⓘ Set out the date on which the application was sent to the court (i.e. the date on which the email was sent, or the date on which the application was posted).

ⓘ Any reply to this application must be sent to the court within 10 days of this application being sent.

## D. THE REPLY

ⓘ If you are the party making this application, do not fill in this part. You should fill in parts A, B and C.

**D1. What is your full name?**

| Name | |
|------|---|
| Middle name | |
| Surname | |
| Trading name or representative capacity (if any) | |

D2. What is your role in this case?

☐ Claimant

☐ Respondent

☐ The person who claimed that the document is confidential

D3. Should the court make an order allowing the sealed envelope to be opened?

☐ Yes

☐ No

D3. If you answered 'no', why should the court not make an order allowing the sealed envelope to be opened?

ⓘ If the party replying to the application objects to the proposed order, they should set out why the court should not make an order allowing the sealed envelope to be opened.

FORM 10D

# The Simple Procedure
# Special Recovery of
# Documents Application

**If you are applying for the sheriff to make orders:**

**If you have been sent this Application:**

This is a Special Recovery of Documents Application.

You can use this Application to ask the court for a special order to recover documents. The court will only grant the Application if it has already made an order to recover documents but that has been unsuccessful.

The special order appoints someone to recover the documents on behalf of the court. The person appointed is normally a solicitor.

This is a Special Recovery of Documents Application.

If the court grants this application then it will make the orders which have been asked for below.

You must fill in part D of this application ('the reply') and return it to court within 10 days of it being sent to you.

The court will then either grant the application and send a special order to recover documents to the parties, refuse the application and make no orders, or order you to appear at a discussion in court where the sheriff will consider whether to make an order.

## A. ABOUT THE CASE

| | |
|---|---|
| Sheriff Court | |
| Claimant | |
| Respondent | |
| Case reference number | |

## B. ABOUT YOU

B1. What is your full name?

| | |
|---|---|
| Name | |
| Middle name | |

| Surname | |
|---|---|

**B2. Which party in this case are you?**

☐ Claimant

☐ Respondent

**C. THE APPLICATION**

ⓘ If you are the party replying to this application, do not fill in this part. You should fill in part D.

**C1. When did the court make an order to recover documents?**

ⓘ Set out the date of the court's order.

| |
|---|

**C2. When did you serve the order to recover documents on the person who possesses the documents?**

ⓘ Set out the date of formal service on that person.

| |
|---|

**C3. Why was the order to recover documents unsuccessful?**

ⓘ Tick the appropriate box.

☐ The person who possesses the documents did not reply to the order.

☐ The person who possesses the documents sent some documents to the court, but these are not all of the documents I want to recover.

☐ I am not satisfied with the explanation given by the person who possesses the documents for not producing them to the court. These are my reasons:

[set out reasons why you are not satisfied with the explanation]

**C4. Who do you want the court to appoint as the commissioner?**

ⓘ The commissioner is the person appointed by the court to carry out the recovery under a special order to recover documents.

ⓘ The commissioner is usually a solicitor, but the court may appoint any suitable person.

ⓘ The court may decide not to appoint the person you propose, and appoint someone else instead.

| Name | |
|---|---|
| Middle name | |
| Surname | |
| Profession | |

C4. When was this application sent to the court?

   ⓘ Set out the date on which the application was sent to the court (i.e. the date on which the email was sent, or the date on which the application was posted).

   ⓘ Any reply to this application must be sent to the court within 10 days of this application being sent.

>  

## D. THE REPLY

   ⓘ If you are the party making this application, do not fill in this part. You should fill in parts A, B and C.

D1. What is your full name?

| | |
|---|---|
| Name | |
| Middle name | |
| Surname | |
| Trading name or representative capacity (if any) | |

D2. Should the court make a special order to recover these documents?

☐   Yes

☐   Yes, but I object to the appointment of the proposed commissioner

☐   No

D3. If you answered 'yes, but I object to the appointment of the proposed commissioner', why should the court not appoint that person as commissioner?

   ⓘ If the party replying to the application objects to the proposed order, they should set out why the court should not appoint that person as commissioner.

>  

**D3. If you answered 'no', why should the court not make a special order to recover these documents?**

ⓘ If the party replying to the application objects to the proposed order, they should set out why the court should not make a special order to recover these documents.

FORM 11A

# The Simple Procedure
# List of Witnesses Form

Before completing this form, you should read Part 11 of the Simple Procedure Rules, which is about witnesses.

This is the List of Witnesses Form. Parties must send a copy to each other and to the court at least 14 days before the hearing.

### A. ABOUT THE CASE

| | |
|---|---|
| Sheriff Court | |
| Claimant | |
| Respondent | |
| Case reference number | |

### B. ABOUT YOU

B1. What is your full name?

| | |
|---|---|
| Name | |
| Middle name | |
| Surname | |
| Trading name or representative capacity (if any) | |

B2. Which party in this case are you?

☐ Claimant

☐ Respondent

### C. LIST OF WITNESSES

ⓘ Set out any witnesses you want to appear at the hearing. You do not need to list yourself or the other party.

ⓘ You may need to cite witnesses using the Witness Citation Form, but you should only cite a witness if you cannot otherwise arrange for that witness to appear at the hearing.

ⓘ Set out the name and address of each witness and explain their relationship to the case. This means the reason why you think this witness's evidence is necessary for the court to make a decision in this case.

ⓘ If you think that you need more than 4 witnesses, please fill out a further List of Witnesses Form and attach it to this one.

## C1. Witness

| | |
|---|---|
| Name of witness | |
| Address of witness | |
| Relationship of the witness to the case | |

## C2. Witness

| | |
|---|---|
| Name of witness | |
| Address of witness | |
| Relationship of the witness to the case | |

## C3. Witness

| | |
|---|---|
| Name of witness | |
| Address of witness | |
| Relationship of the witness to the case | |

## C4. Witness

| Name of witness | |
|---|---|
| Address of witness | |
| Relationship of the witness to the case | |

FORM 11B

# The Simple Procedure
# Witness Citation Notice

You have been cited as a witness in a case in the sheriff court. The details of the case and the date on which you should come to court are below, at Part B.

**It is very important that you attend court and you should note that failure to do so may result in a warrant being granted for your arrest.**

You may claim back money which you have had to spend and any earnings you have lost within certain specified limits, because you have to come to court on the above date. These may be paid to you if you claim within specified time limits. Claims should be made to the person who has asked you to attend court. Proof of any loss of earnings should be given to that person.

If you wish your travelling expenses to be paid before you go to court, you should apply for payment to the person who has asked you to attend court (listed below at C2).

If you:

– would like to know more about being a witness

– are a child under the age of 18

– think you may be a vulnerable witness within the meaning of section 11(1) of the Vulnerable Witnesses (Scotland) Act 2004 (that is someone the court considers may be less able to give their evidence due to mental disorder or fear or distress connected to giving your evidence at the court hearing).

you should contact the person who cited you (listed below at C2) for further information.

If you are a vulnerable witness (including a child under the age of 18) then you should be able to use a special measure (such measures include use of a screen, a live TV link or a supporter, or a commissioner) to help you give evidence.

## A. ABOUT THE CASE

| | |
|---|---|
| Sheriff Court | |
| Claimant | |
| Respondent | |
| Case reference number | |

## B. WHEN AND WHERE YOU MUST COME TO COURT

ⓘ You must come to the court listed below on the date listed below.

The Sheriff Court you must come to is: 

Address 

Postcode 

You must come to the Sheriff Court on this date: 

## C. ABOUT THIS CITATION

ⓘ This part contains information about the party who has cited you as a witness.

### C1. Who formally served this Witness Citation Notice?

Name 

Middle name 

Surname 

Firm or organisation 

Solicitor or sheriff officer 

### C2. Who is citing you as a witness?

ⓘ If the person who cited you is represented by a solicitor, they should list the solicitor's details here. If they do not, they should list their own details.

Name 

Address 

Postcode 

Firm or organisation

FORM 11C
# The Simple Procedure
# Child Witness Notice

This is a Child Witness Notice.

It is used to tell the court that a witness who is to give evidence in the simple procedure case is a child witness (someone who is under 18 when the simple procedure case begins).

It asks the sheriff to authorise the use of special measures to take the child witness's evidence, or to decide that the child witness is to give evidence without any special measures.

## A. ABOUT THE CASE

| | |
|---|---|
| Sheriff Court | |
| Claimant | |
| Respondent | |
| Case reference number | |

## B. ABOUT YOU

### B1. What is your full name?

| | |
|---|---|
| Name | |
| Middle name | |
| Surname | |

### B2. What is your role in this case?

☐ Claimant

☐ Respondent

## C. THE NOTICE

### C1. What is the full name of the child witness?

| | |
|---|---|
| Name | |
| Middle name | |

Surname [                                    ]

C2. What is the child witness's date of birth?

Date of birth [                                    ]

C3. If the child witness is over 18 when this Notice is completed, was the child witness under 18 when the simple procedure case began?

☐   Yes

☐   No

C3. What order should the court make about the child witness?

☐   The court should authorise the use of the special measure(s) mentioned in part D

ⓘ You should also complete parts D and E.

☐   The court should order that the child witness is to give evidence without the benefit of any special measure

ⓘ You should also complete part E.

C4. Why should the court make this order?

ⓘ You should set out the reasons why the court should make this order.

[                                                                  ]

C5. When was this Notice sent to the court?

ⓘ Set out the date on which the notice was sent to the court (i.e. the date on which the email was sent, or the date on which the notice was posted).

[                                                                  ]

## D. THE SPECIAL MEASURES

ⓘ The special measures that the court may make are listed in rule 11.6 of the Simple Procedure Rules.

**D1. What special measures would be most appropriate for taking the evidence of this child witness?**

ⓘ You may select as many special measures as you think are appropriate.

☐ allowing the child witness to give evidence before an independent person

ⓘ This means that the child witness would give evidence before an independent person appointed by the court, rather than coming to court to give evidence.

☐ allowing the child witness to give evidence by live television link

☐ allowing the child witness to use a screen while giving evidence

☐ allowing the child witness to be supported by someone while giving evidence

**D2. Why do you think the special measures you have selected would be most appropriate for taking the evidence of this child witness?**

## E. VIEWS OF THE CHILD WITNESS AND PARENT

ⓘ In completing this Notice, you must take into account the views of the child witness (if the child witness is of sufficient age and maturity to form a view) and the child witness's parent.

ⓘ The parent of a child witness is any person who has parental responsibilities within the meaning of section 1(3) of the Children (Scotland) Act 1995.

ⓘ Section 15(3)(a) of the Vulnerable Witnesses (Scotland) Act 2004 says that a child witness is presumed to be of sufficient age and maturity to form a view if aged 12 or older.

ⓘ Section 15(3)(b) says that if the views of the child witness and the views of the witness's parent are inconsistent, the views of the witness are to be given greater weight.

**E1. Has the child witness expressed a view about how they should give evidence?**

☐ Yes

ⓘ If the answer is 'yes', complete E3.

☐ No

ⓘ If the answer is 'no', complete E2.

**E2. Why has the child witness not expressed a view about how they should give evidence?**

ⓘ Set out why no view has been expressed. For example:

    – the child witness may not be of sufficient age or maturity to do so

    – the child witness may not wish to do so

**E3. What are the views of the child witness?**

ⓘ Set out the views of the child witness. In particular, set out:

    – whether the child witness wishes to use a special measure to give evidence

    – the special measure that the child considers most appropriate

    – whether the child witness wishes to give evidence without the benefit of any
       special measures

**E4. What are the views of the child witness's parent?**

ⓘ Set out the views of the child witness's parent. In particular, set out:

    – whether the parent considers that the child witness should use a special measure
       to give evidence

    – the special measure that the parent considers most appropriate

    – whether the parent considers that the child witness should give evidence without
       the benefit of any special measures

**FORM 11D**
# The Simple Procedure Vulnerable Witness Application

This is a Vulnerable Witness Application.

It is used to ask the court to decide if a witness who is to give evidence in the simple procedure case is a vulnerable witness.

If the sheriff agrees that the witness is a vulnerable witness, it also asks the sheriff to authorise the use of special measures to take the vulnerable witness's evidence.

## A. ABOUT THE CASE

| | |
|---|---|
| Sheriff Court | |
| Claimant | |
| Respondent | |
| Case reference number | |

## B. ABOUT YOU

**B1. What is your full name?**

| | |
|---|---|
| Name | |
| Middle name | |
| Surname | |

**B2. What is your role in this case?**

☐ Claimant

☐ Respondent

## C. THE APPLICATION

**C1. What is the full name of the witness?**

| | |
|---|---|
| Name | |
| Middle name | |

Surname ⌈                                                  ⌉

## C2. Why do you think that the witness is a vulnerable witness?

ⓘ You should set out the reasons why you think the witness is a vulnerable witness.

ⓘ The matters that the court must take into account in deciding whether the witness is a vulnerable witness are set out in section 11(2) of the Vulnerable Witnesses (Scotland) Act 2004.

## C3. When was this Application sent to the court?

ⓘ Set out the date on which the Application was sent to the court (i.e. the date on which the email was sent, or the date on which the notice was posted).

## D. THE SPECIAL MEASURES

ⓘ The special measures that the court may make are listed in rule 11.6 of the Simple Procedure Rules.

## D1. What special measures would be most appropriate for taking the evidence of the witness?

ⓘ You may select as many special measures as you think are appropriate.

☐ allowing the witness to give evidence before an independent person

ⓘ This means that the witness would give evidence before an independent person appointed by the court, rather than coming to court to give evidence.

☐ allowing the witness to give evidence by live television link

☐ allowing the witness to use a screen while giving evidence

☐ allowing the witness to be supported by someone while giving evidence

## D2. Why do you think the special measures you have selected would be most appropriate for taking the evidence of the witness?

## E. VIEWS OF THE WITNESS

&#9432; In completing this Application, you must take into account the views of the witness.

### E1. Has the witness expressed a view about how they should give evidence?

☐   Yes

&#9432; If the answer is 'yes', complete E3.

☐   No

&#9432; If the answer is 'no', complete E2.

### E2. Why has the witness not expressed a view about how they should give evidence?

&#9432; Set out why no view has been expressed. For example, the witness may not wish to do so.

```
```

### E3. What are the views of the witness?

&#9432; Set out the views of the witness. In particular, set out:

  –   whether the witness wishes to use a special measure to give evidence

  –   the special measure that the witness considers most appropriate

```
```

FORM 11E

# The Simple Procedure
# Special Measures Review
# Application

This is a Special Measures Review Application.

It is used where the court has decided that a child witness or a vulnerable witness should use a special measure to give evidence.

Its purpose is to ask the court to change the arrangements that have been made for the witness to give evidence.

## A. ABOUT THE CASE

| | |
|---|---|
| Sheriff Court | |
| Claimant | |
| Respondent | |
| Case reference number | |

## B. ABOUT YOU

B1. What is your full name?

| | |
|---|---|
| Name | |
| Middle name | |
| Surname | |

B2. What is your role in this case?

☐ Claimant

☐ Respondent

## C. ABOUT THE WITNESS

C1. What is the full name of the witness?

| | |
|---|---|
| Name | |
| Middle name | |

Surname [                                                    ]

**C2. Is the witness a child witness or a vulnerable witness?**

☐   Child witness

☐   Vulnerable witness

**C3. What special measures has the court authorised to be used in taking the evidence of the witness?**

ⓘ Select as many special measures as the court has authorised.

☐   allowing the witness to give evidence before an independent person

☐   allowing the witness to give evidence by live television link

☐   allowing the witness to use a screen while giving evidence

☐   allowing the witness to be supported by someone while giving evidence

**D. THE APPLICATION**

**D1. How should the court change the current arrangements?**

ⓘ Set out the changes you want the court to make.

ⓘ The court may:

– vary a special measure

– add a new special measure

– substitute a new special measure for an existing one

– delete a special measure

– revoke the order authorising the use of special measures entirely

[                                                    ]

**D2. Why do you think the proposed changes would be most appropriate for taking the evidence of the witness?**

[                                                    ]

PART 11

**D3. When was this Application sent to the court?**

ⓘ Set out the date on which the Application was sent to the court (i.e. the date on which the email was sent, or the date on which the notice was posted).

---

### E. VIEWS OF THE WITNESS

ⓘ In completing this Application, you must take into account the views of the witness.

ⓘ You only need to complete E4 if the witness is a child witness.

– The parent of a child witness is any person who has parental responsibilities within the meaning of section 1(3) of the Children (Scotland) Act 1995.

– Section 15(3)(a) of the Vulnerable Witnesses (Scotland) Act 2004 says that a child witness is presumed to be of sufficient age and maturity to form a view if aged 12 or older.

– Section 15(3)(b) says that if the views of the child witness and the views of the witness's parent are inconsistent, the views of the witness are to be given greater weight.

**E1. Has the witness expressed a view about the proposed changes to how they should give evidence?**

☐ Yes

ⓘ If the answer is 'yes', complete E3.

☐ No

ⓘ If the answer is 'no', complete E2.

**E2. Why has the witness not expressed a view about the proposed changes to how they should give evidence?**

ⓘ Set out why no view has been expressed. For example:

– a child witness may not be of sufficient age or maturity to do so

– the witness may not wish to do so

**E3. What are the views of the witness?**

ⓘ Set out the views of the witness. In particular, set out whether the witness agrees with the proposed changes.

1303

**E4. If the witness is a child witness, what are the views of the child witness's parent?**

ⓘ Set out the views of the child witness's parent. In particular, set out whether the parent agrees with the proposed changes.

FORM 13A
# The Simple Procedure
# Decision Form

This is the Decision Form. It contains the terms of the decision that the sheriff has made at the end of the simple procedure case. Part 13 of the Simple Procedure Rules is about the decision of the sheriff.

This Decision Form can be used to enforce the decision made by the sheriff. Part 15 of the Simple Procedure Rules is about how to enforce this decision.

---

**THIS EXTRACT DECREE IS WARRANT FOR ALL LAWFUL EXECUTION THEREON.**

Execution of this decree is not lawful:

- within 28 days from the date the Decision Form was sent

- where the decision is being appealed

- where the decision has been recalled.

---

**A. ABOUT THE CASE**

| | |
|---|---|
| **Sheriff Court** | |
| **Claimant** | |
| Address | |
| City | |
| Postcode | |
| **Respondent** | |
| Address | |
| City | |
| Postcode | |
| **Case reference number** | |

**B. THE DECISION OF THE SHERIFF**

ⓘ This part sets out the orders which the sheriff has made when deciding the case.

## C. EXPENSES

ⓘ This part sets out any orders which the sheriff has made about the expenses of the case.

## D. SIGNATURE

Signature of sheriff clerk

Date sent

FORM 13B
# The Simple Procedure
# Application to Recall

Before completing this form, you should read rules 13.5 to 13.7 of the Simple Procedure Rules, which are about recalling a decision.

**If you are applying to have a decision recalled:**

This is an Application to Recall.

You can use this Application to ask the sheriff to recall a decision made because of your failure to attend a hearing or take a step in simple procedure.

If the sheriff made a decision because you did not send a Response Form to court before the last date for a response, you must also include a completed Response Form with this application.

**If you have been sent this application:**

This is an Application to Recall.

If the court grants this application then a decision made in this case may be recalled.

You have received this application because someone has applied to have a decision in a simple procedure case you are involved in recalled.

You must fill in part D of this application ('the reply') and return it to the court within 10 days of it being sent to you. The court will then do one of three things: recall the case, refuse to recall the case, or order a discussion in court.

## A. ABOUT THE CASE

| | |
|---|---|
| Sheriff Court | |
| Claimant | |
| Respondent | |
| Case reference number | |

## B. ABOUT YOU

B1. What is your full name?

| | |
|---|---|
| Name | |
| Middle name | |
| Surname | |

| Trading name or representative capacity (if any) | |
|---|---|

## B2. Which party in this case are you?

☐ Claimant

☐ Respondent

## C. THE APPLICATION

ⓘ If you are the party replying to this application, do not fill in this part. You should fill in part D.

### C1. Why should this case be recalled?

ⓘ The party making the application must set out why the court should recall the case.

| |
|---|
| |

### C2. When was this application sent to the court?

ⓘ Set out the date on which the application was sent to the court (i.e. the date on which the email was sent, or the date on which the application was posted).

ⓘ Any reply to this application must be sent to the court within 10 days of this application being sent.

| |
|---|
| |

## D. THE REPLY

ⓘ If you are the party making this application, do not fill in this part. You should fill in parts A, B and C.

### D1. What is your full name?

| Name | |
|---|---|
| Middle name | |
| Surname | |
| Trading name or representative capacity (if any) | |

### D2. Should this case be recalled?

☐ Yes

☐ No

### D3. If you answered 'no', why should this case not be recalled?

ⓘ If the party replying to the application objects to the case being recalled, they should set out why the court should not recall the case.

FORM 15A

# The Simple Procedure
# Charge to Pay

This is a Charge to Pay. The purpose of this Charge to Pay is to give you one last chance to comply with a decision made in a simple procedure case.

## A. ABOUT THE CASE

| | |
|---|---|
| Sheriff Court | |
| Claimant | |
| Respondent | |
| Case reference number | |

## B. ABOUT THE CHARGE

| | |
|---|---|
| Name of sheriff officer | |
| Address | |
| Witness | |
| Method of formal service | |

## C. ABOUT THE DECISION

ⓘ This Part contains information about the decision which the court made.

ⓘ You must comply with this decision the period set out below or there may be enforcement action taken against you and your property.

ⓘ If you do not comply with this decision, you may have your bank accounts frozen or earnings arrested. If you have debts amounting to over £3,000, you may be sequestrated (made bankrupt).

ⓘ Note that interest will continue to run on any sum set out below until you pay this sum.

| | |
|---|---|
| Date of decision | |

| Details of decision | The sum now due to the claimant is: |
| --- | --- |
| | Principal Sum |
| | Interest to date |
| | Expenses |
| | TOTAL |
| | Less paid |
| | Agent's fee |
| | Expenses of sheriff officer |
| | TOTAL SUM NOW DUE |

## D. THE CHARGE

**YOU ARE CHARGED TO COMPLY WITH THIS DECISION WITHIN** | 14 / 28 days

**IF YOU ARE NOT SURE WHAT TO DO ABOUT THIS CHARGE YOU SHOULD CONSULT A SOLICITOR, CITIZENS ADVICE BUREAU OR OTHER LOCAL ADVICE AGENCY IMMEDIATELY**

FORM 15B

# The Simple Procedure Alternative Decision Application

Before completing this form, you should read rule 15.5 of the Simple Procedure Rules, which is about applying to ask the court to make an alternative decision.

**If you are applying for an alternative order:**

This is an Alternative Decision Application. It can be used when the sheriff made a decision ordering the respondent to deliver something to the claimant or do something for the claimant. If the court alternatively ordered the respondent to pay the claimant a sum of money, then this application can be used to ask the court to make that order.

You must send fill in parts A, B and C of this application and send it to the court and to the other party in this case. So if you are the claimant, it must be sent to the respondent. If you are the respondent it must be sent to the claimant.

## A. ABOUT THE CASE

| | |
|---|---|
| Sheriff Court | |
| Claimant | |
| Respondent | |
| Case reference number | |
| Date of Decision Form | |

## B. ABOUT YOU

B1. What is your full name?

| | |
|---|---|
| Name | |
| Middle name | |
| Surname | |
| Trading name or representative capacity (if any) | |

B2. Which party in this case are you?

☐    Claimant

☐    Respondent

## C. THE APPLICATION

### C1. What alternative order should be made?

ⓘ The party making the application must set out which alternative order for payment
from the Decision Form the court is being asked to make.

 

### C2. Why should this alternative order be made?

ⓘ The party making the application must set out why the court should make that
alternative order for payment

 

### C3. When was this application sent to the court?

ⓘ Set out the date on which the application was sent to the court (i.e. the date on which
the email was sent, or the date on which the application was posted).

FORM 16A

# The Simple Procedure
# Appeal Form

Before completing this form, you should read Part 16 of the Simple Procedure Rules, which is about appeals.

This is an Appeal Form. You can use this to appeal the decision made by the sheriff at the end of a simple procedure case. You may only do this within 28 days from the Decision Form being sent.

## A. ABOUT THE CASE

| | |
|---|---|
| Sheriff Court | |
| Claimant | |
| Respondent | |
| Case reference number | |
| Date of Decision Form | |

## B. ABOUT YOU

### B1. What is your full name?

| | |
|---|---|
| Name | |
| Middle name | |
| Surname | |
| Trading name or representative capacity (if any) | |

### B2. Which party in the simple procedure case were you?

☐ Claimant

☐ Respondent

## C. GROUNDS OF APPEAL

ⓘ Set out the legal points which you want the Sheriff Appeal Court to consider in this appeal.

ⓘ These must be points of law. You cannot appeal simply because you disagree with a
matter of fact which the sheriff made a decision on.

I appeal to the Sheriff Appeal Court on the following points of law:

1.

2.

[...]

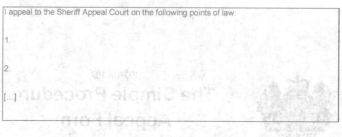

**FORM 16B**

# The Simple Procedure
# Appeal Report

This is an Appeal Report. It sets out the legal questions which the Sheriff Appeal Court will answer in this appeal.

## A. ABOUT THE CASE

| | |
|---|---|
| Sheriff Court | |
| Claimant | |
| Respondent | |
| Case reference number | |
| Date of Decision Form | |
| Date of appeal | |

## B. ABOUT THE DECISION

ⓘ Set out the factual and legal basis for the decision which you came to in this case.

## C. QUESTIONS FOR THE SHERIFF APPEAL COURT

ⓘ Set out the legal questions for the Sheriff Appeal Court to answer in this appeal.

Signature

Sheriff of [sheriffdom] at [sheriff court]

FORM 17A

# The Simple Procedure
# CJEU Reference Form

Before completing this form, you should read rule 17.3 of the Simple Procedure Rules, which is about references to the CJEU.

This is the form of reference for a preliminary ruling of the Court of Justice of the European Union.

## A. ABOUT THE CASE

| | |
|---|---|
| Sheriff Court | |
| Claimant | |
| Respondent | |
| Case reference number | |
| Date of reference | |

## B. THE REFERENCE

ⓘ Set out a clear and succinct statement of the case giving rise to the request for a ruling of the CJEU in order to enable the court to consider and understand the issues of EU law raised and to enable governments of Member States and other interested parties to submit observations.

Include:

- particulars of the parties

- the history of the dispute

- the relevant facts as agreed by the parties or found by the court or (failing such agreement or finding) the contentions of the parties

- the nature of the issues of law and fact between the parties

- the Scots law, so far as relevant

- the Treaty provisions, or other acts, instruments or rules of EU law concerned

- an explanation of why the reference is being made.

## C. THE QUESTIONS

C1. The preliminary ruling of the CJEU is accordingly requested on the following questions:

ⓘ Set out the question(s) on which a ruling is sought, identifying the Treaty provisions, or other acts, instruments or rules of EU law concerned.

FORM 17B

# The Simple Procedure
# Application to Intervene

Before completing this form, you should read rules 17.4 and 17.5 of the Simple Procedure
Rules, which are about interventions by the CEHR and SCHR.

This application is used by the Commission for Equality and Human Rights and the Scottish
Commission for Human Rights to apply to be allowed to intervene in a simple procedure
case.

## A. ABOUT THE CASE

| | |
|---|---|
| Sheriff Court | |
| Claimant | |
| Respondent | |
| Case reference number | |
| Date of application | |

## B. ABOUT THE INTERVENER

B1. Who is the proposed intervener in this case?

☐ The Commission for Equality and Human Rights

☐ The Scottish Commission for Human Rights

## C. ABOUT THE INTERVENTION

C1. Why is the Commission proposing to intervene?

ⓘ Set out the Commission's reasons for believing that the simple procedure case is
relevant to a matter in connection with which the Commission has a function.

**C2. What issue does the Commission want to address?**

ⓘ Set out the issue in the simple procedure case which the Commission wants to address.

**C3. What intervention does the Commission want to make?**

ⓘ Set out the propositions to be advanced by the Commission and the Commission's reasons for believing that they would assist the court.

FORM 17C

# The Simple Procedure
# Invitation to Intervene

This Invitation to Intervene is used by the sheriff to invite the Commission for Equality and Human Rights or the Scottish Human Rights Commission to intervene in a simple procedure case.

## A. ABOUT THE CASE

| | |
|---|---|
| Sheriff Court | |
| Claimant | |
| Respondent | |
| Case reference number | |
| Date of invitation | |

## B. ABOUT THE INVITATION

B1. Who is the sheriff inviting to intervene?

☐  The Commission for Equality and Human Rights

☐  The Scottish Commission for Human Rights

## C. THE INVITATION

C1. What is the simple procedure case about?

ⓘ Set out briefly the facts, procedural history and issues in the simple procedure case.

C2. What is the sheriff inviting the Commission to address in an intervention?

ⓘ Set out the issue(s) in the simple procedure case on which the court would like a submission.

FORM 17D

# The Simple Procedure Application to Change a Damages Management Order

**If you are applying for the sheriff to make orders:**

**If you have been sent this Application:**

This is an Application to Change a Damages Management Order.

It is used where the court has made a damages management order (which is about how a sum of money awarded as damages is to be paid to and managed for a person under a legal disability), but you want the court to change the order.

You must fill in parts A, B and C of this application and send it to the court. If you are one of the parties, you must send a copy to the other party in this case. If you are an interested person, you must send a copy to every party.

This is an Application to Change a Damages Management Order.

If the court grants this application, the damages management order will be changed as proposed in the application.

You have received the application because you are one of the parties in the case.

You must fill in part D of this application ('the reply') and return it to the court within 10 days of it being sent to you.

The court will then either grant the application and send written orders to the parties and the interested person, refuse the application and make no orders, or order you to appear at a discussion in court where the sheriff will consider whether to make any orders.

## A. ABOUT THE CASE

| | |
|---|---|
| Sheriff Court | |
| Claimant | |
| Respondent | |
| Case reference number | |

**B. ABOUT YOU**

B1. What is your full name?

Name

Middle name

Surname

B2. Which is your role in this case?

☐ Claimant

☐ Respondent

☐ Interested person

B3. If you are an interested person, what is your interest in this case?

ⓘ Explain why you have an interest in this case. For example:

– the damages management order might tell you to do certain things

– you might be responsible for looking after the person to whom the damages have been awarded.

**C. THE APPLICATION**

ⓘ If you are replying to this application, do not fill in this part. You should fill in part D.

C1. How should the court change the damages management order?

ⓘ Set out the changes you want the court to make. For example, you could ask the court to:

– appoint someone else to manage the money

– order the money to be paid directly to the person under legal disability.

**C3. Why should the court change the damages management order?**

&#9432; Set out why the court should change the damages management order.

 

**C4. When was this application sent to the court?**

&#9432; Set out the date on which the application was sent to the court (i.e. the date on which the email was sent, or the date on which the application was posted).

&#9432; Any reply to this application must be sent to the court within 10 days of this application being sent.

 

## D. THE REPLY

&#9432; If you are the person making this application, do not fill in this part. You should fill in parts A, B and C.

**D1. What is your full name?**

| | |
|---|---|
| Name | |
| Middle name | |
| Surname | |
| Trading name or representative capacity (if any) | |

**D2. Should the court change the damages management order?**

☐ Yes

☐ No

**D3. If you answered 'no', why should the court not change the damages management order?**

&#9432; If you object to the proposed order, you should set out why the court should not change the damages management order.

 

FORM 17E
# The Simple Procedure
# Application for Instructions
# about a Damages
# Management Order

**If you are applying for the sheriff to make orders:**

This is an Application for Instructions about a Damages Management Order.

It is used where the court has made a damages management order (which is about how a sum of money awarded as damages is to be paid to and managed for a person under a legal disability) and you want the court to tell the person appointed to manage the money how to go about doing that.

You must fill in parts A, B and C of this application and send it to the court. If you are one of the parties, you must send a copy to the other party in this case. If you are an interested person, you must send a copy to every party.

**If you have been sent this Application:**

This is an Application for Instructions about a Damages Management Order.

If the court grants this application, the court will give instructions about how to manage the money to the person appointed to manage it.

You have received the application because you are one of the parties in the case or because you are the guardian appointed to manage the money.

You must fill in part D of this application ('the reply') and return it to the court within 10 days of it being sent to you.

The court will then either grant the application and send written instructions to the parties, the interested person and the sheriff clerk or guardian, refuse the application and make no orders, or order you to appear at a discussion in court where the sheriff will consider whether to give .

## A. ABOUT THE CASE

| | |
|---|---|
| Sheriff Court | |
| Claimant | |
| Respondent | |
| Case reference number | |

**B. ABOUT YOU**

**B1. What is your full name?**

Name

Middle name

Surname

**B2. Which is your role in this case?**

☐  Claimant

☐  Respondent

☐  Interested person

**B3. If you are an interested person, what is your interest in this case?**

ⓘ  Explain why you have an interest in this case. For example:

–  the damages management order might tell you to do certain things

–  you might be responsible for looking after the person to whom the damages have been awarded.

**C. THE APPLICATION**

ⓘ  If you are replying to this application, do not fill in this part. You should fill in part D.

**C1. What instructions about the damages management order should the court give?**

ⓘ  Set out the proposed instructions you want the court to give. For example, you could ask the court to give instructions about how the money is to be spent or invested.

**C3. Why should the court give instructions about the damages management order?**

   ⓘ Set out why the court should give the proposed instructions.

 

**C4. When was this application sent to the court?**

   ⓘ Set out the date on which the application was sent to the court (i.e. the date on which the email was sent, or the date on which the application was posted).

   ⓘ Any reply to this application must be sent to the court within 10 days of this application being sent.

 

**D. THE REPLY**

   ⓘ If you are the person making this application, do not fill in this part. You should fill in parts A, B and C.

**D1. What is your full name?**

| | |
|---|---|
| Name | |
| Middle name | |
| Surname | |
| Trading name or representative capacity (if any) | |

**D2. Should the court give instructions about the damages management order?**

☐   Yes

☐   No

**D3. If you answered 'no', why should the court not give instructions about the damages management order?**

   ⓘ If you object to the proposed instructions, you should set out why the court should not give them.

 

**FORM 17F**

# The Simple Procedure Application for a Child's Property Administration Order

**If you are applying for the sheriff to make orders:**

This is an Application for a Child's Property Administration Order.

It is used where the court has made an order under section 13 of the Children (Scotland) Act 1995 (section 13 is about the payment and management of money to (or for the benefit of) a child).

You must fill in parts A, B and C of this application and send it to the court. If you are one of the parties, you must send a copy to the other party in this case. If you are an interested person, you must send a copy to every party.

**If you have been sent this Application:**

This is an Application for a Child's Property Administration Order.

If the court grants this application, it will make the proposed order which regulates how the child's property is to be administered.

You have received the application because you are one of the parties in the case.

You must fill in part D of this application ('the reply') and return it to the court within 10 days of it being sent to you.

The court will then either grant the application and send written orders to the parties and the interested person, refuse the application and make no orders, or order you to appear at a discussion in court where the sheriff will consider whether to make any orders.

## A. ABOUT THE CASE

| | |
|---|---|
| Sheriff Court | |
| Claimant | |
| Respondent | |
| Case reference number | |

## B. ABOUT YOU

### B1. What is your full name?

Name

Middle name

Surname

### B2. Which is your role in this case?

☐   Claimant

☐   Respondent

☐   Interested person

### B3. If you are an interested person, what is your interest in this case?

ⓘ Explain why you have an interest in this case: see section 11(3) of the Children (Scotland) Act 1995.

## C. THE APPLICATION

ⓘ If you are replying to this application, do not fill in this part. You should fill in part D.

### C1. What order should the court make about administering the child's property?

ⓘ Set out the things you want the Child's Property Administration Order to contain.

### C3. Why should the court make the Child's Property Administration Order?

ⓘ Set out why the court should make the proposed order.

**C4. When was this application sent to the court?**

ⓘ Set out the date on which the application was sent to the court (i.e. the date on which the email was sent, or the date on which the application was posted).

ⓘ Any reply to this application must be sent to the court within 10 days of this application being sent.

<br>

**D. THE REPLY**

ⓘ If you are the person making this application, do not fill in this part. You should fill in parts A, B and C.

**D1. What is your full name?**

| | |
|---|---|
| Name | |
| Middle name | |
| Surname | |
| Trading name or representative capacity (if any) | |

**D2. Should the court make the proposed Child's Property Administration Order?**

☐ Yes

☐ No

**D3. If you answered 'no', why should the court not make the Child's Property Administration Order?**

ⓘ If you object to the proposed order, you should set out why the court should not make it.

<br>

**FORM 19A**

# The Simple Procedure
# Translation Certificate

Before completing this form, you should read Part 19 of the Simple Procedure Rules, which is about international service.

This is a Translation Certificate. It is used to confirm to the court that a document which is formally served in a foreign country has been correctly translated into an official language of the foreign country. It is completed by the translator.

It must be sent to the court at the same time as the Confirmation of Service Notice (or the certificate given by the person who served the document abroad).

## A. ABOUT THE CASE

| | |
|---|---|
| Sheriff Court | |
| Claimant | |
| Respondent | |
| Case reference number | |

## B. ABOUT YOU

### B1. What is your full name?

| | |
|---|---|
| Name | |
| Middle name | |
| Surname | |
| Trading name or representative capacity (if any) | |

### B2. What is your address?

| | |
|---|---|
| Address | |
| Town | |
| Postcode | |

### B3. What are your professional qualifications?

ⓘ Fill in information about your qualifications as a translator.

## C. DECLARATION

ⓘ You must certify that your translation is a correct translation of the Form or Notice.

☐ I certify that the translation of the Form or Notice is a correct translation.

FORM 19B

# The Simple Procedure Method of Service Abroad Certificate

Before completing this form, you should read Part 19 of the Simple Procedure Rules, which is about international service.

This is a Method of Service Abroad Certificate. It is used to tell the court about the way a document has been served in a foreign country. It is only used if no other method of service is available. It must be completed by a person who practises (or has practised) law in that country, or by a representative of that country's government.

## A. ABOUT THE CASE

| | |
|---|---|
| Sheriff Court | |
| Claimant | |
| Respondent | |
| Case reference number | |

## B. ABOUT YOU

B1. What is your full name?

| | |
|---|---|
| Name | |
| Middle name | |
| Surname | |

B2. What is your address?

| | |
|---|---|
| Address | |
| Town | |
| Postcode | |

B3. What is your qualification to provide this certificate?

☐  I practice law in:  [country where Form or Notice served]

☐  I practised law in:  [country where Form or Notice served]

between these dates:  [dates when in practice]

☐  I am a
representative of
the government
of:  [country where Form or Notice served]

## C. ABOUT THE FORMAL SERVICE

### C1. Who was the document served on?

ⓘ You must identify the person on whom it was served.

### C2. Who served it?

ⓘ You must give the following information about the person who served it:

- the person's full name
- the person's address
- the capacity in which the person served the Form or Notice

### C3. How was it served?

ⓘ You must describe the method of service used.

## D. DECLARATION

ⓘ You must certify that the method of service used is in accordance with the law of the country where the document has been served.

☐  I certify that the method by which the document was served is in accordance with the law of the country where it was served.

FORM 20A

# The Simple Procedure Provisional Orders Application

**If you are applying for the sheriff to make orders:**

This is a Provisional Orders Application.

You can use this Application to ask the court to make orders that will protect your position until the sheriff makes a final decision in this case.

If you are asking the court to make a provisional order **without a provisional orders hearing**, you do not have to send the Application to anyone except the court.

Otherwise, you have to send a copy of the Application to the respondent and every interested person as well as sending it to the court.

**If you have been sent this Application:**

This is a Provisional Orders Application.

The claimant has asked the court to make orders to protect the claimant's position until the sheriff makes a final decision in this case.

The sheriff must hear from the claimant, the respondent and any interested person at a provisional orders hearing before deciding whether to make the provisional orders.

## A. ABOUT THE CASE

| | |
|---|---|
| Sheriff Court | |
| Claimant | |
| Respondent | |
| Case reference number | |

## B. ABOUT THE CLAIMANT

B1. What is your full name?

| | |
|---|---|
| Name | |
| Middle name | |
| Surname | |

| Trading name or representative capacity (if any) | |
|---|---|

## C. THE APPLICATION

ⓘ You should complete this Part, Part D and Part F.

ⓘ Only complete Part E if you are asking for an arrestment on the dependence.

**C1. What type of provisional order would you like the court to make?**

☐ **an arrestment on the dependence under section 15A(1) of the Debtors (Scotland) Act 1987**

ⓘ This is an order freezing the respondent's goods or money held by a third party.

☐ **an inhibition on the dependence under section 15A(1) of the Debtors (Scotland) Act 1987**

ⓘ This is an order preventing the respondent from selling their home or other land, or taking out a secured loan.

☐ **an interim attachment under section 9A(1) of the Debt Arrangement and Attachment (Scotland) Act 2002**

ⓘ This is an order preventing the respondent from selling or removing their goods.

**C2. Why should the court make this provisional order?**

ⓘ The court will have to be satisfied about certain matters before it makes the order. The matters that are considered depend on the type of order and on whether you are asking the court to make the order without holding a provisional orders hearing or not.

– If you are asking for arrestment or inhibition on the dependence and you want the court to make a decision about the application without a hearing, see section 15E(2) of the Debtors (Scotland) Act 1987.

– If you are asking for arrestment or inhibition on the dependence and you want the court to make a decision about the application at a hearing, see section 15F(3) of the Debtors (Scotland) Act 1987.

– If you are asking for an interim attachment and you want the court to make a decision without a hearing, see section 9D(2) of the Debt Arrangement and Attachment (Scotland) Act 2002.

– If you are asking for an interim attachment and you want the court to make a decision at a hearing, see section 9E(3) of the Debt Arrangement and Attachment (Scotland) Act 2002.

## D. HOW THE APPLICATION SHOULD BE DEALT WITH

**D1. How do you want the court to deal with your Application?**

☐ I want the court to consider whether to grant the Application without holding a hearing

ⓘ Please complete D2.

☐ I want the court to hold a hearing before deciding whether to grant the Application

**D2. If the court refuses to grant the Application without holding a hearing, what should happen to the Application?**

ⓘ You can decide to go ahead with a hearing where the sheriff will decide whether to grant the Application after hearing from you, the respondent and any interested person. If you do not want a hearing, the Application will be refused.

☐ I want the court to arrange a hearing

☐ I do not want the court to arrange a hearing

## E. ARRESTMENT ON THE DEPENDENCE: INFORMATION ABOUT THIRD PARTY

ⓘ You should only complete this part of the Application if you are asking for an arrestment on the dependence.

ⓘ The third party is the person who holds goods or money that belongs to the respondent.

**E1. Is the third party an individual, a company or an organisation?**

☐ An individual (including a sole trader)

ⓘ Please complete E2.

☐ A company or organisation

ⓘ Please complete E3.

**E2. What is the third party's full name?**

ⓘ If the third party is an individual trading under a business name, please also give that name.

Name

Middle name

Surname

Trading name (if any)

**E3. What is the third party's company name or organisation name?**

ⓘ If the third party is a company (which might be indicated by 'Limited', 'Ltd' or 'plc' after its name), please give the full name of that company and the company registration number.

ⓘ You can check the name of a company on the Companies House website.

| Name | |
|---|---|
| Company type | |
| Company registration number (if limited company or LLP) | |
| Trading name (if any) | |

### E4. What are the third party's contact details?

| Address | |
|---|---|
| City | |
| Postcode | |
| Email address | |

## F. INTERESTED PERSONS

ⓘ This Part tells the court about any person who has an interest in the Application.

ⓘ You do not need to include details for:

– the respondent

– anyone whose details you have given in Part E.

### F1. Does any person have an interest in the Application?

☐ Yes

☐ No

### F2. Is the interested person an individual, a company or an organisation?

☐ An individual (including a sole trader)

ⓘ Please complete F3.

☐ A company or organisation

ⓘ Please complete F4.

### F3. What is the interested person's full name?

ⓘ If the interested person is an individual trading under a business name, please also give that name.

| Name | |
|---|---|
| Middle name | |
| Surname | |
| Trading name (if any) | |

### F4. What is the interested person's company name or organisation name?

(i) If the interested person is a company (which might be indicated by 'Limited', 'Ltd' or 'plc' after its name), please give the full name of that company and the company registration number.

(i) You can check the name of a company on the Companies House website.

Name

Company type

Company registration number (if limited company or LLP)

Trading name (if any)

**F5. What are the interested person's contact details?**

Address

City

Postcode

Email address

FORM 20B

# The Simple Procedure
# Provisional Orders
# Hearing Notice

The claimant has asked the court to make orders to protect the claimant's position until the sheriff makes a final decision in this case.

The sheriff has arranged a hearing about that application. The sheriff has also ordered the claimant to tell you about the date, time and place where the hearing will be held so that you can make your views known to the sheriff.

## A. ABOUT THE CASE

| | |
|---|---|
| Sheriff Court | |
| Claimant | |
| Respondent | |
| Case reference number | |

## B. ABOUT THE RECIPIENT

### B1. Who is this Notice being sent to?

| | |
|---|---|
| Name | |
| Middle name | |
| Surname | |
| Trading name or representative capacity (if any) | |

### B2. What is that person's role in this case?

☐  Respondent

☐  Interested person

## C. ABOUT THE HEARING

### C1. What type of hearing has the sheriff arranged?

☐     A provisional orders hearing

ⓘ   This is a hearing under section 15F of the Debtors (Scotland) Act 1987 or section 9E of the Debt Arrangement and Attachment (Scotland) Act 2002.

☐     A provisional orders review hearing

ⓘ   This is a hearing under section 15K of the Debtors (Scotland) Act 1987 or section 9M of the Debt Arrangement and Attachment (Scotland) Act 2002.

### C2. When will the hearing take place?

Date of hearing

Time of hearing

### C3. Where will the hearing take place?

Place of hearing

FORM 20C

# The Simple Procedure Provisional Orders Reconsideration Application

**If you are applying for the sheriff to reconsider a provisional order:**

This is a Provisional Orders Reconsideration Application.

You can use this Application to ask the court to reconsider a provisional order.

If you are the respondent, you have to send the Application to the court, the claimant and any interested person.

If you are an interested person, you have to send the Application to the court, the claimant, the respondent and any other interested person.

The court will then arrange a provisional orders review hearing. At the hearing, the sheriff must give anyone who was sent the Application an opportunity to be heard before deciding whether to make an order reconsidering the provisional order.

**If you have been sent this Application:**

This is a Provisional Orders Reconsideration Application.

The respondent or an interested person has asked the court to reconsider a provisional order.

The court will arrange a provisional orders review hearing. At the hearing, you will have an opportunity to be heard before the sheriff decides whether to make an order reconsidering the provisional order.

## A. ABOUT THE CASE

| | |
|---|---|
| Sheriff Court | |
| Claimant | |
| Respondent | |
| Case reference number | |

**B. ABOUT YOU**

B1. What is your full name?

Name 

Middle name 

Surname 

B2. What is your role in this case?

☐ Respondent

☐ Interested party

**C. THE APPLICATION**

C1. What type of provisional order would you like the court to reconsider?

☐ an arrestment on the dependence under section 15A(1) of the Debtors (Scotland) Act 1987

ⓘ This is an order freezing the respondent's goods or money held by a third party.

☐ an inhibition on the dependence under section 15A(1) of the Debtors (Scotland) Act 1987

ⓘ This is an order preventing the respondent from selling their home or other land, or taking out a secured loan.

☐ an interim attachment under section 9A(1) of the Debt Arrangement and Attachment (Scotland) Act 2002

ⓘ This is an order preventing the respondent from selling or removing their goods.

C2. When was the provisional order made?

ⓘ Set out the date on which the court made the provisional order?

**C3. What do you want the court to do with the provisional order?**

ⓘ Set out the way in which you want the court to reconsider the provisional order.

— If the order was made under section 15A(1) of the Debtors (Scotland) Act 1987, section 15K of that Act sets out what the court can do on reconsidering it.

— If the order was made under section 9A(1) of the Debt Arrangement and Attachment (Scotland) Act 2002, section 9M of that Act sets out what the court can do on reconsidering it.

**C4. Why should the court reconsider the provisional order?**

ⓘ You must set out why the court should reconsider the provisional order.

FORM 20D

# The Simple Procedure
# Arrestment Notice

This is an Arrestment Notice. It is used when the court makes a provisional order and the provisional order is an arrestment on the dependence.

The purpose of the Arrestment Notice is to inform the third party who holds the respondent's goods or money that they have been frozen by the court. It is formally served on that person by a sheriff officer.

## A. ABOUT THE CASE

| | |
|---|---|
| Sheriff Court | |
| Claimant | |
| Respondent | |
| Case reference number | |

## B. ABOUT THE THIRD PARTY

B1. Is the third party an individual, a company or an organisation?

☐ An individual (including a sole trader)

ⓘ Please complete B2.

☐ A company or organisation

ⓘ Please complete B3.

B2. What is the third party's full name?

ⓘ If the third party is an individual trading under a business name, please also give that name.

| | |
|---|---|
| Name | |
| Middle name | |
| Surname | |
| Trading name (if any) | |

**B3. What is the third party's company name or organisation name?**

ⓘ If the third party is a company (which might be indicated by 'Limited', 'Ltd' or 'plc' after its name), please give the full name of that company and the company registration number.

ⓘ You can check the name of a company on the Companies House website.

| | |
|---|---|
| Name | |
| Company type | |
| Company registration number (if limited company or LLP) | |
| Trading name (if any) | |

**B4. What are the third party's contact details?**

| | |
|---|---|
| Address | |
| City | |
| Postcode | |
| Email address | |

**C. PROTECTED MINIMUM BALANCE**

ⓘ Section 73F of the Debtors (Scotland) Act 1987 prevents the arrestment of money held by a bank or other financial institution below a certain minimum balance if various conditions are met.

ⓘ This Part of the Form identifies whether the Protected Minimum Balance applies to this arrestment.

**C1. Is the respondent an individual?**

☐ Yes

ⓘ Please complete C2.

☐ No

ⓘ The Protected Minimum Balance does not apply. Go to Part D.

**C2. Is the third party a bank or other financial institution?**

ⓘ See section 73F(5) of the Debtors (Scotland) Act 1987 for a definition of bank or other financial institution.

☐ Yes

ⓘ Please complete C3.

☐ No

ⓘ The Protected Minimum Balance does not apply. Go to Part D.

C3. Is the bank account one to which section 73F of the Debtors (Scotland) Act 1987 applies?

ⓘ See section 73F(2).

☐ Yes

ⓘ The Protected Minimum Balance applies. Please complete C4.

☐ No

ⓘ The Protected Minimum Balance does not apply. Go to Part D.

C4. If it applies, what is the Protected Minimum Balance?

ⓘ Insert the Protected Minimum Balance, which is calculated in accordance with section 73F(4).

> Protected Minimum Balance, if applicable.

## D. ABOUT THE ARRESTMENT ON THE DEPENDENCE

| | |
|---|---|
| Date of order for arrestment on the dependence | |
| Name of sheriff officer | |
| Address | |
| Witness | |
| Method of formal service | |
| Date of formal service | |

**IN HER MAJESTY'S NAME AND AUTHORITY AND IN NAME AND AUTHORITY OF THE SHERIFF**, the sheriff officer arrests in your hands:

- any moveable property that belongs to the respondent, and

- the following sum of money, more or less, that is due by you to the respondent or to another person on behalf of the respondent

| Sum arrested | The sum arrested, in excess of the Protected Minimum Balance where applicable. |
|---|---|

## D. DUTIES OF THE THIRD PARTY

D1. Compliance with the arrestment

You must retain anything that has been arrested in your hands under arrestment until one of the following things happens:

- the court makes an order transferring them to the claimant, or

- the court makes another order telling you what to do with them.

ⓘ You should take legal advice before you hand over any goods to the respondent or pay any money to the respondent or someone else on behalf of the respondent.

### D2. Duty of disclosure

ⓘ Section 73G of the Debtors (Scotland) Act 1987 requires you to disclose certain information to the claimant.

You must disclose to the claimant the nature and value of the goods and money which have been attached by this arrestment.

You must do this within the period of 3 weeks beginning with the day on which this arrestment is formally served on you.

You must make your disclosure using the form in Schedule 8 to the Diligence (Scotland) Regulations 2009.

You must also send a copy of the disclosure to:

- the respondent, and

- so far as known to you, any other relevant person.

A relevant person is someone (either solely or in common with the respondent):

- who owns or claims to own the attached goods, or

- to whom the attached money is or is claimed to be due.

ⓘ Failure to comply with this duty may lead to a financial penalty under section 73H of the Debtors (Scotland) Act 1987.

ⓘ Failure to comply may also be dealt with as a contempt of court.

**If you wish further advice, please contact any Citizens Advice Bureau, local advice centre, sheriff clerk or solicitor.**

**FORM 20E**

# The Simple Procedure Confirmation of Formal Service of Arrestment Notice

This is a Confirmation of Formal Service of an Arrestment Notice. It is used to inform the court when and how an Arrestment Notice has been formally served.

It must be completed and sent to the court whenever a sheriff officer formally serves an Arrestment Notice.

## A. ABOUT THE CASE

| | |
|---|---|
| Sheriff Court | |
| Claimant | |
| Respondent | |
| Case reference number | |

## B. ABOUT THE SHERIFF OFFICER

B1. What is your full name?

| | |
|---|---|
| Name | |
| Middle name | |
| Surname | |
| Firm or organisation | |

## C. ABOUT FORMAL SERVICE OF ARRESTMENT NOTICE

C1. Who did you formally serve the Arrestment Notice on?

ⓘ You must identify the person who you were required to serve something on.

C2.How did you formally serve it?

(i) You must describe the method of formal service used.

☐ By a next-day postal service which records delivery

☐ Delivering it personally

☐ Leaving it in the hands of a resident or employee

☐ Depositing it in a home or place of business by letter box or another lawful way

☐ Leaving it at a home or place of business in a way likely to come to the person's attention

☐ Other

(i) If you have selected 'Other' or need to give more details about the manner of formal service, please set this out below.

C3. When did you formally serve it?

(i) You must identify when service was performed.

# SCHEDULE 3

## STANDARD ORDERS

**Paragraph 3(1)**

# The Simple Procedure
# Order of the Sheriff

Response Form received: ordering a case management discussion

The Simple Procedure is a speedy, inexpensive and informal court procedure for settling or determining disputes with a value of **less than £5,000**.

This is an order of the sheriff in a case which you are a party in. You should **read it** and **follow it**.

| | |
|---|---|
| **Sheriff Court:** | |
| **Date of order:** | |
| **Claimant:** | |
| **Respondent:** | |
| **Court ref no:** | |

The responding party has indicated to the court that this claim will be disputed.

The sheriff has considered the Claim Form and the Response Form and has **given the following orders**:–

**Settlement and negotiation**

The claimant and the respondent are **encouraged** to contact each other to seek to settle the case or to narrow the issues in dispute, **before** the hearing date. If the case is settled before the hearing date then the parties must contact the court immediately.

**Case management discussion**

The sheriff would like to discuss this case with **both parties** before ordering a formal court hearing. Both parties are therefore **ordered** to attend a case management discussion in the sheriff court.

The purpose of a case management discussion is to allow the sheriff to discuss the claim and response with both parties and to clarify any concerns which the sheriff has. At the case management discussion, the sheriff will also discuss with both parties their attitudes to negotiation and alternative dispute resolution.

At the case management discussion, the sheriff will give both parties orders in person arranging a hearing at which the case will be considered and their dispute resolved. The sheriff may make a decision at a case management discussion.

**Clarification**

The claimant is **ordered** to write to the court and to the respondent at least **14 days** before the date of the case management conference to clarify these issues:

1. [list]

The responding party is **ordered** to write to the court and to the claimant at least **14 days** before the date of the case management conference to clarify these issues:

1. [list]

**Documents and other evidence**

The claimant is **ordered** to bring the following documents or other evidence to the case management discussion:

1. [list]

The respondent is **ordered** to bring the following documents or other evidence to the case management discussion:

1. [list]

**Date**

Both parties are **ordered** to attend a case management discussion at [sheriff court] on [date] at [time]. Both parties should arrive in good time at the sheriff court building.

At the case management discussion, the sheriff expects both parties to be prepared to discuss the case and to have an open and constructive attitude to the possibility of negotiation or alternative dispute resolution.

**Signed by:**

Sheriff of [sheriffdom] at [sheriff court]

# The Simple Procedure
# Order of the Sheriff

Response Form received: ordering a hearing

The Simple Procedure is a speedy, inexpensive and informal court procedure for settling or determining disputes with a value of **less than £5,000**.

This is an order of the sheriff in a case which you are a party in. You should **read it** and **follow it**.

| | |
|---|---|
| **Sheriff Court:** | |
| **Date of order:** | |
| **Claimant:** | |
| **Respondent:** | |
| **Court ref no:** | |

The respondent has indicated to the court that this claim will be disputed.

The sheriff has considered the Claim Form and the Response Form and has **given the following orders**:—

**Settlement and negotiation**
The claimant and the respondent are **encouraged** to contact each other to seek to settle the case or to narrow the issues in dispute, **before** the hearing date. If the case is settled before the hearing date then the parties must contact the court immediately.

**Documents and other evidence**
The sheriff has considered the evidence and other documents which the claimant thinks would support the claim.

The claimant is **ordered** to **also** lodge the following documents or other evidence at least 14 days before the hearing date, as the sheriff considers them necessary to support their claim:
  1. [list]

The claimant is **ordered** not to lodge the following documents or other evidence, as the sheriff considers them unnecessary to support the claim:
  1. [list]

The sheriff has considered the evidence and other documents which the respondent thinks would support the response.

The respondent is **ordered** to **also** lodge the following documents or other evidence at least 14 days before the hearing date, as the sheriff considers them necessary to support their response:
1. [list]

The respondent is **ordered** not to lodge the following documents or other evidence, as the sheriff considers them unnecessary to support the response:
1. [list]

Both parties are **ordered** to bring two copies of every document that is lodged to the hearing.

**Clarification**

The claimant is **ordered** to write to the court and to the respondent at least **14 days** before the hearing date to clarify these issues:
1. [list]

The respondent is **ordered** to write to the court and to the claimant at least **14 days** before the hearing date to clarify these issues:
1. [list]

**Hearing Date**

Both parties are **ordered** to attend a hearing at [sheriff court] on [date] at [time]. Both parties should arrive in good time at the sheriff court building.

At this hearing, the sheriff will expect both parties to be prepared to argue their case in full. Both parties should be aware that the sheriff may make a decision in their case even if they are not fully prepared to argue their case.

The case may be decided or dismissed in the absence of a party, if that party fails to attend the hearing.

**Signed by:**

Sheriff of [sheriffdom] at [sheriff court]

# The Simple Procedure
# Order of the Sheriff

Response Form received: considering making a decision without a
hearing

The Simple Procedure is a speedy, inexpensive and informal court procedure for settling or
determining disputes with a value of **less than £5,000**.

This is an order of the sheriff in a case which you are a party in. You should **read it** and
**follow it**.

| | |
|---|---|
| **Sheriff Court:** | |
| **Date of order:** | |
| **Claimant:** | |
| **Respondent:** | |
| **Court ref no:** | |

The respodent has indicated to the court that this claim will be disputed.

The sheriff has considered the Claim Form and the Response Form and has **given the
following orders**:–

**Settlement and negotiation**

The claimant and the respondent are **encouraged** to contact each other to seek to settle the
case or to narrow the issues in dispute, **before** the hearing date. If the case is settled before
the hearing date then the parties must contact the court immediately.

**A decision without a hearing**

The sheriff considers that the dispute between the parties is capable of being resolved
without a hearing. This is because the dispute appears only to involve a question of law [*or*
because the dispute appears capable of being resolved based only on consideration of the
documents and other evidence listed in the Claim Form and Response Form]. If the dispute
is resolved without a hearing then the sheriff will give parties an opportunity to write to the
court setting out their arguments in the case in advance of making a decision.

**Opportunity to object**

Both parties are being given an opportunity to object to this dispute being resolved without a
hearing.

Both parties are **ordered** to write to the sheriff by [date] stating whether they are content for a decision to be made without a hearing. If parties are not content for a decision to be made without a hearing, they must set out the reasons why a hearing will be necessary to resolve this dispute.

Parties should be aware that failing to write to the sheriff may result in the sheriff deciding to resolve this dispute without a hearing.

**Next steps**

The sheriff will issue further written orders within 14 days of [date]. These written orders will state whether the sheriff has decided to resolve this dispute without a hearing.

**Signed by:**

Sheriff of [sheriffdom] at [sheriff court]

# The Simple Procedure
# Order of the Sheriff

Response Form received: making a decision without a hearing

The Simple Procedure is a speedy, inexpensive and informal court procedure for settling or determining disputes with a value of **less than £5,000**.

This is an order of the sheriff in a case which you are a party in. You should **read it** and **follow it**.

| | |
|---|---|
| **Sheriff Court:** | |
| **Date of order:** | |
| **Claimant:** | |
| **Respondent:** | |
| **Court ref no:** | |

The sheriff sent the parties written orders stating that the sheriff was considering making a decision in this case without a hearing.

The sheriff has considered the responses received [*or* no responses were received] and has **given the following orders**:–

**Settlement and negotiation**

The claimant and the respondent are **encouraged** to contact each other to seek to settle the case or to narrow the issues in dispute. If the case is settled before the date on which the sheriff intends to make a decision (below) then the parties must contact the court immediately.

**A decision without a hearing**

The sheriff has decided to make a decision in this case without a hearing.

The sheriff will make this decision on [date].

**Clarification**

The claimant is **ordered** to write to the court and to the respondent at least **14 days** before the hearing date to clarify these issues:

2. [list]

The respondent is **ordered** to write to the court and to the claimant at least **14 days** before the hearing date to clarify these issues:

2. [list]

**Notes of argument**

Parties are **ordered** to send the court notes of argument at least 14 days before [date]. These notes should set out any legal points which they wish to make to the sheriff and should comment on any aspect of the evidence which they wish the sheriff to consider.

**Documents and other evidence**

Documents and other evidence may be lodged by sending copies to the sheriff clerk.

The claimant is **ordered** to lodge the following documents or other evidence at least 14 days before the hearing date, as the sheriff considers them necessary to support their claim:

2. [list]

The respondent is **ordered** to lodge the following documents or other evidence at least 14 days before the hearing date, as the sheriff considers them necessary to support their response:

2. [list]

Both parties should be aware that the sheriff may make a decision in this case on [date] even if they do not follow the orders above.

**Signed by:**

Sheriff of [sheriffdom] at [sheriff court]

# The Simple Procedure
# Order of the Sheriff

Transferring a case between courts

The Simple Procedure is a speedy, inexpensive and informal court procedure for settling or determining disputes with a value of **less than £5,000**.

This is an order of the sheriff in a case which you are a party in. You should **read it** and **follow it**.

| | |
|---|---|
| **Sheriff Court:** | |
| **Date of order:** | |
| **Claimant:** | |
| **Respondent:** | |
| **Court ref no:** | |

The sheriff has considered this simple procedure case and has **given the following orders**:-

**Transfer to a different sheriff court**

[The sheriff considers that this claim ought to have been raised in a different sheriff court.]

The case is **ordered** to be transferred to [*name of sheriff court*].

**What happens next**

You will be contacted by the sheriff clerk at [*name of sheriff court*] with the next orders in this case.

| | |
|---|---|
| **Signed by:** | |
| | Sheriff of [sheriffdom] at [sheriff court] |

# The Simple Procedure
# Order of the Sheriff

Unless order

The Simple Procedure is a speedy, inexpensive and informal court procedure for settling or determining disputes with a value of **less than £5,000**.

This is an order of the sheriff in a case which you are a party in. You should **read it** and **follow it**.

| | |
|---|---|
| **Sheriff Court:** | |
| **Date of order:** | |
| **Claimant:** | |
| **Respondent:** | |
| **Court ref no:** | |

**Order**

The sheriff orders [the claimant / the respondent] to take the following step[s] by [date]:
   1.  [list].

**Possibility of dismissal**

The sheriff considers that taking the steps listed above is necessary for the progress of this case. The claimant is **warned** that unless these steps are taken, this case will be **dismissed** without further warning.

If the step[s] listed above are not taken then the sheriff **dismisses** the claim against the responding party.

**Signed by:**

Sheriff of [sheriffdom] at [sheriff court]

# The Simple Procedure
# Order of the Sheriff

Application to Pause

The Simple Procedure is a speedy, inexpensive and informal court procedure for settling or determining disputes with a value of **less than £5,000**.

This is an order of the sheriff in a case which you are a party in. You should **read it** and **follow it**.

**Sheriff Court:**

**Date of order:**

**Claimant:**

**Respondent:**

**Court ref no:**

The court has received an Application to Pause.

The sheriff has considered the Application and has **given the following orders**:–

*[The order below can be used where the sheriff has decided to grant the application, without a discussion in court:]*

**Pausing Order**

The sheriff **orders** the progress of this case to be paused.

This means that all upcoming hearings in this case have been cancelled. No procedural steps may be taken in this case until the case has been restarted. Either party can ask for this to happen by sending an Application to Restart Form to the court and to the other party.

Both parties should be aware that after six months, the sheriff clerk may write to you directing that a particular step should be taken. If this is not done, the claim may be dismissed.

*[The order below can be used where the sheriff has decided to refuse the application, without a discussion in court:]*

**Refusing a Pausing Order**

The sheriff **has not** ordered the progress of this case to be paused.

This means that all upcoming hearings in this case are still to go ahead. Parties may continue to progress this case.

[*The order below can be used where the sheriff has decided that a discussion in court is necessary to decide the application:*]

**Discussion in court**

The sheriff wants to hear from both parties before deciding whether to pause the progress of this case.

Both parties are **ordered** to attend a discussion at [sheriff court] on [date] at [time]. Both parties should arrive in good time at the sheriff court building.

At this discussion, the sheriff will expect both parties to be prepared to discuss whether the progress of the case should be paused. Both parties should be aware that the sheriff may make a decision in their case even where they are not fully prepared to discuss this.

The application may be decided in the absence of a party, if that party fails to attend the discussion.

**Signed by:**

Sheriff of [sheriffdom] at [sheriff court]

# The Simple Procedure
# Order of the Sheriff

Application to Restart

The Simple Procedure is a speedy, inexpensive and informal court procedure for settling or determining disputes with a value of **less than £5,000**.

This is an order of the sheriff in a case which you are a party in. You should **read it** and **follow it**.

| | |
|---|---|
| **Sheriff Court:** | |
| **Date of order:** | |
| **Claimant:** | |
| **Respondent:** | |
| **Court ref no:** | |

The court has received an Application to Restart.

The sheriff has considered the Application and has **given the following orders**:–

*[The order below can be used where the sheriff has decided to grant the application, without a discussion in court:]*

**Restarting Order**

The sheriff **orders** the progress of this case to be restarted.

Both parties are **ordered** to attend a discussion at [sheriff court] on [date] at [time]. Both parties should arrive in good time at the sheriff court building.

*[The order below can be used where the sheriff has decided to refuse the application, without a discussion in court:]*

**Refusing a Restarting Order**

The sheriff **has not** ordered the progress of this case to be restarted.

This means that the progress of the case continues to be paused. There are no upcoming hearings or discussions arranged in this case.

[*The order below can be used where the sheriff has decided that a discussion in court is necessary to decide the application:*]

**Discussion in court**

The sheriff wants to hear from both parties before deciding whether to restart the progress of this case.

Both parties are **ordered** to attend a discussion at [sheriff court] on [date] at [time]. Both parties should arrive in good time at the sheriff court building.

At this discussion, the sheriff will expect both parties to be prepared to discuss whether the progress of the case should be restarted. Both parties should be aware that the sheriff may make a decision in their case even where they are not fully prepared to discuss this.

The application may be decided in the absence of a party, if that party fails to attend the discussion.

**Signed by:**

Sheriff of [sheriffdom] at [sheriff court]

# The Simple Procedure
# Order of the Sheriff

Paused case – unless order

The Simple Procedure is a speedy, inexpensive and informal court procedure for settling or determining disputes with a value of **less than £5,000**.

This is an order of the sheriff in a case which you are a party in. You should **read it** and **follow it**.

| | |
|---|---|
| **Sheriff Court:** | |
| **Date of order:** | |
| **Claimant:** | |
| **Respondent:** | |
| **Court ref no:** | |

The sheriff clerk has presented this case to the sheriff because it has been paused for over 6 months.

The sheriff has considered the case and has **given the following orders**:-

**Possibility of dismissal**

This case has now been paused for over 6 months. Both parties are **warned** that the sheriff will dismiss this claim unless the following steps are taken:

[Both parties / the claimant / the respondent] must write to the sheriff to explain what they would like to happen to this case. If they would like the case to continue to be paused, they must explain why.

[or

The sheriff wants to hear from both parties before deciding what the next steps in this case should be.

Both parties are **ordered** to attend a discussion at [sheriff court] on [date] at [time]. Both parties should arrive in good time at the sheriff court building. At this discussion, the sheriff will expect both parties to be prepared to discuss the progress of the case. ]

**Signed by:**

Sheriff of [sheriffdom] at [sheriff court]

# The Simple Procedure
# Order of the Sheriff

Order to recover documents

The Simple Procedure is a speedy, inexpensive and informal court procedure for settling or determining disputes with a value of **less than £5,000**.

This is an order of the sheriff in a case which you are a party in. You should **read it** and **follow it**.

| | |
|---|---|
| **Sheriff Court:** | |
| **Date of order:** | |
| **Claimant:** | |
| **Respondent:** | |
| **Court ref no:** | |

The court has received a Recovery of Documents Application.

The sheriff has considered the Application and has **given the following orders:-**

**Order to recover documents**

[*This order can be used where the sheriff has decided to grant the application (in whole or in part) without a discussion in court*]

The sheriff **orders** the person mentioned in column 2 of the table below to send the document mentioned in column 1 to the court within [number of days] after this order is formally served.

| Description of document | Name of person who has the document |
|---|---|
| | |
| | |
| | |
| | |

The sheriff also **orders** that person to fill in part A of this order ('the reply') and return it to the court within [number of days] after this order is formally served.

**Refusal of Recovery of Documents Application**

[*This order can be used where the sheriff has decided to refuse the application without a discussion in court*]

The sheriff **refuses to make** an order to recover documents.

**Discussion in court**

[*This order can be used where the sheriff has decided that a discussion in court is necessary to decide the application*]

The sheriff wants to hear from both parties before deciding whether to make an order to recover documents.

Both parties are **ordered** to attend a discussion at [sheriff court] on [date] at [time]. Both parties should arrive in good time at the sheriff court building.

At this discussion, the sheriff will expect both parties to be prepared to discuss whether an order to recover documents should be made. Both parties should be aware that the sheriff may make a decision in their case even where they are not fully prepared to discuss this.

The application may be decided in the absence of a party, if that party fails to attend the discussion.

Signed by:

Sheriff of [sheriffdom] at [sheriff court]

**THE REPLY**
[*for use only where the sheriff makes an order to recover documents*]

**A. ABOUT YOU**

A1. What is your full name?

| | |
|---|---|
| Name | |
| Middle name | |
| Surname | |
| Trading name or representative capacity (if any) | |

**B. DECLARATIONS**

B1. How have you complied with the order to recover documents?

ⓘ  Tick the box next to the appropriate declaration.

☐ I enclose the following documents. They are all the documents in my possession which fall within the description above.

[list documents enclosed with the reply]

☐ I have no documents in my possession which fall within the description above.

**B2. Do you have any additional information about the order to recover documents?**

ⓘ Tick the box next to the appropriate declaration.

☐ I believe that there are other documents which fall within the description above but they are not in my possession. I have the following information about them:

[set out the documents, the date on which you last saw them and the details of the person who you believe possesses them]

☐ I have no additional information about documents which fall within the description above.

**B3. Do you believe that any of the documents that you possess are confidential?**

ⓘ If your answer is yes, you must still send the document to the court. You should:

  – put it in an envelope and seal it

  – mark "CONFIDENTIAL" on the front of the envelope

ⓘ If the party who obtained the order to recover documents wants to open the envelope, the party has to make an application to the court first. You will be told about any application and you can explain to the sheriff why you think the document is confidential before the sheriff decides whether to grant the application.

☐ Yes

☐ No

# The Simple Procedure
# Order of the Sheriff

Special order to recover documents

The Simple Procedure is a speedy, inexpensive and informal court procedure for settling or determining disputes with a value of **less than £5,000**.

This is an order of the sheriff in a case which you are a party in. You should **read it** and **follow it**.

| | |
|---|---|
| **Sheriff Court:** | |
| **Date of order:** | |
| **Claimant:** | |
| **Respondent:** | |
| **Court ref no:** | |

The court has received a Special Recovery of Documents Application.

The sheriff has considered the Application and has **given the following orders:-**

**Special order to recover documents**

[*This order can be used where the sheriff has decided to grant the application (in whole or in part) without a discussion in court*]

The sheriff **grants commission** to [name], solicitor, [address] ('the commissioner') to recover the documents mentioned in column 1 from the person mentioned in column 2.

| Description of document | Name of person who has the document |
|---|---|
| | |
| | |
| | |
| | |

The sheriff also **appoints** the commissioner to send a report to the court, together with any documents recovered, as soon as possible.

**Refusal of Special Recovery of Documents Application**

[*This order can be used where the sheriff has decided to refuse the application without a discussion in court*]

The sheriff **refuses to make** a special order to recover documents.

**Discussion in court**

[*This order can be used where the sheriff has decided that a discussion in court is necessary to decide the application*]

The sheriff wants to hear from both parties before deciding whether to make a special order to recover documents.

Both parties are **ordered** to attend a discussion at [sheriff court] on [date] at [time]. Both parties should arrive in good time at the sheriff court building.

At this discussion, the sheriff will expect both parties to be prepared to discuss whether a special order to recover documents should be made. Both parties should be aware that the sheriff may make a decision in their case even where they are not fully prepared to discuss this.

The application may be decided in the absence of a party, if that party fails to attend the discussion.

**Signed by:**

| |
|---|
| Sheriff of [sheriffdom] at [sheriff court] |

# The Simple Procedure
# Order of the Sheriff

Ordering an expenses hearing

The Simple Procedure is a speedy, inexpensive and informal court procedure for settling or determining disputes with a value of **less than £5,000**.

This is an order of the sheriff in a case which you are a party in. You should **read it** and **follow it**.

| | |
|---|---|
| **Sheriff Court:** | |
| **Date of order:** | |
| **Claimant:** | |
| **Respondent:** | |
| **Court ref no:** | |

The sheriff has decided the case and is going to make an order about expenses. The sheriff has **given the following orders**:–

**Account of expenses**
The sheriff orders the [claimant / respondent] to send an account of expenses to the court and to the other party by [date 4 weeks before the expenses hearing].

**Assessment of expenses**
The sheriff orders the sheriff clerk to assess that account of expenses and send both parties a notice of that assessment by [date 2 weeks before the expenses hearing].

**Expenses hearing**
The sheriff orders both parties to attend an expenses hearing at [sheriff court] on [date] at [time]. Both parties should arrive in good time at the sheriff court building. If either party does not intend to challenge the assessment of expenses made by the sheriff clerk, they should contact the sheriff clerk by [date before the expenses hearing].

A failure to attend the expenses hearing will be considered an acceptance of the expenses as assessed by the sheriff clerk.

**Signed by:**

Sheriff of [sheriffdom] at [sheriff court]

# SHERIFF APPEAL COURT PRACTICE

SHERIFF APPEAL COURT PRACTICE

# SHERIFF APPEAL COURT PRACTICE

Act of Sederunt (Sheriff Appeal Court Rules) 2015
Chapter 1 Citation, Commencement and Interpretation etc.
Chapter 2 Relief for Failure to Comply
Chapter 3 Sanctions for Failure to Comply
Chapter 4 Representation and Support
Chapter 5 Intimation and Lodging Etc.
Chapter 6 Initiation of an Appeal
Chapter 7 Standard Appeal Procedure
Chapter 8 Refusal of Appeal Due to Delay
Chapter 9 Abandonment of Appeal
Chapter 10 Remit to the Court of Session
Chapter 11 Applications for Permission to Appeal to the Court of Session
Chapter 12 Motions: General
Chapter 13 Motions Lodged by Email
Chapter 14 Motions Lodged by Other Means
Chapter 15 Minutes
Chapter 16 Amendment of Pleadings
Chapter 17 Withdrawal of Solicitors
Chapter 18 Caution and Security
Chapter 19 Expenses
Chapter 20 Devolution Issues
Chapter 21 Preliminary References to the CJEU
Chapter 22 Interventions by CEHR and SCHR
Chapter 23 Proof
Chapter 24 Vulnerable Witnesses
Chapter 25 Use of Live Links
Chapter 26 Reporting Restrictions
Chapter 27 Accelerated Appeal Procedure
Chapter 28 Application for New Jury Trial or to Enter Jury Verdict
Chapter 29 Appeals from Summary Causes and Small Claims
Chapter 30 Appeals by Stated Case under Part 15 of the Children's Hearings
    (Scotland) Act 2011
Schedule 1 Administrative Provisions
Schedule 2 Forms

Practice Note No.1 of 2016

# ACT OF SEDERUNT (SHERIFF APPEAL COURT RULES) 2015

## (SSI 2015/356)

# CONTENTS

## PART 1 PRELIMINARY MATTERS
### CHAPTER 1 CITATION, COMMENCEMENT AND INTERPRETATION ETC.
1.1.  Citation and commencement, etc.
1.2.  Interpretation
1.3.  Computation of periods of time
1.4.  Administrative provisions
1.5.  Forms
## PART 2 GENERAL PROVISIONS
### CHAPTER 2 RELIEF FOR FAILURE TO COMPLY
2.1.  Relief for failure to comply with rules
### CHAPTER 3 SANCTIONS FOR FAILURE TO COMPLY
3.1.  Circumstances where a party is in default
3.2.  Sanctions where a party is in default
### CHAPTER 4 REPRESENTATION AND SUPPORT
4.1.  Representation and support
4.2.  Legal representation
4.3.  Lay representation: applications
4.4.  Lay representation: functions, conditions and duties
4.5.  Lay support: applications
4.6.  Lay support: functions, conditions and duties
### CHAPTER 5 INTIMATION AND LODGING ETC.
5.1.  Interpretation of this Chapter
5.2.  Intimation
5.3.  Methods of intimation
5.4.  Methods of intimation: recorded delivery
5.5.  Methods of intimation: by sheriff officer
5.6.  Additional methods of intimation where receiving party represented by solicitor
5.7.  Lodging
## PART 3 INITIATION AND PROGRESS OF AN APPEAL
### CHAPTER 6 INITIATION OF AN APPEAL
6.1.  Application of this Chapter
6.2.  Form of appeal
6.3.  Time for appeal
6.4.  Applications to appeal out of time
6.5.  Order for intimation and answers
6.6.  Initial case management of appeals
6.7.  Provisional orders: representations
### CHAPTER 7 STANDARD APPEAL PROCEDURE
7.1.  Application of this Chapter
7.2.  Timetable in appeal
7.3.  Cross-appeals
7.4.  Urgent disposal

7.5.        Urgent disposal: determination
7.6.        Sist of appeal and variation of timetable
7.7.        Questions about competency
7.8.        Questions about competency: determination
7.9.        Appeal print
7.10.       Appendix to appeal print: contents
7.11.       Appendix to appeal print considered unnecessary
7.12.       Notes of argument
7.13.       Estimates of duration of appeal hearing
7.14.       Procedural hearing
7.15.       Transmission of sheriff court process
7.16.       Extension of notes of evidence
7.17.       Referral to family mediation

PART 4 DISPOSAL OF AN APPEAL
CHAPTER 8 REFUSAL OF APPEAL DUE TO DELAY
8.1.        Application to refuse appeal due to delay
8.2.        Determination of application to refuse appeal due to delay

CHAPTER 9 ABANDONMENT OF APPEAL
9.1.        Application to abandon appeal

CHAPTER 10 REMIT TO THE COURT OF SESSION
10.1.       Application to remit appeal to the Court of Session

CHAPTER 11 APPLICATIONS FOR PERMISSION TO APPEAL TO THE
COURT OF SESSION
11.1.       Application of this Chapter
11.2.       Applications for permission to appeal

PART 5 INCIDENTAL PROCEDURE: STANDARD PROCEDURES
CHAPTER 12 MOTIONS: GENERAL
12.1.       Interpretation
12.2.       Making of motions
12.3.       Oral motions
12.4.       Written motions
12.5.       Provision of email addresses to the Clerk
12.6.       Grounds for written motion
12.7.       Determination of unopposed motions in writing
12.8.       Issuing of orders by email

CHAPTER 13 MOTIONS LODGED BY EMAIL
13.1.       Intimation of motions by email
13.2.       Opposition to motions
13.3.       Consent to motions
13.4.       Lodging unopposed motions
13.5.       Lodging opposed motions by email
13.6.       Variation of periods of intimation

CHAPTER 14 MOTIONS LODGED BY OTHER MEANS
14.1.       Intimation of motions by other means
14.2.       Opposition to motions
14.3.       Consent to motions
14.4.       Lodging of motions
14.5.       Joint motions
14.6.       Hearing of opposed motions

14.7.    Modification of Chapter 5
### CHAPTER 15 MINUTES
15.1.    Application of this Chapter
15.2.    Form and lodging of minute
15.3.    Orders for intimation and answers
15.4.    Consent to minute
15.5.    Minutes of sist and transference
15.6.    Applications to enter process as respondent
### CHAPTER 16 AMENDMENT OF PLEADINGS
16.1.    Amendment of sheriff court pleadings
16.2.    Amendment of note of appeal and answers etc.
### CHAPTER 17 WITHDRAWAL OF SOLICITORS
17.1.    Interpretation of this Chapter
17.2.    Giving notice of withdrawal to the Court
17.3.    Arrangements for peremptory hearing
17.4.    Peremptory hearing
### CHAPTER 18 CAUTION AND SECURITY
18.1.    Application of this Chapter
18.2.    Form of application to find caution or give security
18.3.    Orders for caution or other security: time for compliance
18.4.    Methods of finding caution or giving security
18.5.    Cautioners and other guarantors
18.6.    Form of bond of caution
18.7.    Caution or other security: sufficiency and objections
18.8.    Insolvency or death of cautioner or guarantor
18.9.    Failure to find caution or give security
### CHAPTER 19 EXPENSES
19.1.    Taxation of expenses
19.2.    Additional fee
19.3.    Order to lodge account of expenses
19.4.    Procedure for taxation of expenses
19.5.    Objections to taxed account
19.6.    Decree for expenses in name of solicitor
19.7.    Expenses of curator *ad litem* appointed to a respondent
### PART 6 INCIDENTAL PROCEDURE: SPECIAL PROCEDURES
### CHAPTER 20 DEVOLUTION ISSUES
20.1.    Interpretation
20.2.    Raising a devolution issue
20.3.    Raising a devolution issue: intimation and service
20.4.    Raising a devolution issue: permission to proceed
20.5.    Participation by the relevant authority
20.6.    Reference to the Inner House or Supreme Court
20.7.    Reference to the Inner House or Supreme Court: further procedure
20.8.    Reference to the Inner House or Supreme Court: procedure following determination
### CHAPTER 21 PRELIMINARY REFERENCES TO THE CJEU
21.1.    Interpretation of this Chapter
21.2.    Applications for a reference
21.3.    Preparation of reference

21.4.    Transmission of reference to European Court
21.5.    Sist of appeal

CHAPTER 22 INTERVENTIONS BY CEHR AND SCHR

22.1.    Application and interpretation of this Chapter
22.2.    Applications to intervene
22.3.    Applications to intervene: determination
22.4.    Invitations to intervene
22.5.    Form of intervention

CHAPTER 23 PROOF

23.1.    Taking proof in the course of an appeal
23.2.    Preparation for proof
23.3.    Conduct of proof
23.4.    Administration of oath or affirmation to witnesses
23.5.    Recording of evidence
23.6.    Transcripts of evidence
23.7.    Recording objections where recording of evidence dispensed with

CHAPTER 24 VULNERABLE WITNESSES

24.1.    Interpretation and application of this Chapter
24.2.    Form of notices and applications
24.3.    Determination of notices and applications
24.4.    Determination of notices and applications: supplementary orders
24.5.    Intimation of orders
24.6.    Taking of evidence by commissioner: preparatory steps
24.7.    Taking of evidence by commissioner: interrogatories
24.8.    Taking of evidence by commissioner: conduct of commission
24.9.    Taking of evidence by commissioner: lodging and custody of video record and documents

CHAPTER 25 USE OF LIVE LINKS

25.1.    Interpretation
25.2.    Application for use of live link

CHAPTER 26 REPORTING RESTRICTIONS

26.1.    Interpretation and application of this Chapter
26.2.    Interim orders: notification to interested persons
26.3.    Interim orders: representations
26.4.    Notification of reporting restrictions
26.5.    Applications for variation or revocation

PART 7 SPECIAL APPEAL PROCEEDINGS

CHAPTER 27 ACCELERATED APPEAL PROCEDURE

27.1.    Application of this Chapter
27.2.    Hearing of appeal
27.3.    Application to remove appeal from accelerated appeal procedure

CHAPTER 28 APPLICATION FOR NEW JURY TRIAL OR TO ENTER JURY VERDICT

28.1.    Application of this Chapter
28.2.    Form of application for new trial
28.3.    Application for new trial: restrictions
28.4.    Applications out of time
28.5.    Timetable in application for new trial
28.6.    Sist of application for new trial and variation of timetable

28.7.    Questions about competency of application
28.8.    Questions about competency: determination
28.9.    Appendices to print: contents
28.10.   Appendices to print considered unnecessary
28.11.   Notes of argument
28.12.   Estimates of duration of hearing of application for new trial
28.13.   Procedural hearing
28.14.   Application to enter jury verdict
CHAPTER 29 APPEALS FROM SUMMARY CAUSES AND SMALL CLAIMS
29.1.    Application of this Chapter
29.2.    Transmission of appeal
29.3.    Transmission of appeal: time to pay direction
29.4.    Hearing of appeal
29.5.    Determination of appeal
29.6.    Appeal to the Court of Session: certification
SCHEDULE 1            —        ADMINISTRATIVE PROVISIONS
SCHEDULE 2            —        FORMS

# CHAPTER 1 CITATION, COMMENCEMENT AND INTERPRETATION ETC.

In accordance with section 4 of the Scottish Civil Justice Council and Criminal Legal Assistance Act 2013, the Court of Session has approved draft rules submitted to it by the Scottish Civil Justice Council with such modifications as it thinks appropriate.

The Court of Session therefore makes this Act of Sederunt under the powers conferred by section 14(7) of the Scottish Commission for Human Rights Act 2006, section 104(1) of the Courts Reform (Scotland) Act 2014 and all other powers enabling it to do so.

PART 1

PRELIMINARY MATTERS

Chapter 1

**Citation, Commencement and Interpretation etc.**

## Citation and commencement, etc.

**1.1.**—(1)  This Act of Sederunt may be cited as the Act of Sederunt (Sheriff Appeal Court Rules) 2015.

(2)  It comes into force on 1st January 2016.

(3)  A certified copy is to be inserted in the Books of Sederunt.

## Interpretation

**1.2.**—(1)  In this Act of Sederunt—

"the 2014 Act" means the Courts Reform (Scotland) Act 2014;

"the Clerk" means the Clerk of the Sheriff Appeal Court;

"advocate" means a practising member of the Faculty of Advocates;

"the Court" means the Sheriff Appeal Court;

"grounds of appeal" has the meaning given by rule 6.2(2)(b);

"party litigant" has the meaning given by rule 4.1(2);

"procedural Appeal Sheriff" has the meaning given by paragraph 2(1) of Schedule 1;

"procedural hearing" means a hearing under rule 7.14 or rule 28.13;

"provisional procedural order" means an order under rule 6.6(1);

"sheriff court process" means—

    (a)  the sheriff court process for the cause that is appealed to the Court; or

    (b)  where the cause is recorded in an official book of the sheriff court, a copy of the record in that book certified by the sheriff clerk;

"sheriff's note" means a note setting out the reasons for the decision appealed against;

"solicitor" means a person qualified to practise as a solicitor under section 4 of the Solicitors (Scotland) Act 1980;

"timetable" means a timetable in—

    (a)  Form 7.2 issued under—

        (i)  rule 7.2(1) (timetable in appeal);

> > > (ii) rule 7.6(5)(a) (recall of sist: issuing revised timetable); or
> > >
> > > (iii) rule 7.6(6)(b) (variation of timetable: issuing revised timetable); or
> >
> > (b) Form 28.5 issued under—
> >
> > > (i) rule 28.5(1) (timetable in application for new trial);
> > >
> > > (ii) rule 28.6(6)(a) (recall of sist: issuing revised timetable); or
> > >
> > > (iii) rule 28.6(7)(b) (variation of timetable: issuing revised timetable).
>
> (2) In relation to an application under section 69(1) or 71(2) of the 2014 Act—

> "appeal" includes that application;
> "appellant" includes the applicant;
> "note of appeal" includes an application in Form 28.2 or Form 28.14.

### Computation of periods of time

**1.3.** If any period of time specified in these Rules expires on a Saturday, Sunday or public or court holiday, it is extended to expire on the next day that the office of the Clerk is open for civil business.

### Administrative provisions

**1.4.** Schedule 1 makes provision about administrative arrangements for the Court, including its quorum.

### Forms

**1.5.**—(1) Where there is a reference in these Rules to a form, it is a reference to that form in Schedule 2.

(2) Where these Rules require a form to be used, that form may be varied where the circumstances require it.

# CHAPTER 2 RELIEF FOR FAILURE TO COMPLY

Chapter 2

## Relief for Failure to Comply

### Relief for failure to comply with rules

**2.1.**—(1)  The Court may relieve a party from the consequences of a failure to comply with a provision in these Rules.

(2)  The Court may do so only where the party shows that the failure is due to—
    (a)  mistake;
    (b)  oversight; or
    (c)  any other excusable cause.

(3)  Where relief is granted, the Court may—
    (a)  impose conditions that must be satisfied before relief is granted;
    (b)  make an order to enable the appeal to proceed as if the failure had not occurred.

Chapter 3

## Sanctions for Failure to Comply

### Circumstances where a party is in default

**3.1.** A party is in default if that party fails—
- (a) to comply with the timetable;
- (b) to implement an order of the Court within the period specified in the order;
- (c) to appear or be represented at any hearing; or
- (d) otherwise to comply with any requirement imposed on that party by these Rules.

### Sanctions where a party is in default

**3.2.**—(1) This rule—
- (a) applies where a party is in default; but
- (b) does not apply where a party is in default because the party has failed to comply with rule 17.4(1) (peremptory hearing).

(2) The procedural Appeal Sheriff may make any order to secure the expeditious disposal of the appeal.

(3) In particular, the procedural Appeal Sheriff may—
- (a) refuse the appeal, where the party in default is the appellant;
- (b) allow the appeal, if the condition in paragraph (4) is satisfied, where—
  - (i) the party in default is the sole respondent; or
  - (ii) every respondent is in default.

(4) The condition is that the appellant must show cause why the appeal should be allowed.

Chapter 4

**Representation and Support**

## Representation and support

**4.1.**—(1)  A natural person who is a party to proceedings may appear and act on that party's behalf.

(2)  That person is to be known as a party litigant.

(3)  A party may be represented in any proceedings by—

    (a)  a legal representative (see rule 4.2); or

    (b)  a lay representative (see rule 4.3).

(4)  A lay supporter (see rule 4.5) may assist a party litigant with the conduct of any proceedings.

## Legal representation

**4.2.**  A party is represented by a legal representative if that party is represented by an advocate or a solicitor.

## Lay representation: applications

**4.3.**—(1)  This rule does not apply where any other enactment makes provision for a party to a particular type of case to be represented by a lay representative.

(2)  A party is represented by a lay representative if that party is represented by a person who is not a legal representative.

(3)  A party litigant may apply to the Court for permission to be represented by a lay representative.

(4)  An application is to be—

    (a)  made by motion;

    (b)  accompanied by a document in Form 4.3 signed by the prospective lay representative.

(5)  The Court may grant an application only if it considers that it would assist its consideration of the appeal to do so.

(6)  Where the Court grants permission, it may—

    (a)  do so in respect of one or more specified hearings;

    (b)  withdraw permission of its own accord or on the motion of any party.

## Lay representation: functions, conditions and duties

**4.4.**—(1)  A lay representative may represent a party at a specified hearing for the purpose of making oral submissions on behalf of the party.

(2)  The party must appear along with the lay representative at any hearing where the lay representative is to make oral submissions.

(3)  A party may show any document (including a court document) or communicate any information about the proceedings to that party's lay representative without contravening any prohibition or restriction on disclosure of the document or information.

(4)  Where a document or information is disclosed under paragraph (3), the lay representative is subject to any prohibition or restriction on disclosure in the same way that the party is.

(5)     A lay representative must not receive directly or indirectly from the party any remuneration or other reward for assisting the party.

(6)     Any expenses incurred by a party in connection with a lay representative are not recoverable expenses in the proceedings.

## Lay support: applications

**4.5.**—(1)    A party litigant may apply to the Court for permission for a named person to assist the party litigant in the conduct of proceedings, and such a person is to be known as a lay supporter.

(2)     An application is to be made by motion.

(3)     The Court may refuse an application only if it is of the opinion that—

    (a)    the named person is an unsuitable person to act as a lay supporter (whether generally or in the proceedings concerned); or

    (b)    it would be contrary to the efficient administration of justice to grant it.

(4)     The Court, if satisfied that it would be contrary to the efficient administration of justice for permission to continue, may withdraw permission—

    (a)    of its own accord;

    (b)    on the motion of any party.

## Lay support: functions, conditions and duties

**4.6.**—(1)    A lay supporter may assist a party by accompanying the party at hearings in court or in chambers.

(2)     A lay supporter may, if authorised by the party, assist the party by—

    (a)    providing moral support;

    (b)    helping to manage court documents and other papers;

    (c)    taking notes of the proceedings;

    (d)    quietly advising on—

        (i)    points of law and procedure;

        (ii)    issues which the party litigant might wish to raise with the Court.

(3)     A party may show any document (including a court document) or communicate any information about the proceedings to that party's lay supporter without contravening any prohibition or restriction on disclosure of the document or information.

(4)     Where a document or information is disclosed under paragraph (3), the lay supporter is subject to any prohibition or restriction on disclosure in the same way that the party is.

(5)     A lay supporter must not receive directly or indirectly from the party any remuneration or other reward for assisting the party.

(6)     Any expenses incurred by a party in connection with a lay supporter are not recoverable expenses in the proceedings.

# CHAPTER 5 INTIMATION AND LODGING ETC.

## Chapter 5

## Intimation and Lodging Etc.

### Interpretation of this Chapter

**5.1.**—(1)   In this Chapter—

"first class post" means a postal service which seeks to deliver documents or other things by post no later than the next working day in all or the majority of cases;

"intimating party" means any party who has to give intimation in accordance with rule 5.2(1);

"receiving party" means any party to whom intimation is to be given in accordance with rule 5.2;

"recorded delivery" means a postal service which provides for the delivery of documents or other things by post to be recorded.

(2)   Where this Chapter authorises intimation to be given by electronic means—

(a)   intimation may only be given by this method if the intimating party and the solicitor for the receiving party have notified the Court that they will accept intimation by electronic means at a specified email address;

(b)   the intimation is to be sent to the specified email address of the solicitor for the receiving party.

(3)   Where this Chapter authorises a document to be lodged by electronic means, it is to be sent to the email address of the Court.

### Intimation

**5.2.**—(1)   Unless the Court orders otherwise, where—

(a)   any provision in these Rules requires a party to—

(i)   lodge any document;

(ii)   intimate any other matter; or

(b)   the Court orders a party to intimate something,

intimation is to be given to every other party.

(2)   Where the Court makes an order, the Clerk is to intimate the order to every party.

### Methods of intimation

**5.3.**—(1)   Intimation may be given to a receiving party who is a party litigant by—

(a)   the method specified in rule 5.4;

(b)   any of the methods specified in rule 5.5.

(2)   Intimation may be given to a receiving party who is represented by a solicitor by—

(a)   the method specified in rule 5.4;

(b)   any of the methods specified in rule 5.5;

(c)   any of the methods specified in rule 5.6.

## Methods of intimation: recorded delivery

**5.4.** An intimating party may give intimation by recorded delivery to the receiving party.

## Methods of intimation: by sheriff officer

**5.5.**—(1) A sheriff officer may give intimation on behalf of an intimating party by—

    (a) delivering it personally to the receiving party; or

    (b) leaving it in the hands of—

        (i) a resident at the receiving party's dwelling place; or

        (ii) an employee at the receiving party's place of business.

(2) Where a sheriff officer has been unsuccessful in giving intimation in accordance with paragraph (1), the sheriff officer may give intimation by—

    (a) depositing it in the receiving party's dwelling place or place of business; or

    (b) leaving it at the receiving party's dwelling place or place of business in such a way that it is likely to come to the attention of that party.

## Additional methods of intimation where receiving party represented by solicitor

**5.6.**—(1) An intimating party may give intimation to the solicitor for the receiving party by—

    (a) delivering it personally to the solicitor;

    (b) delivering it to a document exchange of which the solicitor is a member;

    (c) first class post;

    (d) fax;

    (e) electronic means.

(2) Where intimation is given by the method in paragraph (1)(a), (d) or (e) not later than 1700 hours on any day, the date of intimation is that day.

(3) Where intimation is given by the method in—

    (a) paragraph (1)(b) or (c); or

    (b)[1] paragraph 1(a), (d) or (e) after 1700 hours on any day,

the date of intimation is the next day.

## Lodging

**5.7.**—(1) Where any provision in these Rules requires a party to lodge a document, it is to be lodged with the Clerk.

(2) A document may be lodged by—

    (a) delivering it personally to the office of the Clerk;

    (b) delivering it to a document exchange of which the Clerk is a member;

    (c) first class post;

    (d) fax;

    (e) electronic means.

---

[1] As amended by the Act of Sederunt (Rules of the Court of Session, Sheriff Appeal Court Rules and Sheriff Court Rules Amendment) (Sheriff Appeal Court) 2015 (SSI 2015/419) r.19 (effective 1 January 2016; amendment came into force on December 31, 2015 but could not take effect until the commencement of SSI 2015/356 r.5.6(3)(b) on January 1, 2016)).

PART 3

INITIATION AND PROGRESS OF AN APPEAL

Chapter 6

**Initiation of an Appeal**

**Application of this Chapter**

**6.1.** This Chapter applies to an appeal against a decision of a sheriff in civil proceedings except—

(a) an application for a new trial under section 69(1) of the 2014 Act (see Chapter 28);

(b) an application to enter a jury verdict under section 71(2) of the 2014 Act (see Chapter 28);

(c) an appeal under section 38 of the Sheriff Courts (Scotland) Act 1971 (see Chapter 29);

(d) an appeal by stated case under section 163(1), 164(1), 165(1) or 167(1) of the Children's Hearings (Scotland) Act 2011 (see Chapter 30).

(e)[1] an appeal against an interlocutor granting decree of divorce in a simplified divorce application (see rule 33.81 of the Ordinary Cause Rules 1993);

(f)[2] an appeal against an interlocutor granting decree of dissolution of civil partnership in a simplified dissolution of civil partnership application (see rule 33A.74 of the Ordinary Cause Rules 1993).

**Form of appeal**

**6.2.**—(1) An appeal is made by lodging a note of appeal in Form 6.2.

(2) The note of appeal must—

(a) specify—

(i) the decision complained of;

(ii) the date on which the decision was made;

(iii) the date on which it was intimated to the appellant;

(iv) any other relevant information;

(b) state the grounds of appeal in brief specific numbered paragraphs setting out concisely the grounds on which it is proposed that the appeal should be allowed;

(ba)[3] have appended to it a copy of the interlocutor containing the decision appealed against;

---

[1] As inserted by the Act of Sederunt (Rules of the Court of Session, Sheriff Appeal Court Rules and Sheriff Court Rules Amendment) (Sheriff Appeal Court) 2015 (SSI 2015/419) r.19 (effective 1 January 2016; insertion came into force on December 31, 2015 but could not take effect until the commencement of SSI 2015/356 r.5.6(3)(b) on January 1, 2016)).

[2] As inserted by the Act of Sederunt (Rules of the Court of Session, Sheriff Appeal Court Rules and Sheriff Court Rules Amendment) (Sheriff Appeal Court) 2015 (SSI 2015/419) r.19 (effective 1 January 2016; insertion came into force on December 31, 2015 but could not take effect until the commencement of SSI 2015/356 r.5.6(3)(b) on January 1, 2016)).

[3] As inserted by the Act of Sederunt (Sheriff Appeal Court Rules 2015 and Sheriff Court Rules Amendment) (Miscellaneous) 2016 (SSI 2016/194) r.7 (effective 7 July 2016).

(c) where the sheriff's note is available, have appended to it a copy of the note;

(d) where the sheriff's note is not available, indicate whether the appellant—

    (i) has requested that the sheriff writes a note and is awaiting its production;

    (ii) requests that the sheriff write a note; or

    (iii) considers that the appeal is sufficiently urgent that the Court should hear and determine the appeal without the sheriff's note;

(e) state whether, taking into account the matters in rule 6.6(3), the appellant considers that the appeal should be appointed to the standard appeal procedure or to the accelerated appeal procedure;

(f)[1] be signed;

(g) where the appellant is represented by a solicitor, specify the name and business address of the solicitor.

(3) When a note of appeal is lodged, the appellant must lodge a process made up in accordance with paragraph 4 of Schedule 1 (form of process).

### Time for appeal

**6.3.**—(1) An appeal must be made within 28 days after the date on which the decision appealed against was given.

(2) This rule does not apply where the enactment under which the appeal is made specifies a period within which the appeal must be made.

### Applications to appeal out of time

**6.4.**—(1) This rule applies where the enactment under which the appeal is made—

(a) specifies a period within which the appeal must be made; and

(b) provides that a party may apply to the Court to allow an appeal to be made outwith that period.

(2) An application to allow an appeal to be received out of time is to be made by motion.

(3) That motion is to be made when the note of appeal is lodged.

(4) Where a motion to allow an appeal to be received out of time is refused—

(a) the Clerk is to—

    (i) notify the sheriff clerk that leave to appeal out of time has been refused;

    (ii) transmit the note of appeal to the sheriff clerk;

(b) the sheriff clerk is to place the note of appeal in the process.

### Order for intimation and answers

**6.5.**—(1) On the first available court day after being lodged, an appeal is to be brought before the procedural Appeal Sheriff for an order for—

(a) intimation of the appeal, within 7 days after the date of the order, to be given to—

    (i) the respondent;

---

[1] As amended by the Act of Sederunt (Sheriff Appeal Court Rules 2015 and Sheriff Court Rules Amendment) (Miscellaneous) 2016 (SSI 2016/194) r.7 (effective 7 July 2016).

  (ii)  any other person who appears to have an interest in the appeal;
  (b)  any person on whom the appeal is intimated to lodge answers, if so advised, within 14 days after the date of intimation.

(2)  The procedural Appeal Sheriff may vary the periods of 7 days and 14 days mentioned in paragraph (1)—
  (a)  of the procedural Appeal Sheriff's own accord; or
  (b)  on cause shown, on the application of the appellant.

(3)  That application must—
  (a)  be included in the note of appeal;
  (b)  give reasons for varying the period.

(4)  Where an appeal is intimated under this rule, the appellant must lodge a certificate of intimation in Form 6.5 within 14 days after the date of intimation.

### Initial case management of appeals

**6.6.**—(1)  When the procedural Appeal Sheriff makes an order for intimation and answers in accordance with rule 6.5(1), the procedural Appeal Sheriff must also make a provisional procedural order.

(2)  The provisional procedural order must provisionally appoint the appeal to—
  (a)  the standard appeal procedure (see Chapter 7); or
  (b)  the accelerated appeal procedure (see Chapter 27).

(3)  When considering which procedure is appropriate for the appeal, the procedural Appeal Sheriff must take into account—
  (a)  the importance of the appeal;
  (b)  the complexity of the appeal;
  (c)  the novelty of the points of law raised by the appeal; and
  (d)  the presumption in paragraph (4).

(4)  The following categories of appeal are presumed to be appropriate for the accelerated appeal procedure—
  (a)  appeals against a decision of the sheriff to grant decree by default;
  (b)  appeals against a decision of the sheriff to refuse a reponing note.

(5)  A provisional procedural order under this rule is to be intimated at the same time and in the same manner as the order for intimation and answers made in accordance with rule 6.5.

### Provisional orders: representations

**6.7.**[1](1)  Any person to whom a provisional procedural order under rule 6.6 has been intimated may make representations before that order becomes final.

(2)  Representations are to be—
  (a)  made in Form 6.7;
  (b)  lodged within 14 days after the date of intimation of the provisional order.

(2A)  Paragraph (2B) applies where the procedural Appeal Sheriff varies the period of 14 days mentioned in rule 6.5(1)(b) in accordance with rule 6.5(2).

(2B)  The procedural Appeal Sheriff may also vary the period of 14 days mentioned in paragraph (2)(b).

---

[1] As amended by the Act of Sederunt (Sheriff Appeal Court Rules 2015 and Sheriff Court Rules Amendment) (Miscellaneous) 2016 (SSI 2016/194) r.7 (effective 7 July 2016).

(3)  Representations must specify why, taking into account the matters in rule 6.6(3), it is not appropriate for the appeal to proceed in accordance with the provisional procedural order.

(4)  If representations are made, the Clerk is to fix a hearing and intimate the time and date of that hearing to every person to whom the provisional order was intimated.

(5)  At that hearing, the procedural Appeal Sheriff may—

    (a)  confirm the provisional procedural order; or

    (b)  recall the provisional procedural order and make an order appointing the appeal to the standard appeal procedure or the accelerated appeal procedure.

(6)  If no representations are made in accordance with paragraph (2), the provisional procedural order becomes final.

# CHAPTER 7 STANDARD APPEAL PROCEDURE

Chapter 7

## Standard Appeal Procedure

### Application of this Chapter

**7.1.** This Chapter applies to an appeal which has been appointed to proceed under the standard appeal procedure.

### Timetable in appeal

**7.2.**—(1) The Clerk must issue a timetable in Form 7.2 when—

(a) a provisional procedural order appointing the appeal to the standard appeal procedure becomes final or is confirmed; or

(b) the Court makes an order appointing the appeal to the standard appeal procedure under rule 6.7(5)(b).

(2) When the Clerk issues a timetable, the Clerk must also fix a procedural hearing to take place after completion of the procedural steps specified in paragraph (4).

(3) The timetable specifies—

(a) the dates by which parties must comply with those procedural steps;

(b) the date and time of the procedural hearing.

(4) The procedural steps are the steps mentioned in the first column of the following table, provision in respect of which is found in the rule mentioned in the second column—

| Procedural step | Rule |
| --- | --- |
| Cross appeals: lodging of grounds of appeal | 7.3(1) |
| Cross appeals: lodging of answers | 7.3(2) |
| Referral of question about competency of appeal | 7.7(3) |
| Lodging of appeal print | 7.9(1) and (2) |
| Lodging of appendices to appeal print | 7.10(1) |
| Giving notice that the appellant considers appendix unnecessary | 7.11(1) |
| Lodging of notes of argument | 7.12(1) |
| Lodging of estimates of duration of appeal hearing | 7.13 |

### Cross-appeals

**7.3.**—(1)[1] A respondent who seeks to—

(a) appeal against any decision of the sheriff; or

(b) challenge the grounds on which the sheriff made the decision appealed against,

may lodge grounds of appeal in Form 7.3 within 28 days after the timetable is issued under rule 7.2(1).

---

[1] As amended by the Act of Sederunt (Rules of the Court of Session, Sheriff Appeal Court Rules and Sheriff Court Rules Amendment) (Sheriff Appeal Court) 2015 (SSI 2015/419) r.19 (effective 1 January 2016; amendment came into force on 31 December 2015 but could not take effect until the commencement of SSI 2015/356 r.5.6(3)(b) on 1 January 2016)).

(2)   The appellant may lodge answers to the respondent's grounds of appeal within 28 days after the grounds are intimated to the appellant.

## Urgent disposal

7.4.—(1)   The procedural Appeal Sheriff may order urgent disposal of an appeal—

    (a)   of the procedural Appeal Sheriff's own accord; or

    (b)   on the application of the appellant or a respondent.

(2)   Where the appellant or a respondent seeks urgent disposal, an application for urgent disposal is to be made by motion.

(3)   An application may be made—

    (a)   by the appellant, when the note of appeal is lodged;

    (b)   by the respondent, not later than the expiry of the period for lodging answers specified in rule 6.5(1)(b) (order for intimation and answers).

(4)   Where the decision appealed against concerns an order made by the sheriff under section 11(1) of the Children (Scotland) Act 1995 (court orders relating to parental responsibilities etc.), the appellant must seek urgent disposal.

(5)   Where the procedural Appeal Sheriff proposes to order urgent disposal of the procedural Appeal Sheriff's own accord—

    (a)   the Clerk must notify every party to the appeal;

    (b)   any party who objects to urgent disposal may make representations within such time and in such manner as the procedural Appeal Sheriff orders.

## Urgent disposal: determination

7.5.—(1)   Where an application for urgent disposal is opposed, it may only be disposed of after the procedural Appeal Sheriff has heard parties on it.

(2)   Where a party makes representations objecting to urgent disposal in accordance with rule 7.4(5), the procedural Appeal Sheriff must hear parties before ordering urgent disposal.

(3)   At a hearing under paragraph (1) or (2), the parties must provide the procedural Appeal Sheriff with an assessment of the likely duration of the hearing to determine the appeal.

(4)   When ordering urgent disposal of an appeal, the procedural Appeal Sheriff must make an order specifying—

    (a)   the procedure to be followed in the appeal;

    (b)   the periods for complying with each procedural step.

(5)   Accordingly, the following rules apply only to the extent that the procedural Appeal Sheriff specifies in the order made under paragraph (3)—

    (a)   rule 7.2 (timetable in appeal);

    (b)   rule 7.7 (questions about competency of appeal);

    (c)   rule 7.8 (questions about competency: determination);

    (d)   rule 7.9 (appeal print);

    (e)   rule 7.10 (appendices to the appeal print: contents);

    (f)   rule 7.11 (appendices to the appeal print considered unnecessary);

    (g)   rule 7.12 (notes of argument);

    (h)   rule 7.13 (estimates of duration of appeal hearing);

    (i)   rule 7.14 (procedural hearing).

**Sist of appeal and variation of timetable**

7.6.—(1) Any party may apply by motion to—
    (a) sist the appeal for a specified period;
    (b) recall a sist;
    (c) vary the timetable.

(2) An application to sist the appeal or vary the timetable may only be granted on special cause shown.

(3) The procedural Appeal Sheriff may—
    (a) grant the application;
    (b) refuse the application; or
    (c) make an order not sought in the application, where the procedural Appeal Sheriff considers that doing so would secure the expeditious disposal of the appeal.

(4) Where the procedural Appeal Sheriff makes an order sisting the appeal, the Clerk is to discharge the procedural hearing fixed under rule 7.2(2) (timetable: fixing procedural hearing).

(5) When a sist is recalled or expires, the Clerk is to—
    (a) issue a revised timetable in Form 7.2;
    (b) fix a procedural hearing.

(6) Where the procedural Appeal Sheriff makes an order varying the timetable, the Clerk is to—
    (a) discharge the procedural hearing fixed under rule 7.2(2) (timetable: fixing procedural hearing);
    (b) issue a revised timetable in Form 7.2;
    (c) fix a procedural hearing.

**Questions about competency**

7.7.—(1) A question about the competency of an appeal may be referred to the procedural Appeal Sheriff by any respondent.

(2) A question is referred by lodging a reference in Form 7.7.

(3) A question may be referred within 14 days after the timetable is issued under rule 7.2(1).

(4) When a reference is lodged, the Clerk is to fix a hearing and intimate the date and time of that hearing to the parties.

(5) Within 14 days after the date on which the reference is lodged, each party must lodge a note of argument.

(6) That note of argument must—
    (a) give fair notice of the submissions the party intends to make on the question of competency;
    (b) comply with the requirements in rule 7.12(3).

(7) Paragraphs (4) and (5) of rule 7.12 apply to that note of argument.

**Questions about competency: determination**

7.8.—(1) At a hearing on the competency of an appeal, the procedural Appeal Sheriff may—
    (a) refuse the appeal as incompetent;
    (b) find the appeal to be competent;
    (c) reserve the question of competency until the appeal hearing; or
    (d) refer the question of competency to the Court.

(2)   The procedural Appeal Sheriff may make an order as to the expenses of the reference.

(3)   Where the question of competency is referred to the Court, it may—

    (a)   refuse the appeal as incompetent;

    (b)   find the appeal to be competent;

    (c)   reserve the question of competency until the appeal hearing.

(4)   The Court may make an order as to the expenses of the reference.

### Appeal print

**7.9.**[1](1)   The appellant must lodge an appeal print within 21 days after the timetable is issued under rule 7.2(1).

(2)   An appeal print is to contain—

    (a)   the pleadings in the sheriff court process;

    (b)   the interlocutors in the sheriff court process;

    (c)   the sheriff's note setting out the reasons for the decision appealed against, if it is available.

(3)   Where the appeal is directed at the refusal of the sheriff to allow the pleadings to be amended, the appeal print is also to contain the text of the proposed amendment.

### Appendix to appeal print: contents

**7.10.**—(1)   The appellant must lodge an appendix to the appeal print no later than 7 days before the procedural hearing, unless rule 7.11(1) (giving notice that appellant considers appendix unnecessary) is complied with.

(2)   The appendix is to contain—

    (a)   any document lodged in the sheriff court process that is founded upon in the grounds of appeal;

    (b)   the notes of evidence from any proof, if it is sought to submit them for consideration by the Court.

(3)   Where the sheriff's note has not been included in the appeal print and it subsequently becomes available, the appellant must—

    (a)   include it in the appendix where the appendix has not yet been lodged; or

    (b)   lodge a supplementary appendix containing the sheriff's note.

(4)   The parties must—

    (a)   discuss the contents of the appendix;

    (b)   so far as possible, co-operate in making up the appendix.

### Appendix to appeal print considered unnecessary

**7.11.**—(1)   Where the appellant considers that it is not necessary to lodge an appendix, the appellant must, no later than 7 days before the procedural hearing—

    (a)   give written notice of that fact to the Clerk;

    (b)   intimate that notice to every respondent.

---

[1] As substituted by the Act of Sederunt (Rules of the Court of Session, Sheriff Appeal Court Rules and Sheriff Court Rules Amendment) (Sheriff Appeal Court) 2015 (SSI 2015/419) r.19 (effective 1 January 2016; substitution came into force on 31 December 2015 but could not take effect until the commencement of SSI 2015/356 r.5.6(3)(b) on 1 January 2016)).

(2)    Where the appellant complies with paragraph (1), the respondent may apply by motion for an order requiring the appellant to lodge an appendix.

(3)    An application must specify the documents or notes of evidence that the respondent considers should be included in the appendix.

(4)    In disposing of an application, the procedural Appeal Sheriff may—

    (a)    grant the application and make an order requiring the appellant to lodge an appendix;

    (b)    refuse the application and make an order requiring the respondent to lodge an appendix; or

    (c)    refuse the application and make no order.

(5)    Where the procedural Appeal Sheriff makes an order requiring the appellant or the respondent to lodge an appendix, that order must specify—

    (a)    the documents or notes or evidence to be included in the appendix;

    (b)    the time within which the appendix must be lodged.

## Notes of argument

**7.12.**—(1)    The parties must lodge notes of argument no later than 7 days before the procedural hearing.

(2)    A note of argument must summarise briefly the submissions the party intends to develop at the appeal hearing.

(3)    A note of argument must—

    (a)    state, in brief numbered paragraphs, the points that the party intends to make;

    (b)    after each point, identify by means of a page or paragraph reference the relevant passage in any notes of evidence or other document on which the party relies in support of the point;

    (c)    for every authority that is cited—

        (i)    state the proposition of law that the authority demonstrates;

        (ii)    identify the page or paragraph references for the parts of the authority that support the proposition;

    (d)    cite only one authority for each proposition of law, unless additional citation is necessary for a proper presentation of the argument.

(4)    Where a note of argument has been lodged and the party lodging it subsequently becomes aware that an argument in the note is not to be insisted upon, that party must—

    (a)    give written notice of that fact to the Clerk;

    (b)    intimate that notice to every other party.

(5)    Where a party wishes to advance an argument at a hearing that is not contained in that party's note of argument, the party must apply by motion for leave to advance the argument.

## Estimates of duration of appeal hearing

**7.13.**    The parties must lodge estimates of the duration of any appeal hearing required to dispose of the appeal in Form 7.13 not later than 7 days before the procedural hearing.

## Procedural hearing

**7.14.**—(1)    At a procedural hearing, the procedural Appeal Sheriff is to ascertain the state of preparation of the parties, so far as reasonably practicable.

(2)   The procedural Appeal Sheriff may—

    (a)   determine that parties are ready to proceed to an appeal hearing; or

    (b)   determine that further procedure is required.

(3)   Where the procedural Appeal Sheriff determines that parties are ready to proceed—

    (a)   the procedural Appeal Sheriff is to fix an appeal hearing;

    (b)   the Clerk is to intimate the date and time of that hearing to the parties;

    (c)   the procedural Appeal Sheriff may make an order specifying further steps to be taken by the parties before the hearing.

(4)   Where the procedural Appeal Sheriff determines that further procedure is required, the procedural Appeal Sheriff—

    (a)   is to make an order to secure the expeditious disposal of the appeal;

    (b)   may direct the Clerk to fix a further procedural hearing and intimate the date and time of that hearing to parties.

### Transmission of sheriff court process

**7.15.**[1](1)   The procedural Appeal Sheriff may order that the sheriff court process, or any part of it, is to be transmitted to the Clerk—

    (a)   of its own accord;

    (b)   on cause shown, where any party to the appeal applies for such an order by motion.

(2)   Where the procedural Appeal Sheriff makes such an order, the Clerk must send a copy of the order to the sheriff clerk.

(3)   Within 4 days after receipt of the order, the sheriff clerk must—

    (a)   send written notice to each party to the cause;

    (b)   certify on the interlocutor sheet that subparagraph (a) has been complied with;

    (c)   transmit the sheriff court process, or the specified part of it, to the Clerk.

(4)   On receipt of the sheriff court process, the Clerk must—

    (a)   mark the date of receipt on—

        (i)   the interlocutor sheet or the copy record from the sheriff court books, where the entire process is transmitted;

        (ii)   the part of process that has been transmitted, where the procedural Appeal Sheriff has specified that only part of the process is to be transmitted;

    (b)   send written notice of that date to the appellant.

(5)   Where the Clerk or a sheriff clerk fails to comply with this rule—

    (a)   that does not affect the validity of the appeal;

    (b)   the Court may, as it thinks fit, make an order to enable the appeal to proceed as if the failure had not occurred.

### Extension of notes of evidence

**7.16.**—(1)   The parties may agree that, in relation to any particular issue, the decision appealed against is not to be submitted to review.

(2)   It is not necessary to reproduce the notes of evidence or documents relating to that issue.

---

[1] As amended by the Act of Sederunt (Sheriff Appeal Court Rules 2015 and Sheriff Court Rules Amendment) (Miscellaneous) 2016 (SSI 2016/194) r.7 (effective 7 July 2016).

**Referral to family mediation**

**7.17.**—(1)  Where the decision appealed against concerns an order made by the sheriff under section 11(1) of the Children (Scotland) Act 1995 (court orders relating to parental responsibilities etc.), the procedural Appeal Sheriff may refer that matter to a family mediator.

(2)  In this rule, "family mediator" means a person accredited as a mediator in family mediation to an organisation which is concerned with such mediation and which is approved for the purposes of the Civil Evidence (Family Mediation) (Scotland) Act 1995 by the Lord President of the Court of Session.

Chapter 8

**Refusal of Appeal Due to Delay**

**Application to refuse appeal due to delay**

**8.1.**—(1)    Any party may apply to the procedural Appeal Sheriff to refuse the appeal if the conditions in paragraph (2) are met.

(2)    The conditions are that—
   (a)    there has been an inordinate and inexcusable delay by another party or another party's solicitor; and
   (b)    unfairness has resulted from that delay.

(3)    An application is to be made by motion.

(4)    That motion must specify the grounds on which refusal of the appeal is sought.

**Determination of application to refuse appeal due to delay**

**8.2.**—(1)    The procedural Appeal Sheriff may refuse the appeal if the procedural Appeal Sheriff considers that—
   (a)    there has been an inordinate and inexcusable delay on the part of any party or any party's solicitor; and
   (b)    such delay results in unfairness specific to the factual circumstances, including the procedural circumstances, of the appeal.

(2)    The procedural Appeal Sheriff must take into account the procedural consequences of allowing the appeal to proceed for—
   (a)    the parties to the appeal;
   (b)    the efficient disposal of business in the Court.

Chapter 9

## Abandonment of Appeal

### Application to abandon appeal

**9.1.**—(1)    An appellant may apply to the Court to abandon an appeal by lodging a minute of abandonment.

(2)    Where all of the parties consent to the abandonment of the appeal, the Court must refuse the appeal.

(3)    Where the other parties do not consent to the abandonment of the appeal, the Court may—

    (a)    refuse the application;

    (b)    grant the application and refuse the appeal.

(4)    If the Court refuses an appeal under this rule, it may make an order as to the expenses of the appeal.

(5)    If the Court refuses an application, it may make an order as to the expenses of the application.

Chapter 10

## Remit to the Court of Session

### Application to remit appeal to the Court of Session

**10.1.**—(1)  An application under section 112 of the 2014 Act (remit of appeal from the Sheriff Appeal Court to the Court of Session) is to be made by motion.

(2)  Within 4 days after the Court has made an order remitting an appeal to the Court of Session, the Clerk must—

    (a)   give notice of the remit to each party;

    (b)   certify on the interlocutor sheet that subparagraph (a) has been complied with;

    (c)   transmit the process to the Deputy Principal Clerk of Session.

(3)  Failure by the Clerk to comply with paragraph (2)(a) or (b) does not affect the validity of a remit.

# CHAPTER 11 APPLICATIONS FOR PERMISSION TO APPEAL TO THE COURT OF SESSION

Chapter 11

**Applications for Permission to Appeal to the Court of Session**

## Application of this Chapter

**11.1.** This Chapter applies where a party seeks the permission of the Court to appeal to the Court of Session against a decision of the Court constituting final judgment in civil proceedings under section 113 of the 2014 Act.

## Applications for permission to appeal

**11.2.**—(1) An application to the Court for permission to appeal to the Court of Session is to be made in Form 11.2.

(2) Such an application must be lodged within 14 days after the date on which the Court gave its decision on the appeal.

(3) When an application is made, the Clerk is to fix a hearing and intimate the time and date of that hearing to the parties to the appeal.

(4) The hearing is, so far as reasonably practicable, to be before the Appeal Sheriff or Appeal Sheriffs who made the decision in respect of which permission to appeal is sought.

Chapter 11

Applications for Permission to Appeal to the Court of Session

Application of this Chapter

11.1.— This Chapter applies where a party seeks the permission of the Court to
appeal to the Court of Session against a decision of the Lower constituted final Judgment in civil proceedings under section 112 of the 2014 Act.

Applications for permission to appeal

11.2.— (1) An application to the Court for permission to appeal to the Court of
Session is to be made in Form 11.2.

(2) Such an application must be lodged within 14 days after the date on which
the Court gave its decision on the appeal.

(3) When an application is made, the Clerk is to fix a hearing and intimate the
time and date of that hearing to the parties to the appeal.

(4) The hearing is as far as reasonably practicable to be before the Appeal
Sheriff or Appeal Sheriffs who made the decision in respect of which permission to
appeal is sought.

# CHAPTER 12 MOTIONS: GENERAL

## PART 5

## Chapter 12

## Motions: General

### Interpretation

**12.1.**—(1) In this Chapter, Chapter 13 and Chapter 14—

"court day" means a day on which the office of the Clerk is open;
"court day 1" means the court day on which a motion is treated as being intimated under rule 13.1;
"court day 3" means the second court day after court day 1;
"court day 4" means the third court day after court day 1;
"lodging party" means the party lodging the motion;
"receiving party" means a party receiving the intimation of the motion from the lodging party;
"transacting motion business" means—

      (a)   intimating and lodging motions;
      (b)   receiving intimation of motions;
      (c)   intimating consent or opposition to motions;
      (d)   receiving intimation of opposition to motions.

(2)   In this Chapter and Chapter 13, a reference to—

   (a)   the address of a party is a reference to the email address included in the list maintained under rule 12.5(4) of—

      (i)   that party's solicitor; or
      (ii)   that party;

   (b)   the address of the court is a reference to the email address of the court included in that list under rule 12.5(5).

### Making of motions

**12.2.**   A motion may be made—

   (a)   orally, in accordance with rule 12.3; or
   (b)   in writing, in accordance with rule 12.4.

### Oral motions

**12.3.**—(1)   A motion may be made orally during any hearing.

(2)   Such a motion may only be made with leave of the Court.

### Written motions

**12.4.**—(1)   A motion in writing is made by lodging it with the Clerk in accordance with Chapter 13 or Chapter 14.

(2)   Chapter 13 (motions lodged by email) applies where each party to an appeal has provided to the Clerk an email address for the purpose of transacting motion business.

(3)  Chapter 14 (motions lodged by other means) applies where a party to an appeal has not provided to the Clerk an email address for the purpose of transacting motion business.

### Provision of email addresses to the Clerk

**12.5.**—(1)  A solicitor representing a party in an appeal must provide to the Clerk an email address for the purpose of transacting motion business.

(2)  A solicitor who does not have suitable facilities for transacting motion business by email may make a declaration in writing to that effect, which must be—

    (a)  sent to the Clerk; and

    (b)  intimated to each of the other parties to the appeal.

(3)  A party who is not represented by a solicitor may provide to the Clerk an email address for the purpose of transacting motion business.

(4)  The Clerk must maintain a list of the email addresses provided for the purpose of transacting motion business, which must be published in up to date form on the website of the Scottish Courts and Tribunals Service.

(5)  The Clerk must also include on that list an email address of the Court for the purpose of lodging motions.

### Grounds for written motion

**12.6.**  A motion in writing must specify the grounds on which it is made.

### Determination of unopposed motions in writing

**12.7.**—(1)  The Clerk may determine any unopposed motion in writing other than a motion which seeks a final interlocutor.

(2)  Where the Clerk considers that such a motion should not be granted, the Clerk must refer the motion to the procedural Appeal Sheriff.

(3)  The procedural Appeal Sheriff is to determine—

    (a)  a motion referred under paragraph (2);

    (b)  an unopposed motion which seeks a final interlocutor,

in chambers without the appearance of parties, unless the procedural Appeal Sheriff otherwise determines.

### Issuing of orders by email

**12.8.**  Where the Court makes an order determining a motion which was lodged in accordance with Chapter 13, the Clerk must email a copy of the order to the addresses of the lodging party and every receiving party.

## Chapter 13

## Motions Lodged by Email

### Intimation of motions by email

**13.1.**—(1)   The lodging party must give intimation of that party's intention to lodge the motion, and of the terms of the motion, to every other party by sending an email in Form 13.1 (form of motion by email) to the addresses of every party.

(2)   The requirement under paragraph (1) to give intimation of a motion to a party by email does not apply where that party—

    (a)   has not lodged answers within the period of notice for lodging those answers;

    (b)   has withdrawn or is deemed to have withdrawn those answers; or

    (c)   became a party to the appeal by minute, but has withdrawn or is deemed to have withdrawn that minute.

(3)   A motion intimated under this rule must be intimated not later than 1700 hours on a court day.

### Opposition to motions

**13.2.**—(1)   A receiving party must intimate any opposition to a motion by sending an email in Form 13.2 (form of opposition to motion by email) to the address of the lodging party.

(2)   Any opposition to a motion must be intimated to the lodging party not later than 1700 hours on court day 3.

(3)   Late opposition to a motion must be sent to the address of the Court and may only be allowed with the leave of the procedural Appeal Sheriff, on cause shown.

### Consent to motions

**13.3.**   Where a receiving party seeks to consent to a motion, that party may do so by sending an email confirming the consent to the address of the lodging party.

### Lodging unopposed motions

**13.4.**—(1)   This rule applies where no opposition to a motion has been intimated.

(2)   The motion must be lodged by the lodging party not later than 1230 hours on court day 4 by sending an email in Form 13.1 headed "Unopposed motion" to the address of the court.

(3)[1]   That motion is to be determined by 1700 hours on court day 4.

(4)   Where for any reason it is not possible for that motion to be determined in accordance with paragraph (3), the Clerk must advise the parties of that fact and give reasons.

---

[1] As amended by the Act of Sederunt (Rules of the Court of Session, Sheriff Appeal Court Rules and Sheriff Court Rules Amendment) (Sheriff Appeal Court) 2015 (SSI 2015/419) r.19 (effective 1 January 2016; amendment came into force on 31 December 2015 but could not take effect until the commencement of SSI 2015/356 r.5.6(3)(b) on 1 January 2016)).

**Lodging opposed motions by email**

**13.5.**—(1)  This rule applies where opposition to a motion has been intimated.

(2)  The motion must be lodged by the lodging party not later than 1230 hours on court day 4 by—

  (a)  sending an email in Form 13.1 headed "Opposed motion", to the address of the court;

  (b)  attaching to that email the opposition in Form 13.2 intimated by the receiving party to the lodging party.

(3)  That motion is to be heard by the procedural Appeal Sheriff on the first suitable court day after court day 4.

(4)  The Clerk must intimate the date and time of the hearing to the parties.

**Variation of periods of intimation**

**13.6.**  Where—

  (a)  every receiving party in an appeal consents to a shorter period of intimation; or

  (b)  the Court shortens the period of intimation,

the motion may be lodged by the lodging party, or heard or otherwise determined by the Court at an earlier time and date than that which is specified in this Chapter.

Chapter 14

## Motions Lodged by Other Means

### Intimation of motions by other means

**14.1.**—(1)   The lodging party must give intimation of that party's intention to lodge the motion, and of the terms of the motion, to every other party in Form 14.1 (form of motion).

(2)   That intimation must be accompanied by a copy of any document referred to in the motion.

### Opposition to motions

**14.2.**—(1)   A receiving party may oppose a motion by lodging a notice of opposition in Form 14.2 (form of opposition to motion).

(2)   Any notice of opposition must be lodged within 7 days after the date of intimation of the motion.

(3)   The procedural Appeal Sheriff may, on the application of the lodging party—

    (a)   vary the period of 7 days mentioned in paragraph (2); or

    (b)   dispense with intimation on any party.

(4)   An application mentioned in paragraph (3) must—

    (a)   be included in the motion;

    (b)   give reasons for varying the period or dispensing with intimation, as the case may be.

(5)   The procedural Appeal Sheriff may allow a notice of opposition to be lodged late, on cause shown.

### Consent to motions

**14.3.**   Where a receiving party seeks to consent to a motion, that party may do so by lodging a notice to that effect.

### Lodging of motions

**14.4.**—(1)   The motion must be lodged by the lodging party within 5 days after the date of intimation of the motion, unless paragraph (3) applies.

(2)   The lodging party must also lodge—

    (a)   a certificate of intimation in Form 6.5 (certificate of intimation);

    (b)   so far as practicable, any document referred to in the motion that has not already been lodged.

(3)   Where the procedural Appeal Sheriff varies the period for lodging a notice of opposition to a period of 5 days or less, the motion must be lodged no later than the day on which that period expires.

### Joint motions

**14.5.**—(1)   A joint motion by all parties need not be intimated.

(2)   Such a motion is to be lodged by any of the parties.

**Hearing of opposed motions**

**14.6.**—(1)   Where a notice of opposition in Form 14.2 (form of opposition to motion) is lodged, the motion is to be heard by the procedural Appeal Sheriff on the first suitable court day after the lodging of the notice of opposition.

(2)   The Clerk must intimate the date and time of the hearing to the parties.

**Modification of Chapter 5**

**14.7.**   For the purposes of this Chapter, the following provisions in Chapter 5 (intimation and lodging etc.) do not apply—

    (a)   rule 5.6(1)(e) (additional methods of intimation: electronic means);

    (b)   rule 5.7(2)(e) (lodging: electronic means).

# CHAPTER 15 MINUTES

## Chapter 15

## Minutes

### Application of this Chapter

**15.1.** This Chapter applies to any application to the Court that is made by minute, other than a joint minute.

### Form and lodging of minute

**15.2.**—(1) A minute must—

    (a)   specify the order sought from the Court;

    (b)   contain a statement of facts supporting the granting of that order;

    (c)   where appropriate, contain pleas-in-law.

  (2)   A minute is to be lodged in the process of the appeal to which it relates.

### Orders for intimation and answers

**15.3.**—(1) On the first available court day after being lodged, a minute is to be brought before the procedural Appeal Sheriff for an order—

    (a)   for intimation, within 7 days after the date of the order, to—

        (i)   every other party to the appeal;

        (ii)   any other person who appears to have an interest in the minute;

    (b)   for any person on whom the minute is intimated to lodge answers, if so advised, within 14 days after the date of intimation;

    (c)   fixing a hearing on the minute and any answers no sooner than 28 days after the date of the order.

  (2)   The procedural Appeal Sheriff may vary the periods of 7 days, 14 days and 28 days mentioned in paragraph (1)—

    (a)   of the procedural Appeal Sheriff's own accord; or

    (b)   on cause shown, on the application of the applicant.

  (3)   An application mentioned in paragraph (2)(b) must—

    (a)   be included in the minute;

    (b)   give reasons for varying the period.

  (4)   Where a minute is intimated in accordance with an order under this rule, the applicant must lodge a certificate of intimation in Form 6.5 within 14 days after the date of intimation.

### Consent to minute

**15.4.**—(1) Where a person to whom a minute is intimated seeks to consent to the minute, that person may do so by lodging a notice to that effect.

  (2)   Where every person to whom a minute is intimated consents to the minute, the procedural Appeal Sheriff is to determine the minute in chambers without the appearance of those persons, unless the procedural Appeal Sheriff otherwise determines.

### Minutes of sist and transference

**15.5.**—(1) This rule applies where a party to an appeal ("P") dies or comes under legal incapacity while the appeal is depending before the Court.

(2)   Any person who claims to represent P or P's estate may apply to the Court by minute to be sisted as a party to the appeal.

(3)   If no person makes an application under paragraph (2), any other party may apply to the Court by minute to transfer the appeal in favour of or against (as the case may be) the person who represents P or P's estate.

(4)   An application under paragraph (3) must be intimated to the person specified in the minute as representing P or P's estate.

## Applications to enter process as respondent

**15.6.**—(1)   A person on whom the appeal has not been intimated may apply by minute for leave to enter the process as a party minuter and lodge answers.

(2)   A minute under paragraph (1) must specify—

   (a)   the applicant's title and interest to enter the process;

   (b)   the basis for the answers that the applicant proposes to lodge.

(3)   At the hearing fixed under rule 15.3(1)(c), the procedural Appeal Sheriff is to determine whether the applicant has shown title and interest to enter the process.

(4)   If the procedural Appeal Sheriff is satisfied, the procedural Appeal Sheriff may grant the applicant leave to enter the process and lodge answers.

(5)   Where leave is granted, the procedural Appeal Sheriff is to make such further order as the procedural Appeal Sheriff thinks fit.

(6)   In particular, such an order may include an order—

   (a)   varying any timetable;

   (b)   as to the expenses of the application.

# CHAPTER 16 AMENDMENT OF PLEADINGS

## Chapter 16

## Amendment of Pleadings

### Amendment of sheriff court pleadings

**16.1.**—(1)  Any party to an appeal may apply by motion to amend the pleadings in the sheriff court process.

(2)  Where the procedural Appeal Sheriff—

(a)  allows an amendment to the pleadings in the sheriff court process; and

(b)  considers that the amendment makes a material change to the pleadings, the procedural Appeal Sheriff may set aside the decision appealed against and remit the matter to the sheriff for a further hearing.

### Amendment of note of appeal and answers etc.

**16.2.**—(1)  A party who has lodged a document specified in paragraph (2) may apply by motion to amend that document.

(2)  The documents are—

(a)  a note of appeal;

(b)  answers to a note of appeal;

(c)  grounds of appeal in a cross-appeal;

(d)  answers to grounds of appeal in a cross-appeal.

(3)  Such a motion must include the text of the proposed amendment.

(4)  An application under paragraph (1) is to be accompanied by an application to vary the timetable under rule 7.6(1)(c) or rule 28.6(1)(c) (sist of proceedings and variation of timetable) if such an application is necessary.

# CHAPTER 17 WITHDRAWAL OF SOLICITORS

## Chapter 17

## Withdrawal of Solicitors

### Interpretation of this Chapter

**17.1.** In this Chapter, "peremptory hearing" means a hearing at which a party whose solicitor has withdrawn from acting must appear or be represented in order to state whether or not the party intends to proceed.

### Giving notice of withdrawal to the Court

**17.2.**—(1) Where a solicitor withdraws from acting on behalf of a party, the solicitor must give notice in writing to the Clerk and to every other party.

(2) Paragraph (1) does not apply if the solicitor withdraws from acting at a hearing in the presence of the other parties or their representatives.

(3) Paragraph (4) applies if a solicitor who withdraws from acting is aware that the address of the party for whom the solicitor acted has changed from that specified in the instance of the note of appeal or answers to the note of appeal.

(4) The solicitor must disclose to the Clerk and every other party the last known address of the party for whom the solicitor acted.

### Arrangements for peremptory hearing

**17.3.**—(1) On the first available court day after notice is given under rule 17.2(1), the procedural Appeal Sheriff is to make an order—
- (a) ordaining the party whose solicitor has withdrawn from acting to appear or be represented at a peremptory hearing;
- (b) fixing a date and time for the peremptory hearing;
- (c) appointing any other party to the appeal to intimate the order and a notice in Form 17.3 to that party within 7 days after the date of the order.

(2) A peremptory diet is to be fixed no sooner than 14 days after the date on which an order is made under paragraph (1).

(3) The procedural Appeal Sheriff may vary the period of 7 days mentioned in paragraph (1) or the period of 14 days mentioned in paragraph (2)—
- (a) of the procedural Appeal Sheriff's own accord; or
- (b) on cause shown, on the application of any other party to the appeal.

(4) Where any previously fixed hearing is to occur within 14 days after the date on which the procedural Appeal Sheriff is to make an order under paragraph (1), the procedural Appeal Sheriff may continue consideration of the matter to the previously fixed hearing instead of making an order under paragraph (1). (5) Where an order and a notice in Form 17.3 are intimated under this rule, the party appointed to intimate them must lodge a certificate of intimation in Form 6.5—
- (a) within 14 days after the date of intimation; or
- (b) before the peremptory hearing, whichever is sooner.

**Peremptory hearing**

**17.4.**—(1)   At a peremptory hearing, the party whose solicitor has withdrawn from acting must appear or be represented in order to state whether the party intends to proceed.

(2)   Where the party fails to comply with paragraph (1), the Court may make an order mentioned in paragraph (3) only if it is satisfied that the order and notice in Form 17.3 have been intimated to that party.

(3)   The orders are—

    (a)   if the party is the appellant, an order refusing the appeal; or

    (b)   if the party is the respondent and the condition in paragraph (4) is satisfied, an order allowing the appeal.

(4)   The condition is that the appellant must show cause why the appeal should be allowed.

(5)   If the Court is not satisfied that the order and notice in Form 17.3 have been intimated to that party, it may make—

    (a)   an order fixing a further peremptory hearing;

    (b)   any other order that the Court considers appropriate to secure the expeditious disposal of the appeal.

## Chapter 18

### Caution and Security

#### Application of this Chapter

**18.1.** This Chapter applies to any appeal in which the Court has power to order a person to find caution or give other security.

#### Form of application to find caution or give security

**18.2.** An application—

    (a)   for an order for caution or other security;

    (b)   to vary or recall such an order,

is to be made by motion.

#### Orders for caution or other security: time for compliance

**18.3.** Where the Court makes an order for caution or to give other security, the order must specify the period within which caution is to be found or security given.

#### Methods of finding caution or giving security

**18.4.**—(1)   A person who is ordered to find caution must do so by obtaining a bond of caution.

(2)   A person who is ordered to consign a sum of money into court must do so by consignation under the Sheriff Courts Consignations (Scotland) Act 1893 in the name of the Clerk.

(3)   The Court may order a person to give security by—

    (a)   a method other than those mentioned in paragraphs (1) and (2);

    (b)   a combination of two or more methods of security.

(4)   Any document by which an order to find caution or give security is satisfied must be lodged in process.

(5)   A document lodged under paragraph (4) may not be borrowed from process.

#### Cautioners and other guarantors

**18.5.** A bond of caution or other security may only be given by a person who is an authorised person within the meaning of section 31 of the Financial Services and Markets Act 2000.

#### Form of bond of caution

**18.6.**—(1)   A bond of caution must oblige the cautioner to make payment of the sums as validly and in the same manner as the party is obliged.

(2)   In this rule—

"cautioner" includes the cautioner's heirs and executors;

"party" means the person to whom the cautioner is bound, and that person's heirs and successors;

"the sums" are the sums for which the cautioner is bound to the party.

## Caution or other security: sufficiency and objections

**18.7.**—(1)  The Clerk must be satisfied that any document lodged in process under rule 18.4(4) is in proper form.

(2)  A party who is dissatisfied with the sufficiency or form of any document lodged in process under rule 18.4(4) may apply to the Court by motion for an order under rule 18.9 (failure to find caution or give security).

## Insolvency or death of cautioner or guarantor

**18.8.**—(1)  This rule applies where caution has been found by bond of caution or security has been given by guarantee.

(2)  Where one of the events specified in paragraph (3) occurs, the party entitled to benefit from the caution or guarantee may apply to the Court by motion for further caution to be found or further security to be given.

(3)  The events are that the cautioner or guarantor—

    (a)  becomes apparently insolvent within the meaning of section 7 of the Bankruptcy (Scotland) Act 1985;

    (b)  calls a meeting of the cautioner or guarantor's creditors to consider the state of that person's affairs;

    (c)  dies unrepresented;

    (d)  is a company and—

        (i)  an administration, bank administration or building society special administration order has been made in respect of it;

        (ii)  a winding up, bank insolvency or building society insolvency order has been made in respect of it;

        (iii)  a resolution for its voluntary winding up has been passed;

        (iv)  a receiver of all or any part of its undertaking has been appointed;

        (v)  a voluntary arrangement within the meaning of section 1(1) of the Insolvency Act 1986 has been approved under Part I of that Act.

## Failure to find caution or give security

**18.9.**—(1)  Where a person who has been ordered to find caution or give security fails to do so, any other party may apply to the Court by motion for a finding that the person is in default.

(2)  Despite rule 3.1 (circumstances where a party is in default), a person who fails to find caution or give security is only in default if the Court grants a motion under paragraph (1) and makes a finding that the person is in default.

## Chapter 19

### Expenses

**Taxation of expenses**

**19.1.**—(1)  Where the Court makes an order allowing expenses in any appeal, those expenses must be taxed before decree is granted for them.

(2)  This rule does not apply where the Court modifies those expenses to a fixed sum.

**Additional fee**

**19.2.**—(1)  Where the Court makes an order allowing expenses, it may also make an order allowing a percentage increase in the fees authorised in the Act of Sederunt (Fees of Solicitors in the Sheriff Appeal Court) 2015 to reflect the responsibility undertaken by the solicitor in the conduct of the appeal.

(2)  An application for an additional fee is to be made by motion.

(3)  The Court must take the following matters into account in determining what percentage increase, if any, to allow—

    (a)  the complexity of the appeal and the number, difficulty or novelty of the questions raised;

    (b)  the skill, time and labour and specialised knowledge required of the solicitor;

    (c)  the number and importance of any documents prepared;

    (d)  the place and circumstances of the appeal or in which the work of the solicitor in preparation for, and conduct of, the appeal has been carried out;

    (e)  the importance of the appeal or the subject matter of it to the client;

    (f)  the amount or value of money or property involved in the appeal;

    (g)  the steps taken with a view to settling the appeal, limiting the matters in dispute or limiting the scope of any hearing

**Sanction for the employment of counsel**

**19.2A.**—[1](1)  The Court may grant sanction for the employment of counsel to carry out the types of work specified in paragraph (3)—

    (a)  of the Court's own accord; or

    (b)  on the application of any party.

(2)  An application is to be made by motion.

(3)  The types of work are—

    (a)  appearing at any hearing;

    (b)  preparing any document that is to be lodged in relation to the appeal.

(4)  Sanction may be granted before or after the work for which it is sought has been carried out.

---

[1] As inserted by the Act of Sederunt (Rules of the Court of Session, Sheriff Appeal Court Rules and Sheriff Court Rules Amendment) (Sheriff Appeal Court) 2015 (SSI 2015/419) r.19 (effective 1 January 2016; insertion came into force on December 31, 2015 but could not take effect until the commencement of SSI 2015/356 rule 5.6(3)(b) on January 1, 2016)).

(5)   A refusal to grant sanction before work is carried out does not prevent sanction being granted for that work after it has been carried out.

(6)   In granting sanction, the Court may also—

(a)   grant sanction for more than one person to carry out the work;

(b)   impose any restrictions.

## Order to lodge account of expenses

**19.3.**—(1)   This rule applies where a party entitled to expenses has not lodged an account of expenses in process within 4 months after the date of the order about expenses.

(2)   The party found liable in expenses may apply to the Court for an order ordaining the party entitled to expenses to lodge an account of expenses in process.

(3)   An application under paragraph (2) is to be made by motion.

## Procedure for taxation of expenses

**19.4.**—(1)   Where an account of expenses is lodged for taxation, the Clerk must transmit the account and the process to the auditor of court.

(2)   The auditor of court must—

(a)   fix a taxation hearing no sooner than 7 days after the auditor receives the account;

(b)   intimate the date, time and place of the taxation hearing to every party.

(3)   If the auditor reserves consideration of the account at the taxation hearing, the auditor must intimate the auditor's decision to the parties who attended the hearing.

(4)   After the account has been taxed, the auditor must transmit the account and the process, together with the auditor's report, to the Clerk.

(5)   Where no objections are lodged under rule 19.5, the Court may grant decree for the expenses as taxed.

## Objections to taxed account

**19.5.**—(1)   A party may lodge a note of objections to an account as taxed only where the party attended the taxation hearing.

(2)   A note of objections must be lodged within 7 days after—

(a)   the taxation hearing; or

(b)   where the auditor reserved consideration of the account, the date on which the auditor intimates the auditor's decision to the parties.

(3)   The Court is to dispose of the note of objections in a summary manner, with or without answers.

## Decree for expenses in name of solicitor

**19.6.**   The Court may allow a decree for expenses to be extracted in the name of the solicitor who conducted the appeal.

## Expenses of curator ad litem appointed to a respondent

**19.7.**—(1)   This rule applies where a curator ad litem is appointed to any respondent to an appeal.

(2)   The appellant is responsible in the first instance for the payment of the expenses of a curator ad litem mentioned in paragraph (3).

(3)   Those expenses are any fees of the curator ad litem and any outlays incurred by the curator from the date of appointment until any of the following steps occur—

- (a) the lodging of a minute stating that the curator does not intend to lodge answers to the note of appeal;
- (b) the lodging of answers by the curator, or the adoption of answers that have already been lodged;
- (c) the discharge of the curator before either of the steps in subparagraphs (a) or (b) occurs.

# CHAPTER 20 DEVOLUTION ISSUES

PART 6

INCIDENTAL PROCEDURE: SPECIAL PROCEDURES

Chapter 20

## Devolution Issues

### Interpretation

**20.1.** In this Chapter—

"devolution issue" means a devolution issue under—
    (a)   Schedule 6 to the Scotland Act 1998;
    (b)   Schedule 10 to the Northern Ireland Act 1998;
    (c)   Schedule 9 to the Government of Wales Act 2006;
  and any reference to Schedule 6, Schedule 10 or Schedule 9 is a reference to
that Schedule in that Act;
"relevant authority" means—
    (a)   the Advocate General;
    (b)   in the case of a devolution issue under Schedule 6, the Lord
        Advocate;
    (c)   in the case of a devolution issue under Schedule 10, the Attorney
        General for Northern Ireland, and the First Minister and deputy
        First Minister acting jointly;
    (d)   in the case of a devolution issue under Schedule 9, the Counsel
        General to the Welsh Government.

### Raising a devolution issue

**20.2.**—(1)  A devolution issue is raised by specifying a devolution issue in Form 20.2.

(2)  A devolution issue in Form 20.2 is to be lodged—
    (a)   by an appellant, when the note of appeal is lodged;
    (b)   by a respondent, when answers to the note of appeal are lodged,
unless the Court allows an appellant or a respondent to raise a devolution issue at a later stage in proceedings.

(3)  An application to allow a devolution issue to be raised after the note of appeal has been lodged or answers to the note of appeal have been lodged, as the case may be, is to be made by motion.

(4)  The party raising a devolution issue must specify, in sufficient detail to enable the Court to determine whether a devolution issue arises—
    (a)   the facts and circumstances; and
    (b)   the contentions of law,
on the basis of which it is alleged that the devolution issue arises in the appeal.

(5)  The Court may not determine a devolution issue unless permission has been given for the devolution issue to proceed.

### Raising a devolution issue: intimation and service

**20.3.**—(1)  This rule applies to the intimation of a devolution issue on a relevant authority under—

    (a)   paragraph 5 of Schedule 6;

    (b)   paragraph 23 of Schedule 10;

    (c)   paragraph 14(1) of Schedule 9.

(2)   When a devolution issue is raised, the party raising it must intimate the devolution issue to the relevant authority unless the relevant authority is a party to the appeal.

(3)   Within 14 days after intimation, the relevant authority may give notice to the Clerk that it intends to take part in the appeal as a party under—

    (a)   paragraph 6 of Schedule 6;

    (b)   paragraph 24 of Schedule 10;

    (c)   paragraph 14(2) of Schedule 9.

### Raising a devolution issue: permission to proceed

**20.4.**—(1)   When a devolution issue is raised, the Clerk is to fix a hearing and intimate the date and time of that hearing to the parties.

(2)   Within 14 days after the Clerk intimates the date and time of the hearing, each party must lodge a note of argument.

(3)   That note of argument must summarise the submissions the party intends to make on the question of whether a devolution issue arises in the appeal.

(4)   At the hearing, the procedural Appeal Sheriff is to determine whether a devolution issue arises in the appeal.

(5)   Where the procedural Appeal Sheriff determines that a devolution issue arises, the procedural Appeal Sheriff is to grant permission for the devolution issue to proceed.

(6)   Where the procedural Appeal Sheriff determines that no devolution issue arises, the procedural Appeal Sheriff is to refuse permission for the devolution issue to proceed.

(7)   At the hearing the procedural Appeal Sheriff may make any order, including an order concerning expenses.

(8)   In this rule, "party" includes a relevant authority that has given notice to the Clerk that it intends to take part in the appeal as a party.

### Participation by the relevant authority

**20.5.**—(1)   Paragraph (2) applies where a relevant authority has given notice to the Clerk that it intends to take part in the appeal as a party.

(2)   Within 7 days after permission to proceed is given, the relevant authority must lodge a minute containing the relevant authority's written submissions in respect of the devolution issue.

### Reference to the Inner House or Supreme Court

**20.6.**—(1)   This rule applies to the reference of a devolution issue to the Inner House of the Court of Session for determination under—

    (a)   paragraph 7 of Schedule 6;

    (b)   paragraph 25 of Schedule 10;

    (c)   paragraph 15 of Schedule 9.

(2)   This rule also applies where the Court has been required by a relevant authority to refer a devolution issue to the Supreme Court under—

    (a)   paragraph 33 of Schedule 6;

    (b)   paragraph 33 of Schedule 10;

(c)   paragraph 29 of Schedule 9.

(3)   The Court is to make an order concerning the drafting and adjustment of the reference.

(4)   The reference must specify—

(a)   the questions for the Inner House or the Supreme Court;

(b)   the addresses of the parties;

(c)   a concise statement of the background to the matter, including—

(i)   the facts of the case, including any relevant findings of fact; and

(ii)   the main issues in the case and contentions of the parties with regard to them;

(d)   the relevant law including the relevant provisions of the Scotland Act 1998, the Government of Wales Act 2006 or the Northern Ireland Act 1998;

(e)   the reasons why an answer to the questions is considered necessary for the purpose of disposing of the proceedings.

(5)   The reference must have annexed to it—

(a)   a copy of all orders made in the appeal; and

(b)   a copy of any judgments in the proceedings.

(6)   When the reference has been drafted and adjusted, the Court is to make and sign the reference.

(7)   The Clerk must—

(a)   send a copy of the reference to the parties to the proceedings;

(b)   certify on the back of the principal reference that subparagraph (a) has been complied with.

### Reference to the Inner House or Supreme Court: further procedure

**20.7.**—(1)   On a reference being made, the appeal must, unless the Court otherwise orders, be sisted until the devolution issue has been determined.

(2)   Despite a reference being made, the Court continues to have the power to make any interim order required in the interests of the parties.

(3)   The Court may recall a sist for the purpose of making such interim orders.

(4)   On a reference being made the Clerk must send the principal copy of the reference to (as the case may be)—

(a)   the Deputy Principal Clerk of the Court of Session; or

(b)   the Registrar of the Supreme Court (together with 7 copies).

(5)   Unless the Court orders otherwise, the Clerk must not send the principal copy of the reference where an appeal against the making of the reference is pending.

(6)   An appeal is to be treated as pending—

(a)   until the expiry of the time for making that appeal; or

(b)   where an appeal has been made, until that appeal has been determined.

### Reference to the Inner House or Supreme Court: procedure following determination

**20.8.**—(1)   This rule applies where either the Inner House of the Court of Session or the Supreme Court has determined a devolution issue.

(2)   Upon receipt of the determination, the Clerk must place a copy of the determination before the Court.

(3)   The Court may, on the motion of any party or otherwise, order such further procedure as may be required.

(4)  Where the Court makes an order other than on the motion of a party, the Clerk must intimate a copy of the order on all parties to the appeal.

Chapter 21

**Preliminary References to the CJEU**

## Interpretation of this Chapter

**21.1.**   In this Chapter—

"European Court" means the Court of Justice of the European Union;
"reference" means a reference to the European Court for—

   (a)   a preliminary ruling under Article 267 of the Treaty on the Functioning of the European Union;
   (b)   a ruling on the interpretation of the Conventions mentioned in Article 1 of Schedule 2 to the Civil Jurisdiction and Judgments Act 1982 under Article 3 of that Schedule;
   (c)   a preliminary ruling on the interpretation of the instruments mentioned in Article 1 of Schedule 3 to the Contracts (Applicable Law) Act 1990 under Article 2 of that Schedule.

## Applications for a reference

**21.2.**—(1)   An application for a reference by a party is to be made by motion.

(2)   The Court may make a reference of its own accord.

## Preparation of reference

**21.3.**—(1)   Where the Court decides that a reference is to be made, it is to make an order specifying—

   (a)   by whom the reference is to be drafted and adjusted;
   (b)   the periods within which the reference is to be drafted and adjusted.

(2)   A reference is to be drafted in Form 21.3 unless the Court directs otherwise when it makes an order under paragraph (1).

(3)   In drafting and adjusting the reference, parties are to have regard to the Recommendations to national courts and tribunals in relation to the initiation of preliminary ruling proceedings issued by the European Court.

(4)   When the reference has been drafted and any adjustments required by the Court have been made, the Court is to make and sign the reference.

(5)   When the reference is made, the Clerk must notify the parties.

## Transmission of reference to European Court

**21.4.**   A copy of the reference is to be certified by the Clerk and sent to the Registrar of the European Court.

## Sist of appeal

**21.5.**—(1)   When a reference is made, the Court is to sist the appeal until the European Court determines the reference, unless the Court orders otherwise.

(2)   Where an appeal is sisted under paragraph (1), the Court may recall the sist for the purposes of making an interim order.

Chapter 21

Preliminary References to the CJEU

# CHAPTER 22 INTERVENTIONS BY CEHR AND SCHR

## Chapter 22

## Interventions by CEHR and SCHR

### Application and interpretation of this Chapter

**22.1.**—(1)  This Chapter applies to—

    (a)  interventions in legal proceedings by the CEHR under section 30(1) of the Equality Act 2006;

    (b)  interventions in civil proceedings (other than children's hearing proceedings) by the SCHR under section 14(2) of the Scottish Commission for Human Rights Act 2006.

(2)  In this Chapter—

"the CEHR" means the Commission for Equality and Human Rights;

"the SCHR" means the Scottish Commission for Human Rights.

### Applications to intervene

**22.2.**—(1)  An application for leave to intervene is to be made in Form 22.2.

(2)  Such an application is to be lodged in the process of the appeal to which it relates.

(3)  When an intervener lodges an application, rule 5.2(1) applies as if the intervener were a party.

(4)  The parties may request a hearing on the application to intervene within 14 days after the application is lodged.

(5)  Where a hearing is requested—

    (a)  the Court is to appoint a date and time for a hearing;

    (b)  the Clerk must notify the date and time of the hearing to the parties and the applicant.

(6)  Where no hearing is requested, the Court may appoint a date and time for a hearing of its own accord and the Clerk must notify the date and time of the hearing to the parties and the applicant.

### Applications to intervene: determination

**22.3.**—(1)  The Court may determine an application for leave to intervene without a hearing, unless a hearing is fixed under rule 22.2(5) or (6).

(2)  In an application for leave to intervene under section 30(1) of the Equality Act 2006, the Court may grant leave only if it is satisfied that the proposed submissions are likely to assist the Court.

(3)  Where the Court grants leave to intervene, it may impose any conditions that it considers desirable in the interests of justice.

(4)  In particular, the Court may make provision about any additional expenses incurred by the parties as a result of the intervention.

(5)  When an application is determined, the Clerk must notify the parties and the applicant of the outcome.

### Invitations to intervene

**22.4.**—(1)  An invitation to intervene under section 14(2)(b) of the Scottish Commission for Human Rights Act 2006 is to be in Form 22.4.

(2)  The Clerk must send a copy of Form 22.4 to the parties to the proceedings and to the SCHR.

(3)  When the Clerk sends a copy of Form 22.4 to the SCHR, the Clerk must also send—

    (a)  a copy of the note of appeal and any answers to it;

    (b)  the appeal print, if it is available;

    (c)  any other documents relating to the appeal that the Court thinks are relevant.

(4)  Where the Court invites the SCHR to intervene, it may impose any conditions that it considers desirable in the interests of justice.

(5)  In particular, the Court may make provision about any additional expenses incurred by the parties as a result of the intervention.

## Form of intervention

**22.5.**—(1)  An intervention is to be by way of written submission.

(2)  A written submission (including any appendices) must not exceed 5,000 words.

(3)  The intervener must lodge the written submission within such time as the Court may direct.

(4)  In exceptional circumstances, the Court may allow—

    (a)  a written submission exceeding 5,000 words to be made;

    (b)  an oral submission to be made.

(5)  Where the Court allows an oral submission to be made, it is to appoint a date and time for the submission to be made.

(6)  The Clerk must notify that date and time to the parties and the intervener.

# CHAPTER 23 PROOF

## Chapter 23

### Proof

### Taking proof in the course of an appeal

**23.1.**—(1)  If it is considered necessary, proof or additional proof may be ordered—

    (a)  by the procedural Appeal Sheriff at a procedural hearing;

    (b)  by the Court in the course of an appeal hearing.

(2)  Where the procedural Appeal Sheriff orders that proof or additional proof is to be taken—

    (a)  the procedural Appeal Sheriff is to appoint a date and time for a hearing for that to be done;

    (b)  so far as reasonably practicable, the hearing is to be before the procedural Appeal Sheriff who made the order.

(3)  Where the Court orders that proof or additional proof is to be taken, the Court is to—

    (a)  remit the proof to be taken before any Appeal Sheriff;

    (b)  appoint a date and time for a hearing for that to be done;

    (c)  continue the appeal hearing until the Appeal Sheriff reports the proof to the Court.

(4)  Where a hearing is fixed under this rule, the Clerk must notify the date and time of the hearing to the parties.

### Preparation for proof

**23.2.**—(1)  Where a proof or additional proof is ordered, the Appeal Sheriff before whom it is to be taken is to make an order specifying—

    (a)  the witnesses whose evidence is to be taken;

    (b)  how those witnesses are to be cited to the hearing.

(2)  An order under paragraph (1) may include provision as to liability for the fees and expenses of a witness.

### Conduct of proof

**23.3.**  A proof is to be taken continuously so far as possible, but the Appeal Sheriff may adjourn the hearing from time to time.

### Administration of oath or affirmation to witnesses

**23.4.**—(1)  The Appeal Sheriff is to administer the oath to a witness in Form 23.4-A unless the witness elects to affirm.

(2)  Where a witness elects to affirm, the Appeal Sheriff is to administer the affirmation in Form 23.4-B.

### Recording of evidence

**23.5.**—(1)  The evidence given at a hearing is to be recorded, unless the parties agree to dispense with the recording of evidence and the Appeal Sheriff considers that it is appropriate to do so.

(2)  The evidence is to be recorded by—

<ol type="a" start="1">
<li>a shorthand writer to whom the oath de fideli administratione has been administered in connection with the Court; or</li>
<li>by tape recording or other mechanical means approved by the Court.</li>
</ol>

(3)   In the first instance, the solicitors for the parties are personally liable to pay, in equal shares—

<ol type="a" start="1">
<li>the fees of a shorthand writer; or</li>
<li>the fee payable for recording evidence by tape recording or other mechanical means.</li>
</ol>

(4)   The record of evidence is to include—

<ol type="a" start="1">
<li>any objection taken to a question or to the line of evidence;</li>
<li>any submission made in relation to such an objection; and</li>
<li>the ruling of the Appeal Sheriff in relation to the objection and submission.</li>
</ol>

### Transcripts of evidence

**23.6.**—(1)   A transcript of the record of the evidence is to be made only where the Appeal Sheriff orders it to be made.

(2)   In the first instance, the solicitors for the parties are personally liable, in equal shares, for the cost of making the transcript.

(3)   The transcript provided for the use of the Court is to be certified as a faithful record of the evidence by—

<ol type="a" start="1">
<li>the shorthand writer who recorded the evidence; or</li>
<li>where the evidence was recorded by tape recording or other mechanical means, by the person who transcribed the record.</li>
</ol>

(4)   The Appeal Sheriff may alter the transcript where the Appeal Sheriff considers it necessary to do so, but only after hearing parties on the proposed alterations.

(5)   Where the Appeal Sheriff alters the transcript, the Appeal Sheriff is to authenticate the alterations.

(6)   The transcript may only be borrowed from process on cause shown.

(7)   Where a transcript is required for the purpose of an appeal but the Appeal Sheriff has not directed that it be made—

<ol type="a" start="1">
<li>the appellant may request a transcript from the shorthand writer or the person in whose possession the recording of the evidence is;</li>
<li>in the first instance, the solicitor for the appellant is liable for the cost of the transcript;</li>
<li>the appellant must lodge the transcript in process;</li>
<li>any party may obtain a copy by paying the fee of the person who made the transcript.</li>
</ol>

### Recording objections where recording of evidence dispensed with

**23.7.**   Where the recording of evidence has been dispensed with under rule 23.5(1), a party may request that the Appeal Sheriff record in the report of the proof—

<ol type="a" start="1">
<li>any objection taken to a question or to the line of evidence;</li>
<li>any submission made in relation to such an objection; and</li>
<li>the ruling of the Appeal Sheriff in relation to the objection and submission.</li>
</ol>

# CHAPTER 24 VULNERABLE WITNESSES

## Chapter 24

## Vulnerable Witnesses

### Interpretation and application of this Chapter

**24.1.**—(1) This Chapter applies where proof or additional proof is ordered to be taken under rule 23.1(1).

(2) In this Chapter—

"2004 Act" means the Vulnerable Witnesses (Scotland) Act 2004;

"child witness notice" has the meaning given by section 12(2) of the 2004 Act;

"review application" means an application under section 13(1)(a) of the 2004 Act;

"vulnerable witness application" has the meaning given by section 12(6) of the 2004 Act.

### Form of notices and applications

**24.2.**—(1) A child witness notice is to be made in Form 24.2-A.

(2) A vulnerable witness application is to be made in Form 24.2-B.

(3) A review application is to be made—

    (a) in Form 24.2-C; or

    (b) orally, if the Court grants leave.

### Determination of notices and applications

**24.3.**—(1) When a notice or application under this Chapter is lodged, the Court may require any of the parties to provide further information before determining the notice or application.

(2) The Court may—

    (a) determine the notice or application by making an order under section 12(1) or (6) or 13(2) of the 2004 Act without holding a hearing;

    (b) fix a hearing at which parties are to be heard on the notice or application before determining it.

(3) The Court may make an order altering the date of the proof in order that the notice or application may be determined.

### Determination of notices and applications: supplementary orders

**24.4.** Where the Court determines a notice or application under this Chapter and makes an order under section 12(1) or (6) or 13(2) of the 2004 Act, the Court may make further orders to secure the expeditious disposal of the appeal.

### Intimation of orders

**24.5.**—(1) Where the Court makes an order—

    (a) fixing a hearing under rule 24.3(2)(b);

    (b) altering the date of a proof or other hearing under rule 24.3(3); or

    (c) under section 12(1) or (6) or 13(2) of the 2004 Act,

the Clerk is to intimate the order in accordance with this rule.

(2) Intimation is to be given to—

(a) every party to the proceedings; and
(b) any other person named in the order.

(3) Intimation is to be made—
    (a) on the day that the hearing is fixed or the order is made;
    (b) in the manner ordered by the Court.

## Taking of evidence by commissioner: preparatory steps

**24.6.**—(1) This rule applies where the Court authorises the special measure of taking evidence by a commissioner under section 19(1) of the 2004 Act.

(2)[1] The commission is to proceed without interrogatories unless the Court otherwise orders.

(3) The order of the Court authorising the special measure is sufficient authority for citing the vulnerable witness to appear before the commissioner.

(4) The party who cited the vulnerable witness—
    (a) must give the commissioner—
        (i) a certified copy of the order of the Court appointing the commissioner;
        (ii) a copy of the appeal documents;
        (iii) where rule 24.7 applies, the approved interrogatories and cross-interrogatories;
    (b) must instruct the clerk to the commission;
    (c) is responsible in the first instance for the fee of the commissioner and the clerk.

(5) The commissioner is to fix a hearing at which the commission will be carried out.

(6) The commissioner must consult the parties before fixing the hearing.

(7) An application by a party for leave to be present in the room where the commission is carried out is to be made by motion.

(8) In this rule, "appeal documents" means any of the following documents that have been lodged in process by the time the use of the special measure is authorised—
    (a) the note of appeal and answers;
    (b) where there is a cross appeal, the grounds of appeal and answers;
    (c) the appeal print and appendices;
    (d) the notes of argument.

## Taking of evidence by commissioner: interrogatories

**24.7.**—(1) This rule applies where the Court—
    (a) authorises the special measure of taking evidence by a commissioner under section 19(1) of the 2004 Act; and
    (b) orders that interrogatories are to be prepared.

(2) The party who cited the vulnerable witness must lodge draft interrogatories in process.

(3) Any other party may lodge cross-interrogatories.

(4) The parties may adjust their interrogatories and cross-interrogatories.

---

[1] As amended by the Act of Sederunt (Rules of the Court of Session, Sheriff Appeal Court Rules and Sheriff Court Rules Amendment) (Sheriff Appeal Court) 2015 (SSI 2015/419) r.19 (effective 1 January 2016; amendment came into force on December 31, 2015 but could not take effect until the commencement of SSI 2015/356 rule 5.6(3)(b) on January 1, 2016)).

(5)   At the expiry of the adjustment period, the parties must lodge the interrogatories and crossinterrogatories as adjusted in process.

(6)   The Court is to resolve any dispute as to the content of the interrogatories and crossinterrogatories, and approve them.

(7)   When the Court makes an order for interrogatories to be prepared, it is to specify the periods within which parties must comply with the steps in this rule.

## Taking of evidence by commissioner: conduct of commission

**24.8.**—(1)   The commissioner is to administer the oath *de fideli administratione* to the clerk.

(2)   The commissioner is to administer the oath to the vulnerable witness in Form 23.4-A unless the witness elects to affirm.

(3)   Where the witness elects to affirm, the commissioner is to administer the affirmation in Form 23.4-B.

## Taking of evidence by commissioner: lodging and custody of video record and documents

**24.9.**—(1)   The commissioner is to lodge the video record of the commission and any relevant documents with the Clerk.

(2)   When the video record and any relevant document are lodged, the Clerk is to notify every party—

   (a)   that the video record has been lodged;

   (b)   whether any relevant documents have been lodged;

   (c)   of the date on which they were lodged.

(3)   The video record and any relevant documents are to be kept by the Clerk.

(4)   Where the video record has been lodged—

   (a)   the name and address of the vulnerable witness and the record of the witness's evidence are to be treated as being in the knowledge of the parties;

   (b)   the parties need not include—

      (i)   the name of the witness in any list of witnesses; or

      (ii)   the record of evidence in any list of productions.

Chapter 25

## Use of Live Links

### Interpretation

**25.1.**   In this Chapter—

"evidence" means the evidence of—
- (a)   the party; or
- (b)   a person who has been or may be cited to appear before the court as a witness;

"live link" means—
- (a)   a live television link; or
- (b)   where the Court gives permission in accordance with rule 25.2(4), an alternative arrangement;

"submission" means any oral submission which would otherwise be made to the Court by a party or that party's representative, including an oral submission in support of a motion.

### Application for use of live link

**25.2.**—(1)   A party may apply to the Court to use a live link to make a submission or to give evidence.

(2)   An application to use a live link is to be made by motion.

(3)   Where a party seeks to use a live link other than a live television link, the motion must specify the proposed arrangement.

(4)   The Court must not grant a motion to use a live link other than a live television link unless the proposed arrangement meets the requirements in paragraph (5).

(5)   The requirements are that the person using the live link is able to—
- (a)   be seen and heard, or heard, in the courtroom; and
- (b)   see and hear, or hear, the proceedings in the courtroom.

# CHAPTER 26 REPORTING RESTRICTIONS

## Chapter 26

## Reporting Restrictions

### Interpretation and application of this Chapter

**26.1.**—(1)  This Chapter applies to orders which restrict the reporting of proceedings.

(2)  In this Chapter, "interested person" means a person—

(a)  who has asked to see any order made by the Court which restricts the reporting of proceedings, including an interim order; and

(b)  whose name is included on a list kept by the Lord President for the purposes of this Chapter.

### Interim orders: notification to interested persons

**26.2.**—(1)  Where the Court is considering making an order, the Court may make an interim order.

(2)  Where the Court makes an interim order, the Clerk must immediately send a copy of the interim order to any interested person.

(3)  The Court is to specify in the interim order why the Court is considering making an order.

### Interim orders: representations

**26.3.**—(1)  Paragraph (2) applies where the Court has made an interim order.

(2)  An interested person who would be directly affected by the making of an order is to be given an opportunity to make representations to the Court before the order is made.

(3)  Representations are to—

(a)  be made in Form 26.3;

(b)  include reasons why an urgent hearing is necessary, if an urgent hearing is sought;

(c)  be lodged no later than 2 days after the interim order is sent to interested persons in accordance with rule 26.2(2).

(4)  If representations are made—

(a)  the Court is to appoint a date and time for a hearing—

(i)  on the first suitable court day; or

(ii)  where the Court considers that an urgent hearing is necessary, at an earlier date and time;

(b)  the Clerk must—

(i)  notify the date and time of the hearing to the parties to the proceedings and any person who has made representations; and

(ii)  send a copy of the representations to the parties.

(5)  Where no interested person makes representations in accordance with paragraph (3), the Clerk is to put the interim order before the Court in chambers in order that the Court may resume consideration of whether to make an order.

(6)  Where the Court, having resumed consideration, makes no order, it must recall the interim order.

(7)  Where the Court recalls an interim order, the Clerk must immediately notify any interested person.

## Notification of reporting restrictions

**26.4.**—(1)   Where the Court makes an order, the Clerk must immediately—

    (a)   send a copy of the order to any interested person;

    (b)   arrange for the publication of the making of the order on the Scottish Courts and Tribunals Service website.

## Applications for variation or revocation

**26.5.**—(1)   A person aggrieved by an order may apply to the Court for its variation or revocation.

(2)   An application is to be made in Form 26.5.

(3)   When an application is made—

    (a)   the Court is to appoint a date and time for a hearing;

    (b)   the Clerk must—

        (i)   notify the date and time of the hearing to the parties to the proceedings and the applicant; and

        (ii)   send a copy of the application to the parties.

(4)   The hearing is, so far as reasonably practicable, to be before the Appeal Sheriff or Appeal Sheriffs who made the order.

# CHAPTER 27 ACCELERATED APPEAL PROCEDURE

PART 7

SPECIAL APPEAL PROCEEDINGS

Chapter 27

## Accelerated Appeal Procedure

### Application of this Chapter

**27.1.** This Chapter applies to an appeal which has been appointed to proceed under the accelerated appeal procedure.

### Hearing of appeal

**27.2.** The Clerk must fix a hearing and intimate the date and time of that hearing to parties when—

(a) a provisional procedural order appointing the appeal to the accelerated appeal procedure becomes final or is confirmed; or

(b) the Court makes an order appointing the appeal to the accelerated appeal procedure under rule 6.7(5)(b).

### Application to remove appeal from accelerated appeal procedure

**27.3.**—(1) The procedural Appeal Sheriff may—

(a) of the procedural Appeal Sheriff's own accord; or

(b) on the application of any party,

order that an appeal is to proceed under the standard appeal procedure instead of the accelerated appeal procedure.

(1A)[1] An application is to be made by motion.

(2) The procedural Appeal Sheriff may only make such an order if the procedural Appeal Sheriff is satisfied that, taking into account the matters in rule 6.6(3), it is no longer appropriate for the appeal to proceed under the accelerated appeal procedure.

(3) That order must appoint the appeal to proceed under the standard appeal procedure and specify—

(a) the procedure to be followed in the appeal;

(b) the periods for complying with each procedural step.

---

[1] As inserted by the Act of Sederunt (Rules of the Court of Session, Sheriff Appeal Court Rules and Sheriff Court Rules Amendment) (Sheriff Appeal Court) 2015 (SSI 2015/419) r.19 (effective 1 January 2016; insertion came into force on December 31, 2015 but could not take effect until the commencement of SSI 2015/356 rule 5.6(3)(b) on January 1, 2016)).

Part I

SPECIAL APPEAL PROCEDURES

Chapter 27

Accelerated Appeal Procedure

Application of this Chapter

27.1  This Chapter applies to an appeal which has been appointed to proceed under the accelerated appeal procedure.

Hearing of appeal

27.2  The court may, on application, determine the case and time of the hearing to proceed when—

(a)  a provisional timetable for lodging the appeal in the accelerated appeal procedure has been confirmed; or

(b)  the court makes an order appointing the appeal to the accelerated appeal procedure under rule 27.3(1)(b).

Application to remove appeal from accelerated appeal procedure

27.3—(1)  The procedure in any appeal court may—

(a)  be heard on a specified date and time; or

(b)  if the application under rule 27.3(1)(a) is refused or the accelerated appeal procedure.

27.4  An application may be made by motion.

27.5  The accelerated appeal court may make such order as the court in the proceedings considers just and make an order in the course in the proceedings in relation.

27.6  Where there is a genuine need the appeal to proceed under the accelerated appeal procedure.

27.7  Where the court appoints the appeal to proceed under the accelerated appeal procedure the court shall specify—

(a)  the procedure to be followed in the appeal.

(a)  the application for appointment with each procedural step.

# CHAPTER 28 APPLICATION FOR NEW JURY TRIAL OR TO ENTER JURY VERDICT

## Chapter 28

## Application for New Jury Trial or to Enter Jury Verdict

### Application of this Chapter

**28.1.** This Chapter applies to an application—
- (a) for a new trial under section 69(1) of the 2014 Act;
- (b) to enter a verdict under section 71(2) of the 2014 Act.

### Form of application for new trial

**28.2.**—(1) An application for a new trial is to be made in Form 28.2.

(2) Such an application must be made within 7 days after the date on which the jury have returned their verdict.

(3)[1] The application must specify the grounds on which the application is made.

(4) When an application for a new trial is lodged, the party lodging it must also lodge—
- (a) a print containing—
    - (i) the pleadings in the sheriff court process;
    - (ii) the interlocutors in the sheriff court process;
    - (iii) the issues and counter-issues;
- (b) the verdict of the jury;
- (c) any exception and the determination on it of the sheriff presiding at the trial;
- (d) a process made up in accordance with paragraph 4 of Schedule 1 (form of process).

### Application for new trial: restrictions

**28.3.**—(1) An application for a new trial which specifies the ground in section 69(2)(a) of the 2014 Act (misdirection by sheriff) may not be made unless the procedure in rule 36B.8 of the Ordinary Cause Rules 1993 (exceptions to sheriff's charge) has been complied with.

(2) An application for a new trial which specifies the ground in section 69(2)(b) of the 2014 Act (undue admission or rejection of evidence) may not be made unless objection was taken to the admission or rejection of evidence at the trial and recorded in the notes of evidence under the direction of the sheriff presiding at the trial.

(3) An application for a new trial which specifies the ground in section 69(2)(c) of the 2014 Act (verdict contrary to evidence) may not be made unless it sets out in brief specific numbered propositions the reasons the verdict is said to be contrary to the evidence.

---

[1] As amended by the Act of Sederunt (Rules of the Court of Session, Sheriff Appeal Court Rules and Sheriff Court Rules Amendment) (Sheriff Appeal Court) 2015 (SSI 2015/419) r.19 (effective 1 January 2016; amendment came into force on 31 December 2015 but could not take effect until the commencement of SSI 2015/356 r.5.6(3)(b) on 1 January 2016)).

**Applications out of time**

**28.4.**—(1)   An application to allow an application for a new trial to be lodged outwith the period specified in rule 28.2(2) is to be included in the application made under rule 28.2(1).

(2)   Where the procedural Appeal Sheriff allows such an application, the application for a new trial is to be received on such conditions as to expenses or otherwise as the procedural Appeal Sheriff thinks fit.

**Timetable in application for new trial**

**28.5.**—(1)   The Clerk must issue a timetable in Form 28.5 when an application is lodged under rule 28.2(1).

(2)   When the Clerk issues a timetable, the Clerk must also fix a procedural hearing to take place after completion of the procedural steps specified in paragraph (4).

(3)   The timetable specifies—

    (a)   the dates by which parties must comply with those procedural steps;

    (b)   the date and time of the procedural hearing.

(4)   The procedural steps are the steps mentioned in the first column of the following table, provision in respect of which is found in the rule mentioned in the second column—

| Procedural step | Rule |
| --- | --- |
| Referral of question about competency of application | 28.7(3) |
| Lodging of appendices to print | 28.9(1) |
| Giving notice that the applicant considers appendix unnecessary | 28.10(1) |
| Lodging of notes of argument | 28.11(1) |
| Lodging of estimates of duration of hearing of application for new trial | 28.12 |

**Sist of application for new trial and variation of timetable**

**28.6.**—(1)   Any party may apply by motion to—

    (a)   sist the application for a new trial for a specified period;

    (b)   recall a sist;

    (c)   vary the timetable.

(2)   An application is to be determined by the procedural Appeal Sheriff.

(3)   An application to sist the application for a new trial or to vary the timetable may only be granted on special cause shown.

(4)   The procedural Appeal Sheriff may—

    (a)   grant the application;

    (b)   refuse the application; or

    (c)   make an order not sought in the application, where the procedural Appeal Sheriff considers that doing so would secure the expeditious disposal of the appeal.

(5)   Where the procedural Appeal Sheriff makes an order sisting the application for a new trial, the Clerk is to discharge the procedural hearing fixed under rule 28.5(2) (timetable: fixing procedural hearing).

(6)   When a sist is recalled or expires, the Clerk is to—

    (a)   issue a revised timetable in Form 28.5;

    (b)   fix a procedural hearing.

(7)   Where the procedural Appeal Sheriff makes an order varying the timetable, the Clerk is to—

    (a)   discharge the procedural hearing fixed under rule 28.5(2) (timetable: fixing procedural hearing);

    (b)   issue a revised timetable in Form 28.5;

    (c)   fix a procedural hearing.

### Questions about competency of application

**28.7.**—(1)   A question about the competency of an application for a new trial may be referred to the procedural Appeal Sheriff by a party, other than the applicant.

(2)   A question is referred by lodging a reference in Form 28.7.

(3)   A question may be referred within 7 days after the date on which the application for a new trial was lodged.

(4)   Where a reference is lodged, the Clerk is to fix a hearing and intimate the time and date of that hearing to the parties.

(5)   Within 7 days after the date on which the reference is lodged, each party must lodge a note of argument.

(6)   That note of argument must—

    (a)   give fair notice of the submissions the party intends to make on the question of competency;

    (b)   comply with the requirements in rule 28.11(3) (notes of argument).

(7)   Paragraphs (4) and (5) of rule 28.11 apply to a note of argument lodged under paragraph (5).

### Questions about competency: determination

**28.8.**—(1)   At a hearing on the competency of an application for a new trial, the procedural Appeal Sheriff may—

    (a)   refuse the application as incompetent;

    (b)   find the application to be competent;

    (c)   reserve the question of competency until the hearing of the application; or

    (d)   refer the question of competency to the Court.

(2)   The procedural Appeal Sheriff may make an order as to the expenses of the reference.

(3)   Where the question of competency is referred to the Court, it may—

    (a)   refuse the application as incompetent;

    (b)   find the application to be competent;

    (c)   reserve the question of competency until the hearing of the application.

(4)   The Court may make an order as to the expenses of the reference.

### Appendices to print: contents

**28.9.**—(1)   The applicant must lodge an appendix to the print mentioned in rule 28.2(4)(a) no later than 7 days before the procedural hearing, unless rule 28.10(1) (giving notice that applicant considers appendix unnecessary) is complied with.

(2)   The appendix is to contain—

    (a)   any document lodged in the sheriff court process that is founded upon in the application for a new trial;

    (b)   the notes of evidence from the trial, if it is sought to submit them for consideration by the Court.

(3)   Where the sheriff's note has not been included in the print and it subsequently becomes available, the applicant must—

(a)   include it in the appendix where the appendix has not yet been lodged; or

(b)   lodge a supplementary appendix containing the sheriff's note.

(4)   The parties must—

(a)   discuss the contents of the appendix;

(b)   so far as possible, co-operate in making up the appendix.

### Appendices to print considered unnecessary

**28.10.**—(1)   Where the applicant considers that it is not necessary to lodge an appendix, the applicant must, no later than 7 days before the procedural hearing—

(a)   give written notice of that fact to the Clerk;

(b)   intimate that notice to every respondent.

(2)   Where the applicant complies with paragraph (1), the respondent may apply by motion for an order requiring the applicant to lodge an appendix.

(3)   An application under paragraph (2) must specify the documents or notes of evidence that the respondent considers should be included in the appendix.

(4)   In disposing of an application under paragraph (2), the procedural Appeal Sheriff may—

(a)   grant the application and make an order requiring the applicant to lodge an appendix;

(b)   refuse the application and make an order requiring the respondent to lodge an appendix; or

(c)   refuse the application and make no order.

(5)   Where the procedural Appeal Sheriff makes an order requiring the applicant or the respondent to lodge an appendix, that order must specify—

(a)   the documents or notes or evidence to be included in the appendix;

(b)   the time within which the appendix must be lodged.

### Notes of argument

**28.11.**—(1)   The parties must lodge notes of argument no later than 7 days before the procedural hearing.

(2)   A note of argument must summarise briefly the submissions the party intends to develop at the hearing of the application for a new trial.

(3)   A note of argument must—

(a)   state, in brief numbered paragraphs, the points that the party intends to make;

(b)   after each point, identify by means of a page or paragraph reference the relevant passage in any notes of evidence or other document on which the party relies in support of the point;

(c)   for every authority that is cited—

(i)   state the proposition of law that the authority demonstrates;

(ii)   identify the page or paragraph references for the parts of the authority that support the proposition;

(d)   cite only one authority for each proposition of law, unless additional citation is necessary for a proper presentation of the argument.

(4)   Where a note of argument has been lodged and the party lodging it subsequently becomes aware that an argument in the note is not to be insisted upon, that party must—

    (a)   give written notice of that fact to the Clerk;

    (b)   intimate that notice to every other party.

(5)   Where a party wishes to advance an argument at a hearing that is not contained in that party's note of argument, the party must apply by motion for leave to advance the argument.

### Estimates of duration of hearing of application for new trial

**28.12.**   The parties must lodge estimates of the duration of any hearing required to dispose of the application for a new trial in Form 28.12 not later than 7 days before the procedural hearing.

### Procedural hearing

**28.13.**—(1)   At the procedural hearing, the procedural Appeal Sheriff is to ascertain the state of preparation of the parties, so far as reasonably practicable.

(2)   The procedural Appeal Sheriff may—

    (a)   determine that parties are ready to proceed to a hearing of the application for a new trial; or

    (b)   determine that further procedure is required

(3)   Where the procedural Appeal Sheriff determines that parties are ready to proceed—

    (a)   the procedural Appeal Sheriff is to fix a hearing of the application for a new trial;

    (b)   the Clerk is to intimate the date and time of that hearing to the parties;

    (c)   the procedural Appeal Sheriff may make an order specifying further steps to be taken by the parties before the hearing.

(4)   Where the procedural Appeal Sheriff determines that further procedure is required, the procedural Appeal Sheriff—

    (a)   is to make an order to secure the expeditious disposal of the appeal;

    (b)   may direct the Clerk to fix a further procedural hearing and intimate the date and time of that hearing to parties.

### Application to enter jury verdict

**28.14.**—(1)   This rule applies to an application under section 71(2) of the 2014 Act (verdict subject to opinion of the Court).

(2)   Such an application is to be made in Form 28.14.

(3)[1]   When an application is lodged, the party lodging it must also lodge—

    (a)   a print containing—

        (i)   the pleadings in the sheriff court process;

        (ii)   the interlocutors in the sheriff court process;

        (iii)   the issues and counter-issues;

    (b)   the verdict of the jury;

    (c)   any exception and the determination on it of the sheriff presiding at the trial;

---

[1] As amended by the Act of Sederunt (Rules of the Court of Session, Sheriff Appeal Court Rules and Sheriff Court Rules Amendment) (Sheriff Appeal Court) 2015 (SSI 2015/419) r.19 (effective 1 January 2016; amendment came into force on December 31, 2015 but could not take effect until the commencement of SSI 2015/356 rule 5.6(3)(b) on January 1, 2016)).

      (d)   a process made up in accordance with paragraph 4 of Schedule 1 (form of process).

(4)   Unless the procedural Appeal Sheriff otherwise directs—

      (a)   it is not necessary for the purposes of such a motion to print the notes of evidence; but

      (b)   the notes of the sheriff presiding at the trial may be produced at any time if required.

(5)   The procedural Appeal Sheriff may refer an application referred to in paragraph (1) to the Court in cases of complexity or difficulty.

# CHAPTER 29 APPEALS FROM SUMMARY CAUSES AND SMALL CLAIMS

## Chapter 29

## Appeals from Summary Causes and Small Claims

### Application of this Chapter

**29.1.** This Chapter applies to an appeal under section 38 of the Sheriff Courts (Scotland) Act 1971 arising from the decision of a sheriff in proceedings under—

    (a) the Summary Cause Rules 2002;

    (b) the Small Claim Rules 2002.

### Transmission of appeal

**29.2.**—(1)[1] Within 4 days after the sheriff has signed the stated case, the sheriff clerk must—

    (a) send the parties a copy of the stated case;

    (b) transmit to the Clerk—

        (i) the stated case;

        (ii) all documents and productions in the case.

(2) On receipt of the stated case, the Clerk is to fix a hearing and intimate the date, time and place of that hearing to the parties.

### Transmission of appeal: time to pay direction

**29.3.**—(1) Within 4 days after the sheriff states in writing the reasons for the sheriff's original decision in accordance with rule 25.4(4) of the Summary Cause Rules 2002 or rule 23.4(4) of the Small Claim Rules 2002, the sheriff clerk must transmit to the Clerk—

    (a)[1] the appeal in Form 33 of the Summary Cause Rules 2002 or Form 23 of the Small Claim Rules 2002;

    (b) the sheriff's written reasons for the sheriff's original decision.

(2) On receipt of those documents, the Clerk is to fix a hearing and intimate the date, time and place of that hearing to the parties.

### Hearing of appeal

**29.4.**—(1) The Court is to hear parties orally on all matters connected with the appeal, including liability for expenses.

(2) Any party may apply by motion for the question of liability for expenses to be heard after the Court gives its decision on the appeal.

(3) At the hearing, a party may only raise questions of law of which notice has not been given if the Court permits the party to do so.

(4) The Court may permit a party to amend any question of law or to add any new question of law.

(5) Where the Court grants permission under paragraph (3) or (4), it may do so on such conditions as to expenses or otherwise as the Court thinks fit.

---

[1] As substituted by the Act of Sederunt (Sheriff Appeal Court Rules 2015 and Sheriff Court Rules Amendment) (Miscellaneous) 2016 (SSI 2016/194) r.7 (effective 7 July 2016).

## Determination of appeal

**29.5.**—(1)   At the conclusion of the hearing, the Court may either give its decision orally or reserve judgment.

(2)   Where the Court reserves judgment, it must give its decision in writing within 28 days.

(3)   The Court may—

    (a)   adhere to or vary the decision appealed against;

    (b)   recall the decision and substitute another decision for it;

    (c)   remit the matter to the sheriff for further procedure.

(4)   The Court may not remit the matter to the sheriff in order that further evidence may be led.

## Appeal to the Court of Session: certification

**29.6.**—(1)   This rule applies where the Court has determined an appeal arising from the decision of a sheriff in proceedings under the Summary Cause Rules 2002.

(2)   An application under section 38(b) of the Sheriff Courts (Scotland) Act 1971 for a certificate that a cause is suitable for appeal to the Court of Session is to be made in Form 29.6.

(3)   Such an application must be lodged within 14 days after the date on which the Court gave its decision on the appeal.

(4)   An application may only be disposed of after the procedural Appeal Sheriff has heard parties on it.

# CHAPTER 30 APPEALS BY STATED CASE UNDER PART 15 OF THE CHILDREN'S HEARINGS (SCOTLAND) ACT 2011

## Chapter 30

## Appeals by Stated Case under Part 15 of the Children's Hearings (Scotland) Act 2011

### Application and interpretation of this Chapter

**30.1.**—(1)[1] This Chapter applies to an appeal by stated case under section 163(1), 164(1), 165(1) and 167(1) of the Children's Hearings (Scotland) Act 2011.

(2) In this Chapter, "parties" means the parties specified in rule 3.59(2) of the Act of Sederunt (Child Care and Maintenance Rules) 1997.

### Transmission of appeal

**30.2.**—(1)[2] Within 4 days after the sheriff has signed the stated case, the sheriff clerk must—

    (a) send the parties a copy of the stated case;

    (b) transmit to the Clerk—

        (i) the stated case;

        (ii) all documents and productions in the case.

(2) On receipt of the stated case, the Clerk is to fix a hearing and intimate the date, time and place of that hearing to the parties.

### Hearing of appeal

**30.3.**—(1) At the hearing, a party may only raise questions of law or procedural irregularities of which notice has not been given if the Court permits the party to do so.

(2) Where the Court grants permission, it may do so on such conditions as to expenses or otherwise as the Court thinks fit.

### Determination of appeal

**30.4.**—(1) At the conclusion of the hearing, the Court may either give its decision orally or reserve judgment.

(2) Where the Court reserves judgment, it must give its decision in writing within 28 days.

### Leave to appeal to the Court of Session

**30.5.**—(1) This rule applies to applications for leave to appeal to the Court of Session under section 163(2), 164(2) or 165(2) of the Children's Hearings (Scotland) Act 2011.

(2) An application is to be made in Form 30.5.

---

[1] As amended by the Act of Sederunt (Rules of the Court of Session, Sheriff Appeal Court Rules and Sheriff Court Rules Amendment) (Sheriff Appeal Court) 2015 (SSI 2015/419) r.19 (effective 1 January 2016; amendment came into force on December 31, 2015 but could not take effect until the commencement of SSI 2015/356 rule 5.6(3)(b) on January 1, 2016)).

[2] As substituted by the Act of Sederunt (Sheriff Appeal Court Rules 2015 and Sheriff Court Rules Amendment) (Miscellaneous) 2016 (SSI 2016/194) r.7 (effective 7 July 2016).

(3) Such an application must be lodged within 7 days after the date on which the Court gave its decision on the appeal.

(4) On receipt of an application, the Clerk must—

    (a) fix a hearing to take place before the procedural Appeal Sheriff no later than 14 days after the application is received;

    (b) intimate the date, time and place of that hearing to the parties.

# SCHEDULE 1 ADMINISTRATIVE PROVISIONS

## SCHEDULE 1

### ADMINISTRATIVE PROVISIONS

**Rule 1.4**

**Quorum of the Court**

**1.**—(1)  The quorum of the Court for the types of business specified in subparagraph (3) is one Appeal Sheriff.

(2)  The quorum of the Court for any other business is three Appeal Sheriffs.

(3)[1]  The types of business are—

(za)  relieving a party from the consequences of a failure to comply with a provision in these Rules under rule 2.1(1);

(a)  disposing of an application for leave to receive an appeal out of time under rule 6.4(2);

(b)  disposing of an application to abandon an appeal under rule 9.1;

(c)  disposing of an application for permission to appeal to the Court of Session under rule 11.2(1), where the decision in respect of which permission to appeal is sought was made by one Appeal Sheriff;

(d)  a peremptory hearing under rule 17.4;

(da)  disposing of an application for an additional fee under rule 19.2(1), where the order allowing expenses was made by one Appeal Sheriff;

(db)  disposing of an application for sanction for the employment of counsel, unless the application seeks sanction in respect of appearing at a hearing before more than one Appeal Sheriff;

(e)  disposing of an application to ordain a party to lodge an account of expenses under rule 19.3(2);

(ea)  disposing of a note of objections under rule 19.5(3), where the order allowing expenses was made by one Appeal Sheriff;

(f)  disposing of an application to allow a devolution issue to be raised after the note of appeal has been lodged or answers to the note of appeal have been lodged under rule 20.2(3);

(g)  a hearing fixed under Chapter 27 (accelerated appeal procedure);

(h)  a hearing fixed under Chapter 29 (appeals from summary causes and small claims);

(i)  disposing of an application for authority to address the Court in Gaelic or to give oral evidence in Gaelic under paragraph 6 of this Schedule;

(j)  any business where the Rules provide for that business to be disposed of by the procedural Appeal Sheriff.

**Procedural Appeal Sheriff**

**2.**—(1)  Every Appeal Sheriff is a procedural Appeal Sheriff.

(2)  Where the Court considers it appropriate to do so, the Court may dispose of any business where the Rules provide for that business to be disposed of by the procedural Appeal Sheriff.

---

[1] As amended by the Act of Sederunt (Sheriff Appeal Court Rules 2015 and Sheriff Court Rules Amendment) (Miscellaneous) 2016 (SSI 2016/194) r.7 (effective 7 July 2016).

**Signature of interlocutors etc.**

**3.**[1](1)  Any order made by the Court under these Rules is to be contained in an interlocutor.

(2)  An interlocutor is to be signed in accordance with subparagraphs (3) to (5).

(3)  Where the Court is constituted by more than one Appeal Sheriff when an order is made, the interlocutor is to be signed by—

> (a)  the Appeal Sheriff who presided over the Court when the order was made; or
>
> (b)  in the event of the death, disability or absence of that Appeal Sheriff, the next senior Appeal Sheriff who sat on that occasion, after such consultation with the other Appeal Sheriffs who sat as may be necessary.

(4)  Where the Court is constituted by one Appeal Sheriff, the interlocutor is to be signed by that Appeal Sheriff.

(5)  Where the Clerk determines an unopposed motion in writing in accordance with rule 12.7(1), the interlocutor is to be signed by the Clerk unless the procedural Appeal Sheriff directs otherwise.

(5A)  The Clerk may sign any other interlocutor if directed to do so by the procedural Appeal Sheriff.

(5B)  A direction under subparagraph (5A) need not be in writing.

(6)  An interlocutor signed in accordance with subparagraphs (5) and (5A) is to be treated for all purposes as if it had been signed by an Appeal Sheriff.

(7)  An extract of an interlocutor which is not signed in accordance with the provisions of this rule is void and has no effect.

(8)  An interlocutor may, on cause shown, be corrected or altered at any time before extract by—

> (a)  the Appeal Sheriff who signed it;
>
> (b)  in the event of the death, disability or absence of that Appeal Sheriff, by any other Appeal Sheriff;
>
> (c)  where the interlocutor was signed in accordance with subparagraphs (5) and (5A), by any Appeal Sheriff.

**Form of process**

**4.**—(1)[2]  A process must include the following steps of process—

> (a)  a minute of proceedings;
>
> (b)  an inventory of process.

(2)  Any document lodged with the Clerk is to be placed in the process.

**Decrees, extracts and execution**

**5.**[3](1)  In this paragraph, "decree" includes any order or interlocutor which may be extracted.

---

[1]  As amended by the Act of Sederunt (Rules of the Court of Session, Sheriff Appeal Court Rules and Sheriff Court Rules Amendment) (Sheriff Appeal Court) 2015 (SSI 2015/419) r.19 (effective 1 January 2016; amendment came into force on December 31, 2015 but could not take effect until the commencement of SSI 2015/356 rule 5.6(3)(b) on January 1, 2016)).

[2]  As substituted by the Act of Sederunt (Sheriff Appeal Court Rules 2015 and Sheriff Court Rules Amendment) (Miscellaneous) 2016 (SSI 2016/194) r.7 (effective 7 July 2016).

[3]  As amended by the Act of Sederunt (Rules of the Court of Session, Sheriff Appeal Court Rules and Sheriff Court Rules Amendment) (Sheriff Appeal Court) 2015 (SSI 2015/419) r.19 (effective 1 January 2016; amendment came into force on December 31, 2015 but could not take effect until the commencement of SSI 2015/356 rule 5.6(3)(b) on January 1, 2016)).

(2)   A decree may be extracted at any time after whichever is the later of—

   (a)   the expiry of the period within which an application for leave to appeal may be made, if no such application is made;

   (b)   the date on which leave to appeal is refused, if there is no right to appeal from that decision;

   (c)   the expiry of the period within which an appeal may be made, if no such appeal is made;

   (d)   the date on which an appeal is finally disposed of.

(3)   A party may apply by motion to the procedural Appeal Sheriff to allow an extract to be issued earlier than a date referred to in subparagraph (2).

(4)   Nothing in this paragraph affects the power of the Court to supersede extract.

(5)   Where execution may follow on an extract decree, the decree is to include the warrant for execution specified in subparagraph (6).

(6)   That warrant is "This extract is warrant for all lawful execution hereon".

(7)   Where interest is included in or payable under a decree, the rate of interest is 8 per cent a year unless otherwise stated.

## Use of Gaelic

**6.**—(1)   This paragraph applies where the use of Gaelic by a party has been authorised by the sheriff in the proceedings out of which an appeal arises.

(2)   That party may apply by motion for authority to address the Court in Gaelic at—

   (a)   an appeal hearing fixed under rule 7.14(3)(a); or

   (b)   a hearing under rule 29.4.

(3)   Where proof or additional proof is ordered in accordance with rule 23.1 (taking proof in the course of an appeal) and that party wishes to give oral evidence in Gaelic, the party may apply by motion for authority to do so.

(4)   Where the Court grants authority under paragraph (2) or (3), an interpreter is to be provided by the Court.

SCHEDULE 2[1]

FORMS

Form 4.3

Rule 4.3(4)(b)

**Statement of prospective lay representative for appellant or respondent**
IN THE SHERIFF APPEAL COURT
STATEMENT
by
PROSPECTIVE LAY REPRESENTATIVE FOR APPELLANT *[or* RESPOND-
ENT]
in the appeal by *[or* against]
[A.B.] *(designation and address)*
PURSUER and APPELLANT *[or* RESPONDENT]
against *[or* by]
[C.D.] *(designation and address)*
DEFENDER and RESPONDENT *[or* APPELLANT]
Name and address of prospective lay representative who requests to make oral
submissions on behalf of party litigant:
Identify hearing(s) in respect of which permission for lay representation is sought:
The prospective lay representative declares that:
(a)   I have no financial interest in the outcome of the case. *[or*
I have the following financial interest in the outcome of the case: *(state briefly the
financial interest.)*]
(b)   I am not receiving remuneration or other reward directly or indirectly from
       the litigant for my assistance and will not receive directly or indirectly such
       remuneration or other reward from the litigant.
(c)   I accept that documents and information are provided to me by the litigant
       on a confidential basis and I undertake to keep them confidential.
(d)   I have no previous convictions. *[or*
I have the following convictions: *(list the convictions.)*]
(e)   I have not been declared a vexatious litigant under the Vexatious Actions
       (Scotland) Act 1898. *[or*
I was declared a vexatious litigant under the Vexatious Actions (Scotland) Act
1898 on *(date).*]

[X.Y.], Prospective lay representative

Form 6.2

Rule 6.2(1)

**Note of appeal**
APPEAL
to
THE SHERIFF APPEAL COURT
[A.B.] *(designation and address)*
PURSUER and APPELLANT *[or* RESPONDENT]
against

---

[1] As substituted by the Act of Sederunt (Sheriff Appeal Court Rules 2015 and Sheriff Court Rules
Amendment) (Miscellaneous) 2016 (SSI 2016/194) para.7 (effective 7 July 2016).

1469

[C.D.] (*designation and address*)
DEFENDER and RESPONDENT [*or* APPELLANT]
1. The appellant appeals to the Sheriff Appeal Court against the decision of the sheriff at (*place*) (*specify nature of decision*) made on (*date*). The court reference number is (*insert court reference number*).

GROUNDS OF APPEAL

2. (*State briefly (in numbered paragraphs) the ground(s) of appeal.*)

AVAILABILITY OF SHERIFF'S NOTE

3. The sheriff has provided a note setting out the reasons for the decision appealed against, and a copy is appended. [*or*

3. The appellant has requested that the sheriff write a note, but the note is not yet available] [*or*

3. The sheriff has not provided a note setting out the reasons for the decision appealed against, and the appellant requests that the sheriff write a note.] [*or*

3. The sheriff has not provided a note setting out the reasons for the decision appealed against. The appellant considers that the appeal is sufficiently urgent that the Sheriff Appeal Court should hear and determine the appeal without the sheriff's note. (*State briefly (in numbered paragraphs) why the appeal is sufficiently urgent to justify its determination without the sheriff's note.*)]

INITIAL CASE MANAGEMENT: APPELLANT'S VIEWS

4. The appellant considers that the appeal should be appointed to the standard appeal procedure [*or* the accelerated appeal procedure] because:

(*state briefly (in numbered paragraphs) why the appellant considers that the appeal should be appointed to that procedure, taking into account the matters mentioned in rule 6.6(3).*)

IN RESPECT WHEREOF
[A.B.] [*or*[C.D.]], Appellant
[*or* [X.Y.], Solicitor for Appellant
(*insert business address of solicitor)]*
Form 6.5

Rules 6.5(4), 14.4(2), 15.3(4) and 17.3(5)
**Certificate of intimation**
IN THE SHERIFF APPEAL COURT
CERTIFICATE OF INTIMATION
in the appeal by [*or* against]
[A.B.] (*designation and address*)
PURSUER and APPELLANT [*or* RESPONDENT]
against [*or* by]
[C.D.] (*designation and address*)
DEFENDER and RESPONDENT [*or* APPELLANT]

1.  I certify that I gave intimation of (*specify document or other matter to be intimated*) to (*insert name of receiving party*).
2.  Intimation was given by (*specify method of intimation authorised by rule 5.3*).
3.  Intimation was given on (*insert date*).

[A.B.] [*or*[C.D.]], Appellant [*or* Respondent]
[*or* [X.Y.], Solicitor for Appellant [*or* Respondent]
[*or* [P.Q.], Sheriff Officer]
(*insert business address of solicitor or sheriff officer)]*
Form 6.7

Rule 6.7(2)(a)
**Representations about a provisional procedural order**

IN THE SHERIFF APPEAL COURT
REPRESENTATIONS
by
[A.B.] *[or*[C.D.]] (*designation and address*)

RESPONDENT

in the appeal by *[or* against]
[A.B.] (*designation and address*)
PURSUER and APPELLANT *[or* RESPONDENT]
against *[or* by]
[C.D.] (*designation and address*)
DEFENDER and RESPONDENT *[or* APPELLANT]

1. On (*date*) the Sheriff Appeal Court made a provisional procedural order under rule 6.6(1) of the Act of Sederunt (Sheriff Appeal Court Rules) 2015.
2. The respondent is a person to whom the provisional procedural order was intimated.
3. The respondent wishes to make the following representations:

(*state briefly (in numbered paragraphs) the representations.*)

[A.B.] *[or*[C.D.]], Respondent
*[or* [X.Y.], Solicitor for Respondent
(*insert business address of solicitor*)]

Form 7.2

Rules 7.2(1), 7.6(5)(a) and (6)(b)

**Timetable in appeal**
IN THE SHERIFF APPEAL COURT
TIMETABLE IN APPEAL
by *[or* against]
[A.B.] (*designation and address*)
PURSUER and APPELLANT *[or* RESPONDENT]
against *[or* by]
[C.D.] (*designation and address*)
DEFENDER and RESPONDENT *[or* APPELLANT]

Date of issue of timetable: (*date*)

[This is a revised timetable issued under rule 7.6(5)(a) *[or* rule 7.6(6)(b)] which replaces the timetable issued on (*date*).]

1. The respondent may lodge grounds of appeal under rule 7.3(1) not later than (*date*).

*Note:* if grounds of appeal are lodged, the appellant may lodge answers within 28 days after the grounds are intimated, in accordance with rule 7.3(2).

2. The respondent may refer a question of competency under rule 7.7(3) not later than (*date*).

*Note:* if a reference is lodged, parties must lodge notes of argument under rule 7.7(5) within 14 days after the date on which the reference is lodged.

3. The appellant must lodge the appeal print under rule 7.9(1) not later than (*date*).
4. The appellant must lodge the appendix to the appeal print under rule 7.10(1) not later than (*date*).
5. If the appellant does not consider that it is necessary to lodge an appendix to the appeal print, the appellant must lodge written notice under rule 7.11(1) not later than (*date*).
6. The parties must lodge notes of argument under rule 7.12(1) not later than (*date*).
7. The parties must lodge estimates of the duration of any appeal hearing

required to dispose of the appeal under rule 7.13 not later than (*date*).

8.  A procedural hearing will take place at (*place*) on (*date and time*).

Form 7.3

Rule 7.3(1)

**Grounds of appeal in cross-appeal**
IN THE SHERIFF APPEAL COURT
GROUNDs OF APPEAL FOR RESPONDENT
in the appeal by [*or* against]
[A.B.] (*designation and address*)
PURSUER and APPELLANT [*or* RESPONDENT]
against [*or* by]
[C.D.] (*designation and address*)
DEFENDER and RESPONDENT [*or* APPELLANT]

1.  The appellant has appealed to the Sheriff Appeal Court against the decision of the sheriff at (*place*) to (*specify nature of decision*) made on (*date*).

2.  The respondent appeals against the decision of the sheriff at (*place*) to (*specify nature of decision*) made on (*date*). [*or*

2.  The respondent challenges the grounds on which the sheriff made the decision against which the appellant has appealed.]

3.  (*State briefly (in numbered paragraphs) the ground(s) of appeal.*)

[A.B.] [*or*[C.D.]], Respondent
[*or* [X.Y.], Solicitor for Respondent
(*insert business address of solicitor*)]

Form 7.7

Rule 7.7(2)

**Reference of question about competency of appeal**
IN THE SHERIFF APPEAL COURT
REFERENCE OF QUESTION ABOUT COMPETENCY OF APPEAL
by
[A.B.] [*or*[C.D.]] (*designation and address*)

RESPONDENT

in the appeal by [*or* against]
[A.B.] (*designation and address*)
PURSUER and APPELLANT [*or* RESPONDENT]
against [*or* by]
[C.D.] (*designation and address*)
DEFENDER and RESPONDENT [*or* APPELLANT]

1.  The respondent refers the following question about the competency of the appeal to the procedural Appeal Sheriff:

(*state briefly (in numbered paragraphs) the question(s) about the competency of the appeal.*)

2.  (*State briefly (in numbered paragraphs) the grounds for referring the question(s).*)

[A.B.] [*or*[C.D.]], Respondent
[*or* [X.Y.], Solicitor for Respondent
(*insert business address of solicitor*]

Form 7.13

Rule 7.13

**Certificate of estimate of duration of appeal hearing**
IN THE SHERIFF APPEAL COURT
CERTIFICATE OF ESTIMATE OF DURATION OF APPEAL HEARING
in the appeal by [*or* against]

1472

[A.B.] (*designation and address*)

PURSUER and APPELLANT *[or* RESPONDENT]

against *[or* by]

[C.D.] (*designation and address*)

DEFENDER and RESPONDENT *[or* APPELLANT]

I, (*name and designation*) certify that the likely duration of an appeal hearing in this appeal is (*state estimated duration*).

[A.B.] *[or*[C.D.]], Appellant *[or* Respondent]

*[or* [X.Y.], Solicitor for Appellant *[or* Respondent]

(*insert business address of solicitor*)]

Form 11.2

Rule 11.2(1)

**Form of application for permission to appeal to the Court of Session**

IN THE SHERIFF APPEAL COURT

APPLICATION

for

PERMISSION TO APPEAL TO THE COURT OF SESSION

under section 113 of the Courts Reform (Scotland) Act 2014

by

[A.B.] (*designation and address*)

APPLICANT

against

A DECISION OF THE SHERIFF APPEAL COURT

1. On (*date*) the Sheriff Appeal Court (*briefly describe decision in respect of which permission to appeal to the Court of Session is sought.*)

GROUNDS OF APPEAL

2. (*State briefly (in numbered paragraphs) the ground(s).*)

PERMISSION TO APPEAL

3. The appeal raises an important point of principle or practice because (*state briefly the reasons*). *[or*

3. The appeal does not raise an important point of principle or practice but there is some other compelling reason for the Court of Session to hear the appeal because (*state briefly the reasons*).]

[A.B.], Applicant

*[or* [X.Y.], Solicitor for Applicant

(*insert business address of solicitor]*

Form 13.1

Rules 13.1(1), 13.4(2), and 13.5(2)(a)

**Form of motion by email**

**IN THE SHERIFF APPEAL COURT**

**Unopposed [or Opposed] motion**

**To: (email address of the Court)**

1   Case name:

2   Court ref number:

3   Is the case in court in the next 7 days?

4   Solicitors or party lodging motion:

   (a)   Reference:

   (b)   Telephone number:

   (c)   Email address:

5   Lodging motion on behalf of:

6   Motion (in brief terms):

7   Submissions in support of motion (if required):

8    Date of lodging of motion:

9    Intimation made to:

    (a)   Provided email address(es):

    (b)   Additional email address(es) of fee-earner or other person(s) dealing with the case on behalf of a receiving party (if applicable):

10   Date intimations sent:

11   Opposition must be intimated to opponent not later than 1700 hours on:

12   Is motion opposed or unopposed?

13   Has consent to the motion been provided?

14   Document(s) intimated and lodged with motion:

**EXPLANATORY NOTE TO BE ADDED WHERE RECEIVING PARTY IS NOT LEGALLY REPRESENTED**

**OPPOSITION TO THE MOTION MAY BE MADE by completing Form 13.2 (Form of opposition to motion by email) and intimating it to the party intending to lodge the motion (insert email address) on or before the last date for intimating opposition (see paragraph 11 above).**

**IN THE EVENT OF A FORM OF OPPOSITION BEING INTIMATED, the party intending to lodge the motion will lodge an opposed motion and the clerk of the Sheriff Appeal Court will assign a date, time and place for hearing parties on the motion. Intimation of this hearing will be sent to parties by the clerk.**

**IF NO NOTICE OF OPPOSITION IS LODGED, OR IF CONSENT TO THE MOTION IS INTIMATED TO THE PARTY INTENDING TO LODGE THE MOTION, the motion will be considered without the attendance of parties.**

**IF YOU ARE UNCERTAIN WHAT ACTION TO TAKE you should consult a solicitor. You may also obtain advice from a Citizens Advice Bureau or other advice agency.**

Form 13.2

Rules 13.2(1) and 13.5(2)(b)

**Form of opposition to motion by email**
**IN THE SHERIFF APPEAL COURT**

**TO BE INTIMATED TO THE PARTY INTENDING TO LODGE THE MOTION**

1    Case name:

2    Court ref number:

3    Date of intimation of motion:

4    Date of intimation of opposition to motion:

5    Solicitors or party opposing motion:

    (a)   Reference:

    (b)   Telephone number:

    (c)   Email address:

6    Opposing motion on behalf of:

7    Grounds of opposition:

8    Estimated duration of hearing:

Form 14.1

Rule 14.1(1)

**Form of motion**
IN THE SHERIFF APPEAL COURT
MOTION FOR THE APPELLANT *[or* RESPONDENT]
in the appeal by *[or* against]
[A.B.] (*designation and address*)
PURSUER and APPELLANT *[or* RESPONDENT]
against *[or* by]

[C.D.] (*designation and address*)
DEFENDER and RESPONDENT [*or* APPELLANT]

Date: (*insert date of intimation*)

1. The appellant (*or* respondent) moves the Court to (*insert details of the motion*).
2. (*State briefly (in numbered paragraphs) the grounds for the motion*).
3. The last date for lodging opposition to the motion is (*insert last date for lodging opposition*).
4. (Where a copy of a document accompanies the motion in accordance with rule 14.1(2), list the document(s) in question.)

[A.B.] [*or*[C.D.]], Appellant [*or* Respondent]
[*or* [X.Y.], Solicitor for Appellant [*or* Respondent]
(*insert business address of solicitor*)]

**EXPLANATORY NOTE TO BE INSERTED WHERE RECEIVING PARTY IS NOT LEGALLY REPRESENTED.**

**YOU MAY OPPOSE THE MOTION BY COMPLETING FORM 14.2 (Form of Opposition to Motion) and lodging it with the Clerk of the Sheriff Appeal Court.**

**You must do so *on or before* the last date for lodging opposition.**

**IF YOU OPPOSE THE MOTION, the Clerk will arrange a hearing. The Clerk will tell you the date, time and place for the hearing. You will have to attend the hearing or be represented at it.**

**IF YOU DO NOT OPPOSE THE MOTION, the Court may decide how to dispose of the motion without a hearing.**

**IF YOU ARE UNCERTAIN WHAT ACTION TO TAKE, you should consult a solicitor. You may also obtain advice from a Citizens Advice Bureau or other advice agency.**

Form 14.2

Rule 14.2(1)

**Form of opposition to motion**
IN THE SHERIFF APPEAL COURT
OPPOSITION BY APPELLANT [*or* RESPONDENT] TO MOTION
in the appeal by [*or* against]
[A.B.] (*designation and address*)
PURSUER and APPELLANT [*or* RESPONDENT]
against [*or* by]
[C.D.] (*designation and address*)
DEFENDER and RESPONDENT [*or* APPELLANT]

Date of intimation of motion: (*insert date of intimation*)
Date of intimation of opposition to motion: (*insert date of intimation*)

1. The appellant (*or* respondent) opposes the motion by the respondent [*or* appellant].
2. (*State briefly (in numbered paragraphs) the grounds for opposing the motion*).

[A.B.] [*or*[C.D.]], Appellant [*or* Respondent]
[*or* [X.Y.], Solicitor for Appellant [*or* Respondent]
(*insert business address of solicitor*)]

Form 17.3

Rule 17.3(1)(c)

**Notice of peremptory hearing**
IN THE SHERIFF APPEAL COURT
NOTICE OF PEREMPTORY HEARING

in the appeal by *[or* against]
[A.B.] (*designation and address*)
PURSUER and APPELLANT *[or* RESPONDENT]
against *[or* by]
[C.D.] (*designation and address*)
DEFENDER and RESPONDENT *[or* APPELLANT]

1. The Court has been informed that your solicitor no longer represents you.
2. As a result, the Court has made an order that you should attend or be represented at a peremptory hearing at (*insert place*) on (*insert date and time*).
3. At the peremptory hearing, you will have to tell the Court whether you intend to continue with the appeal *[or* your answers to the appeal].

[A.B.] *[or*[C.D.]], Appellant *[or* Respondent]
*[or* [X.Y.], Solicitor for Appellant *[or* Respondent]
(*insert business address of solicitor*)]

**IF YOU ARE UNCERTAIN WHAT ACTION TO TAKE, you should consult a solicitor. You may also obtain advice from a Citizens Advice Bureau or other advice agency.**

Form 20.2

Rule 20.2(1)

**Devolution issue**
IN THE SHERIFF APPEAL COURT
DEVOLUTION ISSUE
in the appeal by *[or* against]
[A.B.] (*designation and address*)
PURSUER and APPELLANT *[or* RESPONDENT]
against *[or* by]
[C.D.] (*designation and address*)
DEFENDER and RESPONDENT *[or* APPELLANT]

The appellant *[or* respondent] wishes to raise a devolution issue in this appeal.
(*State briefly (in numbered paragraphs) the following information—*
(a) the facts and circumstances and contentions on law on the basis of which it is alleged that the devolution issue arises;
(b) details of the relevant law (including the relevant provisions of the *Scotland Act 1998, the Northern Ireland Act 1998 or the Government of Wales Act 2006, as the case may be*).)

[A.B.] *[or*[C.D.]], Appellant *[or* Respondent]
*[or* [X.Y.], Solicitor for Appellant *[or* Respondent]
(*insert business address of solicitor*)]

Form 21.3

Rule 21.3(2)

**Reference to the European Court**
REQUEST
for
PRELIMINARY RULING
of
THE COURT OF JUSTICE OF THE EUROPEAN UNION
from
THE SHERIFF APPEAL COURT IN SCOTLAND
in the appeal by *[or* against]
[A.B.] (*designation and address)*
PURSUER and APPELLANT *[or* RESPONDENT]

against *[or* by]
[C.D.] (*designation and address*)
DEFENDER and RESPONDENT *[or* APPELLANT]

(*Set out a clear and succinct statement of the case giving rise to the request for the ruling of the European Court in order to enable the European Court to consider and understand the issues of EU law raised and to enable governments of Member States and other interested parties to submit observations. The statement of case should include:*

(a)   *particulars of the parties;*
(b)   *the history of the dispute between the parties;*
(c)   *the history of the proceedings;*
(d)   *the relevant facts as agreed by the parties or found by the court or, failing such agreement or finding, the contentions of the parties on such facts;*
(e)   *the nature of the issues of law and fact between the parties;*
(f)   *the Scots law, so far as it is relevant;*
(g)   *the Treaty provisions or other acts, instruments or rules of EU law concerned; and*
(h)   *an explanation of why the reference is being made.*)

The preliminary ruling of the Court of Justice of the European Union is accordingly requested on the following questions:

(*State (in numbered paragraphs) the questions on which the ruling is sought.*)

Dated the (*day*) day of (*month and year*).

Appeal Sheriff

Form 22.2

Rule 22.2(1)

### Application for leave to intervene by CEHR or SCHR
IN THE SHERIFF APPEAL COURT
APPLICATION FOR LEAVE TO INTERVENE
by
THE COMMISSION FOR EQUALITY AND HUMAN RIGHTS ("CEHR")
*[or* THE SCOTTISH COMMISSION FOR HUMAN RIGHTS ("SCHR")]
in the appeal by *[or* against]
[A.B.] (*designation and address*)
PURSUER and APPELLANT *[or* RESPONDENT]
against *[or* by]
[C.D.] (*designation and address*)
DEFENDER and RESPONDENT *[or* APPELLANT]

1. The CEHR *[or* SCHR] seeks leave to intervene in this appeal under section 30(1) of the Equality Act 2006 *[or* section 14(2) of the Scottish Commission for Human Rights Act 2006].

2. The CEHR considers that this appeal is relevant to a matter in connection with which it has a function because:

(*state briefly (in numbered paragraphs) the reasons.*)

*[or* 2. The SCHR considers that an issue arising in this appeal is relevant to its general duty and raises a matter of public interest because:

(*state briefly (in numbered paragraphs) the reasons.*)]

3. The issue in this appeal which the CEHR *[or* SCHR] intends to address is:

(*state briefly (in numbered paragraphs) the reasons.*)

4. The CEHR *[or* SCHR] intends to make the following submission if leave to intervene is granted:

(*state briefly (in numbered paragraphs) a summary of the proposed submissions.*)

[X.Y.], Solicitor for CEHR *[or* SCHR]

Form 22.4

Rule 22.4(1)

### Invitation to the SCHR to intervene
IN THE SHERIFF APPEAL COURT
INVITATION
to
THE SCOTTISH COMMISSION FOR HUMAN RIGHTS ("SCHR")
TO INTERVENE
in the appeal by *[or* against]
[A.B.] *(designation and address)*
PURSUER and APPELLANT *[or* RESPONDENT]
against *[or* by]
[C.D.] *(designation and address)*
DEFENDER and RESPONDENT *[or* APPELLANT]

1. The Sheriff Appeal Court invites the SCHR to intervene in this appeal under section 14(2)(b) of the Scottish Commission for Human Rights Act 2006.

2. *(State briefly (in numbered paragraphs) the procedural history, facts and issues in the appeal.)*

3. The Court seeks a submission from the SCHR on the following issue:
*(state briefly (in numbered paragraphs) the issue.)*

Appeal Sheriff

Form 23.4—A

Rules 23.4(1) and 24.8(2)

### Form of oath for witness
I swear by Almighty God that I will tell the truth, the whole truth and nothing but the truth.

Form 23.4—B

Rules 23.4(2) and 24.8(3)

### Form of affirmation for witness
I solemnly, sincerely and truly declare and affirm that I will tell the truth, the whole truth and nothing but the truth.

Form 24.2—A

Rule 24.2(1)

### Child witness notice
IN THE SHERIFF APPEAL COURT
CHILD WITNESS NOTICE
under section 12 of the Vulnerable Witnesses (Scotland) Act 2004
in the appeal by *[or* against]
[A.B.] *(designation and address)*
PURSUER and APPELLANT *[or* RESPONDENT]
against *[or* by]
[C.D.] *(designation and address)*
DEFENDER and RESPONDENT *[or* APPELLANT]

1. The applicant is the appellant *[or* respondent].

2. The applicant has cited *[or* intends to cite] [E.F.] *(date of birth)* as a witness.

3. [E.F.] is a child witness under section 11 of the Vulnerable Witnesses (Scotland) Act 2004 [and was under the age of eighteen on the date of the commencement of proceedings.]

4. The applicant considers that the following special measure[s] is [are] the most appropriate for the purpose of taking the evidence of [E.F.] *[or* that [E.F.] should give evidence without the benefit of any special measure]:

*(specify any special measure(s) sought).*

5. The reason[s] this [these] special measure[s] is [are] considered the most appropriate is [are] as follows:

*(specify the reason(s) for the special measure(s) sought). [or*

5. The reason[s] it is considered that [E.F.] should give evidence without the benefit of any special measure is [are]:

*(explain why it is felt that no special measures are required).]*

6. [E.F.] and the parent[s] of *[or*[person[s] with parental responsibility for] [E.F.] has [have] expressed the following view[s] on the special measure[s] that is [are] considered most appropriate *[or* the appropriateness of [E.F.] giving evidence without the benefit of any special measure]:

*(specify the view(s) expressed and how they were obtained).*

7. Other information considered relevant to this application is as follows:

*(state briefly any other information relevant to the child witness notice).*

8. The applicant asks the Court to—

(a)    consider this child witness notice; and

(b)    make an order authorising the special measure[s] sought; *[or*

(b)    make an order authorising the giving of evidence by [E.F.] without the benefit of special measures.]

[A.B.] *[or*[C.D.]], Applicant

*[or* [X.Y.], Solicitor for Applicant

*(insert business address of solicitor)]*

Form 24.2—B

Rule 24.2(2)

**Vulnerable witness application**

IN THE SHERIFF APPEAL COURT

VULNERABLE WITNESS APPLICATION

under section 12 of the Vulnerable Witnesses (Scotland) Act 2004

in the appeal by *[or* against]

[A.B.] *(designation and address)*

PURSUER and APPELLANT *[or* RESPONDENT]

against *[or* by]

[C.D.] *(designation and address)*

DEFENDER and RESPONDENT *[or* APPELLANT]

1. The applicant is the appellant *[or* respondent].

2. The applicant has cited *[or* intends to cite] [E.F.] *(date of birth)* as a witness.

3. The applicant considers the [E.F.] is a vulnerable witness under section 11(1)(b) of the Vulnerable Witnesses (Scotland) Act 2004 for the following reasons:

*(specify why the witness is considered to be a vulnerable witness.)*

4. The applicant considers that the following special measure[s] is [are] the most appropriate for the purpose of taking the evidence of [E.F.]:

*(specify any special measure(s) sought.)*

5. The reason[s] this [these] special measure[s] is [are] considered the most appropriate is [are] as follows:

*(specify the reason(s) for the special measure(s) sought.)*

6. [E.F.] has expressed the following view[s] on the special measure[s] that is [are] considered most appropriate:

*(specify the view(s) expressed and how they were obtained.)*

7. Other information considered relevant to this application is as follows:

*(state briefly any other information relevant to the vulnerable witness application.)*

8. The applicant asks the Court to—

1479

(a)    consider this vulnerable witness application; and

(b)    make an order authorising the special measure[s] sought.

[A.B.] *[or*[C.D.]], Applicant

*[or* [X.Y.], Solicitor for Applicant

(*insert business address of solicitor*)]

Form 24.2—C

Rule 24.2(3)(a)

**Application for review of arrangements for vulnerable witness**

IN THE SHERIFF APPEAL COURT

APPLICATION FOR REVIEW OF ARRANGEMENTS FOR VULNERABLE

WITNESSES

under section 13 of the Vulnerable Witnesses (Scotland) Act 2004

in the appeal by *[or* against]

[A.B.] (*designation and address*)

PURSUER and APPELLANT *[or* RESPONDENT]

against *[or* by]

[C.D.] (*designation and address*)

DEFENDER and RESPONDENT *[or* APPELLANT]

1. The applicant is the appellant *[or* respondent].

2. A proof *[or* hearing] is fixed for (*date*) at (*time*).

3. [E.F.] is a witness who is to give evidence at, or for the purposes of, the proof *[or* hearing]. [E.F.] is a child witness *[or* vulnerable witness] under section 11 of the Vulnerable Witnesses (Scotland) Act 2004.

4. The current arrangements for taking the evidence of [E.F.] are (*specify the current arrangements*).

5. The current arrangements should be reviewed because (*specify reasons for review*).

6. [E.F.] [and the parent[s] of *[or* person[s] with parental responsibility for] [E.F.]] has [have] expressed the following view[s] on [the special measure[s] that is [are] considered most appropriate] *[or* the appropriateness of [E.F.] giving evidence without the benefit of any special measure]:

(*specify the view(s) expressed and how they were obtained.*)

7. The applicant seeks (*specify the order sought*).

[A.B.] *[or*[C.D.]], Applicant

*[or* [X.Y.], Solicitor for Applicant

(*insert business address of solicitor*)]

Form 26.3

Rule 26.3(3)(a)

**Representations about a proposed order restricting the reporting of proceedings**

IN THE SHERIFF APPEAL COURT

REPRESENTATIONS

by

[A.B.] (*designation and address*)

APPLICANT

1. On (*date*) the Sheriff Appeal Court made an interim order under rule 26.2(1) of the Act of Sederunt (Sheriff Appeal Court Rules) 2015.

2. The applicant is a person who would be directly affected by an order restricting the reporting of proceedings because:

(*state briefly (in numbered paragraphs) the reasons.*)

3. The applicant wishes to make the following representations:

(*state briefly (in numbered paragraphs) the representations.*)

[4. The applicant seeks an urgent hearing on these representations because:
(*state briefly (in numbered paragraphs) why an urgent hearing is necessary.*)]

[A.B.], Applicant
*[or* [X.Y.], Solicitor for Applicant
(*insert business address of solicitor)]*

Form 26.5

Rule 26.5(2)

## Application for variation or revocation of an order restricting the reporting of proceedings

IN THE SHERIFF APPEAL COURT
APPLICATION
by
[A.B.] (*designation and address*)

APPLICANT

1. On (*date*) the Sheriff Appeal Court made an order restricting the reporting of proceedings in (*name of case (and court reference, if known)*).

2. The applicant seeks variation [or revocation] of the order because:
(*state briefly (in numbered paragraphs) the reasons for the application.*)

[3. The applicant seeks to vary the order by:
(*state briefly (in numbered paragraphs) the proposed variation(s).*)]

[A.B.], Applicant
*[or* [X.Y.], Solicitor for Applicant
(*insert business address of solicitor)]*

Form 28.2

Rule 28.2(1)

### Application for new trial
APPLICATION
to
THE SHERIFF APPEAL COURT
for
A NEW TRIAL
under section 69 of the Courts Reform (Scotland) Act 2014
by
[A.B.] (*designation and address*)

APPLICANT

[C.D.] (*designation and address*)

RESPONDENT

1. On (*date*), a jury trial was held before the Sheriff of Lothian and Borders at Edinburgh in the cause [A.B.] (*designation and address)*, pursuer, against [C.D.] (*designation and address)*, defender. The court reference number is (*insert court reference number*).

2. The verdict of the jury was (*state the verdict returned in accordance with* section 68 of the Courts Reform (Scotland) Act 2014).

3. The applicant applies to the Sheriff Appeal Court for a new trial under section 69(1) of the Court Reform (Scotland) Act 2014.

GROUNDS FOR APPLICATION
(*State briefly (in numbered paragraphs) the ground(s) for the application including references to* section 69(2) of the Court Reform (Scotland) Act 2014).

IN RESPECT WHEREOF
[A.B.], Applicant
*[or* [X.Y.], Solicitor for Applicant
(*insert business address of solicitor)]*

## Form 28.5
Rules 28.5(1), 28.6(6)(a) and (7)(b)
### Timetable in application for new trial
## IN THE SHERIFF APPEAL COURT
## TIMETABLE IN APPLICATION FOR NEW TRIAL
by
[A.B.] (*designation and address*)

**APPLICANT**

against

[C.D.] (*designation and address*)

**RESPONDENT**

Date of issue of timetable: (date)

[This is a revised timetable issued under rule 28.6(6)(a) *[or* rule 28.6(7)(b)] which replaces the timetable issued on (*date*).]

2. The respondent may refer a question of competency under rule 28.7(3) not later than (*date*).

Note: if a reference is lodged, parties must lodge notes of argument under rule 28.7(5) within 7 days after the date on which the reference is lodged.

4. The applicant must lodge the appendix to the print under rule 28.9(1) not later than (*date*).

5. If the applicant does not consider that it is necessary to lodge an appendix to the print, the applicant must lodge written notice under rule 28.10(1) not later than (*date*).

6. The parties must lodge notes of argument under rule 28.11(1) not later than (*date*).

7. The parties must lodge estimates of the duration of any hearing required to dispose of the application for a new trial under rule 28.12 not later than (*date*).

8. A procedural hearing will take place at (*place*) on (*date and time*).

## Form 28.7
Rule 28.7(2)
### Reference of question about competency of application for new trial
## IN THE SHERIFF APPEAL COURT
## REFERENCE OF QUESTION ABOUT COMPETENCY OF APPLICATION FOR NEW TRIAL
by
[C.D.] (*designation and address*)

**RESPONDENT**

in the appeal by

[A.B.] (*designation and address*)

**APPLICANT**

against

[C.D.] (*designation and address*)

**RESPONDENT**

1. The respondent refers the following question about the competency of the application for a new trial to the procedural Appeal Sheriff:

(*state briefly (in numbered paragraphs) the question(s) about the competency of the application for a new trial.*)

2. (*State briefly (in numbered paragraphs) the grounds for referring the question(s).*)

[C.D.], Respondent
*[or* [X.Y.], Solicitor for Respondent
(*insert business address of solicitor*)]

Form 28.12

Rule 28.12

**Certificate of estimate of duration of hearing**
IN THE SHERIFF APPEAL COURT
CERTIFICATE OF ESTIMATE OF DURATION OF HEARING
in the application for a new trial
[A.B.] (*designation and address*)

APPLICANT

[C.D.] (*designation and address*)

RESPONDENT

I, (*name and designation*) certify that the likely duration of a hearing to dispose of this application for a new trial is (*state estimated duration*).

[A.B.], Applicant *[or* Respondent]
*[or* [X.Y.], Solicitor for Applicant *[or* Respondent]
(*insert business address of solicitor*)]

Form 28.14

Rule 28.14(2)

**Application to enter jury verdict**
APPLICATION
to
THE SHERIFF APPEAL COURT
to
ENTER JURY VERDICT
under section 71(2) of the Courts Reform (Scotland) Act 2014
by
[A.B.] (*designation and address*)

APPLICANT

[C.D.] (*designation and address*)

RESPONDENT

1. On (*date*), a jury trial was held before the Sheriff of Lothian and Borders at Edinburgh in the cause [A.B.] (*designation and address*), pursuer, against [C.D.] (*designation and address*), defender. The court reference number is (*insert court reference number*).

2. The verdict of the jury was (*state the verdict returned in accordance with* section 68 of the Courts Reform (Scotland) Act 2014).

3. The applicant applies to the Sheriff Appeal Court for the verdict instead to be entered in the applicant's favour under section 71(2) of the Court Reform (Scotland) Act 2014.

GROUNDS FOR APPLICATION
(*State briefly (in numbered paragraphs) the ground(s) for the application*).

IN RESPECT WHEREOF
[A.B.], Applicant
*[or* [X.Y.], Solicitor for Applicant
(*insert business address of solicitor*)]

Form 29.6

Rule 29.6(2)

**Application for certificate of suitability for appeal to the Court of Session**
IN THE SHERIFF APPEAL COURT
APPLICATION FOR CERTIFICATE OF SUITABILITY FOR APPEAL TO THE
COURT OF SESSION
in the appeal by *[or* against]
[A.B.] (*designation and address*)

PURSUER and APPELLANT *[or* RESPONDENT]
against *[or* by]
[C.D.] (*designation and address*)
DEFENDER and RESPONDENT *[or* APPELLANT]

1. The appellant *[or* respondent] asks the Sheriff Appeal Court to certify that this appeal is suitable for appeal to the Court of Session under section 38(b) of the Sheriff Courts (Scotland) Act 1971.

2. The appellant *[or* respondent] considers that this appeal is suitable for appeal to the Court of Session because:

(*state briefly (in numbered paragraphs) the reasons*).

[A.B.] *[or*[C.D.]], Appellant *[or* Respondent]
*[or* [X.Y.], Solicitor for Appellant *[or* Respondent]
(*insert business address of solicitor)]*

Form 30.5

Rule 30.5(2)

**Application for leave to appeal to the Court of Session**
IN THE SHERIFF APPEAL COURT
APPLICATION FOR LEAVE TO APPEAL TO THE COURT OF SESSION
under
SECTION 163(2) *[or* 164(2)] *[or* 165(2)] OF THE CHILDREN'S HEARINGS
(SCOTLAND) ACT 2011
in the appeal by *[or* against]
[A.B.] (*designation and address*)
PURSUER and APPELLANT *[or* RESPONDENT]
against *[or* by]
[C.D.] (*designation and address*)
DEFENDER and RESPONDENT *[or* APPELLANT]

1. The appellant *[or* respondent] asks the Sheriff Appeal Court to grant leave to appeal to the Court of Session under section 163(2) *[or* 164(2)] *[or* 165(2)] of the Children's Hearings (Scotland) Act 2011.

GROUNDS OF APPEAL

2. (*State briefly (in numbered paragraphs) the point(s) of law or procedural irregularity on which the appeal is to proceed.*)

[A.B.] *[or*[C.D.]], Appellant *[or* Respondent]
*[or* [X.Y.], Solicitor for Appellant *[or* Respondent]
(*insert business address of solicitor)]*"

# PRACTICE NOTE NO. 1 OF 2016

## Contents

Introduction

Part 2: general provisions

    Chapter 3: sanctions for failure to comply

    Rule 4.2: legal representation

Part 3: initiation and progress of an appeal

    Rule 6.2(2)(d): request for sheriff's note

    Rule 6.5(1)(b): answers to note of appeal

    Rule 7.3: cross-appeals

    Rule 7.6: sist or variation of timetable

        Special cause

        Legal aid

    Rule 7.10: appendix to appeal print

        Notes of evidence from proof

        Form of appendix

    Rule 7.12: notes of argument

    Rule 7.13: estimates of length of hearings

    Rule 7.14: procedural hearing

Part 5: incidental procedure: standard procedures

    Chapter 19: expenses

Part 7: special appeal proceedings

    Chapter 28: applications for new trial

    Chapters 29 and 30: appeals by stated case

Schedule 1: administrative provisions

    Paragraph 4: form of process

Miscellaneous procedural matters

    Communication with the Court

        Communication where appeal is not to proceed

    Core bundles

    Authorities

        Contents of bundle of authorities

        Form of bundle of authorities

    Appeal hearings: preparation by the Court

    Documents generally

    Disposal by consent

SCHEDULE

## Introduction

**1.** The purpose of this Practice Note is to set out the practice of the Sheriff Appeal Court ("the Court") in dealing with civil appeals. It comes into force on 29 March 2015.

**2.** This Practice Note follows the general structure of the Sheriff Appeal Court Rules ("the Rules"). Miscellaneous procedural matters are dealt with towards the end. The Court intends to review its practice once it begins to hear appeals. Where no provision is made in the Rules or this Practice Note about any aspect of procedure in relation to civil appeals, practitioners may have regard to the practice of the Court of Session in relation to that type of business.

## Part 2: general provisions

### Chapter 3: sanctions for failure to comply

**3.** Where a party considers that any other party is in default for any of the reasons set out in rule 3.1, that party should bring the matter to the attention of the procedural Appeal Sheriff by lodging a motion in writing.

### Rule 4.2: legal representation

**4.** Where a party is legally represented, it is expected that the advocate or solicitor who will conduct the appeal hearing should appear at the procedural hearing. That person should be authorised to take any necessary decisions on substantive or procedural questions about the appeal. The Court considers that continuity of representation at procedural and appeal hearings is an important factor in minimising late settlements and the discharge of appeal hearings.

## Part 3: initiation and progress of an appeal

### Rule 6.2(2)(d): request for sheriff's note

**5.** Appellants are reminded that it is their responsibility to request a note from the sheriff where one has not already been produced. The note of appeal requires to include information about the availability of the sheriff's note and any steps taken to obtain one.

**6.** Where an appellant fails to take the necessary steps to obtain the sheriff's note and the appeal proceedings are delayed as a result, this may be taken into account in the determination of any question of expenses.

### Rule 6.5(1)(b): answers to note of appeal

**7.** When the procedural Appeal Sheriff makes an order for intimation and answers, any person who receives intimation may lodge answers, if so advised. The lodging of answers makes the Court and all other parties aware of a respondent's case and the Court considers that answers serve an important function in framing a respondent's lines of argument. Accordingly, it considers them to be compulsory where a respondent wishes to oppose an appeal.

**8.** Answers need not be elaborate, but they may mirror the format of the grounds of appeal specified in the note of appeal.

*Rule 7.3: cross-appeals*

**9.** Where the grounds of appeal in a cross-appeal have not been dealt with in the sheriff's note, the respondent should include in the grounds of appeal a request that the sheriff write a further note.

**10.** Where grounds of appeal in a cross-appeal are lodged, it may not be possible for all of the procedural steps to take place in accordance with the timetable issued under rule 7.2. Accordingly, the respondent should discuss with the appellant whether some variation of the timetable is necessary to allow the cross appeal to be taken into account in preparing for the procedural hearing. Where the parties consider that a variation is required as a result of the cross-appeal, a motion under rule 7.6 should be made.

*Rule 7.6: sist or variation of timetable*

**11.** A motion under this rule must, like all motions in writing, specify the grounds on which it is made (rule 12.6). Full details of the grounds on which the motion is based should be given, accompanied where relevant by appropriate evidence. Any such motion should be made as soon as possible after the need for variation or a sist is identified. Variation of the timetable may be either by extension or acceleration.

**12.** A motion to sist must specify the period of sist sought, but parties are reminded that it is for the procedural Appeal Sheriff to determine the period of sist that will be granted. The procedural Appeal Sheriff will seek to avoid any unnecessary delay in carrying out the procedural steps set out in the timetable. Where an appeal is sisted pending the outcome of an application for legal aid, the expectation is that the period of sist will not exceed 6 weeks.

**13.** It should be noted that motions for sist or for variation of the timetable will not be granted, even if made of consent, unless sufficient information to justify them is placed before the procedural Appeal Sheriff. Any party opposing such an application will be required to demonstrate that their opposition is well founded.

Special cause

**14.** A motion to sist the appeal or vary the timetable may only be granted on special cause shown (rule 7.6(2)). The procedural Appeal Sheriff will determine, in the particular circumstances of a case, whether or not special cause has been shown.

**15.** Special cause might arise for example, where there is a need for a party to obtain:

    (a)    transcripts of evidence;

    (b)    legal aid;

    (c)    the sheriff's note, if it cannot be obtained in time to comply with the timetable.

**16.** The procedural Appeal Sheriff may require to hear parties on an unopposed motion to sist the appeal or vary the timetable if:

    (a)    the Scottish Legal Aid Board take issue with what is stated to be the current position in relation to an application for legal aid;

    (b)    the procedural Appeal Sheriff is not satisfied that special cause has been shown.

## Legal aid

**17.** The Court will expect parties to consider at the earliest possible stage whether they may require to apply for legal aid for the appeal. Delay in making an application for legal aid or in then making a motion under this rule may lead to the motion being refused. Generally, the Court will expect parties to adhere to guidance issued by the Scottish Legal Aid Board. Parties are reminded that the Board may make legal aid available for specially urgent work undertaken before a legal aid application is determined. This may obviate the need to sist the appeal or vary the timetable. Further information can be obtained in the Special Urgency Chapter of the Civil Legal Aid Handbook[1].

**18.** Where a party makes a motion under rule 7.6 pending the outcome of an application for legal aid, that party should notify the Board electronically within the same period as that party requires to intimate it to other parties. In specifying the grounds for the motion, the party should set out the current position in relation to the application for legal aid.

### Rule 7.10: appendix to appeal print

**19.** The appendix should be made up in accordance with rule 7.10. However, it should only contain such material as is necessary for understanding the legal issues and the argument to be presented to the Court.

### Notes of evidence from proof

**20.** Where the parties seek to submit the notes of evidence from a proof for consideration by the Court, they are reminded of the terms of rule 29.18(11) of the Ordinary Cause Rules 1993. Where the evidence has been recorded by tape recording, the appellant must request from the sheriff clerk a transcript of the record. In the rare cases where a shorthand writer has been instructed, the appellant must inform the shorthand writer that the notes require to be extended for the purpose of the appeal. If the recording will not be transcribed or the notes will not be extended before the appendix must be lodged, the appellant should inform the Clerk as soon as possible.

### Form of appendix

**21.** The appendix should be paginated, each page being numbered individually and consecutively, with page numbers being inserted in a form which can be clearly distinguished from any other pagination on the document. Where any marking or writing in colour on a document is important, the document should be copied in colour or marked up correctly in colour. Documents which are not easily legible should be transcribed and the transcription placed adjacent to the document transcribed.

**22.** Any questions as to the contents or form of the appendix may be raised with the procedural Appeal Sheriff.

**23.** An appendix which does not conform to rule 7.10 and this Practice Note may be rejected by the Court, which may also find that no expenses are payable, or modify any award of expenses, in respect of the rejected appendix.

**24.** Where documents are included in an appendix unnecessarily, the Court may

---

[1] *http://www.slab.org.uk/handbooks/Civil%20handbook/wwhelp/wwhimpl/js/html/wwhelp.htm#href=Part%20V%20AA%20acs/Part%20V%20AA%20acs.html*

also find that no expenses are payable, or modify any award of expenses, in respect of the appendix.

## Rule 7.12: notes of argument

**25.** Parties are reminded that rule 7.12 makes detailed provision about how notes of argument are to be prepared. A note of argument which does not comply with that rule may be rejected by the Court, which may also find that no expenses are payable, or modify any award of expenses, in respect of the rejected note of argument.

**26.** Any questions as to the form of notes of argument may be raised with the procedural Appeal Sheriff.

**27.** A single date will be specified in the timetable for the lodging of notes of argument. As a matter of good practice, parties should exchange draft versions of their notes of argument in advance of the date referred to in the timetable. Whenever possible, the drafts should be exchanged in sufficient time to enable each party to answer, in its note of argument, the arguments advanced by the other parties.

## Rule 7.13: estimates of length of hearings

**28.** Where a party is legally represented, the certificate of estimate of the length of the hearing in Form 7.13 should be given by the advocate or solicitor who will conduct the appeal hearing. Where a party is not legally represented, it should be given by the party.

**29.** Any estimate exceeding one day should be fully explained in writing.

**30.** The Court expects that persons making oral submissions at an appeal hearing will confine their submissions so as to enable the hearing to be completed within the time indicated in the estimate. If additional time is required, that person must seek the Court's permission.

## Rule 7.14: procedural hearing

**31.** The procedural hearing is an important aspect of the standard appeal procedure. It is intended to be the final procedural step and is dealt with by the procedural Appeal Sheriff.

**32.** The primary purpose of the procedural hearing is to make sure that no case is sent for an appeal hearing (i.e. a hearing on its merits) unless the procedural Appeal Sheriff is satisfied that the parties are prepared for it.

**33.** Where a party is legally represented, the Court expects that the advocate or solicitor who will conduct the appeal hearing should appear at the procedural hearing (see paragraph 4 above).

**34.** At the procedural hearing, the Court expects that parties will be in a position to discuss the issues involved in the appeal and how they can be disposed of. Parties should address the procedural Appeal Sheriff on their state of preparation.

**35.** If the procedural Appeal Sheriff is satisfied that parties are prepared to proceed to an appeal hearing, the procedural Appeal Sheriff will fix the appeal hearing and determine its length.

**36.** If the procedural Appeal Sheriff is not satisfied that parties are prepared to proceed to an appeal hearing, the procedural Appeal Sheriff will make an order to secure the expeditious disposal of the appeal. The procedural Appeal Sheriff may direct the Clerk to fix a further procedural hearing.

**37.**   The Court considers that it is important that further procedural hearings be avoided unless they are necessary. If any difficulty arises in complying with the order of the procedural Appeal Sheriff, the parties should bring this to the attention of the Court. The parties should confirm whether:

(a)   the order has been complied with (and if not, why not);

(b)   further time is required (and if so, why);

(c)   a further hearing is genuinely required.

### Part 5: incidental procedure: standard procedures

*Chapter 19: expenses*

**38.**   The closing submissions for each party in an appeal hearing should deal with expenses: parties should either make their submissions about expenses at that point, or invite the Court to reserve all questions of expenses to a further hearing after it has determined the appeal.

### Part 7: special appeal proceedings

*Chapter 28: applications for new trial*

**39.**   The procedure in an application for a new trial is closely modelled on the standard appeal procedure. Accordingly, the guidance on the standard appeal procedure given in paragraphs 9 to 37 above applies equally (with any necessary modifications of terminology) to applications for a new trial under section 69 of the Courts Reform (Scotland) Act 2014.

*Chapters 29 and 30: appeals by stated case*

**40.**   The procedure for requesting a stated case continues to be governed by the Summary Cause Rules 2002, the Small Claim Rules 2002 or the Act of Sederunt (Child Care and Maintenance Rules) 1997.

**41.**   The Court reminds parties that great care should be taken to focus as precisely as possible the question of law (or procedural irregularity, in Chapter 30 appeals) on which the appeal is to proceed. If an advocate is to be instructed to conduct the appeal before the Court, it may be prudent to consult that advocate about the formulation of the question of law and any proposed adjustments to the draft stated case.

**42.**   Parties are also reminded that the permission of the Court must be obtained if a party wishes at the appeal hearing to raise a question of law of which notice has not been given (see rules 29.4(3) to (5) and 30.3).

**43.**   Where parties disagree about the occurrence of events in the sheriff court proceedings, the Court will normally accept the account of events which is given in the stated case.

## Schedule 1: administrative provisions

### *Paragraph 4: form of process*

**44.** Paragraph 4 prescribes the steps of process that must be included when a process is made up. Styles for each step of process are in the Schedule to this Practice Note. Processes which do not conform substantially to these styles may be rejected by the Court.

## Miscellaneous procedural matters

### *Communication with the Court*

**45.** The Court considers that it is important to avoid unnecessary hearings: hearings in court should not take place unless the matter in issue cannot otherwise be resolved. Hearings can often be avoided by means of email or other communication between solicitors and the Clerk, with the involvement of the procedural Appeal Sheriff where necessary.

### Communication where appeal is not to proceed

**46.** Parties are reminded that those involved in litigation have an obligation to take reasonable care to avoid situations where court time would be wasted. Where a party or that party's legal representative considers that it is likely that the appeal may not proceed, the Clerk must be informed immediately.

### *Core bundles*

**47.** In cases where the appendix comprises more than 500 pages (exclusive of notes of evidence) the appellant should, after consultation with the respondent, also lodge a core bundle. The core bundle should be lodged at least 7 days prior to the procedural hearing. It should contain the documents which are central to the appeal and it should not ordinarily exceed 150 pages. As with the appendix, the core bundle should be paginated, each page being numbered individually and consecutively, with page numbers being inserted in a form which can be clearly distinguished from any other pagination on the document.

**48.** Any questions as to the contents or form of the core bundle may be raised with the procedural Appeal Sheriff.

### *Authorities*

**49.** When an appeal hearing is fixed, the appellant should, after consultation with the respondent, lodge a bundle containing photocopies of the authorities cited in the notes of argument upon which each party will rely at the hearing.

### Contents of bundle of authorities

**50.** The bundle of authorities should not include:
   (a) authorities for propositions not in dispute;
   (b) more than 10 authorities, unless the Court gives permission for additional authorities to be included.

## Form of bundle of authorities

**51.** If a case is reported in Session Cases or the Law Reports published by the Incorporated Council of Law Reporting for England and Wales, it should be cited from those sources. Where a case is not reported in Session Cases or the Law Reports, references to other recognised reports may be given.

**52.** Unreported judgments should only be cited if they contain an authoritative statement of a relevant principle of law not to be found in a reported case or if they are necessary for the understanding of some other authority.

**53.** The bundle of authorities should be assembled in chronological order, with an index page.

**54.** The bundle of authorities should be paginated, each page being numbered individually and consecutively, with page numbers being inserted in a form which can be clearly distinguished from any other pagination on the document.

**55.** The passages on which each party intends to rely (as specified in that party's note of argument) should be marked or highlighted.

**56.** Any questions as to the contents or form of the bundle of authorities may be raised with the procedural Appeal Sheriff.

**57.** A bundle of authorities which does not conform to this Practice Note may be rejected by the Court, which may also find that no expenses are payable, or modify any award of expenses, in respect of the rejected bundle.

**58.** Where authorities are included in a bundle unnecessarily, the Court may also find that no expenses are payable, or modify any award of expenses, in respect of the bundle.

### *Appeal hearings: preparation by the Court*

**59.** Before the appeal hearing, the Appeal Sheriff(s) who will hear the appeal will normally have read:

   (a)   the appeal print;
   (b)   the note of appeal and answers to the note of appeal;
   (c)   any grounds of appeal (and answers) in a cross-appeal;
   (d)   the appendix;
   (e)   parties' notes of argument;
   (f)   any core bundle;
   (g)   the bundle of authorities.

**60.** Accordingly, one copy of each of these documents will be required for each Appeal Sheriff who sits for the appeal hearing. The precise number will depend upon the composition of the Court, which will be confirmed at the procedural hearing.

**61.** Parties will be ordered to lodge these copies by a date specified in the order. That date will be determined by the procedural Appeal Sheriff. Normally these documents will require to be lodged no later than 14 days prior to the hearing.

**62.** The timeous lodging of these copies is critical if the Appeal Sheriffs are to undertake pre-reading in preparation for the appeal hearing. The Court considers that this preparation is essential to the efficient disposal of business. Accordingly, parties and their legal representatives must inform the Clerk at the earliest possible opportunity if any difficulty in complying with the order is anticipated. This will enable the Court to consider whether further orders are required.

*Documents generally*

**63.** Documents, particularly appendices, core bundles and bundles of authorities, must be presented in a form which is robust, manageable and not excessively heavy. All documents must be easily legible.

*Disposal by consent*

**64.** If the parties have reached agreement as to how the appeal should be disposed of, they may prepare and lodge a joint minute setting out that agreement in clear and comprehensive terms. It should include terms as to expenses. It should also state the terms of the interlocutor that the parties wish the Court to pronounce.

**65.** Where the parties have agreed that the appeal should be allowed and the sheriff's decision recalled or varied because it is wrong, the joint minute must also explain why cause has been shown for the appeal to be allowed. Detailed submissions should be made, with appropriate reference to authority.

**66.** Where the parties have agreed that the appeal should be allowed because they wish the sheriff's interlocutor to be recalled or varied for practical reasons (but they do not consider that it was wrong), the joint minute must explain those practical reasons. It must also state that the parties do not seek a determination of the merits of the appeal.

21 March 2016 13

## Schedule

*Style steps of process*

### Style minute of proceedings

IN THE SHERIFF APPEAL COURT

MINUTE OF PROCEEDINGS

in the appeal by

[A.B.] *(designation and address)*

PURSUER and APPELLANT [*or* RESPONDENT]

against

[C.D.] *(designation and address)*

DEFENDER and RESPONDENT [*or* APPELLANT]

*Date*                                                                 *Clerk*

## Style inventory of process

IN THE SHERIFF APPEAL COURT

INVENTORY OF PROCESS

in the appeal by

[A.B.] *(designation and address)*

PURSUER and APPELLANT [*or* RESPONDENT]

against

[C.D.] *(designation and address)*

DEFENDER and RESPONDENT [*or* APPELLANT]

1.  Note of appeal.
2.
3.
4.
5.
6.
7.
8.
9.
10.